PSYCHOLOGY AND LIFE

Thirteenth Edition

PHILIP G. ZIMBARDO

Stanford University

HarperCollinsPublishers

Dedicated to the Zimbardo bambini—Adam (and his music), Tanya (and her writing), Zara (and her drama)—with love and respect for their unique contributions to my life and my psychology.

Sponsoring Editor: Anne Harvey
Development Editor: Becky Kohn
Project Coordination, Text, and Cover Design:
    Proof Positive/Farrowlyne Associates, Inc.
Cover Illustration: Mihail Chemiakin
Photo Researcher: Nina Page
Production Manager: Michael Weinstein
Compositor: Weimer Typesetting Co.
Printer and Binder: Arcata Graphics/Kingsport
Cover Printer: The Lehigh Press, Inc.

For permission to use copyrighted material, grateful acknowledgment is made to the copyright holders on pp. A1–A7, which are hereby made part of this copyright page.

Psychology and Life, Thirteenth Edition

Library of Congress Cataloging-in-Publication Data
    Zimbardo, Philip G.
        Psychology and life/Philip G. Zimbardo—13th ed.
            p.   cm.
        Includes bibliographical references and indexes.
        ISBN 0-673-46509-8 (student edition)

        ISBN 0-673-46621-3 (teacher edition)
        1. Psychology.   I. Title.
        [DNLM: 1. Psychology.   BF 121 Z7ip]
    BF 121.Z54 1991
    150—dc20
                                    91-35357
                                    CIP

91 92 93 94 9 8 7 6 5 4 3 2 1

Brief Contents

DETAILED CONTENTS   iv

PREFACE   xvi

CHAPTER 1   PROBING THE MYSTERIES OF MIND AND BEHAVIOR   1

CHAPTER 2   PSYCHOLOGICAL RESEARCH   26

CHAPTER 3   BIOPSYCHOLOGY AND NEUROSCIENCE   54

CHAPTER 4   MIND, CONSCIOUSNESS, AND ALTERNATE STATES   102

CHAPTER 5   THE DEVELOPING CHILD   134

CHAPTER 6   LIFE-SPAN DEVELOPMENT   178

CHAPTER 7   SENSATION   212

CHAPTER 8   PERCEPTION   254

CHAPTER 9   LEARNING AND BEHAVIOR ANALYSIS   300

CHAPTER 10   REMEMBERING AND FORGETTING   340

CHAPTER 11   COGNITIVE PSYCHOLOGY   378

CHAPTER 12   MOTIVATION   422

CHAPTER 13   EMOTION, STRESS, AND HEALTH PSYCHOLOGY   458

CHAPTER 14   UNDERSTANDING HUMAN PERSONALITY   506

CHAPTER 15   ASSESSING INDIVIDUAL DIFFERENCES   538

CHAPTER 16   SOCIAL PSYCHOLOGY   574

CHAPTER 17   ABNORMAL PSYCHOLOGY   616

CHAPTER 18   THERAPIES FOR PERSONAL CHANGE   660

APPENDIX   Appendix-1

GLOSSARY   G-1

REFERENCES   R-1

ACKNOWLEDGMENTS   A-1

NAME INDEX   NI-1

SUBJECT INDEX   SI-1

Detailed Contents

PREFACE   *xvi*

Chapter 1
Probing the Mysteries of Mind and Behavior   1

PSYCHOLOGY: DEFINITIONS, GOALS, AND TASKS   2
- *DEFINITIONS   3*
- *TIES TO OTHER DISCIPLINES   3*
- *LEVELS OF ANALYSIS   3*
- *THE GOALS OF PSYCHOLOGY   4*
- *WHAT PSYCHOLOGISTS DO: TASKS, SETTINGS, AND ROLES   8*

PSYCHOLOGY'S HISTORICAL FOUNDATIONS   11
- *STRUCTURALISM: THE CONTENTS OF THE MIND   12*
- *FUNCTIONALISM: MINDS WITH A PURPOSE   13*
- *EVOLUTIONISM: NATURAL SELECTION OF SPECIES   13*

CURRENT PSYCHOLOGICAL PERSPECTIVES   14
- *BIOLOGICAL APPROACH   15*
- *PSYCHODYNAMIC APPROACH   15*
- *BEHAVIORISTIC APPROACH   16*
- *COGNITIVE APPROACH   17*
- *HUMANISTIC APPROACH   18*
- *EVOLUTIONARY APPROACH   18*
- *COMPARING PERSPECTIVES: FOCUS ON AGGRESSION   19*

LOOKING AHEAD   21
- *CLOSE-UP: CROSS-CULTURAL PERSPECTIVES ON
  CONTROLLING NATURE   22*

CHAPTER SUMMARY   24

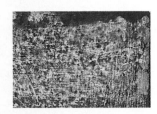

Chapter 2
Psychological Research   26

THE CONTEXT OF DISCOVERY   28
- *BIASES IN RESEARCH   28*
- *THEORIES, HYPOTHESES, AND PARADIGMS   32*

THE CONTEXT OF JUSTIFICATION   33
- *THE SCIENTIFIC METHOD   33*
- *SCIENTIFIC ATTITUDES AND VALUES   33*
- *OBJECTIVITY SAFEGUARDS   34*
- *ACHIEVING RELIABILITY AND VALIDITY   35*

PSYCHOLOGICAL RESEARCH METHODS   36

   PSYCHOLOGICAL MEASUREMENT 36
   CLOSE-UP: PSYCHOLOGY LABORATORY IN THE WILD 40
   CORRELATIONAL METHODS 41
   EXPERIMENTAL METHODS 42
   STATISTICAL ANALYSIS OF DATA 45

ETHICAL ISSUES IN HUMAN AND ANIMAL RESEARCH   46

   INFORMED CONSENT 46
   RISK/GAIN ASSESSMENT 46
   INTENTIONAL DECEPTION 46
   DEBRIEFING 47
   ISSUES IN ANIMAL RESEARCH: SCIENCE, ETHICS, POLITICS 47

BECOMING A WISER RESEARCH CONSUMER   48

   SCIENCE-COATED JOURNALISM 49
   LAUGHING AND CAUSING 49
   CLOSE-UP: THE WAR ON DRUGS 50
   CRITICAL THINKING CONSUMER CHECKLIST 51

CHAPTER SUMMARY   52

Chapter 3

Biopsychology and Neuroscience   54

EVOLUTION, HEREDITY, AND BEHAVIOR   57

   EVOLUTION 57
   HUMAN EVOLUTION 59
   GENES AND BEHAVIOR 61

BRAIN AND BEHAVIOR   63

   CLOSE-UP: THE GENETICS OF ALCOHOLISM 64
   EAVESDROPPING ON THE BRAIN 66
   BRAIN STRUCTURES AND THEIR FUNCTIONS 69

THE ENDOCRINE AND NERVOUS SYSTEMS   76

   GLANDULAR CONTROL OF BEHAVIOR AND INTERNAL PROCESSES 76
   NEURONAL CONTROL OF BEHAVIOR AND INTERNAL PROCESSES 78

THE NERVOUS SYSTEM IN ACTION   81

   THE NEURON 82
   GRADED AND ACTION POTENTIALS 85
   SYNAPTIC TRANSMISSION 87
   NEUROTRANSMITTERS AND THEIR FUNCTIONS 89
   CLOSE-UP: SYNAPTIC TRANSMISSION AND DRUGS: EFFECTS
     OF COCAINE 90
   NEURAL NETWORKS 92

THE NERVOUS SYSTEM AND CONSCIOUS EXPERIENCE   94

   CEREBRAL DOMINANCE 94
   TWO BRAINS OR ONE? 96

OUR RESPONSIVE BRAIN   99

CHAPTER SUMMARY   100

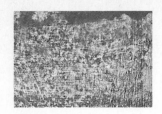

Chapter 4
Mind, Consciousness, and Alternate States

102

BRAIN, MIND, AND SOUL   104
   THE MIND-BODY PROBLEM 105
   PSYCHOLOGY'S CONCEPTION OF THE MIND 105
   THE MIND ACROSS CULTURES 106

THE NATURE OF CONSCIOUSNESS   107
   FUNCTIONS OF CONSCIOUSNESS 107
   LEVELS OF CONSCIOUSNESS 108
   STRUCTURES OF CONSCIOUSNESS 108
   RESEARCH APPROACHES 110

EVERYDAY CHANGES IN CONSCIOUSNESS   111
   DAYDREAMING AND FANTASY 111
   TO SLEEP, PERCHANCE TO DREAM 113

EXTENDED STATES OF CONSCIOUSNESS   122
   LUCID DREAMING 122
   HYPNOSIS 123
   MEDITATION 125
   HALLUCINATIONS 126
   RELIGIOUS ECSTASY 126
   MIND-ALTERING DRUGS 127

POSTSCRIPT: WHY CONSCIOUSNESS?   131

CHAPTER SUMMARY   132

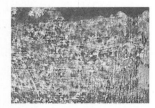

Chapter 5
The Developing Child

134

THE LIFE CYCLE BEGINS   137
   GENETIC INFLUENCES ON BEHAVIOR 137
   SENSORY DEVELOPMENT 142
   THE NATURE-NURTURE CONTROVERSY 143
   CLOSE-UP: DRUG-ADDICTED BABIES 144
   BABIES PREWIRED FOR SURVIVAL 145
   CONTINUITY, STAGES, AND CRITICAL PERIODS 151

ACQUIRING LANGUAGE   153
   INNATE PRECURSORS TO LANGUAGE LEARNING 154
   COMMUNICATION SKILLS 157
   LEARNING WORDS 158
   PUTTING IT ALL TOGETHER: ACQUIRING GRAMMAR 159

COGNITIVE DEVELOPMENT   161
   PIAGET'S INSIGHTS INTO MENTAL GROWTH 161
   MODERN PERSPECTIVES ON COGNITIVE DEVELOPMENT 164

SOCIAL AND EMOTIONAL DEVELOPMENT   168
   SOCIALIZATION 168
   GENDER ROLES 172
   ERIKSON'S PSYCHOSOCIAL STAGES 173

CHAPTER SUMMARY   176

Chapter 6
Life-span Development

178

DEVELOPMENT ACROSS THE LIFE COURSE   180
EARLY LIFE-SPAN THEORIES   *181*
HISTORICAL ANALYSIS OF FAMILIES AND LIFE STAGES   *182*
FAMILIES AND YOUTH AT RISK   *184*

ADOLESCENCE   185
TRANSITION MARKERS AND INITIATION RITES   *185*
THE MYTH OF ADOLESCENT "STORM AND STRESS"   *186*
TASKS OF ADOLESCENCE   *187*
CLOSE-UP: ALCOHOLISM ON CAMPUS   *191*

ADULTHOOD   192
THE TASKS OF ADULTHOOD   *192*
ADULT AGES AND STAGES   *193*
ADULT THINKING   *196*
MORAL DEVELOPMENT   *197*

OLD AGE   200
AGEISM AND MYTHS OF THE AGED   *200*
RESEARCH APPROACHES TO AGING   *201*
NEW PERSPECTIVES ON AGING   *201*
PHYSIOLOGICAL CHANGES   *202*
CLOSE-UP: YOUR DESIGN FOR ELDERLY HABITATS   *203*
COGNITIVE CHANGES   *204*
SOCIAL CHANGES   *206*
PSYCHOPATHOLOGY   *207*
AT LIFE'S END   *208*

CHAPTER SUMMARY   210

Chapter 7
Sensation

212

SENSORY KNOWLEDGE OF OUR WORLD   214
FROM PHYSICAL ENERGY TO MENTAL EVENTS   *215*
PSYCHOPHYSICS   *217*
CONSTRUCTING PSYCHOPHYSICAL SCALES   *221*
SENSORY CODING   *223*
SENSORY ADAPTATION   *223*

THE VISUAL SYSTEM   224
THE HUMAN EYE   *224*
THE PUPIL AND THE LENS   *224*
THE RETINA   *225*
RODS AND CONES   *225*
PATHWAYS TO THE BRAIN   *227*
SEEING COLOR   *229*
SEEING FORM, DEPTH, AND MOVEMENT   *233*

HEARING   239
    THE PHYSICS OF SOUND 239
    PSYCHOLOGICAL DIMENSIONS OF SOUND 240
    THE PHYSIOLOGY OF HEARING 241
    THEORIES OF PITCH PERCEPTION 243
    CLOSE-UP: NOISE POLLUTION FILLS THE AIR 244
    SOUND LOCALIZATION 245

OUR OTHER SENSES   245
    SMELL 246
    TASTE 247
    TOUCH AND SKIN SENSES 248
    PAIN 249

CHAPTER SUMMARY   252

Chapter 8
Perception   254

THE TASK OF PERCEPTION   256

SENSING, PERCEIVING, IDENTIFYING, AND RECOGNIZING   257
    INTERPRETING RETINAL IMAGES 258
    REALITY, AMBIGUITY, AND DISTORTIONS 260
    LESSONS LEARNED FROM ILLUSIONS 262
    THE NURTURE AND NATURE OF PERCEPTION 266

ATTENTIONAL PROCESSES   269
    PREATTENTIVE PROCESSING 269
    FUNCTIONS OF ATTENTION 272
    ATTENTIONAL MECHANISMS 275

ORGANIZATIONAL PROCESSES IN PERCEPTION   278
    REGION SEGREGATION 279
    FIGURE AND GROUND 279
    CLOSURE 280
    PRINCIPLES OF PERCEPTUAL GROUPING 280
    REFERENCE FRAMES 281
    SPATIAL AND TEMPORAL INTEGRATION 282
    MOTION PERCEPTION 283
    DEPTH PERCEPTION 283
    PERCEPTUAL CONSTANCIES 286

IDENTIFICATION AND RECOGNITION PROCESSES   292
    BOTTOM-UP AND TOP-DOWN PROCESSES 292
    RECOGNITION BY COMPONENTS 293
    THE INFLUENCE OF CONTEXTS AND EXPECTATIONS 293
    THE ROLE OF PERSONAL AND SOCIAL FACTORS 295
    CREATIVELY PLAYFUL PERCEPTION 295
    FINAL LESSONS 296

CHAPTER SUMMARY   298

Chapter 9
Learning and Behavior Analysis

300

THE STUDY OF LEARNING 302
WHAT IS LEARNING? 303
BEHAVIORISM AND BEHAVIOR ANALYSIS 304

CLASSICAL CONDITIONING: LEARNING PREDICTABLE SIGNALS 306
PAVLOV'S SURPRISING DISCOVERY 306
BASIC PROCESSES 307
SIGNIFICANCE OF CLASSICAL CONDITIONING 310
THE ROLE OF CONTINGENCY AND INFORMATIVENESS 313
CLOSE-UP: LEARNING TO BE A DRUG ADDICT 314

OPERANT CONDITIONING: LEARNING ABOUT CONSEQUENCES 316
THE LAW OF EFFECT 317
EXPERIMENTAL ANALYSIS OF BEHAVIOR 318
REINFORCEMENT CONTINGENCIES 319
PROPERTIES OF REINFORCERS 323
SHAPING AND CHAINING 325
SCHEDULES OF REINFORCEMENT 325
BIOFEEDBACK: BOOSTING WEAK RESPONSE SIGNALS 327
LEARNED HELPLESSNESS 328

LEARNING, BIOLOGY, AND COGNITION 329
BIOLOGICAL CONSTRAINTS ON LEARNING 330
COGNITIVE INFLUENCES ON LEARNING 332
CONNECTIONIST LEARNING MODELS 335
APPLIED BEHAVIOR ANALYSIS 337

CHAPTER SUMMARY 338

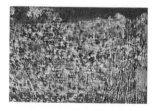

Chapter 10
Remembering and Forgetting

340

WHAT IS MEMORY? 343
TYPES OF MEMORY 343
EBBINGHAUS QUANTIFIES MEMORY 344
IMPLICIT AND EXPLICIT MEMORY 345
ENCODING, STORAGE, AND RETRIEVAL 346
RETRIEVAL METHODS: RECALL AND RECOGNITION 347
AN INFORMATION-PROCESSING VIEW 347
THREE MEMORY SYSTEMS 348

SENSORY MEMORY 349
ENCODING FOR SENSORY MEMORY 349
STORAGE: HOW MUCH AND HOW LONG? 350
TRANSFER TO SHORT-TERM MEMORY 351

SHORT-TERM MEMORY (STM) 352
ENCODING IN STM 353
STORAGE IN STM 353
PROCESSING IN STM 353
RETRIEVAL FROM STM 355

LONG-TERM MEMORY (LTM) 357
 ENCODING FOR LTM 358
 STORAGE IN LTM 360
 RETRIEVAL FROM LTM 362
 DUPLEX MEMORY VERSUS MULTIPLE LEVELS 363

REMEMBERING AS A CONSTRUCTIVE PROCESS 365
 SCHEMAS 366
 EYEWITNESS TESTIMONY 367

WHY WE FORGET 369
 MEMORY TRACES DECAY 369
 INTERFERENCE 369
 RETRIEVAL FAILURES 370
 MOTIVATED FORGETTING 370

THE NEUROBIOLOGY OF MEMORY 371
 THE ANATOMY OF MEMORY 371
 ALZHEIMER'S DISEASE 373
 CELLULAR MECHANISMS OF MEMORY 374
 INTEGRATING THE BIOLOGY AND THE PSYCHOLOGY
  OF MEMORY 375

CHAPTER SUMMARY 376

Chapter 11

Cognitive Processes   378

STUDYING THINKING 380
 THE EMERGENCE OF COGNITIVE PSYCHOLOGY 381
 THE RISE OF COGNITIVE SCIENCE 382

MEASURING THE MIND 384
 INTROSPECTION AND THINK-ALOUD PROTOCOLS 384
 BEHAVIORAL OBSERVATION 385
 MEASURING REACTION TIME 386
 ANALYZING ERRORS 386
 RECORDING EYE MOVEMENTS 387
 READING THE MIND IN BRAIN WAVES 387
 BRAIN IMAGING 390

MENTAL STRUCTURES FOR THINKING 391
 CONCEPTS AND CONCEPT FORMATION 391
 SCHEMAS AND SCRIPTS 395
 VISUAL IMAGERY AND MENTAL MAPS 397

REASONING AND PROBLEM SOLVING 401
 DEDUCTIVE REASONING 401
 INDUCTIVE REASONING 402
 PROBLEM SOLVING 402
 THE BEST SEARCH STRATEGY: ALGORITHMS OR HEURISTICS? 405
 METACOGNITIVE KNOWLEDGE 406
 AN EVOLUTIONARY PSYCHOLOGY PERSPECTIVE 407

JUDGING AND DECIDING 410
 MAKING SENSE OF THE WORLD 410
 PERSEVERANCE OF FALSE BELIEFS 411

SOURCES OF IRRATIONALITY 412
COGNITIVE BIASES 412
THE PSYCHOLOGY OF DECISION MAKING 415
CLOSE-UP: ECOLOGICAL DECISION MAKING 418
CHAPTER SUMMARY 420

Chapter 12
Motivation 422

UNDERSTANDING MOTIVATION 424
FUNCTIONS OF MOTIVATIONAL CONCEPTS 425
MOTIVATIONAL CONCEPTS IN RESEARCH 426

THEORETICAL PERSPECTIVES 428
CONCEPTUAL OVERVIEW 428
INSTINCT THEORY 429
DRIVE THEORY AND LEARNING 430
AROUSAL THEORY 431
HUMANISTIC THEORY OF GROWTH MOTIVATION 433
SOCIAL-COGNITIVE MOTIVATIONAL THEORIES 434

HUNGER AND EATING 436
WHAT REGULATES HUMAN FEEDING PATTERNS? 436
OBESITY AND DIETING 438

SEXUAL MOTIVATION 439
NONHUMAN SEXUAL AROUSAL 439
HUMAN SEXUALITY 440
THE MATING GAME: SEXUAL INVESTMENT STRATEGIES 442
CLOSE-UP: SEXUAL ADDICTION 447

ACHIEVEMENT AND WORK MOTIVATION 449
NEED FOR ACHIEVEMENT 449
INDIVIDUALIST VERSUS COLLECTIVIST CULTURES 451
ATTRIBUTIONS FOR SUCCESS AND FAILURE 451
ATTRIBUTIONAL STYLES: OPTIMISM VERSUS PESSIMISM 452
INTRINSIC VERSUS EXTRINSIC MOTIVATION 454
WORK AND ORGANIZATIONAL PSYCHOLOGY 454

CHAPTER SUMMARY 456

Chapter 13
Emotion, Stress, and Health Psychology 458

EMOTIONS 460
EXPERIENCING EMOTION 461
FUNCTIONS OF EMOTION 464
THEORIES OF EMOTION 465
ARE EMOTIONAL EXPRESSIONS UNIVERSAL? 468

MOOD AND INFORMATION PROCESSING 470

STRESS OF LIVING 472
 SOURCES OF STRESS *473*
 STRESS MODERATOR VARIABLES *477*
 CLOSE-UP: PASSIVE SMOKING *478*
 PHYSIOLOGICAL STRESS REACTIONS *480*
 PSYCHOLOGICAL STRESS REACTIONS *484*

COPING WITH STRESS 487
 COPING STRATEGIES *488*
 MODIFYING COGNITIVE STRATEGIES *489*
 SUPPORTIVENESS OF THE ENVIRONMENT *490*
 STRUCTURING THE PHYSICAL ENVIRONMENT *491*

HEALTH PSYCHOLOGY 492
 THE BIOPSYCHOSOCIAL MODEL OF HEALTH *492*
 THE YIN AND YANG OF HEALTH AND ILLNESS *493*
 HEALTH PROMOTION AND MAINTENANCE *493*
 TREATMENT AND PREVENTION OF ILLNESS *494*
 HEALTHY AGAIN *499*
 CAUSES AND CORRELATES OF HEALTH, ILLNESS,
  AND DYSFUNCTION *501*
 HEALTH CARE SYSTEM AND HEALTH POLICY FORMATION *501*
 A TOAST TO YOUR HEALTH *502*

CHAPTER SUMMARY 504

Chapter 14

Understanding Human Personality   506

THE PSYCHOLOGY OF THE PERSON 509
 STRATEGIES FOR STUDYING PERSONALITY *509*
 THEORIES ABOUT PERSONALITY *511*

TYPE AND TRAIT PERSONALITY THEORIES 511
 CATEGORIZING BY TYPES *511*
 DESCRIBING WITH TRAITS *512*
 ALLPORT'S TRAIT APPROACH *512*
 COMBINING TYPES AND TRAITS *514*
 TRAITS AND HERITABILITY *514*
 THE BIG FIVE *515*
 THE CONSISTENCY PARADOX *516*
 A FRESH LOOK AT TRAITS *518*
 CRITICISMS OF TYPE AND TRAIT THEORIES *518*

PSYCHODYNAMIC THEORIES 519
 FREUDIAN PSYCHOANALYSIS *519*
 POST-FREUDIAN THEORIES *524*

HUMANISTIC THEORIES 525
 ROGERS'S PERSON-CENTERED APPROACH *526*
 CRITICISMS OF HUMANISTIC THEORIES *526*

SOCIAL-LEARNING AND COGNITIVE THEORIES 527
 KELLY'S PERSONAL CONSTRUCT THEORY *527*
 COGNITIVE SOCIAL-LEARNING THEORY: MISCHEL *528*

COGNITIVE SOCIAL-LEARNING THEORY: BANDURA   *529*
CRITICAL EVALUATION OF LEARNING AND
   COGNITIVE THEORIES   *531*

SELF THEORIES   532
SELF AS KNOWER VERSUS KNOWN   *532*
DYNAMIC ASPECTS OF SELF-CONCEPTS   *532*
CRITICAL EVALUATION OF SELF THEORIES   *533*

COMPARING PERSONALITY THEORIES   534
CLOSE-UP: THE ALCOHOLIC PERSONALITY   *534*

CHAPTER SUMMARY   536

Chapter 15

Assessing Individual Differences   538

WHAT IS ASSESSMENT?   540
HISTORY OF ASSESSMENT   *541*
PURPOSES OF ASSESSMENT   *541*

METHODS OF ASSESSMENT   542
BASIC FEATURES OF FORMAL ASSESSMENT   *543*
SOURCES OF INFORMATION   *545*
CLOSE-UP: ALL DRINKERS ARE NOT CREATED EQUAL   *547*

ASSESSING INTELLIGENCE   548
HISTORICAL CONTEXT   *549*
IQ TESTS   *550*
THE USE AND MISUSE OF IQ   *556*

ASSESSING PERSONALITY   562
OBJECTIVE TESTS   *562*
PROJECTIVE TESTS   *566*

ASSESSMENT AND YOU   568
VOCATIONAL INTERESTS AND APTITUDES   *568*
POLITICAL AND ETHICAL ISSUES   *569*

CHAPTER SUMMARY   571

Chapter 16

Social Psychology   574

THE POWER OF THE SITUATION   577
SOCIAL FACILITATION   *577*
SOCIAL ROLES AND RULES   *578*
SOCIAL NORMS   *579*
CONFORMITY VERSUS INDEPENDENCE   *582*
AUTHORITY INFLUENCE   *585*
BYSTANDER INTERVENTION   *592*

Constructing Social Reality   595
   Guiding Beliefs and Expectations *597*
   Cognitive Frameworks *601*
   Social Relevance of Social Psychology's
     Dual Lessons *607*

Solving Social Problems   608
   Environmental Psychology *609*
   Peace Psychology *610*
   Close-Up: Changing Conservation Attitudes
     and Behaviors *612*

Chapter Summary   614

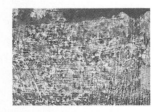

Chapter 17

Abnormal Psychology   616

The Nature of Psychological Disorders   618
   Deciding What Is Abnormal *619*
   Historical Perspectives *621*
   The Etiology of Psychopathology *622*
   Alternative Views *624*

Classifying Psychological Disorders   625
   Goals of Classification *625*
   DSM-III-R *625*

Major Types of Psychological Disorders   628
   Personality Disorders *628*
   Dissociative Disorders *629*
   Anxiety Disorders: Types *632*
   Anxiety Disorders: Causes *635*
   Close-Up: Addicted to Gambling *636*
   Affective Disorders: Types *638*
   Affective Disorders: Causes *639*
   Sex Differences in Depression *643*

Schizophrenic Disorders   645
   Major Types of Schizophrenia *646*
   Causes of Schizophrenia *647*
   Is Schizophrenia Universal? *652*

Judging People as Abnormal   653
   The Problem of Objectivity *653*
   The Problem of Stigma *655*

Chapter Summary   658

Chapter 18
Therapies for Personal Change

660

THE THERAPEUTIC CONTEXT   662

OVERVIEW OF MAJOR THERAPIES   662
ENTERING THERAPY   663
GOALS AND SETTINGS   663
HEALERS AND THERAPISTS   664
HISTORICAL AND CULTURAL CONTEXTS   665

PSYCHODYNAMIC THERAPIES   668

FREUDIAN PSYCHOANALYSIS   668
POST-FREUDIAN THERAPIES   671

BEHAVIOR THERAPIES   673

COUNTERCONDITIONING   674
AVERSION THERAPY   676
CONTINGENCY MANAGEMENT   676
SOCIAL-LEARNING THERAPY   678
GENERALIZATION TECHNIQUES   680

COGNITIVE THERAPIES   682

COGNITIVE BEHAVIOR MODIFICATION   682
CHANGING FALSE BELIEFS   683

EXISTENTIAL-HUMANIST THERAPIES   684

PERSON-CENTERED THERAPY   685
HUMAN-POTENTIAL MOVEMENT   686
GROUP THERAPIES   686
MARITAL AND FAMILY THERAPY   688

BIOMEDICAL THERAPIES   689

PSYCHOSURGERY AND ELECTROCONVULSIVE THERAPY   690
CHEMOTHERAPY   692

DOES THERAPY WORK?   694

EVALUATING THERAPEUTIC EFFECTIVENESS   695
CLOSE-UP: THERAPY FOR DRINKING PROBLEMS: WHAT WORKS?   697
PREVENTION STRATEGIES   699
CLOSE-UP: THE SYSTEM VERSUS THE SCHOOL BULLIES   700

A PERSONAL ENDNOTE   701

CHAPTER SUMMARY   702

APPENDIX: UNDERSTANDING STATISTICS—ANALYZING DATA INTO CONCLUSIONS   Appendix–1

GLOSSARY   G–1

REFERENCES   R–1

ACKNOWLEDGMENTS   A–1

NAME INDEX   NI–1

SUBJECT INDEX   SI–1

Preface

TO THE INSTRUCTOR

Did you know that you have in your hands a little bit of history? *Psychology and Life* is the oldest, continuously selling psychology textbook in existence. Since it first appeared in 1937, *Psychology and Life* has served as the model for all subsequent introductory psychology texts. Before that time, psychology texts reflected the theoretical biases of their authors and were written as much for professionals as for students. Floyd Ruch's 1937 text changed this tradition by presenting an unbiased, eclectic overview of the major fields of psychology, covering the research side of psychology in a way that would interest students and giving the material a practical focus.

I took over authorship of this popular work in 1969 and have written the last six editions. My objective has been to maintain the original perspective while paying close attention to scientific rigor and to psychology's relevance to life concerns. Each edition has integrated new theoretical viewpoints and important current research with classic studies and established principles. This task of integration becomes ever more difficult as more and more information in psychology and related fields becomes available. However, this challenge is a revitalizing learning experience as I approach each new edition of *Psychology and Life*.

WHAT'S NEW AND IMPROVED

To ward off superstition about the 13th edition of this classic text and to convert readers into *triskaidekaphiliacs*—lovers of the number 13—I have more thoroughly revised this edition of *Psychology and Life* than all the previous editions. My efforts have been supported and guided by a new publisher, **HarperCollins,** that offered a new editorial focus on retaining the best of previous editions while improving virtually every aspect of the text. We began work on this edition with the most intensive reviewing process the book has ever received. More than 25 teachers and scholars reviewed the previous edition, and dozens more evaluated drafts of the current edition. In addition to the hundreds of pages of their accumulated critical feedback, the comments of students and colleagues were also extremely helpful. This edition is built on the new foundation these reviewers helped provide, a foundation reflected in the book's organization and pedagogical structure. In addition, every single sentence has been carefully reviewed for its appropriateness, inform-

ativeness, readability, and consistency of style. My goal has been to create an introductory text that is interesting and right, engaging and informative for you and your students. Let's look first at changes in organization and content and then at changes in pedagogy.

NEW ORGANIZATIONAL AND CONTENT FEATURES

The first challenge of revising this text was to present areas of psychology in a sequence that is familiar to most instructors but that is sufficiently flexible to accommodate school terms of different lengths and the varied interests of different teachers and student populations. The second challenge was to do so while building upon the knowledge base of the student reader and while sustaining a meaningful flow and progression of ideas within and across chapters. For example, the book introduces in the opening chapter basic conceptual perspectives that become thematic organizing principles in subsequent chapters, notably in the chapters on motivation, personality, psychopathology, and psychotherapy. Following are some of the additions, improvements, and changes that I most want to call to your attention:

- Evolutionary psychology offers a "new" perspective on many aspects of cognitive, emotional, and behavioral functioning; the topic appears for the first time in this edition, and its predictions and recent research add richness to students' understanding.

- The chapter on research methods (2) has been restructured around the concepts of the Context of Discovery—where good ideas and false beliefs originate and where biased observations can be controlled—and the Context of Justification—where we test and evaluate our hypotheses and determine the validity of our beliefs. A new section on the ethics of research and intervention along with a discussion of animal experimentation in psychology has been added.

- Biopsychology has been moved forward to Chapter 3, it has been expanded, some of its presentation has been simplified, and its relevance to student interests has been emphasized at several points.

- The consciousness chapter (4) is a high interest chapter for students; it offers new research and extended discussion of sleep disorders, dreaming, drugs, and hypnosis. The chapter attempts to provide a conceptual structure for the study of consciousness as a meaningful, distinct domain of psychology.

- A treatment of life-span development in chapters 5 and 6 presents students with the ages, stages, and processes of human development in a way that gives students a feeling for the developing person and not just a presentation of abstract variables and processes; a completely new chapter on adolescence, adulthood, and aging adds much of value to this edition.

- The sensation chapter (7) has been completely rewritten to *explain* complex sensory processes at their physiological level and psychological functioning and not just to describe and list sensory events.

- A new section on *attention* has been added to the chapter on perception (8) to better integrate and elucidate the sequence of perceptual processes.

- The conditioning and learning chapter (9) has been streamlined to highlight important historical developments, key concepts and paradigms, and constraints on the generalizations of behavioral analyses.

- The memory and cognitive processes chapters (10 and 11) have been revised to include new research findings while keeping classic demonstration experiments; sections on amnesia, biology of memory, judgment, and decision making have been updated.

- The motivation chapter (12) includes a new historical overview of theories and approaches and new, expanded coverage of human sexuality, with sensitive discussions of date rape, homosexuality, and sexual addiction.

- Emotions has been combined with stress, coping, and health psychology in Chapter 13 to show their interrelatedness; the sections on stress and health psychology are greatly expanded to include current findings and theories.

- Personality theory and assessment of individual differences are better integrated in chapters 14 and 15; complex conceptual issues are clarified, theories are critiqued, new approaches and major psychological tests are clearly described, and controversial issues related to the abuses of testing are discussed.

- A new chapter on social psychology (16) replaces the previous two-chapter treatment with streamlined, in-depth coverage of the most important concepts emerging from modern social psychology: the power of situational forces, the construction of social reality, and the use of socially relevant research to improve the human condition.

- Major revisions in the psychopathology and therapy chapters (17 and 18) better relate *DSM-III-R* diagnoses to conceptual issues, research, and practical applications, while focusing in more detail on selected types of mental disorders and treatments.

- A new appendix on data analysis and statistics uses, as a unifying case application, actual data from research I did comparing different types of murderers on several psychological dimensions.

NEW PEDAGOGICAL FEATURES

Pedagogy is a funny word; it really refers to all the strategies we adopt as educators to make learning work better for our students. *Pedagogy* is the style one adds to substance that makes a unified whole more than the sum of its parts. It is the way ideas are made palatable and accessible. More than ever before, I have worked hard on the pedagogy of **Psychology and Life** to make this edition "user friendly." What follows are descriptions of changes in the book's pedagogical features:

- This edition enhances student accessibility with high interest features in every chapter, such as many new Opening Cases. These vivid, individual case presentations illustrate basic themes, are referred to in the chapters where relevant, and are designed to grab student attention. For example, a paraplegic mountain climber introduces us to motivation at its most intense level; Howard Hughes's story provides a fascinating study of personality development; Helen Keller's case offers insights on sensation; and a concentration camp survivor's reminder of the basic human curiosity to know and understand all experience, even within the hell of the camps, serves as the introduction to cognitive psychology.

- The former array of Close-Up boxes (popular with students but tangential to the main points of a chapter) has been expanded with two distinctive Close-Ups, featuring either the theme of environmental psychology or of addiction, the latter broadly presented to include drug, alcohol, cigarette, gambling, and sexual addictions. Each Close-Up will present either research, controversy, debate, or a student exercise related to its particular theme. These new Close-Ups directly relate to vital issues in the chapter, focusing on a different perspective of it or using information in the chapter to better inform the student about the issue in the Close-Up. For example, in the chapter on life-span development, students are asked to design part of the living space in a home for the elderly after learning how a business partner used knowledge of the elderly's habits and sensory limitations to design a similar area. In the chapter on cognitive processes, students examine the cognitive process of decision making as they study the debate among environmentalists over the value of darting killer whales for research. In the chapter on research methods, students analyze the "war on drugs," considering how conclusions depend on the way statistics are used or misused. In the therapy chapter, students consider whether alcoholic treatment should involve total abstinence or controlled drinking, in a debate that pits psychologists against the medical establishment, A.A., and religious groups.

- New Interim Summaries now follow almost every first-level heading to give students timely reviews of main ideas before they move on to subsequent sections.
- Recapping Main Points summaries organized around major sections in each chapter help students focus their study efforts.
- Lists of Key Terms and Major Contributors at the end of each chapter include page citations of text sections where the terms are boldfaced for student attention.
- The Glossary has been expanded with the addition of well over 200 terms, the clarification of some definitions, and the identification of prominent contributors.
- Important ideas are previewed and outlined throughout each chapter in ways that promote their encoding and later retrieval.
- This edition uses more examples, metaphors, and analogies than any previous edition to breathe life into abstract concepts.
- We spent much time and creative effort developing an effective art/photo program coordinated to and contributing to the key concepts in every chapter.
- This edition includes elaboration of selected research and photos from appropriate programs in the *Discovering Psychology* TV series, which can be a valuable adjunct to your teaching.

KEEPING UP-TO-DATE

Through my lifelong commitment to teaching, I am able to stay on top of new developments in psychology and to keep in touch with changing student interest. I continue to discover new joys in teaching introductory psychology to large lecture classes (with up to 750 students) as well as in small seminars of a dozen undergraduates. By training graduate teaching assistants in my practicum course on effective teaching, I am forced continually to reevaluate teaching strategies and tactics that will work for a variety of teaching approaches.

Unique to this edition of *Psychology and Life* is my recently completed three-year experience of developing a new television series on psychology. As chief scientific advisor, writer and host of *Discovering Psychology* (produced by Boston public broadcasting station WGBH), I

was able to spend much time thinking about significant ideas, principles, theories, and research in psychology. I spent many hours discussing key subjects with a superb panel of ten scientific advisors who helped sharpen my vision and provided alternative perspectives on ways to present our subject matter to the general public and to students. Devising the means of translating psychology into visual images and words accessible to general audiences has enhanced my ability to communicate these subjects to *my* students and, I believe, to *yours*. I have tried to integrate into this edition of *Psychology and Life* much of what I discovered while developing the 26-program TV series. The end product of all this concentrated effort is, I hope, an accumulation of accessibility, balance, and comprehensiveness.

ACCESSIBILITY, BALANCE, AND COMPREHENSIVENESS

In addition to the organizational and pedagogical improvements already noted, many other features make the information in this text *accessible* to a wide range of student abilities. These features include questions and personal examples in the voice of the author; student exercises; demonstrations; critical thinking exercises; lists of special resources for students; and personal, student-focused information about topics such as psychological testing, health and wellness, sleep disorders, coping with stress, date rape, AIDS, and mental health. *Accessibility* also includes a writing style high in readability and interest level; students will find that this writing style has been a major priority in the revision of *Psychology and Life*.

Balance means many things in an introductory psychology text. A balance of conceptual and theoretical viewpoints is achieved by presenting the five major approaches that guide most psychological thought and practice—cognitive, behavioral, psychodynamic, biopsychological, and humanistic—along with a new approach that is gaining many supporters: evolutionary psychology. These differing perspectives are outlined in Chapter 1 and then reintroduced as organizing themes in many subsequent chapters. The text tries to be eclectic and unbiased in its theoretical orientation by arguing for what is best in each of these approaches while critically evaluating their relevance to various topics and applications.

Balance also means combining the best of the old with the cutting edge of the new. To this end, I have retained those classic studies that form the foundation of much of our knowledge of psychology and joined them with the newest evidence and emerging research paradigms (challenges to Piagetian stages, myths of aging, and the neural network connectionist approach).

The addition of 1100 new references attests to the incorporation of contemporary research. At the same time, this edition provides more historical context than previous ones to enable students to appreciate the intellectual origins of important ideas and controversies in psychology.

Balance also refers to the combining of scientifically rigorous research and lofty theories with practical applications and life-relevant issues. Details of research are highlighted in small modules that distinguish procedure and results from the generalizations made in the running text. At the same time, as the title implies, this text consistently blends psychology and life, the abstract and the pragmatic, the scientific and the applied. One Opening Case shows how pilot error that led to many plane crashes was corrected with the discovery of a psychological illusion affecting pilots under certain flying conditions. A Close-Up describes new research in Sweden that has reduced the extent of school bullying nationwide by changing the social environment that supported such aggression. Another Close-Up details why female college students are more prone to getting drunk than males. Other major text sections are devoted to practical stress-coping strategies and ways to develop a healthy, optimistic outlook.

Psychology and Life is intended to be *comprehensive* enough to satisfy the most discriminating and demanding instructor without being so *pedantic* as to overwhelm the beginning student with excessive detail. Coverage of important topics such as biopsychology, cognitive psychology, attention, cross-cultural approaches, human sexuality, ethics, adulthood, and aging has been expanded. The text spends time explaining critical processes and phenomena rather than merely describing them. An example of this last point can be seen in the new social psychology chapter. It presents adequate evidence, examples, and systematic development of each of three key areas of social psychology. The breadth of the text materials combines with the instructor's class presentations to prepare students to understand what modern psychology is all about or to take any of the next level of psychology courses.

THE TOTAL PSYCHOLOGY AND LIFE TEACHING PROGRAM

A good textbook is only one part of the package of educational materials that makes an introductory psychology course more interesting and valuable for students and more effective and enjoyable for instructors. The introductory psychology course is the most difficult of all courses to teach because of its enormous range of topics, multiple levels of analysis, and initial student misconceptions about the nature of psychology. To make it easier for you and better for your students, the HarperCollins staff has worked with me to prepare a number of valuable ancillary materials.

Instructor's Resource Kit

For new teachers and others interested in improving their teaching effectiveness, this unique instructor's manual offers both general teaching strategies and specific tactics that have been class tested and that work. It provides a detailed compendium of teaching tips, audiovisual resource information for each chapter of the text, elaborate outlines of all the basic information presented in each text chapter, supplementary material for lecture preparation that is not presented in the text or expands on what is in the text, and a set of demonstrations and experiments class tested for use in sections, especially those taught by teaching assistants. This new edition of the Instructor's Resource Kit is coauthored by **Eva Conrad** of San Bernadino Valley College and **Mark Rafter** of Chaffey College.

Test Banks

Two new test banks of over 1800 test questions each are available in hard copy and on computer disk to adopters of *Psychology and Life*. Each set of multiple-choice questions has over 100 items per chapter, with difficulty level, text page citation, and item type noted for each item. The test banks were prepared by **Michael Enzle** of the University of Alberta and by **Sarah Rundle.**

TestMaster Computerized Test Bank

A powerful test-generation system, TestMaster allows instructors to construct test files with multiple-choice and essay questions from the test banks. Questions can be exchanged between the TestMaster program and the instructor's word-processing software. TestMaster is available for IBM, most compatibles, and Macintosh computers.

Transparencies

Your class lectures can be enhanced by the set of more than 100 *overhead transparencies* that accompanies *Psychology and Life*. These transparencies include color graphs, tables, diagrams, and illustrations.

Laser Disc

The HarperCollins *laser disc* contains class demonstration materials and powerful graphics that you can access instantly by following its table of contents and footage index.

Discovering Psychology *Videos*

This set of 26 half-hour videos is available for class use from the Annenberg CPB collection. A free preview cassette with 4 programs can be viewed on request by calling 1-800-LEARNER; in Canada, the number is 416-827-1155.

Discovering Psychology *Telecourse Guides*

For teachers of the *Discovering Psychology Telecourses,* an exceptionally complete *Faculty Guide* and *Student Study Guide* are available that coordinate the video programs and the *Psychology and Life* text. These are available through Adult Learning Services at 1-800-LEARNER.

The Integrator

This chapter-by-chapter cross-referencing guide to all software, media, and print materials has been developed specifically to accompany the 13th edition of *Psychology and Life.* References to the appropriate ancillaries are listed under each major chapter heading.

Student Study Guide and Practice Tests

For students, this workbook, authored by **Grace Galliano** of Kennesaw State College, is designed to aid students in getting the best return on their study time. Each chapter offers two sets of practice tests, with some items taken from the test banks; useful tips on how to approach studying for each chapter; and learning objectives. Research conducted at the University of Vermont on the previous edition of this workbook showed that students assigned to use it averaged grades about 20 percent higher than those in the same introductory psychology class who did not.

For teachers, who might use some or all of the *Discovering Psychology* video series in class or as an out-of-class supplement, a brief video guide has been added to the *Student Study Guide* that gives an overview of each program, lists of key terms and major contributors, sample test items, and references to relevant text sections. It was prepared by **Rose McDermott** of Stanford University with the assistance of **Frank Savage** of De Anza College.

SuperShell II: Computerized Tutorial

Complete with diagnostic and feedback capabilities, the computerized tutorial SuperShell II provides immediate correct answers and it references the text page on which the topic is presented. When students miss a question, the question appears on screen more frequently. A flash-card feature drills students on important terms and concepts. Prepared by **Glenda Smith** of North Harris County College, SuperShell II is available for IBM.

Journey Interactive Software

This unique software provides students with full-color graphic modules on experimental research, the nervous system, learning, development, and psychological assessment. It is available for IBM and Macintosh computers.

PERSONAL ACKNOWLEDGMENTS

Although the Beatles got by with a little help from their friends, I survived the revising and production of this edition of *Psychology and Life* only with a great deal of help from my friends. The enormous task of writing a book of this scope was possible only with the help of many friends, colleagues, students, and the editorial staff of my new publisher, HarperCollins. I gratefully acknowledge their invaluable contributions at every stage of this project, collectively and, now, individually.

Louise Carter, a developmental psychologist by training and a gifted writer, worked closely with me to infuse new vitality into the Opening Cases and the Close-Ups. **William Buskist** (Auburn University), author of his own outstanding introductory psychology textbook, not only provided a most thorough and incisive review of the previous edition, he even volunteered to assist in helping revise the biopsychology and learning chapters. **Carlo Piccione,** a therapist and teacher at Stanford, shared much of his expertise in improving the health psychology chapter.

In the finest academic tradition of teachers learning from students, I learned much that was new and current from gifted graduate students at Stanford University and from the University of California at Berkeley. Their assistance came in many forms, from help on revising chapter sections to providing outlines, references, and critical evaluations. I owe thanks to **David Bryant** (memory), **Eileen Donahue** (personality and assessment), **Barbara Fredrickson** (aging), **Derek Koehler** (judgment), **Jeffrey Miller** (evolutionary psychology), **Donna Mumme** (social-emotional development), **Cheryl Olson** (motivation), **Ruth Polak** (statistics appendix), **Marc Shulz** (abnormal psychology), **Maria Stone** (attention), **Peter Todd** (evolutionary psychology and connectionism), and **Amanda Woodward** (language development).

Advice on new developments in their areas of specialization came from **Kent Harber** (emotions), **Forest Jourdan** (self-efficacy theory), **Angeline Lilliard** (cognitive development), and **Delia Cioffi** (social perception). Organizing references into a coherent bibliography was the much appreciated effort of **Alissa Crovetti, Lunn Lestina, Rose McDermott,** and **Peter Myers. Lyle Brenner** gets credit for helping to organize the Glossary.

From the publisher came an unbridled enthusiasm for making this edition of *Psychology and Life* the best ever. Everyone who had anything to do with the project treated it as if it were a new book that was destined to be a winner. They gave it all the care and sensitive development that is lavished on first editions. **Susan Driscoll,** Vice President and Editor-in-Chief of Behavioral and Social Sciences at the time and, most recently, HarperCollins' new Director of Marketing, set the tone by her total commitment to providing the finest staff and insisting on the highest production values for this new HarperCollins edition of *Psychology and Life.* **Anne Harvey** skillfully orchestrated the many stages, elements, and personnel involved in producing such an imposing product. Credit for the lovely new look goes to Production Manager **Michael Weinstein,** to designer **Kathy Horning,** and to picture editors **Cheryl Kycharzak** and **Carol Parden. Leslie Hawke** perceptively choreographed all the components of the ancillary package into a viable educational program that will facilitate the teaching and learning of psychology. To **Otis Taylor,** Marketing Manager, goes appreciation for all the creativity he has invested in promoting and marketing the book.

The decision to treat this edition of *Psychology and Life* as a new book meant that it underwent extensive developmental editing. I was blessed by being able to work closely with a marvelous editor, **Becky Kohn.** She focused her critical vision on improving the chapter structure, the organization and flow of ideas, and the clarity of style that I hope comes through to the reader. **Sarah Lane** was supposed to be just a copyeditor. However, she added another level of deep editing. Never having taken a psychology course, she was able to bring to the manuscript a fresh perspective that insisted on more examples, clearer definitions, and simpler explanations. I thank them both for their contributions.

Finally, I was aided and abetted throughout this project by the sage advice and wise reviews of colleagues and teachers from all parts of the country. They identified what was good in the previous edition and needed to be retained, what had to go, and what had to be added. I thank each of them, hoping they will recognize how their input has improved my output. Special thanks go to my friend, colleague, and wife, **Christina Maslach,** for always being there when I needed her throughout this long revision process. The reviewers are thanked in alphabetical order:

Mary Alguire, University of Arkansas
Emir Andrews, St. Johns University, Newfoundland
Galen L. Baril, University of Scranton
Ilene Bernstein, University of Washington
Bruce M. Bonger, College of the Holy Cross
Richard W. Bowen, Loyola University, Chicago
Charles L. Brewer, Furman University
Marvin Brown, University of Saskatchewan

Randy Caldwell, San Jose State University
Dennis Cogan, Texas Tech University
Thomas B. Collins, Mankato State University
Imma Curiel, University of Maryland, Baltimore County
Debra J. Elliott, Ohio State University
Roberta A. Eveslage, Johnson County Community College
John L. Fletcher, Southwest Texas State University
Sally A. Frutiger, Denison University
Grace Galliano, Kennesaw State College
Claudia Graham, Wake Technical Community College
Gary Greenberg, Wichita State University
Richard A. Griggs, University of Florida, Gainesville
Lawrence Grimm, University of Illinois, Chicago
Peter Hanford, Indiana University-Purdue University at Indianapolis
Jake W. Jacobs, University of Arizona
Mary L. Jasnoski, George Washington University
Ginny Jelinek, Ohio State University
Carl Johnson, Central Michigan University
Richard A. Kasschau, University of Houston
Mark Koppel, Montclair State College
John Kounios, Tufts University
T. C. Lewandowski, Delaware County Community College
Colin M. MacLeod, University of Toronto, Scarborough
William A. McCormack, San Jose State University
Jerry McCullough, Lenoir Community College
Elizabeth C. McDonel, Indiana University-Purdue University at Indianapolis
Robert W. Newby, Tarleton State University
Thomas Obriemski, University of Denver
Dan Perkins, Richland College
Margaret Philip, Mankato State University
Scott Plous, Wesleyan University
S. Jack Rachman, The University of British Columbia
Franklyn M. Rother, Brookdale Community College
Robert Solso, University of Nevada
David A. Schroeder, University of Arkansas
Marvin W. Schwartz, University of Cincinnati
Colin Silverthorne, University of San Francisco
James R. Speer, Stephen F. Austin State University
Toni L. Strand, Stetson University
Curtis Thomsen, Jersey City State College
Lee Van Scyoc, University of Wisconsin
Roc E. Walley, University of Alberta

Ann Weber, University of North Carolina, Asheville
Linda J. Weldon, Essex Community College
John R. Williams, Westchester Community College
Karen B. Williams, Illinois State University
William H. Zachry, University of Tennessee

Many thanks,

 ## TO THE STUDENT

You are about to embark on an intellectual journey through the many areas of modern psychology, but, before you start out, I want to share with you some important information that will help guide your adventures. The *journey* is a metaphor used throughout **Psychology and Life.** Your teacher serves as the tour director, the text as your tour book, and I, its author, as your local tour guide. The goal of this journey is for you to discover what is known about the most incredible phenomena in the entire universe: the brain, the human mind, and the behavior of all living creatures. Psychology is about understanding the seemingly mysterious processes that give rise to our thoughts, feelings, and actions.

The following pages offer general ideas and specific tips on how to use this book to get the quality grade you deserve for your performance and to get the most from your introduction to psychology.

STUDY STRATEGIES

1. *Set aside sufficient time* for your reading assignments and review of class notes. This text contains much new technical information, many principles to learn, and a whole new glossary of terms that you will have to memorize. To master this material, you will need at least three hours reading time per chapter.

2. *Keep a record of your study time* for this course. Plot the number of hours (in half-hour intervals) you study at each reading session. Chart your time investment on a cumulative graph on which you add each new study time to the previous total on the left-hand axis of the graph and each study session on the base line axis. The chart will provide visual feedback of your progress and show you when you have not been hitting the books as you should.

3. *Be active and space your studying*. Optimal learning occurs when the learner is actively involved with the learning materials. That means reading attentively, listening to lectures mindfully, paraphrasing in your own words what you are reading or hearing, and taking good notes. For the text, underline key sections, write notes to yourself in the margins, and also summarize points that you think might be included on class tests. Research in psychology tells us that it is best to space out your study, doing it regularly rather than cramming just before tests. If you let yourself fall behind, it will be difficult to catch up with all the information in introductory psychology at last minute panic time.

4. *Get study-centered*. Find a place with minimal distractions for studying. Reserve that place for studying, reading, and writing course assignments—and do nothing else there. The place will come to be associated with study activities and you will thus find it easier to work whenever you are seated at your study center.

5. *Encode reading for future testing*. Unlike reading magazines and watching television (which you do usually for their immediate impact), reading textbooks demands that you process the material in a special way. You must continually put the information into a suitable form (encode it) that will enable you to retrieve it when you are asked about it later on class examinations. Encoding means that you summarize key points, rehearse sections (sometimes aloud), and ask questions you want to be able to answer about the contents of a given section of a chapter as you read. You should also take the teacher's perspective, anticipating the kinds of questions she or he is likely to ask, and then make sure you can answer them. Find out the form of the test you will be given in this course—essay, fill in, multiple choice, or true-false. That form will affect the extent to which you focus on the big ideas and on details. Essays and fill-ins ask for *recall*-type memory, while multiple-choice and true-false tests ask for *recognition*-type memory. (Ask the teacher for a sample test to give you a better idea of the kinds of questions for which you need to prepare.)

STUDY TACTICS

1. *Review the outline of the chapter*. It shows you the main topics to be covered, their sequence, and their relationship, giving you an overview of what is to come. The outline at the start of each chapter contains first-level and second-level headings of the major topics. The outline of all the chapters in the Table of Contents at the start of the book also includes the more detailed third- and fourth-level headings. The section headings indicate the structure of the chapter, and they are also

convenient break points, or time-outs, for each of your study periods.

2. *Jump to the end of the chapter to read the Recapping Main Points section.* There you will find the main ideas of the chapter organized under each of the first-level headings, which will give you a clearer sense of what the chapter will be covering.

3. *Skim through the chapter* to get the gist of its contents. Don't stop, don't take notes, and read it as quickly as you can (one hour maximum time allowed).

4. *Finally, dig in* and master the material by actively reading, underlining, taking notes, questioning, rehearsing, and paraphrasing as you go (two hours minimum time expected).

SPECIAL FEATURES TO NOTICE

1. The Opening Cases that start each chapter were written to grab and focus your attention. They present a wide range of vivid, personalized material about people in different types of behavior settings. Each opener illustrates a central theme of the chapter and is typically referred to during the course of the chapter.

2. Interim summaries, Summing Ups, review the key points that you should know in the preceding first-level heading. The final first-level heading does not have its own summary because it is followed by the summary for the entire chapter.

3. Key Terms and Major Contributors are highlighted within the chapter in **boldface type** so they will stand out for you to notice. They are also gathered alphabetically at the end of each chapter along with the page numbers on which they are defined or featured. In addition, all important psychological terms are listed alphabetically at the end of the book and defined in the Glossary, again with the page numbers so you can locate them readily. Any word in boldface type is likely to be test material.

4. The Subject Index and Name Index, appearing at the end of the text, provide you with an alphabetized listing of all terms, subject matter, and people's names that were cited in the text, along with their page citations.

5. The References section, also at the end of the text, presents some bibliographic information on every book, journal article, or media source used to document some point made in the text. It gives you a valuable resource in case you wish to find out more about some topic for a term paper in this or another course or just for your personal interest. A name and date set off by parentheses in text—(Zimbardo, 1992)—identifies the source and publication date of the citation. You will then find the full source information in the References section. Citations with more than two authors list the senior author followed by *et al.*

6. Finally, your study and test performance is likely to be enhanced by using the *Student Study Guide and Practice Tests* that accompanies **Psychology and Life.** It was prepared to give students a boost in studying more efficiently and taking tests more effectively. The study guide contains helpful tips from the senior author—Dr. Grace Galliano—for mastering each chapter, sample practice tests and answers, a guide to each of the video programs, and interesting experiments and demonstrations.

So, there you have it—helpful hints to increase your enjoyment of this special course and to help you get the most out of whatever you put into it.

I value the opportunity your teacher has provided in selecting *Psychology and Life.* You will find it a sourcebook of valuable knowledge about a wide range of topics. Many students have reported that *Psychology and Life* has proven to be an excellent reference manual for term papers and projects in other courses as well. You might consider keeping it in your personal library of valuable resources. However, we must begin at the beginning, with the first steps in our journey.

Phil Zimbardo

Chapter 1

Probing the
Mysteries
of
Mind and Behavior

PSYCHOLOGY: DEFINITIONS, GOALS, AND TASKS 2
  DEFINITIONS
  TIES TO OTHER DISCIPLINES
  LEVELS OF ANALYSIS
  THE GOALS OF PSYCHOLOGY
  WHAT PSYCHOLOGISTS DO: TASKS, SETTINGS, AND ROLES

  INTERIM SUMMARY

PSYCHOLOGY'S HISTORICAL FOUNDATIONS 11
  STRUCTURALISM: THE CONTENTS OF THE MIND
  FUNCTIONALISM: MINDS WITH A PURPOSE
  EVOLUTIONISM: NATURAL SELECTION OF SPECIES

  INTERIM SUMMARY

CURRENT PSYCHOLOGICAL PERSPECTIVES 14
  BIOLOGICAL APPROACH
  PSYCHODYNAMIC APPROACH
  BEHAVIORISTIC APPROACH
  COGNITIVE APPROACH

  HUMANISTIC APPROACH
  EVOLUTIONARY APPROACH
  COMPARING PERSPECTIVES: FOCUS ON AGGRESSION

  INTERIM SUMMARY

LOOKING AHEAD 21

  CLOSE-UP: CROSS-CULTURAL PERSPECTIVES ON CONTROLLING NATURE

RECAPPING MAIN POINTS 24

KEY TERMS 25

MAJOR CONTRIBUTORS 25

As the runners lined up to start the 1986 NCAA 10,000-meter championship, Kathy O. was the odds-on favorite. She had broken high-school track records in three distances and recently set a new American collegiate record for the 10,000-meter race. Her parents, who were always supportive fans, watched from the sidelines. Kathy got off to a slow start, but was only a few paces behind the leaders. Her fans knew she could soon catch up. But this time Kathy didn't bolt to the lead as she had done before. Instead, she veered away from the other runners. Without breaking her stride, she ran off the track, scaled a 7-foot fence, raced down a side street, and jumped off a 50-foot bridge. Ten minutes later, her coach found her on the concrete flood plain of the White River. She had two broken ribs, a punctured lung, and was paralyzed from the waist down. Not only would she never run again, she might never walk again.

What happened to Kathy? Why did she quit the race and nearly self-destruct? As a star athlete and premed student on the Dean's list, she had everything going for her. She had been valedictorian of her high-school class. Teachers and coaches described her as sweet, sensible, diligent, courteous, and religious. Nobody understood her behavior. It didn't make sense.

Kathy's father thought the tragedy "had something to do with the pressure that is put on young people to succeed." Teammates felt the pressure may have come from within Kathy herself. "She was a perfectionist," said one of them. Determined to excel at everything, Kathy had studied relentlessly, even during team workouts.

How did Kathy explain her actions? She told an interviewer that she was overcome by the terrifying fear of failure as she began falling behind in the race. "All of a sudden . . . I just felt like something snapped inside of me." She felt angry and persecuted. These negative reactions were new to Kathy, and made her feel as if she were someone else. "I just wanted to run

away," she recalled. "I don't see how I climbed that fence. . . . I just don't feel like that person was me. I know that sounds strange, but I was just out of control. . . . I was watching everything that was happening and I couldn't stop" (UPI, 12/22/86).

The case of Kathy O. raises fascinating questions for psychology. Personality, social, and developmental psychologists might ask how athletic ability, intelligence, parental support, competition, motivation to achieve, and personality traits combined to make Kathy a superstar in the first place. Clinical psychologists would want to know why something "snapped" inside Kathy at this race, why feelings of anger were so foreign to her, and why she felt persecuted. Those who study the nature of consciousness would try to understand Kathy's perception that she was outside herself, unable to stop her flight toward death. Health psychologists and those who work in the area of sports psychology might try to identify signs of stress and clues in earlier behaviors that could have signaled an impending breakdown. Psychologists who emphasize the biological basis of behavior might consider the role of brain and hormonal factors in her sudden, abnormal reaction. Are there any circumstances under which *you* might quit as Kathy O. did?

We may never completely understand what motivated Kathy's behavior, but psychology provides the tools—research methods—and the scaffolding—theories about the causes of behavior—for exploring basic questions about who we are and why we think, feel, and act as we do. Psychologists are challenged to make sense of cases such as this one that violate ordinary conceptions about human nature. Their motivation is not only intellectual curiosity, but a desire to discover how to help people in ways that might prevent such tragedies in the future.

I want to welcome you to the start of our exciting journey into the realms of the human mind. There are many paths that we must travel to understand "the nature of human nature." We will journey through the inner spaces of brain and mind and the outer dimensions of human behavior. Between those extremes, we shall investigate things that you take for granted, such as how you perceive your world, communicate, learn, think, remember, and even sleep. But we will also detour to try to understand how and why we dream, fall in love, feel shy, act aggressively, and become mentally ill.

Psychology holds the key to a general understanding of how human beings function. While you are discovering what psychologists know about people in general, you can apply that knowledge to change your own behavior, as well as that of other people, for the better. As we progress, you should begin to appreciate more fully how remarkably gifted you are in having at your command so many abilities and skills and you will begin to take even greater control over aspects of your life. Ideally, you will also perceive ways to change society. Many of the urgent issues of our time—global ecological destruction, drug addiction, urban crime, prejudice—benefit from a psychological perspective.

The first goal of *Psychology and Life* is to provide a comprehensive survey of what psychologists have discovered about the workings of the brain, mind, and behavior. The second goal is to show how that knowledge is applied in our everyday lives, and how it can be used wisely to enhance many aspects of the human condition.

The appeal of psychology for me personally has continued to grow over the more than 30 years that I have been an educator and researcher. In recent years there has been a virtual explosion in new information about the basic mechanisms that govern mental and behavioral processes. As new ideas replace or modify old ideas, I am continually intrigued and challenged by the many fascinating pieces of the puzzle of human nature. I hope that by the end of our journey, if you put in the time and effort necessary to qualify as a novice

psychologist, you too will discover the fascination of "people watching." Maybe you will also accept the role of being a source of psychological knowledge, and even comfort, to others.

Foremost in our journey will be a scientific quest for understanding. We shall inquire about the how, what, when, and why of human behavior and about the causes and consequences of behaviors observed in ourselves, other people, and animals, too. We want to know why we think, feel, and behave as we do. What makes each of us uniquely different from all other people? Yet why do we often behave so alike in some situations? Are we molded by heredity, or are we shaped more by personal experiences? How can aggression and altruism, love and hate, and madness and creativity exist side by side in this most complex of creatures—the human animal?

One of America's great writers, Ralph Waldo Emerson, reminds us:

> All persons are puzzles until
> at last we find in some word or
> act the key to the man, to the
> woman: straightway all their past
> words and actions lie in light
> before us.

 ## PSYCHOLOGY: DEFINITIONS, GOALS, AND TASKS

This section will look at some formal definitions of psychology and establish what psychology is all about. We will see how psychology compares to other disciplines that analyze behavior, the brain, and the mind. Then we will preview the five general goals that guide the research and practice of professional psychologists. Finally, we will examine the kinds of tasks that psychologists engage in, the various roles they play, and the settings in which they work.

DEFINITIONS

Psychology is formally defined as the scientific study of the behavior of individuals and their mental processes. Many psychologists seek answers to the fundamental question: What is the nature of human nature? Psychology answers this question by looking at processes that occur within individuals as well as within the physical and social environment. Before considering how psychology is linked to other fields of knowledge, let's examine each part of the definition of psychology—*scientific, behavior, individual, mental.* The *scientific* aspect of psychology requires psychological conclusions to be based on evidence collected following the principles of the scientific method.

The **scientific method** consists of a set of orderly steps used to analyze and solve problems. This method also uses objectively collected information as the factual basis for drawing conclusions. Scientific method relies on *empirical evidence*—data gathered directly by the senses of the observer. Authority and personal beliefs don't determine whether something is true or accepted, but the unbiased methods used to make observations, collect data, and formulate conclusions do verify information. We will elaborate the features of the scientific method more fully in the next chapter when we consider how psychologists conduct their research.

Behavior is the means by which organisms adjust to their environment. Behavior is action. The subject matter of psychology is largely the observable behavior of humans and other species of animals. Smiling, crying, running, hitting, talking, and touching are some obvious examples of behavior we can observe. Psychologists observe how an individual functions, what the individual does, and how the individual goes about doing it within a given behavioral setting and social context. Sociologists study the behavior of people in groups or institutions, while anthropologists focus on the broader context of behavior in different cultures.

The subject of psychological analysis is usually an *individual*—a newborn infant, a teenage athlete, a college student adjusting to life in a dormitory, a man in a mid-life crisis, or a grandmother coping with the stress of raising the "crack baby" of her unmarried, adolescent daughter. However, the subject might also be a chimpanzee learning to use symbols to communicate, a white rat navigating a maze, a hungry pigeon learning to peck a button to deliver food, or a sea slug responding to a danger signal. An individual might be studied in its natural habitat, or in the controlled conditions of a research laboratory. In recent years, researchers have even been studying computer simulations of animal behavior.

The emphasis on studying individual behavior, on investigating observable actions and reactions of organisms, came about as American psychologists in the beginning of this century broke away from earlier traditions. As the field of psychology has matured, it has become clear that we cannot understand human actions without also understanding *mental processes,* the workings of the human mind. Much human activity takes place as private, internal events—thinking, planning, reasoning, creating, and dreaming. Many psychologists believe that mental processes represent the most important aspect of psychological inquiry. Psychological investigators have devised new techniques to study such mental events and processes, as we shall soon see.

TIES TO OTHER DISCIPLINES

Psychology is unique because of its ties with so many different areas of knowledge. It is a social science, a behavioral science, a brain science, a cognitive science, and also a health science. As one of the *social sciences,* psychology draws from economics, political science, sociology, and cultural anthropology. Because it systematically analyzes behavior along with its causes and consequences, psychology is a *behavioral science.* Psychologists share many interests with researchers in *biological sciences,* especially with those who study brain processes and the biochemical bases of behavior. As part of the emerging area of *cognitive science,* psychologists' questions about how the human mind works are related to research and theory in computer science, artificial intelligence, and applied mathematics. As a *health science*—with links to medicine, education, law, and environmental studies—psychology seeks to improve the quality of our individual and collective well-being. Psychology also retains ties to philosophy and areas in the humanities and the arts, such as literature, drama, and religion.

While the remarkable breadth and depth of modern psychology is a source of delight to those who become psychologists, it is often what makes the field a difficult challenge to the student exploring it for the first time. There is so much more to the study of psychology than one expects initially, and there will be so much of value that you can take away from this introduction to psychology.

LEVELS OF ANALYSIS

To investigate an individual's behavior, researchers may use different *levels of analysis*—from the broadest, most global level down to the most minute, specific level. We can compare the broad level to a photograph of a family. In the photograph, we can focus on one individual and even on one feature of that person. Then we can examine even finer details of that feature—for example, we can focus on the pupil of an eye. Similarly, at the broadest level of psychological analysis, researchers investigate the behavior of the whole person within complex social and cultural contexts. This level is the macroscopic or *macro level of analysis* (also known as the *molar level*). On this macro level, for example, researchers may study cross-cultural differences in behavior, violence and terrorism, worker morale and productivity, the origins of prejudice, and symptoms of mental illness. At the next level, the *molecular level of analysis,* many psychologists focus on more narrow, finer units of behavior, such as speed of reacting to a stimulus, eye movements during reading, grammatical errors made by children acquiring language, and hormonal changes during sexual arousal. Researchers can study even smaller units of behavior. At the third level, the microscopic or *micro level of analysis,* researchers work to discover the biological bases of behavior by trying to identify the places in the brain where different types of memories are stored, the biochemical changes that occur during learning, and the sensory paths responsible for vision or hearing. There are no clear boundaries between these three levels of analysis; the differences involve the size and complexity of the units studied. None is better than the others; each yields important information essential for the final composite portrait of human nature that psychologists hope to develop ultimately.

THE GOALS OF PSYCHOLOGY

The goals of the psychologist conducting basic research are to describe, explain, predict, and control behavior. The applied psychologist has a fifth goal—to improve the quality of human life. These goals form the basis of the psychological enterprise. What is involved in trying to achieve each of them?

Describing What Happens

The first task in psychology is to observe behavior carefully and to describe it objectively. Collecting the facts as they exist, and not as one would expect or personally hope they would be, is of utmost importance. This method sounds easy, but because every observer has personal biases, prejudices, and expectations, it is difficult to prevent subjectivity from creeping in and distorting the data.

Data are reports of observations (*data* is the plural, *datum* the singular). **Behavioral data** are reports of observations about the behavior of organisms and the conditions under which the behavior occurs or changes. The specific behavior that is being observed and measured is termed the *response*. A response is triggered by

an environmental condition known as a *stimulus* (the plural of *stimulus* is *stimuli*). Imagine, for example, that you are collecting behavioral data on a baby. You might observe that the baby exhibits a particular response, crying, to the stimulus of a loud noise.

Some stimuli originate in the external environment as sources of physical energy that are detected and responded to by our sense receptors. Other stimuli, such as hormonal changes, creative thoughts, and sexual fantasies, come from within the organism.

Psychologists look for consistent, reliable relationships between stimuli and responses—for example, noise level and study habits. They also look for relationships between sets of particular responses such as having the personality trait of generosity and contributing to charity. Psychologists identify and study these relationships to understand something about the person or organism making the response or about the underlying process that causes or relates responses and stimuli.

Because of our prior experiences, both personal and cultural, we often see in data what we *expect* to see. Consider how sex-typed expectations alter the way American parents perceive their children.

When parents of newborn infants (less than 24 hours old) were asked to describe their babies, they gave very different descriptions depending on the baby's sex. Compared to sons, daughters were rated softer, smaller, weaker, more delicate, and more awkward. Objective measures were then made of the infant's weight, length, state of health, and other attributes relevant to the subjective descriptions. According to these objective criteria, there were no actual differences between the boys and the girls (Rubin et al., 1974).

Within 24 hours of a child's birth, the parents have already begun to see in the child "what is expected to be," not necessarily "what is." Much of what has been found in research about the sexist distortions of reality holds true in studies about the racist distortions of reality as well. We find ways to distort what others do in order to make their actions conform to our beliefs and prejudices.

College students viewed a videotape of two men working on a task. The tape was interrupted after one man shoved the other man. The shove was described as "playful" or "dramatic" by most of the subjects who viewed a white man shove a black man. The identical action was described as "violent" or "aggressive" by most of the subjects who viewed the second tape where a black man shoved a white man (Duncan, 1976).

Even professional observers may fall prey to this tendency to let their perspectives prevent objective observation. However, two procedures help them maintain objectivity. The first safeguard requires that observations be made under carefully controlled and clearly described conditions so that other researchers may repeat the conditions of the experiment. The second requires precise, unambiguous definitions of responses and stimuli so that behavioral data are described, measured, and reported in a consistent fashion. This practice also allows independent observers to repeat the experiment and provides a common basis for understanding the results.

Describing events objectively is not as simple as you might think. For example, how would you describe the action in the photo of the couple? In an objective description you would note gestures, facial expressions, objects, people, and actions being performed. But if you say that a person is showing anger, fear, arrogance, or timidity, you are inferring inner states, not simply describing behavior that you can see. Your descriptions of behavior—your data—can include only external features that can be perceived equally by all, such as what a person said, what movements were made, what score a person got, or how many people indicated agreement with a decision. In objective description, the key is to avoid making inferences about traits and attributes that cannot be seen directly.

Explaining What Happens

While *descriptions* must stick to perceivable information, *explanations* deliberately go beyond what can be observed impartially. We began this chapter by asking for an explanation for why Kathy O. quit the race and nearly destroyed her life. Fans of mystery stories, after figuring out who did it, want to understand the reason why.

In many areas of psychology, the central goal is to find regular patterns in behavioral and mental processes. Psychologists want to discover "how behavior works." Why do we laugh at situations that differ from our expectations of what is coming next? What conditions could lead someone to attempt suicide or commit rape? Understanding such behaviors involves finding out how certain stimuli cause observed responses and discovering relationships between sets of responses. For example, researchers might investigate the links between depression, lack of social support, and suicide. Sometimes this understanding comes from careful observation of many different instances of a phenomena. Master detective Sherlock Holmes made shrewd deductions from scraps of evidence, and Sigmund Freud brilliantly explained irrational behaviors,

An objective description of behavior includes only external features that others can perceive. You could not say whether this couple is happy or sad without making an inference about an inner state.

such as slips of the tongue, after carefully observing many details and their behavioral context.

Correct explanations may also come from research that systematically evaluates alternative views about a psychological event. For example, psychologists might study the conditions under which rewarding an individual's behavior leads to positive change in learning but also has negative effects on learning. However, there is no better path to understanding than that of *informed imagination*, which creatively synthesizes what is known and what is not yet known. A well-trained psychologist can explain observations by using his or her insight into the human experience, along with knowledge of what researchers have uncovered about the phenomenon in question. Sometimes researchers make an *inference*—a logical or reasonable judgment not based on direct observation—about a process that is happening inside an organism. That inferred process helps to make the observed behavior more understandable. Psychologists make inferences about **intervening variables**—inner, unseen conditions that are assumed to function within organisms. These variables may be physiological conditions, such as hunger, or psychological processes, such as fear or creativity. Psychologists conceive of intervening variables to link observable stimulus input with measurable response output.

Suppose your teacher says that to earn a good grade each student must participate regularly in class discussions. Your roommate who is always well prepared for class never raises his hand to answer questions or volunteer information. The teacher chides him for being unmotivated and assumes he is not bright. That same roommate also goes to dances but never asks anyone to dance, doesn't openly defend his point of view when it is challenged by someone less informed, and rarely engages in small talk at the dinner table. What is your diagnosis? What intervening variable might account for this range of responses to this variety of stimuli? How about *shyness?* Like many other people who suffer from intense feelings of shyness, your roommate is unable to behave in desired ways (Cheek, 1989; Zimbardo, 1990). Note that intervening variables are not *interfering variables,* as some students often mistakenly think. Intervening variables play an important role in the process of trying to explain patterns of behavior. An interfering variable is an extraneous variable that distorts or confuses the relationship between the variables being studied, such as noise outside the laboratory when animals are being tested.

Psychological explanations often center on sources of motivation that might account for observed behavior. For example, one explanation for Kathy O.'s behavior may be that a cumulative buildup of pressures to achieve and succeed led her to believe that anything less than perfection was failure. For Kathy, winning was everything. When she thought she was losing the race, she felt frustrated, ashamed, and her self-image declined. Running away from the scene of her perceived failure and attempting to kill herself might have been mindless reactions to these overpowering emotions and motivations. A very different explanation could be generated from a biological perspective. For example, perhaps Kathy was suffering from an undetected physical problem such as a brain tumor.

Any proposed explanation depends on one's perspective and available evidence, but the proposition needs to be validated against systematically collected data that support it or disconfirm alternative explanations. We will see that much psychological research attempts to determine which of several explanations most accurately accounts for a given behavioral pattern.

Predicting What Will Happen

Predictions in psychology are statements about the likelihood that a certain behavior will occur or that a given relationship will be found. While some psychologists believe that explaining a relationship is the primary goal of their field, others argue that psychological study should go further and predict the conditions under which a given behavior will appear or change. These others assert that you cannot be sure your explanation is correct unless you can use it to predict what will happen or what will make it change. When different explanations are put forward to account for some behavior or relationship, they are usually judged by

how well they can make accurate and comprehensive predictions.

Because our well-being and even our survival depend on making accurate predictions about situations that could be dangerous or favorable, we strive to make and find reliable predictions. One form of prediction relies on oracles, astrology, or revelations of presumably gifted people known as psychics or fortune-tellers. However, when this type of prediction is evaluated by statistical analysis, it turns out to be as accurate as random guesses. Of course, many such predictions cannot be proven true or false because they are stated in general and vague terms. Scientific predictions must be worded precisely enough to enable them to be tested and disconfirmed if the evidence is not supportive. A *scientific prediction* is based upon an understanding of the ways events relate to each other, and it suggests what mechanisms link those events to certain predictors. Scientific predictions can then account for changes in situations.

A more common form of prediction than fortune-telling involves applying information about past reactions or events to future situations. Knowing how people behaved in the past—if their behavior was constant—is a good indicator of how they will continue to behave in the future. Often the best source of prediction about behavior in a future situation is information about the behavior of similar people who were in that situation before. This knowledge is known as the base rate prediction. A **base rate** is a statistic that identifies the normal frequency, or probability, of a given event.

When trying to make a prediction about what you are likely to do in a new situation, the base rate is your best bet. For example, what would you do if an authority figure ordered you to deliver an intense electric shock to a nice, middle-aged man? Because you probably have never been in such a situation, you cannot be sure. However, suppose you found out that in an experiment in which this situation actually occurred, two thirds of the participants blindly complied with the instructions (Milgram, 1974)? Now what is your prediction about your own behavior? Although you may be reluctant to acknowledge it, you probably would respond to the special pressures in that situation just as the majority did. In this case, because you cannot predict your behavior based on prior experience, the base rate is the best predictor.

Auto insurance companies use statistical probability to make predictions about how likely it is for members of a certain age group to have accidents. College admissions staff, examining applicants' SAT scores, use statistical probability to predict success in college. Statistics are also helpful to opinion pollsters for predicting election results.

Predictions in psychology also usually recognize that most behavior is influenced by a combination of factors. Some factors operate within the individual, such as genetic makeup, motivation, intelligence level, or self-esteem. These inner determinants of behavior are called **organismic variables;** they tell us something special about the organism. In the case of humans, these determinants are known as **dispositional variables.** Some factors, however, operate externally. Suppose, for example, that someone starts taking drugs because of the pressure of gang members, or that a child tries to please a teacher in order to win a prize, or that a motorist trapped in a traffic jam gets frustrated and hostile. These behaviors are largely influenced by events outside of the person. External influences on behavior are known as **environmental** or **situational variables.**

A *causal prediction* in psychology specifies that some behavior will be changed by the influence of a given stimulus variable. For example, the presence of a stranger is a stimulus that reliably causes human and monkey babies, beyond a certain age, to respond with signs of anxiety. Changes in the observed behavior then are dependent upon variations in the nature of the stimulus, such as the extent of strangeness. Would there be fewer signs of anxiety in a human or monkey baby if the stranger were also a baby rather than an adult, or if the stranger were of the same rather than of a different species? A researcher could manipulate such variations in stimulus conditions and observe their influence on the subject's response. The stimulus condition whose values are free to vary independently of any other variable in the situation is known as the **independent variable.** Any variable whose values are the results of changes in one or more independent variables is known as a **dependent variable.** The independent variable is the *predictor* while the dependent variable is the *predicted response.* Typically, this situation, in which a stimulus causes a response, is known as an $S \rightarrow R$ relationship.

However, often predictions do not specify causation—for example, when your college grades are predicted from your SAT scores. In such cases, where variables are merely associated, the independent variable is still the predictor in the correlation with another response; typically, this is known as an $R = R$ relationship.

Controlling What Happens

For many psychologists, control is the central, most powerful goal. Control means making behavior happen or not happen—starting it, maintaining it, stopping it, and influencing its form, strength, or rate of occurrence. A causal explanation of behavior is convincing if it can

create conditions under which the behavior can be controlled.

Consider smoking as an example. Smoking is a major risk factor in heart disease, cancer, and other illnesses. How does a smoker who wants to live a long, healthy life go about the behavioral task of quitting? Surveys show that the majority of adult smokers in the United States would like to quit, and that many have tried but have failed to kick their addiction. Are they suffering from a lack of "willpower"? Is the nicotine so addictive that withdrawing from it is painful enough to overcome the best of intentions to quit? These explanations are countered by evidence from the Stanford Heart Disease Prevention Program which outlines a plan for smokers to take self-directed control of their smoking behavior (Farquhar, 1978). The plan acknowledges that smoking is a complex behavior controlled by oral satisfaction and nicotine effects. However, the plan also recognizes that people's attitude that smoking is macho or sexy—an attitude developed from pleasurable experiences or from observations of media smoking ads—contributes to the habit. Each factor that contributes to smoking then must be recognized and met by an opposing factor in order for the individual to overcome the habit.

The ability to control behavior is important not only because it validates scientific explanations, but also because it gives psychologists ways of helping people improve their lives. In this respect, psychologists are a rather optimistic group; many believe that virtually any undesired behavior pattern can be modified by the proper *intervention.* Such attempts at control are at the heart of all programs of psychological treatment or therapy.

Serious *ethical issues* can arise, however, when anyone tries to control another person's behavior. Not too long ago, psychotherapists attempted to "cure" homosexual men of their alleged sickness by applying extreme forms of aversive behavior modification. That "treatment" stopped once the scientifically accepted conception of homosexuality was changed from one of sexual *deviance* to one of sexual *preference.* The point is that, until recently, therapists with the best of intentions were intervening in the lives of gay men in ways that now would be considered unethical, if not illegal.

It is interesting to note that understanding—rather than control—tends to be the ultimate goal of psychologists in many Asian and African countries (Nobles, 1972). Critics have argued that the focus on control in western brands of psychology represents a cultural bias dominated by perspectives that emerged from industrialization and colonialism of Europeans, and the mentality of conquest of the frontier in the United States. The control focus of Western psychology has also been depicted more typically as a male perspective that would not have dominated were women more prominent in the development of psychology (Bornstein & Quina, 1988).

Improving the Quality of Life

Many of the findings of psychology are applied to solve human problems. Using psychological knowledge to help improve the quality of people's lives and aid society to function more effectively are the final goals of psychology. Psychology enriches life in profound ways that shape many fundamental ideas and perspectives underlying so-called common sense knowledge. For example, teachers now routinely use positive rewards and incentives rather than punishment and ridicule to motivate their students. In fact, the principle of reinforcement to produce desirable behavioral consequences came from laboratory research on animal learning! Today's parents are more likely to touch, provide intellectual stimulation, and encourage playfulness in their children than parents of earlier generations. The long-term positive effects of such modes of parenting have been documented by psychologists studying human development. Social psychologists in the United States who established principles of group dynamics have contributed in part to the success of Japanese industry. The Japanese workplace has been designed to recognize workers' needs for self-esteem, for sharing in decision making with management, and for taking pride in the product of their labors by working in small supportive groups. Ironically, the Japanese are now importing those ideas back to American businesses, which have been traditionally organized on a model that stresses individual achievement.

WHAT PSYCHOLOGISTS DO: TASKS, SETTINGS, AND ROLES

What is your image of a typical psychologist? What kind of work do psychologists do, and where do they do it? Based on what you have seen on television or read in the media, you may envision a therapist who works in his or her private office treating patients with mental problems. You may label that person a *psychiatrist,* a *psychoanalyst,* or even a *shrink.* But the kinds of tasks that psychologists engage in are much broader than therapy. The roles they play and the settings in which they work are remarkably varied. In this section, we will briefly describe their fields of specialization.

First, some basic distinctions are in order. **Psychiatrists** are medical specialists, with M.D. degrees. They primarily treat people with mental illnesses and work in private practices, clinics, or mental hospitals. They also engage in research to better understand

the nature and treatment of mental illness. Of the many professionals concerned with helping those suffering from mental problems, only psychiatrists can prescribe medication or treatments involving physical-biological methods, such as the use of electroshock therapy for extreme forms of depression. **Clinical psychologists** also treat people with behavior disorders, either in private practices or in clinics and hospitals. Their graduate-level training in psychology earns them a Ph.D. degree. Usually they have a broader background in psychology than psychiatrists do. Clinical psychologists conduct the psychological testing and evaluation for mental hospitals, clinics, schools, courts, and other human services. **Psychoanalysts** are therapists, either psychiatrists or clinical psychologists, with additional specialized training in the principles of psychoanalysis developed by Sigmund Freud and his followers. We will study those principles in our final chapter devoted to psychotherapy.

There are close to 300,000 psychologists worldwide, and one-third of them work in the United States alone. Although the percentage of psychologists in the population is greatest in Western industrialized nations, there is currently a revival or new interest in psychology in many countries—notably in Eastern Europe and China (Rosenzweig, 1984a). As psychology continues to contribute to the scientific and human enterprise, more young people are being drawn to it as a career. The American Psychological Association (APA) is one of the largest professional associations for psychologists, with about 68,320 members as of 1989. The recently formed American Psychological Society (APS) focuses more on scientific aspects of psychology and less on the clinical, treatment side of psychology.

Professional Work Settings

The largest percentage of psychologists (43 percent) work in academic settings (universities, colleges, and medical schools). Nearly one-fourth of psychologists work in a variety of public facilities such as hospitals, clinics, and mental health and counseling centers. As **Figure 1.1** shows, the principal employment setting for many psychologists is business, industry, government, or research. Those in private practice mainly treat patients in their offices or conduct personal consulting services for a variety of clients, such as law firms or marketing and advertising agencies.

Professional Roles

When we look at the areas in which psychologists specialize, as shown in **Figure 1.2,** it is apparent that the majority of psychologists concentrate on the diagnosis and treatment of severe emotional and behavioral problems. *Clinical psychologists* tackle not only mental illness, but also juvenile delinquency, drug addiction, criminal behavior, mental retardation, and marital and family conflict. *Counseling psychologists* are similar to clinical psychologists, but they often work on problems of a less severe nature, and the treatment they provide is usually shorter in duration. *Community psychologists* work in community settings delivering social and psy-

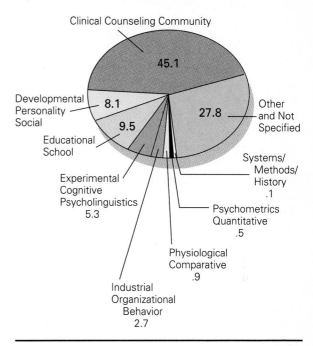

FIGURE 1.2 SPECIALTY AREAS OF PSYCHOLOGISTS

Shown are percentages of psychologists by their areas of specialization, according to a survey of American Psychological Association (APA) members.

chological services to the poor, minorities, immigrants, and to the growing number of homeless people in American cities.

In this course you will become most familiar with psychologists who conduct research. What are some of their specializations and professional roles in psychology?

Biological Psychology Researchers in this specialization study the biological bases of behavior, feelings, and mental processes. They seek to discover how the nervous system and the endocrine system (which controls the flow of hormones), affect learning, memory, emotions, sexual arousal, and other basic processes vital to human and animal functioning. In recent years, the explosion of interest in and research on the brain has helped create a new area of study for researchers from many disciplines: *neuroscience* is the scientific study of the mechanisms that link the brain to the reactions it influences or controls. *Psychopharmacology* is the branch of psychology that investigates the effects of drugs on behavior. These psychologists may work for pharmaceutical companies, testing the behavioral effect

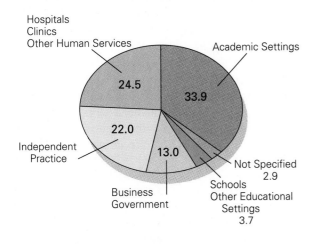

FIGURE 1.1 WORK SETTINGS OF PSYCHOLOGISTS

Shown are percentages of psychologists working in particular settings, according to a survey of American Psychological Association (APA) members holding doctorate degrees in psychology.

of various drugs, but they also conduct basic research to understand the brain mechanisms that cause the special effects of certain drugs. Researchers interested in how heredity contributes to various patterns of behavior and mental functioning work in the area of *behavioral genetics* (Plomin & Rende, 1991).

Experimental Psychology Originally, experimental psychology was restricted to basic experimental research on issues such as learning and conditioning, sensation and perception, motivation and emotion. Experimental psychologists currently work with animals as well as humans in experimental laboratory studies in the hopes of creating general laws of psychology that apply to more than one species. They focus on the effects that stimulus variations have on responding. The goal of their approach is to identify the stimulus conditions under which different individuals behave similarly. The term *experimental* however, is outdated; it now refers to all researchers who use experimental methods, rather than just those who rely on observation and intuition, as we shall see in the next chapter.

Cognitive Psychology Unlike traditional experimental psychologists, cognitive psychologists are primarily interested in organismic rather than stimulus factors. The research of cognitive psychologists focuses on consciousness and on mental processes, such as remembering and forgetting, thinking and communicating, judgment and decision making, reasoning and problem solving. To the extent that human nature is shaped by the processes and products of the mind, cognitive psychologists contribute to a fuller understanding of the human species. In this way, cognitive psychologists share the interests of scholars of philosophy, linguistics, anthropology, and artificial intelligence, who also want to understand how information is represented and processed in the mind. Taken together, these interrelated interests have formed the core of an exciting new area called *cognitive science*.

Developmental Psychology How does human development change over the course of an individual's lifetime? This is the question studied by specialists in developmental psychology. The developmental psychologist focuses on how human functioning changes over time, identifying the factors that shape behavior from birth through childhood, adulthood, and old age.

Personality Psychology What makes each of us unique? What are the distinctive characteristics that create individual differences in the ways people respond to the same stimulus situation? The answers to such questions are the province of personality psychologists who use psychological tests and inventories to assess unique traits and individual differences. These psychologists also advance theories about the origins of personality and the factors that influence the development of personality; so they, too, focus on organismic, or dispositional, variables.

Social Psychology Conformity, compliance, persuasion, aggression, and altruism are just some of the topics social psychologists try to understand. In order to understand how individuals are influenced by other people, the social psychologist studies how behavior and thought are affected by the social context in which stimuli are experienced. They emphasize the power of situational variables in influencing behavior.

Industrial Psychology and Organizational Behavior Psychologists in this area specialize in the relationship between people and their jobs. They work to solve problems related to employee selection, morale, productivity, job enrichment, management effectiveness, and job stresses. A subcategory of industrial psychology—*human factor psychology*—studies the interaction between worker, machines, and working environment. Human factors psychologists study how to make equipment, such as computers, "user friendly" as well as how to design airplane cockpits and automobile display panels for optimal effectiveness by a human operator.

Applied Areas of Psychology Applied psychologists work in a variety of settings. Some study special populations in settings such as schools, prisons, or the military. Others test practical relevance: does the research make a difference in the lives of the people? *Educational* and *school psychologists* study how to improve all aspects of the learning process, with the former working in colleges and universities and the latter working in elementary and secondary schools. These psychologists help design school curricula, teacher training programs, and childcare programs. *Environmental psychologists* may work with architects and urban planners to design housing projects, offices, and shopping centers that meet the needs of the residents and the community. Some environmental psychologists are studying ways to promote behaviors that will conserve energy to help free the United States from reliance on Persian Gulf oil. *Health psychologists* collaborate with medical researchers to understand how different life-styles affect physical health and how to manage or prevent stress. *Forensic psychologists* apply psychological knowledge to human problems in the field of law enforcement. They may work with the courts to determine the mental competency of defendants, counsel inmates in prison rehabilitation programs, or help lawyers with jury selection and with problems such as the unreliability of eyewitness testimony. *Sports psychologists* analyze the performance of athletes and use motivational, cognitive, and behavioral principles to teach them to achieve peak performance levels.

Has your image of psychologists changed? Psychologists are engaged in studying, modifying, preventing, or improving virtually every type of human activity. Knowing what psychology is, what psychologists do, and what their goals are, you are ready to investigate the origins of psychology. Let's examine the history of ideas that form the intellectual foundation of psychology.

SUMMING UP

The four main goals of psychology are (a) to objectively describe the behavior of individuals; (b) to develop an understanding of the causes and consequences of that behavior using explanations that are based on a mix of the best available evidence and creative imagination; (c) to predict accurately if, when, how, and in what form a given behavior will occur; and (d) to demonstrate that it is possible to control a given behavioral response by making it start, stop, or vary in some predictable way. A fifth goal of psychology is more practical and socially relevant—to use psychology in ways that can improve the quality of the lives of individuals and of society in general.

Many of the 300,000 psychologists throughout the world spend their time conducting research. These psychologists concentrate their research in numerous areas of psychology, each having a specific focus: (a) biological psychology—the biological bases of behavior, feelings, and mental processes; (b) experimental psychology—the stimulus conditions under which different individuals behave similarly; (c) cognitive psychology—consciousness and mental processes; (d) developmental psychology—human development across the entire life span; (e) personality psychology—distinct individual characteristics that determine the way different people respond to the same stimulus; (f) social psychology—the way that behavior and thought are affected by social contexts; and (g) industrial psychology—the relationship between people and their jobs. Researchers in applied areas of psychology specialize in educational and school psychology, environmental psychology, health psychology, forensic psychology, or sports psychology, to name only a few areas of applied psychology.

Clinical psychology—the understanding and treatment of psychological disorders—involves both basic research and practical application.

PSYCHOLOGY'S HISTORICAL FOUNDATIONS

"Psychology has a long past, yet its real history is short," wrote one of the first experimental psychologists, Hermann Ebbinghaus (1908). He went on to note that psychology's long past stretches back for thousands of years, but is characterized by little progress or systematic development. Scholars have long asked important questions about human nature—about how people perceive reality, the nature of consciousness, and the origins of madness—but until recently there have been no means for adequately answering them.

Although forms of psychology existed in ancient Indian Yogic traditions, the roots of modern psychology lie in ancient Greece. In the fourth and fifth centuries B.C., the classical philosophers Socrates, Plato, and Aristotle began rational dialogues about how the mind worked, the nature of free will, and the relationship of individual citizens to their community state. While these philosophers and their followers posed fundamental questions about what it means to be a rational, sensitive, responsible human being, the proof for their answers was limited to the power of logic and persuasion. Later, as the doctrines of the Roman Catholic Church spread throughout Europe, theologians taught that the mind and soul had free will (God's gift to humans) and were not subject to the natural laws and principles that determined the actions of physical bodies of all creatures. There could be no scientific psychology until this assumption was challenged.

The formal start of modern psychology can be traced to only a century ago—a short time in human history. In 1879, in Leipzig, Germany, **Wilhelm Wundt,** who was probably the first person to refer to himself as a *psychologist,* founded the first formal laboratory devoted to experimental psychology. Soon afterward, psychological laboratories appeared in universities throughout North America, the first at Johns Hopkins University in 1883. By 1900 there were more than 40 such laboratories (Hilgard, 1986).

Perhaps as a continuing legacy of the Protestant rebellion against the Church of Rome, in the late 1880s German physicists, physiologists, and philosophers began to challenge the notion that the human organism is special in the great chain of being, demonstrating that natural laws determine human actions. Hermann von Helmoltz, trained as a physicist, conducted simple but revealing experiments on perception and the nervous system. He was the first to measure the speed of a nerve impulse. At about the same time, another German, Gustav Fechner, began to study how physical stimulation is translated into sensations that are experienced psychologically. Like Wundt, von Helmoltz and Fechner operated on the assumption that psychological

In 1897, Wilhelm Wundt founded the first formal laboratory devoted to experimental psychology. Here are some of the gadgets he used (*Discovering Psychology,* 1990, Program 1).

processes could be studied objectively by using experimental methods adapted from the natural sciences, such as physics and physiology. They believed in **determinism,** the doctrine that physical, behavioral, and mental events are determined by specific causal factors.

Wundt wrote extensively about the new psychology and trained many young researchers who, in turn, went out to spread the new gospel of scientific psychology. Among his disciples was **Edward Titchener,** who, with his new laboratory at Cornell University, became one of the first American psychologists.

Ideas and intellectual traditions from both philosophy and natural science converged to give rise to the development of the new field of psychology. On this side of the Atlantic, in 1890, a young Harvard philosophy professor who had studied medicine and had strong interests in literature and religion, developed a uniquely American psychological perspective. **William James,** brother of the great novelist Henry James, wrote a two-volume work, *The Principles of Psychology,* which many experts consider to be the most important psychology text ever written. Shortly after, in 1892, G. Stanley Hall founded the American Psychological Association.

Three of the most historically significant approaches to psychology come under the banners of structuralism, functionalism, and evolutionism. While those whose advocated structuralism focused on the structure or mental contents of the mind, psychologists of the functionalist school proposed that what was important to study were the purposes or functions served by given behaviors. Other psychologists believed that to understand behavior, it is necessary to analyze the way that evolutionary forces selected for certain adaptive behaviors and thought processes. Let's examine the differences between these three perspectives.

STRUCTURALISM: THE CONTENTS OF THE MIND

When psychology became a laboratory science organized around experiments, its unique contribution to knowledge was recognized and established. In Wundt's laboratory, subjects made simple responses (saying yes or no, pressing a button) to stimuli they perceived under conditions varied by laboratory instruments. Because the data was collected through systematic, objective procedures, independent observers could replicate the results of these experiments. An emphasis on experimental methods, a concern for precise measurement, and statistical analysis of data characterized Wundt's psychological tradition.

When Edward Titchener brought Wundt's psychology to the United States, he also advocated that psychology study consciousness. How could the elements of mental life be studied? The method of choice at that time was *introspection,* a systematic examination of one's own thoughts and feelings about specific sensory experiences. Titchener emphasized the "what" of mental contents rather than the "why" or "how." His approach came to be known as **structuralism,** the study of the structure of mind and behavior.

Structuralism was based on the presumption that all human mental experience could be understood as the combination of simple events or elements. The goal of this approach was to reveal the underlying structure of the human mind by analyzing all of the basic elements of sensation and other experience that formed an individual's mental life. Many psychologists attacked structuralism on three fronts: (a) it was *reductionistic*

William James
(1842–1910)

because it reduced all complex human experience to simple sensations; (b) it was *elemental* because it sought to combine parts into a whole rather than studying the variety of behaviors directly; and (c) it was *mentalistic* because it studied only verbal reports of human conscious awareness, ignoring the study of subjects who could not describe their introspections, including animals, children, and the mentally disturbed. The major opposition to structuralism came under the American banner of *functionalism*.

FUNCTIONALISM: MINDS WITH A PURPOSE

William James emerged as the champion of American psychology. His broad conception of the many aspects of psychology provided a rich perspective on the phenomena of human experience that psychologists should study. James agreed with Titchener that consciousness was central to the study of psychology, but for James, the study of consciousness was not reduced to elements, contents, and structures—the concerns of structuralists and interior decorators. Instead, consciousness was an ongoing stream, a property of mind in continual interaction with the environment. Human consciousness facilitated one's adjustment to the environment; thus the acts and *functions* of mental processes were of significance, not the contents of the mind. **Functionalism** gave primary importance to learned habits that enabled organisms to adapt to their environment and to function effectively. For functionalists, the key question to be answered by research was "What is the function or purpose of any behavioral act?" The founder of the school of functionalism was American philosopher **John Dewey.** His concern for the practical uses of mental processes led to important contributions in education.

Functionalism was originally a general perspective about the way psychologists should study mind and behavior. It emphasized adaptation to the environment and the practical utility of action through study of an intact, functioning organism interacting with its environment. Functionalists rejected the structuralist notion that the mind should be analyzed in terms of its contents; they sought instead to discover its functions, utilities, and purposes.

Although James believed in the importance of careful observation, he put little value on the rigorous laboratory methods of Wundt. In James' psychology there was a place for emotions, self, will, values, and even religious and mystical experience. His "warm-blooded" psychology recognized a uniqueness in each individual that could not be reduced to formulas or numbers from test results. For James, explanation rather than experimental control was the goal of psychology (Arkin, 1990).

EVOLUTIONISM: NATURAL SELECTION OF SPECIES

Until 1859, there was no coherent scientific account of why we exist and where we came from. The religious doctrine of *creationism* asserted that all species, including humans, were divinely created as separate, unchanging types. In 1859, however, Charles Darwin's theory of evolution by natural selection gave biology the central tool it needed to understand how complex organisms come to exist. The idea of natural selection is really quite simple: those organisms that are better suited to their environments tend to pass on their genes to offspring more successfully than do those organisms with poorer adaptations to changes in their environment. Over many generations, more of the better-suited organisms survive, and their numbers gradually increase. Thus, this cumulative process of mutation and natural selection has produced the great variety of species we observe on earth, with each species incredibly well-adapted to its own environment or ecological niche. **Evolutionism** perceives all species as ever changing, branching lineages. Darwin's theory pushed humans out of the center spotlight of existence by giving them a common ancestry with other animals.

Darwin's theory of evolution pushed humans out of the spotlight by giving them a common ancestry with other animals.

Many psychologists have attempted to distinguish the contributions to human behavior and traits of **nature,** or hereditary influences, from the contributions of **nurture,** or environmental influences. From an evolutionary viewpoint, this distinction seems odd. Nature and nurture are intertwined—our evolved, inherited nature determines how and why environmental influences will affect us throughout our lifetimes. With this insight, evolutionary theory recently has started to influence our understanding of human cognition and motivation through the field of **evolutionary psychology** (to be discussed in the next section). Evolutionary theory continues to play a fundamental role in *comparative psychology,* the study of behavior across different animal species.

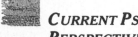

SUMMING UP

We outlined three historically important approaches to the study of psychology: structuralism, functionalism, and evolutionism. Structuralism *had its origins in early laboratory research on the elements that make up the structure or contents of the human mind. It was the "school" of psychology that emerged from Wundt's studies using introspection to investigate how the mind organizes the experiences of the senses. Titchener carried this approach to the United States, but it was attacked as being reductionistic, simplistic, and mentalistic. It also left no place for the study of animal behavior, infants, and others not capable of verbally expressing their experiences.* Functionalism, *as developed by Dewey and James, emphasized the function of or purpose behind any behavioral act. It assumed that the purpose of behavior was to enable each organism to adapt to its environment.* Evolutionism *is the scientific account of how species have survived and are related through natural selection processes, as proposed by Darwin. It too, focuses on how organisms adapt to the challenges of changing environments, but its time frame is millions of years, rather than just that of a human lifetime.*

CURRENT PSYCHOLOGICAL PERSPECTIVES

This final section outlines the perspectives, or conceptual approaches, that dominate contemporary psychology. Each perspective—biological, psychodynamic, behavioristic, cognitive, humanistic, and ev-

olutionary—defines a different area that is important in the study of psychology. These approaches contain points of view and assumptions that influence both what will be studied and how it will be investigated: are humans inherently good or evil? Do people have free will or simply act out a script imposed by their heredity (biological determinism) or their environment (environmental determinism)? Are organisms basically active and creative or reactive and mechanical? Can psychological and social phenomena be explained in terms of physiological processes? Is complex behavior simply the sum of many smaller components or does it have new and different qualities? A psychologist's point of view determines what to look for, where to look, what methods to employ, and what level of analysis to use.

We discussed earlier that the level of analysis may range from micro to macro. The level of analysis also varies in its *temporal* focus, concentrating on either the past, present, or future. Some psychologists look to past experiences to explain present behavior, such as the influence of childhood sexual abuse or parental divorce on adult sexuality. Some psychologists focus on the present situation, observing how the behavior of organisms is shaped by rewards or studying the expression of emotions. Still others study the importance of future events, investigating whether goal setting will influence the educational performance of underachieving students.

The six conceptual approaches can also be understood as *broad conceptual models*—simplified ways of thinking about the basic components of and relationships among phenomena in an area of knowledge. A **model** represents a pattern of relationships found in data or in nature and attempts to duplicate or imitate that pattern in some way. Some models are mechanical, such as those that represent how the ear works. Other models are mathematical, such as those that attempt to depict how certain kinds of decisions are made. Often a model is based on an analogy between the processes to be explained and a system already understood. Early psychologists used the analogy of a telephone switchboard as a model for the way the brain communicates information.

The six conceptual approaches also vary in terms of how specific and precise they try to be and in terms of how much they rely on empirical research findings. Although they are distinctive, at some points they overlap and most psychologists borrow and blend concepts from more than one of these perspectives. Nevertheless, each represents a different approach to the central issues in psychology. In the chapters that follow, we will elaborate in some detail on the contributions of each approach, because taken together, they represent what modern psychology is all about.

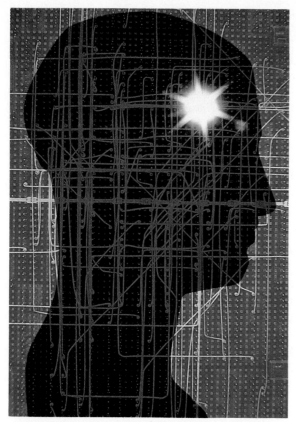

Early psychologists used the analogy of a telephone switchboard as a model for how the brain communicated information.

of researchers is to understand behavior at the most precise micro and molecular levels of analysis.

In the past, this approach was known as *physiological psychology,* but now, with greater focus on unlocking the secrets of brain functioning and the need to integrate many ideas and methods from related areas, these researchers are more likely to refer to themselves as *neuroscientists.* They study processes ranging from the memory circuits in simple organisms such as snails to the way human brains react to surprising stimulus information.

While many such neuroscientists work in university and medical school laboratories, others work in clinical settings. The former might study whether memory in elderly rats can be improved by grafting tissue from the brains of rat fetuses. The latter might study patients suffering a memory loss following an accident or disease. Neuroscientists have won Nobel Prizes in physiology for explaining how we hear (George von Békésy), how the special cells in the eye's retina are designed to perceive different features of the environment (**David Hubel** and Torsten Wiesel), and how the human brain of patients with epilepsy functions when its two halves are split by surgery (**Roger Sperry**). We will have more to say in later chapters about their discoveries.

PSYCHODYNAMIC APPROACH

According to the **psychodynamic approach,** behavior is driven, or motivated, by powerful inner forces. In this view, human actions stem from inherited instincts,

BIOLOGICAL APPROACH

The **biological approach** guides psychologists who search for the causes of behavior in the functioning of genes, the brain, the nervous system, and the endocrine system (controlling hormones). According to this biologically based model, an organism's functioning is explained in terms of underlying physical structures and biochemical processes. All experience and actions are understood as the result of the action of nerve impulses. The triggers for these actions come from chemical and electrical activities taking place within and between nerve cells.

The four assumptions of this approach are that (a) psychological and social phenomena can be understood in terms of biochemical processes; (b) complex phenomena can be understood by analysis, or reduction, into ever smaller, more specific units; (c) all behavior—or behavior potential—is determined by physical structures and largely hereditary processes; and (d) experience can modify behavior by altering these underlying biological structures and processes. The task

Sigmund Freud developed the psychodynamic approach to behavior (*Discovering Psychology,* 1990, Program 18).

biological drives, and attempts to resolve conflicts between personal needs and society's demands to act appropriately—action is the product of inner tension, but the main purpose of our actions is to reduce tension. Motivation is the key concept in the psychodynamic model. Deprivation states, physiological arousal, conflicts, and frustrations provide the power for behavior just as coal fuels a steam locomotive. In this model, the organism stops reacting when its needs are satisfied and its drives reduced.

Psychodynamic principles of motivation were most fully developed by Viennese physician **Sigmund Freud** in the late nineteenth and early twentieth centuries. Freud's ideas grew out of his work with mentally disturbed patients, but he believed that the principles he observed at work with his patients applied to both normal and abnormal behavior. According to Freud's theory, each person is fully determined by a combination of heredity and early childhood experiences. He argued that infants are driven by unlearned instincts for self-preservation and desires for physical pleasure. These primitive impulses are bottled up because they are opposed by taboos of parents and society. The child's personality develops according to the extent to which he or she resolves the conflict between the need to express and the need to inhibit such powerful impulses. Often this early conflict continues to influence behavior and create emotional problems in ways that a person does not understand. Freud's model was the first to recognize that human nature is not always rational; that actions may be driven by motives that are not in conscious awareness. Freud is credited with making the unconscious mind worthy of serious inquiry.

The psychodynamic view of Freud usually adopts a macro level of analysis, viewing a person as pulled and pushed by a complex network of inner and outer forces. The nature of the human organism is portrayed negatively; violence is seen as a natural means of expressing primitive sexual and aggressive urges. This view implies that people need strong societal controls if they are to be saved from their own passions for pleasure and destructiveness.

Freud's ideas have had a greater influence on more areas of psychology than those of any other person. You will encounter different aspects of his contributions as you read about child development, dreaming, forgetting, unconscious motivation, personality, neurotic disorders, and psychoanalytic therapy. His ideas will appear as frequent markers on our psychological journey. But you may be surprised to discover that his ideas were never the result of systematic scientific research. Instead, they were the product of an exceptionally creative mind obsessed with unraveling the deeper mysteries of human thoughts, feelings, and actions. Freud closely observed people—his patients and, most of all, himself. He may have been the world's greatest *egoist,* focusing the spotlight of intense analysis on his every action, from seemingly insignificant slips of the tongue, to fragments of his dreams. Some of the "proofs" of Freud's theories come, not from the laboratory, but from mythology, legend, drama, and archaeology (Gay, 1988).

Many psychologists since Freud have taken the psychodynamic model in new directions. Some neo-Freudian theorists have broadened Freud's theory to include social influences and interactions that occur over a lifetime, not just in infancy.

BEHAVIORISTIC APPROACH

Those who follow the **behavioristic approach** are interested in overt behaviors that can be objectively recorded. They are not concerned with biochemical processes or inner motivations that are inferred "psychic" phenomena. Behaviorally oriented psychologists look to specific, measurable responses—blinking an eye, pressing a lever, or saying yes following an identifiable stimulus (a light or a bell)—for their data.

The main objective of behavioristic analysis is to understand how particular environmental stimuli control particular kinds of behavior, or the *ABCs* of psychology. First, behaviorists analyze the *antecedent* environmental conditions that precede the behavior and "set the stage" for responding or withholding a response. Next they look at the *behavioral response* which is the main object of study—the action to be understood, predicted, and controlled. Finally, they look at the observable *consequences* that follow from the response—its impact on the environment. This level of analysis is molecular.

According to the behavioristic model, behavior is wholly determined by conditions in the environment. People are neither good nor evil but simply reactive to their environment. Their behavior can be changed by the proper arrangement of environmental conditions. Though heredity may place some limits on what environment can accomplish, behavioral psychologists assume that what people become is largely the result of *nurture* (experience), not our inherited nature.

Behaviorists have typically collected their data from controlled laboratory experiments; they may use electronic apparatuses and computers to introduce stimuli and record responses. They insist on very precise definitions of the phenomena studied and rigorous standards of evidence, usually in quantifiable form. Often they study animal subjects because, with animals, control of all the conditions can be much more complete than with human subjects. They assume that the basic processes they investigate with their animal subjects are part of general principles that hold true for different species but that in animals are easier to study.

Behaviorism asserts that only the overt behavior of organisms is the proper subject of scientific study. This view began early in this century with the work of **John B. Watson.** Watson, the first American behaviorist, was influenced by the work of Russian physiologist **Ivan Pavlov.** Pavlov discovered that the physiological response of salivation, thought to be produced only by eating food, could be elicited by the sight or sound of anything that was regularly paired with presentation of the food. Pavlov's primary interest was in the physiology of the learned relationship, known as *conditioning*.

Until Watson, instincts were understood as un observable hereditary mechanisms that could explain personality and behavior. Watson saw that if all behavior could be shown to be the result of learning, it would open up new possibilities for changing undesirable behavior. He believed that mental events could not be studied scientifically, so he exiled introspection and all forms of mental processes from his behaviorist kingdom. He established a new direction in psychology—a search for causes in the environment rather than in a person—and was the first to insist that psychologists study only observable behavior. If Watson laid the groundwork for behaviorism, Harvard's **B. F. Skinner** was the major architect of behaviorism. Until his death in 1990, Skinner's plans and visions shaped behaviorism for many decades. He believed that the house of scientific psychology could accommodate only one tenant—observable behavior. There was no room for brain science or cognitive science or any boarders who made too much noise about motivation, thoughtfulness, or the brain. In Skinner's blueprints, psychology could be described as scientific only if it restricted itself to the study of how behavior operates on the environment and is changed by the consequences it has on the environment.

For much of this century, the behavioristic model has dominated American psychology. Its emphasis on the need for rigorous experimentation and carefully defined variables has influenced most areas of psychology. Although Skinner and his disciples conducted their basic research with animal subjects (mostly pigeons and rats) the principles of behaviorism have been widely applied to human problems. Behaviorist principles have proposed a more humane approach to educating children (through the use of positive reinforcements rather than punishment), developing new therapies for modifying behavior disorders, and helping to create model utopian communities. Skinner's behaviorism has been as practical as it is still provocative—provocative because critics maintain that the narrow view of behaviorism retarded the development of psychology for decades. It did so, they say, by focusing attention and the skills of many researchers away from studying what is the highest expression of the human species—language, thought, and consciousness.

COGNITIVE APPROACH

The "cognitive revolution" in psychology emerges over the past three decades as a direct challenge to the limited perspectives of behaviorism. The centerpiece of the **cognitive approach** is human thought and all the processes of knowing—attending, thinking, remembering, expecting, solving problems, fantasizing, and consciousness. From the cognitive perspective, people act because they think, and people think because they are human beings uniquely equipped to do so due to nature's design of our brains.

In the seventeenth century, the French philosopher René Descartes declared, "I think, therefore I am." This statement expresses a fundamental truth about the nature of human existence—only through the awareness of individual thought processes can people have a sense of personal identity. In the Latin version of Descartes' proclamation, "Cogito ergo sum," *cogito* means "I think." *Cognition* is derived from *cogito*. Personal thoughts give meaning to all experiences and shape perceptions and responses to the world.

According to cognitive psychologists, the processing of information received about a stimulus is at least as important in determining behavior as is the stimulus input itself. These psychologists also assert that humans are not simply reactive creatures in this process but are also active creatures in choosing and creating individual stimulus environments. An individual responds to reality not as it is in the objective world of matter, but as it is in the *subjective reality* of the individual's inner world of thoughts and imagination.

In the cognitive model, behavior is only partly determined by preceding stimulus events and past behavioral consequences, as behaviorists believe. Some of the most significant behavior emerges from totally novel ways of thinking, not from predictable ways used in the past. The ability to imagine options and alternatives that are totally different from what is or was enables people to work toward new futures that transcend the realities of poverty or physical and emotional handicaps. In the cognitive approach, people start life as neither good nor evil, but with potential, in the form of mental templates, to be both good and evil.

Cognitive psychologists of the 1990s are interested in the way people interpret the current stimulus environment. They want to know how people evaluate the various actions they might take and then decide what to do, based on memories of what worked in the past and expectations of future consequences. They view thoughts as both results and causes of overt actions. Feeling regret when you've hurt someone is an example of thought as a result. But apologizing for your actions after feeling regret is an example of thought as a cause. Cognitive psychologists study thought processes at both molecular and macro levels. They may examine patterns of blood flow in the brain during different types of cognitive tasks (molecular), or a student's recollection of an early childhood event (macro).

Psychologist **Herbert Simon** won a Nobel Prize in economics for his research on the way people make decisions under conditions of uncertainty; that is, without all the relevant information. He showed that economic models based on predictions from rational analyses of how people are *supposed* to behave do not work when the situation is unclear. Instead, predictions are improved by psychological, descriptive analysis of the ways people actually behave in those settings. The work of **Albert Bandura** incorporates cognitive events in his explanations of social learning, cognitively based psychotherapy, and even analyses of terrorism (Bandura, 1986; 1990). Many psychologists see the new cognitive orientation as the dominant one in psychology today.

HUMANISTIC APPROACH

Humanistic psychology emerged in the 1950s as an alternative to the pessimism and determinism of the psychodynamic and the behavioristic models. In the humanistic view, people are neither driven by the powerful, instinctive forces postulated by the Freudians, nor manipulated by their environments, as proposed by the behaviorists. Instead, people are active creatures who are innately good and capable of choice. According to the **humanistic approach,** the main task for human beings is to strive for growth and development of their potential.

The humanistic psychologist studies behavior, but not by reducing it to components, elements, and variables in laboratory experiments. Instead, the psychologist looks for patterns in life histories of people. In sharp contrast to the behaviorists, humanistic psychologists focus on the subjective world experienced by the individual, rather than the objective world seen by external observers and researchers. To that extent, they are also considered to be *phenomenologists*, those who study the individual actor's personal view of events. Unlike the cognitively oriented research psychologist who relates inner processes to specific behavioral indi-

cators, humanistic psychologists are more interested in the way these inner processes lead to new insights and value choices.

Humanistic psychologists deal with the whole person, practicing a *holistic* approach to human psychology. They believe that true understanding requires integrating the mind, body, and behavior of the individual with social and cultural forces. Three important contributors to this humanistic perspective were Carl Rogers, Rollo May, and Abraham Maslow. **Carl Rogers** emphasized the individual's natural tendency toward psychological growth and health and the importance of a positive self-concept in this process. **Rollo May** was one of the first psychologists to explore phenomena such as anxiety from the perspective of the individual. May also integrated aspects of existential philosophy into this new psychological approach. (*Existentialism* emphasizes personal decision making and free will in a world without reason or purpose.) **Abraham Maslow** postulated the need for self-actualization and studied the characteristics of people he judged to be self-actualized.

The humanistic approach expands the realm of psychology beyond the confines of science to include valuable lessons from the study of literature, history, and the arts. In this manner, psychology becomes a more complete discipline that balances the empiricism of the sciences with the nonempirical, imaginative approaches of the humanities (Korn, 1985). Many critics of this view see humanism as unscientific, "feel-good, pop psychology." Some humanists respond by advocating a more rigorous approach to the concepts, definitions, and principles central to humanistic approach (Rychlak, 1979). Others argue that their view is the yeast that will help psychology rise above its dismal focus on negative forces and on the animallike aspects of humanity.

EVOLUTIONARY APPROACH

Surprisingly, the evolutionary approach is one of the newest perspectives in the study of psychology. This approach seeks to connect modern psychology to the oldest and most central idea of the life sciences, Darwin's theory of evolution by natural selection. The concept of *behavioral and mental adaptiveness* is the basis for the **evolutionary approach.** This approach assumes that human mental abilities evolved over millions of years to serve particular adaptive purposes, just as our physical abilities did. Postulating the survival purposes for which these abilities evolved and finding empirical evidence to test these hypotheses are the primary tasks of the evolutionary psychologist.

When you see a new device, you probably want to know what it's for and how it works. Evolutionary psychology asks the same two questions about the human mind.

Animals' brains evolve just as other organs do: natural selection shapes their internal structure and functioning to the requirements of their physical and social environment. Brains that generate more adaptive behavior get selected and proliferate. Brains that generate maladaptive behavior die out. Recent advances in evolutionary theory have given researchers a clearer idea of the meaning of behaving adaptively. It does not mean promoting the good of the species or even of the individual. It means only one thing: promoting the replication of the genes carried in the individual and in the individual's offspring and relatives (as described by Richard Dawkins in *The Selfish Gene,* 1976). Behaving adaptively can include sacrificing oneself for one's children or one's siblings, or helping others who may return that help in the future.

Humans spent 99 percent of their evolutionary history as hunter-gatherers living in small groups during the Pleistocene era. Evolutionary psychology uses the rich theoretical framework of evolutionary biology to identify the central adaptive problems that faced this species: avoiding predators and parasites, gathering and exchanging food, finding and retaining mates, and raising healthy children. After identifying the adaptive problems that these evolving protohumans faced, evolutionary psychologists generate inferences about the sorts of mental mechanisms, or psychological adaptations, that might have evolved to solve those problems.

Evolutionary psychologists are trying to develop a complete, unified psychology that embraces all aspects of human life, experience, and behavior. In this framework, neuroscience research into the mechanisms of brain functions can help explain the detailed operation and physical basis of inferred psychological adaptations. Evolutionary theories about why acting deceptively can sometimes have survival utility may help explain psychodynamic forces and why certain motivations are unconscious. Studies of the adaptive functions of different learning mechanisms can enrich behaviorist theories of learning. Studies of the way that certain psychological mechanisms may have evolved to cope with information-processing problems may benefit cognitive psychology. Studies of what humans have evolved to enjoy, value, and overcome during the course of their long struggle for survival may inform humanist concerns about human potential, happiness, and autonomy.

Evolutionary psychology differs from other perspectives most fundamentally in its temporal focus on the extremely long process of evolution as a central explanatory principle. Evolved psychological adaptions cannot really be characterized as good or evil—they are only designs that happened to have been selected in particular environments. As we will see in later chapters, evolution seems to have constructed us with inclinations that we now may value negatively. Research in this field has identified, for example, the male tendency to seek sexual variety, the female tendency to seek mates who are wealthy, or the increased likelihood of stepparents to sexually assault their stepchildren, while favoring their natural children. While one evolutionary theory predicts humans will evolve to be fundamentally selfish and nepotistic (preferring to aid relatives over others), another suggests that altruism is a trait that has an evolutionary advantage (Simon, 1991). The "applied side" of the evolutionary psychology perspective strives to use knowledge about our evolved tendencies to help direct those tendencies in the ways we choose rather than being directed blindly by them (Cosmides and Tooby, 1987).

COMPARING PERSPECTIVES: FOCUS ON AGGRESSION

Each of these six approaches just discussed rests on a different set of assumptions and leads to a different way of looking for answers to questions about behavior. **Table 1.1** summarizes the approaches. As an example, let's briefly compare how psychologists using these models might deal with the question of why people act aggressively. All of the following approaches have been used in the effort to understand the nature of aggression and violence:

- *Biological*—studies the role of particular brain regions in aggression by stimulating different regions and then recording any destructive actions that are elicited. Also analyzes the brains of mass murderers for abnormalities or studies female aggression as related to phases of the menstrual cycle.
- *Psychodynamic*—analyzes aggression as a reaction to frustrations caused by barriers to pleasure, such as poverty or unjust authority. Or views aggression as an adult's displacement of hostility originally felt as a child against his or her parents.
- *Behavioristic*—identifies reinforcements of past aggressive responses, such as extra attention given to a child who hit classmates or siblings. Or asserts that children learn from physically abusive parents to be abusive with their own children.
- *Cognitive*—inquire about the hostile thoughts and fantasies people experience while witnessing violent acts, noting their aggressive imagery and intentions to harm others. Studies the impact of violence in films and video, including

TABLE 1.1   COMPARISON OF SIX APPROACHES TO MODERN PSYCHOLOGY

Approach	View of Human Nature	Determinants of Behavior	Focus of Study	Primary Research Approach Studies
Biological	Passive Mechanistic	Heredity Biochemical processes	Brain and nervous system processes	Biochemical basis of behavior and mental processes
Psychodynamic	Instinct-driven	Heredity Early experiences	Unconscious drives Conflicts	Behavior as overt expression of unconscious motives
Behavioristic	Reactive to stimulation Modifiable	Environment Stimulus conditions	Specific overt responses	Behavior and its stimulus causes and consequences
Cognitive	Creatively active Stimulus reactive	Stimulus conditions Mental processes	Mental processes Language	Inferred mental processes through behavioral indicators
Humanistic	Active Unlimited in potential	Potentially self-directed	Human experience and potentials	Life pattern Values Goals
Evolutionary	Adapted to solving problems of the Pleistocene era	Adaptations and environmental cues for survival	Evolved psychological adaptations	Mental mechanisms in terms of evolved adaptive functions

pornographic violence, on attitudes toward gun control, rape, and war.

- *Humanistic*—looks for personal values and social conditions that foster self-limiting, aggressive perspectives instead of growth-enhancing, sharing experiences.
- *Evolutionary*—considers what Pleistocene era conditions would have made aggression an adaptive behavior. Then identifies psychological mechanisms capable of selectively generating aggressive behavior under those conditions.

It is not only professional psychologists who have theories about why people do what they do. You probably have some convictions about whether behavior is influenced more by heredity or environment, whether people are basically good or evil, and whether or not we have free will. As you read about the findings based on these formal models, keep checking psychologists' conclusions against your own views of behavior. Examine where your personal views came from and think about some ways you might want to broaden or modify them.

SUMMING UP

*We've reviewed the six major approaches that psychologists adopt in studying human and animal behavior as well as the mental and biological processes that underlie that behavior. Each approach takes a unique perspective on what is most important in psychology, what should be investigated, and how and at which level of analysis it should be investigated. Taken together, the approaches represent a composite of the ways we will be looking at the subject matter of **Psychology and Life**.*

The approaches that emphasize inner processes as most critical are the biological, psychodynamic, cognitive, and humanistic. Each focuses on very different internal factors and mechanisms. While the biologically oriented psychologist might study nerve impulses in the brain, the psychodynamic psychologist studies conflicts that are unconscious, the cognitive psychologist investigates thoughts, and the humanist directs primary attention to personal experiences and human potentials. The behavioristic approach focuses on external or environmental determinants of behavior. In one sense, the evolutionary approach is based on inner determinants—inherited adaptive tendencies. But in another sense, it emphasizes the environmental challenges that our ancestors faced successfully and had to survive in order to pass on their genes to us. No one approach is better than the others; they form an array of different angles from which to view psychology.

LOOKING AHEAD

This opening chapter has provided an overview of the entire field of scientific and professional psychology. We have seen that psychologists are interested in understanding the behavioral and mental functioning of individuals as well as using their knowledge to help people, such as the college athlete in the Opening Case whose mental state led to destructive actions. Following Chapter 2, each chapter will focus on one area of contemporary psychology. The researchers, theorists, and practitioners in these areas will share what they are discovering about the relationships among brain, mind, and behavior. Their work seeks to illuminate both what is basic and special about the nature of human nature.

A unique feature of this edition of *Psychology and Life* is the inclusion of special Close-Ups that feature research, theories, and alternative viewpoints on issues related to ecology and addiction. These topics have been chosen because they are areas of great practical concern for people everywhere and, especially, for today's college students. Their complexity also enables them to be used as recurring themes throughout the book that illustrate the application of a range of psychological knowledge and methods to their fuller understanding.

- **Addiction** usually refers to an overdependence of an organism on a drug—alcohol, nicotine, caffeine—but we will define *addiction* more broadly to include other ways people feel compelled to engage in high-risk, "out-of-control" behaviors, such as gambling and sexual addiction.
- **Ecology** is the study of the relationship of organisms to their environment. One aspect of that study is **behavioral ecology,** the extension of ecology to psychology or the transaction between the environment and the *behaviors* of organisms in it. Our ecology Close-Ups will range across the psychological landscape; starting by contrasting views of Western psychologists and indigenous peoples on the control of nature.

Why do people behave aggressively? Each of the six major approaches to modern psychology contributes a perspective to the answer.

CROSS-CULTURAL PERSPECTIVES ON CONTROLLING NATURE

According to Genesis in the Bible, humans "have dominion over the fishes of the sea and over the birds of the air and over every living thing that moves upon the earth." This attitude of separateness from and superiority over nature differs dramatically from the attitudes of people all over the planet who did not emerge from a Judeo-Christian heritage. Contrast the following creation story, told by a Sanpoil chief from the Pacific Northwest, with Genesis. Consider the different human-animal relationship each implies.

> Sweat Lodge was a chief long, long ago; but he wasn't called Sweat Lodge then. He was just called chief. He decided to create all the animals and all the birds. So he created them and named them all. . . . Then he told each one of them: "In times to come, when people have been created, they will send their children out, during the day or during the night, and you will talk with them and tell them what they will be able to do when they grow up (James, 1930).

Native Americans have traditionally followed an elaborate code of respectful behavior toward animals—each animal is believed to have its own spirit, power, and sensitivity—and they have demonstrated a commitment to accommodate and adapt to the environment, taking from it only what they need for survival and looking upon natural resources as precious gifts. In the Native American tradition, anyone who violates these codes risks bad luck, illness, or even death (Nelson, 1989).

Although North America was inhabited for about 25,000 years before the Europeans arrived, there is little evidence that the indigenous people disturbed the land or eliminated any species of animal (*The Harper Atlas of World History*, 1986). Yet, in the comparatively short span of only 500 years, European settlers and their descendants have defoliated immense tracts of forest, degraded agricultural lands, polluted the air and ocean, and driven untold numbers of animal and plant species to extinction (Brown, 1989). While we no longer shoot into herds of buffalo from moving trains for sport, Alaska's fish and game department shoots wolves from aircraft, even as conservationists are trying to restore wolves to the land (Williams, 1989). Even some ecologists, who work tirelessly to preserve the environment, "speak of animals as 'resources,' commodities to be parceled out among groups of 'users'" (Nelson, 1989).

A fundamental belief common to all industrialized nations is that the environment, including outer space, is controllable through technology, and that, indeed, it is human destiny to control it. This orientation toward domination over the environment, rather than accommodation to it, has led people to exploit its limited resources.

In *The Control Revolution* (1986), social scientist James Beniger defines control as "purposive influence toward a predetermined goal." In extolling the virtues of interlinking systems of technical, economic, and information control that have reshaped society in the last century, Beniger points to the control that seems to matter most—control over people. He argues that the great transformation of traditional into modern society was based on the appearance of technical and social systems better able to control or influence human behavior.

This control orientation has led people to exploit one another. Europeans took from Native Americans their land, their freedom, and their way of life. In exchange, they gave them the gun, alcohol, reservations, smallpox, and the assembly line. To the Wasco, a tribe that lived along the Columbia River, the animal spirit Coyote foretold the coming of a pale race with powerful weapons:

> Soon all sorts of strange things will come. No longer will things be as before. No longer will we use these things of ours. Strange people will bring to us everything strange. They will bring to us something—if you just point it at anything moving, that thing will fall down and die (Clark, 1953).

Although when two cultures meet it is not inevitable that one will completely dominate the other, it is inevitable that both will change. Poet Robert Bly reminds us of an ancient reality in which shamans "entered into the realm of the spirits, . . . wrestled with them, outwitted them, and saved people who had become ill through the mischievous activity of those spirits" (1990, p. 60). To ears attuned to beepers and cellular phones, such notions may sound strange. However, some psychologists have begun to listen to the voices of other cultures (Bronstein & Quina, 1988). These voices sensitize us to the realization that control as a scientific goal may result in costs and limitations as well as gains. When interventions designed to modify behavior for the noble ends of science or therapy are perceived as *manipulation* by those who get changed, then the means must be questioned. Recognizing this alternate perspective on the complexity of control broadens and enriches our quest to understand the nature of human nature—and helps to create a psychology of all people.

Before we examine in detail what researchers have found in each of the major areas of psychology, we need to find out the ways that psychologists know what they do about behavior and mental processes. Chapter 2 describes briefly the psychological methods used in research and psychological testing. This chapter also will help you to think more critically about research and what it proves. Like it or not, you are a daily consumer of mass media reports on research findings, some valuable, some worthless, some confusing and misleading. I think that you will become a wiser consumer of research-based conclusions after reading the next chapter.

You're on your way. I hope it will be a worthwhile journey. Be forewarned that, at times, the going will be a little rough and require that you extend yourself. If you do, the journey will become as rewarding as reaching the destination. Let's go, or as the Italians say, "Andiamo!"

Psychology: Definitions, Goals, and Tasks

Psychology is the scientific study of the behavior and mental processes of individuals. The scientific goals of psychology are to describe, predict, explain, and help control behavior. An applied goal is to help improve human functioning. The objective data psychology uses are observable stimuli and responses. Behavior is a function of the characteristics of the individual and the stimulus. The context of the stimulus also influences the behavioral outcome. Psychologists work in a variety of settings and draw on expertise from a range of specialty areas.

Psychology's Historical Foundations

Structuralism emerged from the work of Wundt and Titchener. It emphasized the structure of the mind and behavior built from elemental sensations. Functionalism, developed by Dewey and James, emphasized the purpose behind behavior. Evolutionism, developed by Darwin, focuses on how organisms adapt to the challenges of changing environments over millions of years, and pass on their genes to subsequent generations.

Current Psychological Perspectives

Each of the six approaches to studying psychology differs in its view of human nature, the determinants of behavior, the focus of study, and the primary research approach. The biological perspective studies relationships between behavior and brain mechanisms. The psychodynamic perspective looks at behavior as driven by instinctive forces, inner conflicts, and conscious and unconscious motivations. The behavioristic perspective approaches behavior as determined by external stimulus conditions. The cognitive perspective stresses mental processes that intervene between stimulus input and response initiation. The humanistic perspective emphasizes an individual's inherent capacity to make rational choices. Finally, the evolutionary perspective looks at functioning as having evolved as an adaptation for survival in the environment.

KEY TERMS

addiction, 21
base rate, 6
behavior, 3
behavioral data, 4
behavioral ecology, 21
behaviorism, 17
behavioristic approach, 16
biological approach, 15
clinical psychologists, 8
cognitive approach, 17
dependent variable, 7
determinism, 12
dispositional variable, 7
ecology, 21
environmental variable, 7
evolutionary approach, 18

evolutionary psychology, 14
evolutionism, 13
functionalism, 13
humanistic approach, 18
independent variable, 7
intervening variable, 5
model, 14
nature, 14
nurture, 14
organismic variable, 7
psychoanalysts, 8
psychodynamic approach, 15
psychiatrists, 8
scientific method, 3
situational variable, 7
structuralism, 12

MAJOR CONTRIBUTORS

Bandura, Albert, 18
Dewey, John, 13
Freud, Sigmund, 16
Hubel, David, 15
James, William, 12
Maslow, Abraham, 18
May, Rollo, 18
Pavlov, Ivan, 17

Rogers, Carl, 18
Simon, Herbert, 18
Skinner, B. F., 17
Sperry, Roger, 15
Titchener, Edward, 12
Watson, John B., 17
Wundt, Wilhelm, 11

Chapter 2

Psychological Research

THE CONTEXT OF DISCOVERY   28
  BIASES IN RESEARCH
  THEORIES, HYPOTHESES, AND PARADIGMS

  INTERIM SUMMARY

THE CONTEXT OF JUSTIFICATION   33
  THE SCIENTIFIC METHOD
  SCIENTIFIC ATTITUDES AND VALUES
  OBJECTIVITY SAFEGUARDS
  ACHIEVING RELIABILITY AND VALIDITY

  INTERIM SUMMARY

PSYCHOLOGICAL RESEARCH METHODS   36
  PSYCHOLOGICAL MEASUREMENT
  *CLOSE-UP: PSYCHOLOGY LABORATORY IN THE
    WILD*
  CORRELATIONAL METHODS
  EXPERIMENTAL METHODS
  STATISTICAL ANALYSIS OF DATA

  INTERIM SUMMARY

**ETHICAL ISSUES IN HUMAN AND ANIMAL
RESEARCH**   46
  INFORMED CONSENT
  RISK/GAIN ASSESSMENT
  INTENTIONAL DECEPTION
  DEBRIEFING
  *ISSUES IN ANIMAL RESEARCH: SCIENCE,
    ETHICS, POLITICS*

BECOMING A WISER RESEARCH CONSUMER   48
  SCIENCE-COATED JOURNALISM
  LAUGHING AND CAUSING
  CLOSE-UP: THE WAR ON DRUGS
  CRITICAL THINKING CONSUMER CHECKLIST

RECAPPING MAIN POINTS   52

KEY TERMS   53

MAJOR CONTRIBUTORS   53

I t's cassette magic! One tape guarantees a better sex life; another provides a quick cure for low self-esteem; a third promises safe and effective weight loss. How? All you have to do is *listen*—in bed, while jogging, when doing your homework—to the "restful splash of ocean waves breaking on sandy shores."

These audiotapes contain hidden, "subliminal" messages that supposedly communicate with your subconscious mind, avoiding the usual resistance of your conscious awareness. Sounds like a painless way to a better life, doesn't it? One true believer in the power of these subliminal tapes reported to an

interviewer from *Newsweek* magazine that he became a better salesman after listening to a tape called "Unconditional Love" and stopped losing his hair after playing the "Stop Hair Loss" tape. Although he cannot hear any of the allegedly persuasive messages on the other 15 subliminal tapes he now owns, he is sure that "subliminals are both practical and spiritual" (*Newsweek*, 7/30/90, pp. 60–61).

If these tapes are so powerful, couldn't they be dangerous if they got into the wrong hands? What if unscrupulous influence agents—such as cult leaders, politicians, or advertisers—use these subliminals to penetrate your unconscious with their own hidden messages?

A 1957 study made headlines when, after subliminal messages to "Buy Popcorn" and "Drink Coca-Cola" were flashed on the screen during a movie, food concession sales reportedly increased by 58 percent! *The Wall Street Journal* reported in 1980 that a New Orleans supermarket significantly decreased stealing and cashier shortages after piping the following subliminal message into its Muzak system: "If I steal, I will go to jail." In 1989, the heavy metal band Judas Priest was indicted for re-cording disguised messages on their albums. The group was sued by the parents of two teenagers who had committed suicide after listening to one of their tapes.

Are the claims of the $50 million-a-year subliminal audiotape industry valid? Can their unheard, unseen, brief messages help patients with illnesses as diverse as cancer, high blood pressure, warts, and even AIDS, as they claim? Is there reliable evidence available to consumers before they rush out to buy a set of these "magic" tapes?

Psychologists use a wide variety of methods to answer such questions about behavioral phenomena. As with many other problems, the *assumed* processes of subliminal perception are both silent and invisible. They occur in the brain if at all, but are revealed in our thoughts, feelings, and actions. Like detectives, psychological researchers often solve complex mysteries without ever directly witnessing the phenomena under investigation.

Bertrand Russell, one of the most influential philosophers of our time, proclaimed that, "Psychology is the most important of the sciences . . . all the data upon which our inferences are based are psychological in character. . . ." Let's turn now to discovering *how* psychologists know *what* they know. In this chapter, you will learn some of the methods that psychological researchers use to unravel the secrets of human nature.

What if those tapes really could help cure illness or make your life better? "What if" is to research as a first kiss is to romance. It stimulates a great deal of action that may replace uncertainty with new meaning. Psychologists love to think "what if" thoughts. What if that situation were changed; would she still behave that way? What if he were treated differently; would there be a corresponding change in his attitudes? What if I intervened with a particular kind of therapy; would it make a difference in their behavior? Research is a way to answer such "what if" questions.

This chapter will focus on the kinds of evidence psychological investigators seek as well as on the special procedures they use to gather the facts. Recall that psychology is the *scientific study* of the behavioral and mental functioning of individuals. It is scientific because it uses the principles and practices of the *scientific method*. **Empirical investigation** in any field requires the use of the scientific method to observe, measure, and experiment. This approach contrasts with a theoretical, or explanatory, approach. In this chapter you will discover what is special about the way psychology applies this general approach to its domain of knowledge. How do psychologists measure behavior and design their research? What are the special features of a psychological experiment? How can solid conclusions ever be drawn from the complex and often "fuzzy" phenomena that psychologists study—how you think, feel, and behave?

The final objective of this chapter is to change *you* in a special way. Even if you never do any scientific research in your life, mastering the information in this chapter will be useful. The underlying purpose here is to help improve your *critical thinking skills* by teaching you how to ask the right questions and evaluate the answers about the causes, consequences, and correlates of behavior and psychological phenomena. The mass

media constantly releases stories that begin with, "Research shows that. . . ." The stories often end with direct or implied calls for some citizen action based on that research. By sharpening your intelligent skepticism, you will become a more sophisticated consumer of research-based conclusions that confront you in everyday life, such as the claims for the psychological effects of subliminal tapes.

 ## THE CONTEXT OF DISCOVERY

The research process in psychology, as in all empirical sciences, can be divided into two major categories that usually occur in sequence: getting an idea and then testing it. The **context of discovery** is the initial phase of research during which observations, beliefs, information, and general knowledge lead someone to come up with a new idea or a different way of thinking about phenomena.

BIASES IN RESEARCH

Where do your beliefs about physical reality and human nature originate? Some come from your direct observations of the events, animals, people, and things in the environment around you. Other beliefs come secondhand—from the observations of others, from what you read, or from what you are told by authorities. These diverse sources of information combine to form your personal understanding of different aspects of physical and social reality. Sometimes you may combine them in unique ways that offer an original perspective. The hallmark of the truly creative thinker is the discovery of a new truth that moves society and science in a better direction.

At times what you saw with your own eyes, read, or were told may be incorrect and may distort the truth about some aspect of reality. What distorts the context of discovery for many people?

External Influences

First, there are *external* factors that influence people to accept a particular world view. Culture, authorities, and the media shape an individual's belief system and sense of *subjective reality* that influences his or her perceptions of the world. Culturally imposed systems of belief form the values and ideologies in societies, shaping attitudes about beauty, courage, male and female roles, the origins of good and evil, and illness and health. The mass media also manipulates people's beliefs by presenting sensationalized accounts of rare events and bizarre experiences as if they were factual, substantiated occurrences. The most widely read national tabloids, such as the *National Enquirer,* describe fantastic occurrences—UFO's, extraterrestrial life, mind reading, psychic surgery, reincarnation—as if they had some scientific foundation.

Personal Biases

A second way that the context of discovery becomes murky and distorted is through *internal* psychological processes that are basic to the way individuals function ordinarily. Everyone carries personal biases that may prevent accurate, objective judgments of experiences. A **personal bias** is an error in estimating or evaluating some experience or phenomenon due to the operation of subjective factors. This bias occurs because personal beliefs, personal attributes, or personal past history interfere with accurate perceptions and interpretations of some aspect of reality. For example, tending to rely on faulty memory instead of verifying data can often give an incorrect picture of reality.

Observer Biases

A particular type of personal bias, **observer bias,** is an error in observation that distorts perceptual evidence and that is due to the personal motives and expectations of the viewer. At times, people see and hear what they expect rather than what is. This bias explains how the same evidence can lead different observers to different conclusions. The biases of the observers act as *filters* through which some things are noticed as relevant and significant, while others are ignored as irrelevant and not meaningful. Observational biases come from sources of influence on perceptions, such as culture, gender, age, social class, and education.

Around the turn of the century, a leading psychologist, **Hugo Munsterberg,** gave a speech on peace to a large audience that included many reporters. He summarized the news accounts of what they heard and saw in this way.

> The reporters sat immediately in front of the platform. One man wrote that the audience was so surprised by my speech that it received it in complete silence; another wrote that I was constantly interrupted by loud applause and that at the end of my address the applause continued for minutes. The one wrote that during my opponent's speech I was constantly smiling; the other noticed that

my face remained grave and without a smile. The one said that I grew purple-red from excitement; and the other found that I grew chalk-white. The one told us that my critic, while speaking, walked up and down the large stage; and the other, that he stood all the while at my side and patted me in a fatherly way on the shoulder" (1908, pp. 35–36).

Even scientists can be guilty of this error when their beliefs get in the way of their observations. Recently a team of French researchers declared they had made a remarkable discovery: A substance remained biologically active even when it was so diluted that it disappeared! This strange finding contradicted a basic law of chemistry. It also supported the notion of *homeopathic medicine,* which contends that a person can be cured of disease by taking minute doses of substances that cause its symptoms. However, an investigative team from the science journal *Nature* failed to replicate the findings even in the same French laboratory and with the original researchers' notes and data. The results of the original study are suspicious because the salaries of some of the researchers were paid by a French maker of homeopathic medicines; there may have been bias to find favorable results. Moreover, because the main data involved *personal judgments* about the color of tissue samples, the situation was ripe for biased viewing. "In this kind of experiment, there's a powerful opportunity for observer bias," reported a skeptical investigator from the National Institute of Health. "You're making judgments all the time—how pale something looks, or how red. If you have a concept in mind, you can easily get in trouble" (Revkin, 1989, p. 75).

Expectancy Biases

Another kind of bias that can affect observations of behavior actually triggers the kind of reactions that are being observed. Unintentional **expectancy bias** occurs when a researcher or observer subtly communicates to her subjects the behaviors she expects to find—thereby producing the desired reaction in them. Researchers are human; they tend to see what they expect to see, despite their commitment to objectivity.

Robert Rosenthal has studied this phenomenon of expectancy researcher-caused bias and how it can distort research results.

> College students were hired to be "experimental assistants" in a research project supposedly designed to study if research subjects could accurately rate the success or failure of target people just by looking at their photographs. Their subjects were to rate expressions in the photographs on a scale from + 10 (extreme success) to − 10

(extreme failure). Actually, all the photos had earlier been rated as neutral by other students. The real study manipulated what the research assistants were told about the kind of ratings to expect from their subjects. Half of them were led to believe that the subjects they observed would give ratings that averaged about +5 across all the photos. The other half of the experimental assistants were told to expect average ratings of −5. Both groups of assistants then read the same instructions to their subjects.

Both sets of assistants achieved the results they were expecting. In some subtle, nonverbal way, even though they had read standard instructions and had only watched while the photos were being judged, they had communicated their expectations to their subjects. In turn, the subjects reacted as expected, giving ratings of moderate success or moderate failure according to what their experimental assistant believed was true (Rosenthal, 1966).

This expectation bias distorts the content of discovery. It makes us "discover" only what is already on our minds and not how minds and behavior truly function.

Let's take a demonstration break to illustrate how easy it is to create an observer bias in you. Please look carefully at each of the four drawings in **Figure 2.1**. Then examine **Figure 2.3** on page 32 and note what you see there. *Do not read further.*

Next, ask someone else to assist you by looking first at the four drawings in **Figure 2.2** before turning to describe the target figure in Figure 2.3. This person should not see the drawings in Figure 2.1 nor should you see those in Figure 2.2 before making your final judgment.

Any differences? When viewing the ambiguous Figure 2.3, you should have reported seeing a different figure than your partner did. The four-item set of cartoon figures of people should have given you a perceptual readiness to see a *person* in the ambiguous stimulus figure. However, first viewing the animals in Figure 2.2 sets up an observer bias to see an *animal* in the ambiguous target. If such a brief experience can predispose two observers to see the same figure so differently, you can readily imagine how the life-long effects of cultural experiences or learned prejudices can create major observer biases—and sometimes major disagreements and social conflicts.

FIGURE 2.1 *FOUR STICK FIGURES*

FIGURE 2.2   FOUR STICK FIGURES

Placebo Biases

A special kind of bias exists in many people who have a strong desire to believe that some treatment they receive will have a potent effect on them. This concept originated in medicine to account for cases when a patient's health improved after receiving medication that was chemically inert or treatment that was *nonspecific*. The **placebo effect** refers to an improvement in health or well-being due to the individual's *belief* that the treatment will be effective. In psychology, the placebo effect occurs whenever a behavioral response is influenced by a person's expectation of what to do or how to feel, rather than by the specific intervention or procedures employed to produce that response. (Can you begin to see any connection here with the testimonials for subliminal audiotapes?)

Historical analysis of the healing professions reveals that placebos have been responsible for much of the therapeutic success attributed to all new treatments. Virtually any credible, socially accepted treatment administered in an appropriate context will have a moderate therapeutic success (Frank, 1961; Shapiro, 1971; Shapiro & Morris, 1978). The mere suggestion that someone is being treated for an illness or pain is often sufficient to make the intervention work. Indeed, placebo cures have been effective enough to sustain initial acceptance of many bizarre and even worthless medical treatments within the community of their origin. For example, in ancient Egypt, patients were often treated with medications such as lizard's blood, crocodile dung, powdered donkey's hooves, and remains of mummies. Centuries later, European physicians "cured" their patients by using leeches to suck their blood, making them vomit, freezing them, heating them, and shocking them. Of course, many patients died during these treatments, but those who survived offered vivid personal testimonials to the power of their treatment.

A placebo pill is one of the most powerful drugs a physician can use for treating pain and sickness. Hundreds of studies on numerous ailments show that thousands of patients have reported relief after taking placebos. In some studies, a placebo was shown to be even more effective than a known tranquilizer or a potent painkiller, such as morphine (Haas et al., 1959). Some people even become addicted to their placebos, requiring even larger doses of the imaginary medicine to maintain their state of health. Studies claim that the mere suggestion of a believable treatment will make 25 to 35 percent of the people feel better (Beecher, 1959). So, it appears that about one-third of us are *positive placebo responders*.

In addition to the placebo pill, there is the general effect of all placebo treatments. For example, regardless of the specific type of treatment a patient receives for a mental or behavioral disorder, some improvement will probably occur due to *common factors* in all healing settings. Among these are the expectancy of being cured and the therapist's attention, along with suggestions and persuasion for improvement (Critelli & Neumann, 1984; Fish, 1973).

THEORIES, HYPOTHESES, AND PARADIGMS

Psychological research can be reduced to four general concerns: (a) the stimulus events that cause a particular response to start, stop, or change in quality or quantity; (b) the *structure* of behavior that links certain actions in predictable, orderly ways to other actions; (c) the *relationships* between *internal* psychological processes or physiological mechanisms and *observable* behavior patterns; and (d) the *consequences* that behavior has on the individual's social and physical environment.

Researchers begin with the assumption of **determinism,** the idea that all events, physical, mental, and behavioral, are the result of specific causal factors. These causal factors are limited to those in the individual's environment or within the person. Researchers also assume that behavior and mental processes follow *lawful patterns* of relationships that can be discovered and revealed through research. The ultimate goal of psychology is to discover the basic laws that govern behavioral and mental functioning.

Psychological theories, in general, attempt to understand how brain, mind, behavior, and environment function and how they may be related. Any particular **theory** focuses on a more specific aspect of this broad conception, using a body of interrelated principles to explain or predict some psychological phenomenon.

"We plan to determine, once and for all, if there really ARE any cultural differences between them."

The value of a theory is often measured in terms of the new ideas, or hypotheses, that can be derived from it and tested. A **hypothesis** is a tentative and testable explanation of the relationship between two or more events or variables. A **variable** is any factor that varies in amount or kind. Sexual desire and degree of masculinity or femininity are examples of variables. One's biological sex, on the other hand, is a fixed factor. Hypotheses are often stated as if-then predictions, specifying certain outcomes from specific conditions. Sometimes hypotheses are hunches about what ideas go together, based not on formal theories, but on a psychologist's observations, introspection, creative intuition, or analysis of a pattern of available evidence. In addition, new *technologies* and new *models* also stimulate new psychological discoveries. Often a new method or instrument of observing, recording, or measuring behavior and internal processes will yield new discoveries. For example, the scientific study of sleeping and dreaming opened up only after the development of a technology for recording changes in brain wave patterns that vary as consciousness is altered.

Our understanding of a complex process is also aided by using the correct paradigm. A **paradigm** is a model of the functions and interrelationships of a process. In psychological research, a paradigm is a model of the behavior, mental processes, or physiological processes under study. Sigmund Freud developed a new paradigm for understanding irrational behavior by relating it to unconscious motives or conflicts. Ivan Pavlov provided new insights into the nature of learning

FIGURE 2.3   STIMULUS TARGET

with a paradigm of classical conditioning in which almost any neutral stimulus (such as a bell) could elicit strong physical responses (such as salivating) after pairing it with a biologically powerful stimulus (such as food). Entire fields of knowledge, including psychology, can change directions when new paradigms challenge existing ones. When paradigms shift, revolutions of knowledge usually follow (Kuhn, 1970). However, before a new theory, hypothesis, or paradigm makes a difference in science, it has to undergo an "ordeal of proof." It moves into the public eye where ideas are tested and proven.

SUMMING UP

We have outlined the sources of errors that mar the context of discovery. It is common for our beliefs, motives, and expectations to influence our perception of and interpretation of reality. Our view of reality is not always accurate because we often base our conclusions on evidence subject to personal biases, observer biases, expectancy biases, and placebo effects. Discovering new ideas and understanding psychological phenomena can be hindered by mindless reliance on nonexpert authorities, or the sensationalism and distortion of the mass media. Psychologists use insightful theories, testable hypotheses, new technologies, and creative paradigms to unravel the mysteries of mind and behavior.

 ## THE CONTEXT OF JUSTIFICATION

Psychologists face a difficult challenge when they try to get accurate data and reliable evidence that will generate valid conclusions. They rely on one ally to make success possible: the scientific method. Psychologists also rely on a wide variety of methods to measure different aspects of the particular psychological phenomena they wish to understand.

THE SCIENTIFIC METHOD

We have seen that different people can interpret the same situation differently, and even our own observations can be distorted by our personal biases, prejudices, and expectations. However, researchers want accurate evidence and they want to minimize errors in drawing conclusions. The scientific method helps them achieve these goals.

The **scientific method** is a general set of procedures for gathering and interpreting evidence in ways that limit sources of errors and yield dependable conclusions. The scientific method also demands special attitudes and values on the part of research scientists. Psychology is considered a science to the extent that it follows the rules established by the scientific method.

SCIENTIFIC ATTITUDES AND VALUES

Scientists are motivated by a *curiosity* about the unknown and the uncertain. They seek to discover lawful, orderly patterns of relationships in the phenomena they investigate. But they are aware of the many disguises that nature may use to conceal truths. So the scientific method demands a *critical* and *skeptical* attitude toward any conclusion until it has been duplicated repeatedly by independent investigators. *Open-mindedness* serves two purposes. First, it makes truth provisional, ever ready to be modified by new data. Second, an open-minded orientation makes researchers willing to evaluate seriously claims for phenomena that they may not personally believe or accept, such as extrasensory perception (ESP). Secrecy is banned from the research procedure because all data and methods must eventually be open for *public verifiability;* that is, other researchers must have the opportunity to inspect, criticize, replicate, or disprove the data and methods. We noted earlier how the criteria of public verifiability was applied in the case of the research on homeopathic medicine.

Scientific knowledge is based on respect for empirical evidence obtained through controlled observation and careful measurement. When good data clash with the opinions of experts, in the realms of science, data win. Data must be collected by special methods that eliminate or correct the subjective influences and biases of researchers. Descriptions of the data, results, and the methods for collecting the data are kept separate from any inferences and conclusions about the meaning of the evidence. In scientific publications, each part of an investigation is reported in a distinct section to allow readers to distinguish the objective features of the data from subjective interpretation by the researchers. Finally, there is a demand that research be published in order to add to the cumulative body of knowledge about the topic studied, as well as to enable other investigators to replicate the findings.

The broader significance of the scientific method for any society that values truth and freedom was eloquently stated by philosophers Cohen and Nagel (1934) over 50 years ago. The force of their argument is even more powerful today as science and technology play even greater roles in our lives now than they did in the past.

> Scientific method is the only effective way of strengthening the love of truth. It develops the intellectual courage to face difficulties and to overcome illusions that are pleasant temporarily but destructive ultimately. It settles differences without any external force by appealing to our common rational nature . . . because it requires detachment, disinterestedness, and it is the finest flower and test of a liberal civilization (pp. 402–403).

OBJECTIVITY SAFEGUARDS

Since subjectivity must be minimized in the data collection and analysis phases of scientific research, procedural safeguards are used to increase objectivity. These safeguards include (a) keeping complete records of observations and data analyses in a form that other researchers can understand and evaluate, (b) standardizing all procedures, (c) using operational definitions, and (d) minimizing personal biases and controlling potential flaws or confounds that limit the interpretation of the results. The first of these safeguards needs no explanation, but we need to clarify the other three.

Standardization

Standardization means using uniform, consistent procedures in all phases of data collection. Instructions must be delivered in the same way to each person each time the test, interview, or experiment is conducted. Having results printed or recorded helps ensure their comparability in different times and places and with different subjects and researchers. All features of the test or experimental situation should be sufficiently standardized so that all research participants experience exactly the same experimental conditions. This standardization means asking questions in the same way and scoring responses according to preestablished rules.

Operational Definitions

How much is "many"? How sweet is "sweet nectar" to a hummingbird? How violent is "aggression"? How active is "sexually active"? Scientists in all areas have a basic problem to solve: how to translate concepts that have meaning for them into concepts that have a commonly accepted meaning for anyone using them. The strategy for standardizing the meaning of concepts is called *operationalization*. An **operational definition** standardizes meaning by defining a concept in terms of specific operations or procedures used to measure it or to determine its presence. An operational definition avoids the ambiguity of everyday descriptive terms and ensures that both the stimulus variables and the response variables are observable events. Furthermore, this definition allows both research participants and researchers to understand clearly how a given concept is being used. Take the case of a woman who described herself as "not sexually active" on a researcher's form not long ago—even though she had gonorrhea. Asked to explain, she insisted that she wasn't "active" in bed at all. "I just lie there," she said.

Many psychological concepts also have familiar, everyday meanings. Consider *anxiety, conflict, love, shyness,* and *hunger.* These terms may lead to ambiguity and confusion when they are used in psychological research and reported in the mass media—another important reason to use operational definitions. For example, hunger might be operationally defined as "24 hours without food," or "15-percent loss of body weight in a given time period."

> To compare evidence with theory requires that you measure the ingredients of your theory. For ingredients like weight or speed it's clear what you measure, but what would you measure if you wanted to understand political instability? Somehow, you would have to design a series of actual operations that yield a suitable measurement— i.e., you must operationalize the ingredients of theory (Diamond, 1987, p. 35).

Avoiding Bias, Controlling Confounds

Biases are to research conclusions what pebbles are to a hiker's shoe. However they got there, they spoil the journey and can even interfere with reaching the destination. Good research keeps them out, minimizes them, or takes account of them by means of statistical adjustments during data analysis. In psychological research, uncorrected sources of unintentional bias can make a

How would you characterize the behavior of the girl in this picture? She probably appears shy to you. Shyness can be operationalized in many different ways including failure to make eye contact and percentage of time the child is silent, looks down, or is distant from the mother. Shyness also can be operationalized in terms of ratings made by the child's parents, teachers, or peers.

actually received the treatment than for those in the control condition who were merely expecting to receive it but did not.

Another type of general response bias occurs when research subjects change the way they behave simply because they are aware of being observed or tested. For example, subjects may feel special about being chosen to participate in a study and thus act differently than they would ordinarily. An experimenter might then mistakenly conclude that their reactions were caused by the manipulation of the specific *independent variable* instead of an extraneous variable.

When something other than what an experimenter purposely introduces into a research setting changes a subject's behavior and adds confusion to the interpretation of the data, it is called a **confounding variable.** Flawed research jeopardizes the simple, straightforward interpretation of a study's findings. When the real cause of some observed behavioral effect is confounded, instead of explaining the cause in terms of the hypothesis being tested, the research suggests other interpretations. The more **alternative explanations** there might be for a given result, the less confidence we have in our initial hypothesis. Because human and animal behaviors are complex and often have multiple causes, good research design involves anticipating possible confounds and devising strategies for eliminating them. Similar to defensive strategies in sports, good research designs anticipate what the other team might do and set plans to counteract it. For each anticipated confounding variable, a procedural control is needed to rule out the alternative explanations it raises. We will consider examples of typical confounds that researchers face when we focus on types of measurement psychologists use in their research.

study scientifically worthless. *Standardized procedures* help avoid bias by keeping constant the important elements of the research.

Researchers also use various *control procedures* to test their hypotheses in a fair, error-free way. Even with standardized procedures, bias can inadvertently be introduced into research. Researcher-caused bias can be controlled in several ways. Bias based on the expectations of experimenters can be eliminated by keeping both subjects and experimental assistants unaware of, or blind to, which subjects get which treatment. This is called a **double-blind control** condition. Potential bias is further reduced by not allowing the researcher to enter the testing room during data collection. When placebo effects might possibly occur, researchers employ a **placebo control.** The effect of the treatment must be shown to be significantly greater for those who

ACHIEVING RELIABILITY AND VALIDITY

The goal of psychological research is to generate findings that are both reliable and valid. **Reliability** refers to the consistency or dependability of behavioral data resulting from psychological testing or experimental research. A reliable result is one that will be repeated under similar conditions of testing at different times. A reliable measuring instrument or device yields comparable scores when utilized repeatedly. As we will see in Chapter 15, there are a number of ways to assess just how reliable a psychological test is.

Reliability is enhanced when (a) the research, test, or measurement conditions are standardized; (b) enough observations are made or responses are measured so that atypical ones do not distort the overall effect, and (c) factors that might cause the data to vary in unsystematic ways are anticipated and controlled.

Validity means that the information produced by research or testing accurately measures the psychological variable or quality it is intended to measure. A valid test enables the tester to make predictions from the test scores about performance in another situation where the ability being measured by the test is significant. For example, SAT scores are a fairly valid predictor of college grades, in general (assuming one's level of academic motivation does not change dramatically between high school and college). But SAT scores are not valid for predicting how creative, popular, or healthy you will be.

Serious misuse of psychological information occurs when test results that are valid for one group or one type of prediction are used as the basis for evaluating another group's performance. This misuse has been found in some tests of intelligence and achievement developed only on subjects who were white, male, or native speakers but then used to assess nonwhites, females, and the foreign born. Another problem of validity arises when the content of tests is designed to favor individuals with a particular background or type of experience.

"Find out who set up this experiment. It seems that half of the patients were given a placebo, and the other half were given a different placebo."

 SUMMING UP

We have seen that psychological researchers use the scientific method for testing ideas developed within the context of discovery. The scientific method encourages intellectual curiosity, open-minded skepticism, and a reliance on empirical data rather than on authority as the foundation of scientific knowledge. The scientific method also establishes a set of procedures to increase objectivity and reduce errors and bias in research-based conclusions. Findings are made more reliable through standardizing the administration of all parts of a study, operationally defining key concepts, and safeguarding against confounding variables by using special control procedures.

PSYCHOLOGICAL RESEARCH METHODS

Research begins with defining objectively and describing precisely the phenomenon of interest. The focus of this first phase is on discovering the relevant factors and determining how they might be measured or manipulated. After this phase, the researcher wants to know which variables are related to one another, to what extent they are correlated, and whether they can be used to make accurate predictions. To find out if one variable is causally related to another, researchers turn to a special kind of investigation that relies on experimental

methods. This section outlines some basic methods of psychological measurement that use *descriptive research* techniques, examines how psychologists use *correlational* and *experimental* methods, and finally considers the important role of *statistical analysis* of data.

PSYCHOLOGICAL MEASUREMENT

Because psychological processes are so varied and complex, they pose major challenges to researchers who want to measure them. The first challenge is to access the psychological phenomenon one wants to understand. Although some actions and processes are easily seen, many, such as anxiety or dreaming, are not. Thus, one task for a psychological researcher is to make the unseen visible, to make internal events and processes external, and to make private experiences public. Many methods are available for accomplishing this task, each with its particular advantages and disadvantages. A second challenge is to find the right measure—the best *outcome variable*—to assess the psychological phenomenon described in the theory or hypothesis.

All attempts at measurement use some procedure for assigning numbers to, or *quantifying*, different levels, sizes, intensities, or amounts of a variable. Some measures may be physical, such as the speed at which a subject reacts to a red light, while others are scaled along a continuum that orders the variable in some systematic way: "How often do you feel shy when you are alone with someone of the opposite sex? Always? Almost always? Sometimes? Hardly ever? Never?" Other measures take qualitative answers, such as statements of one's feelings, and code them into categories that can be quantified. Assigning numbers to variables increases the precision of scientific communication procedures and results.

We will review three important methods of measurement that are part of the descriptive research techniques psychologists use: self-reports, behavior analysis, and physiological measures.

Self-report Measures

Sometimes researchers are interested in what people think and feel, as well as in what they do. Sometimes, they might want information about behaviors that are very difficult or impossible to observe, such as sexual activities or criminal acts. In these cases, investigations rely on verbal reports. **Self-report measures** are verbal answers, either written or spoken, to questions the researcher poses. Sometimes these answers are taken at face value, as in the case of *opinion surveys*. Sometimes they are interpreted in terms of other information known about the subjects, such as test scores, the evaluations of teachers or other kinds of measurement. Often one person's self-report is compared to those of others responding to the same questions or tasks.

Self-reports are the primary method for getting information about beliefs, attitudes, feelings, motives, and personality. However, there are limits to their usefulness and there are problems with their validation. Obviously, self-reports cannot be used with preverbal children, illiterate adults, foreigners, some mentally disturbed people, and animals. Even when verbal reports can be used, they may not be accurate. Subjects may not remember clearly what they actually experienced or misunderstand the questions. One confounding variable in the use of verbal reports is social desirability—people may give false or misleading answers to create a favorable impression of themselves. They may be embarrassed to report their true feelings.

Self-reports include questionnaires, surveys, and interviews. A *questionnaire* is a written set of questions, ranging in content from questions of fact ("Are you a registered voter?") to questions about past or present behavior ("How much do you smoke?"). It may also include questions about attitudes and feelings ("How satisfied are you with your present job?"). *Open-ended* questions allow respondents to answer freely in their own words. Questions may also have a number of *fixed alternatives* such as *yes, no,* and *undecided*.

Questionnaires are used in *survey research*, which is a way to gather information efficiently from a large number of people. In a *survey*, a standardized set of questions is given to a large number of participants, either by mail, by telephone, or face-to-face. Unlike the

census, which tries to survey the entire population, a sample survey collects information from a carefully selected group of people who are believed to have attributes that are representative of the entire population from which the sample is drawn. One example of a sample survey is a public opinion poll; its conclusions about national opinions are often based on a sample of about 1500 people.

There is always the risk of error in sampling a population. Most polls carry a standard warning label about the margins for error. Often the margin of error is about 3 percent, which means that the data is accurate within 3 percent, plus or minus, of the values presented. (A value reported at 30 percent with a margin of error of 3 could actually be as high as 33 percent or as low as 27 percent.)

An *interview* is a face-to-face dialogue between a researcher and an individual for the purpose of obtaining detailed information. Instead of being completely standardized, as a questionnaire is, an interview is *interactive*. An interviewer may vary the questioning to follow up on something the respondent said. Good interviewers are also sensitive to the process of the social interaction as well as to the information revealed. They are trained to establish *rapport,* a positive social relationship with the respondent that encourages trust and the sharing of personal information.

Interviews can generate invalid data. Respondents who are aware of the interviewer's purpose may lie or alter the truth to get a job, to get discharged from a mental hospital, or to accomplish any other goal they may have. The interview situation also allows personal biases and prejudices to affect how the interviewer asks questions and how the respondent answers them.

Behavioral Measures

Although psychological researchers are interested in behavior, the kind of behavior they are interested in varies dramatically. They may be interested in studying a rat running a maze, a child drawing a picture, a student memorizing a poem, or a worker repeatedly performing a task. **Behavioral measures** are ways to study overt actions and observable and recordable reactions.

One of the primary ways to study what people do is *observation*. Researchers use observation in a planned, precise, and systematic manner. For example, researchers often document behavior samples on videotape for later analysis.

Direct observations are those made with the "naked eye." The behavior under investigation is clearly visible and overt and can be easily recorded. For example, in a study of communication patterns, a researcher might ask a group of students to discuss a controversial issue while he or she makes direct observations about who

By standing behind a one-way mirror, a researcher can watch a child at play and record his or her observations without influencing or interfering with the child's behavior.

starts the discussion, who changes the topic, who speaks, and so forth. In a laboratory experiment on emotions, a researcher could observe a subject's facial expressions as the subject looked at emotionally arousing stimuli.

In *naturalistic observations,* some naturally occurring behavior is viewed by a researcher who makes no attempt to change or interfere with it. For example, a researcher behind a one-way mirror might observe the play of children who are not aware of being observed. From observations about each child's interaction patterns, the researcher might make inferences about sociability or relationships with adults. (See photo of Harvard University researcher Jerome Kagan.)

When studying behavior in a laboratory setting, a researcher is unable to observe the long-term effects that one's natural habitat has in shaping complex patterns of behavior. One of the most valuable examples of naturalistic observation conducted in the field is the work of **Jane Goodall** (1986). Goodall has spent many years studying patterns of behavior among chimpanzees in Gombe on Lake Tanganyika in Africa. The focus of her research is the insight chimpanzee behavior might shed on the evolutionary development of certain forms of human behavior, especially aggression. Goodall's exhaustive observational analysis of every aspect of chimpanzee behavior began over 25 years ago and continues today, even though it was originally scheduled to last for only ten years. Goodall notes that had she ended her research after ten years, she would not have drawn the correct conclusions.

> We would have observed many similarities in their behavior and ours, but we would have been left with the impression that chimpanzees were far more peaceable than humans. Because we were able to continue beyond the first decade, we could document the division of a social group and observe the violent aggression that broke out between newly separated factions. We discovered that in certain circumstances the chimpanzees may kill and even cannibalize individuals of their own kind. On the other side of the coin, we have learned of the extraordinarily enduring affectionate bonds between family members . . . advanced cognitive abilities, [and the development of] cultural traditions . . . (Goodall, 1986, pp. 3–4).

In the early stages of an investigation, naturalistic observation is especially useful. It is used to help discover the extent of a phenomenon or to get an idea of what the important variables and relationships might be. The data from naturalistic observation often provide clues for an investigator to use in formulating a specific hypothesis to be tested or other research methods. Some kinds of human behavior can be studied only through naturalistic observation, because it would be unethical or impractical to do otherwise. For example, it would be unethical to experiment with severe deprivation in early life to see its effects on a child's later development.

While observations usually focus on the *process* of behavior, some researchers focus on the *products* of behavior. In an experiment on learning, for instance, a researcher might observe how many times a subject rehearsed a list of words (process) and then how many words the subject remembered on a final test (product). Or the researcher might observe behavioral products that were generated in the past or made for purposes other than research. Personal documents, such as autobiographies, letters, diaries, drawings, and speeches can yield other valuable background information.

Behavioral observations are improved with technology that permits more precise measurement, such as stop-action photography which can document rapidly

Jane Goodall's continuing study of chimpanzees in Gombe on Lake Tanganyika in Africa is one of the most well-known examples of naturalistic observation conducted in the field.

changing behavior. Among other things, stop-action photography has been used in studies of the way subtle changes in facial expressions of mothers and their babies become synchronized and similar over time. Another useful technology is high output responding. In a test that measured the performance of hungry pigeons, high output responding permitted researchers to measure how pigeons learned to peck a button that triggers delivery of food pellets. At times the pigeons worked at the rate of 4500 responses per hour (Ferster and Skinner, 1957), a rate that would have been impossible to observe without the aid of technology.

Physiological Measures

How does a researcher know what the brain is doing when someone is asleep or solving a problem? Special instruments are available to show these internal reactions in a measurable form. For example, by amplifying the brain's electrical signals and recording them on a computerized graph or by monitoring the blood flow in the brain, it is possible to get a picture of someone's state of mental activity. The *electroencephalogram* (EEG) permits researchers to record patterns of brainwave activity. Researchers then study how these patterns vary as consciousness is altered when a subject goes from a state of wakefulness to sleeping and dreaming. At a more precise level of micro analysis, researchers interested in discovering how information is processed in specialized cells in the brain can do so by implanting minute electrodes into single brain cells and recording their pattern of activity. One disadvantage of such technology is that it is *invasive* (it invades one's awareness and modifies their usual reactions)—because the equipment is attached to the research subjects, they are prevented from moving about freely and acting as they might ordinarily.

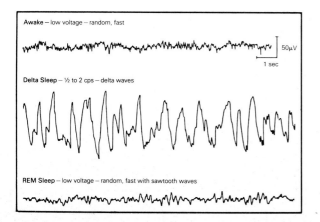

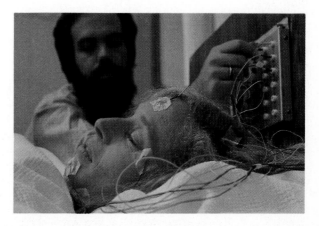

By connecting subjects to EEG machines, scientists can study the activity of the brain during sleep.

PSYCHOLOGY LABORATORY IN THE WILD

Morning breezes ripple the tall, golden grass in Tanzania's Mikumi National Park. A troop of 70 yellow baboons moves slowly up the sparsely wooded hillside. Some animals groom each other and others feed, alone or in groups. Their fur is the same color as the grass, and the untrained eye might miss them altogether if it weren't for the human in their midst: psychologist Sam Wasser, lean and bearded. He follows a small group of animals, marking a data sheet on his clipboard, checking and resetting his stopwatch. Wasser pauses and lowers his binoculars. His baboons have stopped and are catching bugs only a few feet in front of him.

Suddenly, five female baboons rush another female, grunting loudly and snapping at her. She tries to fight back, but the odds are against her, and she retreats to the base of a nearby baobab tree. The episode is over in less than a minute. If you hadn't witnessed it directly, you never would have known that anything had happened. Brittle grass crunches under Wasser's boot. A giraffe grazes at the bottom of a neighboring hill. A herd of zebra meanders through miombo woodland half a mile away.

To Wasser, however, the attack, which he refers to as a "coalition," fits into an intricate pattern of behaviors in which social stress helps to regulate the timing and distribution of births in the troop. He knows that Haki, the victim crouched beneath the baobab, is pregnant. Pregnant baboons, simi-

lar to pregnant humans, are sensitive to stress. During the preceding week, Haki has been attacked more than ten times by groups of females, many of them also pregnant, and Wasser expects the stress generated by the attacks might make her lose her unborn baby.

Since the late 1970s, Wasser has been one of a handful of psychologists who conduct naturalistic observations of primates in the wild. By working with noncaptive subjects, he hopes to build an ecologically valid model of social and reproductive behavior as it occurs in the animals' natural habitat.

Wasser proposes that the female reproductive system is acutely sensitive to information from both the social and physical environments. When environmental conditions are harsh enough to threaten an infant's chances of survival *and* when circumstances are unlikely to improve in the future, Wasser predicts that a female's reproductive capacity may shut down

temporarily, terminating a pregnancy or preventing conception altogether.

Female attack coalitions occur primarily when a large number of females are in reproductive synchrony. If too many births occur in a single season, competition for resources could threaten the lives of the weaker ones. The coalitions, which occur at different stages of the reproductive cycle, keep birth cohorts at a size where demand for resources will not exceed supply. Attacks during pregnancy can lead to spontaneous abortion, prematurity, and low birth weight. Mid-ranking mothers can increase their own infants' chances of survival by eliminating the competition before it becomes too strong, attacking low-ranking mothers and their babies. Wasser has recorded two infanticides and has watched the steady decline of several mother-infant pairs under siege (Wasser & Starling, 1988).

The ethological approach to research has attracted considerable attention over the past two decades. Psychologists realized that the very act of *controlling* environmental conditions in the lab could elicit behaviors that never occur under ordinary circumstances. Wasser does not have that problem. Because he uses an ecologically valid methodology, he feels confident that the behaviors he observes are not artifices of his experimental procedure. He is now extending the implications of his model for human infertility, miscarriage, abortion, and premature birth (Wasser, 1990).

A new use of EEG recordings is mapping the response to surprise. How do our brains react to a stimulus that appears unexpectedly?

Neuroscientist **Emanual Donchin** uses a particular type of brain wave—the P300 wave—to assess the emotional response triggered by a surprising event. A research subject responds by pressing one button when a male name appears on the computer screen, a second when a female name appears. Because most of the names are male, the appearance of a female name is unexpected. This stimulus event triggers a specific change in brain activity, known as event-related potential. It is a brain-wave that reaches a peak about 300 milliseconds after the surprising event but does not occur in response to expected stimuli. Donchin notes that "by looking at changes in brain activity in relation to psychological processes we are trying to understand better the relationship between the mind and the brain" (*Discovering Psychology*, 1990, Program 1).

CORRELATIONAL METHODS

Is intelligence associated with creativity? Are optimistic people healthier than pessimists? What is the link between social isolation and madness? Is there a relationship between being easily hypnotized and being conforming? These are a few of the questions we will answer in later chapters using the results of research based on correlational methods. Psychologists use correlational methods when they want to determine to what extent two variables, traits, or attributes are related.

To determine the precise degree of correlation that exists between two variables, psychologists use two sets of scores to compute a statistical measure known as the **correlation coefficient** (r). This value can vary between $+1.0$ and -1.0 where $+1.0$ is a perfect positive correlation, -1.0 is a perfect negative correlation, and 0.0 means there is no correlation at all. A positive correlation coefficient means that as one set of scores increases, a second set also increases. The reverse is true with negative correlations; the second set of scores goes in the opposite direction to the values of the first scores. Correlations that are closer to zero mean that there is a weak relationship or no relationship between scores on two measures. As the correlation coefficient gets stronger, closer to the $+/-1.0$ maximum, predictions about one set of scores based upon information about the other set of scores (for the other characteristic) become increasingly more accurate.

For example, a researcher exploring the relationship between worker productivity and stress might measure how much stress people are experiencing in their lives and how well they are performing at work. *Stress* might be operationally defined as scores on a stress questionnaire. *Job productivity* might be defined as the number of units of a given product that a worker produces each day. The researcher could then measure each variable for many different workers and compute the correlation coefficient between them. A strongly negative score would mean that as stress goes up, productivity goes down. Knowing someone's life stress score would then allow the researcher to make a reasonable prediction about that person's productivity.

The researcher could go the next step and say that the way to increase productivity would be to lower stress. This assessment is incorrect. A strong correlation only indicates that two sets of data covary in a systematic way; the correlation does not ensure that one of them causes the other. *Correlation does not imply causation.* The correlation could reflect any one of several cause and effect possibilities or none.

For example, a negative stress and work productivity correlation might mean that (a) stress at home carries over to cause people to do poorly at work, (b) poor job productivity makes people experience more stress, or (c) those with a certain personality style are more likely to experience stress and also to perform poorly on the job. (Note that in the last case, a third variable is causing the other two to vary.) Consider another example: there is a strong correlation between contraceptive use in Taiwan and the number of electrical appliances in Taiwanese homes. Given this finding, would you expect contraceptive use to increase if the government gave away radios and popcorn machines? The answer would be yes only if the two variables are related causally. In actuality, a third set of variables—education and social class—is responsible for both phenomena (Li, 1975). Can you see how?

When a correlation exists between two events or measures, they may be related only by *coincidence*. For example, the migration of birds and whales might occur every year around the time of your birthday. But it is a coincidence that your birthday falls at a time when birds and whales migrate. As obvious as this seems, people often fail to recognize the possibility that coincidence rather than causation or correlation is operating.

Another example of coincidental correlation is the supposed connection between the power blackout in New York City in 1965 and the reported jump in the birth rate nine months later. "New Yorkers are very romantic. It was the candlelight," said one new father. An official for a planned parenthood group offered the explanation that, because of the blackout, "All the substitutes for sex—meetings, lectures, card parties, theaters, saloons—were eliminated that night. What else could they do?" (*The New York Times*, 8/11/66). The same correlation is often reported after major blizzards and other disasters in many parts of the world. "Quake May Have Caused Baby Boom in Bay Area," was a recent headline in San Francisco's *Chronicle* (7/17/90). However, when anyone takes the time to compare these apparently dramatic birth rate increases with the ordinary seasonal variations in birth over many years in local hospitals, the correlation turns out to be coincidence masquerading as a causation.

Correlations, because of the way data are collected, may also be spurious, biased, or false. For example, Arizona and Florida have the highest incidence of respiratory illness and arthritis in the country. This occurrence is not due to the fact that there is something unhealthful about Arizona and Florida. The correlation is due to the fact that these states include great numbers of the elderly who are especially susceptible to these diseases. Although correlational studies have the advantage of being able to establish relationships between variables that cannot be manipulated in experiments, we must always be cautious when interpreting them.

Because correlations are relationships between sets of measurements usually taken of many people, predictions based on them are *group* predictions. Correlations are rarely accurate predictions for *individuals*. For example, the high positive correlation repeatedly found between heavy smoking and incidence of lung cancer indicates that there will be more cancer among heavy smokers than among nonsmokers. It does not tell us whether any particular heavy smoker will get cancer or whether a given nonsmoker will remain healthy.

Two research approaches that make use of correlational methods are psychological tests and cross-cultural research. A *psychological test* is a measuring instrument used to assess an individual's standing, relative to others, on some mental or behavioral characteristic such as intelligence, personality, vocational interests, aptitudes, or scholastic achievement. Each test consists of a set of questions, problems, or activities. The responses are assumed to be indicators of a particular psychological function. The use of group tests permits information to be obtained quickly and efficiently from large numbers of people. Typically, test performance is used to predict how a person will probably behave in a particular situation—for example, SAT scores are used as predictors of grades in college.

Cross-cultural research is used to discover whether behavior found in one culture also occurs in other cultures. In this type of research, the unit of analysis is a whole culture or society rather than an individual. However, the data consist of observations of individual reactions (Brislin, 1981). The cross-cultural method has been used to compare diverse sexual patterns, perceptual differences in reactions to illusions,

and cultural factors that influence productivity (Hofstede, 1980). A recent summary of more than 100 cross-cultural studies points to a basic distinction between societies throughout the world, namely whether they are *individualistic* or *collectivist* (Triandis, 1990). Individualistic societies stress the individual as the most important unit; they value competition, individual achievement, and personal fulfillment. In contrast, collectivist societies place the greatest value on social group, family, community, or tribe. Cooperation, sharing, altruism, and the social good are the main values that guide collectivist societies. These two fundamentally different orientations influence a wide range of behavioral patterns. For example, in one study, a researcher tested his hypothesis about the relationship between societal life-styles and conformity by comparing people from a hunting society (the Inuit) with people from an agricultural society (the Temne in Africa). He found a tendency toward conformity on a standardized test in the agricultural society whose members learned to cooperate and depended on each other for their food. Conformity scores were lower in the hunting society where food gathering was an individual activity and required independence and self-reliance (Berry, 1967). Around the world, individualistic or collectivist societies are unequally distributed; 70 percent of societies are collectivist and only 30 percent are individualistic. Because most of modern psychology is based on research conducted in individualistic societies in North America and Europe, it becomes questionable how far the conclusions of this research can be generalized.

EXPERIMENTAL METHODS

Experimental methods are used to discover causal relationships between variables specified by the hypothesis being tested. The method of choice when a researcher is searching for the causes of a behavior is the controlled experiment. In a **controlled experiment,** observations of specific behavior are made under systematically varied conditions. An experimenter manipulates a stimulus and measures its effects on one or more behavioral outcomes. The stimulus or stimulus condition that is systematically manipulated or varied by the experimenter is known as the *independent variable.* That aspect of a subject's behavior or experience that is observed or measured as a predicted change resulting from the manipulation of the independent variable is known as the *dependent variable.* All conditions—except the independent variable—are held *constant* or accounted for in other ways. Research subjects must be *randomly assigned,* by chance procedures, to an **experimental condition** (exposed to the independent variable or treatment) or to a **control condition** (not exposed to the experimental treatment).

In the ideal experiment, all confounding variables, extraneous conditions, and personal biases are eliminated so that all alternative explanations (other than the one proposed by the experimental hypothesis) can be ruled out. This is a difficult task. It is achieved through standardized procedures, random assignment of research subjects to the experimental control conditions, and the use of appropriate control procedures to rule out observer and research biases.

Randomization is a critical feature of experimental methods. This chance assignment to experimental and control conditions makes the two groups similar in important ways at the start of an experiment because each group has the same probability of being in the treatment condition as in the control condition. If outcome differences are found between the two conditions, the researcher can be more confident that they were caused by treatment or intervention rather than by already existing differences. Another key feature of experimental methods is providing a comparison for an obtained result. Once, when I asked my young daughter if she loved her older sister, she asked, "Compared to what?" That question is one that must be asked—and satisfactorily answered—before we can really understand what a research finding means. The data from the control condition serve as this comparison or baseline against which the experimental effect is evaluated.

So what is the first question you should ask when you read that a recent study shows that "more than three-quarters of a group of people trying to quit smoking were able to win with the help of nicotine patches" (*The New York Times*, 4/29/90)? Compared to what? In the placebo control group that wore nicotine-free patches, a full 39 percent also stopped smoking! Moreover, the longer they wore these medically useless patches, the more likely they were to quit smoking (Abelin, et al., 1989). So the nicotine patch was an effective treatment, but more than half of its cure was due to the placebo effect of expecting that it would work.

Sometimes such comparisons are not made with a separate control group that did not receive the treatment. Instead, comparisons might be made to a group that received a different level of the experimental treatment. Or the behavior of an experimental subject before getting the treatment might be compared to his behavior after. In what is known as an **A-B-A design,** subjects first experience the baseline, or control condition (A), then experience the experimental treatment (B), and then go back to the baseline (A).

This A-B-A design was used by an investigator who wanted to test the hypothesis that making children feel anonymous would increase their level of aggression when the situation provided an opportunity. Grade-school children were invited to a Halloween party where a variety of games were available, both those that invited aggressive and non-aggressive play. In the baseline condition (A), the children played without wearing Halloween costumes. Then in the treatment condition (B), they put on costumes and continued to play the games of their choice. Finally, in a return to the baseline condition (A), they were told the costumes had to be returned but they could continue playing without them. The results supported the experimenter's hypothesis, as you can see in **Figure 2.4.** Across the three conditions that were otherwise constant, the same children were much more aggressive when they were anonymous than when they were identifiable. (Fraser, 1974.)

Another form of control in scientific experiments is the use of controlled procedures—methods that attempt to hold constant all variables and conditions other than those related to the hypothesis being tested. (We mentioned this kind of control earlier as one way in which

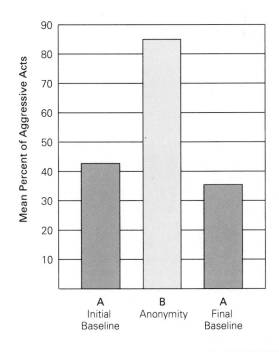

FIGURE 2.4   *AGGRESSION VERSUS REWARDS*

The effects of being anonymous are dramatic—aggression is much higher in the anonymous condition.

objectivity is promoted through the scientific method.) In an experiment, all instructions, room temperature, tasks, the way the researcher is dressed, time allotted, how the responses are recorded, and many more details of the experimental situation need to be similar for all subjects to ensure that their experience is the same. The only difference in their experiences is that introduced by the independent variable.

What are the limits and disadvantages of psychologists relying on the experimental method? First, during an experiment, behavior is often studied in an artificial environment, one in which the situational factors are controlled so heavily that the environment may distort the behavior from the way it would occur naturally. Second, research subjects typically know they are in an experiment and are being tested and measured. They may react to this awareness by trying to please the researcher, attempting to "psych out" the research purpose, or changing their behavior from what it would be if they were unaware of being monitored. Critics claim that much of the richness and complexity of natural

behavior patterns are lost in controlled experiments, sacrificed to the simplicity of dealing with only one or a few variables and responses. Third, some people challenge experimental research on ethical grounds. In the next section, we will consider some of the ethical issues raised by research.

But first, we have to go back to the beginning. We are now ready to answer the question raised in our opening case: Do the subliminal audio tapes influence mental states and behavior as their advocates claim? Our answer comes from experimental methods used to test the hypothesis (see **Figure 2.5**).

Recently, a team of experimenters set out to determine the effectiveness of listening to commercially available audiotapes designed to improve self-esteem or memory. The subjects were 78 men and women volunteers, ranging from 18 to 60 years of age. After a pretest session in which their initial self-esteem and memory were measured on standard psychological tests and questionnaires,

FIGURE 2.5 *EXPERIMENTAL DESIGN FOR TESTING HYPOTHESES ABOUT THE EFFECTIVENESS OF SUBLIMINAL AUDIOTAPES*

In this simplified version of the experiment, a sample of people is drawn from a larger, general population. They are given a series of pretest measures and randomly assigned either to receiving subliminal tapes with either memory or self-esteem messages or to receiving a control tape. They are then given posttests that objectively assess any changes in memory and self-esteem—the dependent variables. The study found no significant effects of subliminal persuasion.

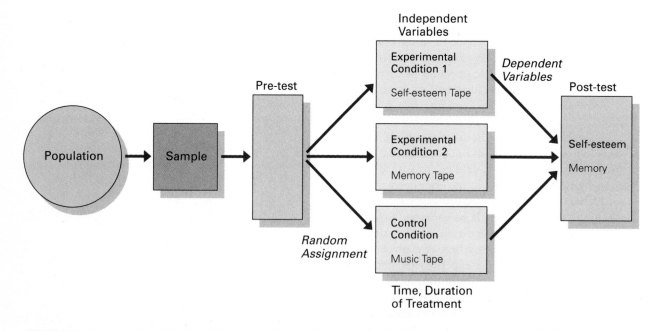

the subjects were randomly assigned to two conditions. Half of them received subliminal memory tapes, while the others received subliminal self-esteem tapes. They listened regularly to the tapes for a five-week period and then returned to the laboratory for a posttest session to evaluate their memories (using four memory tests) and self-esteem (using three self-esteem scales). The researchers were blind to which subjects received which treatment (Greenwald, et al., 1991).

Did the tapes boost self-esteem and enhance memory? The results from this controlled experiment indicate that there was *no significant improvement* shown on any of the objective measures of either self-esteem or memory. However, one very powerful effect did emerge: the placebo effect of expecting to be helped. Anticipating this effect, the researchers had added another independent variable. Half the subjects in each group received memory tapes that were mismarked "self-esteem" and the others received self-esteem tapes in memory boxes. Subjects believed their self-esteem improved if they received tapes with that label or felt that their memory improved if their tapes were labeled "memory"—even when they had been listening to the other tape! The findings are best described by researcher **Anthony Greenwald** as "what you expect is what you believe but not necessarily what you get."

So, buyer beware of personal testimonials for subliminal self-help tapes that offer nothing more than placebo effects. Here is one instance where experimental research clearly contradicts what individuals believe is the psychological effect of a treatment—they believe in the treatment because they do not systematically and objectively evaluate its effectiveness.

STATISTICAL ANALYSIS OF DATA

A full description of how psychologists analyze their data using statistical methods is given in the appendix to this chapter, *Understanding Statistics*. It should be read in conjunction with the chapter. An overview of the major points is given here as a summary for classes in which the appendix is not assigned.

Psychologists use statistics to make sense of the data they collect. They also use statistics to provide the quantitative foundation for the conclusions they draw. **Descriptive statistics** are used to describe numerically sets of data collected from research subjects and to describe relationships among two or more variables. Descriptive statistics indicate what scores are most typical, or average, and also how *variable,*

or dispersed, the rest of the scores are from the average score.

Measures of *central tendency* give a single, representative score that can be used as an index of the most typical score obtained by a group. The measures of central tendency are the mode, the median, and the mean. The **mode** is the average score that occurs most often. The **median** is the middlemost average score—half the scores are above and half below the mode. The **mean** is the most useful measure of central tendency because it is the average score (of a distribution of scores) which takes account of the size of each individual score. The mean is computed by adding the sum of the scores and dividing by the total number of scores.

Measures of *variability* indicate how close together or spread apart the scores in a distribution are. Two measures of variability are the **range,** the highest and lowest scores, and the **standard deviation,** the average distance each score is from the mean of all scores.

Inferential statistics are used to determine what conclusions can be drawn about a given population from the sample data collected. A difference between two sets of data is said to be statistically significant if the probability that the difference is due to chance is less than 5 percent. That effect—less than five times out of 100—is the acceptable standard in psychology for determining whether a result is significant. If so, a researcher can conclude that, because it was not due to chance or random factors, the results obtained are more likely to have occurred as the consequence of the intervention, or independent, variable.

SUMMING UP

By quantifying measures of behavior and mental processes, psychologists gain greater precision in describing and communicating research results. Psychologists measure variables by using verbal self-reports, overt behavioral responses, and physiological responses. Each has advantages and also some disadvantages that researchers must take into account. The use of new technologies for videotaping, brain mapping, and computerized analyses enables researchers to study more subtle and complex behavior.

After describing the variables of interest, researchers use correlational and experimental methods to understand, predict, and help control behavior. Correlational methods are best for the early stages of research; they help us discover which variables are related and how strongly they are related. Experimental methods are designed for testing hypotheses about the causal relationship between two variables. Correlational studies use sets of scores from psycho-

logical tests, questionnaires, surveys, interviews, and observations to quantify the degree of relationship, generating a correlation coefficient statistic. Strong correlations allow predictions of behavior, but these never can be used as statements of causation, because two correlated variables can be related in many different ways. The key components of a controlled experiment are systematic variation of the independent variable, control of extraneous variables, random assignment of subjects to treatment and control conditions, standardized testing procedures, and precise measurement of behavioral outcomes. Using the experimental method, researchers found no support for claims of the power of subliminal self-help tapes.

Research-based conclusions in psychology are made after statistical analysis of the data is completed. After making a descriptive summary of the data in terms of average scores and the variability of scores, researchers use inferential statistics to determine the extent to which obtained results differ from those that would be expected by chance alone. A difference is considered statistically significant if it occurs by chance less than five times in 100 trials—a probability of less than 5 percent.

ETHICAL ISSUES IN HUMAN AND ANIMAL RESEARCH

In the study that tested the effectiveness of subliminal messages, the researchers deceived the participants by mislabeling the tapes. They did so to see if the subjects' expectations would lead them to believe that the messages were helpful even if objective measures of memory and self-esteem showed no improvement. Deceiving people is always unethical, but in this case, how else could researchers assess the placebo effect of false beliefs held by the subjects? How would you weigh the *potential gains* of a research project against the *certain costs* it incurs to those who are subjected to procedures that are risky, painful, stressful, or deceptive?

Respect for the basic rights of humans and animals who participate in psychological research is a fundamental obligation of all researchers. To guarantee that these rights are honored, special committees oversee every research proposal, imposing strict guidelines issued by the U.S. Department of Health and Human Services. Psychology departments at universities and colleges, hospitals, and research institutes each have review panels that approve and reject proposals for human and animal research. In a sense, these institutional review boards try to adjust the balance of power be-

tween experimenters and research participants. The American Psychological Association (1982) has established detailed guidelines for ethical standards for researchers. What are some of those guidelines and ethical concerns?

INFORMED CONSENT

Typically all research on human subjects begins with a full description of the procedures, potential risks, and expected benefits that subjects will experience. Before beginning the research, subjects are given this information and asked to sign statements indicating that they give their *informed consent* to participate. The subjects are assured in advance that they may leave an experiment any time they wish, without penalty, and are given the names and phone numbers of officials to contact if they have any grievances.

RISK/GAIN ASSESSMENT

Most psychology experiments carry little risk to the subjects, especially where participants are merely asked to perform routine tasks. However, some experiments that study more personal aspects of human nature— such as emotional reactions, self-images, conformity, stress, or aggression—can be upsetting or psychologically disturbing. Therefore, whenever a researcher conducts such a study, it is important that he or she includes, as a basic feature of the research process, procedures designed to protect the subjects' physical and psychological well-being (Diener & Crandall, 1978). Risks must be minimized, subjects must be informed of the risks, and suitable precautions must be taken to deal with strong reactions by the subjects. Where any risk is involved, it is carefully weighed by each institutional review panel in terms of its necessity for achieving the benefits to science, to the society, and even to the participants of the study. Similar precautions are to be exercised in animal research, where the humane and considerate treatment of all animal subjects is now clearly recognized as essential.

INTENTIONAL DECEPTION

For some kinds of research it is not possible to tell the subjects the whole story in advance without biasing the results. If you were studying the effects of deception on subjects in an experiment, for example, you could not tell them what you were studying because then they would not be able to react to being deceived. However, many critics argue that deception is never justified in research because it violates the basic right of informed consent (Korn, 1987). Others assert that the immorality of any deception does harm to the subjects, the profession of psychology, and to society (Baumrind, 1985). On the other side of the controversy, some researchers who use deception have argued that the harm is exaggerated and that follow-up studies typically reveal that most subjects enjoyed participating and report having acquired important self-knowledge, especially when the study dealt with personally experiencing the "darker side of human nature."

Perhaps the most controversial study in psychology was one in which subjects were made to think they should follow the orders of an authority figure who instructed them to deliver painful shocks to another subject. In fact, they were not actually hurting the victim, although they did not know this. In this study of blind obedience to authority, the subjects were quite torn between honoring their research commitment by doing as they were told and quitting the experiment (Milgram, 1974). The researcher reported that over 80 percent of the subjects were "very glad" or "glad" to have been in the study, only 1 percent said they were "sorry" or "very sorry" and the rest were neither glad nor sorry to have participated (Milgram, 1977).

Yet, if even one subject feels harmed by participating in a deception experiment, doesn't that make it unethical? Alternatives to deception research are being put into practice wherever possible and safeguards are instituted to reduce the potential risks. In risky experiments, the review committee may impose constraints, insist on monitoring initial demonstrations of the procedure, or deny approval (Steininger et al., 1984).

DEBRIEFING

Participation in psychological research should always be a mutual exchange of information between researcher and subject. The researcher may learn something new about a behavioral phenomenon from the subject's reactions, while the subject should be informed of the purpose, hypothesis, anticipated results, and expected benefits of the study. At the end of an experiment, each subject must be given a careful **debriefing,** in which the researcher provides as much information about the study as possible and makes sure that no one leaves feeling confused, upset, or embarrassed. If it was necessary to mislead the subjects during any stage of the research, the experimenter carefully explains the reasons for this deception. In addition, the privacy of subjects is protected; all records of their behavior are kept strictly confidential or any public sharing of them must be approved by the subjects. Finally, subjects have the right to withdraw their data if they feel they have been misused or their rights abused in any way.

ISSUES IN ANIMAL RESEARCH: SCIENCE, ETHICS, POLITICS

Should animals be used in psychological and medical research? Before we consider the pro and con sides of this heated issue, let's first outline some reasons that psychologists use animal subjects in their research. First, it is more possible to distinguish between heredity and environment factors that influence performance and brain functioning in animals bred and reared under controlled conditions than it ever could be in humans. Second, since many species breed more rapidly than do humans, studies of developmental processes that occur over many generations are possible. Third, in some species, basic processes—such as sensation, learning, memory, and even social status—are comparable to those in humans. Since in animals they occur in less complex forms that can be more readily investigated, animal models of these processes shed light on human functioning. Fourth, other psychologists study animal behavior, not for what it may reveal about humans, but to better understand general laws of behavior that are true across species or simply to learn about a given animal species. Much of the psychological knowledge that we will study in our journey has come from research that investigated the mental, physiological, and behavioral functioning of animals.

In recent years, concern over the care and treatment of animals used in psychological and biomedical research has led to strict guidelines that researchers must follow in order to receive research funds and conduct their research. Laboratory facilities must have adequate space, be well maintained, and use qualified staff to care for the animals. The health of the animals and their general well-being also is monitored. Every effort must be made to minimize pain and discomfort and to seek alternative procedures that are not stressful.

None of these precautions and procedures matter now to animal rights activists. The dominant goal of this large, politically powerful group is "to stop the exploitation of animals for any purpose, and in particular, to abolish animal experimentation altogether" (McCabe, 1990). While some of these individuals push for restrictive state and federal legislation to inhibit and prohibit much animal research, others have taken more direct action. The Animal Liberation Front takes credit for "liberating" research animals from many laboratories and for breaking into the labs, trashing them, and even burning some to the ground (*U.S. News & World Report,* 8/31/87). Such terrorist acts have interfered with and, in many cases, halted basic biomedical research. Some of this animal research "is essential if the progress that has been made in the prevention, treatment, and cure of ailments that cause human suffering is to continue" (Kaplan, 1988, p. 839).

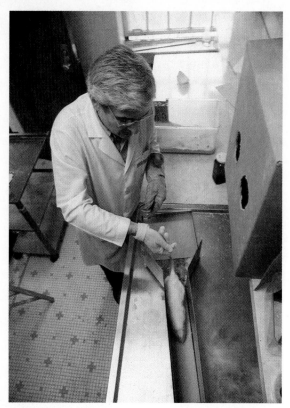

Rats are often used for experiments because the experimental variables are easy to control for them and we know their genetic history.

such as rabies, distemper, and anthrax, are preventing suffering and untimely deaths in billions of domestic animals. Psychological researchers have shown how to alleviate the stresses of confinement experienced by zoo animals. Their studies of animal learning and social organization have led to the improved design of enclosures and animal facilities that promote good health (Nicoll et al., 1988).

Citizens must inform themselves with accurate information about the total costs and benefits to humans and to animals of animal research before deciding to take political, legal, or destructive actions to stop it. In a democracy, as in scientific endeavors, rational information should guide decisions.

 ## BECOMING A WISER RESEARCH CONSUMER

This chapter has emphasized an appreciation of the methods, approaches, and values that form the scientific foundation of psychology. It has also highlighted the need to be critically aware of sources of error in conclusions that are reported to be based on research. In this final section, we will focus on the kinds of critical thinking skills you need to become a wiser consumer of psychological knowledge.

Honing these "thinking tools" is essential for any responsible person in a dynamic society such as ours— one so rich in information and so filled with claims of truth, with false "common sense" myths, and with biased conclusions that serve special interests. Analytical skills enable the individual to begin to assess the plausibility of claims made about "what research shows." They encourage an open-minded skepticism about proofs and conclusions based solely on the opinions of "experts." They provide means for adjusting the confidence one has in personal testimonials and eyewitness observations—even one's own. To be a critical thinker is to go beyond the information as given and to delve beneath slick appearances, with the goal of understanding the substance without being seduced solely by style and image.

Because psychology is so much a part of our everyday lives and is often misrepresented in the media, professional psychologists are extremely concerned about communicating accurate information to the public about what is known and about how one can go about evaluating its validity. Most psychology in the public domain comes not from the books, articles, and reports of accredited psychologists. Rather, this information comes from the mass media, newspaper and magazine articles, TV and radio shows, pop psychology and self-help books, and the "pseudosciences industry"

The debate over animal testing goes beyond issues of ethics in research. It centers on society's recognition of the contributions that scientific research with animals, and with humans, makes daily to the health and well-being of humans and animals alike. How would safe medicines or vaccines that protect us from deadly and contagious diseases have been developed without animal research and human clinical trials? The benefits of animal research include discovery and testing of drugs that treat anxiety, mental illnesses, and Parkinson's disease; new knowledge about drug addiction; rehabilitation of neuromuscular disorders; and currently work on the desperately sought cure for AIDS (Miller, 1985).

Animal activists claim that not a single medical advance has depended on animal experimentation. Oxford professor of physiology, Colin Blakemore, rebuts their assertion as "nonsense." He says, "I cannot think of a single advance that has not depended on animals at some stage" (*Science,* 8/31/90, p. 981). A different perspective on the debate comes from a catalog of benefits that animal research has made to animals. On a worldwide basis, immunizations for various animal diseases, (astrology, psychic surgery, subliminal mind control, and "New Age" gimmicks).

A major goal of education is to provide the learner with an understanding of how the world functions and of how to separate superstition and irrational beliefs from fact and reason. In general, the more formally educated someone is, the less that person believes in occult, miracles, and the paranormal. However, national public opinion surveys reveal that for a large percentage of the 25 million U.S. adults without high-school diplomas, the world is a confusing and threatening place that operates in incomprehensible ways. They feel that they are controlled by fate and can do little to control their lives. It follows that they are inclined to believe in lucky numbers, cosmic signs, omens, horoscopes, and mystical forces. A large percentage of them believe that "Scientific researchers have a power that makes them dangerous." Even more agree that "The only way we can know what is going on is to rely on leaders and experts who can be trusted" (J. D. Miller, 1987). Such beliefs, sometimes shared by more educated people, indicate that our schools have failed to provide the conceptual framework for separating superstition and science fiction from scientific understanding and fact.

The multimillion-dollar *pseudoscience industry* sells its diverse products to the legions of "true believers" who come prepared to accept the unexplained, the unevaluated, and the unproven. It is not surprising that many cult leaders find willing recruits to their never-ending array of social-political-religious movements. Common to many such cults are attacks on the rational, scientific foundation of our knowledge about the world. Cult leaders, such as Reverend Moon, ask their followers "not to question with your mind but to think with your heart," and to practice "authority surrender"—unquestioning trust in *their* authority. Since hearts play no documented role in comprehension, and unjust authorities can mislead and betray our trust, it becomes vital to cultivate an open-minded skepticism about others who want to totally structure our view of reality.

Psychological claims are an unavoidable aspect of the daily life of any thinking, feeling, and acting person in our psychologically sophisticated society. Every day you address the same issues psychologists do: you ask questions about your own behavior or that of other people, you seek answers in your theories or observations of what "authorities" say, and you check out the answers against the evidence available to you.

Studying psychology will help you make wiser decisions based on evidence gathered either by you or by others. Some of these decisions are the everyday ones about which products to buy or services to use. Others are more substantial—affecting your entire life-style and perhaps even the life of this planet.

SCIENCE-COATED JOURNALISM

When you read that a toothpaste is "37 percent more effective," do you run out and buy some, or do you ask, "Compared to what?" Compared to not brushing at all or to brushing with sugar, maybe? When you learn from an ad that 4 out of 5 doctors recommend Brand X aspirin, do you want to know if the sample size for this research was only five doctors? While these instances may seem extreme, we are asked to believe many such claims, not only by advertisers, but by journalists and all sorts of pop-psych practitioners as well.

Recently, a report about sexual behavior that made national headlines was found to be based on faulty sampling procedures. According to the conclusions of the Hite Report (contained in the popular book, *Woman and Love,* by Shere Hite, 1987), 98 percent of married women reported they were dissatisfied with some aspect of their marriages, and three-fourths of these married women had engaged in extramarital affairs as a result. These and other sensational findings were based on data from a reasonably large sample of 4500 American women, ages 14 to 85. However, when the same questions were posed to another sample of women by ABC News and *The Washington Post,* the results were quite different. Only 7 percent reported having affairs, and the majority, 93 percent, were emotionally satisfied with their relationships (*The Washington Post,* 10/27/87).

Which report about the mental, emotional, and social state of women in modern times is true? The answer lies in *how* the data were gathered. The Hite Report used a *convenience sample* of women in church and political groups who answered researcher Hite's mail survey anonymously. But they represented only a 4-percent return of the 100,000 questionnaires mailed out. Their answers hardly can be taken as representative of U.S. women's attitudes and marital relationships. Unhappily married women or those with more active fantasy lives may have been more likely to take the time to answer. The survey conducted to check the validity of the Hite Report used a random sampling procedure with only 1505 participants. To assure that all groups were proportionally represented, subjects were selected according to U.S. Census figures on age, education, race, and sex. The Hite Report, similar to many reports that misuse surveys, is a case of science-coated journalism. Statistics are used to convey the aura of science, but the methods employed to collect them are so flawed that the statistics are worthless.

LAUGHING AND CAUSING

A miracle cure for a usually incurable, crippling spinal disease was reported by **Norman Cousins,** editor of

THE WAR ON DRUGS

Addiction

In September of 1990, U.S. President George Bush and antidrug czar William Bennett presented an upbeat report on the first year of the Bush administration's "war on drugs." One study they cited found *decreases* in cocaine and marijuana use (*U.P.I.*, 9/4/90), and another reported a reduction in the number of hospital emergency room records that mentioned cocaine or heroin. Bennett "attributed the gains, in part, to Bush's leadership and the American people's resolve" (*U.P.I.*, 9/5/90).

At the same time, the Drug Policy Foundation, an international group seeking alternatives to the current drug war approach taken by the administration cited *increases* in drug-related crimes, an overloaded criminal justice system, a heroin comeback, and underfunded treatment programs. They used this evidence to back up their contention that the drug war was failing and that other strategies needed to be developed.

Both sides claimed that the data supported their conclusions. How can you, as a wise consumer of research, evaluate these conflicting assertions?

First, *define the problem* as clearly and simply as possible: The U.S. government conducted a one-year, $9.5 billion experiment in which more than 70 percent of the funds were earmarked for "get-tough" law enforcement. Did this intervention show evidence of lowering recruitment of new drug takers, cutting the incidence of chronic drug addiction, and reducing the negative effects of drug use in our society? Next, *operationally define* a set of dependent variables that measure the harm posed to society by drug abuse. You might come up with some of the following: incidence of new drug addicts, rates of needle-transmitted AIDS and HIV infection, incidence of newborns showing opiate withdrawal symptoms at birth, incidence of drug-related homicides, dollar cost of imprisoning drug addicts and pushers, and number of lung cancer deaths attributed to smoking (tobacco is one of the most lethal drugs). The "drug problem" is so vaguely defined and multifaceted that, through careful selection and emphasis, you might find strong empirical support for any position.

Let's look more closely at some of the evidence in this case. Bush and Bennett reported decreases in drug use, but failed to mention that use of illicit drugs in the United States has *decreased* steadily since 1979 (*National Institute on Drug Abuse*, 1989). In this historical context, a one-year continuation of a ten-year trend hardly seems like a major victory for their war on drugs. And while emergency rooms treated 4 percent fewer cases involving cocaine, cocaine-related deaths actually increased by 11 percent in the same year (*U.P.I.*, 9/5/90).

The Drug Policy Foundation has also been known to select data that suit its purposes. At the 1989 launch of the war on drugs, it used the same measure cited by Bush and Bennett—emergency room records of drug abuse—to counter the Administration's claim that expanding prison capacity by 85 percent would ease the drug crisis. Emergency rooms had reported a 121 percent increase in drug-related cases at the same time that, under the Reagan administration, prison populations almost doubled (*The Drug Policy Letter,* Sept.–Oct. 1989). Although the Foundation correctly reported an increase in drug-related crime (based on drug-related arrests), that increase does not prove that the war on drugs is a failure. The argument is circular, and could be used by either side. The "experiment" is working as planned if there are more drug-related arrests, court hearings, or incarcerations for drug-related offenses. It is not working to reduce the incidence of taking drugs in the first place, it is only increasing the criminal justice counterattack.

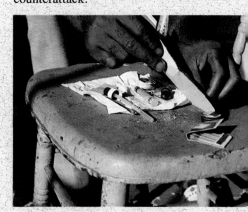

What would it take to convince *you* that a government policy decreased drug-related harm to society? What would you find more compelling—a series of raids on marijuana farms in Oregon or a decrease in the rate of HIV infection in newborns? Think the problem through as though *you* were designing the experiment.

Consider the appropriateness of the study's timespan. Many of the important questions about drugs and behavior—or any major social-economic problem—cannot be answered by a short-term study. While you can tell almost immediately if flea-bombing your apartment worked, the effects of

Saturday Review. He cured himself. He did so by laughing. His self-prescribed laughter therapy came from watching videos of "Candid Camera" episodes and old Marx Brothers movies. His account was detailed in 1979 in a best-selling book, *Anatomy of an Illness,* and laughter therapy soon became popular. Before using Cousins's treatment for your ailments, however, you should ask "Was that all there was to it?"

The answer is no. There were many other possible ingredients in Cousins's self-therapy program. Before we can be sure that laughter alone is the active ingredient in this new treatment, it is necessary to separate its effects from all the other possible sources of influence on Cousins's state of mind and health. Among the other independent variables in his situation were massive intravenous doses of vitamin C, a treatment plan supervised by his physician, library research on his illness, and a well-developed optimism and a strong will to live.

It may be that the cure was influenced by the total combination of these factors, and none of them alone might be sufficient to improve one's well-being. Having a clinic simply prescribe funny movies for patients might not be health enhancing if the critical variable is the patient's sense of personal control over sickness.

With so many factors at work at the same time, can we single out funny movies and recommend them as therapy for others? They may work only when part of a treatment package that includes some of those other ingredients. It might also be that laughter therapy works only for certain people—maybe for optimists, for positive placebo responders, or for those suffering from certain kinds of medical problems. It is difficult to assert that one factor is the cause of an effect when there are so many others operating simultaneously. In this case, systematic experimentation could isolate the causal factors from the extraneous ones. In a later chapter on health psychology, we will review some of the positive evidence for the therapeutic effects of humor and laughter.

CRITICAL THINKING CONSUMER CHECKLIST

Here are some general rules to keep in mind in order to be a more sophisticated shopper as you go through the supermarket of knowledge:

- Avoid the inference that correlation is causation.
- Ask that critical terms and key concepts be defined operationally so that there can be consensus about their meanings.
- Consider first how to disprove a theory, hypothesis, or belief before seeking confirming evidence, which is easy to find when you're looking for a justification.
- Don't buy into personal testimonials and case studies that don't offer objective data of how typical they are, their comparative base rates, and any special conditions associated with their success and failure.
- Always search for alternative explanations to the obvious ones proposed, especially when the explanations benefit the proposer.
- Recognize how personal biases can distort perceptions of reality.
- Be suspicious of simple answers to complex questions or single causes and cures for complex effects and problems.
- Question any statement about the effectiveness of some treatment, intervention, or product by finding the comparative basis for the effect: compared to what?
- Allow yourself cognitive flexibility in recognizing that most conclusions are tentative and not certain; seek new evidence that decreases your uncertainty while keeping yourself open to change and revision.
- Be sensitive to the fallacy of explaining social and psychological problems, such as poverty, in terms of the special features of *people* alleged to cause them rather than to the *situations* that influence their behavior.
- Challenge authority that is unjust, uses personal opinion in place of evidence for conclusions, and is not open to constructive criticism.

Some of these points about how we interpret evidence presented in the media are illustrated in the Close-Up on page 50.

RECAPPING MAIN POINTS

The Context of Discovery

In the discovery phase of research, observations, beliefs, and information lead to a new way of thinking about a phenomenon. The researcher verbalizes an idea to be tested as a theory, hypothesis, or paradigm. The discovery phase may be distorted by external or internal influences on the researcher. There are three kinds of bias: personal, observer, and expectancy.

The Context of Justification

Justification is the phase in which ideas are tested and disconfirmed or proven to some degree of certainty. To test their ideas, researchers use the scientific method, a set of procedures for gathering and interpreting evidence in ways that limit errors. Researchers maintain objectivity in part by keeping complete records, standardizing procedures, using operational definitions, minimizing biases, and controlling flaws. A reliable research result is one that can be repeated in similar conditions at different times by independent investigators.

Psychological Research Methods

Descriptive research techniques include self-reports, behavior analysis, physiological measures, questionnaires, surveys, interviews, and psychological tests. Correlational research methods determine if and how two variables are related. Experimental research methods determine whether causal relationships exist between variables specified by the hypothesis being tested. Correlations do not imply causation. Descriptive statistics describe sets of data and the relationships among two or more variables. Inferential statistics determine what conclusions can be drawn legitimately about a given population from the sample data.

Ethical Issues in Human and Animal Research

Respect for the basic rights of humans and animal subjects in psychological research is the obligation of all researchers. A variety of safeguards have been enacted to guarantee ethical and humane treatment.

Becoming a Wiser Research Consumer

Becoming a wise research consumer involves learning how to think critically and knowing how to evaluate claims about what research shows.

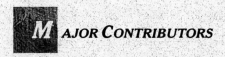

KEY TERMS

A-B-A design, 43

alternative explanations, 35

behavioral measures, 37

confounding variable, 35

context of discovery, 28

control condition, 42

controlled experiment, 42

correlation coefficient, 41

cross-cultural research, 42

debriefing, 47

descriptive statistics, 45

determinism, 32

double-blind control, 35

empirical investigation, 28

expectancy bias, 29

experimental condition, 42

hypothesis, 32

mean, 45

median, 45

mode, 45

observer bias, 29

operational definition, 34

paradigm, 32

personal bias, 29

placebo control, 35

placebo effect, 31

randomization, 43

range, 45

reliability, 35

scientific method, 33

self-report measures, 37

standard deviation, 45

standardization, 34

theory, 32

validity, 36

variable, 32

MAJOR CONTRIBUTORS

Cousins, Norman, 49

Donchin, Emanual, 41

Goodall, Jane, 38

Greenwald, Anthony, 45

Munsterberg, Hugo, 29

Rosenthal, Robert, 29

Chapter 3

Biopsychology
and
Neuroscience

EVOLUTION, HEREDITY, AND BEHAVIOR   57
   EVOLUTION
   HUMAN EVOLUTION
   GENES AND BEHAVIOR

   ■ INTERIM SUMMARY

BRAIN AND BEHAVIOR   63
   CLOSE-UP: THE GENETICS OF ALCOHOLISM
   EAVESDROPPING ON THE BRAIN
   BRAIN STRUCTURES AND THEIR FUNCTIONS

   ■ INTERIM SUMMARY

THE ENDOCRINE AND NERVOUS SYSTEMS   76
   GLANDULAR CONTROL OF BEHAVIOR AND
     INTERNAL PROCESSES
   NEURONAL CONTROL OF BEHAVIOR AND
     INTERNAL PROCESSES

   ■ INTERIM SUMMARY

THE NERVOUS SYSTEM IN ACTION   81
   THE NEURON
   GRADED AND ACTION POTENTIALS
   SYNAPTIC TRANSMISSION
   NEUROTRANSMITTERS AND THEIR FUNCTIONS
   CLOSE-UP: SYNAPTIC TRANSMISSION AND DRUGS:
     EFFECTS OF COCAINE
   NEURAL NETWORKS

   ■ INTERIM SUMMARY

**THE NERVOUS SYSTEM AND CONSCIOUS
EXPERIENCE**   94
   CEREBRAL DOMINANCE
   TWO BRAINS OR ONE?

   ■ INTERIM SUMMARY

OUR RESPONSIVE BRAIN   99

RECAPPING MAIN POINTS   100

KEY TERMS   101

MAJOR CONTRIBUTORS   101

ive-and-a-half weeks before her twins were due, Christine felt the first sharp pains of labor. Her husband drove her to the hospital where, for 16 hours, the two of them followed the breathing instructions given to them during their natural childbirth class. Then a fetal monitor showed that the heartbeat of one of the babies was weakening. Doctors quickly performed a cesarean section. Within minutes, Nicole, at 4 pounds, and Alexis, at 3 pounds 14 ounces, had entered the world.

Immediately after birth, Nicole and Alexis joined half a dozen other babies in the Neonatal Intensive Care Unit. For two-and-a-half weeks, electronic devices monitored their vital signs. Experienced nurses tended to their physical needs and held them frequently. Christine spent a good part of each day with her babies, holding and rocking them and feeding them her breast milk from bottles, awaiting the day when she could actually breast-feed them. Wearing diapers barely the size of cocktail napkins, the twins looked fragile and unfinished. With no layers of baby fat, every little rib in their bodies showed.

Had Nicole and Alexis been born 20 years earlier, their first few weeks of life would have been quite different. Until the late 1970s, prematurely born infants were touched as little as possible. Parents and medical personnel feared that any unnecessary contact with the outside world might harm the babies. Fortunately for Nicole and Alexis, we now know better.

Research with infant rats and humans has led scientists to conclude that brain functioning can be altered by touch, and that, for newborns, touch is essential for normal growth and development. Biologist **Saul Schanberg** found that when rat pups were removed from their mothers, the levels of an enzyme important for growth decreased dramatically (Schanberg et al., 1990). The longer they were deprived of maternal contact, the less responsive the pups became. The effects of maternal deprivation could be reversed in only two ways: by returning them to the mother, who immediately started licking them, or by having a researcher vigorously stroke them with a small paintbrush. Schanberg (1990) concluded that, "The need for a mother's touch is really brain based. It isn't just nice to have it. It's a requirement for the normal development and growth of the baby."

This research with animals led psychologist **Tiffany Field,** who had collaborated with Schanberg (Field & Schanberg, 1990), to conduct studies of prematurely born human infants. Her research team randomly selected 20 preemies to receive periodic massages throughout the day, while 20 others received normal hospital treatment in the intensive care unit—treatment which did not include massages. According to Field, "The premature babies who were massaged for 45 minutes a day for ten days before they were discharged gained 47 percent more weight than the babies who did not get massaged. They were more active. They were more alert." Eight months later, the massaged babies had maintained their weight advantage and were also more advanced in motor, cognitive, and emotional development (Field, 1990). This research is being extended and replicated in larger samples of preemies in order to establish the power of human touch on biological and psychological health.

In the United States, more than 0.25 million infants are born prematurely each year. Those who are touched and cuddled leave the hospital several days sooner than usual, reducing care costs by about $3,000 per child. Unfortunately, not all hospitals

Tiffany Field (*Discovering Psychology,* 1990, Program 3)

apply what scientists have learned about the positive effect of early touch on development. If they did, the lives of thousands of children would be improved, saving billions of dollars each year—both very practical benefits of this basic research.

When Nicole and Alexis left the hospital, they were still rather small, but were developing so well that the doctors felt confident they would be all right. At home, the babies shared a crib in the living room, where relatives and friends who remarked on their tiny size were encouraged to pick up the babies gently and cuddle them. Christine and her husband were acutely aware that providing such physical stimulation is apparently critical for optimal development of the brain and, in turn, the mental and physical processes the brain controls.

When fully matured, the brain weighs only 3 pounds, less than Nicole and Alexis did at birth. But, despite its small weight and even though it is made up of the same basic chemical molecules found throughout the universe, the brain is the most complex structure in the known universe. This little biocomputer contains more cells than there are stars in our entire galaxy— over 100 billion nerve cells—designed to communicate and store information. What is even more difficult to comprehend is that within this biochemical structure is the basis for communicating all the information that is ever possible for the brightest of us to know or the most sensitive of us to experience. Because of our brains, each of us is a self-contained miracle, able to do many things more easily and more automatically than even the most powerful computers.

The human brain, which has developed over millions of evolutionary years, is the subject of study for a new breed of researchers in the rapidly emerging field of *neuroscience,* a multidisciplinary attempt to understand the functioning of the nervous system. The psychologists in neuroscience are also identified as researchers in *biopsychology,* a rapidly growing area of psychology that studies the relationship among biology,

behavior, and environment. These psychologists believe that everything the brain does is ultimately caused by physical, chemical, or biological events taking place in specific regions of the brain. The first task of biopsychologists is to *reduce* behavioral phenomena to the smallest units in the biochemical mechanisms that underlie the actions of all living creatures. Once they have an elemental understanding of the biological substrate, they move on to the more difficult task of *synthesizing* the complex repertoire of human actions. The ultimate question for biopsychologists is how the human mind emerges from this mass of tangled organic tissue.

Many questions arise as we charge the brain with the task of understanding itself. How does the biological machinery of the brain and its connections to the rest of the nervous system—the spinal column and the nerves of the body—become the basis for intelligent life? How can a series of on-off electrical impulses within the brain's nerve cells, and the flow of chemical transmitter substances between these cells, be the basis for our every thought, dream, feeling, motive, and action? How can an organ that does not generate enough energy to illuminate an ordinary light bulb be the most powerful creative and destructive force on earth?

Then there is the grand illusion fostered by the brain: each human mind comes to believe that *it* is more powerful than the combined, emerging properties of all the brain's structure and functions. The conscious aspect of mind—the sense of self that looks out at the world and in at its own thoughts and mortality—seems to exist independently of its biology, which it perceives as inferior. But when brain cells are destroyed by disease, drugs, and accidents, we are suddenly reminded of the biological basis of the human mind. In such cases, we are forced to recognize the physical matter from which sensation and language, learning and memory, passion and pain, and human reason and madness spring forth.

The goal of this chapter is to make you aware of the way psychology as a discipline investigates the relationship of biological systems to the outside world. First, we will learn how evolution and heredity determine our biology and behavior. We will then see how laboratory and clinical research provide a view into the workings of the brain, the nervous system, and the endocrine system. We will examine some intriguing relationships among these biological functions and some aspects of the human experience of consciousness. Finally, we will consider how touch and other stimulation can actually modify the brain—which will explain why we perceive the brain as responsive and dynamic.

For many students, this chapter will pose a greater challenge than the rest of *Psychology and Life.* It requires that you learn some anatomy and many new terms that seem far removed from the information you may have expected to get from an introduction to psychology. However, understanding your biological nature will enable you to appreciate more fully the complex interplay among the brain, mind, behavior, and environment that creates the unique experience of being human. And that experience is what your journey in life is all about.

EVOLUTION, HEREDITY, AND BEHAVIOR

Before we can even begin to appreciate the brain's involvement in our behavior and thought processes, we need to ask two questions: How did this marvelous piece of biology come to be and why are the brains of all species, although similar, so different? The answers to these questions will provide us a powerful perspective from which we can appreciate the significance in everyday life of the brain and the nervous system. The first question will lead us to consider **evolution,** the theory that, over time, organisms originate and adapt to their unique environments through the interaction of

Charles Darwin
(1809–1882)

biological and environmental variables (outlined in Chapter 1). The second question will lead us to consider **heredity,** the biological transmission of traits from parent to offspring.

EVOLUTION

About 50 years before Wilhelm Wundt established psychology's first experimental laboratory, **Charles Darwin,** fresh out of college with a degree in theology, set sail on a 5-year cruise that would change his life—and the history of science—forever. In 1831 the *H. M. S. Beagle,* an ocean research vessel, set sail from the shores of England to survey the coast of South America. During the trip, Darwin collected everything that crossed his path: marine animals, birds, insects, plants, fossils, seashells, and rocks. His extensive notes became the foundation for his books on topics ranging from geology to emotion to zoology. The book for which he is most remembered is *On the Origin of Species,* published in 1859. In this work, Darwin set forth science's grandest theory: the evolution of life on planet earth.

While he was at sea, Darwin only briefly entertained some of the ideas that lead to evolution. What made him develop this idea into a theory? For years after his return to England, he marveled at the differences among his specimens and reread and revised his notes countless times. Darwin argued theory and data for long hours with other naturalists. He even began to dabble in *selective breeding,* a procedure for purposely mating plants and animals to produce offspring that possess specific and highly desirable traits.

It was Darwin's research into selective breeding that eventually gave rise to some of his most important ideas on evolution. He began to think that some analogous mechanism in nature might be responsible for the ways different species either adapted to their environment or became extinct. After all, if humans could *select* for specific traits in breeding animals and plants, why couldn't nature, in all its grandeur and power, do the same? Thinking along these lines eventually led Darwin to the conclusion that, in a species' struggle for existence, some characteristics are favored and *preserved* by nature while others are not favored and *destroyed*. The result of this process, he wrote, "would be the formation of a new species" (Darwin, 1887).

Natural Selection

Darwin called his theory—that some members of a species tend to produce more offspring than others—the theory of **natural selection.** Organisms well adapted to their environment, whatever it happens to be, will produce more offspring than those less well adapted. Over time, those organisms possessing traits more favorable for survival will become more numerous than those not possessing those traits. In evolutionary terms, an individual's success is measured only by the number of offspring he or she produces. Let's look at a specific example.

One of the many places that Darwin visited on his voyage was the Galapagos Islands, a volcanic archipelago off the west coast of South America. These islands are a haven for diverse forms of wildlife, including 13 species of finches, now known as *Darwin's Finches.* How did so many different species of finches come to inhabit the islands? They couldn't have migrated from the mainland, for those species don't exist there. The answer to the question is found in natural selection. Apparently, long ago, a small flock of finches found their way to one of the islands; they mated among themselves and eventually their number multiplied. Food resources and living conditions—*habitats*—vary considerably from island to island. Some of the islands are lush with berries and seeds, others are covered with cacti, and others have plenty of insects. Over time, some finches migrated to different islands in the archipelago. What happened next is the process of natural selection. Birds that migrated to islands rich in berries and seeds survived and reproduced *only* if they had thick beaks. On those islands, birds with thinner, more pointed beaks, unsuitable for crushing or breaking open seeds, died. Birds that migrated to insect-rich islands survived and reproduced *only* if they had thinner, more pointed beaks. There, birds with thick beaks, not selected for eating insects, died. The environment of each island determined which finches would live and reproduce and which would perish, leaving no offspring. The diversity of habitats on these islands permitted the different species of Darwin's Finches to evolve from the original ancestral group.

Recent research has shown that natural selection can have dramatic effects, even in the short run. In a series of studies by **Peter Grant** (1986), involving one species of Darwin's Finches, records were kept of rainfall, food supply, and the population size of these finches on one of the Galapagos Islands. In 1976, the population numbered well over 1000 birds. The following year brought a murderous drought that wiped out most of the food supply. The smallest seeds were the first to be depleted, leaving only larger and tougher seeds. That year the finch population decreased by more than 80 percent. However, smaller finches with smaller beaks died at a higher frequency than larger finches with thicker beaks. Consequently, and as Darwin would have predicted, the larger birds became more numerous in the following years. Why? Because only they, with their larger bodies and thicker beaks, were fit enough to respond to the environmental change caused by the drought. Interestingly, in 1983, rain was plentiful, and seeds, especially the smaller ones, became abundant. As a result, smaller birds outsurvived larger birds, probably because their beaks were better suited for pecking the smaller seeds. As Grant's study shows, while evolutionary effects occur over a very long time frame, natural selection can have noticeable effects even over short periods.

Variation and Competition

Although the environment is the driving force behind natural selection, it is not the only factor. Two other factors, variation and competition, also play key roles.

Variation refers to differences in biological and psychological traits among individuals within a given population. Some people are big and strong; others are intelligent; and still others are big, strong, *and* intelligent. Each finch species studied by Grant differed from the others in its **phenotype,** the many features by which an individual is recognized. These phenotypes included physical traits (beak size) and behavioral traits (ability to crack different kinds of seeds). The differences among the finches went deeper than outward appearances and seed-cracking abilities. Each finch also possessed a different **genotype,** or genetic structure inherited from its parents. Genotypes determine the extent to which the environment can influence an organism's development and behavior. Any organism's phenotype is determined by one and only one process: the interaction of the organism's genotype with the environment. Ultimately, natural selection operates at the level of the genotype; if the phenotype is not well adapted to an environment, then neither is the particular genotype that gave rise to it.

During times of drought and scarcity of small seeds, larger birds outsurvived and outreproduced smaller birds. Had there been no phenotypic variation among the finches, no differences among the finches in terms of their physical traits and abilities, none or all would have survived. But because there was phenotypic variation, and because that variation was genetically based, the larger finches had a *selective advantage* and they survived and reproduced. When environmental conditions reversed and small seeds became more plentiful, birds with the smaller phenotype had a selective advantage. Then the smaller phenotypes were better suited to the environment, and the larger birds, carrying the corresponding genotype, were selected against.

Because members of the same species occupy the same ecological niche, strong competition for food, territory, and mates occurs. This means that for every seed consumed by one finch, there is that much less food for other finches. A small piece of real estate protected by one bird is that much less territory that can be occupied by another. In times of food scarcity, competition gets even tougher, and only those with the fittest phenotype will survive and pass along the corresponding genotype to the next generation. **Figure 3.1** is a simplified model of natural selection, including how variation and competition are involved in the selection of the fittest phenotypes.

HUMAN EVOLUTION

What sort of role, if any, has natural selection played in human evolution? We sometimes forget that, first and foremost, we are biological creatures. Occasionally, we are reminded of this fact, when we become ill or have to visit the dentist to have a cavity filled. For the most part, however, the comforts of modern culture dispose us to take our biology for granted. As in Darwin's times, some people still argue that natural selection applies to animals, but not to us. We seldom appreciate that our life-style, with all of its conveniences and luxuries, is the result of the natural selection of certain genotypes passed along to us from our ancient ancestors.

Through the combined efforts of hundreds of naturalists, biologists, anthropologists, and geneticists, we now know that, in the evolution of our species, natural selection favored two adaptations—bipedalism and encephalization. Together, they made possible the rise of human civilization. **Bipedalism** refers to the ability to walk upright and **encephalization** refers to increases in brain size. These two adaptations are responsible for most, if not all, of the other major advances in human evolution, including cultural development (see **Figure 3.2**). As our ancestors evolved the ability to walk upright, they were able to explore new environments and exploit new resources. As brain size increased, our ancestors became more intelligent and developed capac-

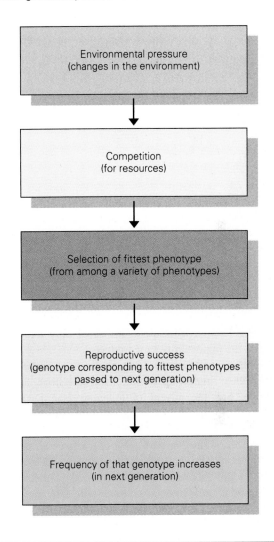

FIGURE 3.1 HOW NATURAL SELECTION WORKS

Environmental changes create competition for resources among species members. Only those individuals possessing characteristics instrumental in coping with these changes will survive and reproduce. The next generation will have a greater number of individuals possessing these genetically based traits.

Environmental pressure
(changes in the environment)

Competition
(for resources)

Selection of fittest phenotype
(from among a variety of phenotypes)

Reproductive success
(genotype corresponding to fittest phenotypes passed to next generation)

Frequency of that genotype increases
(in next generation)

ities for complex thinking, reasoning, memory, and planning. (However, the evolution of a bigger brain did not guarantee that humans would become more intelligent—what was important was the kind of tissue that developed and expanded within the brain.) Because the opposable thumb evolved, humans fashioned and used tools. They developed simple strategies for hunting big game, and they used fire for heating and cooking. The genotype coding for intelligent and mobile phenotypes slowly squeezed other, less well-adapted genotypes

FIGURE 3.2

APPROXIMATE TIME LINE FOR THE MAJOR EVENTS IN HUMAN EVOLUTION

Bipedalism freed the hands for grasping and tool use. Encephalization provided the capacity for higher cognitive processes such as abstract thinking and reasoning. These two adaptations probably led to the other major advances in our evolution.

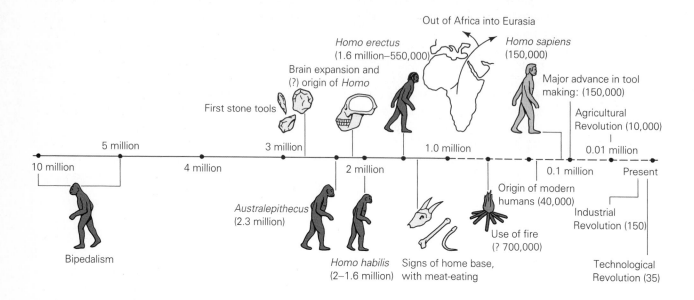

from the human gene pool, affording only intelligent bipeds the opportunity to reproduce.

After bipedalism and encephalization, perhaps the other most important evolutionary milestone for our species was the advent of *language* (see Diamond, 1990). The capacity for language, of course, stemmed directly from encephalization. If bipedalism and encephalization are the cornerstones upon which modern civilization is built, then language is the tool by which cultures are fashioned and refashioned. Think of the tremendous adaptive advantages that language conferred upon early humans. Simple instructions for making tools, finding a good hunting or fishing spot, and avoiding danger would save time, effort, and lives. Conversation, even humor, would strengthen further the social bonds among members of a naturally gregarious species. Most importantly, the advent of language, particularly the written word, would provide for the transmission of accumulated wisdom, from one generation to future generations. Language is the basis for *cultural evolution,* which is the tendency of cultures to respond adaptively to environmental change through learning. Cultural evolution gives rise to major advances in toolmaking, to improved agricultural practices, and to the development and refinement of industry and technology. In short, cultural evolution is critical to the development

and maintenance of the kinds of life-styles enjoyed by our species today.

In contrast to biological evolution, cultural evolution allows our species to make very rapid adjustments to changes in environmental conditions. Instead of taking thousands, even millions, of years for an adaptation to evolve, adaptations may appear within a single generation. As the basic unit of biological evolution is the gene, the basic unit of cultural evolution is the written or spoken word. But cultural evolution *does* have a genetic basis; without genotype coding for the capacities to learn and to think abstractly, cultural evolution would not occur. Culture—including art, literature, music, scientific knowledge, and philanthropic activities—is possible only because of the human genotype. The influence of genes on our behavioral and cognitive abilities explains why psychologists are so keenly interested in genetics.

The marvelous piece of biology we call the brain exists because it was favored by natural selection in our ancient ancestors' quest for survival. Our brains differ from those of other species for much the same reason (Harvey & Krebs, 1990). The earliest humans lived and survived in an environment different from those of other species so their brains evolved differently to meet the needs of their unique environment.

Genotype coding for the capacity to learn and think abstractly has made cultural evolution possible. These are Native American petroglyphs.

GENES AND BEHAVIOR

You have learned that, in the struggle for existence, environment determines a genotype's ability to live. Now let's briefly consider how the genes themselves are related to behavior. You differ from your parents in part because you grew up and continue to live in different environments than they did. However, you differ from them also because you possess a different combination of genes than they do. Your mother and father have endowed you with a part of what their parents, grandparents, and all past generations of their family lines have given them, resulting in a unique biological blueprint and timetable for your development. The study of heredity—the inheritance of physical and psychological traits from ancestors—is called **genetics.**

Basic Genetics

In the nucleus of each of our cells is genetic material called DNA (deoxyribonucleic acid). DNA contains the instructions for the production of proteins. These proteins regulate the body's physiological processes and the expression of phenotypic traits: body build, physical strength, intelligence, and many behavior patterns. DNA is organized into tiny units called **genes** that are found on rodlike structures, known as *chromosomes*.

At the very instant you were conceived, you inherited from your parents 46 chromosomes—23 from mom and 23 from dad. Each of these chromosomes contains thousands of genes—the union of a sperm and egg will result in only one of many billion possible gene combinations. Although you have a full 50 percent of your genes in common with your brothers or sisters, your set of genes is unique unless you have an identical twin. The difference in your genes is one reason why you differ, physically and behaviorally, from your brothers and sisters. (The other reason is that you do not live in exactly the same environment as they do.)

The **sex chromosomes** are those that contain genes coding for development of male or female physical characteristics. You inherited an *X* chromosome from your mother and either an *X* or a *Y* chromosome from your father. An XX combination codes for development of female characteristics; an XY combination codes for development of male characteristics. Consider, for a moment, the psychological implication of this one factor of your biology. How your parents reared you; how your relatives, friends, teachers, and others treat you; whether you can bear children; the kinds of athletic, social, and occupational opportunities afforded you; and even your self-perception stem, by and large, from this one very critical genetic factor. Is your psychology—how you get along in the world—rooted in your biology? Whether we answer this question in terms of your behavior, cognition, social perception, or physical appearance, the answer is an unequivocal yes.

Remember, though, that genes do not code for destinies; they code for potential. Although only women can bear children, they do so by choice. Just because you're tall doesn't mean you will play basketball. Also keep in mind that it is not only genetic factors that determine who you are. Physical size, for example, is determined jointly by genetic factors and nutritional environment. Physical strength can be developed in both males and females through special exercise

We have significant genetic similarities to our parents, making us like them in many ways.

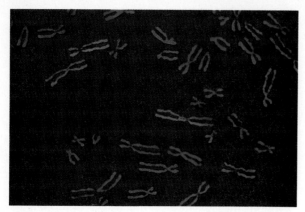

Human chromosomes

programs. Intellectual growth is determined by both genetic potential and educational experiences. Neither genes nor the environment alone determines who you are or what kind of person you ultimately become. Genes only control the range of effects that the environment can have in shaping your phenotype.

Genetics and Psychology

The task for psychologists is to determine what environments help people develop their full potential. Consider, for example, people with Down's Syndrome. *Down's Syndrome* is caused by an extra chromosome in the 21st pair (resulting in three chromosomes instead of two in the pair). It is characterized by impaired psychomotor and physical development as well as mental retardation. (The majority of Down's Syndrome babies are born to mothers over the age of 40.) Without intervention from psychologists and other skilled professionals, people with this disorder depend almost wholly on others to fulfill their basic needs. However, special educational programs can train persons with Down's Syndrome to care for themselves, hold simple jobs, and establish a small degree of personal independence that would otherwise be impossible.

The behavior of persons with Down's Syndrome can be modified through training. This fact underscores an important relationship that is emerging between psychology and genetics. Scientists and applied researchers in both fields have united forces in an interdisciplinary effort to accomplish two goals: to understand how genes influence behavior and to determine how environmental variables (training programs, diet, and social interactions) can be used to modify behavior that has a strong genetic basis. **Human behavior genetics** is a relatively new field uniting both geneticists and psychologists interested in determining the genetic basis of behavioral

traits and functioning, such as intelligence, mental disorders, and altruism (Fuller, 1982; Plomin & Rende, 1991). Much of the research conducted by behavior geneticists involves selective breeding, similar to the research once practiced by Darwin. (Recall that selective breeding is the artificial selection of specific phenotypic traits.) They also investigate the inheritance of certain behavioral traits, such as intelligence, among individuals who vary in their degree of genetic similarity. Psychologists working in the field of **developmental disabilities** are primarily responsible for designing programs to improve the quality of life for individuals born with genetically based disorders.

Genetic research over the past two decades has brought us to a threshold of understanding once thought impossible. We are on the verge of being able to map all of the human genes and use that knowledge to improve our quality of life by gigantic leaps (Delisi, 1988). *Genetic mapping* is the attempt to decipher the DNA code for each of our estimated 100,000 genes. Once these codes are broken—once we know which genes give rise to which traits—scientists will be able to conduct more accurate diagnostic tests for genetically based disorders. In the past 20 years, the genes involved in juvenile diabetes, some forms of cancer, arthritis, blindness, and manic-depressive disorder have been identified. Identifying defective genetic coding is the first step in developing effective intervention and treatment programs. For example, since 1970, regular diagnostic tests for Tay-Sachs disease (which involves massive neurological damage and usually ends in death before the age of 4) have been routinely performed on persons believed to be at risk for this disorder. Since the tests have been conducted, the incidence of Tay-Sachs has plummeted by over 90 percent (*Consumer Reports,* 1990). The test warns couples of the possibility that their children may be born with the disorder, allowing them to make an enlightened decision about whether to have children. With increased knowledge of how genes contribute to the development of physical and psychological traits, it may soon be possible to provide gene therapy for people with certain medical and psychological disorders (Anderson, 1984). Already researchers have found ways to produce human insulin and vaccines from genes to use in the treatment of diseases; use of genetic materials to treat some immune system disorders appears likely in the next few years. Other research has demonstrated that gene therapy is highly effective in treating cancerous tumors in mice. Based on this success, similar research with humans is expected to begin soon (Culliton, 1990). And if these advances are not amazing enough, research is currently under way that may soon provide for the actual replacement or repair of defective genes.

As we learn more and more about genes and their relationship to behavior and psychological disorders, psychologists will likely be called on even further to provide guidance about the way that knowledge might be put to its most effective use (Wingerson, 1990).

![icon] **SUMMING UP**

Species originate and change over time because of natural selection, which is the tendency of organisms to reproduce differently due to the interaction of phenotypic traits with the environment. Because members of a species vary in their biological and behavioral characteristics and because that variation is genetically based, changes in environmental conditions may favor organisms possessing special characteristics. In terms of the evolution of our species, natural selection has favored two adaptations: bipedalism and encephalization. These adaptations are responsible for subsequent evolutionary advances, including language and culture.

The basic unit of evolution is the gene—a small unit of DNA found along chromosomes. Genes alone do not determine the specific nature of a phenotype. Rather, genes set the range of effects that environmental factors can have in influencing expression of phenotypic traits. Because behavior is determined by both genetic and environmental variables, psychologists and geneticists have united to accomplish two goals: to understand better how genetic variables influence behavior and to use that knowledge to improve the quality of life. Advances in genetic mapping promise to provide researchers with surer diagnoses of genetically based disorders, which will lead to more effective clinical treatments.

BRAIN AND BEHAVIOR

Long before Darwin made preparations for his trip aboard the *Beagle*, scientists, philosophers, and others debated the role that the brain and nervous system play in everyday life. One of the most important figures in the history of brain studies was the French philosopher **René Descartes** (1596–1650). He was important because he proposed what at that time was a very new and a very radical idea: the human body is an "animal machine" that can be understood scientifically—by discovering natural laws through empirical observation. He raised purely *physiological* questions, questions about body mechanics and motion that led him to speculate about the forces that control human action. Basi-

cally, Descartes argued that human action is a mechanical reflex to environmental stimulation. He explained that physical energy excites a sense organ. When stimulated, the sense organ transmits this excitation to the brain in the form of "animal spirits." The brain then transmits the animal spirits to the appropriate set of muscles, setting in motion a reflex. Today, the idea of reflexive behavior is something that most of us, especially psychologists, take for granted. In the seventeenth century, the idea had serious implications that could have angered religious leaders. At the time, the prevailing religious dogma taught that humans were special, endowed by a higher agency with the power of free agency. Descartes' idea of reflexive behavior, however, implied that humans were no different than animals.

But Descartes did believe that humans and animals were different. He believed that, unlike animals,

René Descartes
(1596–1650)

THE GENETICS OF ALCOHOLISM

Addiction

"My mother didn't answer the door when I came to pick her up for Christmas dinner. She was passed out on the floor next to an empty bottle. It was classic. Thirty years earlier, the same thing had happened with my grandmother. Back then my mother said, 'If I ever get to be like grandma, I want you to tell me.' Sometimes I wonder: Should I tell my son the same thing?"

This 42-year-old college professor is not an alcoholic. But his mother wasn't an alcoholic at 42 either. Over the years, her drinking increased; then she was involved in a fender-bender after which she was arrested for driving while intoxicated. The Christmas incident was one of several binges that the family wanted to overlook.

We know that half of all the alcohol drunk in the United States is consumed by only ten percent of the population and that individual differences in the frequency and total amount of alcohol drunk as well as reactions to heavy drinking are determined by many factors. What does it mean to have a predisposition for alcoholism and what factors—genetic, biological, sociocultural, and environmental—influence how that tendency expresses itself?

Many different fields of research in brain and behavioral sciences contribute etiologic information about alcoholism—information about the causes of alcoholism. Knowledge about the relative contributions of biological and environmental factors to alcohol dependence comes from studies of human families and from research on animals.

Psychologists compare the concordance rates of alcoholism in *monozygotic* twins (those who are genetically identical) and *dizygotic* twins (those who, like siblings, share only half their genes). When both members of a pair of twins have the same diagnosis—alcoholic or nonalcoholic—they are concordant for alcoholism. If one twin is alcoholic and the other is not, they are discordant for alcoholism. All major studies of alcoholism in twins have found that monozygotic (MZ) twins are more

similar in both being alcoholic or both being nonalcoholic than dizygotic (DZ) twins (*Alcohol & Health,* 1990). It is important to note, however, that the MZ twins' concordance rates, although higher than those for DZ twins, show a wide range from a low of 26 percent in one study (Hrubec & Omenn, 1981) to a very high 74 percent in an earlier study (Kaij, 1960). This variability in concordance rates (using reliable mea-

sures) suggests that environmental factors can strongly influence whether a person with a genetic predisposition will become an alcoholic.

A second line of research compares children reared by alcoholic adoptive parents and those raised by alcoholic biological parents. While children reared by alcoholic adoptive parents are at no greater risk of becoming alcoholics than anyone else, the children of alcoholic biological parents are more likely than others to abuse alcohol—even when they are reared apart from their parents since infancy and placed in stable homes (Cloninger, 1987). Such findings tend to implicate the effects of genetic predispositions. However, environment does play an important role when a child is reared in a "provocative environment." The risk of alcoholism increases significantly among adopted sons living with fathers who drink heavily and are in unskilled occupations. When the adopted son comes from a biologically alcoholic parent and is reared in a similarly provocative milieu, the chances of severe alcohol abuse more than double.

Curiously, the genetic patterning of alcoholism is different for women than it is for men. This difference is related to two different types of alcoholism. Type 1 involves the inability to stop binges once begun but the ability to abstain for long periods. Type 2 involves those who have persistent alcohol-seeking behaviors and an inability to abstain. Although both types of alcoholism are common in men, women predominantly develop Type 1 alcoholism, and men who are being treated in hospitals for severe alcoholism are largely Type 2. These subgroups of alcoholics differ in their neurophysiological and neurochemical reactions to various types of stimulation from their environment. New theorizing links such reactions both to genetic predispositions and to personality variables. We will examine the personality types linked to different patterns of alcoholic addiction in a later chapter.

Biopsychologists are trying to find biological markers to help them identify individuals likely to develop problems with alcohol. *Markers* are any measurable indicators that reliably predict the behavior or reaction under investigation; they may be precursors or correlates of the event but not necessarily the causes of the event. As

the search for markers continues, researchers are also learning how environmental factors can modify the extent to which genetic similarity determines drinking habits. In an Australian study of almost 2000 pairs of female twins, married twins were much less similar to one another in their alcohol consumption patterns than were unmarried twins (Heath et al., 1989). This finding suggests that something about the experience of marriage decreased the degree to which genetic factors influenced drinking. It might also be hypothesized that unmarried twins were more likely to have lower levels of social support than married twins and we

know that social isolation is causally related to many forms of pathological behavior, among them alcoholism.

Will the professor continue his family's legacy of alcohol problems? Today's science cannot answer that question with certainty, but many researchers are working to discover the extent to which genetic and environmental factors contribute to this widespread, self-destructive behavior. Once we can identify people whose genes predispose them to alcoholism, we will be able to learn much more about how the interplay of biology and environment contribute to an addiction to alcohol.

humans have souls that guide their actions, enabling them to make rational choices between right and wrong. Because animals do not possess souls, he argued, they cannot be aware of their actions; their behavior is wholly mechanistic and they are driven completely by primitive needs.

Although Descartes' idea of a soul kept him in good graces with the church, we know that it was wrong: our actions are mediated by the brain. But just because he was wrong about the soul, we shouldn't dismiss Descartes' other ideas as being wrong also. In fact, it was those other ideas—that the human body is subject to scientific study, that behavior is a response to environmental stimulation, and that the brain is somehow involved in that response—that eventually led subsequent researchers to study further the relation between the brain and behavior.

Descartes was way ahead of his time; discoveries relating the brain and nervous system did not come for another 140 years. In 1811, researchers discovered that there are two basic types of nerves: *sensory* and *motor*. Almost 40 years later, in 1838, **Johannes Müller** formulated his *doctrine of specific nerve energies,* which states that one's sensory experience (of seeing and hearing, for example) is determined not by the stimulus input but by the specific part of the nervous system activated by that input. In 1861, **Paul Broca** discovered that damage to the left side of the brain impairs language abilities, the first suggestion of a connection between brain structure and brain function. Descartes'

notion of the reflex did not have valid scientific support until 1906 when **Sir Charles Sherrington** discovered that reflexes are composed of direct connections between sensory and motor nerve fibers at the level of the spinal cord. Sherrington also developed the idea that the nervous system involves both *excitatory* (increasing neural activity) and *inhibitory* (decreasing neural activity) processes. And it was also not until this century that scientists knew anything at all about the basic unit of the nervous system, the neuron. In 1933, Santiago Ramón y Cajal theorized that the nervous system is comprised of neurons; 20 years later, with the aid of the electron microscope, other scientists proved his ideas. Since then, our understanding of the brain and nervous system has mushroomed. In 1948, Canadian psychologist **Donald Hebb** proposed that the brain is not merely a mass of tissue but a highly integrated series of structures, or "cell assemblies," that perform specific functions.

Today, neuroscience is one of the most rapidly growing areas of science. Time between important discoveries is now measured by weeks, sometimes even days. What is permitting such rapid advances in neuroscience? Broadly speaking, the answer to that question is *cultural evolution*. Knowledge and wisdom acquired over hundreds of years of science, in combination with advances in research technology, has given today's neuroscientists both the intellectual resources and the technological wizardry necessary for eavesdropping on the brain.

Phineas Gage

was a changed man, as his doctor's account makes clear:

> His physical health is good, and I am inclined to say that he has recovered. Has no pain in [his] head, but says it has a queer feeling which he is not able to describe. . . . His contractors, who regarded him as the most efficient and capable foreman in their employ previous to his injury, considered the change in his mind so marked that they could not give him his place again. He is fitful, irreverent, indulging at times in the grossest profanity (which was not previously his custom). . . . Previous to his injury . . . he possessed a well-balanced mind, and was looked upon by those who knew him as a shrewd, smart businessman, very energetic and persistent in executing all his plans of operation. In this regard his mind was radically changed, so decidedly that his friends and acquaintances said he was "no longer Gage" (Bigelow, 1850, pp. 13–22).

At about the same time that Gage was convalescing from his injury, Paul Broca, French neurosurgeon, was studying the brain's role in language. His first laboratory research in this area involved an autopsy of a man whose name was derived from the only word he had been able to speak, "Tan." Broca found that the left front portion of Tan's brain had been severely damaged. This finding led Broca to study the brains of other persons who suffered from language impairments. In each case, Broca's work revealed similar damage to the same area of the brain. He concluded that language ability depended on the functioning of structures in a specific region of the brain.

Lesions

As the remarkable story of Gage and word of Broca's carefully conducted laboratory research spread, more and more researchers began to wonder about the functions the brain plays in helping people to manage their day-to-day affairs. But some of these researchers did not stop at studying the effects of accidental brain damage on behavior; they began, with considerable deliberation and skill, to lesion (destroy sections of) the brains of otherwise intact animals (typically rats and other small creatures) and then to systematically measure the outcomes.

The problem with studying accidentally damaged brains, of course, is that researchers have no control over the location, extent of the damage, or its other related complications (infection, blood loss, traumas). If science were going to produce a well-founded understanding of the brain and its relationship to behavioral

EAVESDROPPING ON THE BRAIN

Neuroscientists have four ways of plumbing the depths of the brain to uncover its secrets: studying patients suffering from brain damage, chemically or electrically producing lesions at specific brain sites, electrically stimulating and recording brain activity, and using computer-driven scanning devices to "photograph" the brain. Each of these techniques serves a dual function: first, to produce new knowledge about the structure, organization, and biochemical basis of normal brain functions; and second, to diagnose brain disease and dysfunctions and then clinically evaluate therapeutic effects of specific treatments.

Brain Damage

In September 1848, *Phineas Gage,* a 25-year-old railroad worker in Vermont, was tamping a charge of black powder into a hole drilled deep into a rock in preparation for blasting. The powder exploded unexpectedly, blowing the tamping iron, over 3 feet long and weighing 13 pounds, right through Gage's head. Still conscious, Gage was taken by wagon to his hotel, where he was able to walk upstairs. The physician who attended him noted that the hole in Gage's skull was 3 inches wide, with shreds of brain all around it. He dressed the wound. Two days later, Gage became delirious and remained near death for the next two weeks, but he eventually healed. Incredibly, Gage lived for another 12 years.

Gage's physical impairment was remarkably slight: he lost vision in his left eye, and the left side of his face was partially paralyzed, but his posture, movement, and speech were all unimpaired. Yet, psychologically, he and cognitive functioning, Broca's colleagues needed a better method. Instead of waiting for patients with brain damage to show up in hospital labs, researchers asked, "Why not deliberately produce carefully placed lesions in the brains of experimental research subjects?" Although we can now appreciate the ethical implications of this question, early neuroscientists believed this was a good strategy.

Lesions are carefully inflicted injuries to specific brain areas. Researchers create three types of lesions: they either surgically remove specific brain areas, cut the neural connections to those areas, or destroy those areas through application of intense levels of heat, cold, or electricity or through laser surgery. Our conception of the brain has been radically changed as researchers have repeatedly compared and coordinated the results of lesioning experiments on animals with the growing body of clinical findings on the effects of brain damage on human behavior. Knowledge of brain functions gained from laboratory studies has also been supplemented by observation of the effects of lesions used for medical therapy. For example, a type of lesion used widely with epileptic patients involves severing the nerve fibers connecting the two hemispheres, or sides, of the brain. In addition to easing the suffering of patients, these types of studies have also revealed to us important information about the brain's role in everyday conscious experience, a topic we will take up at the end of this chapter.

Electrical Stimulation and Recording

Before the Canadian neurosurgeon **Wilder Penfield** operated on the brain of a patient suffering from epileptic seizures, he made a map of the cortex so that he could localize the origin of the seizures and leave unharmed other areas vital to the patient's functioning. His mapmaking tool was an **electrode,** a thin

Wilder Penfield
(1891–1976)

wire through which small amounts of precisely regulated electrical current could pass. As Penfield touched one cortical surface after another with this surgical wand, the conscious patient (under local anesthesia only, since there are no pain receptors in the brain itself) reacted in various ways. When stimulating some sites, Penfield observed motor reactions of hand clenching and arm raising; when touching others, he witnessed "experiential responses" as the patient vividly recalled past events or had sudden feelings (such as fear, loneliness, or elation) with a dèjá vu familiarity about them. As if he had pushed an electronic memory button, Penfield touched memories stored silently for years in the deep recesses of his patient's brain (Penfield & Baldwin, 1952). Penfield's explorations of the surface of the brain, together with many subsequent studies, have permitted researchers to draw precise maps of the brain's surface.

In the mid-1950s, **Walter Hess** pioneered the use of electrical stimulation to probe structures deeper in the brain. For example, Hess put electrodes deep into specific parts of the brain of a freely moving cat. By pressing a button, he could then send a small electrical current to the brain at the point of the electrode. Hess carefully recorded the behavioral consequences of stimulating each of 4500 brain sites in nearly 500 cats. Electrical stimulation of certain regions of the brain led the otherwise gentle cats to bristle with rage and hurl themselves upon a nearby object—which, in the early days, was sometimes the startled experimenter! Sleep, sexual arousal, anxiety, or terror could be provoked by the flick of the switch—and turned off just as abruptly.

Other neuroresearchers discovered another application of the new electrode technology. Instead of electrically stimulating the brain, they simply used electrodes to record the electrical activity of the brain as it occurred in response to environmental stimulation.

The brain's electrical output can be monitored in two ways. First, by inserting ultrasensitive microelectrodes into the brain, researchers can record the electrical activity of a single brain cell. Usually, invertebrates, such as the seaslug *Aplysia,* are used in this kind of research because they have relatively few neurons and the neurons they have are large enough to be easily identified, enabling researchers to record the electrical activity within each nerve cell. Such recordings will eventually illuminate the fundamental mechanisms used to process information in human brains as well. Second, by placing a number of electrodes on the surface of the head, researchers can record larger, integrated patterns of electrical activity. These electrodes transmit signals regarding the brain's electrical activity to a machine called an electroencephalograph. In turn, the machine produces an **electroencephalogram (EEG),** or an amplified tracing of the activity. An EEG is used to study the brain during states of arousal and has been particularly useful in helping researchers study processes involved in sleeping and dreaming. In one recent experiment, changing aspects of human thought were detected by 124 EEG sensors applied to the scalps of each subject. In the split second *before* they were to respond behaviorally, the subjects' brains showed activity in brain areas that would be activated during execution of the task—suggesting mental rehearsal prior to acting (Givens, 1989; Barinaga, 1990).

By developing a large set of brain electrical-activity data from healthy people and from people with various brain and psychiatric disorders, ranging in age from 6- to 90-years-old, researchers are now able to diagnose brain dysfunctions reliably. Using just a single 60-minute EEG sample, researchers and clinicians can perform computer-assisted diagnosis and classification of different disorders with accuracy—a process known as *neurometrics* (John et al., 1988).

Brain Scans

The most exciting technological innovations for studying the brain are machines originally developed to help neurosurgeons detect brain abnormalities, such as tumors or damage caused by strokes or diseases. These machines, or brain scanners, produce images of different regions of the living brain. Research using brain scans does not require surgery or other intrusive proce-

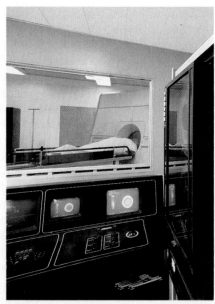

CT scans allow neuroscientists and neurosurgeons to produce computer-enhanced images of the brain to help them understand brain structures and their relationship to behavior.

dures that may damage brain tissue. Three brain scanning devices are currently used.

Perhaps the most widely used scanner is the computerized tomography scanner, better known as the **CT scanner.** The CT scanner projects X rays through the head at various angles. A computer then calculates the amount of radiation passing through the brain from the various angles and integrates that information into an image that can be seen on a monitor. By looking at the image, researchers can locate abnormalities in brain tissue, which permits them to link brain structure to the psychological symptoms exhibited by the individual.

An even more powerful scanner is the positron emission tomography scanner, or **PET scanner.** In PET research, subjects are given different kinds of radioactive (but safe) substances that eventually travel to the brain, where they are taken up by active brain cells. Recording instruments outside the skull can detect the radioactivity emitted by the cells that are active during different cognitive or behavioral activities. This information is then fed into a computer that constructs a dynamic portrait of the brain and projects it onto a monitor, showing where different types of neural activity are actually occurring.

Another new technology allowing brain researchers and neurosurgeons to explore the living brain is *magnetic resonance imaging,* or **MRI.** MRI uses magnetic fields and radio waves to generate pulses of energy within the brain. By tuning the pulse to different frequencies, some atoms line up with the magnetic field. When the magnetic pulse is turned off, the atoms vibrate (resonate) as they return to their original positions. These vibrations are picked up by special radio receivers that channel information about the vibrations into a computer. In turn, the computer generates maps of the locations of different atoms in areas of the brain. These maps enable researchers to see which cells are functioning normally and which are not. In addition, researchers can use the maps to study the different kinds of activity taking place in specific areas of the brain or the spinal cord in response to various types of physical and psychological stimulation.

Brain imaging is a very promising tool for achieving a better understanding of normal brain structure, physiology, chemistry, and functional organization. By directly imaging the brain's structure and the biochemical processes underlying psychological disorders, we can learn how to evaluate and better design the medications used to treat those disorders (Andreason, 1988). Three hundred years have passed since Descartes sat in his candle-lit study and theorized how the brain functions; over 100 years have passed since Broca discovered in his crude autopsy of Tan that brain regions seem

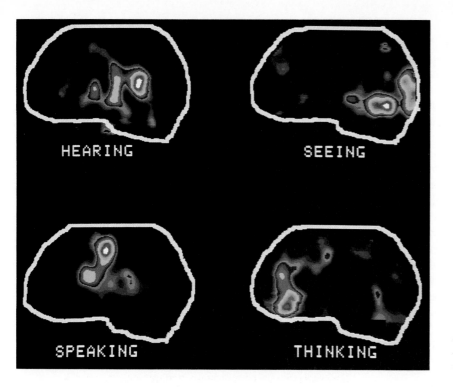

These PET scans show that different tasks stimulate neural activity in distinct regions of the brain.

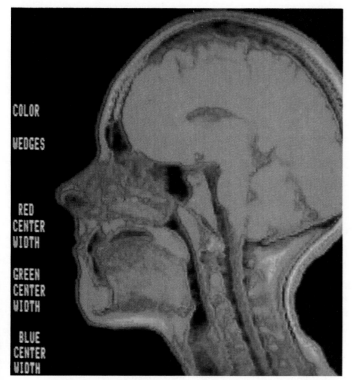

Magnetic resonance imaging (MRI) produces this color-enhanced profile of a normal brain. MRI uses a combination of radio waves and a strong magnetic field to view soft tissue. This technique provides a truer image than other imaging techniques.

to be linked to specific functions. In the time since these developments, cultural evolution has provided neuroscientists with the kinds of technology necessary to reveal some of the brain's most important secrets. The remainder of the chapter describes some of these secrets and discusses how they are related to our behavior, our thinking, and, in short, our psychology.

BRAIN STRUCTURES AND THEIR FUNCTIONS

The development of the brain in members of any species follows strict genetic coding for the hardwiring of certain basic neural circuits. The way the brain forms and separates into divisions is similar in many species; but the higher the species is on the evolutionary scale, the larger and more complex the brain becomes and the more sophisticated the functions it can perform become. In the human brain, the genetic instructions lead to a remarkably precise, efficient communication and computational system unmatched by any other species.

Environmental stimulation is necessary to fine-tune the brain. Without this stimulation, many brain structures will not develop properly. Enriched early experience has been shown to develop superior adult learners and physically change the human brain (Rosenzweig, 1984).

The brains of human beings have three interconnected layers, each corresponding to different epochs in our evolutionary history (MacLean, 1977). In the deepest recesses of the brain, in a region called the *central core,* are structures involved primarily with autonomic processes such as heart rate, breathing, swallowing, and digestion. Enveloping the central core is the *limbic system,* which is involved with emotional and sexual behaviors as well as with eating, drinking, and aggression. Wrapped around these two "primitive" brains is the pinnacle of human evolution: the *cerebral cortex.* For each of us, the universe of the human mind exists in this region, just beneath the scalp. Without the cerebral cortex we would be no different from the lowliest of animal species. With it, we can design new ways to challenge the limits imposed by heredity on our human nature. The cerebral cortex integrates sensory information, coordinates our movements, and facilitates abstract thinking and reasoning (see **Figure 3.3**).

The structures of the brain perform specific activities that can be divided into five general categories: (a) internal regulation, (b) reproduction, (c) sensation, (d) motion, and (e) adaptation to changing environmental conditions. The first two are the brain's way of controlling bodily processes that keep us alive, well, and prepared to reproduce and nourish offspring. The third activity enables the brain to make contact with the outside world by processing sensory information from receptors located throughout the body. The brain also monitors internal sensations that provide information about balance, gravity, movements of limbs, and orientation. Some neuroscientists believe that the fourth activity, motion, is the major role of the brain. The brain must get the muscles to move so that an organism can effect changes in its environment to produce desired consequences. As "a mechanism for governing motor activity," the brain's "primary function is essentially the transforming of sensory patterns into patterns of motor coordination" (Sperry, 1952, p. 297). The final function—adapting to the environment—involves the brain's remarkable ability to modify itself as it learns, stores what it has experienced, and directs new actions based on feedback from the consequences of its previous actions. Let's look more closely at the three major brain regions that regulate these numerous activities, beginning with the central core.

FIGURE 3.3

THE CENTRAL CORE, LIMBIC SYSTEM, AND CEREBRAL CORTEX

From an evolutionary perspective, the central core is the oldest part of the brain; the limbic system evolved next; and the cerebral cortex is the most recent achievement in brain evolution.

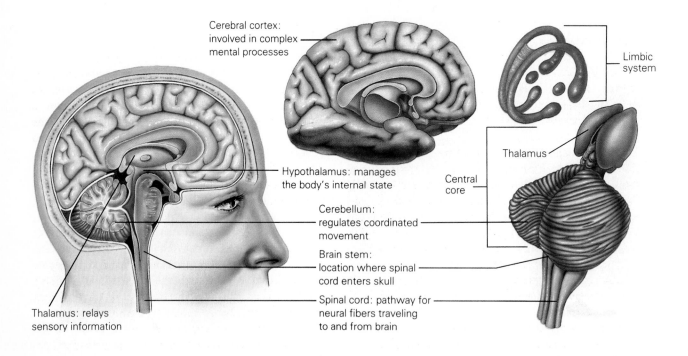

Cerebral cortex: involved in complex mental processes

Limbic system

Hypothalamus: manages the body's internal state

Thalamus

Cerebellum: regulates coordinated movement

Central core

Brain stem: location where spinal cord enters skull

Spinal cord: pathway for neural fibers traveling to and from brain

Thalamus: relays sensory information

FIGURE 3.4   THE STRUCTURES OF THE CENTRAL CORE

The structures of the central core are primarily involved with basic life processes: breathing, pulse, arousal, movement, balance, and rudimentary processing of sensory information.

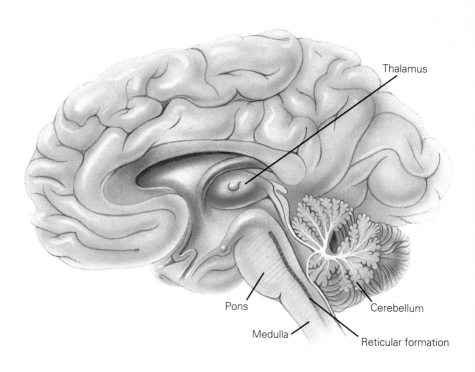

Thalamus

Pons

Medulla

Cerebellum

Reticular formation

The Central Core

The **central core** is found in all vertebrate species. It contains five structures that collectively regulate the internal state of the body (see **Figure 3.4**). The **medulla,** located at the very top of the spinal cord, is the center for breathing, waking, sleeping, and the beating of the heart. Because these processes are essential for life, damage to the medulla can be fatal. Nerve fibers ascending from the body and descending from the brain cross over at the medulla, which means that the left side of the body is linked to the right side of the brain and the right side of the body is connected to the left side of the brain. Directly above the medulla is the **pons,** which is involved in dreaming and in waking from sleep. The **reticular formation** is a dense network of nerve cells situated between the medulla and pons. It serves as the brain's sentinel. It arouses the cerebral cortex to attend to new stimulation and keeps the brain alert even during sleep. Massive damage to this area often results in a coma. The reticular formation has long tracts of fibers that run to the **thalamus,** a relay station

that channels incoming sensory information to the appropriate area of the cerebral cortex, where that information is then processed. For example, the thalamus relays information from the eyes to the visual cortex, a portion of the cortex located at the very rear of the head. The **cerebellum,** attached to the brain stem at the base of the skull, coordinates bodily movements, controls posture, and maintains equilibrium. Damage to the cerebellum interrupts the flow of otherwise smooth movement, causing it to appear uncoordinated and jerky.

The Limbic System

The central core is found in all vertebrates, but only mammals are equipped with the more recently evolved limbic system. The **limbic system** mediates motivated behaviors, emotional states, and memory processes. It also regulates body temperature, blood pressure, and blood-sugar level and performs other housekeeping activities. The limbic system comprises three structures:

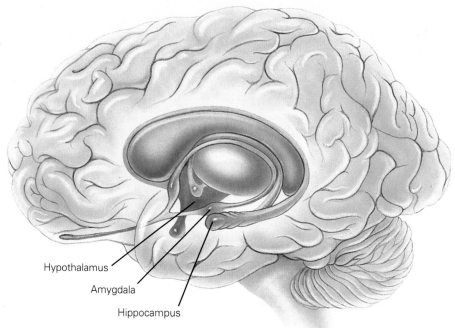

FIGURE 3.5 *THE LIMBIC SYSTEM*

The structures of the limbic system, which are present only in mammals, are involved with motivated behavior, emotional states, and memory processes.

Hypothalamus

Amygdala

Hippocampus

the hippocampus, amygdala, and hypothalamus (see **Figure 3.5**).

The **hippocampus,** which is the largest of the limbic system structures, plays an important role in memory—especially in long-term storage of information (Galluscio, 1990). Damage to the hippocampus does not impair the learning of new information, but it does impair the ability to remember it. Thus, if you were in an accident and sustained damage to your hippocampus, you would still be able to learn new tasks, but you would not be able to remember having done so! In other words, your life would always be in the present: everything you learn today, you would have to relearn tomorrow. Evidence for the hippocampus's role in memory is derived mostly from clinical evidence, notably from studies of a patient, H. M., perhaps psychology's most famous subject.

> When he was 27, H. M. underwent surgery in an attempt to reduce the frequency and severity of his epileptic seizures. During the operation, parts of his hippocampus were accidentally removed. As a result, H. M. could only recall the very distant past; his ability to put new information into

long-term memory was gone. Long after his surgery, he continued to believe he was living in 1953, which was the year the operation was performed. However, and for some unknown reason, comparable damage to the hippocampus in other animals, such as rhesus monkeys, does not result in the same degree of memory impairment (Salmon et al., 1987).

The **amygdala** is known best for its role in aggression, although it is also involved in feeding, drinking, and sexual behaviors. Studies with several animal species, including humans, have shown that lesioning the amygdala has a calming effect on otherwise mean-spirited individuals. In some cases, animals who have undergone amygdalectomies (surgical removal of the amygdala) show bizarre sexual behavior, attempting to copulate with just about any available partner. In one early experiment, a cat was observed trying to copulate with a dog, a chicken, and a monkey (Schreiner & Kling, 1953).

The **hypothalamus** is one of the smallest structures in the brain, yet it plays a vital role in many of our most important daily actions. It is actually composed of several nuclei, small bundles of neurons that regulate physiological processes involved in motivated behavior (including eating, drinking, temperature regulation, and sexual arousal). The hypothalamus also regulates the activities of the endocrine system, which secretes hormones. The hypothalamus basically maintains the body's internal equilibrium. When the body's energy reserves are low, the hypothalamus is involved in stimulating the organism to find food and to eat. When body temperature drops, the hypothalamus causes blood-vessel constriction, or minute involuntary movements we commonly refer to as the "shivers." This bodily thermostatic function is a form of **homeostasis,** maintaining an internal balance or equilibrium.

The Cerebral Cortex

When someone says that you "really have brains," he or she is referring to your cerebral cortex. In humans, the **cerebral cortex** dwarfs the rest of the brain, occupying two-thirds of its total mass. Its role is to regulate the brain's higher cognitive and emotional functions.

The cerebral cortex is divided into two almost symmetrical halves, the **cerebral hemispheres,** each mediating different cognitive and emotional functions. The *left cerebral hemisphere* is involved with spontaneous use of language (both written and spoken), integration of complex movement, memory for words and numbers, and anxiety and positive emotions. The *right cerebral hemisphere* regulates memory for music and geometric patterns, facial recognition, and feelings of negative emotions. The two hemispheres are connected by a thick mass of nerve fibers, collectively referred to as the **corpus callosum.** This pathway sends messages back and forth between the hemispheres.

Neuroscientists have mapped each hemisphere using two important landmarks as their guides. One deep groove, called the *central fissure,* divides each hemisphere vertically, and a second similar groove, called the *lateral fissure,* divides each hemisphere horizontally (see **Figure 3.6**). These vertical and horizontal divisions create four areas, or brain lobes, in each hemisphere. Each of these lobes serves specific functions. The *frontal lobe,* which is involved with motor control

---

FIGURE 3.6   THE CEREBRAL CORTEX

Each of the two hemispheres of the cerebral cortex has four lobes. Different sensory and motor functions have been associated with specific parts of each lobe.

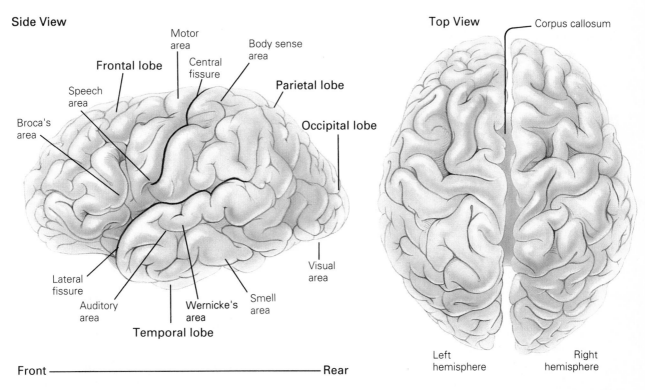

and cognitive activities, such as planning, making decisions, setting goals, and relating the present to the future through purposeful behavior, is located above the lateral fissure and in front of the central fissure. Accidents that damage the frontal lobes can have devastating effects on human action and personality—as in the case of Phineas Gage. The *parietal lobe* is involved with controlling incoming sensory information and is located directly behind the central fissure, toward the top of the head. The *occipital lobe,* the final destination for visual information, is located at the back of the head. The *temporal lobe,* where auditory information is processed, is found below the lateral fissure, on the sides of each cerebral hemisphere.

It would be misleading to say that one specific lobe alone controls any one specific function by itself. The structures of the brain perform their duties in concert,

working smoothly as an integrated unit, similar to a symphony orchestra. Whether you are doing the dishes, solving a calculus problem, or carrying on a conversation with a friend, your brain works as a unified whole, each lobe interacting and cooperating with the others. Nevertheless, neuroscientists can identify specific functions of areas of the four lobes of the cortex that are necessary for specific functions, such as vision, hearing, language, and memory.

The actions of the body's voluntary muscles, of which there are more than 600, are controlled by the **motor cortex,** located just in front of the central fissure in the frontal lobes. Muscles in the lower part of the body, for example the toes, are controlled by neurons in the top part of the motor cortex. Muscles in the upper part of the body, such as the throat, are controlled by neurons in the lower part of the motor cortex. As you

---

| **FIGURE 3.7** | *THE MOTOR CORTEX* |

Different parts of the body are more or less sensitive to environmental stimulation and brain control. Sensitivity in a particular region of the body is related to the amount of space in the cerebral cortex devoted to that region. In this figure, the body is drawn so that size of body parts is relative to the cortical space devoted to them. The larger the body part in the drawing, the greater its sensitivity to environmental stimulation and the greater the brain's control over its movement.

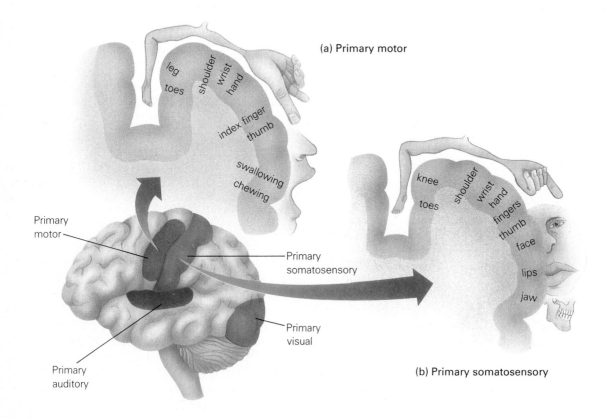

can see in **Figure 3.7,** the upper parts of the body receive far more detailed motor instructions than the lower parts. In fact, the two largest areas of the motor cortex are devoted to the fingers—especially the thumb—and to the muscles involved in speech, reflecting the importance in human activity of manipulating objects, using tools, eating, and talking. Remember that commands from one side of the brain are directed to muscles on the opposite side of the body. So, the motor cortex in the right hemisphere of your brain controls the muscles in your left foot.

The **somatosensory cortex** is located just behind the central fissure in the left and right parietal lobes. This part of the cortex processes information about temperature, touch, body position, and pain. Similar to the motor cortex, the upper part of the sensory cortex relates to the lower parts of the body, and the lower part to the upper parts of the body. Most of the area of the sensory cortex is devoted to the lips, tongue, thumb, and index fingers—the parts of the body that provide the most important sensory input (see Figure 3.7). Similar to the motor cortex, the right half of the somatosensory cortex communicates with the left side of the body and the left half with the right side of the body.

Auditory information is processed in the **auditory cortex,** which is in the two temporal lobes. The auditory cortex in *each* hemisphere receives information from *both* ears. One area of the auditory cortex is involved in the *production* of language and a different area is involved with language *comprehension*. Visual input is processed at the back of the brain in the **visual cortex,** located in the occipital lobes. Here the greatest area is devoted to input from the center part of the retina at the back of the eye, the area that transmits the most detailed visual information.

Not all of the cerebral cortex is devoted to processing sensory information and commanding the muscles to action. In fact, the majority of it is involved in *integrating* information. Processes, such as planning and decision making, are believed to occur in all the areas of the cortex *not* labeled in Figure 3.6, or the **association cortex.** Animals located on higher rungs of the evolutionary ladder have more of their cortexes devoted to association areas than lower animals do. This difference in the relative size of association areas reflects a physiological, structural difference among animals, but it also reflects a behavioral difference. For example, humans, at the top of the evolutionary ladder, show greater *flexibility* in behavior because their genotypes code for proportionately more of their cortexes to be devoted to association areas.

How do these different areas of the brain work in unison? Consider, as an example, the biology of speak-

FIGURE 3.8 **HOW A WRITTEN WORD IS SPOKEN**

Nerve impulses, laden with information about the written word, are sent by the retinas to the visual cortex via the thalamus. The visual cortex then sends the nerve impulses to an area in the rear of the temporal lobe, the angular gyrus, where visual coding for the word (the arrangements of letters and their shapes, etc.) is compared to its accoustical coding (the way it sounds). Once the proper accoustical code is located, it is relayed to an area of the auditory cortex known as Wernicke's area. Here it is encoded and interpreted. Nerve impulses are then sent to Broca's area which sends the message to the motor cortex. The motor cortex puts the word in your mouth by stimulating the lips, tongue, and larynx to act in synchrony.

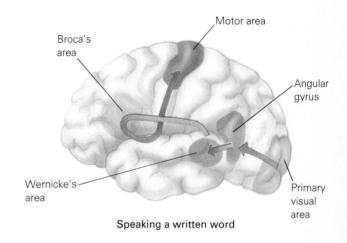

Speaking a written word

ing a written word (see **Figure 3.8**). Imagine that your psychology instructor hands you a piece of paper with the word *chocolate* written on it, and he or she asks you to say the word aloud. Saying the word *chocolate* is probably a very easy thing for you to imagine yourself doing, if only because you have probably said the word many times before. But the biological processes involved in the action are subtle and complex. Neuroscience can break down your verbal behavior into numerous steps. First, the visual stimulus (the written word *chocolate*) is detected by the nerve cells in the retinas of your eyes, which send nerve impulses to the visual cortex (via the thalamus). The visual cortex then sends nerve impulses to an area in the rear of the temporal lobe (called the angular gyrus) where visual coding for the word is compared to its acoustical coding. Once the proper acoustical code is located, it is relayed to an area of the auditory cortex known as *Wernicke's* *area,* where it is decoded and interpreted. ("Ah! delicious! In fact, I'd like some now. But wait, I am supposed to be dieting.") Nerve impulses are then sent to Broca's area, which, in turn, sends a message to the motor cortex, stimulating the lips, tongue, and larynx to produce the word *chocolate.*

That's a lot of mental effort for just one word. Now imagine what you require of your brain every time you read aloud a book or even a billboard. The truly amazing thing is that your brain responds effortlessly and intelligently, translating thousands of scribbles and marks on paper into a biological code, informing other brain areas about what's going on, and finally, putting words in your mouth (Montgomery, 1990).

SUMMING UP

Descartes' speculation that the human body is governed by natural laws and that the brain is somehow involved in regulating behavior laid the foundation for modern neuroscience. Neuroscience is a multidisciplinary approach to understanding the relation between brain and behavior. Modern neuroscientists use four methods of research in this area: studying patients suffering from brain damage, chemically or electrically producing lesions at specific brain sites, electrically stimulating and recording brain activity, and using computer-driven scanning devices to photograph the brain. Precise use of these methods has permitted neuroscientists to make important discoveries about the way brain structures process information, generate thoughts, and coordinate complex behavior patterns.

The brain is divided into three integrated layers—the central core, the limbic system, and the cerebral cortex. The central core is the oldest part of the human brain and is chiefly responsible for life-sustaining functions: breathing, digestion, and heart rate. Encircling the central core are the structures of the limbic system, which are involved in storage of long-term information, aggression, eating and drinking, and sexual behavior. The most recently evolved area of the brain is the cerebral cortex, which surrounds the central core and limbic system and accounts for most of the brain's mass. The cerebral cortex is divided into two roughly symmetrical halves called hemispheres. Different areas of the cortex process different kinds of environmental stimulation or initiate movement. But the brain functions as an integrated whole; no one brain region operates independently of the others.

THE ENDOCRINE AND NERVOUS SYSTEMS

Think of someone you know—perhaps your closest friend. For whatever reason, this person has come to play a significant role in your life. He or she can make you smile and laugh, keep you company when you're feeling lonely, cause you to question your motives for taking a certain course of action, and make you angry sometimes and joyful other times. The relationship you have with this person can be traced to your experiences together, but the ways your friend makes you feel, think, or act is more than the mere sum of your interactions with each other. How you react to your friend is largely influenced by the way your brain processes information about his or her actions and by the way your brain tells your body and mind to respond. In more technical terms, your response to environmental stimulation is mediated by an electrochemical communications system, whose job it is to relay sensory information to the brain and, in turn, relay behavioral information from your brain to various parts of your body.

We actually have two distinct and highly complex communication systems. One system, the **endocrine system,** is a network of glands that manufacture and secrete chemical messengers called **hormones** into the bloodstream (see **Figure 3.9**). The other system, the *nervous system,* is a massive network of nerve cells that rapidly relays messages to and from the brain using different kinds of chemical messengers that are called *neurotransmitters.*

GLANDULAR CONTROL OF BEHAVIOR AND INTERNAL PROCESSES

Hormones are important in everyday functioning, although they are more vitally important at some stages of life and in some situations than others. Hormones are involved in a wide array of bodily functions and behaviors. They influence your body growth; initiate, maintain, and stop development of primary and secondary sexual characteristics; moderate levels of arousal and awareness; serve as the basis for mood changes; and regulate metabolism, the rate at which the body uses its energy stores. The endocrine system promotes the survival of an *organism* by helping fight infections and disease. It advances the survival of the *species* through regulation of sexual arousal, production of reproductive cells, and production of milk in nursing mothers.

Endocrine glands respond to the levels of chemicals in the bloodstream or are stimulated by other hormones or by nerve impulses from the brain. Hormones are then

FIGURE 3.9   ENDOCRINE GLANDS IN FEMALES AND MALES

The pituitary gland is shown at the far right; it is the master gland that regulates the glands shown at the left. The pituitary gland is under the control of the hypothalamus, an important structure in the limbic system.

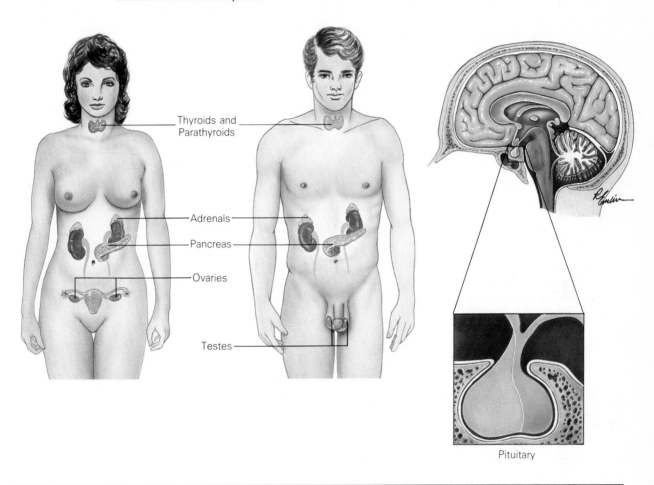

Thyroids and Parathyroids

Adrenals

Pancreas

Ovaries

Testes

Pituitary

---

secreted into the blood and travel to distant target cells with specific receptors; hormones exert their influence on the body's program of chemical regulation only at the places that are genetically predetermined to respond to them. In influencing diverse, but specific, target organs or tissue, hormones can regulate such an enormous range of biochemical processes that they have been called "the messengers of life" (Crapo, 1985). This multiple-action communication system allows for control of slow, continuous processes such as maintenance of blood-sugar levels and calcium levels, metabolism of carbohydrates, and general body growth. But what happens during sudden crises? For example, what happens to your body when you see a child run out in front of your car? The endocrine system releases the hormone adrenaline into the bloodstream, which energizes your body so that you can respond quickly to avert disaster.

A similar process happens when you are frightened. Suddenly, you become tremendously alert, your muscles tense, readying you to spring into action: to fight or to flee.

Hormones are produced in several different regions of the body. These hormone "factories" make a variety of hormones, each of which regulates different bodily processes, as outlined in **Table 3.1.** Let's examine the most significant of these hormones.

In charge of the endocrine system is the *hypothalamus,* a bundle of small nuclei that reside at the brain's base. The hypothalamus is an important relay station among other parts of the brain, the endocrine system, and the central nervous system. Specialized cells in the hypothalamus receive messages from other brain cells commanding it to release a number of different hormones to the pituitary gland, where they either

These Glands:	Produce Hormones that Regulate:
Hypothalamus	Release of Pituitary Hormones
Anterior Pituitary	Testes and Ovaries Breast Milk Production Metabolism Reactions to Stress
Posterior Pituitary	Water Conservation Breast Milk Excretion Uterus Contraction
Thyroid	Metabolism Growth and Development
Parathyroid	Calcium Levels
Gut	Digestion
Pancreas	Glucose Metabolism
Adrenals	Fight or Flight Responses Metabolism Sexual Desire in Women
Ovaries	Development of Female Sexual Traits Ova Production
Testes	Development of Male Sexual Traits Sperm Production Sexual Desire in Men

stimulate or inhibit the release of other hormones.

The **pituitary gland** is often called the "master gland," because it secretes about ten different kinds of hormones that influence the secretions of all the other endocrine glands as well as a hormone that influences growth. The absence of this growth hormone results in dwarfism; its excess results in gigantic growth. In males, pituitary secretions activate the testes to secrete **testosterone,** which stimulates production of sperm. The pituitary gland is also involved in the development of male secondary sexual characteristics, such as facial hair, voice changes, and physical maturation. Testosterone may even increase aggression and sexual desire. In females, a pituitary hormone stimulates production of **estrogen,** which is essential to the hormonal chain reaction that triggers the release of ova from a female's ovaries, making her fertile. Certain birth-control pills work by blocking the mechanism in the pituitary gland that controls this hormone flow, thus preventing the ova from being fertilized.

NEURONAL CONTROL OF BEHAVIOR AND INTERNAL PROCESSES

The body's other communication system, the nervous system, is more extensive and acts more quickly than the endocrine system. The nervous system is composed of billions of highly specialized nerve cells, or *neurons* that are organized either into densely packed clusters called nuclei or into pathways (some of which are very extensive) called *nerve fibers*. The major task of the nuclei is to process information; the chief job of nerve fibers is to relay information to and from these nuclei. We have already discussed these nuclei in detail—they make up the brain. To a lesser degree, nuclei are found outside the brain, mainly along the spinal cord where they receive and relay sensory and motor information to and from the brain.

The brain and the nerve fibers that are found throughout the body constitute the nervous system. The nervous system is subdivided into two major divisions:

FIGURE 3.10 *PHYSICAL ORGANIZATION OF THE HUMAN NERVOUS SYSTEM*

The sensory and motor nerve fibers that constitute the peripheral nervous system are linked to the brain by the spinal cord.

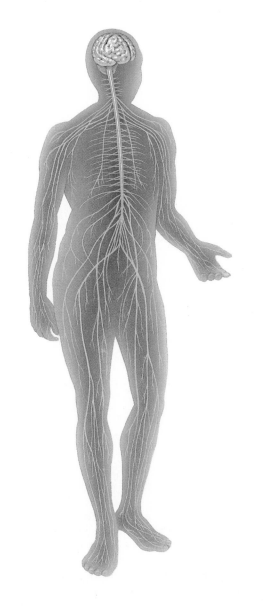

the **central nervous system** (CNS) and the **peripheral nervous system** (PNS). The CNS is composed of all the neurons in the brain and spinal cord; the PNS is made up of all the neurons forming the nerve fibers that connect the CNS to the body. **Figures 3.10** and **3.12** show the relationship of the CNS to the PNS.

The job of the CNS is to integrate and coordinate all bodily functions, process all incoming neural mes-

sages, and send out commands to different parts of the body, depending upon the environmental situation. The CNS sends and receives neural messages through the *spinal cord,* a trunkline of neurons that connects the brain to the PNS. The trunkline itself is housed in a hollow portion of the spinal cord called the spinal column. Spinal nerves branch out from the spinal cord between each pair of vertebrae in the spinal column, eventually connecting with sensory receptors throughout the body and with muscles and glands. The spinal cord also coordinates the activity of the left and right sides of the body and is responsible for simple reflexes that do not involve the brain. For example, an organism whose spinal cord has been severed from its brain can still withdraw its limb from a painful stimulus. Though normally the brain is notified of such action, the organism can complete the action without directions from above. Damage to the nerves of the spinal cord can result in paralysis of the legs or trunk, as seen in paraplegic individuals. The extent of paralysis depends on how high up on the spinal cord the damage occurred.

Despite its commanding position, the CNS is isolated from any direct contact with the outside world. It is the role of the PNS to provide the CNS with information from sensory receptors, such as those found in the eyes and ears, and to relay commands from the brain to the body's organs and muscles. The PNS is actually composed of two subdivisions of nerve fibers (see **Figure 3.11**). The **somatic nervous system** regulates the actions of the body's skeletal muscles. For example, right now I am typing these words on a microcomputer. Movement of my fingers over the keyboard is managed by my somatic nervous system. As I think about what it is that I want to say, my brain sends commands to my fingers to press certain keys. Simultaneously, the fingers send feedback about their position and movement to the brain. When I strike the wrong kee (as I often do when tired), the somatic nervous system informs the brain, which then issues the necessary correction, and, in a fraction of a second, I delete the mistake and hit the right key.

The other subdivision of the PNS is the **autonomic nervous system** (ANS), which sustains basic life processes. This system is on the job 24 hours a day, regulating bodily processes that we usually don't consciously control, such as respiration, digestion, and arousal. It must work even when the individual is asleep, and it sustains life processes during anesthesia and prolonged coma states. The autonomic nervous system deals with survival matters of two kinds: those involving threats to the organism and those involving bodily maintenance. To accomplish these tasks, the autonomic nervous system is further subdivided into the sympathetic and parasympathetic nervous system

FIGURE 3.11 *HIERARCHICAL ORGANIZATION OF THE HUMAN NERVOUS SYSTEM*

The central nervous system is composed of the brain and the spinal cord; the peripheral nervous system is divided according to function; the somatic nervous system controls voluntary actions; and the autonomic nervous system regulates internal processes. The autonomic nervous system is subdivided into two systems: The sympathetic nervous system governs behavior in emergency situations, and the parasympathetic nervous system regulates behavior and internal processes in routine circumstances.

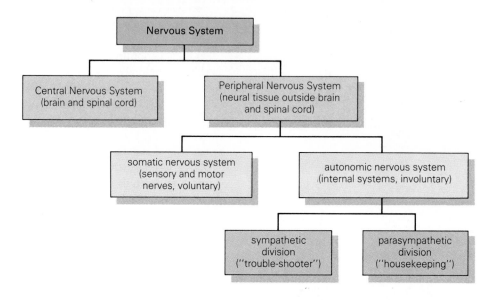

(see Figure 3.11). These divisions essentially work together "in opposition" to accomplish their tasks. The **sympathetic division** governs responses to emergency situations, when large amounts of energy must be mobilized and behavior initiated with split-second timing. The **parasympathetic division** monitors the routine operation of the body's internal functions. The sympathetic division can be regarded as a troubleshooter—in an emergency or stressful situation, it arouses the brain structures for "fight or flight." Digestion stops, blood flows away from internal organs to the muscles, oxygen transfer increases, heart rate increases, and the endocrine system is stimulated to facilitate motor responses. After the danger is over, the parasympathetic division takes charge to decelerate these processes, and the individual begins to calm down. Digestion resumes, heartbeat slows, and breathing is relaxed. Basically, the parasympathetic division carries out the body's nonemergency housekeeping chores, such as elimination of bodily wastes, protection of the visual system (through tears and pupil constriction), and long-term conservation of body energy. The separate duties of the sympathetic and parasympathetic nervous systems are illustrated in Figure 3.12.

SUMMING UP

Both the endocrine system and the nervous system function as communications systems. The endocrine system is a slow-acting system of glands that produce and secrete chemical substances called hormones into the blood stream. Hormones are involved in body growth, development of primary and secondary sexual characteristics, metabolism, digestion, and arousal. The endocrine system is controlled by the hypothalamus, which receives messages from higher-order brain centers about when and how to stimulate the pituitary gland. The pituitary gland then secretes the appropriate hormone, which, in turn, stimulates one or more of the other endocrine glands into operation. Two of the more important hormones are estrogen, which triggers the release of ova, and testosterone, which stimulates production of sperm.

The nervous system is composed of billions of neurons and is divided into two major subdivisions: the CNS, which is composed of the brain and spinal cord, and the PNS, which is composed of all the neu-

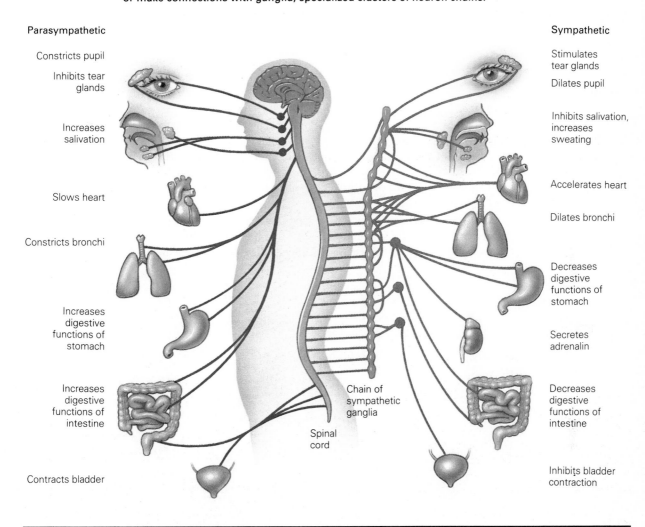

FIGURE 3.12   *THE AUTONOMIC NERVOUS SYSTEM*

The parasympathetic nervous system, which regulates day-to-day internal processes and behavior, is shown on the left. The sympathetic nervous system, which regulates internal processes and behavior in stressful situations, is shown on the right. Note that, on their way to and from the spinal cord, the nerve fibers of the sympathetic nervous system innervate, or make connections with ganglia, specialized clusters of neuron chains.

Parasympathetic

Constricts pupil

Inhibits tear glands

Increases salivation

Slows heart

Constricts bronchi

Increases digestive functions of stomach

Increases digestive functions of intestine

Contracts bladder

Sympathetic

Stimulates tear glands

Dilates pupil

Inhibits salivation, increases sweating

Accelerates heart

Dilates bronchi

Decreases digestive functions of stomach

Secretes adrenalin

Decreases digestive functions of intestine

Inhibits bladder contraction

Chain of sympathetic ganglia

Spinal cord

rons connecting the CNS to the body. The PNS is further divided into two subdivisions: the somatic nervous system, which regulates the body's skeletal muscles, and the autonomic nervous system, which governs basic life-support processes. The sympathetic division of the autonomic nervous system springs into action during times of stress and emergency, and the parasympathetic division operates under more routine circumstances.

THE NERVOUS SYSTEM IN ACTION

To interact with the world, we depend more on the nervous system than we do the endocrine system. Although both systems are critical to our ability to live the way we do, the nervous system allows us to sense and to respond to the outside world. For that reason, one of the major goals of early physiologists was to understand better how the nervous system operates. In large measure, modern neuroscientists have accomplished this goal, although they continue to work on finding smaller pieces of the puzzle. Our objective in this section is to analyze and understand how all the information available to our senses is ultimately communicated throughout our body and brain by nerve impulses. We begin by discussing the properties of the basic unit of the nervous system, the neuron.

THE NEURON

A **neuron** is a cell specialized to receive, process, and/or transmit information to other cells within the body. Neurons vary in shape, size, chemical composition, and function—over 200 different types have been identified in mammal brains—but all neurons have the same basic structure (see **Figure 3.13**).

At birth, or shortly afterward, your brain will have all the neurons it is ever going to have. Unlike the brains of fish, amphibians, and birds, in which new neurons appear even in adults, the human brain has a fixed number of neurons. This stable set of neurons may be essen-

tial for the *continuity* of learning and memory over a long lifetime (Rakic, 1985). However, human neurons die in astonishing numbers—somewhere in the neighborhood of 10,000 each and every day of your life! Fortunately, because we start out with so many neurons, we will lose less than two percent of our original supply in 70 years. The deteriorated brain functioning that sometimes occurs in old age is usually not a result of the decrease in the number of neurons but an effect of destructive changes within the neurons themselves or in the chemical substances that carry signals between neurons.

Understanding how individual neurons function is important because it has the potential for opening up new directions in the use of therapeutic drugs and genetic engineering to control nerve transmission. With such new directions usually comes the betterment of human lives.

Neurons typically take in information at one end and send out messages from the other. The part of the cell that receives incoming signals is a set of branched fibers called **dendrites,** which extend outward from the

---

FIGURE 3.13   *TWO DIFFERENT KINDS OF NEURONS*

Note the differences in shape and dendritic branching.

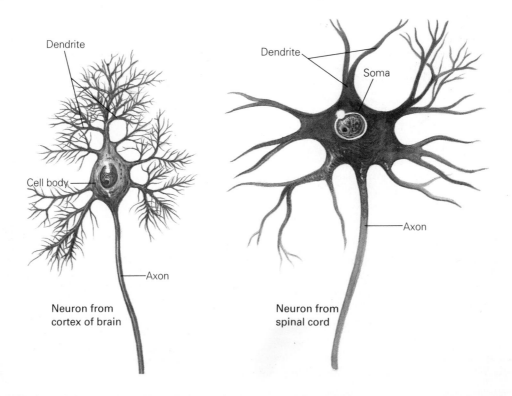

Dendrite

Cell body

Axon

Neuron from cortex of brain

Dendrite

Soma

Axon

Neuron from spinal cord

---

cell body. The basic job of the dendrites is to receive stimulation from other neurons or sense receptors. The cell body, or **soma,** contains the nucleus of the cell and the cytoplasm that sustains its life. The soma integrates information about the stimulation received from the dendrites (or in some cases received directly from another neuron) and passes it on to a single, extended fiber, the **axon.** In turn, the axon conducts this information along its length, which, in the spinal cord, can be several feet long and, in the brain, less than a millimeter. At the other end of axons are swollen, bulblike structures called **terminal buttons** through which the neuron is able to stimulate nearby glands, muscles, or other neurons. Neurons transmit information in only one direction: from the dendrites through the soma to the axon to the terminal buttons—this is known as the **law of forward conduction** (see **Figure 3.14**).

In general, there are three major classes of neurons. **Sensory neurons,** also called *afferent neurons,* carry messages from sense receptor cells toward the central nervous system. Receptor cells are highly specialized cells that are sensitive to light, sound, and body position. **Motor neurons,** also called *efferent neurons,* carry messages away from the central nervous system toward the muscles and glands. Sensory neurons rarely communicate directly with motor neurons, however.

Most of the billions of neurons in the brain are **interneurons,** which relay messages from sensory neurons to other interneurons or to motor neurons. For every motor neuron in the body there are as many as 5000 interneurons in the great intermediate network that forms the computational system of the brain (Nauta & Feirtag, 1979).

As an example of how these three kinds of neurons work together, consider the pain withdrawal reflex (see **Figure 3.15**). When pain receptors near the skin's surface are stimulated by a sharp object, they send messages via sensory neurons to an interneuron in the spinal cord. The interneuron responds by stimulating motor neurons, which, in turn, excite muscles in the appropriate area of the body to pull away from the pain-producing object. It is only *after* this sequence of neuronal events has taken place and the body has been moved away from the stimulating object, that the brain is informed of the situation. In cases such as this, where survival depends on swift action, our sensation and subsequent perception of pain often occurs after we have physically responded to the danger. Of course, then the information from the incident is stored in the brain's memory system so that the next time we avoid the potentially dangerous object altogether before it can begin to hurt us.

<table>
<tr><td>**FIGURE 3.14**</td><td>*THE MAJOR STRUCTURES OF THE NEURON*</td></tr>
</table>

The neuron receives nerve impulses through its dendrites. It then sends the nerve impulses through its axon to the terminal buttons where neurotransmitters are released to stimulate other neurons.

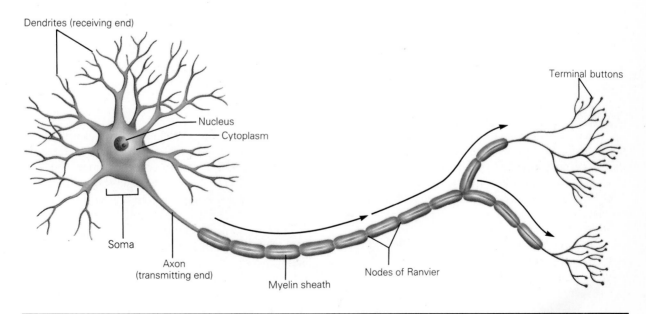

Dendrites (receiving end)

Terminal buttons

Nucleus
Cytoplasm

Soma

Axon
(transmitting end)

Myelin sheath

Nodes of Ranvier

FIGURE 3.15

THE PAIN WITHDRAWAL REFLEX

The pain withdrawal reflex shown here involves only three neurons: a sensory neuron, a motor neuron, and an interneuron.

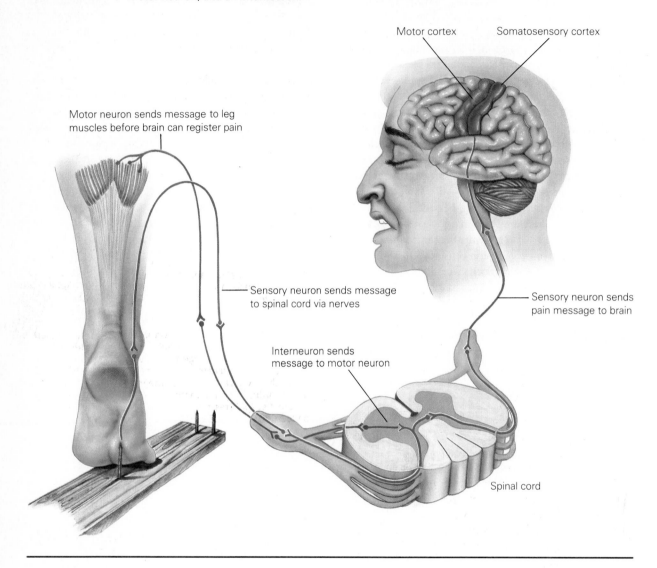

Motor cortex

Somatosensory cortex

Motor neuron sends message to leg muscles before brain can register pain

Sensory neuron sends message to spinal cord via nerves

Sensory neuron sends pain message to brain

Interneuron sends message to motor neuron

Spinal cord

Interspersed among the brain's vast web of neurons are about ten times as many **glial cells (glia).** The word *glia* is derived from the Greek word for *glue*, which gives you a hint of one of the major duties performed by these cells: they bind neurons to each other (although not so close that they actually touch). In vertebrates, glial cells also have several other important functions. Their first function is garbage removal. When neurons are damaged and die, glial cells in the area multiply and clean up the cellular junk left behind; they can also take up excess chemical substances at the gaps between neurons. Their second function is insulation. Glial cells form an insulating cover, called a *myelin sheath*, around some types of axons. This fatty insulation greatly increases the speed of nerve signal conduction. The third function of glial cells is to prevent poisonous substances in the blood from reaching the delicate cells of the brain. Specialized glial cells, called astrocytes, make up a *blood-brain barrier*, forming a continuous envelope of fatty material around the blood vessels in the brain. Substances that are not soluble in fat do not dissolve through this barrier, and since many poisons and other harmful substances are not fat soluble, they cannot penetrate the barrier to reach the brain.

GRADED AND ACTION POTENTIALS

How is the violent discharge of an electric eel when disturbed by an intruder similar to the gentle lullaby of a mother putting her baby to sleep? Both are the outcomes of the same kind of electrochemical signals used by the nervous system to process and transmit information. Both electrical messages involve changes in the electrical activity of a single neuron. These changes are caused by the flow of electrically charged particles, called *ions,* through the neuron's membrane, a thin "skin" separating the cell's internal and external environments.

Think of a nerve fiber as macaroni, filled with salt water and proteins, floating in a salty soup. The soup and the fluid in the macaroni both contain ions—atoms of sodium (NA+), chloride (CL−), calcium (CA+), and potassium (K+)—that have either positive (+) or negative (−) charges. The membrane, or the surface of the macaroni, plays a critical role in keeping the ingredients of the two fluids apart or letting them mix a little. In other words, the membrane determines the *polarity* of the macaroni's (or cell's) fluid, or its electrical state in relation to the soup (or outside fluid). When a cell is inactive, or in a *polarized* state, there are about ten times as many potassium ions inside as there are sodium outside. (Think of the ions being kept "poles apart.") Even in a polarized state, the fluid inside a neuron has a slightly negative voltage relative to the fluid outside. In a polarized or resting state, the neuron is simply prepared to respond; whether it actually does or not depends upon the activity of its neighboring neurons. It is similar to a battery ready to be used.

The membrane is not a perfect barrier; it is semipermeable. It "leaks" a little, allowing some sodium ions to slip in while some potassium ions slip out. To correct for this, nature has provided transport mechanisms within the membrane that pump out sodium and pump in potassium. The nervous system uses a great deal of energy to maintain this polarized state of readiness for every neuron in the body (Kalat, 1984).

When a neuron is stimulated, it becomes less negatively charged, or *depolarized,* and starts producing its own electrical signals. In a depolarized state, ions flow in and out of the neuron through the membrane. All neural messages in all organisms are initiated by this process of ion flow; it is the basis of all sensation, experience, thought, and action. The neuron's universal language consists of two basic types of electrical signals: graded potentials and action potentials.

The Graded Potential

A **graded potential** is produced by the external physical stimulation of the dendrite or soma and varies in size according to the magnitude of the stimulus. The more intense the stimulation, the larger the graded potential. For example, in sensory receptors, such as the retina of the eye, light is converted or transduced into a graded potential (often called a receptor potential). The size of this potential will depend upon how intense or bright the light is. Graded potentials are only useful as short-term, local signals within the neuron, usually between the dendrite and axon, because they weaken over long distances. Graded potentials can only have a significant influence on overall nervous system activity when they are of sufficient strength to cause the cell membrane to depolarize suddenly to a certain critical level or threshold (see **Figure 3.16**).

FIGURE 3.16   GRADED ACTION POTENTIALS

A graded action potential is caused when one neuron stimulates the dendrite or soma of another neuron. The graded potential increases with the intensity of the stimulation. Because they weaken over distance, graded potentials serve only as localized signals within the neuron, usually between the dendrite and the axon. However, if the graded potential is of sufficient intensity when it reaches the axon, the cell membrane will depolarize and give rise to an action potential. The action potential is propagated along the axon in an all-or-nothing fashion; once its threshold is met, it will travel at a constant speed down the axon regardless of the intensity of the originating stimulus. Its final destination is the terminal button where it stimulates release of chemical messengers called neurotransmitters.

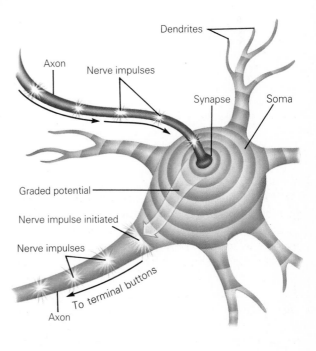

The Action Potential

When one neuron stimulates another to the point that its threshold is met or exceeded, a dramatic event takes place: the nerve impulse or **action potential** is generated along the axon. The action potential is caused by the chemical and electrical changes that occur within the neuron when its state is changed from being polarized (slightly negative) to being depolarized (slightly positive). In other words, when a neuron is depolarized, the fluid inside becomes more positively charged relative to that outside the neuron (see **Figure 3.17**).

Unlike the graded potential, whose intensity is directly proportional to the intensity of the stimulus, the action potential is unaffected by properties of the stimulus. The action potential is said to obey the **all-or-none law:** The speed with which the action potential travels along the axon is unaffected by increases in the size or intensity of stimulation beyond the threshold level. Once the threshold level is reached by the incoming, graded potential, a uniform and complete action potential is generated. If the threshold is not reached, no action potential happens. In this way, propagation of an action potential along the axon is analogous to flushing a toilet: no matter how hard you press the lever beyond some minimal level, the speed of the water into the toilet bowl and down the drain is the same.

A second important characteristic of the action potential is that its speed or size will not decline with the length of the axon: The action potential just keeps moving along at the same speed until it reaches its final destination, the terminal buttons. In this sense, the action potential is said to be *self-propagating;* once started, it needs no outside stimulation to keep itself moving. It's similar to a lit fuse on a firecracker.

A third characteristic of the action potential is actually a feature of the neuron in which the action potential is occurring. Just after an action potential is finished and the neuron is attempting to return to its polarized state, further stimulation, no matter how intense, cannot cause another action potential to be generated (see Figure 3.17). This period of total unresponsiveness lasts only 0.5 to 2 milliseconds and is called the absolute **refractory period.** Have you ever tried to flush the toilet, while it is filling back up with water? There must be a critical level of water for the toilet to flush again. Similarly, in order for a neuron to be able to generate another action potential, it must "reset" itself and await simulation beyond its threshold. However, when the neuron is in the process of returning to its polarized state, very strong stimulation will cause it to fire again. This *relative refractory period* lasts for a few milliseconds before the threshold returns to normal.

How can this uniform, all-or-none, action potential transmit information about differences in intensity of stimulation? A more intense stimulus does two things to make its presence known to the nervous system. First, it triggers more frequent action potentials in each neuron (faster rate). Second, it also triggers action potentials in more neurons (greater quantity). Somewhere in the brain this information about rate and quantity is combined and encoded, resulting in an appropriate reaction to an ever-varying outer world.

Different neurons conduct action potentials along their axons at different speeds; the fastest have signals that move at the rate of 200 meters per second, the slowest plod along at 10 centimeters per second (Bullock et al., 1977). The axons of the faster neurons are covered with a myelin sheath, making this part of the neuron resemble long beads on a string. The tiny breaks between the beads are called *nodes of Ranvier* (see Figure 3.14). In neurons having myelinated axons, the action potential literally skips along from one node to the next. Damage to the myelin sheath throws off the delicate timing of the action potential and causes serious problems. Multiple sclerosis (MS) is a devastating disorder caused by deterioration of the myelin sheath.

FIGURE 3.17   *TIMETABLE FOR ELECTRICAL CHANGES IN THE NEURON DURING AN ACTION POTENTIAL*

Sodium ions entering the neuron cause its electrical potential to change from slightly negative during its polarized or resting state to slightly positive during depolarization. Once the neuron is depolarized, it enters a brief refractory period during which further stimulation will not produce another action potential. Another action potential can occur only after the ionic balance between the inside and the outside of the cell is restored.

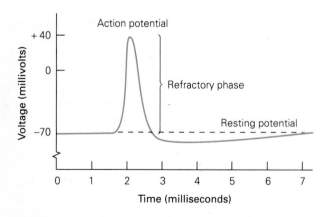

It is characterized by double vision, tremors, and eventually paralysis. In MS, specialized cells from the body's immune system actually attack myelinated neurons, exposing the axon and disrupting normal synaptic transmission (Joyce, 1990).

The key to understanding how the action potential is generated along the axon is understanding the properties of the neuron's cell membrane. All electrical signaling in the nervous system involves the flow of ions through ion channels in the cell membrane (Catterall, 1984; Hille, 1984). **Ion channels** are excitable portions of the cell membrane that produce and change electrical signals. They do so by opening or closing *pores,* tiny tunnels in the membrane, which selectively permit certain ions to flow in and out. Three positively charged ions (sodium, potassium, and calcium) and one negatively charged ion (chloride), appear to be the ones moving through these channels. The signal-processing property of neurons is determined by how many ion channels are packed into a given area in each part of the cell and the type of ion involved.

The high density of sodium channels in the part of the axon nearest the soma reduces the threshold for generating the action potential and typically starts the impulse on its way. The way is slow if the axon is not myelinated, because there are relatively few sodium channels operating; but it becomes speedy with myelinated axons because of their great density of sodium channels. The most sodium channels are found at the nodes of Ranvier where the electrical signals literally jump from node to node. Why? Because the great concentration of sodium channels at these nodes requires fewer ions to move into the cell while moving the action potential down the axon. Thus the action potential can buzz along with little time lost in ion exchange or cost in metabolic energy.

While sodium is rushing into the neuron, potassium and chloride are rushing out through their own channels. As a result, the inside of the neuron becomes positive relative to the outside, meaning the neuron has become fully depolarized. How does the neuron return to its original resting state of polarization? The microscopic transport mechanisms embedded in the cell membrane work to reestablish ionic equilibrium by pumping sodium out of the cell, and potassium and chloride back into the cell. (These are the same transport mechanisms or pumps that also help the neuron maintain its resting state.)

SYNAPTIC TRANSMISSION

There is more to the action potential than its leapfrog journey down the axon. When this train of impulses finally arrives at the terminal, there is no direct connection to the next destination—no two neurons ever touch. So, somehow, there must be an indirect connection with the next impulse train. Action potentials set off the activity at a **synapse,** a junction of two or more neurons. Once the action potential reaches the terminal button, it sets in motion a series of truly remarkable events called **synaptic transmission,** which is the relaying of information from one neuron to another across the synaptic gap (see **Figure 3.18**). Four basic steps are involved in synaptic transmission. First, upon arriving at the terminal button, the action potential causes small round packets called *synaptic vesicles* to move toward and affix themselves to the interior membrane of the terminal button. The action potential also opens calcium ion channels that admit positive ions into the terminal button. Inside each vesicle are **neurotransmitters,** biochemical substances whose function is to stimulate other neurons. Second, *synaptic* vesicles rupture, spilling the neurotransmitters into the *synaptic cleft,* the tiny space separating the *presynaptic membrane* (the terminal button of the sending neuron) from the *postsynaptic membrane* (the surface of a dendrite or soma of a receiving neuron). Researchers believe that the influx of positive ions through the calcium channels causes the rupture of the synaptic vesicles and the release of whatever neurotransmitters they contain (Zucker & Lando, 1986). Third, neurotransmitters are dispersed rapidly across the synaptic cleft to the postsynaptic membrane. And fourth, the neurotransmitters attach themselves to *receptor molecules* embedded in the postsynaptic membrane.

The neurotransmitters will bind themselves to the receptor molecules under only two conditions: First, no other neurotransmitters or other chemical substances must be attached to the receptor molecule. Second, the shape of the neurotransmitter must match the shape of the receptor molecule—as precisely as a key fits into a keyhole. If neither condition is met, the neurotransmitter will not attach itself to the receptor molecule, and therefore it will not be able to stimulate the postsynaptic membrane. If the neurotransmitter does become attached to the receptor molecule, then it may initiate a graded potential, and the message it contains is passed on to the next synaptic gap and on and on. Once the neurotransmitter has completed its job, it detaches itself from the receptor molecule and drifts back into the synaptic gap. There it is either decomposed through enzymatic action or reabsorbed into the presynaptic terminal button for reuse with the next graded potential.

So far we have a system for generating action, but what about inaction? How is some of our behavior inhibited, prevented from being activated? Synapses come in two types. In *excitatory* synapses, the binding of the neurotransmitter to receptor molecules causes the

FIGURE 3.18   SYNAPTIC TRANSMISSION

The action potential in the presynaptic neuron causes neurotransmitters to be released into the synaptic gap. Once across the gap, they stimulate receptor molecules embedded in the membrane of the postsynaptic neuron.

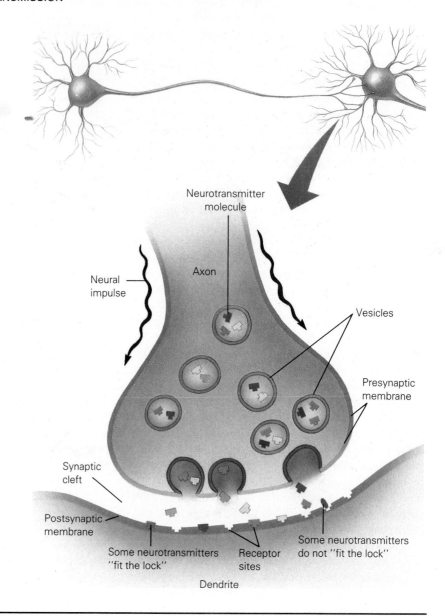

Neurotransmitter molecule

Neural impulse

Axon

Vesicles

Presynaptic membrane

Synaptic cleft

Postsynaptic membrane

Some neurotransmitters "fit the lock"

Receptor sites

Some neurotransmitters do not "fit the lock"

Dendrite

postsynaptic neuron to generate action potentials or generate them at a higher rate. In *inhibitory* synapses, the binding of the neurotransmitter to receptor molecules causes the postsynaptic neuron not to generate action potentials or to generate them at lower rates. Interestingly, it is *not* the neurotransmitter that determines whether the postsynaptic neuron will be excited or inhibited. Instead, it is the nature of the receptor molecule that determines what the effect will be. The same neurotransmitter may be excitatory at one synapse but inhibitory at another, depending on whether the receptor excites or inhibits nerve signals.

A single neuron may have synapses with thousands of other neurons. Whether that postsynaptic neuron will generate action potentials and at what rate it will generate them is determined by the sum of all the excitatory and inhibitory effects acting on it. If the majority of its synapses are excitatory, then it will generate action potentials when stimulated. If the majority of its synapses are inhibitory, then it will not generate action potentials.

You may be wondering why we have taken you so deep into the caverns of the nervous system. After all, this is a psychology course, and psychology is supposed to be about behavior and thinking and emotion. In fact, synapses are the biological medium in which all of these activities occur. If you change the normal activity of the synapse, then you change how people behave, how they think, and how they feel. Understanding the functioning of the synapse has led to tremendous advances in our understanding of learning and memory, emotion, psychological disorders, drug addiction and, in general, the chemical formula for mental health. There is good reason to believe that the synapse is the space where evolution has etched one of its most significant contributions to humanity (Rose, 1973).

NEUROTRANSMITTERS AND THEIR FUNCTIONS

More than 60 different chemical substances are known or suspected to function as neurotransmitters in the brain. To qualify as a neurotransmitter, a substance must meet a set of technical criteria. It must be manufactured in the presynaptic terminal button and must be released when an action potential reaches that terminal. Its presence in the synaptic cleft must produce a biological response in the postsynaptic membrane and, if its release is prevented, no subsequent responses can occur. Six substances that qualify as neurotransmitters have been studied intensely, largely because they have been found to play such an important role in the daily functioning of the brain. These six are acetylcholine, GABA, dopamine, norepinephrine, serotonin, and endorphins.

Acetylcholine is found in both the central and peripheral nervous systems. In the brain, it appears to be involved with memory processes. Memory loss among patients suffering from Alzheimer's disease, a degenerative disease that is increasingly common among older persons, is believed to be caused by the deterioration of neurons that secrete acetylcholine. Acetylcholine is also excitatory at junctions between nerves and muscles, where it causes muscles to contract. A number of toxins affect the synaptic actions of acetylcholine. For example, botulinum toxin, which is often found in food that has been preserved incorrectly, poisons an individual by preventing release of acetylcholine in the respiratory system. This poisoning, known as *botulism,* can cause death by suffocation. Curare, a poison Amazon Indians use on the tips of their blowgun darts, produces a similar effect, paralyzing lung muscles.

GABA (gamma-amino butyric acid) is affected by a variety of depressants, chemical compounds that reduce central nervous system activity. For example, barbiturates are believed to bind to receptor molecules sensitive to GABA, causing sedation. This effect implies that low levels of GABA may be responsible for anxiety (Paul et al., 1986).

The *catecholamines* are a class of chemical substances that include two important neurotransmitters, *dopamine* and *norepinephrine*. Both have been shown to play prominent roles in psychological disorders, such as schizophrenia and mood disturbances. Norepinephrine appears to be involved in some forms of depression. Drugs that increase brain levels of this neurotransmitter also elevate mood and relieve depression. Higher than normal levels of dopamine have been found in persons with schizophrenia. As you might expect, one way to treat people with this disorder is to give them a drug that decreases brain levels of dopamine. In the early days of drug therapy, an interesting but unfortunate problem arose: high doses of the drug used to treat schizophrenia produced symptoms of Parkinson's disease, a progressive and ultimately fatal disorder involving disruption of motor functioning. (Parkinson's disease is caused by deterioration of neurons that manufacture most of the brain's dopamine.) This important finding led to research that improved drug therapy for schizophrenics and to research that focused on drugs that could be used in the treatment of Parkinson's disease.

Another important neurotransmitter is *serotonin*. All serotonin-producing neurons are located in the brain stem, which is involved with arousal and many autonomic processes. Hallucinogenic drugs such as LSD (lysergic acid diethylamide) appear to have profound effects on these serotonin neurons by influencing one kind of postsynaptic receptor molecule to which they attach (Jacobs, 1987). By exerting their influence on these receptors, hallucinogens produce vivid and bizarre sensory experiences, some of which last for hours.

The *endorphins* are a very interesting group of chemical substances that are usually classified as neuromodulators instead of neurotransmitters. A **neuromodulator** is any substance that modifies or modulates the activities of the postsynaptic neuron. Endorphins were discovered fairly recently during experiments on morphine conducted by Candace Pert and Solomon Snyder (1973). Pert and Snyder found that morphine (which is derived from the opium poppy) binds to specific receptor sites in the brain. Quite logically, they reasoned that morphine exerts its pain-relieving and euphoric effects at these sites.

But why should morphine have its own receptor sites in our brains? In fact, the brain produces its own morphinelike substances. Researchers have discovered a number of chemical brain substances that have binding sites on receptors in the limbic system and that produce effects similar to those of morphine (Hughes et al. 1975). **Endorphins,** for example, are naturally occurring, morphinelike chemicals produced in the brain that play an important role in the control of emotional behaviors (anxiety, fear, tension, pleasure) and pain. Endorphins have been called "nature's link between pleasure and pain," and their study is helping us understand more about the nature of drug addiction.

An interesting research paradigm has been developed for the study of the painkilling effects of chemicals suspected to be one of the endorphins. *Naloxone* is a drug that has only one known effect; it blocks morphine and endorphins from binding to receptors (Hopson, 1988). Any procedure that

reduces pain by stimulating release of endorphins becomes ineffective when naloxone is administered. So researchers concluded that endorphins are involved in pain mediation, because when naloxone was administered, along with the medical treatment designed to reduce pain, no pain medication effects were observed. By using this "negative method," researchers have implicated release of endorphins as being at least partially responsible for the pain-reducing effects of acupuncture (Watkins & Mayer, 1982) and even for placebos (Fields & Levine, 1984).

Addiction

SYNAPTIC TRANSMISSION AND DRUGS: EFFECTS OF COCAINE

The last 30 years have witnessed an explosion of worldwide drug use and abuse. Drug addiction, which we will read about in the next chapter, is a growing social and economic problem costing taxpayers in the United States and Canada billions of dollars each year. This dollar cost cannot even begin to reflect the tremendous personal losses incurred by abusers, addicts, and their families. Because of the criminal activity associated with the need to support expensive drug habits, addiction is putting a severe strain on the legal and penal systems as well as on our health care system. An interest in reducing drug addiction has led to increased research aimed at understanding its biological bases—at discovering the specific brain systems responsible for the variety of pleasurable effects and negative withdrawal effects experienced by drug users. Much of the research to date has

been conducted on those drugs that are being abused most widely, for example, cocaine.

Over the past ten years, cocaine addiction has evolved from a very rare problem to one of the greatest national health concerns. One report estimates that one in two Americans between the ages of 25 and 30—as many as 25 million Americans—have tried cocaine. While 5 to 10 million people use cocaine on a monthly basis, as many as 3 million cocaine abusers are estimated to be in need of treatment—six times the number of heroin addicts (Gawin, 1991; Ray & Ksir, 1987). Although cocaine abuse has only recently developed into a national epidemic, the drug has been around for a very long time. However, *crack cocaine* is a fairly new variation of the drug. Crack cocaine is an incredibly powerful—and dangerous—central nervous system stimulant.

Crack is made by mixing cocaine with water and baking soda. When the mixture dries, it forms a rock or crystal that may be smoked. Many people prefer crack to regular cocaine because it is cheaper and more available and because smoking cocaine provides a much more rapid and powerful high than snorting cocaine does. The reason it does is that the surface area of the lungs is larger than that of the mucus membranes of the nose, and so it permits more of the drug to enter the central nervous system. Intravenous injection of cocaine produces even more powerful effects, but is not as popular because people are afraid of needles, infections, and AIDS transmission.

Cocaine is one of the most powerful reinforcers known in humans and animals. Experimental animals will press a lever thousands of times for a single dose of cocaine, and they will work incessantly to obtain continuous, rapid intravenous administration of the drug for several weeks—until they die (Johanson & Fischman, 1989). In humans, cocaine produces profound euphoria, well-being, and alertness. It magnifies the intensity of almost all known pleasures except for those associated with eating, which, in fact, are diminished. Cocaine and crack users find the effects of the drug so rewarding that they use it more and more and eventually may become addicted to it. Chronic drug addiction is maintained in part by the psychological symptoms of drug withdrawal—unpleasant mood states and cravings for drug euphoria. The earlier distinction between psychological and physiological addiction and dependence has been replaced by the World Health Organization with the term *neuroadaptation* to indicate the more typical combination of both consequences of chronic drug use.

About 10 to 15 percent of initial cocaine users (snorters) become abusers. We don't yet know why some users progress to addiction and others stop experimenting with cocaine. However, once addiction develops, the typical pattern is high-dose, long-duration binging, with repeated use of cocaine every 10 to 30 minutes for 4 to 24 hours until the supply runs out. Binges, which average from one to seven a week, are followed by several days of abstinence. Addicts report that, during binges, everything in life, except the cocaine euphoria, loses its significance—including one's very survival.

Abstaining from cocaine results in a three-phase pattern: an initial *crash* of mood and energy, intense craving, depression, and anxiety; a *withdrawal* phase a few days later when all normal pleasurable experiences are diminished; and an *extinction* phase when craving is gradually reduced as the learned associations of cues conditioned to taking cocaine are weak-

ened. From 30 to 90 percent of cocaine abusers who remain in drug treatment programs cease cocaine use. Those programs usually combine psychotherapy with pharmacological interventions designed to break the binging cycles and to prevent relapse.

How can cocaine have such powerful control over otherwise rational individuals? The answer is found in the way the drug interacts with the central nervous system. Cocaine (and amphetamines) produces pleasure or reward by increasing the activity of certain brain neurotransmitters. Specifically, after being released at the synapse, cocaine inhibits the reuptake of dopamine and the neurotransmitters norepinephrine and serotonin. This means that nerve signal activity continues, causing continual, heightened activity among the neurons meeting at these synapses (Ritz et al., 1987). The brain experiences or interprets this increased activity as pleasur-

able, and any actions that led to it are reinforced. Ultimately, then, the lure of cocaine resides in the action at the synapse. Long-term cocaine abuse generates neurophysiological changes in brain systems that regulate the psychological processes associated with feelings of pleasure. Cocaine works on the human mind by changing the pattern of synaptic transmission in the brain. Research is showing that virtually all drugs exert their psychological and physiological effects by altering the activity of synapses, either by blocking or enhancing the release of certain neurotransmitters or by affecting how they bind to specific postsynaptic drug receptors in the brain. This knowledge has come from "basic animal research, thus underscoring the value of basic research directed at unraveling the neurophysiological mysteries of human experiences of pleasure and pain" (Gawin, 1991, p. 1585).

NEURAL NETWORKS

You now know how the nervous system relays information between cells, but it must do much more to generate organized and complex reactions of thought, feeling, and action. The other major task of the nervous system is to process a wealth of information in an integrated fashion; this means that it must be able to handle large amounts of information coming and going simultaneously between a large number of structures. At the most basic level of processing there is the combination of graded potentials in the cell body and the modification of synaptic transmission to inhibit or increase nerve cell activity. Higher levels of information processing require **neural networks,** circuits or systems of neurons that are functioning together to perform tasks that individual cells cannot carry out alone. We have already looked at one of the simplest neural networks, the pain-withdrawal reflex (review Figure 3.15).

Neural networks follow a basic principle of nature: all life processes are organized *hierarchically.* In other words, simpler units, structures, and processes are organized into levels of ever greater complexity, with higher ones exercising some control over lower ones. At each level of complexity there are limits and constraints that can be overcome only by a more complex system (Jacob, 1977). Just as new capabilities become available at each level from molecule to cell to organ to organism, new potential for information processing becomes available with increasingly complex neural networks.

Because neural networks in humans can be so complex, scientists often study the neural networks of simple organisms such as invertebrates. This research helps them understand the biological basis of more complex behavior. A favorite subject of study has been the large sea snail, *Aplysia,* because its relatively few neurons are large enough to be identified so that they can be traced and so that "wiring diagrams" can be worked out for given types of behavior. For example, *Aplysia's* heart rate is controlled by a simple neural network involving only a few cells: some excite it to pump and others inhibit it. These cells are command cells, individual cells at a critical position to control other cells and, thus, to trigger entire behavioral sequences.

A more complex neural network is found in *Aplysia's* gill-withdrawal reflex, a defensive response that protects organs vital to its survival. Tactile stimuli applied to the siphon of *Aplysia* at first elicit gill withdrawal. With repeated stimulation, however, the gill-withdrawal response *habituates:* it becomes weaker and weaker until it is not made at all. Yet if a strong stimulus is now applied to another part of the body, the gill-withdrawal reflex returns. This effect is called *dishabituation.*

Eric Kandel with Aplysia

When **Eric Kandel** and his associates searched for the biochemical basis of this gill-withdrawal reflex, they found that, because of the action of a particular neural network during habituation, a smaller amount of neurotransmitter (serotonin) than usual was being released (Kandel, 1979). This finding is important because it identifies a specific biochemical mechanism that explains a simple learned behavior, habituation of the gill-withdrawal reflex (see **Figure 3.19**).

SUMMING UP
The neuron is the basic unit of the nervous system. Its function is to receive, process, and relay information to other cells, glands, or muscles. Neurons relay information in only one direction: from the dendrites through the cell body to the axon to the terminal buttons. Sensory neurons receive messages from specialized receptor cells and send them toward the central nervous system. Motor neurons channel messages from the brain away from the central nervous system to muscles and glands. Interneurons relay information from sensory neurons to other interneurons or to motor neurons. Glial cells help bind neurons together; they also perform basic housekeeping duties for the cell and the synapse.

Within a neuron, information is passed from the dendrites to the soma in the form of graded potentials, which are proportional in size to the intensity of the stimulus causing them. Once the graded potential exceeds a specific threshold, an action potential, which obeys the all-or-none law, is sent along the axon to the terminal buttons. Action potentials are actually caused by the opening of special ion cells that allow sodium ions to enter the cell and potassium and chloride ions to leave. The arrival of the action potential at the terminal buttons causes neurotransmitters to be released into the synaptic cleft. Once across the cleft, they can become lodged in the receptor molecules found in the postsynaptic membrane. The effects of these neurotransmitters—whether they excite or inhibit the postsynaptic membrane—depend upon the nature of the receptor molecule. Of the more than 60 known neurotransmitter substances, six have been particularly well researched. Each of these neurotransmitters is involved with specific functions of the brain and with behavior. Drugs affect behavior and cognition by influencing synaptic transmission.

Neural networks are involved in higher-level processing of information. Because they possess large but relatively few neurons, invertebrates such as Aplysia are ideal subjects for the study of simple neural networks. In his research with Aplysia, Kandel discovered all the components of a neural network that serves as the basis for a form of simple learning involving habituation of the gill-withdrawal reflex. Such findings are apt to lead to future research involving more complex neural networks and correspondingly more complex behavior.

FIGURE 3.19 NEURAL NETWORK FOR THE GILL WITHDRAWAL REFLEX IN APLYSIA

The top left drawing shows the sea slug in its normal state. The top right drawing shows it with the gill withdrawn. The schematic diagram represents the neural network controlling the reflex. The sensory neurons involved are indicated by a single line, but each of the motor and interneurons is shown.

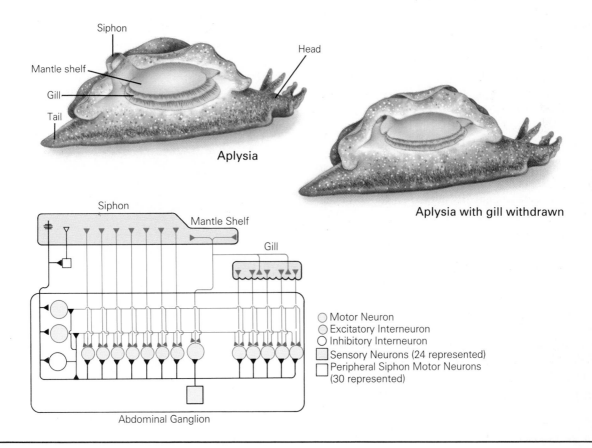

Siphon
Mantle shelf
Gill
Tail
Head
Aplysia
Aplysia with gill withdrawn

Siphon
Mantle Shelf
Gill

○ Motor Neuron
○ Excitatory Interneuron
○ Inhibitory Interneuron
□ Sensory Neurons (24 represented)
□ Peripheral Siphon Motor Neurons (30 represented)

Abdominal Ganglion

THE NERVOUS SYSTEM AND CONSCIOUS EXPERIENCE

Understanding what neuroscience has to say about the operation of the nervous system is important because the nervous system is the basis for all of our conscious experience. Anything that changes how the nervous system operates also changes normal consciousness—sensing, perceiving, thinking, and behaving are all affected, and usually for the worse. In the next chapter, we will focus our attention on the realm of consciousness, but first we want to inquire about some links between the biology of the brain and the nervous system and the human experience of consciousness.

We now know that the part of the brain responsible for consciousness is the cerebral cortex. And, interestingly enough, each hemisphere of the cortex appears to be involved in regulating different aspects of conscious experience. How does this occur?

CEREBRAL DOMINANCE

If you were a neuroscientist investigating the functions of the cerebral hemispheres, what might you conclude from these three clues?

1. Patients suffering strokes that paralyze the right side of their bodies often develop speech disturbances.
2. Patients suffering strokes that damage the left hemisphere often develop problems in using and understanding language. (Recall Paul Broca's early findings.)
3. The left hemisphere is usually slightly larger than the right one (Galaburda et al., 1978).

Though the two hemispheres appear to be physically similar, both clinical and experimental evidence clearly indicates dissimilarity in their functions. In fact, each hemisphere tends to dominate the control of different functions. **Cerebral dominance** is the term for the command of one cerebral hemisphere over bodily movements and speech. For the vast majority of right-handed people, language-related functions are dominated by the left hemisphere (a smaller majority of left handers is also left-hemisphere dominant for language). This dominance explains why the left hemisphere is usually larger and why damage to it may cause language disorders. It also explains why people suffering paralysis on the right side due to a stroke may have speech problems—right-side paralysis indicates that the damage was to the left side of the brain (the effects are contralateral, to the opposite side of the body).

Neuroscientists have found that only about five percent of right-handers and 15 percent of left-handers have

speech controlled by the right hemisphere, while another 15 percent of left-handers have language functions occurring in both sides of the brain. Persons with right-brain dominance in language functions are at higher risk to develop disorders interfering with language-related functions such as reading. Interestingly, males are more likely than females to be left-handed and also to have more speech-related learning disorders.

Much of our knowledge about cerebral dominance derives from observing people who have suffered brain damage on one side or whose cerebral hemispheres could not communicate with each other (see **Figure 3.20**). Patients with right-hemisphere damage are more likely to have perceptual and attentional problems, possibly including serious difficulties in spatial orientation. For example, they may feel lost in a previously familiar place or be unable to fit geometric shapes together. Patients with right-hemisphere damage in the right parietal lobe may show a syndrome in which they totally ignore the left side of their bodies and left visual fields—eating only what is on the right side of a plate of food, for example.

FIGURE 3.20 THE EFFECTS OF DAMAGE TO ONE SIDE OF THE BRAIN

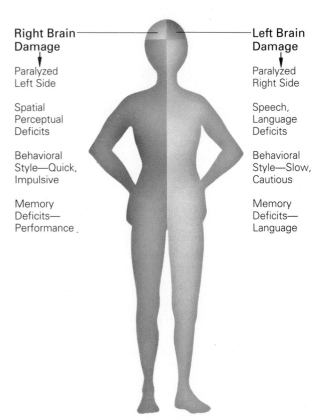

Right Brain Damage
Paralyzed Left Side
Spatial Perceptual Deficits
Behavioral Style—Quick, Impulsive
Memory Deficits— Performance

Left Brain Damage
Paralyzed Right Side
Speech, Language Deficits
Behavioral Style—Slow, Cautious
Memory Deficits— Language

FIGURE 3.21   SPECIALIZATION OF THE CEREBRAL HEMISPHERES

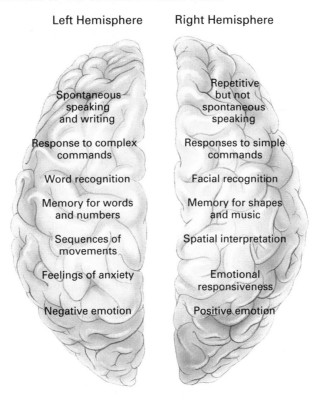

Left Hemisphere   Right Hemisphere

Spontaneous speaking and writing

Response to complex commands

Word recognition

Memory for words and numbers

Sequences of movements

Feelings of anxiety

Negative emotion

Repetitive but not spontaneous speaking

Responses to simple commands

Facial recognition

Memory for shapes and music

Spatial interpretation

Emotional responsiveness

Positive emotion

In general, studies of healthy individuals have shown that the left side of the brain is more involved in controlling verbal activities, and the right side is more important in directing visual-spatial activities. However, the two hemispheres often make different contributions to the same function. For example, both hemispheres contribute to language and memory functions, to perceptual-cognitive functions, and to emotional functions (see **Figure 3.21**). As evidence for this generalization, consider a study in which subjects were given tasks requiring a series of split-second decisions and actions while brain-wave recordings were taken of the electrical activity of both hemispheres. Brain-wave activity rapidly bustled back and forth between the two hemispheres, depending on the kind of judgment and response being made at the moment. The researchers referred to this shifting pattern of brain-wave activity as "shadows of thought" (Gevins et al., 1983).

Canadian psychologist **Doreen Kimura** has found that there are *gender differences* in the size of each hemisphere and in how the left hemisphere is organized to control language abilities. In females, the left hemisphere appears to be larger; in men, it is the right hemisphere that is larger. This corresponds roughly to gender differences in language (controlled by the left hemisphere) and spatial abilities (controlled by the right hemisphere): Women tend to outperform men in verbal tasks and men do better in spatial tasks. Kimura's work with brain-damaged persons shows that women tend to suffer speech impairments when the front portion of the left hemisphere is damaged. For men, similar problems arise when the rear portion of the left hemisphere is damaged. Why the left hemisphere is organized differently for men and women is not exactly clear, although Kimura believes that hormonal influences during brain development may play a role (Holloway, 1990).

Early neuroscientists concluded that left hemisphere language functions would be found only in humans. We now know that this is not the case. For example, the development of a canary's songs is controlled by the left side of its brain. Also, rats handled frequently when young were found to have stored early experiences in the right hemisphere of their brains. As adults, these rats were less aggressive than those rats not given early handling. This effect was eliminated in animals that had the right hemispheres of their brains removed. Such research has led investigators to conclude that "no animal species, no matter how humble, lacks cerebral dominance" (Geschwind, cited in Marks, 1981).

TWO BRAINS OR ONE?

That we have two cerebral hemispheres, each of which appears to have different functions, raises an intriguing question: Would each half of the brain be able to act as a separate conscious mind if it were separated from the other in some way? The chance to investigate this possibility has been provided by a treatment for severe epilepsy in which surgeons sever the corpus callosum—that bundle of about 200 million nerve fibers that transfers information back and forth between the two hemispheres (see **Figure 3.22**). The goal of this surgery is to prevent the violent electrical rhythms that accompany epileptic seizures from crossing between the hemispheres (Wilson et al., 1977). The operation is usually successful and a patient's subsequent behavior in most circumstances appears normal. Patients who undergo this type of surgery are often referred to as split-brain patients.

What gave researchers the idea that the two hemispheres may be able to function independently? When sensory input from the eyes, for example, is registered by the receptors, it automatically goes across to the opposite side of the brain (right eye to left hemisphere; left eye to right hemisphere). However, the information is shared by both hemispheres through the corpus callosum (see **Figure 3.23**). So when they can coordinate input from both eyes, split-brain patients can function without problems. But when given special tasks that present separate information to each eye or each hand, the effects of the split-brain surgery are quite dramatically not normal.

The first split-brain operations on human patients were performed by neurosurgeon William Van Wagener in the early 1940s (Van Wagener & Herren, 1940). Over a decade later, experimenters cut the corpus callosum in animals and then trained the subjects in visual discrimination tasks with one eye covered. When the eye patch was switched to the other eye, the animals took as long to learn the tasks as they had the first time. The one side of the brain had not learned anything from the experience given to the other side (Myers & Sperry, 1958).

To test the capabilities of the separated hemispheres of epileptic patients, **Roger Sperry** (1968) and **Michael Gazzaniga** (1970) devised situations that could allow visual information to be presented separately to each hemisphere (see **Figure 3.24**).

> The researchers found that the left hemisphere was superior to the right hemisphere in problems involving language or requiring logic and sequential or analytic processing of concepts. The left hemisphere could "talk back" to the researchers while the right hemisphere could not. Communication with the right hemisphere was achieved by confronting it with manual tasks involving identification, matching, or assembly of objects—tasks that did not require the use of words. The right hemisphere turned out to be better than the left at solving problems involving spatial relationships and at pattern recognition. However, it could only add up to 10 and was about at the level of a 2-year-old in the use and comprehension of word combinations.

The two hemispheres also seemed to have different "styles" for processing the same information. For example, on matching tasks, the left hemisphere matched objects analytically and verbally—by similarity in function. The right hemisphere matched things that looked alike or fit together to form a whole pattern. Thus, when pictures of a hat, a knife, and a fork were presented only to the left hemisphere, a split-brain subject asked to match the correct one with a picture of cake on a plate would report, "You eat cake with a fork and knife." When the test stimuli were presented to the right hemisphere, the same patient might match the hat with the cake since the items were similar in shape (Levy & Trevarthen, 1976).

| FIGURE 3.22 | THE CORPUS CALLOSUM |

The corpus callosum is a massive network of nerve fibers that channels information between the two hemispheres. Severing the corpus callosum impairs the communication process.

Corpus callosum

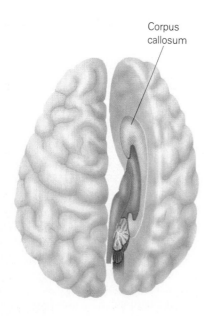

FIGURE 3.23   THE NEURAL PATHWAYS FOR VISUAL INFORMATION

The neural pathways for visual information coming from inside portions of each eye cross from one side of the brain to the other at the corpus callosum. The pathways carrying information from the outside portions of each eye do not cross over. The ultimate destination of all visual information is the visual cortex. Severing the corpus callosum prevents information selectively displayed in the right visual field from entering the left hemisphere where it would be integrated with language formation.

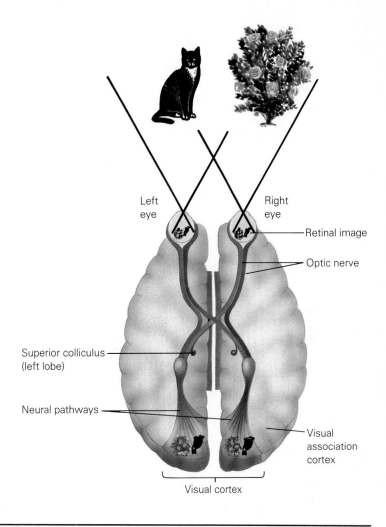

Left eye

Right eye

Retinal image

Optic nerve

Superior colliculus (left lobe)

Neural pathways

Visual association cortex

Visual cortex

The brain is designed to function as a whole with a vast, precise communication network integrating both hemispheres. When the hemispheres are disconnected, the result is two separate brains and a *duality of consciousness*. Each hemisphere can respond independently and simultaneously when stimuli are presented separately to each side. When stimuli are presented to only one side, responses are either emotional or analytic, depending on which hemisphere gets the task of interpreting the message. Lacking language competence, however, the disconnected human right hemisphere has limited and vastly inferior visual-spatial skills as compared to the cognitive skills of the left hemisphere. The right hemisphere has failed to develop not only language facility but also a range of mental processes necessary for comprehension and understanding of both external and internal events.

Consider the following demonstration of a split-brain subject using his left half brain to account for the activity of his left hand, which was being guided by his right half brain.

A snow scene was presented to the right hemisphere and a picture of a chicken claw was simultaneously presented to the left hemisphere. The subject selected, from an array of objects, those that "went with" each of the two scenes. With his right hand, the patient pointed to a chicken head; with his left hand he pointed to a shovel. The patient reported that the shovel was needed to clean out the chicken shed (rather than to shovel snow). Since the left brain was not privy to what the right brain "saw" because of the severed corpus callosum, it needed to explain why the left

FIGURE 3.24   *COORDINATION BETWEEN EYE AND HAND*

Coordination between eye and hand is normal if a split-brain patient uses the left hand to find and match an object that appears in the left visual field because both are registered in the right hemisphere. However, when asked to use the right hand to match an object seen in the left visual field, the patient cannot do so because sensory messages from the right hand are going to the left cerebral hemisphere, and there is no longer a connection between the two hemispheres. Here the cup is misperceived as matching the pear.

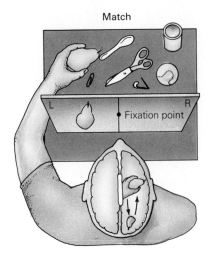

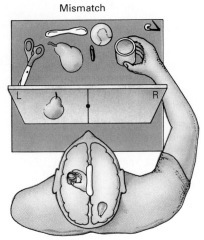

Match

Mismatch

hand was pointing at a shovel when the only picture the left hemisphere was aware of seeing was a chicken claw. The left brain's cognitive system provided a theory to make sense of the behavior of different parts of its body. It appears that the dominant left hemisphere interprets the meaning of overt behaviors, emotional responses, and the experiences of the right hemisphere (Gazzaniga, 1985).

We must be cautious, however, about generalizing such findings from split-brain patients into a basic view of the way that normal brains function. Does the brain function holistically as a uniform central command system, or is it organized according to specialized functions for each hemisphere? A number of investigators propose that the human mind is neither a single entity nor even a dual entity but rather a confederation of multiple mind modules. These "miniminds" are each specialized to process almost automatically a specific kind of information, such as spelling or arithmetic. The input from these many separate modules is then synthesized and coordinated for action by central, executive processors (Fodor, 1983; Hinton & Anderson, 1981; Ornstein, 1986). Some researchers and practitioners have gone beyond theory to develop techniques designed to enhance right hemisphere functioning in the hope of boosting creativity (Buzan, 1976; Edwards, 1979).

Other neuroscientists and psychologists are skeptical about the importance and validity of hemispheric specialization. Despite the striking fact that the human

brain is not completely symmetrical, these investigators still suspect that any asymmetries are explainable in terms of specialized processes located in each hemisphere (Efron, 1990). Ideally, the debate between these two views of the brain will generate a fuller understanding of how our brain works so effectively. It should also provide insights into why the human brain sometimes fails to function rationally or wisely.

SUMMING UP

The cerebral cortex is the basis of consciousness. If it didn't exist or if it were different in the slightest of ways, our conscious experience of the world would be changed. The cerebral cortex is divided into two halves or hemispheres by the corpus callosum. Although the hemispheres are physically symmetrical, their functions are not. Language, memory for words and numbers, word recognition, feelings of anxiety, and negative emotions are regulated by the left hemisphere. The right hemisphere controls spatial interpretation, facial recognition, memory for shapes and music, and positive emotions. The two hemispheres can be physically disconnected by surgically severing the corpus callosum. As long as stimuli are presented to the visual or auditory fields of both hemispheres, the brain will continue to work as an integrated whole. But when stimuli are selectively presented to the visual or auditory field of only one hemisphere, the other one is neither aware of that stimulation nor of the kind of cognitive activities that are taking place in the other hemisphere. (However, the left hemisphere often constructs explanations and theories to account for reactions generated by stimulating the right hemisphere.) Severing the corpus callosum, then, creates two brains, each capable of independent functions.

 ## OUR RESPONSIVE BRAIN

In this chapter, we have peeked at a small bit of the marvelous 3-pound universe that is our brain. It is one thing to recognize that the brain controls behavior and our mental processes, but quite another to understand *how* it serves all those functions that we take for granted when it functions normally and what happens when it doesn't. Neuroscientists are engaged in this fascinating quest to understand the interplay between brain, hormones, behavior, experience, and environment.

We began our study of the biology of behavior with the example of how touch can have a biological effect in transforming the growth of premature infants (for more on the effects of touch, see Brown, 1984, and Gunzenhauser, 1990). This positive effect of physical stimulation on bodily growth is mediated by changes in brain functioning. The massaged babies gained more weight than the unstimulated control infants (despite similar formula and calorie intake), they became more physically active, and their sleep patterns changed. These stimulated babies showed significantly higher catecholamine levels, releasing more of several neurotransmitters. The key to weight gain in both premature human infants and rat pups deprived of a mother's touch is stimulating the activity of a special brain enzyme (ODC) which synthesizes growth proteins that are essential for normal development. While deprivation of mother contact shuts down the growth hormone, massaging the infants maintains the brain's release of the hormone (Field & Schanberg, 1990). So here is a clear case where the brain's functioning is modified in profound ways by external stimulation. Also, it has been found that therapeutic touch profoundly improves the mental and physical health of the elderly (Fanslow, 1984).

Much new research, across a wide range of species, is demonstrating that the brain is a *dynamic* system capable of changing itself—both its functions and its physical structure—in response to various kinds of stimulation and environmental challenges (Fernald, 1984; Sapolsky, 1990). We are thus led to a new perspective about the nature of the brain. In addition to the well-known *behaving brain* which controls behavior, there is the *responsive brain* which is changed by the behavior it generates and by environmental stimulation. This capacity for its own internal modification makes the complex human brain the most dynamic, responsive system on the planet (Rosenzweig, 1984b).

Evolution, Heredity, and Behavior

Species originate and change over time because of natural selection. In the evolution of humans, bipedalism and encephalization were responsible for subsequent advances including language and culture. The basic unit of evolution is the gene. Genes determine the range of effects that environmental factors can have in influencing expression of phenotypic traits.

Brain and Behavior

Neuroscientists use four methods to research the relation between brain and behavior: studying brain damaged patients, producing lesions at specific brain sites, electrically stimulating and recording brain activity, and scanning the brain with computerized devices. The brain consists of three integrated layers: central core, limbic system, and cerebral cortex. The central core is responsible for breathing, digestion, and heart rate. The limbic system is involved in long-term memory, aggression, eating, drinking, and sexual behavior. The cerebral cortex consists of two hemispheres—different areas of the cortex process different kinds of stimulation, form associations, or initiate movement.

The Endocrine and Nervous Systems

The endocrine system produces and secretes hormones into the blood stream. Hormones help regulate growth, primary and secondary sexual characteristics, metabolism, digestion, and arousal. The hypothalamus controls the endocrine system by stimulating the pituitary gland. The pituitary gland then secretes the appropriate hormone to stimulate one or more of the other endocrine glands.

The brain and the spinal cord make up the central nervous system (CNS). The peripheral nervous system (PNS) is composed of all neurons connecting the CNS to the body. The PNS consists of the somatic nervous system, which regulates the body's skeletal muscles, and the autonomic nervous system (ANS), which regulates life support processes. The sympathetic division of the ANS is active during stress. Its parasympathetic division operates under routine circumstances.

The Nervous System in Action

The neuron, the basic unit of the nervous system, receives, processes, and relays information to other cells, glands, and muscles. Neurons relay information in a fixed direction from the dendrites through the cell body to the axon to the terminal buttons. Sensory neurons receive messages from specialized receptor cells and send them toward the CNS. Motor neurons channel messages away from the CNS to muscles and glands. Interneurons relay information from sensory neurons to other interneurons or motor neurons.

Information passes from dendrites to the soma in the form of graded potentials. Once the graded potential exceeds a specific threshold, an action potential is sent along the axon to the terminal buttons. Action potentials are caused when the opening of ion cells allows an exchange of positive and negative ions across the cell membrane. Neurotransmitters are released into the synaptic gap. Once across the gap, they lodge in the receptor molecules of the postsynaptic membrane. Whether these neurotransmitters excite or inhibit the membrane depends on the nature of the receptor molecule.

The Nervous System and Conscious Experience

The cerebral cortex is the basis of consciousness. Language, word, and number memory; anxiety; and negative emotions are regulated by the left hemisphere. The right hemisphere controls spatial interpretation, facial recognition, memory for shapes and music, and positive emotions. If the hemispheres are surgically severed, each functions independently of the other and is not aware of stimulation or cognitive activities that affect the other.

The behaving brain initiates and controls behavior. The responsive brain's functions and structure are changed by stimulation from the environment and from its own behavior.

Our Responsive Brain

Research has shown that the brain's functioning is modified in profound ways by external stimulation. New research is showing that the brain is a dynamic system, responsive to environmental stimulation and capable of self-modification.

KEY TERMS

action potential, 86
all-or-none law, 86
amygdala, 72
association cortex, 75
auditory cortex, 75
autonomic nervous system (ANS), 79
axon, 83
bipedalism, 59
central core, 71
central nervous system (CNS), 79
cerebellum, 71
cerebral cortex, 73
cerebral dominance, 94
cerebral hemispheres, 73
corpus callosum, 73
CT scanner, 68
dendrite, 82
developmental disability, 62
electrode, 67
electroencephalogram (EEG), 68
encephalization, 59
endocrine system, 76
endorphin, 89
estrogen, 78

evolution, 57
gene, 61
genetics, 61
genotype, 58
glial cells (glia), 84
graded potential, 85
heredity, 57
hippocampus, 72
homeostasis, 73
hormone, 76
human behavior genetics, 62
hypothalamus, 72
interneuron, 83
ion channel, 87
law of forward conduction, 83
lesion, 67
limbic system, 71
medulla, 71
motor cortex, 74
motor neuron, 83
MRI, 68
natural selection, 58
neural network, 92
neuromodulator, 89

neuron, 82
neurotransmitter, 87
parasympathetic division, 80
peripheral nervous system (PNS), 79
PET scanner, 68
phenotype, 58
pituitary gland, 78
pons, 71
refractory period, 86
reticular formation, 71
sensory neuron, 83
sex chromosome, 61
soma, 83
somatic nervous system, 79
somatosensory cortex, 75
sympathetic division, 80
synapse, 87
synaptic transmission, 87
terminal button, 83
testosterone, 78
thalamus, 71
visual cortex, 75

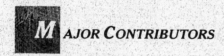

MAJOR CONTRIBUTORS

Broca, Paul, 65
Darwin, Charles, 57
Descartes, René, 63
Field, Tiffany, 55
Gazzaniga, Michael, 96

Grant, Peter, 58
Hebb, Donald, 65
Hess, Walter, 67
Kandel, Eric, 92
Kimura, Doreen, 95

Müller, Johannes, 65
Penfield, Wilder, 67
Schanberg, Saul, 55
Sherrington, Sir Charles, 65
Sperry, Roger, 96

Chapter 4

Mind, Consciousness, and Alternate States

BRAIN, MIND, AND SOUL   104
   THE MIND-BODY PROBLEM
   PSYCHOLOGY'S CONCEPTION OF THE MIND
   THE MIND ACROSS CULTURES

THE NATURE OF CONSCIOUSNESS   107
   FUNCTIONS OF CONSCIOUSNESS
   LEVELS OF CONSCIOUSNESS
   STRUCTURES OF CONSCIOUSNESS
   RESEARCH APPROACHES

   ■ INTERIM SUMMARY

EVERYDAY CHANGES IN CONSCIOUSNESS   111
   DAYDREAMING AND FANTASY
   TO SLEEP, PERCHANCE TO DREAM

   ■ INTERIM SUMMARY

EXTENDED STATES OF CONSCIOUSNESS   122
   LUCID DREAMING
   HYPNOSIS
   MEDITATION
   HALLUCINATIONS
   RELIGIOUS ECSTASY
   MIND-ALTERING DRUGS

POSTSCRIPT: WHY CONSCIOUSNESS?   131

RECAPPING MAIN POINTS   132

KEY TERMS   133

MAJOR CONTRIBUTORS   133

"One hundred, 99, 98, 97 . . ." Karen counted as the anesthetic flowed from the needle to her vein. Geometric patterns oscillated wildly before her. "Ninety-two, 91, 9. . . ." Darkness descended. Sensation and awareness shut down. Karen's surgery began.

Karen hadn't worried about this operation—it was only minor surgery to remove a cyst in her mouth. Minutes into the operation, however, the surgeon exclaimed, "Why, this may not be a cyst at all. It may be cancer!" Fortunately, the biopsy proved him wrong. In the recovery room he told Karen, who was still groggy and slightly nauseated, that everything was fine; the operation was a complete success.

That night, Karen felt anxious and had trouble falling asleep. She started crying for no apparent reason. Finally, when she did fall asleep, she dreamed about a puppy she couldn't get because of her allergy to dogs. She awoke feeling sad and was depressed all day. At first, Karen attributed her bad mood to her dream. But when all attempts to restore her usual good spirits failed and her depression worsened, Karen sought professional help.

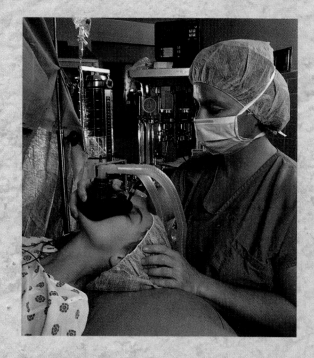

A therapist hypnotized Karen and then asked her to lift her hand if something was disturbing her. Karen's hand rose, and the therapist suggested that she report what was disturbing her. Karen exclaimed, "The cyst may be cancerous!"

After receiving assurances that the cyst was benign, Karen's depression lifted. Consciously, Karen had not understood the source of her anxiety. But even in an unconscious, anesthetized state, some part of her mind had comprehended the surgeon's words. The dire meaning of that information became psychologically traumatic to Karen.

Karen's case is not unusual. Accumulating evidence indicates that many patients who are fully anesthetized and have no conscious recall of their operation may still hear what is going on during their surgery. Our hearing sensitivity appears to remain on alert even under adequate anesthesia. The reasons for this auditory alertness may be deeply rooted in our evolutionary history—animals in the open had to respond swiftly to possible danger sounds even when asleep. Whatever the reason, highly specialized cells in the auditory nerve make signals passing along it exceptionally clear and hard to block out with anesthetics. Because of this sensitivity, even casual remarks in the operating room can be dangerous. "I think they can kill people, if you want to know the truth," said a researcher in the department of anesthesiology at a California medical center. "I've seen cardiac arrests during surgery that can't be explained except by comments made around the operating table" (Rymer, 1987, p. 19).

The possibility that patients might experience auditory awareness during general anesthesia has led to research and stimulated considerable controversy among psychologists and physicians (Bitner, 1983; Cheek, 1979; Cherkin & Harrour, 1971; Guerra & Aldrete, 1980; Millar & Watkinson, 1983). Negative messages have been shown to induce anxiety following surgery (Levinson, 1967), as in Karen's case. On the positive side, encouraging messages during surgery have been linked to shorter hospital stays and decreased needs for postoperative painkilling medication (Hutchins, 1961; Pearson, 1961). This phenomenon is not always replicable, and it requires carefully designed and well-controlled procedures to rule out alternative explanations.

Karen's case introduces us to the complexities of human consciousness. Her ordinary state of conscious awareness was altered in many ways: by drugs, by sleeping and dreaming, and by hypnosis. Her waking thoughts and moods were influenced by memories and impulses that she may not have been able to acknowledge, such as her frustrated desire for a puppy and her fear of cancer. Even when her body was immobilized by a general anesthetic, her brain was still subconsciously processing environmental stimuli. Karen fits the description French physiologist Claude Bernard gave of patients who received the paralyzing drug curare. He called them "sensitive beings locked in immobile bodies."

What is ordinary conscious awareness? What determines the contents of our consciousness, and why do we need it? What happens to stimulus events that our sense organs detect but our brains fail to notice? Can unconscious mental events really influence our thoughts, emotions, and behavior, as they seemed to do for Karen? How does consciousness change over the course of a day-night cycle, and how can we intentionally alter our state of consciousness? The budding psychologist in you should want to know how private, internal states of mind can be studied scientifically.

Our search for answers to these questions puts the *human mind* in the spotlight. Attention, awareness, and conscious and unconscious information processing are all functions of mind that take place somewhere in the brain and have a powerful impact on all that we think, feel, and do.

At the end of the previous chapter, we began to examine brain mechanisms involved in some alterations of consciousness. We considered the effects on the brain of psychoactive drugs and of operations that sever the connections between the cortical hemispheres. In this chapter, we continue our exploration of the mind by first

reflecting on an ages-old problem for philosophers, psychologists, and neuroscientists: What is the relationship between brain and mind? Next, we will analyze the nature of consciousness—its functions, levels, and different structures. Then we will shift to the regular mental changes we all experience during daydreaming, fantasizing, sleeping, and night dreaming. Finally, we will look at how consciousness is altered dramatically by hypnosis, meditation, religious rituals, and certain drugs.

 ## BRAIN, MIND, AND SOUL

Throughout human history, people have tried to account for human behavior. Our early ancestors traced the causes of human actions to their *anima,* or inner life force, and the operation of outer spiritual forces—divine and demonic—that they believed existed in nature. In these *animistic* explanations of behavior, the same kinds of spiritual forces guided all creatures of nature. An individual's spirit, or soul, was assumed to be separate from the body, doing all those things that make people human: seeing, talking, remembering, and feeling. It controlled the person. When evil spirits entered a person's body, they could cause disease or bizarre behavior. Puncturing the person's skull allowed these evil spirits to escape. When the spirit left, whether it had been good or evil, the person could do nothing, and the body died. This notion of spirit is similar to how some people today conceptualize the mind.

Across the centuries, philosophers, such as those from ancient Greece and from Renaissance Europe, have debated over the relationship between brain and mind—the sources of all actions and thoughts. A review of this debate will be a useful starting point for learning about human consciousness.

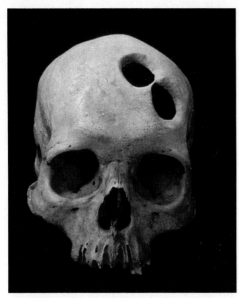

Trephination—perforating the skull with a sharp instrument—was long thought to be a means of treating mental disorders. The process was originally believed to drive out the evil spirits causing the disturbance.

THE MIND-BODY PROBLEM

The problem of the relationship between the mind and the brain has long perplexed serious thinkers and defied easy solutions. On one side of the debate are those who hold that the *mind* does not exist: they believe the term is merely a popular way of referring to what the brain does. It is only the *brain,* they say, that thinks about the brain's activities, just as a computer's diagnostic programs check on its own circuits and functioning. On the other side are those who believe that *mind* is more than just a convenient term for *thoughtful reflection;* they believe that mind and consciousness are central to what it means to be human.

Plato was one of the first Greek philosophers to try to distinguish between notions of mind and body. In his view, the mind and its mental processes were absolutely distinct from the physical aspects of body and brain. Plato gave the mind a special position. He believed it went beyond the directly sensed physical world to consider abstractions and "ideal realities," and he speculated that the mind survived the death of the body. Plato's view became known as *dualism.* **Dualism** proposes that the mind is fundamentally different from and independent of the brain: the mind and brain are dual aspects of human nature.

With the rise of the Roman Empire, philosophical analyses of such matters were set aside in favor of military, legal, and technological matters for several thousand years. Later, the ideas of Plato and other Greek thinkers were further suppressed by the spread of Christianity, which insisted that belief in the nonphysical soul was a matter of uncontested faith and not an issue open to debate. It was not until the Renaissance that a renewed appreciation for scientific, rational inquiry sparked efforts to understand the nature of the mind.

In the mid-1600s, the French philosopher and mathematician **René Descartes** advanced the radical new theory that the body was an "animal machine." Its workings could be studied scientifically by *reducing* all sensations and actions to their underlying physical components. In this *mechanistic approach,* animal behaviors and some basic human behaviors are reflex reactions to physical energies exciting the senses. It follows from Descartes's theory that, as a machine, the body can't be subject to moral principles, so, other human behaviors—reasoning, decision making, and thinking about oneself, for example—are based on the operation of the soul, or human mind. Descartes's dualistic view enabled him to resolve the dilemmas he faced as a devoutly religious Catholic (who believed in the spiritual soul), a rational thinker (who believed in the ephemeral mind), and a scientific observer (who believed in the mechanistic view of perception and reflex actions).

In opposition to dualism was **monism,** which proposes that mind and brain are one—that mental phenomena are nothing but the products of the brain. Monists contend that mind and its mental states are reducible, in principle, to brain states; that is, all thought and action have a physical, material base (Churchland, 1986).

PSYCHOLOGY'S CONCEPTION OF THE MIND

Throughout psychology's short history, there has been an ongoing, vigorous tug-of-war between dualists and monists. As psychology gradually diverged from philosophy in the early 1800s it became "the science of the mind." Wundt and Titchener used introspection to discover the contents of the conscious mind, and William James observed his own stream of consciousness. In fact, James asserted on the very first page of his 1890 classic text that "Psychology [is] the description and explanation of 'consciousness' as such."

Watson's objective behaviorism dismissed these psychologists' introspection and stream of consciousness studies as unscientific, substituting their methods with research on directly observable behavior and observations of learned habits of responding. During the decades that behaviorism dominated American psychology, psychology lost not only its mind but its brain, as behaviorists focused solely on external behavior.

In the 1960s, psychology reexamined the mind-body debate. Cognitive psychologists and psycholinguists studying thought and communication examined the workings of the mind and its mental products. Humanist psychologists, focusing on processes of self-knowledge and self-actualization, actually made the foundation of their entire discipline the study of the human mind.

However, the emergence of brain sciences led biologically oriented psychologists to champion a monist position. They believed that the brain alone sits at the head of the table of life and that mind and brain are identical. "The mind is nothing but the brain. . . . We can give a complete account of man in purely physiochemical terms" within a "purely electrochemical account of the workings of the brain," asserted one such psychologist (Armstrong, 1968). However, if mind has no role in this life's drama, then consciousness also must exit the scene. Nobel Laureate Sir John Eccles (1964) proclaimed, "We can, in principle, explain all our input-output performance in terms of activity of neuronal circuits and consequently, consciousness seems to be absolutely unnecessary!"

This narrow view of consciousness was challenged by the research of Roger Sperry and Michael Gazzaniga in which surgical disconnections of the cerebral hemispheres created a duality of conscious experience in patients (see Chapter 3). Out of this research came a new perspective, called the **emergent-interaction theory** of mind-brain relationships. This theory asserts that (a) brain activities give rise to mental states, but these mental states are different from, more than, and not reducible to brain states; (b) the mind and conscious experience are dynamic, *emergent* properties of brain activity (as water is an emergent property of hydrogen and oxygen molecules); (c) the phenomenon of "inner experience" is a high-order emergent property of the brain's hierarchical organization of control and regulation; (d) brain and mind *interact,* so, while the brain acts on the mind, the mind acts on the brain to govern, rule, and direct neural and chemical events; and (e) the conscious mind exerts top-level causal influence over the brain in directing and controlling behavior.

Although this new form of dualism is not compatible with the perspectives of most neuroscientists, it is with the perspectives of many psychologists, and it is the one we shall utilize in our exploration of consciousness and mental phenomena. According to Roger Sperry (1976, 1987), this view fuses science and our common experience:

> The mind has been restored to the brain of experimental science. . . . The subjective is no longer outside the mainstream of objective science, nor

something that will eventually be reducible in principle to neurophysiology. . . . Scientific theory has become squared finally with the impression of common experience: we do in fact use the mind to initiate and control our physical actions (1986, p. 166).

Although we shall treat the concept of mind as a valid psychological process, it should be clear that it is not possible to prove or disprove either scientifically or logically the existence of the mind. Since the mind is by definition something we each experience subjectively, research can only discover reflections of it in its assumed activities. Research cannot uncover the existence of the mind in any direct way. While we are aware of the *products* of mind and consciousness, we cannot perceive the *processes* that give rise to our attention, awareness, and personal experience of consciousness. So, accepting the existence of the mind—at least your own—remains a matter of faith.

THE MIND ACROSS CULTURES

Our bias toward Western ideas often leads us to overlook those of other cultures. Before the Greek philosophers debated mind-body questions, views of the mind already existed in the philosophies and religions of many cultures. Let's consider briefly a Chinese and an Indian view of the mind before moving on to study the nature of consciousness and its various forms.

The ancient Chinese did not believe in a mind-body dualism; there was no mind, only the organic body. Mental and physical activities were attributed to the actions of the internal organs, just as mental disorders and physical ailments were the products of imbalances in these organs. Treatment for all ailments consisted of herbal drugs and acupuncture to alter the functioning of specific internal organs and return the person to a holistic balance. This organic outlook is deeply ingrained in Chinese thought and in the thinking of many other East Asian cultures.

Indian views of the mind are diametrically different. According to the teachings of Buddhism, the visible universe is an illusion of the senses; the world is nothing but mind; and the mind of the individual is part of the collective, universal mind. Excessive mental activity distracts one from focusing on inner experience and allowing mind to rise above sensory experience. Meditation is a life-long exercise in discovering how to remove the mind from distractions and illusions, allowing it to roam freely and discover wisdom. To become an enlightened being requires the control of bodily yearnings, stopping the ordinary experiences of the senses and mind, and discovering how to see things in their true light.

THE NATURE OF CONSCIOUSNESS

A penny for your thoughts. What sort of response allows you to collect on such an offer? The person making it expects you to describe the current contents of your consciousness, that part of the mind of which you are aware. Think of *consciousness* as the front page of the mind and *attention* as the lead story. Awareness is the knowledge that the story is in the newspaper of your mind. Ordinary waking consciousness includes the immediate mental experiences comprising your perceptions, thoughts, feelings, and desires at a given moment—all the mental activity on which you are focusing your attention. You are conscious of focusing attention not just on what you are doing but on the fact that you are doing it and, at times, on the realization that others are observing, evaluating, and reacting to what you are doing. A *sense of self* comes out of this experience of watching ourselves from this privileged "insider" position. Taken together, these various mental activities form the *contents* of consciousness—all the experiences we are consciously aware of at a particular time.

There is more to consciousness than its contents. Sometimes, we use the term *consciousness* to refer to a general *state of mind* rather than to its specific contents. In sum, **consciousness** can mean simply that you are aware of the general condition of your mind, or are aware of particular mental contents, or are self-aware.

What functions does consciousness serve? What are the different levels at which consciousness operates? What is the structure of consciousness that includes all those processes of which we are *not aware*? Finally, how do psychologists study such private experiences as consciousness, attention, and awareness? These are the questions we will now consider.

FUNCTIONS OF CONSCIOUSNESS

Why does consciousness exist—what purpose does it serve? The general functions of consciousness are to aide our survival and enable us to construct both personal realities and culturally shared realities.

Aiding Survival

From a biological perspective, consciousness probably evolved because it helped individuals make sense of environmental information and use that information in planning the most appropriate and effective actions. Usually we are faced with a sensory-information overload. William James described the massive amount of information that strikes our sensory receptors as a "blooming, buzzing confusion" assailing us from all sides. Consciousness helps us adapt to our environment by making sense of this "profusion of confusion" in three ways.

Restrictive Function   First, it reduces the flow of stimulus input by restricting what we notice and to what we pay attention. This *restrictive function* of consciousness tunes out much of the information that is not relevant to our immediate goals and purposes. All that is evaluated as "irrelevant" becomes background noise to be ignored while we focus conscious awareness on "relevant" input, the *signal* we wish to process and respond to.

Selective Storage Function   Second, consciousness helps us select and store personally meaningful stimuli from the flow of all relevant environmental input. It selects stimuli with the highest priority at any given moment. After the stream of all sensory input is perceptually processed into a smaller number of recognizable patterns and categories, consciousness serves as a mental storage shelf and display stand for those special stimuli we want to analyze, interpret, and act upon (Duncan & Humphries, 1989; Marcel, 1983). This *selective storage function* of consciousness allows us to form and retain a mental representation—a *short-term memory*—of the stimulus after it is no longer physically present. (Atkinson & Shiffrin, 1969).

Planning or Executive Control Function   The third function of consciousness is to make us stop, think, consider alternatives based on past knowledge, and imagine various consequences. This *planning or executive control function* enables us to suppress strong desires when they conflict with moral, ethical, or practical concerns. Without this kind of consciousness, you would immediately eat a juicy and poisonous mushroom when you were hungry if it was the first food you saw. Because consciousness gives us a broad *time perspective* in which to frame potential actions, we are able to call upon abstract representations of the past and the future to influence our current decisions. You are able to recall a television program about the dangerous properties of certain mushrooms which influences you to pass up the mushroom and buy a sandwich at the corner deli. For all these reasons, consciousness gives us far more potential than other species have for flexible, appropriate responses to the changing demands in our lives (Ornstein, 1986; Rozin, 1976).

Personal and Cultural Constructions of Reality

No two people interpret every situation in exactly the same way. Your *personal construction of reality* is your unique interpretation of a current situation based on a broader scheme or model that includes your general knowledge, memories of past experiences, current needs, values, beliefs, and future goals. Each person attends more to certain features of the stimulus environment than to others precisely because her or his personal construction of reality has been formed from a selection of unique inputs. When your personal construction of reality remains relatively stable, your *sense of self* is given unity and continuity over time and across situations. Some psychologists believe that at the core of the *unique personality* that differentiates each of us is our personal construction of reality.

Individual differences in personal constructions of reality are even greater when people have grown up in different cultures, lived in different environments within a culture, or faced different survival tasks. The opposite is also true—because the people of a given culture share many of the same experiences, they often have similar constructions of reality. *Cultural constructions of reality* are ways of thinking about the world that are shared by most members of a particular group of people. When a member of a culture develops a personal construction of reality that fits in with the cultural construction, it is affirmed by the culture and, at the same time, it affirms the cultural construction. This mutual affirmation of conscious constructions of reality is known as **consensual validation** (Natsoulas, 1978; Rozin & Fallon, 1987).

LEVELS OF CONSCIOUSNESS

What are you doing at this moment? What were you just thinking? What is the effect of my asking you these questions? You should have been aware that you were reading a section of the consciousness chapter in your **Psychology and Life** textbook. Perhaps you were thinking about when you rejected someone or were rejected. Surely my questions made you aware that you were aware of something. Psychologists identify three different levels of consciousness. They correspond roughly to (a) a basic level of awareness of the world; (b) a second level of reflection on what we are aware of; and (c) a top level of awareness of ourselves as conscious, reflective individuals (Hilgard, 1980; Natsoulas, 1981; Tulving, 1985).

At the basic level, consciousness is being aware that we are perceiving and reacting to available perceptual information. At the second level, consciousness relies on symbolic knowledge to free us from the constraints of real objects and present events—it gives us *imagination*. We can contemplate and manipulate objects in their absence, visualize new forms and uses for the familiar, plan utopias, and invent new products. The top level of consciousness is **self-awareness,** cognizance

that personally experienced events have an *autobiographical* character. Self-awareness gives us our sense of personal history and identity. At this level of consciousness, if we have personally experienced an orderly, predictable world, we come to expect it, and this expectation equips us to choose the best present actions and plans for the future (Lachman & Naus, 1984).

A fascinating illustration of the *absence* of self-awareness is the case of patient N. N., who suffered a head injury to the frontal lobes of his cortex. (Recall that the frontal lobes direct planning functions and handle time-based experiences.)

> N. N. is conscious, remembers many things about the world, can solve problems in a flexible, symbolic way, has good language skills and general knowledge. Although he has a sense of clock time, he has no sense of personal time perspective—no awareness of his own autobiography over time. He does not know what he did yesterday or what he will do tomorrow. When asked questions about his activities, he reports his mind is blank—he feels as if he is looking for a piece of furniture in an empty room. He lives in a state of "permanent present" without any anxiety over his inability to experience an awareness of his relationship to past and future events (Tulving, 1984).

STRUCTURES OF CONSCIOUSNESS

Clearly, consciousness is crucial to the control of our behavior. But is behavior controlled only by mental processes of which we are consciously aware? Were you aware of your heartbeat just now? Probably not; its control is part of *nonconscious processes*. Were you thinking about your last vacation or the author of *Hamlet*? Again, probably not; control of those kinds of thoughts are part of *preconscious memories*. Were you aware of background noises, such as a clock ticking, traffic, and a neon light buzzing? You couldn't be and still pay full attention to the meaning of the material in this chapter, because awareness of nonrelevant stimuli is part of *subconscious awareness*. Finally, are you aware of how some of your early life experiences, sexual desires, and feelings of aggression affect what you say and do now? According to psychodynamic analysis, awareness of these strong, disruptive emotions is blocked by powerful forces that are part of the *unconscious*.

Nonconscious Processes

Nonconscious processes involve information not represented in either consciousness or memory but that still influences fundamental bodily or mental activities. An example of nonconscious processes at work is the regulation of blood pressure, in which physiological information is detected and changes are acted on continually without our awareness. Another is the basic perception of *figure and ground,* as you can see in the left-hand image of **Figure 4.1.** We instantly separate the figure from its background, but we are unaware of the organizing processes that give rise to this perceptual response. We only become aware of the fact that such processes must be going on behind the scenes when we look at an ambiguous drawing, such as the right-hand image, and have to search for a recognizable figure.

Preconscious Memories

Memories accessible to consciousness only after something calls our attention to them are known as **preconscious memories.** The storehouse of memory is filled with an incredible amount of information, such as your general knowledge of language, sports, or geography; recollections of all your personally experienced events; and the procedures for skilled performance, such as riding a bike or even dressing yourself. Preconscious memories function silently in the backgrounds of our minds until needed or stimulated, until something interferes with our usual performance, or until we are trying to teach others what we know how to do automatically, such as tying shoelaces.

Subconscious Awareness

We put much of the stimulation around us out of our minds in order to focus attention on a small part of it. Nevertheless, a great deal of it still gets registered and evaluated at some level below that of conscious awareness. **Subconscious awareness** involves processing information not currently in consciousness but retrievable from memory by special recall or attention-getting procedures. Much research indicates that we are influenced by stimuli not perceived consciously (Kihlstrom, 1987). For example, at a noisy party, you might focus attention on your attractive date, seemingly oblivious to a nearby conversation—until you overhear your name mentioned. Suddenly, you are aware that you must have been monitoring the conversation to detect that special signal amid the noise. In the case that opened the chapter, Karen's depression was the result of a subconscious process; once it was brought into her consciousness by hypnotic therapy, she could recognize it and deal with it appropriately.

The Unconscious

Although we use the term *unconscious* to refer to someone who has fainted, fallen into a coma, or undergone general anesthesia, the term has a special meaning in psychology. In psychoanalytic theory, which was developed by **Sigmund Freud,** the **unconscious** refers to mental processes that keep out of conscious awareness any information that would cause extreme anxiety if recognized. Such processes are assumed to stem from the need to *repress* traumatic memories and taboo desires. Freud believed that when the content of original, unacceptable ideas or motives are *repressed*—put out of consciousness—the strong feelings associated with the

FIGURE 4.1   *A. Standard Figure Ground Stimulus*
B. Ambiguous Stimulus

A.

B.

thoughts still remain and show up in various forms. One of Freud's contributions was discovering how much adult behavior is influenced by unconscious processes that originate in early life.

In passing, we must briefly note the historical background in which Freud's theory of the unconscious was presented. From the time when the English philosopher John Locke (1690) wrote his classic text on the mind, *An Essay on Human Understanding,* most thinkers firmly believed that rational beings had access to all the activities of their own minds. Freud's initial hypothesis about the existence of unconscious mental processes was an outrage at the time (Dennett, 1987).

RESEARCH APPROACHES

Psychologists have developed a variety of techniques to study different aspects of consciousness, attention, and awareness. We will look at a few here to give you a sense of how it has been possible to study such subjective phenomena.

Researchers use a new variation on *introspection* as an exploratory procedure to map the workings of the mind. Subjects are asked to speak aloud as they work through puzzles, try to operate an unfamiliar machine, or carry out other kinds of complex tasks. They report in as much detail as possible the sequence of thoughts they experience while solving the problem or completing the task. Their reports, called **think-aloud protocols,** are used to document the mental strategies employed to do the task and the ways knowledge is represented by the subject and to analyze the discrepancies between task performance and awareness of how it is carried out (Ericsson & Simon, 1984; Newell & Simon, 1972).

In the **experience-sampling method,** subjects wearing electronic pagers are asked to write down or describe to a portable tape recorder what they are feeling and thinking whenever the pager signals. A radio transmitter activates the pager at various random times each day for a week or more (Emmons, 1987; Hurlburt, 1979). Whenever the pager signals, subjects may also be asked to respond to questions, such as "How well were you concentrating?" In this way, researchers can keep a running record of people's thoughts, awareness, and attention foci as they go about their everyday lives (Csikszentmihalyi, 1990).

In the **dichotic listening task,** a subject listens through stereo earphones to two different channels of input while being instructed to *attend* to just one channel (Broadbent, 1954). To increase selective listening, the subject is further told to repeat the input aloud as it enters the attended ear; that is, to "shadow" it while ignoring the other story. It is not surprising that subjects

do not remember information presented to the unattended ear. What is remarkable is that they don't even notice major changes in that input—when the tape is played backward or the language changes from English to German. They *do* notice changes in pitch—when a speaker's voice switches from male to female (Cherry, 1953)—and special signals, such as their own names. Gross physical features of the unattended message receive perceptual analysis, apparently at a *subconscious* level of awareness, but the meaning does not get through into consciousness.

> In an experiment on subconscious sentence comprehension, subjects in the dichotic listening task heard ambiguous sentences in the *attended* channel, such as "He put out the lantern to signal the attack." In the second, unattended channel the experimental group received information that clarified the ambiguity, such as the meaning of *put out:* "He extinguished the lantern." The controls heard sentences unrelated to those in the attended channel. Although members of the experimental group could not report what was presented through the unattended channel, they did favor those interpretations of the meaning of the sentences that were suggested in the unattended channel significantly more than the control group did. So, for example, they would say the lantern was extinguished while the control subjects would more often say it was put outside. Thus, it is concluded that the *unattended signal* does get through and is processed all the way up to the semantic level of comprehension, but it is not consciously recognized (Lackner & Garrett, 1973).

In Chapter 1 we noted that a specific brain wave pattern, the *P-300 wave form,* is used as an index of surprise or violation of expectation. It signals that a novel, unexpected stimulus is being registered by the brain even before the person is consciously aware of its presence and can respond behaviorally to it. These and a host of other new techniques are allowing psychological researchers to fulfill their desire to explore the secret world of other people's consciousness—the same desire that motivated Wundt, Titchener, and James a century earlier. Those three pioneers of psychology would surely approve the following sentiment expressed by a present-day researcher of human thinking processes: "Of all the mysteries of nature, none is greater than that of consciousness. Intimately familiar to all of us, our capacity to contemplate the universe and to apprehend the infinity of space and time, and our knowledge that we can do so, have continued to resist analysis and elude understanding" (Tulving, 1985).

SUMMING UP

In this section we examined the functions, levels, and structures of consciousness. We also looked at approaches to research on consciousness. Consciousness aids our survival in several ways. By restricting input, selectively storing currently relevant information, and using past and current knowledge to plan future actions, it allows us to make intentional, flexible responses. It also enables individuals to construct models of their reality and communities to construct culturally shared representations of reality. There are at least three different levels of consciousness: (a) a basic level of world awareness, (b) a level of reflection about what we are aware of, and (c) a top level of self-consciousness. Structures of consciousness can influence our behavior, thoughts, and feelings. These structures include nonconscious processes that automatically regulate bodily functions and perceptual decisions, preconscious memories, subconscious awareness (retrievable only with special procedures), and the unconscious, as hypothesized by Freud to be both the dynamic process for generating repression and the storehouse for all repressed thoughts. Research designed to observe these private events of consciousness employs new variations on introspection, such as think-aloud protocols and experience sampling. The dichotic listening task detects the effects on consciousness of attentional focus, while physiological measures index brain-mind signals during sleep, surprise, and other aspects of consciousness.

EVERYDAY CHANGES IN CONSCIOUSNESS

Watch children stand on their heads or spin around in order to make themselves dizzy and then ask them why they do it. "So everything looks funny." "It feels weird." "To see things tumble around in my head." Answers such as these support the belief that "human beings are born with a drive to experience modes of awareness other than the normal waking one; from very young ages, children experiment with techniques to change consciousness" (Weil, 1977, p. 37).

As they grow older, some people continue these mind experiments by taking drugs (including alcohol and caffeine) that alter their ordinary awareness. Some people purposely change their consciousness through religious ecstasy, meditation, or hypnosis. We all change our consciousness every time we daydream, have fantasies, or slip from wakefulness into sleep and have night dreams. In this section we will look at everyday changes in consciousness that are unavoidable, occur naturally, and play important functions in our lives.

DAYDREAMING AND FANTASY

Imagine that you have just won millions of dollars in the lottery. What will you do with all your tax-free money? Next, imagine that it's finals time, and, as you begin to take each exam, you see that every question is about something you know really well. You ace exam after exam, ending up with 20 units of straight A's and praise from everyone. While we're playing mind games, imagine that the person you find most desirable in the whole world says, "Yes, of course" to your every request.

Daydreaming is a mild form of consciousness alteration that involves a shift of attention away from the immediate situation or task to thoughts that are elicited in a semiautomatic way, either spontaneously or inten-

From a very young age, children experiment with ways to change consciousness.

tionally. Daydreams include fantasies and thoughts focused on current concerns. Daydreaming occurs when people are alone, relaxed, engaged in a boring or routine task, or just about to fall asleep. People are least likely to daydream just after awakening or when eating (Singer, 1966, 1975).

Do you daydream? You have plenty of company if you do. In one sample of 240 respondents with some college education, ages 18 to 50, 96 percent reported daydreaming daily. Young adults, ages 18 to 29, reported the most daydreaming; there was a significant decline with age (Singer & McCraven, 1961).

Although many people enjoy daydreaming and consider it a normal human function, for many years experts considered it a bad habit—a sign of laziness, infantile wish fulfillment, and mental failure to separate reality from fantasy. As recently as the middle of this century, educational psychologists cautioned that children who were permitted to daydream could develop neuroses and even schizophrenia!

Today, experts believe that daydreaming serves valuable functions and that it is often healthy for children and adults alike (Klinger, 1987). Current research using the experience-sampling method suggests that most daydreams dwell on practical and current concerns,

Daydreaming is common among people of all ages. It provides a means of transcending time and space.

everyday tasks, future goals (trivial or significant), and interpersonal relationships. Daydreaming reminds us to plan for things to come, helps us solve problems, and gives us creative time-outs from routine mental activities.

What triggers daydreams? Usually the trigger is a cue from the environment or our own thoughts in the form of words or pictures. The cue automatically activates a mental association with current concerns. Emotionally tinged cues are the most effective in sparking daydreams. However, we may also deliberately initiate daydreams to relieve the tedium of a boring lecture or job or to prepare ourselves for a particular task. One study revealed that more than 80 percent of lifeguards and truck drivers daydream at times to ease their boredom at work (Klinger, 1987). Sports psychologists often have athletes deliberately daydream as part of visualization training, and soldiers going into battle may prepare themselves by daydreaming the hated enemy (Keen, 1986).

Surprisingly, sexual and violent daydreams account for only a small percentage of all daydreams. The combined results from many studies show that explicitly sexual daydreams average only about 5 percent of the total, while violent fantasies are even less frequent. Even more unexpected is the finding that sexual fantasies are most typical during sexual activity. The most common fantasy is having sex with someone other than the actual partner. Others include having sex in a more romantic setting, having sex with more than one partner, and forcing a partner to have sex or being forced into sex (Pelletier & Herold, 1983). Men tend to have more reality-based sexual daydreams whereas women tend more toward purely imaginative situations. In general, sexually explicit fantasies enhance sexual pleasure.

A daydream questionnaire, the *Imaginal Processes Inventory,* is used to study differences in the kinds of daydreamers. This inventory was developed by **Jerome Singer,** the most influential pioneer in modern daydreaming research, and his colleague, John Antrobus. It reveals that daydreamers differ from one another in three ways. They vary in how many vivid, enjoyable daydreams they have regularly, how many of their daydreams are ridden with guilt or fear, and how easily they are distracted or can maintain their attention (Singer & Antrobus, 1966).

When we *fantasize* about what might be, we are not necessarily escaping from life. Instead, we may be confronting the mysteries of life with wonder and respect and working through actual difficulties. Regardless of how realistic our fantasies may be and how pertinent they may be to our lives, daydreams are rarely as vivid and compelling as night dreams.

To Sleep, Perchance to Dream

Every day of our lives, we ride on a consciousness roller coaster that careens through alert wakefulness to drowsiness, light sleep, deep sleep, dreaming (which sometimes includes nightmares), light sleep again, near awakeness, and, finally, full alertness once more. A third of your life is spent sleeping, when your muscles are in a state of "benign paralysis" and your brain is humming with varied activity. We take this daily dramatic alteration of our consciousness for granted because it generally happens spontaneously.

We slip in and out of different states of consciousness as a natural consequence of light cycles and patterns of wakefulness and sleep. These ordinary fluctuations in consciousness are part of the rhythm of nature, yet they are expressed at the micro level of the activity of single brain cells and neural networks that control sleeping and waking processes.

Circadian Rhythms

All creatures are influenced by nature's rhythms; humans are attuned to a time cycle known as **circadian rhythms,** patterns that repeat approximately every 24 hours. An individual's circadian rhythm corresponds to daily changes in the physiological activities of his or her nervous system. Arousal levels, metabolism, heart rate, body temperature, and hormonal activity ebb and flow according to the ticking of the individual's internal clock. For the most part, these human activities reach their peak during the day—usually during the afternoon—and hit their low point at night while we sleep. However, the clock the body uses to measure time is not the same clock we use to keep our daily appointments. Our appointment clocks run on a 24-hour schedule. The biological clock controlling circadian rhythms operates on a 25-hour cycle. We know this from studies of persons who are forbidden access to timekeeping devices. If you were to seal yourself off from the rest of the world in a darkened room and without a watch, your body would soon come under the control of its own natural circadian rhythm.

Circadian rhythms are very sensitive to environmental change. Anything that throws off our natural biological clocks affects how we feel and act. Think of how you feel the day after an all-night study session. Perhaps the most dramatic example of how changes in daily routine affect circadian rhythms is air travel. When people fly across many time zones, they may experience *jet lag,* a condition whose symptoms include fatigue, irresistible sleepiness, and subsequent unusual sleep-wake schedules. Jet lag occurs because the internal circadian rhythm is out of phase with the normal temporal environment. For example, your body says it's

2:00 A.M. when local time is noon. Jet lag fatigue is a special problem for flight crews and is responsible for pilot errors that cause airplane accidents (Coleman, 1986).

What variables influence jet lag? The direction of travel and the number of time zones passed through are the most important variables. Traveling eastbound creates greater jet lag than does westbound flight since our biological clocks can be extended more readily than shortened as required on eastbound trips (it is easier to stay awake longer than it is to fall asleep sooner). When healthy volunteer subjects were flown back and forth between Europe and the United States, their peak performance on standard tasks was reached within 2 to 4 days after westbound flights but 9 days after eastbound travel!

The Technology of Sleep and Dreams

About a third of our circadian rhythm is devoted to that period of quiescence called sleep. Most of what we know about sleep concerns the electrical activities of the brain. The methodological breakthrough for the study of sleep came in 1937 with the development of a technology that records brain-wave activity of the sleeper in the form of an electroencephalogram (EEG). The EEG provided an objective, ongoing measure of the way brain activity varies when people are awake or asleep. With the EEG, researchers discovered that brain waves change in form at the onset of sleep and show further systematic, predictable changes during the entire sleep period (Loomis et al., 1937).

The next significant discovery in sleep research was that bursts of **rapid eye movement** (REM) occur at periodic intervals during sleep (Aserinsky & Kleitman, 1953). The time when a sleeper is not showing REM is known as **non-REM sleep** (NREM). During a study, sleepers were awakened and asked to describe their mental activity during REM sleep or NREM sleep. The NREM reports were filled with brief descriptions of ordinary daily activities, similar to waking thoughts. But the REM reports were qualitatively different; they were vivid, fanciful, bizarre scenes from incomplete plots—in essence, dreams. Adult subjects in sleep laboratories were found to have four or five distinct dreams every night. So, rapid eye movements (REM) are reliable behavioral signs that a sleeper's mental activity is centered around dreaming. Many investigators were excited by this new objective pathway into a previously hidden side of human activity (Dement & Kleitman, 1957). Since then, researchers in sleep laboratories throughout the world have tried to add to our understanding of this nightly alteration of human consciousness.

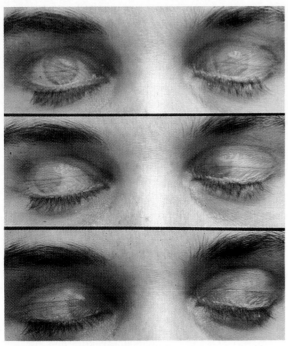

This double exposure photograph shows the rapid eye movements associated with dreaming.

The Sleep Cycle

Imagine that you are preparing to "hit the sack." As you undress, an EEG records that your brain waves are moving along at a rate of about 14 cycles per second (cps). Once you are comfortably in bed, you begin to relax and your brain waves begin to slow down to a rate of about 8 to 12 cps. Soon you are asleep, which will reflect even further changes in the EEG. In fact, over the course of the night, your sleep cycle will cross several stages, each of which shows a distinct EEG pattern. In Stage 1 sleep, the EEG shows brain waves of about 3 to 7 cps. During Stage 2, the EEG is characterized by *sleep spindles,* minute bursts of electrical activity of 12 to 16 cps. In the next two stages (3 and 4) of sleep, you enter into a very deep state of relaxed sleep. Your brain waves slow to about 1 to 2 cps, and your breathing and heart rate decrease. In Stage 5, the electrical activity of your brain increases; your EEG looks very similar to those recorded during stages 1 and 2. It is during this stage that you will experience REM sleep, during which your eyes will move rapidly back and forth and you will begin to dream (see **Figure 4.2**). (Because the EEG pattern during REM sleep resembles that of an awake person, REM sleep was originally termed *paradoxical sleep.*)

Cycling through the first four stages of sleep, which are NREM sleep, requires about 90 minutes. Next, Stage 5 sleep lasts for about 10 minutes. Over the course

of a night's sleep, you pass through this 100-minute cycle four to six times. With each cycle, the amount of time you spend in deep sleep (stages 3 and 4) decreases, and the amount of time you spend in REM sleep increases. During the last cycle, you may spend as much time as an hour in REM sleep.

Humans and most other animals have regular sleep-wake cycles, orderly stages of sleep, and a standard ratio of REM to NREM sleep. The sleep-wake cycle has been found to correspond with activity in specific areas of the brain, such as certain brainstem neurons and cells in the thalamus—the principal gateway to the cerebral cortex (Steriade & McCauley, 1990). Sleep-wake cycles are affected also by the release of chemicals that influence sleeping and waking (Maugh, 1982). For instance, sleep is promoted when large amounts of the hormone melatonin are released from the pineal gland (Binkley, 1979), and serotonin seems to be involved with changes in arousal levels.

If you were to be deprived of REM sleep for a night, you would find that you would have more REM sleep than usual the next night. Perhaps we need to sleep only to get REM sleep rather than simply to rest our weary bodies and minds. A number of interesting, but not yet fully demonstrated, benefits have been attributed to REM sleep. For example, it appears that, during infancy, REM sleep is responsible for establishing the pathways between our nerves and muscles that enable us to move our eyes. REM sleep may also establish functional structures in the brain, such as those involving the learning of motor skills. REM sleep can also play a role in the maintenance of mood and emotion, and it may be required for storing memories and fitting recent experiences into networks of previous beliefs or memories (Cartwright, 1978; Dement, 1976).

Sleep Patterns

For a young adult living on a conventional sleep-wake cycle without sleep complaints, the pattern of sleep follows a standard schedule. Sleep is entered through NREM sleep, REM sleep follows about 80 to 90 minutes later, and the two stages alternate throughout the night in 90-minute cycles. In the first third of the night, slow brain wave sleep predominates; REM sleep predominates in the last third. The percent of time spent at each of the four sleep stages varies according to this pattern: Stage 1—2 to 5 percent; Stage 2—45 to 55 percent; Stage 3—3 to 8 percent; and Stage 4—10 to 15 percent. Thus, NREM sleep accounts for 75 to 80 percent of total sleep time, while REM sleep makes up 20 to 25 percent of sleep time (Carskadon & Dement, 1989).

The length of nocturnal sleep depends on many factors. The two most general factors are a genetic *sleep need* which is programmed into each species and, most importantly for humans, *volitional* determinants. People actively control sleep length in a number of ways, such as by staying up late and using alarm clocks. Sleep duration is also controlled by circadian rhythms; that is, *when* one goes to sleep influences sleep duration because REM sleep increases with length of sleep. REM sleep depends on reaching the peak circadian time.

What accounts for variations in amount of sleep? Individuals who sleep longer than average are found to be more nervous and worrisome, artistic, creative, and nonconforming. Short sleepers tend to be more energetic and extroverted (Hartmann, 1973). Strenuous physical activity during the day increases the amount of time spent in the slow-wave sleep of Stage 4, but it doesn't affect REM time (Horn, 1988). Mental problems seem to have a great effect on extending

REM sleep—severe psychological depression exerts a variety of influences on sleep patterns, according to recent research from the sleep laboratory of **Rosalind Cartwright,** a leader in the field.

> The researcher compared sleep and dream patterns among divorcing people who were depressed over it, with divorcing people who were not depressed and with happily married people. The depressed divorcing subjects showed sleep abnormalities typical for severely depressed people: an initial REM period that is too early (20 to 65 minutes instead of the norm of about 90 minutes after sleep onset); REM that lasts too long (20 to 30 minutes instead of 5 to 10 minutes); and REM periods that vary more in their duration and that contain more than the usual amount of rapid eye movements. The content of their dreams also differed in unhealthy ways from those not so troubled. The dreams of the depressed people studied were "stuck in the past," allowing no working through of problems, new roles, and future possibilities, as occurred in the dreams of the happier people (Cartwright, 1984).

Of further interest is the dramatic change in patterns of sleep that occurs over an individual's lifetime (shown in **Figure 4.3**). We start out in this world sleeping for about 16 hours a day, with nearly half of that time spent in REM sleep. By the time we are old, we sleep very little and spend only about 15 percent of the time in REM sleep. Young adults typically sleep 7 to 8 hours, with about 20 percent REM.

Why Sleep?

Because humans and other mammals exhibit regular sleep-wake cycles, orderly stages of sleep, and a standard ratio of REM to NREM sleep, there would appear to be both an evolutionary basis and a biological need for sleep. Why do we sleep as we do and what functions does sleep serve?

The two most general functions for sleep may be *conservation* and *restoration*. Sleep may have evolved because it enabled animals to *conserve* energy at times when there was no need to forage for food, search for mates, or work (Allison & Cicchetti, 1976; Cartwright, 1982; Webb, 1974). On the other hand, sleep also enables the body to engage in housekeeping functions and to *restore* itself in any of several ways. During sleep, neurotransmitters may be synthesized to compensate for the quantities used in daily activities and postsynaptic receptors may be returned to their optimal level of sensitivity (Stern & Morgane, 1974). A different function is proposed by Francis Crick (Nobel Prize winner for unraveling the structure of DNA) and mathematician

---

FIGURE 4.2   *EEG PATTERNS REFLECTING THE STAGES OF A REGULAR NIGHT'S SLEEP*

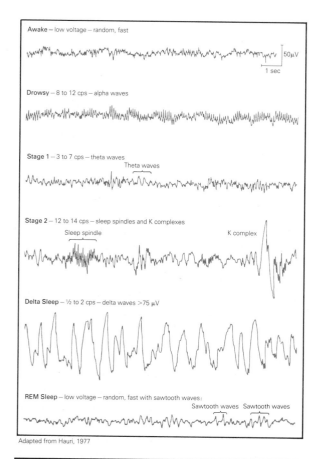

Awake — low voltage — random, fast

50μV
1 sec

Drowsy — 8 to 12 cps — alpha waves

Stage 1 — 3 to 7 cps — theta waves
Theta waves

Stage 2 — 12 to 14 cps — sleep spindles and K complexes
Sleep spindle   K complex

Delta Sleep — ½ to 2 cps — delta waves >75 μV

REM Sleep — low voltage — random, fast with sawtooth waves
Sawtooth waves   Sawtooth waves

Adapted from Hauri, 1977

FIGURE 4.3   PATTERNS OF HUMAN SLEEP OVER A LIFETIME

The graph shows changes with age in total amounts of daily REM and NREM sleep and percentage of REM sleep. Note that the amount of REM sleep decreases considerably over the years, while NREM diminishes less sharply.

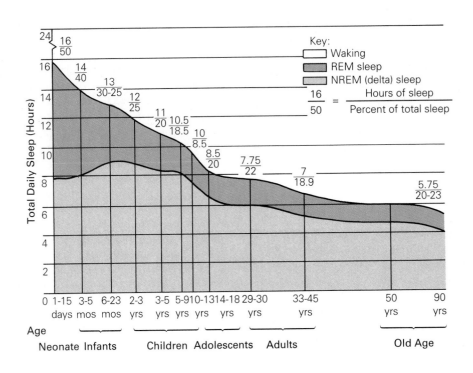

Graeme Mithison who believe that sleep and dreams help the brain to flush out the day's accumulation of unwanted and useless information. Dreams may also serve to reduce fantasy and obsession, thereby minimizing bizarre connections among our many memories (Crick & Mithison, 1983).

William Shakespeare proposed a somewhat more elegantly stated hypothesis: "Sleep knits up the ravelled sleeve of care." During sleep, unravelled material—new information that doesn't fit in properly and loose ends of information—may be integrated or eliminated. According to sleep researcher Ernest Hartmann, "In the morning, sleep has done its thing. If you're in good shape your sleeve has been restored for the next day's wear" (*Discovering Psychology*, 1990, program 13).

Sleep Disorders

For millions of Americans, sleep disorders pose a persistent, serious burden that can disrupt marriages, interfere with careers, and even result in death. This alarming conclusion was recently presented at a hearing of the United States Congress by sleep researcher **William Dement,** Chair of the National Commission on Sleep Disorders Research (A. P., 9/26/90). A colleague added, "Inadequate sleep is a major cause of human error, and at least as important as drugs, alcohol, and equipment failure" in workplace accidents (Dinges, quoted in A. P., 9/26/90, *San Francisco Chronicle,* p. 2). It is estimated that more than 100 million Americans get insufficient sleep. Of those whose work schedules include night shifts, more than half nod off at least once a week on the job. In fact, according to recent studies, some of the world's most serious accidents—Three Mile Island, Chernobyl, Bhopal, and the Exxon Valdez Disaster—have occurred during late evening hours. People have speculated that these accidents occurred because key personnel failed to function optimally as a result of insufficient sleep. What are some types of sleep disorders that can result in tragic outcomes? Some of the disorders are biological, and others are more psychological in origin; we will sample both kinds because of their importance in many students' lives.

Insomnia   When people are dissatisfied with their amount or quality of sleep, they are suffering from **insomnia.** This chronic failure to get adequate sleep is characterized by an inability to fall asleep quickly, frequent arousals during sleep, and/or early morning awakening (Bootzin & Nicasio, 1978). Insomnia is a complex disorder caused by a variety of psychological, environmental, and biological factors (Borkovec, 1982). However, when insomniacs are studied in sleep laboratories, the objective quantity and quality of their actual sleep varies considerably, from disturbed sleep to normal sleep. Research has revealed that many insomniacs who complain of lack of sleep actually show completely normal patterns of sleep—a condition described as *subjective insomnia.* Equally curious is the finding that some people who show detectable sleep disturbances report no complaints of insomnia (Trinder, 1988). The discrepancies may result from differences in the way people recall and interpret a state of light sleep. For example, they may recall light sleep as much more frequent and distressing than it was and have no memory of having slept deeply.

Narcolepsy and Sleep Apnea   Two unusual sleep disorders that can wreak havoc on the lives of those afflicted are narcolepsy and sleep apnea. **Narcolepsy** is a sleep disorder characterized by a periodic compulsion to sleep during the daytime. It is often combined with *cataplexy,* a total loss of muscle control brought on by emotional excitement (such as laughing, anger, fear, surprise, or hunger) that causes the afflicted to fall down suddenly. When they fall asleep, narcoleptics enter REM sleep almost immediately. This rush to REM causes them to experience—and be aware of—vivid hallucinations or images of their dreams that break into daytime consciousness. Recently, it has been discovered that certain species of dogs also suffer from narcolepsy; in addition to the sudden onset of sleep, these dogs experience severe symptoms of sudden muscle paralysis. Because narcolepsy runs in families, scientists assume the disease has a genetic basis. The search is underway for drugs that can control the symptoms of the disorder without undesirable side effects, but none has yet been discovered. In the meantime, narcoleptics can benefit most from recognizing the nature of their disease and belonging to a social support group. In the United States, about 10 of every 10,000 individuals are afflicted with the disease, and many of these people remain undiagnosed long after they first notice its symptoms (Guilleminault et al., 1989; Joyce, 1990).

Sleep apnea is an upper respiratory sleep disorder in which the person stops breathing while asleep. When this happens, the blood's oxygen level drops and emergency hormones are secreted, causing the sleeper to awaken, to begin breathing again, and then to fall back to sleep. While most of us have a few such apnea episodes a night, someone with sleep apnea disorder can have hundreds of such cycles every night. Apnea during sleep is frequent in premature infants who sometimes need physical stimulation to start breathing again. Because of their underdeveloped respiratory system, these infants must remain attached to monitors in intensive care nurseries as long as the problem continues.

Sometimes apnea episodes frighten the sleeper, but often they are so brief that the sleeper fails to attribute accumulating sleepiness to them. (Guilleminault, 1989). Consider the case of one of my colleagues.

> This highly productive, famous researcher, who is usually intense and very dedicated to his work, begin thinking that he was losing interest in psychology because he started dozing during research meetings and lectures. He could not keep his eyes open when reading research reports and, especially, student dissertations. He was suffering from undetected sleep apnea and mistakenly attributed his daytime sleepiness to boredom (while others may have attributed it to laziness or indifference to their work). When his wife made him aware of his nighttime behavior which was disturbing her, he went to a sleep disorder clinic for observation. There he was fitted with a device to give him more oxygen while sleeping and another to adjust his jaw to permit him to breath better during the night. Fortunately, he is now sleeping better, staying awake during my lectures and those of his other colleagues, and keeping his students active doing research and publishing. His case illustrates how a biologically based sleep disorder can begin to have negative psychological and social effects in many areas of life. In other similar cases, people have lost their jobs, friends, and even spouses because their daytime behavior was so disrupted by their nighttime disorder (Zimbardo, personal communication, 1991).

Daytime Sleepiness   Sleepiness is an inevitable consequence of not getting enough nocturnal sleep that is experienced by many people. However, *excessive daytime sleepiness* is a persistent problem that qualifies as a sleep disorder because it is a physiological state not remedied by simply getting more sleep. About 4 to 5 percent of the general population surveyed reports excessive daytime sleepiness, and excessive sleepiness is the major complaint of the majority of patients evaluated at U. S. sleep disorder centers (Roth et al, 1989). This sleepiness causes diminished alertness, delayed reaction times, and impaired performance of motor and cognitive tasks. The consequences can be a loss of psychological and physical well-being, life-threatening accidents, and untold costs in lost productivity and associated medical bills. Nearly half the patients with excessive sleepiness report automobile accidents, more than half have had job accidents, some serious.

In preparing *Sleep Alert,* a documentary film on this sleep deprivation disorder, psychologist **James Maas** reported that "there are some people who are literally walking zombies." He learned of airline pilots who reported falling asleep on the job for short naps only to find the rest of the crew napping when they awoke. Impaired judgment in police officers and medical interns was also shown to be a consequence of excessive sleepiness. High school and college students also typically suffer from excessive sleepiness. They get an average of only six hours of sleep a night when they need about 10 hours to function optimally. Maas reports that as many as 30 percent of high school students fall asleep in class once a week. Can't boring lectures, overheated rooms, heavy meals, or monotonous tasks be the cause of this sleepiness? No, say the experts. These conditions only unmask the presence of physiological sleepiness; they do not cause it (Roth et al., 1989). Although the cause of daytime sleepiness is not simply insufficient sleep—tension, worry, depression, and agitation are often responsible—learning how to get longer, more restful sleep can reduce its undesirable symptoms.

▭▬▭▬▭▬▭▬ Need help with a chronic sleep disorder? The following organizations offer assistance to individuals who suffer from persistent sleep problems:

- American Sleep Disorders Association, 685 2nd Street, SW, Rochester, Minnesota 55902
- Sleep Disorders Center, TD-114, Stanford University School of Medicine, Stanford, California 94305 ▬▭▬▭

Dreams: Theater of the Mind

During every ordinary night of your life, you experience the most bizarre event staged by the human mind—the dream. Vivid, colorful, completely nonsensical hallucinations characterized by complex miniplots that transform time, sequence, and place occupy the theater of your sleep. Dreamers may float or fly or feel as immobile as sacks of potatoes while some kind of danger swiftly approaches. They may talk, hear sounds, and experience sexual excitement, but they can't smell, taste, or feel pain. Overall, dreams are best character-

ized as theater of the absurd—chaotic dramas that appear illogical when analyzed in the rational mindset of our waking hours.

Freud called dreams "transient psychoses" and models of "everynight madness." He also called them "the royal road to understanding the unconscious." In the past few decades, a new path to understanding the interaction of the brain's biology and the mind's psychology has been worn. Once only the province of prophets, psychics and psychoanalysts, dreams have become a vital area of study for scientific researchers. Dream research got its impetus from sleep laboratory findings that correlated rapid eye movements, unique EEG patterns, and the sleeper's report of having dreamed. Since then, researchers have explored and charted many fascinating aspects of this "ordinary" variation in consciousness. They want to know where dreams come from and where they go. Why can't we remember them better? How can we see and hear clearly and move effortlessly in our dreams without any sensory stimulation or motor involvement? Why do we dream in symbols and metaphors? What do dreams tell us about the mind of the dreamer? Let's try to answer some of these questions.

Although dreams are primarily REM phenomena, some dreaming (of a different quality) also takes place during non-REM periods. Dreaming associated with NREM states is less likely to contain dramatic story content. It is full of specific thoughts but has little sensory imagery. Subjects recall a much higher percentage of REM dreams than NREM dreams, as shown in ten different studies that used a variety of definitions of dreaming (Freeman, 1972). NREM dreaming is enhanced in those with sleep disorders and in normal sleepers during the very late morning hours (Kondo et al., 1989). (See **Figure 4.4.**)

Age and Gender Effects We know from recent dream research that dreams are influenced by age and that they bear the clear stamp of gender. There seems to be a developmental timetable for dreaming that follows the same lines and operates at the same rate as the timetable for the development of intelligence. This conclusion emerges from studies where children between the ages of 3 and 9 were awakened from sleep on successive nights and asked what they remembered. The youngest children reported frozen scenes of static, storybooklike images. By the age of 5 or 6, children have dreams that are stories with action and movement. But not until age 7 or 8 do children star in their dreams, and not until age 8 or 9 do they begin dreaming as adults do. Some developmental researchers believe that this sequence in dream development depends on the maturation of the brain. That maturation makes possible the

FIGURE 4.4   SLEEP AND DREAM CYCLES

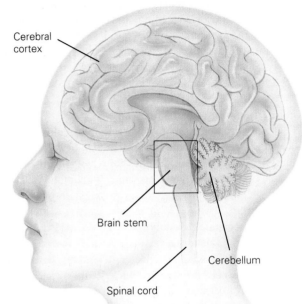

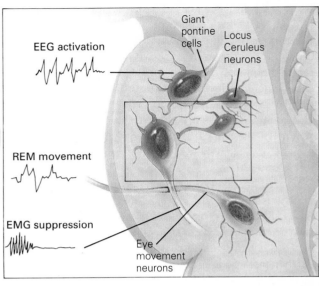

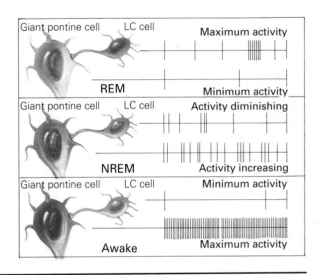

In the brainstem, a group of giant cells called the *pontine reticular formation* is involved in the generation of REM sleep. Just prior to and during REM sleep, the activity of these pontine cells greatly increases and excites eye movement neurons. The activity of another nearby group of cells, locus ceruleus or LC cells, that affects muscle tone via the cerebral cortex diminishes. During NREM sleep and wakefulness, the LC cells inhibit the pontines, suggesting that the two cell groups act reciprocally.

use of symbols and the ability to analyze concepts and weave them into novel patterns.

In keeping with some of the gender-based training of our culture, men and women typically have different dream content. Men's dreams tend to be more active and include more fighting, male antagonists, mechanical images, traveling, and explicit sex. Men dream about being naked in public places and about finding money more often than women do. The dreams of women feature more conversations, emotions, interior

scenes, and plots in which they are pursued or endangered. However, the sexual revolution is showing up in womens' dreams in the form of more outdoor activity and torrid sex (Begley, 1989).

Freudian Dream Analysis   Sigmund Freud made the analysis of dreams the cornerstone of psychoanalysis with his classic book, *The Interpretation of Dreams* (1900). "When the work of interpretation has been completed, we perceive that a dream is the fulfillment of a wish," he wrote. Freud saw dreams as symbolic expressions of powerful, unconscious, repressed wishes. These wishes appear only in disguised form because they harbor forbidden desires, such as sexual yearning for the parent of the opposite sex. The two dynamic forces operating in dreams are, thus, the wish and the *censor,* a defense against the wish. The censor transforms the hidden meaning, or **latent content,** of the dream into **manifest content,** that which appears to the dreamer after a distortion process that Freud referred to as **dream work.** The manifest content is the acceptable version of the story; the latent content represents the socially or personally unacceptable version but also the true, "uncut" one.

In the Freudian perspective, the two main functions of dreams are to guard sleep and to serve as sources of wish fulfillment. They guard sleep by draining off psychic tensions created during the day, and they allow the dreamer to work through unconscious desires. To the therapist who uses dream analysis to understand and treat a patient's problems, dreams reveal the patient's unconscious wishes, the fears attached to those wishes, and the characteristic defenses the patient employs to handle the resulting psychic conflict between the wishes and the fears.

In Freudian dream analysis, the symbols and metaphors that appear are always subject to interpretation within the context of the person's dream. Nevertheless, Freud did propose some universal symbols, many of a sexual nature, that usually have the same meanings from dream to dream. All elongated objects, for example, such as sticks, tree trunks, and umbrellas, represent the male organ.

> Boxes, cases, chests, cupboards and ovens represent the uterus, and also hollow objects, ships, and vessels of all kinds. Rooms in dreams are usually women; if the various ways in and out of them are represented, this interpretation is scarcely open to doubt. . . . A dream of going through a suite of rooms is a brothel or harem dream. . . . It is highly probable that all complicated machinery and apparatus occurring in dreams stand for the genitals (and as a rule male ones). . . (Freud, 1900, pp. 354–356).

Activation-Synthesis Theory of Dreaming The Freudian view is facing its severest challenge from a new biologically based theory that states that all dreams begin with random electrical discharges from deep within the brain. The signals emerge from a primitive part of the brain, the *brain stem,* and then stimulate higher areas of the brain's cortex. These electrical discharges are automatically *activated* about every 90 minutes and stay activated for 30 minutes or so—a time period equivalent to REM sleep periods. They are sent to the forebrain and association areas of the cortex, where they trigger memories and connections with the dreamer's past experiences. There are no logical connections, no intrinsic meaning, and no coherent patterns to these random bursts of electrical signals. However, the brain/mind handles this strange event by doing what it is designed to do best: it tries to make sense of all input it receives, to impose order on chaos, and to *synthesize* separate bursts of electrical stimulation into a coherent story by creating a dream.

The proponents of this controversial theory, **Robert McCarley** and **J. Allen Hobson** (1977), argue that REM sleep furnishes the brain with an internal source of activation, when external stimulation is tuned down, in order to promote the growth and development of the brain. This view does not say the content of dreams is meaningless, only that their source is random stimulation and not unconscious wishes. Hobson (1988) claims that the meaning is added as a kind of brainstorm afterthought. He writes that because the brain is so "inexorably bent upon the quest for meaning," it makes sense out of totally random signals by investing them with meaning. That meaning comes from the dreamer's current needs and concerns, past experiences, and expectations. Notice the connection between this interpretation of dreams and the view of Michael Gazzaniger, presented in the previous chapter, that in split-brain patients the left hemisphere of the brain tries to make sense of the activities controlled by the silent right hemisphere.

The activation-synthesis approach helps explain many of the mysteries of sleep we posed earlier. The "stuff" of dreams may be a brain chemical, *acetylcholine,* which is turned on by one set of neurons in the brain stem during REM. Those neurons are "on" only when the others, which trigger the release of *serotonin* and *norepinephrine,* are "off." Those brain chemicals are necessary to store memories. We forget some 95 percent of our dreams because they are only stored temporarily in our short-term memory. They cannot be "printed" to more permanent memory because serotonin and norepinephrine are shut off during the dream. Our dreams are vivid but devoid of smells and tastes because only visual neurons are stimulated by the electrical discharges during REM. We dream with such rich, vivid images because the brain uses symbols and metaphors to store higher-order knowledge; the dream is simply utilizing this storehouse of material to find some preexisting meaning in the madness of chaotic brain discharges. Our eyes move, but our other muscles do not, during REM sleep because of the action of groups of cells in the brain stem that make up the pontine reticular system (see Figure 4.4).

"The golden arches! The golden arches got me!"

Unique to the dream state then are the dual processes of *distributed activation* across the cortex—which ordinarily executes perceptual, cognitive, and motor responses in the waking state—and *massive inhibition* of sensory and proprioceptive inputs. The results of these processes are thought and dreams without physical action or speech. New views assume that there is a common set of processing modules in the brain that produces both dreaming and waking perceptions (Steriade & McCarley, 1990). By better understanding the mechanisms of dreaming, we can enhance our knowledge of waking aspects of imagery and conscious thought processes (Antrobus, 1991).

Nightmares　When a dream frightens you by making you feel helpless or out of control, you are having a nightmare. Although relatively infrequent (occurring only a few times a year), nightmares can be terrifying, especially for children. Typically, nightmares are triggered by stress, especially fear of harm and being deserted. Being stabbed, shot, hurled off a cliff, or chased by a predator are some of the feared events experienced in nightmares. People who have experienced traumatic events, such as rape or war, may have repetitive night-

mares that force them to relive some aspects of their trauma. Although the distinguishing feature of most nightmares is the dreamer's sense of being endangered, the nightmares of new parents involve their babies.

Some psychologists believe that nightmares resemble ordinary dreams in that they are reflections of the mind's attempt to make connections between various experiences and to solve current problems. Those who suffer from nightmares more frequently (on a weekly basis) are typically sensitive, easily hurt, empathic, artistic, aware of their inner feelings, and more vulnerable to some types of mental illness. These people also have more of a tendency to get so caught up in their daydreams that they aren't sure whether or not they are real.

A fitting conclusion to this section is provided by Hobson's view that "the most important thing is that sleep research reminds us once again that mind and body are one. Even in sleep and dreaming, they cannot be divorced" (quoted in Kiester, 1980, p. 43).

SUMMING UP

In this section, we saw that everyday changes in consciousness include daydreaming, fantasy, sleeping, dreaming, and nightmares. Daydreaming is a common, mild consciousness alteration that works by shifting attention away from a current situation to practical personal concerns or future goals. Fantasies are vivid images of desired, imagined states, such as being rich, successful, sexually attractive, or powerful.

Many changes in consciousness correspond to the body's timetable or circadian rhythm and to physiological activities occurring in the nervous system. Daily stresses, physical exertion, and traveling across time zones are examples of the kinds of activities that can disrupt circadian rhythms. For all of us, sleep represents an important change in consciousness. Sleep is characterized by a reliable series of changes in the brain's electrical activities. These changes can be described in terms of five sleep stages, which we cycle through several times during a night's sleep. Stage 5, REM sleep, is significant because of the corresponding heightened electrical activity that occurs in the brain and because dreams occur primarily in this stage. Sleep researchers believe that sleep may serve several functions: the conservation of energy during times when it is not needed and the restoration of resources used by the nervous system. The standard sleep cycle follows predictable patterns of alternating between REM and NREM sleep throughout the night.

Sleep duration is determined by a genetically based need for sleep as well as by environmental, personality, and learned factors. Sleep disorders, which are surprisingly common and costly to the individual and society, result in complaints of poor quality of sleep or lack of adequate sleep. Among the major types of sleep disorders are insomnia, narcolepsy, sleep apnea, and excessive daytime sleepiness.

Dreams are the most common variations of consciousness. Vivid dreaming occurs during REM sleep, which is brought on by nerve cell signals in the brain stem. Dreams are influenced by age—their content becomes more complex, active, and personalized as an individual's brain matures. Dreams are also influenced by different gender-socialization experiences. In Freudian interpretation, dreams are manifestations of psychologically significant unconscious wishes. The dream censor allows these wishes to manifest themselves in disguised forms only. A competing activation-synthesis theory argues that dreams are biologically based, caused by the random activation of nerve discharges from the brain stem, which the mind then tries to make sense of and synthesize into a coherent story. Nightmares, which center on themes of helplessness and loss of control, occur during times of stress. When they become persistent, they are related to personality factors and traumas.

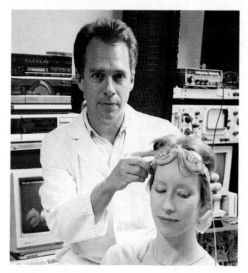

Stephen LaBerge

EXTENDED STATES OF CONSCIOUSNESS

In every society, people have been dissatisfied with purely ordinary transformations of their waking consciousness. They have developed practices that take them beyond familiar forms of consciousness to experiences of extended states of consciousness. Some of these practices are individual, such as taking recreational drugs. Others are shared attempts to transcend the normal boundaries of conscious experience, such as certain religious practices, meditation, and reduced sensory stimulation. Psychological researchers and therapists have also developed procedures for deliberately altering states of consciousness, such as training people to control their dreams or using hypnosis to modify ordinary mental and emotional processes.

LUCID DREAMING

Is it possible to be aware that one is dreaming? Proponents of the theory of **lucid dreaming** argue that being consciously aware that one is dreaming is a learnable

skill (perfected with regular practice) that enables dreamers to control the direction of their dreams (Garfield, 1975; LaBerge, 1985). In laboratory sleep research, dreamers wear specially designed goggles that detect their rapid eye movements when they are having a dream. When the goggles detect REM sleep, they begin to flash a red light in subjects' eyes. The subjects had learned previously that the red light was a cue for becoming consciously aware that they were dreaming. This procedure is being used both in laboratory studies and with volunteers at home. Once aware of dreaming, yet still not awake, sleepers move into a state of lucid dreaming in which they are able to take control of their dreams, directing them according to their personal goals and making their outcomes fit their current needs. The ability to have lucid dreams reportedly increases with one's intention to do so, belief that most people can do so with practice, learning to detect the first signs of a dream, and regular practice of the lucid dream induction techniques (LaBerge & Rheingold, 1990).

The idea of consciously controlling one's dreams is very controversial. Therapists who use dream analysis as part of their understanding of a patient's problems oppose such procedures because they feel that they distort the natural process of dreaming. On the other side, researchers such as **Stephen LaBerge** argue that gaining control over events previously thought to be uncontrollable is healthy because it enhances self-confidence and generates positive experiences for the individual. (If you are interested in learning more about experiencing lucid dreaming, you can contact the Lucidity Institute, Box 2364, Stanford, California 94309.)

HYPNOSIS

Most people find hypnosis fascinating. As portrayed in popular films, the hypnotist need only speak a few words in order to cause major changes in the behavior of the hypnotic subject. We feel uneasy about the perceived power of hypnotists over their subjects; but is this view of hypnotists accurate? What is hypnosis, what are its important features, and what are some of its valid psychological uses?

Hypnosis is a term derived from *Hypnos,* the name of the Greek god of sleep. Sleep plays no part in hypnosis, except in a subject's *appearance* of being in a deeply relaxed, sleeplike state, in some cases. If a subject were in fact asleep, he or she would not respond to hypnosis. There are many different theories about what hypnosis is and how it works. A broad definition of hypnosis is that it is an alternate state of awareness induced by a variety of techniques and characterized by the special ability some people have to respond to suggestion with changes in perception, memory, motivation, and sense of self-control (Orne, 1980). In the hypnotic state, the subject experiences heightened responsiveness to the hypnotist's suggestions. Not only does a hypnotic subject follow suggestions but often feels that his or her behavior is performed without intention or any conscious effort.

Hypnotizability

Most dramatic stage performances of hypnosis give the impression that the power of hypnosis lies with the hypnotist. However, the real star is the person who is hypnotized. The hypnotist is only a coach or experienced travel guide who shows the way. In fact, some individuals can even practice self-hypnosis, or *autohypnosis*.

The single most important factor in hypnosis is a participant's ability or "talent" to become hypnotized. **Hypnotizability** represents the degree to which an individual is responsive to standardized suggestions to experience hypnotic reactions. There are wide *individual differences* in this susceptibility, varying from a complete lack of responsiveness to any suggestion to total responsiveness to virtually every suggestion. A highly hypnotizable person may respond to suggestions to change motor reactions, experience hallucinations, have amnesia for important memories, and become insensitive to powerful pain stimuli.

Figure 4.5 shows the percentage of college-age subjects at various levels of hypnotizability the first time they were given a hypnotic induction test. This objective measure of hypnotizability is the most important single predictor of a person's responsiveness to a variety of hypnotic phenomena. For example, high scorers are more likely than low scorers to experience pain

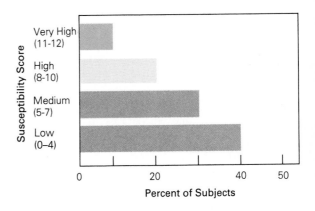

FIGURE 4.5 *LEVEL OF HYPNOSIS AT FIRST INDUCTION*

The graph shows the results for 533 subjects hypnotized for the first time. Hypnotizability was measured on the Stanford Hypnotic Susceptibility Scale which consists of 12 items.

relief as a result of hypnosis *(hypnotic analgesia)* and to respond to hypnotic suggestions to have perceptual distortions of various kinds.

Hypnotizability is a relatively stable attribute. An adult's scores remain about the same when measured various times over a 10-year period (Morgan et al., 1974). In fact, when 50 men and women were retested 25 years after their first hypnotizability assessment (as college students), the results indicated a remarkably high correlation coefficient of .71 (Piccione et al., 1989). Children tend to be more suggestible than adults; hypnotic responsiveness peaks just before adolescence and declines thereafter. There is some evidence for genetic determinants of hypnotizability because the scores of identical twins are more similar than are those of fraternal twins (Morgan et al., 1970).

Although hypnotizability is relatively stable, it is surprisingly not correlated with any personality trait. It is not the result of gullibility or conformity, and it is not an attempt at role playing or a reaction to the social demands of the situation (Fromm & Shor, 1979). Hypnotizability is a unique cognitive ability—a special aspect of the human imagination. It develops early in life along with the sense of being able to become completely absorbed in an experience. A hypnotizable person is one who is capable of deep involvement in the imaginative-feeling areas of experience, such as in reading novels or listening to music. Hypnotizability may also involve a willingness to suspend ordinary reality. Under hypnosis, highly hypnotizable subjects can so vividly imagine a scene suggested to them that it seems as if it were actually happening at that moment (J. R. Hilgard, 1970, 1979). A hypnotizable person can be hypnotized by anyone he or she is willing to respond to, while someone unhypnotizable will *not* respond to the tactics of the most skilled hypnotist.

Induction of Hypnosis

Hypnosis begins with *hypnotic induction,* a preliminary set of activities that prepare a participant for the alternate state of awareness that accompanies hypnosis. Induction activities involve suggestions to imagine certain experiences or to visualize events and reactions. When practiced repeatedly, the hypnotic induction procedure functions as a learned signal. Induction minimizes distractions and encourages the subject to concentrate only on suggested stimuli and believe that he or she is about to enter a special state of consciousness.

The typical induction procedure uses suggestions for deep relaxation, but some people can become hypnotized with an active, alert induction—even suggesting that the subject imagine jogging or riding a bicycle. A child in the dentist's chair can be hypnotized while his or her attention is directed to vivid stories or to imagining the exciting adventures of a favorite TV character. Meanwhile, the dentist drills and fills cavities, using no anesthesia, but the child feels no pain (Banyai & E. Hilgard, 1976). Responsiveness to hypnotic suggestion can be slightly enhanced with intensive practice as well as with sensory deprivation or drugs, such as LSD or mescaline (Diamond, 1974; Sanders & Reyhen, 1969; Sjoberg & Hollister, 1965). These procedures do

not transform unsusceptible subjects into highly responsive ones, however.

Altered Personal Reality Under Hypnosis

It is necessary to maintain a scientific skepticism about the claims made about hypnosis, especially when they are based on individual case reports or research lacking proper control conditions (Barber, 1969). Researchers disagree about the psychological mechanisms involved in hypnosis (Fromm & Shor, 1979). Some argue that hypnosis is nothing more than heightened motivation (Barber, 1976), and others believe it is only social role playing, a kind of *placebo response* of trying to please the hypnotist (Sarbin & Coe, 1972). However, research has shown that the specific effects hypnosis produces in deeply hypnotized subjects is distinguishable from both the expectancy effects of placebo responding and general suggestibility effects (Evans, 1989).

A reliable body of empirical evidence bolstered by expert opinion strongly suggests that hypnosis can exert a powerful influence on many psychological and bodily functions (Bowers, 1976; Burrows & Dennerstein, 1980; E. Hilgard, 1968, 1973). One of the most valuable uses of hypnosis has been in therapy with patients who develop multiple personalities. (This use is discussed in Chapter 18.) Let's briefly review several interesting aspects of hypnosis: pain control and dissociation.

Pain Control

One of the most common and undisputed values of hypnosis is its effect on pain. Our minds can amplify pain stimuli through anticipation and fear; we can also diminish the psychological component of pain with hypnosis. Pain control is accomplished through a variety of hypnotic suggestions: distraction from the pain stimulus, imagining the part of the body in pain as nonorganic (made of wood or plastic) or as separate from the rest of the body, taking one's mind on a vacation from the body, and distorting time in various ways. Hypnosis has proven especially valuable to surgery patients who cannot tolerate anesthesia, to extreme burn patients, to mothers in natural childbirth, and to cancer patients learning to endure the pain associated with the disease and its treatment. Self-hypnosis is the best approach to controlling pain because patients can then exert control over their pain whenever it arises. In a recent study of 86 women with metastatic cancer, those using self-hypnosis for pain control reported having only half the pain as others (Spiegel, 1989).

To demonstrate that hypnotic pain control is more than a placebo expectancy effect or a heightened moti-

In this demonstration of hypnotic pain control, the self-hypnotized female student reports feeling no pain from the ice water. The male student's pain escalates rapidly until he cannot tolerate it and pulls his arm away (*Discovering Psychology,* 1990, Program 4).

vation, researchers conducted this well-controlled experiment:

> Excruciating muscle pain was delivered to volunteer subjects during three experimental sessions: (a) with highly motivating instructions; (b) following the induction of hypnotic analgesia; and (c) after ingesting a placebo capsule described as painkilling medication. Half of the 24 subjects were highly hypnotizable and the rest scored low on the hypnotizable scale. The placebo was administered in double-blind fashion. Experimenter expectancy was also manipulated by deceiving the experimenter into believing that hypnotic analgesia worked for all subjects. This was done by using a pretest trial in which the pain-stimulus intensity level was secretly turned down for the low hypnotizable subjects. The placebo pill significantly reduced pain in all subjects, beyond the level of the motivating instructions. In addition, *expecting* hypnosis to reduce pain also had a significant effect on all subjects—the placebo expectancy effect of hypnosis.

> However, pain tolerance for the highly hypnotizable subjects during the hypnotic analgesia induction period was significantly greater than for the low hypnotizables and for any of the other conditions. The authors attribute this added effect of hypnotic pain control to the ability of highly hypnotizable subjects to experience *dissociation* (McGlashan, et al., 1969).

Dissociation

Psychologists use the term **dissociation** for the functioning of consciousness at *different levels,* either without awareness or without a complete transfer of information from one level of the mind to another. Some highly suggestible individuals are especially responsive to stored information that is not directly accessible during their conscious awareness. While they are in the hypnotic trance state, they function at two levels of consciousness: (a) a full, but hypnotic, consciousness of the suggested experience and (b) a concealed, nonconscious awareness. Such highly hypnotizable subjects can sometimes reveal this hidden level of their consciousness if they are instructed to engage in *automatic writing,* a process in which a person writes meaningful words without a conscious awareness of what he or she is writing. *Automatic talking* occurs when a person's cognitive system reports on itself without a conscious awareness of what is occurring.

A pioneering researcher in hypnosis, **Ernest Hilgard** (1977), has coined the term *hidden observer* to refer to the unconscious awareness of personal knowl-

edge. This phenomenon was first observed in hypnotic subjects who reported feeling no pain when subjected to a painful stimulus and told they would feel nothing. They were then told that a hidden part of them knew what was going on in their bodies and could report it accurately. Then some of these subjects processed the pain experience and reported pain intensity levels closer to those of individuals not hypnotized (see Kihlstrom, 1985).

We can appreciate from these statements by a college student subject in hidden observer research how consciousness can travel on parallel tracks:

> The hidden observer and the hypnotized part are both all of me, but the hidden observer is more aware and reported honestly what was there. The hypnotized part of me just wasn't aware of the pain. In hypnosis I kept my mind and body separate, and my mind was wandering to other places—I was not aware of the pain in my arm. When the hidden observer was called up, the hypnotized part had to step back for a minute and let the hidden part tell the truth (Knox et al., 1974, p. 845, 846).

This dual consciousness revealed by the hidden observer phenomenon should remind you of the split-brain research, where the left brain reports on the activities of the silent right brain. Dissociation can occur also in individuals experiencing religious ecstasy, taking psychedelic drugs, and suffering from certain forms of mental illness. The most remarkable illustrations of dissociation at work are in cases of multiple personality disorders. These dissociation phenomena reveal the complex capabilities of the human mind, which can function simultaneously at conscious and nonconscious levels.

MEDITATION

Many religions and traditional psychologies of the East work to direct consciousness away from immediate worldly concerns, external stimulation, and action. They seek to achieve an inner focus on the mental and spiritual self. **Meditation** is a form of consciousness change designed to enhance self-knowledge and well-being by reducing self-awareness. During meditation, a person focuses on and regulates breathing, assumes certain bodily positions (yogic positions), minimizes external stimulation, and either generates specific mental images or frees the mind of all thought.

One consequence of meditation is mental and bodily *relaxation.* Meditation reduces anxiety, especially in those who function in stress-filled environments (Benson, 1975; Shapiro, 1985). However, meditative practices can function as more than valuable time-outs from tension. When practiced regularly, some forms of meditation serve the functions of *heightening* consciousness, achieving *enlightenment* by enabling the individual to see familiar things in new ways, and freeing perception and thought from the restrictions of automatic, well-learned patterns. When practiced regularly, meditation is said to lead to *mindful awareness* in one's daily life. Mindfulness of the routine activity of breathing especially creates a sense of peace. One of the foremost Buddhist teachers of meditation, Nhat Hanh (1991), recommends awareness of breathing and simple appreciation of our surroundings and minute daily acts as a path to psychological equilibrium.

Meditative practices were given a boost in western countries when the Beatles followed a guru to India and proclaimed the virtues of meditation. Although many music fans rushed to follow in the footsteps of the Fab Four, the practice of using meditation to achieve peace of mind, a sense of connectedness with the world, and spiritual awakening requires neither group participation nor a group leader. Any individual who is sufficiently motivated to try modifying the standard operating procedures of his or her consciousness can effectively practice meditation. There is some controversy over the measurable effects of meditation. Advocates claim wide-ranging positive influences while opponents report no reliable experimental evidence that regular meditation leads to a heightened state of consciousness (Holmes, 1984).

HALLUCINATIONS

Under unusual circumstances, a distortion in consciousness occurs during which the individual sees or hears things that are not really present. **Hallucinations** are vivid perceptions that occur in the absence of objective stimulation; they are a mental construction of an individual's altered reality. They differ from *illusions,* which are perceptual distortions of real stimuli and are experienced by most people.

Hallucinations can occur during high fever, epilepsy, and migraine headaches. They also occur in cases of severe mental disorders when patients respond to private mental events as if they were external sensory stimuli. Hallucinations have been associated with heightened arousal states and religious ecstasies as well. In fact, in some cultures and circumstances, hallucinations are interpreted as mystical insights that confer special status on the visionary. So, in different settings, the same vivid perception of direct contact with spiritual forces may be deprecated as a sign of mental illness or respected as a sign of special gifts.

Evaluation of such mental states often depends as much on the judgment of observers as on the content of the perceptual experience itself.

Hallucinations may be induced by psychoactive drugs, such as LSD and peyote, as well as by withdrawal from alcohol in severe cases of alcoholism (these hallucinations are known as *delirium tremens,* "the DTs"). For the most part, however, chemically induced hallucinations are not regarded as "true" hallucinations because they are direct effects of the drug on the brain rather than part of a new view of reality that a person is creating.

Some psychologists wonder why we do not hallucinate all the time. They believe that the ability to hallucinate is always present in each of us but normally inhibited by interaction with sensory input, by our constant reality checks, and by feedback from the environment. When sensory input and feedback are lacking and there is no way to test our ideas against outer reality, hallucinations are more likely. They are also fostered by heightened arousal, states of intense need, or the inability to suppress threatening thoughts.

Many instances of altered states of consciousness are reported following overstimulating experiences, such as mob riots, religious revival meetings, prolonged dancing (such as that done by the religious sect of whirling Dervishes), extreme fright or panic, trance states, and moments of extreme emotion.

Because the complex functioning of the brain requires some constant level of external stimulation, when it is lacking the brain manufactures its own. Some subjects, when kept in a special environment that minimizes all sensory stimulation, show a tendency to hallucinate. *Sensory isolation* "destructures the environment" and may force subjects to try to restore meaning and stable orientation to a situation. Hallucinations may be a way of reconstructing a reality in accordance with one's personality, past experiences, and the demands of the present experimental setting (Zubeck et al., 1961; Suedfeld, 1980).

RELIGIOUS ECSTASY

Meditation, prayer, fasting, and spiritual communication all contribute to having a *religious experience*. For William James, the religious experience constituted a unique psychological experience (James, 1917). He believed that religious experience is characterized by a sense of oneness and relatedness of events, of realness and vividness of experiences, and an inability to communicate in ordinary language the nature of the whole experience. For many people, religious experiences are clearly not part of their ordinary consciousness, especially when they are intense.

There are few religious experiences more intense than those of the Holy Ghost People of Appalachia. Their beliefs and practices create a unique form of consciousness that enables them to do some remarkable things. At church services they handle deadly poisonous snakes, drink strychnine poison, handle fire, and speak in imaginary languages. To prepare for these experiences, they listen to long sermons and participate in loud, insistent singing and wild spinning and dancing:

> The enthusiasm may verge on violence . . . Members wail and shake and lapse into the unintelligible, ecstatic "new tongues" of glossolalia [artificial speech with no linguistic content]. Each member has his or her own style of speaking. . . . The ecstasy spreads like contagion. . . . Their hands are definitely cold, even after handling fire. This would correspond with research in trance states involved in other religious cultures. It would also account for the vagueness of memory, almost sensory amnesia, that researchers have reported in serpent handlers as well as fire handlers (Watterlond, 1983, pp. 53, 56).

Psychological research on serpent-handling religious group members has found them to be generally well-adjusted people who receive powerful social and psychological support from being part of their religious group. Participating in the "signs of the spirits" gives them a "personal reward equalled in no other aspect of their lives" (Watterlond, 1983).

MIND-ALTERING DRUGS

Since ancient times, people have taken drugs that altered their perception of reality. There is archaeological evidence for the uninterrupted use of sophora seed (mescal bean) for over 10,000 years in the southwestern United States and Mexico, from the ninth millennium BC to the nineteenth century AD. Ancient Americans smoked sophora to bring about ecstatic hallucinatory visions. Sophora was later replaced by the more benign peyote cactus, which is still used in the sacred rituals of many Native American tribes.

Today, drugs are associated less with sacred communal rituals than with recreational pleasure. Individuals throughout the world take various drugs to relax, cope with stress, avoid facing the unpleasantness of current realities, feel comfortable in social situations, or experience an alternate state of consciousness. Using drugs to alter consciousness was popularized by the publication of *The Doors of Perception* by Aldous Huxley (1954). Huxley took mescaline as an experiment on his own consciousness. He wanted to test the validity of poet William Blake's assertion in *The Marriage of Heaven and Hell* (1793): "If the doors of perception were cleansed every thing would appear to man as it is, infinite. For man has closed himself up, till he sees all thro' narrow chinks of his concern."

A few decades after Huxley's book appeared, nearly 55 percent of American high-school seniors (in annual surveys of over 16,000 students) reported using one or more illegal drugs in their senior year. Although this figure has declined steadily since 1982 (to about 38

Rayford Dunn was bitten on his hand by a cottonmouth moments after this picture was taken in Kingston, Georgia. Not only did he go out to eat afterward, he returned to church the next day and handled a rattler and a water moccasin without getting bitten. However, some believers have died from poisonous snake bites.

percent in 1987), the number of adolescents addicted to drugs has reached epidemic proportions (Johnston et al., 1989). It is interesting to note that males are more likely to use drugs and to know more users than females (Brunswick, 1980).

Recreational drug use has become a serious social problem. With addiction to illegal drugs come crime and crime-related problems that plague all levels of society. A Gallup poll of U. S. adults in April 1990 found that drugs and drug abuse were considered by far "the most important problem facing the country today."

Dependence and Addiction

Psychoactive drugs are chemicals that affect mental processes and behavior by temporarily changing conscious awareness. Once in the brain, they may attach themselves to synaptic receptors, blocking or stimulating certain reactions. By doing so, they profoundly alter the brain's communication system, affecting perception, memory, mood, and behavior. However, continued use of a given drug lessens its effect on the nervous system. A reduced effectiveness with repeated use is called **tolerance.** As tolerance develops, greater dosages are required to achieve the same effect. Hand-in-hand with tolerance is **physiological dependence,** a process in which the body becomes adjusted to and dependent on the substance, in part because neurotransmitters are depleted by the frequent presence of the drug. The tragic outcome of tolerance and dependence is **addiction.** A person who is addicted requires the drug in his or her body and suffers painful **withdrawal symptoms** (shakes, sweats, nausea, and, in the case of alcohol withdrawal, even death) if the drug is not present.

When an individual finds the use of a drug so desirable or pleasurable that a *craving* develops, with or without addiction, it is known as **psychological dependence.** Psychological dependence can occur with any drug—including caffeine and nicotine. We noted in Chapter 3 that a new term, neuroadaptation, is being used for both kinds of dependence—physiological and psychological—because it is often difficult to separate their interrelated effects. The result of drug dependence is that a person's life-style comes to revolve around drug use so wholly that his or her capacity to function is limited or impaired. In addition, the expense involved in maintaining a drug habit of daily—and increasing—amounts often drives an addict to robbery, assault, prostitution, or drug peddling. One of the gravest dangers currently facing addicts is the threat of getting AIDS through sharing hypodermic needles—intravenous drug users can unknowingly inject themselves with drops of bodily fluid from others who have this deadly immune deficiency disease.

Teenagers who use drugs to relieve emotional distress and to cope with daily stressors suffer long-term negative consequences.

An eight-year study of teenage drug use starting in 1976, with 1634 junior high school students from Los Angeles, collected complete annual data on 739 subjects. While fewer than 10 percent of those studied were regular or chronic drug users, fewer than 10 percent reported not using any drugs. The results can be grouped into four major findings:
- Daily drug use had a negative impact on personal and social adjustment, disrupting relationships, reducing educational potential, increasing nonviolent crime, and encouraging disorganized thinking.
- Hard drugs, such as stimulants and narcotics, increased suicidal and self-destructive thoughts while reducing social support, thereby promoting loneliness.
- Drug effects varied with type of drug and mixed use of drugs, so that cocaine increased confrontations and weakened close relationships, but the combination of hard drugs and cigarettes was most damaging to psychological and physical health.
- Surprisingly, teenagers who used alcohol moderately and no other drugs "showed increased social integration and increased self-esteem." These students may have been better adjusted to begin with than their peers (Newcomb & Bentler, 1988).

Varieties of Psychoactive Drugs

A summary of common psychoactive drugs is listed in **Table 4.1.** We noted in the previous chapter how drugs have differing effects on the central nervous system, stimulating, depressing, or altering neurotransmission. Here we will summarize some of the major psychological experiences created by these drugs and the conditions under which they are taken.

The most dramatic changes in consciousness are produced by drugs known as *hallucinogens,* or *psychedelics;* these drugs alter both perceptions of the external environment and inner awareness. As the name implies, these drugs often create hallucinations and a loss of the boundary between self and all that is nonself. Hallucinogenic drugs, such as LSD, act in the brain at specific receptor sites for the chemical neurotransmitter serotonin (Jacobs, 1987). The four most commonly known hallucinogens are *mescaline* (from cactus plants), *psilocybin* (from a mushroom), and *LSD and PCP,* which are synthesized in chemical laboratories. Of these,

TABLE 4.1 PSYCHOACTIVE DRUGS: USES, DURATION, AND DEPENDENCIES

	Medical Uses	Duration of Effect (hours)	Dependence Psychological	Dependence Physiological
Opiates (Narcotics)				
Morphine	Painkiller, cough suppressant	3–6	High	High
Heroin	Under investigation	3–6	High	High
Codeine	Painkiller, cough suppressant	3–6	Moderate	Moderate
Hallucinogens				
LSD	None	8–12	None	Unknown
PCP (Phencyclidine)	Veterinary anesthetic	Varies	Unknown	High
Mescaline (Peyote)	None	8–12	None	Unknown
Psilocybin	None	4–6	Unknown	Unknown
Cannabis (Marijuana)	Nausea associated with chemotherapy	2–4	Unknown	Moderate
Depressants				
Barbiturates (e.g., Seconal)	Sedative, sleeping pill, anesthetic, anticonvulsant	1–16	Moderate–High	Moderate–High
Benzodiazepines (e.g., Valium)	Antianxiety, sedative, sleeping pill, anticonvulsant	4–8	Low–Moderate	Low–Moderate
Alcohol	Antiseptic	1–5	Moderate	Moderate
Stimulants				
Amphetamines	Hyperkinesis, narcolepsy, weight control	2 to 4	High	High
Cocaine	Local anesthetic	1 to 2	High	High
Nicotine	Nicotine gum for cessation of smoking habit	Varies	Low–High	Low–High
Caffeine	Weight control, stimulant in acute respiratory failure, analgesic	4 to 6	Unknown	Unknown

young people are most likely to abuse PCP, or *angel dust*. PCP produces a strange dissociative reaction in which the user becomes insensitive to pain, becomes confused, and feels apart from his or her surroundings.

Cannabis is a plant with psychoactive effects. Its active ingredient is *THC,* found in both *hashish* (the solidified resin of the plant) and *marijuana* (the dried leaves and flowers of the plant). The experience derived from inhaling THC depends on its dose—small doses create mild, pleasurable highs, and high doses result in long hallucinogenic reactions. The positive reports from regular users include changes at a sensory and perceptual level—notably, euphoria, well-being, distortions of space and time, and, occasionally, out-of-body experiences. However, depending on the social context and other factors, the effects may be negative—fear, anxiety, and confusion. Because motor coordination is impaired with marijuana use, those who work or drive under its influence suffer more industrial and auto ac-

cidents (Jones & Lovinger, 1985). Cannabinoids, the active chemicals in marijuana, work by binding to specific receptors in the brain that are designed to be activated only by that drug. Researchers have found that these cannabinoid receptors are particularly common in the hippocampus, the brain region involved in memory. Recently, a gene has been isolated and cloned that gives rise to the receptor molecules that cannabinoids bind to in the brain. This discovery should stimulate new research on cannabis, known as the "assassin of youth."

Opiates, such as *heroin,* suppress physical sensation and response to stimulation. The initial effect of an intravenous injection of heroin is a rush of pleasure— feelings of euphoria supplant all worries and awareness of bodily needs. There are no resulting major changes in consciousness, but serious addiction is likely once a person begins to inject heroin.

The *depressants* include *barbiturates*—most notably *alcohol.* These drugs tend to depress (slow down) the mental and physical activity of the body by inhibiting or decreasing the transmission of nerve impulses in the central nervous system. High dosages of barbiturates induce sleep but reduce the time spent in REM sleep. After the withdrawal of barbiturates which were given over prolonged periods, extended REM periods are punctuated by frightening nightmares. Overdoses of barbiturates lead to loss of all sensations and coma. More deaths are caused by overdoses of barbiturates, taken either accidentally or with suicidal intent, than any other poison (Kolb, 1973). One of the most subtly addictive depressants is *valium,* which is prescribed as a tranquilizer to reduce temporary anxiety. Valium often becomes a permanent habit that is very difficult to kick.

Alcohol was apparently one of the first psychoactive substances used extensively by our ancestors. Under its influence, some people become silly, boisterous, friendly, and talkative; others become abusive and violent; still others become quietly depressed. At small dosages, alcohol can induce relaxation and slightly improve an adult's speed of reaction. However, the body can break down alcohol at the rate of only approximately one ounce per hour, and greater amounts consumed in a short time period overtax the central nervous system. Driving fatalities and accidents occur six times more often to individuals with 0.10 percent alcohol in their bloodstream than to those with half that amount. Another way alcohol intoxication contributes to accidents is by dilating the pupils, thereby causing night vision problems that drunk drivers are not aware of having. When the level of alcohol in the blood reaches 0.15 percent, there are gross negative effects on thinking, memory, and judgment along with emotional instability and motor incoordination.

In our culture, we spend millions of dollars annually on advertisements glorifying the social and personal benefits of drinking beer and whiskey. Throughout the United States, drinking is a vital part of a young adult's social life. It is no wonder that we have a problem with excess consumption of alcohol. Alcohol-related automobile accidents are the leading cause of death among people between the ages of 15 and 25. When the amount and frequency of drinking alcohol interferes with job performance, impairs social and family relationships, and creates serious health problems, the diagnosis of *alcoholism* is appropriate. Physical dependence, tolerance, and addiction all develop with prolonged heavy drinking. For some individuals, the problem of alcoholism is associated with an inability to abstain from drinking. For others, alcoholism manifests itself as an inability to stop drinking once the person takes a few drinks (Cloninger, 1987).

Stimulants, such as *amphetamines* and *cocaine,* have three major effects that users seek. These are increased self-confidence, greater energy and hyperalertness, and mood alterations that approach euphoria. Heavy users experience frightening hallucinations and develop beliefs that others are out to harm them. These beliefs are known as *paranoid delusions.* A special danger with cocaine use is the contrast between euphoric highs and very depressive lows. This leads users to uncontrollably increase the frequency of drug use and the dosage. One survey of 1212 cocaine users who went to the hospital for a variety of reasons found that about 20 percent had severe seizures and impaired psychological functioning (Petit, 1987).

A new, particularly destructive street drug is *crack,* a highly purified form of cocaine. It produces a swift high that wears off quickly. Because it is sold in small, cheap quantities that are readily available to the young and the poor, crack is destroying social communities. Despite the well-publicized deaths of prominent ath-

In our drug-using culture, the line between use and abuse is easy to cross for many who become addicted.

letes from crack overdoses, there is little evidence that its use is declining at this time.

Two stimulants that we rarely think of as psychoactive drugs are *caffeine* and *nicotine*. As you may know from experience, within 10 minutes, two cups of strong coffee or tea administer enough caffeine to have a profound effect on heart, blood, and circulatory functions. They can also disturb your sleep.

Certain Native American shamans used high concentrations of nicotine to attain mystical states or trances. Unlike some modern users, however, the shamans believed that nicotine was addictive, and they carefully chose when to be under its influence. Is nicotine really addictive? Definitely. Like all addictive drugs, nicotine mimics natural chemicals released by the brain. These chemicals stimulate receptors that make us feel good whenever we have done something right—a phenomenon that aids our survival. Unfortunately, nicotine teases those same brain receptors into responding as if it were good for us to be smoking. By short-circuiting our brains, nicotine shortens our lives as well. The total negative impact of nicotine on health is greater than that of all other psychoactive drugs combined, including heroin, cocaine, and alcohol. The U. S. Public Health Service attributes 350,000 deaths annually to cigarettes. While smoking is the leading cause of preventable sickness and death, it is both legal and actively promoted—$2.7 billion are spent annually on its advertising and promotion. Although antismoking campaigns have been somewhat effective in reducing the overall level of smoking in the United States, some 54 million Americans are still smoking. Of the million people who start smoking each year, the majority of them are under 14, female, and members of a racial minority (Goodkind, 1989).

POSTSCRIPT: WHY CONSCIOUSNESS?

It is reasonable to reflect briefly on the ordinary, fundamental nature as well as the extraordinary capacities of human consciousness. Why do we have a conscious mind, and why do we sometimes try to alter it?

The evolution of the human brain permitted survival of those of our forebears who could cope with a hostile environment, even when their sensory and physical abilities were not adequate. They compensated for their relative lack of highly specialized sense receptors, strength, speed, protective coloration, or safe habitat by developing a unique set of mental skills. Humans became capable of *symbolic representation* of the outer world and of their own actions—enabling them to remember, plan, predict, and anticipate (Craik, 1943). Instead of merely reacting to stimuli in the physical present or to biological needs, *Homo sapiens'* complex brain was able to model its world; to imagine how present realities could be transformed into alternative scenarios.

This symbolic representation was a tremendous new survival tool. The capacity to deal with objective reality in the here-and-now was expanded by the capacity to bring back lessons from the past (memory) and to imagine future options (foresight). A brain that can deal with both objective and subjective realities needs a mechanism to keep track of the focus of attention. It must know whether the source of the stimulation being processed consists of external objects and events or internal thoughts and concepts. That part of the brain is the *conscious mind*.

The prominence of *Homo sapiens* among all other creatures may be attributed to the development of a human intelligence and consciousness that was forged in the crucible of competition with the most hostile force in its evolutionary environment—*other humans*. The origin of the human mind may have evolved as a consequence of the extreme *sociability* of our ancestors, perhaps originally as a group defense against predators and to create more efficient exploitation of resources. However, close group living then created new demands for cooperative as well as competitive abilities with other humans. Natural selection favored those who could think, plan, and imagine alternative realities that could promote both bonding with kin and victory over adversaries. Those who developed language and tools won the grand prize of survival of the fittest mind—and, fortunately, passed it on to us (Lewin, 1987).

If the *mind* is the sum of the integrative mental activities to which brain processes give rise, then *consciousness* is the mind's *active construction of incoming information into a coherent, stable, organized pattern of symbols*. This construction makes sense of a confusing world, imposes order on chaos, and finds meaning even in nonsensical events (Johnson-Laird, 1983).

So why did we ever become dissatisfied with our everyday working minds and seek to alter our consciousness? Ordinarily, our primary focus is on meeting the immediate demands of tasks and situations facing us. This focus forces our attention to serve as an ever-shifting searchlight illuminating relevant dimensions of our current experience. However, we are aware of these reality-based constraints on our consciousness. We realize they limit the range and depth of our experience and do not allow us to fulfill our vast intellectual potential. Perhaps, at times, we all long to reach beyond the confines of ordinary reality (Targ & Harary, 1984). The human need to expand consciousness is the mental equivalent of learning to walk erect when it is easier to crawl and of seeking the uncertainty of freedom instead of settling for the security of the status quo. Extending our consciousness broadens the universal experience of what it means to be a thoughtful human being.

Brain, Mind, and Soul

A continuing debate in psychology and philosophy has centered on the relationship between mind and body, or between the physical brain and the ephemeral mind. Dualism considers them separate; monism postulates they are one. The emergent-interaction approach offers a reconciliation of the two postures by proposing that brain activities give rise to mental states that are emergent properties of the brain's hierarchical organization, that brain and mind interact, and that the mind can exert causal influences over the brain in controlling behavior. Different cultures have various beliefs about what the mind is.

The Nature of Consciousness

Consciousness is an awareness of the mind's functioning and its contents. Consciousness aids our survival and enables us to construct both personal and culturally shared realities. Three levels of consciousness are (1) a basic awareness of the world, (2) a reflection on what we are aware of, and (3) self-awareness. The structure of consciousness involves nonconscious processes, preconscious memories, subconscious awareness, the unconscious, and conscious awareness. Many different research techniques are employed to study different aspects of consciousness. These include think-aloud protocols, experience sampling, and dichotic listening tasks.

Everyday Changes in Consciousness

Ordinary alterations of consciousness include daydreaming, fantasy, sleep, and dreams. Daydreaming is a common experience when attention is shifted from the immediate situation to other thoughts that are elicited semiautomatically. Both genetic and volitional factors determine the length of sleep for humans. Sleep patterns change with age. Babies sleep about 16 hours each day, with nearly half of that time in REM sleep. By old age, sleep may last fewer than 6 hours, only 15 percent of which is REM. REM sleep is signalled by rapid eye movements and accompanied by vivid dreaming. About one-fourth of sleep is REM, coming in 4 or 5 separate dream episodes. Sleep disorders are more common than usually recognized, especially among overactive people. Insomnia, narcolepsy, and sleep apnea can be modified with medical and psychological therapy.

Freud proposed that the content of dream is unconscious material stimulated by the day's events. The activation-synthesis dream theory challenges Freud's psychodynamic approach with a purely biological explanation.

Extended States of Consciousness

Lucid dreaming is an awareness that one is dreaming in an attempt to control the dream.

Hypnosis is an alternate state of consciousness characterized by the ability of hypnotizable people to respond to suggestions from the hypnotizer with changes in perception, motivation, memory, and self-control. Pain control is one of the major benefits of hypnosis. Meditation changes conscious functioning by ritual practices that focus attention away from external concerns to inner experience that may enhance self-knowledge.

Hallucinations are vivid perceptions that occur in the absence of objective stimulation. Psychoactive drugs affect mental processes by temporarily changing consciousness as they modify CNS activity. Among the psychoactive drugs that alter consciousness are hallucinogens, stimulants, opiates, and depressants, including alcohol, caffeine, and nicotine.

KEY TERMS

addiction, 128

circadian rhythms, 113

consciousness, 107

consensual validation, 108

daydreaming, 111

dichotic listening task, 110

dissociation, 125

dream work, 120

dualism, 105

emergent-interaction theory, 106

experience-sampling method, 110

hallucination, 126

hypnosis, 123

hypnotizability, 123

insomnia, 117

latent content, 120

lucid dreaming, 122

manifest content, 120

meditation, 125

monism, 105

narcolepsy, 117

non-REM sleep (NREM), 113

nonconscious processes, 108

physiological dependence, 128

preconscious memories, 109

psychoactive drug, 128

psychological dependence, 128

rapid eye movement (REM), 113

self-awareness, 108

sleep apnea, 117

subconscious awareness, 109

think-aloud protocols, 110

tolerance, 128

unconscious, 109

withdrawal symptoms, 128

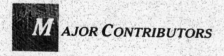

MAJOR CONTRIBUTORS

Cartwright, Rosalind, 115

Dement, William, 116

Descartes, René, 105

Freud, Sigmund, 109

Hilgard, Ernest, 125

Hobson, J. Allen, 120

LaBerge, Stephen, 122

McCarley, Robert, 120

Maas, James, 118

Singer, Jerome, 112

Chapter 5

The Developing Child

THE LIFE CYCLE BEGINS   137
   GENETIC INFLUENCES ON BEHAVIOR
   SENSORY DEVELOPMENT
   THE NATURE-NURTURE CONTROVERSY
   CLOSE-UP: DRUG-ADDICTED BABIES
   BABIES PREWIRED FOR SURVIVAL
   CONTINUITY, STAGES, AND CRITICAL PERIODS

   ▩ INTERIM SUMMARY

ACQUIRING LANGUAGE   153
   INNATE PRECURSORS TO LANGUAGE LEARNING
   COMMUNICATION SKILLS
   LEARNING WORDS
   PUTTING IT ALL TOGETHER: ACQUIRING
      GRAMMAR

   ▩ INTERIM SUMMARY

COGNITIVE DEVELOPMENT   161
   PIAGET'S INSIGHTS INTO MENTAL GROWTH
   MODERN PERSPECTIVES ON COGNITIVE
      DEVELOPMENT

   ▩ INTERIM SUMMARY

SOCIAL AND EMOTIONAL DEVELOPMENT   168
   SOCIALIZATION
   GENDER ROLES
   ERIKSON'S PSYCHOSOCIAL STAGES

RECAPPING MAIN POINTS   176

KEY TERMS   177

MAJOR CONTRIBUTORS   177

1984. The tiny figures in buntings are not quite three weeks old. They lie in their crib on their stomachs, in mirror image positions—a small fist inches from each mouth, one head turned to the right, the other to the left. Nicole wakes up first. She lies there, quite content, listening to her mother in the kitchen. Ten minutes later, Alexis awakens. Almost immediately, she begins to howl. The babies' mother runs in from the kitchen, picks up Alexis, and reaches for a clean diaper.

Nicole and Alexis are genetically identical, the products of a fertilized ovum that split sometime in the first two weeks of prenatal life. However, because of their positions on the placenta, Nicole was always first to get the nutrients that support prenatal growth. Thus, at birth she weighed 4 pounds; Alexis weighed a little less. Although no one can tell the girls apart when they are dressed identically, there are some important differences between the babies.

1985. Much to her mother's dismay, Alexis starts climbing on chairs as soon as she learns to crawl. Nicole follows suit in a couple of days. Alexis takes her first step on her first birthday. Friends and relatives clap and cheer. Nicole watches. In less than a week, she is walking too. After her morning Cheerios, Alexis sits in her daddy's lap and opens her mouth wide for bites of his scrambled eggs. She never seems to get enough. When anyone offers eggs to Nicole, she turns away and grimaces. She sticks to Cheerios.

1986. When Alexis and Nicole are 19 months old, their mother goes away for four days. This is the first time she has ever left her daughters for more than a day. The girls accompany their father to the hospital where their mother and a newborn baby, Mikey, are waiting. Nicole greets her mom with a big smile and a hug, as though nothing has happened. Alexis looks away, fidgets, and shows little emotion.

1987. Both girls are wild about clothes. Sometimes they empty their drawers and closet and put on several layers of socks, blouses, skirts, and hats. Then they stand before their mother's full-length mirror and admire their fashions. Alexis claims pink and green are her favorite colors and is very possessive about them. Nicole likes purple, but allows Alexis to wear "her color" if she wants.

Nicole likes sleeping alone, while Alexis often gets anxious if she feels she has lost track of her sister—even in her sleep. Sometimes Alexis wakes up in the night. "I had a bad dream," she cries. "I lost 'cole and I couldn't find her anywhere." Together or apart, they sleep in identical, sometimes mirror-image, positions.

When they work at their little table, Alexis scribbles intently on sheets of paper, "writing" letters and stories that she later dictates to her mother. Nicole is more interested in three-dimensional art projects—sculpting Play-Doh into intricate shapes and making collages out of objects she finds outdoors and in the house. Nicole still sucks her thumb and likes to stay close to her Mom. She also loves to climb on the tire swing in the backyard, and she begs to be pushed "higher, higher." Alexis prefers to watch.

1990. Although Alexis sometimes eats up to three times as much as Nicole, their weight never differs by more than 4 ounces. (Nicole is heavier). Nicole loves fruits and vegetables. Alexis prefers eggs and meat. Nicole takes violin lessons and practices every day. Alexis would like to take lessons too, but she doesn't want to practice. While Nicole practices, Alexis reads. She can read anything, even the instructions for the family's new laptop computer. When Nicole picks up a book, she looks first at the pictures and then reads each word carefully.

On vacation, Alexis likes to sleep with her aunt and grandma. Nicole prefers to stay with her mother. When Nicole is nearby, Alexis is theatrical and outgoing, but when she's on her own she seems more withdrawn. Nicole is more self-contained than Alexis and seems less dependent on social approval. Alexis reacts immediately and intensely to everything that happens, her emotions seemingly just beneath her skin. Nicole is more likely to watch and wait passively, not revealing what she is feeling.

At the end of each day, the girls brush their teeth (which grew at the same time but on opposite sides of their mouths). After listening to a bedtime story, Alexis and Nicole climb into their beds and curl up in those same mirror-image identical positions. Their parents wonder what other aspects of their development will be identical and which will be shaped by unique experiences they will have in school and outside the home.

Although Alexis and Nicole developed from the same egg and sperm, the preceding excerpts from their baby book illustrate how very different they already were three weeks after birth and what unique personality traits and behaviors each was exhibiting six years later. How is it possible that two people with identical origins could develop so differently?

This chapter begins our study of **developmental psychology,** the branch of psychology that is concerned with the changes in physical and psychological functioning that occur during the processes and stages of growth, from conception across the entire life span. The task of developmental psychologists is to find out how organisms change over time. They study the ages and stages of development at which different abilities and functions first appear and observe how they are modified. Developmental psychologists are concerned with many of the questions raised by the example of Nicole and Alexis—questions about the effects on development of genetics, brain maturation, psychological environment, and experience.

In studies of development, the usual independent variable is *age;* the dependent variable is the behavior being studied at various ages. But age is really an indicator of underlying physiological and psychological processes that are presumed to be taking place and caus-

ing, or making possible, the changes in observed behavior. So age is also called an *index variable,* a variable that indicates the presence of other variables but does not *cause* them to occur. Psychologists make a distinction between **chronological age**—the number of months or years since birth, which they usually use as their independent variable—and **developmental age**—the chronological age at which most children show a particular level of physical or mental development. For example, a 3-year-old child who has verbal skills typical of most 5 year olds is said to have a developmental age of 5 for verbal skills.

We will focus on psychological development that takes place during the early years of infancy and childhood. It is in this period that the transformations are rapid and varied. Our plan is to understand how an apparently "know-nothing" newborn becomes such a competent, mentally sophisticated organism in such a relatively brief period. We will explore how the child functions and changes in many ways—perceptually, cognitively, linguistically, socially, and emotionally. The next chapter will extend and broaden our perspective on development by examining the major psychological changes and challenges unique to each successive period of life, from adolescence through adulthood to old age.

THE LIFE CYCLE BEGINS

An energetic sperm cell finds a receptive egg cell. They unite, and, after nine months of gestation in the mother's womb, they become a newborn human being. This marvelous transformation is guided by principles of evolution and shaped by individual genetic influences. We will begin by reviewing some of the ways human development is influenced by genetic instructions and examining evidence that these genetic instructions enable the human brain to start functioning much earlier in prenatal development than most of us realize. Then we'll consider whether heredity or environment plays a greater role in human development—there must be some adaptive reason that, of any species, human infants have the longest and most dependent relationship with their caregivers.

GENETIC INFLUENCES ON BEHAVIOR

Your body build, behavior, and development were all determined, to some extent, at the moment the genetic material in sperm and egg cells of your parents united. Your genetic inheritance imposes certain constraints, but it also makes possible for you certain behaviors that are not possible for members of other species. Specifically, what constitutes the genetic inheritance of humans?

Chromosomes and Genes

Chromosomes are double strands of DNA (deoxyribonucleic acid) in the nucleus of cells. DNA is a long molecule whose appearance is similar to that of a twisted rope ladder, technically known as a *double helix*. Each rung of this DNA ladder is composed of two chemicals selected from a group of four possibilities: *adenine (As), cytosine (Cs), guanine (Gs),* and *thymine (Ts)*. These pairings of chemicals are known as *nucleotide base pairs*.

All normal human body cells have 46 chromosomes. As cells divide, each chromosome strand splits down the middle, and half of the chromosomes go to each new cell. Each half then acts as a template for the missing half, replacing the missing cells with materials in the surrounding tissue. However, **germ cells**—spermatozoa in the male sperm and ova in the female egg—maintain only 23 chromosomes—they remain at half strength in their final division. Thus, when male and female germ cells unite, they form 23 pairs to provide the 46 chromosomes that later will be found in a child's body cells. The outcome of this process is that the child receives half its chromosomes— a random selection—from each parent. In both males and females, 22 pairs are the same; the twenty-third pair determines the sex of the child. Males have one X chromosome and one smaller Y chromosome, or an XY pair. Females have two X chromosomes, or an XX pair.

Genes are segments along the chromosome strands that contain the "blueprints" or instructions for the development of our physical characteristics and even some of our psychological attributes. Genes determine not only *what* characteristics we will develop but also *when*. These instructions are carried out through the *synthesis of proteins,* when the genes arrange and sequence the nucleotide base pairs that form a protein-making code. If any of the codes are incorrect, then the genes will synthesize the wrong kind of protein. The result of incorrect codes might be a genetic disease that impairs normal functioning or even premature death.

A baby born with the normal complement of 46 chromosomes has as many as 100,000 genes in each of its many body cells. A full set of genes—all of the genes inherited from both parents—is an organism's *genotype*. The set of characteristics an organism actually develops—observable features, such as body build and eye color—is called its *phenotype*. Most of the genetic component deals with characteristics that are specific to each species, the rest with individual differences within that species. It is not always possible to tell the genotype from the phenotype, but, as we noted in Chapter 3, the field of research known as *behavior genetics* attempts to identify the genetic bases of behavioral traits, such as intelligence and personality (Fuller, 1982).

Research in behavior genetics has determined that most human characteristics in which heredity plays a role are **polygenic,** or dependent on a combination of genes. In other words, the mere presence of a gene may not indicate that a certain human characteristic will develop. Instead, the development of that characteristic may be determined by the combination of that gene with one or more others. Genes that are always expressed when they are present in an individual, regardless of their combination with another gene, are called *dominant genes*. Genes that are expressed only when paired with a similar gene are called *recessive genes*. For example, an individual who has a gene for brown eyes, a dominant gene, will always have brown eyes, whether that gene pairs with a blue-eye gene or a brown-eye gene. However, an individual who has a gene for blue eyes, a recessive gene, will only have blue eyes if that gene pairs with another blue-eyed gene. All-or-nothing characteristics, such as eye color, are controlled by either a single gene or by a pair of genes, depending on whether the characteristic is dominant or recessive. Characteristics that vary in degree, such as height, are thought to be controlled by several genes. Complex characteristics, including some psychological attributes such as emotionality, are surely controlled or influenced by the interaction of many groups of genes.

Only about 10 percent of the genes we inherit will be used in the course of our lives. The unused genetic potential in our genotype is similar to a trust fund, available only if our usually constant environment changes in significant ways. If that environment does change, those who possess a genetic trust fund with the "right stuff" will be able to adapt to the change and pass on these environmentally appropriate genes to the next generation.

When the environmental requirements are specific and predictable, genes rigidly program behavior. The result is *stereotyped,* unlearned behavioral patterns. Animals that are higher on the *phylogenetic,* or animal development, scale face more varied environmental challenges. Through experience and learning, they have replaced the stereotyped behavior patterns seen in lower animals with more complex and flexible patterns. In humans, an almost limitless diversity of behavioral traits can emerge as genetic predispositions and interact with experience across the varied physical, social, and cultural environments in which we function.

There are many events that occur after a gene organizes the protein molecules and before the structure of an organ is finalized or any given behavioral ability emerges. Environmental influences—from biological to physical and social—help determine the outcome of each of these intermediate events. For example, the very first event in the long process of development is that neighboring genes regulate whether a particular gene will be turned "on or off." During the first months of pregnancy, environmental factors such as malnutrition, radiation, or drugs can prevent the normal formation of organs and body structures. In the early 1960s, several hundred women took a tranquilizer called *thalidomide* in early pregnancy to prevent morning sickness and insomnia. The unanticipated side effect was that the drug "turned off" normal fetal growth of limbs. These mothers gave birth to babies whose arms and legs had not developed beyond stumps.

Understanding the gene-environment-behavior pathway has led to a remarkably simple treatment for one kind of mental deficiency, *phenylketonuria,* or *PKU.* A PKU infant lacks the genetic material to produce an enzyme that metabolizes the amino acid *phenylalanine.* Because of this deficiency, phenylalanine accumulates in the infant's nervous system and interferes with normal growth and brain development. Changing the infant's diet to eliminate or greatly reduce food substances containing phenylalanine (such as lettuce) counteracts the genetic predisposition, and intellectual development moves into the normal range (Koch et al., 1963).

The Native American use of back cradles delays the age at which infants learn to walk. However, the development of walking in Native American infants will follow the same time-ordered sequence as in other infants.

Physical Growth and Maturation

The blueprint provided by the genes directs the physical development of an organism in a predictable sequence. The blueprint is responsible also for the appearance of certain behaviors at roughly the same time for all normal members of a species (as we noted with twins Nicole and Alexis), although there are some cultural variations. Some basic survival behaviors, such as sucking, are unlearned. Others follow inner promptings but need a bit of refinement, which comes through experience. For example, most children sit without support by 7 months of age, pull themselves up to a standing position a month or two later, and walk soon after their first birthday. Once the underlying physical structures are sufficiently developed, proficiency in these behaviors requires only a minimally adequate environment and a little practice. On the other hand, these behaviors can't be speeded up by earlier efforts. They seem to "unfold from within," following an inner, genetically determined timetable that is characteristic for the species.

Maturation refers to the process of growth typical of all members of a species who are reared in the species' usual habitat. Maturation describes the systematic changes occurring over time in bodily functioning and behavior, that are influenced by (a) genetic factors; (b) chemical factors in the prenatal and postnatal environments (nutritive or toxic influences); and (c) sensory factors that are *constant* for all members of the species—such as the force of gravity or basic social contacts (Hebb, 1966). Excluded from this view of maturation are the effects of *variable sensory experiences,* those experiences that vary in kind and degree from one member of the species to another and abnormal physical and psychological events that are described as traumatic (Rabinowitz, 1987).

The characteristic maturational sequences of physical and mental growth are determined by the interaction of inherited biological boundaries and environmental inputs that are normal for a given species. For example, in the sequence for locomotion, as shown in **Figure 5.1,** a child learns to walk without special training. Development of walking follows a fixed, time-ordered sequence that is typical of all physically capable members of our species. In cultures where there is more physical stimulation, children begin to walk sooner. The Native American practice of carrying babies in tightly bound back cradles retards walking, but once released, the child goes through the same sequence. An infant must suffer frustration during early attempts to walk, yet the infant persists. Ultimately the child reaps the evolutionary reward of greater flexibility and adaptability than is possible with crawling.

Genetic factors are believed to instigate the maturational changes that make an individual ready for new experiences and learning. However, certain kinds of experience may influence physiological functioning and thus biological development (Gottleib, 1983). The influence of maturation is most apparent in early development, but it continues throughout life. Maturation in the nervous system changes the amount and type of sleep we need at different stages of life; maturation in the endocrine system brings on the rapid development of

---

FIGURE 5.1   *MATURATIONAL TIMETABLE FOR LOCOMOTION*

The development of walking requires no special teaching. It follows a fixed time-ordered sequence that is typical of all physically capable members of our species. In cultures where there is more stimulation, children begin to walk sooner (Shirley, 1931).

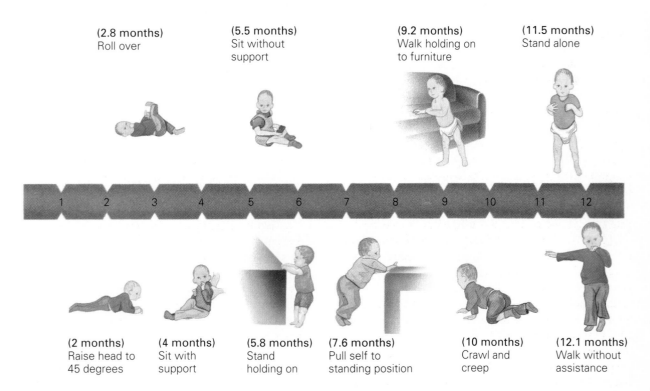

(2.8 months)
Roll over

(5.5 months)
Sit without support

(9.2 months)
Walk holding on to furniture

(11.5 months)
Stand alone

1   2   3   4   5   6   7   8   9   10   11   12

(2 months)
Raise head to 45 degrees

(4 months)
Sit with support

(5.8 months)
Stand holding on

(7.6 months)
Pull self to standing position

(10 months)
Crawl and creep

(12.1 months)
Walk without assistance

the sex organs and secondary sex characteristics at puberty. Different aspects of development follow different maturational timetables.

The earliest behavior of any kind is the heartbeat. It begins in the *prenatal period,* before birth, when the embryo is about 3 weeks old and a sixth of an inch long. Responses to stimulation have been observed as early as the sixth week, when the embryo is not yet an inch long. Spontaneous movements are observed by the eighth week (Carmichael, 1970; Humphrey, 1970).

After the eighth week the developing embryo is called a *fetus.* The mother feels fetal movements in about the sixteenth week after conception, although these movements may be heard with a stethoscope a week or two earlier. In the sixteenth week, the fetus is about 7 inches long (the average length at birth is 20 inches). As the brain grows in utero, it generates new neurons at the rate of 250,000 per minute, reaching a full complement of over 100 billion neurons by birth (Cowan, 1979). In humans and many other mammals, this cell proliferation and migration of neurons to their correct locations takes place prenatally, while the development of the branching processes of axons and dendrites largely occurs after birth (Kolb, 1989). The sequence of brain development, from 25 days to nine months, is shown in **Figure 5.2.**

FIGURE 5.2   *THE DEVELOPMENT OF THE HUMAN BRAIN*

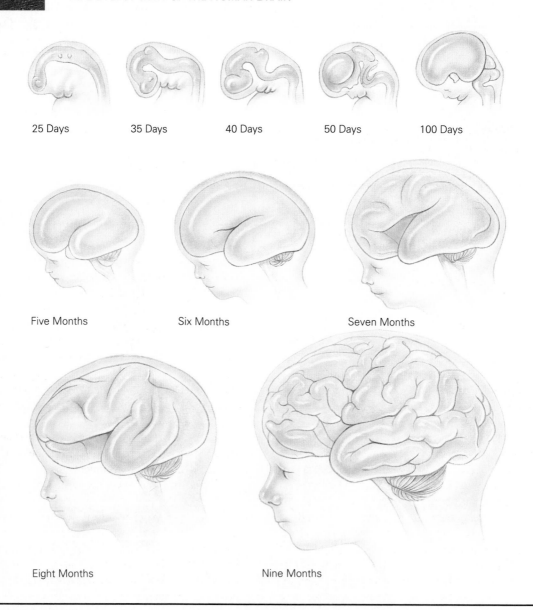

25 Days   35 Days   40 Days   50 Days   100 Days

Five Months   Six Months   Seven Months

Eight Months   Nine Months

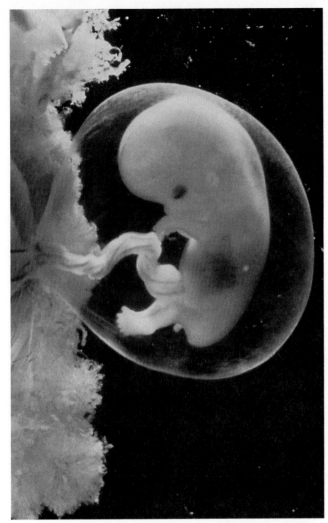

As the brain grows in the developing fetus, it generates 250,000 new neurons per minute.

FIGURE 5.3   *NEURAL GROWTH IN THE FIRST YEAR OF LIFE*

Neural growth occurs very rapidly in the first year of life. It is much faster than overall physical growth. By contrast, genital maturation does not occur until adolescence.

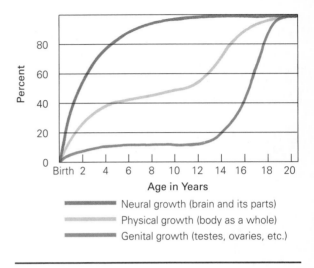

Neural growth (brain and its parts)
Physical growth (body as a whole)
Genital growth (testes, ovaries, etc.)

Constitutional Factors

By birth, or soon afterward, genetic and early environmental influences result in the development of basic physical and psychological characteristics, such as body build, predispositions to certain physical and mental illnesses, and *temperament* (personality style). These **constitutional factors** are basic physiological and psychological tendencies resulting from the interaction of genetically determined characteristics, or *endowment*, with early life experiences and environmental influences. Because they are largely hereditary, constitutional factors remain fairly consistent throughout a person's lifetime. Constitutional factors are apparent even in a newborn child's body type, characteristic physiological functioning, and basic reaction tendencies. For example, some babies are more sensitive to stimulation than others—some have a high energy level and some are placid and not easily upset. Basic reaction tendencies such as these may affect the way children interact with their environment and, thus, what they will experience and how they will develop (Miyake et al., 1985).

Harvard researcher **Jerome Kagan** has shown that about 10 to 15 percent of infants are "born shy" or "born bold" (Kagan & Snidman, 1991; Kagan & Reznick, 1986). They differ in sensitivity to physical and social stimulation—the shy baby is more easily frightened and less socially responsive. People are less likely

Babies seem to be all head. At birth a baby's head is already about 60 percent of its adult size and measures a quarter of the whole body length (Bayley, 1956). The neural tissue of the brain (the total mass of brain cells) grows at an astonishing rate, increasing by 50 percent in the first two years and 80 percent above birth size in the next two and leveling off by about 11 years of age. An infant's body weight doubles in the first six months and triples by the first birthday; by the age of 2, a child's trunk is about half of its adult length.

Genital development follows a very different developmental program. Genital tissue shows little change until the teenage years, and then develops rapidly to adult proportions. **Figure 5.3** shows the systematic, though different, patterns of growth for neural and genital tissues, compared with overall body growth.

to interact and be playful with the shy baby, accentuating the child's initial disposition. However, experience and special training can modify the way a constitutional factor is expressed.

Genetically shy monkey temperament is being studied by researcher **Steven Suomi** (1990), who sees many parallels with shy children. When faced with challenges, these monkeys exhibit consistent behavior patterns; they cling to their mother, do not explore, are easily frightened by strangers, and are tense in posture, very cautious, and very vigilant. They seem to have brain alarm systems that are easily triggered to release hormones into the bloodstream, causing respiration and heart rate to accelerate and pupils to dilate. Blood testing established that the shy trait was inherited, and it was apparent that shy mothers tended to have shy babies. To modify the behavior pattern, the research team arranged for foster parenting by nonshy, supportive, calm mothers and nurturing grandmothers, which has worked to help shy youngsters handle social threats with greater confidence.

When developmental psychologists speak of *environmental* effects, they often mean factors such as culture, childrearing methods, parental attitudes, and educational opportunities that shape the child's mental and behavioral development. All these environmental effects exist independently of the child and contribute to his or her development in ways that can be modified relatively easily. A family can move from one neighborhood (or country) to another. Parents can try new techniques of discipline or socialization. A child can change teachers, classrooms, or schools.

Steven Suomi (*Discovering Psychology*, 1990, Program 5)

Every aspect of a child's prenatal environment is mediated by the biological-chemical connection to the mother. Experiences that are initiated outside the mother (for example, exposure to heat in a sauna, or eating highly seasoned foods) become internalized and are transmitted to her developing fetus. Maternal drug use is among the most devastating of these prenatal experiences.

SENSORY DEVELOPMENT

William James, the foremost American psychologist at the turn of the century, believed that the human infant was a totally helpless and confused organism. After experiencing the tranquility of life in the womb, the infant was assailed on all sides by sudden bursts of stimulation—the world was "one great blooming, buzzing confusion." In 1928, John Watson, the founder of behaviorism, described the human infant as "a lively, squirming bit of flesh, capable of making a few simple responses." As recently as 1964, the author of a medical textbook proclaimed that the newborn could not focus its eyes or respond to sounds and did not possess consciousness.

These individuals were more wrong than they could begin to imagine. For the past two decades, research from psychological and medical experiments in laboratories across the United States and many other countries has pointed to an inescapable conclusion: babies come into the world with the ability to do all sorts of amazing mental and perceptual feats. Moments out of the womb, infants begin to reveal that they are precocious, sophisticated, and friendly.

A few minutes after birth, a newborn's eyes are alert, turning in the direction of a voice and searching inquisitively for the source of certain sounds that it prefers. The baby stretches out an exploratory hand.

Babies are also born with prejudices. New research shows that they perceive much more than we ever thought they did and that they have distinct preferences for smells, sounds, and sights. As early as 12 hours after birth they show distinct signs of pleasure at the taste of sugar water or vanilla, and they smile when they smell banana essence. Infants prefer salted to unsalted cereal, even when they had virtually no prior experience with salted foods (Bernstein, 1990; Harris et al., 1990). But they recoil from the taste of lemon or shrimp or from the smell of rotten eggs. Their hearing functions even before birth, so they are prepared to respond to certain sounds when they are born. They prefer female voices, are attentive to clicking sounds, fall asleep to the beating of a heart, and recognize their mothers' speech a few weeks after birth. Some of these auditory preferences are probably due to the embryo's familiarity with

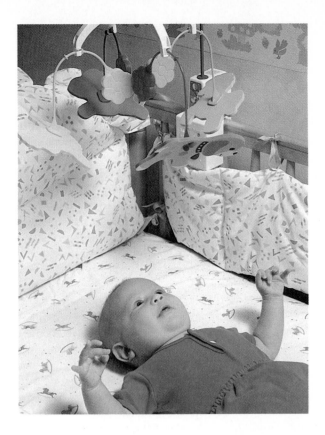

such sounds, having experienced them in the uterine environment.

Vision is less well developed than the other senses at birth; indeed, babies are born "legally blind" with a visual acuity of about 20/500. There are three related reasons for this initially blurred vision: poor optics, not enough cones, and not enough neurons. Good vision—sensitivity to contrast, visual acuity, and color discrimination—requires that a great many photoreceptor cone cells function in the fovea of the eye's retina and that the optics of the eye develop appropriately. "Front-end" information losses are due to the immaturity of these components of the infant's visual system. On the "back-end," good vision requires numerous connections between the neurons in the visual cortex of the brain. At birth, not enough of these connections are laid down. However, these immature systems develop very rapidly, and as they do, the baby's visual capacities become evident (Banks & Bennett, 1988). Early on, infants can perceive large objects that display a great deal of contrast. A 1-month-old child can detect contours of a head at close distances; at 7 weeks the baby can scan the interior features of the mother's face, and as the mother talks the baby can scan her eyes. As early

as 2 months of age, the baby begins to see a world of color, differentiating patterns of white, red, orange, and blue. At 3 months, the baby can perceive depth and is well on the way to enjoying the visual abilities of adults.

THE NATURE-NURTURE CONTROVERSY

To what extent is human behavior determined by heredity (nature), and to what extent is it a product of learned experiences (nurture)? The **nature-nurture controversy** is a long-standing debate among philosophers, psychologists, and educators over the relative importance of heredity and learning. Are infants born with capabilities and skills that are refined with experience, or are they born "dumb," ready only to be smartened up by their contact with society and learned experiences? For centuries, both sides of the debate have been hotly defended. To appreciate one of the classic elements in this controversy, we must go back in time to a curious event that took place in the year 1800.

At the end of the eighteenth century, the new science of "mental medicine," an early version of modern psychology, had begun to capture the interest of learned people. These people debated the true nature of the human species, the influences of the mind on behavior, and the differences between humans and animals. On one side of the debate were those who believed that the human infant is born without knowledge or skills— experience, in the form of human learning, etches messages on the blank tablet—or *tabula rasa*—of the infant's unformed mind. This view, proposed by British philosopher **John Locke,** is known as *empiricism.* It credits human development to experience. What directs human development is the stimulation people received as they are *nurtured.*

Among the scholars opposing empiricism was French philosopher **Jean Rousseau.** He argued the *nativist* view that *nature,* or what we bring into the world from our evolutionary legacy, is the mold that shapes development. People are, at birth, "noble savages," he argued, likely to be spoiled or corrupted by contact with society (Cranston, 1991).

The nature-nurture debate was intensified by the discovery of a wild boy who had apparently been raised by animals in the forests around the village of Aveyron, France. This 12-year-old, uncivilized, *feral* (wild) child, who became known as the Wild Boy of Aveyron, was thought to hold the answers to these profound questions about human nature.

A young doctor, **Jean Marie Itard,** accepted the challenge of trying to civilize and educate the Wild Boy of Aveyron, whom he named Victor. At first, Itard's intensive training program seemed to be working; Victor became affectionate and well-mannered and learned

DRUG-ADDICTED BABIES

Based on a 1988 survey of 36 hospitals, Dr. Ira Chasnoff, director of the National Association for Perinatal Addiction Research and Education, estimates that each year 375,000 babies are prenatally exposed to illicit drugs. This figure may be an underestimate because many mothers are reluctant to disclose their drug habits, and drug testing is not a universal procedure in obstetrical wards (Chasnoff et al., 1989).

The Federal Department of Health and Human Services estimates that by the year 2000, about four million children whose mothers used cocaine during pregnancy will require specialized medical and educational services costing billions of dollars (Hamilton, 1990). Since the cocaine derivative *crack* was first introduced, in some inner-city hospitals the rate of low-birth-weight deliveries has increased by as much as 60 percent (The Drug Policy Letter, 1990, p. 6).

Like alcohol, heroin, and other drugs, cocaine travels through the placenta and can affect fetal development directly. In adults, cocaine causes blood vessels to constrict; in pregnant women, cocaine restricts placental blood flow and oxygen to the fetus. If severe oxygen deprivation results, blood vessels in the fetus's brain may burst. Such prenatal strokes can lead to lifelong physical and mental handicaps (Chasnoff, 1985). Restricted blood flow may also explain the high incidence of miscarriage and premature delivery among mothers who use co-

caine. Those who continue to use the drug throughout pregnancy have four times the normal risk of delivering a low-birth-weight baby. All low-birth-weight premature infants are at risk for having learning problems, cognitive deficits, and difficulties in behavioral adjustment (Gross, 1990; Neligan et al.,

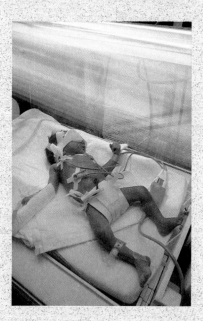

1976; Scott, 1987). These adverse consequences increase in the face of poverty and drug-related complications. From 25 to 30 percent of infants prenatally exposed to cocaine experience preterm delivery, low birth weight, and/or growth retardation (Chasnoff, 1985).

Addicts often give birth to drug-dependent babies. For a cocaine-addicted newborn, the first two to three weeks of life are spent in the agony of drug withdrawal. Some of these babies are sluggish and depressed while others are jit-

tery and easily excitable. Once provoked, they are almost impossible to calm. Later, the child may experience such symptoms as hyperactivity, mental retardation, impaired motor and cognitive skills, short attention span, speech problems, apathy, aggression, and emotional flattening (Hamilton, 1990; Quindlen, 1990). Even worse, some of these addicted babies also have AIDS because their mothers had sex with afflicted partners in exchange for crack, or shared contaminated needles when shooting drugs.

When cocaine-exposed babies reach school age, they require a great deal of individual attention and feel overwhelmed in settings with too much activity or too many people. A Los Angeles Public School program for drug-exposed children has found a few strategies that help: early intervention; slow introduction of new concepts; and a great deal of nurturing and one-on-one attention from adults. Such attention, however, is expensive. In 1990, the program cost $15,000 a year for each child as compared to $4000 for children in the regular school program (Hamilton, 1990), and with cutbacks in educational budgets it is unlikely such costly programs will survive.

Victor, The Wild Boy of Aveyron

to follow instructions. After five years, however, progress stopped, and the teacher reluctantly called an end to the experiment (Itard, reprinted, 1962).

To this day, the controversy persists about what this curious case study actually revealed. Did nature or nurture fail? Perhaps Victor had been abandoned as an infant because he was developmentally disabled. If that were the case, any training would have only limited success. If not, would modern training procedures have helped the boy develop more fully than Itard's methods? One authority on Victor's story, Harlan Lane (1976, 1986), believes that the case shows clearly the devastating effects of social isolation or, conversely, the vital role of early social contact on communication and mental growth. Outside of society, says Lane, we are nothing more than "ignoble savages."

Today, thanks to the work of many researchers and scholars, we know that the extreme positions of Locke and Rousseau do injustice to the richness of human behavior. Almost any complex action is shaped both by an individual's biological inheritance and by personal experience, including learning. Heredity and environment have a continuing mutual influence on each other: each makes possible certain further advances in the other, but each also limits the other's contributions. We have noted the negative effect low birth weight has on physical and mental development. Two types of environmental intervention can dramatically modify this poor head start in life: physical stimulation via touch (as noted in Chapter 3) and early education and parent training. In a pioneering nationwide study of nearly

1000 tiny infants over the first three years of life, low-birth-weight babies randomly assigned to the intensive intervention program exhibited major improvements in intelligence scores and reduced behavioral problems (Gross, 1990).

Heredity sets a *reaction range* of potential; experience determines where in that range any individual will be. For example, your heredity determines how tall you can grow; how tall you actually become depends partly on nutrition, an environmental factor. **Figure 5.4** (page 146) illustrates the interaction of height and favorableness of environment for groups of children with different genotypes for height. Similarly, your level of mental ability seems to depend on both genetic potential, early stimulation, and environmental opportunity. In almost every instance we examine, *nature and nurture interact*. Nature provides the raw materials, and nurture affects how genes "play out" their potential.

Genetic influences have been found for many psychological characteristics. For example, certain reading disabilities appear to have a significant genetic component (De Fries & Decker, 1982). Boys are four times more likely than girls to be affected by **developmental dyslexia,** a specific reading disability that often involves transposition of letters and/or numbers and difficulty knowing right from left and up from down. (Findings with regard to genetics, personality, and intelligence will be presented in Chapters 14 and 15.) Although the debate continues, most investigators are now more interested in identifying *how* heredity and environment and their interaction contribute to development than in trying to weigh their relative importance.

BABIES PREWIRED FOR SURVIVAL

Research in the past two decades has challenged Locke's blank slate view of the newborn mind. Babies apparently start life already equipped with remarkable know-how, and they can use many of their senses to take in information and react to it. They might be thought of as prewired "friendly computers," well suited to respond to adult caregivers and to influence their social environments.

How do babies organize their early experiences and what can they do? These questions are at the core of an explosion of research on the *infancy period,* which lasts for about the first 18 months of life while the child is incapable of speech (the Latin meaning of the word *infancy* is *incapable of speech*). Much of this research is focused on the *neonate,* the newborn baby up to a month old (see **Table 5.1** for an outline of the early stages of child development).

FIGURE 5.4 REACTION RANGES FOR HEIGHT AS A FUNCTION OF ENVIRONMENT

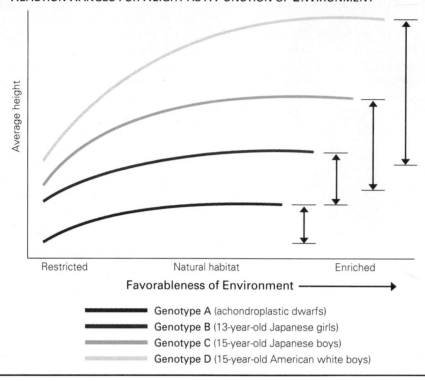

Genotype A (achondroplastic dwarfs)
Genotype B (13-year-old Japanese girls)
Genotype C (15-year-old Japanese boys)
Genotype D (15-year-old American white boys)

TABLE 5.1 STAGES IN EARLY LIFE-SPAN DEVELOPMENT

Stage	Age Period	Some Major Characteristics
Prenatal Stage	Conception to birth	Physical development
Infancy	Birth at full term to about 18 months	Locomotion; rudimentary language; social attachment
Early Childhood	About 18 months to about 6 years	Well-established language; gender typing; group play; ends with "readiness" for schooling
Late Childhood	About 6 years to about 13 years	Many cognitive processes become adult except in speed of operation; team play

Responding and Adapting

Even within the first few hours of life, a newborn infant, given an appropriate stimulus, is capable of a variety of responses. If placed upon the mother's abdomen, the baby will usually make crawling motions. The baby will also turn its head toward anything that strokes its cheek—a nipple or a finger—and begin to suck it. Sucking is the only behavior that is common among all mammals (Blass & Teicher, 1980). *Sucking* is an exceedingly complex, but already highly developed, behavior pattern involving intricate coordination of tongue and swallowing movements, synchronization of the baby's breathing with the sucking and swallowing sequence, and tactile stimulation from the nipple. Yet it appears that most babies know how to do it from the start. Sucking is an adaptable behavior that can be changed by its *consequences*. The rapidity of sucking, for example, is dependent on the sweetness of the fluid being received. The sweeter the fluid, the more continuously—and also the more forcefully—an infant will suck (Lipsitt et al., 1976). In fact, the sucking rate even depends on the pattern of sweetness over time, rather than simply on the absolute amount of sweetness at the moment.

A group of newborns who were given a sucrose-sweetened solution through an automated nipple apparatus responded at the average rate of 55 sucks per minute, compared with 46 sucks per minute for a group that received water. A third group, which had sucrose first and then water, matched the rate of the first group while it was getting sucrose; but when the sucrose changed to water, the group's rate fell below that of the water-only group. Not only did this group respond differently to the different tastes, but the experience of the sweet solution in the preceding 5 minutes weakened its response to the water solution (Kobre & Lipsitt, 1972).

Infants apparently come into the world preprogrammed to like and seek pleasurable sensations, such as sweetness, and to avoid or escape unpleasant stimulation, such as loud noises, bright lights, strong odors, and painful stimuli. However, human infants younger than three weeks do not respond to possible *negative* effects of sucking. Sucking seems to serve as an end in itself, as evidenced by the fact that babies are so unresponsive to formula alterations that are bitter or salty and that they can continue to suck, become sick, and even die from accidental substitutions of salt for sugar (Blass & Teicher, 1980).

A 2-hour-old infant begins to extract cause and effect relationships from experience with signals that reliably predict pleasurable events, such as getting a few drops of sweet liquid. The infant's response to conditioning implies that a simple memory system must be operating and, further, that expectations and inferences are being formed.

Elliott Blass (1990) and his research team at Johns Hopkins University started their study of the abilities of newborn babies with baby rats. They wanted to know how newborn rats, which are blind and deaf, learn to find their mother's nipple. Smell is the key—baby rats move towards a familiar odor when they search for a nipple. When the mother's nipple is washed, making it lose its odor, the rats don't attach. After a tasteless, lemon-scented fluid is injected into the mother's amniotic fluid during pregnancy, newborn rats will attach to her nipple only if it smells like lemon. Even more fascinating is Blass' finding that when the rats mature, this learned preference for lemon scent extends to their choice of a sexual partner—they will select a rat with a lemon scent.

Researchers began studying human newborns after their studies with rats. They taught newborns only 2 to 48 hours old to *anticipate* the pleasurable sensation of the sweet taste of sucrose.

When they stroked the baby's forehead and gave it the sugar water, it extended its tongue and became calm. Soon, just stroking alone would cause

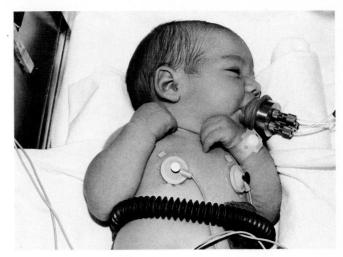

Infant with Lipsitt sucking device

the baby to turn its head in the direction the sweet fluid was delivered—in anticipation of good times past. What do you predict happened when the stroking was not followed by sucrose? The babies got upset. Almost all (seven of eight) newborns cried when the sweets failed to show up, while few cried (1 of 16) in the control group not conditioned to expect sucrose after stroking. It is as if the babies were responding emotionally to a violation of a reliable relationship that had been established.

When the researchers tried different sounds instead of the stroking as the signal for the sucrose, they were surprised to find that only the click of a castanet became associated with the sweet liquid. The babies ignored a *psst* sound and the *ting* of a triangle; they became calm and inactive when they heard a *shhh* sound. Click sounds are the primary form of communication between mammals and their infants. Clicks, kisses, and clucks are the natural sounds heard around maternity wards; babies are thus prepared to respond exclusively to certain sounds that caregivers ordinarily make (Blass, 1990).

It seems that babies start to build up their knowledge of the world by extracting relations between related sensory events. Through interactions of inherited response tendencies and learned experiences, babies, in time, become competent survivors able to learn vast amounts of information.

Interacting Socially

Babies are designed to be sociable. They prefer human voices to other sounds and human faces to most other patterns (Fantz, 1963). When only a week old,

Newborns respond to the looks and words of their parents. They send out messages to their caregivers in return.

some babies can distinguish their mothers' voices from the voices of other women. In another week, babies can perceive their mothers' voices and faces as part of a total unit and will get upset when experimenters pair the mothers' faces with the voices of strangers (Carpenter, 1973).

Babies not only respond to, but also interact with, their caregivers. High-speed film studies of this interaction reveal a remarkable degree of *synchronicity*—the gazing, vocalizing, touching, and smiling of mothers and infants are closely coordinated (Martin, 1981; Trevarthen, 1977). Babies respond and learn, but they also send out messages to those willing to listen to and love them. Not only are the behaviors of mothers and infants linked in a socially dynamic fashion but their feelings are also matched (Fogel, 1991). A 3-month-old infant may laugh when its mother laughs and frown or cry in response to her negative show of affect (Tronick et al., 1980).

In general, developmental psychologists studying what babies can do are becoming ever more impressed with how precocious, or smart for their age, they are. They seem to come equipped to accomplish three basic tasks of survival: (a) sustenance (feeding), (b) maintenance of contact with people (for protection and care), and (c) defense against harmful stimuli (withdrawing from pain or threat). These tasks require perceptual skills, some ability to understand experiences with people and objects, and basic thinking skills that combine information from different senses (von Hofsten & Lindhagen, 1979). Some investigators have concluded that children are born with the ability to distinguish among experiences and to put this information into separate categories. This ability to categorize the flow of conscious experience is essential for building a knowledge base (Masters, 1981).

But how do we know what babies can do, feel, and think? There are two answers to this question. First,

Researcher Alan Fogel has shown that an infant can match its mother's emotions.

TABLE 5.2   NORMS FOR INFANT MENTAL AND MOTOR DEVELOPMENT *(based on the Bayley Scales)*

One Month
Responds to sound

Becomes quiet when picked up

Follows a moving person with eyes

Retains a large easily grasped object placed in hand

Vocalizes occasionally

Two Months
Smiles socially

Engages in anticipatory excitement (to feeding, being held)

Recognizes mother

Inspects surroundings

Blinks to object or shadow (flinches)

Lifts head and holds it erect and steady

Three Months
Vocalizes to the smiles and talk of an adult

Searches for sound

Makes anticipatory adjustments to lifting

Reacts to disappearance of adult's face

Sits with support, head steady

Four Months
Head follows dangling ring, vanishing spoon, and ball moved across table

Inspects and fingers own hands

Shows awareness of strange situations

Picks up cube with palm grasp

Sits with slight support

Five Months
Discriminates strange from familiar persons

Makes distinctive vocalizations (e.g., pleasure, eagerness, satisfaction)

Makes effort to sit independently

Turns from back to side

Has partial use of thumb in grasp

Six Months
Reaches persistently, picks up cube deftly

Transfers objects hand to hand

Lifts cup and bangs it

Smiles at mirror image and likes frolicking

Reaches unilaterally for small object

Seven Months
Makes playful responses to mirror

Retains two of three cubes offered

Sits alone steadily and well

Shows clear thumb opposition in grasp

Scoops up pellet from table

Eight Months
Vocalizes four different syllables (such as *da-da, me, no*)

Listens selectively to familiar words

Rings bell purposively

Attempts to obtain three presented cubes

Shows early stepping movements (prewalking progression)

This table shows the average age at which each behavior is performed up to 8 months. Individual differences in rate of development are considerable, but most infants follow this sequence.

developmental psychologists engage in research investigations to observe, compare, and test children (and adults) at different ages. Second, they use the infant's physical reactions as indices of internal processes. Let's see how each of these methodologies works to generate the evidence on which modern developmental psychology rests.

Normative and Longitudinal Investigations

Normative investigations seek to describe a characteristic of a specific age or developmental stage. By systematically testing individuals of different ages, researchers can determine developmental landmarks, such as those listed in **Table 5.2.** The data provide *norms*, standard patterns of development or achievement, based on observation of many children during the first eight months after their births. The data indicate the average age at which the behaviors were performed. Thus a child's performance can be diagnosed in terms of its position relative to the standard for the typical individual at the same age. Extreme deviations on some behaviors are predictive of abnormal development. In short, a norm provides a standard basis for comparison not only between individuals but also between groups.

Developmental psychologists use several other types of time-based, research designs to understand possible mechanisms of change and causal influences on behavior. Most characteristic of their approach is the **longitudinal design,** in which the same individuals are repeatedly observed and tested over time, often for many years. An advantage of longitudinal research is that, because the subjects have lived through the same socioeconomic period, age-related changes cannot be confused with variations in differing societal circumstances. But there are several disadvantages. The results can be generalized only to a very limited group: those born at the same time period of the data collection. Also, longitudinal design is costly, it is difficult to keep track of the subjects over extended time periods in a society that is so highly mobile, and data are easily lost due to subject attrition.

> One of the most ambitious longitudinal studies is the study of geniuses, begun by Lewis Terman soon after World War I and still going on 60 years later through the work of psychologists at Stanford University. Over 1500 boys and girls, in grades three through eight (born about 1910), were selected on the basis of high intelligence scores (in the genius range). They have been tested at regular intervals ever since—first, to see how they compared to youngsters in general, later to see if their intellectual superiority would be maintained over the years, and then to discover the conditions and experiences that contributed to life satisfaction and to different styles of handling important life problems. About 75 percent of those still living continue to return questionnaires every ten years (Terman, 1925; Terman & Oden, 1947, 1959).

Most research on development uses a **cross-sectional design,** in which groups of subjects, of different chronological ages, are observed and compared at one and the same time. A researcher can then draw conclusions about behavioral differences that may be related to those age differences. In experiments using a cross-sectional design, those in the experimental group receive a particular treatment or stimulus condition, while those in the control group—subjects of the same age distribution—are not exposed to the independent variable. Using a cross-sectional design, researchers can investigate an entire age range at one time. The disadvantage of cross-sectional design comes from comparing individuals who differ by year of their birth as well as by their chronological age differences. Age-related changes are confounded by differences in the social or political conditions experienced by different *birth cohorts* (those born in the same year). Thus, a study comparing samples of 10 and 18 year olds now might differ from that of 10 and 18 year olds who grew up in the 1970s in ways related to their different eras as well as to their developmental stages.

The best features of cross-sectional and longitudinal approaches are combined in **sequential design.** In this method, subjects span a certain, small age range. The subjects are grouped according to the years of their births, and the groups are observed repeatedly over several years. For example, a sequential design study might start in 1992 with four birth cohorts of children ages 5 (1987), 4 (1988), 3 (1989), and 2 (1990), tested each year for three years. By choosing cohorts whose ages will overlap during the course of the study, a researcher avoids the problems of both the cross-sectional and the longitudinal approaches: age and time-of-birth effects and lack of generalizability.

Indices of Internal Processes

Modern developmental researchers discover what babies see, think, and feel by noting what infants can do and then inferring the meaning that certain patterns of behavior have for those infants. Infants move their eyes to look at things, reach out to touch objects, and suck liquids. Researchers use these simple behaviors to index their abilities, capacities, and psychological states. But how?

One of the most useful research paradigms is that of *habituation*. Experimenters record whether an infant looks at one stimulus more than another as an indication that the infant can perceive the difference between them. Too much of the same stimulus quickly loses its appeal to babies who soon stop responding to it. This decrease in response to any repeatedly presented event is known as **habituation.** It is a basic response process found in most species and is especially evident in newborns. **Dishabituation** occurs when, after the baby has habituated to a familiar stimulus, another stimulus is presented to which the infant responds. This new attentional focus reveals that the baby perceives it to be different from the previous stimulus. Researchers use the babies' looking time and reaching as dependent measures of attention, preference, or perceptual ability. Changes in sucking rate can also show that infants detect various tastes or, indeed, any stimuli associated

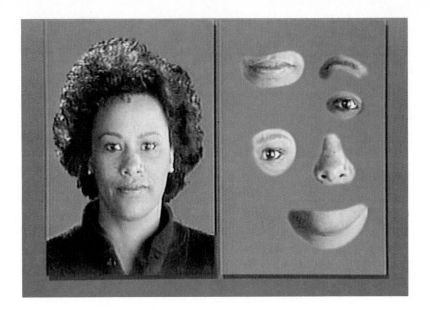

Shown are Fantz stimuli; babies prefer the complete face to the one in disarray (*Discovering Psychology,* 1990, Program 5).

with or signalling soon-to-come pleasures. In addition to recording these simple responses and others, such as smiling, crying, and sticking the tongue out, devices can record electrical responses from specific brain regions, degree of dilation of the pupil of the eye, or heart rate. Each of these responses tells the researcher something about the babies' responses to different events.

For example, in 1958, **Robert Fantz** began to study babies' preferential looking and fascination with novelty as a form of silent speech. He observed that babies preferred objects with contours to those that were plain, complex ones to simple ones, and whole faces to faces with features in disarray. This breakthrough in understanding soon led other researchers to discover just how active the minds of infants and young children really are.

CONTINUITY, STAGES, AND CRITICAL PERIODS

An important issue in developmental psychology is the extent to which development is characterized by *continuity* or *discontinuity*. Some psychologists take the position that development is essentially continuous; they believe it occurs through the accumulation of *quantitative* changes. According to this view, we become more skillful in thinking, talking, or using our muscles in much the same way that we become taller—through the cumulative action of the same continuing processes. In contrast, other psychologists see development as a succession of reorganizations—behavior is *qualitatively* different in different *age-specific life periods*. In this view, particular aspects of development are discontinuous, although development, as a whole, is a continuous process. Thus, newborns are seen not as less dependent on the mother than they were before birth (a quantitative change) but as dependent in different ways. They exhibit a physical dependence that is different and a new dimension of psychological dependence (qualitative changes).

Psychologists who believe development is discontinuous look for and theorize about **developmental stages,** qualitatively different levels of development. They believe that different behaviors appear at different ages or life periods, because different underlying processes are operating during those periods. The term *stage* is reserved for an interval of time in which there are some observed qualitative differences in physical, mental, or behavioral functioning.

The concept of stages implies a progression toward an expected end state (Cairns & Valsinger, 1984). Developmental stages are assumed to occur always in the same sequence; each stage is a necessary building block for the next. Children may go through the stages at different rates but not in different orders. A recent cross-sectional study of the activity of the cerebral hemispheres reveals the existence of both continuity and discontinuity but each occurs on a different side of the brain (Thatcher et al., 1987). The EEG patterns of activity in the right and left hemispheres was studied in more than 500 subjects ranging in age from 2 months to early adulthood. As can be seen in **Figure 5.5,** the left hemisphere develops in sudden growth spurts, while the changes in the right hemisphere occur gradually and continuously across this age range. The timing of the abrupt EEG changes in the left hemisphere overlaps the timing of Piaget's theorized stages of cognitive devel-

FIGURE 5.5 *EEG ACTIVITY IN THE CEREBRAL HEMISPHERES*

The graph shows the findings of research on 577 children, ages 2 months to early adulthood. The electrical activity in the right (front-white) and left (rear-black) hemispheres at each age period is compared to an adult comprehension level. While the development shown in the right hemisphere is continuous, there are growth spurts and discontinuities in the left hemisphere at early ages that correspond to Piaget's cognitive development stages.

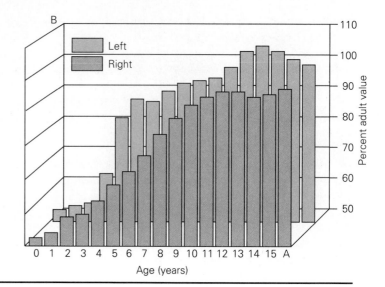

opment—stages that would have to involve differential degrees of left hemisphere development.

Related to the concept of developmental stages is the concept of critical periods. A **critical period** is a sensitive time during development when an organism is optimally ready to acquire a particular behavior if certain stimuli and experiences occur. If those stimuli and experiences do not occur, the organism does not develop the behavior at that time and it will have a difficult time doing so later. Research attempts to determine whether certain experiences must occur in the early years for normal development to proceed. Experimental evidence supports the idea that critical periods for certain functions occur in animals and humans. For example, salamander tadpoles usually start swimming immediately upon birth. If they are prevented from swimming during their first eight days (by being kept in an anesthetizing solution), they swim normally as soon as they are released. However, if they are kept in the solution four or five days longer, they are never able to swim; the critical period has passed (Carmichael, 1926). Likewise, dogs and monkeys raised in isolation for a few months after birth behave in bizarre ways throughout their lives, even if they are later reared with other normal animals (Scott, 1963).

Malnutrition can impair mental capacities permanently if it occurs shortly before birth and for a few months thereafter (when the brain is growing rapidly) but not when it occurs later in life (Wurtman, 1982). Children raised in institutions with minimal social attachments to adult caretakers show attentional and so-

cial problems in school even when they are adopted after the age of 4 years into caring families (Tizard & Hodge, 1978). From these findings, it seems reasonable to conclude that there are times in the early life of most organisms when optimum development is vulnerable to critical-period effects. There is one startling exception to this rule; it comes in the area of *intellectual development*. Although children's intellectual development is sensitive to environmental change, deprivation in early years does not necessarily cause permanent handicaps (see Rutter, 1979). We attribute the development of intelligence in the face of adversity to the "plasticity," or adaptability, of the human brain (Kolb, 1989). The fascinating case of a tragically abused girl, *Genie*, "the wild child of California," illustrates both the critical-period effect on language development and the human ability to overcome early intellectual deficits (Pines, 1981).

> In 1970, a mistreated girl of 13 was found in California. She had been isolated in a small dark room by her father and had not heard human speech since infancy. She was a pitiful, malnourished, unsocialized creature of only 59 pounds, unable to stand erect or to speak. She had been kept naked and harnessed in nearly total isolation, forced to sleep in a straitjacket in a caged crib, and forbidden to make any noise or to have anyone speak to her. Her mother, nearly blind and unable to take care of her daughter, was terrified of her violent, disturbed husband. Eventually, she ran away with the child.

When first tested, Genie scored at the level of normal 1 year olds. But under the guidance and intensive training of a young UCLA researcher, Susan Curtiss, and other teachers, Genie made rapid progress in many areas of functioning. Her performance on many tests that did not require verbal abilities increased consistently over the years; her IQ score nearly doubled from 38 in 1971 to 74 in 1977 (which is still well below the average of 100). Although she learned many hundreds of words and could communicate effectively, Genie seemed to have passed the critical period for language acquisition. She never asked questions, and because she could not understand grammatical principles that put order and meaning in language, her speech was similar to a garbled telegram. Genie's right brain activities had not been impaired by her years of deprivation, but the development of her left hemisphere had been seriously limited by her failure to use language for all those years. Despite training and practice, normal language development would now be unlikely. (A full account of Genie's story is found in *Genie: A Psycholinguistic Study of a Modern-day "Wild Child"* by Susan Curtiss, 1977.)

SUMMING UP

Developmental psychologists study the processes and changes that accompany different ages and stages of human development, from conception through infancy and childhood and throughout the entire life span. The major independent variable is time, or the age of the organism being studied. A major concern of psychologists is understanding the contributions of genetics to what makes us human, unique, and different from others of our species, and to what goes wrong in our functioning. Physical growth and the development of many abilities follow a genetically based timetable of maturation, but early chemical and sensory experience also plays a role in maturation. Environmental inputs can modify, to some extent, genetically inherited predispositions, such as shyness and height. The sensory systems that are most well developed at or soon after birth are hearing, smell, and touch, with fine distinctions being made by the neonate. Vision, however, develops more slowly.

The nature-nurture controversy is an old, but continuing, debate about what is more vital to human development: what we bring into the world or what the world brings to us. Early nineteenth-century thinkers argued that the case of the Wild Boy of Av-eyron demonstrated what the lack of human nurturing means for humans. Others felt that the case showed that nature provides many skills that are essential for survival. Current wisdom suggests that nature and nurture always interact to determine any complex behavioral pattern. Infants are born with many abilities and active minds prewired to survive by getting nourishment, defending against harm, and making social contact with adult caregivers. Researchers have studied the behavior of infants through normative investigations that establish standards of behavior typical for each age period; research using longitudinal, cross-sectional, and sequential designs; and studies of overt behaviors, such as sucking, looking, and touching, that index the baby's preferences, feelings, and mental functioning.

While some developmental psychologists argue that development is continuous over time, others take the discontinuity view that specific functions are qualitatively different at different age periods. The latter also outline a series of stages that all children must go through in a fixed sequence to achieve optimal performance; there are optimal times or critical periods when the organism is most ready to profit from appropriate stimulation, and when, if it is severely deprived, it will suffer handicaps. The case of Genie illustrates what can happen to an individual who has missed the critical period for language acquisition.

ACQUIRING LANGUAGE

Imagine that you lived in a country where no one could translate for you or teach you the language. Would you be able to learn this foreign language—let's call it language Z—on your own? How would you figure out what language Z words meant and the grammatical rules by which the language was organized? How soon might you become fluent? Could you learn the rules of polite conversation? Figuring out a new language without a translator is a problem of epic proportions.

Infants, who know no language at all, are faced with an even bigger problem and yet, in the span of only a few years, with little formal instruction, and often in spite of faulty or incomplete information, young children become fluent speakers of any language they hear spoken, provided they are given the opportunity to speak. By the time they are 6 years old, children can analyze language into its minimal, separable units of sound and meaning, use rules they have discovered by themselves for combining sounds into words and words into meaningful sentences, and take an active part in coherent conversations. To acquire all of these abilities in just a few short years, infants and young children must be excellent language learners.

A study of people whose first language is **American Sign Language** (ASL) supports the point. ASL is the language of the hearing-impaired community in the United States. It is a true language, with its own system of symbols and grammar. Many of the adults who use ASL as their main language first learned ASL at different ages. Until recently, the hearing-impaired did not uniformly learn ASL as a matter of course—many were taught to lip-read and use vocal speech instead. Also, many hearing-impaired children are born to hearing parents who do not know ASL. Researchers used the fact that many ASL speakers learned at different ages to study language acquisition (see **Figure 5.6**).

Researchers identified hearing-impaired adults who had been fluent signers of ASL for many years. Some of these signers had been exposed to ASL since birth, others did not encounter it until they started school at 5, and still others hadn't encountered ASL until they were teenagers. Even though all of the signers were able to use ASL

FIGURE 5.6   *GIRL USING ASL*

quite fluently, there were differences in their abilities to use it in very complex ways. Adults who had used ASL since birth or early childhood were much better at complex language tasks than adults who had started learning ASL later, even though all of the adults studied had been signers for 30 years or more (Newport, 1990).

In a follow-up study, the researchers did a similar analysis of people who learned English as a second language. In second-language learning, there was a clear advantage for those who had started learning English at a young age. Thus, it seems that infancy and early childhood are the peak years for learning language, whether it be a first or second language (Newport, 1990).

Why is it that infants are such expert language learners? Part of the answer to this question is that infants are born with some important language learning abilities. However, as we shall see, this innate language readiness is only part of the answer, since social factors in conversational language and children's cognitive ability to learn new rules also play major roles in language acquisition.

INNATE PRECURSORS TO LANGUAGE LEARNING

Depending on where a child happens to be born, he or she may end up as a native speaker of any one of about 4000 of the world's different languages. While linguists agree that the ability to learn language is biologically based—that we are born with an innate language capacity or universal grammar—there is no universal language. This means that the predisposition to learn language must be remarkably flexible as well as strong (Meier, 1991). There are five factors that many developmental linguists point to as especially important in language mastery by children: their high level of social interest, their speech perception and speech production abilities, their language acquisition device, and finally, the time they spent listening to their mothers' sounds while still in utero. Let's see how each of these factors contributes to making children language experts so quickly.

Social Interest

Infants are social beings. To newborns, humans are very interesting and emotionally important stimuli, more so than anything else that infants encounter. For example, studies show that infants prefer stimuli that have many rounded contours and edges and that move and emit sounds—in other words, objects that look and act similar to people. Without this interest in social interaction and in communicating with others, there would be no motivation for children to learn language.

Moreover, language acquisition is dependent on children's participation in a supportive social environment. This dependence of language acquisition on social interaction is seen in the case study of a boy with normal hearing who was born to hearing-impaired parents.

The parents spoke only in American Sign Language but exposed their child to a daily diet of television viewing where he heard people talking; but because he was sickly and confined to his home, the only real people he had contact with were his parents. By the age of 3 he was able to use sign language fluently—but could not speak or understand spoken English. The researcher concluded that a child can learn a language only if there are chances for interaction with real people who speak the language (Moskowitz, 1978).

Speech Perception Abilities

Except for children born with hearing deficits, all infants can hear many of the sound contrasts that languages use to distinguish between different meanings. In English, *bit* and *pit* have different meanings. We know that they are different words because we can hear the difference between *b-* and *p-*, which are different **phonemes,** or minimal, meaningful sound units. There are about 45 distinct phonemes in English. Researchers using the habituation paradigm to study perception of speech sounds in infants from 1 to 4 months of age have shown that newborns can distinguish all of them.

Infants were given special pacifier nipples that electronically recorded their rate of spontaneous sucking (babies this age will suck, even when they are not being fed). Then the infants heard synthetic speech sounds, for example *ba ba ba ba ba,* which were *contingent* on their sucking; that is, every time an infant sucked, he or she heard a *ba.* After a while, babies became bored with the sound (became habituated to it), and their rate of sucking decreased. Then the researchers played the infants a test stimulus: either a *ba ba ba* sound or a *pa pa pa* sound. Infants who heard *pa pa pa* dishabituated—they started sucking more rapidly, presumably to hear the new sound more. Infants who continued to hear *ba ba ba,* however, did not increase their rate of sucking. Thus, newborns showed sensitivity to the change in phoneme (Eimas et al., 1971).

Moreover, recent studies have shown that infants can hear sound differences that their parents can't. No language uses all of the speech sound contrasts that can be made. A well-known example is the lack of differentiation between the English *r* and *l* in Japanese. Native speakers of Japanese often have a very hard time

hearing the difference between these sounds when they study English. English speakers are also plagued with this problem when they learn new languages: there are a number of sound contrasts that are used in other languages that adult English speakers have a very hard time hearing. Several such contrasts are used in Hindi.

The researcher, Janet Werker, measured the ability of infants learning English and Hindi as well as adults who spoke English and Hindi to hear the differences between the Hindi phonemes. She found that all of the infants, regardless of which language they were learning, could hear the differences until the age of 8 months. However, of the infants older than 8 months and of the adults, only the Hindi-speaking subjects could hear the Hindi contrasts. Thus, infants start out with sensitivities to sounds that they lose if these contrasts are not used in their language (Werker & Lalonde, 1988).

Speech Production Abilities

In addition to their abilities to perceive speech sounds, infants have a biological predisposition to make certain sounds that will later be used in language. The basic apparatus for speech production (the vocal tract) is inborn. Moreover, well before they begin to use true words, infants *babble*, making speechlike sounds, such as *mamama* or *bububu,* and the age of onset of babbling seems to be biologically determined.

Because babbling consists of syllabic vocal sequences, such as *mamama* and *bububu,* it sounds somewhat languagelike. It is also characterized as having an onset at well-defined ages (from 7 to 10 months), with characteristic stages and special features. Indeed, some linguists have argued that babblings are the direct precursors of speech sounds. Specifically, they suggest that a baby babbles all sounds in all languages, and the repertoire is eventually narrowed down only to those sounds found in the language he or she learns (Mowrer, 1960). This view is not entirely accurate because a baby does not babble certain speech sounds (consonant clusters such as *str* in *strong* and *xth* in *sixth.* In addition, some sounds (*r* and *l,* for example) are present in babbling but not in a child's first words. Babbling allows children learning spoken languages to practice making sounds with the vocal apparatus, grouping the sounds into sequences, and adding intonation to those sequences (Clark & Clark, 1977).

New research on the babbling of hearing-impaired children who were exposed to signed languages from birth provides evidence that babbling serves a more significant function in language development. Babbling is not merely a speech-based phenomenon tied to maturation of the vocal cords and mouth muscles responsible for speaking and to speech modalities in the brain. Rather, babbling is tied to the abstract structure of language and to an expressive capacity that is capable of processing different types of signals, either spoken or signed. Hearing-impaired babies of hearing-impaired parents babble with their hands in the same rhythmic, repetitive fashion in which hearing infants babble vocally.

> Data were collected from 5 children at three age periods (10, 12, and 14 months); two were hearing-impaired infants of hearing-impaired parents acquiring ASL and three were hearing infants of hearing parents acquiring spoken language. Videotapes were made of all types of hand gestures and vocal activities of these subjects during several taping sessions. They were analyzed and coded reliably for being gestures (such as pointing at things) and syllabic manual babbling (a reduced set of combinations of phonetic units that had an organization seen only in signed languages and without an external referent or meaning).
>
> Hearing and hearing-impaired children produced similar types and amounts of gestures but differed dramatically in producing manual babbling. The hearing-impaired infants used an organized set of 13 different handshapes repeatedly. This manual babbling accounted for up to 71 percent of their manual activity by age 14 months, but only 15 percent for the hearing infants. Because manual babbling shares the basic features of vocal babbling, "babbling is thus the mechanism by which infants discover the map between the structure of language and the means for producing this structure" (Petitto & Marentette, 1991, p. 1495).

LAD: The Language Acquisition Device

Finally, many theorists have agreed that, in addition to these innate abilities, there is a biologically based **language acquisition device** (LAD) that plays a major role in children's language learning. Psycholinguist **Noam Chomsky** (1965, 1975), the proponent of LAD, argues that children are born with biologically predetermined mental structures that facilitate the comprehension and production of speech. LAD limits the hypotheses children generate about the grammar of language, narrowing their possible language options and making it easier for them to discover grammatical patterns and relationships.

There are three lines of evidence for LAD. First, virtually all human beings (except those with extreme impairments or who experienced early social deprivation) learn language very quickly. Second, they do so based on input that does not provide enough information to allow them to learn how to extract grammatical rules.

Finally, parental feedback is not sufficient to teach children grammatical rules.

Parents tend to correct children's utterances on the basis of their *truth value* rather than on their accurate grammatical quality. When a child says, "One, two, I have two foots!" the mother may respond enthusiastically, "That's right! You really know how to count now." The mother is unlikely to frown and say, "No, silly, you have two FEET, not two foots!" However, when children utter a grammatically correct but factually incorrect sentence, they are likely to be corrected. For example, when a child calls a muffin a *cookie,* he is likely to hear his mother say, "No, that's not a cookie. It's a muffin" (Brown & Hanlon, 1970). Neither learned imitation nor parental correction, then, can explain grammatical development very well. Moreover, many aspects of language emerge and evolve at particular periods—critical language acquisition periods—that correspond more closely with physical and cognitive maturation than with particular learning experiences (Lenneberg, 1969).

Prenatal Listening Experience

One final factor that favors early language acquisition is prenatal listening experience. Until recently, researchers have assumed that experience with language begins at birth. A compelling series of studies, however, challenges this assumption, suggesting that babies listen to sounds while they are still *in utero*. Researchers used rate of sucking as a dependent measure of preferences for sounds heard in the womb.

> In the first study, mothers-to-be read aloud from a storybook, twice a day during the last two months of pregnancy. A day or two after birth, their babies were tested for story preferences. The infants were given a nonnutritive nipple to suck. If the infant sped up her rate of sucking, a tape of one story was played, and if she slowed down her rate of sucking, another story was played. One story was the same as the story the infant had heard prenatally, while the other was a new story. In order to control for effects of particular rates of sucking, half of the infants heard the "familiar" story when they sped up and half heard it when they slowed down. The researchers found that infants adjusted their rate of sucking in order to hear the story their mothers had read aloud during pregnancy. This means that they preferred listening to stories they had heard in utero, showing that they must have been listening (DeCasper and Spence, 1986).

But what exactly do fetuses hear? After all, they are immersed in water, and there are competing bodily noises that may block out incoming sound. Using paradigms such as the one described above, the research team explored this question by examining other neonatal listening preferences. They found that, although infants prefer to listen to their mothers' voices over the voices of other women, they show no such preference for their fathers' voices (DeCasper & Prescott, 1983). This difference occurs because mothers' voices are audible to the fetus in utero, but outside voices are not. In another study, researchers compared infants' preference for normal speech to speech that had been filtered so that no words were audible, leaving only the intonation. If the speaker was a stranger, infants preferred the clear, unmuffled version. However, if the tape was of the infants' mothers, infants showed no preference for the unmuffled version. The researchers concluded that infants may like muffled maternal speech equally well early on because it sounds similar to what they heard *in utero* (Spence & DeCasper, 1987). While it is true that listening begins before birth, the speech that fetuses hear may be muffled and, thus, lacking much of the information that is available to infants once they are born.

In spite of all these early factors that contribute to the relative ease with which infants master language, there is still much work for the prelinguistic infant to do. The next sections outline some of the accomplishments children must achieve: development of communication skills, word learning, and the acquisition of grammatical rules. These three areas roughly correspond to the academic disciplines of phonology, syntax, semantics, and pragmatics (see **Table 5.3**).

COMMUNICATION SKILLS

Without language you can't communicate abstract ideas, but by using nonverbal gestures you can indicate you are hungry or tired; prelinguistic infants use nonverbal means to communicate. They cry when distressed and coo and smile when pleased. At first, infant communication relies greatly on parents as interpreters, but over time, children take on more of the communication burden. Infants use the words they learn to build more sophisticated ways to communicate.

Parents work to keep their infants' interest and to introduce them to language. When adults speak to infants and young children they use a special form that differs from adult speech: an exaggerated, high-pitched intonation known as **motherese.** This way of speaking appears to serve a number of functions, among them to get and hold the infants' attention, communicate affect, and mark turn-taking in parent-infant dialogues. A recent study demonstrates that infants prefer motherese to other kinds of speech.

A sample of 48 4-month-old infants listened to tape-recorded speech samples of other mothers talking to their babies, and these infants also heard

---

TABLE 5.3   *THE STRUCTURE OF LANGUAGE*

Grammar is the field of study that seeks to describe the way language is structured and used. It includes several domains:

   Phonology—the study of the way sounds are put together to form words.

   A **phoneme** is the smallest unit of speech that distinguishes between any two utterances. For example, *b* and *p* distinguish *bin* from *pin.*

   Phonetics is the study and classification of speech sounds.

   Syntax—the way in which words are strung together to form sentences. For example, subject (I) + verb (like) + object (you) is a standard English word order.

   A **morpheme** is the minimum distinctive unit of grammar that cannot be divided without losing its meaning. The word *bins* has two morphemes, *bin* and *s,* indicating the plural.

   Semantics—the study of the meanings of words and their changes over time. **Lexical meaning** is the dictionary meaning of a word. Meaning is sometimes conveyed by the *context* of a word in a sentence ("Run *fast*" versus "Make the knot *fast*") or the *inflection* with which it is spoken (try emphasizing different words in *a white house cat*).

   Pragmatics—rules for participating in conversations; social conventions for communicating, sequencing sentences, and responding appropriately to others.

adult-directed speech by the same women. The infants' preferences were measured by the number of times they turned their heads in the direction of one of these types of speech stimuli. The majority of infants revealed a clear preference for motherese by turning more often to listen to its high intonation (Fernald, 1985).

So one way that motherese helps infants to acquire language is by keeping them interested in and attentive to the things that their parents say to them. Furthermore, motherese intonations contain affective messages without words. Parents use rising intonation to engage babies' attention, falling intonation to comfort them, and short staccato bursts as prohibitions. Research by **Anne Fernald** and her colleagues shows that parents in many different cultures use these patterns and that babies understand them, even if they are not in their native tongue (Fernald et al., 1989).

Probably without realizing it, parents work to introduce their infants to language by engaging them in proto-dialogues. At first, these dialogues are very one sided; parents will talk and pause at certain points to let infants respond. Parents will accept as valid responses anything the babies do, even burping or sneezing.

As babies get older, parents become more demanding conversational partners, requiring at first that babies verbalize, later that they use actual words, and later still that they use words relevant to the topic at hand. This pattern of gradually increasing demands on the child and decreasing parental support is called *scaffolding*. With this experience, young children become less reliant on their parents as interpreters of communication. The infants learn to use gestures (pointing) and nonverbal vocalizations (whining) to communicate their desires and interests. Eventually, children use their first

Anne Fernald (*Discovering Psychology,* 1990, Program 5)

words for making assertions and requests; they seem to use their very first words to communicate messages to others (Greenfield & Smith, 1976).

Beyond these early communicative skills, there are more skills and knowledge that children must acquire to become fully competent communicators. Adult language users are unaware that they coordinate many different kinds of information in order to communicate effectively. Adults know the "rules" of verbal exchange—they know how to partake in conversations, that people take turns talking and listening, and that new utterances should relate to previous turns. And they appreciate that the rules for conversations differ from the rules for lectures or sermons. In addition, adult speakers are able to make their attempts at communication successful by using a number of different devices (such as body language, intonation, and facial expressions). They also use feedback that they get from listeners to inform their strategies for communication and thus make communication successful. This skill requires the speaker to take the perspective of the listener—for preschoolers, conversations are often separate monologues, similar to trains on parallel tracks, crossing over occasionally (Stone & Church, 1957).

LEARNING WORDS

An important project for children in their first few years of life is acquiring a basic vocabulary. Imagine a straightforward word learning situation: a child and her father are looking at some toys on a table and the father points at one and says, "That's a ball." First, the child must decide what the new word is. Unlike in written language, in spoken language there are seldom any gaps between words. Thus, determining whether the sound unit is *ball* instead of *aball* or *Thatsa* is no trivial achievement. Once she has pulled out the new word, the child must decide to which piece of the world it applies. Again, this is no easy feat. In the situation described, *That's a ball* could mean *table full of toys, the red one, mine all mine,* or *should we play with these?* as well as *that particular object is a ball.*

In spite of these complications, young children are excellent word learners. By the age of 6, the average child is estimated to understand 14,000 words (Templin, 1957). Assuming that most of these words are learned between the ages of 18 months and 6 years, this works out to about nine new words a day, or almost one word per waking hour (Carey, 1978). The cumulative growth of a child's vocabulary is shown in **Figure 5.7.**

Initially, during the *one-word phase,* children use only one word at a time. These first single words are usually concrete nouns or verbs. Children use them to

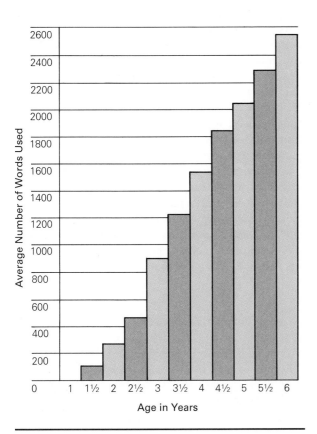

FIGURE 5.7 CHILDREN'S GROWTH IN VOCABULARY

The number of words a child can use increases rapidly between the ages of 1½ and 6. This study shows children's average vocabularies at intervals of six months. *Source:* B. A. Moskowitz, "The Acquisition of Language," *Scientific American,* Inc. All rights reserved. Reprinted by permission.

At around 18 months, children's word learning often takes off at an amazing rate. At this age, children might point to every object in a room and ask, "What's that?" Researchers have called this phase the *naming explosion* because children begin to acquire new words, especially names for objects, at a rapidly increasing rate.

Parents help in early word learning. They provide many opportunities for children to encounter new words. The nature of these opportunities differs from culture to culture. Middle-class U.S. parents often teach their children the names for objects by reading them picture books and playing naming games with them. By contrast, in the Kaluli culture of Papua New Guinea, parents teach their children the honorific titles of their relatives and social regulation terms (Schieffelin, 1985). Consider the task facing Chinese children who learn nearly 3000 Chinese characters and their combinations in thousands of words—some of which are selected for their sound and others for their meaning. Rote memorization during the first six years of elementary school is the only sure avenue to correct pronunciation and understanding (Stevenson, 1990).

Learning the names for objects is only the first stage of language learning. As children grow older, they begin to express more abstract meanings, going beyond talking about their physical world to begin talking about their psychological world as well. For example, around the age of 2, children begin to use words such as *dream, forget, pretend, believe, guess,* and *hope,* as they talk about internal states (Shatz et al., 1983). They also refer to emotional states with words such as *happy, sad,* and *angry.* Finally, after cognitive advances that occur later in childhood, they understand and use abstract words such as *truth, justice,* and *idea.*

PUTTING IT ALL TOGETHER: ACQUIRING GRAMMAR

As adult users of language, we know how to combine words into meaningful larger units. Combining words greatly increases the number of meanings and the level of complexity of those meanings. For example, "Christina put the package in Phil's box" and "Phil put the box in Christina's package" use the same words but have very different meanings. As anyone who has learned a second language will attest, languages differ considerably in how they combine word units to make grammatical sentences. For example, in English, the typical ordering of units in a sentence is subject-verb-object, but, in Japanese, the ordering is subject-object-verb.

During the *one-word stage,* the child actively develops hypotheses about the way to combine words into

name objects that move, make a noise, or can be manipulated—such as, mama, ball, and dog. During the one-word phase, children sometimes *overextend* words, using them incorrectly to cover a wide range of objects. For example, they may use the word *dog* to refer to all animals or the word *moon* to refer to all round objects, including clocks and coins. Perhaps, when children overextend words, they are not labeling the object but commenting on it. Thus, the child who points to a clock and says, "Moon," may not mean, "That is a moon" but "That looks like a moon" or "My, how moonlike!" Another possible explanation for overextensions is that children are doing the best they can with limited vocabularies. If a child doesn't know the words for *cow, sheep,* and *pig,* he may use *dog,* not because he thinks that cows are dogs but because it's the closest word he has for a four-legged animal; it fits better than *table.*

sentences. After the naming explosion, which occurs between 18 months and 2 years, children begin to use their one-word utterances in sequence to convey more complex meanings. By combining words into two-word utterances, children can communicate more meaning than simple identification. For adults to understand two-word utterances, they must know the context in which the words are spoken. "Tanya ball," for example, could mean, "Tanya wants the ball" or "Tanya throws the ball." At this *two-word stage,* children across widely differing language communities tend to break down the world into similar linguistic categories with two-word utterances. For instance, ten children speaking different languages (English, Samoan, Finnish, Hebrew, and Swedish) were found to talk mostly about three categories: movers, movable objects, and locations (Braine, 1976). When Tanya kicks a ball, for example, the mover is Tanya and the movable object is ball. Tanya then verbalizes the sequence "Tanya ball."

After two words, sequence size continues to increase. From the two-word stage on into early multiword sentences, children's speech is *telegraphic:* filled with short, simple sequences or sentences, using many content words (mostly nouns and verbs) but lacking tense endings and plurals. Telegraphic speech also lacks function words, such as *the, and,* and *of,* which help express the relationships between words and which the language user adds in a predictable order as she matures. For example, "Bill hit ball window break" is a telegraphic message.

In addition to learning how to fill out the full grammatical form of sentences, children must learn how to put words together. For example, by the age of 2, English-speaking children have learned that word order is important and that the three critical elements are actor-action-object, usually arranged in that order. However, young children make word order too important—by ignoring the function words, they typically misinterpret "Mary was followed by her little lamb to school" as *Mary* (actor) *followed* (action) *her lamb* (object). Children must also learn how to rearrange the elements of a statement to form questions and negatives. To make a sentence negative, young children may simply put a no in front of it: "No the sun is shining." Later, they learn where to insert the negative: "The sun is not shining."

An additional grammatical skill that children need to acquire is using morphemes, such as *-'s, -ed,* and *-ing,* to mark certain kinds of meaning, such as possession (Maria's), past tense (danced), and continuing action (still laughing). From a study of the regular error patterns of children at each stage of language development, it is apparent that they try out hypotheses about the way grammatical morphemes should be used. Sometimes, of course, their hypotheses are wrong.

One very common error is **overregularization,** in which a rule is applied too widely, resulting in incorrect linguistic forms. For example, once children learn the past-tense rule (adding *-ed* to the verb), they add *-ed* to all verbs, forming words such as *doed* and *breaked.* As children learn the rule for plurals (adding the sound *-s* or *-z* to the end of a word), they again overextend the rule, creating words such as *foots* and *mouses.* Overregularization is an especially interesting error to psycholinguists, because it usually appears *after* children have learned and used the correct forms of verbs and nouns. The children first use the correct verb forms (for example, *came* and *went*) apparently because they learned them as separate vocabulary items; but when they learn the general rule for the past tense, they immediately extend it to all verbs, even to words that are exceptions to the rule—words that they previously used correctly. To researchers, such mistakes are evidence that language learning depends on acquiring *general rules of grammar,* rather than just imitating what adults say (Slobin, 1979). So, for developmental psychologists interested in language acquisition, the common errors of childhood are more than sources of amusement; they offer exciting glimpses into the complex mental processes that underlie all human speech.

SUMMING UP

Although language learning presents children with a host of problems to solve, they meet this challenge readily. They are master language learners because they come into the world prepared with innately based precursors to language, supportive social contexts, and the cognitive abilities to solve problems and learn rules. Some psycholinguists assume that language acquisition relies on an inborn language-acquisition device, a basic mental structure that limits the hypotheses about possible word arrangements and sequences. Nurture adds to these inherited gifts of nature in the form of culture and parental stimulation and interchange. Experience and practice overcome the complexity of learning a language's specific rules of grammar as well as the rules that govern conversations. There are fixed stages of word learning that proceed from a preverbal babbling stage, to a one-word stage, to a two-word stage, and finally to the limitless utterances of short sentences in the telegraphic stage. Psycholinguists learn about the hypotheses children are entertaining and about their complex thought processes by studying the mistakes children make in sending and receiving verbal messages. Language development and cognitive development are thus entwined.

COGNITIVE DEVELOPMENT

How and when do children begin to reason, think, plan strategies, and solve problems? How does the way a child understands physical and social reality change at different developmental ages? **Cognitive development** is the study of the processes and products of the mind as they emerge and change over time. Although largely focused on intelligent aspects of "higher mental processes," the study of cognitive development is broad enough to include social cognition and social communication (thoughts about other people and the way one relates to them). Cognitive development is also concerned with the child's theory of mind. Do children know objects still exist even when they can't see them? Do they know that it is possible to believe in ideas that aren't true and that people, but not objects, have desires and dreams? Developmental psychologists want to know the way children think and what they think.

There are two dominant views on the nature of the human cognitive system. The *information-processing approach* uses computer information-processing as the model for how people think and deal with information. The *cognitive-development view* derives from the pioneering work of the late Swiss psychologist **Jean Piaget.**

PIAGET'S INSIGHTS INTO MENTAL GROWTH

No one has contributed more to our knowledge of the ways that children think, reason, and solve problems than Jean Piaget. For nearly 50 years, he observed children's intellectual development. Perhaps Piaget's interest in cognitive development grew out of his own intellectually active youth: as a child, Piaget studied mollusks; in 1910, at age 14, he was published for the first time; at 16 he became the curator of a museum; and in later years he worked as a biologist. His training in biological methods of observation helped him investigate human cognition as a form of biological adaptation. Piaget saw the human mind as an active biological system that seeks, selects, interprets, and reorganizes environmental information to fit with or adjust to its own existing mental structures.

Piaget began his quest to understand the nature of the child's mind by carefully observing the behavior of his own three children. He would pose problems to them, observe their responses, slightly alter the situations, and once again observe their responses. Piaget used simple demonstrations and sensitive interviews with his own children and with other children to generate complex theories about early mental development.

How does a child transform specific, concrete information gathered through sensory experience into general, abstract concepts that are not limited to any immediate stimulus situation? To answer this question, Piaget studied the ways children perceive certain situations and the ways they come to know about physical reality. His interest was not in the amount of information children possessed but in the ways their thinking and inner representations of outer reality changed at different stages in their development.

There are three key components of Piaget's approach to cognitive development: (a) schemes; (b) assimilation and accommodation; and (c) the four stages of cognitive growth.

Schemes

A 3-month-old infant thinks and knows about the world in very practical, hands-on, mouth-on motor-action responses to sensory stimulation. This infant cognition involves sensorimotor intelligence, rather than symbolic representation. According to Piaget, sensorimotor intelligence consists of **schemes,** mental structures or programs that guide sensorimotor sequences, such as sucking, looking, grasping, and pushing. Schemes are enduring abilities and dispositions to carry out specific kinds of action sequences that aid the child's adaptation to its environment—with little or no thought as we know it. With practice, elementary schemes are combined, integrated, and differentiated into ever more complex, diverse action patterns, as when a child pushes away undesired objects to seize a desired one behind them. At first, these sensorimotor sequences are dependent on the physical presence of objects that can be sucked, or watched, or grasped, for example. But thereafter, mental structures increasingly incorporate *symbolic representations* of outer reality. As they do, the child performs more complex mental operations (Gallagher & Reid, 1981; Piaget, 1977).

Assimilation and Accommodation

According to Piaget, there are two basic processes at work in cognitive growth, assimilation and accommodation. In assimilation, the new is changed to fit the known; in accommodation, the known is changed to fit the new. **Assimilation** modifies new environmental information to fit into what is already known. External sensory data coming into the child are changed in line with existing internal, cognitive-structural units of its sensorimotor schemes. **Accommodation** restructures or modifies the child's existing schemes so that new information can fit in better. Consider the transitions a baby must make from sucking at mother's breast, to sucking the nipple of a bottle, to sipping through a straw, and then to drinking from a cup. The initial sucking response is a reflex action present at birth, but it must be modified somewhat so that the child's mouth fits the

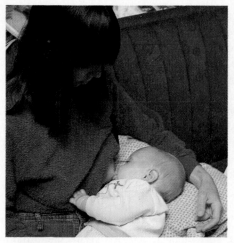

Although an infant will begin to suck a bottle just the way he or she sucked a breast (assimilation), the infant will soon discover that some changes are necessary (accommodation). The child will make an even greater accommodation in the transitions from bottle to straw to cup.

shape and size of the mother's nipple. In adapting to a bottle, an infant still uses many parts of the sequence unchanged (assimilation), but he must grasp and draw on the rubber nipple somewhat differently than before and learn to hold the bottle at an appropriate angle (accommodation). The steps from bottle to straw to cup require more accommodation, but still rely on earlier skills of sucking and swallowing fluids at particular rates.

Piaget saw cognitive development as the result of constant interweaving of assimilation and accommodation in an upward spiraling process. Assimilation keeps and adds to what exists, thereby connecting the present with the past. Accommodation results from new problems posed by the environment. These *discrepancies* between the child's old ideas and new experiences are an important motivator of changes in cognitive development. They force a child to develop more adaptive inner structures and processes, that, in turn, permit creative and appropriate action to meet future challenges. Both assimilation and accommodation are needed, but they are needed in balance. Through these two processes, children's behavior and knowledge becomes less dependent on concrete external reality, coming to rely more on abstract thought. Mental growth always follows the path from reliance on *appearances* to reliance on *rules* and from the concrete and physical to the abstract and symbolic.

Stages in Cognitive Development

There are four qualitatively different Piagetian stages of cognitive growth: the *sensorimotor stage* (infancy), the *preoperational stage* (early childhood), the

concrete operational stage (middle childhood), and the *formal operational stage* (adolescence). Distinct cognition styles emerge at each stage in this progression from sensory-based reaction to reflective, logical thought. All children are assumed to progress through these stages in the same sequence, although one child may take longer to pass through a given stage than another.

Sensorimotor Stage (Roughly from birth to age 2.) So many new cognitive achievements appear during the first two years of a child's life that Piaget subdivided this first stage of sensorimotor cognitive development into six substages. We will summarize only the two main trends in this period: changes in how the infant interacts with its environment and the infant's understanding of object permanence.

In the early months, an infant knows only "in the sense of recognizing or anticipating familiar, recurring objects and happenings, and 'thinks' in the sense of behaving towards them . . . in predictable, organized, and often adaptive ways" (Flavell, 1985, p. 13). During the first year, the sensorimotor sequences are improved, combined, coordinated, and integrated (sucking and grasping, looking and manipulating, for example). They become more varied as the infant tests different aspects of the environment, discovers that her actions have an effect on external outer events, and begins to perform what appear to be intentional, directed behaviors toward clear goals. But in the sensorimotor period, the child is tied to her immediate environment and motor-action schemes because she lacks the cognitive ability to represent objects symbolically.

The most important cognitive acquisition of the infancy period is the ability to form mental representations of absent objects—those with which the child is not in direct sensorimotor contact. By the end of the second year, the child has developed this ability. **Object permanence** refers to a child's perceptions that objects exist and behave independently of her actions or awareness. In the first months of life, Nicole and Alexis would follow objects with their eyes, but when the objects disappeared from view, the girls turned away as if the objects had also disappeared from their minds. Around 3 months of age, however, they would keep looking at the place where the objects had disappeared from view. If their mother exited their bedroom through one door and returned soon after through another, they would show signs of surprise. Clearly, something new was going on in their minds; perceptually absent objects were being actively represented mentally. These observations are supported by a considerable body of experimental research on children's visual tracking and surprise responses to objects that move, disappear behind a screen, and reappear in expected or unexpected locations. The results indicate that object permanence develops gradually during this first stage of cognitive development and is solidly formed before age 2 (Flavell, 1985).

Preoperational Stage   (Roughly from 2 to 7 years of age.) The big cognitive advance in this next developmental stage is the consolidation of representational thought—the ability to represent objects mentally that are not physically present. Although representational thought begins in the sensorimotor period, it becomes fully functioning in the preoperational stage. Except for this development, Piaget characterizes the preoperational stage according to what the child can't do, such as solve problems using logical operations. Three of the most interesting features of the child's mind in this period are egocentrism (self-centered focus), the inability to distinguish mental from physical worlds, and centration (focus on only central features of objects).

At the preoperational stage, young children can imagine a world from only one perspective—their own *egocentric* point of view. This egocentrism is evident during their conversations with other children, when they often look as if they are talking to themselves, rather than interacting. **Egocentrism** refers to children's inability to take the perspective of another person or to imagine a scene from any perspective other than their own. Piaget showed children a three-dimensional, three-mountain scene and asked them to describe what a teddy bear standing on the far side would see; his subjects could not describe this scene from that other perspective accurately until about age 7 (Piaget & Inhelder, 1967). In later research, however, when looking at scenes more familiar to them, children of 3 and 4

were able to turn movable images to show someone else's view, though they still did poorly with a stationary scene such as the one Piaget used (Borke, 1975).

The child is unable to distinguish her or his mental world from the physical world. We can see this in their tendency to physicalize mental phenomena, such as when they say that dreams are pictures on the walls that everyone can see. We can also see this in their *animistic thinking*—attributing life and mental processes to physical, inanimate objects and events. Thus, clouds cover the sun "on purpose" because "we ought to go to sleep" (Piaget, 1929). Animism gets carried over into adult thinking in some cultures' spiritual beliefs: many American Indian cultures perceive everything in nature as part of "one great system of all-conscious and interrelated life" (Cushing, 1974).

Children at the preoperational stage typically ignore the less noticeable features of objects because they are captivated by more perceptually striking features. A child's central focus on a single perceptual factor is called **centration.** Piaget's classic demonstration of a child's inability to understand that a given amount of a substance does not change when it is poured into containers of various sizes and shapes illustrates the phenomenon of centration.

> When an equal amount of lemonade is poured into two glasses, children of ages 5, 6, and 7 all report that the glasses contain the same amount; but when the lemonade from one glass is poured into a tall, thin glass, they have differing opinions. The 5 year olds know that the lemonade in the tall glass is the same lemonade (qualitative identity), but they believe that somehow it has become more. The 6 year olds are uncertain about the nature of the changed quantity, but also say the tall glass has more. The 7 year olds know there is no difference between the amounts. The younger children still rely on appearance; the older ones rely on a rule. They also take into account two dimensions—height and width—while the younger children center on a single, perceptually salient dimension—the height of the glass— which is usually a cue for "more."

Concrete Operational Stage   (Roughly from 7 to 11 years of age.) At this stage, the child is capable of *mental operations* but still cannot reason abstractly. The deficiencies of the earlier stages no longer operate as long as the child is dealing with concrete, perceptually visible objects. For example, if a child sees that Adam is taller than Zara and, later, that Zara is taller than Tanya, the child can reason that Adam is the tallest of the three. But if the information about their relative

This 5-year-old girl is aware that the two containers have the same amount of colored liquid. However, when the liquid from one is poured into a taller container, she indicates that there is more liquid in the taller one. She has not yet grasped the concept of conservation.

heights is presented to the child verbally and he is not permitted to directly observe their height, he cannot make the correct conclusion. However, at this stage, children begin to break through their centration, decentering from one physically obvious characteristic to take a second one into account.

The 7 year olds in the lemonade study had mastered the concept of what Piaget called **conservation:** physical properties do not change when nothing is added to them or taken away from them, even though their appearance changes. The lemonade example showed an understanding of conservation of volume; children at this stage also develop an understanding of conservation of area, number, and shape.

Although these children learn to use logic and inference in solving concrete problems, the symbols they use in reasoning are still symbols for concrete objects and events and not abstractions. The limitations of their thinking are shown in the familiar game of Twenty Questions, the goal of which is to determine the identity of an object by asking the fewest possible questions of the person who thinks up the object. A child of 7 or 8 usually sticks to very specific questions, such as "Is it a bird?" or "Is it a cat?" Children at the concrete operational stage usually don't ask abstract questions, such as "Does it fly?" or "Does it hunt?"

Formal Operational Stage (Roughly from age 11 on.) In this final stage of cognitive growth, thinking becomes abstract. Adolescents can see how their particular reality is only one of several imaginable realities, and they begin to ponder deep questions of truth, jus-

tice, and existence. Most young adolescents have acquired all the mental structures needed to go from being naive thinkers to experts. The approach of adolescents and adults to the Twenty Questions game demonstrates their ability to use abstractions and to adopt an information-processing strategy that is not merely random guesswork. They impose their own structures on the task, starting with broad categories and then formulating and testing hypotheses in the light of their knowledge of categories and relationships. Their questioning moves from general categories ("Is it an animal?") to subcategories ("Does it fly?") and then to specific guesses ("Is it a bird?") (Bruner et al., 1966).

MODERN PERSPECTIVES ON COGNITIVE DEVELOPMENT

Piaget's theory of the dynamic interplay of assimilation and accommodation is generally accepted as a valid account of the way a child's mind develops. The developmental sequences he identified have also been supported by other researchers. Piaget's *stage* approach to cognitive development is the model many developmental psychologists rely on to understand how other mental and behavioral processes develop. We noted earlier that there is some evidence that the left cerebral hemisphere shows EEG activity in growth spurts around the ages that correspond with some of Piaget's stages (Thatcher et al., 1987).

However, contemporary researchers have come up with new and better ways of studying the development of the child's cognitive abilities. Their research has shown that children are much more intellectually sophisticated at each stage than Piaget realized. Investigators are also challenging his theory of the sensorimotor foundations of thought (J. Mandler, 1990) and turning more to information-processing models of cognitive development (Siegler, 1986). This new research benefits from the use of superior technology, more valid index variables, and cross-sectional experimental research designs involving many children.

New Views of Perceptual and Conceptual Development

The following conclusions about perceptual and conceptual development are emerging from recent experimental research:

- There is a greater degree of order, organization, and coherence in the perceptual experience of the infant and young child than Piaget realized. Infants are sensitive to much visual, auditory, and tactile information about objects and events in their physical world and are able to coordinate sensory input from different senses.
- Infants can develop a conception of objects and events, represent them in their absence, and recall objects seen in the past, and may have the capacity for conceptual thinking not based solely on sensorimotor schemes.
- Piaget did not distinguish between *performance* (doing) and *competence* (knowing) and, therefore, assumed that failure to perform verbally or behaviorally was evidence of a lack of underlying cognitive competence. On some of his tasks, the young child may not have understood his verbal instructions or may not have had sufficient motivation to carry out the complex routine required. Newer research shows that the difference of conceptual understanding between preoperational and concrete operational children may actually be a difference in immediate, or short-term memory (Case, 1985). Children at the preoperational stage are unable to perform tasks that overload their more limited memory system, even when they understand the basic concepts involved in the task.
- New research designs and improved index variables, such as habituation-dishabituation, are showing that infants know much more than they can tell us and that young children think in ways not always reflected on certain test measures. When the situation and task are changed, it appears that children in the preoperational period can do what they are not supposed to: break through their egocentrism, differentiate physical and mental worlds, and decenter their perceptions.

In one study, 1-month-old infants were habituated to sucking on pacifiers with either bumpy or smooth surfaces, but they weren't allowed to see them. When the pacifiers were removed and the infants were shown both kinds of pacifiers, they looked longer at the type of pacifier they had felt tactually in their mouths (Meltzoff & Borton, 1979; Walker-Andrews & Gibson, 1986). This is clear evidence for very early sensory coordination and visual recognition of objects felt but never seen.

Infants as young as 3 months see objects as solid and as having boundaries; they can discriminate these objects from their backgrounds.

In another experiment, a stick was moved repeatedly back and forth behind a block of wood until habituation occurred. Then the subjects were shown two displays of sticks moving as before but missing the block. One display consisted of a solid stick; the other display consisted of two sticks, one above and one below where the solid block used to be (see **Figure 5.8**). Which display did the babies prefer? They preferred the broken rod to the more familiar, habituated, whole stick. Thus they can determine object boundaries by perceiving relative motion (Kellman & Spelke, 1983; Spelke, 1988).

We now know that infants as young as 3 months old, and perhaps younger, have already developed the concept of object permanence. They apparently understand the basic principle that solid objects cannot pass through other solid objects; when they think they perceive such an event, they let researchers know it is impossible. This important finding has been shown repeatedly with different tasks devised by University of Illinois researcher **Renée Baillergeon** (Buy-ay-zhon)

Renée Baillergeon (*Discovering Psychology,* 1990, Program 5)

FIGURE 5.8   *Task Stimuli Used to Demonstrate That Infants Perceive Objects and Boundaries*

Three-month-old infants can develop concepts of objects and object boundaries as shown by their preferences in a habituation paradigm. They habituate to the top display of a rod moving behind a block. Then they are tested with each of the two lower displays: the moving rod without the block in front and two pieces of moving rods that appear as parts of the rod seen above and below the block before. The infants continue to habituate to the whole rod, instead preferring to look at the "novel" broken rod. They show no preference for either kind of stationary rod after seeing a stationary rod behind the block. Can you explain what this preference means in terms of forming concepts of objects at this age?

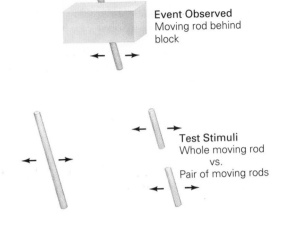

Event Observed
Moving rod behind block

Test Stimuli
Whole moving rod
vs.
Pair of moving rods

(1987a, 1987b). During one task, subjects demonstrated surprise when observing sequences of events that are possible and impossible.

> The infants sat in front of a large display box. Directly before them was a small screen; to the left of the screen was a long ramp. The infants watched the following event: the screen was raised (so the infants could see there was nothing behind it) and then lowered; a toy car was pushed onto the ramp; the car rolled down the ramp and across the display box, disappearing as it shot behind the screen, reappearing at the end of the screen, and finally exiting the display box to the right (see **Figure 5.9**).
>
> After the infants habituated to this event, they saw two test events. These events were identical to the habituation event except that, in both test events, a box was placed behind the screen so that, when the screen was raised, it revealed the box. The only difference between the test events was the location of the box behind the screen. In the *possible event* the box was placed at the back of the display box, behind the tracks of the car, so the car could roll freely through the display. In the *impossible event,* the box was placed on top of the tracks so that it blocked the car's path; but, during the event, the car still appeared to roll freely through it. The infants showed more surprise and looked longer at this impossible event. (See *Discovering Psychology,* 1990, program 5.)

Further evidence of conceptual functioning during the sensorimotor stage is seen when 9-month-old children imitate actions they saw performed a day earlier. After having seen an experimenter perform an unusual action on a novel object—pressing a recessed button that made a beeping sound come from a box—the subjects were able to reproduce the action 24 hours later. The subjects recalled a pattern of events that they had not practiced (Meltzoff, 1988).

Evidence that preoperational children are not totally egocentric is apparent when they can take the perspective of others if the task is simplified. When shown a card with a horse on one side and an elephant on the other, they can say that the experimenter sitting across from them sees the elephant while they are seeing the horse (Masangkay et al., 1974). Children can also adapt their communication to different types of listeners. When a 4 year old tells a 2 year old about a toy, she uses shorter, simpler utterances than she does when telling a peer or adult about that toy (Shatz & Gilman, 1973).

Children in this stage can differentiate mental and physical worlds if the right questions are asked of them. When shown a photo of two boys, one thinking about a cookie and one holding a cookie, children can tell which boy can actually eat the cookie (Wellman & Estes, 1986). A related study showed that these preoperational children can decenter their perceptions by sometimes focusing on less perceptually salient physical features of stimuli. Children at this young age preferred to describe people according to their mental states, rather than their

FIGURE 5.9   A SCHEMATIC REPRESENTATION OF HABITUATION AND TEST EVENTS

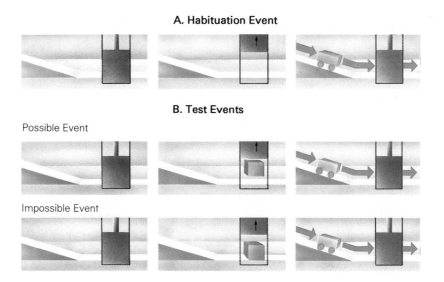

A. Habituation Event

B. Test Events

Possible Event

Impossible Event

physical actions; when shown drawings that illustrated both they would be less likely to say, "He's wiping up his spilled milk" than "He's feeling sad about his spilled milk" (Lillard & Flavell, 1990).

The Child's Mind as Computer

Some developmental psychologists modify Piaget's stages to fit this new evidence. Others reject the stage approach altogether. They prefer an *information-processing approach* that looks at the child's mind as a complex cognitive system, analogous to a high-speed digital computer (Siegler, 1986). According to this model, information is taken in from the environment, identified, and temporarily stored in short-term memory. Some of it is then sent to more permanent storage in long-term memory for later retrieval. From this perspective, a major difference between child and adult cognition lies in memory functioning. As early limitations on memory are overcome, the child is able to demonstrate better his or her conceptual abilities. Some investigators argue that cognitive development is a *continuous process* because memory limitations are overcome gradually, continuously improving cognitive functioning. Others believe that changes in *memory capacity* are not continuous but follow a stagelike, discontinuous pattern (Case, 1985; Fischer, 1980). The information-processing approach is leading some researchers to study the kinds of rules children use to solve conceptual problems, the knowledge they possess within specific domains, and the way they organize existing knowledge into coherent subroutines for dealing with their perceptual and cognitive worlds (Chi & Koeske, 1983; Flavell, 1985; Rozin, 1976; J. Mandler, 1988, 1990). These researchers are forcing the field of developmental psychology to reformulate long-held ideas about the child's mind and the way it develops into the most dynamic, creative thinking machine on the planet.

SUMMING UP

Through careful, intensive observations of individual children at different ages, Piaget formulated significant views about the way the infant's mind develops and the child's conceptual abilities emerge and expand. His key ideas center on the development of schemes (sensory-action programs that guide specific behaviors), assimilation (which fits new input into existing mental structures), accommodation (which changes current aspects of thinking to fit new input), and the four-stage theory of discontinuous cognitive development. The earliest sensorimotor stage is one in which infants are assumed to know and think in very limited ways and to be perceptual-behaving creatures rather than conceptual ones. In the preoperational stage, the ability to represent absent events becomes well organized. During the concrete operational stage, earlier mental deficiencies wane. The child can perform a range of mental operations involving concrete, but not symbolic, thoughts. The final stage of formal operations involves acquiring all the mental structures necessary to become an expert thinker—to reason logically and abstractly.

Many features of Piaget's theories and observations are being challenged by current investigators who are using new technology along with improved research designs. There is now evidence that perceptual and conceptual functioning occur at much earlier ages and that the sensorimotor stage may not be a necessary first stage of cognitive development. Debate continues over the merits of a discontinuous stage model versus a continuous information-processing model of cognitive development.

SOCIAL AND EMOTIONAL DEVELOPMENT

A child competent in language and cognitive skills would still be deficient without appropriate social and emotional reactions and capabilities. Children do not thrive only by becoming smarter about the nature of physical reality. Their basic survival depends on forming meaningful, effective relationships with other people. They need to learn and internalize sets of rules that their society has adopted to govern much of the personal behavior and social transactions of its members. They must be in touch with their own feelings and respond perceptively to the feelings of others.

One way in which children have a significant impact on their social environment is by smiling. "Smile and the world smiles back" is an aphorism that many parents and teachers encourage children to put into practice. We smile not only as a sign of positive affect but also because of "audience effects." In many situations, smiles are more expressed by adults when others are watching than when there is no audience for the facial expression (Fridlund, 1990). Similar effects have been demonstrated recently among 10-month-old infants.

> Videotapes were made and analyzed of infants playing with toys in a laboratory while their mothers either watched them attentively or were inattentive (reading magazines) according to a

prearranged sequence. The mother's attentiveness was an audience cue for a smile; if she looked at the baby when the infant glanced at her, the baby smiled, but if she was inattentive, the baby usually turned back to the toys without smiling. The only behavior that was affected by the mother's attention was the frequency with which the infant smiled in the mother's direction. These and other results lead to the conclusion that "smiling is partially dependent on the infant's appraisal of the social context and partially independent of emotion at this early point in development" (Jones et al., 1991, p. 49).

SOCIALIZATION

Socialization is the life-long process of shaping an individual's behavior patterns, values, standards, skills, attitudes, and motives to conform to those regarded as desirable in a particular society (Hetherington & Parke, 1975). Many people are involved in this process—mother, father, siblings, relatives, friends, and teachers. Institutions, such as schools, churches, and legal systems, exert pressure on the individual to adopt socially approved values and to comply with given standards of conduct. The family, however, is the most influential shaper and regulator of socialization. The family helps the individual form basic patterns of responsiveness to others, which, in turn, form the basis of the individual's lifelong style of relating to other people.

Parental socializing goals for their children range from behavioral compliance with specific social rules—saying "please" and "thank you" and not talking with a mouth full of food—to internalizing general social values—being cooperative, honest, and responsible. Overall, parents are interested in fostering the optimal development of their children so that as adults they will be able to function within the framework of their particular culture and time. Our society, for example, values the ability to form bonds of intimacy and stability with others (Maccoby & Martin, 1983).

Attachment and Social Support

Social development begins with the establishment of a close emotional relationship between a child and a mother, father, or other regular caregiver. This intense, enduring, social-emotional relationship is called **attachment.** Attachment behaviors appear to occur instinctively in many species. Among rats, for example, the mother's licking of the newborn or eating of the placenta activates hormones that prime her to provide care and protection for her young (Pedersen & Blass, 1982). In other species, the infant automatically forms an attachment to the first moving object it sees or hears

(Johnson & Gottlieb, 1981). When this attachment occurs rapidly and during a critical period of development, when it cannot easily be modified, and when it has a lasting effect on later social behavior, the process is called **imprinting.** The response in newly hatched ducklings to their mother's movements is a classic example of imprinting. Because the mother is usually the first moving object the infant sees, the infant usually imprints on and becomes attached to an appropriate adult member of its species. What happens if the species-appropriate mother is not available during the critical imprinting period? Young geese raised by a human will imprint on the human instead of on one of their own kind, as demonstrated by ethologist Konrad Lorenz (1937). A monkey raised by a dog will become more strongly attached to its foster canine mother than to other monkeys (Mason & Kenney, 1974).

Human infants and human caregivers may have similar instinctive attachment behaviors. In the 1970s, it was reported that human mothers were more likely to "bond" with their babies if they were allowed to see and hold the babies immediately after delivery (Klaus & Kennell, 1976). Researchers proposed that childbirth activated bonding hormones in the mothers. Although later research has shown that physical contact immediately after delivery is neither critical for nor enough to stimulate human attachment, the idea that early attachment right after birth is a good idea has changed standard delivery procedures in many hospitals. Today most healthy newborns are placed on top of their mothers'

Konrad Lorenz, the researcher who pioneered in the study of imprinting, graphically demonstrates what can happen when young animals become imprinted on someone other than their mother.

bellies to bond. Hormones alone cannot account for attachment, and human babies also cannot rely on their own locomotor capacities to achieve closeness to and get attention from a caregiver. Human babies do, however, seem to have built-in behaviors that signal to others to respond to them (Campos et al., 1983). Smiling, crying, and vocalizing are examples of these *proximity-promoting signals*. Successful attachment, of course, depends not only on an infant's ability to emit these signals but also on an adult's tendency to respond to the signals. Who can resist a baby's smile? According to **John Bowlby** (1973), an influential theorist on human attachment, infants will form attachments to individuals who consistently and appropriately respond to their signals.

Once established, secure attachment has powerful, lasting, beneficial effects; it provides a psychological home base from which an individual can explore the physical and social environment. Secure attachment to valued adult models who offer dependable social support enables the child to learn a variety of prosocial behaviors (taking turns, sharing, cooperating), to take risks, to venture into novel situations, and to seek and accept intimacy in personal relationships.

Assessing Attachment We can infer a child's development of attachment from several behaviors. The child seeks to be near the caregiver, uses the caregiver as a secure base when exploring unfamiliar situations, clings to the caregiver when afraid, and resists separation from the caregiver (Brackbill, 1979). Psychologists have been able to use these behaviors to assess attachment relationships in very young children. One of the most widely used research procedures for assessing attachment is the *Strange Situation Test* developed by **Mary Ainsworth** and her colleagues (Ainsworth et al., 1978).

> In the first of several standard episodes, the child is brought into an unfamiliar room filled with toys. With mother present, the child is encouraged to explore the room and to play. After several minutes, a stranger comes in, talks to the mother, and approaches the child. Next, the mother exits the room. After this brief separation, the mother returns, there is a reunion with her child, and the stranger leaves. The researchers record the child's behaviors at separation and reunion.

The researchers have found that children's responses fall into three or, perhaps, four general categories. *Securely attached* children show some distress when the parent leaves the room; seek proximity, comfort, and contact upon reunion, and then gradually return to play. *Insecurely attached-avoidant* children seem aloof and may actively avoid and ignore the parent upon her return. *Insecurely attached-ambivalent* children become quite upset and anxious when the parent leaves; at reunion they cannot be comforted and they show anger and resistance to the parent but, at the same time, express a desire for contact. More recently, another classification has been added to describe children who act dazed and confused upon reunion. After the parent's return, these *insecurely attached-disorganized* children may stop moving completely or show contradictory behavior patterns, such as gazing away while in contact with the parent (Main et al., 1985). The unresolved controversy surrounding this line of research is whether these behavior patterns seen in infants at 12 and 18 months of age are stable over time. In other words, do insecurely attached infants become insecurely attached preschoolers and perhaps even insecurely attached adults? Some researchers have found evidence that these attachment patterns do reflect stable personality characteristics, while others argue that the methods of assessing attachment, both in infancy and in later childhood or adulthood, are questionable.

Why Form Attachments? The evolutionary explanation for attachment assumes that infants who formed close attachments to parents and got their needed social-emotional support were more likely to survive and to pass their genes on to future generations than were infants not able to form such protective attachments. Attached infants are less at risk for being killed by predators, getting lost, suffering exposure or hunger, or receiving injuries from members of their own species.

The basic first attachment is the way young animals establish their identification as members of their species. Sigmund Freud and many other psychologists have argued that babies become attached to their parents because the parents provide them with food—their most basic physical need. This is called *the cupboard theory* of attachment. Think about your experiences with infants. Does the cupboard explanation seem satisfactory? You can probably think of many times when infants seem to be very interested in developing social relationships and participating in playful interactions with people who have never given them food.

Harry Harlow (1965) did not believe that the cupboard theory completely explained the motivation for and importance of attachment. He set out to test the cupboard theory of attachment against his own hypothesis that infants might also attach to those who provide "contact comfort." Harlow separated macaque monkeys from their mothers at birth and placed them in cages where they had access to two artificial "mothers": a wire one and a terry cloth one. Harlow found that the baby monkeys nestled close to the terry cloth mother and spent little time on the wire one. They did this even when only the wire mother gave milk! The baby monkeys also used the cloth mother as a source of comfort when frightened and as a base of operations when exploring new stimuli. When a fear stimulus (for example, a toy bear beating a drum) was introduced, the baby monkeys would run to the cloth mother. When novel and intriguing stimuli were introduced, the baby monkeys would gradually venture out to explore and then return to the terry cloth mother before exploring further. When new stimuli were presented in the terry cloth mother's absence, the monkeys would often freeze in a crouched position or run from object to object screaming and crying. The infant monkeys became attached to and actually preferred the mother that provided **contact comfort** over the one that provided food (Harlow & Zimmerman, 1958).

Observations of human infants have also demonstrated the critical value of contact comfort. A lack of close, loving relationships in infancy has been shown in many studies to affect physical growth and even survival. In 1915, a doctor at Johns Hopkins Hospital reported that, despite adequate physical care, 90 percent of the infants admitted to orphanages in Baltimore died within the first year. Studies of hospitalized infants over the next 30 years found that, despite adequate nutrition, the children often developed respiratory infections and fevers of unknown origin, failed to gain weight, and even showed signs of physiological deterioration, such as diarrhea, decrease in muscle tone, and eating difficulties (see Bowlby, 1969; Sherrod et al., 1978). Another study of infants in foundling homes in the United States and Canada reported evidence of severe emotional and physical disorders as well as high mortality rates, despite good food and medical care (Spitz & Wolf, 1946). The negative effects of early institutionalization hold true for high-stress, hostile family environments. In family environments marked by emotional detachment and hostility, children are found to weigh less and to have retarded bone development. They begin to grow when they are removed from the hostile environment, but their growth again becomes stunted if they are returned to it—a phenomenon that is known as **psychosocial dwarfism** (Gardner, 1972). Negative environments, however, affect not only physical development but also social development.

In one study of ten abused toddlers, ages 1 to 3 years, researchers found that the children did not respond appropriately when a peer was in distress. When another child is upset and crying, toddlers will normally respond by showing concern, empathy, or sadness. By contrast, the abused children were more likely to respond with fear, anger, or physical attacks (Main & George, 1985).

In the theory of attachment developed by John Bowlby (1973), early infant-mother bonding is necessary for the development of normal social relationships. Although attachment is necessary, it is not a sufficient condition for social development—something more is needed. Further studies by Harlow and his colleagues found that the monkeys' formation of a strong attachment to the mother substitute was not sufficient for healthy social development. At first, the experimenters thought the young monkeys with terry cloth mothers were developing normally, but a very different picture emerged when it was time for the female monkeys who had been raised in this way to become mothers. If these monkeys had been deprived of chances to interact with other responsive monkeys in their early lives, they had trouble forming normal social and sexual relationships in adulthood. Despite elaborate arrangements, it took many months for them to conceive; success was finally achieved with only 4 of the 18.

> After the birth of her baby, the first of these un-mothered mothers ignored her infant and sat relatively motionless at one side of the living cage, staring fixedly into space hour after hour. If a human observer approached and threatened either the baby or the mother, there was no counter-threat. As the infant matured and became mobile, it made continual, desperate attempts to effect maternal contact. These attempts were consistently repulsed by the mother. She would brush the baby away or restrain it by pushing the baby's face to the woven-wire floor (Harlow, 1965, pp. 256–257).

When the other "motherless" monkeys gave birth after having been artificially inseminated, most were either indifferent or unresponsive to their babies or brutalized them, biting off their fingers or toes, pounding them, and nearly killing them until human caretakers intervened. One of the most interesting findings was that, despite the consistent punishment, the babies persisted in their attempts to make maternal contact. In the end, "it was a case of the baby adopting the mother, not the mother adopting the baby" (Harlow, 1965, p. 259). Fortunately, with successive pregnancies, the maternal behavior of these mothers improved so that this brutal behavior was no longer the norm for this group of monkeys. In subsequent studies, researchers found that the monkeys who had only terry cloth mothers showed adequate, but considerably delayed, heterosexual adjustment if they were given ample opportunity to interact with other infant monkeys as they were growing up

(Harlow & Harlow, 1966). Younger, normally reared monkeys served as "peer therapists" when paired with the unattached, socially deprived monkeys, helping them to attain a more normal mode of social functioning (Suomi & Harlow, 1972).

Primate researcher Stephen Suomi (1987; 1990) has shown that putting emotionally vulnerable infant monkeys in the foster care of supportive mothers virtually turns their lives around. Suomi notes how monkeys put in the care of mothers who are known to be particularly loving and attentive are transformed from marginal members of the monkey troop into bold, outgoing young males who are among the first to leave the troop at puberty to work their way into a new troop. This *cross-fostering* gives them coping skills and information essential for recruiting support from other monkeys and for maintaining a high social status in the group. (See *Discovering Psychology,* 1990, program 5.)

The development of normal socialization and communication in monkeys and human children—learning essential social skills, putting them into practice, and being reinforced for using them appropriately—seems to require interaction with other members of the species. We also know that the early proximity of the child to the biological mother is *not* necessary for attachment and healthy social development (Rutter, 1979). Positive bonds can be formed with any caregiver who is comforting, interacts actively, and is responsive to a baby's signals (Ainsworth, 1973). Indeed, mother-child bonding is strong when these three "quality of care" conditions exist and weak when they don't. On the other hand, the importance of early attachments and strong, loving relationships with a mother or another caregiver, should not be underestimated.

A tragedy is occurring now in institutions in Romania where as many as 40,000 homeless infants and children have been kept under the worst possible conditions. Many of these children are called "nonrecoverables"; a more accurate translation is "lost forever." Totalitarian dictator Nicolae Ceaușescu (overthrown in 1990) started a campaign to increase Romania's population, at any cost. The country's extremely poor economic conditions caused such hardships that many mothers abandoned the babies they had conceived in response to Ceaușescu's campaign. Many of these children who were left in state institutions "appear to suffer chiefly from isolation and neglect. . . . Babies may have been born normal but arrive at the orphanage totally unresponsive, the result of never having been shown affection or being touched." Western relief workers have found "children tied to their beds, starving and filthy. Often, the children have never been touched or held. No one has talked to them. They rock back and forth, staring blankly, or cower in the presence of strangers" (Sachs, 1991, p. A-12). It is doubtful whether any form of intervention can overcome this early trauma of having no attachment to a caring adult.

Most research clearly shows that chronic stress in early life can slow physical, mental, and social development, producing lasting handicaps (Kagan & Klein, 1973). Yet there are almost always some children who are resilient to the consequences of severe life stress and deprivation, who somehow transcend their traumatic early life experiences (Garmezy, 1976; Skolnick, 1986). Why? The presence of strong attachment relationships in these children's lives may be part of the answer.

> A longitudinal study of a group of 690 Hawaiian children from very poor families followed their development from soon after conception to age 20. In their life of poverty, these children experienced many stressful events, and one in five developed serious behavior problems at some time during the 20-year period. Boys suffered most from illnesses, learning problems, and problems in controlling aggression; girls suffered most from dependency problems. Those who were the resilient children, the "invulnerables," showed effective coping patterns and were physically robust, very active, and responsive to other people. Furthermore, they had developed a sense of self-confidence and coherence in their positive relationships with their families. Strong bonds had been forged between them and their primary caregivers. They had rarely been separated from their families, had been given much attention, and were part of a multigenerational social support network that included grandparents, family, and neighbors (Werner & Smith, 1982).

A close interactive relationship with loving adults is a child's first step toward healthy physical growth and normal socialization. As the original attachment to the primary caregiver extends to other family members, they too become models for new ways of thinking and behaving. From these early attachments, a child develops the tendency to adapt to the needs of others.

GENDER ROLES

Males and females are different. Not only do they have different physical characteristics, but they often behave in different ways and play different roles in society. While some of these differences are linked to biology, many are the results of socialization. How do boys and girls learn the different expectations their culture has of them? The answer begins with the differences between sex, gender, gender identity, and gender roles.

Sex refers to the biologically based characteristics that distinguish males and females. These characteristics include different reproductive functions and differences in hormones and anatomy. These differences are universal, biologically determined, and unchanged by social influence. Over time, they have also led to the development of some traditional social roles—for example, since women can breastfeed their babies, prehistoric peoples may have determined that women should also remain close to home, caring for children, while the men hunted for food (Rossi, 1984).

After infancy, boys are more physically active and aggressive than girls. All over the world, boys are more likely than girls to engage in rough play. This difference is partly related to sex hormones—biological factors can create behavioral dispositions (Maccoby, 1980). We know that sex hormones affect social play because observations of young male and female rats and monkeys reveal the same behavioral differences found in humans (Meany, 1988). Male animals engage in vigorous forms of physical play that require gross motor activity. Female animals engage in activities that require precise motor skills.

In contrast to biological sex, **gender** is a psychological phenomenon referring to learned, sex-related behaviors and attitudes. Cultures vary in how strongly gender is linked to daily activities and in the amount of tolerance for what is perceived as cross-gender behavior. **Gender identity** is an individual's sense of maleness or femaleness; it includes awareness and acceptance of one's sex. Some individuals, such as transsexuals, feel a conflict between sex and gender identity. A sense of gender identity is important to a child's psychological well-being. Some theorists believe that children inherently value what is similar to them and, therefore, seek out sex-appropriate activities (Kohlberg, 1966).

Gender roles are patterns of behavior regarded as appropriate for males and females in a particular society. They provide the basic definitions of *masculinity* and *femininity*. Much of what we consider masculine or feminine is shaped by our culture (Williams, 1983). Children learn the gender roles of their cultures in many ways. Adults reward them for gender-appropriate behavior and punish them for actions that are gender-inappropriate. Boys, in particular, receive strong negative responses from their fathers when they engage in cross-gender behavior (Langlois & Downs, 1980). Also, children often imitate the behavior of people around them or of people in movies or books. Finally, children also develop beliefs in limiting rules about gender roles ("girls can't be soldiers").

Gender-role socialization begins at birth. In one study, parents described their newborn daughters, using words such as *little, delicate, beautiful,* and *weak.* By

contrast, parents described their newborn sons as *firm, alert, strong,* and *coordinated.* The babies actually showed no differences in height, weight, or health (Rubin et al., 1974). The differences in the responses of these parents seems to be based on *gender-role stereotypes.* Parents dress their sons and daughters differently, give them different kinds of toys to play with, and communicate with them differently (Reingold & Cook, 1975). For example, parents hold their sons more often, give them more physical stimulation, and pay more attention to their vocalizations and signals for food (Parke & Sawin, 1976; Yarrow, 1975). These effects have also been demonstrated in controlled research studies.

Parents seem to be the key socializers of gender roles. Recently, however, researchers have begun to examine the importance of peers in the development of gender differentiation and identification. Apparently, the effects of gender labeling are more powerful for children than adults (Stern & Karraker, 1989). Children between the ages of 2 and 6 seem to have more extreme and inflexible perceptions of gender than do adults. The children's extreme reactions may be linked to the fact that they are at the age when they try to establish their own gender identity.

Eleanor Maccoby argues that parents do not stamp in gender roles (1988). She has found evidence that play styles and toy preferences are not highly correlated with parental preferences or roles. Maccoby believes that many of the differences in gender behavior among children are the results of peer relationships. Because of gender-role socialization, boys and girls grow up in different psychological environments that shape their views of the world and their ways of dealing with problems. Young children are segregationists—they seek out peers of the same sex even when adults

are not supervising them or in spite of adult encouragement for mixed-group play.

A variety of socializing agents—parents, teachers, peers, and the media—consistently and subtly reinforce gender stereotypes. **Jeanne Block** (1983) concludes that parents give their girls "roots" to build homes and families, but they give their boys "wings" to soar to new adventures. Can these gender-based behaviors ever change?

ERIKSON'S PSYCHOSOCIAL STAGES

As a middle-aged immigrant to America, **Erik Erikson** (1963) became aware of conflicts he faced because of his new status. His awareness caused him to reflect on the many such conflicts all individuals face in the life-long process of development. His reflection ultimately resulted in a new way of thinking about human development in terms of a sequence of conflicts and challenges that emerge at many stages in the life course, from infancy to old age. **Psychosocial stages** are successive orientations toward oneself and toward others that influence personality growth across the entire life span. Each stage requires a new level of social interaction; success or failure in achieving it can change the course of subsequent development in a positive or negative direction. Unlike other theorists who believed development took place during infancy and early childhood, Erikson saw development as continuing throughout life.

Erikson identified eight psychosocial stages in the life cycle. At each stage, a particular conflict comes into focus, as shown in **Table 5.4.** Although the conflict continues in different forms and is never resolved once and for all, it needs to be sufficiently resolved at a given

TABLE 5.4   ERIKSON'S PSYCHOSOCIAL STAGES

Approximate Age	Crisis	Adequate Resolution	Inadequate Resolution
0–1½	Trust vs. mistrust	Basic sense of safety	Insecurity, anxiety
1½–3	Autonomy vs. self-doubt	Perception of self as agent capable of controlling own body and making things happen	Feelings of inadequacy to control events
3–6	Initiative vs. guilt	Confidence in oneself as initiator, creator	Feelings of lack of self-worth
6–puberty	Competence vs. inferiority	Adequacy in basic social and intellectual skills	Lack of self-confidence, feelings of failure
Adolescent	Identity vs. role confusion	Comfortable sense of self as a person	Sense of self as fragmented; shifting, unclear sense of self
Early adult	Intimacy vs. isolation	Capacity for closeness and commitment to another	Feeling of aloneness, separation; denial of need for closeness
Middle adult	Generativity vs. stagnation	Focus of concern beyond oneself to family, society, future generations	Self-indulgent concerns; lack of future orientation
Later adult	Ego-integrity vs. despair	Sense of wholeness, basic satisfaction with life	Feelings of futility, disappointment

stage if an individual is to cope successfully with the conflicts of later stages.

For example, in the first stage, an infant needs to develop a basic sense of trust in the environment through interaction with caregivers. Trust is a natural accompaniment to a strong attachment relationship with a parent who provides food, warmth, and the comfort of physical closeness. But a child whose basic needs are not met, who experiences inconsistent handling, lack of physical closeness and warmth, and the frequent absence of a caring adult, may develop a pervasive sense of mistrust, insecurity, and anxiety. This child will not be prepared for the second stage which requires the individual to be adventurous.

With the development of walking and the beginnings of language, there is an expansion of a child's exploration and manipulation of objects (and sometimes people). With these activities should come a comfortable sense of autonomy and of being a capable and worthy person. Excessive restriction or criticism at this second stage of development may lead instead to self-doubts, while demands beyond the child's ability, as in too-early or too-severe toilet training, can discourage the individual's efforts to persevere in mastering new tasks. They also can lead to stormy scenes of confrontation, disrupting the close, supportive parent-child relationship that is needed to encourage the child to accept risks and meet new challenges. The 2 year old who insists that a particular ritual be followed or demands the right to do something without help is acting out of a need to affirm his or her autonomy and adequacy. Toward the end of the preschool period, a child who has developed a basic sense of trust, first in the immediate environment and then in himself or herself, has become a person who can now initiate both intellectual and motor activities. The ways that parents respond to the child's self-initiated activities either encourage the sense of freedom and self-confidence needed for the next stage or produce guilt and feelings of being an inept intruder in an adult world.

During the elementary-school years, the child who has successfully resolved the crises of the earlier stages is ready to go beyond random exploring and testing to the systematic development of competencies. School and sports offer arenas for learning intellectual and motor skills, and interaction with peers offers an arena for developing social skills. Other opportunities develop through special lessons, organized group activities, and perseverance of individual interests. Successful efforts in these pursuits lead to feelings of competence. Some youngsters, however, become spectators rather than performers or experience enough failure to give them a sense of inferiority, leaving them unable to meet the demands of the next life stages. Erikson's formulation has been widely accepted, because it looks at the life cycle as a whole, putting both changes and overall continuity into perspective. The first four stages are part of a child's socialization; the last four are landmarks in an adult's continuing socialization. We will examine these last four stages in the next chapter as we try to understand some of the significant forces that shape human development during adolescence, adulthood, and old age.

RECAPPING MAIN POINTS

The Life Cycle Begins

Developmental psychologists study human development throughout the life span. Physical and mental development depend on both genetic factors and environmental inputs. The nature-nurture controversy is an old, continuing debate about whether heredity or environment is more important in human development. There are two basic approaches to development theory: continuity and discontinuity. Many aspects of development depend on stimulation at an optimal time.

Acquiring Language

Children are master language-learners. Some researchers believe that we have an inborn language acquisition device. Culture and parental interaction are essential parts of the language acquisition process. Word learning proceeds from preverbal babbling, to the one-word stage, to the two-word stage, and then on to forming short sentences. Language development and cognitive development are intertwined.

Cognitive Development

Piaget's key ideas about cognitive development include development of schemes, assimilation, accommodation, and the four-stage theory of discontinuous cognitive development. The four stages are sensorimotor, preoperational, concrete operational, and formal operational. Many of Piaget's theories are now being challenged by ingenious research paradigms. However, they still hold a critical place in our understanding of cognitive development.

Social and Emotional Development

Socialization is the process whereby we acquire values, standards, skills, attitudes, and motives to conform to those considered desirable in our society. Socialization begins with an infant's attachment to a caregiver. Failure to make this attachment leads to numerous physical and psychological problems. Gender is a psychological phenomenon referring to learned, sex-related behavior and attitudes. Gender-role socialization begins at birth. A variety of socializing agents reinforce gender stereotypes. Erikson believed that socialization takes place in a series of psychosocial stages from infancy to old age.

K EY TERMS

accommodation, 161

American Sign Language (ASL), 154

assimilation, 161

attachment, 168

centration, 163

chromosome, 137

chronological age, 136

cognitive development, 161

conservation, 164

constitutional factor, 141

contact comfort, 170

critical period, 152

cross-sectional design, 150

developmental age, 136

developmental dyslexia, 145

developmental psychology, 136

developmental stages, 151

dishabituation, 150

egocentrism, 163

gender, 172

gender identity, 172

gender role, 172

gene, 137

germ cell, 137

habituation, 150

imprinting, 169

language acquisition device (LAD), 156

longitudinal design, 150

maturation, 139

motherese, 157

nature-nurture controversy, 143

normative investigations, 149

object permanence, 163

overregularization, 160

phoneme, 155

polygenic, 137

psychosocial dwarfism, 170

psychosocial stages, 173

schemes, 161

sequential design, 150

sex, 172

socialization, 168

M AJOR CONTRIBUTORS

Ainsworth, Mary, 169

Baillargeon, Renée, 165

Blass, Elliott, 147

Block, Jeanne, 173

Bowlby, John, 169

Chomsky, Noam, 156

Erikson, Erik, 173

Fantz, Robert, 151

Fernald, Anne, 158

Harlow, Harry, 170

Itard, Jean Marie, 143

Kagan, Jerome, 141

Locke, John, 143

Maccoby, Eleanor, 173

Piaget, Jean, 161

Rousseau, Jean, 143

Suomi, Steven, 142

Chapter 6

Life-span Development

DEVELOPMENT ACROSS THE LIFE COURSE   180
  EARLY LIFE-SPAN THEORIES
  *HISTORICAL ANALYSIS OF FAMILIES AND LIFE
    STAGES*
  FAMILIES AND YOUTH AT RISK

  INTERIM SUMMARY

ADOLESCENCE   185
  TRANSITION MARKERS AND INITIATION RITES
  THE MYTH OF ADOLESCENT "STORM AND STRESS"
  TASKS OF ADOLESCENCE
  CLOSE-UP: ALCOHOLISM ON CAMPUS

  INTERIM SUMMARY

ADULTHOOD   192
  THE TASKS OF ADULTHOOD
  ADULT AGES AND STAGES
  ADULT THINKING
  MORAL DEVELOPMENT

  INTERIM SUMMARY

OLD AGE   200
  AGEISM AND MYTHS OF THE AGED
  RESEARCH APPROACHES TO AGING
  NEW PERSPECTIVES ON AGING
  PHYSIOLOGICAL CHANGES
  CLOSE-UP: YOUR DESIGN FOR ELDERLY HABITATS
  COGNITIVE CHANGES
  SOCIAL CHANGES
  PSYCHOPATHOLOGY
  AT LIFE'S END

RECAPPING MAIN POINTS   210

KEY TERMS   211

MAJOR CONTRIBUTORS   211

"**M**om, cut it out! Mothers don't ask those questions." Brad is watching his mother roll out dough for pumpkin pies. He walks to the counter and pours himself a cup of coffee. Any other mother would hand her son some money and tell him to have a good time. His mother wants to know if he uses condoms.

"I'm sorry." Brad's mother Susan stops rolling and brushes a strand of hair from her eyes. "It's just that your father has been so stressed lately that I didn't know if he would get around to it."

"Mom, it's none of your business."

Susan looks at Brad until he looks away. Then she says evenly, "Like it or not, your life is my business. Sure, I feel awkward bringing it up, but I'd feel a whole lot worse if you got AIDS just because you weren't careful."

"Look, I'm not gay. I don't do drugs. I only go out with nice girls. You don't need to worry. Anyway, you weren't so careful when you were my age." Brad immediately wishes he hadn't said that. He knows his mother was pregnant with him her senior year of high school.

"Times were different then," Susan says softly. "I know you must get tired of hearing that, but we weren't dealing with an invisible, fatal disease. *Anyone* can have AIDS." Susan walks around the counter and stands in front of her son. "No matter *how* nice she seems!"

"So when is Gram getting here?" Anything to end this tiresome conversation.

"Didn't I tell you?" Susan grins—she's relieved too. "Your grandmother won't be with us this Thanksgiving. She's in China, leading one of her Adventures for Seniors tours. I just wish *my* mother was doing as well."

"What's with Nana?"

"She just sits in front of the tube all day. She wouldn't let us pick her up until after her soaps."

"Nana was always the life of the party!"

"When Papa died, some part of Nana went away too." Susan sighs. "She says she has no reason to live, but she won't move out of her house or even discuss other options."

Susan sets the pies on the baking rack, then catches a glimpse of her reflection in the glass door of the oven. No, she definitely is not as young as she used to be. There are more wrinkles around her eyes, like Nana's. Susan sees her mother's face as a map of where her own is headed, a continent of rivers, streams, and tributaries. Sure, everybody gets older. But so soon?

Brad clears his throat. "These days, I've been worried about Dad. He seems so sad and remote."

"I know; he says he doesn't feel he's making a real difference with his life."

"Maybe he's going through some kind of mid-life crisis."

"You sound like Gram. Before she left, she said, 'Watch out, Susie. He'll quit his job or have an affair. Either way, you lose.' But I don't think so."

"What do you think?"

"I think it's time for a change. He's burned out on law; I'm burned out on social work. Maybe we should join the Peace Corps."

The interaction between mother and son raises a number of issues that clearly go beyond the concerns prevalent in early childhood phases of development. The tasks that face the maturing adolescent differ from those facing adults. An adolescent such as Brad must go through the process of developing a sense of personal identity and separateness from parents—a process that will result in mature independence and, ideally, lead to a new relationship with his parents. Adults such as Susan have to make the transition from earlier dependence on their parents and on institutional supports (such as college) to becoming responsible for their own well-being and that of others who may come to depend on them. They must also deal with intimate relationships (such as Susan's relationships with Brad and her husband) that change over time. With old age, comes either the opportunity for self-exploration and reflection, guided by a sense of wisdom and resulting in feelings of contentment (as in the case of adventure-bound Gram) or a time to lament unrealized potential, illness, loss, and impoverishment (as represented by the home-bound Nana in our family scenario).

Each of the stages of life are played out against a background of ever-changing values and social-economic-political patterns. For example, in the United States, the extreme conformity and conservatism of the 1950s sowed the seeds of the adolescent revolution of the 1960s and early 1970s. The resulting sexual freedom was bolstered by the development of birth control technology; but that freedom is challenged in the 1990s by the fear of widespread, sexually-transmitted diseases, especially AIDS. Fear of disease, widespread drug use, increased crime, teenage pregnancy, and the emergence of a new underclass of homeless poor may spark a conservative backlash to the free-thinking experimental mood of the 1960s and 1970s (Shinn & Weitzman, 1990). Patriotic fever, unthinking obedience to authority, traditional values, and a baby boom characterized the decades that followed the conclusion of the Second World War. We all experience similar developmental stages in our lives, however, the manifestation of these stages differs widely from generation to generation as social, political, and economic currents guide the flow of human development. A significant feature of human development everywhere in the world is individ-

ual *resiliency*. **Resiliency** is successful adaptation in the face of extremely challenging or threatening circumstances (Dugan & Coles, 1989). This resiliency takes three forms: good life outcomes for high-risk children; good functioning under adverse, stressful conditions; and recovery from trauma or disasters.

This chapter begins with a discussion of the later stages of Erikson's psychosocial approach to life-span development. We will put the concept of family and life stages into a historical perspective and consider the crises facing many modern families and especially children and adults who must survive below the poverty level. Then we will examine selected aspects of adolescent development. After analyzing the major developmental tasks facing adults and aspects of adult thinking and moral reasoning, we will move on to consider what it means to age well.

DEVELOPMENT ACROSS THE LIFE COURSE

Life-span development explores the continuities, stabilities, and changes in physical and psychological processes that characterize human functioning from conception through the final phases of life (Honzik, 1984). Though childhood years are formative, we have a remarkable capacity for change across the entire life span (Brim & Kagan, 1980). The long-term effects of early infant and childhood experiences are highly variable and continue to be influenced by later experiences (Henderson, 1980; Simmel, 1980).

After childhood come choices about intimate relationships, sexual partners, education, careers, marriage, family, and leisure time. Obligations and commitments multiply as time seems to become scarcer. There never is enough time to get everything done and our time is usually spent doing what we perceive *we have to do,* rather than what *we want to do.* We begin to live for the future and we become nostalgic about the ever-distancing past. For many of us, the delight of being absorbed in the present (which we felt as children) is lost forever as coping with life's daily hassles becomes a more pressing concern. Old age either brings with it new stresses or new challenges; how they are resolved frames the retrospective portrait of one's life.

Most theorists who influenced the study of individual development, such as Sigmund Freud and Jean Piaget, focused only on early life periods. They assumed that the burden of development is carried on only through adolescence; after that the person and the psyche were set for life and would experience only a few more important changes. New research, however, is challenging long-held notions about the insignificance of adult midlife and the irreversible decline of biological and psychological functioning in the elderly. Out of this research has emerged the basic premise of **life-span developmental psychology:** that personality, mental functioning, and other vital aspects of human nature continue to develop and change throughout the entire life cycle.

EARLY LIFE-SPAN THEORIES

Study of the unique features of life development stages was most strongly championed by **Erik Erikson** (1963). Two other influential theorists on stages of life-long development, Carl Jung and Charlotte Buhler, have made important contributions to the field.

Erikson's Later Psychosocial Stages

Erikson, who was trained by Anna Freud (Sigmund's daughter), focused on the relationship between psyche and society—on the ego within the broader context provided by each person's culture. His insights into the crises of identity that people experience as they mature came out of his immigrant experience of U.S. society and they were refined by his work with Native Americans and returning World War II veterans.

Recall that Erikson identified eight stages of psychosocial development, from birth to late adulthood, during which the individual is challenged by a specific crisis or conflict. Each of Erikson's stages is defined by the *developmental tasks* it presents the individual. The developmental task of each stage is to come to terms with both of its opposite demands—self and the world—balancing or integrating them. This is shown in **Table 6.1.** (Note that the full table is on page 174.)

Erikson believes that the essential crisis of *adolescence* is discovering one's true *identity* amid the confusion created by playing many different roles for the different audiences in an expanding social world. Resolving this crisis helps the individual to develop a sense of a coherent self; failing to do so adequately may result in a self-image that lacks a central stable core. The essential crisis for the *young adult* is to resolve the conflict between *intimacy* and *isolation*—to develop the capacity to make full emotional, moral, and sexual commitments to other people. Making that kind of commitment requires that the individual compromise some personal preferences, accept some responsibilities, and yield some degree of privacy and independence. Failure to resolve this crisis adequately leads to isolation and the inability to connect to others in psychologically meaningful ways. (We will see throughout our journey in *Psychology and Life* that much research supports the conclusion that anything that *isolates* us from sources of social support—from a reliable network of friends and family—puts us at risk for a host of physical ills, mental problems, and even social pathologies.)

TABLE 6.1	ERIKSON'S LATER PSYCHOSOCIAL STAGES (ADOLESCENCE TO LATER ADULT)		
Approximate Age	**Crisis**	**Adequate Resolution**	**Inadequate Resolution**
Adolescent	Identity vs. role confusion	Comfortable sense of self as a person	Sense of self as fragmented; shifting, unclear sense of self
Early adult	Intimacy vs. isolation	Capacity for closeness and commitment to another	Feeling of aloneness, separation; denial of need for closeness
Middle adult	Generativity vs. stagnation	Focus of concern beyond oneself to family, society, future generations	Self-indulgent concerns; lack of future orientation
Later adult	Ego-integrity vs. despair	Sense of wholeness, basic satisfaction with life	Feelings of futility, disappointment

The next major opportunity for growth occurs during *adult midlife* and is known as *generativity*. People in their 30s and 40s move beyond a focus on self and partner to broaden commitments to family, work, society, and future generations. Those who haven't resolved earlier life stage crises of identity and intimacy, however, may experience a mid-life crisis. These people are still self-indulgent, question past decisions and goals, want to give up commitments for one last fling, and pursue freedom at the expense of security. (Brad's parents, who were considering dropping out of their regular jobs to join the Peace Corps, were experiencing mid-life crises.)

Awareness of one's mortality and changes in body, behavior, and social roles sets the stage for Erikson's final stage: *late adulthood*. The crisis at this stage is the conflict between *ego-integrity* and *despair*. Resolving the crises at each of the earlier stages prepares the older adult to resolve the crisis of late adulthood—to look back without regrets and to enjoy a sense of wholeness. When previous crises are left unresolved, aspirations remain unfulfilled, and the individual experiences futility, despair, and self-depreciation. The overall result is that the individual fails to solve the crisis at this final developmental stage as well. Many elderly men, confronted by this ultimate failure, choose to end their lives, rather than continue to experience such pain (see Chapter 17).

Erikson's stage model emerged from his study of biographies, in-depth interviews, and personal experiences. In later sections, we will examine other sources of evidence for the validity of his model of adult development. As pertinent as Erikson's formulation may be to Western societies which prize individuality and ego autonomy, however, it may accurately describe the lives of people in societies that are based on principles of *collective organization* that minimize individual initiative and a focus on self (Triandis, 1991). Similarly, cultures with strong religious values that severely limit the experiences of women, such as some Moslem or Hindu cultures, force women to confront a different set of developmental crises than males of those societies (see Bond, 1988; Dhruvarajan, 1990; Shweder & Bourne, 1982).

Jung's Outward-Inward Directedness

Carl Jung challenged his mentor Sigmund Freud with the hypothesis that adulthood, not childhood, represents the most significant phase of psychological growth for the self. Jung believed that a sense of self does not even become established until adolescence when societal prohibitions and limitations are imposed, challenged, obeyed, internalized, and when they conflict with the emerging self-concept (Jung, 1935). He identified two major periods for self-development: *Youth*

(puberty to about age 35) when values expand in an *outward direction* and *adulthood* (ages 35–40 to old age) when values are focused in an *inward direction*.

In youth, an individual must confront issues of sexuality, make connections with others, and make a place in the world—all of which direct the individual's focus outward. With adulthood comes the full flowering of the human potential. It is a time to develop a more refined sense of spirituality and commitments to life and to a smaller circle of loved ones. It is also a time to explore one's values, culture, and even death. Jung believed that the changes in adulthood, although they are not as obvious, are more profound and broad than the swift changes in infancy and early childhood.

Buhler's Reproductive Phases

Charlotte Buhler (1968) developed the concept of the cycle of *reproductive activities*. Her model of life-span development asserts that psychosocial phases of life parallel biological phases of life. Initial phases of psychological expansion in the early periods of life are followed by their culmination and contraction in midlife. The underlying biological phases of those psychosocial phases are *progressive growth* (birth to age 15), *emergence of sexual reproductive capacity* (ages 15–25), *stability* (ages 25–45), *loss of reproductive capacity* (ages 45–65), and *biological decline* (age 65 to death).

The value of Buhler's approach lies in its recognition that, for many people, life is organized around reproductive activities. However, this organization seems more true for women than for men and for people who have chosen lives of celibacy. The biological age periods that Buhler outlined have also changed since she formulated her theory—girls are able to conceive much earlier than age 15, men don't lose their reproductive capacity by age 65, and biological decline now sets in well past age 70.

Each of these theories about life-span development agrees that human development over the course of life is *not* synonymous with growth. First we experience **psychological adolescing,** emerging into full adulthood and realizing the full potential of our humanity. As we come toward the end of life we experience **biological senescing,** becoming biologically older. The study of adulthood incorporates this distinctive coexistence of growth and decline and the challenge of adapting to continual change.

HISTORICAL ANALYSIS OF FAMILIES AND LIFE STAGES

While psychological researchers interested in child and adult development gather their data from observations, interviews, surveys, biographies, and controlled experiments, a new source of evidence enriches our view of human developmental patterns—historical analysis. Only recently has the **historical approach** emerged as a major way of gaining information about development. An interesting aspect of this approach is that *time* is the primary independent variable in the study of development, while *time perspective* is what historians are uniquely qualified to offer.

History puts human affairs into perspective. Developmental psychologists generally portray the child as an isolated entity for professional study. On the other hand, historical analysis studies individual development in a social, economic, and political context (Furstenberg, 1985). Historical analysis of the family includes both cross-sectional and longitudinal research—historians examine the individual nuclear family as well as its relationship to extended kinships and to the larger social community. Family histories demonstrate how families are influenced by major social forces at a particular historical period and, in turn, how families then become active agents of subsequent social change (Smuts & Hagen, 1985). Historical analysis also reveals how society and science interact to define and to set norms for various stages of life while influencing family practices, such as those defining roles for mothers and those governing the care of elderly parents. With a historical perspective, it is possible to see how social and legal policies that affect families and their members are themselves influenced by the historical circumstances of an era. For example, rigid, authoritarian child-rearing practices are traced to times of evangelical religious fervor. The current phenomenon of latchkey kids is a complex consequence of high divorce rates, smaller family size, absence of extended families, and working parents.

Using the historical perspective, developmental psychologists have come to see that the transitions of individual life patterns—entering school, work, and marriage—are synchronized to collective changes taking place within the family. We now also know that transitions of individuals and families are better understood within the broader historical circumstances of the time. For example, because of current social values, you will probably make your decision about whether to marry or to have children later in your life than your parents did. Your decision to go away to college or to seek a job in another city reflects current individualistic and achievement values of U.S. society and it creates the empty-nest syndrome for your parents in their middle age. This syndrome is not found in other cultures where children stay close to their parents throughout their lives.

Changing Conceptions of Childhood

Prior to the sixteenth century, most children older than 6 years of age were considered small adults and were expected to perform as adults whenever their competencies allowed it. During this grim period of history, parents and employers had virtually unlimited power over children; children were abused, abandoned, sold as slaves, and mutilated (McCoy, 1988; Pappas, 1983).

From the sixteenth through the eighteenth centuries, children were considered *chattel*, family property useful for doing family work and for supporting parents. In those times of high infant and child mortality, adults considered young children to be interchangeable and replaceable—children's individual identities weren't acknowledged; all that mattered was their ability to contribute to the welfare of the family. Children were expected to assume adult responsibilities as soon as they were physically able. Not until increased industrialization, during the nineteenth-century Industrial Revolution, reduced the need for children as cheap sources of labor was adolescence "invented" and then the concept was developed only to keep young people out of a competitive job market (Krett, 1977). Eventually, children began to be treated as *valuable* and also as *vulnerable* property by parents, schools, and society. During the 1800s, people began to perceive that many conditions associated with industrialization, urbanization, and immigration were threatening to children. These concerns led to child labor laws, compulsory education, and juvenile court systems.

During the first half of the twentieth century, children became valued as potential persons. Child-oriented family life emerged along with external sources of influence on child care, such as developmental psychology and juvenile courts. But the child's status as a person did not receive societal acknowledgement until the second half of this century. The emerging status of *child as person* afforded children legal rights including protection from abuse and neglect, due process in juvenile courts, and self-determination. Children are now recognized as competent persons worthy of considerable freedom (Horowitz, 1984).

Changes in U.S. attitudes towards children have been influenced by many factors: economic events, changes in attitudes towards work and education, improved childbearing, lower mortality rates, changing state interests, decisions made in activist courts, and the development of professions that support the rights of children. However, at this point in history, further advances in securing the person status of children require greater contribution by psychologists. As a science, psychology can provide empirical evidence of children's readiness or capacities for self-determination and develop the best practices for achieving self-determination within a context of nurturing support and protection. "As a human service profession, psychology is capable of translating its knowledge base into support for a positive ideology of children that involves them in establishing their rights. Psychology has a preeminent responsibility to assist persons toward higher levels of self-determination and personhood" (Hart, 1991, pp. 57–58).

FAMILIES AND YOUTH AT RISK

Traditionally, psychologists have focused their attention on the developing individual as distinct from the social-economic-health context in which the child or adult functions. The assumption has been that those environments were relatively normal or similar enough for those people being studied that they could be ignored or discounted as significant contributors to variations in psychological development. Sociologists were assigned the task of exploring how family disintegration, poverty, and social alienation affect development. Current trends in the United States and in many countries throughout the world make it impossible for developmental psychologists not to consider the exceptional circumstances in which many children, adolescents, and adults are forced to live and that continually put their very sanity, safety, and survival at risk (Dryfoss, 1990).

Historical analysis is encouraging in that it reveals that treatment of children and adolescents has continually improved over the centuries. However, many current indicators suggest that the 1980 decade was terrible for youth and many families and that conditions will worsen in the 1990s. More American children today than at the start of the last decade are likely to be poor, pregnant, in jail, hungry, homeless, suffering from psychological problems, or dead from violence and preventable diseases. These conclusions emerge from a number of recent nationwide surveys (Center for the Study of Social Policy, 1991; National Center for Health Statistics, 1990; National Association of Children's Hospitals and Related Institutions, 1989; Carnegie Foundation Study of the Condition of Teaching, 1988; *The Health of America's Children*, 1988).

Consider the following evidence for the decline in the quality of life of America's youth and their families:

- Low birth weight, affecting 270,000 infants annually, doubles or triples the risk of chronic handicap, such as mental retardation, deafness, and blindness. The major cause of low birth weight is lack of or delayed prenatal care. In 1985, three of every ten women of all races in the United States did not receive adequate prenatal care; the figure escalates to one in every two for African-American women.
- Hundreds of thousands of children who survive until school age will suffer from some sort of developmental disability as a result of having eaten lead-contaminated paint chips or from having been born to crack cocaine-addicted mothers. Thousands more will be malnourished or physically or sexually abused. Child abuse and neglect cases increased by 55 percent between 1981 and 1985. Nationwide, 68 percent of teachers report the existence of undernourished children in their schools; 69 percent have said that the poor health of their students poses a problem in the classroom; and 89 percent of teachers report that there are abused or neglected children in their schools.
- The most recent census figures show that 20 percent of children in the United States live in families with incomes below the poverty line. Family poverty is an extension of the social and economic changes affecting families in all income classes (Bane & Ellwood, 1989).
- The teenage suicide rate has doubled in the past two decades. Teenage violent deaths increased by 12 percent between 1984 and 1988; juvenile incarceration rates increased by 41 percent between 1979 and 1987; and more than 50,000 juveniles are currently serving time in some kind of penal institution.
- Births to unmarried women increased dramatically in 1985, with 22 percent of all births, and 51 percent of all nonwhite births, occurring to unmarried women, many of whom were in their teens.
- One in every five children under age 18 has a learning, emotional, behavioral, or developmental problem that researchers trace to the continuing dissolution of the two-parent family.

Patterns of development of deprived and abused people may be very different from those patterns of people who researchers have systematically studied.

These serious psychological problems, which affect an estimated 10 million American children, are linked primarily to "negative family dynamics," which include parents' divorce, single parent situations, conflict-filled environments, and sub-poverty level households run by single parents with little education. Many of these problems are not diagnosed, and even when they are, only a fourth of the afflicted children receive any special educational help in school.

• It is estimated that one-third of the growing population of homeless people in cities throughout the United States are families who live in shelters or on the streets. There may be as many as 750,000 homeless children in this country. Today's homeless are not only more numerous than in the past; they are also much younger and include more women, minorities, veterans, and former mental patients (Shinn & Weitzman, 1990). Homeless children suffer specific physical, psychological, academic, and emotional damage due to the unstable, hostile circumstances accompanying homelessness (Molnar et al., 1990).

The development of many people in the United States and worldwide is impaired in ways that are not under their control. Contemporary problems facing children, adolescents, adults, and families have an adverse effect on their physical and psychological well-being, the extent of which we have not yet been able to measure. Major reforms are clearly needed to institute and coordinate better health-care, welfare programs, and social policy; but there is another important conclusion from these statistics. Developmental psychologists typically analyze life stages by focusing on a typical or average individual. Their analysis usually does not include exceptions to the norm, even though patterns of development for deprived and abused people may be very different from those for the people researchers have systematically studied. Only new research will tell us if this is so.

SUMMING UP

The field of developmental psychology has broadened its perspective to recognize the continuing challenges and changes that mark the entire life span. Life-span theorist Erikson identified the psychosocial tasks that accompany each of the four later life stages, from adolescence through late adulthood. Jung emphasized the contrasting foci of youth on outward experience and of adulthood on inward experience. Buhler focused on the concordance between biological reproductive stages and developmental stages.

Another new direction in developmental psychology is the use of historical analysis to provide a fuller context for understanding the individual development of children and family life. From application of this approach, we learn that, until recently, children were perceived as property, to be used and abused by parents and employers. While conditions for children have greatly improved since the sixteenth century, a brief survey of current conditions for children offers a pessimistic view: children are still at risk for developing many psychological and physical problems.

ADOLESCENCE

Adolescence is commonly defined as the stage of life that begins at the onset of *puberty*, when sexual maturity, or the ability to reproduce, is attained. However, where adolescence ends and adulthood begins is not so clear. Much of the difficulty of defining the span of adolescence is attributed to variations among cultures—although the physical changes that take place at this stage are universal, the social and psychological dimensions of the adolescent experience are highly dependent on the cultural context.

TRANSITION MARKERS AND INITIATION RITES

Can you identify a time when you were aware that you were becoming an adolescent? Most nonindustrial societies do not identify an actual adolescent stage as we know it. Instead, many such societies have *rites of passage* or **initiation rites.** These rituals usually take place around puberty and serve as a public acknowledgment of the transition from childhood to adulthood. The rites themselves vary widely from extremely painful ordeals to periods of instruction in sexual and cultural practices or periods of seclusion involving survival ordeals. Rites involving genital operations or forms of physical scarring or tattooing give initiates permanent physical markers of adult status. Separate rites are carried out for males and females, reflecting the clear separation of gender roles in these cultures. Whatever form they take, such rites are usually highly dramatic and memorable ceremonies in which young initiates symbolically give up their childhood roles and accept the full privileges and responsibilities of adulthood.

Why do many initiation ceremonies involve some form of ordeal or torture, especially of male children? Cross-cultural studies of these practices by cultural anthropologists have suggested several interesting hypotheses about their psychological (or psychoanalytic) meaning. Before entering adult status, male children must resolve several forms of *power problems*. They must identify themselves with powerful males rather than harbor any impulses of violence toward adult males, especially their fathers. This process is known as "identification with the aggressor." Young males also need to give up being dependent on and too physically (or sexually) close to their mothers, so that they are not ambivalent about their male status, and so that they are unlikely to violate incest taboos (DeVos & Hippler, 1969). Another hypothesis proposes that initiation rituals involve some form of genital organ mutilation so that children of both sexes perceive adult sexual organs as symbols of power and align themselves with the power of same-sex adults, keeping that power away from the other sex (Bettleheim, 1962).

In many traditional societies, then, the period of adolescence as a transition between childhood and adulthood lasts for only the few hours or the few months of the rite of passage. Once individuals have passed through that period, there is no ambiguity about their status—they are adults and the ties to their childhood have been severed. In our society there are few transition rituals to help children clearly mark their new adolescent status or for adolescents to know when they have become young adults.

The adolescent stage is a time in which childhood dependence on parents and other adults is replaced by independence and self-definition. In U.S. society adolescence can extend for more than a decade, through the teens to the mid-20s, until adult roles begin, and it has no clearly defined beginning or end. The legal system defines adult status according to age; but different legal ages exist for "adult" activities, such as drinking alcohol in public, driving, engaging in sex, marrying without parental consent, joining the military, and voting.

Similarly, social events, such as graduation from high school (or college, or graduate school), moving out of the family home, the establishment of financial independence, and marriage, have been used to mark the beginning of adulthood. Even religious rituals, such as confirmation or the Hebrew bar mitzvah (for males) and bat mitzvah (for females), are not lasting indicators of adulthood for the 13-year-old initiate.

THE MYTH OF ADOLESCENT "STORM AND STRESS"

Adolescents in modern Western society are faced with choosing among a wide variety of possible roles and values. Although they experience parental, peer, and social pressures to adopt certain roles, these influences may provide different and sometimes conflicting ideals. It is ultimately up to each person to forge a personal *identity,* to choose principles and values, and to elect

Many cultures have initiation rites that signal a child's passage into adulthood. Shown above left is a bar mitzvah, a Jewish ceremony marking a boy's 13th birthday. The photo at left records the puberty rites of the White Mountain Apaches of Arizona. At right is the initiation ceremony of a young Lamaist monk.

what life direction to pursue. Given the complexity and rapid social change characteristic of Western society, it is not surprising that the formation of a stable adult identity can be a slow and difficult process. Recognition of these difficulties has contributed to the view that adolescence is a time of inevitable stress and turmoil. While adolescence can be stressful, most adolescents succeed in making the transition to adulthood without undue trauma.

The traditional "storm and stress" view of adolescence holds that it is a uniquely tumultuous period of life, characterized by extreme mood swings and unpredictable, difficult behavior. This view can be traced back to Romantic writers of the late eighteenth and early nineteenth centuries, such as Goethe. More recently, the storm and stress conception of adolescence was strongly propounded by **G. Stanley Hall,** the first psychologist of the modern era to write at length about adolescent development (1904). Following Hall, the major proponents of this view have been psychoanalytic theorists working within the Freudian tradition (for example, Blos, 1967; A. Freud, 1946, 1958). Some of them have argued that not only is extreme turmoil a normal part of adolescence but that failure to exhibit such turmoil is a sign of arrested development. **Anna Freud** writes that "to be normal during the adolescent period is by itself abnormal" (1958, p. 275).

Two early pioneers in cultural anthropology, **Margaret Mead** (1928) and **Ruth Benedict** (1938), argued that the storm and stress theory is not applicable to many non-Western cultures. They described cultures where children gradually take on more and more adult responsibilities without any sudden stressful transition or period of indecision and turmoil. It was not until large studies were undertaken of representative adolescents in this society, however, that the turmoil theory finally began to be widely questioned within psychology. The results of such studies have been consistent: few adolescents experience the inner turmoil and unpredictable behavior ascribed to them (Offer, et al., 1981a; Oldham, 1978). Offer and his colleagues asked over 20,000 adolescents about their personal experiences. The researchers concluded that normal adolescents "function well, enjoy good relationships with their families and friends, and accept the values of the larger society" (1981 a, p. 116). See **Table 6.2** for a summary of some of the key findings of this ambitious project.

There also appears to be much more consistency in personality development from early adolescence to adulthood than the traditional turmoil theory would predict. Good adjustment in adolescence tends to predict good adjustment in adulthood, and, although adolescence is experienced by many young people as a stressful period, those few adolescents who experience

TABLE 6.2	THE PSYCHOLOGICAL SELF OF THE NORMAL ADOLESCENT

Item	Percentage of Adolescents Endorsing Each Item
I feel relaxed under normal circumstances.	91
I enjoy life.	90
Usually I control myself.	90
I feel strong and healthy.	86
Most of the time I am happy.	85
Even when I am sad I can enjoy a good joke.	83

serious trauma during the period are likely to continue doing so as they move into adulthood (Bachman et al., 1979; Offer & Offer, 1975; Vaillant, 1977). A recent study clearly points to the strong pathway between adolescent conduct problems and subsequent adult criminality.

> A large-scale longitudinal study of adolescents (ages 10–13) attending school in a typical Swedish town compared their conduct status (from teachers' reports) and biological functioning with the likelihood of their having criminal records or other adjustment problems as young adults (ages 18–26). Among the boys, those who showed early aggressiveness, restlessness (hyperactivity), and low levels of adrenaline were significantly more likely to develop into adults who would commit registered criminal offenses. In addition, a more severe pattern of early maladjustment is correlated with other adult adjustment problems as well, such as alcohol abuse and being under psychiatric care. **Figure 6.1** shows the extent to which early aggressiveness is linked to adult criminality (Magnusson, 1987; Magnusson & Bergman, 1990).

TASKS OF ADOLESCENCE

Of all the issues that are important in adolescence, we will focus on three developmental tasks that commonly confront adolescents in Western society: (a) coming to terms with physical maturity and adult sexuality; (b) redefining social roles, including achieving autonomy from parents; and (c) deciding upon occupational goals.

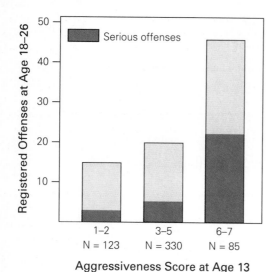

FIGURE 6.1   ADOLESCENT AGGRESSION AND ADULT CRIMINALITY

This chart shows percentages of individuals who achieved various ratings of aggressiveness at the age of 13 and who were registered for criminal offenses at the ages of 18 to 26.

Each of these issues is a component of the central task of establishing an *integrated identity.* Consistent with Erikson's (1968) description of the social context of identity, each of these issues can be looked at as a different way in which young people define themselves in relation to others.

Puberty and Sexuality

The first concrete indicator of the end of childhood is the *pubescent growth spurt.* Two to three years after the onset of the growth spurt, **puberty,** or sexual maturity, is reached. (The Latin word *puberty* means *covered with hair* and signifies the growth of hair on the arms and legs, under the arms, and in the genital areas.) Puberty for males begins with the production of live sperm, while for girls it begins at **menarche,** the onset of menstruation. In the United States, the average time for menarche is between the ages of 12 and 13, although the normal range extends from 11 to 15. For boys, the production of live sperm, accompanied by the ability to ejaculate, first occurs, on the average, at about 14 years, but, again, there is considerable variation in this timing.

Part of achieving a personal identity involves coming to terms with one's physical self by developing a realistic, yet accepting image of physical appearance.

Although attractiveness has been found to have an influence on the way we view each other at all ages (Hatfield & Sprecher, 1986), during adolescence, an individual becomes increasingly self-focused on appearance. The term **body image** refers to the way one subjectively views one's appearance. This image is dependent not only on measurable features, such as height and weight, but also on other people's assessments and on cultural standards of physical beauty. During adolescence, dramatic physical changes and heightened emphasis on peer acceptance (especially peers of the opposite sex) can lead to an increased, if not excessive, concern with one's body image.

Approximately 44 percent of American adolescent girls and 23 percent of boys claimed that they "frequently felt ugly and unattractive" (Offer et al., 1981a). Even more striking, in another study, physical appearance was the biggest source of concern for a group of 240 high-school students (Eme et al., 1979). Again, most of the females in the sample reported being particularly concerned with their appearances. The self-concepts of girls are closely tied to perceptions of their physical attractiveness, while boys seem to be more concerned with their physical prowess, athletic ability, and effectiveness (Lerner et al., 1976). These differences probably mirror a cultural preoccupation with female beauty and male strength, but, because not all adolescents can embody the cultural stereotypes of attractiveness, it is not surprising that this preoccupation can become a major source of concern. However, researchers find that young adolescence appears to be the peak period of such concern, and that, over time, adolescents appear to become more accepting of their appearances. Nonetheless, the attainment of acceptable body images can be a difficult task, especially for adolescent females. Some develop serious eating disorders, such as *anorexia,* which involves self-starvation, and *bulimia,* which involves binging and purging.

A new awareness of sexual feelings and impulses accompanies physical maturity. In one large study of American adolescents, the majority of adolescent males and females said that they often think about sex (Offer et al., 1981a). Although they think about sex, many adolescents still lack adequate knowledge or have misconceptions about sex and sexuality. Because sex is a topic parents find difficult to discuss with their children, adolescents tend to be secretive about their sexual feelings and experiences. Few families encourage open communication about sexual issues. Sex education in junior and senior high schools tends to focus solely on the biology of sex and on the negative aspects of sex, such as sexually transmitted diseases and unwanted pregnancy. For all of these reasons, early sexual feelings and experiences can make many adolescents feel confused and anxious. These uncomfortable feelings can make it particularly difficult for a young person to reconcile conflicts between peer and parental pressures. The development of a sexual identity that defines sexual orientation and guides sexual behavior thus becomes an important task of adolescence.

In early adolescence, masturbation is the most common expression of sexual impulses. About 50 percent of boys and 37 percent of girls report masturbating by the age of 13; 80 percent of boys and 69 percent of girls report masturbating by the age of 18 or 19 (Hass, 1979; Sorensen, 1973). Homosexual experiences are also common in adolescence. Between 14 and 17 percent of teenage boys report some homosexual experiences, although the actual rate may be considerably higher. The rate is about half as high for adolescent girls (Hass, 1979; Sorensen, 1973). The vast majority of adolescents who have homosexual experiences develop an exclusively heterosexual orientation.

Exclusively homosexual feelings are typically much more difficult to resolve during adolescence. While most gays and lesbians first become aware of their sexual orientation in early adolescence, many do not attain positive sexual identities until their middle or late 20s (Riddle & Morin, 1977). The time lag undoubtedly reflects the relative lack of social support for homosexual orientation and exemplifies the importance of society's role in all aspects of identity development.

The proportion of adolescents engaging in sexual intercourse has risen substantially in the last 20 years. Most of this increase is attributable to a dramatic increase in the numbers of adolescent girls becoming sexually active. Coupled with this increase is a trend toward acceptance of nonmarital sex within romantic relationships. It is estimated that at least half of all young people have engaged in intercourse before age 18, and about 75 percent have done so by the age of 20 (Chilman, 1983; London et al., 1989).

About 60 percent of males ages 15 to 19 report having had sexual intercourse—the percentages are higher for black males than hispanic or white males as shown in **Table 6.3.** By age 19, between 82 and 96 percent (depending on race and ethnic background) of these unmarried males report having had intercourse.

There is evidence that the initial sexual experiences of males and females differ substantially. The vast majority of females become sexually involved with individuals with whom they are in love. In contrast, for most adolescent males, personal relationships appear to be less important than the sexual act itself—the average male reports no emotional involvement with his first sexual partner (Miller & Simon, 1980).

Developing a sexual identity involves more than recognizing and accepting one's sexual orientation and gaining sexual experience. Adolescents must develop and then rely on personal values to guide their sexual activity. The development of values can involve a re-evaluation of peer and parental moral values—values that previously may have been accepted unquestioningly. For those adolescents who do choose to become sexually active, the challenge is to conduct their sexual relationships in a responsible fashion. Sexual responsibility entails taking into consideration the present and future consequences of one's actions as well as being sensitive to the needs of one's partner and oneself. One of the greatest challenges in developing a sexual identity is to formulate, and act in accordance with, a personally meaningful sexual ethic. Such an ethic reflects one's

TABLE 6.3 PERCENTAGES OF NEVER-MARRIED MALES AGES 15–19 WHO HAVE HAD SEXUAL INTERCOURSE (1988)

Age	All races (N = 1,880)	Black (N = 676)	Hispanic (N = 385)	White (N = 752)
15–19	60.4	80.6	59.7	56.8
15	32.6	68.6	32.8	25.6
16	49.9	70.1	47.2	46.7
17	65.6	89.6	87.6	59.1
18	71.6	82.5	52.8	71.4
19	85.7	95.9	82.2	84.5

Note: Percentages are not cumulative across ages within racial categories. "All races" includes blacks, whites, Hispanics, and others. For each age except 19 years, racial differences were significant at $p < 0.001$; for the "All races" group, age differences were significant at $p < 0.001$.

personal standards, morals, and preferences and is based on a realistic understanding of the consequences of sexual behavior. While this task may take many years to complete, it is in adolescence that the foundations of a healthy sexual identity are established. The high incidence of teenage pregnancy and sexually transmitted diseases suggests that many adolescents become sexually active before they are capable of shouldering the corresponding responsibilities. For instance, it is estimated that more than one-third of adolescent females who are sexually active (outside of marriage) become pregnant before the age of 19 (Zelnick & Kantner, 1980).

Social Relationships

Family ties are stretched as the adolescent spends more time outside the home. In U.S. society, this change typically means that the adolescent experiences less structure and adult guidance, is exposed to new and perhaps conflicting values, and develops a strong need for peer support and acceptance. Adolescents report spending more than four times as much time talking to peers as adults and also a preference for talking to their peers (Csikszentmihalyi et al., 1977). It is with their peers that adolescents refine their social skills and try out different social roles and behaviors. Through this process, they gradually define the social component of their developing identities, identifying the kind of people they choose to be and the kind of relationships they choose to pursue. Peers become an increasingly important source of social contact and emotional support; but it appears that, as needs for close friendships and peer acceptance become greater, there is also an increase in the anxiety that may become associated with being rejected. Conformity to peer values and behaviors rises to a peak around ages 12 and 13. Concerns with peer acceptance and popularity are particularly strong for females who appear to be more focused upon social relations than their male counterparts; but females are less likely to conform to group pressures to engage in antisocial behaviors than are males (Berndt, 1979). Loneliness also becomes significant at this age; between 15 and 25 percent of adolescents report feeling very lonely (Offer et al., 1981a). Shyness reaches its highest level in early teenage years as desire for social acceptance markedly increases (Zimbardo, 1990).

Engaging in behaviors that parents do not approve of can be a concrete means of establishing independence from them and affirming solidarity with peers. While adolescents may differ greatly from their parents in preferences for music, fashion, and other issues of personal taste, their fundamental values tend to remain similar to those of their parents (Conger, 1991). When conflict does arise, it is often related to relatively super-ficial aspects of adolescent culture. However, conflict sometimes centers on more significant problem behaviors, such as drinking, illicit drug use, and sexual activity. **Richard Jessor,** a noted authority on adolescent problem behavior, suggests that coming to terms with alcohol, drugs, and sex has emerged as a new developmental task that all adolescents face as part of the normal process of growing up in contemporary U.S. society (1982, p. 297).

The dual forces of parents and peers at times exhibit conflicting influences on adolescents, and this conflict can fuel the dynamic process of separating from parents and becoming increasingly identified with peers. In general, however, parents and peers may be seen as serving complementary functions and fulfilling different needs in the lives of adolescents (Davis, 1985). Identity development ultimately involves establishing independent commitments that are sensitive to parental *and* peer environments but are not mere reflections of either. However, among poor children from the inner city, those who cope well have at least one significant adult role model (Carnegie Quarterly, 1990). Similarly, peer support is vital for adolescents who get little support from absent, neglectful, abusive, or harshly critical parents.

Occupational Choice

According to Erikson, deciding upon a vocational commitment is the hallmark of adolescent identity formation. The ubiquitous question, "What are you going to be when you grow up?" reflects the common assumption that occupation largely determines a person's identity. Selecting an occupation involves tasks central to all aspects of identity formation: appraisal of one's abilities and interests, awareness of realistic alternatives, and the ability to make and follow through on a choice. Prior to high school, few young people are concerned with issues such as occupational choice. During the high-school years, concern with future vocations and life-styles increases. Through vocational choice, adolescents can both differentiate themselves from and affirm their acceptance of parental and social values. The resulting sense of continuity and connectedness to one's social environment is critical to achieving a sense of consistent individual identity.

Many personal factors have been found to influence vocational aspirations and achievement, but the clearest factor is socioeconomic background. Adolescents from families of higher socioeconomic status are more likely to pursue and complete postsecondary education, and to have higher levels of occupational aspiration and achievement. Middle-class and upper middle-class parents tend to encourage higher achievement motivation

ALCOHOLISM ON CAMPUS

Addiction

A month into his sophomore year, a Yale student died of alcohol poisoning (Gibson, 1990). After participating in a fraternity pledge ritual that required him to drink beer for an hour-and-half, a Hofstra student fell out of a fifth-story window and broke almost every bone in his body (Associated Press, 1/3/91). In a highly publicized legal case in New Hampshire, the "presence of alcohol" was judged a significant factor in the decision to convict a Dartmouth man of sexually assaulting a female student (Weiss, 1991). These dramatic cases are not rare; rather they are signs of the widespread effects that alcoholism is having on many college students.

Since the mid-1970s, the University of Michigan's Institute for Social Research has tracked patterns of alcohol and drug use among high school and college students. From 1975 to 1989, overall illicit drug use by high school seniors declined slightly from 55 to 51 percent, and cigarette smoking went down from 74 to 66 percent. But alcohol consumption remained the same for the entire period: between 91 and 93 percent of graduating seniors reported drinking alcohol in the preceding 12 months. In 1989, one-third said they consumed five or more drinks in a row in the preceding two weeks (University of Michigan Institute for Social Research, 1990).

These high-school students take their drinking habits to college where 70 to 95 percent of students drink, and 15 to 25 percent can be classified as "heavy or problem drinkers" (Baer et al., 1991).

While alcohol problems in older adults are linked to long-term physical dependence, heavy drinking among college students is more likely to result in emergency room visits because of overdose complications and serious accidents (Morrison, 1990). Accidents involving alcohol are the leading cause of death in 16 to 24 year olds (NIAAA, 1984).

Until recently, college administrators preferred to look the other way. Because alcohol is so readily

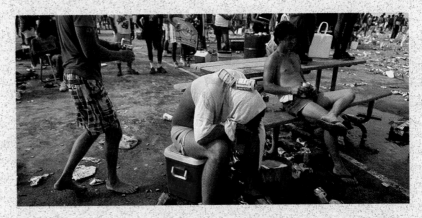

available, no-drinking policies are hard to enforce. Colleges have been reluctant to support programs that teach moderate, responsible drinking—in part because they fear the public will view such support as an endorsement of underage drinking.

Most campus alcohol programs, therefore, serve purely informational functions. Information alone, however, does not work because students rarely identify themselves as problem drinkers (Goodstadt, 1986). Even when changes in attitudes and knowledge are achieved, drinking behavior is unaffected.

At the University of Washington, a pragmatic skills-training program is getting some results. Research indicated that four techniques helped people abstain or moderate their drinking: self-monitoring; understanding the behavioral effects of various blood-alcohol levels; evaluating common drinking situations; and planning strategies to deal with potentially high-risk drinking situations (Alden, 1988; Sanchez-Craig et al., 1984). Using these findings as a basis for the program, psychologist **Alan Marlatt** and his colleagues started teaching students how to moderate their drinking.

The program rests on two assumptions: (a) moderating alcohol consumption significantly reduces the risks of accidents, hangovers, and embarrassment and (b) the effects of alcohol in social settings depend more on one's *beliefs* about such effects than on the pharmacological properties of the drug. For a demonstration of the second point, students go to the University's "bar lab," a dimly lit, fully equipped bar in the psychology building. They believe they are there to undergo tests for alcohol sensitivity. As the subjects wait for their drinks to take effect, a party atmosphere develops in the lab and students report feeling intoxicated.

Then they are told that their drinks contained no alcohol.

In other sessions, students rehearse strategies for coping with social pressure, setting limits, pacing their drinking, and calculating blood-alcohol levels. If they drink in order to relax, they are encouraged to explore alternative techniques, such as exercise or meditation.

In pilot experiments, alcohol consumption decreased substantially by the end of the eight-week course. More significantly, students maintained lower drinking levels for two years after completing the program. If alcohol use is a problem in your school, you might want to consider involving other students and faculty in developing a similar program that meets the particular needs of your student population.

in their children, but they also act as models of higher career success and have the economic resources to provide educational opportunities unavailable to children from less privileged backgrounds.

Educational and occupational choices made in later adolescence can have a profound effect on future options; but, as with all aspects of identity, occupational identity is best conceived of in the context of the whole life cycle. The key is a flexibility and a willingness to explore new directions based on a sense of self-confidence that is developed during successful negotiation through the demands of adolescence.

SUMMING UP

In our society, adolescence is a vaguely defined period between childhood and adulthood, marked by the onset of puberty. In other societies, dramatic initiation rites more clearly define the transition between childhood and adulthood, but individuals in these societies do not actually go through an adolescent stage. Despite reports of the turmoil experienced in adolescence, evidence from self-reports of U.S. adolescents and of individuals in other cultures reveals little evidence that this period is a time of "storm and stress"; most adolescents report being relatively satisfied with their lives. However, an over-concern about appearance and social rejection is common among adolescents, as are shyness, feelings of loneliness, and eating disorders.

The adolescent is challenged to resolve three primary issues: sexuality, social relationships between parents and peers, and occupation selection. Alcohol abuse is one of the problems facing college students, many of whom drink to excess. New programs based on psychological principles are proving effective in training students to control their drinking.

ADULTHOOD

The transition into young adulthood is marked by decisions about advanced education, vocation, intimate relationships, and marriage. What are the tasks of adulthood and what form does cognitive development take over the course of adulthood?

THE TASKS OF ADULTHOOD

According to Freud, despite the many variations in adult life-styles, adult development is driven by two basic needs: *Lieben und Arbeiten,* or *love and work.* Abraham Maslow (1968) described these needs as *love* and *belonging* which, when satisfied, develop into the needs for *success* and *esteem.* Other theorists describe these basic needs as *affiliation* or *social acceptance* needs and *achievement* or *competence* needs. Recall that, for Erikson, the comparable needs are *intimacy* and *generativity.*

Erikson described **intimacy** as the capacity to make a full commitment—sexual, emotional, and moral—to another person. Intimacy, which can occur in both friendships and romantic relationships, requires openness, courage, ethical strength, and usually some sacrifice and compromise of one's personal preferences.

Erikson perceived young adults as consolidating clear and comfortable senses of their identity in preparation for embracing the risks and potentials of intimacy. However, the sequence from identity to intimacy that Erikson described may not accurately reflect present-day realities. The trend in recent years has been for young adults to live together before marrying. As a result, they tend to marry later in life than people did in the past. These societal developments suggest that many individuals today must struggle with identity issues, such as vocational choice, at the same time that they are dealing with intimacy issues.

In addition, marriage, which is the prototype of the successful resolution of the search for intimacy, today often occurs more than once. In fact, married adults are now divorcing at a rate four times greater than adults did 50 years ago. The current prevalence of divorce and separation leads many adults to reexamine their conceptions of, and capacity for, intimacy at later points in the life cycle. A major factor in the rising divorce rate is that spouses have higher expectations for each other and of what constitutes an ideal marriage and family structure (Cleek & Pearson, 1985). However, there is evidence that communication and affection between modern spouses is substantially better than it was in earlier times (Caplow, 1982). Of course, social factors also contribute, such as the easing of divorce laws, a change in attitudes of tolerance for divorce, and an increase in options for men and women after divorce. This is another example of the way social trends affect the course of psychosocial development.

Those who meet the challenges of identity and intimacy successfully usually move on to *generativity.*

In recent years, growing tolerance for divorce has led many adults to change their ideas about traditional marriage. Communication and affection between modern spouses has also changed—improving over earlier times. Shown here on their wedding day are Ril and Sayoko Bandy with Ril's children from a previous marriage.

This is a commitment beyond oneself to family, work, society, or future generations—typically a crucial step in development in one's 30s and 40s. Those who have not successfully resolved the crises of identity and intimacy may still be trying to do so at these ages, perhaps with an increasing sense of insecurity and failure.

A crisis that develops at this middle stage of life is the struggle between the desire for *security,* with its comforting stability and predictability, and the desire for *freedom,* with its exciting potential for adventure and new experiences. In many traditional marriages, women have given up much more of their personal freedom and autonomy than men in the hope of achieving security, which is often illusory and short-lived.

ADULT AGES AND STAGES

Researchers point out that adults are continually exploring options for security, commitment, work, and social acceptance, while, at the same time, seeking greater change, risks, and openness. They reexamine their earlier choices in light of new knowledge, recommitting to them, modifying them, or abandoning them. Life-span developmental researcher **Daniel Levinson** (1978, 1986) outlines the chronological periods in adulthood that correspond to the critical transitions that occur in the building, evaluating, and rebuilding of life structures. As **Table 6.4** shows, adulthood transitions involve periods of questioning, choice, and change.

Systematic studies of personality development in adulthood are comparatively recent and are still mapping unmarked territory. In addition to the work of Levinson, we can point out that of psychoanalytically oriented **George Vaillant** (1977).

For men, the 20s seem to be a period of hope, optimism, and independence, during which they take full responsibility for themselves and for their choice of life-style. Early in the 30s, they may experience a period of reassessment, questioning basic directions set in the 20s and either affirming them or adjusting course to follow new quests. The late 30s are often a time of consolidation and satisfaction. Between 40 and 50 what has come to be known as mid-life crisis may occur, during which past choices and present contributions and commitments are questioned. Life is half over—has freedom been sacrificed for security? Has intimacy been traded for career success? Men become concerned about genuine identity, a later version of adolescents' search for identity. Depending on the way they adapt to the stress of this inner turmoil, adult men may renew commitments, make changes, or become resigned to unfulfilling life situations.

TABLE 6.4   LEVINSON'S STAGES OF ADULTHOOD

Ages 17 to 22	*Early Adult Transition* Leave adolescence, make preliminary choice for adult life.
Ages 22 to 28	*Entering the Adult World* Initial choices in love, occupation, friendship, values, life-style.
Ages 28 to 33	*Age 30 Transition* Change in life structure. Either a moderate change or, more often, a severe and stressful crisis.
Ages 33 to 40	*Settling Down* Establish a niche in society, progress on a timetable, in both family and career accomplishments.
Ages 40 to 45	*Mid-life Transition* Life structure comes into question. Usually a time of crisis in the meaning, direction, and value of each person's life. Neglected parts of the self (talents, desires, aspirations) seek expression.
Ages 45 to 50	*Entering Middle Adulthood* Choices must be made and a new life structure formed. Person must commit to new tasks.
Ages 50 to 55	*Age 50 Transition* Further questioning and modification of the life structure. Men who did not have a crisis at age 40 are likely to have one now.
Ages 55 to 60	*Culmination of Middle Adulthood* Build a new life structure. Can be time of great fulfillment.
Ages 60 to 65	*Late Adult Transition* Reappraisal of life. Moments of pride in achievement are interspersed with periods of despair.
Ages 65 to 80	*Late Adulthood* Make peace with oneself and others. Fewer illusions, broader perspective on life.
Age 80 plus	*Late Late Adulthood* Final transition. Prepare for death.

George Vaillant studied the personality development of 95 highly intelligent men through interviews and observations over a 30-year period following their graduations from college in the mid-1930s. Many of the men showed great changes over time, and their later behavior was often quite different from their behavior in college. The interviews covered the topics of physical health, social relationships, and career achievement. At the end of the 30-year period, the 30 men with the best outcomes and the 30 with the worst outcomes were identified and compared in a number of ways, including in terms of their ma-

turity as defined by Erikson's psychosocial stages. **Table 6.5** compares the scores of the two groups on several items that revealed psychosocial maturity.

By middle life, the best-outcome men were carrying out generativity tasks, assuming responsibility for others and contributing in some way to the world. Their maturity even seemed to be associated with the adjustment of their children—the more mature fathers were more able to give children the help they needed in adjusting to the world. In a supplementary study of 57 members of the sample, the ongoing importance of the ca-

	Best Outcomes (30 men)	Worst Outcomes (30 men)
Childhood environment poor	17%	47%
Pessimism, self-doubt, passivity, and fear of sex at 50	3%	50%
Personality integration rated in bottom fifth percentile during college	0	33%
Subjects whose career choice reflected identification with father	60%	27%
Dominated by mother in adult life	0	40%
Failure to marry by 30	3%	37%
Bleak friendship patterns at 50	0	57%
Current job has little supervisory responsibility	20%	93%
Children's outcome described as good or excellent	66%	23%

pacity for intimacy was confirmed. The purpose of the study was to predict psychosocial adjustment in middle age from measures of social motivation 17 years earlier. The best predictor of mental, physical, and social adjustment was intimacy motivation, "a recurrent preference or readiness for experiences of close, warm, and communicative interpersonal exchange" (Vaillant, 1977, p. 587). The two areas of adjustment that were most highly correlated with intimacy motivation were enjoyment of job and marital satisfaction (McAdams & Vaillant, 1982).

In general, less is known about the adult personality development of women. In light of changing sex roles over the last few decades, a central issue for adult women has become the integration of occupational and family aspirations. Not surprisingly, greater uncertainty about vocational choice is expressed by women than by men. One study found among women whose vocation was exclusively homemaking, feelings of social isolation, frustration, and some guilt for not pursuing goals for which their education had prepared them (Sheehy, 1976). Other research has found that women who have families and work outside the home tend to be more

satisfied with their lives than either single working women or married homemakers (Crosby, 1982).

Some researchers argue that personality development through the adult years continues to progress differently for men and women. This occurs because of their basically different earlier socialization—toward *separateness* for men and *attachment* for women. Each of these trends is one-sided, given evidence that, in mid-life, many men and women try to establish a better balance, the men moving toward more attachment, the women toward greater self-identity (Gilligan, 1982).

Many developmental theorists have proposed that the quality of adult relationships and social functioning can be traced to the quality of parent-child relationships, especially in the early years of life (Ainsworth, 1989; Hartup, 1989; Hazen & Shaver, 1987). Freud described the mother-child unit as the most critical for adult development: "unique, without parallel, established unalterably for a whole lifetime as the first and strongest love-object and as the prototype of all later love relations—for both sexes" (1949, p. 45).

To evaluate the effects of early life experiences on subsequent adult development, it is necessary to do *longitudinal prospective research*, in which data about early

"It just doesn't look like the usual case of midlife crisis, Dr. Elmark."

relationships is collected when the subjects are children. Instead, much research has been of a retrospective nature, assessing the childhood rearing patterns and parent-child relationships of adult subjects. Such research may provide biased, or misremembered accounts. A recent study has carefully examined the childhood antecedents of social accomplishment of mid-life adults by using a prospective longitudinal design on a large sample of children. The social accomplishment that the researcher measured was a subject's capacity to maintain a marriage, a family, and outside friendships (based on Vaillant's study, 1977).

> The study began in 1951 with interviews of 379 mothers about the child-rearing practices they used with their 5-year-old kindergartners. Additional data about the social and personal adjustment of each child (202 boys, and 177 girls from both working class and middle-class backgrounds) were collected from the kindergarten teachers. Until the children turned 18, researchers also made measures of sources of family stress including divorce, death, hospitalization, and moving.
>
> When these subjects turned 41, those who could be contacted completed questionnaires and interviews. The final sample consisted of 76 married or previously married white subjects—33 men and 43 women—primarily from middle-class backgrounds. Measures of social adjustment were taken in the form of reports about various aspects of each subject's life history including marriage, divorce, friendships, and the quality of personal

relationships. Other measures taken included physical health, life satisfaction, feelings of stress and well-being, and psychosocial generativity—concern for and commitment to the next generation.

The key finding in this study was that the mothers' reports of feelings of warmth felt and expressed for their 5-year-old child were significantly associated with the child's conventional social accomplishment more than three decades later. Adults with warm, affectionate mothers or fathers were able to sustain long and relatively happy marriages, raise children, and be involved with friends at mid-life. Contrary to expectations, parental harmony did not relate to social accomplishment in the adults, nor did having a difficult childhood. Socially accomplished adults were emotionally stable, active, reliable, and self-disciplined. Compared to the subjects who tested low on this measure of conventional social adjustment, the socially accomplished subjects had higher levels of psychological well-being, had less strain, and showed a greater sense of generativity. In addition, those whose marriages and family lives were working best were also more committed to and involved with their life work (Franz et al., 1991).

ADULT THINKING

Adults' thinking differs from adolescents' in several distinctive ways. In the process of meeting the tasks of adulthood, adults change their style of thinking to become more highly focused and channeled in specific directions. They must more often take into account the differing perspectives of people from a wider range of ages and backgrounds than they did as adolescents. They must discover how to negotiate disputes and resolve conflicts through compromise, bargaining, and generating alternative goals or paths.

Recall that, according to Piaget, the final stage of cognitive development is that of *formal operational thought,* achieved in adolescence through maturation and educational experience. Formal thinking enables one to reason logically, use abstract thought to solve general problems, and consider hypothetical possibilities in given types of structured systems. But most of the everyday, practical problems of adults occur in ambiguous, unstructured social and work relationships. Dealing with these unknowns and partial truths with formal thought is too limiting and rigid. What adult life requires is a more dynamic, less abstract, and less absolute way of thinking that can deal with inconsistencies, contradictions, and ambiguities. This pragmatic, world-wise cognitive style that adults use is referred to as **postformal thought** (Basseches, 1984; Labovie-Vief, 1985).

K. Warner Schaie (1982), one of the leading researchers on adult thinking, suggested that the cognitive style of adults occurs in stages. **Table 6.6** outlines the five stages of cognitive development across the life course. Through adolescence, the person acquires information and techniques for solving problems that are generic and not typically relevant to personal life situations. In *early adulthood* this "liberal arts" knowledge gives way at the *achieving stage* to a focus on information used for more narrowly defined, self-relevant purposes, such as achieving specific goals. With *middle adulthood* comes the *responsible stage,* a broadening of this "entrepreneurial" style of personal goal-seeking to a focus on responsibilities to others, especially to family and community. For some people in this mid-adult period, the feeling of responsibility extends to a deeper, more complex concern for social welfare and for harmony between social, political, and occupational groups. Schaie identifies this deeper level as the *executive stage,* where the person thinks in terms of obligations and commitments to larger systems. Finally, during *late adulthood,* the individual refocuses cognitive style inward to make sense of his or her own life and, simultaneously, outward to deal with broad issues, such as the meaning of life and death, and concerns about the survival of the planet. At this *reintegrative stage,* the individual develops a thinking style that is best characterized as evidence of *wisdom.*

One of the hallmarks of adult thinking is the development of higher levels of moral reasoning. Although these higher levels of moral reasoning are increasingly more abstract in cognitive terms, they are believed to be propelled by the practical necessity for sustained responsibility for the welfare of others and also by the experience of having to make irreversible moral choices (Kohlberg, 1973).

MORAL DEVELOPMENT

Morality is a system of beliefs, values, and underlying judgments about the rightness or wrongness of human acts. Developing an understanding and internalization of morality is an important part of socialization. Parents and society want children to become adults who accept their moral value system and whose behavior is guided by moral principles. There is an important difference, however, between moral understanding and moral behavior.

Moral Reasoning

Piaget (1960) sought to tie the development of moral judgment to a child's general cognitive development, as discussed in Chapter 5. As the child progresses through the stages of cognitive growth, he or she assigns differing relative weights to the *consequences* of an act and to the actor's *intentions*. For example, to the *preoperational* child, someone who breaks ten cups accidentally is "naughtier" than someone who breaks one cup intentionally. As the child gets older, the actor's intentions weigh more heavily in the judgment of morality. The best-known psychological approach to moral development was created by **Lawrence Kohlberg** (1964, 1981). Kohlberg, who based his theory on Piaget's earlier work, focused on the stages of development of *moral reasoning*. Each stage is characterized by a different basis for making moral judgments. **Table 6.7** summarizes the seven stages proposed by Kohlberg.

As you can see, the lowest level of moral reasoning is based on self-interest, while higher levels center on social good, regardless of personal gain. The cosmic orientation of stage 7 is very rare, but it is presented as an ideal upper limit. To measure the kinds of moral reasoning that people use at these different stages, Kohlberg used a series of moral dilemmas that pit different moral principles against one another.

In one dilemma, a man named Heinz is trying to help his wife obtain a certain drug needed to treat

TABLE 6.6	SCHAIE'S STAGES OF COGNITIVE DEVELOPMENT

Childhood and Adolescence	Early Adulthood	Middle Adulthood	Late Adulthood
Acquisition (Piaget's four stages)	Achieving (goal-directed learning)	Responsible (concern for others)	Reintegrative (wisdom)
		Executive (concern for social systems)	

TABLE 6.7   KOHLBERG'S STAGES OF MORAL REASONING

Levels and Stages	Reasons for Moral Behavior
I Preconventional Morality	
Stage 1 Pleasure/pain orientation	To avoid pain or not to get caught
Stage 2 Cost-benefit orientation; reciprocity—an eye for an eye	To get rewards
II Conventional Morality	
Stage 3 Good child orientation	To gain acceptance and avoid disapproval
Stage 4 Law and order orientation	To follow rules, avoid censure by authorities
III Principled Morality	
Stage 5 Social contract orientation	To promote the society's welfare
Stage 6 Ethical principle orientation	To achieve justice and avoid self-condemnation
Stage 7 Cosmic orientation	To be true to universal principles and feel oneself part of a cosmic direction that transcends social norms

her cancer. An unscrupulous druggist will only sell it to Heinz for ten times more than what the druggist paid. This is much more money than Heinz has and more than he can raise. Heinz becomes desperate, breaks into the druggist's store and steals the drug for his wife. Should Heinz have done that? Why? An interviewer probes the subject for the reasons for the decision and then scores the answers.

The scoring is based on the reasons the person gives for the decision and not on the decision that is made. For example, a subject who says that the man should steal the drug because of his obligation to his dying wife or that he should not steal the drug because of his obligation to uphold the law of society (despite his personal feelings about saving his wife's life) is expressing concern about meeting *established obligations* and is scored at stage 4.

There are four principles governing Kohlberg's moral stage model: (a) an individual can be at one and only one of these stages at a given time; (b) everyone goes through the stages in a fixed order; (c) each stage is more comprehensive and complex than the preceding; and (d) the same stages occur in every culture. These principles apply more clearly to the first three stages of moral reasoning than they do to the last four. Stages 1 to 3 are traversed by all people over the course of normal cognitive development; almost all children reach stage 3 by the age of 13. The stages are acquired in

order, and each can be seen to be more cognitively sophisticated than the preceding. Acquisition of these stages generally parallels the development of stages of cognitive ability proposed by Piaget. In contrast, not all people attain stages 4 to 7; in fact, many adults never reach stage 5, and only a few go beyond it. The higher stages are not associated with any particular age or type of cognitive achievement. Sometimes adults who have attained a higher stage drop back a stage or two under certain circumstances. The content of the stages themselves appears to be somewhat more subjective, and it is harder to understand each successive stage as more comprehensive and sophisticated than the preceding. For example, "avoiding self-condemnation," the basis for moral judgments at stage 6, does not seem obviously more sophisticated than "promoting society's welfare," the basis for judgments at stage 5. In addition, the higher stages are not found in all cultures and appear to be associated with education and verbal ability in our own culture, features which should not necessarily be prerequisites for moral achievement (Rest & Thoma, 1986).

Kohlberg's stages of moral reasoning have generated considerable controversy. Some of this controversy has arisen from concerns about the universality of the stages, especially the higher stages, which sometimes are not found at all in cultures that do not emphasize a high degree of abstraction and education (Gibbs, 1977; Simpson 1974). Especially controversial is the early claim Kohlberg made that women lag behind men in moral development, typically stopping at a less advanced level than men do. Finally, many researchers have questioned his decision to study moral *reasoning* instead of moral *action;* these critics believe that what people *say* and what they *do* when faced with moral choices often differ (Kurtines & Greif, 1974). Let's examine more closely these last two criticisms.

Controversy: Gender Differences in Moral Judgment

There has been considerable controversy over the question of gender differences in moral reasoning. In early experiments, Kohlberg (1969) and others using his measurement paradigm (Alker & Poppen, 1973) found that most men reach stage 4, a law-and-order orientation, while most women remain at stage 3, where moral reasoning involves living up to the expectations of others. This conclusion is challenged by some researchers. **Carol Gilligan** (1982) has proposed that Kohlberg's finding that women's morality is less fully developed than men can be explained by the fact that his coding scheme is biased in favor of men. His original work was developed from observations of boys only. Gilligan believes that women develop *differently,* not *less* morally. She proposes that women's moral development is based on a standard of *caring for others* and progresses to a stage of self-realization, whereas men base their reasoning on a standard of *justice.* Other researchers dispute whether gender differences in moral reasoning really exist at all (Baumrind, 1986). An extensive review of the empirical literature shows that gender differences in moral reasoning are rarely found, and, when they are found, they are explained by the male subjects in a particular study having a higher average education level than the female subjects (Walker, 1984). At the same time, there are studies that indicate that women may call more on rationales for their moral decisions that involve maintaining harmony in their social relationships. Men are more likely to call on the need to maintain justice; in addition, men may refer more to fairness (Lyons, 1983). These possibly different orientations may not necessarily correspond to women and men scoring differently on Kohlberg's scale or other moral reasoning scales (Gibbs et al., 1984; Lyons, 1983). The jury is still out on this complex issue.

Moral Action

Of course, these intriguing sex differences in moral judgment or orientation may have absolutely nothing to do with moral behavior. The majority of studies of gender differences in prosocial or moral behaviors have found no consistent gender differences (Eisenberg & Mussen, 1989; Radke-Yarrow et al., 1983). In addition, very different patterns of moral reasoning and understanding may lead to the same moral behaviors. Furthermore, one's level of moral understanding may have little to do with one's display of moral action.

> In the 1920s, a team of Yale University behaviorists set out to study moral knowledge and its relation to moral behavior in children ages 6 to 14. They administered tests of moral knowledge to large numbers of children and observed their behavior in situations where there was a chance to be either honest or dishonest. The data were unexpected. Most children were honest in some situations and dishonest in others. Instead of being guided by a general trait of honesty or dishonesty, behavior seemed to depend more on the situation—how attractive the reward was and how likely the children were to get caught. Also, moral or immoral behavior showed little relation to moral knowledge, which was generally high, and there was no evidence of greater moral development with age. These experimenters concluded that, although moral knowledge may be stable, moral behavior is not a stable quality in people; rather it is a response that varies with the *demands of the situation* (Hartshorne & May, 1928).

Kohlberg's theory of moral development does not address human motivation to act morally because he was interested in the cognitive aspect of moral reasoning and not of behavior. However, if we want to understand moral development more completely, we must consider what it is that motivates people to behave honestly, cooperatively, or altruistically. Several groups of psychologists recently have begun to investigate the emotional and social roots of morality. **Martin Hoffman** (1987), among others, argues that emotions within the child, especially *empathy,* may provide the motivation for moral behavior. Observational studies reveal that children experience empathy at very young ages, and some researchers believe that empathy may actually be an innate response such as sucking or crying.

Empathy is the condition of feeling someone else's emotion. Feeling another person's distress may trigger a sympathetic response. First, children feel distress with and then sorrow for another individual. Children then may want to reduce these unpleasant feelings, and they discover that acting positively towards the distressed person helps accomplish this. Young children are capable of positive social behaviors designed to help or comfort others in apparent distress. Many psychologists now believe these types of behaviors signal the start of moral development. Empathy may represent part of the foundation for future moral behavior.

Thus, we need a new theory of moral development that integrates patterns of moral reasoning with the motivational and social conditions under which moral behaviors, such as altruism, are enacted at various stages in human development (Zahn-Waxler & Radke-Yarrow, 1982).

 ### SUMMING UP

Life-span theorists have proposed models of adult personality, cognition, and moral reasoning developmental stages. Different investigators agree that the main needs and tasks of adulthood are organized around love, affiliation, social acceptance, and intimacy, on one side, and work, success, esteem, and generativity, on the other. Changing social values and standards are modifying traditional views regarding marriage, family, and divorce. A major change in adult thinking is the emergence of postformal thinking which is pragmatic, problem oriented, socially sensitive, and flexible to cope with the ambiguities of adult life.

Moral reasoning follows a clear stage model of development at the lower levels, but it doesn't for the hypothesized higher levels. Controversy exists about the nature of gender differences in moral reasoning; some investigators have responded to research that has shown differences between the moral levels of men and women by arguing that females are more responsive to social obligations (which gives them lower scores on the scale) than males who are focused more on the issue of justice as the moral code of their reasoning. More research is needed on moral behavior—on the conditions under which children and adults behave in moral or immoral ways, regardless of the underlying cognitive aspects of their moral reasoning.

OLD AGE

One of the fastest-growing special fields in psychology is **behavioral gerontology,** the study of all the psychological aspects of aging and of the elderly. One reason for this growth area is revealed by national *demographics,* the study of populations. At the beginning of this century, only 3 percent of the U.S. population was over 65. Today that figure is about 13 percent, and, when the baby-boom generation reaches old age, nearly a quarter of our population will be in this oldest group. The projection for the year 2030 (when today's college students will be around 60 years old) is that more than 80 million Americans will be over 60 years of age. That is more than the number expected to be under 20 years of age—a dramatic reversal of all previous demographics

(Pifer & Bronte, 1986). With such drastic changes occurring in the age distribution of our society, it is more essential than ever for us to understand the nature of aging as well as the particular abilities and needs of the elderly.

AGEISM AND MYTHS OF THE AGED

Ageism is the term for prejudice against older people. Ageism leads to discrimination against the elderly that limits their opportunities, isolates them, and fosters negative self-images about them. Our society values growth, strength, and physical appearance and worships youthfulness; the enemy—getting old—is marked by signs of decline and weakness (Butler & Lewis, 1982). Even undergraduate psychology texts have been found guilty of ageism. A survey of 139 texts written over the past 40 years reveals that many of the texts failed to cover the period of late adulthood or presented stereotypical views of the elderly (Whitbourne & Hulicka, 1990). But a more dramatic instance of ageism is shown in the personal experiences of a reporter who deliberately "turned old" for a while.

> **Pat Moore** disguised herself as an 85-year-old woman and wandered the streets of over 100 American cities to discover what it means to be old in America. Clouded contact lenses and earplugs diminished her vision and hearing; bindings on her legs made walking difficult; and taped fin-

At left is Pat Moore; in the photo on the right, she is disguised as an elderly woman. (*Discovering Psychology,* 1990, Program 18).

gers had the dexterity of arthritic ones. This "little old lady" struggled to survive in a world designed for the young, strong, and agile. She couldn't open jars, hold pens, read labels, or climb up bus steps. The world of speed, noise, and shadows frightened her. When she needed assistance, few ever offered it. She was often ridiculed for being old and vulnerable and was even violently attacked by a gang of adolescents (Moore in *Discovering Psychology,* 1990, Program 18).

Old age does increase susceptibility to illness. Even so, it is crucial to distinguish changes associated with normal aging—changes most people can expect as they grow old—from those associated with disease or illness. Making this distinction is not as simple as it sounds. At one time, it was a commonly held myth that anyone would become senile if he or she lived long enough. Now, most severe cognitive deficits are attributed to specific age-related diseases—some of which are avoidable or treatable—rather than to natural consequences of the aging process. Is it true that "You can't teach an old dog new tricks," "Old people lose their sexuality," and "Old people are typically abandoned by their children"? A few myths about aging are partially borne out by scientific data, but most are not.

The boundaries between what we consider normal age changes and what we consider the effects of disease and illness are changing with our expanding medical knowledge. Indeed, we now know that most cognitive abilities do not show major or significant decline under ordinary circumstances of aging. In this final section of our study of development, let's examine normal aging.

RESEARCH APPROACHES TO AGING

As you learn about psychological research on aging, be inquisitive about the sources of data you encounter. Most often, what you will be interested in are *age changes*—the way people change as they grow older. Usually, however, empirical data demonstrate *age differences*—the way people of different ages differ from one another. Why is this so? Cross-sectional research designs are more commonly used than longitudinal research. Age differences uncovered in cross-sectional studies sometimes reflect age-changes, but sometimes they do not. They may instead represent *cohort effects,* that is, differences between people born at different times in history, rather than differences in what the same people at different chronological ages can do.

Consider an imaginary study on computer literacy as an example of the way research can be misleading. You sit people of varying ages in front of word processors. Then you ask the subjects to perform basic word processing tasks. You discover that the older a subject

is the worse he or she performs the task. Are you willing to conclude that, as people age, they lose their abilities to use computers? Certainly not. Many older generations did not have access to such technology until they were well into their adult years, if ever. You, by contrast, are more than likely computer literate. As you can see, the critical difference is not the age of the person but the experience of the different cohorts. Does a study compare individuals of different age groups? If so, it informs us only of differences or similarities between younger people and older people. Does a study compare assessments of the same individuals over time? If so, it can inform us about how people change or remain the same as they age. It is important to interpret data on aging cautiously. By simply finding out if a particular study employed longitudinal or cross-sectional design, you will already know a great deal about the usefulness of the data collected. According to K. Warner Schaie (1989, p. 487), "Only longitudinal data permit investigation of individual differences in antecedent variables that can differentiate those persons that experience early decrement from others who maintain high levels of functioning well into very advanced age."

NEW PERSPECTIVES ON AGING

Aging can mean different things depending on what perspective you take. From a biological perspective, aging typically means decline: energy reserves are reduced, cells decay, and muscle tone diminishes. From a psychological perspective, however, aging is not synonymous with decline. Many aspects of the human condition improve with age. The lifelong accumulation of experience, for example, may culminate in wisdom in old age. One recent theoretical approach to studying change and stability views development—at any age—in terms of the joint occurrence of gains and losses (Baltes, 1987). For example, as a child gains the ability to talk, to some extent she loses the ability to get what she wants by simply crying or fussing. In old age, a person may lose energy reserve but gain an ability to control emotional experiences and thereby conserve energy. Viewed in this way, we can expect two kinds of changes—gains and losses—as we grow older. If experiencing both gains and losses is typical, then what would be a good strategy for dealing with life's changes?

Successful aging might consist of making the most of gains while minimizing the impact of the losses that accompany normal aging. This strategy for successful aging, proposed by psychologists **Margaret Baltes** and **Paul Baltes,** is called **selective optimization with compensation** (Baltes, M., 1986; Baltes, P., 1987). *Selective* means that people scale down the number and extent of their goals for themselves. *Optimization* refers to people exercising or training themselves in areas that are of highest priority to them. *Compensation* means that people use alternative ways to deal with losses, for example, choosing age-friendly environments. While this general strategy of adapting to losses and taking advantage of gains may be universal, each individual's adaptations will likely take on quite different forms.

Many older people have discovered particular strategies that help them age successfully. What about those who might experience trouble or personal difficulty in aging? In our youthcentric society, many beliefs about growing old are based more on folklore than on sound empirical evidence. What happens if people arrive at old age believing these myths? Might there be a way to generate more positive approaches to growing old? Consider yourself a consultant of sorts: How might you advise an older person—a grandparent, a neighbor, or yourself in 50 years? Could you suggest ways to live well by taking advantage of remaining abilities and gains, at the same time minimizing the impact of losses? How might you design or envision a more age-friendly world? What kinds of structural improvements do we need to make in our environments and in our society to create a better habitat in which you can grow old successfully?

PHYSIOLOGICAL CHANGES

Some of the most obvious changes that occur with age concern people's physical appearances and abilities. As we grow older, we can expect our skin to wrinkle, our hair to thin and gray, and our height to decrease an inch or two. Because our hearts and lungs operate less efficiently with age, we can expect decreased physical stamina. We can also expect some of our senses to dull. These changes do not appear suddenly at age 65. They occur gradually, beginning as soon as early adulthood. Below are some common age-related sensory and physical changes, their effects, and some ways people effectively deal with them.

Vision

The vast majority of people over 65 experience some loss of visual ability. Without corrective lenses, half of the elderly would be considered legally blind. With age, the lenses of people's eyes become less flexible and yellowed. The rigidity of the lens can make seeing things at close range difficult. Lens rigidity also affects dark adaptation, making night vision more difficult for older people. The yellowing of the lens is thought to be responsible for diminished color vision experienced by some older people. Colors of lower wavelengths—violets, blues, and greens—are particu-

larly hard for some elderly people to discriminate. They also have difficulty identifying objects within dark shadows. Most normal visual changes in old age can be aided with corrective lenses. An elderly person may find glasses helpful for night driving or bifocals useful for close work such as reading.

Hearing

Hearing loss is common among those 60 and older. The average old person will have difficulty hearing high frequency sounds (this impairment is greater for men than for women). So, older people can have a hard time understanding speech—particularly that spoken by high-pitched voices. (Oddly enough, with age, people's speaking voices increase in pitch due to stiffening of the vocal cords.) Deficits in hearing can be quite gradual and hard for an individual to notice until they are extreme. In addition, even when the person becomes aware of it, he or she may wish to deny it because it is perceived as an undesirable sign of old age.

Hearing loss that remains undetected or denied, however, can have far-reaching implications (Maher & Ross, 1984; Manschreck, 1989). An elderly person may think that those around him are whispering so that he won't be able to hear them converse. If this is how someone makes sense of his inability to understand other people's speech, it is easy to see how mild paranoia can develop. It is not uncommon for nursing home residents to exhibit mild paranoid symptoms. By reasoning logically from her initial false premise that the problem is in the social interaction rather than in her hearing

YOUR DESIGN FOR ELDERLY HABITATS

Maye is preparing to send her mother, who has Alzheimer's disease, to a nearby nursing home. She wants her mother to have maximum freedom and self-sufficiency and still get help with her perceptual, cognitive, and physical impairments. Maye has read some research on the importance of elderly people maintaining a sense of control and personal responsibility in their lives, especially when living in the alien environment of nursing homes. Senior citizens who have little or no control over their environment are likely to feel helpless and depressed, and rapid physical decline often accompanies these negative feelings (Schultz, 1976). For people of reduced competence, small improvements in the environment can enhance their quality of life (Lawton, 1977). Maye wants to select an institution designed to maintain her mother's sense of self-control and control of her environment (Rodin & Langer, 1977; Rodin et al., 1982).

Imagine that you are an interior designer. Your firm has accepted a contract to remodel a nursing home. You recently designed a day-care center for infants and toddlers, so you are accustomed to considering special needs in your design. For this job, one of your partners has already prepared plans for the dining room and kitchenette areas. You will be responsible for the halls and bedrooms.

The director of the nursing home describes for you the people who will use and live in the facility. Their memories are so poor that the hospital environment may seem unfamiliar to them every morning. They have trouble with complex tasks because they can't remember the proper *sequence* of actions. They wander and often get disoriented, finding themselves in a dead-end hallway when they were on the way to lunch. They are sensitive to glare, and typically have impaired vision. They often become agitated—by noise, too much activity, or frustration at their diminished condition.

Your partner is M. P. Calkins, a pioneer in the design of habitats for the elderly and for those suffering from **dementia**—loss of intellectual capacity due to organic brain disorders (1988). He has

placed the dining area at one end of a large pod onto which all bedrooms in the unit open. It is visually distinguished from the larger space by low, carpeted walls, railings, and columns, enabling residents to orient themselves to this important activity space as soon as they leave their rooms. The light color of tables and chairs make them easy to distinguish from the darker floor. To facilitate mealtime conversations and keep stimulation to a manageable level, each table seats between two and six people, with each individual's personal space clearly defined. Attractive, dark placemats provide a helpful contrast to the raised edges of lightly colored, oversized plates and bowls. Cups have two handles, and the silverware is heavy, well-balanced, and large enough to grip firmly. There is plenty of space between tables for wheelchairs and walkers. Next to the dining area, the residents can prepare snacks and make coffee in the kitchenette. Food is clearly labeled, and locations for dishes and cookware are indicated by bold, attractive diagrams. The padded vinyl floor is claret—a dark, solid color that permits residents to distinguish dropped utensils, food, or liquids. The round-edged counters are three inches below standard height, and large, comfortable handles open under-the-counter cabinets. To eliminate shadows, bright lights

203

hang on the underside of upper cabinets. Stove timers automatically turn off the burners. Potentially dangerous utensils and appliances are kept in discreetly locked cabinets. A buzzer at the edge of the counter can be used to summon an aide to supervise dangerous or complicated tasks. Although the residents' capacities are limited, this living environment is designed to enhance the independence and dignity of those who live in it (Calkins, 1988).

Maye is favorably impressed with what the nursing home director has described to her, but she won't make a final decision until she sees your plans. As an exercise in environmental design, formulate how your bedroom and hallway plans will accommodate the needs of physically, cognitively, and perceptually impaired residents. Your goal is to modify the environment to fit the capabilities and needs of the elderly who can then enjoy living there. Please take some time to reflect on and outline your design.

loss, an elderly person may begin to believe that others are out to get her. In a controlled laboratory study, similar paranoidlike reactions occurred in young, healthy college student subjects if they experienced hearing deficits without being aware of the true source of their problem. They had been hypnotized to have temporary partial hearing loss with amnesia for the hypnotic suggestion. When others in the room could not be clearly understood, each of the experimental subjects began to respond with suspicion, hostility, and eventually with paranoidlike thinking. Their reactions were reversed with debriefing (Zimbardo et al., 1981).

Thus, it may well be that the prevalence of paranoid thinking among institutionalized elderly is not so much a function of changes in mental functioning due to aging as it is a function of undetected hearing loss. This hearing loss may trigger the cognitive-social process of *misattributing* the causes of others' behavior to their evil intentions. Hearing loss, however, is more easily corrected at the first symptoms with the help of *hearing aid therapy* than it is later with psychotherapy. Hearing aids can compensate for much hearing loss. Speaking in lower tones, enunciating clearly, and reducing background noise can also help older people understand your speech better, reducing the chance for paranoidlike behavior to develop.

Sexual Functioning

One myth about aging is that old people can't or shouldn't be sexual. While some age-related changes affect sexual functioning, belief in a myth such as this can be a greater obstacle to having a satisfying sex life in old age than actual physical limitations. Although sex loses its reproductive functions in old age, it does not lose its capacity to provide pleasure. Indeed, sex is one of life's "healthy pleasures" which should be practiced with regularity whenever possible to enhance successful aging since it is arousing, provides aerobic exercise, stimulates fantasy, and is a form of social interaction (Ornstein & Sobel, 1989). There is no age—for women or for men—at which orgasm ceases. The most notice-able change older women experience after menopause (the cessation of menstruation and ovulation) is less natural lubrication and less fatty tissue surrounding the vagina and clitoris. These changes could result in soreness, but the problem can be prevented easily by using added lubrication. In general, there is less known about how men's sexual functioning changes with age. Older men seem to place less emphasis on ejaculation as the primary means of achieving sexual pleasure. Consequently, older men can maintain their erections longer, which can lead to greater sexual satisfaction for both partners. Sexuality is one clear domain where experience and experimentation can compensate for minor physical changes or general losses in physical stamina.

COGNITIVE CHANGES

One of the great fears about aging is that it is accompanied by the loss of cognitive abilities: thinking productively and creatively, remembering, planning, and making good decisions. Is this fear justified?

Intelligence

There is little evidence to support the notion that general cognitive abilities decline among the healthy elderly. Only about 5 percent of us will become senile and experience major losses in cognitive functioning. The majority of us will experience more difficulty in forming new associations, and we can expect to acquire new information more slowly by the time we are in our 70s or 80s, but we really will undergo no dramatic changes in the way we think and remember. One of the simplest forms of learning, Pavlovian conditioning, declines with age starting around age 40; the decline is also found in other species, such as cats and rabbits (Woodruf-Pak, 1988).

There is even evidence that some aspects of intellectual functioning are superior in older people. For instance, psychologists are now exploring age-related gains in **wisdom**—expertise in the fundamental pragmatics of life (Baltes, 1990). When age-related decline in cognitive functioning occurs, it is usually limited to only some abilities. IQ test scores do decline with age, but that is only because education influences IQ scores and each successive generation is better educated—the historical cohort effect mentioned before. When intelligence is separated into the components that make up our verbal abilities, or *crystallized intelligence,* and those that are part of our ability to learn quickly and thoroughly, or *fluid intelligence,* only fluid intelligence shows slight decline with age (Botwinick, 1977).

Individuals vary greatly in their later life intellectual performance. Some people, such as elderly Supreme Court Justices and important senior contributors to cultural and political life, do not show any decline until their 80s or later. Elderly people who pursue high levels of environmental stimulation, including both formal and informal education, tend to maintain high levels of cognitive abilities. Diversity in cognitive functioning among older individuals leads psychologists to reject claims that cognitive decline in old age is caused by systematic physiological decay of the central nervous system. Instead, it appears that *disuse,* rather

than decay, may be responsible for isolated deficits in intellectual performance. "Use it or lose it," is the motto of the wise elderly. It is even possible to learn how to reuse it after not using it, as research shows.

The cognitive functioning of 229 community-dwelling elderly people in good health (aged 64 to 95) was assessed over a 14-year period. Individuals were classified into two groups: those who had declined (122) and those who had remained stable (107) in inductive reasoning and spatial orientation abilities. Subjects were then assigned to 5-hour training programs on either ability. The study employed a pretest-treatment-posttest control group design: All subjects took pretests and posttests for both inductive reasoning and spatial orientation, and each training group served as a treatment control for the other group. Results show that (a) cognitive training techniques can reverse reliably documented decline over a 14-year period in a substantial number of older adults (up to 50 percent of subjects experienced com-

Elderly people who pursue high levels of environmental stimulation tend to maintain higher levels of cognitive abilities.

plete remediation of their decline in ability); (b) such reversals can be documented for both inductive reasoning and spatial orientation; and (c) training procedures also enhance the performance of many older people who have remained stable in their abilities (Schaie & Willis, 1986).

Showing that reliably demonstrated decline can indeed be reversed has theoretical importance. It raises grave doubts about the universality of intellectual decline due to physiological decay in advanced age. Instead, these data and a body of related research support the view that cognitive deficits in aging are attributable to disuse and can be modified in many of the elderly through specialized educational training.

Memory

A common complaint among the elderly is the feeling that their ability to remember things is not as good as it used to be. While trying to evaluate these complaints, psychologists have learned that not all memory systems show deficits with age. As yet, they have also been unable to come up with an adequate explanation for the mechanisms that underlie memory impairment in old age (Light, 1991). On a number of tests of memory, adults over 60 perform worse than young adults in their 20s (Hutsch & Dixon, 1990; West, 1986). Memory difficulties appear primarily in that part of the memory system known as *short-term*, or *working memory*, where new memories are processed and stored for less than a minute (Poon, 1985). Aging does not seem to diminish *long-term memory* (access to their knowledge store or information about events that occurred long ago). In a study of name and face recognition, middle-aged adults could identify 90 percent of their high school classmates in yearbooks 35 years after graduation, while older adults were still able to recognize 70 to 80 percent of their classmates some 50 years later (Bahrick et al., 1975).

There are many different theories about the effects of age on memory. Some theories focus on differences between old and young people in their efforts to organize and encode the information that is to be remembered later, others point to the elderly's reduced attentional capacity, and still others suggest that the elderly's belief that their memory is poor may impair performance. However, a recent review of all the research designed to assess alternative explanations for age-related differences in memory concludes that none of the explanations offers an adequate account of the evidence (Light, 1991).

Other theories look to differences in the brain. There are two general ways in which age-related, neurobiological changes might result in impaired memory.

The first is cell loss or decay in the brain itself. The second is deficiencies in the biochemicals, or neurotransmitters, that flow through the brain. Research shows that both the mechanics of the brain and its fuel system are implicated in memory ability. If the brain mechanisms responsible for memory are intact in older people, but these mechanisms are not optimally fueled by neuroendocrine systems, then memory impairment might be lessened by increasing neurotransmitter levels. A recent study has shown that long-term memory was enhanced among elderly subjects who were given drinks containing *glucose* (which helps the brain to utilize neuroendocrines). This suggests that neuroendocrine systems may be responsible for memory loss and that pharmacological treatment may improve memory in the elderly (Manning et al., 1990). Another, quite controversial, approach to counteracting memory impairment in the aged involves **fetal brain transplant.** Neuron-rich, developing tissue from the brains of aborted fetuses is transplanted directly into the brains of the elderly. This experimental technique is being used with patients severely affected with Parkinson's disease to improve the dopamine transmission in the dopamine-depleted region of their brain (Lindvall et al., 1990). Exploratory research with this technique has yielded promising results of improved functioning in transplant recipients (Gage, 1990). However, ethical and political concerns are limiting its utility, and more successful experimental tests are required before neural transplantation can be considered a viable therapeutic procedure (Freed, 1990; Sladek & Shoulson, 1988).

Both cognitive theories and neurobiological theories of memory changes related to aging are being vigorously investigated at this time. The hope is to improve not only our general understanding of the nature of human memory and the aging process but to develop strategies and procedures for preventing memory impairment.

We may summarize what is known about the six variables that predict favorable cognitive aging as follows: (a) absence of cardiovascular and other chronic diseases; (b) favorable environment aided by higher levels of social-economic status; (c) involvement in a complex and intellectually stimulating environment; (d) having a flexible personality style at mid-life; (e) having a spouse with a high level of cognitive functioning; and (f) maintaining a level of perceptual processing speed (Schaie, 1989).

SOCIAL CHANGES

One unfortunate consequence of living a long life is that you can expect to outlive some of your friends and family members. Also, some older people find it difficult to get out to socialize with friends and family because their mobility is restricted by illness or disability. Given these considerations, it is not surprising that people become less socially active in old age. This finding is well-established, supported by both cross-sectional and longitudinal studies. Yet, rates of social contact in late life decrease more substantially than can be explained solely by the deaths of friends and loved ones and reduced mobility (as was the case with Nana in our Opening Case scenario). One early explanation assumed that the elderly voluntarily withdraw from society in symbolic preparation for death (Cumming & Henry, 1961). This *disengagement theory* suggested that the elderly's weakened emotional attachments to other people were general, universal, and inevitable.

The disengagement view of social aging has been largely discredited for a number of reasons. The first reason is that it fails to acknowledge that, even though older people limit many types of social contact, they do remain vitally involved with some people—particularly family members and long-time friends. Feelings of social connectedness in these relationships may actually increase with age. Interestingly, having one intimate relationship (with either a friend or family member) has been found to be more important in promoting older people's health, well-being, and longevity than having dozens of casual friends. Having a pet seems to have similar benefits (Siegel, 1990). The second reason the disengagement view has been criticized is that older people are not emotionless or emotionally withdrawn as the disengagement view implies (Levenson et al., 1991; Malatesta & Kalnok, 1984). There is even some evidence that, in old age, emotions become more central determinants of people's social preferences (Frederickson & Carstensen, 1990). One new theory suggests that, as people age, they become more selective in choosing their social partners; that is, they sift through their various interpersonal relationships and maintain only their most rewarding ones. Such selectivity can account for overall reductions in rates of social contact. *Selective social interaction* may also be a practical means by which people can regulate their emotional experiences and conserve their physical energy, according to researcher **Laura Carstensen** (1987, 1991).

PSYCHOPATHOLOGY

The incidence rates for most functional mental disorders appear to be *lowest* after age 65, with the exception of perhaps depression and the dementias, such as Alzheimer's disease (Kay & Bergmann, 1982). The normal course of aging does not necessarily or usually entail worsened mental health.

Depression has long been assumed to be the most common psychological disorder among the elderly, with risk of onset increasing steadily as people age. Recent epidemiological studies, however, have called this assumption into question. Some studies suggest that initial onset of major depression is less prevalent among those 65 and older than in younger groups (Robins et al., 1984). At any rate, depression presents a major problem for many older people: It is the number one reason for psychiatric hospitalization in old age. Depression often accompanies the dependence and helplessness caused by many illnesses. Yet this is true at any age. In fact, older people seem *less* susceptible to depression as a result of physical disability than are middle-aged people. Perhaps this is so because older adults come to expect some degree of dependence in old age.

The suicide rate among older white males is the highest of any age or racial group. Contrary to common belief, these older suicide victims seldom take their lives because they are desperately ill, in debt, or socially isolated. The majority of these suicides can be traced to mental health problems. A recent study in Cook County (which includes Chicago and surrounding suburban areas) found that, while relatively few suicide victims had experienced recent stressful life events, 65 percent had been chronically depressed and 19 percent were alcoholic. These men were usually not receiving psychiatric treatment. Moreover, surviving relatives nearly always professed surprise at the suicides even though half the victims had spoken of suicide in the previous six months (research by D. Clark, reported in the Associated Press, 1991). Clearly, depression and

As people age, they become more selective in choosing their companions, maintaining only the most rewarding social contacts.

mention of suicide in the elderly should be taken as serious danger signs that warrant intervention.

Alzheimer's disease is the most common form of dementia, characterized by gradual loss of memory and deterioration of personality. It is a chronic organic brain syndrome that afflicts about 5 percent of Americans over 65 and 20 percent of those over 80. The causes of Alzheimer's disease are not yet known, and there is no known cure. Its onset is deceptively mild—in early stages the only observable symptom may be memory impairment. However, its course is one of steady deterioration: victims may show gradual personality changes, such as apathy, lack of spontaneity, and withdrawal from social interactions. In advanced stages, people with Alzheimer's disease may become completely mute and inattentive, even forgetting the names of their spouses and children. In these final stages, Alzheimer patients can become incapable of caring for themselves, lose memory for who they are, and eventually die.

AT LIFE'S END

For all of us, death is inevitable, and yet, while medical advances cannot prevent death, they have changed our manner of dying. Chronic illnesses now constitute the major causes of death. So, for most people, dying will now be a lengthy process. Preparing for our deaths and responding to the deaths of others are parts of life that psychologists want to understand so that they may help people through them.

Dying a Good Death

According to some theorists, notably **Elisabeth Kubler-Ross,** all dying patients go through the same series of *emotional stages* (Kubler-Ross, 1969, 1975). The first is *denial*. This initial stage may actually help the person to maintain hope by avoiding overwhelming grief. The second stage is *anger*. This anger arises from the loss of personal control over present and future life plans. The third stage is *bargaining*. At this stage, a dying person, for example, might make an agreement with God in exchange for a little more time. The fourth stage is *depression*. This depression may arise from an anticipated or actual turn for the worse. The final stage is *acceptance*. With enough time and emotional support from caring family, friends, or institutional caregivers, people can work through their anguish and calmly accept their impending death. Kubler-Ross believes that, if people accept their own death, it is easier for them to die in peace and dignity—essentially to die the "good death."

Other researchers studying the reactions of dying

people have observed more fluidity and complexity than is suggested by this fixed-stage model. Denial, anger, and depression may reappear at different times during the dying process, depending on the context of the death and if an illness such as cancer or AIDS is involved (Kastenbaum, 1986). These emotional reactions vary according to the perceived stigma of one's illness, the social support during treatment, and whether there is progressive, steady decline or periodic improvement. Still others suggest that people's responses to their own terminal illnesses remain fairly constant and do not proceed through stages at all. Regardless of these challenges to the universality of her five-stage model, Kubler-Ross' work provides useful insights into the psychology of dying and has helped health-care professionals compassionately assist the dying with this ultimate life transition.

Another way to characterize the dying process is in terms of the physical and socioemotional needs of dying people (Schulz, 1978). The single most important need may be the alleviation of physical pain. Drug therapy is the most common treatment, although surgical procedures are also used. Dying people (as well as their families and friends) also have a number of social and emotional needs that have to be acknowledged. The need to maintain a sense of dignity and self-worth can be met, in part, by allowing dying people control over the course of their treatments. Needs for social closeness and emotional support can be satisfied by involving family members in the treatment process and by allowing dying people ample private time with their loved ones. Often the needs of the chronically ill can be better met in hospices, which create homelike atmospheres, than in hospitals. The primary goal of the **hospice approach** is to make the process of dying more humane than it can be in institutional settings.

Bereavement

The impact of death does not end when a person dies. Family and friends cope with their own feelings of grief and bereavement for months or even years after the death of someone close to them. Loss of a spouse after decades of marriage can be particularly traumatic; it actually substantially increases illness and mortality rates. Compared to the general population, widows and widowers have two times as many diseases as do those of the same age who are single or married (Stroebe et al., 1982). Because women typically live longer, and marry men older than themselves, losing a spouse is much more common for women than for men. Yet there is some evidence that the stress of losing a spouse is harder on men than on women. Research also indicates that intense grief may actually alter the immune systems.

These women, newly widowed, have joined a support group to help them with their losses.

The immune system functioning of 15 healthy men (aged 33 to 76) whose wives were diagnosed with terminal cancer were examined over the course of bereavement. Lymphocyte function was assessed while their wives were still alive, and again at two and at fourteen months after their wives had died. As predicted, compared to the prebereavement period, each man showed sup-

pressed lymphocyte function, especially during the two months following his wife's death. These findings are consistent with a hypothesis that changes in the immune system following bereavement are related to the increased mortality of bereaved widowers (Schliefer et al., 1983).

Although susceptibility to illness tends to increase during bereavement, the actual number of widows and widowers who "die of a broken heart" is fairly small. Most recover from their grief and return to their normal—and sometimes stronger—selves.

Some investigators have identified distinct *stages of mourning* (Kalish, 1985). The first *shock* stage is followed by the *longing* phase of desire to be with the deceased. The third major reaction is the *depression* stage with despair at the loss, sometimes combined with irrational anger and confusion. Finally, the last stage of mourning is the *recovery* phase when the death is put into a meaningful perspective.

With anticipated deaths (as opposed to sudden, accidental deaths), people have time to prepare for the inevitable endings of their important relationships with others and work through *anticipatory grief*. Preparing for such endings might entail sharing innermost feelings and spending quality time together. There is some evidence that, after a partner has died, these last interactions represent what a survivor remembers about his or her relationship with the deceased (Fredrickson, 1990).

A memory of the deceased individual lives on in all those who were somehow touched by his or her presence. It is in this sense that we can say that the human life cycle is neverending.

Development Across the Life Course

Developmental psychologists now recognize that development occurs throughout the entire life span. Three important psychologists who have contributed theories about development over the whole life course are Erikson, Jung, and Buhler. Historical analysis provides a fuller context for understanding how social forces contribute to shaping an individual's development. Until recently, children were treated as property to be used or abused. Many youths now face a hostile economic and social environment which puts them at risk for psychological and social problems.

Adolescence

Adolescence is a vaguely defined period between childhood and adulthood, often marked by the onset of puberty. Research shows that most adolescents are satisfied with their lives but that they are overconcerned about their appearance and social acceptance. Shyness, loneliness, and eating disorders are frequently problems among adolescents. Adolescents must develop a personal identity through accepting their sexuality, forming comfortable social relationships with parents and peers, and choosing an occupation. Alcohol abuse has become a common problem among high school and college students.

Adulthood

The central concerns of adulthood are organized around two groups of needs. The first includes love, affiliation, social acceptance, and intimacy. The second group includes work, success, esteem, and generativity. Adult thought shows the emergence of postformal thinking. Moral reasoning in adults shows a clear stage model of development at the lower levels but not for hypothesized higher levels. There is considerable debate over possible gender differences in moral reasoning.

Old Age

Successful aging can be characterized by people optimizing their functioning in select domains that are of highest priority to them and compensating for losses by using substitute behaviors. Age-related declines in cognitive functioning are typically evident in only some abilities; individuals vary greatly in intellectual performance as they grow old. Declines in performance can often be reversed with educational training. This suggests that isolated cognitive deficits are caused by disuse rather than by decay of the central nervous system. People become less and less socially active as they grow older. It appears that as people age they selectively maintain only those relationships that matter most to them. Emotional closeness within these select relationships may even increase with age. Most people will die in old age from chronic illnesses of long duration. Kubler-Ross suggests that the process of dying involves five emotional stages: denial, anger, bargaining, depression, and finally, acceptance. While these stages should not be considered fixed or universal, they offer insight into people's psychological responses to their own mortality and impending death.

KEY TERMS

adolescence, 185
ageism, 200
Alzheimer's disease, 208
behavioral gerontology, 200
biological senescing, 182
body image, 188
dementia, 203
empathy, 199
fetal brain transplant, 206
historical approach, 183
hospice approach, 208
initiation rites, 185
intimacy, 192

life-span development, 180
life-span developmental psychology, 181
menarche, 188
morality, 197
postformal thought, 197
psychological adolescing, 182
puberty, 188
resiliency, 180
selective optimization with compensation, 201
wisdom, 204

MAJOR CONTRIBUTORS

Baltes, Margaret, 201
Baltes, Paul, 201
Benedict, Ruth, 187
Buhler, Charlotte, 182
Carstensen, Laura, 207
Erikson, Erik, 181
Freud, Anna, 187
Gilligan, Carol, 199
Hall, G. Stanley, 187
Hoffman, Martin, 199

Jessor, Richard, 190
Jung, Carl, 182
Kohlberg, Lawrence, 197
Kubler-Ross, Elisabeth, 208
Levinson, Daniel, 193
Marlatt, Alan, 191
Mead, Margaret, 187
Moore, Pat, 200
Schaie, K. Warner, 197
Vaillant, George, 193

Chapter 7

Sensation

SENSORY KNOWLEDGE OF OUR WORLD 214
  FROM PHYSICAL ENERGY TO MENTAL EVENTS
  PSYCHOPHYSICS
  CONSTRUCTING PSYCHOPHYSICAL SCALES
  SENSORY CODING
  SENSORY ADAPTATION

  █ INTERIM SUMMARY

THE VISUAL SYSTEM 224
  THE HUMAN EYE
  THE PUPIL AND THE LENS
  THE RETINA
  RODS AND CONES
  PATHWAYS TO THE BRAIN
  SEEING COLOR
  SEEING FORM, DEPTH, AND MOVEMENT

  █ INTERIM SUMMARY

HEARING 239
  THE PHYSICS OF SOUND
  PSYCHOLOGICAL DIMENSIONS OF SOUND
  THE PHYSIOLOGY OF HEARING
  THEORIES OF PITCH PERCEPTION
  CLOSE-UP: NOISE POLLUTION FILLS THE AIR
  SOUND LOCALIZATION

  █ INTERIM SUMMARY

OUR OTHER SENSES 245
  SMELL
  TASTE
  TOUCH AND SKIN SENSES
  PAIN

RECAPPING MAIN POINTS 252

KEY TERMS 253

MAJOR CONTRIBUTORS 253

ive months before her second birthday, **Helen Keller** was stricken with a mysterious illness that deprived her of both sight and hearing. Helen's other senses became highly developed—a phenomenon experienced by many people who suffer long-term sensory deprivation—and her sensory experiences were eloquently documented: "I cannot recall what happened during the first months after my illness. I only know that I sat in my mother's lap or clung to her dress as she went about her household duties. My hands felt every object and observed every motion, and in this way I learned to know many things. . . . Sometimes I stood between two persons who were conversing and touched their lips. I could not understand, and was vexed" (Keller, 1902, pp. 26–27).

In her seventh year, Helen Keller became the pupil of Annie Sullivan, a young woman whose vision was partially impaired. In letters to a matron at the Perkins School in Boston where Annie had been educated, she wrote of the pleasure Helen derived from her remaining senses: "On entering a greenhouse her countenance becomes radiant, and she will tell the names of the flowers with which she is familiar, by the sense of smell alone. . . . She enjoys in anticipation the scent of a rose or a violet; and if she is promised a bouquet of these flowers, a peculiarly happy expression lights her face. . . ." (Sullivan, 1954, p. 294).

Helen herself wrote about the way her sense of smell gave her advance warning of storms. "I notice first a throb of expectancy, a slight quiver, a concentration in my nostrils. As the storm draws near my nostrils dilate, the better to receive the flood of earth odors which seem to multiply and extend, until I feel the splash of rain against my cheek. As the tempest departs, receding farther and farther, the odors fade, become fainter and fainter, and die away beyond the bar of space" (Keller, in Ackerman, 1990, p. 44).

Annie Sullivan reported that Helen's "whole body is so finely organized that she seems to use it as a medium for bringing herself into closer relations with her fellow creatures." Annie was puzzled at first by Helen's "inexplicable mental faculty" to pick up emotions and physical sensations. She soon realized, though, that Helen had developed an exquisite sensitivity to the muscular variations of those around her. "One day, while she was out walking with her mother, . . . a boy threw a torpedo, which startled Mrs. Keller. Helen felt the change in her mother's movements instantly, and asked, 'What are we afraid of?' " (Sullivan, 1954, pp. 294–295). During a hearing test, Helen astonished a roomful of people when "she would turn her head, smile, and act as though she had heard what was said." However, when Annie let go of Helen's hand and moved to the opposite side of the room, Helen remained motionless for the rest of the test (Sullivan, 1908, p. 295).

Although she could neither see nor hear, Helen Keller extracted a great deal of sensory information from the world. She did not perceive color, light, and sound through the ordinary channels. Instead, she "heard" symphonies by placing her hands on a radio to feel the vibrations, and she "saw" where a person had been by picking up the scent of his or her clothes. Her ability to compensate for her sensory disabilities hints at the intricate coordination within human sensory systems and the interaction of sensory and brain processes. It also makes us aware of the extent to which our senses work in unison to weave experience of the world around us into the fabric of our very being.

The moving story of Helen Keller raises a fundamental question: How does the brain—locked in the dark, silent chamber of the skull—experience the blaze of color in a Van Gogh painting, the booming melody of Beethoven's Ninth Symphony, the refreshing taste of watermelon on a hot day, the soft touch of a lover's lips, the fragrance of a field of wildflowers in the springtime, and the pain of disease and illness that afflicts each of us at some time? Our task in this chapter is to discover how our brains and bodies make contact with the world of sensation that is continually present around us. We want to know how evolution has designed our sense receptors to detect the many different types of energy sources in the external environment and the sensory signals that emerge from within our bodies. How does the brain make sense of the many types and intensities of stimulation we constantly receive?

This chapter deals with **sensory processes,** the systems associated with the sense organs and peripheral aspects of the nervous system that put us in direct contact with sources of stimulation. Sensation involves the basic elements of experience—the *bottom-up* processing of detectable input. The next chapter deals with the processes associated with higher level activity of the central nervous system, the *perceptual processes*—the *top-down* identification, interpretation, integration, and classification of sensory experience. We will begin this chapter with a discussion of those features of sensory processing that are common to all of our senses. We will also examine how psychological researchers measure and quantify our sensory experiences. Then we will consider the functioning of specific **sensory modalities,** such as vision and hearing.

However, before beginning this journey into the world of sensation, we should pause to reflect on the dual functions of our senses: *survival* and *sensuality.* Our senses help us survive by sounding alarms of danger, priming us to take swift actions to ward off hazards and by directing us toward agreeable sensations, such as tasty foods, which are healthy, and sexual touch, which promotes procreation. Our senses also provide us with sensuality. **Sensuality** is the quality of being devoted to the gratification of the senses; it entails enjoying the experiences that are appealing to the eye, the ear, touch, taste, and smell. Our academic focus will be on detailing the mechanisms that underlie sensory processes. Your personal focus might include exercises to enrich your enjoyment of everyday life, to help you discover the healthy pleasures of sensuality, and to teach you to take new delight in the world of sounds, colors, smells, tastes, and touch (Ornstein & Sobel, 1990). Your role model might be Helen Keller who has been considered one of the world's greatest *sensuits* because she rejoiced so greatly in her sensory experiences (Ackerman, 1990).

SENSORY KNOWLEDGE OF OUR WORLD

Ordinarily, our experience of external reality is relatively accurate and error-free; it has to be so that we can survive. We need food to sustain us, shelter to protect us, interactions with other people to fulfill our social needs, and awareness of danger to keep us out of harm's way. To meet these needs, we must get reliable information about the world we live in. All species have

Your author appears to defy the laws of gravity by floating in air. This perceptual illusion is created by the mirror reflection of the right side of his body which obscures the fact that his left leg is planted firmly on the ground (*Discovering Psychology,* 1990, Program 7).

To hunt small flying objects at night, bats rely on the sensory system of echolocation, a kind of sonar. Bats emit high-frequency sounds that bounce off insects, revealing their locations so the bats can find them.

developed some kind of specialized *information-gathering apparatus*. We humans lack the acute senses that other species have perfected, such as the vision of hawks, the hearing of bats, or the sense of smell of rodents. Instead, we have developed complex sensory organs and additional neural apparatuses that enable us to process a wider range of more complex sensory input than any other creature.

Seeing is believing. We automatically assume that what we see with our own eyes is what truly exists in the physical structure of the external world. Do our senses accurately interpret reality? The relation between what exists and what we see—or hear, touch, smell, taste, or feel—is not simple.

Sensation is the process by which a stimulated sensory receptor gives rise to neural impulses that result in an elementary experience of feeling, or awareness, of conditions inside or outside the body. **Perception** is the elaboration, interpretation, and assignment of meaning to a sensory experience. The boundaries between sensation and perception are not distinctly drawn; however, most psychologists treat sensation as a primitive, data-based experience generated by the activities of receptors, and they treat perception as a brain-based interpretation of sensory input.

The study of sensation and perception has had a prominent place since the earliest history of experimental psychology. We saw in Chapter 1 that Wundt (1896, 1907) proposed that sensations and feelings are the elementary processes from which complex experiences are built. E. B. Titchener (1898) brought this view to

the United States, giving sensation a central place in his introspective examination of the contents of consciousness. Introspection was replaced by a broader cognitive approach to sensation concerned with the way the processing of stimuli guides the perceiver's behavior (Coren & Ward, 1989).

Now sensory psychologists work along with physiologists, biologists, geneticists, and neurologists to map the process by which physical energy from the external world is transformed into sensations that result in our ten senses: vision, hearing, smell, taste, touch, warmth, cold, equilibrium, kinesthesis, and pain. Later in this chapter, we will discuss the mechanisms underlying some of these senses, but first let's consider how sensory psychologists study sensation.

FROM PHYSICAL ENERGY TO MENTAL EVENTS

At the heart of sensation lies a profound mystery: How do physical energies give rise to psychological experiences? Stimulus energy arrives at our sensory receptors as physical energy of some kind. There it is converted into electrochemical signals that the nervous system can transmit—still physical energy but coded by our nervous system so that when the signal reaches the cerebral cortex, we have a sensation of a particular type. The study of sensation is the study of the translation of physical energy into neural processes.

Transduction is the process that converts one form of physical energy, such as light, to another form, such as neural impulses. Although the essence of this conversion remains a mystery, research has taught us a great deal about how and where it happens and what physical and psychological processes affect it.

The field of sensory psychology has two main branches: *sensory physiology* and *psychophysics*. **Sensory physiology** is the study of the way biological mechanisms convert physical events into neural events. Its goal is to discover what happens at a neural level in the chain of events from physical energy to sensory experience. Sensory psychologists are primarily interested in discovering the way transduction works in the receptors themselves. They try to determine how electrochemical activity in the nervous system gives rise to sensations of different quality (red rather than green) and different quantity (loud rather than soft).

All sensory systems share at least three components: (a) a *stimulus detector unit,* consisting of a specialized sensory receptor neuron; (b) an *initial receiving center,* where the convergent information from different detector units is assembled by neurons at this level, and (c) one or more *secondary receiving/integrating centers,* where neurons receive and process information from groups of the initial receiver neurons. The interaction of a variety of these secondary centers generates perceptual experiences. The secondary centers in the sensing chain often add to the information received by sensations from other sources as well as prior information from relevant past experiences.

The trigger for any sensing system is the detection by a sensory neuron of an environmental event, or *stimulus*. This stimulus detector converts the physical form of the sensory signal into an *action potential,* or nerve impulse. The action potential then codes the sensory event into cellular signals that can be processed by the nervous system. These cellular signals travel along the sensory neuron to the receiving center specialized for each form of sensation. At this stage, information is extracted about the basic qualities of the stimulus, such as its size, intensity, shape, and distance. The secondary processing centers receive this information and more, combining it into more complex codes that are passed on to the neurons in specific areas of the sensory and association cortex of the brain. While the sensory systems process information coming *into* the brain, processes known as **afferent systems,** the motor systems process information *going out* from the brain to muscles and glands, processes known as **efferent systems.**

There are four basic types of sensory receptors, each designed to detect a particular kind of stimulus energy (**Table 7.1** summarizes the stimuli and receptors for each of the human senses):

- *photoreceptors*—detect the light that results in vision,
- *chemoreceptors*—detect the chemical stimuli that result in taste and smell,
- *mechanoreceptors*—detect the movements of receptor cells that result in hearing and touch sensations,
- *thermoreceptors*—detect the temperature changes that result in the sensations of warmth and cold.

TABLE 7.1 HUMAN SENSORY SYSTEM: FUNDAMENTAL FEATURES

Sense	Stimulus	Sense Organ	Receptor	Sensation
Sight	Light waves	Eye	Rods and cones of retina	Colors, patterns, textures
Hearing	Sound waves	Ear	Hair cells of the basilar membrane	Noises, tones
Skin sensations	External contact	Skin	Nerve endings in skin (Ruffini corpuscles, Merkel disks, Pacinian corpuscles)	Touch, pain, warmth, cold
Smell	Volatile substances	Nose	Hair cells of olfactory epithelium	Odors (musky, flowery, burnt, minty)
Taste	Soluble substances	Tongue	Taste buds of tongue	Flavors (sweet, sour, salty, bitter)
Equilibrium	Mechanical and gravitational forces	Inner ear	Hair cells of semi-circular canals and vestibule	Spatial movement gravitational pull

PSYCHOPHYSICS

How loud must a fire alarm at a factory be in order for workers to hear it over the din of the machinery? How bright does a warning light on a pilot's control panel have to be to appear twice as bright as the other lights? How loud can a motorcycle be before its driver should be cited for noise pollution? Practical questions such as these often arise when people are making decisions about safety regulations, product design, and legal issues. To answer them, we must somehow be able to measure the intensity of sensory experiences. This task is accomplished by relating these psychological experiences to an amount of physical stimulation. It is the central task of **psychophysics,** the study of lawful correlations between physical stimuli and the behavior or mental experiences the stimuli evoke. Psychophysics represents the oldest field of the science of psychology (Levine & Shefner, 1981).

The most significant figure in the history of psychophysics was the German physicist, **Gustav Fechner** (1801–1887) who taught at the University of Leipzig (along with Wilhelm Wundt). He coined the term *psychophysics* and provided an objective measure and a set of procedures to relate the intensity of a physical stimulus—measured in physical units—to the magnitude of the sensory experience—measured in psychological units (Fechner, *Elements of Psychophysics,* 1860). Fechner believed that psychophysics was the key to understanding the relationships between bodily functions—the detection by sense receptors of physical stimuli—and mental functions—the sensations experienced and reported (Marshall, 1987).

Fechner's psychophysical techniques measure the strength of sensations experienced by an alert, normal organism in response to stimuli of different strengths. Whether the stimuli are for light, sound, taste, odor, or touch, the techniques for measuring them are the same: determining thresholds and constructing psychophysical scales relating strength of sensation to strength of stimuli. Two kinds of thresholds can be measured by these techniques: *absolute thresholds* and *difference thresholds*.

Absolute Thresholds

What is the smallest, weakest stimulus energy that an organism can detect? How dim can a light be, for instance, and still be visible? How soft can a tone be and still be heard? These questions refer to the **absolute threshold** for different types of stimulation—the minimum amount of physical energy needed to produce a sensory experience.

Researchers measure absolute thresholds psychophysically by asking vigilant observers to perform detection tasks, such as trying to see a dim light in a dark room or trying to hear a soft sound in a quiet room. During a series of many *trials,* the stimulus is presented at varying intensities, and on each trial the observers indicate whether they were aware of it. (If you've ever had your hearing evaluated, you participated in an absolute threshold test.)

The results of an absolute threshold study can be summarized in a **psychometric function:** a graph that shows the percentage of detections (plotted on the vertical axis, or Y-axis) of each stimulus intensity (plotted on the horizontal axis, or X-axis). A typical psychometric function is shown in **Figure 7.1.** For very dim lights, which are clearly below threshold, detection is at 0 percent; for bright lights, which are clearly above threshold, detection is at 100 percent. If there were a single, true absolute threshold, you would expect the transition from 0 to 100 percent detection to be very sharp, occurring right at the point where the intensity reached the threshold; but this does not happen. Instead, the psychometric curve is usually a smooth S-shaped curve, in which there is a region of transition from no detection to occasional detection to detection all the time.

According to the classical view of absolute thresholds, stimuli below the threshold produce no sensation; stimuli above it do. However, because a stimulus does not suddenly become clearly detectable at a specific point, a person's absolute threshold is more accurately defined as the intensity at which the stimulus is detected half of the time over many trials. The usual practice is to define the threshold arbitrarily as the intensity level at which the psychometric function crosses 50 percent detection. The operational definition of absolute threshold is *the stimulus level at which a sensory signal is detected half the time.* Thresholds for different sense modalities can be measured in the same way, simply by changing the stimulus dimension. **Table 7.2** shows absolute threshold levels for several familiar natural stimuli.

Under some circumstances, people behave as though they have seen or heard something even when their detection performance has indicated a stimulus below the sensory threshold (Dixon, 1971). This phenomenon is known as **subliminal perception** (*sub* means below; *limen* refers to the threshold. Regardless of what pop psychologists may assert, subliminal messages that are below recognition threshold do *not* have a demonstrable effect of influencing behavior—a message concealed in a television commercial won't influence you to buy a given product. There is little practical value in using subliminal visuals for social influence (Moore, 1982). However, in precisely controlled laboratory research, subliminals have been shown to influence judgments of emotion stimuli (Greenwald et al.,

FIGURE 7.1   CALCULATION OF ABSOLUTE THRESHOLDS

Because a stimulus does not become suddenly detectable at a certain point, absolute threshold is defined as the intensity at which the stimulus is detected half of the time over many trials.

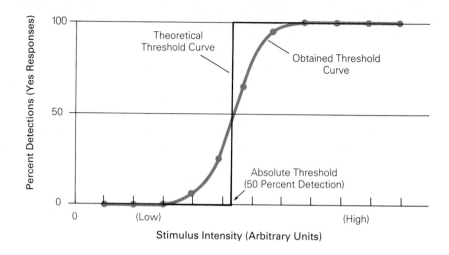

1989; Marcel, 1983); affect evaluations of target people and events (Erdley & D'Agostino, 1988; Devine, 1989); and increase anxiety of subjects (Robles et al., 1987). Subliminals seem to work by *priming* the unaware viewer's memory or emotions to react more swiftly or to employ prior stored experiences to react to currently presented stimuli.

TABLE 7.2   APPROXIMATE THRESHOLDS OF FAMILIAR EVENTS

Sense Modality	Detection Threshold
Light	A candle flame seen at 30 miles on a dark clear night
Sound	The tick of a watch under quiet conditions at 20 feet
Taste	One teaspoon of sugar in 2 gallons of water
Smell	One drop of perfume diffused into the entire volume of a 3-room apartment
Touch	The wing of a bee falling on your cheek from a distance of 1 centimeter

Response Bias

Threshold measurements can be affected by a **response bias,** the systematic tendency for an observer to favor responding in a particular way due to factors unrelated to the sensory features of the stimulus. For example, someone could overrespond *yes* in a detection task because she wanted to be selected for a job requiring acute sensitivity, while someone else might favor *no* if he thought that response would get him out of a dangerous assignment given only to those with acute sensitivity. Response biases are most likely to arise in situations that have important consequences for an observer's life. (Response biases are *not* the same as experimental artifacts, procedural errors that come from inadvertently cueing the subject about how to respond, which is what happened when Helen Keller did well while holding Annie Sullivan's hand during her hearing test and remarkably poorly when Annie moved away.)

Why does someone's detection threshold become distorted by response bias? At least three sources for the bias have been identified: desire, expectation, and habit. When we want a particular outcome, we are more likely to give whatever response will achieve that desired objective—"I didn't see anything, officer" is likely if we want to avoid getting involved; "Yes, I'm sure he's the one," is a more probable response if we want to be in line for a reward. Our expectations, or knowledge, of stimulus probabilities may also influence our readiness to report a sensory event—we are more likely to detect and report as a submarine the weak blip on a sonar scope if we are on a cruiser during wartime than if we are on a yacht during peacetime. Finally, people develop habits of responding—some people chronically answer *yes* and some *no*. This learned habit of biased responding means that under conditions of *uncertainty* some people will overreport the presence of a stimulus event while others will consistently underreport it.

How can researchers detect such biases during tests on absolute thresholds? Researchers use *catch trials* to find out whether response biases are operating in sensory detection tasks. On a few of the trials, they present no stimulus to *catch* the subject with a bias to respond *yes*. The researchers then adjust the threshold estimate of the real stimulus according to how often such false alarms occur. What would you do to catch a subject who overuses *no* when there is a stimulus present?

Signal Detection Theory

The **theory of signal detection** (TSD) is a systematic approach to the problem of response bias. This theory is an alternative to the classical approach to psychophysics (Green & Swets, 1966). Instead of focusing strictly on sensory processes, signal detection theory emphasizes the process of making a *judgment* about the presence or absence of stimulus events. Whereas classical psychophysics conceptualized a single absolute threshold, TSD identifies two distinct processes in sensory detection: (a) an initial *sensory process,* which reflects the subject's sensitivity to the strength of the stimulus—the *signal strength*—and (b) a subsequent separate *decision process,* which reflects the subject's response biases. These biases are sources of *noise strength* in the system and lead to inaccurate estimates of the signal. The task then is to identify the signal accurately by accounting for the biasing influences of the background noise.

TSD offers a procedure for measuring thresholds that can measure both the sensory and decision processes at once. The measurement procedure is actually just an extension of the idea of catch trials. The basic design is given in **Figure 7.2.** A weak stimulus is presented in half the trials; no stimulus is presented in the other half. In each trial, subjects respond by saying *yes* if they think the signal was present and *no* if they think it wasn't. As shown in matrix A of the figure, each response is scored as a hit, a miss, a false alarm, or a correct rejection, depending on whether a signal was, in fact, presented and whether the observer responded accurately.

An observer who is a *yea sayer* (chronically answers *yes*) will give a high number of hits but will also have a high number of false alarms, as shown in matrix B; one who is a *nay sayer* will give a lower number of hits but also a lower number of false alarms, as shown in matrix C. Combining the percentages of hits and false alarms creates a mathematical relationship that differentiates sensory responses from response biases. This procedure makes it possible to find out whether two observers have the same sensitivity despite large differences in response bias.

According to the theory of signal detection, any stimulus event (signal or noise) produces some neural activity in the sensory system. In deciding whether a stimulus was present, the observer compares the sensory value in the neural system with some personally set response criterion. If the response of the sensory process exceeds that critical amount, the observer responds *yes;* if not, *no.* Thus, in TSD, the discrete threshold appears in the decision process instead of in the sensory process.

FIGURE 7.2   THE THEORY OF SIGNAL DETECTION

Matrix A shows the possible outcomes when a subject is asked if a target stimulus occurred on a given trial. Matrices B and C show the typical responses of a *yea sayer* and a *nay sayer.*

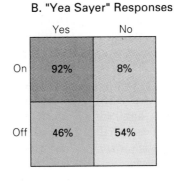

The response criterion reflects the observer's strategy for responding in a particular situation. By providing a way of separating sensory process from response bias, the theory of signal detection allows an experimenter to identify and separate the roles of the sensory stimulus and the individual's criterion level, or response bias, in producing the final response.

The TSD approach now dominates modern psychophysics. As a matter of fact, it provides a model of decision making that can be used in other contexts as well. Many everyday decisions involve different rewards for every hit and correct rejection and penalties for every miss and false alarm; decisions are likely to be biased by the schedule of anticipated gains and losses. Such a detection matrix is called a *payoff matrix*. If saying *yes* when a stimulus is really present will result in a large gain, and if saying *no* when it is present will probably result in a great loss then a *yes* bias will rule. For example, a surgeon can be biased in favor of operating for a possible malignant condition if he charges a big fee for the surgery or if he fears that a patient will die if the malignant condition is present. The payoff matrix is different for the patient; if the malignant condition is not present, the decision to operate is a costly false alarm. Thus, the decision maker must consider the available evidence, the relative costs of each type of error, and the relative gains from each type of correct decision. More conservative decisions result when there is a high cost for a false alarm and a low cost for a miss. Can you think of an example of a risky decision encouraged by the payoff matrix even when supporting evidence might be absent?

Difference Thresholds

Suppose you are a programmer inventing a new video game. You have decided to use bars to represent the enemy spaceships that have been captured; each time a ship is downed, the striker's bar gets a little longer. You want the players to be able to tell which of the two bars is longer so they will know who is winning, but you also want the additions to the bar length to be small enough so that as many spaceships as possible can be represented. To do this, you need to determine the **difference threshold,** the smallest physical difference between two stimuli that can still be recognized as a difference.

You would determine a difference threshold in much the same way that you would determine an absolute threshold, except that for the difference threshold procedure you would use a pair of stimuli on each trial and ask your subjects whether the two stimuli were different instead of just asking whether a stimulus was present. For the video game problem, you would show your subjects two bars on each trial, one of some standard length and one just a bit longer. For each pair, the

observer would say *same* or *different*. After many such trials, you would plot a psychometric function by graphing the percent of *different* responses on the vertical axis as a function of the actual differences in length which you would plot on the horizontal axis. The difference threshold is the length difference at which the curve crosses the 50-percent value. Thus, the difference threshold is operationally defined as *the point at which the stimuli are recognized as different half of the time* (on 50 percent of the trials). This difference threshold value is known as the **just noticeable difference,** or JND. The JND, which was designed by Fechner, is a quantitative unit for measuring the magnitude of a sensation or the sensed difference between any two sensations. How does this psychological series of JNDs change with physical changes in stimulus intensity? What mathematical function relates physical to psychological change?

Suppose you perform your experiment with a standard bar length of 10 millimeters, using increases of varying amounts. You find the difference threshold to be about 1 millimeter—you know that a 10-millimeter bar will be detected as different from an 11-millimeter bar 50 percent of the time. Can you go ahead and design your video-game display now?

Unfortunately, you're not ready yet, because the difference threshold is not the same for long and short bars. With a standard bar of 20 millimeters, for instance, you would have had to add about 2 millimeters to get a just noticeable difference; with a bar of 40 millimeters, however, you would need to add 4 millimeters. **Figure 7.3** shows some examples of JNDs with bars of several lengths: the JNDs increase steadily as the length of the standard bar increases.

What does remain the same for both long and short bars is the *ratio* of the size of the increase that produces a just noticeable difference to the length of the standard bar. For example, *1 mm/10 mm = 0.1; 2 mm/20 mm = 0.1*. In 1834, **Ernst Weber** discovered this relationship and found that it held for a wide range of stimulus dimensions. The only difference he found between stimulus dimensions was the particular value of the ratio. He summarized all his findings in a single equation now called **Weber's law:** *the JND between stimuli is a constant fraction of the intensity of the standard stimulus.* Thus, the bigger or more intense the standard stimulus, the larger the increment needed in order to get a just noticeable difference; or, the smaller or weaker the standard stimulus, the less the increase needed before a JND is found. A few drops of water added to a test tube are more likely to be noticed than the same amount added to a jug. This is a very general property of all sensory systems. The formula for Weber's law is $\Delta I/I = k$, where I is the intensity of the standard; ΔI, or Delta I, is the size of the increase that produces a

FIGURE 7.3   *JUST NOTICEABLE DIFFERENCES AND WEBER'S LAW*

The longer the standard bar, the greater the amount you must add (ΔL) to see a just noticeable difference. The difference threshold is the added length detected on half the trials. In plotting these increments against standard bars of increasing length, the proportion stays the same—the amount added is always one-tenth of the standard length. The relationship is linear, producing a straight line on the graph. We can predict that the ΔL for a bar length of 5 will be 0.5.

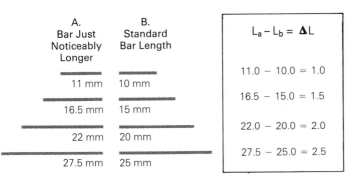

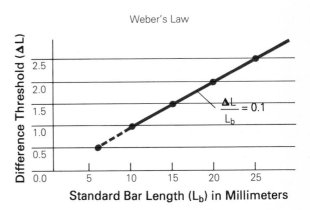

A. Bar Just Noticeably Longer	B. Standard Bar Length	$L_a - L_b = \Delta L$
11 mm	10 mm	$11.0 - 10.0 = 1.0$
16.5 mm	15 mm	$16.5 - 15.0 = 1.5$
22 mm	20 mm	$22.0 - 20.0 = 2.0$
27.5 mm	25 mm	$27.5 - 25.0 = 2.5$

JND; and *k* is the constant ratio for the particular stimulus dimension, or *Weber's constant*. Weber's law provides a good approximation, but not a perfect fit to experimental data, of how the size of JND increases with intensity. We see in **Table 7.3** that Weber's constant has different values for different sensory dimensions—there is greater sensitivity as the value becomes smaller. So this table tells us that we can differentiate two sound frequencies more precisely than light intensities, which, in turn, are detectable with a smaller JND than odor or taste modalities are. (Work through the bar length example plotted in Figure 7.3 to be sure you understand what a JND is, what Weber's law is, and how they are related.)

TABLE 7.3   *WEBER'S CONSTANT VALUES FOR SELECTED STIMULUS DIMENSIONS*

Stimulus Dimension	Weber's Constant
Sound frequency	.003
Light intensity	.01
Odor concentration	.07
Pressure intensity	.14
Sound intensity	.15
Taste concentration	.20

CONSTRUCTING PSYCHOPHYSICAL SCALES

You are already familiar with physical scales—the metric scale for lengths and the Fahrenheit and Celsius scales for temperature, to name just a few. Could such scales be used directly for measuring psychological sensations? According to Weber's law, they couldn't because the psychological differences between 1 and 2 inches is much bigger than the psychological difference between 101 and 102 inches while the physical difference is the same. So, for example, while a person would be able to detect the difference between 1° C and 2° C much more easily than the difference between 22° C and 23° C, the actual difference in both cases is the same: 1° C.

One approach to constructing psychophysical scales is based on treating JNDs as psychologically equal intervals. After all, they are equal in the sense of being just noticeably different from neighboring stimuli, so it would make sense to assume that JNDs are the psychological units of sensation. Using our bar-length example, the 1-mm difference between 10-mm and 11-mm bars is perceived as the same as the 1.5-mm difference between bars of 15 mm and 16.5 mm and the 2-mm difference between bars that are 20 mm and 22 mm long. Together with Weber's law, this finding implies that equal increases in the physical intensity of the stimulus will produce sensations that rise rapidly at first and then more and more slowly, as shown in **Figure 7.4.** This was the relationship proposed by Gustav Fechner in 1860; it is expressed mathematically in an

FIGURE 7.4

FECHNER'S LOGARITHMIC PSYCHOPHYSICAL SCALE

According to Fechner's equation which is based on just noticeable differences, sensation units first increase rapidly with equal increases in stimulus intensity but then increase more and more slowly. (Adding one candle to two candles increases the brightness you see much more than adding one candle to 100 candles.)

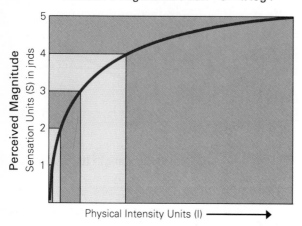

Fechner's Logarithmic Law $S = k \log I$

Perceived Magnitude Sensation Units (S) in jnds

Physical Intensity Units (I) ⟶

---

equation known as **Fechner's law:** $S = k \log I$, where S is the magnitude of the sensory experience, I is the physical intensity, and k is a constant for the dimension being scaled. According to Fechner's law, a person's experience of sensory intensity increases *arithmetically* (2, 3, 4) as the stimulus intensity increases *geometrically* (2, 4, 8). Thus, within limits, sensory experience is proportional to the logarithm of stimulus intensity. This logarithmic equation represents one form of mathematical relationship between psychology and physics—between sensory experience and physical reality. The Weber-Fechner law of psychophysics states that the intensity of subjective sensation increases arithmetically as the physical stimulus increases geometrically.

A hundred years after Fechner's work on psychophysical scales, psychologist **S. S. Stevens** devised a different method of constructing psychophysical scales, and he obtained a different answer. Using a method called **magnitude estimation,** he asked observers to assign numbers to their sensations. Observers were presented with an initial stimulus—for instance, a light of some known intensity—and asked to assign a value to it—say, 10. They were then presented with another light at a different magnitude and told that if they perceived it as twice as bright, they should call it 20. If it were half as bright, they should call it 5, and so on. When Stevens constructed psychological scales in this

---

manner, he found that the results could be described by a mathematical equation known as a *power function:* $S = kI^b$, where S is (again) the magnitude of the sensory experience, I is (again) the physical intensity of the stimulus, k is a constant (not Fechner's constant), and b is an exponent that varies for different sensory dimensions. **Figure 7.5** shows psychophysical curves for brightness and electrical shock, where the exponents are very different. Doubling the physical intensity of a light less than doubles the sensation of brightness, which is qualitatively consistent with Fechner's law. As you might guess, however, doubling the magnitude of an electrical shock more than doubles its corresponding sensation. Fechner's law cannot predict such a result.

Stevens's approach has proved to be very useful, because almost any psychological dimension can be readily scaled in this way. Psychologists have used magnitude estimation to construct psychological scales for everything from pitch and length to beauty, the seriousness of crimes, and the goodness of Swedish monarchs (Stevens, 1961, 1962, 1975). Stevens's direct method of magnitude estimation proved to be very convenient and more useful than the Fechner formula when adapted

FIGURE 7.5

STEVENS'S POWER LAW

According to Stevens's equation which is based on direct judgments of sensory magnitude, the psychophysical curve is different for different stimuli. For brightness, the curve is similar to Fechner's. However, for a stimulus such as electric shock, slight increases in physical intensity produce greater and greater sensations of pain.

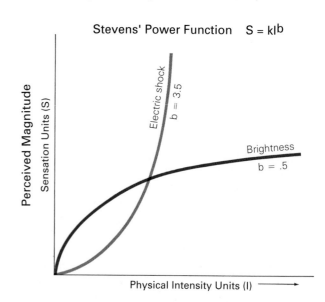

Stevens' Power Function $S = kI^b$

Perceived Magnitude Sensation Units (S)

Electric shock $b = 3.5$

Brightness $b = .5$

Physical Intensity Units (I) ⟶

to data outside the province of purely sensory estimations. However, the Stevens power law is not, as he claimed, a direct measure of sensation (Savage, 1970).

Although similar equations express the relationships between stimuli and sensations in the various sensory modalities, each sense responds to a different kind of stimulus energy, and through the operation of its own ingenious physiological mechanisms, provides us with different qualities of sensory experience. Before turning to examine the special features of each of our different sensory modalities, there are two more common aspects of all sensory processing to consider: sensory coding and sensory adaptation.

SENSORY CODING

In Chapter 3, we noted that the brain differentiates signals for light and sound not from their different sensory codes but from the different receptors that are stimulated by each type of physical energy. Those receptors respond by sending that sensory information to specific sensory areas of the cortex. This currently accepted biological view of sensation was first stated in the doctrine of specific nerve energies by **Johannes Müller** in 1825. In Chapter 3, we also noted that all information coming into and out of the brain's neurons takes only one form: a bioelectrical coding of neural discharges that operates as a series of on-off signals. How then does the brain capture the quality and intensity of sensory experiences, which we know vary so enormously within and between each of our senses?

What is the physiological mechanism by which we come to experience the quality and intensity of the many stimuli that bombard us every moment? How was Helen Keller able to detect the subtle nuances of events from their smell or feel? The primary way stimulus *intensity* is coded across all sensations is in terms of the *rate of neural impulses*. For example, a light touch on the skin will generate a series of electrical impulses in nerve fibers at that point. As the pressure is increased, the impulses increase in their *frequency* of firing, but do not change their basic form. Thus, for all modalities, our perceived magnitude of stimulus intensity is a function of the rate of neural firing. A second way that intensity is coded is by the regularity in the *temporal patterning* of these nerve impulses. At weak intensities, the firing is spaced and irregular, but as the intensity increases, the patterning becomes not only more closely spaced but more constant.

The coding for *sensory qualities* of our different sense modalities takes place according to brain codes in the specific neural pathways activated by each sense. Within any one sense, the variations in quality depend both on the specific neurons that are activated within that sense receptor and on the particular patterning of neural activity associated with each type of sensation. For example, some nerve fibers in the tongue respond more strongly to bitter tastes than to sweet, sour, and salt tastes. Thus **sensory coding** for each sense depends on both *specificity* and *patterning*.

SENSORY ADAPTATION

The main role of our stimulus detectors is to announce changes in some feature of the external world. Each new event is brought by the stimulus detectors into the total information pool we use to interpret the momentary status of our sensory field. The great quantity of new incoming stimuli would overwhelm our ability to deal with old sensations were it not for a specially evolved function of all sensory systems: *adaptation*. **Sensory adaptation** is the diminishing responsiveness of sensory systems to prolonged stimulus input. As our response to old stimuli fades quickly over time, we are able to be continually refreshed in our quest to experience the vibrant world of sensory impressions all about us. **Figure 7.6** illustrates a typical adaptation to a maintained stimulus.

FIGURE 7.6   SENSORY ADAPTATION

Initial response to the onset of a stimulus is vigorous, but as the stimulus is maintained, the receptor adapts to it. This adaptation is reflected by the diminishing activity in the nerve fiber over time. The low level of activity (of which we are not usually aware) is immediately modified with the offset of the maintained stimulus. Brief, periodic stimuli cause the receptor to respond fully each time without any adaptation.

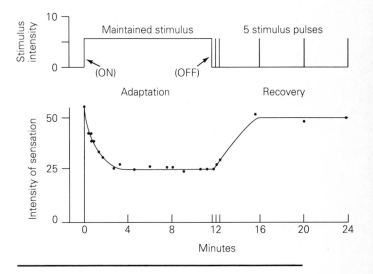

SUMMING UP

Sensation involves all the sensory processes that put us in direct contact with the physical energies of our world. This first stage in the overall process of perception detects the basic intensities and qualities of stimuli that are picked up by the many sense receptors throughout the body. Translating physical energy of stimuli into neural codes via transduction is the process that produces sensation.

Sensory physiologists study the origins of sensory experience. Psychophysicists look at the measurable relationships between psychological responses and physical stimuli. The precise assessment of the way physical and mental processes are related in sensation was pioneered by Fechner.

Vital to the study of sensation is the determination of absolute thresholds, difference thresholds, and just noticeable differences between stimuli. To correct for response biases that affect the measurement of thresholds, the theory of signal detection uses methods that separate sensory processes from decision processes (where response biases operate). Weber's law states that the JND is a constant ratio of the standard stimulus intensity, and Fechner's law states that sensory experience is related to intensity as a logarithmic function. In contrast, Stevens proposed magnitude estimation to derive power functions relating magnitude of sensation to stimulus intensity. Sensory coding uses frequency or rate of neural firing and the patterning of neural impulses to convey information about stimulus intensity. Sensory quality is coded by means of the specificity of neurons activated in sense receptors and the patterning of neural impulses in sensory pathways to the cortex. Sensory adaptation is an essential design feature of all sensory systems enabling sensory fibers to fade out responsiveness to prolonged stimuli in order to be ready to process new stimulus signals.

THE VISUAL SYSTEM

Vision is the most complex, highly developed, and important sense for humans and most other mobile creatures; animals with good vision have an enormous evolutionary advantage. Good vision helps animals detect their prey or predators from a distance. Vision enables humans to be aware of changing features in the physical environment and to adapt their behavior accordingly. With the help of microscopes and telescopes, vision allows us to probe the secrets of nature and to see minute molecules and the vast expanse of our galaxy. Vision is the most well studied of all the sense modalities.

THE HUMAN EYE

The eye is the camera for the brain's motion pictures of the world (see **Figure 7.7**). A camera views the world through a lens that gathers and focuses light. The eye also gathers and focuses light—light enters the *cornea,* a transparent bulge on the front of the eye that is filled with a clear liquid called the *aqueous humor;* next it passes through the *pupil,* an opening in the opaque *iris.* To focus a camera, we move its lens closer to or further from the object viewed. To focus the eye, a rubbery, bean-shaped crystalline *lens* changes its shape, thinning to focus on distant objects and thickening to focus on near ones. To control the amount of light coming into a camera, we vary the opening of the lens (the f-stop). In the eye, the muscular disk of the iris changes the size of the pupil, the aperture through which light passes into the eyeball. At the back of a camera body is the photosensitive film that records the variations in light that have come through the lens. Similarly, in the eye, light travels through the *vitreous humor,* finally striking the *retina,* a thin sheet that lines the rear wall of the eyeball.

As you can see, the processes of a camera and the eye are very similar. Now let's examine the components of the vision process in more detail.

THE PUPIL AND THE LENS

The pupil is the opening in the iris through which light passes. The iris makes the pupil dilate or constrict to control the amount of light entering the eyeball. Pupil size doesn't only vary in response to light variations, however. Psychological factors can also affect pupil dilation—positive emotional reactions dilate the pupil and negative ones constrict it. When you look at pictures of people you find very attractive, for example, your pupils may expand by about 30 percent. Pupil size also reflects mental effort, decreasing when concentration is intense. Any of these changes in pupil size are involuntary and occur without your awareness (Hess, 1972).

The lens of the eye focuses light on the retina, reversing and inverting the light pattern as it does so. The lens is particularly important because of its variable focusing ability for near and far objects. The ciliary muscles can change the thickness of the lens and, hence, its optical properties in a process called **accommodation.**

FIGURE 7.7   STRUCTURE OF THE HUMAN EYE

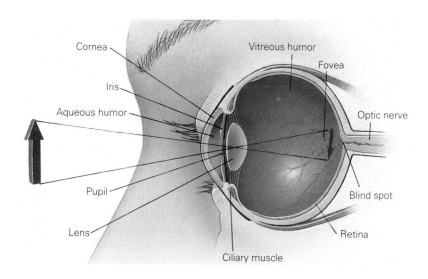

Many people suffer from accommodation problems. For example, people who are nearsighted—who have *myopia*—cannot focus distant objects properly, while those who are farsighted cannot focus on nearby objects. The lens starts off as clear, transparent, and convex. As people age, however, the lens becomes more amber tinted, opaque, and flattened, and it loses its elasticity. The effect of some of these changes is that the lens cannot become thick enough for close vision. When people pass the 45-year mark, the blur point—the closest point at which they can focus clearly—gets progressively farther away. When this happens, people who have never needed glasses before begin to need them for reading and other close work; people who already wear glasses may need *bifocals*—glasses that provide a nearer focus on the bottom half and a far one on the upper half.

THE RETINA

We look with our eyes but see with our brains. The eye gathers light, focuses it, and sends a neural signal on its way for subsequent processing into a visual image. The eye's critical function is to convert the information about the world from light waves into neural signals the brain can process. This happens in the **retina** at the back of the eye, where integration of the input also begins. Under the microscope, we see the retina's highly organized, layered structure. The retina has five types of neurons (each with its own layer): (a) the *rods* and *cones,* (b) the *bipolar neurons,* (c) the *ganglion cells,* (d) the *horizontal* cells, and (e) the *amacrine* cells. The first three types of neurons are arranged in a hierarchical pattern that achieves divergent processing of incoming light, thus maximizing its detection. The last two types of neurons in the retina are inhibitory cells that restrict the spread of the visual signal within the retina.

RODS AND CONES

The basic conversion from light energy to neural responses is performed in the retina by **photoreceptors**—receptor cells sensitive to light. These photoreceptors, rods and cones, are uniquely placed in the visual system between the outer world ablaze with light and the inner, dark world of neural processing and visual sensation. Because we sometimes operate in darkness and sometimes in bright light, nature has provided two different ways of processing light stimuli: the 125 million thin **rods** "see in the dark" and report what they detect in black and white; the seven million fat **cones** "view" the bright, color-filled day. The cone cells are each specialized to detect either blue, red, or green hues. When the rods and cones are functioning in tandem, we get information about the size, shape, edges, boundaries, and color of whatever is in our focus of vision (see **Figure 7.8**). In the very center of the retina is a small region called the **fovea** that contains nothing but densely packed cones—it's rod free. The fovea is the area of your sharpest vision—both color and spatial detail are most accurately detected there.

Bipolar and Ganglion Cells

The responses of many nearby receptors are gathered by the retina's bipolar and ganglion cells. The **bipolar cells** are nerve cells that combine impulses from many receptors and send the results to ganglion cells. They have a single dendrite with branched endings and one axon and terminal button. Each **ganglion cell** then integrates the impulses from many bipolar cells into a single firing rate. The cones in the central fovea send their impulses to the ganglion cells in that region while, further out on the periphery of the retina, rods and cones converge on the same bipolar and gan-

glion cells. The axons of the ganglion cells make up the optic nerve, which carries this visual information out of the eye and back toward the brain.

Finding Your Blind Spot

An interesting curiosity in the anatomical design of the retina exists where the optic nerve leaves the eye. This region, called the optic disk or *blind spot* contains no receptor cells at all. You do not experience blindness there, except under very special circumstances because (a) the blind spots of the two eyes are so positioned that receptors in each eye register what is missed in the other, and (b) the brain "fills in" this region with appropriate sensory qualities just as it does for the shadows of the blood vessels in the retina.

To find your blind spot, you will have to look at **Figure 7.9** under special viewing conditions. Hold this book at arm's length, close your right eye, and fixate on the bank figure with your left eye as you bring the book slowly closer. When the dollar sign is in your blind spot,

---

| **FIGURE 7.8** | RETINAL PATHWAYS |

This is a stylized and greatly simplified diagram showing the pathways that connect three of the layers of nerve cells in the retina. Incoming light passes through all these layers to reach the receptors at the back of the eyeball which are pointed away from the source of light. Note that the bipolar cells gather impulses from more than one receptor cell and send the results to several ganglion cells. Nerve impulses (blue arrows) from the ganglion cells leave the eye via the optic nerve and travel to the next relay point.

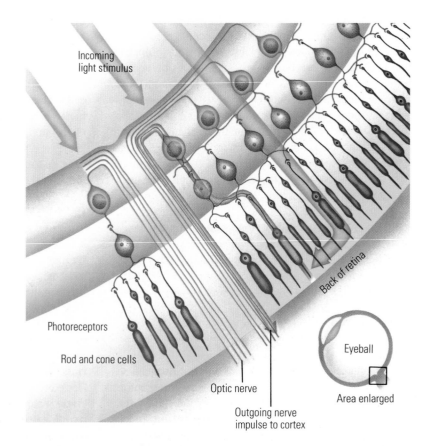

Incoming light stimulus

Back of retina

Photoreceptors

Rod and cone cells

Eyeball

Optic nerve

Area enlarged

Outgoing nerve impulse to cortex

FIGURE 7.9   FIND YOUR BLIND SPOT

Bank

it will disappear, but you will experience no gaping hole in your visual field. Instead, your visual system fills in this area with the background whiteness of the surrounding area so you "see" the whiteness, which isn't there, while failing to see your money, which you should have put in the bank before you lost it!

To convince yourself that higher brain processes "fill in" the missing part of the visual field with appropriate information, close your right eye again and focus on the cross in Figure 7.9 as you bring the book closer to you. This time, the gap in the line will disappear and be filled in with a line that completes the broken one. At least in your blind spot, what you see with your own eye may be a false view of reality. (Some people draw the analogy between this visual blind spot and the mental and emotional blind spots of prejudice; can you see the parallels?)

PATHWAYS TO THE BRAIN

At the back of the brain is a special area for the processing of the neural coded information coming from the eyes. It is the part of the occipital cortex known as the primary **visual cortex,** or *striate cortex.* The visual cortex displays a remarkably orderly layering of neurons that is unrivaled anywhere else in the entire nervous system. While the rest of the cerebral cortex has about six layers identifiable by the numbers of their neurons, the visual cortex in humans and monkeys has 12 distinct layers that help in the complex processing required by visual information. The many cortical neurons in these 12 layers are further organized into *vertical columns.* Each of these columns appears to perform a specific processing task, passing its products on to another cortical column (by means of synaptic relays). Curiously, any given vertical column—whether in the brains of monkeys, cats, rats, or humans—has the same relatively small number of cells. The difference in processing ca-

pacity of the brains of these species comes from the number of cortical columns and the number of nerve fibers linking columns with cortical regions. In humans, these numbers are obviously greater than they are in rats, for example.

Optic Nerve and Optic Tract

Nerve impulses leaving the retina project to at least six parts of the brain, some in the cortex and some in subcortical regions. The bundled axons of the ganglion cells forming the **optic nerve** first travel to the base of the *hypothalamus* where they come together in the *optic chiasma,* which resembles the Greek letter X (*chi,* pronounced *kye*). In humans, the axons in the optic nerve are divided into two bundles at the optic chiasma; a bundle from the inner half of each eye crosses over to the other side to continue its journey toward the back of the brain, as shown in **Figure 7.10** on the next page. From the optic chiasma there are two separate pathways on each side. The axon bundles separate and are called the *optic tract.* Visual information is divided between two way stations: the *lateral geniculate nucleus* and the *superior colliculus.*

Lateral Geniculate Nucleus The major pathway goes first to the **lateral geniculate nucleus** of the thalamus and then to the region of the visual cortex in each of the cerebral hemispheres at the rear of the brain. At the synapses in the lateral geniculate nucleus, influences from other brain regions, such as the *reticular activating system,* are believed to interact with the impulses coming from the eyes before they are finally sent to the primary visual areas in the cortex.

Superior Colliculus The small pathway from the optic chiasma goes to the **superior colliculus,** a cluster of nerve cell bodies in the midbrain region of the brain stem. It has recently been discovered that the superior colliculus has a very important function that gives the organism flexibility in orienting to multiple sensory stimulation from the environment. The superior colliculus serves as a sensorimotor center that integrates sensory input of different types, such as sound and light, with motor responses that orient the eyes, ears, and head toward a wide variety of environmental cues (Meredith & Stein, 1985). In addition, this nerve cell cluster also controls the pupil to open in dim light and to close in bright light.

The recent discovery of some of the functions of the superior colliculus has not helped to resolve the debate over the existence of two separate but parallel visual systems. Some researchers believe that the superior colliculus operates as a "second visual system," performing functions that differ distinctly from the pri-

FIGURE 7.10 PATHWAYS IN THE HUMAN VISUAL SYSTEM

The diagram shows the way light from the visual field projects onto the two retinas and shows the routes by which neural messages from the retina are sent to the two visual centers of each hemisphere.

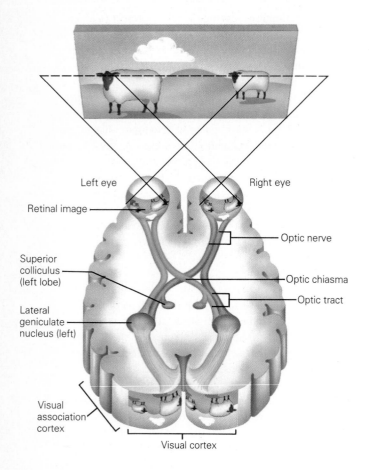

Left eye

Right eye

Retinal image

Optic nerve

Superior colliculus (left lobe)

Optic chiasma

Optic tract

Lateral geniculate nucleus (left)

Visual association cortex

Visual cortex

The following case study vividly illustrates this fascinating phenomenon.

When Don was 14 years old, he began to have severe, prolonged headaches. Right before a headache, Don would see in his left visual field a flashing oval light and then a blank white region with colored fringes around it. Within 15 minutes, the headache would begin on the right side of his head. It would be followed by vomiting, increased blindness in the left visual field, and up to two full days of no sleep. As Don grew older, these attacks became increasingly frequent despite his doctors' attempts to treat them. Finally, when Don was 34, he decided to have an operation in which a neurosurgeon would remove a small portion of his right occipital cortex in an attempt to correct the problem.

The surgery permanently cured Don's headaches but he was left totally blind in the left half of his visual field because the region removed contained the primary visual cortex for the left visual field. When a bright spot of light was shown directly to the left of his fixation point, for example, he was simply unaware of its presence.

On an informed hunch, however, a group of psychologists asked Don to guess the location of the spot of light by pointing with his left index finger. The results were remarkable; Don was nearly as accurate at locating the spot in this "blind" left field as he was at locating spots in the right visual field which he saw clearly! Further experiments showed that he could also guess whether a line in his "blind" field was vertical or horizontal and whether a figure presented there was an *X* or an *O*. Throughout the tests, Don was completely unaware of the presence of the spots, lines, or figures. He claimed he was merely guessing. When shown videotapes of his testing, Don was openly astonished to see himself pointing to lights he hadn't seen (Weiskrantz et al., 1974).

Don's "vision" has been aptly dubbed *blindsight,* visually guided behavior that identifies the location of stimuli projected to the blind area of an eye's retina without an individual's conscious awareness of seeing any object there. Blindsight sounds like a contradiction in terms, but we know that the detailed processing of visual input that occurs in the visual cortex is only the final stage of the overall process of converting light waves to conscious vision. An earlier, nonconscious stage of processing—and perhaps the place in the brain where it may occur—is revealed by Don's case. Comparable results have since been found in tests

mary visual system that is located in the pathways between the geniculate nucleus and the visual cortex. In this view, the "first visual system" is concerned with *pattern recognition*—how things look; the subcortical activities of the superior colliculus's "second visual system" are responsible for *place recognition*—where things are (Bridgeman, 1983; Poppel, 1977; Schneider, 1969).

How did this debate come about? It all began with the discovery of the phenomenon known as **blindsight,** visually guided behavior that takes place without conscious awareness in patients whose visual cortexes have been surgically removed. These individuals know where objects are even though they cannot recognize them. Supposedly, blindsight occurs in the superior colliculus.

on several other patients with similar damage in the visual cortex (Perenin & Jeannerod, 1975).

Don's experience raises a fundamental question about the way humans and animals make contact with their sensory environment. In lower animals, such as squirrels, the superior colliculus is the place where all visual information is interpreted; they have no visual cortex. When the visual cortex is removed in other animals, they can still perform many visual tasks in its absence, relying on the more primitive visual processing center below the level of the cortex. This lower center evidently developed earlier in the evolutionary process and still retains sensory abilities that were lost as humans developed more complex brains. Although contributing basic information about where objects are in the visual scene, this lower visual center does so below the level of consciousness.

Opponents of the dual visual-system hypothesis argue that the blindsight phenomenon can be attributed to factors other than subcortical processing of visual input (Campion et al., 1983). They claim further that visual information about both pattern and place recognition is processed in the human brain either by the visual cortex entirely or with the assistance of cortical mechanisms that operate after it but not separate from it. Resolution of this exciting controversy over whether we see with one or two visual systems awaits new sources of data (Weiskrantz, 1990).

Isaac Newton showed that white light passing through a prism yields a rainbow of all colors of the spectrum.

SEEING COLOR

One of the most remarkable features of the human visual system is that our experiences of form, color, position, and depth are based on processing the same sensory information in different ways. However, if you observed the nerve impulses carrying various informa-

Sir Isaac Newton

tion about the external world, they would look identical. How do the transformations in processing occur that enable us to see form, color, position, and depth?

Physical objects and beams of light seem to have the marvelous property of being painted with color, but the red Valentines, green fir trees, blue oceans, and rainbows that you see are actually colorless. Despite appearances, color does not exist in the objects you see; it only exists in the mind. One of the first to argue this view was **Sir Isaac Newton** in 1671:

> For the rays [of light], to speak properly, are not colored. In them there is nothing else than a certain power and disposition to stir up a sensation of this or that color. For as sound, in a bell or musical string or other sounding body, is nothing but a trembling motion, and in the air nothing but that motion propagated from the object, . . . so colors in the object are nothing but a disposition to reflect this or that sort of ray more copiously than the rest. . . .

Newton, who discovered the laws of motion and of gravity, also discovered that when white light is shined through a prism it separates into a rainbow of colors: the *visible spectrum.*

Color is a psychological property of your sensory experience, created when your brain processes the information coded in the light source. Although the processes involved are fairly complex, color vision is one of the best understood aspects of our visual experience.

Wavelengths and Hues

Visible light is a kind of energy that our sensory receptors can detect. The light we see is just a small portion of a physical dimension called the *electromagnetic spectrum,* which also includes X rays, microwaves, radio waves, and TV waves. Because we have no receptors sensitive to these light waves, we cannot detect them without the help of special detection instruments—X-ray cameras, radios, and television sets— that convert them into signals we can see or hear.

All electromagnetic energy comes in tiny, indivisible units called *photons.* The only physical property that distinguishes one photon from another is its *wavelength,* measured in units of distance of the wavelike propagation of a photon along its path. Wavelengths of visible light are measured in *nanometers* (billionths of a meter). What we see as light is the range of wavelengths from 400 to about 700 nanometers. Each color you see is the result of experiencing light rays of a particular physical wavelength, for example, violet-blue at the lower level and red-orange at the higher level. White sunlight combines all these wavelengths in equal amounts. A prism separates them into their distinctive wavelengths. So, light is described physically in terms of wavelengths, not colors; colors exist only in your experience.

All experiences of color can be described in terms of three basic dimensions of our perception of light: hue, saturation, and brightness. **Hue** is the dimension that captures the essential color of a light in terms of the wavelength entering the eye. In pure lights that contain only one wavelength (such as a laser beam) the psychological experience of hue corresponds directly to the physical dimension of the light's wavelength. **Saturation** is the psychological dimension that captures the purity and vividness of color sensations. Undiluted colors have the most saturation; muted, muddy, and pastel colors have intermediate amounts of saturation; and grays have zero saturation. **Brightness** is the dimension of color experience that captures the intensity of light. White has the most brightness; black has the least. When colors are analyzed along these three dimensions, a remarkable finding emerges: humans are capable of visually discriminating about 5 million different colors! However, most people can identify only 150 to 200 colors.

Our perception of color of any one object depends on our comparisons with the colors of other objects in the scene as well as on the remembered colors of certain objects and the names we have for different colors. Although there is a high degree of agreement across different cultures in naming colors, interesting differences exist. For example, the Japanese only recently introduced a word into their language for *blue;* previously, the word *aoi* stood for the range of colors from green and blue to violet. By contrast, the Maori of New Zealand have a great many different color names for shades of red that match subtle differences in the changing colors of fruits and flowers as they mature and fade and for different conditions of blood.

Now we are ready to return to the puzzle of the prism's rainbow. To answer the question of how all colors combine to form white light, we need to refer to the *color circle* in **Figure 7.11.** It shows the hues arranged in a circle, according to their perceived similarity, with those that are most similar in adjacent positions. Their order mirrors the order of hues in the spectrum. Four hues are unique—red, yellow, green, and blue—because they are not combinations of other hues as are all the rest. These unique, pure hues are equally spaced. Colors that are directly opposite are **complementary colors;** when they stimulate the same part of the retina simultaneously, their added effects yield *white light* (at the center of the color circle). This phenomenon is called *additive color mixture.* Yellow

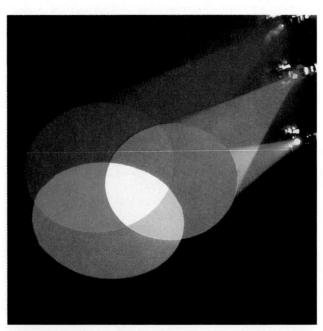

Any two unique hues yield the complement of a third color, but the combination of the three wavelengths produces white light.

FIGURE 7.11   THE COLOR CIRCLE

Colors are arranged by their similarity. Complementary colors are placed directly opposite each other. Mixing complementary colors yields a neutral gray or white light at the center. The numbers next to each hue are the wavelength values for spectral colors, those colors within our region of visual sensitivity. Nonspectral hues are obtained by mixing short and long spectral wavelengths.

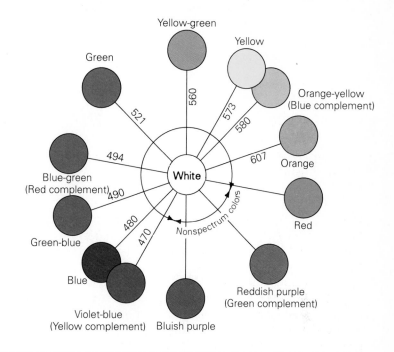

and blue *lights,* for example, produce an additive color mixture. However, yellow and blue *paints* produce green. When paint or crayon pigments are mixed, some wavelengths of light are absorbed or subtracted from the light. This phenomenon is called *subtractive color mixture*. The remaining reflected wavelength the eye sees gives the painted object the color we perceive.

Now you have the elements to understand why combining spectral hues forms white light. Through the phenomenon of additive color mixture, combining any two of the hues red, green, and blue will form a complement; green and red will form yellow, for example. However, mixing all the unique hues yields white light, as shown in the photo on this page.

Another interesting aspect of complementary colors is what happens after you stare at a brightly colored object for a while and then turn away to look at a blank surface. You will see its complementary color as a *visual afterimage*. Since seeing is sometimes believing, try the Patriotism Test in **Figure 7.12** before continuing. Surprised? Do it again; but this time just close your eyes after fixating on the green-yellow-black flag, and see if you have an "internalized" sense of patriotism. Can you explain why you saw what you did?

Afterimages (or aftereffects) may be negative, or positive. *Negative afterimages* are the opposite or the reverse of the original experience, as in the flag exam-

ple; they are more common and last longer. *Positive afterimages* are caused by a continuation of the receptor and neural processing following stimulation; they are rare and brief. An example of positive afterimages is what happens when you look at the light of a flashbulb.

Not everyone sees colors in the same way; some people are born with a color deficiency. *Color blindness* is the partial or total inability to distinguish colors. The negative afterimage effect of viewing the green, yellow, and black flag will not work if you are color-blind. Color blindness is usually a sex-linked hereditary defect associated with a gene on the X chromosome. Males more readily develop this recessive trait than females, because they have a single X chromosome; females would need to have it on both X chromosomes to become color-blind. Estimates of color blindness among Caucasian males are about 10 percent, but less than 0.5 percent for females.

There are different forms of color-blindness. People with color weakness can't distinguish pale colors, such as pink or tan. Most typical color blindness involves trouble distinguishing red from green, especially at weak saturations. Those who confuse yellows and blues are rare—about one or two people per thousand. Rarest of all are those who see no color at all and see only variations in brightness. Only about 500 cases of this total color blindness have ever been reported.

FIGURE 7.12 COLOR AFTERIMAGES: THE PATRIOTISM TEST

Stare at the dot in the center of the green, black, and yellow flag for at least 30 seconds. Then fixate on the center of a sheet of white paper or a blank wall.

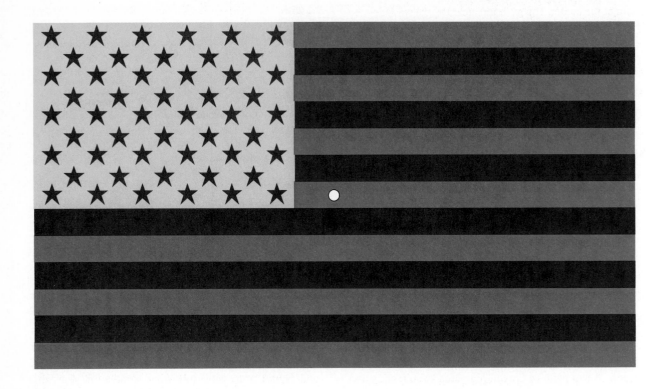

To see whether you have a major color deficiency, look at **Figure 7.13** and note what you see. If you see the numbers 12 and 5 in the pattern of dots, your color vision is probably normal. If you see something else, you are probably at least partially color blind. (Try the test on others as well—particularly people you know who are color blind—to find out what they see.)

Theories of Color Vision

What theories have psychologists proposed to account for how we see color? We will consider the two most prominent models: *trichromatic theory* and *opponent-process theory.*

The first scientific theory of color vision was proposed by Sir Thomas Young around 1800. He suggested that there were three types of color receptors in the normal human eye that produced psychologically primary color sensations: red, green, and blue (he did not include yellow). All other colors, he believed, were combinations of these three primaries. Young's theory was later refined and extended by Hermann von Helm-

holtz and came to be known as the Young-Helmholtz **trichromatic theory.**

Trichromatic theory was widely accepted for a long time, because it provided a plausible explanation for the production of people's color sensations and for color blindness (according to the theory, color-blind people had only one or two kinds of receptors); but other facts and observations were not as well explained by the theory. Why did adaptation to one color produce color afterimages that had the complementary hue? Why did color-blind people always fail to distinguish *pairs* of colors: red and green or blue and yellow?

Answers to these questions became the cornerstones for a second theory of color vision proposed by **Ewald Hering** in the late 1800s. According to his *opponent-process theory,* all color experiences arise from three underlying systems, each of which includes two opponent elements: red versus green, blue versus yellow, or black (no color) versus white (all colors). Hering theorized that colors produced complementary afterimages because one element of the system became fatigued (from overstimulation) and, thus, increased the relative contribution of its opponent element. In Hering's theory, types of color blindness came in pairs because the color system was actually built from pairs of opposites, not from single primary colors.

For many years, scientists argued about which theory was correct. Eventually, scientists recognized that the theories were not really in conflict; they simply described two different stages of processing that corresponded to successive physiological structures in the visual system (Hurvich & Jameson, 1957). We know now that there are, indeed, three types of cones—each of which is most sensitive to light at a particular wavelength—and they work very much as predicted by the original Young-Helmholtz trichromatic theory. One type of cone responds most vigorously to short wavelengths of light (seen as blue), a second type to medium wavelengths (seen as green), and a third to long wavelengths (seen as red). The responses of these cone types correspond to the three primary colors in the Young-Helmholtz theory. People who are color-blind lack one or more of these three types of receptor cones.

The retinal ganglion cells then combine the outputs of these three cone types in different ways, in accordance with Hering's opponent-process theory (R. De Valois & Jacobs, 1968). According to the modern version

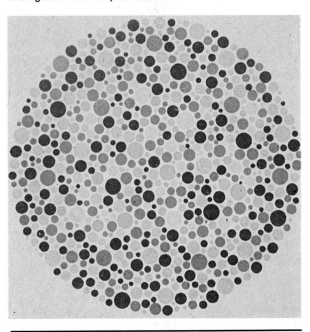

FIGURE 7.13   *THE ISHIHANI COLOR BLINDNESS TEST*

A person who cannot discriminate between red and green colors will not be able to identify the number hidden in the figure. What do you see?

of **opponent-process theory,** as supported by **Leo Hurvich** and **Dorothea Jameson** (1974), the two members of each color pair work in opposition (are opponents) by means of neural inhibition. Some cells are excited by light that produces sensations of red and are inhibited by light that produces sensations of green. Other cells in the system do the opposite: they are excited by light that looks green and are inhibited by light that looks red. Together, these two types of ganglion cells form the physiological basis of the red/green opponent-process system. Other ganglion cells make up the blue/yellow opponent system. The black/white system contributes to our perception of color saturation and brightness.

Molecular Basis of Color Vision

Recent discoveries from genetics and neurobiology laboratories support psychological theories about the way color vision functions. We perceive different colors by analyzing the inputs from cones that are sensitive to either red, green, or blue light. Each cone contains pigments that detect one of these three kinds of light. The colors we see depend on how strongly light entering the eye excites each of these three types of cone cells. Using the powerful tools of molecular genetics, researchers have isolated and identified the genes that direct the development of the three color vision proteins (Nathans et al., 1986).

Other vision researchers have developed a technique for analyzing the electrical activity of a single cone cell from the retinas of macaque monkeys and humans (which are quite similar).

> Single cone cells were "sucked up" into a special hollow glass tube that is less than 1/25th the diameter of a human hair. Light of various wavelengths was shone on the tube and the strength of electrical signals emitted from the cone cell was amplified and measured. Using this technique, the researchers found that some cells were tuned to respond maximally to light wavelengths of 435 nanometers (blue cells), others to 535 nm (green cells), and others to 570 nm (red cells). Now researchers are trying to identify the biochemical activities of these cells that are triggered by light and start the process of transduction of external energy into neural energy that underlies our visual sensation (Baylor, 1987).

SEEING FORM, DEPTH, AND MOVEMENT

Seeing the world of color is only a small part of the complex task facing the visual system which must also detect the form or shape of objects, their depth or distance, and their movement in space. The main reason

Wearing lenses that displace the visual field by 20° to the left side, this college quarterback consistently overthrows his receiver by about 20°. After adjusting to this visual distortion, he is able to hit his target. When the lenses are removed, his throws are 20° off in the opposite direction, revealing the overcompensation of his brain and kinesthetic system (*Discovering Psychology*, 1990, Program 7).

for developing a complex visual system that can accomplish these tasks in the blink of an eye is not to appreciate the beauty of a sunset or your lover's eyes but to visually guide your movement toward desirable objects and away from undesirable ones. The visual system must also be coordinated to a motor action system so that you can accurately reach and grasp, pucker your lips for a kiss, and run in the right direction. In this final section on the visual system, we will briefly touch on the highlights of new research that is now providing answers to questions about vision that have puzzled scientists and philosophers for centuries.

Our visual system consists of several separate and independent subsystems that analyze different aspects of the same retinal image. Evidence that subdivisions of the visual system are responsible for particular visual abilities came from patients with various types of strokes. Some suffered surprisingly selective visual losses, such as the loss of color discrimination but not of form perception, the loss of motion perception but not of color and form perception, or the loss of the ability to recognize familiar faces but not of other visual abilities. These clinical studies are now supported by anatomical, physiological, and psychological experiments. They clearly indicate that there is a subdivision of functions at all levels of processing information within the visual pathway from retina to cortex. Distinct sets of neurons have unique properties that generate the perceptions of color, form, contrast, movement, and texture (Livingstone & Hubel, 1988). Although our final perception is of a unified visual scene, our vision

of it is accompanied by a host of entirely separate channels in our visual system that, under normal conditions, are ultimately coordinated.

Let's consider the information we use to perceive the shape and form of objects in space and then examine the way the visual system enables us to transform that stimulus input into the "right" neural codes for accurate identification of its properties.

Contrast Effects

Any typical visual field consists of many shapes, colors, and textures that impinge on the retina. How do we see what is important? First, we must separate figures from their background so that we can make subsequent detailed analysis of their properties. This *figure-ground segregation* occurs largely automatically at the earliest stages of processing. Still, a visual scene filled with figures is quite complex. The key to perceiving different objects in space is finding *contrasts* in brightness to form boundaries and distinct edges that give objects shape, size, and orientation in space. The visual system accentuates the edges between objects to make them stand out clearly by searching for contrasts.

A patch of gray appears lighter against a dark background than it does against a light background, as shown in **Figure 7.14**. This brightness contrast effect makes the response to a constant stimulus greater as the intensity difference between it and its background increases. In the retina, adjacent areas are accentuated by this brightness contrast effect, causing perceived boundaries between surfaces to be sharpened.

The power of edges to define a visual field is seen in the two rectangular surfaces in **Figure 7.15**. Rectangle A and rectangle B seem similar—they both have dark right halves and light left halves. To prove that the right half of rectangle A is darker than the left half, place a pencil along the center of the rectangle. Note the brightness difference on either side of the pencil. To prove that your perception of the world can be distorted, place the pencil along the center of rectangle B. Visual magic! The difference between the left and right halves has vanished (as seems to be happening in U.S. politics). A light meter moved across rectangle A records the sharp change in light intensity at the midpoint of the rectangle; but the bottom rectangle is shown to have the same light intensity throughout except at the midpoint between the two halves where there is a gradual shift toward brighter on the left side and darker on the right. The midpoint border creates a false impression of contrast that fools your visual system into seeing a difference where there is none.

Receptive Fields and Feature-detectors

The cells at each level in the visual pathway respond *selectively* only to a particular part of the visual

FIGURE 7.14 **BRIGHTNESS CONTRAST**

These four (objectively) identical gray squares are set on different backgrounds. As you can see, the lighter the background, the darker the gray squares appear.

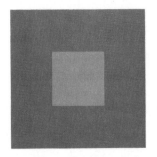

FIGURE 7.15 **THE ILLUSION OF CONTOUR**

Put a pencil or a straightedge down the center divide between the left and right sections of A. Then do the same for B. What happens to the difference between the left and right segments of each?

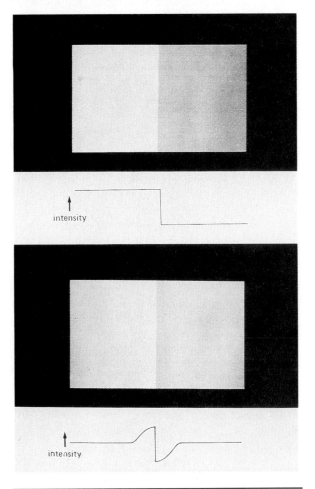

field. We noted earlier that each retinal ganglion cell integrates the information about light patterns that comes from many receptor cells. When microrecordings are made of the electrical activity of single ganglion cells, the firing rate, or frequency with which they discharge impulses, is changed by the presentation of a visual stimulus with specific properties. The area of a cell that is affected selectively—gets excited or inhibited—by a particular property of a visual stimulus is known as the **receptive field.**

Receptive fields of retinal ganglion cells are of two types: (a) those in which stimulation in the center produces excitation while stimulation in the surrounding part produces inhibition and (b) those with the opposite organization—an inhibitory center and an excitatory surround. Ganglion cells respond to the *differences* in stimulation coming from their center and the surround. They are most excited by *stimulus contrast;* those with *on* centers fire most strongly to a bright spot surrounded by a dark border while those with *off* centers fire most vigorously to a dark spot surrounded by a light border. Uniform illumination causes the center and surround to cancel each other's activity—the cell is not as excited by uniform illumination as it is by a spot or bar of light.

When a receptor cell is stimulated by light it transmits information in two directions: upward to the brain and sideways to neighboring receptor cells. What are sent out to adjacent cells are impulses that *inhibit* the transmission of receptor cells. This sideways suppression of other receptor cells, called **lateral inhibition,** is the basis for the brightness contrast effect we have previously noted. As one receptor is excited by an intense amount of light, it inhibits neighboring cells from being excited by the stimulus. Lateral inhibition exaggerates the difference between them, generating messages to the brain that there is more contrast than actually exists.

David Hubel and **Thorsten Weisel,** sensory physiologists at Harvard University, pioneered the study of the receptive fields of cells in the visual cortex, and, in 1981, they won a Nobel prize for their work. They recorded the firing rates from single cells in the visual cortex of cats in response to moving spots and bars in the visual field. When Hubel and Weisel mapped out the receptive fields of these cortical cells, they found both excitatory and inhibitory regions, as in the case of the retinal ganglion cells; but they found that the receptive fields of the cortical cells were almost always elongated rather than round. As a result, these cortical cells were strongly excited (or inhibited) by bars of light or by edges in their "favorite" orientation (Hubel & Weisel, 1962, 1979). Because these cortical cells were simply and directly related to specific receptive fields, Hubel and Weisel called them *simple cells*. Their output, in turn, is processed by other, more complex types of cortical cells (see **Figure 7.16**).

When the electrical activity of single cells in the visual cortex was recorded in response to stimulation of different types, a surprising discovery emerged. Some cells responded to lines, some to edges, some to particular positions or orientations of a stimulus, some to particular shapes, and some to movement in a particular direction. Within their receptive fields, these cortical cells responded only to patterns of specific shapes and angles of orientation.

One way to think about this finding is that the brain is designed to extract certain simple features from the complex stimuli that bombard the visual system. Lines,

edges, angles, and corners are the effective stimuli for cortical cells. Thus, simple cortical cells in the visual cortex might respond to a triangle by detecting the sides. Some of the cells would detect horizontal lines and others would detect straight lines at 60°. More complex cortical cells might detect 60° corners. The information from the different cells would then be combined as the stimulus that would activate a triangle detector somewhere in a higher level of brain processing.

Hubel and Weisel called these cortical cells **feature-detection cells** because they responded most strongly by discharging impulses when specific stimulus features were present in their receptive fields. Each feature detector cell was assumed to abstract a particular aspect of a total pattern of stimulation from the visual field to which it was specifically sensitive. Recent research indicates that individual cells, as well as clusters of cells throughout the visual pathway, are sensitive to specific visual inputs—some to one color and not another, some to depth, some to the orientation of lines, and some to motion.

A **feature-detection model** postulates that these feature detectors are arranged hierarchically—the simple input from lower centers is combined and expanded at each successive stage along the visual pathway. While there is some evidence to support this view, the theory does not explain the whole story. Rather than merely responding to simple bars that have the same contrast, most cortical cells are even more sensitive to successive, *contrasting* bands of dark and light. This research by **Russell De Valois** and **Karen De Valois** (1980) has

---

FIGURE 7.16   *RECEPTIVE FIELDS OF GANGLION AND CORTICAL CELLS*

The receptive field of a cell is the area in the visual field from which it receives stimulation. The receptive fields of the ganglion cells in the retina are circular (A, B); those of the simplest cells in the visual cortex are elongated in a particular orientation (C, D, E, F). In both cases, the cell responding to the receptive field is excited by light in the regions marked with plus signs and inhibited by light in the regions marked with minus signs.

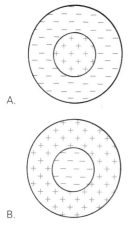

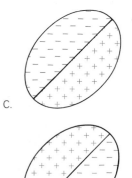

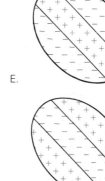

generated the **spatial-frequency model** of the way patterns and shapes are perceived. The model suggests that our nervous system constructs visual scenes by transforming visual images into an alternate representation that is mathematically equivalent to describing them in terms of light and dark. Any image that is composed of patterns of dark-light variations can be analyzed according to the number of its dark-light cycles over a given distance of visual space—its *spatial frequency*. These spatial frequencies can be analyzed mathematically by a procedure called Fourier analysis; the analysis yields a measure of the sensitivity of the visual system (Campbell & Robson, 1968). Research evidence suggests that the human visual system may analyze visual scenes by actually performing some kind of Fourier analysis on the patterns of dark-light cycles it detects (Blakemore & Campbell, 1969). Sets of cortical cells may be organized into channels that are tuned to respond to different spatial frequencies. Some channels, specific to low frequencies, pick up blobs of light, others detect high frequencies, and others are specific for frequencies in between. Together, they provide all the information needed to represent a visual scene by combining the range of spatial frequencies that define its dark-light pattern. Any two-dimensional pattern—from an American flag to a photograph of Groucho Marx—can be analyzed mathematically and broken down into computer codes as the sum of its many spatial frequencies (measured as sine-wave gratings or alternating light-dark stripes). **Figure 7.17** of Groucho Marx reveals what you would see of him with only low spatial frequencies—the overall shape in the blurry picture, A.

The high spatial frequencies are responsible for the sharp edges and fine detail in the outline picture, B. What we ordinarily see is the combination of all spatial frequencies, as in picture C.

What Neurons "See," the Brain Perceives

Do we really know that what these nerve cells in the visual system are responding to affects what the brain perceives and how we behave? In the last few years the answer to this question has been *yes*. New research has shown that the patterns of light and dark picked up by receptors in the eye are transformed into electrical signals that the brain interprets and uses to trigger appropriate action in the perceiving organism. Stimulating distinct circuits of receptive fields of neurons in the visual cortex not only excites the neurons but also causes certain perceptions to occur (Newsome & Pare, 1988).

> Rhesus monkeys had been trained to make a specific response to a visual display of dots moving in a certain direction on a television screen. If they correctly identified the direction of movement—as up or down, for example—they were rewarded. During the experiment, researchers directly stimulated those cortical neurons that were sensitive to a given direction of motion in the visual field. When cells sensitive to upward movement were electrically stimulated, the monkeys would often "report" upward movement of the random dots. Thus, if random dot patterns were being shown to the monkeys, they responded

---

FIGURE 7.17   HIGH AND LOW SPATIAL FREQUENCIES

Detection of only low spatial frequencies would give us the blurry view in A. Detection of only the high spatial frequencies would give us the outline view in B. Normal detection of all frequencies gives us the full view in C.

A.   B.   C.

behaviorally as if the dots were moving in the direction of the preferred receptive field of the stimulated neurons. If the upward preferred direction was being stimulated, the monkeys reported upward movement even when the actual movement of the dots was downward. This is the first study to demonstrate a causal connection between neuronal activity of cells in the visual cortex and perceptually judged direction of movement (Salzman et al., 1990).

From Attention to Action

Finally, we come back to the survival issues raised earlier: how are the objects of our attention chosen and how are our eyes and hands directed to move them? The ordinary ability of many animals—especially humans—to reach out, grasp, and manipulate perceived objects is a feat of biological engineering that is unmatched by state-of-the-art robots. Apparently, we are able to perform these feats because of specialized cells in the central nervous system. Some of the cells are involved in directing our attention to certain objects, others in moving the eyes to the object of most interest, and still others in generating limb movements to grasp and manipulate the object.

After the first stage of processing where *figure-ground separation* occurs, comes the second stage where selecting objects or special features of forms occurs. At this *attentional stage* perception operates serially by focusing on one or two objects at a time. While attention at a *psychological level* facilitates behavioral responses and access to memory (to be discussed in detail in the next chapter), attention at a *neurophysiological level* can have powerful effects on the responses of individual neurons. It can enhance neuronal responses to attended items and suppress responses to unattended items in the visual system and other sensory systems as well.

Special neurons in the rear of the *parietal cortex* appear to be important for spatial attention. These neurons respond most strongly when the subject attends to a specific location in space, but they respond weakly when the subject ignores objects in the preferred receptive field. These findings lead some researchers to describe these neuronal cells as having an *attention field* rather than a receptive field (Wise & Desimone, 1988). Lesions in this brain region impair humans' ability to shift their attention from one location to another.

In another visual pathway in the *temporal cortex,* neurons have such large receptive fields that many different stimuli will typically fall within them. When a monkey subject restricts its attention to just one of these stimuli, the response of the receptive field of the neuron is determined by the attended stimulus. For example, if the monkey focuses its attention on green stimuli when red and green stimuli appear together at different locations, a neuron that normally responds to red stimuli will fire only weakly, if at all. Neurons thus selectively process information about attended stimuli at different locations and also about attended features of a single stimulus, boosting responsiveness to them at the expense of the unattended stimuli and features.

Once attention focuses the brain's information processing system on the object, a number of other processes are called into play. *Gaze control* directs eye movement to scrutinize the target; *limb movement control* directs arms, hands, and mouth toward the target; and *body movement control* directs the body toward targets out of reach and away from feared targets. These actions are largely controlled by neurons in the *motor cortex,* which have been shown to begin discharging impulses before the first muscle activity starts to move the limbs. The neurophysiology of these motor responses has also been described in detail.

Researchers in this field of *behavioral neurophysiology* are now developing models of the neural networks involved in visually guided movement. Their challenging task is to demonstrate how one's accumulated *experience*—learning and memory—adjusts and maintains the consistency between sensory input maps and the motor output maps. These models will both increase our basic understanding of how we are able to act so accurately on the basis of what we perceive. It will also have practical utility for clinical interventions with patients suffering from problems of visual-movement impairments (Wise & Desimone, 1988).

SUMMING UP

The visual system, the most thoroughly studied of any sensory system, is investigated with many approaches: anatomical, physiological, neurophysiological, genetic, and psychological. In the eye, light energy is converted to neural impulses by photoreceptors in the retina: the rods and cones. Ganglion cells in the retina integrate the input from several receptors and bipolar cells; their axons form the optic nerves, which meet at the optic chiasma. From there, a small pathway goes to the superior colliculus, where some information about the location of the stimulus object is processed (and where blindsight may occur). A large pathway goes by way of the lateral geniculate nucleus to the visual cortex, where information about color and detail is processed.

The stimulus for color is the wavelength of light— the visible portion of the electromagnetic spectrum. Color sensations differ in hue, saturation, and brightness. Current color vision theory combines the Young-

Helmholtz trichromatic theory (receptor processing) and the opponent-process theory (ganglion cell processing). Researchers have now isolated and identified the human genes that direct the development of the three proteins responsible for color vision. Contrasts in brightness form boundaries and distinct edges that give objects size, shape, and orientation in space. Cells in the retina, as well as higher centers in the visual pathway and cortex, have receptive fields that respond maximally to specific types of stimulus features.

Researchers disagree about whether spatial information is detected by feature detectors or analyzed as spatial frequency patterns. Detection of spatial frequencies is studied by analysis of patterns of light-dark cycles known as sine-wave gratings. New research demonstrates that stimulating receptive fields of visual neurons causes perceptual judgments; the brain starts perceiving what the neuron is "seeing." The complex processes involved in attending to selected stimuli and coordinating movements toward target stimuli are being illuminated by investigators in the new field of behavioral neurophysiology.

 # HEARING

Similar to vision, audition, or hearing, provides us with reliable spatial information over extended distances. However, hearing may be even more important than vision in orienting us toward distant events. We often hear stimuli before we see them, particularly if they take place behind us or on the other side of opaque objects such as walls. Although vision is better than hearing for identifying an object once it is in the field of view, we often see the object only because we have used our ears to point our eyes in the right direction.

Besides orienting us, hearing plays a crucial role in our understanding of spoken language; it is the principal sensory modality for human communication. People who lack the capacity to hear are excluded from much normal human interaction and may suffer psychological problems associated with feelings of frustration, rejection, and isolation as a result. People can usually tell right away that someone is visually impaired so they are able to make adjustments in their behavior (i.e. verbally describing an incident to a visually impaired person who can't see it); hearing impairments, however, often go unrecognized even by the individual who is experiencing the impairment if the onset is gradual. Depression and paranoid disorders may accompany undetected loss of hearing (Post, 1980; Zimbardo et al., 1981). The importance of hearing and the tragedy of its loss is captured in this eloquent description:

The world will still make sense to someone who is blind or armless or minus a nose. But if you lose your sense of hearing, a crucial thread dissolves and you lose track of life's logic. You become cut off from the daily commerce of the world, as if you were a root buried beneath the soil (Ackerman, 1990, p. 175).

THE PHYSICS OF SOUND

Clap your hands together. Whistle. Tap your pencil on the table. Why do these actions create sounds? The reason is that they cause objects to vibrate. The vibrational energy is transmitted to the surrounding medium—usually air—as the vibrating objects push the molecules of the medium back and forth. The resulting slight changes in pressure spread outward from the vibrating objects in the form of sound waves traveling at a rate of about 1100 feet per second. Sound cannot be created in a true vacuum (such as outer space) because there are no air molecules in a vacuum for vibrating objects to move.

Air pressure changes—changes in the density of air molecules in space—travel in waves, as shown in **Figure 7.18.** These particular waves, called *sine waves,* are similar to the ones we discussed in connection with spatial frequencies in vision.

A sine wave has two basic physical properties that determine how it sounds to us: frequency and amplitude. *Frequency* measures the number of cycles the wave completes in a given amount of time. A cycle, as indi-

FIGURE 7.18   *SOUND WAVES*

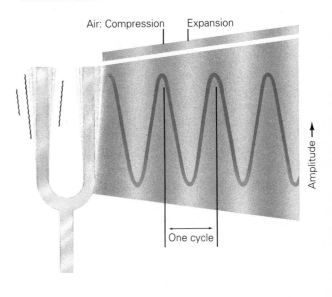

cated in Figure 7.18, is the left-to-right distance from the peak in one wave to the peak in the next wave. Sound frequency is usually expressed in cycles per second (cps) or **Hertz** (Hz). *Amplitude* measures the physical property of strength of the sound wave, as shown in its peak-to-valley height. Amplitude is defined in units of sound pressure or energy.

Sounds produced by a single sine wave, such as those made by tuning forks, are called *pure tones*. A pure tone has only one frequency and one amplitude. Most sounds in the real world are not pure tones as they are produced by complex waves containing a combination of frequencies and amplitudes. We hear differing qualities of sounds (clarinet versus piano, for example) because most sounds contain differing combinations of frequencies and amplitudes.

PSYCHOLOGICAL DIMENSIONS OF SOUND

The three dimensions of the sounds we experience are pitch, loudness, and quality. Though you already know a bit about the characteristics of the sound waves that produce these experiences, we need to take a closer look at the way we sense each of these physical qualities.

Pitch

Pitch is the highness or lowness of a sound determined by the sound's frequency; high frequencies produce high pitch, and low frequencies produce low pitch. The full range of human sensitivity to pure tones extends from frequencies as low as 20 cps to frequencies as high as 20,000 cps. (Frequencies below 20 Hz may be experienced through touch as vibrations rather than as sound.) Out of the full range of frequencies to which we are sensitive, the corresponding notes on a piano cover only the range from about 30 Hz to 4000 Hz.

The psychophysical relationship between pitch and frequency is not a linear one: at the low end of the frequency scale, increasing the frequency by just a few cps raises the pitch quite noticeably; but at the high end of frequency, we require a much bigger increase in order to hear the difference in pitch. For example, the two lowest notes on a piano differ by only 1.6 Hz whereas the two highest ones differ by 235 Hz—a difference that is more than 140 times greater than the difference between the two lowest notes. This relationship between pitch and sound frequency is described by *Fechner's logarithmic law*.

Loudness

The **loudness,** or physical intensity, of a sound is determined by its amplitude; sound waves with large amplitudes are experienced as loud and those with small amplitudes as soft. The human auditory system is sensitive to an enormous range of physical intensities—

people can hear sounds across a wide range of loudness. The auditory system is sensitive enough to hear the tick of a wristwatch at 20 feet; this is the system's absolute threshold—if it were more sensitive, we would hear the blood flowing in our ears. At the other extreme, a jet airliner taking off 100 yards away is so loud that it is painful. In terms of physical units of sound pressure, the jet produces a sound wave with more than a billion times the energy of the ticking watch.

Because the range of hearing is so great, physical intensities of sound are usually expressed in ratios rather than absolute amounts; loudness is measured in units called **decibels** (db). **Figure 7.19** shows the loud-

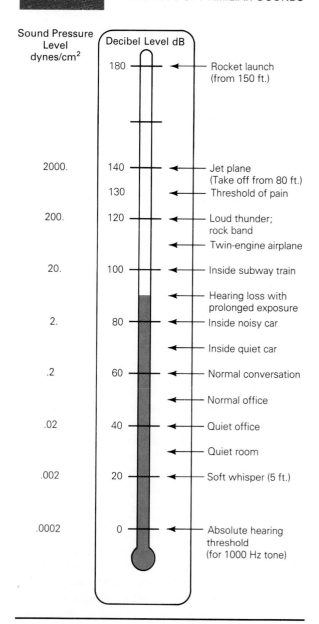

| FIGURE 7.19 | *LOUDNESS OF FAMILIAR SOUNDS* |

ness of some representative natural sounds in decibel units. It also shows the corresponding sound pressures for comparison. Notice that sounds louder than about 90 db can produce hearing loss, depending on how long one is exposed to them.

Timbre

The **timbre** of a sound reflects the quality of complexity of its sound wave. A complex sound can be analyzed as a sum of many different pure tones, each with a different amplitude and frequency. **Figure 7.20** shows the complex waveforms that correspond to several familiar sounds. The graph in the figure shows the sound spectrum for middle C on a piano—the range of all the frequencies actually present in that note and their amplitudes.

In a complex tone such as middle C, the lowest frequency (about 256 Hz) is responsible for the pitch we hear; it is called the *fundamental.* The higher frequencies are called *harmonics,* or overtones, and are simple multiples of the fundamental. The complete sound we hear is produced by the total effect of the fundamental and the harmonics shown in the spectrum. If pure tones at these frequencies and intensities were added together, the result would sound the same to us as middle C on a piano. Amazingly, the human ear actually analyzes complex waves by breaking them down into these component waves.

The sounds that we call *noise* do not have the clear, simple structures of fundamental frequencies and harmonics. Noise contains many frequencies that are not systematically related to each other. For instance, the static noise you hear between radio stations contains energy at all audible frequencies; you perceive it as having no pitch because it has no fundamental frequency.

THE PHYSIOLOGY OF HEARING

Now that we know something about our psychological experiences of sound and how they correspond psychophysically to the stimuli for sound, let's see how those experiences arise from physiological activity in the auditory system. First we will look at the way the ear works; then we will consider some theories about how pitch experiences are coded in the auditory system.

The Auditory System

In order for people to hear, four basic energy transformations must take place: (a) airborne sound waves must get translated into fluid waves within the cochlea of the ear, (b) the fluid waves must then stimulate mechanical vibrations of the basilar membrane, (c) these vibrations must be connected into electrical impulses, and (d) the impulses must travel to the auditory cortex.

FIGURE 7.20 **WAVEFORMS OF FAMILIAR SOUNDS**

Below the complex waveforms of five familiar sounds is the sound spectrum for middle C on the piano. The basic wavelength is produced by the fundamental, in this case at 256 cycles, but the strings are also vibrating at several higher frequencies that produce the jaggedness of the wave pattern. These additional frequencies are identified in the sound spectrum.

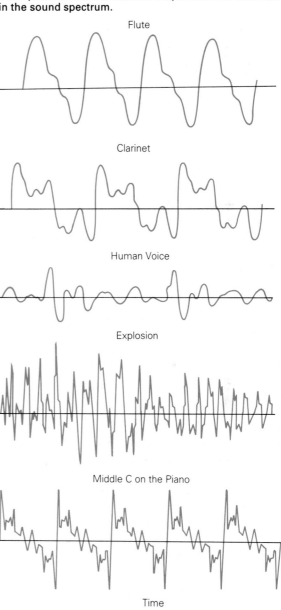

Let's examine each of these transformations in greater detail.

In the first transformation, vibrating air molecules enter the ears (see **Figure 7.21**). Some sound enters the external canal of the ear directly and some enters after having been reflected off the *external ear*, or *pinna*. The sound wave travels along the canal through the outer ear until it reaches the end of the canal. There it encounters a thin membrane called the eardrum, or *tympanic membrane*. The sound wave's pressure variations set the eardrum into motion. The eardrum transmits the vibrations from the outer ear into the middle ear, a chamber that contains the three smallest bones in the human body: the *hammer*, the *anvil*, and the *stirrup*.

These bones form a mechanical chain that transmits and concentrates the vibrations from the eardrum to the primary organ of hearing, the *cochlea*, which is located in the *inner ear*.

In the second transformation, which occurs in the cochlea, the airborne sound wave becomes "seaborne." The **cochlea** is a fluid-filled, coiled tube that has a membrane known as the **basilar membrane** running down its middle and along its length. When the stirrup vibrates against the oval window at the base of the cochlea, the fluid in the cochlea is set into wave motion. This fluid wave travels down the length of the coiled tube, around the end, and back to the base on the other side of the basilar membrane, where it is absorbed by

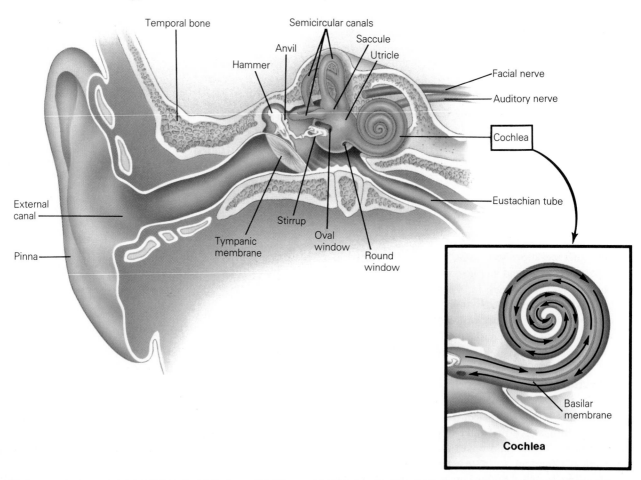

| FIGURE 7.21 | *STRUCTURE OF THE HUMAN EAR* |

Sound waves are channeled by the external ear, or pinna, through the external canal, causing the tympanic membrane to vibrate. This vibration activates the tiny bones of the inner ear—the hammer, anvil, and stirrup. Their mechanical vibrations are passed along from the oval window to the cochlea where they set in motion the fluid in its canal. Tiny hair cells lining the coiled basilar membrane within the cochlea bend as the fluid moves, stimulating nerve endings attached to them. The mechanical energy is then transformed into neural energy and sent to the brain via the auditory nerve.

the round window. As the fluid moves, it causes the basilar membrane to move in a wavelike motion; this motion bends the tiny hair cells connected to it.

In the third transformation, the wavelike motion of the basilar membrane bends the tiny hair cells connected to the membrane. As the hair cells bend, they stimulate nerve endings, transforming the mechanical vibrations of the basilar membrane into neural activity.

Finally, in the fourth transformation, nerve impulses leave the cochlea in a bundle of fibers called the **auditory nerve.** These fibers meet in the *cochlear nucleus* of the brain stem. Similar to the crossing over of nerves in the visual system, stimulation from one ear goes to both sides of the brain. Auditory signals pass through a series of other nuclei on their way to the **auditory cortex** in the temporal lobes of the cerebral hemispheres. The higher order processing of these signals begins in the auditory cortex.

The four transformations occur in fully functioning auditory systems. However, millions of people may suffer from some form of hearing impairment. There are two general types of hearing impairment, each caused by a defect in one or more of the components of the auditory system. The less serious type of impairment is *conduction deafness,* a problem in the conduction of the air vibrations to the cochlea. Often in this type of impairment, the bones in the middle ear are not functioning properly, a problem that may be corrected in microsurgery by insertion of an artificial anvil or stirrup. The more serious type of impairment is *nerve deafness,* a defect in the neural mechanisms that create nerve impulses in the ear or relay them to the auditory cortex. Obviously, damage to the auditory cortex can also create nerve deafness. Currently, there are no known ways to modify nerve deafness.

THEORIES OF PITCH PERCEPTION

To explain how the auditory system converts sound waves into sensations of pitch, two distinct theories have been proposed: *place theory* and *frequency theory.*

Place theory was initially proposed by **Hermann von Helmholtz** in the 1800s and was later modified, elaborated, and tested by **Georg von Békésy,** who won a Nobel prize for this work in 1961. **Place theory** proposes that pitch perception depends on which part of the receptor is stimulated. It is based on the fact that the basilar membrane moves when sound waves are conducted through the inner ear. Different frequencies produce most movement at particular locations along the basilar membrane. For high-frequency tones, the wave motion is greatest at the base of the cochlea, where the oval and round windows are located. For low-frequency tones, the greatest wave motion of the basilar membrane

is at the opposite end. So, place theory states that perception of pitch depends upon the specific place on the basilar membrane where the greatest stimulation occurs. Thus the place of greatest movement could be the code for pitch that is used by the nervous system.

The second theory, **frequency theory,** explains pitch by the timing of neural responses. Its main hypothesis is that neurons fire only at a certain phase in each cycle of the sine wave—perhaps at the peaks. Their firing rate is determined by a tone's frequency. This *rate of firing* is the code for pitch. One problem with this theory is that individual neurons cannot fire rapidly enough to represent high pitch sounds, because none of them can fire more than 2000 times per second. This limitation makes it impossible for one neuron to distinguish sounds above 2000 Hz, which of course, our auditory system can do quite well. This limitation is overcome by the **volley principle** which explains what might happen when the peaks in a sound wave come too rapidly for any single neuron to fire in response to each peak. As shown in **Figure 7.22,** several neurons in a combined action, or volley, could fire at the frequency that matched the stimulus tone (Wever, 1949).

As with the trichromatic and opponent-process theories of color vision, the place and frequency theories of pitch perception were long thought to be in direct conflict. Recently, it has become clear that both are correct, each accounting for only a portion of the audible frequency range. Frequency theory accounts well for

---

FIGURE 7.22   THE VOLLEY PRINCIPLE

The total collective activity of the auditory (black) nerve cells has a pattern that corresponds to the input sound wave (red) even though each individual fiber may not be firing fast enough to follow the sound wave pattern.

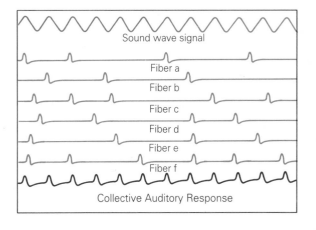

NOISE POLLUTION FILLS THE AIR

During the 1980s, the California communities of Monterey, Beverly Hills, and Del Mar banned the use of leaf blowers. In other towns, residents still put up with these motorized rake substitutes that blast bystanders with sounds as loud as 91 decibels—about the same loudness as Niagara Falls (Carlton, 1990). Ninety-one dbs is a level that can cause auditory damage.

In San Francisco, problems with noise pollution have become so serious that the police force has a special noise abatement unit. When noise cops respond to citizens' complaints, they turn on their computers and measure the decibel level of the offending sounds. If it's more than 5 decibels over the background noise, they issue warnings. A second violation merits a citation. If the source of the noise is a night club, its operating permit may even be revoked (Krieger, 1990).

Why all this fuss about noise? Prolonged exposure to intense sounds can produce permanent hearing loss. Impairment depends both on the duration and intensity of a sound. A sudden explosion at 200 dbs can cause massive damage in a fraction of a second, but routine, continued exposure to sounds more than and even less than 100 dbs can also cause significant hearing impairment. Many people report *stimulation deafness* for up to several hours after listening to a rock concert in an enclosed area. Rock musicians may suffer more permanent hearing loss because they are exposed to intense sound levels so frequently.

Rock musicians are not the only ones adversely affected by the noise levels in modern society. While the majority of 70 year olds living near the Sudanese-Ethiopian border could hear a whisper from 100 yards away (Krieger, 1990), about one in four Americans over 65 needs a hearing aid to detect whispers across the room (Clayman, 1989).

Sustained exposure to loud noises damages the sensitive hair cells that convert the motion of the basilar membrane into neural impulses. Once damaged, these cells do not regenerate, and they cannot be surgically repaired. Short exposure to very loud sounds—a jackhammer at 3 feet, a jet engine at 100 feet, or a rock concert from the front row—can cause damage in less than half an hour. Short blasts

of loud but less intense sounds, such as those caused by a power mower (about 85 db), may be safe but earplugs are advised. The federal government regulates the maximum noise exposure allowed in the workplace. While the limit for 90 db noise is 8 hours a day, workers cannot legally be exposed to 110 dbs for longer than half an hour daily.

Loud noise primarily affects sensitivity to high frequencies (at or above 4000 cps). With age, almost everyone in our noisy society loses some ability to hear at these frequencies. The data from Africa suggest that this loss may not be a physiological consequence of aging but could be the cumulative effect of a lifetime's exposure to environmental noise. If so, those who want to preserve their hearing might consider cleaning up their yards the old fashioned way—with a rake.

coding frequencies below about 5000 Hz; at higher frequencies neurons cannot fire quickly and precisely enough to code a signal adequately, even in volley. Place theory accounts well for perception of pitch at frequencies above 1000 Hz. Below 1000 cps, the entire basilar membrane vibrates so broadly it cannot provide to the neural receptors a signal that is distinctive enough to be used as a means of distinguishing pitch. Between 1000 and 5000 Hz both mechanisms can operate. As in the case of the competing color theories, the two pitch theories have proven to be compatible. Each offers a good explanation of part of the puzzle. A complex sensory task is divided between two systems that, together, offer greater sensory precision than either system alone could provide.

What is the evolutionary significance of an auditory system designed for greatest precision within the 1000 and 5000 Hz range of sounds? The auditory system may well have evolved for hearing the human voice, because speech frequency has a considerable overlap with these auditory perception frequencies in its range of generating sound and because the shape of the auditory canal magnifies sounds within the range of human speech.

SOUND LOCALIZATION

Porpoises and bats do not use vision to locate objects in dark waters or dark caves. Instead, they use *echolocation*—they emit high-pitch sounds that bounce off objects, giving them feedback about the objects' distances, locations, sizes, textures, and movements. Although we humans lack this special ability, we do use sounds to determine the location of objects in space, especially when seeing them is difficult. We do so through two mechanisms: relative timing of sounds to each ear and relative pitch of sound from each ear.

The first mechanism involves neurons that compare the relative times when incoming sound reaches each ear. A sound on your right side, for example, reaches the right ear before the left. Neurons are arranged in rows, so that every other row is stimulated by one of the two ears. Another set of neurons compares the times when these rows are stimulated and computes the relative arrival times of sounds to each ear. This mechanism is quite sensitive, detecting differences in arrival times as small as one/ten millionth of a second, under ideal conditions.

The second mechanism relies on the principle that, as sound travels around your head, it changes ever so slightly in pitch. Another set of detector neurons compares the relative pitch of sounds from each ear, providing a second source of information about the location of a target sound. Can you figure out a weakness in both

of these sound localization systems? What happens when a sound is directly in front of or behind you and equidistant between your ears? With your eyes closed, you cannot tell its exact location. So, you automatically move your head or rather your ears to position them to perform their sound localization in the way for which they were designed.

SUMMING UP

Audition (hearing) is produced by sound waves that vary in frequency, amplitude, and complexity. Our sensations of sound vary in pitch, loudness, and timbre (quality). In the cochlea, sound waves are transformed into fluid waves that move the basilar membrane. When the tiny hairs on the basilar membrane bend in response to this movement, they stimulate neural impulses that are sent along to the auditory cortex.

Place theory accounts best for the coding of high frequencies; together, frequency theory and the volley principle account best for the coding of low frequencies. While conductance deafness may be corrected, nerve deafness, which involves defects in neural transmission of sound codes, cannot. Temporary deafness is experienced with exposure to intense sounds, such as those at a rock concert. Prolonged exposure to sources of noise pollution diminishes hearing ability and can lead to permanent hearing impairment. Localizing sounds in space involves the interplay of two neuronal mechanisms that compute the relative timing of sounds coming to each ear and the relative pitch of sounds from each ear.

OUR OTHER SENSES

Vision and hearing are the senses that have been studied the most because they are the most important to us. However, we depend on many other senses, too. We will chose our discussion of sense modalities with a brief analysis of some essential features of the human senses of smell, taste, touch, and pain. Before doing so, we'll briefly consider two other vital senses of which we are often less aware: the *vestibular sense* and the *kinesthetic sense*.

To move around purposefully in our environment we need constant information about where our limbs and other body parts are in relation to each other and to objects in the environment. Without this knowledge, even our simplest actions would be hopelessly uncoordinated. The **vestibular sense** tells us how our bodies—especially our heads—are oriented in the world with respect to gravity. It also tells us when we are moving or, more precisely, when the direction or rate of our motion is changing.

The receptors for this information are tiny hairs in fluid-filled sacs and canals in the inner ear; the hairs bend when the fluid moves and presses on them, which is what happens when we turn our heads quickly. The *saccule* and *utricle* shown in Figure 7.21 tell us about acceleration or deceleration. The three canals, called the *semicircular canals,* are at right angles to each other and, thus, can tell us about motion in any direction. They inform us how our heads are moving when we turn, nod, or tilt them. The vestibular sense also helps us keep ourselves upright. People who lose their vestibular sense because of accidents or disease are initially quite disoriented and prone to falling and dizziness. However, most of these people eventually compensate by relying more heavily on visual information. *Motion sickness* can occur when the signals from the visual system conflict with those from the vestibular system. Feeling nauseous when reading in a moving car is common because the visual signal is of a stationary object, while the vestibular signal is of movement. Drivers rarely get motion sickness because they are seeing and also feeling motion.

Whether we are standing erect, riding bicycles, drawing pictures, removing splinters with tweezers, or making love, our brains need to have accurate information about the current positions and movement of our body parts relative to each other. The **kinesthetic sense** (also called kinesthesis) provides constant sensory feedback about what the body is doing during motor activities. Without it, we would be unable to coordinate most of the voluntary movements we make so effortlessly.

We have two potential sources of kinesthetic information: receptors in the joints and receptors in the muscles and tendons. Receptors that lie in the joints respond to pressures that accompany different positions of the limbs and to pressure changes that accompany movements of the joints. Receptors in the muscles and tendons that hold bones together respond to changes in tension that accompany muscle shortening and lengthening and tendons. They are involved in motor control and coordination but tell us little about body position.

SMELL

The sense of smell involves a sequence of biochemical activities that trigger the firing of action potentials. The first stage of this sequence consists of the interaction of odors with receptor proteins on the membrane of tiny hairs in the nose (*olfactory cilia*). Only eight molecules of a substance are required to initiate one of these nerve impulses, but at least 40 nerve endings must be stimulated before the organism can smell the substance. Once initiated, these nerve impulses convey odor information to the **olfactory bulb,** located just above the receptors and just below the frontal lobes of the cortex. Odor stimuli may start the process of smell by stimulating an influx of chemical substances into ion channels in olfactory neurons, which, as you may recall from Chapter 3, triggers an action potential (Restrepo et al., 1990).

The brain center that is specialized to process information about smell is the *rhinencephalon,* one of the oldest parts of the brain. Several facts have led researchers to conclude that smell is our most primitive sense. First, the human rhinencephalon looks very similar to that of other organisms—for example, the lizard—suggesting that the sense evolved long before major differences among organisms began to evolve. Second, while sensory signals from all other sense modalities pass through the relay station of the thalamus before going on to their destination in the sensory cortex, smell signals do not. Instead, they go directly to the brain's smell center.

Smell presumably evolved as a system for detecting and locating food (Moncrieff, 1951). It is also used for detecting potential sources of danger. Because smell is a distance sense—organisms do not have to come into direct contact with other organisms in order to smell them—it is particularly useful for alerting organisms to danger. In addition, smell can be a powerful form of active communication. Members of some species communicate with each other by secreting and detecting chemical signals called *pheromones*. **Pheromones** are chemical substances used as communication within a given species to signal sexual receptivity, danger, territorial boundaries, and food sources. Worker ants and bees use pheromone signals to let others in their colony or hive know where they found a food source (Marler & Hamilton, 1966).

The significance of the sense of smell varies greatly across species. Dogs, rats, insects, and many other creatures for whom smell is central to survival have a far keener sense of smell than we do; thus, relatively more of their brain area is devoted to smell. Humans primarily seem to use the sense of smell in conjunction with taste to seek and sample food, but there is some evidence that humans may also secrete and sense sexual pheromones. Particularly suggestive is the fact that, over time, menstrual cycles of close friends in women's dormitories have been shown to fall into a pattern of synchrony. This phenomenon is known as the *McClintock effect* (McClintock, 1971). Humans give off scents that carry signals to other humans that affect

Wine tasters are able to make subtle and complex taste distinctions. They rely on smell as well as taste.

their physiological responses. It has been reported that about a fourth of the people with smell disorders find that their sex drive disappears (Henkin, in Ackerman, 1990).

An ongoing program of research conducted jointly at the Monell Chemical Senses Center and the University of Pennsylvania Medical School has found that women who have regular sexual activity with men are more likely to have normal menstrual cycles, fewer infertility problems, and a milder menopause than women who are celibate or have irregular sexual relationships. It may be the smell of male sweat, however, and not sexual activity that is the secret causal ingredient influencing the female endocrine system. One study has shown that an extract of male underarm secretions dabbed on female subjects' upper lips has positive health effects similar to those found in subjects who have regular sexual intercourse (Cutler et al., 1986). In related research, female subjects who received similar applications of female sweat began to synchronize their menstrual cycles after only a few months. Those in a control condition showed no such synchronization (Preti et al., 1986).

TASTE

Although food and wine gourmets are capable of making remarkably subtle and complex taste distinctions, many of their sensations are really smells and not tastes. Taste and smell work together closely when food is actually being eaten. In fact, when you have a cold, food seems tasteless because your nasal passages are blocked and you can't smell the food. Demonstrate this principle for yourself: hold your nose and try to tell the dif-

ference between foods of similar texture but different tastes, such as pieces of apple and raw potato.

There are only four true, or primary, taste qualities: sweet, sour, bitter, and saline (salty). These qualities define your *taste space* (analogous to color space) in which the primary tastes are positioned at the corners of a prism (as shown in **Figure 7.23**) and various taste combinations lie within its boundaries.

The taste receptor cells are gathered in clusters called the **taste buds**. From the tops of these cells come small tendrils, or *papillae,* similar to shoots of a plant, that have the taste receptor sites embedded in them. They are distributed in the mouth cavity, particularly on the upper side of the tongue, as shown in **Figure 7.24.** Sensitivity to sweetness is greatest at the tip of the tongue; to sourness on the edges; and to bitterness at the back. Sensitivity to saltiness is spread over the whole surface. Taste is also mediated by three of the *cranial nerves,* which activate different parts of the tongue, mouth, and throat.

The tendrils and their taste receptors can be damaged by many things we put in our mouths, such as alcohol, cigarette smoke, and acids. Fortunately, our

FIGURE 7.23   *TASTE SPACE*

Shown are the four primary tastes and the names of substances in which each taste predominates. Although different parts of the tongue and mouth are more sensitive to one taste or another, individual taste receptors seem to respond to all tastes in varying proportions.

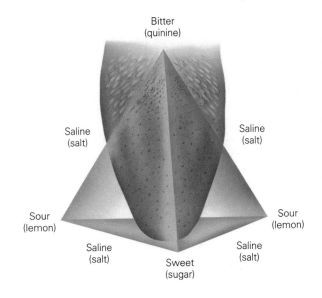

FIGURE 7.24   RECEPTORS FOR TASTE

Part A shows the distribution of the papillae on the upper side of the tongue. Part B shows a single papilla enlarged so that the individual taste buds are visible. Part C shows one of the taste buds enlarged.

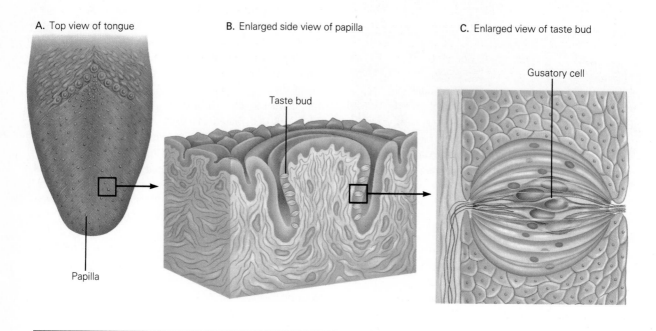

A. Top view of tongue

Papilla

B. Enlarged side view of papilla

Taste bud

C. Enlarged view of taste bud

Gusatory cell

taste receptors get replaced every few days—even more frequently than smell receptors. Indeed, the taste system is the most resistant to damage of all our sensory systems; it is extremely rare for anyone to suffer a total, permanent taste loss (Bartoshuk, 1990).

Single-cell recordings of taste receptors show that individual receptors respond somewhat to all the taste stimuli. Tastes seem to be coded in terms of relative activity in the different types of receptors. For instance, all receptors fire to both salt solutions and sweet solutions, but some fire more to one, and some fire more to the other (Pfaffman, 1959).

Taste sensitivity is exaggerated in infants and decreases with age. Many elderly people who complain that food has lost its taste really mean that they have lost much of their sensory ability to detect differences in the taste and smell qualities of food.

TOUCH AND SKIN SENSES

The skin is a remarkably versatile organ. In addition to protecting us against surface injury, holding in body fluids, and helping regulate body temperature, it contains nerve endings that produce sensations of pressure, warmth, and cold when they are stimulated by contact with external objects. These sensations are called the **cutaneous senses** (skin senses). Their importance to an organisms's survival is obvious.

The skin's sensitivity to pressure varies tremendously over the body. For example, we are ten times more accurate in sensing the position of stimulation on our fingertips than the position of stimulation on our backs. The variation in sensitivity of different body regions is shown by the greater density of nerve endings in these regions and also in the greater amount of sensory cortex devoted to them. In Chapter 3, we learned that our sensitivity is greatest where we need it most—on our faces, tongues, and hands. Precise sensory feedback from these parts of the body permits effective eating, speaking, and grasping.

One aspect of cutaneous sensitivity plays a central role in human relationships, emotions, and sexuality: *touch*. Through touch we communicate to others our desire to give or receive comfort, support, love, and passion. Our language reflects the importance of touch—it is filled with touch metaphors: it is good to "be in touch with your feelings," to be "touched by kindness," to show a "touch of class," and to have "that personal touch"; but it is bad to be "touchy" and terrible to be "untouchable." Touch is the primary stimulus for sexual arousal in humans. However, where you get touched or touch someone else makes a difference; those areas of the skin surface that are especially sensitive to stimulation and give rise to erotic or sexual sensations are called **erogenous zones.** Other touch-sensitive erotic areas vary in their arousal potential for different individuals depending on learned associations and the concentration of sensory receptors in the areas.

In Chapter 3, we reported research by Tiffany Field on the positive effects of touch (in the form of massage) for premature babies—massaged babies not only grew faster than untouched preemies but their mental development was also enhanced by the touch. Comparable research with rats shows that vigorous stimulation releases growth hormones and activates the growth enzyme ODC (onithine decarboxylase) in the brain and other vital organs. Deprivation of touch stimulation has been shown to stunt the growth of rat babies and human children. Moreover, in studies at McGill University, rat pups that were handled daily in their early lives showed a life-long enhancement of many aspects of their health. Compared to control animals, the stimulated pups were more resistant to stress and grew old more gracefully, sustaining more brain cells and better memory than unstimulated pups (Meany et al., 1988). The practical message is clear: touch those you care about often and encourage others to touch you—it not only feels good, it's healthy for you and for them (Lynch, 1979; Montague, 1986).

PAIN

The final sense we will examine is the most puzzling of all—our sense of pain. Pain is the universal complaint of the human condition—from the pain associated with birth to the periodic pain of teething, injury, sickness, menstruation, and headache and to chronic pain such as arthritis, lower back pain, and pain with unknown origins. About one third of Americans are estimated to suffer from persistent or recurring pain (Wallis, 1984). Between 60 and 90 percent of cancer patients experience great pain. One hundred million Americans experience back pain, 90 million are debilitated by arthritic pain, and more than 40 million suffer annually from headaches. Medical treatment for pain and the resulting lost workdays are estimated to cost more than $55 billion annually in the United States alone (Kraus, 1990). Depression and even suicide can result from the seemingly endless nagging of chronic pain.

What is pain? If it is so awful, why do we need it? What can be done to control it? **Pain** is the body's response to stimulation from noxious stimuli—those that are intense enough to cause tissue damage or threaten to do so. The pain response is complex, involv-ing a remarkable interplay between chemical reactions at the site of the pain stimulus, nerve impulses to and from the spinal cord and brain, and a number of psychological and cultural factors. Simply put, pain is a hurt we feel. "It is always more than a distressing sensation. It is useful to think of pain as a person's emotional experience of a distressing sensation; thus, morale and mood can be as important as the intensity of the feeling itself in determining the degree of pain" (Brody, 1986, p. 1).

Acute pain is studied experimentally in laboratories with paid volunteers who experience varying degrees of a precisely regulated stimulus, such as heat applied briefly to a small area of the skin. This procedure can test a subject's *tolerance* for pain as well as measure the sensory and subjective responses to it—without causing any damage to the skin tissue. In some cases, a human subject's nerve impulses are monitored by passing a slender recording sensor through the skin into the nerve fiber itself. This enables the researcher to listen to signals being sent by cells in the peripheral nervous system to the brain. *Chronic pain* is typically studied in hospital research clinics as part of the treatment program to find new ways to alleviate it.

Almost all animals are born with some type of pain defense system that triggers automatic withdrawal reflexes to certain stimulus events. When the stimulus intensity reaches threshold, organisms respond by escaping—if they can. In addition, they quickly learn to identify painful stimulus situations, avoiding them whenever possible.

You might think that it would be nice never to experience pain. Actually, such a condition would be deadly. People born with congenital insensitivity to pain feel no hurt, but their bodies often become scarred and their limbs often become deformed from injuries that they could have avoided had their brains been able to warn them of danger. In fact, because of their failure to notice and respond to tissue-damaging stimuli, they tend to die young (Manfredi et al., 1981). Their experience makes us aware that pain serves as an essential defense signal—it warns us of potential harm. In this way, it helps us to survive in hostile environments and to cope with sickness and injury.

People can suffer from two kinds of pain: *nociceptive* and *neuropathic.* **Nociceptive pain** is the negative feeling induced by a noxious external stimulus; for example, the feeling you have when you touch a hot stove with your hand. Specialized nerve endings in the skin send the pain message up your arm, through the spinal cord, and into your brain which issues the "pull away" command. By pulling away, you can make this type of pain stop. **Neuropathic pain** is caused by the abnormal functioning or overactivity of nerves. It comes from injury or disease of nerves caused by accidents or cancer, for example. Drugs and other therapies that calm the nerves can relieve much of this type of pain.

Pain Mechanisms

It has been difficult to learn how the pain system works because of the complexity of the interconnections and pathways involved in the perception of pain and also because of the fact that much pain involves psychological factors as well as purely stimulus factors. Scientists have only recently been able to identify the specific sets of nerves that respond to pain-producing stimuli. They have learned that some nerves respond only to temperature, others to chemicals, some to mechanical stimuli, and still others to combinations of pain-producing stimuli. These nerves set off action potentials that eventually get to the brain. This network of pain fibers is a fine meshwork that covers your entire body; there are about 6,000 of these nerve fibers in one square millimeter of the cornea of your eye.

Although researchers have no clue yet about how the brain interprets the neural signals it receives as pain, they have been able to map the actual procedure involved in signaling the brain. Powerful chemicals are stored in or near free nerve endings. When an injury occurs, the chemicals at the site of injury are released, and the nerves transmit impulses to the spinal cord. Peripheral nerve fibers send pain signals to the central nervous system by two pathways: a fast-conducting set of nerve fibers that are covered with a myelin sheeting and slower, smaller nerve fibers without any myelin coating. From the spinal cord, the impulses are relayed to the thalamus and then to the cerebral cortex, where the location and intensity of the pain are identified, the significance of the injury is evaluated, and action plans are formulated (McKean, 1986).

New research has used both PET scans and magnetic-resonance imaging (MRI) to discover where in the brain pain is represented. In experimental studies with healthy, awake volunteers subjected to nociceptive heat pain, the researchers found that pain information is *not* distributed over large areas of the cortex. Instead, signals of pain intensity are processed by specific sites in the parietal and frontal cortical areas. Emotional reactions to pain are processed in a different region—by the limbic system (Talbot et al., 1991).

One of the strategies adopted by the brain is to send white blood cells to the area of injury to fight infection. The brain also releases *endorphins*—the brain's own morphine (see page 89). Endorphins produce analgesia (pain reduction) by reducing sensitivity to pain stimuli. They appear to be responsible for the pain relief achieved by acupuncture and direct electrical stimula-

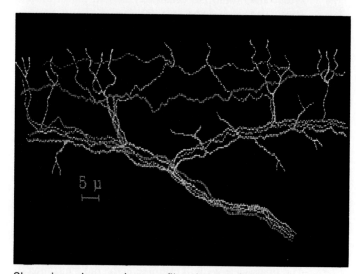

Shown is a microscopic nerve fiber that was filled with fluorescent dye so that it could be photographed. Also shown is a computerized simulation of nerve fibers. Each color responds to different pain-producing stimuli.

tion of the brain stem (Hosobuchi et al., 1979). People who suffer from chronic pain that is not relieved by standard medical treatments have abnormally low concentrations of endorphins in their cerebrospinal fluid (Akil, 1978).

One theory about the way pain may be modulated is the **gate-control theory,** developed by **Ronald Melzack** (1973, 1980), which assumes that the nervous system is able to process only a limited amount of sensory information at any one time. If too much information is being sent through, certain cells in the spinal cord act as neurological gates, interrupting and blocking some pain signals and letting others get through to the brain. Small fibers in the spine open these gates when signals from injured tissues are received, while the large fibers of the spine close the gates, shutting down the pain response. Treatment for chronic pain sometimes involves electrical stimulation designed to activate the gate-closing function of the large neural fibers. Other sensory influences that close the pain gates may include massaging of the hurt area, the emotional arousal accompanying competition, and distracting mental activities.

The Psychology of Pain

Our emotional reactions, context factors, and our interpretation of the situation can be as important as the actual physical stimuli in determining how much pain we experience. In fact, the sensation of pain may not be directly related to the intensity of the noxious stimulus at all or even to its presence or absence.

The importance of central processes in the experience of pain is shown in two extreme cases—one where there is pain but there is no physical stimulus for it and another where there is no pain but there is an intensely painful stimulus. For example, up to 10 percent of people who have limbs amputated report extreme or chronic pain in the limb that is no longer there—the **phantom limb phenomenon.** The perceived reality of a phantom limb may show that the unique experiences of one's body are invested with emotional tone and cognitive meaning (Melzack, 1989). In contrast, some individuals taking part in religious rituals are able to block out pain while participating in activities involving intense stimulation, such as walking on a bed of hot coals or having their bodies pierced with needles.

The sensation of pain may not be directly related to the intensity of the stimulus. Individuals taking part in religious rituals, such as walking on a bed of coals, are able to block out pain.

Much research points to the conclusion that the pain one feels is affected by the meaning one attaches to the experience, culturally learned habits, social support and attention, and learned gender roles (Weisenberg, 1977). Because pain is in part a psychological response, it can be modified by treatments that make use of mental processes, such as hypnosis, deep relaxation, and thought-distraction procedures. The Lamaze method of preparation for childbirth without anesthetics, reduces the woman's intense labor pains by combining several of these methods. Lamaze breathing exercises aid relaxation and focus attention away from the pain area. The use of distracting, pleasant images, massage that creates a gentle counter-stimulation, and the social support of a coaching spouse or friend all work to give a prospective mother a greater sense of control over this painful situation. Research has shown that such techniques increase the subject's pain tolerance in other experiences as well. For example, pregnant women who have received Lamaze training are able to keep their hands immersed in ice water longer than they were before the training (Worthington et al., 1983).

One of the most potent of all treatments for pain is placebo therapy (Fish, 1973). Pain can be relieved by drugs *expected* to be painkillers that are, in fact, inert substances with no medicinal value. Believing that a particular treatment will lead to pain reduction is sufficient to bring about major psychological and physiological relief in many people. It appears that belief, as well as perception of pain, can trigger the release of pain-killing endorphins in the brain. Recent evidence suggests that the one third of the population who are positive placebo responders may have higher concentrations of endorphins than other people do (Levine et al., 1978).

The way you perceive your pain, what you communicate about it to others, and even the way you respond to pain-relieving treatments may reveal more about your psychological state—about the kind of inferences you are making—than about the intensity of the pain stimulus. What you perceive may be different from, and even independent of, what you sense—as we will see in our study of the psychology of perception.

Sensory Knowledge of Our World

Sensation is the first stage in the process of perception; it translates the physical energy of stimuli into neural codes via transduction. Psychophysics investigates psychological responses to physiological stimuli. To study sensation, researchers measure absolute thresholds, difference thresholds, and just noticeable differences between stimuli. Signal detection corrects for response biases that affect the measurement of thresholds. Weber, Fechner, and Stevens each proposed different ways to measure the magnitude of sensation.

During sensory coding, the rate of neural firing and the pattern of neural impulses conveys information about stimulus intensity. Sensory quality is coded by specific neurons that are activated in sense receptors and by patterns of neural impulses in sensory pathways to the cortex. Sensory adaptation enables sensory fibers to fade responsiveness to prolonged stimuli and receive new stimulus signals.

The Visual System

Photoreceptors in the retina, rods, and cones convert light energy into neural impulses. Ganglion cells in the retina integrate input from several receptors and bipolar cells. Their axons form the optic nerves that meet at the optic chiasma. Some information about the stimulus location is processed in the superior colliculus. Information about color and detail is processed in the visual cortex.

The wavelength of light is the stimulus for color. Color sensations differ in hue, saturation, and brightness. Contrasts in brightness form boundaries and distinct edges that give objects size, shape, and spatial orientation.

Color vision theory combines the trichromatic theory of three color receptors with the opponent-process theory of color systems composed of opponent elements. Detection of stimulus features occurs through the action of feature detection cells in the retina and higher visual centers and the analysis of spatial frequencies of light-dark cycles. Research shows that stimulating receptive fields of visual neurons causes perceptual judgments.

Hearing

Hearing is produced by sound waves that vary in frequency, amplitude, and complexity. In the cochlea, sound waves are transformed into fluid waves that move the basilar membrane. Hairs on the basilar membrane stimulate neural impulses that are sent to the auditory cortex. Place theory explains the coding of high frequencies and frequency theory explains the coding of low frequencies. Conductance deafness may be corrected but nerve deafness cannot. Exposure to intense sounds may cause temporary hearing impairment. Two neuronal mechanisms compute the relative timing and pitch of sounds coming to each ear.

Our Other Senses

The vestibular sense gives information about the direction and rate of body motion. The kinesthetic sense gives information about the position of body parts and helps coordinate motion. Olfaction (smell) and gustation (taste) respond to the chemical properties of substances and work together when people are seeking and sampling food. Olfaction is accomplished by odor-sensitive cells deep in the nasal passages. Pheromones are chemical signals detected by smell. Taste receptors are taste buds embedded in papillae, mostly in the tongue. The cutaneous (skin) senses give sensations of pressure and temperature. Pain is the body's response to potentially harmful stimuli. The physiological response to pain involves chemical reactions at the site of the pain stimulus and nerve impulses moving between the brain and the spinal cord. Pain is in part a psychological response that can be modified by treatments that emphasize mental processes and thought distraction.

KEY TERMS

absolute threshold, 217
accommodation, 224
afferent systems, 216
auditory cortex, 243
auditory nerve, 243
basilar membrane, 242
bipolar cell, 226
blindsight, 228
brightness, 230
cochlea, 242
complementary colors, 230
cones, 225
cutaneous senses, 248
decibel (db), 240
difference threshold, 220
efferent systems, 216
erogenous zones, 249
feature-detection cells, 236
feature-detection model, 236
Fechner's law, 222
fovea, 226
frequency theory, 243
ganglion cell, 226
gate-control theory, 250
Hertz (Hz), 240

hue, 230
just noticeable difference
   (JND), 220
kinesthetic sense, 246
lateral inhibition, 235
lateral geniculate nucleus, 227
loudness, 240
magnitude estimation, 222
neuropathic pain, 249
nociceptive pain, 249
olfactory bulb, 246
opponent-process theory, 233
optic nerve, 227
pain, 249
perception, 215
phantom limb phenomenon,
   251
pheromones, 246
photoreceptor, 225
pitch, 240
place theory, 243
psychometric function, 217
psychophysics, 217
receptive field, 235
response bias, 218

retina, 225
rods, 225
saturation, 230
sensation, 215
sensory adaptation, 223
sensory coding, 223
sensory modalities, 214
sensory physiology, 216
sensory processes, 214
sensuality, 214
spatial-frequency model, 237
subliminal perception, 217
superior colliculus, 227
taste buds, 247
theory of signal detection
   (TSD), 219
timbre, 241
transduction, 215
trichromatic theory, 232
vestibular sense, 245
visual cortex, 227
volley principle, 243
Weber's law, 220

MAJOR CONTRIBUTORS

De Valois, Karen, 236
De Valois, Russell, 236
Fechner, Gustav, 217
Hering, Ewald, 232
Hubel, David, 236
Hurvich, Leo, 233

Jameson, Dorothea, 233
Keller, Helen, 213
Melzack, Ronald, 250
Müller, Johannes, 223
Newton, Sir Isaac, 229
Stevens, S. S., 222

von Békésy, Georg, 243
von Helmholtz, Hermann, 243
Weber, Ernst, 220
Weisel, Thorsten, 236

Chapter 8

Perception

THE TASK OF PERCEPTION   256

SENSING, PERCEIVING, IDENTIFYING, AND RECOGNIZING   257
  INTERPRETING RETINAL IMAGES
  REALITY, AMBIGUITY, AND DISTORTIONS
  LESSONS LEARNED FROM ILLUSIONS
  THE NURTURE AND NATURE OF PERCEPTION

  ▥ *INTERIM SUMMARY*

ATTENTIONAL PROCESSES   269
  PREATTENTIVE PROCESSING
  FUNCTIONS OF ATTENTION
  ATTENTIONAL MECHANISMS

  ▥ *INTERIM SUMMARY*

ORGANIZATIONAL PROCESSES IN PERCEPTION   278
  REGION SEGREGATION
  FIGURE AND GROUND
  CLOSURE
  PRINCIPLES OF PERCEPTUAL GROUPING

REFERENCE FRAMES
SPATIAL AND TEMPORAL INTEGRATION
MOTION PERCEPTION
DEPTH PERCEPTION
PERCEPTUAL CONSTANCIES

  ▥ *INTERIM SUMMARY*

IDENTIFICATION AND RECOGNITION PROCESSES   292
  BOTTOM-UP AND TOP-DOWN PROCESSES
  RECOGNITION BY COMPONENTS
  THE INFLUENCE OF CONTEXTS AND
    EXPECTATIONS
  THE ROLE OF PERSONAL AND SOCIAL FACTORS
  CREATIVELY PLAYFUL PERCEPTION
  FINAL LESSONS

RECAPPING MAIN POINTS   298

KEY TERMS   299

MAJOR CONTRIBUTORS   299

One night in late 1965, a United Airlines Boeing 727 started a steady descent to Chicago's O'Hare Airport from an altitude of 22,000 feet. Nineteen miles off the shore of Lake Michigan, the plane plunged into the lake.

One month later, also at night, an American Airlines Boeing 727, preparing to land at Kentucky's Boone County Airport, followed the thread of the Ohio River toward the runway which began at the river's steep south bank. The plane never touched down. It crashed into the bank, 12 feet below the runway.

One night in early 1966, an Al Nippon Airlines Boeing 727 headed toward Tokyo Bay. The pilot could see the lights of Tokyo and Yokohama clearly. He requested and received permission to approach using visual cues rather than relying exclusively on the plane's instruments. The pilot had not even let down the wheels or extended the flaps when, six-and-a-half miles from the runway, the plane dove into Tokyo Bay at a speed of 240 knots.

Preliminary analyses of these and other similar cases showed that all the accidents occurred at night, under clear weather conditions, with the planes flying over a dark area of water or land. In every case, irregular patterns of light (as opposed to grids of neatly intersecting lines of street lights) in the distance had been visible to the pilots.

Flight simulator (*Discovering Psychology,* 1990, Program 19)

In a way, the new Boeing 727 design was partly responsible for the accidents, because it was so well engineered. In earlier, less stable models, feedback from vibrations and sounds and kinesthetic sensations would have warned the pilots that they were descending too rapidly. However, it was more than an improved design that had caused the accidents.

Using a flight simulator, engineering psychologist **Conrad Kraft** found that an error in the pilot's visual perception was responsible for each of the accidents. Pilots making a visually guided approach over a dark terrain relied on the relatively constant visual angle between their planes and the distant light patterns in determining their altitudes. If they were approaching flat terrain, their altitude estimates were generally correct, but if the terrain sloped upwards, with the farthest lights higher than the closer ones, even the most experienced pilots descended to dangerously low altitudes. With no visual information from the "dark hole" below them, the pilots overestimated their distance from the ground and inappropriately adjusted their descent angles.

Why didn't the pilots also use their altimeters? When landing an airplane, a pilot must monitor several functions simultaneously—speed, engine power, altitude, direction—while responding to air traffic controller directions and watching for other aircraft. With all of these responsibilities, especially when visibility is good, pilots may fail to check their altimeters.

After Dr. Kraft solved the mystery of the accidents, commercial airlines around the world informed pilots of the conditions under which they might misjudge altitude on approach to landing. Psychologists such as Dr. Kraft study perception in order to learn how the body's major sensory systems help (and sometimes trick) us in gathering information about the environments in which we live and work.

How do we organize and interpret the many sources of stimulus input coming from all of our sensory systems into our brain? How do we form mental representations of external objects and events taking place? The eye is more than a camera photographing lights; the ear is more than a microphone recording sounds. Sensation is what gets the show started, but something is needed to make it meaningful and interesting to us, and, most important, to make it possible for us to respond effectively to what we are experiencing. We may look with our eyes and listen with our ears, but we see and hear with our minds and brains.

Most of the time, sensing and perceiving occur so effortlessly, continuously, and automatically that we take them for granted. They typically give us an accurate, or *veridical,* view of reality. The perceptual distortion experienced by the ill-fated pilots is one exception to this rule of the trustworthiness of perception. In this chapter, we will lift the hood from the perceptual apparatus to discover how it drives our perceptions so well. In doing so, we will learn some of the ways that we make sense of the host of messages sent from sense receptors to the brain and back to response systems for action. We will also learn how the mind interprets external reality and goes beyond the physics of sensation to design its own imaginative and personalized views of reality.

THE TASK OF PERCEPTION

Look around the room you are in, first by moving your head slowly and then by moving it quickly. Did any objects move? Shut this book, rotate it, and open it again. Hold the book at arm's length and then move it toward your face. Did any images in the book change shape or size? Probably not, but why are you so sure? According to the sensory information from your retina there were many objects moving and changing. How can you be so confident that the movement was a function of your body or eyes and not a property of the objects you saw? How do you know that the book or your hand did not go through size and shape transformations that corresponded to the changing images they projected onto the retina as they moved? During this exercise, were you looking out at the world, or was the world looking in at you?

We might say that the role of perception is to make *sense* of sensation. Making sense means going beyond processing sensory input to create a personal understanding of our experienced physical world. It involves many different mental processes including synthesizing elements into combinations; judging sizes, shapes, distances, intensities, and pitches; estimating the unknown or uncertain from known features; remembering past experiences with given perceptual stimuli, comparing different stimuli currently being experienced; and associating perceived qualities of stimuli with appropriate ways of responding to them. Every action of perception then becomes a series of very complex *computational* problems to be solved by the perceiving person.

The task of perception is to extract the continuously changing, often chaotic, *sensory input* from external energy sources (for example, light and sound waves) and organize it into stable, orderly *percepts* of meaningful objects that are relevant to a perceiver. A **percept** is what is perceived—the phenomenological or experienced outcome of the process of perception. It is *not* a physical object nor its image in a receptor but, rather, the psychological product of perceptual activity. Perception must discover what features of the world are *invariant,* fixed, and unchanging by using sensory input that is variable and a perceiver whose eyes and body are often in motion.

Psychologists who study perception come to this field from many directions (Banks & Krajicek, 1991). Some are interested in it from a *neuroscience perspective,* using a molecular level of analysis. They track sensory stimuli through the sensory receptors, pathways in the brain, and areas of the brain involved in sensory recognition, sensory association, and sensory response. Others want to understand perception at a broader level by discovering the principles governing certain perceptual phenomena, such as the way we perceive motion and depth. Researchers from the field of *artificial intelligence* (AI) are bringing new conceptual tools to the study of perception as they distinguish between the biological hardware of perception and the rules that specify how each perceptual process works. A third basic approach to perception comes from the descendants of what is known as the *Gestalt tradition,* which constitutes modern perceptual psychology. These researchers study the laws of perceptual organization and the units of perception. We will examine the contributions of each of these approaches to perception.

Other psychologists are interested in the relationships between perception and other processes that influence it (such as attention, memory, cognition, and motivation) or that are influenced by it (such as learning and social interaction). For example, researchers have discovered relationships between vision problems in childhood and adolescence and subsequent learning problems and juvenile delinquency (Dowis, 1984; Harris, 1989; Snow, 1983).

Finally, because perception is the way we make contact with our social and physical worlds, many psychologists apply perceptual knowledge and theory to the development of improved technology. During the development of flight simulators, robots, and NASA's space-vehicle workstations, psychologists worked with engineers to help them apply perceptual theory in the creation of their designs. So, too, improvements in telephone reception, television viewing, and prosthetic devices that aid hearing- and vision-impaired people have come from knowledge of the psychology of hearing and vision.

SENSING, PERCEIVING, IDENTIFYING, AND RECOGNIZING

In this section, we will distinguish among three different stages in the overall process of perception, examine how we interpret the images that appear unannounced on our retinas, and play some tricks on your perceiving mind.

The term *perception,* in its broad usage, means the overall process of *apprehending* objects and events in the external environment; to sense them, understand them, identify and label them, and to prepare to react to them. The process of perception is best understood when we divide it into three stages: sensation, perception, and identification/recognition of objects.

Sensation refers to the first stage in which physical energy in the world, such as light and sound waves, is *transduced* (converted) into neural activity of cortical cells that codes information about the way the receptor organs are being stimulated. Even at this early point in the neurological journey, stimulus selection and transformation are occurring. Retinal cells are emphasizing borders, edges, and differences in light while not getting

excited by unchanging, constant stimulation. Meanwhile, cortical cells are extracting features and spatial frequency information from the input they get from the ganglion cells of the retina.

Perception, in its narrow usage, refers to the next stage in which an internal representation of an object is formed and a percept of the external stimulus is developed. The representation provides a working description of the perceiver's external environment. Stimuli picked up by lower-order detectors are organized and modified by higher-order brain processes into patterns and forms that are recognizable. For example, three straight lines of the same size identified by cortical cells soon become recognized as the percepts 1—1, H, Δ, or III, depending on other information provided by the context.

Perceptual processes also may involve our estimations of an object's likely size, shape, movement, distance, and orientation. Those estimates are based on mental computations that integrate our past knowledge with the present evidence received from our senses and with the stimulus within its perceptual context. Perception involves *synthesis* (integration and combination) of simple sensory features, such as colors, edges, and lines, into the percept of an object that can be recognized later.

You will understand better what perception does by considering the strange case study of **Dr. Richard,** whose brain damage left his sensation intact but altered his perceptual processes.

Dr. Richard was a psychologist with considerable training and experience in introspection. This special skill enabled him to make a unique and valuable contribution to psychology. However, tragically, he suffered brain damage that altered his visual experience of the world. Fortunately, the damage did not affect the centers of his brain responsible for speech, so he was able to describe his subsequent unusual visual experiences quite clearly. In general terms, the brain damage seemed to have affected his ability to put sensory data together properly. For example, Dr. Richard reported that if he saw a complex object, such as a person, and there were several other people nearby in his visual field, he sometimes saw the different parts of the person as separate parts not belonging together in a single form. If the person then moved, so that all parts went in the same direction, Dr. Richard would then see them as one complete person. Without some common factor—such as like motion—to help "glue" things together, he tended to see a confusion of separate objects, all of which were simultaneously present in his field of view but which he did not experience as going together in the same way as he would have before the neurological damage occurred.

Sometimes perceiving a common element would result in absurd configurations. He would frequently see objects of the same color, such as a banana, a lemon, and a canary, going together even if they were separated in space. People in crowds would go together if they were wearing the same colored clothing. At other times, however, Dr. Richard had difficulty combining the sound and sight of the same event. When someone was singing, he might see a mouth move and hear a song, but it was as if the sound had been dubbed with the wrong tape in a foreign movie. Dr. Richard's experiences of his environment during such episodes were disjointed, fragmented, and bizarre—quite unlike what he had been used to before his problems began (Marcel, 1983).

There was nothing wrong with Dr. Richard's eyes or with his ability to *analyze* the properties of stimulus objects—he saw the parts and qualities of objects accurately. Rather, his problem lay in *perceptual synthesis*—putting the bits and pieces of sensory information together properly to form a unified, coherent perception of a single event in the visual scene. His case makes salient the distinction between sensory and perceptual processes. It also serves to remind us that both sensory analysis and perceptual synthesis must be going on all the time even though we are unaware of the way they are or even that they are. (For other cases in which neurological damage affects different aspects of percep-

tion, you might enjoy reading the superbly written clinical tales of Dr. Oliver Sachs in *The Man Who Mistook His Wife for a Hat and Other Clinical Tales*, 1985.)

Identification and recognition, the third stage in this sequence, assigns meaning to the percepts. Circular objects "become" baseballs, coins, clocks, oranges, and moons; people may be identified as friend or foe, pretty or ugly, movie star or rock star. At this stage, the perceptual question, "What does the object look like?" changes to a question of identification—"What is this object?"—and to a question of recognition—"What is the object's function?" The product of recognition is a person's reported percept, which is the only data we have available to assess a viewer's perceptual experience. To identify and recognize what something is, what it is called, and how best to respond to it involves cognitive processes, which include our theories, memories, values, beliefs, and attitudes concerning the object.

Perception and the combined processes of identification/recognition work so swiftly and seemingly automatically that they typically mesh smoothly together in our everyday lives, but, conceptually, they are different. Recognition is a matter of attaching a label to an object, deciding what it is, and comparing the object percept to a memory representation. Dividing the global process of perception into the stages of sensation, perception, and identification/recognition emphasizes the parts of this complex process. Throughout the rest of this chapter we will use perception in its narrower sense, that of going beyond sensory information to provide a meaningful awareness and knowledge of the world of objects, actors, and episodes. Thus, we will focus on the second and third steps in the overall perceptual process.

INTERPRETING RETINAL IMAGES

Imagine you are the person in **Figure 8.1.** You are sitting in an easy chair with your feet up. Light is reflected from the objects in the room and some of the light enters your eye, forming an image on your retina. Also in Figure 8.1 you can see what would appear to your left eye as you sat in the room. (The bump on the right is your nose, and the hands and feet at the bottom are your own.) How does this retinal image compare with the environment that produced it?

One very important difference is that the retinal image at the back of your eyeball is *two-dimensional* whereas the environment is *three-dimensional*. This difference produces many other differences that you may not notice without looking carefully. For instance, compare the shapes of the physical objects out there in the world with the shapes of their corresponding retinal images. Look at Figure 8.1 again. The table, rug, window, and picture in the real-world scene are all rectan-

When sensory and perceptual processes do not work together in perceptual synthesis, the world appears to be fragmented and disjointed.

FIGURE 8.1   INTERPRETING RETINAL IMAGES

A. Physical Object (Distal Stimulus)

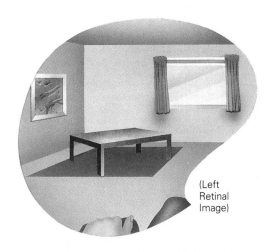

(Left Retinal Image)

B. Optical Image (Proximal Stimulus)

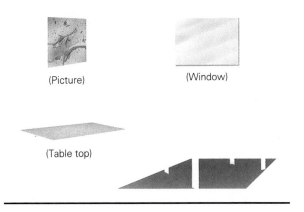

(Picture)   (Window)

(Table top)

gular, but only the image of the window actually produces a rectangle in your retinal image. The image of the picture is a trapezoid, the image of the table top is an irregular four-sided figure, and the image of the rug is actually three separate regions with more than 20 different sides! How do you manage to see all of these objects as simple, standard rectangles when your retinal images of them are so different?

Notice also that many parts of what you perceive in the room are not actually present in your retinal image at all. For instance, you perceive the vertical edge between the two walls as going all the way to the floor, but your retinal image of that edge stops at the table-top. Similarly, in your retinal image parts of the rug are hidden behind the table, the stool, and your feet; yet this does not keep you from correctly perceiving the rug as a single, unbroken rectangle. In fact, when you consider all the differences between the environmental objects and the images of them on your retina, you may be surprised that you can perceive the scene as well as you do.

The differences between a physical object in the world and its optical image on your retina are so profound and important that psychologists distinguish carefully between them as two different stimuli for perception. The physical object in the world is called the **distal stimulus** (distant from the observer) and the optical image on the retina is called the **proximal stimulus** (proximate or near to the observer), as shown in **Figure 8.2.**

The critical point of our discussion can now be restated more concisely: what you *perceive* corresponds to the *distal stimulus*—the "real" object in the environment—whereas the stimulus from which you must derive your information is the *proximal stimulus*—the image on the retina. The major computational task of perception can be thought of as the process of determining the distal stimulus from information contained in the proximal stimulus.

The distinction between proximal and distal stimuli applies to all kinds of perception, not just to vision. Auditory images—the patterns of sound waves that enter your ears—differ from the physical objects that produce them. Even tactile images—the patterns of pressure and temperature that you feel on your skin as you actively explore objects with your hands—are not the same as the physical objects that cause them. In each case, perception involves processes that somehow use information in the proximal stimulus to tell you about properties of the distal stimulus.

There is much more to perceiving a scene, however, than just determining the *physical properties* of the distal stimulus. You see objects as familiar and meaningful: a window, a picture, a table, and a rug. Besides

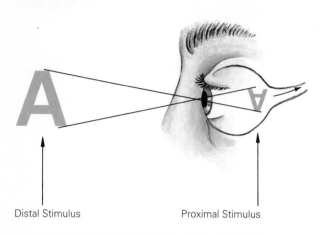

FIGURE 8.2   DISTAL AND PROXIMAL STIMULUS

Distal Stimulus   Proximal Stimulus

accurately perceiving the shapes and colors of the objects, you *interpret* them in terms of your past experience with similar objects. This process of identification and recognition is also part of what you do automatically and almost constantly as you go about perceiving your environment.

To illustrate the distinction among the three stages in perceiving, let's examine one of the objects in the scene from Figure 8.1: the picture hanging on the wall. In the *sensory stage,* this picture corresponds to a two-dimensional trapezoid in your retinal image; the top and bottom sides converge toward the right and the left and right sides are different in length. In the *perceptual stage,* you see this trapezoid as a rectangle turned away from you in three-dimensional space. You perceive the top and bottom sides as parallel, but receding into the distance toward the right; you perceive the left and right sides as equal in length. In the *recognition stage,* you recognize this rectangular object as a *picture.*

Figure 8.3 is a flow chart illustrating this sequence of events. The processes that take information from one stage to the next are shown as arrows between the boxes. Taking sensory data into the system by receptors and sending it upward for extraction and analysis of relevant information is called **bottom-up processing.** Bottom-up processes are those that are anchored in empirical reality and deal with bits of information and the transformation of concrete, physical features of stimuli into physiological codes and ultimately into abstract representations. At the same time, however, the opposite process is also occurring; **top-down processing** involves a perceiver's past experience, knowledge, expectations, memory, motivations, cultural background, and language in the interpretation of the object of per-

ception. With top-down processes, higher mental functioning affects how we understand the nature of the objects and events we perceive. The two types of processes usually interact as we perceive our environment.

REALITY, AMBIGUITY, AND DISTORTIONS

A primary goal of perception is to get an accurate "fix" on the world—to recognize predators and prey and sources of danger and pleasure that guide behavior in appropriate ways. Survival depends on accurate perceptions of objects and events in our environment, but the environment is not always easy to "read." Take a look at the photo of black and white splotches in **Figure 8.4.** What is it? Try to extract the stimulus figure from the background. Try to see a dalmatian taking a walk. The dog is hard to find because it blends with the background. (Hint: the dog is on the right side of the figure with its head pointed toward the center.)

The world is filled with ambiguous data that lead to uncertainty and, at times, danger. Potential prey hide behind screens of protective coloration just as soldiers hide their lethal presence with camouflage. Some foods taste good, such as sugar or salt, but they aren't good for one's health; other foods look innocent, but they can be deadly, such as certain mushrooms and berries. We learn not to trust appearances entirely and to supplement what our senses tell us with our other knowledge. For example, when you are driving on a hot highway, you might see water puddles shimmering on the road ahead. The puddles vanish when you get to the spot where you thought they were. The image of the puddles is caused by heat rays bouncing off the black asphalt surface that bend the light rays coming to your retina.

When your senses deceive you into experiencing a stimulus pattern in a manner that is demonstrably incorrect, you are experiencing an **illusion.** The word *illusion* shares the root in *ludicrous*—both stem from the Latin *illudere* which means *to mock at.* Your misinterpretation of the sensory stimulus is shared by most people in the same perceptual situation because it is a function of distortions in the usual information we receive from a sensory pattern. Typically, illusions become more common when the stimulus situation is *ambiguous,* critical information is missing, elements are in unexpected relationships, and usual patterns are not apparent.

Your view of reality may also be distorted by three other processes. A **hallucination** is a false perception that is a personal distortion of reality *not shared* by others in the same situation. A hallucinating person hears voices and may see images that are not sensory based. Hallucination occurs during a state of altered

FIGURE 8.3   *SENSATION, PERCEPTION, AND IDENTIFICATION/RECOGNITION STAGES*

The diagram outlines the processes that give rise to the transformation of incoming information at the stages of sensation, perception, and identification/recognition. Bottom-up processing occurs when the perceptual representation is derived from the information available in the sensory input. Top-down processing occurs when the perceptual representation is affected by an individual's prior knowledge, motivations, expectations, and other aspects of higher mental functioning.

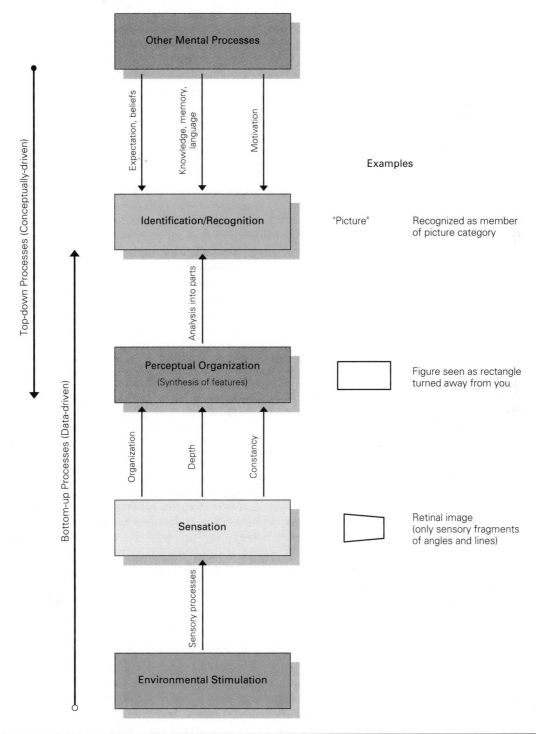

FIGURE 8.4   AMBIGUOUS PICTURE

consciousness caused by certain mental disorders, such as schizophrenia, brain diseases, alcohol intoxication, psychedelic drugs, hypnotic suggestions, and religious ecstasy. A **delusion** is a strongly held, false belief that resists change despite evidence of its irrational basis. Delusions may be distorted ideas about oneself, others, or the environment. Delusions of persecution, jealousy, and grandeur are common in some paranoid conditions as well as in some types of racial prejudice. Finally, a last type of reality distortion comes from the mind's tendency to filter out information that is threatening to one's self-esteem. This **self-deception** is a form of lying to oneself for the benefit of maintaining a positive self-image. When overused, such deception becomes a *denial* of potential dangers to one's health and well-being that are better handled by some form of direct confrontation (Goleman, 1987).

By studying hallucinations, delusions, and self-deception, psychologists learn something about the personality, conflicts, and motivations of the individuals who experience them. We find out when, why, and how normal, higher cognitive functioning can break down. This information, in turn, provides researchers with insights into the nature of normal functioning. From these studies, psychologists hope to learn about perceptual processes under normal conditions when they do lead to accurate perception of distal objects.

LESSONS LEARNED FROM ILLUSIONS

Psychologists who study perception love ambiguities and the illusions they generate. Since the first scientific analysis of illusions was published by **J. J. Oppel** in

1854, literally thousands of articles have been written about illusions in nature, sensation, perception, and art. Oppel's modest contribution to the study of illusions was a simple array of lines that appeared longer when divided into segments than when only the end lines were present:

versus

Oppel called his work the study of *geometrical optical illusions*. Illusions point out the discrepancy between percept and reality—between the marvelously complex sensory and perceptual processes that are evolution's masterpiece and the ease with which they can be fooled by a simple arrangement of lines. Illusions can demonstrate the abstract conceptual distinctions between sensation, perception, and identification and can help us understand some fundamental properties of perception (Cohen & Girgus, 1978).

First examine an illusion that works at the sensation level: the *Hermann grid* in **Figure 8.5.** As you stare at the center of the grid, dark, fuzzy spots appear at the intersections of the white bars. Now focus closely on one intersection; the spot vanishes. Indeed, as you shift focus, you transform the spots into little dancing dots. How do you do that, you wonder? The answer lies in something you read about in the last chapter—*lateral inhibition*. Assume the stimulus is registered by ganglion retinal cells, two of which have their receptive fields drawn in the lower corner of the grid. The receptive field at the center of the intersection has two white bars projecting through its surround while the neighboring receptive field has only one. The cell at the center, therefore, receives more light and can respond at a lower level because of the greater lateral inhibition by the surround. Its reduced response shows up as a dark spot in its center. When you focus at the intersection, you place the image in the center of your fovea, which is where the retina has its maximum sensitivity (because of the concentration of cone cells). The fovea also has many ganglion cells, but they are different from those elsewhere in the retina. The fovea's receptive fields are smaller; hence, they will fall entirely within the intersection, both center and surround. There is no lateral inhibition caused by the surrounding black squares— therefore there are no more black spots. Illusions at this level generally occur because the arrangement of a stimulus array stimulates receptor processes in an unusual way that generates a distorted image.

To study illusions that reveal the operations of perception and identification, psychologists rely on ambiguous figures—stimulus patterns that can be seen in two or more distinct ways. **Ambiguity** is an important con-

<table><tr><td>FIGURE 8.5</td><td>THE HERMANN GRID</td></tr></table>

This Hermann Grid has two ganglion cell receptive fields projected on it. It is an example of an illusion at the sensory stage.

black objects with a white area between them. The Necker cube can be seen as a three-dimensional hollow cube either *below* you and angled to your left or *above* you and angled toward your right. With both vase and cube, the ambiguous alternatives are different physical arrangements of objects in three-dimensional space, both resulting from the same stimulus image. Because it cannot recognize both alternatives at the same time, your perceptual system has jumped to a decision about

<table><tr><td>FIGURE 8.6</td><td>A. PERCEPTUAL ILLUSIONS
B. RECOGNITION ILLUSION</td></tr></table>

A.

Vase or Faces?

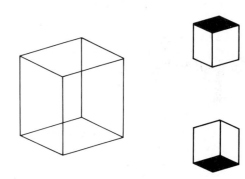

The Necker Cube: Above or Below?

B.

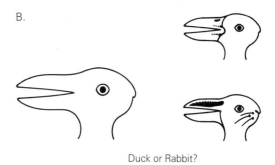

Duck or Rabbit?

cept in understanding perception because it shows that a *single image* at the sensory level can result in *multiple interpretations* at the perceptual and identification levels.

Sometimes ambiguity arises in the perception stage when an object can be interpreted as two or more different objects in the environment. Ambiguity can also arise in the identification/recognition stage when the object being perceived can be interpreted as belonging to different categories.

Figure 8.6 shows three examples of ambiguous figures. Each figure is accompanied by two unambiguous but conflicting interpretations. Look at each image until you can see the two alternative interpretations. Notice that once you have seen both of them, your perception flips back and forth between them as you look at the ambiguous figure. This perceptual *instability* of ambiguous figures is one of their most important characteristics.

The vase/faces and the Necker cube are examples of ambiguity in the perception stage. You have two different perceptions of objects in space relative to you, the observer. The vase/faces can be seen as either a central white object on a black background or as two how to synthesize the elements into a whole on the basis of attending to certain local features.

The duck/rabbit figure is an example of ambiguity in the recognition stage. It is perceived as the same physical shape in both interpretations; the ambiguity arises in determining the kind of object it represents and in how best to classify it given the mixed set of information available.

One of the most fundamental properties of normal human perception is the tendency to transform ambi-guity and uncertainty about the environment into a clear interpretation that we can act upon with confidence. In a world filled with variability and change, our percep-tual system must meet the challenges of discovering invariance and instability.

Perceptual illusions make us aware of two consid-erations: the active role the mind plays in structuring our view of the world, and the effects of *context* on the way we perceive stimuli within it. Examine the classic illusions in **Figure 8.7.** Psychologists have discovered

FIGURE 8.7   *SIX ILLUSIONS TO TEASE YOUR BRAIN*

A. Use a ruler to answer each question.

Which is larger: the brim or the top hat?

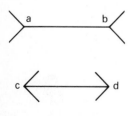

Top Hat Illusion

Is the diagonal line broken?

Poggendorf Illusion

B. Which of the boxes are the same size as the standard box? Which are definitely smaller or larger? Measure them to discover a powerful illusory effect.

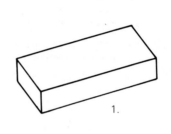

1.

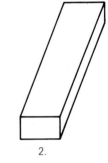

2.

Which central circle is bigger?

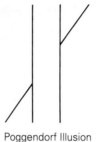

Ebbinghaus Illusion

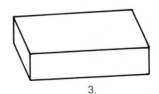

Standard

Which horizontal line is longer?

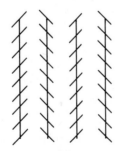

Müller–Lyer Illusion

Are the vertical lines parallel?

Zöllner Illusion

3.

4.

many such illusions not only in vision but also in other sensory modalities (Bregman, 1982; Shepard & Jordan, 1984). These illusions occur because the central nervous system does not simply record events. Instead, the system involves complex processes for detecting, integrating, and interpreting information about the world in terms of what we already know and expect; thus, what we "see" goes beyond present physical stimulus properties. The fact that these processes usually occur effortlessly and are helpful in decoding the world around us does not mean that they are simple or error-free.

Ambiguity in Art

The ambiguous figures that psychologists developed served as catalysts for several prominent modern artists who became fascinated with the complex, dynamic visual experiences the figures created for the viewers. These artists have used perceptual ambiguity as the central artistic device in many of their works of art. On this page, you will find three examples. The first, by *Victor Vasarely,* produces depth reversals similar to the Necker cube. The corners of the surfaces can be seen either as coming out toward you or going away from you. The next, by *M. C. Escher,* is based on figure/ground reversals similar to the vase/faces. In *Sky and Water,* Escher has created an ambiguous mosaic of interweaving fish and birds at the center where you tend to see the fish or the birds but not both. Toward the top and bottom of the work, the figures become gradually less ambiguous. Notice that after you look at the unambiguous birds at the top, you tend to see birds rather than fish in the ambiguous center section; but after you

look at the unambiguous fish at the bottom, you tend to see fish rather than birds in the center section. This tendency demonstrates the influence of context on your perception, a topic we will discuss later in more detail.

The final example is *Slave Market with the Disappearing Bust of Voltaire* by *Salvador Dali.* This work reveals a more complex ambiguity in which a whole section of the picture must be radically reorganized and reinterpreted to allow perception of the "hidden" bust of the French philosopher-writer Voltaire. The white

Paintings by Victor Vasarely (top), M. C. Escher (left), and Salvador Dali

sky under the lower arch is Voltaire's forehead and hair; the white portions of the two ladies' dresses are his cheeks, nose, and chin. (If you have trouble seeing him, try squinting, holding the book at arm's length, or taking off your glasses.) Once you have seen the bust of Voltaire in this picture, however, you will never be able to look at it without knowing where this Frenchman is hiding.

Illusions in Reality

Are illusions just peculiar arrangements of lines, colors, and shapes used by artists and psychologists to plague unsuspecting people? Hardly. Illusions are a basic part of our everyday life. They are an inescapable aspect of the subjective reality we each construct with our personal experiences, learning, and motivation. Even though we may recognize an illusion, it can continue to occur and fool us again and again.

You've seen the sun rise and set even though you know that the sun is sitting out there in the center of its solar system absolutely still. You can appreciate why it was such an extraordinary feat of courage for Christopher Columbus and other voyagers to deny the obvious illusion that the earth was flat and sail off toward one of its apparent edges. When a full moon is overhead it seems to follow you wherever you go even though you know the moon isn't chasing you. What you are experiencing is an illusion created by the great distance of the moon from your eye. When they reach the earth, the moon's light rays are essentially parallel and perpendicular to your direction of travel no matter where you go.

People can control illusions to achieve desired effects. Architects and interior designers use principles of perception to create objects in space that seem larger or smaller than they really are. A small apartment becomes more spacious when it is painted with light colors and sparsely furnished with low, small couches, chairs, and tables in the center of the room instead of against the walls. Psychologists working with NASA in the U.S. space program have researched the effects of environment on perception in order to design space capsules that have pleasant sensory qualities. Set and lighting directors of movies and theatrical productions purposely create illusions on film and on stage.

The everyday use of illusion can be seen in our choices of cosmetics and clothing (Dackman, 1986). We choose light-colored clothing with horizontal stripes to make our bodies seem larger and dark-colored clothing with vertical stripes to make our bodies seem slimmer. Illusions also appear in more tragic contexts, as we noted in our opening case. In the continual process of resolving the discrepancy between the distal stimulus (external reality) and the proximal stimulus

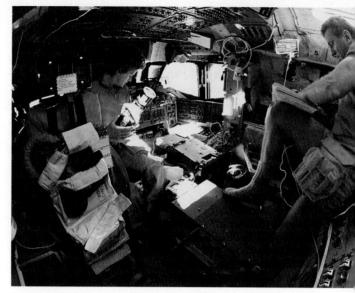

Psychologists have researched the effects of environment on perception in order to design space capsules that have pleasant sensory qualities.

(receptor reality), we establish personal perceptions (phenomenological reality) that guide decisions and behavior—for better or for worse. The way we go about resolving that discrepancy has long been a source of controversy among psychologists.

THE NURTURE AND NATURE OF PERCEPTION

Recall the debate between the *nativists,* who argued that all knowledge of the external world comes through the senses in a direct way that is interpreted by innate mechanisms—the nature view—and the *empiricists,* who held that most perceptual knowledge is learned through experience with the environment—the nurture view. These alternative views about the way in which the mind develops have also played an important role in theories of perception.

Advocates of both the heredity and environment positions assumed that some perceptual attributes, such as color and brightness, were built into the sensory system. Their disagreement was over the mechanisms for perceiving *relational* qualities, such as the size and location of objects in space (Hochberg, 1988). We will begin with the dominant approach perception has followed for about a hundred years, as represented by the experiential theory of Hermann von Helmholtz. We will contrast this with several newer views—the view of James Gibson and the Gestalt approach—that propose innate bases for perception. Finally, we will consider the newest theoretical view of perception—that provided by investigators in the area of artificial intelligence.

Helmholtz's Classical Theory

Hermann von Helmholtz (1866) argued for the importance of *experience* in perception. His theory emphasized the role of mental processes in interpreting the often ambiguous stimulus arrays that excite the nervous system. An observer makes sense of the proximal stimulus by using prior knowledge of the environment. On the basis of this experience, the observer makes hypotheses, or inferences, about the way things really are. Perception is thus an *inductive* process, moving from specific images to inferences (reasonable hunches) about the general class of objects or events that the images might represent. Since this process takes place out of our conscious awareness, Helmholtz termed it **unconscious inference.** Ordinarily, these inferential processes work well and generate veridical perceptions of reality. However, perceptual illusions can result when unusual circumstances in the stimulus array or viewing position allow multiple interpretations of the same stimulus or favor an old, familiar interpretation when a new one is required.

Basically, Helmholtz's classical theory broke perception down into two stages. In the first, *analytic* stage, the sense organs analyze the physical world into fundamental sensations. In the second, *synthetic* stage, we integrate and synthesize these sensory elements into perceptions of objects and their properties. Helmholtz's theory proposes that we learn how to interpret sensations on the basis of our experience with the world; our interpretations are, in effect, hypotheses about our perceptions.

This notion of perception as hypothesis is currently part of a general class of perceptual theories based on visual information-processing strategies. One such theory stresses the importance of human transactions with the environment as the basis for developing perception hypotheses. It is called, appropriately, **transactional perception** (Ames, 1951).

Gibson's Ecological Optics

The modern nativists, following in the path of the famous British philosophers Locke, Berkeley, and Hume, argue for innately determined sensory processes that enable an observer to perceive an object's size, shape, and distance. One proponent of this view, **James Gibson** (1966, 1979), searched for the aspects of the proximal stimulus that provide information about the distal stimulus. According to Gibson, the answer to the question "How do we learn about our world?" is simple. We directly pick up information about the invariant properties of the environment. There is no need to take raw sensations into account or to look for higher level systems of perceptual inference—perception is direct. Not only do we have information about the retinal color, size, and shape of each object, we also have information about the relative positions, sizes, and shapes of these objects and even about our own position with respect to these objects. While the retinal size and shape of each object changes, depending on the object's distance and on the viewing angle, these changes are not random. Such changes are systematic, and certain properties of objects remain invariant under all such changes of viewing angles and viewing distances. Our visual system is tuned to detect such invariances because we have evolved in the environment in which these invariances were important for our survival (Palmer, 1981).

Much of the earlier laboratory research on perception involved having subjects sit in one place while viewing simple, unmoving stimuli under highly restricted and artificial conditions. Gibson and others argued that perceptual systems evolved in organisms who were on the move—seeking food, water, mates, and shelter—in a complex and changing environment (Gibson, 1979; Pittenger, 1988; Shaw & Turvey, 1981; Shepard, 1984). Instead of trying to understand perception as a result of an organisms's structure, Gibson proposed that it could be better understood through an analysis of the immediately surrounding environment (or its ecology). As one writer put it, Gibson's approach was, "Ask not what's inside your head, but what your head's inside of" (Mace, 1977). In effect, Gibson's **theory of ecological optics** is concerned with the perceived stimuli rather than with the mechanisms by which we perceive the stimuli. This approach was a radical departure from all previous theories. Gibson's ideas emphasized perceiving as *active exploration* of the environment. When an observer is *moving* in the world, the pattern of stimulation on the retina is constantly changing over time as well as space. Gibson stressed the richness of this optical flow in perceptual events. The theory of ecological optics tried to specify the information about the environment that was available to the eyes of a moving observer. It had little to say about optical illusions because, according to Gibson, such illusions only occur when the viewing conditions are constrained and unnatural and the stimuli are artificially constructed in the laboratory. In the real world, subjects would have a lot more information available to them about the nature of ambiguous stimuli.

The Gestalt Approach

Founded in Germany in the second decade of this century, **Gestalt psychology** maintained that psychological phenomena could be understood only when viewed as organized, structured *wholes* and not when broken down into primitive perceptual elements (by introspective analysis). The term *Gestalt* roughly means *form, whole, configuration,* or *essence.* It challenged atomistic views of psychology, as proposed by the structuralists and behaviorists, by arguing that the whole is more than the sum of its parts. For example, a particular melody is perceived as a whole tune even though it is composed of separate notes. Gestalt psychologists argued further that we perceive the world of objects as whole units because the cortex is organized to function that way; it coordinates incoming stimuli that have interacted within a complex field of forces. This nativist approach proposed that we organize sensory information the way we do because it is the most economical, simple way to organize the sensory input for our brain, given the structure and physiology of the brain. The main exponents of Gestalt psychology were **Kurt Koffka** (1935), **Wolfgang Kohler** (1929), and **Max Wertheimer** (1923).

Although Gestalt psychology has ceased to exist as a separate school of psychology, some of its basic ideas and questions are still being actively studied by researchers in perception and other areas of psychology. You should note that Gibson's ecological perception shares with the Gestalt viewpoint the belief that perception is determined directly by the stimulus configuration presented to the viewer, and both reject any view of perception as being mediated by constructions built up from sensory elements.

The AI Approach

Proponents of the artificial intelligence or **AI approach** divide the study of perception into three levels of analysis: hardware or neurophysiological mechanisms; rules or algorithms for operation that specify the processes of perception; and the theory of the task that perception must perform or an analysis of the physical properties of the world that allow us to perceive (Banks & Krajicek, 1991). Together, these three levels would constitute a complete theory of perception. However, as yet, there is not sufficient integration between them. Neuroscientists are working at the first level, followers of Gibson function at the third level, and most of the work of AI researchers is directed at the second, computational level. AI models of perception have generally focused on the perceptual processes that operate on stimulus information, without reference to the underlying biological hardware. AI models focus on two main issues; the mechanisms necessary to pick up the information contained in the stimulus and the kinds of inferences and probability estimates observers engage in to make interpretations and conclusions about what is being perceived (Bennett et al., 1989).

Current positions on perception are incorporating the best of these approaches. Following the insights provided by Gibson, many researchers are well aware of the need to study the ecological constraints on perception and the dynamic nature of the sensory information available to the brain (Shaw & Turvey, 1981; Cutting, 1981; Pittenger, 1988). Yet, most of the researchers do not believe that perception is direct and immediate, as Gibson and some Gestalt psychologists claimed. They compare the process of perception to conceptual problem solving (Beck, 1982; Kanitza, 1979; Pomerantz & Cubovy, 1986; Rock, 1982, 1986; Shepp & Ballisteros, 1989). New approaches emphasize both the role of past experience (as Helmholtz did) and the role of simplicity and economy (as Gestalt psychologists did) in perceptual organization, while recognizing the value of the AI approach in developing testable models of the functional properties of the process of perceiving.

SUMMING UP

Perception extracts the continuously changing, often chaotic, sensory input from external energy sources and organizes it into stable, orderly percepts of meaningful objects. The proximal stimulus is the pattern of neural activity in a receptor; the distal stimulus is the actual physical object out there in the world. Perceptual processes allow us to construct, identify, and recognize the physical objects (distal stimuli) from the information available to us in the form of neural activity in the receptors (proximal stimuli). The term perception *is often used to refer to the overall process of apprehending objects and events in the external environment; that process can be divided into three parts: sensation in which physical energy is transformed into the neural activity of cortical cells; perception (in its narrow usage) during which features encoded at the sensory stage are organized and combined into percepts; and the identification/recognition stage involving memory and providing us with a mental representation of a familiar, meaningful object.*

Although perception is usually accurate, it can fail when the sensory data are incomplete or ambiguous. Illusions occur when your senses deceive you into experiencing an incorrect stimulus pattern. Psychologists study illusions because the failures of the human perceptual system provide us with useful insights into the mechanisms that normally result in accurate perception. Some illusions can be explained by simple sensory mechanisms; others occur because the same image can be interpreted as two or more different objects in the environment, requiring explanation at the perceptual organization or at the identification stage. Illusions are used by artists as well as designers and others to alter the impressions created by a given stimulus array.

Helmholtz argued for the importance of experience in perception. He took the empiricist position that we learn to make sense of proximal stimuli by using our prior experience with the world. Gibson, a nativist, believed that information available to us in the proximal stimulus unambiguously and directly determines the distal stimulus because we are "tuned" to detect certain invariances in our environment. Gestalt psychologists believed that we organize stimulus information as whole units and not as sensory elements because our brain is designed to function in this integrated, coordinated fashion. The AI approach differs from that of Gibson and the Gestalt view in specifying three different levels of analysis, and in emphasizing the complex processes of inference and probability estimates that take place during the process of perception.

ATTENTIONAL PROCESSES

When your teacher asks you to pay attention, what exactly does he mean? Obviously, you are familiar with the term *attention* as it is used in everyday speech. You believe that paying attention is, to some extent, under voluntary control—you can *choose* to pay attention. You've noticed that you better comprehend the material when you pay attention to the lesson. You also know that sometimes, no matter how hard you try, you just don't seem to be able to pay attention—you are distracted. **Distraction** means you are unable to focus your perceptual processing on the sights and sounds that are relevant to a task in the current situation because of interference from competing thoughts, images, and irrelevant sensory stimuli.

What does attention really do for us, and how does it do it? One way to find out what attention does is to ask what we know about objects or events after we have *not* attended to them consciously. Why does paying attention improve your comprehension of material? What exactly does attention contribute to the processing of information? These questions will be considered in detail in the first two parts of this section. Then we will turn to another set of questions: How much control do we have over attention? Why is it hard to pay attention sometimes? How successful are we at directing attention or dividing it between several tasks?

Attention appears to serve divergent functions related to perception, cognition, and consciousness. Some researchers now believe that we have several kinds of attention, each with its own mechanisms and functions (Posner, 1990). This issue has not yet been resolved, in part because of different methods researchers use to study attention. We'll look at some of these methods as we consider basic conceptual problems that arise when psychologists focus their attention on understanding the nature of attention, especially as it works in perception.

PREATTENTIVE PROCESSING

If you listened to your teacher's advice and paid attention to the lesson, how much would you be able to tell about a conversation going on at the same time between your classmates seated next to you or about a passerby outside the window if someone suddenly asked you? While you probably would not know the content of the conversation, you would be able to tell whether the voices were male or female. Similarly, you would not be able to remember or identify the person who passed by, but you would probably be aware of movement outside.

Even though conscious memory and recognition of objects require attention, quite complex processing of information does go on without our awareness and without attention. This earlier stage of processing is called **preattentive processing** because it operates on sensory inputs before we attend to them, as they first come into the brain from the sensory receptors. The simple demonstration in **Figure 8.8** will give you a rough idea of what can and cannot be processed without attention (adapted from Rock & Gutman, 1981).

Our memory for the attended (red) shapes in the figure is much better than memory for the unattended shapes. However, we remember some basic features of the unattended shapes, such as their color and whether they were drawn continuously or had gaps. It is as though our visual system extracted some of the simple features of the unattended objects but never quite managed to put them together to form whole percepts.

Early in visual processing, raw materials or basic stimulus features—edges, lines, contours, and color—are extracted from the patterns of light energy striking the retina. These features are then combined into percepts that enter consciousness. Many researchers now believe that putting these features together into a complete percept requires attention (Treisman, 1988, 1986; Treisman & Gelade, 1980).

We can illustrate the importance of attention for integrating features into composites that we recognize as whole units (based on experiments by Beck, 1982; Julesz, 1982; and Treisman, 1988). When asked to locate boundaries between regions of a scene, subjects report that the boundaries "pop out" when they are defined by a difference in a single simple feature, such as color, curved vs. straight line shape, or orientation of

FIGURE 8.8

AN EXAMPLE OF OVERLAPPING FIGURES

Cover the right part of the figure with a piece of paper. Look at the pictures of overlapping colored shapes on the left side of the figure. Try to attend to the red shapes only and rate them according to how appealing they seem to you. Next, cover the left side of the figure and uncover the right side. Now test your memory for the red (attended) figures and the blue and green (unattended) figures. Put a check mark next to each figure you definitely recall seeing on the left. How well do you remember the attended versus the unattended shapes?

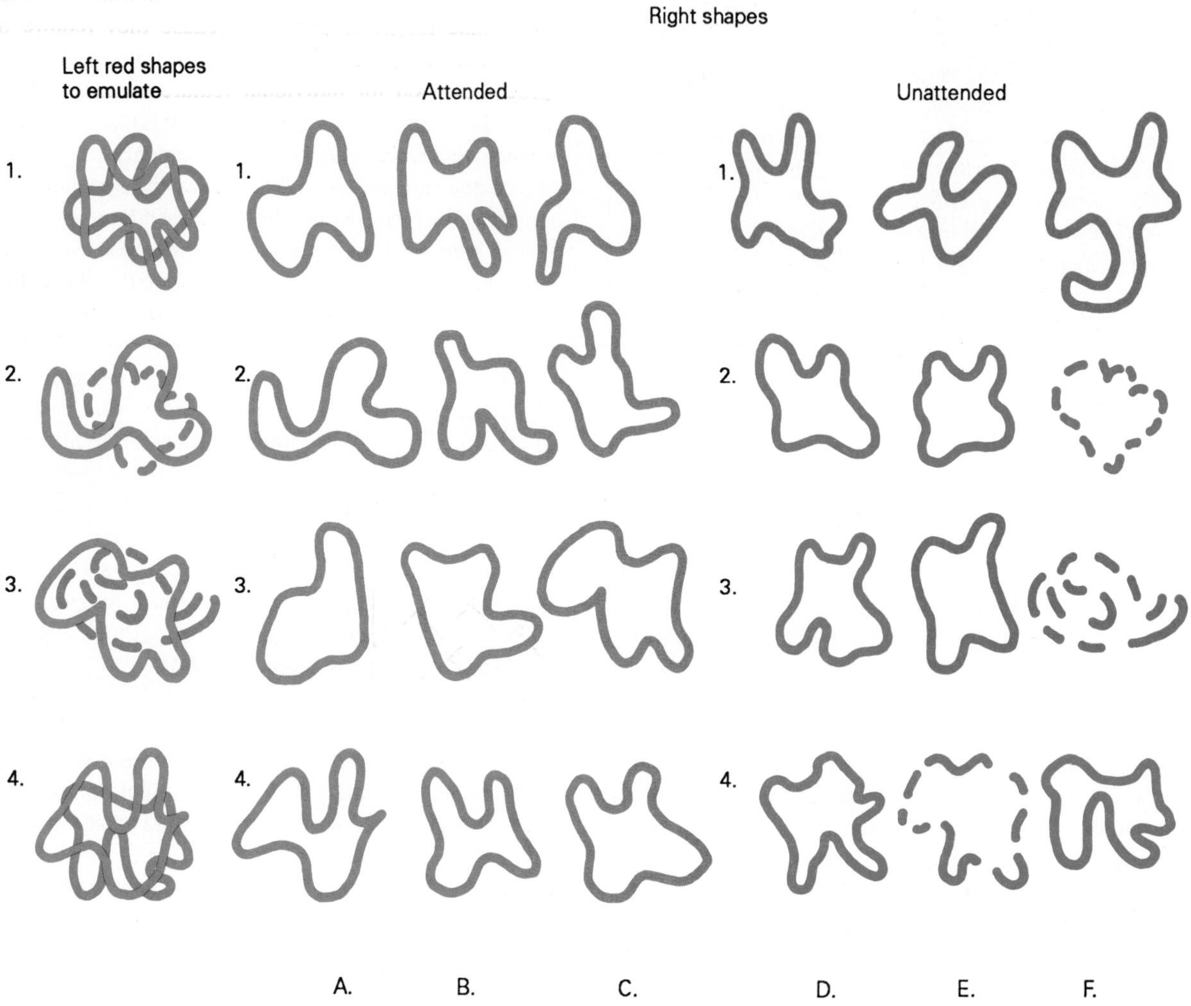

Right shapes

Left red shapes to emulate — Attended — Unattended

A.   B.   C.   D.   E.   F.

lines (vertical vs. horizontal), as shown in A of **Figure 8.9.** The boundaries of red and blue and of V's and O's in B are distinct. In contrast, the boundaries between red V's or blue O's and red O's or blue V's in C must be sought out with more mental effort. While boundaries based on a single feature emerge *preattentively*, boundaries that are defined by a combination of features do not, since combining features requires attention.

When scenes such as those in Figure 8.9 are flashed very briefly, subjects are much more accurate at locating single-feature boundaries than the feature-combination boundaries. Even when such scenes are allowed to stay in view and response time is measured, subjects locate single-feature boundaries faster.

A stronger demonstration of the role of attention in proper feature combination comes by diverting or overloading attention. Under such circumstances, errors in feature combinations often occur; the perceptual mistakes we make are called **illusory conjunctions.**

Illusory conjunctions result when three colored letters with digits on both sides of them are flashed briefly (for less than one-fifth of a second).

5 X O T 7

The subjects' task is to report the digits first and then to report all of the color-letter combinations. On a third of the trials, subjects report seeing the wrong color-letter combination. For example, they report a red X instead of a blue X or a red O. They rarely make the mistake of reporting any colors or letters that were not present in the display, such as a yellow X or a blue Z.

Subjects were also likely to report that they saw a dollar sign ($) in the briefly flashed display containing S's and line segments shown in **Figure 8.10.** The same effect was obtained even when the display contained S's and triangles. This result demonstrates that the subjects did not combine the lines of the triangles right away; the lines were floating unattached at some stage of perceptual processing, and one of the lines could be borrowed by the visual system to form the vertical bar in the dollar sign (Treisman & Gelade, 1980).

These results also suggest that *combinations* of features take longer to process because they require the involvement of attention in addition to preattentive processes used for individual feature identification. If selective attention to objects is disrupted or prevented, people are likely to make mistakes of a certain type—they are likely to get the individual features right but put them together into illusory combinations.

If we make so many mistakes when putting the features together without attention in the laboratory, why don't we make many more mistakes of this type when our attention is often diverted and overloaded in

---

FIGURE 8.9   *Locating Boundaries Between Regions of a Scene*

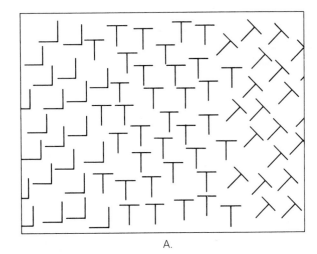

A.

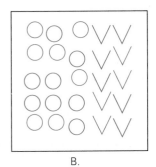

B.

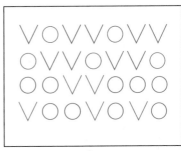

C.

FIGURE 8.10 COMBINATIONS OF FEATURES

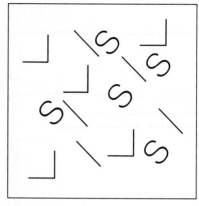 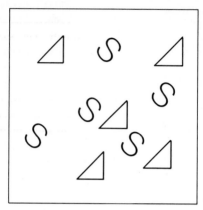 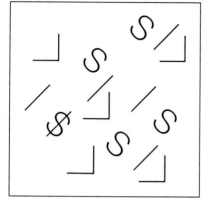

Actually Observed   Reported with Illusory $

the real world? Researcher **Anne Treisman** argues that most stimuli we process are familiar and sufficiently different from one another so that there are a limited number of sensible ways to combine their various features. Even when we have not attended as carefully as necessary for accurate integration of features, our knowledge of familiar perceptual stimuli allows us to guess how their features ought to be combined. These guesses, or perceptual hypotheses, are usually correct, which means that we construct some of our percepts by combining preattentive perception of single stimulus features with memory for familiar, similar whole figures.

FUNCTIONS OF ATTENTION

Treisman's view that attention is required to put features together is popular, but it is not accepted universally. Some researchers believe that combination of single features is completed without the involvement of attention. They say that attention only brings the finished percept into conscious awareness or allows the selection of the appropriate response to the perceived stimulus.

Psychologists have proposed several important functions for attention in the complex interrelated processes of perceiving, responding, and consciously remembering sensory and perceptual information. We will review three of these functions: stimulus filter, response selector, and gateway to conscious processing of information.

Attention as Sensory Filter: Early Feature Selection

The experiments mentioned on preattentive processing strongly suggest the possibility that one function of attention is to select some part of the sensory input for further processing. The modern version of this view was introduced by British psychologist **Donald Broadbent** in his book, *Perception and Communication,* published in 1958.

Broadbent was the first to say the mind is a *communications channel*—similar to a telephone line or a computer link—that actively processes and transmits information. The amount of information the channel can handle accurately at any one time is severely limited. Therefore, people must focus on one source of information at a time. When they need to attend to more than one source, the efficiency of information processing is restricted by the limited ability of attention to switch back and forth among the sources.

Imagine listening to a lecture while people on both sides of you are engaged in conversations. What do you hear, understand, and remember? You will probably be able to stay tuned to the lecturer if the material is interesting or important for tomorrow's exam—you will ignore your neighbors as long as they don't get too loud. However, if the lecture is boring and irrelevant to your goals, and one of the conversations concerns your best friend and the other is about sex, chances are that you'll lose track of the lecture and attend to what is happening around you. You will not be able to listen carefully to all three sources of input simultaneously or even to two of them at once. You must *selectively attend* to only one at a time if you are to fully understand and remember anything.

Broadbent and many other investigators have simulated this selective attention phenomenon in the laboratory with a technique called **dichotic listening.**

> A subject wearing earphones listens to two tape-recorded messages played at the same time—a different message is played into each ear. The subject is instructed to repeat only one of the two messages to the experimenter, while ignoring whatever is presented to the other ear. This procedure is called *shadowing* the attended message (see **Figure 8.11**).

Subjects in shadowing experiments remember the attended message and do not remember the ignored message. Subjects usually do not even notice major alterations in the ignored message, such as changing the language from English to German or playing the tape backward. However, subjects do notice marked physical changes, for example, substantially raising the pitch by

changing the speaker's voice from male to female (Cherry, 1953).

Gross physical features of the unattended message receive perceptual analysis, apparently below the level of consciousness, but most meaning does not get through. The first experiments on attention involved auditory modality; more recent studies demonstrate similar effects in visual modality. You have already encountered some of these demonstrations in the segment on preattentive processing (Rock & Gutman, 1981; Beck, 1982; Treisman & Gelade, 1980).

In light of results such as these, Broadbent conceived of attention as a *selective filter* that deals with the overwhelming flow of incoming sensory information by blocking out the unwanted sensory input and passing on specific desired input. The filter resembles a tuning dial on a radio or TV, which lets you receive only one of the many available programs at a time. The tuning dial can get you whatever program happens to be on Channel 10, but it cannot guarantee that the program will be a football game. So too, Broadbent's attentional filter can select on the basis of rough physical properties—such as whether the message is heard in the left or the right ear or whether the message is given in a woman's voice or a man's—but it can't automatically select a message on a particular topic. More conceptual aspects of the message, such as the language in which it is phrased or the meaning it conveys, have to be determined by the more complete processing that takes place after the input enters into consciousness.

According to Broadbent's theory, as a communication channel the mind has only *limited capacity* to carry out complete processing. It requires that attention strictly regulate the flow of information from sensory input to consciousness. However, attention creates a bottleneck in the flow of information through the cognitive system, filtering out some information and allowing other information to continue. The filter theory of attention asserted that the selection occurs early on in the process, before the input's meaning is accessed.

Selection theory was first challenged when it was discovered that some subjects were perceiving things they would not have been able to if attention had been totally filtering all ignored material.

> In dichotic listening tasks, subjects sometimes did notice their own names and other personally relevant information contained in the message they were instructed to ignore (Cherry, 1953). When a story being shadowed in one ear was switched to the unattended ear and replaced by a new story, some subjects continued to report words from the original story which was then entering the suppos-

---

FIGURE 8.11   *DICHOTIC LISTENING TASK*

A subject hears different digits presented simultaneously to each ear: 2 (left), 7 (right), 6 (left), 9 (right), 1 (left), and 5 (right). He reports hearing the correct sets—261 and 795. However, when instructed to attend only to the right ear input, the subject reports hearing only 795.

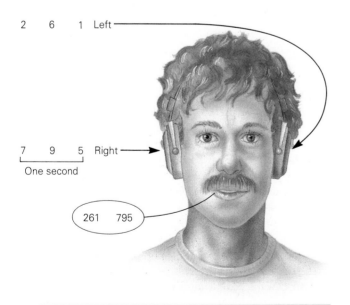

2   6   1   Left

7   9   5   Right

One second

261   795

edly ignored ear. The subjects did so even though they had been accurately following the instruction about which ear to shadow (Treisman, 1960).

Apparently, subjects were intrigued by the meaning and continuity of the particular message they had been shadowing, which momentarily distracted them from the attended channel. Some meaningful analysis of the ignored channel must have been taking place—otherwise, subjects would not have known that the message on that channel was the continuation of the message they had been shadowing.

Research such as this forced researchers to conclude that attention is not an exclusive feature as filter theory postulated. Anne Treisman subsequently proposed the *attenuation theory* of attention as a modification to the filtering theory (Treisman, 1964b; Norman, 1968). In the attenuation theory, ignored information gets some higher-level, meaningful analysis, but the analysis is only partial, is not guaranteed, and frequently does not reach consciousness. The attended channel still receives far more processing than the unattended channel—attention is necessary to guarantee that pieces of sensory input will be put together properly into coherent meaningful percepts. This modified version is now the more widely held view of early feature selection.

Attention and Response Selection: Late Feature Selection

What evidence do we have that unattended information is not processed completely? All we can conclude from the demonstration (and its supporting research) described in Figure 8.8, is that people *are not consciously aware* of the shapes of the unattended figures. How do we know that our visual system did not put these shapes together correctly and completely without our awareness? According to some new research, a nonconscious awareness of unattended information may be occurring (Allport et al., 1985).

> Look at **Figure 8.12.** Try to read the red letters in each column. Disregard the overlapping green letters. Did you notice that one of the columns is harder to read? Which one? Now look carefully at the green letters. In the first column, there is no relationship between the green letters and the red letters. However, in the second list, beginning with the second red letter, each red letter is the same as the green letter above it. A number of experiments show that subjects take longer to read the second list (Tipper & Driver, 1988; Driver & Tipper, 1989).

According to the authors of such experiments, subjects take longer to read the second column because they

First read aloud the red letters in column one as quickly as possible, disregarding the green. Next, quickly read the red letters in column two, also disregarding the green. Which took longer?

Column One   Column Two

actually process the green letters unconsciously and have to inhibit or prevent themselves from responding to them. When, after having inhibited a particular letter, subjects are asked to respond to it, they are slowed down because they have to unblock or disinhibit the letter and make it available for response. For example, when you read the first red letter in the second row, you had to ignore, or inhibit, a green H. The second red letter in the row happens to be the letter H. Thus, when you try to read the red H, you have to unblock, or disinhibit, the letter H. Nothing similar to this happens when you read the first row of letters; the red letters in this row never appear as green letters.

This and similar experiments demonstrate that just because something did not enter our consciousness does not mean it was not processed completely. The late selection view hypothesizes that all sensory inputs may be processed completely without attention (Deutch & Deutch, 1963; Driver & Tipper, 1989).

According to the late selection view, we are limited not on the stimulus input side but rather on the response output side. If you were asked to pick up four objects at once, you would have difficulty since your response is limited by having only two hands. Evidence about your limited response does not mean you haven't noticed all four objects. We cannot respond to many stimuli simultaneously; survival depends on being able to respond correctly and swiftly to only the most important stimuli. The late selection view suggests that we need attention not because we are limited in the amount of information we can process but because we are limited in the number of responses we can make at a given time.

There is no question that *selection of responses,* or late selection, does occur, particularly when the stimuli are few and familiar and have been processed many times before in the past (Posner, 1986). The more familiar we are with a stimulus, the more likely we are to process it relatively automatically, outside conscious awareness and attention. The fewer stimuli we see or hear, the more likely we are to process all of them completely. There still is question about whether and when selection of input, or early selection, occurs (Lambert, 1985; Treisman, 1988; Yantis & Johnson, 1990). Many investigators now wonder exactly what constitutes *early* and what constitutes *late* selective processing and await new research to clarify the distinction.

Attention as the Gateway to Consciousness

Of all the things that happen around us, we actually become aware of only those on which we focus attention. When we select something to attend to, either because of its striking characteristics or its relevance to a goal, we inevitably ignore many other possibilities. You can think of attention as the bridge over which pieces of the external world—the pieces selectively focused on—are carried over into the subjective world of consciousness (Carver & Schneider, 1981; Posner, 1982, 1986). Attention is also frequently described as a spotlight that illuminates certain portions of its surroundings (Briand & Klein, 1988; Eriksen & Yeh, 1985).

What does conscious attentional processing achieve for us? Its most significant function is permitting percepts that enter consciousness to be stored as memories for later conscious recollection. While information that does not reach consciousness can also be stored and may even influence later behavior, people have great difficulty explicitly remembering information that did

Once you learn how to roller skate you don't need to think about how to do it. This routinizing makes your supply of mental energy go further when attending to other events.

not receive conscious processing (Jacoby et al., 1989; Richardson-Klavehn & Bjork, 1988; Schacter, 1989). So, the information will not be available as conscious memories that can be used intentionally in current thinking, planning, and communicating. Conscious processing, on the other hand, allows new ideas to be developed about the material that is attended (Baddeley, 1986; Mullin & Egeth, 1989; Nissen & Bullemer, 1987).

ATTENTIONAL MECHANISMS

We have considered three possible functions of attention: selection of input for further processing, selecting responses, and providing conscious access to parts of the sensory input. Now we need to consider the way attention works. In principle, there are two possible ways for attention to do its work. First, attention may *facilitate* the stimulus processing, response selection, or conscious access of the *relevant* information. Second, attention may hinder undesired processing—it may *inhibit* the processing of, responses to, or conscious access to *irrelevant* information. Most researchers now believe that attention employs both mechanisms but, perhaps, at different times in the course of processing or for different tasks (Posner, 1990). These two mechanisms function through the processes of resource allocation and automaticity.

Resource Allocation

What we selectively attend to and how much control we have over our attention depends on a number of external and internal factors. We attend to environmental stimuli that are intense, novel, changing, and unexpected or that stand out as salient or special (Berlyne, 1950, 1951, 1958; Kahneman, 1973; Yantis & Jonides, 1984). Consider the techniques advertisers regularly employ to capture your attention. Notice, for example, that the sound tracks that accompany TV advertisements are often louder than the regular programming. Advertisers are aware of the paradigms of habituation and dishabituation, so important for modern developmental researchers interested in discovering what babies know (Chapter 5). Even at a very early age, infants habituate to the old, tuning out familiar objects and repetitive events and tuning in to whatever is new. It is reasonable to conclude that humans and most animals come equipped to attend to all signals from their environment that carry some potentially significant information for their survival—to approach the good and avoid or flee the bad. Familiar stimuli that no longer signal significant consequences are rerouted to an attentional sidetrack. This allows the new and significant events to have unimpeded access to the main attentional express track. Advertising messages that are louder than other programming are, thus, more likely to command your attention.

Not only unfamiliar stimuli but current physiological conditions as well can direct our attention. For example, hunger makes us notice newspaper ads for food or restaurants. Listening to a charismatic speaker, watching an exciting movie, reading an absorbing novel, and playing video games are attention capturing and, hence, attention restricting. Furthermore, past experience, special interest, or expertise in a given area carries with it not just an expanded knowledge base but a greater sensitivity to particular stimuli, events, and relationships as well. Such sensitivity is seen in the fabulous detective work of Sherlock Holmes, who noticed the significance of details that others overlooked, or in the ability of an experienced bird watcher to spot rare birds that others do not notice. Perception psychologist James Gibson (1966) called this type of sensitivity "the education of attention."

When people do two or more things at once, attention focused on one task hurts performance on the other (Navon, 1979; Hirst et al., 1980). You can prove this phenomenon for yourself. When jogging with a friend, ask him or her to divide 86 by 14 or to tell you how many windows there are in his or her family home. Chances are, your friend will slow down or stop jogging altogether while trying to answer the question. This shows that an important mechanism of attention is to select specific tasks to perform and also to keep us from switching to a new task before the old one is satisfactorily completed. Our ability to perform several tasks at

once while successfully disregarding another is quite limited, as you might expect both from your personal experience and from the studies we have been discussing.

Thus, some researchers refer to attention as a *limited processing resource* (Kahneman, 1973; Navon & Gopher, 1979). As is the case with natural resources, the supply of processing resources is limited at any given time. Each task uses up a certain amount of the supply. When you try to perform several tasks at once, the amount of processing resources the tasks require may exceed what is available. You then have to divide attention between several tasks. Allocating more resources to one of the tasks will diminish the performance on the others. As you practice a given task and become more adept at it, you free up more processing resources which you can then apply to other tasks. However, several different pools of resources may exist. Whether or not two tasks can be performed at the same time without interference depends on whether performance of these tasks requires use of the same pool of resources. This condition is shown in an experiment with a researcher's secretary.

The secretary, a very skilled typist, was asked to perform several tasks at once. She was asked to shadow a speech while continuing to type visually presented words. When the speech had no relation

Some people are very confident in their ability to attend to more than one stimulus at the same time.

to the typed material, she had no trouble performing both tasks at the same time. However, if the speech consisted of single letters, shadowing became very difficult, although typing was unaffected. The secretary also had difficulty spelling words that were presented to her via earphones, and her spelling task interfered with her typing (Shaffer, 1975).

These results are explained by the attentional resource theory. Since the subject was highly practiced at typing and since shadowing a speech and typing probably do not share the same pool of resources, the subject was able to perform two tasks at once. Her performance deteriorated when the tasks tapped into the same cognitive resource pool—when a similar type of information processing had to be used for both the typing task and the competing task. Since the secretary was more practiced at typing than at shadowing, the shadowing was impaired more than the typing.

Automaticity

Highly practiced cognitive and motor tasks, such as typing, reading, or riding a bicycle, are of great interest to psychologists studying attention. Initially, learning such tasks requires a great deal of concentrated effort. A beginner must attend to every little detail when learning to read, type, ride a bike, or drive a car. However, with practice, performance of the task becomes automatic. **Automaticity** refers to one or more of the following conditions in the performance of a task: (a) the processing becomes seemingly effortless; (b) it can be triggered, carried out, and completed without any degree of conscious attention; and (c) other tasks can be performed concurrently without interference (Logan, 1980; Shiffrin & Schneider, 1977).

A good illustration of automaticity in reading is a *Stroop task*—in which a subject must name the ink color of a word without reading the word itself. A Stroop task is shown in **Figure 8.13.** Follow the instructions given. You will probably discover that you cannot stop yourself from reading the word, even though reading it interferes with the task of naming the ink color. In the Stroop task, reading satisfies two out of three criteria for automaticity—it is carried out without attention and it appears to be effortless. However, the last criterion is violated—it does interfere with the naming of ink color. The studies on automaticity demonstrate that much of the processing that normally requires attention can eventually be done preattentively. Perhaps, there is no sharp boundary between preattentive and attentive processing, and, with enough practice, elaborate preattentive processing is possible (Shiffrin & Schneider, 1977).

FIGURE 8.13	THE STROOP TASK

Perform the following two tasks:
1. Time yourself as you read aloud all the words, ignoring the colors in which they are printed.
2. Time yourself as you read the colors, ignoring what the words say.

    You probably did the first task quickly and effortlessly, with little or no thought. The second required your full conscious attention because you had to deal with cognitive interference.

PURPLE	BLUE	RED
GREEN	YELLOW	ORANGE
RED	BLACK	**BLUE**
ORANGE	**GREEN**	BROWN
BLUE	YELLOW	PURPLE

SUMMING UP

Attention refers to our ability to focus selectively on part of a sensory input. Survival depends on this ability—we must be able to deal successfully with input that is currently significant or meaningful to us, setting aside the many stimuli that do not have immediate significance. Preattentive processing is that early stage of perceptual processing of sensory input that occurs without involving attention. Preattentive processing seems to be limited to registering simple elementary features, such as colors, orientations of lines, or edges. Properly combining such elementary features into perceptual objects may not occur without attentional focus. Illusory conjunctions are perceptual errors that occur when the primitive features of objects, such as their color and shape, are not combined correctly by the visual system.

Attention may serve one or more of the following functions: the successful synthesis of simple perceptual features into perceptual objects; the process of making the appropriate response selection; and the control of conscious access to sensory and perceptual information stored in memory. The sensory filter function of attention (first described by Broadbent), has been studied using the dichotic listening task. In the early stimulus selection theory, attention is required for proper synthesis of sensory information and for the complete semantic processing of the input. Late selection theory holds that unattended information is processed completely, but that attention is necessary to ensure that response is limited to the attended stimuli because we cannot usually respond to more than one source of stimulation at a time. Finally, attention may also serve as the gateway to consciousness, providing us conscious access to the attended information while blocking the unattended information from reaching our consciousness.

Attention serves these functions by inhibiting the processing of, responses to, or conscious access to unattended input and by facilitating the processing of, responses to, or conscious access to attended stimuli. These dual mechanisms are probably employed at different stages of processing or for different purposes. With voluntary control over attention we can allocate it at will to any perceptual event, but certain physical characteristics of objects, such as exceptional brightness or sudden movement, capture our attention automatically. Attention also helps to manage our limited mental processing resources. High levels of practice on a particular task result in automaticity and improve the efficiency with which we can access limited resources. Automaticity involves effortless processing, minimal or no attention, and performance of concurrent tasks without interference.

ORGANIZATIONAL PROCESSES IN PERCEPTION

Vision is the most important and complex perceptual system in humans and most other mammals. In this chapter, our discussion is generally about vision because vision has been more intensively studied than the other modalities, and on the printed page it is easier to provide visual demonstrations. In this section, we will explore what is known about several kinds of processes that transform sensory information into perception of real-world objects.

Imagine how confusing the world would be if we were unable to put together and organize the information available from the output of our millions of retinal receptors. We would experience a kaleidoscope of disconnected bits of color moving and swirling before our eyes. (Dr. Richard was able to put parts together, although sometimes he did it incorrectly.) The processes

that put sensory information together to give us the perception of coherence are referred to collectively as processes of **perceptual organization.** We have seen that what a person experiences as a result of such perceptual processing is called a percept.

For example, your percept of the two-dimensional geometric design in **Figure 8.14** is probably three diagonal rows of figures, the first being composed of squares, the second of arrowheads, and the third of diamonds. Nothing seems remarkable about this until you analyze all the organizational processing that you must be performing to see the design in this way. Many of the organizational processes we will be discussing in this section were first described by Gestalt theorists

FIGURE 8.14 *PERCEPT OF A TWO-DIMENSIONAL GEOMETRIC DESIGN*

What is your percept of the geometrical design in A? B represents the mosaic pattern that stimulus A makes on your retina.

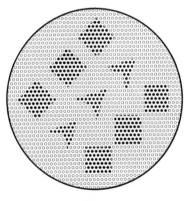

A.

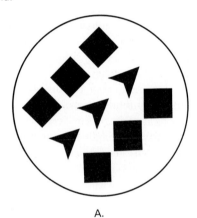

B.

who argued that what we perceive depends on laws of organization, or simple rules by which we perceive shapes and forms.

REGION SEGREGATION

Consider your initial sensory response to Figure 8.14. Because your retina is composed of many separate receptors, your eye responds to this stimulus pattern with a mosaic of millions of independent neural responses coding the amount of light falling on tiny areas of your retina. This mosaic pattern is also shown in Figure 8.14. The first task of perceptual organization is to determine which of these tiny areas belong with which others. In other words, the outputs of the separate receptors must be combined into larger regions that are uniform in their properties.

The primary information for this region segregation process comes from color and texture. An abrupt change in color (hue, saturation, or brightness) signifies the presence of a boundary between two regions. Abrupt changes in texture can also mark boundaries between visibly different regions. Finding these boundaries is the first step in organizational processing.

Many researchers now believe that the cells in the visual cortex, discovered by Hubel and Wiesel (see Chapter 7), are involved in these region-segregating processes (Marr, 1982). Some cells have elongated receptive fields that are ideally suited for detecting boundaries between regions that differ in color. Others have receptive fields that seem to detect little bars or lines such as those that occur in grassy fields, wood grains, and woven fabrics. These cortical line-detector cells

may be responsible for our ability to discriminate between regions that have different textures (Beck, 1972, 1982; Julesz, 1981).

FIGURE AND GROUND

As a result of region segregation, the stimulus in Figure 8.14 has now been divided into thirteen regions: twelve small dark ones and a single large light one. You can now think of each of these regions as a unified entity, such as thirteen separate pieces of glass combined in a stained-glass window. Another organizational process divides the regions into figures and background. A **figure** is seen as an objectlike region in the forefront, and **ground** is seen as the backdrop against which the figures stand out. In Figure 8.14, you probably see the dark regions as figures and the light region as ground. However, you can also see this stimulus pattern differently by reversing figure and ground, much as you did with the ambiguous vase/faces drawing and the Escher art. To do this, try to see the white region as a large white sheet of paper that has nine holes cut in it through which you can see a black background.

Notice that when you perceive a region as a figure, the boundaries between light and dark are interpreted as edges or contours that belong to the figure. In contrast, the ground seems to extend behind these edges rather than stopping at them.

The tendency to perceive a figure as being in *front* of a ground is very strong. In fact, you can even get this effect in a stimulus when the perceived figure doesn't actually exist! In the first image of **Figure 8.15,** you probably perceive a fir tree set against a ground contain-

---

FIGURE 8.15   SUBJECTIVE CONTOURS THAT FIT THE ANGLES OF YOUR MIND

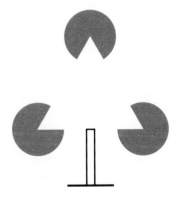
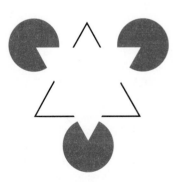

ing several red circles on a white surface. Notice, however, that there is no fir tree shape; the figure consists only of three solid red figures and a base of lines. You see the illusory white triangle in front because the straight edges of the red shapes are aligned in a way that suggests a solid white triangle. To see an illusory six-pointed star, look at the other image in Figure 8.15.

In this example, there seem to be three levels of figure/ground organization: the white fir tree, the red circles, and the larger white surface behind everything else. Notice that, perceptually, you divide the white area in the stimulus into two different regions: the white triangle and the white ground. Where this division occurs, you perceive illusory **subjective contours** which, in fact, exist not in the distal stimulus but only in your subjective experience.

CLOSURE

Your perception of the white triangle in these figures also demonstrates another powerful organizing process: *closure*. **Closure** makes you see incomplete figures as complete. Though the stimulus gives you only the angles, your perceptual system supplies the edges in between that make the figure a complete fir tree. The law of closure describes an innate tendency to perceive stimuli as complete, balanced, and symmetrical, even when there are gaps, some imbalance, and asymmetry.

PRINCIPLES OF PERCEPTUAL GROUPING

In Figure 8.14, you perceive the nine distinct figural regions as being grouped together in three distinct rows, each composed of three identical shapes placed along a diagonal line. How does you visual system accomplish this **perceptual grouping,** and what factors control it?

The problem of grouping was first studied extensively by Gestalt psychologist Max Wertheimer (1923). Wertheimer presented subjects with arrays of simple geometric figures. By varying a single factor and observing how it affected the way people perceived the structure of the array, he was able to formulate a set of laws of grouping. Several of these laws are illustrated in **Figure 8.16.** In section A, there is an array of equally spaced circles that is ambiguous in its grouping—you can see it equally well as either rows or columns of dots. However, when the spacing is changed slightly so that the horizontal distances between adjacent dots are less than the vertical distances, as shown in B, you see the array unambiguously as organized into horizontal rows; when the spacing is changed so that the vertical distances are less as shown in C, you see the array as organized into vertical columns. Together, these three groupings illustrate Wertheimer's

FIGURE 8.16   GROUPING PHENOMENA

We perceive each array from B through G as being organized in a particular way, according to different Gestalt principles of grouping.

law of proximity: all else being equal, the nearest (most proximal) elements are grouped together.

In D, the color of the dots instead of their spacing has been varied. Although there is equal spacing between the dots, your visual system automatically organizes this stimulus into rows because of their *similar color.* You see the dots in E as being organized into columns because of *similar size,* and you see the dots in F as being organized into rows because of *similar shape* and *orientation.* These grouping effects can be summarized by the **law of similarity:** all else being equal, the most similar elements are grouped together.

When elements in the visual field are moving, similarity of motion also produces a powerful grouping. The **law of common fate** states that, all else being equal, elements moving in the same direction and at the same rate are grouped together. If the dots in every other column of G were moving upward, as indicated by the blurring, you would group the image into columns because of their similarity in motion. You get this effect at a ballet when several dancers move in a pattern different from the others. Remember Dr. Richard's observation that an object in his visual field became organized properly when it moved as a whole. His experience was evidence of the powerful organizing effect of common fate.

The Gestalt grouping laws operate only when two or more elements are simultaneously present in a visual field. The Gestaltists interpreted such results to mean that the whole stimulus pattern is somehow determining the organization of its own parts; in other words, the *whole percept* is different from the mere collection of its *parts*. Perceiving the whole—the Gestalt—was itself more basic and took place at the same time or earlier than the perception of its elements.

Once a given region has been segregated and selected as a figure against a ground, the boundaries must be further organized into specific *shapes*. You might think that this task would require nothing more than perceiving all the edges of a figure, but the Gestaltists showed that visual organization is far more complex. If a whole shape were merely the sum of its edges, then all shapes having the same number of edges would be equally easy to perceive. In reality, organizational processes in shape perception are also sensitive to something the Gestaltists called **figural goodness,** a concept that includes perceived simplicity, symmetry, and regularity. **Figure 8.17** shows several figures that exhibit a range of figural goodness even though each has the same number of sides. Figure A is the "best" figure (or most standard looking) and Figure E is the "worst" (or least standard looking).

Experiments have shown that "good" figures are more easily and accurately perceived, remembered, and described than "bad" ones (Garner, 1974). Such results suggest that shapes of "good" figures can be coded more rapidly and economically by the visual system than those of "bad" figures. In fact, the visual system sometimes tends to see a single "bad" figure as being composed of two overlapping "good" ones, as shown in **Figure 8.18.**

Is there a more general way of stating the various grouping laws we have just discussed? We have mentioned the law of proximity, the law of similarity, the

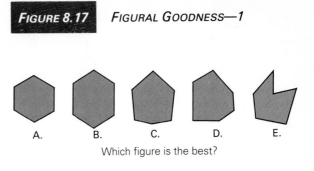

FIGURE 8.17 FIGURAL GOODNESS—1

A. B. C. D. E.
Which figure is the best?

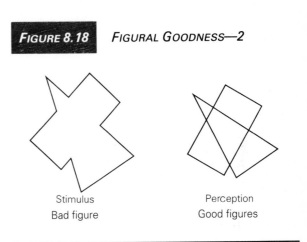

FIGURE 8.18 FIGURAL GOODNESS—2

Stimulus
Bad figure

Perception
Good figures

law of common fate, and the law of symmetry, or figural goodness. Gestalt psychologists believed that all of these laws are just particular examples of a general principle, the **law of pragnanz,** that states that the simplest organization requiring the least cognitive effort will always emerge. Perhaps the most general Gestalt principle is this: We perceive the simplest organization that fits the stimulus pattern—the *minimum principle of perception.*

REFERENCE FRAMES

Higher levels of organization are achieved when the shapes of figures are perceived relative to **reference frames** established by the spatial and temporal context. The perceptual effects of reference frames are demonstrated in **Figure 8.19:** if you saw the left-hand image in A by itself, it would resemble a diamond, whereas the right-hand image would resemble a square. When you see these images as parts of diagonal rows, as shown in B, the shapes reverse: the line composed of diamonds resembles a tilted column of squares and the line composed of squares resembles a tilted column of diamonds. The shapes of the images look different when

FIGURE 8.19   REFERENCE FRAMES

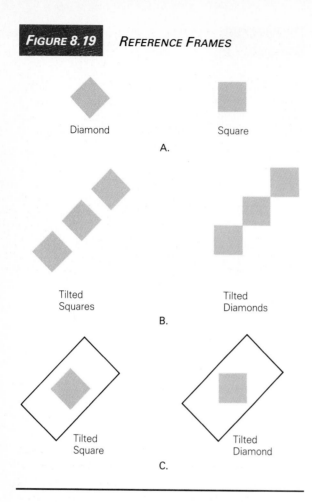

Diamond   Square

A.

Tilted Squares   Tilted Diamonds

B.

Tilted Square   Tilted Diamond

C.

You must be able to integrate your perceptions from these restricted glimpses of the world from one moment to the next. As you fixate on different parts of the same figure, what you see in your present fixation is somehow properly integrated with what you saw in the last one, which was properly integrated with the one before that, and so on. If this phenomenon were not true, you would not perceive the same objects in successive views; you would see a hodgepodge of unrelated and overlapping shapes.

The process of putting together visual information from one fixation to the next in both space and time is absolutely critical for useful perception. The world around you is so much larger than a single field of view that you could never know about the spatial layout of your surroundings without organizational processes that integrate the visual information from many eye fixations into a single continuing episode of related images (Hochberg, 1968; Parks, 1965).

Complex objects often require several eye fixations before you can build up a complete spatial interpretation, even when the objects are small enough to fit into a single field of view. One interesting consequence of the way we put together the information from different fixations is that we are able to perceive "impossible" objects, such as the one in **Figure 8.20.** For example,

FIGURE 8.20   IMPOSSIBLE FIGURES

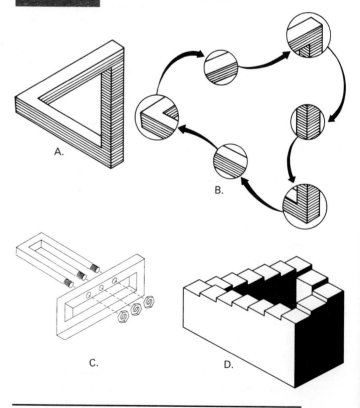

A.

B.

C.   D.

they are in diagonal rows because the orientation of each image is seen in relation to the reference frame established by the whole row (Palmer, 1984, 1989). In effect, you see the shapes of the images as you would if the rows were vertical instead of diagonal (turn the book 45 degrees clockwise to see this phenomenon).

There are other ways to establish a contextual reference frame that has the same effect. These same images appear inside of rectangular frames tilted 45 degrees in C of Figure 8.19. If you cover the frames, the left image resembles a diamond and the right one a square. When you uncover the frames, the left one changes into a square and the right one into a diamond.

SPATIAL AND TEMPORAL INTEGRATION

Reference frames are just one example of the visual system's tendency to organize individual parts in relation to larger spatial contexts. In fact, even the whole visual field at any moment is seldom perceived as ending at the edges of our vision. Instead, we perceive it as a restricted glimpse of a large visual world extending in all directions to unseen areas of the environment.

each fixation of corners and sides provides an interpretation that is consistent with an object that seems to be a three-dimensional triangle (image A); but when you try to integrate them into a coherent whole, the pieces just don't fit together properly (image B). Image C has two arms that somehow turn into 3 prongs right before your vigilant gaze, and the perpetual staircase in image D forever ascends or descends.

MOTION PERCEPTION

Although most of the visible environment is usually stationary, certain kinds of objects are not. Those that move tend to be especially significant to us because they are likely to be potential predators, prey, enemies, mates, or dangerous objects. Being able to perceive motion is critical for survival.

It is tempting to think that all of our motion perception can be accounted for by "motion-detector" cells in our brains, as described in the last chapter. Unfortunately, motion perception is a far more complicated affair, requiring that higher levels of perceptual organization in the brain integrate and interpret the responses of different retinal cells over time.

Similar to orientation, motion is not perceived absolutely but relative to a reference frame. If you sit in a darkened room and fixate on a stationary spot of light inside a lighted rectangle that is moving very slowly back and forth, you will perceive instead a *moving* dot going back and forth within a *stationary* rectangle. This illusion, called **induced motion,** occurs even when your eyes are quite still and fixated on the dot. Your motion-detector cells are not firing at all in response to the stationary dot, but presumably, are firing in response to the moving lines of the rectangle creating the perception of motion. To see the dot as moving requires some higher level of perceptual organization in which the dot and its supposed motion are perceived within the reference frame provided by the rectangle.

There seems to be a strong tendency for the visual system to take a larger, surrounding figure as the reference frame for a smaller figure inside it. You have probably experienced induced motion many times without knowing it. The moon (which is nearly stationary) frequently looks as if it is moving through a cloud when, in fact, it is the cloud that is moving past the moon. The surrounding cloud induces perceived movement in the moon just as the rectangle does in the dot (Rock, 1982, 1986).

Sometimes, when you are moving, you might experience the illusion that components of the visual field are moving. Have you ever been in a train that started moving very slowly? Didn't it seem as if the pillars on the station platform or a stationary train next to you

The moon appears to move through the clouds when, actually, it is the clouds that are moving rapidly.

might be moving backward instead? Another movement illusion that demonstrates the existence of some higher-level organizing processes for motion perception is called **apparent motion.** The simplest form of apparent motion, the **phi phenomenon,** occurs when two stationary spots of light in different positions in the visual field are turned on and off alternately at a rate of about 4 to 5 times per second. This effect occurs on outdoor advertising signs and in disco light displays. Even at this relatively slow rate of alternation, it appears that a single light is moving back and forth between the two spots. There are multiple ways to conceive of the path that leads from the location of the first dot to the location of the second dot. Yet, human observers normally see only the simplest path: a straight line (Shepard, 1984; Cutting & Proffitt, 1986).

All the organizational processes we have discussed so far explain how humans can see a unified world in the successive, partial, and unorganized patterns of stimulation that affect our sensory organs. Unlike Dr. Richard, we are able to synthesize the many bits of sensory information we receive to make sense of them. There is no question that our brains perform this synthesis very well, but perception psychologists are still trying to figure out the way brains do it.

DEPTH PERCEPTION

Until now, we have considered only two-dimensional patterns on flat surfaces. Everyday perceiving, however, involves objects in three-dimensional space. Perceiving all three spatial dimensions is absolutely vital for you to approach what you want, such as good food and interesting people, and avoid what is dangerous, such as speeding cars. This perception requires accurate information about *depth* (the distance from you to an object) as well as about its *direction* from you. Your ears can help in determining direction, but they are not much help in determining depth.

Seeing how far away an object is may not seem to be much of a problem, but have you ever tried to figure out how the visual system does it? Keep in mind that the visual system must rely on retinal images that have only two spatial dimensions—vertical and horizontal. The visual system has no third dimension for depth.

To illustrate the problem of having a 2-D retina doing a 3-D job, consider the situation shown in **Figure 8.21.** When a spot of light stimulates the retina at point a, how do you know whether it came from position a1 or a2? In fact, it could have come from *anywhere* along line A because light from any point on that line projects onto the same retinal cell. Similarly, all points on line B project onto the single retinal point b. To make matters worse, a straight line connecting any point on line A to any point on line B (a_1 to b_2 or a_2 to b_1, for example) would produce the same image on the retina. The net result is that the image on your retina is ambiguous in depth: it could have been produced by objects at any one of several different distances. For this reason, the same retinal image can be given many different perceptual interpretations.

The ambiguity of the Necker cube on page 263 results from this ambiguity in depth. The fact that you can be fooled under certain circumstances, shows that depth perception requires an *interpretation* of sensory input and that this interpretation can be wrong. Your interpretation relies on many different information sources about distance (often called *depth cues*), among them binocular cues, motion cues, and pictorial cues.

Binocular Cues

Have you ever wondered why you have two eyes instead of just one? The second eye is more than just a spare—it provides some of the best, most compelling information about depth. The two sources of binocular depth information are *binocular disparity* and *convergence*.

Because the eyes are about two to three inches apart horizontally, they receive slightly different views of the world. To convince yourself of this, try the following experiment. First, close your left eye and use the right one to line up your two index fingers with some small object in the distance, holding one finger at arm's length and the other about a foot in front of your face. Now, keeping your fingers stationary, close your right eye and open the left one while continuing to fixate on the distant object. What happened to the position of your two fingers? The second eye does not see them

FIGURE 8.21   DEPTH AMBIGUITY

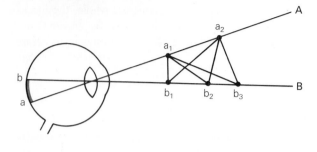

lined up with the distant object because it gets a slightly different view.

This displacement between the horizontal positions of corresponding images in your two eyes is called *binocular disparity*. It provides depth information because the amount of disparity, or difference, depends on the relative distance of objects from you. For instance, when you switched eyes, the closer finger was displaced farther to the side than was the distant finger.

When you look at the world with both eyes open, most objects that you see stimulate different positions on your two retinas. The object you directly focus on projects onto the two foveae. Any other objects that happen to be at that same distance from you will also project onto corresponding retinal positions in the two eyes, but all other objects will actually produce images at different places on the two retinas because of binocular disparity. If the disparity between corresponding images in the two retinas is small enough, the visual system is able to fuse them into a perception of a single object in depth. However, if the images are too far apart, as when you cross your eyes, you actually see the double images.

When you stop to think about it, what your visual system does is pretty amazing: it takes two different retinal images, compares them for horizontal displacement of corresponding parts (binocular disparity), and produces a unitary perception of a single object in depth. In effect, the visual system interprets horizontal displacement between the two images as depth in the three-dimensional world.

Other binocular information about depth comes from *convergence*. The two eyes turn inward to some extent whenever they are fixated on an object (see **Figure 8.22**). When the object is very close—a few inches in front of your face—the eyes must turn toward each other quite a bit for the same image to fall on both foveae. You can actually see the eyes converge if you watch a friend focus first on a distant object and then on one a foot or so away.

FIGURE 8.22   CONVERGENCE CUES TO DEPTH

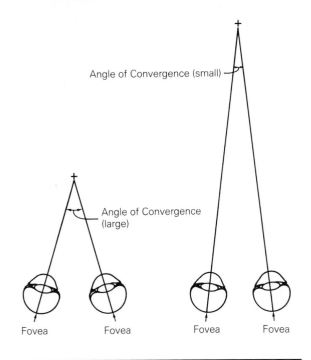

Convergence information sent back to the brain from the eye muscles is useful for depth perception only up to about 10 feet, however. At greater distances the angular differences are too small to detect, because the eyes are nearly parallel when you fixate on a distant object.

Motion Cues

To see how motion produces depth information, try the following demonstration. Close one eye, line up your two index fingers with some distant object as you did before, and then move your head to the side while fixating on the distant object and keeping your fingers still. As you move your head, you see both your fingers move, but the close finger seems to move farther and faster than the more distant one. The fixated object does not move at all. This source of information about depth is called **relative motion parallax.**

Motion parallax provides information about depth because, as you move, the relative distances of objects in the real world determine the amount and direction of their relative motion in your retinal image of the scene. When you are moving in a stationary environment, the speed and direction of motion of points in your retinal image depends on their distance in depth relative to the fixated point (which does not move).

Pictorial Cues

Further sources of information about depth are available from even just one eye and no motion of the head. These sources are called *pictorial cues,* because they include the kinds of depth information found in pictures. Artists who create pictures in what appear to be three dimensions (on the two dimensions of a piece of paper or canvas) make skilled use of pictorial cues.

Interposition, or *occlusion,* arises when an opaque object blocks the light coming toward your eye from an object behind it so that only the front object is fully present in your retinal image. Interposition gives you depth information indicating that the occluded object is farther away than the occluding one. Opaque surfaces block light, creating shadows, producing more depth information about three-dimensional shape and about the position of the light source.

Three additional sources of pictorial information are all related to the way light projects from a three-dimensional world onto a two-dimensional surface such as the retina: relative size, linear perspective, and texture gradients. Relative size involves a basic rule of light projection: objects of the same size at different distances project images of different sizes on the retina. The closest one projects the largest image and the farthest one the smallest image. This rule is called the *size/distance relation.* The size/distance relation makes *relative size* a cue for depth perception. *Linear perspective* is a depth cue that also depends on the size/distance relation. When parallel lines (by definition separated along their lengths by the same distance) recede into the distance, they converge toward a point on the horizon in your retinal image. This very important fact was discovered around 1400 by Italian Renaissance artists who were then able to paint depth compellingly for the first time (Vasari, 1967). Prior to their discovery, artists had incorporated in their paintings information from interposition, shadows, and relative size, but they had been unable to depict realistic scenes that showed objects at various distances. Application of Euclidean theorems of geometry to create illusionistic effects (as first devised by Brunelleschi) had a great impact on the history of Western art (Kemp, 1990). The third kind of pictorial depth cue comes from Gibson's *texture gradients.* Images of uniform texture are smaller at greater than closer distances because they are projected onto smaller areas of the retina. The wheat field in **Figure 8.23** is an example of the way texture is used as a depth cue. The gradients result from the size/distance relation but are applied to textures of surfaces rather than to edges. Although the texture of a surface, such as a rug or tile floor, is actually uniform, the size/distance relation requires that its texture elements that are far away appear smaller than those that are closer.

FIGURE 8.23 *EXAMPLES OF TEXTURE AS A DEPTH CUE*

The wheat field is a natural example of the way texture is used as a depth cue. Notice the way wheat slants. The geometric design uses the same principles.

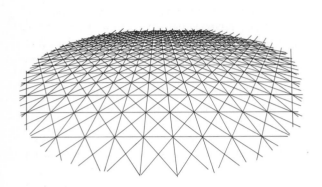

By now, it should be clear that there are many sources of depth information. Under normal viewing conditions, however, information from these sources comes together in a single, coherent three-dimensional interpretation of the environment. You experience depth, not the different cues to depth that existed in the proximal stimulus. In other words, you don't perceive double images, differential motion, interposition, shadows, relative size, or convergence of parallel lines, even though all these factors are constantly present in the patterns of light that enter your eyes (unless you are an art student especially sensitive to drawing perspective). Rather, your visual system uses these sources of information automatically, without your conscious awareness, to make the complex computations that give you a perception of depth in the three-dimensional environment, which is what you consciously experience.

It may even be true that your depth perception processes are at work when you don't consciously experience depth. This idea underlies the usual explanation of the *Ponzo illusion* (see **Figure 8.24**). The upper line looks longer because you unconsciously interpret the converging sides according to linear perspective as parallel lines receding into the distance, similar to railroad tracks. Thus, you unconsciously process the upper line as though it were farther away, so you see it as longer—a farther object would have to be longer than

a nearer one for both to produce retinal images of the same size. The illusion is created by the converging lines that add a dimension of depth and by the distance cue.

PERCEPTUAL CONSTANCIES

The goal of perception is to obtain information about the world around us not about images on our sensory organs. We have already shown a number of ways in which the human visual system meets this goal by going beyond the information it is given directly. Another very important way it meets the goal is by perceiving an unchanging world despite the constant changes that occur in viewing conditions, creating different patterns of stimulation on the retina.

Put this book down on the table, then move your head closer to it so that it's just a few inches away. Then move your head back to a normal reading distance. Although the book stimulated a much larger part of your retina when it was up close than when it was far away, you saw the book's size as constant.

Now set the book upright and try tilting your head clockwise. When you do this, the image of the book rotates counterclockwise on your retina, but you still perceive the book to be upright: its perceived orientation is *constant*. In general, then, you see the world as

FIGURE 8.24   *THE PONZO ILLUSION*

The converging lines add a dimension of depth, and, therefore, the distance cue makes the top line appear larger than the bottom line, even though they are actually the same length.

invariant, constant, and *stable* despite changes in the stimulation of your sensory receptors. Psychologists refer to this general phenomenon as **perceptual constancy.** Roughly speaking, it means that you perceive the properties of the distal stimuli, which are generally constant, rather than the properties of proximal stimuli, which change every time you move your eyes or head. For survival it is critical that we perceive constant and stable properties of continuing objects in the world despite the enormous variations in the properties of the light patterns that stimulate our eyes. Without constancy, our eyes really wouldn't do us much good, because we wouldn't be seeing the world out there but only the images on the backs of our eyes. The task of perception is to discover *invariant* properties of our environment despite the *variations* in our retinal impressions of them.

Under extreme conditions, perceptual constancy nearly always breaks down. For example, when you look at people from the top of a skyscraper, they resem-

ble ants. However, under normal circumstances, constancy holds over almost all visible properties. In this section we will discuss only three such properties in which constancy has been intensively studied: size, shape, and orientation.

Size and Shape Constancy

What determines your perception of the size of an object? In part, you perceive an object's actual size on the basis of the size of its retinal image. However, the demonstration with your book shows that the size of the retinal image depends on both the actual size of the book and its *distance* from the eye. Because of this relation between size and distance (the same one we discussed in the section on depth perception), the perceptual system must determine an object's actual size by combining information from the size of its retinal image with other information about its distance. As you now know, information about distance is available from a variety of depth cues. Your visual system combines that information with retinal information about image size to yield a perception of an object size that usually corresponds to the actual size of the distal stimulus. **Size constancy** refers to this ability to perceive the true size of an object despite variations in the size of its retinal image.

The theory that size constancy is achieved by comparing retinal size to distance was first proposed by Helmholtz (Cutting, 1987). He called the perceptual process that makes the comparison *unconscious inference.* It is a process of inference because the visual system must figure out, or infer, the size of an object by combining several different kinds of information. It is unconscious because the observer is not aware of knowing the size/distance relation or of using it to perceive objective size. Unconscious inferences about the true sizes of objects seem to be made rapidly, automatically, and without conscious effort of any sort—a major achievement in our perceptual processing of information.

If the size of an object is perceived by taking distance cues into account, then we should be fooled about size whenever we are fooled about distance. One such illusion occurs in the Ames room shown in **Figure 8.25.** In comparison to his four-foot daughter Tanya, your six-foot-tall author looks quite short in the left corner of this room, but he looks enormous in the right corner. The reason for this illusion is that you perceive the room to be rectangular, with the two back corners equally distant from you. Thus you perceive my actual size as being consistent with the size of the images on your retina in both cases. In fact, however, I am not at the same distance, because the Ames room creates a clever illusion. It appears to be a rectangular room, but

FIGURE 8.25   THE AMES ROOM

A.

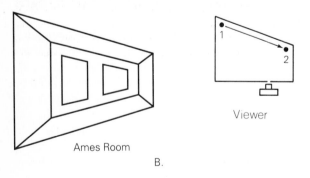

Ames Room

Viewer

B.

it is actually made from nonrectangular surfaces at odd angles in depth and height as you can see in the drawings that accompany the photos. Any person on the right will make a larger retinal image because he or she is twice as close to the observer.

Another way that the perceptual system can infer objective size is by using prior knowledge about the characteristic size of similarly shaped objects. For instance, once you recognize the shape of a house, a tree, or a dog, you have a pretty good idea of how big each is, even without knowing its distance from you. Most of the time your perception is correct, but, as movie directors are well aware, miniature scenery constructed to scale can give you a perception of normally sized real objects. Universal Studios in Hollywood uses the following trick in its set for Westerns. The set consists of an average street in a typical western town. However, the doors on one side of the street are much smaller than the doors on the other side of the street. When shooting the scenes of the westerns, directors position male actors on the side of the street with small doors. This makes them look bigger. Female actors, on the other hand, get filmed on the other side of the street, against the background of large doors, which make them look petite.

Sometimes shape information is not sufficient to produce accurate perception of size, especially when past experience does not give you a knowledge of what familiar objects look like at extreme distances. This phenomenon happened to a man named Kenge of the equatorial Africa Pygmy culture. Kenge had lived in dense tropical forests all his life. He was accustomed to using sound cues to guide his hunting. Kenge had occasion, one day, to travel by car for the first time across an open plain with anthropologist Colin Turnbull. Later, the anthropologist described Kenge's reactions.

> Kenge looked over the plains and down to where a herd of about a hundred buffalo were grazing some miles away. He asked me what kind of *insects* they were, and I told him they were buffalo, twice as big as the forest buffalo known to him. He laughed loudly and told me not to tell such stupid stories, and asked me again what kind of insects they were. He then talked to himself, for want of more intelligent company, and tried to liken the buffalo to the various beetles and ants with which he was familiar.
>
> He was still doing this when we got into the car and drove down to where the animals were grazing. He watched them getting larger and larger, and though he was as courageous as any Pygmy, he moved over and sat close to me and muttered that it was witchcraft. . . . Finally, when

The two little men may not look it, but they are exactly the same size. Most people see the little man on the right as smaller because they unconsciously use distance to judge the size of something familiar.

and as the fast-moving car approached them and Kenge's retinal images got larger and larger, he had the frightening illusion that the animals were changing in size. We can assume that, with further experience, he would have come to see them as Turnbull did.

Shape constancy is closely related to size constancy. You perceive an object's actual shape correctly even when it is slanted away from you, making the shape of the retinal image substantially different from that of the object itself. For instance, a circle tipped away from you projects an elliptical image onto your retina; a rectangle tipped away projects a trapezoidal image (see **Figure 8.26**). Yet you usually perceive the shapes accurately as a circle and a rectangle slanted away in space. When there is good depth information available from binocular disparity, motion parallax, or even pictorial cues, your visual system can determine an object's true shape simply by taking your distance from its different parts into account.

Orientation Constancy

When you tilted your head to the side in viewing your book, the world did not seem to tilt; only your own head did. Orientation constancy is our ability to recognize the true orientation of the figure in the real world, even though its orientation in the retinal image is changed. This form of constancy, too, results from a process of unconscious inference. Information about the orientation of an object in the environment is inferred from the orientation of its retinal image. In addition, head tilt is taken into account, largely through the vestibular system in your inner ear (discussed in Chapter 7). By using the output of the vestibular system with retinal orientation, your visual system is usually able to give you a perception of the orientation of an object in the environment.

Field Dependence Versus Independence   In familiar environments, prior knowledge provides additional information about objective orientation. While we are good at recognizing simple and familiar objects, complex and unfamiliar figures are not as recognizable, es-

he realized that they were real buffalo he was no longer afraid, but what puzzled him still was why they had been so small, and whether they *really* had been small and had so suddenly grown larger, or whether it had been some kind of trickery (Turnbull, 1961, p. 305).

In this unfamiliar perceptual environment, Kenge first tried to fit his novel perceptions into a familiar context, by assuming the tiny, distant specks he saw were insects. With no previous experience seeing buffalo at a distance, he had no basis for size constancy,

---

SHAPE CONSTANCY

As a coin is rotated, its image becomes an ellipse that grows narrower and narrower until it becomes a thin rectangle, an ellipse again, and then a circle. At each orientation, however, it is still perceived as a circular coin.

pecially when they are seen in unusual orientations. Can you recognize the shape in **Figure 8.27**?

When a figure is complex and consists of subparts, each part must be rotated mentally. It may not be possible to rotate so many parts at the same time (Rock, 1986). So, while one part is undergoing rotation, another part may still be perceived as unrotated. Look at the two upside-down pictures of former British Prime Minister Margaret Thatcher on this page before reading further. You can probably tell that one of them has been altered slightly around the eyes and mouth, but the two pictures look pretty similar. Now turn the book upside down and look again. The same pictures look extraordinarily different now. One is still Margaret Thatcher, but the other is a ghoulish monster that not even her mother could love! Your failure to see that obvious difference before turning the book upside down may be due to your inability to rotate all of the parts of the face at the same time. It is also a function of years of perceptual training to see the world right side up and to perceive faces in their visual orientation. Try this Thatcher test with young children to determine whether they detect the ghoul more quickly than adults do.

There are significant *individual differences* among people in reconciling contradictory data—some rely more heavily on internal vestibular information and others more heavily on visual information from the external environment. Are you the sort of person who has a strong interpersonal orientation and is emotionally open? Do you prefer nonsocial situations in which you

Which photo was taken after Margaret Thatcher resigned? Turn the book around for a different orientation.

can keep your emotions pretty much to yourself? Psychologists have found that your answer could probably be predicted from your performance on perceptual tests related to orientation perception. A personality dimension, called **field dependence,** has been proposed to reflect a person's preference for depending on external versus internal sources of information in both perceptual and social situations (Witkin & Goodenough, 1977).

The primary test for field dependence in perception requires subjects to judge when lines are vertical (aligned with gravity) in situations in which there is conflicting visual information. In one version of the test—the *rod-and-frame test*—subjects are shown a tilted rod inside a tilted frame with no other visual information. They are asked to adjust the tilt of the rod so that it is upright with respect to gravity. Some people are able to do this quite accurately despite the tilt of the frame. These people are called *field independent* because they seem to rely almost exclusively on *internal* bodily information provided by their vestibular and kinesthetic systems to define *vertical* and are able to ignore contradictory information from the visually tilted frame. Other people, however, adjust the rod so that it is strongly tilted toward the orientation of the frame. These people are called *field dependent* because they seem to *depend* more upon the *external* field information provided by the frame and less on internal information.

A number of studies have investigated the relation between field dependence and field independence in perceptual and social situations. In one such study, subjects were asked by an interviewer to talk about a topic that interested them. In one condition, the interviewer kept silent during the subject's response; in the other, the same interviewer gave feedback ("uh huh" or

FIGURE 8.27   *AFRICA ROTATED 90°*

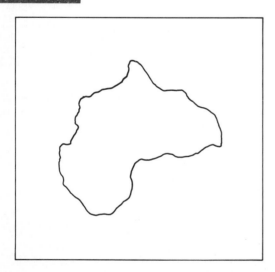

"yeah") during the response. Field-dependent subjects produced less verbal output in the silent condition than in the feedback condition, whereas field-independent subjects were not much affected by the interviewer's reactions. Later, when filling out questionnaires, field-dependent subjects more often agreed with the statement "I think I might have done a little better if the interviewer had told me at times just how I was doing," whereas field-independent subjects tended to agree with the statement "I don't think it made much difference one way or the other that the interviewer didn't tell me how I was doing during the interview" (Gates, 1971).

An interesting extension of this result to therapist-patient interactions is a finding based on analysis of therapy-session transcripts. Therapists ask more specific questions and give more support in sessions with their field-dependent patients than in sessions with their field-independent patients, even though they are unaware of this perceptual difference between the two kinds of patients (Witkin et al., 1977).

Many such studies have led to the conclusion that people shown to be field-dependent in a perceptual task tend to (a) make greater use of social feedback in ambiguous situations; (b) be more attentive to social cues; (c) be more interested in other people; (d) be emotionally open; (e) like social situations; and (f) choose careers in welfare, humanitarian, and helping professions. Field-independent people tend to (a) rely less on social feedback; (b) be generally less sensitive to social cues; (c) be more impersonal; (d) keep their emotions to themselves; (e) be less gregarious; and (f) choose careers in mathematical, scientific, and analytic professions (Witkin & Goodenough, 1977).

The correspondence between people's social preferences and their behavior on the rod-and-frame test suggests that we each have our own unique cognitive style that determines how we seek, acquire, and evaluate information about our environment, both physical and social (G. Klein, 1970).

SUMMING UP

The processes that put sensory information together to give us the perception of a coherent scene over the visual field are called the processes of perceptual organization. At the sensory stage, abrupt changes in color and texture result in region segregation—deciding which parts of visual field belong together. A further distinction that emerges is that between the figure (object-like regions) and ground (background against which the figures stand out).

Sometimes, we even perceive figures that are physically not there—such as illusory contours. Illusory contours demonstrate another important principle in perceptual organization—the principle of closure. We tend to perceive whole figures, complete disconnected borders, and fill in occluded parts. Several disjoint figures or parts may be perceived as a group if they are close to each other (the law of proximity), similar to each other (the law of similarity), move together (the law of common fate), or if they form a "good" figure (the law of symmetry). An underlying principle for the grouping laws has been suggested by Gestalt psychologists; the simplicity or pragnanz principle states that the simplest configuration requiring least cognitive effort will emerge.

The spatial and temporal context in which the figures occur establishes a reference frame, and the figures are perceived relative to their reference frames. The role of reference frames is particularly evident in motion perception. We assume larger objects are stationary, and we perceive the motion of smaller objects relative to the larger ones. Apparent motion occurs when two stationary spots of light are turned on and off in different positions in the visual field at given rates. Both the reference frame effects and the existence of apparent motion demonstrate the contribution of higher level perceptual processes to motion perception.

The most striking difference between the retinal image and the percept is that the retinal image is two-dimensional whereas the percept is three-dimensional. Depth perception requires interpretation of sensory input, and this interpretation relies on a number of depth cues, such as binocular cues, motion parallax, and pictorial cues. These factors affect the retinal image of the object, yet we correctly perceive the unchanging distal object; this paradox is the phenomenon of perceptual constancy. We have constancy for size, shape, and orientation of objects, as well as for other aspects of perception, such as brightness. Our ability to recognize a figure in unusual orientations is limited by our familiarity with the figure and especially by the figure's complexity. Simple figures are easily recognized in unfamiliar orientations; complex figures are harder to recognize. When a figure consists of multiple parts, the human perceptual system is not able to rotate all of the parts at the same time. Individual differences exist in the extent to which people are field dependent or field independent in their perception of stimuli. This personality difference shown in perceptual tasks is also revealed in social and emotional responding.

IDENTIFICATION AND RECOGNITION PROCESSES

You can think of all the perceptual processes described so far as providing reasonably accurate knowledge about physical properties of the distal stimulus—the position, size, shape, texture, and color of three-dimensional objects in a three-dimensional environment. With just this knowledge and some basic motor skills, you would be able to walk around without bumping into objects, manipulate objects that are small and light enough to move, and make accurate models of the objects that you perceive. However, you would not know what these objects were and whether you had seen them before. Your experience would resemble a visit to an alien planet where all the objects were new to you; you would not know what to eat, what to put on your head, what to run away from, and what to date.

To get information about the objects you perceive, you need to be able to identify or recognize them as something you have seen before and as members of the meaningful categories that you know about from experience. Identification and recognition attach meaning to percepts.

BOTTOM-UP AND TOP-DOWN PROCESSES

Identifying objects implies matching what you see against your stored knowledge. The processes of bringing in and organizing information from the environment are often called *data-driven* or bottom-up processes, because they are guided by sensory information—the raw data of direct experience. Sensations of visual features and perceptions of organized objects are largely the result of bottom-up processes. However, even at this level of hard evidence of sensory images, what your senses detect of all available environmental stimulation is heavily influenced by *attention,* as we noted earlier.

Processes that originate in the mind/brain and influence the selection, organization, or interpretation of sensory data are called *conceptually-driven* (or hypothesis-driven) or top-down processes. Abstract thoughts, prior knowledge, beliefs, values, and other aspects of an individual's higher mental processes control the way incoming stimulation is managed and even what qualifies as relevant (review Figure 8.3).

The importance of top-down processes can be illustrated by drawings known as *Droodles* (Price, 1953, 1980). Without the labels, these drawings are seen as meaningless doodles. However, once the drawings are identified, you can easily find meaning in them (see **Figure 8.28**). Clinical psychologists make use of our ability to use labels in order to organize our percepts; one striking example of this usage involves Rorschach

FIGURE 8.28   DROODLES

Do you see a woman scrubbing the floor (A) and a giraffe's neck (B)? Each of these figures can be seen as representing something familiar to us, although this perceptual recognition usually does not occur until some identifying information is provided.

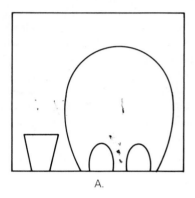

A.

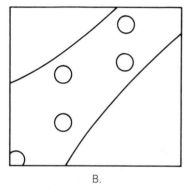

B.

inkblots, ambiguous images onto which people project meaning as dictated by their current motives and conflicts (see Chapter 15, p. 566).

Identification and recognition give our experiences continuity over time and across situations. The third stage of perceiving is a process in which memory, conceptual analysis, expectation, motivation, personality characteristics, and social experience are all involved in the comprehension of what is being perceived. To perception this stage adds *conception*—mental activity—and to facts it adds *meaning*.

Psychologists are trying to figure out the process that leads from the finished percept to the recognition and identification of a particular object. In addition, psychologists are interested in the way we classify patterns into particular categories and in the way identification is affected by expectations, contexts, and personal and social motivation factors.

RECOGNITION BY COMPONENTS

How do we recognize objects? What makes us decide that a grey, oddly shaped, medium sized, furry thing is actually a cat? Presumably, we have a memory representation of a cat, and the identification process consists of matching such a memory representation to the newly constructed percept and deciding that they are the same. Because computer scientists are attempting to teach computerized robots to recognize objects, they are especially interested in how these matches between memory representation and percept are accomplished. One possibility is that the memory representations of various objects consist of components and information about the way these components are attached to each other. Several different theories exist about the nature of such components (Biederman, 1985, 1987; Cooper, 1989; Marr & Nishihara, 1978). See, for example, **Figure 8.29.**

After the percept is constructed from primitive features, such as colors or edges, it also gets divided up into components, such as cylinders, cubes, and pyramids of various sizes. Then the components of the memory representation of the object get matched against the components of the percept. If a close match is found, the object is identified or recognized.

THE INFLUENCE OF CONTEXTS AND EXPECTATIONS

Have you ever had the experience of seeing people you knew in places where you didn't expect to see them, such as in the wrong city or the wrong social group? It takes much longer to recognize them in such situations, and sometimes you aren't even sure that you really know them. The problem is not that they look any different but that the *context* is wrong; you didn't *expect* them to be there. The spatial and temporal context in which objects are recognized provides an important source of information for classifying because once you have identified the context, you have expectations about what objects you are and are not likely to see nearby (Biederman, 1989).

Perceptual identification depends on your expectations as well as on the physical properties of the objects you see—*object identification is a constructive, interpretive process.* Depending on what you already know, where you are, what else you see around you, and

FIGURE 8.29 RECOGNITION BY COMPONENTS

Suggested components of 3-dimensional objects and examples of how they may combine. In the top half of the figure, each 3-D object is constructed of cylinders of different sizes. In the bottom half of the figure, several different building blocks are combined to form familiar objects.

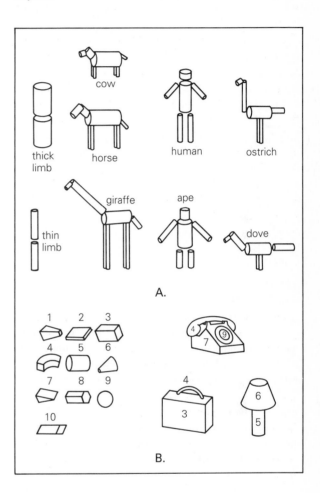

your expectations from context, the identification you make will vary. Read the following words.

They say *THE CAT,* right? Now look again at the middle letter of each word. Physically, these two letters are exactly the same, yet you perceived the first as an H and the second as an A. Why? Clearly, your perception was affected by what you know about words in English. The context provided by T__E makes an H highly likely and an A unlikely, whereas the reverse is true of the context of C__T (Selfridge, 1955).

Schemas

To account for contextual effects, it has been suggested that interpretation of perceptual data depends on complex information structures in memory. Instead of storing information in memory in isolated bits, we organize our knowledge of the world into integrated packages—clusters of information called *schemas*. A **schema** is a cognitive structure that represents knowledge about a concept or about a type of stimulus, including its attributes (characteristics) and the relations among those attributes (Fiske & Taylor, 1991). Schemas reflect an important function of the human mind. They reveal the way perception of reality is actively constructed through the interplay of external stimulus information and the personal experiences and knowledge that we bring into every perceptual setting. Schemas are made up of information from different sources organized around various topics, themes, and types. We have schemas about dating, college lectures, restaurants, and good friends, for example. Schemas may organize information according to objects, activities, people, or ideas that usually are found together or share some basic features.

Schemas not only are a source of factual knowledge in relevant situations, they are a source of expectations. Once formed, they exert powerful influences on the way we *predict* what objects are *likely* to be present in a given context. We then use both these expectations and sensory and perceptual information to recognize the objects in the visual field. All this happens very quickly, automatically, and preconsciously. We will have a more detailed look in later chapters at the influence of schemas in remembering and thinking.

Perceptual Set

Another aspect of the influence of context and expectation on your perception (and response) is set. **Set** is a temporary readiness to perceive or react to a stimulus in a particular way. There are three types of set: motor, mental, and perceptual. A *motor set* is a readiness to make a quick, prepared response. A runner trains by perfecting a motor set to come out of the blocks as fast as possible at the sound of the starting gun. A *mental set* is a readiness to deal with a situation, such as a problem-solving task or a game, in a way determined by learned rules, instructions, expectations, or habitual tendencies. A mental set can actually prevent you from solving a problem when the old rules don't seem to fit the new situation, as we'll see when we study

problem solving in a later chapter. However, set can facilitate responding by inhibiting irrelevant or wrong responses. Game-show contestants who compete to answer first typically reveal the operation of this set. A *perceptual set* is a readiness to detect a particular stimulus in a given context—a new mother is perceptually set to hear the cries of her child. Often, a perceptual set leads you to see an ambiguous stimulus as the one you are expecting.

a. FOX; OWL; SNAKE; TURKEY; SWAN; D?CK

b. BOB; RAY; DAVE; BILL; HENRY; D?CK

Look at the series of words in row a. Have a friend look at the words in row b at the same time. If you both have to call out the missing letter in the same ambiguous stimulus D?CK, will the differences in your perceptual sets make a difference in your responses? Definitely. Test it yourself.

Labels can provide a context that gives a perceptual set for an ambiguous figure. We have seen how meaningless droodles turn into meaningful objects. Look carefully at the picture of the woman in **Figure 8.30A** on this page; have a friend examine **Figure 8.30B** on page 296. Next, together look at **Figure 8.30C** on page 297—what do each of you see? Did the prior exposure to the unambiguous pictures with their labels have any effect on either perception of the ambiguous image?

This demonstration shows how easy it is for people to develop different views of the same person or object given prior conditions that create different sets. Mental and perceptual sets can also act as a part of social attitudes or can bias how we interpret some part of our world.

FIGURE 8.30   *A. Young Beauty*

The Role of Personal and Social Factors

Each of us brings more to the act of perceiving our world than sensory receptors; we each carry a unique history, sets of personal experiences, needs, styles of coping, and personality. These social characteristics affect our perception which takes place in social contexts. These variables also enter into the top-down processes that can come to influence our perception, especially when the stimulus is somewhat ambiguous or lacks clarity.

There are many ways in which social variables may influence perception. Broad cultural influences set basic, accepted social categories that determine standards for beauty, fear, appropriateness, or unacceptability. Socially learned attitudes can function as anchors or standards by which new inputs are often evaluated without conscious awareness of their biasing influence (Deregowski, 1980). It is not surprising that the way an individual classifies objects and events in the environment can also be affected by the ways other similar people classify the same things. After all, we humans are social creatures who depend on interactions with others for many of our most significant experiences and for much of our information.

A tragic example of how visual functioning may be affected by personal experiences comes from a study of 30 Cambodian female refugees who appeared to be blind, but who, upon examination, had no physiological basis for the visual loss. They were suffering *psychosomatic blindness* brought about by harrowing wartime trauma. Ninety percent of these refugees reported loss of from one to ten close family members and all had experienced forced labor, starvation, and dangerous escapes to refugee camps in Thailand. They coped with their stressful experiences in part by blocking out visual perception of the external world (Rozee & Van Boemel, 1989).

This dramatic reaction to trauma can be viewed as the extreme of a personality dimension—*leveling versus sharpening*—that psychologists have related to a variety of perceptual tasks. Leveling and sharpening are two poles on the dimension of *cognitive style*. Levelers tend to smooth over what seems irregular, novel, or unusual and omit details in order to give a more homogenous and less incongruous interpretation of the stimulus event. Levelers are also more likely to miss subtle differences—their perceptions are dominated by similarities apparently because their perceptual processing is too much influenced by memory of what has gone before. By contrast, when given a task with a sequence of gradually changing stimuli, sharpeners see the elements of each stimulus display as independent of what went before, accentuating and overemphasizing details. They

tend to perceive the elements of a situation more accurately than do levelers, but they may miss the forest by focusing too closely on the trees.

People who typically deal with threats by denying their potential significance or who avoid noticing or classifying them as threats are termed *repressors*. At the opposite end of this continuum are *sensitizers* who tend to be especially vigilant, perceiving subtle, disguised cues of potential approaching threats. The *repressor-sensitizer continuum* is related to a variety of cognitive-perceptual behaviors (Ericksen, 1966). For example, when shown very sexually explicit pictures, repressors look very little and recall much less than sensitizers (Luborsky et al., 1965). Such differences probably arise from the ways the two groups use attentional processes: the sensitizers have developed a more active scanning and searching attention than the repressors.

Many interesting findings have emerged from attempts to understand the process of perception in terms of the people who use it or to "put the person back into perception." However, there is yet to emerge a comprehensive theory that integrates the complex network of processes involved in perception, cognition, and personality.

Creatively Playful Perception

Because of our ability to go beyond the sensory gifts that evolution has bestowed on our species, we can become more creative in the way we perceive the world.

Is this figure possible?

Our role model is not a perfectly programmed computerized robot with exceptional sensory acuity; instead, it is Pablo Picasso. Picasso's genius was, in part, attributable to his enormous talent for "playful perception." This artist could free himself from the bonds of perceptual and mental sets to see not the old in the new but the new in the old, the novel in the familiar, and the unusual figure concealed within the familiar ground.

Perceptual creativity involves experiencing the world in ways that are imaginative, personally enriching, and fun (as illustrated in Herbert Leff's original work, 1984). You can accomplish perceptual creativity by consciously directing your attention and full awareness to the objects and activities around you. Your goal is to become more flexible in what you allow yourself to perceive and think, remaining open to yet another alternative response to a situation.

I can think of no better way to conclude this rather formal presentation of the psychology of perception than by proposing ten suggestions for playfully enhancing your powers of perception:

- Imagine everyone you meet is really a machine designed to look humanoid, and all machines are really people designed to look inanimate.
- Notice all wholes as ready to come apart into separately functioning pieces that can make it on their own.
- Imagine that your mental clock is hooked up to a video recorder that can rewind, fast forward, and freeze time.
- Recognize that most objects around you have a "family resemblance" to other objects.
- View the world as if you were an animal or a home appliance.

FIGURE 8.30   *B. OLD HAG*

- Consider one new use for each object you view (use a tennis racket to drain cooked spaghetti).
- Suspend the law of causality so that events just happen, while coincidence and chance rule over causes and effects.
- Dream up alternative meanings for the objects and events in your life.
- Discover something really interesting about activities and people you used to find boring.
- Violate some of the assumptions that you and others have about what you would and wouldn't do (without engaging in a dangerous activity).

FINAL LESSONS

The important lessons to be learned from the classification dimension of the overall perceptual experience can now be summarized broadly. The top-down effects of expectations, personality, and social influence variables all highlight the same important fact: perceptual experience in response to a stimulus event is a response of the whole person. In addition to the information provided when your sensory receptors are stimulated, your final perception depends on who you are, whom you are with, and what you expect, want, and value.

FIGURE 8.30   *C. NOW WHAT DO YOU SEE?*

The interaction of top-down and bottom-up processes also means that perception is an act of constructing reality to fit one's assumptions about how reality probably is or should be. A perceiver often plays two different roles that we can compare to gambling and interior design. As a *gambler*, a perceiver is willing to bet that the present input can be understood in terms of past knowledge and personal theories; but a gambler may not know "when to hold 'em" and "when to fold 'em," as the song goes. A perceiver can also resemble a *compulsive interior decorator,* constantly rearranging the stimuli so that they fit better and are more coherent. Incongruity and messy perceptions are rejected in favor of those with clear, clean, consistent lines.

If perceiving were completely *data-driven,* we would all be bound to the same mundane, concrete reality of the here and now. We could register experience but not profit from it on later occasions, nor would we see the world differently under different personal circumstances. If processing in perception were completely *hypothesis-driven,* however, we would each be lost in our fantasy worlds of what we expect and hope to perceive. A proper balance between the two extremes achieves the basic goal of perception: to experience what is out there in a way that maximally serves our needs as biological and social beings moving about and adapting to our physical and social environment.

The Task of Perception

Our perceptual systems do not simply record information about the external world but actively organize and interpret information as well. Knowledge about perceptual illusions can give us clues about normal organizing processes. Perception is a constructive process of going beyond sensory stimulation to discover what objects exist in the world around us. The task of perception is to determine what the distal (external) stimulus is from the information contained in the proximal (sensory) stimulus.

Sensing, Perceiving, Identifying, and Recognizing

At the sensory level of processing, physical energy is detected and transformed into neural energy and sensory experience. At the perceptual level, brain processes organize sensations into coherent images and give us perception of objects and patterns. At the level of identification, percepts of objects are compared to memory representations in order to be recognized as familiar and meaningful objects. Perception is a three-stage process consisting of a sensory stage, a perceptual organization stage, and an identification and recognition stage. Ambiguity may arise when the same sensory information is organized into different percepts. It is also possible for the same percepts to be interpreted or identified differently.

Attentional Processes

Attention refers to our ability to select part of the sensory input and disregard the rest. Attention may serve several functions. It may be necessary for successful synthesis of sensory information into perceptual objects (early selection view); for making sure that we respond only to the most important stimuli (late selection view); or for providing conscious access to the attended, most important stimuli. Attention may accomplish its tasks either by suppressing the processing of irrelevant, unattended stimuli (inhibition) or by facilitating the processing of the relevant, attended stimuli (facilitation). Without attention, only simple physical characteristics of objects, such as color or loudness of pitch, reach our consciousness. Attention also guarantees that simple physical properties of ob-

jects will be combined correctly and that this information, as well as information about an object's identity, will reach consciousness. Our ability to pay attention to several sources of stimulation at once is severely limited. It depends on (a) whether the tasks involved make use of the same processing resources and (b) to what extent each of these tasks can be carried out automatically.

Organizational Processes in Perception

Organizational processes provide percepts consistent with the sensory data. These processes segregate our percepts into regions and organize them into figures that stand out against the ground. We tend to see incomplete figures as wholes; group items by similarity; and see "good" figures more readily.

We tend to organize and interpret parts in relation to the spatial and temporal context in which we experience them. We also tend to see a reference frame as stationary and the parts within it as moving, regardless of the actual sensory stimulus. In converting the two-dimensional information on the retina to a perception of three-dimensional space, the visual system gauges object size and distance: distance is interpreted on the basis of known size and size is interpreted on the basis of various distance cues. We tend to perceive objects as retaining the same size, shape, and orientation. Prior knowledge normally reinforces these and other constancies in perception; under extreme conditions, perceptual constancy may break down.

Identification and Recognition Processes

During the final stage of perceptual processing—identification and recognition of objects—percepts are given meaning through processes that draw on memory, expectation, motivation, and personality characteristics. Expectations, schemas, and perceptual sets may guide recognition of incomplete or ambiguous data in one direction rather than another equally possible one. Personality characteristics, motives, and social influences contribute to the meanings of perceptual data and may lead us to distort the data. Perception, thus, depends on who we are, what we know and expect, and the nature of the sensory stimulus.

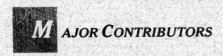KEY TERMS

AI approach, 268
ambiguity, 262
apparent motion, 283
automaticity, 277
bottom-up processing, 260
closure, 280
delusion, 262
dichotic listening, 273
distal stimulus, 259
distraction, 269
field dependence, 290
figural goodness, 281
figure, 279
Gestalt psychology, 267
ground, 279
hallucination, 260
identification and recognition, 258
illusion, 260
illusory conjunctions, 271
induced motion, 283
interposition, 285
law of common fate, 281
law of pragnanz, 281

law of proximity, 280
law of similarity, 281
percept, 256
perception, 257
perceptual constancy, 287
perceptual grouping, 280
perceptual organization, 278
phi phenomenon, 283
preattentive processing, 269
proximal stimulus, 259
reference frames, 281
relative motion parallax, 285
schema, 294
self-deception, 262
sensation, 257
set, 294
shape constancy, 289
size constancy, 287
subjective contours, 280
theory of ecological optics, 267
top-down processing, 260
transactional perception, 267
unconscious inference, 267

MAJOR CONTRIBUTORS

Broadbent, Donald, 272
Gibson, James, 267
von Helmholtz, Hermann, 267
Koffka, Kurt, 268
Kohler, Wolfgang, 268

Kraft, Conrad, 255
Oppel, J. J., 262
Richard, Dr., 257
Treisman, Anne, 272
Wertheimer, Max, 268

Chapter 9

Learning
and
Behavior Analysis

THE STUDY OF LEARNING   302
  WHAT IS LEARNING?
  BEHAVIORISM AND BEHAVIOR ANALYSIS

  ■ *INTERIM SUMMARY*

**CLASSICAL CONDITIONING: LEARNING
PREDICTABLE SIGNALS**   306
  PAVLOV'S SURPRISING DISCOVERY
  BASIC PROCESSES
  SIGNIFICANCE OF CLASSICAL CONDITIONING
  *THE ROLE OF CONTINGENCY AND
    INFORMATIVENESS*
  CLOSE-UP: LEARNING TO BE A DRUG ADDICT

  ■ *INTERIM SUMMARY*

**OPERANT CONDITIONING: LEARNING ABOUT
CONSEQUENCES**   316
  THE LAW OF EFFECT
  EXPERIMENTAL ANALYSIS OF BEHAVIOR
  REINFORCEMENT CONTINGENCIES

PROPERTIES OF REINFORCERS
SHAPING AND CHAINING
SCHEDULES OF REINFORCEMENT
*BIOFEEDBACK: BOOSTING WEAK RESPONSE
  SIGNALS*
LEARNED HELPLESSNESS

  ■ *INTERIM SUMMARY*

LEARNING, BIOLOGY, AND COGNITION   329
  BIOLOGICAL CONSTRAINTS ON LEARNING
  COGNITIVE INFLUENCES ON LEARNING
  CONNECTIONIST LEARNING MODELS
  APPLIED BEHAVIOR ANALYSIS

RECAPPING MAIN POINTS   338

KEY TERMS   339

MAJOR CONTRIBUTORS   339

During a routine checkup, the doctor finds that your blood pressure is dangerously high. She explains that untreated hypertension can lead to heart failure, stroke, kidney damage, retinal damage, and even seizures. You are not overweight or diabetic, and you reassure the doctor that you don't smoke or drink. Yes, life's a little stressful, especially since school, work, and family concerns all make demands on you at the same time, but you can't do much about that right now. The doctor tells you that she is putting you on an antihypertensive drug. You express concern about side effects—you know someone who became impotent when he took the same drug. The doctor says not to worry—side effects should give you little trouble after the first few weeks. To your relief, after a short time, your blood pressure returns to normal.

Unbeknownst to you, a few weeks after you started taking the drug, your doctor replaced the real medication with a placebo—in this case, a drug that has no actual physiological effect. Today, use of the placebo is one of the most promising developments in modern medicine. In a recent set of experiments, researchers **Robert Ader** and Anthony Suchman found that hypertensive patients who were taken off medication while continuing to be treated with placebos maintained healthy blood pressures longer than patients who did not get placebos (Ader & Suchman, 1991; Suchman & Ader, 1989).

How can an inert pill cure hypertension? After repeated exposures to the real drug, the physical ritual involved in taking

Robert Ader (*Discovering Psychology,* 1990, Program 8).

the drug became associated with the physiological changes involved in lowering blood pressure. Patients did not have to learn consciously that a medication reduced the force of the heartbeat, increased salts and water excreted in urine, or dilated blood vessels. Instead, through repeated association of these effects with the act of taking the medicine, subjects' bodies became conditioned to respond appropriately, even after the active ingredients were withdrawn. The medicine-taking ritual alone initiated the body's conditioned responses. However, it did so only after the medicine had been taken with the belief that it was effective medicine, and the entire procedure of medicine taking (pharmacotherapy) became part of this placebo effect. Although side effects as well as positive changes could become conditioned to a placebo, the side effects would likely diminish in time as other, stronger stimuli elicited incompatible responses.

In an earlier experiment, Ader and colleague Nathan Cohen demonstrated that some functioning of the immune system could be controlled by psychological factors (Ader & Cohen, 1981). They taught one group of rats to associate sweet-tasting saccharin with weakened immunity by giving them a drug that depressed the immune system after giving them saccharin. A control group received only the saccharin. Later, when both groups of rats were given only saccharin, the animals that had originally received saccharin *and* the drug still produced significantly fewer antibodies to foreign cells than those that had been given only saccharin. The learned association alone was sufficient to elicit suppression of the immune system, making them vulnerable to a range of diseases. The learning effect was so powerful that, later in the study, some of the rats died after drinking only the saccharin solution. (See *Discovering Psychology,* Program 8.)

Until recently, it was assumed that immunological reactions—rapid production of antibodies to counterattack substances that invade and damage the organism—were automatic, biological processes that occurred without any involvement of the central nervous system. It is now clear that the vital immune system is under both psychological and biological control. In other words, our brains and bodies learn

messages from the environment that can enhance or diminish our health. Usually this learning occurs unconsciously, but, by understanding how it works, psychological researchers can develop strategies for teaching us how to learn the right messages about resisting disease and to block the wrong ones about vulnerability to disease. Pharmaceutical companies will not be happy about these results. Periodic substitution of placebos for potent drugs could enable patients to maintain therapeutic effects with only minimal levels of medication and much reduced side effects. It is possible that, soon, modern medicine will be applying basic principles of learning theory to help us teach our bodies how to stay healthy.

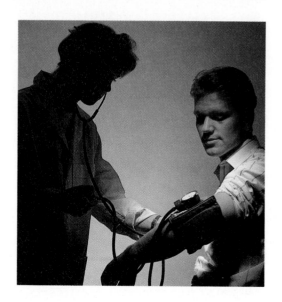

 ## THE STUDY OF LEARNING

Psychologists have long been interested in conditioning, or the ways in which events, stimuli, and behavior become associated with one another. Although the study of conditioning is historically rooted in the study of animal behavior, research over the last two decades shows that conditioning applies equally well to humans.

Psychologists have explored two basic types of conditioning: classical conditioning and operant conditioning. In classical conditioning, two stimuli become associated in such a way that the occurrence of one reliably predicts the occurrence of the other. In our opening example, ingestion of the drug—and later the placebo—became associated with the absence of physiological symptoms related to high blood pressure. The placebo was a stimulus that came to influence bodily changes that previously had been produced only by the drug. In operant conditioning, behavior becomes associated with its consequences. For people addicted to smoking, inhaling cigarette smoke is associated with a pleasurable sensation, and the reactions of the nervous system are associated with the nicotine. It is difficult to break this habit because of these conditioned associa-

tions as well as the physiological dependence on the drug's direct effect—when a smoker has gone without a cigarette for a long period, smoking will relieve negative withdrawal symptoms. The behavioral act of smoking gets conditioned to both the learned pleasurable sensations and the reduction of the negative symptoms associated with withdrawal. Cigarette smoking thus becomes a learned psychological and physiological addiction.

In this chapter, we will examine the ways researchers have studied these two kinds of conditioning and the conclusions their scientific investigations have drawn about how we learn important information that helps us to survive and prosper. We will also examine a growing body of evidence that shows the complexity of what we assume to be simple kinds of learning. Finally, we will note how the procedures used to study the learning process have become powerful tools also used to investigate the effects of many different variables on behavior and mental processes.

Before we begin our study of learning in earnest, let's consider the significance of learning from an *evo-*

lutionary perspective. Learning is as much a product of our genetic endowment as any other phenotype. Similar to physical phenotypes, learning is influenced by experience; that is, nature does not bequeath us a fixed tendency to learn only certain things. Instead, we inherit a *capacity* for learning. Whether that capacity is realized—and to what extent—depends on the individual. While most of us have similar capacities for learning, we learn different things and in different degrees because of our unique individual life experiences. Sociobiologist David Barash expressed the matter eloquently when he wrote, "It may well be true that we are born able to lead a thousand different lives, but it is no less true that we die having lived just one" (1979, p. 1).

There can be little doubt that our capacity for learning is what separates us from our fellow creatures. The capacity for learning varies among animal species according to their genetic blueprint (Mayr, 1974). Some creatures, such as reptiles and amphibians, do not benefit much from interactions with the environment. For them life is a series of rigid stimulus-response patterns. Their survival depends on living in a relatively *constant habitat* in which their responses to specific environmental events get them what is needed or away from what

must be avoided. For animals higher on the evolutionary ladder, such as monkeys and humans, genes play much less of a role in determining specific behavior-environment interactions and allow for greater *plasticity,* or variability, in learning. These animals are able to learn according to the ways in which their behavior produces changes in their environment.

Since the turn of the century, U.S. psychologists have been fascinated by learning, probably because it reflects the democratic and capitalistic ideal that people can shape their lives by their actions (meaning their hard work); they are not limited by factors such as biology and family history; and they can aspire to better lives, regardless of their origins. This perspective on learning is unique to psychology in the United States. Psychologists all over the world have realized that learning may be linked to the development of maladaptive behaviors. The same person who learned how to use the rules of logic could learn to be superstitious, develop phobias, and adopt irrational beliefs that form the basis of madness. So, at the heart of much that is human nature—for better or for worse—is the psychology of learning.

WHAT IS LEARNING?

Learning is a process that results in a relatively permanent change in behavior or behavior potential and that is based on experience. Let's look more closely at the three critical parts of this definition.

A Change in Behavior or Behavior Potential

It is obvious that learning has taken place when you are able to demonstrate the results, such as drive a car or earn a high score on a test. Learning is not observed directly but is inferred from changes in observable behavior. Learning is apparent from improvements in your **performance.** Often, however, your performance doesn't show everything that you have learned. The test questions may be unfair, or you may do poorly because test anxiety interferes. When your motivation is either very weak or very strong, performance may not be a good indicator of learning. Sometimes, too, you have acquired general attitudes such as an *appreciation* of modern art or an *understanding* of Eastern philosophy, that may not be apparent in your measurable actions. In such instances, you have learned a *potential for behavior change* because you have learned attitudes and values that can influence the kind of books you read or the way you spend your leisure time, for example. Learning involves change in behavior potential because we may know and learn much that does not show up in specific performances. This is an example of the **learning-performance distinction**—the difference between

THE FAR SIDE By GARY LARSON

"Stimulus, response! Stimulus, response! Don't you ever *think*?"

what has been learned and what is expressed in overt behavior.

If performance (behavior) is the primary index of learning, how can we discover what infants or animals know when they can't tell us, what mental patients know when they won't tell us, and what shy people know when they are too anxious to tell us? Researchers must devise special testing procedures to make external, observable, and measurable the silent knowledge and learning hidden within an organism. Indeed, it is the creative task of most psychological researchers to find ways to measure and quantify external indices of internal changes within the organisms they study.

Learning is not observed directly but is inferred from changes in observable behavior. We should, however, be careful not to infer learning from all changes in behavior or behavior potential. Sometimes behavior changes occur for reasons other than learning. Some changes are due to physical maturation or the development of the brain as the organism ages. Other changes occur because of disease, illness, brain damage, or the effects of drugs. Similarly, you must have noticed that your performance in many areas is lowered by fatigue, boredom, and anxiety, while it is boosted by encouraging reactions of teammates, an inspirational pep talk, and especially attractive incentives. These biological and motivational variables affect performance of what has been learned but not learning itself.

A Relatively Permanent Change

To qualify as learned, a change in behavior or behavior potential must be relatively permanent. Once you learn to swim, you will probably always be able to do so. Some changes in behavior, however, are transitory and not learned. For example, your pupils dilate or contract as the brightness of light changes. This change in behavior is a *reflex* that is dependent on the effects a given stimulus has on your nervous system. On the other hand, much of your learning, especially knowledge of ideas, is eventually forgotten or changed by what you learn later; learned changes may not necessarily last forever.

A Process Based on Experience

Learning can take place only through experience. Experience includes taking in information (and evaluating and transforming it) and making responses that affect the environment. Psychologists are especially interested in discovering what aspects of behavior can be changed through experience and *how* such changes come about. Some lasting changes in behavior require a combination of experience and maturational readiness. For example, consider the timetable that determines when an infant is ready to crawl, stand, walk, run, and

be toilet trained. No amount of training or practice will produce those behaviors before the child has matured sufficiently.

Under most circumstances, learning can be said to have taken place when the three conditions we have outlined exist. However, sometimes it is not obvious to the person or observers that these conditions are present. For example, changes in physiological responses, such as those in the immune system, can only be monitored with technical equipment. Learning of a broad rather than specific nature—such as adopting a value system of respect for authority or love of one's country—is very difficult to measure. Finally, what constitutes experience varies from person to person. We say that prejudice is learned by experience, but that experience may consist of accepting biased views held by other people and not of personal negative contact with the targets of that prejudice. Similarly, a phobic fear of snakes, for example, may be learned but not based on actual experience with snakes. These exceptions or extensions of the definition of learning highlight the need for researchers to be precise when determining the conditions associated with different types of learning.

BEHAVIORISM AND BEHAVIOR ANALYSIS

Much of modern psychology's view of learning finds its roots in the work of **John Watson** (1878–1958). As you might recall from Chapter 1, Watson founded the school of psychology known as *behaviorism*. For nearly fifty years, American psychology was dominated by the behaviorist tradition expressed in Watson's 1913 article *Psychology as the Behaviorist Sees It*. Watson was influential in advancing the assumptions and methods of behavior theory into many areas of psychological re-

J. B. Watson

search—most notably, the field of learning. His early work on the way rats learn to solve mazes used a method that other researchers readily adopted; later, he adapted Ivan Pavlov's conditional response as the unit of learned habit (which we will soon study). In perhaps his most influential work, *Psychology from the Standpoint of a Behaviorist*, Watson (1919) argued that introspection—verbal reports of sensations, images, and feelings—was *not* an acceptable means of studying behavior because it was too subjective. After all, psychology is a science, and the hallmark of science is objective methodology. What, then, should be the subject matter of psychology? Watson's answer was *observable behavior*. In Watson's words, "States of consciousness, like the so-called phenomena of spiritualism, are not objectively verifiable and for that reason can never become data for science" (Watson, 1919, p. 1). In Watson's view, then, behavior—not mental states—was the only acceptable subject matter for psychology.

Watson's ideas had direct influence on a young man who went on to become one of the most famous psychologists of his time. **B. F. Skinner** (1904–1990) began his graduate study in psychology at Harvard after reading Watson's 1924 book *Behaviorism*. During his career, Skinner pioneered a new brand of behaviorism known as *radical behaviorism*. Skinner's complaint against internal states and mental events dealt not so much with their legitimacy as data as with their legitimacy as *causes of behavior* (Skinner, 1990). In Skinner's view, mental events, such as thinking and imaging, do not cause behavior. Rather, they are examples of behavior that are caused by environmental stimuli. Suppose that we deprive a pigeon of food for 24 hours, place it in an apparatus where it can obtain food by pecking a small disk, and find that it soon does. Skinner would say that the bird's behavior is explained by food deprivation, an event that was manipulated environmentally. He would also say that it adds nothing to our account to say that the bird pecked the disk because it was hungry or that it did so because it wanted to get the food. The animal's behavior can be explained by an environmental event—deprivation. The subjective feeling of hunger, which cannot be directly observed or measured, is not a cause of the behavior but the result of deprivation. So, too, the behavior of pecking the disk with its consequence of getting food is a result of the initial deprivation followed by the *consequences* on the environment of the animal's actions.

Behaviorism serves as the philosophical cornerstone of **behavior analysis,** the area of psychology that focuses on discovering environmental determinants of learning and behavior. In general, behavior analysts argue that human nature can be fully understood only by using extensions of the methods and principles of natural science—especially physics. The task is to discover the regularities in human action that are universal, occurring to all types of people and other animal species under comparable situations. Although experience changes people's actions, the actual changes follow orderly principles. Identifying these principles will achieve the primary goal of behavior analysis: to explain behavior in terms of its controlling variables. It is the relationship between behavior and environmental events and not the relationship between behavior and mental events that concerns the behaviorists. The causes of behavior are found solely in the environment.

Behavior analysts approach their work with two basic assumptions: (a) learning is largely due to the processes involved in classical and operant conditioning and (b) the behavior of humans and other animal species can be explained by the same general laws of learning. First, the two types of conditioning are sufficient to explain most or all of human and animal behavior. Second, in the language of classical and operant conditioning, learning occurs under two conditions: (a) when two environmental stimuli coincide so that the presence of one reliably predicts the presence of the other and (b) when behavior produces a change in the organism's environment.

Although the behavioristic position has yielded many valuable explanations of human nature, we will see that it has been challenged by other psychologists who insist on keeping a thinking brain and a rational mind in control of the behaving body.

SUMMING UP

Learning may be defined as a relatively permanent change in behavior or behavior potential based on experience. Our capacity for learning depends upon both our genetic heritage and the nature of our environment. The study of learning has been dominated by the behavioristic approach as represented in the work of Watson, Pavlov, and, more recently, Skinner. Behaviorism serves as the philosophical bedrock of behavior analysis, the area of psychology that focuses on discovering the environmental determinants of learning and behavior. Behavior analysts operate under two general assumptions. First, learning can be explained according to the processes involved in classical and operant conditioning. Second, the behavior of all organisms can be described by the same general laws of learning. Behavior analysis has recently come under attack from psychologists who have shown that learning is determined both by biological and cognitive factors in addition to environmental ones.

CLASSICAL CONDITIONING: LEARNING PREDICTABLE SIGNALS

In the story that began our chapter, we saw how the body can become conditioned to respond to particular stimuli based on an association with specific events. The beneficial effects of a drug became associated with the act of taking a particular pill, even when that pill contained no medically active ingredients. This type of conditioning is known as **classical conditioning,** a form of basic learning in which one stimulus or event predicts the occurrence of another stimulus or event. The organism learns a new *association* between two stimuli—a neutral stimulus (that did not previously elicit the response) and a more powerful stimulus (that elicits the response by itself). Following conditioning, the formerly neutral stimulus elicits a new response that is very similar to the original response. This simple pairing of events we experience in our environment has profound implications.

PAVLOV'S SURPRISING DISCOVERY

The Russian physiologist **Ivan Pavlov** (1849–1936) is credited with discovering the basic principles of classical conditioning. Pavlov did not set out to study classical conditioning or any other psychological phenomenon. He happened upon classical conditioning while conducting research on digestion, research for which he won a Nobel Prize in 1904.

Pavlov had devised a technique to study digestive processes in dogs by implanting tubes in their glands and digestive organs to divert bodily secretions to containers outside their bodies so that the secretions could be measured and analyzed. To produce these secretions, Pavlov's assistants put meat powder into the dogs' mouths. After repeating this procedure a number of times, Pavlov observed an unexpected behavior in his dogs—they salivated *before* the powder was put in their mouths! They would start salivating at the mere sight of the food and, later, at the sight of the assistant who brought the food or even at the sound of the assistant's footsteps. Indeed, any stimulus that regularly preceded the presentation of food came to elicit salivation. Quite by accident, Pavlov had discovered that learning may result from two stimuli becoming associated with each other.

To Pavlov, this finding did not make sense, at least in a purely physiological point of view. After all, why should stimuli *unrelated* to a given stimulus (eating) come to elicit the same kind of behavior (salivation) that the stimulus (eating) does? Salivating to footstep sounds had no apparent survival value, for example. Pavlov believed that other principles had to be at work. It has been said that "chance favors the prepared mind," and Pavlov was ready to realize the significance of these "psychic secretions," as he called them. He ignored the advice of the great physiologist of the time, Sir Charles Sherrington, that he should abandon his foolish investigation. Pavlov, at that point a distinguished, middle-aged physiologist, became consumed by his unusual finding. He abandoned his work on digestion and, in so doing, changed the course of psychology forever (Pavlov, 1928).

The behavior Pavlov studied was the reflex. A **reflex** is an unlearned response, such as salivation, pupil contraction, knee jerks, or eye blinking, that is naturally elicited by specific stimuli that have biological relevance for the organism. Simply put, a reflex is an elicited behavior that promotes biological adaptation to a changing environment. For example, salivation, the reflex Pavlov studied, helps digestion. After conditioning, organisms make reflexive responses to new stimuli having no such original biological relevance for them.

Pavlov was among the best of the early researchers. He knew that, in order to discover what was causing his dogs to salivate, he would have to manipulate various

To study classical conditioning, Pavlov placed his dogs in a restraining apparatus. The dogs were then presented with a neutral stimulus, such as a tone. Through its association with food, the neutral stimulus became a conditional stimulus, eliciting salivation.

aspects of his experimental setting and observe what effects, if any, would follow. His strategy was elegant and simple. He first placed a dog in a restraining harness. At regular intervals, a tone was sounded and the dog was given a bit of food. As you might imagine, the dog's first reaction to the tone was only an *orienting response*—the dog pricked its ears and moved its head to locate the source of the sound. However, with *repeated pairings* of the tone and the food, the orienting response stopped, and salivation began. What Pavlov observed in his earlier research was no accident, the phenomenon could be replicated under controlled conditions. A neutral stimulus—such as the tone—when paired with another, more relevant stimulus—such as food—will eventually elicit a response very similar to the original reflex—such as salivation.

The main features of Pavlov's classical conditioning procedure are illustrated in **Figure 9.1.** Any stimulus, such as food, that naturally elicits a reflexive behavior is called an **unconditional stimulus** (UCS) because learning is not a necessary condition for the stimulus to control the behavior. The behavior elicited by the unconditional stimulus is called the **unconditional response** (UCR). During conditioning trials, a neutral stimulus, such as a tone, is repeatedly paired with the unconditional stimulus so that it predictably follows the neutral stimulus. After several trials, the tone is presented alone. Now it elicits the same response as the UCS does—in this case, salivation. The tone stimulus has acquired some of the power to influence behavior that was originally limited to the unconditional stimulus. The neutral stimulus paired with the unconditional stimulus is now called the **conditional stimulus** (CS) because its power to elicit behavior is *conditional* upon its association with the UCS. The reflexive behavior elicited by the CS is called the **conditional response** (CR). In other words, nature provides the UCS-UCR connections, but the learning produced by classical conditioning creates the CS-CR connection.

Pavlov's careful laboratory experiments showed how otherwise neutral stimuli could come to exert powerful control over reflexive behavior. He used many stimuli, such as metronome ticking, lights, and tones, to demonstrate that virtually any of them could become substitutes for biologically significant unconditional stimuli. Pavlov's work was important because it demonstrated a new behavioral phenomenon. However, Pavlov was not content to stop his research there. For the remainder of his life, he continued to search for the variables that influence classically conditioned behavior. His research uncovered a number of important processes involved in classical conditioning, most of which are still being studied by modern psychologists.

FIGURE 9.1 BASIC FEATURES OF CLASSICAL CONDITIONING

Before conditioning, the unconditional stimulus (UCS) naturally elicits the unconditional response (UCR). A neutral stimulus, such as a tone, has no eliciting effect. During conditioning, the neutral stimulus is paired with the UCS. Through its association with the UCS, the neutral stimulus becomes a conditional stimulus (CS) and elicits a conditional response (CR) that is similar to the UCR.

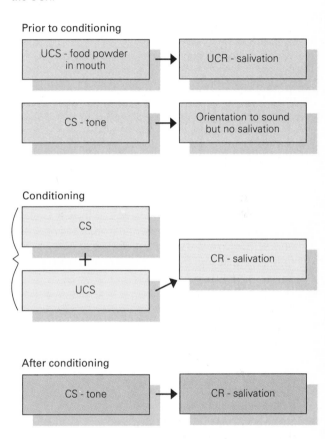

Classical conditioning is also called *Pavlovian conditioning* because of Pavlov's discovery of the phenomena of conditioning and his dedication to tracking down the variables that influence it. It is to these phenomena that we now turn.

BASIC PROCESSES

What conditions are optimal for classical conditioning? This general question has been asked in many different ways and answered in literally thousands of different studies. The answers provide clues to the fundamental processes underlying learning. In this section, we will review what is known about these processes.

Acquisition

In general, the CS and UCS must be paired several times before the CS reliably elicits a CR. **Acquisition** refers to the process at the beginning of a classical conditioning experiment by which the CR is first elicited and gradually increases in frequency over repeated trials. The far left panel in **Figure 9.2** shows the acquisition phase of a hypothetical experiment. At first, very few CRs are elicited by the CS. With continued CS-UCS pairings, however, the CR is elicited with increasing frequency, and a conditioned response is acquired by the organism.

In studying conditioning, an experimenter may vary several aspects of Pavlov's procedure, such as the number of trials an organism receives, the time interval between successive trials, the time interval between the CS and UCS, and the intensity or quality of either or both stimuli. Variations in these and other aspects of the situation are the *independent variables*. The four major *dependent variables* that index the effectiveness of the conditioning are (a) the *amplitude* (or the strength) of the CR; (b) the *latency* (or time delay) between when the CS is presented and the CR is made; (c) the *rate* at which (or how often) the CR is elicited; (d) and the *persistence* of the CR (or how long the CR continues to be elicited by the CS) in the absence of the UCS. This last measure is very important in conditioning; it is also known as **resistance to extinction.**

In conditioning, as in telling a good joke, *timing* is critical. The CS and UCS must be presented close enough in time to be perceived by the organism as being related. Four temporal patterns between the two stimuli have been studied, as shown in **Figure 9.3.** The most widely used type of conditioning is called *forward conditioning,* in which the CS comes on prior to and stays on until the UCS is presented, overlapping it. In *trace conditioning,* the CS is turned off just before the UCS is presented. *Trace* refers to the memory that the organism must have of the CS which is no longer present when the UCS appears. In *simultaneous conditioning,* both the CS and UCS are presented at the same time. Finally, in the case of *backward conditioning,* the CS is presented after the UCS.

Conditioning is usually better with a short interval between the CS and UCS. The range of time intervals between the CS and UCS that will produce the best conditioning depends upon the response being conditioned. For motor and skeletal responses, such as eye blinks, a short interval of a second or less is best. For visceral responses, such as heart rate and salivation, however, longer intervals of 5 to 15 seconds work best. Conditioned fear usually requires longer intervals of

---

FIGURE 9.2 *ACQUISITION, EXTINCTION, AND SPONTANEOUS RECOVERY IN CLASSICAL CONDITIONING*

During acquisition (CS + UCS), the strength of the CR increases rapidly. During extinction, when the UCS no longer follows the CS, the strength of the CR drops to zero. The CR may reappear after a brief rest period, even when the UCS is still not presented. The reappearance of the CS is called "spontaneous recovery."

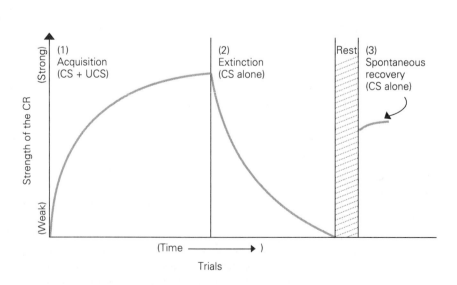

FIGURE 9.3

FOUR VARIATIONS OF THE CS-UCS TEMPORAL ARRANGEMENT IN CLASSICAL CONDITIONING

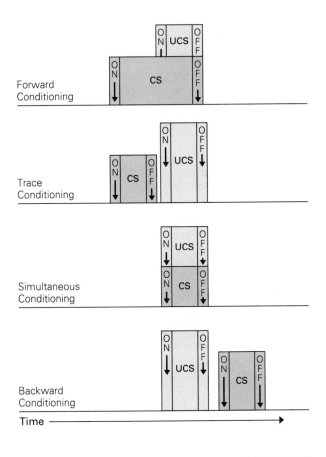

(Rescorla, 1972; Rescorla & Wagner, 1972). In real life, as in the conditioning laboratory, the key to developing a strong conditional response is to increase the signal-to-noise ratio of the CS by making it a stronger signal than all other competing events—background stimuli or irrelevant noise.

Extinction and Spontaneous Recovery

Once a conditional response is acquired, does it last forever? When the UCS no longer follows the CS, the CR becomes weaker over time and eventually stops occurring. When the CR no longer occurs in the presence of the CS (and absence of UCS), **extinction** is said to have occurred (see Figure 9.2, second panel from left). Conditional responses, then, are not necessarily a permanent aspect of the organism's behavioral repertoire. However, the CR will reappear in a weak form when the CS is presented alone again (see Figure 9.2, far right panel). Pavlov referred to this sudden reappearance of the CR after a rest period, or time-out, without further exposure to the UCS as **spontaneous recovery.**

With further postextinction training (further pairings of CS and US), the CR gets rapidly stronger. This more rapid relearning is an instance of **savings:** less time is *required* to reacquire the response than to acquire it originally, so some of the original conditioning must be retained by the organism even after experimental extinction appears to have eliminated the CR. In other words, extinction has only weakened its performance, not wiped out the original learning.

Stimulus Generalization

Once a CR has been conditioned to a particular CS, similar stimuli may also elicit the response. For example, if conditioning was to a high frequency tone, a lower tone may also elicit the response. A child bitten by a big dog is likely to respond with fear even to smaller dogs. This automatic extension of responding to stimuli that have never been paired with the original UCS is called **stimulus generalization.** The more similar the new stimulus is to the original CS, the stronger the response will be. When response strength is measured for each of a series of increasingly dissimilar stimuli along a given dimension, as shown in **Figure 9.4,** a *generalization gradient,* or slope, is found.

Because important stimuli rarely occur in exactly the same form every time in nature, stimulus generalization builds in a similarity safety factor by extending the range of learning beyond the original specific experience. With this feature, new but comparable events can be recognized as having the same meaning or behavioral significance despite apparent differences. For example, a predator can make a different sound or be seen

many seconds or even minutes to develop.

Conditioning is generally poor with a simultaneous procedure and very poor with a backward procedure. Evidence of backward conditioning may appear after a few pairings but disappear with extended training as the animal learns that the CS is followed by a period free of the UCS. In both cases, conditioning is weak because the CS does not actually signal the onset of the UCS.

Conditioning occurs most rapidly when the CS stands out against the many other stimuli that are also present. Thus, a stimulus will be more readily noticed the more *intense* it is and the more it *contrasts* with other stimuli. Either a strong, novel stimulus in an unfamiliar situation or a strong, familiar stimulus in a novel context leads to good conditioning (Kalat, 1974; Lubow et al., 1976). In general, the feature of the CS that most facilitates conditioning is its *informativeness*—its reliability in predicting the onset of the UCS from a different angle and still be recognized and responded to quickly.

Stimulus Discrimination

Though stimuli similar to the original CS may elicit a similar response, it is possible for an organism to respond only to one particular CS and not to respond to other stimuli, regardless of how similar they are. **Stimulus discrimination** is the process by which an organism learns to respond differently to stimuli that are distinct from the CS on some dimension (for example, differences in hue or in pitch). An organism's discrimination among similar stimuli (tones of 1000, 1200, and 1500 cps, for example) is sharpened with discrimination training in which only one of them (1200 cps, for example) predicts the UCS and in which the others are repeatedly presented without it. Early in conditioning, stimuli similar to the CS will elicit a similar response, though not quite as strong. As discrimination training proceeds, the responses to the other, dissimilar stimuli weaken: the organism gradually learns which event-signal predicts the onset of the UCS and which signals do not.

For optimum adaptation, the initial perceptual tendency to generalize and respond to all somewhat similar stimuli needs to give way to discrimination among them, with responses only to those that are, in fact, followed by the UCS. Ideally, then, conditioning is a process in which discrimination ultimately wins over generalization; but it is a balancing act between these two counteracting tendencies of being overresponsive and overselective.

SIGNIFICANCE OF CLASSICAL CONDITIONING

Pavlov's work helps us understand significant everyday behavior. Many of the emotions we experience and many of our attitudes can be explained by classical conditioning. Let's take a closer look at how classical conditioning can help us understand emotion and attitude development.

Fear Conditioning

Pavlov's conditioning with meat powder is an example of *appetitive conditioning*—conditioning in which UCS is of positive value to an organism—related to its appetites. However, classical conditioning may also involve an aversive, painful UCS. *Aversive conditioning* occurs when the CS predicts the presentation of an aversive UCS, such as electrical shock. An organism's natural response to such stimuli is reflexive behavior that reduces the intensity of the UCS or removes it entirely. Through its association with the UCS, the CS also comes to elicit these kinds of responses when it is

---

FIGURE 9.4   STIMULUS GENERALIZATION GRADIENTS

After conditioning to a medium green stimulus, the subject responds almost as strongly to stimuli of similar hues, as shown by the flat generalization gradient in panel A. When the subject is exposed to a broader range of colored stimuli, responses grow weaker as the color becomes increasingly dissimilar to the training stimulus. The generalization gradient becomes very steep, as shown in panel B. The experimenter could change the generalization gradient shown in panel A to resemble the one in panel C by giving the subject discrimination training. In this case, the medium green stimulus would be continually paired with the UCS but stimuli of all other hues would not.

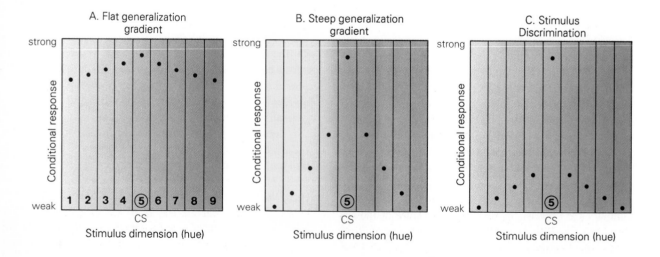

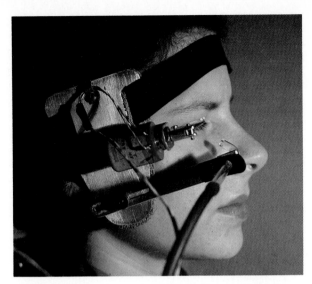

In eyelid conditioning, a puff of air to the eye (UCS) forces an eyeblink or lid closure (UCR). When a tone (CS) is paired with the air puff, it soon elicits the eyeblink (CR).

presented later independently of the UCS. In *eyelid conditioning,* a puff of air to the eye (UCS) forces an eyeblink or lid closure (UCR). When a tone (CS) is paired with the airpuff, it soon elicits the eyeblink (CR).

This simple procedure for classically conditioning the eyelid closure response has been used in the study of the neurobiological circuits of the brain systems involved in each of the components of the overall response—response to the air puff, to the tone, and to the stored memory trace of the CS-UCS connection as conditioning develops (Thompson, 1986). It is also being used to compare the effects of age differences in learning and memory of humans, rabbits, and other mammals (Woodruf-Pak & Thompson, 1988).

An important discovery from aversive conditioning studies has been that the organism learns not only a specific conditional muscle response but a *generalized fear reaction* as well. The subject learns a specific response to a stimulus and re-evaluates the previously neutral stimulus as affectively negative. Withdrawal from the negative stimulus is accompanied by reactions of the autonomic nervous system—changes in heart rate, respiration, and electrical resistance of the skin (the galvanic skin response, or GSR). These changes become part of an overall conditional fear response.

Interestingly, when strong fear is involved, conditioning may take place after only *one* pairing of a neutral stimulus with the UCS. Traumatic events in our lives that may occur only once can condition us to respond with strong physical, emotional, and cognitive reactions that are highly resistant to extinction. Conditional fear is often easy to acquire and difficult to extinguish. For example, I have a friend who was in a bad car accident during a rain storm. Now, every time it begins to rain while he is driving, he becomes panic-stricken, sometimes to the extent that he has to pull over and wait the storm out. On one occasion he even crawled into the back seat and laid on the floor, face down, until the rain subsided.

A classic study of conditional fear in a human being was conducted by psychologists John Watson and Rosalie Rayner with an infant named Albert.

Watson and Rayner (1920) trained Albert to fear a white rat he had initially liked by pairing its appearance with an aversive UCS—a loud gong struck just behind him. The unconditional startle response and the emotional distress to the noxious noise was the basis of Albert's learning to react with fear to the appearance of the white rat. His fear was developed in just seven conditioning trials. The emotional conditioning was then extended to behavioral conditioning when Albert learned to escape from the feared stimulus. The infant's learned fear then generalized to other furry objects, such as a rabbit, a dog, and even a Santa Claus mask! [In the early days of psychology, careful attention to possible harmful effects of experiments on subjects was sometimes lacking. In fact, Albert's mother, a wet nurse at the hospital where the study was conducted, took him away before the researchers could remove the experimentally conditioned fear. So we don't know whatever happened to *Little Albert* (Harris, 1979).]

We know now that conditioned fear is highly resistant to extinction. Even if the overt components of muscle reaction eventually disappear, the reactions of the autonomic nervous system continue. This leaves an individual vulnerable to arousal by the old signals, sometimes without awareness of why the reaction is occurring. Conditional fear reactions may persist for years, even when the original frightening UCS is never again experienced, as shown in the following study.

During World War II, the signal used to call sailors to battle stations aboard U.S. Navy ships was a gong sounding at the rate of 100 rings a minute. To personnel on board, the sound was associated with danger; thus, it became a CS for strong emotional arousal. Fifteen years after the war, a study was conducted on the emotional reactions of hospitalized Navy and Army veterans to a series of 20 different auditory stimuli. Although none of the sounds were current signals for danger, the sound of the old "call to battle stations" still produced strong emotional arousal in the Navy veterans who had previously experienced that

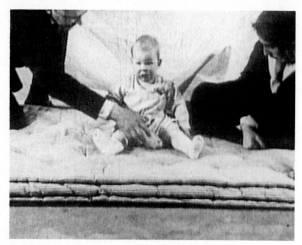

John Watson and Rosalie Rayner conditioned Little Albert to fear small, furry objects (*Discovering Psychology,* 1990).

association. Their response to the former danger signal, as determined by galvanic-skin-response measures, was significantly greater than that of the Army veterans (Edwards & Acker, 1962).

All of us retain learned readiness to respond with fear, joy, or other emotions to old signals (often from our childhood) that aren't appropriate or valid in our current situation. When we are unaware of their origins, these once reasonable fear reactions may be interpreted as anxiety, and we get more upset because we seem to be reacting irrationally without adequate cause or reason (Dollard & Miller, 1950). Aversive conditioning has been used as part of therapeutic programs to stop undesirable behavior, as we shall see in Chapter 18.

Conditioned Social Behavior

Many of our *attitudes* have been formed by conditioning processes that take place without our awareness (Staats & Staats, 1958). Attitudes are often defined as an individual's learned tendencies to respond behaviorally, emotionally, and cognitively to particular target stimuli, such as people, ideas, or objects, with a positive or negative evaluation. Stimuli may acquire their power to elicit attitudinal responses by being paired with UCSs that elicit emotional or affective responses. Words, symbols, and pictures that naturally elicit strong positive responses will become conditional arousers of similarly positive reactions. This principle has been applied by advertisers and promoters who want us to like their products enough that we will purchase them.

In one research study, researchers demonstrated that pairing food words with meaningless trigrams such as *jik* or *daz*, led to attitudes toward the trigrams that were more positive among college students who were

food deprived than among those who had eaten (Staats et al., 1972). In another study, trigrams were paired with items that were of negative interest to students. The students then evaluated these trigrams as unpleasant (Staats et al., 1973). A large body of research shows that social behavior—aggression, altruism, persuasion, cooperation, and competition—can be studied as a response system formed through classical conditioning (Lott & Lott, 1985; Weiss et al., 1971).

The ability of neutral stimuli to acquire through conditioning the power to elicit strong responses automatically makes us all vulnerable to our emotions and attitudes. Although there are some limitations to this process—to be discussed later—the tremendous implications of the ease with which conditioning takes place should not escape you. A very powerful conclusion has emerged from the many years of psychological research on conditioning: *Virtually any stimulus you can perceive can be associated with almost any response so that you learn to value, desire, or fear the stimulus.* (For notable exceptions, see the last section of this chapter on biological constraints.) We learn to use information about impending events to help us make preparatory responses; we prepare for the future on the basis of our conditioning history. Even our immune system, as you will recall from our opening story in this chapter, is influenced by classical conditioning and conditioning can kill, as shown in *Learning to Be a Drug Addict* on page 314.

Fifteen years after World War II, Navy veterans still responded to auditory stimuli that resembled battleship gongs as if they were current danger signals.

When the dogs were jumping across the barrier regularly, Rescorla randomly divided his subjects into two groups and subjected them to another training procedure. Each group was exposed to a different CS-UCS relation where the CS was a tone and the UCS was a shock. To the Random Group, the UCS was delivered randomly and independently of the CS. Thus, the UCS was as likely to be delivered in the absence of the CS as it was in its presence, which means that the CS had no predictive value. For the Contingency Group, however, the UCS always followed the CS. Thus, for this group, the sounding of the tone was a reliable predictor of the delivery of the shock.

Once this training was complete, the dogs were put back into the shuttlebox but this time with a twist. Now, the tone used in the second training procedure occasionally sounded, signalling shock. What would the dogs do? According to Rescorla, if Pavlov was correct, both groups of dogs should show about the same amount of conditioned fear in the presence of the tone—dogs in both groups should jump with about the same frequency because the *temporal contiguity* between the CS and UCS was the same for both groups. However, if classical conditioning is dependent upon a *contingent CS-UCS relation* in addition to contiguity, then dogs in the Contingency Group should jump more frequently than the other group.

THE ROLE OF CONTINGENCY AND INFORMATIVENESS

So far, we have *described* classical conditioning, but we have not yet *explained* it. Pavlov believed that classical conditioning was due to the mere pairing of the CS and the UCS. In his view, to classically condition a response the CS and the UCS must occur close together in time, that is, be *temporally contiguous*. Pavlov's theory dominated classical conditioning until the mid 1960s when **Robert Rescorla** (1966) conducted a very telling experiment using dogs as subjects. Rescorla placed dogs in one side of a shuttlebox (see **Figure 9.5**). Occasionally they would be given unsignaled electric shocks through the grid floor. Rescorla had trained his animals to jump the barrier that divided the box in half. If they did not jump, they received a shock; if they did jump, the shock was postponed. Rescorla used the frequency with which dogs jumped the barrier as a measure of fear conditioning. The more often they jumped the greater the amount of fear conditioning.

FIGURE 9.5   *A SHUTTLEBOX*

Rescorla used the frequency with which dogs jumped over a barrier as a measure of fear conditioning.

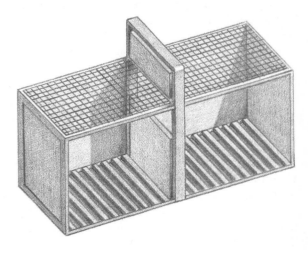

LEARNING TO BE A DRUG ADDICT

Addiction

A man's body lay in a Manhattan alley, a half-empty syringe dangling from his arm. Cause of death? The coroner called it an overdose, but the man had ordinarily shot up far greater doses than the one that had supposedly killed him. This sort of incident had happened before, and it baffled investigators. How could an addict with high drug tolerance die of an overdose when he didn't even get a full hit?

Psychologist **Shepard Siegel** thought something else might be happening. Studies of rats had convinced him that *tolerance*—decreased responsiveness to a drug after repeated use—involved more than just *physiological* changes in the brain. He thought *learning*—an association of the drug with the physical setting and rituals normally associated with its use—also contributed to tolerance.

Some time ago, Pavlov (1927) and later his colleague Bykov (1957) pointed out that tolerance to opiates can develop when an individual anticipates the pharmacological action of a drug. Perhaps with advance notice—provided by the conditional stimulus associated with the ritual of injection—the body somehow learns to protect itself by preventing the drug from having its usual effect. In settings ordinarily associated with drug use, the body physiologically prepares itself for the drug's expected effects. Over time, larger doses are needed to achieve the desired effect.

In one study, Siegel classically conditioned rats to expect *heroin*

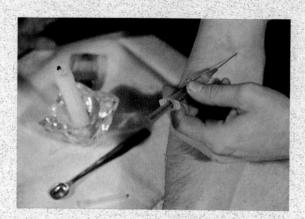

injections (UCS) in one setting (CS_1) and *dextrose* (sweet sugar) solution injections in a different setting (CS_2) (Siegel et al., 1982). In the first phase of training, all rats developed heroin tolerance. On the test day, all subjects received a larger-than-usual dose of heroin—nearly twice the previous amount. Half of them received it in the setting where heroin was expected; the other half received it in the setting where dextrose solutions had been given during conditioning. More than twice as many rats died in the dextrose-solution setting when heroin was *not* expected as when it was expected in the usual heroin setting—82 percent versus 31 percent! Those receiving heroin in the usual setting had valid expectations and were more prepared for this potentially dangerous situation, perhaps by initiating a physiological response that countered the drug's typical effects.

In order to find out if a similar process might operate in humans, Siegel and a colleague interviewed heroin addicts who had come close

to death from supposed overdoses. In seven out of ten cases, the addicts had been shooting up in a new and unfamiliar setting (Siegel, 1984). Although this natural experiment provides no conclusive data, it suggests that a dose for which an addict has developed tolerance in one setting may become an overdose in an unfamiliar setting. Conditioned cues may be powerful elicitors of a learned tolerance response. Without this protective reaction, the drug's effects could be more potent than usual, increasing the addict's susceptibility to overdose and death.

Rescorla's results, shown in **Figure 9.6,** indicate that Pavlov's explanation of classical conditioning is inadequate. Dogs exposed to the *contingent* (predictable) CS-UCS relation jumped more frequently in the presence of the tone than did dogs exposed only to the *contiguous* (associated) CS-UCS relation. Thus, in addition to contiguity, it appears that the CS *must reliably predict* the occurrence of the UCS in order for classical conditioning to occur. This finding makes considerable sense (Rescorla, 1988). After all, in natural situations, where learning enables organisms to adapt to changes in their environment, stimuli come in clusters and not in neat, simple units as they do in traditional laboratory experiments. To survive, the animal must be able to detect which of all the available stimuli signal rewards and which signal danger.

Although Rescorla's work demonstrated that contingency plays a crucial role in classical conditioning, other researchers wondered if there was more to the story. One such researcher was **Leon Kamin,** who conducted an experiment equally as ingenious as that of Rescorla's (see **Figure 9.7**).

Kamin's study involved two groups of rats. The experimental group was first trained to press a lever in the presence of a tone (CS) to avoid shock

(UCS). Next, a second CS—a light—was added; now the UCS was preceded by two CSs: the tone (CS$_1$) and the light (CS$_2$). The control group was exposed only to this sequence of tone-light-shock; it never experienced the tone alone as a predictor of shock delivery. Kamin then tested both groups of rats for fear conditioning to the light alone or to the tone alone. If contingency is sufficient to explain classical conditioning, then both groups of rats should have responded in equal amounts to the light and the tone.

Interestingly, that is not what Kamin found. The experimental rats responded to the tone but not the light, whereas control rats responded equally to both the tone and the light. Kamin explained his results in terms of the *informativeness* of the conditional stimuli. For experimental rats, the previous conditioning to the tone in the first

FIGURE 9.6

THE ROLE OF CONTINGENCY IN CLASSICAL CONDITIONING

Rescorla showed that dogs trained under the contingent CS-UCS relation showed more jumping (and thus conditioned fear) than did dogs trained under the contiguous but noncontingent CS-UCS relation. The arrows indicate the onset and offset of the CS tone.

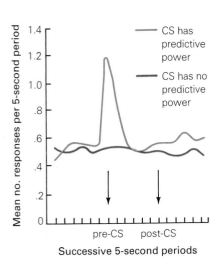

FIGURE 9.7

KAMIN'S PROCEDURE FOR PRODUCING THE BLOCKING EFFECT

Rats in the experimental group were first trained to respond to a tone (CS1). Next they were trained to both a tone (CS1) and a light (CS2). Rats in the control group were trained only to the compound light and tone (CS). When tested for conditioning to light alone and to tone alone, only the control rats responded to both stimuli. According to Kamin, experimental rats did not respond to the light because it contained no new information predicting the occurrence of the UCS. The tone's effect blocked the light's effect.

Experimental group	Control group
Training	
Phase 1.	
CS$_1$	
UCS ⟶ CR	Ø
Phase 2.	
CS$_1$	CS$_1$
CS$_2$	CS$_2$
UCS ⟶ CR	UCS ⟶ CR
Testing	
CS$_1$ ⟶ CR	CS$_1$ ⟶ CR
CS$_2$ ⟶ No CR	CS$_2$ ⟶ CR

CS$_1$ = tone   CS$_2$ = light

phase of the experiment, blocked any subsequent conditioning that could occur to the light. In other words, the previous experience with the tone overshadowed the significance of the light as a predictor of the UCS. From the rat's point of view, the light may as well not have existed; it provided no additional information beyond that already given by the tone. The ability of the first CS to reduce the informativeness of the second CS because of previous experience with the UCS is called **blocking.** For control rats, both the light and the tone were equally informative—the rats had no previous experience with either CS so that one would reduce the informativeness of the other.

Classical conditioning, then, is much more complex than Pavlov originally theorized. Simply pairing a neutral stimulus with a UCS will not result in classical conditioning. For a neutral stimulus to become a CS, it must satisfy two other criteria beside contiguity. First, it must reliably predict the occurrence of the CS (there must be a *contingent relationship* between the CS and the UCS). Second, the CS must also be *informative*. If two CSs are equally predictive, as was the case for Kamin's experimental rats, then the CS that is more informative will become the more potent CS. Kamin's study showed that once an organism learns about the UCS on the basis of one dependable signal, it does not bother to learn about other stimuli that are also consistently present, presumably because their information is redundant. The power of any particular neutral stimulus to become a CS thus depends on the presence of other stimuli that could also serve as potential signals.

SUMMING UP

One widely used procedure for investigating learning, especially how organisms learn about the relationships between stimulus events in their environment, is classical conditioning. In this procedure, developed by Pavlov, a biologically significant stimulus, called an unconditional stimulus (UCS), elicits a reflex, called an unconditional response (UCR). A neutral stimulus that is then paired repeatedly with the UCS becomes a conditional stimulus (CS), which elicits a similar response, called the conditional response (CR). However, if the UCS no longer follows the CS, extinction, or disappearance, of the CR occurs. After a rest period, though, spontaneous recovery may occur—the CR partially returns when the CS is presented alone again. Stimuli similar to the CS also elicit the CR; this phenomenon is called stimulus generalization. If these stimuli are not followed by the

UCS, stimulus discrimination occurs—the organism stops responding to the irrelevant stimuli and responds only to the original CS. For classical conditioning to occur, two criteria must be met. First, Rescorla's research showed there must be a contingent relation between the CS and UCS—the CS must reliably predict the occurrence of the UCS. Second, the CS also must be informative. If two CSs are equally predictive, as in Kamin's experiment, then the more informative CS will become the better predictor of the presentation of the UCS, and responding will be directed toward only that CS. Classical conditioning is a powerful means by which we learn to respond emotionally to a host of desirable or fearful stimuli; it is also a way in which certain attitudes are formed.

OPERANT CONDITIONING: LEARNING ABOUT CONSEQUENCES

At about the same time that Pavlov was using classical conditioning to induce Russian dogs to salivate to the sound of a bell, **Edward L. Thorndike** (1898) was watching American cats trying to escape from puzzle boxes (see **Figure 9.8**). He reported his observations

---

FIGURE 9.8   *A THORNDIKE PUZZLE BOX*

To get out of the puzzle box and obtain food, Thorndike's cat had to loosen a bolt, bar, or loop that would release a weight that would then pull the door open.

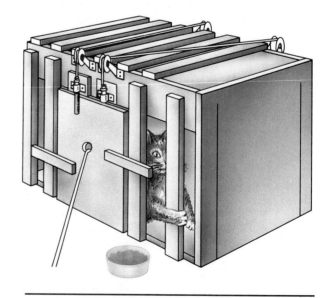

---

and inferences about the kind of learning he believed was taking place in his subjects:

> When put into the box, the cat shows evident signs of discomfort and develops an impulse to escape from confinement. It tries to squeeze through any opening; it claws and bites at the bars or wire; it thrusts its paws out through any opening and claws at everything it reaches. . . . It does not pay very much attention to the food outside (the reward for the hungry cat) but seems simply to strive instinctively to escape from confinement. The vigor with which it struggles is extraordinary. For eight or ten minutes it will claw and bite and squeeze incessantly. . . . Whether the impulse to struggle be due to an instinctive reaction to confinement or to an association, it is likely to succeed in letting the cat out of the box. The cat that is clawing all over the box in [its] impulsive struggle will probably claw the string or loop or button so as to open the door. And gradually all the other unsuccessful impulses will be *stamped out* and the particular impulse leading to the successful act will be *stamped in* by the resulting pleasure, until, after many trials, the cat will, when put in the box, immediately claw the button or loop in a definite way (Thorndike, 1898, p. 13).

What did Thorndike's cats learn that was different from what Pavlov's dogs had learned? According to Thorndike's procedure, learning was an association not between two stimuli but between stimuli in the situation and a response that a subject learned to make: a *stimulus-response* (S-R) *connection*. Thorndike believed that responses repeatedly followed by reward brought satisfaction, and were strengthened, or stamped in, while nonrewarded responses were weakened, or stamped out. Thorndike's conditioning procedure allowed an animal to respond freely, but only one of its responses would have a satisfying consequence.

THE LAW OF EFFECT

According to Thorndike's "connectionist" theory, the learning of reinforced S-R connections occurs gradually and automatically in a mechanistic way as the animal experiences the consequences of its actions through blind *trial-and-error*. Gradually, the behaviors that have satisfying consequences increase in frequency; they eventually become the dominant response when the animal is placed in the puzzle box. Thorndike referred to this relationship between behavior and its consequences as the **law of effect.**

The law of effect has an important conceptual parallel to *natural selection* in evolution (Skinner, 1981).

BIZARRO   By DAN PIRARO

For both, the environment acts as the agent of selection. In natural selection, the environment determines which genes become more frequent in future populations. Similarly, the law of effect describes how environmental changes produced by behavior increase the frequency of that behavior in the future. Behaviors leading to satisfying or rewarding consequences are selected; they are likely to occur more frequently in the future than behaviors leading to unsatisfying or punishing consequences.

Thorndike believed that the law of effect was also applicable to human learning. His ideas had a major impact on the educational psychology of his time, even though he believed that learning involved trial-and-error without conscious thought. By the 1950s, over a thousand research reports a year on factors influencing animal learning were being published. These researchers generally assumed that elementary processes of learning were *conserved across species,* which meant that, from the lowest to the highest level animal species, these processes were comparable in their basic features. Complex forms of learning represented combinations and elaborations of these simpler processes. The study of animal learning was easier and allowed greater control over relevant variables than did the study of human learning. In most cases, the ultimate hope was that this basic research with simpler animals would shed more light on the mysteries of human learning—on how we have earned the many *habits* that formed our behavioral repertoires.

EXPERIMENTAL ANALYSIS OF BEHAVIOR

B. F. Skinner embraced Thorndike's view that environmental consequences influenced the responses that preceded them, but he rejected all assumptions about satisfaction and about S-R habits being learned and any interpretation that resorted to inferences about an organism's intentions, purposes, or goals. What an animal wanted was not important.

> A natural datum in a science of behavior is the probability that a given bit of behavior will occur at a given time. An experimental analysis deals with that probability in terms of frequency or rate of responding. . . . The task of an experimental analysis is to discover all the variables of which probability of response is a function (Skinner, 1966, pp. 213–214).

The **experimental analysis of behavior** means discovering, by systematic variation of stimulus conditions, all the ways that various kinds of environmental conditions affect the probability that a given response will occur. Skinner's analysis is experimental rather than theoretical—theorists are guided by derivations and predictions about behavior from their theories, but empiricists, such as Skinner, advocate the bottom-up approach, starting with the collection and evaluation of data within the context of an experiment. Skinner refused to make inferences about what happens inside an organism. No intervening variables are assumed; in his analysis inner conditions such as hunger are defined operationally, in terms of the procedures an experimenter can carry out—for example, deprivation of food for 24 hours. While approaching food and eating it can be observed and recorded, desire for food or pleasure at receiving it cannot.

To analyze behavior experimentally, Skinner developed operant conditioning procedures in which he manipulated the consequences of an organism's behavior in order to see what effect it had on subsequent behavior. An **operant** is any behavior that is *emitted* by an organism and can be characterized in terms of the observable effects it has on the environment. Literally, *operant* means *affecting the environment,* or operating on it (Skinner, 1938). Operants are *not elicited* by specific stimuli as classically conditioned behaviors are. Pigeons peck, rats search for food, babies cry and coo, some people gesture while talking, and others stutter or say *like* and *you know* frequently. The probability of

these behaviors occurring in the future can be increased or decreased by manipulating the effects they have on the environment. Operant conditioning, then, modifies the probability of different rates of operant behavior as a function of the environmental consequences they produce.

Behavior analysts manipulate contingencies of reinforcement to study behavior. Usually, this manipulation occurs within the highly controlled environment of a special apparatus invented by Skinner: the *operant chamber* (Baron et al., 1991, in press). **Figure 9.9** shows how the operant chamber works.

In many operant experiments, the cumulative recorder is used to record the animal's responding and

An operant conditioning laboratory

FIGURE 9.9   *OPERANT CHAMBER AND CUMULATIVE RECORDER*

In the operant chamber typical of those used with rats, presses on the lever are followed by delivery of a food pellet. Each response moves the pen one step vertically along a sheet of moving paper. The steeper the response record, the greater the rate of responding.

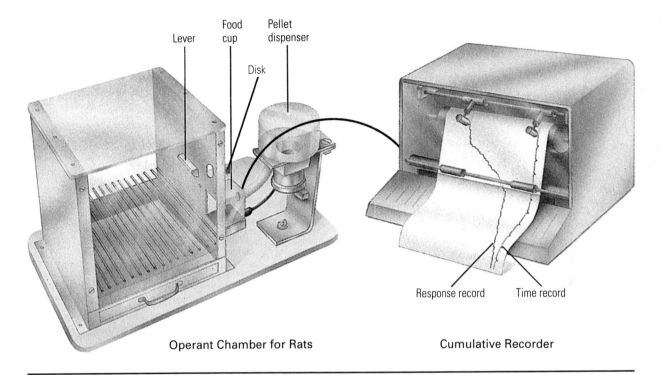

Operant Chamber for Rats   Cumulative Recorder

delivery of reinforcers. Each response "steps" a pen vertically across paper that is being rotated outward by a small moving drum. The greater the animal's response rate, the steeper the line drawn by the pen. Delivery of reinforcers is denoted by tiny hash marks drawn downward from this line.

REINFORCEMENT CONTINGENCIES

A **reinforcement contingency** is a consistent relationship between a response and the changes in the environment that it produces. For example, a pigeon's pecking (the response) is generally followed by the presentation of grain (the corresponding change in the environment). This consistent relationship, or reinforcement contingency, will usually be accompanied by an increase in the rate of pecking. For delivery of grain to increase *only* the probability of pecking, it must be contingent *only* on the pecking response—it must occur regularly after that response but not after other responses, such as turning or scratching.

Based on Skinner's work, modern behavior analysts seek to understand behavior wholly in terms of reinforcement contingencies. The primary goal of behavior analysis is to understand complex behavior in terms of the reinforcement contingencies that engender and maintain it. Behavior analysts have been successful in applying their understanding of reinforcement contingencies to a wide variety of everyday situations: programmed learning in schools, behavior modification in therapy, and even the training of porpoises and whales in zoos. Let's take a closer look at how reinforcement contingencies operate.

Consequences of Behaving

Significant events that can strengthen an organism's responses if they are contingently related are called *reinforcers*. Reinforcers are always defined empirically—in terms of their effects on changing the probability of a response. Reinforcers in operant conditioning differ from unconditional stimuli in classical conditioning only because of the variations between the

Cindy and Diego have been trained through operant conditioning techniques to leap over hurdles at Sea World.

procedures used in each form of conditioning and not because of any special properties of the stimuli themselves. A **positive reinforcer** is any stimulus that—when made contingent upon a behavior—increases the probability of that behavior over time. The delivery of a positive reinforcer contingent upon a response is called *positive reinforcement.* A food pellet positively reinforces a rat to press a lever. Getting a laugh positively reinforces a human to tell a joke. Your attention positively reinforces your professor to lecture.

Because behavior that produces desirable consequences is reinforced and repeated, we can use this principle to find out what is desirable for organisms that can't tell us, such as newborn babies. Newborn infants younger than three days of age have been shown to learn a response (sucking on a non-nutritive nipple in certain ways) that gives them the opportunity to hear their mothers' voices instead of hearing the voice of another female. The evidence shows that newborns can discriminate between speakers and prefer their own mothers' voices and that operant conditioning can be used to assess such perceptual and motivational capacities (DeCasper & Fifer, 1980). (In Chapter 5, we described many uses of behavior analysis by developmental psychologists using the habituation paradigm and rates of responding in sucking or heart rate changes.)

A **negative reinforcer** is any stimulus that—when removed, reduced, or prevented—increases the probability of a given response over time. The removal, reduction, or prevention of a negative reinforcer following a response is called *negative reinforcement.* Using an umbrella to prevent getting wet during a downpour is a common example of a behavior that is maintained by negative reinforcement. The negative reinforcer, rain, is avoided by using an umbrella. An automobile seat belt

buzzer also serves a negative reinforcing function; its annoying sound is terminated when the driver buckles up.

To clearly distinguish between positive and negative reinforcement, try to remember the following: Both positive and negative reinforcement *increase* the probability of the response that precedes them. Positive reinforcement increases response probability by the presentation of a positive stimulus following a response; negative reinforcement does the same in reverse through the removal, reduction, or prevention of a negative stimulus following a response. In the umbrella example, staying dry is a positive stimulus that positively reinforces you to use an umbrella; the rain is a negative stimulus that negatively reinforces you to use an umbrella.

Positive and negative reinforcement explain how new behaviors are acquired and old ones maintained. Suppose, however, that you wanted to eliminate an existing operant? How would you do it? One way would be to use **operant extinction,** a procedure in which delivery of a positive reinforcer is withheld. If the behavior does not produce any consequences, it returns to the level it was before operant conditioning—in other words, it is *extinguished.* For example, smiling and nodding are behaviors that may reinforce your professor to look at you often. Withholding of those reinforcers will decrease the probability of the professor looking at you as often. Have you ever had the experience of dropping

Kicking a vending machine would be reinforced if candy or soda came out as a result.

a few coins into a vending machine and getting nothing in return? If you kicked the machine and your soda or candy then came out, kicking would be reinforced. However, if your kicking produced no soda or candy and only a sore foot, kicking would quickly be extinguished.

An unwanted response is extinguished only if all reinforcers can really be withheld. Complete withholding is difficult outside the laboratory where many aspects of a person's environment are not under the control of readily identifiable reinforcers. Extinction is, thus, more likely to occur when withholding of reinforcers is combined with positive reinforcement to increase the probability of the desired response. Clowning in class to get attention is most likely to stop if the student finds that it doesn't work any more (extinction) and discovers that other, more socially approved behaviors do elicit attention (positive reinforcement).

Punishment

Another technique for decreasing the probability of a response is punishment. A **punisher** is any stimulus that—when it is made contingent upon a response—decreases the probability of that response over time. *Punishment* is the delivery of a punisher following a response. Touching a hot stove, for example, produces pain that punishes the preceding response so that you are less likely next time to touch the stove. Responses that are punished immediately tend to decrease in frequency, however, responses that produce delayed aversive consequences are only suppressed. When a formerly punished response no longer produces aversive consequences, it tends to increase in frequency to pre-punishment levels.

Although punishment and negative reinforcement are closely related operations, they differ in important ways. A good way to differentiate them is to think of each in terms of its effects on behavior. Punishment, by definition, always *reduces* the probability of a response occurring again; negative reinforcement, by definition, always *increases* the probability of a response recurring. For example, some people get severe headaches after drinking caffeinated beverages. The headache is the stimulus that *punishes* and reduces the behavior of drinking coffee. However, once the headache is present, people often will take aspirin or another pain reliever to eliminate the headache. The aspirin's analgesic effect is the stimulus that *negatively reinforces* the behavior of ingesting aspirin.

A word of caution is in order regarding the *use* and *abuse* of punishment in family and institutional settings. To eliminate undesired behaviors, it is always preferable to reinforce the alternative, desired behavior than it is to punish the undesired behavior. When reinforcement

The punishment of the pain resulting from touching a hot stove decreases the probability that the child will do it again.

is not possible or does not stop the negative action swiftly enough and punishment is the only alternative, psychological research shows that punishment should meet a number of conditions. It should be swift and brief; be administered right after the response occurs; be limited in intensity; be specific to responses and never to the person's character; be limited to the situation where the response occurs; give no mixed messages to the person being punished; and consist of *penalties* instead of physical *pain* (Walters & Grusec, 1977).

Serious long-term problems arise with the use of punishment to control human behavior because the conditions just mentioned are rarely met by angry parents and emotional teachers. Children are punished often and hard—federal surveys reveal that corporal punishment is meted out 3 million times a year in our schools—mostly to elementary school boys and disproportionately to African Americans "by teachers or administrators wielding wooden paddles to whack students across their buttocks" (Schmidt, 1987). Although parents and school officials say corporal punishment is essential to maintain discipline and order at home and in school, its presence means that they do not understand how to motivate or reward children in positive ways. Punishment is often counterproductive, suppressing the punished response only in the presence of authority and causing physical harm, emotional scars, stigmatization (when given in public), and hatred for the institution in which it is experienced. Worst of all, the physically punished child learns that physical aggression is an acceptable means of controlling the behavior of others (Bongiovani, 1977; Hyman, reported in Schmidt, 1977).

Behavior analysts assume that any behavior that persists does so because that behavior results in reinforcement. Any behavior, they argue—even irrational or bizarre behavior—can be understood by discovering what the reinforcement or payoff is. Sometimes, behaviors may be maintained by reinforcers different from those involved in the original conditioning. For example, symptoms of mental or physical disorders are sometimes maintained because the person gets attention and sympathy and is excused from normal responsibilities. These *secondary gains* reinforce irrational and sometimes self-destructive behavior. Can you see how shy behaviors can be maintained through reinforcement even though the shy person would prefer not to be shy?

Three-term Contingency

Organisms learn not only *to* behave but also *how to* behave in certain situations. Through their associations with reinforcement or punishment, certain stimuli that precede a particular response, or **discriminative stimuli,** later come to set the occasion for that behavior. Discriminative stimuli do *not* signal other stimuli as CSs in classical conditioning do. Through experience with different stimuli and behavioral consequences, organisms learn that in the presence of some stimuli but not others their behavior is likely to have a particular effect on the environment. For example, in the presence of a green street light, the act of crossing an intersection in a motor vehicle is reinforced. When the light is red, however, such behavior may be punished—it may result in a traffic ticket or an accident. (I became aware of the discriminatively learned nature of street light colors when in Naples, Italy, I was nearly run over by drivers who simply did not stop or even slow down when their light was red unless a police officer was at the corner—their discriminative stimulus.)

Skinner referred to the sequence of discriminative stimulus-behavior-consequence as the **three-term**

 TABLE 9.1 THE THREE-TERM CONTINGENCY: RELATIONSHIPS AMONG DISCRIMINATIVE STIMULI BEHAVIOR, AND CONSEQUENCES

	Discriminative Stimulus (S^D)	Emitted Response (R)	Stimulus Consequence (S)
1. Positive Reinforcement: A response in the presence of an effective signal (S^D) produces the desired consequence. This response increases.	Soft-drink machine	Put coin in slot	Get drink
2. Negative Reinforcement (escape): An unpleasant situation is escaped from by an operant response. This escape response increases.	Heat	Fan oneself	Escape from heat
3. Negative Reinforcement (avoidance): A stimulus signals the organism that an unpleasant event will occur soon. An appropriate response avoids its occurrence. This avoidance response increases.	Sound of seatbelt buzzer	Buckle up	Avoid aversive noise
4. Extinction Training: An operant response is not followed by a reinforcer. It decreases in rate.	None or S^{Δ}	Clowning behavior	No one notices and response becomes frequent
5. Punishment: A response is followed by an aversive stimulus. The response is eliminated or suppressed.	Attractive matchbox	Play with matches	Get burned or get caught and spanked

contingency and believed that it could explain most human action (Skinner, 1953). **Table 9.1** describes how the three-term contingency might explain several different kinds of human behavior.

Skinner's belief that human behavior can be explained by the three-term contingency was based on work with laboratory rats and pigeons. Under laboratory conditions, manipulating the consequences of behavior in the presence of discriminative stimuli can exert powerful control over that behavior (Mazur, 1990). For example, a pigeon might be given grain after pecking a disk in the presence of a green light but not a red light. The green light is a discriminative stimulus that sets the occasion for pecking; the red is a discriminative stimulus that sets the occasion for *not* pecking. The green light is a *positive discriminative stimulus* or S^D (pronounced *ess dee*). The red light is a *negative discriminative stimulus* or S^Δ (pronounced *ess Delta*).

Organisms learn quickly to discriminate between these two conditions, responding regularly in the presence of S^Ds and not responding in the presence of S^Δs. By manipulating the components of the three-term contingency, we can exert powerful stimulus control over our own behavior as well as that of others.

Organisms also learn to *generalize responses* to other stimuli that resemble the S^D. Once a response has been reinforced in the presence of one discriminative stimulus, a similar stimulus can become a discriminative stimulus for that same response. For example, pigeons trained to peck a disk in the presence of a green light, will also peck the disk in the presence of lights that are lighter or darker shades of green than the original discriminative stimulus. This kind of generalization is at the heart of some of life's most embarrassing moments. Have you ever had the experience when walking down the street of thinking you see someone you know? After waving or calling to the person, you realize that he or she is a complete stranger.

PROPERTIES OF REINFORCERS

Whether through discrimination or generalization, the three-term contingency describes the conditions under which behavior is controlled by a particular stimuli. Such control is acquired through the repeated association of behavior producing reinforcing or punishing consequences in the presence of those stimuli.

Reinforcers have a number of interesting and complex properties. They can start out as weak and become strong, can be learned through experience rather than biologically determined, and can be activities rather than objects. In some situations, even powerful reinforcers may not be enough to change a dominant behavior pattern (in this case, we would say that the consequences were not actually reinforcers).

Reinforcers and punishers are the power brokers of operant conditioning—they change or maintain behavior. Contingent reinforcement strengthens responding; contingent punishment suppresses responding. When stimuli are presented *noncontingently,* their presence has little effect on behavior—for example, when a parent praises your bad work as well as your good efforts or a teacher is overly critical regardless of the quality of your performance. Such noncontingent consequences reveal more to us about the attributes of the loving parent or hostile teacher than about your performance.

Humans, unlike most other species, can learn even when behavioral consequences are not apparently immediate but delayed. You typically get feedback on examination performance days after you study for and take the test, but if the feedback is positive, the response of studying for the next test is likely to be strengthened. Although your test score is the reinforcer of interest in testing situations, taking a test does have other consequences. For example, you don't need to wait to get your test back to know that you answered some of the questions right. The fact that you can respond to a test question quickly and without a great deal of deliberation serves to reinforce your studying and test-taking behavior. If you have another test before you get the results of the previous test, you are likely to approach studying for it in the same way you did the first one.

Conditioned Reinforcers

In operant conditioning, otherwise neutral stimuli paired with primary reinforcers, such as food and water, can become **conditioned reinforcers** for operant responses. When they do, they can come to serve as ends in themselves. In fact, a great deal of human behavior is influenced less by biologically significant primary reinforcers than by a wide variety of conditioned reinforcers. Money, grades, praise, smiles of approval, gold stars, and various kinds of status symbols are among the many potent conditioned reinforcers that influence much of our learning and behavior. When a conditioned reinforcer controls a wide range of responses, it is said to be a *generalized conditioned reinforcer*. Money, for example, controls so much human behavior because it can be traded for many significant events in our lives. It is a reinforcer that can maintain a high level of responding even when a person hoards it and never exchanges it for property and pleasures of the mind or flesh.

Virtually any stimulus can become a conditioned reinforcer by being paired with a primary reinforcer. In one experiment, simple tokens were used as conditioned reinforcers with animal learners.

> In an early study, chimps were trained to learn how to solve problems with edible raisins as primary reinforcers. Then tokens were delivered

Inedible tokens can be used as conditioned reinforcers with animals. In one study, chimps deposited tokens in a "chimp-o-mat" in exchange for raisins.

along with the raisins. When only the tokens were presented, the chimps continued working for their "money" because they could later deposit their hard-earned tokens in a "chimp-o-mat" designed to exchange tokens for the raisins (Cowles, 1937).

Teachers and experimenters often find secondary conditioned reinforcers more effective and easier to use than primary reinforcers because (a) few primary reinforcers are available in the classroom, whereas almost any stimulus event that is under control of a teacher can be used as a conditioned reinforcer; (b) they can be dispensed rapidly; (c) they are portable; and (d) their reinforcing effect may be more immediate since it depends only on the perception of receiving them and not on biological processing as in the case of primary reinforcers (food).

In some institutions, *token economies* have been set up based on these principles. Desired behaviors (grooming or taking medication, for example) are explicitly defined, and token payoffs are given by the staff when they are performed. These tokens can later be exchanged by the patients for a wide array of rewards and privileges (Ayllon & Azrin, 1965; Holden, 1978). These systems of reinforcement are especially effective in modifying patients' behaviors regarding self-care, upkeep of their environment, and, most importantly, frequency of their positive social interactions.

Preferred Activities as Positive Reinforcers

Positive reinforcers in the laboratory are usually substances such as food or water. However, outside the laboratory there are many more behavior reinforcers in operation. We know that nursery-school children enjoy running and shouting much more than sitting still and listening to someone talk. What would happen if the opportunity to run and shout were made contingent on a period of sitting still first? Would there be an increase in the sitting-still behavior? The answer is yes. In a classic study, when pleas, punishment, and a bit of screaming proved unsuccessful, a teacher reprogrammed her classroom contingencies. The procedure the teacher used may seem unusual, but it worked.

> Short periods during which the children sat quietly in their chairs facing the blackboard were occasionally followed by the sound of a bell and the instruction, "Run and scream." The students immediately jumped out of their chairs and ran around the room screaming and having a good time. After a few minutes, another signal alerted them to stop and return to their chairs. Later in the study, the children were given the opportunity to earn tokens for engaging in low-probability behaviors, such as practicing arithmetic. The children could use the tokens to buy the opportunity to participate in high-probability activities, such as playing with toys. With this kind of procedure, control was virtually perfect after a few days (Homme et al., 1963).

The principle that a more preferred activity can be used to reinforce a less preferred one is called the **Premack principle,** after its discoverer **David Premack** (1965). He found that water-deprived rats learned to increase their running in an exercise wheel when running was followed by an opportunity to drink. Other rats that were not thirsty but exercise-deprived would learn to increase their drinking when that response was followed by a chance to run. According to the Premack principle, a reinforcer may be any event or activity that is valued by the organism. The Premack principle is often used by parents and teachers to get children to engage in low-probability activities. For a socially outgoing child, playing with friends can reinforce the less pleasant task of finishing homework first. For a shy child, reading a new book can be used to reinforce the less preferred activity of playing with other children. Whatever activity is valued can be used as a reinforcer and thus increase the probability of engaging in an activity that is not currently valued. Over time, there is the possibility that the less-favored activities will come to be valued as exposure to them leads to discovery of their intrinsic worth.

The Premack principle is enormously useful for *self-management*. If you wish you could get your studying done early in the evening before you get tired but you are easily distracted, try promising yourself a half-hour break to engage in an activity you really want to do—but *only* after you have studied for a given period of time or have read a given number of pages. A Premack moral is that pleasure before study makes study a pain; pleasure after study makes study a gain.

SHAPING AND CHAINING

Similar to classical conditioning, operant conditioning does not usually occur in one trial. Reinforcing behavior only once or even twice in the presence of a discriminative stimulus is usually not sufficient to produce learning. In the laboratory, behavior analysts train new behaviors with a method called **shaping by successive approximations,** which means reinforcing any responses that successively approximate and ultimately match the desired response.

Suppose that you wish to train an animal—a rat—to press a lever in an operant chamber. The rat has learned to use its paws in many ways, but it probably has never pressed a lever before. First, you deprive the rat of food for a day. (Without deprivation, food is not likely to serve as a reinforcer.) Next, you teach it to eat food from the food hopper in an operant chamber. When the rat is properly motivated and has learned where the food is located, you can begin the actual shaping process. You start by making delivery of food contingent upon specific aspects of the rat's behavior, such as orienting itself toward the lever. Next, food is delivered only as the rat moves closer and closer to the lever. Soon, the requirement for reinforcement is actually to touch the lever. Finally, the rat must depress the lever for food to be delivered. Now the rat is ready to be left on its own; it has learned that it can produce food by pressing the lever.

Shaping is a procedure for changing behavior in small steps that successively approximate the desired terminal stage performance. When shaping begins, any element of the target response is reinforced. When this element occurs regularly, only responses more like the final goal response are reinforced. By carefully combining *differential reinforcement* for the currently correct response (rather than any of the former responses) with gradual raising of the criteria for desired performance, an experimenter can shape the desired, higher-level action.

Shaping is not effective on nonhuman animals alone; it has important practical applications for human behavior as well. Consider the following example involving a young schizophrenic child.

> The patient was a 3-year-old boy who was diagnosed as having childhood schizophrenia. He lacked normal social and verbal behavior, and was given to ungovernable tantrums and self-destructive actions. After a cataract operation, he refused to wear the glasses that were essential for the development of normal vision. So, first, he was given a bit of candy or fruit at the clicking sound of a toy noisemaker; through its association with food, the sound became a conditioned reinforcer. Then, training began with empty eyeglass frames. At first, the noisemaker was sounded after the child picked up the glasses. Soon, though, it sounded only when the child held the glasses and, later, only when he carried them. Slowly and through successive approximations, the boy was rewarded for bringing the frames closer to his eyes. After a few weeks, he was putting the empty frames on his head at odd angles and, finally, he was wearing them in the proper manner. With further training, the child learned to wear his glasses up to 12 hours a day (Wolf et al., 1964).

In everyday life, you can rarely get by with a single response to a situation. Usually, you must perform long sequences of actions to complete a behavioral episode. You write essays that consist of many strings of responses, your teacher delivers a lecture that involves many different responses, and any sports skill you've acquired is composed of a host of components. To teach a sequence of actions, you could use a technique called **chaining,** a procedure in which each response in a sequence is followed by a conditioned reinforcer and the final response is followed by a primary reinforcer. In chaining, the last response of the sequence is reinforced (with the primary reinforcer) first. This final response then becomes a conditioned reinforcer for the response that occurs just before it. Each link in the behavior chain serves as a *discriminative stimulus* for the next response in line and as a *conditioned reinforcer* for the response that immediately precedes it. Consider, for example, the chain of behaviors involved in eating. How would you go about teaching a child to eat with the proper utensils? Three separate actions are involved in this operant chain: putting food onto the spoon, raising the spoon to the mouth, and inserting the spoon into the mouth. First, by reinforcing the last behavior in the chain, you would actually put food into the child's mouth. Next, you would reward lifting the spoon (you would have already placed food onto the spoon for the child). Putting food into the mouth reinforces the action of lifting the spoon and serves as a discriminative stimulus for chewing. Only after the child has learned to lift the spoon and insert it into his or her mouth, is the child actually trained to put food onto the spoon.

SCHEDULES OF REINFORCEMENT

In the laboratory, shaping and chaining are used by behavior analysts to train new behaviors in their subjects. By systematically manipulating the consequences of an organism's behavior in the presence of discriminative stimuli, new patterns of responding, some of them quite complex, can be created and studied. The basic principles of operant behavior that we have discussed so far—reinforcement, punishment, and extinction—were each discovered and subsequently studied with variations of this simple approach. The most commonly used variation is to expose subjects to different **schedules of reinforcement,** in which reinforcement (or punishment) is dependent on either the number of responses emitted or a single response made after a given time interval has elapsed. So, instead of getting one unit of reward for one unit of response every time, different patterns of responding are required to get that same unit of reward. Sometimes many responses are necessary to get it or one response will get the prize but only after a given time period since the last reward. Different reinforcement schedules have different effects on behavior. Let's take a closer look at how these schedules operate and how they influence behavior.

Sometimes when you raise your hand in class, the teacher calls on you and sometimes not. The best batters in baseball hit .300 for an entire season, which means that their attempts at hitting succeed only three times out of ten, but on any given day they might get four hits in four at bats. Some slot machine players continue to put coins in the one-armed bandits even though the reinforcers are delivered only rarely. Obviously, behavior is not always followed by reinforcement or by punishment. The relationship between behavior and reinforcement may vary according to a variety of *patterns* or *schedules,* four of which we discuss below.

There is a legendary story about the way the first schedule of reinforcement was accidentally discovered by young B. F. Skinner. It seems that one weekend he was secluded in his laboratory with not enough of a food-reward supply for his hard-working rats. He economized by giving the rats pellets after every two responses rather than after each one. From the rats' points of view, half the time they responded they got reinforcers and half the time they did not. Under this condition of partial, or intermittent, reinforcement, the rats still acquired the operant response, although more slowly than usual. What do you predict happened when these animals underwent extinction training and their responses were now followed by no pellets at all? How did the extinction curve of these partially reinforced subjects look compared to those who were reinforced on a one-to-one schedule? The animals trained under partial reinforcement continued to respond longer and more vigorously than did the rats who had gotten payoffs after every response. Half as many experiences of the response-reinforcer contingency had produced a more durable response! The **partial reinforcement effect** is now a widely established principle: responses acquired under schedules of partial reinforcement are more resistant to extinction than those acquired with continuous reinforcement (Bitterman, 1975). To keep a learned response going for a long time in the absence of rewards, researchers deliver reinforcement during training occasionally but not continuously.

The discovery of the effectiveness of partial reinforcement led to extensive study of the effects of different reinforcement schedules on human and animal behavior (see **Figure 9.10**). Reinforcers can be delivered according to either a *ratio schedule,* after a certain number of responses, or an *interval schedule,* after the first response following a specified interval of time. In each case, there can be either a constant, or *fixed,* pattern of reinforcement or an irregular, or *variable,* pattern of reinforcement, making four major types of schedules in all. Even when the amount and kind of reinforcement are the same and deprivation is constant, performance will vary enormously according to the schedule on which reinforcers are given (Ferster et al., 1975).

Fixed-ratio (FR) Schedules

In *fixed-ratio schedules,* the reinforcer comes after the organism has emitted a fixed number of responses. When reinforcement follows one response, the schedule is called an FR-1 schedule. When the first 24 responses are unreinforced and reinforcement follows only every twenty-fifth response the schedule is an FR-25 schedule. The FR-1 schedule, or *continuous reinforcement schedule,* is the most efficient for rapidly shaping an

FIGURE 9.10 *REINFORCEMENT SCHEDULES*

These different patterns of behavior are produced by four simple schedules of reinforcement. The hash marks indicate when reinforcement is delivered.

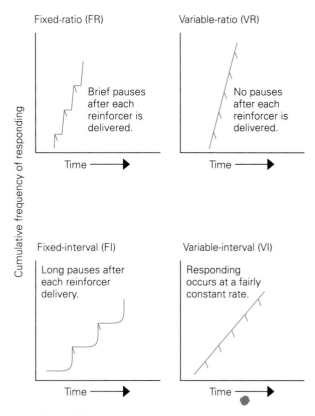

"FR 25! Pass it on!"

animal to acquire a new response. FR schedules generate high rates of responding because there is a direct correlation between responding and reinforcement—the more responses the more often reinforcement is delivered. When workers get paid once after making or selling a given total number of units, FR schedules are in operation. The higher the ratio, the more rapid the responding but also the longer the pause after each reinforcement. Stretching the ratio too thin by requiring a great many responses for reinforcement without first shaping the organism to emit that many responses may lead to extinction.

Variable-ratio (VR) Schedules

In a *variable-ratio schedule,* the number of responses required for reinforcement varies from one reinforcer delivery to the next. A VR-10 schedule means that, on the average, reinforcement follows every tenth response; but it might come after only one response or after twenty responses. Variable-ratio schedules generate the highest rate of responding and the greatest resistance to extinction, especially when the VR value is large. A pigeon on a VR-110 schedule will respond with up to 12,000 pecks per hour and will continue responding for hours even with no reinforcement. Keep in mind, though, that the pigeon's behavior was shaped—at first, it was exposed to low VR values (for example, VR-5) and, then, to increasingly larger values. Gambling would seem to be under the control of VR schedules. The response of dropping coins in slot machines is maintained at a high, steady level by the payoff that is delivered only after an unknown, variable number of coins has been deposited. VR schedules leave us guessing when the reward will come—we gamble that it will be after the next response and not much later.

Fixed-interval (FI) Schedules

On a *fixed-interval schedule,* a reinforcer is delivered for the first response made after a fixed period of time has elapsed. On an FI-10 schedule, the subject, after receiving any one reinforcer, will have to wait at least ten seconds before another response is reinforced. Other responses in between, before the time interval has elapsed, have no programmed consequences—they do not count toward reinforcement. Response patterns under FI schedules show a scalloped pattern. Immediately after each reinforced response, the animal makes few if any responses—it takes a time out without making meaningful responses. As time passes, the animal responds more and more until, eventually, it is payoff time.

Variable-interval (VI) Schedules

With *variable-interval schedules,* the first response after a variable period of time has elapsed from the last reinforcement is reinforced. On a VI-20 schedule, reinforcers are delivered, on the average, once every 20 seconds. Thus, a response after 10 seconds is sometimes followed by a reinforcer, but sometimes 30 seconds must pass before a response is reinforced. Responses during the intervening interval have no effect on reinforcement. No wonder this schedule generates a low but very stable response rate. Extinction under VI schedules is gradual and much slower than under fixed-interval schedules. Although there is a steady decline in responding without reinforcement, subjects trained under a long VI schedule continue to respond for long periods. In one case, a pigeon pecked 18,000 times during the first 4 hours after reinforcement stopped and required 168 hours before its responding extinguished completely (Ferster & Skinner, 1957). Such persistence of performance during extinction is one of the most powerful effects of partial reinforcement schedules.

BIOFEEDBACK: BOOSTING WEAK RESPONSE SIGNALS

Imagine that your task is to help someone learn how to make baskets from the foul line. Your task sounds relatively straightforward; however, there is a catch: you are blindfolded. How will you give your pupil the feedback needed to correct misses or reinforce hits? Now, remove the blindfold. Is there any difference in the procedure or the outcome? You can now verbalize what is needed to help the shooter sink the ball in the hoop.

How can we extend the free-throw metaphor to learning to control heart rate, blood pressure, and brain waves? It is possible to learn to control involuntary behaviors that are otherwise controlled by the autonomic nervous system. **Biofeedback training** is a procedure for providing clear external signals of ordinarily weak or internal responses to make an individual aware of those responses. When you are blindfolded, you can't easily increase the basketball player's free-throw percentage. However, when you can see that the player's

After five years flat on her back in the hospital, Sue Strong used biofeedback to learn to increase her blood pressure to the point where she could sit up. She was also helped by a monkey who had been operantly shaped to comb her hair, feed her, turn book pages, and make other responses Sue could not do on her own because of paralysis.

shooting arm doesn't fully extend after the shot, you can make some necessary suggestions. Similarly, in biofeedback training, the subject can "see" his or her own bodily reactions which are monitored and amplified by special equipment that transforms them into lights and sound cues of varying intensity. The subject's task is then to control the level of these external cues; for example, a subject might have to keep lit a light on a meter or maintain a tone at a given intensity. Achieving control of the level of the cues is the reinforcer. In biofeedback, as in basketball, the reinforcer is rarely a tangible substance but more often the personal pride or sense of accomplishment that accompanies meeting the criterion reaction.

Biofeedback, as pioneered by psychologist **Neal Miller** (1978), has helped many people gain control over a variety of nonconscious biological processes. When combined with other behavioral techniques, biofeedback is useful in the treatment of many conditions, such as headaches, neuromuscular disorders, hypertension, hypotension, Raynaud's disease, and fecal incontinence (Olton et al., 1980). Biofeedback has made some dramatic changes in severely handicapped patients, as in the case of Sue Strong. A physical condition made it impossible for her to sit up without fainting; when she would try, her blood pressure would suddenly plummet. Biofeedback enabled Strong to monitor her blood pressure and learn how to increase it gradually to the point where she no longer fainted. Thanks to biofeedback, patients who had been immobilized on their backs for years now can sit up and function more effectively (Miller, 1985).

LEARNED HELPLESSNESS

We've noted that contingency between responding and reinforcement increases desirable responding, while response-contingent punishment suppresses undesirable responding. What happens when the individual gets punished arbitrarily regardless of the response? Imagine that, after years of raising your hand in class to get the teacher's attention, you take a class in which the teacher makes fun of you for raising your hand, suggesting that you must think you are in elementary school. In addition, the teacher never calls on you, no matter how you signal that you want to ask or answer a question. What do you do? One simple answer is that you give up—you stop trying to get the teacher's attention. Because environmental consequences do not seem to be related in any contingent or meaningful way to what you do, you stop trying to control them. This passive resignation that follows prolonged, noncontingent, inescapable punishment is termed **learned helplessness.**

Learned helplessness was discovered by **Martin Seligman** and **Steven Maier** (1967) in a study on dogs who received painful, unavoidable shocks. Some of them could escape these shocks by learning to press a switch that stopped the shock (negative reinforcement). However, others continued to get shocked no matter what response they made (noncontingent punishment). In the next phase, each dog was put into a shuttlebox (similar to the one used by Rescorla, p. 313). The dogs could escape the shocks on the grid floor by jumping over the small hurdle between the two compartments of the box. Just before a shock was given, a tone sounded (the conditional stimulus). Some of the dogs—those who had learned to escape before by pressing the switch—soon learned that tone reliably predicted shock and escaped to the safe side of the box as soon as the tone signal came on. The dogs who had been exposed previously to noncontingent punishment, however, did not escape the painful shocks, even when it was possible and easy to do so. Instead, they crouched, barked, or shook with fear; they seemed to have given up.

The passively resigned dogs' impaired performance included three components: *motivational deficits*—they were slow to initiate known actions; *emotional deficits*—they appeared rigid, listless, frightened, and distressed; and *cognitive deficits*—they demonstrated poor learning in new situations where simple new responding would be reinforced. Even when these sad dogs were repeatedly dragged over the hurdle to the safe side of the box, they did not learn to jump over on their own (Maier & Seligman, 1976).

There are some obvious parallels between learned helplessness in animals and depression in humans (Seligman, 1975). However, in the case of humans, we must consider cognitive factors—the ways in which they interpret situations of noncontingency. Do humans attribute failure to personal factors or to situational features? How important is it for them to have a sense of control over their outcomes (Abramson et al., 1978)? We will answer these questions in Chapter 17 when we investigate clinical depression.

SUMMING UP

Drawing from his research on cats in puzzle boxes, Thorndike formulated his law of effect: Behavior that produces "satisfying" outcomes tends to be repeated. Skinner incorporated the law of effect into his study of operant conditioning. Emitted behaviors are called operants *because they operate on or change the environment. Skinner's analytic approach centers on manipulating contingencies of reinforcement and observing the effects on behavior. A positive reinforcer is any stimulus that, when made contingent upon a behavior, increases the probability of that behavior over time. A negative reinforcer is any stimulus that, when removed, reduced, or prevented following a response, increases the probability of that response over time. Two ways to reduce or eliminate behavior are extinction, or the withholding of a positive or negative reinforcer, and punishment, or the delivery of an aversive stimulus contingent upon responding. Based on his work, Skinner argued that behavior could be explained in terms of the three-term contingency: Manipulating the consequences for behaving in the presence of discriminative stimuli results in powerful control over behavior.*

Primary reinforcers are biologically important stimuli that function as reinforcers even though an organism may have had no previous experience with them. Conditioned reinforcers are learned; for humans, they include money, praise, and status symbols. New complex responses may be learned by shaping or chaining procedures. A desired response may be shaped through successive reinforcement of closer approximations of the desired response. A chain of responses may be taught by making completion of each link a conditioned reinforcer for the response that comes before it and a discriminative stimulus for the next one in the chain. Partial or intermittent reinforcement leads to greater resistance to extinction than continuous reinforcement. Behavior is affected by schedules of reinforcement that may be fixed or that vary in the number of responses or in the temporal patterning of reinforcers. On ratio schedules, reinforcers are delivered after a certain number of responses that may be constant (fixed) or irregular (variable). On interval schedules, reinforcers are delivered after a specified interval of time that may also be fixed or variable.

Biofeedback is a procedure for changing behavior. It amplifies usually weak or nonobservable responses so they can be reinforced. Biofeedback has been used successfully to help people control pulse rate, blood pressure, and migraine headaches.

When punishment is noncontingent on behavior but occurs regardless of what the organism does, a state of learned helplessness may emerge. The learned helplessness syndrome includes the triad of deficits in motivation, emotion, and cognition; it also has parallels to states of human depression.

LEARNING, BIOLOGY, AND COGNITION

The bulk of research on animal learning has focused on arbitrarily chosen responses to conveniently available stimuli in artificial laboratory environments. The laboratory approach was adopted purposely by researchers who believed that the laws of learning they uncovered would be powerful general principles of behavior for all organisms and all types of learning. Critics have argued that traditional behavior theory did not do justice to the conception of humans as controllers of their own lives; personal autonomy, inner directedness, or reason-based actions had no rightful place in this view of learning (Schwartz & Lacy, 1982). In addition, central to the approach of operant conditioners was the assumption that the specific responses, discriminative stimuli, and reinforcers used in their studies were all arbitrarily chosen merely to demonstrate the power of the general principles of learning. They had no intrinsic value to the organism but were determined operationally according to what worked in the laboratory control of behavior.

Curiously, the contemporary view that a single, general account of the associationist principles of learning is common to humans and all animals was first proposed centuries ago by English philosopher David Hume in 1771. Hume reasoned that "any theory by which we explain the operations of the understanding, or the origin and connexion of the passions in man, will acquire additional authority, if we find that the same theory is requisite to explain the same phenomena in all other animals" (Hume, 1977/1951, p. 104).

The appealing simplicity of such a view has come under attack in the last three decades as psychologists have discovered certain *constraints*, or limitations, on the generality of the findings regarding conditioning. Some constraints are imposed by the biological makeup of the organism and the environmental habitats to which particular species must normally adapt (Leger, 1991, in press). Other constraints are imposed by the fact that animal learners can think, reason, interpret, and attribute meaning and causality to stimulus events and to behavior. The operation of these cognitive processes serves to make conditioning less mechanical and more flexible than originally believed—making possible more complex kinds of learning than those envisioned in the simpler views of conditioning.

BIOLOGICAL CONSTRAINTS ON LEARNING

Organisms that survive the particular challenges their ancestors faced pass on their genotypes to future generations. In order to fit a given ecological niche, each species must develop certain behavioral repertoires that aid survival. For instance, birds living on steep cliffs must make nests in such a way that their eggs won't roll out; the offspring of those that make the wrong kind of nests die and fail to pass on their genes. Some animals develop particular sense modalities (eagles have superior vision and bats have excellent hearing), and others develop special response capabilities, such as speed or strength, suggesting that different species may have different capabilities for learning in a given situation—notably the habitat in which their species usually functions. Some relationships between CSs and UCSs, or behavior and its consequences, may be more difficult for some organisms to learn than others, depending on their relevance to survival.

Biological constraints on learning are any limitations on learning imposed by a species' genetic endowment. These constraints can apply to the animal's sensory, behavioral, and cognitive capacities. Biological constraints challenge assumptions of the traditional behavior-analytic approach; they suggest that the principles of conditioning cannot be universally applied to all species across all situations and that not all reinforcement contingencies work equally well to produce learning in any given species. If they must take into account the natural environments of different species and their genetic makeup, the laws of learning are neither universal nor even very general. There are two areas of research showing that behavior-environment relations can be *biased* by an organism's genotype: species-specific behavior and taste-aversion learning.

Species-specific Behavior

You have seen animals performing tricks on television, in the circus, or at zoos or fairs. Some animals play baseball or Ping-Pong and others drive tiny race cars. For years, **Keller Breland** and **Marion Breland** had used operant conditioning techniques to train thousands of animals from many different species to perform a remarkable array of such behaviors. The

Brelands had believed that general principles derived from laboratory research using virtually any type of response or reward could be directly applied to the control of animal behavior outside the laboratory.

At some point after their training, however, some of their animals began to "misbehave." For example, a raccoon was trained, after great difficulty, to pick up a coin, put it into a toy bank, and collect an edible reinforcer. The raccoon, however, would not immediately deposit the coin. Later, when there were two coins to be deposited, conditioning broke down completely— the raccoon would not give up the coins at all. Instead, it would rub the coins together, dip them into the bank, and then pull them back out. (Such behavior seems strange until you consider that raccoons often engage in rubbing and washing behaviors as they remove the outer shells of a favorite food, crayfish.) Similarly, when pigs were given the task of putting their hard-earned tokens into a large piggy bank, they instead would drop the coins onto the floor, root (poke at) them with their snouts, and toss them into the air. (Pigs root and shake their food as natural part of their inherited food-getting repertoire.)

This experience convinced the Brelands that, even when animals have learned to make operant responses perfectly, the newly "learned behavior drifts toward instinctual behavior" over time. They termed this tendency **instinctual drift** (Breland & Breland, 1951, 1961). The behavior of their animals is not explainable by the three-term contingency; but it is understandable, if we consider the species-specific tendencies imposed by an inherited genotype—raccoons naturally rub objects together before eating them and pigs naturally root their food as they eat it. These tendencies override the temporary changes in behavior brought about by operant conditioning. In fact, the inherited behavioral pattern is incompatible with the operant conditioning task. The tokens might have elicited the natural response of the animal to food in the way a CS does a CR. The animals' misbehaviors were a manifestation of the embedding of classical conditioning (involving natural, biologically significant relationships) in an operant conditioning procedure designed to teach new contingencies present in the response-token-food sequence. The intrusion of competing contingencies occurs when an animal responds to the token (CS) as if it were food (UCS) and not simply a conditioned reinforcer for the preceding operant response.

To demonstrate that operant conditioning principles hold even for pigs, what change might you suggest to the animal trainer? If the token were paired with a water reward for a thirsty pig, it would then not be rooted as food but would be deposited in the bank as a valuable commodity—dare we say a *liquid asset*?

Taste-aversion Learning

As a child, I once got sick after eating pork and beans in the grade-school lunch room. Although no one else got ill from the meal, I immediately attributed my sickness to the strong smelling, foul tasting food and not to a stomach virus or to any other factor present in the lunch room setting. For years, the very smell of pork and beans triggered a reaction of nausea. My bean-bias is not strange—humans and many other animals readily form an association between illness and a small class of likely causes: food. Did we learn this bias or is it a part of the genetic endowment? Let's look to the laboratory for a clue.

Taste-aversion learning, or the tendency to associate a substance's taste with illness caused by eating that substance, represents a genetic bias in learning. Indeed, studies of taste aversion seem to violate usual principles of conditioning but make sense when viewed as part of a species' adaptiveness to its natural environment. Suppose that a rat eats poisoned bait and many hours later becomes ill but survives. After only this one pairing and despite the long interval (up to 12 hours) between tasting the food (CS) and experiencing poisoned-based illness (UCS), the rat learns to avoid other foods with that specific flavor. There is no principle in classical conditioning that can adequately explain such one-trial learning and why such a long CS-UCS interval is effective in eliciting a CR.

Interestingly enough, other stimuli present at the same time are not avoided later—only those associated with *taste,* as shown in a study by the psychologist who first discovered the phenomenon of taste-aversion learning, **John Garcia.**

Garcia and his colleague, Robert Koelling (1966), designed an ingenious study to demonstrate that some CS-UCS combinations can and some cannot be classically conditioned in particular species of animals. In this study, rats were shown to learn an association between the flavor of a liquid and later illness but not between flavor and simultaneous pain. They also demonstrated the capacity to associate the cues of sound and light with shock-produced pain but not with illness.

In phase 1, thirsty rats were first familiarized with the experimental situation in which licking a tube produced three CSs: saccharine-flavored water, noise, and bright light. In phase 2, when the rats licked the tube, half of them received only the tasty water and half received only the noise, light, and plain water. Each of these two groups was again divided: half of each group was also given electric shocks that produced pain, and half was given X-ray radiation that produced nausea and illness.

The amount of water drunk by the rats in phase 1 was compared with their drinking in phase 2 when pain and illness were involved (see **Figure 9.11**). Big reductions in drinking occurred when flavor was associated with illness (taste aversion) and when noise and light were associated with pain. However, there was little change in behavior under the other two conditions—when flavor predicted pain or when the "bright-noisy water" predicted illness. This experimental design generated the conclusion that rats show taste aversion by avoiding a sweet-tasting (usually preferred) saccharine water when it predicts illness. The pattern of results suggests that rats have an inborn bias to associate particular stimuli with particular consequences (Garcia & Koelling, 1966).

Even without conditioning, most animals show *bait shyness,* an unlearned reluctance to sample new foods or even familiar food in a strange environment. Of all the stimuli available to them, animals seem to use the sensory cues—of taste, smell, or appearance—that are most adaptive in their natural environments for responding to potential edible or dangerous foods. Evolution has provided organisms with a survival mechanism for avoiding foods that are toxic and thus illness-producing, and perhaps all unfamiliar foods are responded to as potentially toxic until proven otherwise.

FIGURE 9.11   *INBORN BIAS*

Results from Garcia and Koelling's study (1966) showed that rats possess an inborn bias to associate certain cues with certain outcomes. Rats avoided saccharin-flavored water when it predicted illness but not when it predicted shock. Similarly, rats avoided the "bright-noisy water" when it predicted shock but not when it predicted illness.

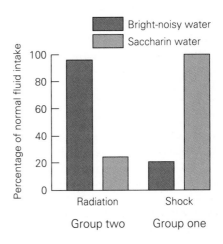

Several recent programs of research illustrate the practical application of the principles discovered about conditioned food aversions to coyotes and cancer patients. To stop coyotes from killing sheep (and sheep ranchers from shooting coyotes), John Garcia and colleagues have put toxic lamb burgers wrapped in sheep fur on the outskirts of fenced-in areas of sheep ranches. The coyotes who eat these lamb burgers get sick, vomit, and develop an instant distaste for lamb meat. Their subsequent disgust at the mere sight of sheep makes them back away from them instead of attacking. This type of taste-aversion learning depends on the powerful feedback from the animal's nervous system, which occurs without awareness and does not even depend on memory to be effective. In another experiment, animals taste a special food, are put to sleep under deep anesthesia, and are given a drug that produces nausea. When awake and exposed to the food they had tasted just before the anesthesia, the animals recoil and avoid it (Garcia, 1990).

Cancer patients often develop aversions to normal foods in their diets to such an extent that they become anorexic and malnourished. Their aversions are, in part, a serious consequence of their chemotherapy treatments, which produce nausea and which often follow meals. Researchers are working to prevent the development of aversions to nutritive foods—necessary in the diets of children with cancer—by arranging for meals not to be given just before the chemotherapy and by presenting the children with a "scapegoat" aversion. They are given candies or ice cream of unusual flavors to eat before the treatments so that the taste aversion becomes conditioned only to those special flavors. Extension of this practical solution to cancer may be a lifesaver for some cancer patients (Bernstein, 1988).

Some instances of conditioning, then, depend not only on the relationship between stimuli and behavior, as was long thought, but also on the way an organism is genetically predisposed toward stimuli in its environment (Barker et al., 1978). What any organism can and cannot readily learn in a given setting is as much a product of its evolutionary history as it is a product of reinforcement contingencies.

COGNITIVE INFLUENCES ON LEARNING

Despite Skinner's insistence on building a psychology of learning based solely on observable events, cognitive processes are significant in many kinds of learning. *Cognition* is any mental activity involved in the representation and processing of knowledge. Cognitive activities include thinking, remembering, perceiving, and using language. Although the next two chapters are devoted to cognitive psychology, here we will discuss briefly how cognitive processes influence learning.

Observational Learning

If important stimuli carry information for us, then we must be able to pay attention to them and decode their meaning. Observational responses can be made through any sense modality and are reinforced by the information obtained. When are you most likely to make observational rather than action responses? Unless you enjoy risk taking, chances are that you look before you leap into new ventures and uncertain situations. Recognizing the right cues enables you to behave appropriately and avoid embarrassment.

Much social learning occurs in situations where learning would not be predicted by traditional conditioning theory, because a learner has made no active response and has received no tangible reinforcer. The individual has simply watched another person exhibiting behavior that was reinforced or punished and later behaved in exactly the same way or refrained from doing so. **Observational learning** is the type of learning that occurs when someone uses observations of another person's actions and their consequences to guide his or her future actions. Observational learning results in the formation of certain expectations. In essence, after observing a model, you may think to yourself, "If I do exactly what she does, I will get the same reinforcer or avoid the same punisher." For example, the 3-year-old boy who imitates his mother baking cookies does so because he expects that he will "have fun just like Mommy."

A classic demonstration of observational learning occurred in the laboratory of **Albert Bandura.** After watching adult models punching, hitting, and kicking a large plastic *BoBo* doll, the children in the experiment later showed a greater frequency of the same behaviors than did children in control conditions who had not observed the aggressive models (Bandura et al., 1963). Subsequent studies showed that children imitated such behaviors just from watching filmed sequences of models, even when the models were cartoon characters.

There is little question now that we learn much—both prosocial (helping) and antisocial (hurting) behaviors—through observation of models, but what variables are important in determining which models will be most likely to influence us? Although this is a complex issue to resolve, the following general conclusions appear warranted (Baldwin & Baldwin, 1986; Bandura, 1977a). A model's observed behavior will be most influential when (a) it is seen as having reinforcing consequences; (b) the model is perceived positively, liked, and respected; (c) there are perceived similarities between features and traits of the model and the observer; (d) the observer is rewarded for paying attention to the model's behavior; (e) the model's behavior is visible and salient—it stands out as a clear figure against the background of competing models; and (f) it is within

The coyote is showing species-specific disgust responses to the carcass of a prey after having been exposed to taste-aversion conditioning.

the observer's range of competence to imitate the behavior.

The capacity to learn from watching as well as from doing is extremely useful. It enables us to acquire large, integrated patterns of behavior without going through the tedious trial-and-error process of gradually eliminating wrong responses and acquiring the right ones. Observational learning also enables us to profit from the mistakes and successes of others. How to recognize snakes or mushrooms that are poisonous or how to protect our eyes during a solar eclipse are examples of dangerous lessons better learned through observation than experience.

As you might expect, given Bandura's findings and the great amount of time most of us spend watching television, much psychological research has been directed at assessing the behavioral impact that TV's modeled behavior has on viewers (Huston, 1985; Williams, 1986). Because of the high level of violence in U.S. society, there is concern over the possible influence of televised violence. Does exposure to acts of violence—murder, rape, assault, robbery, terrorism, and suicide—increase the probability that viewers will imitate them? The conclusion from psychological research is yes—it does for some people (Milavsky et al., 1982; National Institutes of Mental Health Report, 1982). In controlled laboratory studies, the two major effects of filmed violence were a reduction in emotional arousal and distress at viewing violence, or *psychic numbing,* and an increase in the likelihood of engaging in aggressive behavior (Murray & Kippax, 1979).

Because much behavior is under the control of thoughts and internalized images, a cognitive analysis of behavior has been very influential in guiding new forms of therapy. *Cognitive behavior-modification* involves the use of cognitive principles to modify behavior patterns that are undesirable for clients. Bandura's work (1986) has been influential in redirecting approaches that were originally limited to behavior change principles to a broader conception that integrates cognitive and behavior change. Getting patients to restructure their thinking about distressing situations, relationships with other people, memories of past ex-periences, and personal goals is proving effective in helping them overcome certain types of mental disorders. In Chapter 18 we will describe this therapy in detail.

Rule Learning

Smoking is dangerous to your health; do not smoke. To reduce the risk of AIDS, practice safe sex. These are just two of many recommendations that attempt to influence our behavior. Watching models may help us to learn some information faster or better, but verbal instructions can serve as rules that guide our actions in a wider variety of situations, especially those we have never personally observed. *Rules* are guidelines for behavior in certain situations that are verbally encoded as instructions, suggestions, commands, hints, proverbs, and morality tales. Rules are essentially discriminative stimuli. **Rule learning** involves recognizing the contexts in which rules are relevant and perceiving the consequences for obeying or violating them. Through rules, a society passes along its accumulated wisdom and prejudices to future generations. Rules help its members behave appropriately as they attempt to acquire reinforcers and avoid punishers. The most powerful rules, however, are those that are *internalized*—self-instructions regarding what one can and cannot do. Attempts to change the negative behavior patterns of ineffective, shy, aggressive, or neurotic people often involve teaching them to modify patterns of limiting rules they impose on themselves (Martin & Pear, 1983). Behaviorists argue that rule-controlled behavior is under reinforcement contingencies that support formulating the rules and following the rules, so it is not a challenge to their viewpoint (Zettle, 1990).

Cognitive Maps

The importance of cognitive processes in learning was demonstrated by psychologist **Edward C. Tolman** (1886–1959). He accepted the behaviorists' idea that psychologists must study observable behavior, but he created many situations in which mechanical, one-to-one associations between specific stimuli and responses could not explain the behavior that he observed. Tolman

FIGURE 9.12   USE OF COGNITIVE MAPS IN MAZE LEARNING

Subjects preferred the direct path (path 1) when it was open. With a block at A, they preferred path 2. When a block was placed at B, the rats usually chose path 3. Their behavior seemed to indicate that they had a cognitive map of the best way to get the food.

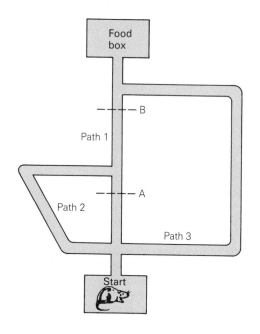

that particular response was never previously reinforced (Tolman & Honzig, 1930). **Figure 9.12** shows the arrangement of one such maze. Rats behaved as if they were responding to an internal cognitive map, rather than blindly exploring different parts of the maze through trial-and-error. More recent experiments on cognitive maps in rats, chimpanzees, and humans have confirmed Tolman's earlier findings (Menzel, 1978; Moar, 1980; Olton, 1979). Organisms learn the general layout of their environment by exploration, even if they are not reinforced for learning particular paths. In fact, when foraging animals have found food in one spot, they tend to seek it elsewhere and not return to the original site for a while.

Tolman's results showed that learning is neither blind nor simple. Conditioning involves more than forming an association between sets of stimuli or between responses and reinforcers. It includes the learning of expectancies, predictions, and information evaluation—cognitive factors—as well as learning about other facets of the total behavioral context (Balsam & Tomie, 1985).

Insight Learning

Based on his experiments with cats, Thorndike believed that all learning depended on trial-and-error. His conclusion supported educational practices of the time, which emphasized rote practice and were not concerned with what learners might be perceiving and understanding. A young German psychologist in the Gestalt tradition, **Wolfgang Köhler,** challenged Thorndike's view of learning. He pointed out that, although the cats could only have escaped by the means they used, many puzzles in real life have meaningful internal relationships providing clues to the appropriate responses. Sometimes these puzzles require putting known facts together in new ways; sometimes they enable one to formulate hypotheses to test new theories that make sense of partial knowledge.

During World War I, Köhler was on Tenerife Island off the coast of Africa. Because chimpanzees were available on the island, Köhler used them as subjects

(1948) claimed that learning probably involved two components: a **cognitive map,** or inner representation of the learning situation as a whole, and an *expectancy* about the consequences of one's actions.

To show that animals are capable of learning more than just a fixed response stamped in by reinforcement, Tolman and his students performed a series of studies on *place learning*. They demonstrated that, in a maze, when an original goal-path is blocked, an animal will take the shortest detour around the barrier, even though

A pigeon is initially baffled but then uses a box to get a banana that is out of reach.

for his research on problem solving. He put them in enclosed areas where tasty morsels were in sight but out of reach—suspended high up or placed a few feet outside the enclosure. Typically, his subjects would first try unsuccessfully to reach the food directly and then stop and survey the situation. After a period of time, and often suddenly, they would try an approach based on a novel way of using the objects at hand: they would drag a box under the fruit and climb onto it to reach the prize (later, when the fruit was hung higher, they reached it by piling boxes on top of each other) and they would rake in the food placed outside the enclosure with a stick, or they would use the short, accessible stick to rake in a longer stick that could do the job (Köhler, 1925).

Köhler concluded that, whether an organism will solve a problem by trial-and-error or by **insight**—a sudden understanding of the relationships among elements in the situation for the solution to a particular goal—depends on (a) whether there are relationships in the problem that can be discovered and (b) whether they are within the cognitive capacity of the organism. Even if the latch in Thorndike's puzzle boxes had not been out of sight, the cats might not have had the ability to understand its mechanism by looking at it.

Conditioning in the laboratory provides little opportunity for subjects to make much use of the full range of their higher cognitive processes, but, even

there, the subject is clearly an active processor of information, scanning the environment for significant events, storing experience in memory, integrating and organizing this stored information in useful ways, and drawing on appropriate parts of that information to decide on the best response to the current situation. According to the cognitive view, changes in behavior are manifestations of cognitive processes that also change the way some organisms think about their environment and understand themselves.

In the past two decades, there has been a significant shift among psychologists from the behavioral viewpoint toward cognitive approaches to learning. At the same time, there has been an increased recognition of the significance of evolutionary and neurological processes in learning (Garcia & Garcia y Robertson, 1985; McGaugh et al., 1985; Thompson, 1986).

CONNECTIONIST LEARNING MODELS

Another area of learning theory that has made a surge of progress in the past few years is the development of *learning models,* hypothesized systems that try to rigorously describe the processes and structures involved in learning. These models can be used to gain understanding and make predictions about what and how humans and animals will learn in different situations. The concern with the *how* of learning is one of the features that sets these models apart from the learning paradigms of the behaviorists, which typically just say *what* and *when* learning occurs. Because these learning models actually hypothesize the way learning can take place, researchers can write computer programs that model the proposed learning processes. This new approach allows great flexibility in both the testing of and modifying of the hypothetical models. While the ideas involved in some modern learning models are not new, the use of computers in psychology has recently spurred the study of learning models.

One of the major classes of learning models being investigated is known as **connectionism,** which deals with the learning of *connections* between components of thought, such as concepts and sensations. Connectionist models consist of a collection of units—representing concepts, parts of concepts, or sensations—and connections or links between these units—representing the relations between the various concepts and sensations. Each connection has a certain strength associated with it, corresponding to the strength of the relationship between the items it connects. If the connection strength between a unit that corresponds to the concept *chocolate* and a unit that corresponds to the sensation *delicious* is positive, then *chocolate* and *delicious* are positively associated with each other—in other words, *chocolate* implies *delicious*. On the other hand, if the connection strength between a unit that corresponds to *pork and beans* and the *delicious* unit is negative, then there is a negative association between these two notions, and *pork and beans* implies *not delicious*. The bigger the connection strengths, positive or negative, the more strongly the relation between the two concepts is implied. If the connection strength between a *water* unit and the *delicious* unit is zero, then there's no particular association or implication between water and what it tastes like.

A connectionist model can have many such conceptual units with connections of various strengths between them, capturing the associations and implications between the collection of concepts and sensations represented. The connectionist learning model also specifies how those *connection strengths are acquired.* The simplest type of learning rule we might think of to change connection strengths between conceptual units in our model is purely associational, just as we saw in classical conditioning. So, whenever two units are "on" simultaneously—that is, whenever their two concepts are both true at about the same time—we will positively strengthen the connection between them. For instance, whenever we have *chocolate* that is *delicious,* we strengthen the positive connection between these two concepts. Soon, we will have learned that chocolate is, in fact, delicious. Such learning is often called *Hebbian learning* after **Donald Hebb,** who proposed it in a general form (Hebb, 1949). If we apply this type of learning model to the case of bells, buzzers, and shocks, we can easily model how an animal might build up associations between conditional stimuli (the bell or buzzer) and unconditional stimuli (the shock) and its unconditional response.

While Hebbian learning is a useful beginning for modeling some forms of conditioning, it errs by building up associations between *any* conceptual units that happen to be "on" close together in time. For example, imagine that a tone and a shock are presented together. A learning model using a Hebbian learning rule will come to associate these two sensations with each other, as expected. Now, imagine that a tone and a light are paired with the shock. Hebbian learning will continue to take place, this time also strengthening the association between the light and the shock, since they occur near in time to each other. Thus, the model will predict that a tone implies the shock *and* a light implies the shock. As we saw in the blocking experiments, however, animals do not learn this second association; they pick up only the first association. The Hebbian model of animal learning fails in this case, and we need to find a new learning rule to explain this blocking situation.

Our new learning rule comes from the notion of *informativeness* of the CS, which we saw was critical for classical conditioning. We will change the interpretation of the interaction of units in the model slightly; now, instead of merely associating pairs of concepts or sensations, we will use the connections between units to *predict* some concept or sensation given the presence of others. The connection between the tone unit and the shock unit represents the prediction about whether a tone will be followed by a shock; if there is a strong positive connection between the two, then a tone will predict a shock, but if there is a zero-strength connection between them, then hearing a tone neither implies a shock nor guarantees that there won't be one. The learning rule we will use strengthens the connection between two present concepts or sensations whenever the prediction about the second one is wrong (see **Figure 9.13**).

For example, imagine that the model begins with zero-strength connections between a tone unit and a shock unit, and between a light unit and the same shock unit. If we present the model with a tone, the connection from the tone unit to the shock unit is zero, and the model will not predict that a shock is about to happen. When we turn on the tone unit to correspond to a shock sensation, the model now realizes that it has made a mistake in its prediction, and the new learning rule will cause the strength between the tone unit and the shock unit to be increased. After we do this tone-shock pairing a few times, the strength of the connection between the two corresponding units will be great enough that the next time we present the model with a tone, it will predict a shock. When the shock occurs, however, it will not be a surprise, and no further learning will take place. If we then turn on the tone and light units together, the tone-shock connection will still predict a shock, and when we produce the shock, no learning will take place, and there will be no change in the connection strength between the light and the shock units. In this case, the light sensation is *not informative* and so its association is not learned. In this way, we have achieved *blocking* with our new learning rule, and we've added another degree of realism to our learning model (Rescorla & Wagner, 1972).

Because this new learning rule only causes a change in the connection strengths, which is what learning is primarily, when the model makes a mistake in its prediction about the world, it is known as *error-correcting,* or error-minimizing, learning. It is often called the *delta rule* because it deals with the difference, or delta, between predictions and reality (Rumelhart & McClelland, 1986). The delta rule can model a variety of learning situations, but it is still quite limited. For instance, imagine that you want to train an animal to respond to expect food *either* when a light comes on *or* when a bell is rung but *not* when both the light and bell

FIGURE 9.13   CONNECTIONISM

In a complex connectionist network, a subject can expect food in response to a light stimulus or a bell stimulus but not both. The complex network includes the AND unit in the center which comes on when both the light and the bell are perceived, turning off the food expectation unit (hence the strong negative connection from it to the top unit). An extended version of error-correcting learning (the generalized Delta rule) is necessary to learn the proper connections in such a network.

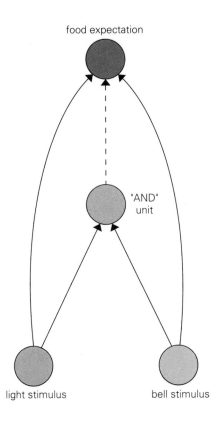

food expectation

"AND" unit

light stimulus   bell stimulus

occur together. You cannot merely have a connectionist model using the delta rule that learns a positive connection from a light unit to a food unit and from a bell unit to the same food unit, because then food will be predicted for either stimulus *and* for both. In fact, you need a more powerful learning rule that is able to create *new conceptual units* to help solve difficult learning situations. For instance, if you had a learning rule that could invent a new conceptual unit that only came "on" when both the bell and light were on and that had a strong negative connection to the food unit, this model would predict no food when both the bell and the light were witnessed.

Until fairly recently, there was no known learning rule that could solve such a problem of *conceptual restructuring*. Now, however, the *generalized delta rule* (Rumelhart & McClelland, 1986), among others, allows this more flexible type of learning and has spurred the recent interest in *connectionist learning models*. These powerful new models are giving us greater insight into the way people and animals learn about their worlds. They are extending our understanding and appreciation of the realm of learning research previously amassed, and may even suggest new future directions.

APPLIED BEHAVIOR ANALYSIS

The final point to be made in this chapter is that behavior-analytic methodology is used routinely by many different kinds of researchers to investigate a broad range of topics. The behavior-analytic method is a tool for

- Studying the learning capacities of a species by defining the variables and conditions that favor or disfavor learning and using the results to infer the capabilities of a particular type of organism;
- Studying the memory capacities of a species by assessing performance on recognition tasks and other behavioral tests;
- Determining the sensory and perceptual capacities of a species through discrimination learning tasks and habituation-dishabituation paradigms;
- Getting animals, infants, and people without language to tell us what they know and experience when such knowledge is otherwise "behaviorally silent"; and
- Uncovering the relationships between brain structure, brain function, and behavior.

Our understanding of how humans and animals learn has come a long way from the early studies of Pavlov, Thorndike, and Skinner. The basic principles of conditioning and learning are being extended in many exciting new directions. The search for the biological bases of learning and the interest in the cognitive dimension of human learning have expanded. The new evolutionary perspective adds another dimension. We are also witnessing a wider, practical utilization of learning theory in psychotherapy, programs for stress reduction, and health management. In addition, there are many applications of learning theory (LTE) to situations that occur in everyday life. LTE has been used in homes, sports arenas, businesses, supermarkets, industry, transit systems, television, and school systems (Krasner, 1985).

RECAPPING MAIN POINTS

The Study of Learning

The capacity for learning depends on genetic heritage and environmental influences. The study of learning has been dominated by behaviorism. Behaviorists believe that learning can be explained by the processes involved in classical and operant conditioning. They also believe that the same principles of learning apply to all organisms. Recently, challengers to the behaviorist view have shown that learning is determined by a combination of biological, cognitive, and environmental factors.

Classical Conditioning

Classical conditioning, discovered by Pavlov, is widely used for investigating relationships between stimulus events. In classical conditioning, an unconditional stimulus (UCS) stimulates an unconditional response (UCR). A neutral stimulus paired with the UCS becomes a conditional stimulus (CS) which elicits a similar response, called the conditional response (CR). Extinction occurs when the UCS no longer follows the CS. Stimulus generalization is the phenomenon whereby stimuli similar to the CS elicit the CR. For classical conditioning to occur, there must be a contingent relationship between the CS and UCS. The CS must be informative as well as predictive.

Operant Conditioning

Thorndike's law of effect states that satisfying outcomes tend to be repeated. Skinner's behavior analytic approach centers on manipulating contingencies of reinforcement and observing the effects on behavior. There are two kinds of reinforcers: negative and positive. Withholding a reinforcer and punishment are the two ways of eliminating a behavior. According to Skinner, behavior can be explained by the three-term contingency of discriminative stimulus-behavior-consequence.

Primary reinforcers are stimuli that function as reinforcers even when an organism has not had previous experience with them. Conditioned reinforcers are learned. Complex responses may be learned through chaining or shaping. Partial or intermittent reinforcement leads to greater resistance to extinction than does continuous reinforcement. Behavior is affected by schedules to reinforcement that may be varied or fixed and delivered in intervals or in ratios.

Biofeedback is a procedure for changing behavior by amplifying weak or nonobservable responses so they can be reinforced. Learned helplessness occurs when there is a noncontingent relationship between behavior and environmental consequences.

Learning, Biology, and Cognition

Several lines of research evidence suggest that learning is constrained by genetic heritage and cognitive abilities. The species-specific repertoires of different organisms, adaptive in their natural environments, make some CS-UCS and response-reinforcement connections easier to learn than others. They may even prevent conditioning from occurring in laboratory settings. Cognitive influences on learning are shown in observational learning, rule learning, and insight learning. People (and some animals) can learn through observation. Rule learning is another type of cognitive learning. The most powerful rules are those internalized as one's own rules. Current research on conditioning and learning reveals that organisms can do much more than learn specific responses and associations among concrete events. They can also learn abstract, symbolic associations, general response patterns, rules, and an understanding of the meanings of relationships connecting stimuli to responses. Behavior-analytic procedures have many applications outside of the laboratory in everyday life. Researchers currently use these procedures and paradigms in studies of memory, sensation, perception, language, and brain structure and function.

KEY TERMS

acquisition, 308

behavior analysis, 305

biofeedback training, 327

biological constraints on learning, 330

blocking, 316

chaining, 325

classical conditioning, 306

cognitive map, 334

conditional response (CR), 307

conditional stimulus (CS), 307

conditioned reinforcers, 323

connectionism, 335

discriminative stimuli, 322

experimental analysis of behavior, 318

extinction, 309

insight, 335

instinctual drift, 330

law of effect, 317

learned helplessness, 328

learning, 303

learning-performance distinction, 303

negative reinforcer, 320

observational learning, 332

operant, 318

operant extinction, 320

partial reinforcement effect, 326

performance, 303

positive reinforcer, 320

Premack principle, 324

punisher, 321

reflex, 306

reinforcement contingency, 319

resistance to extinction, 308

rule learning, 333

savings, 309

schedules of reinforcement, 325

shaping by successive approximations, 325

spontaneous recovery, 309

stimulus discrimination, 310

stimulus generalization, 309

taste-aversion learning, 331

three-term contingency, 322

unconditional response (UCR), 307

unconditional stimulus (UCS), 307

MAJOR CONTRIBUTORS

Ader, Robert, 301

Bandura, Albert, 332

Breland, Keller, 330

Breland, Marion, 330

Garcia, John, 331

Hebb, Donald, 336

Kamin, Leon, 315

Köhler, Wolfgang, 334

Maier, Steven, 328

Miller, Neal, 328

Pavlov, Ivan, 306

Premack, David, 324

Rescorla, Robert, 313

Seligman, Martin, 328

Siegel, Shepard, 314

Skinner, B. F., 305

Thorndike, Edward L., 316

Tolman, Edward C., 333

Watson, John, 304

Chapter 10

Remembering and Forgetting

WHAT IS MEMORY?   343
  TYPES OF MEMORY
  EBBINGHAUS QUANTIFIES MEMORY
  IMPLICIT AND EXPLICIT MEMORY
  ENCODING, STORAGE, AND RETRIEVAL
  RETRIEVAL METHODS: RECALL AND
    RECOGNITION
  AN INFORMATION-PROCESSING VIEW
  THREE MEMORY SYSTEMS

  ■ INTERIM SUMMARY

SENSORY MEMORY   349
  ENCODING FOR SENSORY MEMORY
  STORAGE: HOW MUCH AND HOW LONG?
  TRANSFER TO SHORT-TERM MEMORY

  ■ INTERIM SUMMARY

SHORT-TERM MEMORY (STM)   352
  ENCODING IN STM
  STORAGE IN STM
  PROCESSING IN STM
  RETRIEVAL FROM STM

  ■ INTERIM SUMMARY

LONG-TERM MEMORY (LTM)   357
  ENCODING FOR LTM
  STORAGE IN LTM
  RETRIEVAL FROM LTM
  DUPLEX MEMORY VERSUS MULTIPLE LEVELS

  ■ INTERIM SUMMARY

**REMEMBERING AS A CONSTRUCTIVE
PROCESS**   365
  SCHEMAS
  EYEWITNESS TESTIMONY

  ■ INTERIM SUMMARY

WHY WE FORGET   369
  MEMORY TRACES DECAY
  INTERFERENCE
  RETRIEVAL FAILURES
  MOTIVATED FORGETTING

  ■ INTERIM SUMMARY

THE NEUROBIOLOGY OF MEMORY   371
  THE ANATOMY OF MEMORY
  ALZHEIMER'S DISEASE
  CELLULAR MECHANISMS OF MEMORY
  INTEGRATING THE BIOLOGY AND THE
    PSYCHOLOGY OF MEMORY

RECAPPING MAIN POINTS   376

KEY TERMS   377

MAJOR CONTRIBUTORS   377

In 1960, Nick A., a young Air Force radar technician, experienced a freak injury that permanently changed his life. Nick had been sitting at his desk while his roommate played with a miniature fencing foil. Then, suddenly, Nick stood up and turned around—just as his buddy happened to lunge with the sword. The foil pierced Nick's right nostril and continued to cut into the left side of his brain.

The accident left Nick seriously disoriented. His worst problem was *amnesia*, the failure of memory over a prolonged period. He had trouble remembering anything that had happened since his injury—a memory failure for recent events *after* an amnesia-causing trauma is known as **anterograde amnesia.** Nick also had no memory for anything that had happened in the two years before the accident—a memory failure for events *prior* to an amnesia-causing trauma is known as **retrograde amnesia.** Perhaps what was most disturbing was that when Nick talked about his situation, he sounded completely objective and impersonal, referring to himself as "the injured person."

After a year in the hospital, Nick moved in with his mother. For a couple of years, his intellectual performance improved dramatically. His memory for many events that occurred between 1958 and 1960 gradually returned, but he could not recall what had happened—to him or to the world—since his accident. Memories that normally recede into a distant past were, for Nick, more vivid than anything that had happened in the years since his injury.

Today, Nick still has many problems. Because of his amnesia, he forgets many events immediately after they happen. After he reads a few paragraphs of writing, the first sentences slip from his memory. He cannot remember the plot of a television show unless, during commercials, he actively thinks about and rehearses what he was just watching. Cooking is a major challenge for Nick—he says, "If I have two things on the stove, I can't remember how long each one is supposed to cook, or how long they've been on." As you might expect, Nick often eats cold cereal.

Nick still remembers *how* to do things—*procedural knowledge*—but he cannot remember the *what* of specific facts—*declarative knowledge*. For example, he remembers how to mix, stir, and bake the ingredients in a recipe, but he forgets what the ingredients are. Nick's retention of procedural knowledge enables him to acquire some new information by relating it to motor skills or procedures—he has worked out routines that give the illusion of a kind of memory he has not known for three decades.

Because Nick has presented psychologists and psychiatrists with an unfortunate "natural" experiment, his functioning has been studied extensively, notably by memory researcher **Larry Squire.** He scores above average on intelligence tests and performs at normal levels on tests of perceptual ability, problem-solving, calculating, language, and motor functions. His memory, however, is highly selective, being most severe for verbal material (Kaushall et al., 1981; Squire, 1986; Squire et al., 1989).

Brain scans initially suggested that Nick's injury was limited to a small area on the left side of his brain. Recently, however, MRI revealed three major areas of damage. One of these, in his right temporal lobe, probably occurred during surgery that was performed shortly after his accident. After comparing Nick's injuries with those of other amnesia patients, neurologists hypothesize that memory loss such as Nick's may occur when several brain structures are damaged at once. They do not know if such severe amnesia would result from injury in only one site (Squire et al., 1989).

Since 1982, Nick has lived alone, although his mother continues to help him. Despite being unemployed since the accident and living a solitary existence, Nick maintains a positive attitude. Because he cannot store new memories within his brain, Nick collects photos and mementos of his experiences. With these physical representations of trips, hobbies, and places, Nick creates an external memory—a vital stage show—that captures fragments of the life that his brain stopped recording when he was only 22 years old.

In Nick's case, we recognize the powerful influence that an ordinary process such as remembering has on our lives. Anything that interferes with the way our memory normally works not only changes how we think and behave but also may alter our emotions and even change our personalities. Try to imagine what it would be like if you suddenly had no memory for your past— no memory of people you have known or of events that have happened to you. Without such "time anchors," how would you maintain a sense of who you are—of self-identity? Suppose, like Nick, you lost the ability to form new memories. How would your life be altered?

Research on people suffering from amnesia is just one way psychologists are trying to understand the complex mechanisms of memory. More often, researchers study the way people with normal memories store the enormous amount of information that they acquire, the way people retrieve that information from memory when they need it, and the way people sometimes cannot find what they have stored in their vast memories.

When someone cannot remember a past event, is the memory truly lost, or is it simply not accessible at that time? Failure to retrieve information about a past event may be the result of either psychological or physical factors. When former President Ronald Reagan said to congressional investigating committees that he did not remember conversations with his staff about arms deals with Iran and funds for the Nicaraguan Contras, many people questioned his memory. One elderly doctor wrote that Reagan's problem may have been a natural consequence of old age: "In the elderly, recent memory begins to fail. His staff may brief him immediately before a press conference, but in a few minutes he could honestly forget almost everything that had been prepared: 'At my age [74] I can go into the next room to get something, only to find when I get there that I have forgotten my original purpose' " (quoted in Reston, *The New York Times,* December 24, 1986). Of course, it may well have been that Reagan's failure of memory was psychologically motivated—he may have wanted to forget events that were personally distressing.

Memory failures raise questions about what memory is and what role it plays in our lives. What good would all your learning be were it not for a brain that could store its lessons and a mental system that could call them up upon demand—for example, during a multiple-choice examination? It is estimated that the average human mind can store 100 trillion bits of information, yet, sometimes, we can't recall where the car keys are, or we forget a promise to call home. We all would like to be able to improve our memories—for trivial information, names, faces, musical tunes, and funny jokes—and, so, some psychologists are engaged in developing techniques for memory enhancement.

For research psychologists and neuroscientists, memory has deeper significance because it underlies so much of our behavior and our humanity. Try to think of any activity that does not require the use of memory in some form or another. It's not easy to come up with an example, is it? Memory raises a variety of issues for psychologists in many different areas. Psychologists who study social relations consider how people remember the traits and behaviors of others in order to form coherent mental representations of their social environments. Psychologists who study thinking and reasoning need to know how memory affects people's ability to solve problems or reason logically. Developmental psychologists are concerned with when in life memory begins to help a person structure his or her world; they also want to find ways to help the elderly cope with declining memory skills. Since so much of what we do depends on memory, memory has become a separate field of study. Psychologists have come to see that our thoughts and dreams and our sense of who we are are defined by our memories of past experiences.

In this chapter you will learn what psychology has discovered about memory and how it works. Ideally, you will gain an appreciation for how wonderful a skill memory is.

 ## WHAT IS MEMORY?

Memory is the mental capacity to store and, later, recall or recognize events that were previously experienced. For most cognitive psychologists, **memory** is an active mental system that receives, encodes, modifies, and retrieves information. Memory also refers to *what* is retained—the total body of remembered experience as well as a specific event that is recalled. We use the term **remembering** to mean either *retaining* or *recalling experiences*.

Behaviorists study stimulus input and response output, but they neglect what happens *between* these processes. The associations formed between stimulus events and responses are themselves units of memory. An organism without a capacity for memory is not able to use associations; he or she can't profit from experience or training to predict what will be.

Memory differs from a photo or documentary film in that memories are rarely exact copies of earlier experiences, as photographs and film frames are. What you remember is influenced by many factors—some operating at the time of the original event, others operating when you're storing the information for later use, and still others operating when you're recalling the original information. Your memories can also be affected by your physical health, attention, emotions, and prejudices. The net effect of the many influences on your memory is that you remember a collage of the events you experience, second-hand descriptions of events, your expectations, your fantasies, and even your sense of what is socially desirable. So, your most vivid memories may actually be distortions of what really happened. Perhaps you even remember being somewhere you never were but only heard about. Instead of thinking of your memory as a log of events, think of it

as a library of your personal history. As Nick's case suggests, memories help you define yourself, connect your present thoughts and actions to your roots, and prepare for a meaningful future.

In this chapter we will use an *information-processing view of memory*. This approach outlines three types of mental processes that transform the sensory stimuli and the thoughts and feelings we experience into remembered bits of information. It also proposes that each of us has not one but three different memory systems. We shall also be concerned with how memories are *constructed* and how and why we forget. Finally, we will look at the biological reality of memory, outlining some new insights coming from neurobiologists who are charting the brain's hardware and the chemistry of memory. Now, where were we going to begin? Oh, yes. . . .

TYPES OF MEMORY

Your long-term memory stores more than sensory information about your world; it also stores internally generated information, such as creative thoughts, opinions, and values. How is all this information represented in the storehouse of memory? There are actually two main varieties of memory—procedural and declarative—each distinguished by the kind of information it holds.

Do you remember how Nick's amnesia was selective? After his accident, he could store *procedural knowledge*—ways to do things, such as brush his teeth or cook. He could *not* retain *declarative knowledge*—facts about events since his accident, about how they were related, and about what they meant. Cases such as Nick's have led to the conclusion that procedural (skill) knowledge and declarative (fact) knowledge must somehow be stored differently.

Procedural Memory

Procedural memory is the way we remember how things get done. It is used to acquire, retain, and employ perceptual, cognitive, and motor skills (Anderson, 1982; Tulving, 1983). Skill memories are memories of *actions,* such as bicycle riding or tying shoelaces. They are acquired by practice and observation of models, and they are difficult to learn but even harder to forget (Bandura, 1986). Skill memories are consciously recalled only during early phases of performance. Experts perform their skilled tasks without conscious recall of the appropriate skill memories. In fact, experts are often unable to consciously think through their tasks without hindering their performance—try to explain how to tie a shoelace or how to swim. It's easier to perform the task than describe how to do it.

Declarative Memory

Unlike procedural memory, **declarative memory** —the way we recall explicit information—involves some degree of conscious effort. There is another important difference between the two types of memory.

Procedural memory is thought to be a capacity of subcortical areas in the evolutionarily old brain. The declarative memory system evolved more recently, built upon the primitive base. This difference may account for the fact that both human and animal babies develop skill memories earlier than fact memories.

> Young monkeys were tested at different ages on both a skill-acquisition task and a simple memory-association task. At 3 months of age, they were as proficient as adults on the skill task but could not do the other task until they were 6 months old and did not develop adult proficiency at it until they were almost 2 years old (Mishkin, 1982).

There are two different types of declarative memory: semantic and episodic. This distinction was first proposed by Canadian psychologist **Endel Tulving** (1972).

Semantic Memory   **Semantic memory** is the generic, categorical memory that stores the basic *meanings* of words and concepts without reference to their time and place in experience. It more closely resembles an encyclopedia than an autobiography. The meaning-based relationships in your semantic memory are organized around abstract and conceptual information. Among other information, your semantic memory includes generic facts (true for others, regardless of personal experience) about grammar, musical composition, and scientific principles. For example, the formula $E = MC^2$ is stored in semantic memory. Nick's semantic memory for information learned before his accident, and to a large extent for information learned after, was apparently unaffected by his accident.

Episodic Memory   This second variety of declarative memory storage involves remembering events that have been personally experienced. **Episodic memory** stores autobiographical information—an individual's own perceptual experiences—along with some *temporal coding* (or time tags) to identify when the event occurred and some *content* coding for where it took place. For example, memories of a happiest birthday or of a first love affair are stored in episodic memory. Nick suffered from impaired episodic memory for events he experienced after his accident.

Successful recall of much of the factual information you have learned in college can also involve episodic

memory because many events, formulas, and concepts are stored, in part, according to a variety of personally relevant context features. For example, in trying to answer a particular test question, you remember which course the material came from; whether you heard the information during a lecture, read it in the class textbook, or discussed it in a study group and whether you recorded it in your notes.

EBBINGHAUS QUANTIFIES MEMORY

The first significant study providing a truly quantitative measure of memory was published in 1885 by the German psychologist **Hermann Ebbinghaus.** He was the pioneering force in the experimental investigation of human verbal memory. How he conducted his research is as interesting as what his research found.

> Ebbinghaus used nonsense syllables—meaning-less three-letter units consisting of a vowel between two consonants, such as *CEG* or *DAX*. He used nonsense syllables, rather than meaningful three-letter words, because he hoped to obtain a "pure" measure of memory—one uncontaminated by previous learning or associations that the person might bring to the experimental memory task.

Not only was Ebbinghaus the researcher, he was also his own subject. He performed all the research tasks himself and then measured his own performance. The task he assigned himself was *serial learning,* or memorization of a set of items. Ebbinghaus chose to use *rote learning,* memorization by mechanical repetition, to perform the task.

Ebbinghaus started the study by examining a list of the nonsense syllables. He read through the items one at a time until he finished the list. Then he read through the list again in the same order and again until he could recite all the items in the correct order—the *criterion performance.* Then he distracted himself from rehearsing the list by forcing himself to learn many other lists. Next, instead of trying to recall all the items on the original list, Ebbinghaus measured his memory by seeing how many trials it took him to *relearn* the original list. If he took fewer trials to relearn it than he had to learn it, he had *saved* information from his original study.

> For example, if Ebbinghaus took 12 trials to learn a list and 9 trials to relearn it several days later, his savings score for that elapsed time would be 25% (12 trials − 9 trials = 3 trials; 3 trials ÷ 12 trials = 25%). Using this **savings method,** Ebbinghaus recorded the degree of memory lost after different time intervals. The curve he obtained is shown in **Figure 10.1.** As you can see, he found a rapid initial loss of memory, followed by a gradually declining rate of loss. Ebbinghaus's curve is typical of results from experiments on rote memory of meaningless material.

FIGURE 10.1 EBBINGHAUS'S FORGETTING CURVE

The curve shows how many nonsense syllables individuals using the savings method can remember when tested over a 30-day period. The curve decreases rapidly and then reaches a plateau.

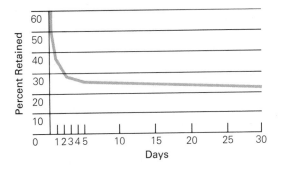

Following Ebbinghaus's lead, for many decades psychologists studied verbal learning by observing subjects learning nonsense syllables. This research was based on the assumption that there was only one kind of remembering. By studying memory in as "pure" a form as possible, *uncontaminated by meaning,* researchers hoped to find basic principles that could then be used to understand more complex examples of remembering.

Although Ebbinghaus's general experimental approach to studying memory proved valuable, it also may have done a disservice to psychology by relegating meaning to the status of a confounding variable rather than treating it as the most significant aspect of memory. The study of the memory of *meaningful* material was neglected until the 1950s when theorists began to use computers to simulate psychological processes in memory, language understanding, and reading comprehension. Today, this type of study has become an important branch of memory research.

IMPLICIT AND EXPLICIT MEMORY

Semantic and episodic memories are what we usually think of when we talk about memory—the conscious recollection of knowledge and our past experiences. However, what we have learned from past experiences can sometimes be expressed nonconsciously. In recent years, the study of nonconscious memory has received much attention. **Implicit memory** is the learning that emerges from experiences you are unaware of that improve your performance on a task (Roediger, 1990). This is a nonconscious form of memory because you need not explicitly remember the original learning event that is influencing your current performance. One example of a task involving implicit memory that has been studied in detail is word-fragment completion. In this task, people are presented with word fragments, such as _ss_ss_n, and asked to fill in the blanks with the letters that will make it a word. What researchers have found is that people are much more likely to solve this fragment correctly if they have recently seen the word *assassin* in a list, whether they remember having seen the word or not. This kind of improvement on a task is known as a **priming effect** (Schacter, 1987).

Interestingly, amnesiacs, such as Nick, display normal implicit memory. In other words, amnesiacs benefit from learning experiences as much as normal subjects when their memory is tested with an implicit task, such as word-fragment completion (Graf et al., 1984). Implicit memory has even been demonstrated in otherwise normal patients suffering from anesthesia-induced anterograde amnesia (for recent events) which clearly demonstrates the distinction between explicit, or conscious, memory and implicit, or nonconscious, memory (Kihlstrom et al., 1990). Although amnesiacs are not able to consciously recall their past experiences, they are nevertheless affected by them and do show that they have learned from them. What is it they have learned? Psychologists disagree about what produces implicit memory. Some believe that it reflects the residual activation of the memory system and is only a temporary benefit to performance on tasks that require memory. Others believe it may reflect a separate memory system that encodes perceptual events and helps a person perceive more quickly and accurately after the events (Tulving & Schacter, 1990).

ENCODING, STORAGE, AND RETRIEVAL

No matter what type of memory it involves, being able to recall an experience at some later time requires the operation of three mental processes: encoding, storage, and retrieval. **Encoding** is the translation of incoming stimulus energy into a unique neural code that your brain can process. **Storage** is the retention over time of encoded material. **Retrieval** is the recovery at a later time of the stored information. In computer terminology, encoding, storage, and retrieval are processes that put information into the computer's hard drive, hold it there, and later allow the computer operator to access it.

Encoding requires that you first select some stimulus event from among the huge array of inputs nearly always available to you. Then you must identify the distinctive features of that experienced event. Both bottom-up and top-down processing are involved here; you react to the sensory features of the stimulus and bring to bear all you know about similar stimuli and the beliefs and attitudes you have formed about them (see Chapter 8 for a discussion of bottom-up and top-down processing).

Is the event a sound, a visual image, or a smell? If it's a sound, is it loud, soft, or harsh? Does it fit with other sounds into some pattern that forms a name, a melody, or a cry for help? Is it a sound you have heard before? During encoding, you try to tag an experience with a variety of labels. Some of these labels are specific and unique—"It's Adam Z." Others put the event into a general category or class—"He's a rock musician." This encoding process is usually so automatic and rapid that you are unaware you are doing it.

A further encoding process relates the new input to other information you already possess or to goals or purposes for which it might later prove relevant. This process is called **elaboration.** Retention is better when you can link new information with what you already know. Some researchers believe that you remember re-

Psychologists suggest that units of information are stored in our brains as memories in much the same way that bits of information are stored in a computer's data bank.

lationships between single memories by forming *networks* of ideas that link together the information you know. Memories that are connected to other information are much more usable than isolated memory units.

Storage retains encoded information over some period of time. Encoded information tends to be lost when it cannot be linked to already stored information, or if it is not periodically practiced or used. The more often some bit of information is rehearsed, the more likely it is to be retained. Researchers are just now uncovering the neurophysiological changes in certain neuronal synapses and other biochemical processes that are associated with information storage.

Minds, similar to libraries, must rely upon proper encoding and systematic storage to be useful. When you read for fun, you make no special effort to organize the ideas for later retrieval. If you use that same process with information units in this text, making no effort to organize what you take in, you'll be in trouble when test time comes. Good encoding and storage organize information so that it will be easy to find when you need it.

Retrieval is the payoff for all your earlier effort. When it works, it enables you to gain access—sometimes in a split second—to information you stored earlier. Can you remember what comes before storage: decoding or encoding? The answer is simple to retrieve now, but will you still be able to retrieve *encoding* as swiftly and with as much confidence when you are tested on this chapter's contents days or weeks from now? Discovering *how* you are able to retrieve one specific bit of information from the vast quantity of information in your memory storehouse is a challenge facing psychologists who want to know how memory works and how it can be improved.

We saw in Chapter 8 that perceptual processes can alter sensory information and that past memories can sometimes distort perception. In this chapter, we will see that there is a continuing interplay between what we perceive and what we remember. This interaction among encoding, storage, and retrieval is complex, and disturbances that occur during any one of these processes will affect what we remember. The whole system is further complicated by the fact that encoding, storage, and retrieval processes take place in each of three basic memory systems. Before we turn to examine what these memory systems do, take a moment to answer the questions that follow:

1. What is your social security number? What is your best friend's?
2. What was your first-grade teacher's name and eye color? What is the name and eye color of your current psychology instructor?
3. Name the title, edition, and author of this textbook.
4. Can you form an image of this page when you close your eyes?
5. When did you *first* experience the emotion of guilt? When was the *last* time you told your parents that you loved them?
6. Do you know the difference between iconic and echoic sensory information storage?
7. What is the significance of *Rosebud* in the movie *Citizen Kane*?
8. What are the connections among former Red Sox star Ted Williams, .406, and neckties?

Was your recall quick and certain on some items and incomplete and vague on others? Were there some answers you didn't remember but might have known once? Were there some events you had experienced but didn't remember, because you didn't see them as significant at the time? Was your memory for negative emotional experiences similar to your ability to recall dates and places? Would questions phrased differently have helped you remember better? Are there answers you are sure you do not know? This experience of getting to know your own memory and retrieval mechanisms will help clarify some of the abstract discussions of the memory types and processes that follow.

RETRIEVAL METHODS: RECALL AND RECOGNITION

You might assume that you either know something or you don't and that any method of testing what you know will give the same results. Not so. The two most common testing methods—recall and recognition—give quite different results.

Recall means reproducing the information to which you were previously exposed. "What are the three memory systems?" is a recall question. **Recognition** means realizing that a certain stimulus event is one you have seen or heard before. "Which is the term for a visual sensory memory: (a) echo; (b) engram; (c) icon; or (d) abstract code?" is a recognition question. By giving different retrieval cues, these two methods call for different mental processes.

When trying to identify a criminal, the police would be using the recall method if they asked the victim to describe, from memory, some of the perpetrator's distinguishing features: "Did you notice anything unusual about the attacker?" They would be using the recognition method if they showed the victim photos, one at a time, from a file of criminal suspects, or if they asked the victim to identify the perpetrator in a police lineup.

Both recall and recognition require a search using given cues. However, recall questions usually give fewer and less specific cues than recognition questions. There is another important difference between recognition and recall. For recognition, you need simply to match a remembered stimulus against a present perception; both the stimulus and perception are in your consciousness. For recall, however, you must reconstruct from memory something that is not in the present environment and then describe it well enough so that an observer can be sure, from your words or drawings, that it really is in your mind.

It is hardly surprising, therefore, that you can usually recognize far more than you can recall, that most students find true-false or multiple-choice tests (recognition) easier than fill-in-the-blank tests (recall), and that recognition tests usually lead to better test performance. It is important to note, however, that as the incorrect alternatives become more similar to the correct answer, recognition becomes more difficult, and recall can actually be easier.

AN INFORMATION-PROCESSING VIEW

Psychologists used to be content to analyze behavior solely in terms of its relationship to stimulus inputs. Psychologists cared very little about what activities were occurring in the "black box" of the mind into which stimuli went and out of which responses came. Today, psychologists studying memory and other mental processes view the mind as an information-processing *system*. They find it helpful to talk about mental processes in the language of computer programming and functioning because it enables them to break down the complex process of remembering into simpler subprocesses or stages.

Using the analogy between the brain and a computer, psychologists suggest that units of information are stored in our brains as memories in much the same way that bits of information are stored in a computer's data bank. However, the human mind operates in more complex and subtle ways than any computer. A digital computer processes one bit of information at a time, using transistors that respond to only two signals: 1 (on) and 0 (off). A brain, however, uses graded and changing signals and processes many different kinds of information at the same time. Digesting one piece of information at a time, as a digital computer does, is called *serial processing*. Digesting different types of information at the same time, as a human does, is known as *parallel processing*. (Computer engineers have recently developed reliable parallel-processing computers.)

Humans and computers also differ in the stability of their memories. A computer does not spontaneously add to or modify its stored memories. The trillions of synapses in the brain that vary in their excitability-inhibitory strengths permit processing far more complex than that provided by any computer so far (Sinclair, 1983). On the other hand, the brain's memory units are not as stable and unchanging as those of computer memory. The very act of recalling information changes a memory in some way.

Clearly there are significant differences between a computer and the human brain. Nonetheless, borrowing from computer science has helped researchers formulate hypotheses about remembering and forgetting that can be tested experimentally on humans.

THREE MEMORY SYSTEMS

There is much that psychologists do not know about memory. They are fairly confident, however, that, within the overall system of remembering and recalling information, there are three memory systems: sensory memory, short-term memory, and long-term memory. *Sensory memory* preserves fleeting impressions of sensory stimuli—sights, sounds, smells, and textures—for only a second or two. *Short-term memory* includes recollections of what we have recently perceived; such limited information lasts only up to 20 seconds unless it receives special attention. *Long-term memory* preserves information for retrieval at any later time—up to an entire lifetime. Information in long-term memory constitutes our knowledge about the world.

Imagine that, as you are passing a movie theater, you notice the odor of popcorn and hear loud sounds from inside (*fleeting sensory memories*). When you get home you decide to check the time of the next show, so you look up the theater's number and then dial the seven digits. Your *short-term memory* holds these digits for the brief period between when you look up the number and when you dial it; if the line is busy, you will have to work at remembering the number or have to look it up again. Once the theater's message machine gives you the show times, you rehearse them. Then you can rely on your *long-term memory* to get you to the show on time.

The three memory systems are also thought of as *stages* in the sequence of processing information. They differ, not only in how much information they can hold and how long they can hold it, but also in the way they process it. Memories that get into long-term storage have passed through the sensory and short-term stages first. In each stage, the information is processed in ways that make it eligible for the next stage. Sense impressions become ideas or images; these, in turn, are organized into patterns that fit into existing networks in long-term memory.

Keep in mind that memory is not a *thing* but a *process*. This distinction explains why *remembering* is a better term to use than *memory*. The three systems or stages of remembering are conceptual models of the way psychologists believe we process incoming information, retain it, and then later use it. Psychologists do not know whether these stages involve physically separate brain areas. The stages seem to be functionally distinct subsystems within the overall system of remembering and recalling information. By finding out how information is processed in each subsystem, psychologists hope to understand why some conditions help us remember experiences, even trivial ones, while other conditions make us forget even important experiences. **Figure 10.2** shows the hypothesized flow of information into and among these subsystems.

SUMMING UP
We have noted that memory is the process by which we take in and later reproduce information. Memory can be procedural or declarative. Declarative memory is further divided into semantic memory and episodic memory. Implicit memory is a nonconscious form of memory exhibited in the enhanced performance on various cognitive tasks that follow a learning event that is not consciously remembered.

The act of remembering can be divided into three stages. Encoding is the process whereby information about a stimulus is coded into memory. This process links new experiences to those already in memory. Storage is the process of retaining information over time—an active process in which experiences are constantly reorganized, edited, and updated. Retrieval is

FIGURE 10.2   A MODEL OF THE HUMAN MEMORY SYSTEM

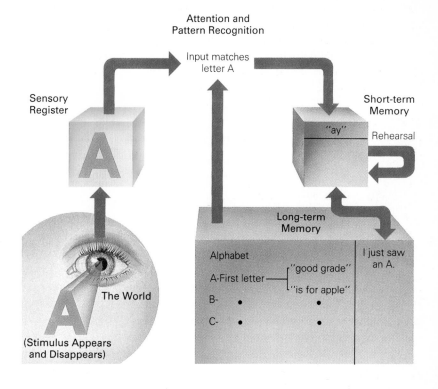

the process of gaining access to previously stored information. Two common methods of retrieval are recall and recognition. An information-processing model has guided much of psychology's study of memory. This model identifies three memory systems: sensory memory, short-term memory, and long-term memory.

SENSORY MEMORY

A **sensory memory**—also called a **sensory register**—is an impression formed from input of any of the senses. Sensory memory represents a primitive kind of memory that occurs *after* sensation but *before* a stimulus is assigned to some category during the process of *pattern recognition*. Psychologists believe that sensory memory, which is the first stage of most information-processing models of human memory, is a register for each sense and holds appropriate incoming stimulus information for a brief interval. It holds this information in a form that faithfully reproduces the original stimulus. That form is called *pre-categorical,* because it takes place prior to the process of categorization (Crowder & Morton, 1969).

Psychologists know more about visual and auditory memories than those of other senses (although the senses of taste and smell are obviously of great importance for survival among free-ranging animal species). A visual memory, or **icon,** lasts about one-half second. An auditory memory, or **echo,** lasts several seconds (Neisser, 1967). You can easily demonstrate the difference between the sensory registers for yourself. When you turn off a radio, the sounds of the music literally echo in your head for a while after the sound is gone, but if you pull down a window shade, the scene outside is gone almost at once.

What would happen if icons and echoes did not occur? Without them, we could see and hear stimuli only at the moment they were physically present, which would not be long enough for recognition to occur. These sensory registers are essential to hold input until it is recognized and passed on for further processing.

ENCODING FOR SENSORY MEMORY

To enter the sensory register, the physical stimuli that impinge on your sensory receptors must be encoded into the biochemical processes that give rise to sensations and perceptions. Even at the first stage, *selectivity* is occurring. Stimuli of vital importance to organisms take priority over others that aren't as important—for example, soldiers who are focusing on detecting enemy gunners may be unaware of the pain from their wounds. Through **sensory gating,** which is directed by processes in the brain, information in one sensory channel is boosted while information in another is suppressed or disregarded.

STORAGE: HOW MUCH AND HOW LONG?

Though fleeting, your sensory storage capacity is large—more than all your senses can process at one time. Early researchers, because of the methodology they used, underestimated the amount of stimuli that could actually be stored during this brief interval. They asked subjects to look at a visual display of nine items for a fraction of a second and then recall as much of the display as they could. With this method, called a **whole-report procedure,** subjects could report only about four items of the nine they saw. Psychologists assumed that the subjects' performances reflected the limits of their immediate memory spans.

> D J B
> X H G
> C L Y

A young researcher named **George Sperling** suspected that the number of items recalled might not be an accurate indication of the number that actually had entered the sensory memory. In 1960, he devised an ingenious method—the **partial-report procedure**—to test his hypothesis.

> Sperling flashed the same arrays of three sets of three consonants for the same amount of time (one twentieth of a second) but now asked his subjects to report only one row rather than the whole pattern. A signal of a high, medium, or low tone was sounded immediately *after* the presentation to indicate which row from the entire set the subjects were to report. He found that, regardless of which row he asked for, the subjects' recall was nearly *perfect*. Sperling took this to indicate that all the items must have gotten into the sensory memory. When, next, three rows of four items were flashed to other subjects, the subjects were 76 percent accurate in their reports—indicating again that there were nine items (9 ÷ 12 = 75%) available in sensory memory for immediate recall (Sperling, 1960, 1963).

What happens if the identification signal is not immediate but slightly delayed? **Figure 10.3** shows that,

FIGURE 10.3   RECALL BY THE PARTIAL-REPORT METHOD

The dots in the solid line show the average number of items four subjects recalled using the partial-report method, both immediately after presentation and at three later times. For comparison, the dotted line shows the number of items recalled by the whole-report method (Adapted from Sperling).

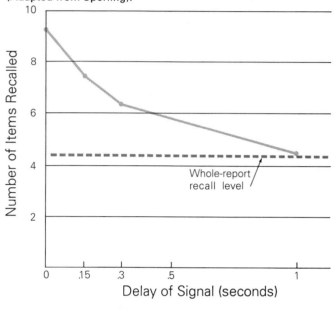

as the delay interval increases from zero seconds to one second, the number of items accurately reported declines steadily. Sperling's experiments demonstrate that immediate visual storage is quite accurate, but that the image or *trace* of the stimulus decays very rapidly. With the whole-report method, however, the short duration of iconic memory is taken up while the person is reporting three to four letters. After that time, information about the rest of the letters—which has been registered in sensory memory—has been lost.

Psychologists assumed that storage loss occurred because, after the visual stimulus ended, the contents of the memory trace began to decay. However, subsequent research on iconic memory has revealed that the visual persistence of a stimulus after it is no longer present is due to ongoing neural processes that are triggered by the *onset* of the stimulation and continue for a given, brief duration of about 100 milliseconds (Di-Lollo, 1980). Using Sperling's procedure, other researchers have shown that in auditory memory, too, more information is available than people can typically report (Darwin et al., 1972). Echoic memories may be necessary to process many subtle, simultaneously presented aspects of speech, such as intonation and emphasis.

Would it be better if sensory memories lasted longer so that we would have more time to process them? Not really. New information is constantly coming in, and it must also be processed. Sensory memories last just long enough to give a sense of continuity but not long enough to interfere with new sensory impressions.

The rapid decay of sensory memories ensures that sensory registers are available for new inputs. There is another way that sensory registers are cleared: new inputs that are similar can erase iconic and echoic representations.

> In one study, two rows of letters were flashed briefly, and 100 milliseconds later, a circle was flashed where one of the letters had been. Normally, all the letters would have been seen 100 milliseconds after presentation, but, instead of seeing all the letters with a circle around one of them, the subjects saw the two rows with the circle *in place* of one of the letters (Averbach & Coriell, 1961).

What happened in the study was that a stimulus following another of a similar kind erased or masked the preceding one; this phenomenon is known as **backward masking** (see **Figure 10.4**). Backward masking is simply an interference with the ongoing perceiving process. It is an unusual experience in that what comes later prevents what came earlier from being recognized and remembered.

At the first stage of information processing there is a race against the clock to complete pattern recognition and other coding before the sensory memory fades away. Because of stimulus trace decay and backward masking, most sensory inputs lose that race and fail to make it out of the sensory register into either short-term or long-term memory.

TRANSFER TO SHORT-TERM MEMORY

Though sensory gating has kept some stimulus input from being translated into sensations and perceptions, you still receive far more sensory information than you can remember or than you can use if you do remember. Actually, only a tiny fraction of what you sense stays with you permanently, as you may have discovered when you tried to remember everything you saw and heard on an exciting trip. How do sensory memories move into short-term memory?

The only way to move sensory memories into short-term memory is to *attend* to them. Of the vast range of sense impressions you experience and retain briefly in your sensory memory, only those to which you attend become eligible for more lasting memory. **Selective attention**—being aware of only part of the available sensory input—is a familiar experience for you. At a party you can participate intelligently in only one conversation at a time; you manage to tune out the others going on around you. In a student dorm a half-dozen stereos may be blasting away at once, and, although all are detected by the receptors in your ears, you can hear the music you want to hear. If you become engaged in an animated conversation, you can selectively attend to the conversation, pushing the music to the background of your attentional focus, even though it is as loud as ever. Similarly, parents can detect their baby's cry over the noise of a houseful of guests who may not register the crying at all. Through selective attention we can choose which inputs to focus upon. Only those inputs that somehow command attention become candidates for further processing and storage in short-term memory.

As we saw in earlier chapters, the global process of taking in sensory input actually involves three stages: transforming stimulus energy into sensory data (sensation), organizing data from individual receptors into groupings (perception), and classifying new information in long-term memory through top-down processes. This third perceptual stage includes pattern recognition and incorporates influences from expectations or personal needs.

What kinds of information have the best chance of receiving attention and getting into short-term memory? In general, familiar information will make it into this stage of processing most easily. For example, a pseudoword such as *eetpnvma* will not be processed as well as a real word such as *pavement,* even though both

---

FIGURE 10.4　SEQUENCE OF EVENTS IN BACKWARD MASKING

In backward masking, a stimulus that appears in the same position as one just perceived (here the letter *Q*) masks or blocks it from being perceived. It is an anomaly that a later event blocks out an earlier one.

Display On:　　　A X Q P N B L M
　　　　　　　　V T C H R E V K

Display Off:

Mask On:　　　　　　　○

What a Person Sees:　A X ○ P N B L M
(Q Is Masked)　　　　V T C H R E V K

contain the same letters. Similarly, it is hard for people growing up in Western cultures to remember music with the tonal scales of Southeast Asian traditional music. However, the principle of familiarity does not always hold. When something is repeated so often that it becomes boring—when familiarity breeds information contempt—we become habituated to it and tune out the stimulus.

You may recall Donchin's research (presented back in Chapter One) in which the P-300 EEG wave detected that the brain prepares to receive an unconsciously expected stimulus. Wouldn't it follow then that we are more likely to remember vivid, bizarre variations within a known, established structure—a purple dog, a two-headed cow, a joke with a surprise ending? Also, because we are subjective human information processors, wouldn't we be more likely to notice and recall events of personal significance to us?

The representation of information in some encoded form in storage is called a **memory code.** When there is no memory code already in long-term memory that matches or relates to a new stimulus, encoding for short-term memory is harder, takes longer, and is less likely to occur. Thus, it is easier to remember new information if you can relate it to something you already know or associate it with something bizarrely memorable. The concept of memory code may help explain why you probably have so few memories of your earliest years—you had very few memories already stored that could help you in encoding new experiences.

SUMMING UP

Sensory memory is the first stage of information processing in memory. In sensory memory, each sense briefly retains incoming stimuli. A visual sensory memory is called an icon and an auditory sensory memory is called an echo. Both represent precategorical memories and both retain unanalyzed sensory information. Information is encoded in sensory memory as physical stimuli impinge on sensory receptors. Sensory gating is a process by which our sensory apparatus responds more strongly to important stimuli and less strongly to personally irrelevant ones. Sensory memory does not store information for long but it has a large capacity, as indicated by results of Sperling's partial-report procedure and related techniques. Information decays in visual sensory memory in about a second, but it may last in auditory memory for up to four seconds. New inputs also replace old ones, causing even more rapid loss of information.

Only a small fraction of the vast information stored in sensory memory can be transferred to short-term memory. In order for an input to be transferred, you must attend to it. You can selectively attend to just a few inputs to accommodate them in a short-term store. You must also recognize an input in order to transfer it from sensory memory. Familiar, recognizable patterns are most likely to make it into short-term memory. As you shall see, the short-term store is a critical stage in memory because it is the workbench of the mind.

SHORT-TERM MEMORY (STM)

A stimulus that has been recognized is likely to be transferred to **short-term memory** (STM). STM occurs between the fleeting events of sensory memory and the more permanent storage of long-term memory. A number of interesting characteristics distinguish this memory-processing phase.

Short-term memory has a very *limited capacity.* Much less information is stored in this stage than in either of the other two stages. It also has a *short retention duration:* what is stored is lost after about 18–20 seconds unless it is held in consciousness. But short-term memory is the only memory stage in which conscious processing of material takes place, and material held in it survives as long as it is held in conscious attention—far beyond the 20-second limit when material is held without attention. This is why short-term memory is also called **working memory**—material transferred to it from either sensory or long-term memory (both of them nonconscious) can be worked over, thought about, and organized.

Short-term memory is part of our psychological present. It is what sets a context for new events and links separate episodes together into a continuing story. It enables us to maintain and continually update our representation of a changing situation and to keep track of the topics during a conversation.

Short-term memory gives a context for both comprehension and new perceptions. For example, suppose a waiter carrying a tray of used dishes passes your table while you are deeply engaged in conversation. A minute or so later, you hear an enormous crash. You know that you have not just heard a falling tree or a car accident; you immediately interpret the sound as the crashing of dishes from that waiter's tray. In this example, short-term memory is using information from a recent event and from long-term memory about the sounds of different types of events to help you interpret a new current perception (Baddeley & Hitch, 1974).

Encoding in STM

Information enters short-term memory as organized images and patterns that are usually recognized as familiar and meaningful. Verbal patterns entering short-term memory usually seem to be held there in *acoustic* form—according to the way they sound—even when they come through an individual's eyes rather than ears. We know this from research in which subjects were asked to recall lists of letters immediately after seeing them. Errors of recall tended to be confusions of letters that *sounded* similar, rather than letters that looked similar. For example, the letter *D* was confused with the similar-sounding *T* rather than with the more similar-looking *O* (Conrad, 1964). Our use of an acoustic code in short-term memory may be tied to our preference for verbal rehearsal of information. This characteristic obviously does not pertain to the short-term memory system of nonverbal creatures.

You may be wondering how hearing-impaired people can manage if short-term memory uses acoustic encoding. Apparently the hearing-impaired use two alternatives to the acoustic coding most hearing people use. They rely on *visual encoding* (identifying letters, words, and sign-language symbols) and, to a lesser extent, on *semantic encoding* (identifying the categories or classes to which visually observed events belong). The basis for this deduction comes from the nature of the errors they make in controlled experimental trials: confusing items that are similar in appearance or in meaning instead of similar in sound (Bullugi et al., 1975; Frumkin & Anisfeld, 1977). Even though hearing persons generally rely on acoustic encoding in short-term memory, there is evidence that they, too, sometimes rely on visual and semantic encoding (Conrad, 1972).

Storage in STM

The limited, brief storage capacity for short-term memory is called **immediate memory span.** When the items to be remembered are *unrelated,* the capacity of short-term memory seems to be between five and nine bits of information—about seven (plus or minus two) familiar items: letters, words, numbers, or almost any kind of meaningful item. When you try to force more than about seven items into short-term memory, earlier items are lost to accommodate more recent ones. This displacement process is similar to laying out seven 1-foot bricks on a 7-foot table. When an eighth brick is pushed on at one end, the brick at the opposite end is pushed off the table. What is so special about that number SEVEN?

The power of the number seven knows no cultural bounds. For example, when African tribal histo-

rians tell stories of their ancestors, they may be able to recite by heart 12,000-word tales, such as *The Mwindo Epic*. However, these ancestral histories usually go back only seven generations. Anthropologists have noted that these oral historians usually stop after tracing back their roots for seven generations, explaining that before that first generation, the Primal Ancestor "came from heaven" (D'Azevedo, 1962).

The special relevance of seven to our purposes is that human memory seems bound by that number. Read the following list of random numbers once, cover them, and write down as many as you can in the order they appear.

8 1 7 3 6 4 9 4 2 8 5

How many did you get correct?

Now read the following list of random letters and perform the same memory test.

J M R S O F L P T Z B

How many did you get correct?

If your short-term memory is similar to that of most others, you probably recalled about seven numbers and seven letters. Some people will recall five units, some as many as nine—that is, seven, plus or minus two. You will discover the same principle operating with recall of lists of random words or names.

Processing in STM

There are two important ways to increase the limited capacity of short-term storage so that more of the information there can be transferred into long-term memory. These two methods are *chunking* and *rehearsal*. You already use them, and now you'll discover why they help you.

Chunking

A **chunk** is a meaningful unit of information. A chunk can be a single letter or number, a group of letters or other items, or even a group of words or an entire sentence. For example, the sequence 1-9-8-4 consists of four digits that could constitute four chunks—about half of what your short-term memory can hold. However, if you see the digits as a year or the title of George Orwell's book—1984—they constitute only one chunk, leaving you much more capacity for other chunks of information. **Chunking** is the process of recoding single items by grouping them on the basis of similarity or some other organizing principle or by combining them into larger patterns based on information stored in long-term memory.

A good listener uses the process of chunking while listening to a lecture.

See how many chunks you find in this sequence of 20 numbers: 19411914186518121776. You can answer "Twenty" if you see the sequence as a list of unrelated digits, or "Five" if you break down the sequence into the dates of major wars in U.S. history. If you do the latter, it's easy for you to recall all the digits in proper sequence after one quick glance. It would be impossible for you to remember them all from a short exposure if you saw them as 20 unrelated items. Your memory span can always be greatly increased if you can discover how to organize the available body of information into smaller chunks. A famous subject, S. F., was able to memorize 84 digits by grouping them as racing times (S. F. was an avid runner). His huge memory span, however, just encompassed digits and did not transfer to letters or other material.

You can also structure incoming information according to its personal meaning to you (linking it to the ages of friends and relatives, for example); or you can match new stimuli with various codes that have been stored in your long-term memory. Thus your ability to remember the sequence ERATVCIAFBIGMUSA will be improved if you chunk the sequence: ERA-TV-CIA-FBI-GM-USA (Bower, 1972). Even if you can't link new stimuli to rules, meanings, or codes in your long-term memory, you still can use chunking. You can simply *group* the items in a rhythmical pattern or temporal group (181379256460 could become 181, pause, 379, pause, 256, pause, 460).

Rehearsal

We have already mentioned the usefulness of repeating the digits of a telephone number to keep them in mind. This memorization technique is called **maintenance rehearsal.** The fate of unrehearsed information was demonstrated in an ingenious experiment.

Subjects heard three consonants, such as F, C, and V. They had to recall those consonants when given a signal after a variable interval of time, ranging from 3 to 18 seconds. To prevent rehearsal, a *distractor task* was put between the stimulus input and the recall signal—the subjects were given a three-digit number and told to count backward from it by threes until the recall signal was presented. Many different consonant sets were given and several short delays were used over a series of trials with a number of subjects.

As shown in **Figure 10.5,** recall got increasingly poorer as the time required to retain the information got longer. After even 3 seconds, there was considerable memory loss, and, by 18 seconds, loss was nearly total. In the absence of an opportunity to rehearse the information, short-term recall was impaired with the passage of time (Peterson & Peterson, 1959).

Recall suffered from not being able to rehearse the new information. It also suffered from interference from the competing information of the distractor task. (Interference as a cause of forgetting will be discussed later in this chapter.)

Rehearsal keeps information in working memory and prevents competing inputs from pushing it out; but maintenance rehearsal is not an efficient way to transfer information to long-term memory. To make sure that information is transferred, you need to engage in **elaborative rehearsal,** a process in which the information is not just repeated but actively analyzed and related to already-stored knowledge. This process happens when you note that the telephone number 358-9211 can also be thought of as *3 + 5 = 8* and *9 + 2 = 11*. This elaboration depends upon your having addition rules and summations stored in and transferred from long-term memory. If you do, then you can find patterns and meanings in otherwise unrelated and meaningless items. Similarly, once you have learned the rules of syntax—how words can be arranged to form acceptable sentences—you can group the words in English sentences into chunks. We will have more to say about elaborative rehearsal later when we discuss encoding for long-term memory.

The limited capacity of short-term memory is one of the fundamental and stable features of the human memory system. However, there are memory experts

FIGURE 10.5 SHORT-TERM RECALL WITHOUT REHEARSAL

When the interval between stimulus presentation and recall was filled with a brief distracting task, recall became poorer as the interval grew longer.

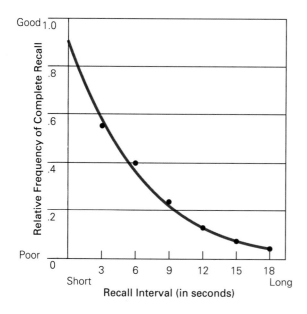

S. F.'s protocols provided the key to his mental wizardry. Because he was a long-distance runner, S. F. noticed that many of the random numbers could be grouped into running times for different distances. For instance, he would recode the sequence 3, 4, 9, 2, 5, 6, 1, 4, 9, 3, 5 as 3:49.2, near record mile; 56:14, 10-mile time; 9:35, slow 2 miles." Later, S. F. also used ages, years of special events, and special numerical patterns to chunk the random digits. In this way, he was able to use his long-term memory to convert long strings of random input into manageable and meaningful chunks. S. F.'s memory for letters was still only seven, plus or minus two, because he had not developed any chunking strategies to recall alphabet strings (Chase & Ericsson, 1981; Ericsson & Chase, 1982).

RETRIEVAL FROM STM

You now know something about how to get approximately seven chunks of information into your short-term memory, but how do you get them out? Getting them out is the problem of *retrieval*. Retrieval from short-term memory has been studied experimentally by **Saul Sternberg** (1966, 1969). Although the task he asked his subjects to perform was quite simple, the results of his study revealed in detail how items seem to be retrieved from short-term memory.

On each of many trials, subjects were given a memory set consisting of from one to six items—for instance, the digits 5, 2, 9, 4, and 6. From trial to trial, the list would vary in terms of which digits and how many were shown. After presenting each set, Sternberg immediately presented a single test "probe"—a digit that the subjects had to determine either had been or had not been a part of the memory set just presented. Because the size of the set was less than the capacity of short-term memory, subjects could easily perform the task without error.

The dependent variable was, therefore, not accuracy but *speed of recognition*. How quickly could subjects press a *yes* button to indicate that they had seen the test item in the memory set or a *no* button to indicate they were sure that they had not seen it? *Reaction time* was used to discover the mental activities that were occurring as subjects searched their short-term memories. Three components of the retrieval process were assumed to make up this reaction time—the subject (a) perceived and encoded the test stimulus ("it's a six"); (b) matched the test stimulus against the

who can remember long strings of numbers after a single presentation or multiply large numbers in their heads in a few seconds. Apparently, part of their secret is learning to shift information back and forth between short-term and long-term memory. To see how this skill might be developed, cognitive psychologist William Chase worked with a student identified as S. F.

At the beginning, S. F. could repeat only the standard seven numbers in proper sequence, but after two-and-a-half years of practice (an hour a day, two to five days a week), he could recall up to 80 digits or reproduce perfectly a matrix of 50 numbers—and do so more quickly than lifelong memory experts.

S. F. was neither coached nor given special training. He merely put in hundreds of hours of practice listening to random digits being read one per second and then recalling them in order. When he reported them correctly, another digit was added on the next trial; if he was incorrect, one digit was dropped on the next trial. After each trial, S. F. gave a verbal report (a protocol) of his thought process.

items in the stored memory set (5, 2, 9, 4, 6); and (c) made a recognition response by pressing either the *yes* button (in example) or the *no* button (had the set been 5, 2, 9, 4, 7).

Sternberg believed that short-term memory might be scanned using any of three possible search strategies (as shown in **Figure 10.6**):

1. *Parallel-processing scanning*. The entire stored set would be treated as a composite, and separate digits would be examined simultaneously, all in parallel. With this strategy, it would take no longer to search big sets than it would short ones, and reaction time would be the same regardless of the number of digits searched.

2. *Serial self-terminating scanning*. Each digit would be examined one at a time until the test probe digit was found. The search would then be terminated. With this process, longer lists would require more search time. In addition, it would take more time for a *no* response than it would for a *yes* response, because the subject would stop searching as soon as a match (*yes*) was found but would have to scan all the digits in the set before deciding *no*.

3. *Serial-exhaustive scanning*. The digits in the stored memory set would be scanned separately and the entire set would be examined before a *yes* or a *no* response was made. In this case, longer lists would have a slower reaction time,

---

FIGURE 10.6   *RETRIEVAL FROM SHORT-TERM MEMORY*

Reaction time for retrieval from short-term memory increases with the length of the memory set and is the same for *no* and *yes* responses, as predicted for serial exhaustive processing.

Predictions

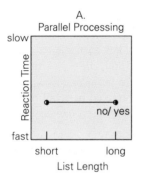

A.
Parallel Processing

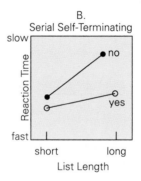

B.
Serial Self-Terminating

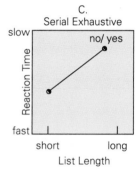

C.
Serial Exhaustive

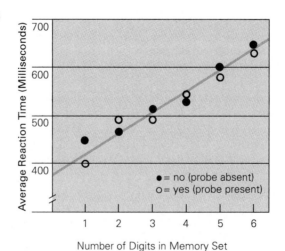

Results

but *yes* and *no* responses would take equal time.

As you can see in Figure 10.6, the results fit the memory scanning prediction of a *serial-exhaustive search*. It took subjects more time to recognize test stimuli from longer memory sets, but it took them the same time to give a *yes* as a *no* response. Sternberg figured that it took about 400 milliseconds to encode the test stimulus and make a response and then about 35 milliseconds more to compare the stimulus to each item in the memory set. In a single second, a person could make about 30 such comparisons. With such fast scanning, that person could afford the time it took to conduct an exhaustive search before deciding what he or she really remembered.

Although other researchers have suggested that the Sternberg finding can be reinterpreted in terms of a parallel model (Townsend, 1972; Wingfield, 1973), Sternberg's work has been very influential in our understanding of retrieval from STM. His work not only shows how items were retrieved from short-term memory but also how effectively reaction time can be used to test theories about mental processes.

SUMMING UP

We have seen that short-term memory is the link between the rapidly changing sensory memory and our permanent store of long-term knowledge. Short-term memory has, however, a very limited capacity, and its information is lost after 20 seconds unless it is actively rehearsed. Short-term memory is also known as working memory because it is the stage at which conscious processing of material takes place. Information enters short-term memory as organized patterns from sensory memory. Verbal information is usually encoded in an acoustic form, even when it is read silently from a visual display. People are capable of encoding information in visual and semantic forms as well. The immediate memory span is the limited capacity of short-term memory; it consists of about seven chunks, plus or minus two. A chunk is a coherent, meaningful pattern of information.

The capacity of short-term memory can be increased by chunking and rehearsing information. Chunking is the process of recombining single items into larger, meaningful groups that are stored in STM as single units. Maintenance rehearsal is the simple repetition of items in short-term memory and serves to keep information there indefinitely. In order to transfer items from short-term to long-term memory, however, a person must engage in elaborative re-hearsal, a process whereby information is analyzed and related to the contents of general knowledge. Retrieval from short-term memory is a serial-exhaustive search process, as first established by Sternberg who found that the time a person takes to retrieve an item from short-term memory increases with the number of items in short-term memory, regardless of whether the test probe was or was not part of the stored set.

LONG-TERM MEMORY (LTM)

My wife's grandmother vividly recalls the 1906 San Francisco earthquake and subsequent fire. She remembers exactly how she felt as she and the other children scrambled to fetch water from the bay to drench big, burlap bags. Her father took the bags she soaked and draped them over the roof, hoping to save their home from the hungry flames. For this 96-year-old woman, the San Francisco earthquake of 1989 had little impact. Nothing could ever rekindle the terror and excitement she had felt as a young girl watching her city being leveled to the ground.

Somehow, despite all the experiences and thoughts she has had in the 84 years since the earthquake, my wife's grandmother has maintained her memories of 1906. This is the miracle of long-term memory, our third memory system. **Long-term memory** (LTM) is the storehouse of all the experiences, events, information, emotions, skills, words, categories, rules, and judgments that have been transferred into it from sensory and short-term memories. LTM constitutes each person's total knowledge of the world and of the self. This memory system enables you to do much more than just retain a record of past events or thoughts. Material in long-term memory helps you deal with and store new information through *top-down processing*. It also makes it possible for you to solve new problems, reason, keep future appointments, and apply a variety of rules to the manipulation of abstract symbols—to think about situations you have never experienced, or to create.

Given the amount of information stored in long-term memory, it is a marvel that it is so accessible. You can often get the exact information you want in a split second: Who discovered classical conditioning? Name a play by Shakespeare. Your responses to these challenges probably came effortlessly because of several special features of long-term memory: (a) words and concepts have been stored in it or encoded by their *meanings*, which have given them links to many other stored items; (b) the knowledge in your long-term memory is stored in a well-organized, orderly fashion; and (c) many alternative cues are stored to help you retrieve exactly what you want from all that is there.

ENCODING FOR LTM

We have seen that short-term memory is similar to an office in-basket. Items are stored in your short-term memory sequentially in a temporal order according to their arrival. Long-term memory, by contrast, more closely resembles a set of file cabinets or a library. Items are stored according to their meanings and all items are cataloged and cross-referenced. There are consequently many indexes to help you retrieve most items from your brain.

Meaningful Organization

The role that meaningful organization plays in long-term storage is demonstrated when you remember the gist or sense of an idea rather than the actual sentence you heard. For example, if you hear the sentence, "Mary picked up the book," and later hear, "The book was picked up by Mary," you might think that the second sentence was the same as the one you heard earlier, because the meaning was the same even though the form was different.

Research has shown that information about the *meanings* of sentences is more likely to be stored than the exact structures of the sentences (Bransford & Franks, 1971). Moreover, if you do not understand the meaning of a sentence or paragraph, you will be unable to organize it into a memorable unit of information. Even descriptions of common events can't be properly understood and remembered without sufficient organizational cues. Read the following passage and then write down as much as you can recall. Then, read the passage's title, which was "misplaced" on the next page. You might also test your friends' recall with and without the title (Bransford & Johnson, 1972, 1973).

> The procedure is actually quite simple. First you arrange items into different groups. (Of course one pile may be sufficient depending on the amount there is to do.) If you have to go somewhere else because of lack of facilities you'd better do so; otherwise, you are pretty well set. It is important not to overdo things. That is, it is better to do too few things at once than too many. In the short run, this may not seem important, but complications can easily arise. A mistake can be expensive as well. At first, the whole procedure will seem complicated. Soon, however, it will become just another facet of life. It is difficult to foresee any end to the necessity for this task in the immediate future, but then, one never can tell. After the procedure is completed, arrange the materials into different groups again. Then you can put them into their appropriate places. Eventually they will be used once more and the whole cycle

Participants in a knowledge bowl need to draw on their long-term memories to answer the varied questions they are asked.

will have to be repeated; however, that is part of life.

Chunking and elaborative rehearsal are helpful in preparing material for long-term storage because they organize the material and make it more meaningful. When you are not limited to the 20 seconds of short-term memory, but can study material in front of you that you want to remember, there are several other things you can do to organize the material and give it meaning.

For example, you may make sense of new information by putting it in a category you already have, transforming it into something familiar, or organizing it in some other way that is meaningful to you. Suppose, for example, you are asked to learn the following list of words for later recall and are told that you may recall them in any order. (This task is called *free recall*.)

house	yellow
tree	green
bird	nest
dog	tiger
grass	tent
purple	shoe
horse	

How might you begin? You could first note that the list has 13 items and then see how many fit into different categories: animals—4; living places—4, if you include *tree;* colors—3; and so on. Or you could encode this input by grouping pairs together: tree-house; bird-nest; green-grass; horse-shoe; and yellow-tiger.

According to researchers, older children recall such lists better than younger ones, because they are more likely to organize the items in pairs or group them by category. Most third-graders use only maintenance rehearsal—simply repeating the items. When the younger children are taught to look for ways to organize the items, their recall becomes as good as that of the older children (Ornstein & Naus, 1978).

Material can usually be meaningfully organized in more than one way. Sometimes you encode by noticing the structure already imposed on the material, such as the different levels of headings in this chapter. Other times you may impose your own organization by outlining the main points and subpoints or by fitting new items into a structure of knowledge you already have. You may also organize material on the basis of relevant personal experiences or physical reminders. Recall that Nick collected mementos as physical reminders of his experiences.

Mnemonics

To help yourself remember, you can draw on special mental strategies called mnemonics (from the Greek word meaning *to remember*). **Mnemonics** are short, verbal devices that encode a long series of facts by associating them with familiar and previously encoded information. Mnemonics are especially useful in *rote memorization*. A graduate psychology student at Kansas State University set a *Guiness World Book* record by memorizing 31,811 digits of *pi*. He learned as many as 6000 digits a day, all of which he could recall nine months later without practice and several years later with practice. How did he do it? Practice and mnemonics. Let's examine three types of mnemonics that the student used: natural language mediators, the method of loci, and visual imagery.

Natural language mediators are word meanings or spelling patterns already stored in long-term memory that can be associated with new information. For example, you might encode the paired nonsense syllables *vol-tur* by associating them with *vulture*. You might remember more complex material or a list of unrelated words by making up a story that connects the parts into a coherent whole. Associations that use *rhyming* or jingle mnemonics, can also help you remember. When does the letter I come before and when after the letter E? "I before E, except after C or in rhyming with A, as in neighbor and weigh." Even though the encoded item is then longer than the original one, your recall is better because you remember those mediators easily, and they, in turn, lead you to the material you need to retrieve (Montague et al., 1966).

Another common mnemonic strategy is the *method of loci*. The singular of *loci* is *locus*, and it means *place*. The method of loci is a means of remembering the order of a list of names or objects by associating them with

some sequence of places with which you are familiar. To remember a list of people you are meeting, you might mentally put each one sequentially in a separate room in your house; to remember their names, you mentally go through your house and find the name associated with each spot.

Visual imagery is one of the most effective forms of encoding, perhaps because it gives you codes for both verbal and visual memories simultaneously (Paivio, 1968). You remember words by associating them with visual images—the more vivid and distinctive the images the better. For example, if you wanted to remember the pair *cat-bicycle,* you might conjure up an image of a cat riding on a bicycle to deliver pizzas. Delayed recall is enhanced when you encode the separate bits of information into a creative, bizarre story line (Bower, 1972).

Other mnemonic devices use organizational schemes or strategies that rely on word or sound associations or that put the items into a pattern that is easy to remember. There are two major types of mnemonic devices that use organizational strategies. In the *acrostic-like mnemonic,* the first letters of each word cue a response. For example, a mnemonic to remember the colors of the spectrum in their proper sequence becomes a person's name. Roy G. Biv (red, orange, yellow, green, blue, indigo, violet). Similarly, the familiar Every Good Boy Does Fine is an acrostic mnemonic for remembering the musical notes on the treble clef: E, G, B, D, F.

In *acronym mnemonics,* each letter of a word stands for a name or other piece of information. HOMES is the acronym for the Great Lakes: Huron, Ontario,

Leading memory researcher Gordon Bower has investigated the effects on memory of visual imagery (*Discovering Psychology,* 1990, Program 9).

The title of the passage on page 358 is "Procedure for Washing Clothes."

Michigan, Erie, Superior. In the order of their locations, from west to east, try: Sergeant Major Hates Eating Onions.

Encoding Specificity

Your method of organizing material in the encoding stage directly affects not only how the material is stored but, equally important, what cues will work when you want to retrieve it. The close relationship among encoding, storage, and retrieval is called the **encoding specificity principle** (Tulving & Thomson, 1973). The better the match between your organization for encoding and the cues you are likely to be given later, the better your recall will be. For example, if you memorize the word *jam* in the context of *traffic jam*, you will have trouble recognizing it when its context is changed to *strawberry jam*. If you expect essay questions on a test, during encoding you should look for and try to remember general information about abstract relationships, implications, and conceptual analysis, because that is probably what you will be asked to retrieve. If you expect multiple-choice questions, you should pay more attention to specific, concrete, right-or-wrong factual details, comparisons, and distinctions.

The encoding specificity principle also means that when you are learning new material, you will be encoding details about the circumstances around you at the time you are encoding—the principle of **context dependence.** Your learning can provide additional retrieval cues if you are in similar circumstances when you try to retrieve the material you have studied. The power of such context dependence was demonstrated by the finding that divers who learned material underwater remembered it better when tested underwater, even when the material had nothing to do with water or diving (Baddeley, 1982). Context dependence is one reason that studying in a noisy environment may not help your retrieval when you will be tested in a quiet room. (One of my students took this principle to heart and studied for his final exam in the lecture hall where he was to take the exam.)

What you learn when you are in a particular emotional or physical state will be recalled best when you are in that same state. This principle is known as **state dependence.** Put differently, retrieval will be better if there is no big change in your physical or psychological state between the time of learning and the time of retrieval. We should add, however, that the research evidence for state dependent learning and memory is equivocal.

STORAGE IN LTM

The storehouse of LTM is filled with the names of sensations, world facts, your opinions and values, and dates and places important to you. It is your personal museum. How are all these different kinds of information represented in this LTM storage?

Information Representation

We know that information in LTM is stored in organized patterns, with networks of meaningfully related concepts and multiple connections for many—perhaps all—chunks of knowledge. From the functional differences among our three types of memories—procedural, semantic, and episodic—we guess that there is probably a difference in the ways or places these chunks are stored. Also, one memory ability can be lost and another retained so they must be structurally different as well as functionally different. We know that in LTM there must also be representations of past sensory experiences (sights, sounds, and smells, for example), emotional experiences, experiences of movement (as in skill learning), and even episodes of interpersonal experiences. These representations are not only stored, but stored with interconnections (Forgas, 1982). Because of the enormous complexities involved, we know little about the way all forms of the experiences we remember are actually represented in long-term memory. Psychologists have put forth three hypotheses about the ways that people represent ideas and experiences in long-term memory. These three are propositional storage, dual-code memory, and eidetic imagery.

Propositional Storage Researchers who study the comprehension and memory of verbal material have hypothesized that memory code is verbal—that people store representations of ideas in some type of linguistic code. The smallest unit of meaning that people store is called a **proposition.** A proposition is an idea that expresses a relationship between concepts, objects, or events; to express that relationship, the proposition is comprised of a subject and a predicate. "People drink water" and "Grandparents spoil children" are examples of propositions. As you can see, propositions are not facts—they are merely assertions that can be judged to be true or false.

Although we just defined *proposition* in terms of language, psychologists assume that propositions are represented in our minds in a nonlinguistic form. These psychologists believe that a single proposition (the deep structure of meaning) can be expressed in numerous linguistic forms (the surface structures of meaning), but that the proposition, which is the "meaning atom" or smallest unit of meaning, is actually an abstract code. For example, the meaning conveyed by the sentence "They drank water" is also conveyed by the sentences "They imbibed H_2O" and "They swallowed the liquid that comes out of a faucet." All of the sentences are different, but they all mean the same thing because they are all based on the same abstract proposition. We have no other way to represent that proposition consciously except in language.

According to some theorists, networks of propositions form the structural building blocks of LTM. These semantic (meaning) networks enable us to locate stored information, alter it, or add to it (Anderson, 1976). It is not always easy, however, to retrieve information stored in LTM. It takes longer to understand the meaning of sentences containing more propositions, even when the number of words in the sentences is the same (Kintsch, 1974). Researchers have also shown that when subjects are asked to remember a set of interrelated sentences, the more propositions there are related to a given concept, the longer it takes to recall any one of those propositions (Anderson & Bower, 1973). These two facts provide evidence for the importance of propositions in our thought processes.

Dual-code Memory Other investigators believe that people use visual codes in addition to verbal ones for storing memories. This hypothesis is known as the **dual-code model** of memory (Begg & Paivio, 1969; Paivio, 1983). According to this view, sensory information and concrete sentences are more likely to be stored as images, while abstract sentences are coded verbally. Verbal codes cannot act as indexes or reference pegs for visual codes. One version of this dual-code theory asserts that images reside in a visual buffer—a spatial medium—where they can be worked on and transformed in various ways (for example, rotated or scanned) by other cognitive processes (Kosslyn, 1983).

Researchers continue to debate what memory codes are used to represent information. Some argue that a single code is used in propositional networks (Anderson, 1978). Others believe that a memory system using the same code for all informational input would not be efficient (Kosslyn, 1983). Some psychologists have proposed that memory uses different types of codes to represent different types of information (Day, 1986)—for example, propositional networks are used to encode test information (Anderson & Bower, 1973), and mental images are used for maps (B. Tversky, 1981) and mentally rotating complex figures (Cooper & Shepard, 1973). It seems that the answer to the debate is that both propositions and images represent information, but at different times and for different processing demands.

Eidetic Imagery Actual images may be stored in memory. We know this because of the phenomenon of photographic memory, known technically as **eidetic imagery.** Research subjects who claim to have eidetic imagery report seeing a whole stimulus picture in front of their closed eyes as if they were experiencing it directly rather than scanning memory for traces of it. Instead of asking subjects to describe pictures they have

been shown, researchers now use a more demanding test for eidetic imagery. Researchers show subjects two pictures in succession, each meaningless by itself, but together forming a meaningful composite. The subjects must hold the two images in visual memory in enough detail so the images will fuse to form a single picture that is not predictable from either part alone. As the test progresses, the pictures become more complex. When tested with this method, only a small number of people qualify as true "eidetikers" (Gummerman et al., 1972; Leask et al., 1969)—only about 5 percent of those studied (Gray & Gummerman, 1975).

> One unusual case is that of a woman, Elizabeth, who appeared to have an amazing degree of eidetic imagery. She passed all tests the researchers developed to challenge the existence of her photographic memory. In the most stringent test, Elizabeth saw a special complex pattern of a million dots with one eye, then up to several hours later looked at another seemingly random dot array. She was able to fuse the earlier image with the currently perceived one to form a 3-D picture. Normally this feat can be accomplished only by looking at the two images at the same time with special 3-D glasses. Elizabeth must have had the ability to retain the first image in long-term memory and retrieve it on demand. There may be other people with her remarkable type of memory who have not yet been studied, but even this one rare case forces us to acknowledge the possibility of vivid visual memory storage (Stromeyer & Psotka, 1970).

Additional evidence for eidetic imagery comes from ordinary honey bees! For most animals, remembering the cues that identify a desirable food source is of great significance; learning specific food cues is essential for survival. Honey bees store information about their food sources in constellations of associated features. If a single feature of a food source is changed (for example, a flower's odor), the bees must forget everything else they know about the flower in order to relearn its shape, color, and other features, even though these other features have not changed (Gould & Marler, 1984). In a well-controlled study, honey bees were given a reward of sugar when they responded differently to complex colored patterns. The results revealed that bees remember shapes "photographically." They are able to store complex patterns, not as isolated features, but as low-resolution eidetic images of the total pattern of colored shapes. The data suggest that bees remember the spatial relationship of elements in each pattern (Gould, 1985).

Much remains to be learned about the structures and networks involved in memory storage. It is clear, however, that the computer models of memory proposed until now are much simpler than the rich reality of personal memory.

Odor Recognition

For some, it is the smell of baking bread or chestnuts roasting on an open fire; for me, it's the fragrance of tomato sauce simmering for our family's Sunday pasta dinner. What is the smell that brings back a flood of childhood memories for you? Unlike visual and auditory memories, odor memories uniquely recreate significant past episodes in your life. In his novel, *Remembrance of Things Past*, French author Marcel Proust describes how the aroma and flavor of a morsel of food triggered long-forgotten memories of his childhood: "When from a long-distant past nothing subsists, . . . the smell and taste of things . . . bear unfaltering, in the tiny and almost impalpable drop of their essence, the vast structure of recollection."

While we can have vivid, long-lasting *recognition* of odors, we have at best limited *recall* of odors. You can recall the size, color, and shape of a banana, but you cannot conjure up its odor sensation. There is no controllable recall of odor perceptions because the primary function of the sense of smell is to respond immediately to odors when they are experienced—not to permit later recall for the purpose of cognitive analysis (Engen, 1987). **Figure 10.7** compares the special strength of odor memories—both natural episodic odors and laboratory-presented odors—with visual memory for pictures.

It has been shown that mice have an odor-recognition system that is acquired in only one-trial learning. This pheromone memory enables a female to recognize her stud male's odor which helps sustain her pregnancy (Brennan et al., 1990).

RETRIEVAL FROM LTM

Some researchers believe that information is never lost from long-term memory. They argue that all information encoded in long-term memory is stored there permanently. Retrieval failures, however, occur when the appropriate retrieval location or pathway for a given memory is forgotten (Linton, 1975). A great deal of research has focused on the retrieval process and on the cues that are most effective for locating specific memories among the massive number held in long-term storage.

The stimuli available to us as we search for a memory are known as **retrieval cues.** These cues may be provided externally, such as questions on a quiz (What memory principles do you associate with the research of Sternberg and Sperling?) or generated internally

FIGURE 10.7 **THE SPECIAL STRENGTH OF ODOR MEMORY**

The relative permanence of the ability to recognize a given odor is apparent when one compares it to recognition memory for pictures. The recognition of episodic odors (those associated with significant experiences) remains close to initial strength as time passes. By comparison, one's ability to recognize pictures shown in a laboratory experiment, while as strong as odor recognition initially, decreases rapidly. Laboratory odors are not recognized well after a minimal time interval but show little long-term loss.

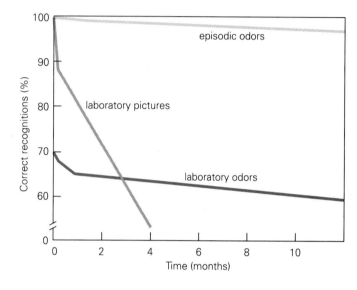

(Where have I met her before?). In the same way that the correct call number will get us the library book we want, a suitable retrieval cue will unlock the particular stored memory we are seeking. We have already mentioned the importance of encoding specificity for retrieval—remembered material is much more accessible if it has been encoded in accordance with the retrieval cues that you have available. As we have seen, cues can be provided both by the content of a stimulus and by the context during encoding. If the content and context are the same during your learning and during your memory search, you will have better access to what you learned.

Since information is organized in LTM storage, it is not surprising that cues based on *organization* can also help you retrieve what you know.

> In one study, subjects were given a list of words to memorize for free recall. The words were arranged by categories; a label preceded each category of words. The category labels were not mentioned in instructions—subjects were simply

told to memorize the words. During the recall test, half the subjects were given the category labels as retrieval cues, while the other subjects were asked only to recall as many items as they could. Recall was much better for the subjects given the category labels as retrieval cues.

In the second recall test, both groups were given the category retrieval cues, and they remembered equally well. The information had evidently been available in the long-term memory store of all the subjects, but was just not as accessible without the retrieval cues to help locate the items (Tulving & Pearlstone, 1966).

Other research has shown that recall is aided by organization, whether the organization is imposed by the experimenter or generated by the subject (Mandler, 1972).

Even with good cues, not all stored content is equally accessible, as you know only too well. In the case of familiar, well-learned information, more as-

pects of it have been stored and more connections between it and the many different parts of the memory network have been established, so a number of cues can give you access to it. On the other hand, when trying to find the one key that will unlock a less-familiar memory, you may have to use special search strategies.

DUPLEX MEMORY VERSUS MULTIPLE LEVELS

Most of the information in this chapter about memory is based on a single theory about short- and long-term memory: The **duplex theory of memory.** This theory assumes a flow of information from temporary sensory memory to short-term memory and, finally, to long-term memory (Atkinson & Shiffrin, 1968). Duplex theory focuses primarily on the differences between short-term memory and long-term memory. **Figure 10.8** presents an elaborate version of this theory, with a summary of the main features we have discussed.

Although the duplex theory is widely accepted, it has also been challenged. One alternative theory is that

---

FIGURE 10.8   THE MAIN FEATURES OF THE DUPLEX MEMORY SYSTEM

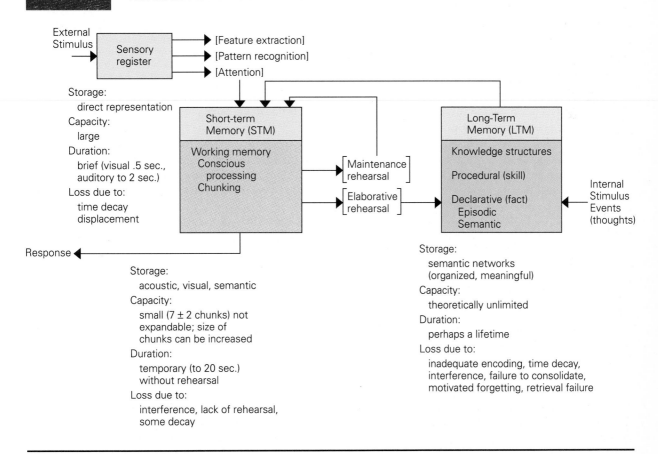

there may be a single system of memory with variations in levels of processing: deeper processing involves more analysis, interpretation, comparison, and elaboration, and so it results in better and longer memory. This view is called the **levels-of-processing theory** (Craik & Lockhart, 1972; Lockhart & Craik, 1990).

According to the levels-of-processing theory, the word *memory* can be processed at three levels: (a) physical, in terms of its appearance and the size and shape of the letters; (b) acoustic, involving the sound combinations that distinguish it from similar-sounding words (such as *memo*); and (c) semantic, according to its meaning. Levels-of-processing theorists claim that these processes differ in depth. It takes little mental work to process input at a physical level, more at an acoustic level, and still more at a semantic level. Moreover, within any of these three levels of processing, there can also be more variations in depth. For example, it should now require deeper processing for you to complete the sentence "Memory means . . ." than it did before you started this chapter, because the word is now linked to many more concepts and associations.

One way that level of processing is shown to influence memory comes from research on subjects working on tasks that require either low-level processing or deep processing. Those subjects who simply read sentences and rated their pleasantness recalled more total words from the sentences (deep processing) than did subjects who read the same sentences but focused on counting the number of *e* letters in them (shallow processing) (Jenkins, 1978).

This levels-of-processing view is important because of the emphasis it places on the varying depths at which information can be processed. However, it is unlikely to replace the duplex theory. A major problem with the levels-of-processing theory is that it is often difficult to determine in advance whether a task will require deep or shallow processing. Moreover, the duplex memory theory is bolstered by evidence from studies of amnesia, brain responses, and serial position effects. Let's briefly review this evidence.

The first evidence is that amnesiacs such as Nick retain long-term memory for events prior to the brain injury and short-term memory for events currently taking place, but have no ability to transfer new information from short-term to long-term memory. Others with amnesia have shown more impairment of long-term than short-term memory, suggesting that there are two memory systems (Milner, 1966; Wingfield & Byrnes, 1981).

A second source of support for the theory that there is a separate short-term memory system comes from a physiological study of brain responses during a test of recall. A unique brain wave form (a particular evoked potential) was found to be related to recall in a standard task that measured memory for very recent events within the short-term memory period. The researchers interpreted this result as evidence for a memory storage system that holds incoming information for a short time (Chapman et al., 1978). We will also see in a later section that different biochemical processes seem to operate in temporary storage as opposed to permanent storage.

The third type of evidence supporting a dual memory system comes from studies of the **serial position effect** in episodic memory. When a subject is free to recall, in any order, unrelated items presented for memorization, he or she recalls best those at the beginning and end of the list, as shown in **Figure 10.9.** Presumably, the subject would have processed all items at the same level in this case. The greater recall of items at the beginning and end of lists could be explained, however, by the existence of two memory systems. At recall time, the items at the beginning of the list would have been transferred to long-term storage and those at the end would still be in short-term memory. Those in the

---

FIGURE 10.9 **THE SERIAL POSITION EFFECT**

The graph shows the effects of a distracting task performed between the presentation of the list and the request for recall. The items on the beginning of the list are recalled best regardless of the delay-distraction. The items at the end are recalled well without delay-distraction but gradually worse as the delay-distraction is lengthened. The poorer recall at the middle of the list is due to the serial position effect (After Glanzer & Cunitz, 1966).

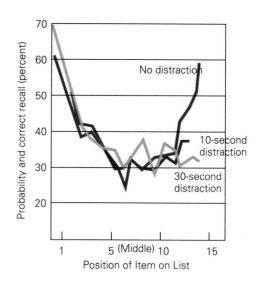

middle would have neither advantage, and their recall would be further hampered by interference from items before and after. This interpretation of the results is bolstered when subjects are given a distracting task after exposure to the list but before the testing: subjects recall the items in the last part of the list as poorly as those in the middle of the list, whereas they remember early items as well as ever (Glanzer & Cunitz, 1966; Postman & Phillips, 1965).

Having a poorer memory for the middle position of any series is a general phenomenon that occurs even when different types of materials are presented and when different modes of presentation are used (Roediger & Crowder, 1976). When learning the alphabet, children make most errors on the middle letters (I to M). Most spelling errors also occur in the middle of words. College students fail more exam items on material from the middle of a lecture than on material from the start or end of the lecture (Holen & Oaster, 1976; Jensen, 1962). So now you know what to devote some extra time and effort to—hit that middle! (You might also take note that this chapter is in about the middle of *Psychology and Life,* making it more difficult to remember its contents on a final examination that covers all the course material.)

SUMMING UP

Long-term memory is the permanent store of one's experiences, knowledge, and skills. Information transferred from STM is encoded into LTM by its meaning and associations to other pieces of information already there. Thus, we retain more about the meanings of sentences than we do about the actual words or sentence structures. Encoding is facilitated by organization strategies. Thinking of relationships between separate concepts is a good way to ensure that each will make it into long-term memory. Mnemonics are special strategies for associating new information with already familiar information. The way one encodes something also affects its retrieval. The encoding specificity principle states that when retrieval cues match the organization of encoding, recall will be better. Therefore, one's recall is improved to the extent that one is able to reinstate the organization used at the time of encoding.

There are several theories concerning how information is represented in LTM. One theory holds that ideas are stored as propositions that express the relation between concepts. Propositions can be organized into large networks that store huge amounts of information. The dual-code theory proposes that there are two forms of storage, a verbal code and a visual code.

Abstract information might be stored as propositions, but visual and spatial information would be stored as mental images. Odor memory endures much longer than visual memory although, unlike visual memory, it is limited to the function of odor recognition. The levels-of-processing theory proposes that there is a single memory system but that the level to which inputs are processed varies: material may be analyzed at the physical, acoustic, or semantic level. The durability and retrievability of information from memory increases with the depth to which that information was originally processed. Although the levels-of-processing theory points out that memory is a process, evidence from studies of amnesiacs and from studies of the serial position seem to support the duplex theory of memory.

REMEMBERING AS A CONSTRUCTIVE PROCESS

We have been talking as if we simply store and remember varying amounts of the information we receive. Sometimes what we remember is either more than or different from what we actually experienced. Laboratory studies about the way people process and remember meaningful material have forced psychologists to begin to conceptualize remembering as a continuation of the active, constructive process of perception. According to this new view, as we organize material to make it meaningful, we frequently add details to make it more complete or change it to make it fit better with other, already existing information in our personal memory store. As first noted by psychologist **Jerome Bruner,** when we construct memories, we "go beyond the information given" (1973).

Adding new information to what we take in is a constructive process that happens when the given information seems incomplete and we fill in the rest to make a "good figure." We saw this in our perception study of incomplete visual figures. This completion process may involve putting material into a context that makes sense to us or making inferences about events preceding an experienced action, unstated motives of the actors, or expected outcomes. For example, you see two friends parting and hear one say, "Between 8:00 and 8:30." Later on, you may "remember" hearing the friends planning their next meeting, although the time you heard one give may have referred to when the mail carrier empties the mailbox.

Changing information to make it conform to knowledge already in memory is a distortion process. When a new idea or experience is incompatible with your values, beliefs, or strongly felt emotions, you may alter it to be more consistent with your worldview or self-concept. You also reconstruct your memories to make them consistent with your current emotional state, or mood. Leading memory researcher **Gordon Bower** (1981) has demonstrated that people who are depressed tend to remember more sad events from the past than happy ones. Likewise, happy people tend to remember more happy than sad experiences. In part, this tendency is due to the *encoding specificity principle*. When you're happy, your mood serves as a retrieval cue for happy information and it biases recall toward positive events.

Distortion can occur at the encoding stage (when the material is first processed), at the retrieval stage, and perhaps even in between, during storage, as apparent inconsistencies and contradictions are managed. Usually we are quite unaware of such changes and confidently believe that our memory is an accurate record of what took place (Spiro, 1977).

SCHEMAS

The study of constructive processes is one of the most exciting new directions in memory research. It focuses on the way people organize, interpret, and retain meaningful input. The study is guided by the following general principle: *How and what you remember is determined by who you are and what you already know.* In other words, a person brings more to every situation than his or her memory recording device. What is perceived and remembered is a function of the individual's past history, current values, and future expectations, as well as the nature of the stimulus being committed to memory.

Much of what we know seems to be stored as **schemas,** general conceptual frameworks or clusters of knowledge and preconceptions regarding certain objects, people, and situations. Schemas are "knowledge packages" that provide expectations about the attributes we will find in future examples of various concepts and categories. For example, for a student, the term *registration day* probably conjures up a schema that includes scenes of hassle, long lines, delay, and frustration. For a political candidate, however, the schema for *registration day* might include feelings of nervousness and excitement and scenes of photographers, large crowds, and campaign posters.

Many of the constructions and distortions that occur when we remember new information are the result of interpreting that information in the light of expectations we have from existing schema. Cues in the present input steer us to a particular schema and we proceed to fill in the rest of the picture from schema-relevant information.

The importance of schemas in helping us organize and make sense of details—and remember them—has been shown in many studies, a few of which are described here.

> In one study, subjects listened to a story that included the following sentences: "Now three sturdy sisters sought proof. Forging along, sometimes through calm vastness, yet more often over turbulent peaks and valleys, days became weeks as many doubters spread fearful rumors about the edge. . . ."
>
> Those subjects who were given no title for this story had more difficulty remembering it than those subjects in a second group who were told before hearing the story that its title was "Columbus Discovering America." The latter group recalled much more of the story, evidently because the title brought to mind a well-known schema that provided a meaningful context for the ambiguously presented information (Dooling & Lachman, 1971).

Story titles give us schemas that help us make sense of elements in the plot and enable us to remember relevant sections of the story. When the elements don't fit with the title, reconstructive memory has trouble, as seen in the following study.

> While some subjects read a story titled "Watching a Peace March from the Fortieth Floor," other subjects read the exact same story but retitled "A Space Trip to an Inhabited Planet." Most of the story was ambiguous enough to fit under either title, but one sentence fit only the space trip title: "The landing was gentle, and luckily the atmosphere was such that no special suits had to be worn."
>
> More than half of those who were given the space trip title remembered this sentence, but only a few remembered it from the "peace march" story. The titles seemed to have activated different schemas. For one schema, the critical sentence fit, was interpreted as relevant, and was remembered; for the other, it had no meaning and was lost or not retrievable (Bransford & Johnson, 1972).

We also have people-related schemas that can influence what we perceive and remember about people who are described to us (Cantor & Mischel, 1979b). For example, most of us have schemas for Communists, cult leaders, environmentalists, and used-car salesmen. If a person we do not know is described as belonging to one of these categories, our schemas lead us to assume that the person has particular personality characteristics, and they lead us to have an emotional reaction to the person, either approving or disapproving. In addition, when we hear details about someone we do not know, we remember more of the details if we can relate them to an appropriate organizing schema.

> Subjects were presented with a list of behaviors (such as *ate lunch in the park, rented an apartment near work*). Some of the subjects were told that this was a memory experiment and that they should try to remember as much of the information as possible. Other subjects were told that this was an experiment about the way people form impressions of others and that they should form an impression (or schema) of the person who supposedly engaged in all of the behaviors.
>
> After a short delay, all subjects were asked to recall as many of the behaviors as possible. The subjects who had processed the information in terms of a schema about a certain kind of person (thus, in more depth) remembered more than did those who tried to remember the same information as unrelated items on a list (Hamilton et al., 1980).

When we try to recall information that is not consistent with a schema we have formed about certain individuals, our memory may distort the input to make it more schema-consistent. For example, if we are told that two people are arguing a great deal during their courtship, but a year later hear that the people are happily married to each other, we are either likely to forget about the disagreements we heard they were having or else we are suspicious of their "happy" marriage. Either distortion permits a memory consistent with our schema. When the same early information about disagreement is followed by a report of an unhappy marriage, we tend to remember the disagreement quite accurately (Spiro, 1977).

The same distortion process is probably at work when people have difficulty learning and fairly representing an opponent's point of view. In political arguments, both sides tend to remember the opposing viewpoint as oversimplified, less rational, and more extreme than their own, thereby achieving a more comfortable overall perspective of the problem and their relation to it. Although the study of constructive processes in memory has only recently become popular in memory research, it was actually begun over 50 years ago by British psychologist **Sir Frederic Bartlett** who described his work in his classic book, *Remembering* (1932). Bartlett focused on the kinds of constructions that take place when people try to remember material that is unfamiliar to them. He observed the way British undergraduates transmitted and remembered simple stories whose themes and wording were taken from an-

other culture. His most famous story was "The War of the Ghosts," an American Indian tale.

Bartlett used two procedures to study the way his subjects transformed this story into a coherent narrative that made sense to them. In *serial reproduction,* one person would read the story and tell it from memory to a second person, who communicated it to a third, and so on. In *repeated reproduction,* the same person would retell the story from memory over a number of repeated sessions (in some cases years apart). In both cases, memory was very inaccurate; the recalled story that emerged was often quite different from the original story that was read.

Bartlett found that constructive processes were intervening between input and output. The original story was evidently unclear to the subjects because of their lack of cultural understanding. The subjects unknowingly changed details to fit their own schemas so that the story would make sense to them.

The distortions Bartlett found involved three kinds of constructive processes: (a) *leveling*—simplifying the story; (b) *sharpening*—highlighting and overemphasizing certain details; and (c) *assimilation*—changing the details to better fit the subject's own background or knowledge.

Our selective and constructive memory "is part of the basic human impulse to have a meaningful and acceptable past, a *story,* that tells us who we are, where we come from. . . . How and what we remember is influenced by our environment, or culture. Conversely, the memories of individuals are part of what makes up a culture, are the seeds of history and myth" (Pearce, 1988, p. 17).

EYEWITNESS TESTIMONY

Juries tend to give much weight to the testimony of witnesses who are "at the scene" and report on what they see "with their own eyes"; but if memory is reconstructed to fit our schemas, how far should the memory of such witnesses be trusted? The ease with which we can be misled into "remembering" false information has been amply demonstrated in the laboratory research of **Elizabeth Loftus** (1979, 1984) and her colleagues. During the research, bright college students with good memories were misled into "recalling" that, "at the scene," a *yield* sign was a *stop* sign, that a nonexistent barn existed, and that a *green* stoplight was shining *red.*

The basic research design used in these studies typically involved two groups of students, both of which viewed the same stimulus materials on film or slides. Members of the experimental group later received information designed to "contaminate" their memories— indirect suggestions that certain events happened or

The way in which a witness is questioned about an event can affect his or her recall.

certain actions occurred. For example, they might have heard another "witness" report something about a man's mustache when, in fact, the man had no mustache. Although many subjects resisted being misled, a significant proportion integrated the new information into their memory representations and confidently reported the nonexistent mustache, barn, and stop sign as part of what they actually saw "with their own eyes."

The way in which a witness is questioned about an event can affect his or her recall. Sometimes words used in questioning suggest a particular interpretation. These words then function as misleading retrieval cues.

> In one study, people were shown a film of an automobile accident and were asked to estimate the speeds of the cars involved; however, some people were asked, "How fast were the cars going when they smashed into each other?" while others were asked, "How fast were the cars going when they contacted each other?" When *smash* was used in the question, the eyewitnesses reported that the cars had been going over 40 miles per hour. Those same cars were reported to be going 30 miles per hour by eyewitnesses who had been asked the *contact* question. About a week later, all the eyewitnesses were asked, "Did you see any broken glass?" In fact, no broken glass had appeared in the film. However, of the eyewitnesses who had been asked the *smash* question the week before, about a third reported that there had been broken glass. Only 14 percent of the *contact* eyewitnesses said they had seen broken glass. Clearly, the type of verb used in the original question altered people's memories of what they had witnessed. More-

over, these witnesses had filled in the gaps with plausible details that fit the general context suggested by the verb (Loftus, 1979).

This line of research has practical, applied value and also contributes to basic knowledge. The issue that is involved in these findings is of central importance to both psychologists and professionals working in the legal system. The process by which a person perceives an event, encodes that information, and recalls it at a later time is at the heart of psychological interest in learning and memory. From the legal perspective, the limitations of the memory process and the perceptual and cognitive biases that may be involved can have profound implications for the use of eyewitness testimony in courtroom trials. Memory researchers are using this research paradigm to discover how memories are changed by subsequent information—are they lost, suppressed, or blended? Researchers are also testing variables that extend or limit the general conclusion that "misleading mentions may make memories mucky" (see Bekerian & Bowers, 1983; McCloskey & Egeth, 1983). Memory distortion is a critical issue affecting legal testimony by children, especially when there is the possibility of sexual abuse and allegations of subsequent coaching by interviewers. Finally, lawyers can use information about memory distortion to learn how to elicit the responses they want from witnesses.

Human capacity for constructive memory not only increases the difficulty of getting accurate eyewitness testimony but also shields people from some truths they do not want to accept—it makes bigots more bigoted as corrective information gets distorted, and it makes all of us more likely to disregard new details in familiar contexts, when we remember what we expect rather than what exists.

Despite its faults, constructive memory is an enormously positive feature of creative minds at work. More often than not, it helps us to make sense of our uncertain world by providing the right context in which to understand, interpret, remember, and act on minimal or fragmentary evidence. Without it, our memories would be little more than transcription services that would be unable to assign any special significance to our many experiences.

SUMMING UP
We have emphasized that remembering is a constructive process. When the information we were originally given is incomplete or not fully understandable, we frequently add to it; we make inferences and assumptions that allow us to retain a more complete and organized memory. Schema are knowledge struc-

tures that summarize our knowledge within a limited domain. They are used to interpret events and serve as a source of expectations when learning something new. They also help us recall information by providing a framework for us to use in evaluating experiences. Schema tend to induce three processes in remembering: leveling or simplification, sharpening or highlighting, and assimilation or changing details to fit one's schema. The constructive quality of memory has implications for eyewitness testimony. People are susceptible to biases when trying to recall past events, especially details about those events. Recall is affected by information people learn after an event. Recall also depends a great deal on the retrieval cues that lawyers offer to witnesses in their questions.

WHY WE FORGET

We all remember an enormous amount of material over long periods of time. College students can accurately recall details about the births of younger siblings even when those events occurred 16 years earlier (Sheingold & Tenney, 1982). Conductor Arturo Toscanini, even at an advanced age, supposedly knew "by heart every note of every instrument of about 250 symphonic works and the words and music of about 100 operas" (Marek, 1975).

Knowledge in semantic memory is retrieved even better than knowledge in episodic memory, regardless of the time lapsed since the actual experience of the knowledge. In semantic memory, you will retain generalizations longer than details. For long-term retention, as for efficient encoding and retrieval, meaningful organization seems to be the key.

However, even well-learned material may be irretrievable over time. We forget much of what we have learned. Why? In this section, we will explore the following four perspectives on forgetting (each one offers an explanation for what has happened to stored infor-

mation when we can't remember it): (a) *Decay*—stored information is lost over time, similar to the colors of a picture bleached by the sun; (b) *Interference*—stored information is blocked by similar inputs, as when multiple exposures of a negative interfere with the clarity of the original image; (c) *Retrieval Failure*—stored information can't be located, as when you can't find your car in a huge parking lot; and (d) *Motivated Forgetting*—stored information is hidden from consciousness for some personal reason, as when you forget the name of someone you don't like.

MEMORY TRACES DECAY

Some early psychologists theorized that we forget because we suffer gradual storage loss; the memory traces decay over time, just as batteries lose their charge. However, to prove that decay is to blame for forgetting, research would have had to show that: (a) no mental activity that could change or interfere with the memories occurs between original learning and recall and (b) decayed memories are, in fact, gone from the brain and not merely inaccessible for some reason. Although it seems plausible that decay is partly responsible for the inability to remember material learned long ago, all we can say with certainty is that decay is an important factor in sensory memory loss and in short-term memory loss when all maintenance rehearsal is prevented.

In fact, some memories do not seem to become weaker over time. Recall that learned motor skills are retained for many years even with no practice. Once you learn to swim, you never forget how. In addition, trivia and irrelevant information, such as song titles and commercial jingles, seem to persist in memory, as do memories of odors from childhood.

INTERFERENCE

We never learn anything in a vacuum; we have other experiences before and after we learn new material. Both our learning and our retention of new material are

affected by these interferences from other experiences, as demonstrated by the serial-position effect when end list input interferes with middle list recall. **Proactive interference** (*pro* means *forward acting*) refers to the phenomenon that occurs when the vocabulary list you learned yesterday interferes with your learning of today's list. **Retroactive interference** (*retro* means *backward acting*) describes what happens when studying today's list interferes with your memory for yesterday's list.

There are three general principles governing interference. First, the greater the *similarity* between two sets of material the greater the interference between them—two vocabulary lists in the same foreign language would interfere with each other more than a vocabulary list and a set of chemical formulas. Second, meaningless material is more vulnerable to interference than meaningful material. Third, the more difficult the distracting task between learning and recall the more it will interfere with memory of material learned earlier.

Ebbinghaus, after learning dozens of lists of nonsense syllables, found himself forgetting about 65 percent of the new ones he was learning. Fifty years later, students at Northwestern University who studied Ebbinghaus's lists had the same experience—after many trials with many lists, what the students had learned earlier interfered proactively with their recall of current lists (Underwood, 1948, 1949).

The most obvious prediction that emerges from interference theory is that information undisturbed by new material will be recalled best. A classic study by Jenkins and Dallenbach (1924) provided support for this hypothesis. Subjects who went to sleep immediately after learning new material recalled it better the next morning than those who spent the same amount of time after learning performing their usual activities. Another finding from interference research is that short-term memory seems most vulnerable to interference. Evidence from the studies of the serial position effect suggests that once material is firmly encoded in long-term memory, it is less subject to interference from later material.

RETRIEVAL FAILURES

An apparent memory loss often turns out to be only a failure of retrieval. A question worded a little differently will guide us to the information, or a question requiring only recognition will reveal knowledge that we could not access and reproduce by recall. The Northwestern students who were having trouble recalling Ebbinghaus's lists often remembered better when retrieval cues were given. But even the best retrieval cues will not help if a person didn't store the material

properly, just as a book not listed in the card catalog will not be retrievable even if it is on a shelf somewhere in the library. In any case, it seems clear that much of our failure to remember reflects poor encoding or inadequate retrieval cues rather than loss of memory. Failure to call up a memory is never positive proof that the memory is not there.

Why do we forget the names of many of our high school classmates or even college teachers whom we meet in town away from school? One reason is that the social context in which we met those people originally is changed and with that change we have lost the *social-context retrieval cues* we used to form memories for those acquaintances (Reiser et al., 1985). Memories of people are formed around the social contexts in which they were encountered, and only later with more interaction, do we add secondary retrieval cues based on the personality traits and personal attributes of those people (Bond & Brockett, 1987).

MOTIVATED FORGETTING

On September 22, 1969, 8-year-old Susan Nason vanished from her northern California neighborhood. For 20 years, no one knew what had happened to her. Then, in 1989, Susie's friend, Eileen Franklin-Lipsker, contacted county investigators. Eileen told them that, with the help of psychotherapy, she had recalled a long-repressed, horrifying memory about what had happened to Susan. She had returned to California from her new home in Switzerland to testify against Susan's murderer.

On that autumn day two decades earlier, Eileen had witnessed her father sexually assault her friend and then bludgeon her to death with a rock (Marcus, 1990). He had threatened to kill Eileen if she ever told anyone. Eileen remembered that her father hid the body in a remote wooded area. After weeks of searching, investigators found the girl's remains near where Eileen thought the incident had occurred.

In a Redwood City courtroom in late 1990, Eileen testified about the murder she had witnessed. She also testified that, when she was a child, her father had beaten and sexually molested her, and that once he had even held her down while a friend of his raped her. She said that the memory of the murder was triggered by a profound moment of eye contact with her daughter who reminded her of Susie. Suddenly, gazing into the eyes of her little girl, she remembered the look in Susie's eyes during her father's brutal assault.

Newspapers reported that "the testimony of memory experts played a key role in the trial, which some believe may give more credence to other victims of violence who have repressed memories . . ." (Work-

Eileen Franklin-Lipsker

man, 1990). After less than eight hours of deliberation, the jury found Eileen's father guilty. He was sentenced to life imprisonment by a judge who called him "a depraved and wicked man" (*San Francisco Chronicle*, January 30, 1991).

In cases of psychologically caused amnesia, such as this one, the forgotten material is retained but blocked from retrieval. Not until an effective retrieval cue is experienced does the traumatic memory come flooding back. We sometimes forget because we do not want to remember certain memories that are frightening, painful, or personally degrading.

Sigmund Freud (1923) first perceived memory and forgetting as dynamic processes that enable us to maintain a sense of self-integrity. Research on childhood memories recalled by adults found that, in general, unpleasant events were more often forgotten than pleasant events (Waldvogel, 1948). We all forget some ideas we do not want to recognize as part of us, appointments we do not want to keep, names of people we do not like, and past events that threaten our basic sense of self or security. Freud gave the label **repression** to the mental process by which we protect ourselves from unacceptable or painful memories, pushing them out of consciousness.

Our motivational needs not only prevent retrieval of certain memories but even change the tone and content of memories that we do retrieve. A study of early recollections revealed that many memories judged as traumatic by the researchers were selectively recoded as neutral or even pleasant by the subjects during recall. Evidently, we can reconstruct our early childhood so that we remember the "good old days" not the way they were but the way they should have been (Kihlstrom & Harackiewicz, 1982).

SUMMING UP

Some early psychologists theorized that people forget because memories gradually decay over time. But research has never demonstrated any evidence of people forgetting in the absence of intervening mental activity. Without such evidence, the theory can't be proved. More widely held views attribute forgetting to interference. Proactive interference is the negative impact on memory of earlier learning; retroactive interference is the negative impact of later learning. These theories are supported by evidence that people tend to forget learned material more when they are active in the time between learning and recall than when they sleep. Not all forgetting reflects the loss of information from memory; forgetting can sometimes be a failure of retrieval. Items that once could not be recalled may eventually be remembered in the presence of more effective retrieval cues. Freud believed that retrieval failure may be, in some cases, motivated by a desire to avoid painful memories. In his theory, repression is a process that prevents unacceptable information from being admitted to consciousness.

THE NEUROBIOLOGY OF MEMORY

Psychologists study memory at the macro level, as a whole behavior. They create theoretical models of an information-processing organism that forms, associates, and holds learned experiences. They test their theories with behavioral data from a variety of laboratory experiments. Neuroscientists also seek to unlock the mysteries of memory. Their general strategy for understanding the mechanisms of memory is to study how experience modifies various components of the nervous system. Two of the many tactics that emerge from this more molecular level of analysis are studying the anatomy of memory—where the brain forms and stores memories—and analyzing the changes in synapses and neurons that are assumed to constitute memory. Let's examine some of the evidence being uncovered by neuroscientists.

THE ANATOMY OF MEMORY

In addition to encoding genetic information in the DNA of every cell nucleus, nature encodes experiential information in the neurons of the brain. The general term for this coding of acquired information in the brain is the **engram** or **memory trace.** The sum of a person's store of engrams is the biological substrate of human memory and the foundation upon which each human being's uniqueness rests.

Where in the vast galaxy of the brain are these memory traces to be found? Are they localized in particular brain regions or are they distributed throughout many different areas? The search for the engram was begun many years ago by physiological psychologist **Karl Lashley** (1929, 1950). He trained rats to learn mazes, removed portions of their cerebral cortexes, and then retested their memories for the mazes. He found that memory impairment from brain lesioning was proportional to the amount of tissue that was removed. The impairment grew worse as more of the cortex was damaged. However, memory was not affected by *where* in the brain the tissue was removed. Lashley gave up in disappointment, prematurely concluding that the elusive engram did not exist in any localized regions of the brain but was widely distributed throughout the entire brain.

We now know that Lashley was partly correct—and partly incorrect. Maze learning, which involves spatial, visual, and olfactory signals, is complex and memory for complex sets of information *is* distributed across many neural systems. However, memory for each specific type of sensory information and memory for discrete types of knowledge are separately processed and localized in limited regions of the brain. Modern neuroscientists are now able to trace the neural circuitry that is necessary and sufficient for a particular type of learning—and for its remembrance.

There are four major brain structures involved in memory: (a) the *cerebellum* (essential for procedural memory, memories acquired by repetition, and classically conditioned responses); (b) the *striatum* (a complex of structures in the forebrain—the likely basis for habit formation and for stimulus-response connections); (c) the *cerebral cortex* (for sensory memories and associations between sensations); and (d) the *amygdala* and *hypothalamus* (largely responsible for declarative memory of facts, dates, and names and also for memories of emotional significance). Other parts of the brain, such as the thalamus, the basal forebrain, and the prefrontal cortex, are involved also as way stations for the formation of particular types of memory (see **Figure 10.10**).

FIGURE 10.10 *BRAIN STRUCTURES INVOLVED IN MEMORY*

This simplified diagram shows some of the main structures of the brain that are involved in the formation, storage, and retrieval of memories.

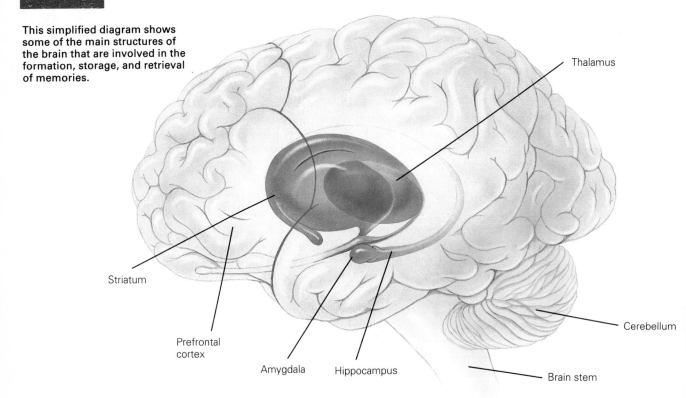

Clinical and experimental evidence makes it apparent that memory is resident in brain tissue. When something is learned and remembered, evidence shows that there is a permanent change that takes place in a given brain process located in one or more regions of the brain. One example of this evidence is the work of surgeon **Wilder Penfield** with a teenage epileptic patient. Penfield performed surgery on the young woman to create a map of her cortex. He used an electrode probe to apply electrical impulses to different areas of her brain. As Penfield touched one part of her brain, the patient screamed in horror. The surgeon had activated a terrifying childhood memory with the electric pulses surging through certain nerve cells.

Neuropsychologist **Richard Thompson** (1987) has been investigating the anatomy of memory for the past 20 years and claims to have found the engram—at least one of them. He uses Pavlovian eyelid conditioning in rabbits as a model for an organism's adaptive behavioral responding to known brain circuits. Thompson conditions rabbits to blink when they hear a tone that signals that an air puff will shoot at their eyes. He has discovered that a lesion of only one cubic millimeter of cell tissue in the cerebellum of a rabbit causes permanent loss of the conditioned eyeblink. (The *cerebellum* is found to play an essential role in both the learning and memory of specific conditioned responses to aversive events.) The memory deficit is highly specific to that learned association—the animal can still hear the tone, respond to the air puff, and learn the conditioned response in the other eye, but it can't relearn the response in the first eye.

The entire circuitry for learning and storing this simple conditioned response has been traced to specific nuclei in and around the cerebellum. In more complex conditioning, as when the subject learns to remember that there is a delay between the tone and the air puff, circuits in the hippocampus also become involved (McCormick & Thompson, 1984).

The hippocampus and amygdala are currently believed to be involved in encoding stimulus inputs, while the cerebral cortex is probably the storage center of long-term memory (McGaugh et al., 1985). Studies of human patients with amnesia have identified the important role of the hippocampus in encoding new fact memories. Comparable memory deficits are found in monkeys with lesions in the hippocampus and amygdala (Mishkin et al., 1984).

Some researchers are studying memory in cortical networks by stimulating or blocking smell memory. The olfactory system is unique among the senses because it has fairly direct connections to the hippocampus, amygdala, and the thalamus. This fact may account for the power of certain odors to evoke strong childhood memories in humans. Remarkable parallels occur between the smell memory of rats and humans. Lesions that separate the olfactory system and the hippocampus in rats produce forgetting for learned odors similar to the amnesia experienced by humans, such as Nick, who have suffered damage to their temporal lobe and hippocampus (Lynch, 1986).

Other research supports theories that the brain organizes memory functions around two different systems for information storage. The distinction we encountered earlier between procedural (skill) and declarative (fact) knowledge is supported by a variety of experiments with patients who experienced temporarily impaired memories as a result of electroconvulsive shock therapy and with brain-lesioned monkeys (Squire, 1986; Thompson, 1986; Mishkin & Appenszeller, 1987).

Skill learning and stimulus-response habits appear to be more primitive than fact, or cognitive, learning in the evolution of learning systems. Skill learning may involve a collection of special purpose abilities that are stored in structures evolutionarily even more primitive than the limbic system (which includes the amygdala and hippocampus). These structures are not affected by brain damage to higher level brain centers. In an extensive series of well-controlled experiments with monkeys, **Mortimer Mishkin** and his associates have convincingly demonstrated that different neural systems underlie memories for information and memories for simple habits (Mishkin & Petri, 1984). While fact learning seems to be centered in the hippocampus and amygdala, skill learning may be located in the *basal ganglia striatum* (a group of cell bodies in the forebrain).

The hippocampus is also implicated in another vital aspect of memory we have not yet mentioned—the way stored information and new information are connected. Memory is not fixed at the time of learning but is gradually transformed into a durable long-term memory code by the dynamic process known as **consolidation** (Hebb, 1949; McGaugh & Herz, 1972). This stabilizing or consolidating of memories can proceed for as long as several years in humans and for weeks in lower animals. It is the mechanism for the transition from short-term to long-term memory and is currently hypothesized to occur in the hippocampus.

ALZHEIMER'S DISEASE

Further evidence of the hippocampus's importance to memory comes from the tragic disorder **Alzheimer's disease.** This disease strikes more than 10 percent of people over the age of 65 and almost half of those over 85. The disease is marked by a gradual, but ultimately severe, decline in intellectual ability and memory. The symptoms of Alzheimer's are alarming: once independent and competent individuals begin to lose the ability to take care of themselves. In large part, this loss is due to a deficit of short-term memory, as sufferers forget things after only a few minutes. Similar to Nick, patients cannot hold onto plans, forget what they are doing midway through an activity, and have trouble learning new information. But Alzheimer's patients also suffer from an increasingly debilitating loss of past knowledge. Patients slowly forget how to perform skills they have performed most of their lives, including how to drive a car, cook, and care for themselves. In late stages of the disease, patients may even fail to remember who family members are or even forget their own identity. The loss of past memories in addition to the disruption of new learning sets Alzheimer's disease apart from other amnesia syndromes.

Alzheimer's disease is clearly linked to degeneration of the hippocampus and related areas of the midbrain. Autopsies have shown that up to three quarters of the neurons in these areas may be lost in Alzheimer's patients and the remaining neurons damaged. Massive tangles of fibers appear in the cell bodies, and there is a decline in production of the neurotransmitters necessary for neurons to communicate with one another. Such degeneration of the hippocampus is not a necessary part of growing older, and Alzheimer's may have a genetic cause. However, the disorder points out the importance of the hippocampal system in the encoding and storage of new memories. Moreover, it suggests that these structures may also play a role in the act of retrieval as well, because of Alzheimer's devastating effects on old memories.

CELLULAR MECHANISMS OF MEMORY

Neuroscientists now generally accept that human memory involves changes in the physiology and/or structure of synaptic membranes (Lynch, 1986)—neural impulses that signal specific experiences modify subgroups of the many billions of synapses in the cortex (see **Figure 10.11**). In this view of the biology of memory, the chemistry of memory must be able to modify irreversibly the structure of a small group of synaptic contacts on a single cell—without affecting neighboring units.

Researchers have reached this conclusion by using high frequency stimulation of inputs to the hippocampus. This stimulation increased memory strength for new learning for 32 months. This technique, called **long-term potentiation,** was found to cause changes in the shapes of synapses, to lead to the formation of new synaptic contacts on nerve cells, and to increase the number of receptors for the neurotransmitter *glutamate* used by the hippocampus (McGaugh et al., 1985).

This long-lasting potentiation effect alters cortical synapses through several chemical processes triggered by neural impulses (or the experimental high-frequency stimulation). One such chemical process appears to involve the sudden increase in *calcium* within neurons. Calcium activates a special kind of enzyme called *calpain,* which causes the breakdown of parts of the cell membrane by influencing a protein, *fodrin,* in the spine of the neuron. The result is a change in the shape of the dendritic spines, thus forming new receptors on the membrane which make it more sensitive to subsequent signals from connecting neurons. Calpain's effects are permanent and irreversible, thus making it ideal for pro-

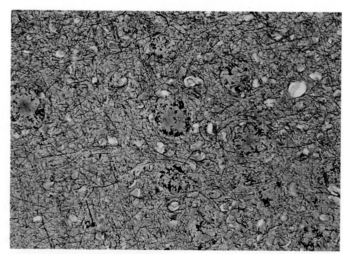

Alzheimer's disease is characterized by emotional and behavioral abnormalities and intellectual deterioration including memory loss.

ducing long-lasting changes in cellular chemistry and anatomy.

In addition, inputs to neurons also increase levels of neurotransmitters, the chemical messengers by which neurons communicate with one another. New evidence shows that neurons maintain a number of neurotransmitters, each independently regulated (Black et al., 1987). Learning modifies the levels of these neurotransmitters.

INTEGRATING THE BIOLOGY AND THE PSYCHOLOGY OF MEMORY

Understanding the human mind is the central goal of much psychological research. The learning and memory of experiences fills our minds with ideas that give meaning to our existence and purpose to our actions. There can be no mind without memory and no sense of human consciousness without mind. The psychological study of memory in the laboratory and in real life has provided new insights into the multiplicity of systems and operations involved in processing information into memory codes. Theoretical speculations on the part of cognitive psychologists about the dual coding of short-term and long-term memory and distinctions among procedural, semantic, and episodic memory have now been confirmed by the research of neurobiologists and neuropsychologists. These investigators study the brain as the biological substrate of the mind and memory as "the essential brain substrate for all higher mental processes" (Thompson, 1984). Despite differences in the way each of these disciplines approaches the study of memory, there is a new level of cooperation and integration between them. The ultimate goal of cognitive psychologists, neurobiologists, and neuropsychologists is to be able to provide formal descriptions of cognition, underlying brain systems, and the neurons and cellular events within these systems (Squire, 1986). A memory may be vulnerable to distortion and loss over time, and we could all improve the ways we commit information to memory; but, to psychologists, memory is the "Queen of the Cognitive Sciences" and, to poets, the very crux of being human.

FIGURE 10.11   *HOW MEMORIES ARE FORMED*

A nerve spine in the hippocampus changes shape after receiving the type of stimulation that occurs during a learning experience. Below left, the first of several bursts of electricity causes a chemical neurotransmitter to be released from a neighboring neuron onto the receptors of the nerve spine shown here. Calcium enters the cell. The calcium activates calpain (orange), an otherwise dormant enzyme, which begins to degrade fodrin, the structural material of the spine. With additional bursts of electricity, the fodrin continues to break down, and more receptors appear, below right. More receptors result in a greater influx of calcium, and therefore more calpain activation and even greater fodrin degradation. With significant loss of structural material, the spine changes shape. A new spine may also begin to extend through the membrane. These permanent changes result in new connections between neurons in the brain, a plausible explanation for memory.

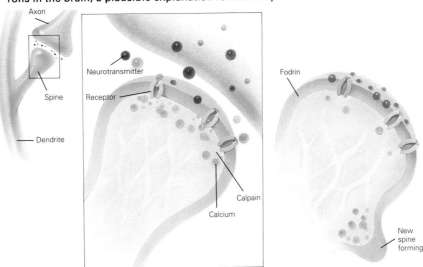

What Is Memory?

Cognitive psychologists study how remembering is a way of processing information. They view it as a three-stage process in which information that arrives through our senses is encoded, stored, and later retrieved. Three separate memory systems have been proposed: sensory, short-term, and long-term.

Sensory Memory

In encoding for sensory memory, stimulus energy is changed to a neural code. Sensory memory has a large capacity but a very short duration. Attention and pattern recognition help sensory information to get into short-term memory.

Short-term Memory

Short-term memory (STM) has a limited capacity (7 +/− 2 items), and lasts only briefly without rehearsal. STM, as part of our psychological present, is also called working memory. Material may be transferred to it from either sensory or long-term memory; information can be consciously processed only in STM.

Verbal information entering STM from sensory memory is usually encoded acoustically. Its capacity can be increased by chunking unrelated items into meaningful groups. Maintenance rehearsal extends the duration of material in STM indefinitely; elaborative rehearsal prepares it for long-term storage.

Long-term Memory

Long-term memory (LTM) constitutes our total knowledge of the world and of the self; it is nearly unlimited in capacity. Meaningful organization is the key to encoding for LTM: the more familiar the material and the better the organization, the better the retention.

The more specifically material is encoded in terms of expected retrieval cues, the more efficient later retrieval will be, if the same cues are available at retrieval. Similarity in context between learning and retrieval also aids retrieval.

Three kinds of memory content are procedural, semantic, and episodic memory. Procedural memory is memory for skills—how things get done. Semantic memory is memory for the basic meaning of words and concepts. Episodic memory is concerned with memory of events that have been personally experienced; it stores autobiographical information.

Investigators disagree about the number of memory codes—whether only verbal, both verbal and visual, or some other combination or relationship.

There is also disagreement about whether there are actually three different memory systems (sensory, short-term, and long-term) or whether there is only one memory and we simply process memories at different levels, using varying depths of processing.

Remembering as a Constructive Process

Remembering is not simply recording but a constructive and a selective process. We remember what we want to and what we are prepared to remember based on our cultural and personal history. Schemas play a major role in constructive memory processes. Schemas are cognitive clusters built up from earlier experience that provide expectations and a context for interpreting new information and, thus, influence what is remembered.

Information or misinformation provided during retrieval can bias our recall without our realizing it, making eyewitness testimony unreliable when contaminated by after-the-fact input.

Why We Forget

Explanations for forgetting include decay, interference, retrieval failures, and motivated forgetting. Each one is shown to play a role in some specific instances of forgetting.

The Neurobiology of Memory

Study of the neurobiology of memory is concentrated in three areas: identification of brain structures involved in the formation and storage of memories, analysis of the synaptic and neuronal changes assumed to underlie memory, and discovery of the physiological systems that regulate or modify memory storage.

Different brain structures (including the hippocampus, the amygdala, the cerebellum, and the cerebral cortex) have been shown to be involved in different types of memory, in the formation of new memories, and storage of old memories. It appears that memory may involve lasting changes in the membranes of neurons at some synapses and in levels of neurotransmitters. Hormones such as epinephrine may play a role in regulating memory.

Cognitive psychologists and neurobiologists are working together to crack the secrets of memory, which will stand as one of the major accomplishments of modern science.

KEY TERMS

Alzheimer's disease, 373
anterograde amnesia, 341
backward masking, 351
chunk, 353
chunking, 353
consolidation, 373
context dependence, 360
declarative memory, 344
dual-code model, 361
duplex theory of memory, 363
echo, 349
eidetic imagery, 361
elaboration, 346
elaborative rehearsal, 354
encoding, 346
encoding specificity principle, 360
engram, 371
episodic memory, 344
icon, 349

immediate memory span, 353
implicit memory, 345
levels-of-processing theory, 364
long-term memory (LTM), 357
long-term potentiation, 374
maintenance rehearsal, 354
memory, 343
memory code, 352
memory trace, 371
mnemonics, 359
partial-report procedure, 350
priming effect, 345
proactive interference, 370
procedural memory, 343
proposition, 360
recall, 347
recognition, 347
remembering, 343
repression, 371

retrieval, 346
retrieval cues, 362
retroactive interference, 370
retrograde amnesia, 341
savings method, 345
schema, 366
selective attention, 351
semantic memory, 344
sensory gating, 350
sensory memory, 349
sensory register, 349
serial position effect, 364
short-term memory (STM), 352
state dependence, 360
storage, 346
whole-report procedure, 350
working memory, 352

MAJOR CONTRIBUTORS

Bartlett, Sir Frederic, 367
Bower, Gordon, 366
Bruner, Jerome, 365
Ebbinghaus, Hermann, 344
Freud, Sigmund, 371

Lashley, Karl, 372
Loftus, Elizabeth, 367
Mishkin, Mortimer, 373
Penfield, Wilder, 373
Sperling, George, 350

Squire, Larry, 341
Sternberg, Saul, 355
Thompson, Richard, 373
Tulving, Endel, 344

Chapter 11

Cognitive
Processes

STUDYING THINKING   380
   THE EMERGENCE OF COGNITIVE PSYCHOLOGY
   THE RISE OF COGNITIVE SCIENCE

   ■ INTERIM SUMMARY

MEASURING THE MIND   384
   INTROSPECTION AND THINK-ALOUD PROTOCOLS
   BEHAVIORAL OBSERVATION
   MEASURING REACTION TIME
   ANALYZING ERRORS
   RECORDING EYE MOVEMENTS
   READING THE MIND IN BRAIN WAVES
   BRAIN IMAGING

   ■ INTERIM SUMMARY

MENTAL STRUCTURES FOR THINKING   391
   CONCEPTS AND CONCEPT FORMATION
   SCHEMAS AND SCRIPTS
   VISUAL IMAGERY AND MENTAL MAPS

   ■ INTERIM SUMMARY

REASONING AND PROBLEM SOLVING   401
   DEDUCTIVE REASONING
   INDUCTIVE REASONING
   PROBLEM SOLVING
   THE BEST SEARCH STRATEGY: ALGORITHMS OR
     HEURISTICS?
   METACOGNITIVE KNOWLEDGE
   AN EVOLUTIONARY PSYCHOLOGY PERSPECTIVE

   ■ INTERIM SUMMARY

JUDGING AND DECIDING   410
   MAKING SENSE OF THE WORLD
   PERSEVERANCE OF FALSE BELIEFS
   SOURCES OF IRRATIONALITY
   COGNITIVE BIASES
   THE PSYCHOLOGY OF DECISION MAKING
   CLOSE-UP: ECOLOGICAL DECISION MAKING

RECAPPING MAIN POINTS   420

KEY TERMS   421

MAJOR CONTRIBUTORS   421

At the age of 16, Edith Eva Eger's world turned upside down. She and her family were suddenly arrested and interned in Auschwitz, a Nazi concentration camp in Poland. Shortly after they arrived at Auschwitz, her mother was sent to the gas chamber. Before she was taken away, she urged Edith and her sister to live their lives fully: "Remember," she said, "what you put inside your brain, no one can take away" (Eger, 1990, p. 6).

In the horror-filled existence of concentration camp life, Edith found that the basic logic of the world was reversed. The notions of good behavior she had learned growing up "were replaced by a kind of animal quiver, which instantly smelled out danger and acted to deflect it." Matters of life and death were decided as casually as flipping a coin—you could be sent to the "showers of death" for having a loosely tied shoelace.

After years of being brutalized, the camp inmates longed for freedom, yet, paradoxically, also dreaded it. When their liberators arrived, some prisoners "rushed forward but most retreated and even returned to their barracks."

Edith was a fortunate survivor. She later married, emigrated to the United States, and became a clinical psychologist. Recently, at age 61, Dr. Eger's need to understand the twisted reality of the camps caused her to return to Auschwitz. "I came to mourn the dead and celebrate the living. I also needed to formally put an end to the denial that I had been a victim and to assign guilt to the oppressor" (Eger, 1990, p. 6). For many years, she had denied the horrible truths of her camp experiences, but, eventually, denial was unacceptable to her. By reliving the events of her incarceration and forcing herself to think about the meaning of that horror, Dr. Eger believes she has become better able to help others understand events that seem inexplicable in the context of their everyday lives.

The fundamental human desire to comprehend the nature of one's existence that motivated Dr. Eger was eloquently described by another survivor of Auschwitz, Italian writer Primo Levi. He reports, "It might be surprising that in the camps one of the most frequent states of mind was curiosity. And yet, besides being frightened, humiliated, and desperate, we were curious: hungry for bread and also to understand. The world around us was upside down and somebody must have turned it upside down . . . to twist that which was straight, to befoul that which was clean" (Levi, 1985, p. 99).

Edith took her mother's last words to heart. No one can take away what she has "put inside her brain." By becoming a psychotherapist, Dr. Eger chose a career in which she helps others cope with personal realities that defy rational explanation. Noting that today's college students have little knowledge of the Holocaust, she hopes "that some day, when they are ready, my grandchildren will have the curiosity to ask their grandmother questions about the time when the world was upside down. So that if it starts tilting again, they and millions of others can redress it before it is too late" (Eger, 1990, p. 9).

Philosopher René Descartes said, *"Cogito ergo sum"*—I think, therefore, I am. Dr. Eger's story forces us to add the postscript, "I am human, therefore I *must think*." Even in the hell of a concentration camp, the human mind still insists on knowing the *why* of such evil. We appear to be driven by a basic need to understand the nature of our existence and to try to comprehend the causes of our thoughts, feelings, and actions. We have looked at consciousness, learning, and memory. Now we are prepared to understand how humans think, reason, judge, decide, and solve life's many problems and puzzles.

> There is more to be gained from studying how the mind functions than just the satisfaction of scientific curiosity. As Nobel Prize winning psychologist and computer scientist Herbert Simon said, "The human mind is the resource that human beings apply to the world of work; it is therefore required for productivity increases in the post-industrial world" (1985, pp. 2, 9).

STUDYING THINKING

Thinking turns violations of moral codes into *guilt,* inappropriate or stupid deeds into *shame,* and accomplishments into *pride.* Only humans have the capacity to go beyond the perception of what is here and now to think about what was, will be, might be, and should be. Thinking provides the context for our perception, the purposes for our learning, and the meaning for our memories. Thoughts developed in the inner universe of our minds enable us to form abstract working models of our physical and social worlds. We then use these personal mental representations of reality to reshape and sometimes improve aspects of that world (Hunt, 1982).

We tend to take thinking for granted because it's something we do continually most of our waking hours. However, when we witness a child's joy at solving a puzzle or read a detective story in which the sleuth combines a few scraps of apparently trivial clues into a brilliant solution of the crime, we are forced to acknowledge the intellectual triumph of thinking. We are also reminded of the power of human thought when we see it diminished under the influence of drugs, distorted by extreme stress and some forms of mental illness, or destroyed by brain damage.

The study of thinking is the study of all the higher mental processes. **Cognition** is a general term for all forms of knowing. As **Figure 11.1** shows, these forms of knowing include attending, remembering, reasoning, imagining, planning, deciding, judging, and problem solving.

A cognition is a bit of information, a thought unit, or an idea. Cognition includes both contents and processes. The contents of cognitive processes are concepts, facts, propositions, rules, and memories. Some *cognitive processes* mentally represent the world around us, such as those that classify information and interpret experiences; others are internally focused, such as those in our dreams and fantasies. Knowledge-based processes of the mind make sense of the neurally coded signals coming from the eye and other sensory systems.

We will begin with an analysis of the ways in which researchers try to measure the inner, private processes involved in cognitive functioning. We will then outline some of the models and basic ideas of information processing that are being used to account for the way we think, comprehend, and reason; in short, the way we come to understand ourselves. Finally, we will examine basic topics in cognitive psychology that are generating much of the basic research and application today: reasoning, problem solving, and decision making and judging.

© 1985 BLOOM COUNTY, Washington Post Writers Group. Reprinted with permission.

FIGURE 11.1 THE DOMAIN OF COGNITIVE PSYCHOLOGY

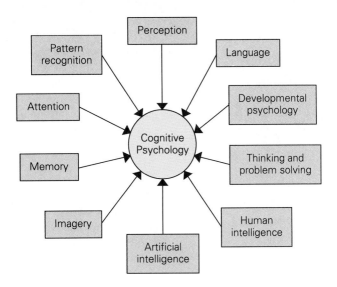

THE EMERGENCE OF COGNITIVE PSYCHOLOGY

Cognitive psychology is the scientific study of mental processes and mental structures. Cognitive psychologists investigate the ways people absorb, transform, and manipulate information. The study of cognitive processes is taking place in many areas of psychology, and cognitive psychology has moved to the very core of modern psychology.

Although it seems obvious that thinking and using knowledge should occupy a central position in psychology, it was not always so. During the decades when psychology was entrenched in *behaviorism,* the discipline focused on examining the organism's behavioral reactions to the external world; thinking minds were banished from behaviorist laboratories. A *science of the mind* became possible in the 1950s when researchers and scholars from different fields began to seek an understanding of the inner, private information processing that occurs out of sight but that gives observed behavior its direction, meaning, and coherence. This shift in focus began with the convergence of an unlikely threesome of new approaches involving computers, children, and communication.

The modern conception of a computer as a general-purpose logic machine with built-in intelligence, able to operate flexibly on internal instructions, came from the vision of a brilliant young mathematician, **John Von Neumann.** In 1945, he boldly drew comparisons between the electronic circuits of a new digital computer and the brain's neurons and between the computer pro-

gram and the brain's memory. His vision was based on the work of neurophysiologist Warren McCulloch who had just published a description of the functioning of the human brain (Heppenheimer, 1990). Researchers **Herbert Simon** and **Allen Newell** developed computer programs to simulate human problem solving, thereby providing new ways of studying mental processes (Newell, Shaw, & Simon, *Elements of a Theory of Human Problem Solving,* 1958). Simon is reputed to have told his 1955 class at the Carnegie Institute of Technology that, over the Christmas break, he and Newell had "invented a thinking machine." The next year, their computer, named *Johniac* in honor of John Von Neumann, worked out a proof of a mathematical theorem. If computers could process symbols in this reasoning exercise, then the human minds that designed them should be studied by psychologists as symbol-processing devices.

Around the same time, developmental psychologist **Jean Piaget** was pioneering a successful way to infer the mental processes children go through to understand physical realities (Piaget, *The Construction of Reality in the Child,* 1954). As we saw in Chapter 5, his notion of stages of cognitive development was based on observations of the kinds of mental tasks that children of different ages were capable of performing.

Finally, and also at about the same time, linguistic researcher **Noam Chomsky** studied language as part of a unique cognitive system for comprehension and production of symbols (Chomsky, *Syntactic Structures,* 1957). Chomsky postulated that an innate language

Noam Chomsky

acquisition device, LAD, made it possible for young children to understand the basic rules of grammar in the absence of any formal education or systematic reinforcement.

These three new approaches to human thought involving computers, children, and communication boosted the scientific legitimacy of research on all forms of higher mental processes. Since then, cognitive theory has developed into the foundation of the psychology of the 1990s (Mayer, 1981; Solso, 1991).

THE RISE OF COGNITIVE SCIENCE

Cognitive science is an interdisciplinary field being developed as a broad approach to studying the variety of systems and processes that manipulate information. As depicted in **Figure 11.2,** cognitive science draws on

 THE DOMAIN OF COGNITIVE SCIENCE

The domain of cognitive science occupies the intersection of cognitive psychology, computer science (artificial intelligence), and neuroscience.

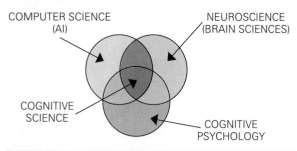

the three major overlapping disciplines of cognitive psychology, computer science, and neuroscience (Farah, 1984). Cognitive science also receives input from philosophy, economics, and cultural anthropology. A cognitive-literary analysis of the way the human mind constructs and understands stories, drama, myths, and rituals—acts of imagination that give meaning to human existence—has also been developed (Bruner, 1986). Cognitive science seeks to explore the classic questions of Western thought: What is knowledge, and how is it represented in the mind (Gardner, 1985)?

The Information-processing Model

Researchers studying the way information is represented and processed try to understand cognitive processes by building *conceptual models*. A **cognitive model** is an explanatory metaphor that describes how information is detected, stored, and used by people and machines. It is a hypothetical explanation that uses known metaphors to understand complex mental processes. Cognitive models are useful ways of thinking about specific phenomena because they can guide new research and make sense of existing knowledge. However, regardless of how correct a model may seem, it must stand the data test; new research can cause it to be modified or discarded.

The basic approach taken by most psychologists studying cognitive processes is represented by the **information-processing model.** This model proposes that thinking and all other forms of cognition—such as memory, perception, or the structure of knowledge—can be understood by analyzing them into component parts. Incoming information goes through a series of stages that are arranged in a processing hierarchy from simpler to more complex. As the information passes through the overall system of brain/mind, different subsystems process it in ways that enable complex input to be decoded, simplified, and understood on its own terms, and then responded to appropriately—with the formulation of thoughts, memories, feelings, and/or actions. Just as automobiles are built one step at a time, cognition might also be conceptualized as an assembly line process, building from primitive stages, such as basic sensations and perception, to more complex stages, such as naming, classifying, inferring, reasoning, decision making, and problem solving. However, unlike the automobile assembly line, the human mind works on parallel paths simultaneously. The mind also is capable of making remote associations between thought units and of coming up with novel concepts and links between them that have never before been processed.

"No good. It's still not worrying about how it's doing."

processing model based on the digital computer, ignoring what was known about neuronal signal processing in the brain. On the other hand, researchers in neuroscience have worked to analyze minute levels of brain functioning. Now the work of cognitive scientists and neuroscientists is converging into the new field of **cognitive neuroscience** which seeks to integrate what is known at the microscopic and molecular levels of single neurons and neuronal networks with the systems level represented by behavior (Churchland & Sejnowski, 1988).

Cognitive neuroscientists develop and test *brain models* that simplify the complex processes involved when the brain accomplishes specific processing tasks. These models may enable researchers to discover the rules and principles that govern the brain's *computational solutions* to the various problems it encounters.

Among these simplified brain models are those described as connectionist models (introduced in Chapter 9). Many theories state that the mind processes information in a serial, or sequential, fashion. The connectionist approach, however, assumes that the mind is made up of a very large set of simple processing units, or nodes, that are linked in a huge network that can process different information at the same time. **Parallel distributed processing models** (PDP), which are also known as connectionist models, show that information is processed in a massively distributed, interactive, parallel system that can carry out various activities simultaneously by exciting or inhibiting the connections between processing units. The PDP model is being developed and tested by **David Rumelhart** and his associates (Rumelhart et al., 1986).

Artificial Intelligence

Researchers in the field of computer science, who seek to make machines do the kind of thinking human minds do, work in the area of **artificial intelligence,** or AI. AI theories are *computer programs,* the software that is tested by the outcomes generated when a program is run on the computer. However, AI is not the study of computers as much as the study of intelligence in thought and action. Computers are only the *tools* that AI researchers use to study the human mind. AI research is concerned with thinking in general, with the way symbols are manipulated and combined according to the instructions expressed in the language of computer programs.

The main theoretical construct of AI is *representation*—the way a programmed system constructs, adapts, and uses its inner representations to interpret and change its world. A programmed AI computer may even be thought of as a *subjective system,* vulnerable to illusions and errors just as humans are.

Cognitive Neuroscience

The recent explosion of research in the many areas that comprise neuroscience has enhanced our understanding of the structure of the brain at cellular and molecular levels. However, we still do not know how the nervous system functions at a macro or systems level to enable us to see, hear, learn, remember, and think. Cognitive scientists have tended to rely on a symbol-

David Rumelhart

SUMMING UP

A basic function of the human mind is to create abstract representations of the physical and social worlds in which we live. The study of cognitive psychology includes looking at the mental processes and mental structures that enable us to think, reason, make inferences and decisions, solve problems, and use language. Cognition is the general term for all forms of knowing. Cognitive psychologists generally use an information-processing approach to analyze information into components that are processed in stages or sequences. Cognitive psychology has come to replace behaviorism as the core area of U.S. psychology. It began to emerge in the 1950s with the triple developments of digital computers and programs that can manipulate symbols; the study of the way knowledge develops in children; and the analysis of language acquisition as an innate symbolic manipulating system.

Cognitive science is a new interdisciplinary field of study that utilizes the expertise of cognitive psychologists and researchers in the brain sciences and computer science to study the way the brain and mind use knowledge to guide thought and action. Investigators in artificial intelligence are developing computer programs that mimic aspects of human thought and other aspects of higher mental processing of information. Cognitive neuroscience is another promising new area of study. It attempts to bridge the gap in our understanding between the molecular level of analysis of neuron functioning and the macro level of systems analysis of behavioral functioning. It does so, in part, by developing simplifying models of the brain that reveal how the brain solves specific computational problems and by testing them with computer simulations.

MEASURING THE MIND

If your thinking is an internal, subjective process that only you can experience, how can it ever be studied scientifically? A number of general approaches and specific methods have been developed to assess that which is not directly observable. In a sense, these approaches and methods all share the goal of putting a measure to the mind or focusing a beacon to illuminate human thought. In this section, we will briefly review some of the most important traditional methods and a few of the newest techniques of studying the mind. These methods and techniques include a refined method of introspection, behavioral observations, measuring reaction time, analyzing errors, recording eye and muscle movements, measuring brain-wave patterns, and brain visualization.

INTROSPECTION AND THINK-ALOUD PROTOCOLS

As we saw in Chapter 1, *introspection* was developed by Wilhelm Wundt in the late 1800s. It involved training people to analyze the contents of their own consciousness into component parts, such as sensations, images, and feelings. Although it yielded catalogs of the elements of consciousness, the introspective approach provided no clues about the actual sequences of mental processes in life situations. When the introspections of two people differed in the same situation, there was no empirical way to resolve the discrepancy between them. Moreover, many of your mental processes are not even available for your own conscious inspection. Often you are simply not aware of the *process* of thinking—only of its *product*—so trying to introspect on the way you think is similar to looking under the hood of a stalled car when you don't know how an engine works. In the five seconds or so that it took you to read that last sentence, you identified the letters and words, retrieved the stored meaning of each of them, and (I hope!) comprehended the meaning of the sentence. You even began to store that unit of information under different retrieval labels for ready access should it appear on a test. Do you know *how* you did *what* you just did so efficiently?

For an example of the method of introspection, consider your thoughts as you answer the following questions as quickly as possible. (The answers are on page 385.)

- What animal's name begins with the letter I?
- What series of letters comes after BCZYMCDYXN? (Hint: the first subset ends at M.)

How did you find an answer for each question? Could you follow your thoughts in both cases? If your thought processes were different in each instance, why?

Introspection can be used to supplement other methods, but it can never work as a technique for studying cognition. Recently, however, researchers have found a way to use introspection as an *exploratory procedure* to help map out more precise research. During the process of working on a task, experimental subjects describe what they are doing and why. Researchers use their reports, called **think-aloud protocols,** to infer the mental strategies the subjects employed to do the task and the ways the subjects represented knowledge.

An example of a think-aloud protocol is found in Chapter 10 in the case of a subject who could remember a sequence of 80 digits. Another example, an investigation of the way people plan everyday shopping trips, follows.

> Subjects were presented with a map of the city identifying several stores and businesses. They were assigned several items to purchase and required to plan a day's shopping trip, thinking aloud while they planned. From the protocols, the researchers discovered that planning is not a logical, organized, hierarchical process. Instead, it is an opportunistic process: A person follows many trains of thought simultaneously, jumping back and forth while discovering information that is relevant to one line of thought or another (Hayes-Roth & Hayes-Roth, 1979).

This jumping around contrasts sharply with the models of planning that are built into robots or computerized decision aids for business. Those models set up planning in a very systematic manner with main points and subpoints recognized and treated in a logical fashion. The think-aloud protocols show how people *actually* proceed instead of how a purely logical approach assumes they *ought* to behave. Such protocols have been collected in a wide variety of studies; they have proven especially useful in studying the cognitive processes involved in problem solving.

BEHAVIORAL OBSERVATION

A basic task of much psychological research is to infer internal states and processes from observations of external behavior. If we know the context in which the behavior occurred, we can theorize about the affective, motivational, or cognitive determinants of that behavior. Crying at a funeral is evidence of grief, while crying at a prize ceremony is evidence of great joy.

Answers to the questions on page 384:

- There aren't many animals whose names begin with I—two are *ibis* and *impala*.
- The next series of letters would be DEXWO. Some letters are ascending and others are descending in alphabetical order.

A direct test of the acquisition of an early kind of symbolic understanding used observations of children's behavior as they looked for a hidden object in a room after having seen where the object was hidden in a small-scale model of the room. Researchers wanted to determine at what age a child comes to understand that the model represents or is a symbol for something else. Researcher **Judy DeLoache** (1987) devised an ingenious way to identify such information.

> The child is placed in an experimental situation that requires two responses. First, the child must retrieve a toy from its observed hiding place in a scale model of the room (Snoopy is hidden behind a pillow on a couch). This task is simply an act of memory. Then the child must retrieve an analogous large size object hidden in a corresponding place in a full size room. Here the task is to combine memory of the first event with inferences about the symbolic equivalence of the scale model to the real environment.
>
> Two and a half year olds do as well as 3 year olds on the memory task, but most of them fail the second symbolic task, searching the room without any systematic pattern. In contrast, just six months older, almost all of the 3 year olds are able to solve the problem by using symbolic representation to guide their reality search (DeLoache, 1990).

The context in which behavior occurs can tell us something about the internal states and processes the behavior reflects.

Judy DeLoache (*Discovering Psychology,* 1990, Program 5)

MEASURING REACTION TIME

The elapsed time between the presentation of some stimulus or signal and a subject's response to it is known as **reaction time.** In Chapter 10, we saw that Robert Sternberg (1969) used measurement of reaction time to infer that retrieval from short-term memory involved a *serial exhaustive search* of all items in a remembered list. Reaction time is one of the most basic measurements that cognitive psychologists use to assess mental responding on different tasks. They then infer underlying differences in the thought processes involved in generating those responses, with slower reaction times indicative of more complex mental processing.

For example, it has been found that *simple reaction time,* the single response to a single stimulus, is shorter than *discrimination reaction time,* in which different stimuli are presented and the subject responds only to a designated one. *Choice reaction time,* in which a different response must be made for each of several different stimuli, is the longest. Adopting the principle that complex mental processes take more time, researchers today are using reaction time in a number of research designs to infer the occurrence of various cognitive processes.

The reaction-time technique is also being used to assess the steps involved in understanding the meaning of words that we read.

> In one situation, a subject who was seated before a video screen saw pairs of words appear and had to decide as quickly as possible if they belonged to the same semantic (meaning) category. The subject pressed one button if they were judged "same" and another if they were "different." Reaction time measurement began with the second word in the sequence and ended with the subject's response. For example, when the pair *cow-tiger*

appeared, the subject responded "same," requiring about three fourths of a second to do so.

> After responding to several pairs, the word *banana* appeared alone on the screen, followed less than a second later by *apple.* The subject's response—"same"—required a fifth of a second *less* than when the word pairs were presented together (Hunt, 1982).

From this finding, the researcher concluded that one of the mental processes included in a subject's reaction time involved looking up the meaning of each word in the "word dictionary" stored in long-term memory. When the first word of the pair appeared early, its meaning already must have been retrieved before the second appeared, thus shortening the time required to decide if the words were similar.

ANALYZING ERRORS

Cognitive psychologists assume that errors, such as reaching an incorrect conclusion, making an illogical inference, or remembering something incorrectly, are probably not random but reflect systematic properties of the thought processes involved. Analysis of thought errors can give us clues about these properties. Sigmund Freud (1904) pioneered the analysis of speech errors—slips of the tongue—to detect latent sexual or hostile impulses. For example, a competitor pretending to like you might say, "I'm pleased to *beat* you" instead of "I'm pleased to *meet* you." In such cases the true intention slips past the conscious censor we all use to suppress socially inappropriate thoughts.

Current researchers are extending Freud's focus on the *motivational* basis for verbal errors by looking for their *cognitive* basis. They believe that some slips arise merely from lapses of attention to the specifics of what is being said; others reveal a mental competition between similar verbal choices. People often say, "I'd be *interesting* in . . ." instead of the correct "I'd be *interested* in. . . ." The sentence structure allows the two suffixes *-ing* and *-ed* to be exchanged if the person's attention is not focused (and he or she is a bit self-centered).

A *spoonerism* is the exchange of the initial phonetic elements of two or more words in a phrase or sentence. The term derives its name from Reverend W. A. Spooner of Oxford University who made many such remarkable exchanges. When tongue-lashing a lazy student for wasting the term, Reverend Spooner said, "You have tasted the whole worm!" Spoonerisms show that whole phrases and sentences are mentally planned in advance of their being said. Cognitive psychologists are making detailed analyses of the conditions and structures of thought and language that facilitate such error production (Norman, 1981, 1983).

Slips of the tongue also provide evidence of the way the human mind represents language structures. For example, an English-language speaker might exchange initial consonants—"tips of the slung" for "slips of the tongue"—but never would say, "stip the of tlung," which would violate several grammatical rules (Fromkin, 1980). Verbal errors are never considered to be random; they provide clues to the structure and function of the mind.

Another view about the way verbal errors arise—and what studying them reveals—is found in **spreading activation theory.** According to this theory, a person's mental dictionary is organized into a network so that each word is interconnected with many others that are similar in meaning, sound, or grammar. As the person prepares to speak, relevant parts of the network become activated, causing a "vibration" of the web that spreads to closely related words. The word with the highest total activation is then selected. Problems arise when competing choices have activation levels that are almost equal (Hillis, 1985).

RECORDING EYE MOVEMENTS

Much of our thinking involves gathering information from the environment. One of the primary ways we do this is through our eyes. Monitoring the way people move their eyes—what they look at when viewing a picture, a person, or a passage of text—and for how long they look can provide a rich source of data about ongoing thought processes. A record of a reader's eye fixations also provides information about the cognitive processes taking place as the reader tries to comprehend the content of a verbal message.

One study used these two similar sets of sentences:

I: It was dark and stormy the night the millionaire was murdered. The killer left no clues for the police to follow.
II: It was dark and stormy the night the millionaire died. The killer left no clues for the police to follow.

Researchers asked each subject to read either the first or second sentence pair. The researchers measured the time the subject took to read it. They found that the second pair took about a half second longer to read than the first, generally because the reader had to make an inference. Since the cause of death was not mentioned in the first sentence of the second pair, the reader had to con-

nect *the killer* in the second sentence to the death in the first sentence by inferring *murder*. No such inference was required in the first pair since the word *murder* implied that there was a killer involved.

In addition to this reaction-time analysis, the researchers used a special apparatus to examine each subject's eye movements while reading the sentences. They found that most of the extra time spent on the second pair was taken up in longer eye fixations on the words *killer* and *died*. These eye-movement patterns supported the hypothesis that an inference was being made about the meaning of the word *killer* during the reading of the second pair of sentences but not the first. The subject's eye movements provided a "window" into the private thoughts of a mind-at-work (Just & Carpenter, 1981).

In another demonstration of the way cognitive psychologists go about describing and validating internal representations, a reader had to continually coordinate perception of letters, words, and phrases with cognitive information accessed from memory about word meanings, grammar, and intentions of the author. At the same time, the reader coded the material for future use. One model of reading comprehension was tested with a special apparatus that unobtrusively measures eye movements and eye fixations during reading (Just & Carpenter, 1982, 1987).

College students read scientific text from *Newsweek* and *Time* magazines while their eye movements were recorded. The data were number of milliseconds of time spent fixating on each word. The evidence supports predictions from the cognitive model that there is a greater processing load when readers are confronted with uncommon words, have to integrate information from important clauses, and have to make inferences at the end of sentences. One student's sample performance is shown in **Figure 11.3.** You can see the amount of time spent viewing each word.

READING THE MIND IN BRAIN WAVES

Sensory stimuli elicit electrical waves in the brain that can be measured at the scalp. A brain wave evoked by stimulus events is called an **evoked potential,** or an *event-related potential* (ERP), to distinguish it from the spontaneous electrical activity that is going on all the time in the living brain. It appears that an ERP first reflects properties of the stimulus, such as its intensity, but then begins to reflect cognitive processes, such as

FIGURE 11.3 EYE FIXATIONS DURING READING

This figure shows eye fixations of a college student reading a scientific passage. Gazes within each sentence are sequentially numbered above the fixated words with the durations (in msec.) indicated below the sequence number.

1	2	3	4	5	6	7
1566	267	400	83	267	617	767
Flywheels	are	one	of the	oldest	mechanical	devices

8	9	1	2	3	5	4	6
450	450	400	616	517	684	250	317
known to	man.	Every	internal-	combustion	engine		contains

7	8		9	10	11	12
617	1116		367	467	483	450
a small	flywheel	that	converts	the	jerky	motion	of the pistons

13	14	15	16	17	18	19	20	21
383	284	383	317	283	533	50	366	566
into	the	smooth	flow	of	energy	that	powers	the	drive	shaft.

the person's evaluation of the stimulus. For example, the evoked potential is larger for the last word in the sentence "He took a sip from the *computer*" because it is more unusual and unexpected than the word *glass* might be (Donchin, 1975; Woods et al., 1980). One component of ERPs is a brain response that is measured to determine attention and detection of low probability events—surprises. It is also measured as an index of the mental workload involved in certain tasks—such as those performed by air traffic controllers. This brain response is called the *P-300 component* because it is a *positive* waveform that peaks 300 milliseconds after a stimulus event (Donchin, 1985).

Brain waves can help us read the mind in other ways. Electroencephalograms (EEGs), described in Chapter 3, are used to probe the relationship between the functioning of the two cerebral hemispheres in mental tasks. For example, it has been found that tasks with attentional demands are reflected in EEG alpha waves with middle frequencies (8 to 15 Hz), while cognitive and emotional tasks are reflected in higher frequency beta waves (16 to 24 Hz). Moreover, alpha-wave activity is sensitive to the type of attentional task. It is greater for tasks, such as mental arithmetic, that require a focus on internal processes than it is for tasks that require monitoring of environmental stimuli (Ray & Cole, 1985).

There are several other applications of measurement of the electrical activity of the brain to index mental processes. One research program has found that each of the cerebral hemispheres picks up different emotional reactions. The left frontal region is involved with positive affect, while the right frontal region processes negative affect. People who are *repressors* maintain a coping style in which their verbal reports of feeling "good" or "calm" are contradicted by autonomic arousal responses associated with stress. Repressors may maintain this cognitive-affective dissociation through deficits in transferring affective information from the right hemisphere to the left (Davidson, 1983).

Another research program uses recordings from many electrodes placed on the scalp to measure the rapidly changing patterns of brain electrical activity that occur prior to a subject's overt response to a cue. The human brain seems to "program" different regions or subsystems in anticipation of the need to process certain types of information and take certain kinds of action. Analyses of the brain wave patterns of these *preparatory sets* enable researchers to predict whether a response will be accurate or inaccurate. Performance is likely to be inaccurate when these preparatory sets are incomplete or incorrect—when the mind is not properly prepared to direct the correct response (Gevins et al., 1987).

E. R. John and his associates have developed a practical way to read the mind through EEG patterns (1988). By comparing the brain electrical activity of healthy people, ages 6 to 90, with those of individuals suffering from disorders of brain functioning, mental illness, and cognitive impairments, it is possible to make accurate diagnoses of the nature and severity of many types of brain dysfunctions. **Figure 11.4** shows a

FIGURE 11.4   EEG BRAIN MAPS USED FOR DIAGNOSES

The figure shows brain mapping by multiple EEG scalp recordings that are averaged over a large sample of normally functioning people and then compared to the EEG recordings from the same brain sites of those with various mental problems and brain dysfunctions. The columns show different brain wave frequencies, and the four rows show the EEG data for each of these frequencies in samples of normal adults and those with alcoholism, schizophrenia, and a cognitive impairment. Deviations from the dark color pattern of the normal group are indicated by lighter reds and blues. Diagnosis of individuals can be made by comparing their EEG patterns with those from a variety of samples that differ in brain/mind dysfunctions.

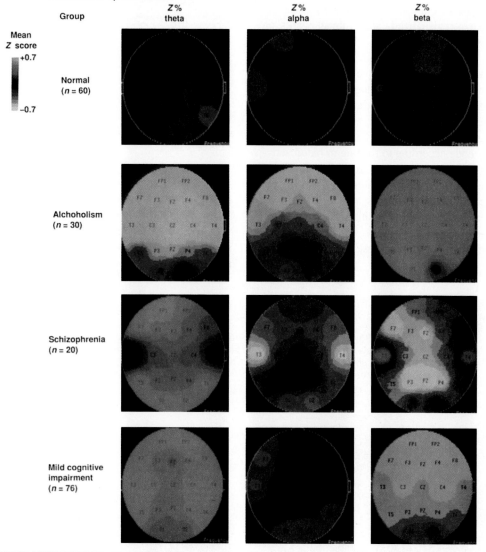

series of "head maps" of the average EEGs of normal subjects and the EEGs of comparison subjects with alcoholism, schizophrenia, and a mild cognitive impairment. The power of each of three different bands of EEG waves are converted to a color code so that normal is the dark color and deviations from normal are toward blue or, in the opposite direction, toward red. The extent and brain location of each type of dysfunction can be read from such comparative maps. Thus, any new, undiagnosed patient's EEG pattern can be computed relative to these group norms. Then, a diagnosis can be made.

BRAIN IMAGING

In the past decade, technological breakthroughs have made it possible to map brain structure and function in normal human beings while they perform mental tasks. These brain imaging techniques include those discussed in Chapter 3: CAT and PET scans and magnetic resonance imaging (MRI). Researcher **Michael Posner** (1990) is using PET to study basic cognitive processing during reading and imaging. He uses cognitive theory to guide his hypotheses and then traces the predicted operations to specific brain structures and processes that can be imaged, or visualized, as a subject works on particular cognitive tasks.

Another cognitive researcher, **Endel Tulving** (1989), is using a different technique for imaging brain functions, the pattern of cerebral blood flow in different regions of the brain. A radioactive tracer is injected into the bloodstream of an alert person, and special sensors detect its flow through the brain. Each tiny area is assigned a color code according to the rate of blood activity there, and it is portrayed in a computer-generated visual mosaic. **Figure 11.5** illustrates two brain images of regional cerebral blood flow as a subject performs two tasks: thinking about events in his episodic memory and then in his semantic memory. While some brain regions are active during the first task, they become less

Michael Posner (*Discovering Psychology*, 1990, Program 10)

so and others take over during the second memory task. These results are brain-based evidence for Tulving's cognitive model about the different types of memory, which we discussed in the last chapter.

| FIGURE 11.5 | BRAIN IMAGES OF REGIONAL CEREBRAL BLOOD FLOW |

Cerebral blood-flow patterns differ in episodic and semantic retrieval. The brain image on the left shows recently acquired semantic knowledge (news about elections). The brain image on the right shows a recently experienced personal episode (thinking about an outing of a few days before).

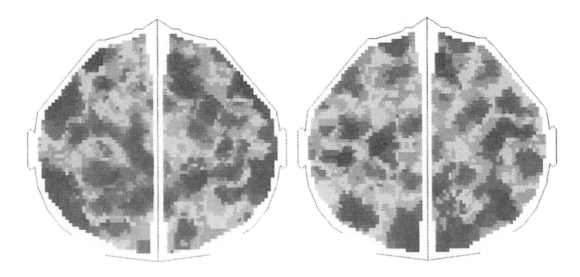

SUMMING UP

Cognitive researchers employ a variety of techniques to test their models and hypotheses. Their goal is to make public and visible the private mental world of thoughts, images, and the representation of reality. Introspection has been revived in a more useful format: think-aloud protocols. These protocols require subjects to verbalize their thoughts as they work on a cognitive task. As in other areas of psychology, behavioral observations are used to index internal processes. Search behavior, facial expressions, and attentional focus are observed to study complex processes such as symbolic representation of reality. Recording eye movements and fixation is useful in detecting reading comprehension difficulties and is a way to test cognitive models of reading. Reaction time is one of the most common dependent variables in cognitive psychology. It assumes that greater cognitive complexity is reflected in longer reaction times. Error analysis is used to study cognitive and linguistic rules that are violated when a speech error is made.

In the search to understand mental functioning, cognitive neuroscientists have gone directly to the brain to map its structure and activity during mental tasks. Single evoked potentials can provide evidence of surprise and other aspects of information processing, while broad EEG patterns can reveal how the brain prepares to respond to a cue or abnormal functioning. New techniques of brain imaging, such as PET scans and cerebral flow mapping, are allowing scientists to literally peer into the alert brain as it learns, thinks, and remembers.

MENTAL STRUCTURES FOR THINKING

Recall from the last chapter that the act of remembering usually involves top-down processing of stored information. The sensory input is matched against our mental structures or internal representations. This matching enables us to identify the input as new or familiar, dangerous or desired, and useful or irrelevant—which guides our actions. This process of basic pattern recognition helps new input get past the sensory register into short-term memory. Once there, further organizing processes help us store it more permanently in long-term memory. Pattern recognition and the later organizational processing, in turn, are the first stages of our higher mental processes—the beginnings of *thinking*. They go beyond the information contained in the sen-

sory input by using stored knowledge to interpret it (Bruner, 1973).

Human thought processes are at the upper end of the information-processing sequence, building on the more fundamental components of lower order cognitions, such as pattern recognition, perceptual analysis, and memory. What happens when we reach that ultimate stage of information processing called thinking? **Thinking** is a complex mental process of forming a new representation by transforming available information. That transformation involves the interaction of many mental attributes, such as inferring, abstracting, reasoning, imagining, judging, problem solving, and, at times, creativity. From the perspective of cognitive psychology, thinking has three general features: it occurs in the mind but is inferred from observable behavior, it is a process that manipulates knowledge in a person's cognitive system, and it is directed toward finding solutions to problems facing the individual (Mayer, 1983).

As we store information from our encounters with people, objects, events, and the environment, we build an abstract working model in our minds to represent their important features. We also begin to develop generalizations based on specific instances, along with rules and principles about how our physical, biological, and social worlds function. Some obvious examples of these generalizations are "You don't eat dessert before the main course" and "Someone who smiles at you is more approachable than a frowner."

Thinking relies on a variety of mental structures. These structures include concepts, schemas, scripts, and visual imagery. Let's examine how we utilize them to form thoughts.

CONCEPTS AND CONCEPT FORMATION

Imagine taking medicine that continually clears your brain of all old thoughts, so that every object and every event looks new to you and seems unrelated to anything that has happened before. The medicine would give you a fresh, new view of the world. However, you would also lose information that is vital for survival and personal happiness; you would not distinguish between sources of danger and pleasure, friends and foes, and fantasies and reality-based, probable consequences. In a world of perpetual novelty, with no way to classify information, you could not build on your experience one day for more effective behavior the next. Fortunately, you have the capacity to respond to stimuli as instances of categories that you have formed through your experiences. This ability to *categorize individual experiences*—to take the same action toward them or give them the same label—is regarded as one of the most

A concept is a mental event that represents a category or class of objects. The concept of *flower* encompasses many different flowers.

basic abilities of thinking organisms (Mervis & Rosch, 1981).

The categories we form, which are mental representations of kinds of related items that are grouped in some way, are called **concepts.** Concepts are the building blocks of thinking. They enable us to organize knowledge in systematic ways. Concepts may represent *objects, activities,* or *living organisms.* Concepts may also represent *properties,* such as *red* or *large, abstractions,* such as *truth* or *love,* and *relations,* such as *smarter than,* which tells us about a difference between two organisms but does not tell us about either of the individuals being compared (Smith & Medin, 1981). Because they can never be observed directly, concepts, as mental structures, must be discovered through research or invented by psychological theories.

A basic task of thinking is concept learning or **concept formation**—identifying the stimuli properties that are common to a class of objects or ideas. We live in a world filled with untold numbers of individual events from which we are continually extracting information about how to combine them into an ever smaller, simpler set that we can manage mentally. The mind lives by the principle of **cognitive economy,** minimizing the amount of time and effort required to process information. We learn not only features that form concepts, such as the colors of traffic lights, but also *conceptual rules* by which these features are related. For example, consider traffic light rules: If red, stop; if yellow, slow down and prepare to stop; if green, go. It is amazing how many conceptual rules we learn, store, retrieve on demand, and use to direct our interactions with people and the environment (Haygood & Bourne, 1965).

Critical Features Versus Prototypes

What is the unit of information that is stored in memory when we form a concept? Psychologists have not yet agreed on the unit. Currently, two competing theories attempt to account for the form in which information is stored.

The **critical feature** approach suggests that we store definitions or lists of critical features that are necessary and sufficient conditions for a concept to be included in a category. A concept is a member of the category if, and only if, it has every feature on the list.

The **prototype** approach suggests that categories are structured around an ideal or most representative instance which is called a prototype (Rosch, 1973). A concept is classified as a member of a category if it is more similar to the prototype of that category than it is to the prototype of any other category. Prototype theories assume that a prototype of *averaged features* is stored along with some allowable variations of its features. A stimulus might not fit precisely within the limits of a stored category but would still be classified as belonging to it if its variation from the prototype was within an acceptable range. For example, although the following fonts are very different, we still recognize them as belonging to the same category of the letter Z.

It appears that we use both methods of storing concepts—critical features and prototypes—but we use each for different kinds of concepts. Concepts in science are often based on definitions of critical features. For

example, *mammals* are defined as vertebrates that nurse their young. The boundaries between mammals and nonmammals are well defined, and a list of critical features seems to work to distinguish among them. How is the concept *bird* defined? The dictionary defines a *bird* as "a warm-blooded vertebrate with feathers and wings." However, *bird* is a fuzzy concept because it has no well-defined boundaries between some members of its class (Zadeh, 1965). Some aspects of the definition don't fit every type of bird (especially a Larry Bird of the Boston Celtics). If you were asked to build a cage for a bird, you would probably construct a cage that would be far too small for an ostrich or a penguin, both of which are birds. Your concept of bird seems to include something about *typicality*—the most typical member of the class—which goes beyond the list of critical features that qualifies creatures for birdhood.

Many of our concepts in everyday life are like this. We can identify clusters of properties that are shared by different instances of a concept, but there may be no one property that all instances show. We consider some instances as more representative of a concept—more typical of our mental prototype—than others.

Research studies show that people respond more quickly to typical members of a category than to its more unusual ones. Reaction time to determine whether a robin is a bird is quicker than reaction time to determine whether an ostrich is a bird, because robins resemble the prototype of a bird more than ostriches do (Kintsch, 1981; Rosch et al., 1976). One reason reaction time is faster for prototypes is that a prototype is formed on the basis of frequently experienced features. These features and their relations are stored in memory, and the more often they are perceived the stronger their overall memory strength is. Thus, the prototype can be rapidly accessed and recalled.

The police use the general principle of the prototype when helping witnesses identify criminal suspects. They prepare a prototype face made of plastic overlays of different facial features (from a commercially prepared "identikit"). The witness then is asked to modify the prototype model until it is most similar to the suspect's face. Psychological researchers have used the overlay technique to study memory for prototypes. Subjects study a series of "exemplar faces" that vary from prototype, as shown in **Figure 11.6.**

FIGURE 11.6

A. PROTOTYPE FACE AND EXEMPLAR FACES
B. CONFIDENCE RATINGS FOR PROTOTYPE, OLD ITEMS, AND NEW ITEMS

The 75-percent face has all the features of the prototype face except the mouth; the 50-percent face has different hair and eyes; the 25-percent face has only the eyes in common and the 0-percent face has no features in common.

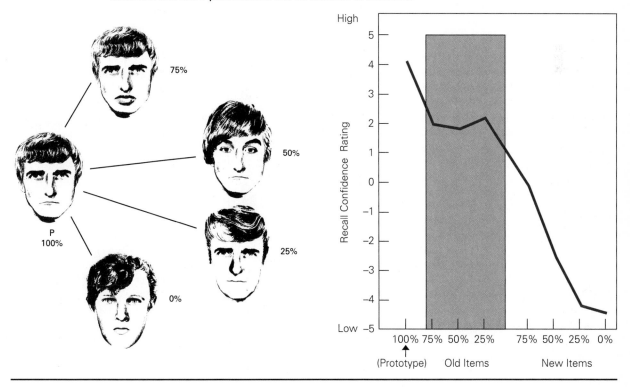

Subjects were shown a set of 12 exemplar faces made from three prototype faces. Then they saw a second group of faces: some of the original exemplar faces, some new ones that were made to differ from the prototype, and the original prototype face, which they had never seen. The subjects' task was to rate their confidence in having seen each face before, during the first presentation. Three results clearly emerge, as seen in the chart in Figure 11.6.

Recall confidence was equally high for all the old items even if they had only a 25 percent similarity to the prototype. The new items were accurately identified as unfamiliar, but false confidence in a feeling of having seen them was greater as the items more resembled the prototype. Finally, the highest level of confidence was for the prototype face itself—although the subjects had never seen it before.

The subjects' reaction is known as **pseudo-memory,** recall of a *new* stimulus because its attributes were stored in memory (Solso & McCarthy, 1981). In-fants also assign prototypes special status by recognizing prototypical category members even when they have never seen them before—a case of "baby pseudo-memories" (Younger & Gotlieb, 1988).

If we tend to perceive and remember prototypical faces better than atypical faces, then which should we evaluate as more attractive? A recent study tested the nonobvious prediction that we prefer prototypically average faces over attractive individual faces.

The researchers photographed hundreds of male and female college students. From the photos, they randomly selected 96 faces. Each individual face was used to create a composite face through computer processing. These computer-generated composite faces were created by combining either 2, 4, 8, 16, or 32 faces. The individual photos and their composite photos were presented in random order to 300 college student raters of both sexes (see **Figure 11.7**). The college students were asked to rate the photos on their physical attractiveness.

The results were the same for both male and female faces and for male and female raters. The composite faces were judged as significantly more attractive than

FIGURE 11.7 **COMPOSITE FACES**

The faces from left to right represent six different composite sets. Faces from top to bottom represent composite levels of 8 faces, 16 faces, and 32 faces.

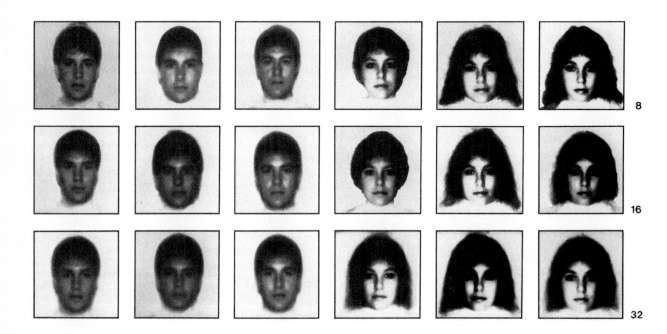

8

16

32

the individual faces. This effect occurred when the composites consisted of an average of 16 and 32 faces but not for lesser composite levels. Only rarely was any individual face evaluated as more attractive than the composite. The authors of this study argue that these findings are consistent with both evolutionary pressures that favor characteristics close to the average of the population rather than "deviant" features and also cognitive processes that favor responding to prototypical category members (Langlois & Roggman, 1991).

Hierarchies and Basic Levels

Concepts are often organized in *hierarchies,* from general to specific, as seen in **Figure 11.8.** The broad category of *animal* has several subcategories, such as *bird* and *fish,* which in turn are subdivided into their instances, such as *canary, ostrich, shark,* and *salmon,* for example. The animal category is itself a subcategory of the still larger category of *living beings.* These concepts and categories are arranged in a hierarchy of levels, with the most general and abstract at the top and the most specific and concrete at the bottom. They are also linked to many other concepts: some birds are *edible,* some are *endangered,* some are *national symbols.*

There seems to be a level in such hierarchies at which people best categorize and think about objects. That level—the **basic level**—can be retrieved from memory most quickly and used most efficiently. For example, the chair at your desk belongs to three obvious levels in a conceptual hierarchy: *furniture, chair,* and *desk chair.* The lower level category, *desk chair,* would provide more detail than you generally need, whereas the higher level category, *furniture,* would not be precise enough. When spontaneously identifying it, you would be more likely to call it a *chair* than a *piece of furniture* or a *desk chair.* If you were shown a picture of it, your reaction time would be faster if you were asked to verify that it was a chair than if you were asked to verify that it was a piece of furniture (Rosch, 1978). It is now believed that our dependence on basic levels of concepts is another fundamental aspect of thought.

SCHEMAS AND SCRIPTS

You are already familiar with the important concept of **schema,** a general cluster of stored knowledge that represents knowledge about a concept or type of stimulus,

---

FIGURE 11.8   *HIERARCHICALLY ORGANIZED STRUCTURE OF CONCEPTS*

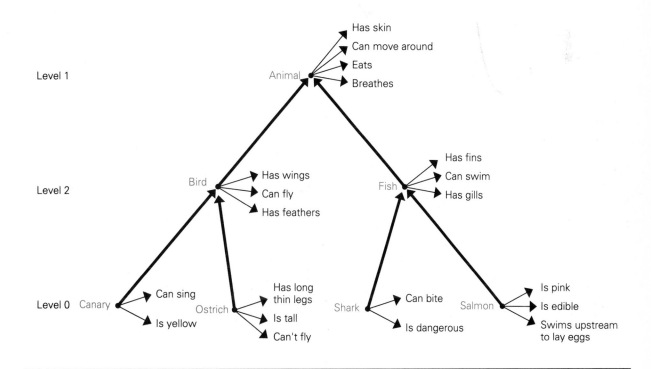

along with its attributes and the relations that exist among the stimuli. We have seen how schemas influence what we perceive and remember by facilitating top-down, or conceptually driven, processing of information. How do schemas function as structures for thinking?

Schemas include expectations about what attributes and effects are typical for particular concepts or categories. New information, which is often incomplete or ambiguous, makes more sense when we can relate it to existing knowledge in our stored schemas. So we may say that, in addition to the functions of encoding new information (interpreting and organizing it) and influencing memory for old information, schemas also enable us to make inferences about missing information. What can you infer about the statement, "Tanya was upset to discover, upon opening the basket, that she'd forgotten the salt." With no further information, you can infer a great deal about this event that is not explicit in the description given. Salt implies that the basket is a picnic basket. The fact that Tanya is upset that the salt is missing suggests that the food in the basket is food that is usually salted, such as hardboiled eggs and vegetables. You automatically know what other foods might be included and, equally important, what definitely is not: everything in the world that is larger than a picnic basket and everything that would be inappropriate to take on a picnic—from a boa constrictor to bronze-plated baby shoes. The body of information you now have has been organized around a "picnic-basket" schema. By relating the statement about Tanya to your preestablished picnic-basket schema, you understand the statement better.

According to researchers David Rumelhart and Don Norman, schemas are the primary units of meaning in the human information-processing system (1975). In their view, the mind is a network of interrelated schemas, in which parts of schemas are themselves schemas. Comprehension of new information seems to occur through integrating consistent new input with what we already know and/or through overcoming the discrepancy between new input and stored schemas by changing a knowledge structure or by changing or ignoring the new input.

What do the following sentences mean to you?

• The notes were sour because the seam was split.

• The haystack was important because the cloth ripped.

Taken alone, these sentences make little sense. What notes are being referred to, what is the seam, and how does a split seam cause sour notes? Why should ripped cloth make a haystack important?

Now, how does your thinking change with the addition of two words: *bagpipes* and *parachute*? Presto! The sentences suddenly become understandable. The notes were sour because the seam in the bag of the bagpipe was split. If you were falling from a plane in a torn parachute, the haystack could save your life. The sentences became comprehensible when you could integrate them into what you already knew—into appropriate schemas. They would remain confusing to anyone who did not know what a bagpipe or a parachute was.

Thinking, similar to perceiving and remembering, is a *constructive process* in which we draw on our existing mental structures to make as much sense as possible out of new information. Once we interpret information as belonging to a particular schema, we may unwittingly change the information in our internal representation of it. To see how this transformation can occur, read the following passage:

> Chief resident Jones adjusted his face mask while anxiously surveying a pale figure secured to the long gleaming table before him. One swift stroke of his small, sharp instrument and a thin red line appeared. Then the eager young assistant carefully extended the opening as another aide pushed aside glistening surface fat so that the vital parts were laid bare. Everyone stared in horror at the ugly growth too large for removal. He now knew it was pointless to continue.

Stop! Without looking back please complete the following exercise:

Circle below the words that appeared in the passage.

**patient   scalpel   blood   tumor
cancer   nurse   disease   surgery**

Most of the subjects that read this passage circled the words *patient, scalpel,* and *tumor*. However, none of the words were there! Interpreting the story as a medical story made it more understandable, but also resulted in inaccurate recall (Lachman et al., 1979). Once they had related the story to their schema for hospital surgery, the subjects "remembered" labels from their schema that were not present in what they had read. Drawing on a schema not only gave the subjects an existing mental structure to tie the new material to but also led them to change the information to make it more consistent with their *schema-based expectations*.

We have schemas not only about objects and environmental events but also about persons, roles, and ourselves. *Person schemas* contain information about particular people as well as people in general and their traits, goals, and ideas about what causes them to behave as they do. *Role schemas* include expected behaviors that are appropriate for a person in a particular social setting, such as a doctor, a waiter, or a parent. *Self schemas* are the conceptions we have of ourselves that guide the way we process all self-relevant information, such as shyness, generosity, and femininity (Fiske & Taylor, 1991).

An event schema or **script** is a cluster of knowledge about sequences of interrelated, specific events and actions expected to occur in a certain way in particular settings. A *script* is to *procedural knowledge* (how) what a *schema* is to *declarative knowledge* (what). We have scripts for going to a restaurant, using the library, listening to a lecture, and going on a first date. In other cultures, some scripts differ from ours, such as the scripts that govern gift-giving and gift-receiving, funerals, and ways to treat women.

Similar to a script in a play, a mental script outlines the "proper" sequence in which actions and reactions are expected to happen in given settings. When all people in a given setting follow similar scripts, they all feel comfortable because they have comprehended the "meaning" of that situation in the same way and have the same expectations for each other (Abelson, 1981; Schank & Abelson, 1977). When all people do not follow similar scripts, however, they are made uncomfortable by the script "violation" and may have difficulty understanding why the scene was "misplaced." In some cases, scripts are so different that they result in traumatic or even life-threatening situations. For example, in the case of date rape, the perpetrator's script suggests that his victim means *yes* when she says *no* and that she wants to be physically overpowered and seduced so that she doesn't feel responsible for the sexual act. The victim's script, however, asserts that the perpetrator is assaulting her against her wish, that she is in danger, and that the experience is traumatic and terrifying.

We have trouble comprehending situations that do not fit scripted patterns. We are uncomfortable when we encounter new information that either does not fit readily into our mental structures or that contradicts them. One way to reduce the discrepancy between new stimuli and existing structures is to enlarge and change our mental structures in appropriate ways to make a broader understanding possible. This process of *accommodation* begins in infancy and continues as long as we increase our knowledge and competence in any field. Being open to new possibilities that challenge old actualities is the way the mind matures. Mental flexibility means adjusting schemas and scripts to fit new ideas and experiences. By contrast, mental rigidity means forcing the new into old molds, and merely making exceptions for events that don't fit the rule, without ever changing the basic rule for using the schema or the script.

VISUAL IMAGERY AND MENTAL MAPS

Do you think only in words or do you sometimes think in pictures and spatial relationships? Although you may not actually store visual memories in visual codes, you clearly are able to use imagery in your thinking. *Visual mental imagery* is a review of information previously perceived and stored in memory. It takes place in the absence of appropriate immediate sensory input and relies on internal representations of events and concepts in visual forms. Many psychologists believe that visual thought differs from verbal thought (Kosslyn, 1983; Paivio, 1983).

History is full of examples of famous discoveries made on the basis of mental imagery. For example, the discoverer of the chemical structure of benzene, F. A. Kekulé, often conjured up mental images of dancing atoms that fastened themselves into chains of molecules. His discovery of the benzene ring occurred in a dream in which a snakelike chain molecule suddenly grabbed its own tail, thus forming a ring. Albert Einstein claimed to have thought entirely in terms of visual images, translating his findings into mathematical symbols and words only after the work of visually based discovery was finished. Michael Faraday, who discovered many properties of magnetism, knew little about mathematics, but he was able to work by placing the supposed properties of magnetic fields in a visual image of relationships (**Roger Shepard,** 1978).

Evidence of the psychological reality of mental images is provided in the following study that shows the behavioral consequences of images.

> Each student was shown examples of the letter R and its mirror image that had been rotated various amounts, from 0 to 180 degrees (see **Figure 11.9**). As the letter appeared, the student had to identify it as either the normal R or its mirror image. The reaction time taken to make that decision was longer the more the figure had been rotated. This finding indicated that a subject was imagining the figure in his or her "mind's eye" and rotating the image into an upright position, before deciding whether the figure was an R or a mirror image. Such results support the idea that thinking processes using visual imagery are similar to the processes involved in visually perceiving real-world objects (Shepard & Cooper, 1982).

Not only are the processes (of using visual imagery and visually perceiving real-world objects) similar but also the way people scan their mental images of objects and scan the actual perceived objects.

In one study, subjects first memorized pictures of complex objects, such as a motorboat (see **Figure**

FIGURE 11.9 ROTATED R USED TO ASSESS MENTAL IMAGERY

Subjects presented with these figures in random order were asked to say, as quickly as possible, whether each figure was a normal R or a mirror image. The more the figure was rotated from upright, the longer the reaction time was.

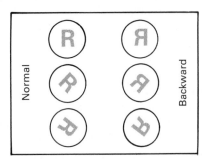

11.10). Then they were asked to recall their visual images of the boat and focus on one spot—for example, the motor. When asked if the picture contained another object—a windshield or an anchor, for example (both were present)—they took longer to "see" the anchor than the windshield, which was only half as far away as the anchor from the motor. The researcher regarded the reaction-time difference as evidence of the visual scanning times required to examine the objects at different physical distances in their mental images (Kosslyn, 1980).

Many problems cannot be solved by visual imagery, as you will discover by trying to meet the following challenge (Adams, 1979):

Imagine that you have a large piece of blank paper. In your mind, fold it in half (making two layers), fold it in half again (four layers), and continue folding it over 50 times. About how thick is the paper when you are done?

The actual answer is about 50 million miles (2^{50} × 0.028, the thickness of this paper), approximately half the distance between the earth and the sun. Your estimate was probably far from right. Why? You probably visualized the piece of paper, imagined folding it once and then twice, and then extrapolated the result to 50 folds. However, the effect of folding the paper 50 times, doubling the thickness each time, was so large that the problem had to be translated into mathematical symbols to be solved.

Visual thought adds complexity and richness to our thinking, as do forms of thought that involve the other senses: sound, taste, smell, and touch. Visual thinking can be very useful in solving problems in which relationships can be grasped more clearly in diagram form than in words. Visual thought, for example, is useful in spatial or geographical relationships. A cognitive representation of physical space is called a **mental map,** or *cognitive map*. Learning theorist **Edward Tolman** was the first to hypothesize that people form mental maps of their environment as they learn their way through life's mazes, and these internal maps guide their future actions toward desired goals (see Chapter 9). Cognitive maps help people get where they want to go. They also enable them to give directions to someone else. By using cognitive maps, people can move through their homes with their eyes closed or go to familiar destinations even when their usual routes are blocked (Hart & Moore, 1973; Thorndyke & Hayes-Roth, 1978).

Try answering the following questions:

• Which is farther north: Seattle or Montreal?
• Which is farthest west: the entrance to the Panama Canal from the Atlantic Ocean (Caribbean side) or the entrance from the Pacific Ocean (Gulf of Panama side)?

To find the answers to these questions, you must use a mental representation of the spatial environment as you have personally experienced it, remember it from

FIGURE 11.10 VISUAL SCANNING OF MENTAL IMAGES

Subjects studied a picture of a boat and then were asked to look at the motor in their own image of the boat. While doing so, they were asked whether the boat had a windshield or an anchor. The faster response to the windshield, which was closer than the anchor, was taken as evidence that they were scanning their visual images.

a map you have seen, or reconstruct it from separate bits of information that you possess. Although everybody seems to develop cognitive maps to navigate through the complex environments in which they live, these maps can sometimes be misleading. Did you know that Seattle is farther north than Montreal? Most people miss this one because they think of Canada as north of the United States and don't realize how far south the border drops around the Great Lakes. Did you realize that the Atlantic Ocean is actually more westerly than the Pacific Ocean at the Panama Canal entrances? Most people are surprised at such information because their mental maps of Central America distort the sharp eastward curve of both coastlines to make them more vertical (B. Tversky, 1981). Similarly, on the mental maps of Parisians, the Seine River curves only gently through Paris instead of curving more sharply as it actually does. Thus, some Parisians misjudge places that are on the Right Bank of the Seine as being on the Left Bank (Milgram & Jodelet, 1976).

Mental maps seem to reflect our subjective impressions of physical reality. They often mirror the distorted view we have developed about the world from our personal or cultural egocentric perspective. A case in point is world-scale cognitive maps. If you were asked to draw a world map, where would you begin and how would you represent the size, shape, and relations between various countries? This task was given to nearly 4000 students from 71 cities in 49 countries as part of an international study of the way people of different nationalities visualize the world. The goal of the study was to broaden understanding of cultural differences and to promote world peace. Among other information, the study found that the majority of maps had a Eurocentric world view—Europe was placed in the center of the map and the other countries were arranged around it (probably due to the dominance for many centuries of Eurocentric maps in geography books). However, the study also yielded many instances of culture-biased maps, such as the one by a Chicago student in **Figure 11.11** and that of an Australian student in **Figure 11.12.** In addition, American students did poorly on this task, misrepresenting the placement of countries, while students from the Soviet Union and Hungary made the most accurately detailed maps (Saarinen, 1987).

FIGURE 11.11   *CHICAGOCENTRIC VIEW OF THE WORLD*

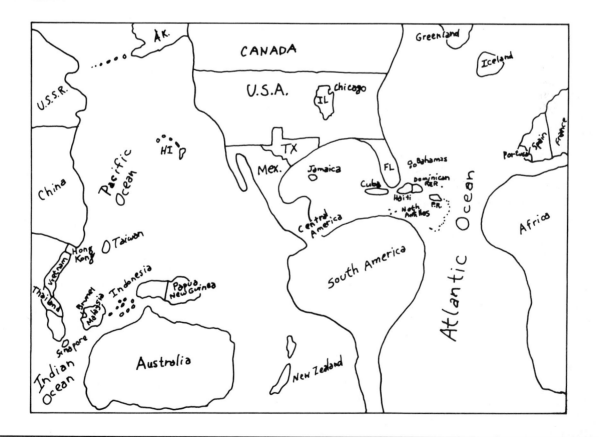

FIGURE 11.12 AN AUSTRALOCENTRIC VIEW OF THE WORLD

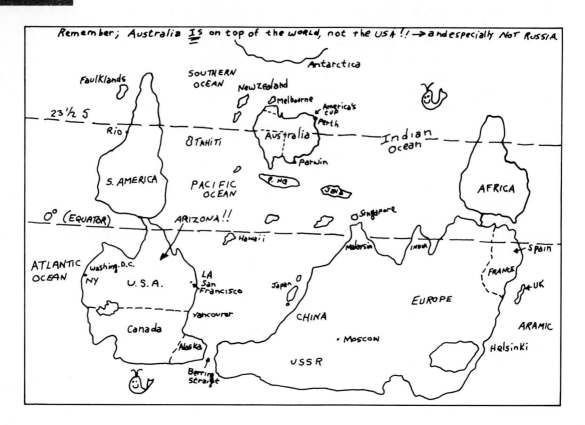

SUMMING UP

Thinking is a higher-order mental process that goes beyond the information given by sensory processing. Thinking transforms available information into new abstract representations. Human thought relies on many types of mental structures. One of the most basic abilities of thinking organisms is categorizing individual experiences. Concepts, the building blocks of thinking, are mental representations that group related items in particular ways. We form concepts by identifying those properties that are common to a class of objects or ideas. This process is part of the mind's attempt to ensure cognitive economy—to minimize processing time and effort whenever possible. Conceptual rules specify how we think the features of concepts are related. We store their critical features as definitions of some types of concepts, such as well-defined scientific concepts. For concepts with ill-defined boundaries, we seem to store the prototypical or the most average instance of the concept. We respond to prototypes more quickly and recall them with more confidence than nonprototypical instances. Concepts are often arranged in hierarchies, from general to specific, and there is an optimal level of describing a complex concept, the basic level, to which we respond most effectively.

Other mental structures that guide thinking are the knowledge packages of schemas and scripts. They help to encode and store information in memory and also to form expectations about appropriate attributes and effects of concepts. Scripts are event schemas, organized knowledge about expected sequences of action in given settings. In addition to these verbal thinking structures, we rely on visual imagery which adds further richness to thinking. Mental maps are cognitive representations of physical space. They are useful in learning our way around our immediate environment and reveal our personal and cultural view of geography. Taken together, these mental structures form the basis of how we think so efficiently.

REASONING AND PROBLEM SOLVING

Our thoughts range between two extremes: the autistic and the realistic. **Autistic thinking** is a personal, idiosyncratic process involving fantasy, daydreaming, unconscious reactions, and ideas that are not testable by external reality criteria. This type of individualized thought is part of most creative acts. However, when it generates delusions and hallucinations, it can be evidence that the individual has lost touch with reality and is suffering from some type of mental illness. Autistic thinking is always top-down processing. **Realistic thinking,** by contrast, requires that ideas be fit into the reality of situational demands, time constraints, operational rules, and personal resources. Thinking realistically involves frequent checks on reality and tests that measure the appropriateness and correctness of one's ideas against some acceptable standard.

Reasoning is a process of realistic, goal-directed thinking in which conclusions are drawn from a set of facts. In reasoning, information from the environment and stored information are used in accordance with a set of rules (either formal or informal) for transforming information. There are two types of reasoning: deductive and inductive.

DEDUCTIVE REASONING

Deductive reasoning is drawing a conclusion that follows logically according to established rules from two or more statements, or premises. More than 2000 years ago, Aristotle introduced the form of deductive reasoning known as the **syllogism,** which has three components: a major premise, a minor premise, and a conclusion. He also developed rules for syllogistic reasoning—if these rules are adhered to, the conclusion will be drawn *validly* from the premises. Consider the following example:

Major premise: All people are thinking creatures
Minor premise: Descartes was a person
Valid conclusion: Therefore, Descartes was a thinking creature
Invalid conclusion: Therefore, all thinking creatures are Descartes.

If the conclusion is not derived by the rules of logic it is *invalid*, as shown in the second conclusion of the example. You immediately knew the second conclusion was invalid—evidence that deductive reasoning is a fundamental part of reasoning ability (Ripps, 1983).

Validity and truth need to be distinguished in syllogistic thinking. If one of the premises is false, then the conclusion must also be false even though it can be drawn validly from them. If the conclusion is not logically derived from the premises, it is invalid even if it is true. Consider the following examples that mix truth and validity.

Major premise: Some psychologists study cognitions
Minor premise: Some cognitions are about women

True but invalid conclusion: Some psychologists are women

Major premise: All women have cognitions
Minor premise: All cognitions are intelligent

False but valid conclusion: All women have intelligent cognitions.

Cognitive psychologists study the errors people make in logic and syllogistic reasoning in order to understand their mental representations of premises and conclusions (Johnson-Laird & Byrne, 1989). Some errors occur because the individual's personal beliefs about the premises and conclusions get in the way of logic. People tend to judge as valid those conclusions with which they agree and as invalid those with which they don't (Janis & Frick, 1943). The **belief-bias effect** occurs when a person's prior knowledge, attitudes, or values distort the reasoning process by influencing the

person to accept as valid those arguments that are invalid but believed to be true or as invalid those arguments that are believed to be false (Evans et al., 1983).

INDUCTIVE REASONING

Inductive reasoning is a form of reasoning that uses available evidence to generate a conclusion about the likelihood of something. The process of inductive reasoning involves constructing a hypothesis based on limited evidence and then testing it against other evidence. The hypothesis is not drawn inescapably from the logical structure of the argument as it is in deductive reasoning. Rather, inductive reasoning requires leaps from data to decisions. These leaps are accomplished by integrating past experience, perceptual sensitivity, weighted value of the importance of each element of evidence, and a dash of creativity. Most scientific reasoning is inductive.

After solving a difficult mystery, Sherlock Holmes frequently exclaims to his sidekick, "It's a matter of deduction, my dear Dr. Watson." In fact, Holmes's solutions involve shrewd *induction*—he pieces together shreds of data into a compelling web of evidence that eventually supports his hypothesis about the agent of and motive for the crime. Inductive reasoning plays a key role in helping all of us solve many of the problems we face.

PROBLEM SOLVING

What goes on four legs in the morning, on two legs at noon, and on three legs in the twilight? According to Greek mythology, this was the riddle posed by the Sphinx, an evil creature who threatened to hold the people of Thebes in tyranny until Oedipus could solve the riddle. To break the code, Oedipus had to recognize elements of the riddle as metaphors. Morning, noon, and twilight represented different periods in a human life. A baby crawls and so has four *legs*, an adult walks on two legs, and an older person walks on two legs but uses a cane, making a total of three legs. Oedipus's solution to the riddle was *Man*. (A modern Sphinx might hold out for *Humans* throughout the life cycle.)

While our daily problems may not seem as monumental as the one faced by young Oedipus, problem-solving activity is a basic part of our everyday existence. We continually come up against problems that require solutions: how to manage work and tasks within a limited time frame, how to succeed at a job interview, how to break off an intimate relationship, how to conserve energy, how to avoid sexually transmitted diseases, to name a few. For psychologists, **problem solving** is thinking that is directed toward solving specific prob-

lems and that moves from an initial state to a goal state by means of a set of mental operations.

Many problems are discrepancies between what you know and what you need to know. When you solve a problem, you reduce that discrepancy by finding a way to get the missing information. To get into the spirit of problem solving yourself, try the problems in **Figure 11.13** (the answers are on page 404).

In information-processing terms, a problem has three parts: (a) an *initial state*—the incomplete information you start with that perhaps corresponds to some unsatisfactory set of conditions in the world; (b) a *goal state*—the set of information or state of the world you hope to achieve; and (c) a *set of operations*—the steps you must take to move from an initial state to a goal state (Newell & Simon, 1972). Together, these three parts define the problem space. You can think of solving a problem as walking through a maze (the problem space) from where you are (the initial state) to where you want to be (the goal state), making a series of turns (the allowable operations).

Well-defined and Ill-defined Problems

There is an important distinction between well-defined and ill-defined problems (Simon, 1973). A *well-defined problem* is similar to an algebra problem in which the initial state, the goal state, and the operations are all clearly specified. The task is simply to discover how to use allowable known operations to get the answer. By contrast, an *ill-defined problem* is similar to designing a home, writing a novel, or finding a cure for AIDS; the initial state, the goal state, and/or the opera-

Designing a building is an example of an ill-defined problem. The architects must determine the function, location, and capacity of the building and then draw the plans.

FIGURE 11.13 *A. CAN YOU SOLVE IT?*

A. Can you connect all the dots in the pattern by drawing four straight, connected lines without lifting your pen from the paper?
B. A prankster has put 3 ping-pong balls into a 6-foot long pipe that is standing vertically in the corner of the physics lab, fastened to the floor. How would you get the ping-pong balls out?
C. The checkerboard shown has had 2 corner pieces cut out, leaving 62 squares. You have 31 dominoes, each of which covers exactly 2 checkerboard squares. Can you use them to cover the whole checkerboard?
D. You are in the situation depicted and given the task of tying 2 strings together. If you hold one, the other is out of reach. Can you do it?
E. You are given the objects shown (2 candles, tacks, string, matches in a matchbox). The task is to mount a lighted candle on the door. Can you do it?
F. You are given 3 "water-jar" problems. Using only the 3 containers (water supply is unlimited), can you obtain the exact amount specified in each case?

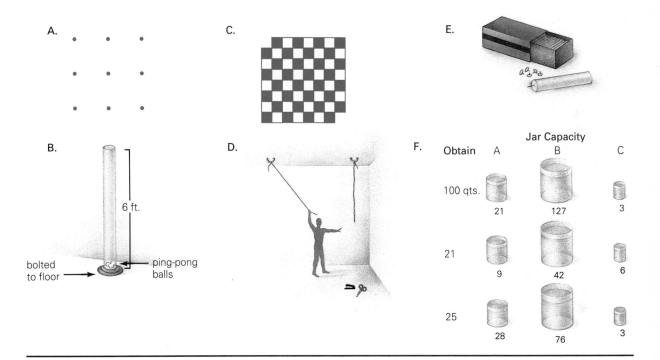

tions may be unclear and vaguely specified. In such cases, the problem solver's major task is first to define exactly what the problem is—to make explicit a beginning, an ideal solution, and the possible means to achieve it. Once that is done, the task becomes a well-defined problem that can be solved by finding a sequence of operations that will, in fact, achieve an acceptable solution.

As we accumulate knowledge, have more abilities, and understand better how to solve problems, problems that may still be ill-defined for others become more well-defined for us. The "I can't" lament of the three-year-old child facing the problem of carrying four liquid-filled glasses becomes the older child's confident solution: "It's a cinch! I'll use a tray."

Understanding the Problem

Setting up an internal representation of the problem space—specifying all the elements in it—is not an automatic process. Often it requires finding the appropriate schema from analogous previous tasks or situations. On the other hand, existing schemas can be restricting when the new problem calls for a new solution.

If you solved the problems in Figure 11.13, you recognized the importance of an accurate internal representation of the problem space. To connect the nine dots, you had to realize that nothing in the instructions limited you to the area of the dots themselves. To get the Ping-Pong balls out of the pipe, you had to realize that the solution did not involve reaching into the pipe. In the checkerboard problem, you had to realize that

FIGURE 11.13   B. SOLUTIONS TO THE PROBLEMS

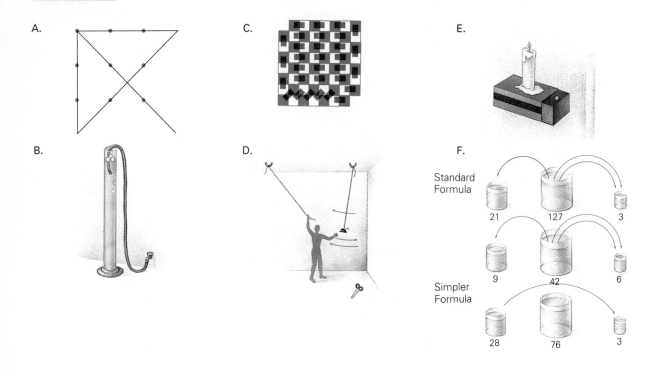

A.

B.

C.

D.

E.

F.

Standard
Formula

21   127   3

9   42   6

Simpler
Formula

28   76   3

you could use the domino at any angle to cover any two squares, regardless of their color. To connect the two strings, you had to see one of the tools on the floor as a weight. To mount the candle on the door, you had to alter your usual perspective and perceive the matchbox as a platform instead of as a container and you had to perceive the candle as a tool as well as the object to be mounted on the door.

Mental Sets: Enhancers and Inhibitors

The last two problems show a phenomenon called *functional fixedness* (Duncker, 1945; Maier, 1931). **Functional fixedness** is a mental block that adversely affects problem solving and creativity by inhibiting the perception of a new function for an object that was previously associated with some other purpose. You put your conceptual "blinders" on and use only your familiar schemas, which shows again the power of schemas to guide or misguide perception of reality.

Another kind of mental rigidity may have hampered your solution of the water-jar problem. If you had

discovered in the first two problems the conceptual rule that B − A − 2(C) = answer, you probably tried the same formula for the third problem and found it didn't work. Actually, simply filling jar A and pouring off enough to fill jar C would have left you with the right amount. If you were using the other formula, you probably did not notice this simpler possibility—your previous success with the other rule would have given you a *mental set*. A **mental set** is a preexisting state of mind, habit, or attitude that can enhance the quality and speed of perceiving and problem solving under some conditions, but inhibit or distort the quality of our mental activities at times when old ways of thinking and acting are nonproductive in new situations. Having a mental set, or readiness, to respond to new problems by using the same procedure, rules, or formula that worked in the past is known as the *Einstellung effect* (Luchins, 1942). The term was coined by Gestalt psychologists who studied problem solving in terms of the way a task and its elements are perceived. Much problem solving involves "breaking set"—temporarily giving up reliance on past learning and mental habits for fullest participation in the stimulus array of the present moment in order to view options from a new perspective.

Another restrictive mental set is the tendency to take a safe course and stick with the "tried and true" instead of trying to see things with fresh eyes and find better ways of proceeding. Sometimes this tendency is simply habit, but sometimes it is the result of a fear of making a mistake or being criticized. Children are sometimes more creative problem solvers than adults, because they are not constrained by existing mental sets or schemas and have not yet been socialized away from fantasy toward logical, linear forms of thought. (See Adams, 1979; Sinnott, 1989 for a more detailed discussion of how you can learn to be a more creative problem solver.)

Another approach to improving problem solving contrasts *descriptive thinking*—how computers and people solve problems—with *prescriptive thinking*—how people *ought* to solve problems (Levine, 1987). People need to be taught ways to avoid pitfalls in reasoning and to be sensitive to perceptual sets and biases. They also need to adhere to the following prescriptive principles for solving problems—although some of them seem obvious, they are not routinely employed; when they are they can improve problem-solving success.

- Formulate a plan. Make it sufficiently concrete to be action-oriented and sufficiently abstract to generalize beyond specific, limited applications.
- Work in an organized way.
- Work, at first, with simpler versions of complex problems.
- Mentally rehearse taking the right action. This visual imaging can be especially helpful when you are learning motor habits.
- Engage in the problem intimately and with enthusiasm; give it time and energy.
- Try to overcome dispositional fallacies, such as starting out by feeling you're inadequate to the task ("I'm not good at numbers," "Women can't work with machines," and "Men aren't good at interpersonal problems").

Table 11.1 offers additional tips for improving your cognitive skill functioning.

THE BEST SEARCH STRATEGY: ALGORITHMS OR HEURISTICS?

After the problem space is known, the problem is well defined but not yet solved. Solving the problem requires using the operations to get from the initial state to the path.

TABLE 11.1 TIPS FOR IMPROVING COGNITIVE SKILLS

Applications of basic principles for developing your cognitive skills can be summarized as follows (Anderson, 1981, 1982):

1. Space your practice. In learning a new skill, regularly practice a short time each day, trying to complete a unit of study or one action pattern at one occasion. One early study found that four hours a day practice on Morse code netted results as good as did seven hours a day (Bray, 1948).

2. Master the subskills. Many skills have component parts. Develop these to the point where they are automatic so you don't have to attend to them. Then start focusing on the next higher level and, finally, on the overall skill.

3. Internalize an ideal model. Observe the correct performance of an expert role model so you can get a good picture of what you are trying to achieve. Then monitor your own performance, noting explicitly how it compares with that of your model. When children learn to play the violin by the Suzuki method, they listen to the music, become familiar with the way it should sound, and then try to match their own performances to that model.

4. Seek immediate feedback and use it immediately. Get knowledge as quickly as you can about the quality of your performance—if possible while the feeling of your action is still in your working memory. Then try to use the feedback while it is still in your working memory. Skill at video games can be acquired quickly because of the immediate electronic feedback and the opportunity to use that feedback to alter responding. Having sports and motor performances videotaped for detailed analysis is another way to use feedback to enhance performance.

5. Anticipate initial frustrations, setbacks, and plateaus in performance. Overcoming them requires persistence, practice, renewed effort, and a sense of one's self-efficacy in achieving preset goals.

One search strategy is an **algorithm,** a methodical, step-by-step procedure for solving problems that guarantees that eventually, with sufficient time and patience, a solution will be found. For example, there are 120 possible combinations of the letters *otrhs;* you could try each one to find the only combination that is also a word: *short.* For an eight-letter group such as *teralbay,* there would be 40,320 possible combinations (8 × 7 × 6 × 5 × 4 × 3 × 2 × 1). A search of all the combinations would eventually reveal the solution, but the search would be long and tedious. Luckily, there is an alternative approach that we can use to solve a great many problems every day. In problem solving, just as in making judgments, we can use a **heuristic,** which is an informal rule of thumb that provides shortcuts, reducing complex problem solving to more simple judgmental operations. Heuristics are general strategies that have often worked in similar situations in the past and may work also in the present case. For example, a heuristic that can help you solve the word jumble of *teralbay* is "Look for short words that could be made from some of the letters and then see if the other letters fit around them." Using such a strategy, you might generate *ably* (tear*ably*?), *able* (ray*table*?), and *tray* (la*tray*be?). By using this particular search strategy, you would probably not need to try more than a few of the possibilities before you came up with the solution: *betrayal* (Glass et al., 1979).

Using a heuristic does not guarantee that a solution will be found; using an algorithm, tedious though it might be, does. Heuristics do work often enough; as we use them, we gradually learn which ones to depend on in which situations. One way experience helps us become better problem solvers is by teaching us when and how to use heuristics appropriately. When there are few possible combinations of elements, use an algorithm to reduce them to the solution; when there are a great many, go for the heuristic. This last statement is itself one kind of heuristic that can guide rational problem-solving strategies.

METACOGNITIVE KNOWLEDGE

One way that experts differ from novices in solving problems is in their metacognitive knowledge. **Metacognitive knowledge** is awareness of what one already knows—the level of comprehension of current information about the task, situation, and options—and one's assessment of personal resources for dealing with the immediate problem. Metacognitive processes enable people to monitor their own mental activities—what they are learning and understanding in a given situation.

They enable people to analyze what they need to know, predict the outcome of different strategies (and check the results later), and evaluate their progress. You use your metacognitive knowledge when you organize your studying differently for a multiple-choice exam than for an essay exam or when you decide which options to take on an essay exam and how much time to devote to each part, according to the points it is worth.

When you are dealing with a task, your metacognitive knowledge search leads you to (a) evaluate your own skills and physical and mental states as well as those of others involved; (b) search your stored knowledge for various possible strategies and evaluate them; (c) decide how much knowledge you have and how much you still need; and (d) assess how much attention to pay to incoming information. These four variables—person, task knowledge, strategy, and sensitivity—may act separately to influence your decisions, but more often they interact (Brown & DeLoache, 1978).

John Flavell (1979, 1981) is a pioneering theorist and researcher in metacognition. He believes that a better understanding of the way metacognitive knowledge develops and is used or misused will help greatly in teaching children and adults to gather information and evaluate the strategies they are using.

Metacognitive knowledge may include self-knowledge and knowledge of the nature of different tasks, different situations, different types of people, and different possible strategies. This knowledge is translated into appropriate action when supplemented by (a) an awareness of reasonable cognitive goals for the contemplated action, (b) an adoption of workable strategies to go from knowledge to goal attainment, and (c) utilization of self-monitoring during an activity to know one is on the right track.

The implications of research on metacognitive processes are profound. To become proficient, you need to go beyond learning specific knowledge and skills. You must become aware—and maintain a continuing awareness—of what you know and can do, where you are in a sequence, and when procedures should be modified to meet the special requirements of the problem. Children should be encouraged early to start dealing with problems by analyzing what they already know about similar problems, where they are deficient, and what a successful solution might look like. They also need to be taught to keep monitoring their progress (or lack of it) to detect confusion in themselves or in information sources and to recognize when they need additional information or resources. Novices become experts—and learners become their own teachers—when they take charge of their own search for knowledge (Scardamalia & Bereiter, 1985).

AN EVOLUTIONARY PSYCHOLOGY PERSPECTIVE

Whenever we analyze behavior, thought, or problem solving as rational or irrational, we are likely to lose sight of its functional basis: whether or not it is *adaptive*. The human mind evolved to promote survival and reproduction. Seeing our cognitive foibles as some kind of deviation from a purely logical, rational ideal keeps us from understanding adaptive functions.

The view that the mind behaves in a rational fashion, following logical rules, has been supported by the *computational model* of cognition. Researchers wrote programs that simulated the mind, and they used those programs to try to tackle different computational problems, from mathematical word problems to playing chess. From the computational model perspective, human deviations into *irrationality* were seen as the result of computational limitations, such as too little memory or not enough processing time—similar to the hardware limits on your personal computer. It was assumed that these constraints prevent the mind from performing the otherwise completely logical information processing it was designed to do.

However, it soon became clear that it was impossible to write a general-purpose, rational problem-solving program. Too many different tricks and techniques were needed for reasoning in specific domains that did not transfer to others. In fact, an enormous amount of information was necessary to create a model of cognition that was able to operate in even a single highly-restricted domain, such as chess playing or programming a robot to pick up a target object within a set. Researchers in artificial intelligence and cognitive science who had been trying to write general purpose reasoning programs gave up the quest for a general intelligence system and began to concentrate instead on restricted, domain-specific models that used a large amount of information that was dependent on a given task.

Similarly, according to the evolutionary view of human cognition, our minds did not evolve to be general-purpose information processors that could solve any problem we faced. As the computer modelers found out, applying general approaches is just not a practical way to solve the wide variety of specific problems. Instead, the mind evolved as a set of separate domain-specific information processing modules, each meant to apply only to certain situations that have survival or reproductive consequences. Furthermore, each module uses a body of information specifically needed in those situations to produce adaptive behavior.

According to this new view, the human mind resembles a *confederacy* of semi-independent modules that can work on their own within a centrally organized plan of action. These *multiminds* are designed to function swiftly and automatically as fixed reactions, special talents, and practiced skills in response to very specific stimulus situations. They get the job done even before we have had time to think it through, as in a well-practiced gymnastic routine or arpeggio on a piano. This new view of the mind is being developed in many fields, including philosophy (Dennett, 1978), artificial intelligence (Hinton & Anderson, 1981), cognitive science (Fodor, 1983), linguistics (Chomsky, 1984), neuroscience (Gazzaniga, 1985), and psychology (Ornstein, 1986).

Let's examine how one of these proposed modules might operate to solve certain types of problems. The **Darwinian algorithms** (as named by Cosmides, 1989) are mental shortcuts related to specific aspects of survival or reproduction. Some of them come into play when you are trying to negotiate a swap of resources with another individual. A completely separate module would be used if you were looking for hiding places when fleeing from danger. In the first case, you would use specific information about bargaining to evaluate how much someone wants what you have and how much he values what he has. In the second case, you would use information about paths, routes, vantage points, and speeds of pursuit.

From this evolutionary viewpoint, behavior that seems irrational could be the result of Darwinian algorithms operating in a situation they did not evolve to handle. For instance, our modules for dealing with aggression from other humans evolved hundreds of thousands of years ago when the biggest threat could be a long, drawn-out, painful fight with fists, stones, or clubs. There was probably plenty of opportunity to stop and evaluate what you'd gotten yourself into and decide to quit or negotiate a solution. In modern society, however, with the availability of handguns, the modules for aggressive confrontation can prove very maladaptive, and trivial disagreements can result in death.

Seemingly irrational behavior can also prove, on closer analysis, to be the adaptive strategy. Consider the actions of a rabbit fleeing a fox across a field. The most "rational" behavior for the rabbit might seem to be to head straight for the nearest bush and stay on that course until reaching it. However, rabbits trying to escape from a predator zigzag in an unpredictable pattern, which gets them to shelter more slowly than a straight line would (**Figure 11.14**). Why should rabbits adapt this unpredictable pattern (called *Protean strategy*)? Their behavior is, in fact, more adaptive than the straight-line path. If the rabbit were to follow a straight path, the pursuing predator would be able to determine

FIGURE 11.14   *THE VIRTUE OF BEING AN UNPREDICTABLE PREY*

The unpredictable zigzag escape pattern is typical of rabbits pursued by a predator.

a precise location at which to intercept the rabbit as it runs. By taking an unpredictable path to safety, the rabbit foils its predator's ability to predict its course and, thus, evades capture. The rabbit's seemingly irrational behavior proves to be the adaptive response we would expect natural selection to produce. (Another example of nature selecting for an unpredictable reaction pattern is shown in **Figure 11.15**.)

Adaptive behavior can also help explain why our approach to solving logical reasoning tasks is not always apparently rational. If our minds were general-purpose, rational information processors, we could reason logically in any domain equally well because logical rules are independent of the meaning of their symbols. However, experimental evidence shows that we are better at solving the same type of problems when they are presented in some domains than in others.

For example, consider the following problem. You've been hired by a bar to enforce the following drinking-age law: If a person is drinking beer, then he or she must be over 21 years old. There are four people drinking in the bar, and each one has a card that tells her age on one side, and what she is drinking on the other side. The sides of the cards you can see are labelled "drinking soda," "drinking beer," "26 years

old," and "17 years old." Which of these cards would you need to turn over to see if anyone is violating the law? Only two: just check the cards marked "drinking beer" and "17 years old." It is relatively easy to figure out why this is the solution.

Now consider a different but similar problem. This time, you've been hired by a high school to check student records to see whether they conform to the following rule: If a person received a *D* rating (written on the front of the record sheet), then the record must be coded *4* (on the back). You have the records of four students, each of which has her letter rating on one side and her corresponding numeric code on the other side. On the sides of the records facing you, you see *F, D, 4,* and *2*. Which of these four records do you have to turn over to see if they violate the rule you are enforcing? The answer in this case is the second and fourth records, marked *D* and *2*. The form of the problem is *if P, then Q*—so look for P on one side, and then look for Q on the other side. This leads you to select D to see if it has a 4 on the other side. However, the problem also implies that *if P, then not Q*. This implication leads you to look at the 2 to make sure it has a letter other than D on the other side. You don't test the rule by the 4 card because other grades could also be linked to 4—the rule said

FIGURE 11.15 **THE ADVANTAGE OF AN UNPREDICTABLE ATTACK STRATEGY**

A mongoose can kill a cobra by swiftly jumping around it in an unpredictable pattern that prevents the cobra from executing a planned strike at the mongoose.

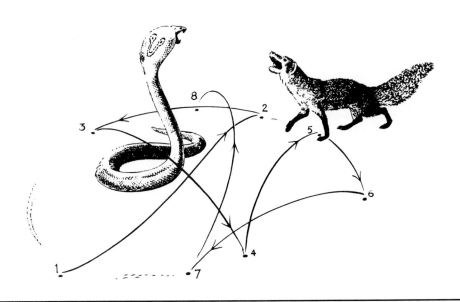

only that D implies 4, not that 4 implies only D. If you are similar to the typical subject in many studies with similar problems, you may have had a harder time with the second problem than you did with the first. Why?

The second logical reasoning task, known generally as the *Wason Selection Task,* was exactly the same in structure as the first one. Only the domains were different. Yet people find the first one much easier to solve correctly. Evolutionary psychologist **Leda Cosmides** (1989) has analyzed this task across many domains, familiar and unfamiliar, and concluded that people find this reasoning problem easiest when it involves a *social contract* where we are looking for cheaters. Why? Because such situations invoke a Darwinian algorithm that evolved specifically to reason about *social exchange;* the algorithm is tuned to the task of making sure that these exchanges go fairly (for us at least) and that we are not cheated. Keeping others from taking advantage of us in social situations is an important adaptive problem our ancestors had to solve again and again, and so we would expect that a specific mental mechanism has evolved to guide our behavior in such circumstances. The first problem involves a social exchange: we are looking for people violating the social contract concerning who can drink. The second problem, though, is just an abstract situation in which we are looking for mistakes, and, therefore, our cheater-detection Darwinian algorithm is not brought into play, and we do much more poorly. The difference in problem-solving behavior between different domains does not fit the definition of rationality, but it is readily understandable in terms of domain-specific adaptive functions when viewed from the perspective of evolutionary psychology.

SUMMING UP

The extremes of human reasoning are autistic and realistic. The first is idiosyncratic, without reference to external validity checks; the second is governed by reality constraints. In between the two lies the territory where most reasoning takes place. Deductive reasoning involves drawing conclusions from premises on the basis of rules of logic. Valid conclusions from syllogisms follow inescapably from major and minor premises if we reason correctly. Validity and truth of conclusions are not the same; sometimes our beliefs bias reasoning so that we falsely believe as valid those statements we favor and as invalid those that are contrary to our beliefs. Inductive reasoning involves inferring a conclusion from evidence on the basis of its likelihood or probability. Hypothesis formation and testing in science are typically based on inductive reasoning.

When solving problems, we must define the initial state, the goal state, and the operations that can get us from the first to the second—a difficult task in ill-defined problems. Functional fixedness and other mental sets can hamper creative problem solving and require attempts at breaking set. Algorithms ensure an eventual solution if there is one, but are impractical in many cases. Heuristics are mental shortcuts that often help us reach a solution quickly. We also rely on metacognitive knowledge that provides a background mental picture of the task at hand and of the skills and background we use to solve it. Evolutionary psychology shows us that it is more useful to explore the possible adaptive functions originally served by cognitive processes than it is to label them as rational or irrational. Unpredictable behavior may be quite rational, as in the case when it helps an animal escape a predator or a predator catch its prey. Evolutionary psychology also suggests that the mind developed not as a general information processor but rather as a host of specific modules, each designed to serve a specific adaptive function related to survival and reproduction.

JUDGING AND DECIDING

We live in a world of *uncertainty*. We can never be completely confident in our predictions about how people will behave or how events will unfold. Despite this uncertainty, we are constantly called upon to make personal, economic, and political decisions that have enormous impacts on our lives. Are there accepted guidelines or models for making good decisions? When scientists, physicians, lawyers, politicians, stockbrokers, and parents make their decisions, what procedures do they follow in order to get the best possible outcomes? In this section, we will see that decision making is always subjective, often error-prone, and sometimes irrational. In addition, we will see that human intuition can be fallible, at times leading us to make obvious mistakes. By recognizing the underlying cognitive mechanisms that guide our choices, however, we have an opportunity to improve our decision making.

Psychologists often distinguish between judgment and decision making. **Judgment** is the process by which we form opinions, reach conclusions, and make critical evaluations of events and people on the basis of available information. Judgments are also the product or the conclusion of that mental process. We often make judgments spontaneously, without prompting. **Decision making,** on the other hand, is the process of choosing between alternatives, selecting and rejecting available options. Judgment and decision making are interrelated processes. For example, you might meet someone at a party, and, after a brief discussion and a dance together, *judge* the person to be intelligent, interesting, honest, and sincere. You might then *decide* to spend most of your party time with that person and to arrange a date for the next weekend.

Behind apparently ordinary, routine social interactions lie a host of cognitive processes and strategies. You are not aware of many of the processes that generally operate smoothly on what you think and how you act. However, under some circumstances, these cognitive processes can lead you astray. In these special cases, you might make erroneous inferences from the evidence; generate faulty, irrational judgments; or use a process that leads your decisions away from an objectively ideal alternative. Awareness of such mental traps is the first step in avoiding them.

MAKING SENSE OF THE WORLD

Our everyday world is a complicated place, and we often must rely on relevant knowledge we have accumulated previously to guide our behavior. Unlike Dr. Eger, whose experience in the chaos of a concentration camp had no parallels in her experience, most of the situations in which we find ourselves share basic properties with previous situations we have encountered. The theories we have developed through a wide variety of experiences can help us to understand novel events and new information. For example, as a student you have attended a great number of classes, and your memory of these experiences will guide how you behave on the first day of a new class. Using your previous knowledge simplifies matters—you do not need to relearn the guidelines for class behavior every time you begin a new course.

Our judgments are based on **inference,** the reasoning process of drawing a conclusion on the basis of a sample of evidence or on the basis of prior beliefs and theories. We employ a variety of *inferential strategies* to simplify the inferences we make. Ordinarily these strategies serve us well. In some circumstances, however, we misapply these strategies to new data. In particular, when faced with new information that is inconsistent with previous knowledge, we are often too ready to try to fit it into an established theory rather than considering the possibility that the theory itself requires revision.

Some psychologists believe that people are "cognitive misers," always trying to minimize mental effort whenever sustained attention, comprehension, or analysis is required (Taylor, 1980). People habitually use *mental shortcuts* to make up their minds quickly, easily, and with maximum confidence (Kahneman et al., 1982). They are often too ready to be led astray by their theories about what *ought* to be and their values, ignoring data about what really is (Nisbett & Ross, 1980). These psychologists believe the human information processor is fallible; it is susceptible to systematic errors that can be studied to determine the mental processes involved in judgments and decisions.

It is important to be aware that people can sometimes be misled by the very same cognitive processes that work remarkably effectively in most situations. However, just because these processes can sometimes lead us to apparently irrational conclusions, they are not themselves irrational—it might, for example, make more sense to use a mental shortcut that usually works than to employ a more ideal approach that always yields the correct answer but does so at the price of a great deal of time and mental effort. Just as the process of learning can also cause us to "mislearn" phobias and superstitions, the processes of inferential judgment can have costs as well as benefits.

It is cognitively efficient to identify a few significant, stable characteristics around which to organize our initial reactions of others, but we may form overgeneralized stereotypes that are based on minimal, faulty, or false information. These stereotypes may then influence the way we behave toward other people and, in turn, the way they behave toward us. For example, if you are told that someone you are about to meet is schizophrenic, you are likely to form an emotional impression that is different from the impression you would have formed had you not been given the label—regardless of the person's behavior (Fiske & Pavelchak, 1986).

Forming such initial impressions based on minimal information would not present a problem if the impressions were subsequently revised on the basis of new information about the object of our judgment. Often, though, our theories are slow to change in the light of new data. Why are initial impressions so persistent over time and so resistant to new information and contradictory data? What are the forces that exert a distorting influence on the way we interpret the evidence of our senses, the memories we retrieve, and the decisions we make?

PERSEVERANCE OF FALSE BELIEFS

In Chapter 5, we saw that Piaget characterized cognitive development in children as the interweaving of the dual processes of *assimilation* and *accommodation*. A child interprets the new by assimilating it into known categories and accommodating old mental structures to new information. So, too, the adult mind must decide again and again when new data supports (or can be stretched to fit) old theories and when old theories must be changed because new data just doesn't fit. The proper balance between the processes of accommodation and assimilation enables us to make optimal use of past knowledge, experience, and personal theories without forfeiting the opportunity to learn something new about how our physical, biological, and social worlds work.

We often continue to persevere in beliefs, theories, and ways of doing things because we *assimilate* data or new experiences in a *biased* fashion (Ross & Lepper, 1980). Data consistent with our beliefs are given little attention before they are filed away mentally as evidence supporting our views because they are expected. Any ambiguity in the data is resolved, often without full awareness, in terms of our existing beliefs. Our attention is drawn, quite naturally, to aspects of the data that are incongruent and may challenge our theories, and we devote our efforts to reinterpreting and explaining this information within the context of our theories. This process is known as **biased assimilation.** Using our current theories to explain new data is a reasonable approach, and in fact, we would not be able to understand new information at all without interpreting it in terms of previous knowledge. The problem is that, if our initial belief is wrong, new information which should help us to correct the mistake may be taken instead as evidence *supporting* the first impression.

Adding to this problem is the fact that we have control over what information we receive. We may choose to ask questions in such a way that they are bound to yield the answer we want (Snyder & Swann, 1978a). What answer will an interviewer elicit when she asks, "Are you prepared to work hard at this job?" of a candidate desperate for work? Can you imagine anyone ever saying, "No"? In addition, we usually associate with and seek out others who share our points of view. We expose ourselves to people and information that reinforce what we want to believe (Festinger, 1957; Olson & Zanna, 1979). As a result of this **selective exposure,** we notice and process more data that support than that disconfirm our beliefs. An expectation from our personal theories can also serve as a *self-fulfilling prophecy* about future events, becoming true because we create the circumstances that make their fulfillment inevitable (Snyder, 1984).

Our tendency to cling to initial theories can lead to *overconfidence* in the truth of our beliefs because it causes us to underestimate the probability that these beliefs could be wrong.

> Consider a study in which college students living in dormitories were asked to predict the behavior of their roommates. They were asked to predict, for instance, whether their roommates would keep or turn in a five-dollar bill found on the floor of a local campus eatery and how their roommates would respond to a hypothetical choice between two magazine subscriptions. When compared to the actual responses of their roommates, subjects' predictions were overconfident; subjects believed their predictions would be correct significantly more of the time than they actually were (Dunning et al., 1990).

Overconfidence can also lead people to overestimate their abilities. When asked about their driving skills and safety, for example, people typically judged themselves to be better drivers than 85 percent of all the people they knew. Subjects believed they were safer drivers than the majority, which, statistically speaking, they all couldn't be (Sevnson, 1981). Similarly, 94 percent of all college professors claim that the work they do is above average (Cross, 1977). Researchers are currently debating vigorously about whether this overconfidence does more harm than good (Taylor & Brown, 1988). On one hand, having an inflated sense of confidence may encourage persistence and help you to accomplish feats you normally might not try. On the other hand, underestimating your chances of being a victim of a violent crime or contracting a sexually transmitted disease may prevent you from taking action to avoid such undesirable outcomes. Unrealistic optimism about future life events can get you in trouble when you do not have the resources to cope effectively with those events (Weinstein, 1980).

SOURCES OF IRRATIONALITY

How have social scientists explained apparent lapses into irrationality? At least three explanations have been advanced: the masses, the passions, and biases.

The ancient Greek philosopher Plato and the more contemporary sociologist LeBon (1895–1960) both believed that individual reasoning is undermined when faced with the common influences of the masses. Under the influence of a crowd, an individual ceases to think logically and succumbs to the disordered thinking of "mob psychology."

A different view emerges from the distinction between human reason and animal appetites or passions. When driven by desires that demand immediate gratification, people cease to be rational. Freudian theory argues that sexual and aggressive instincts and the unconscious exercise a powerful motivational influence on perception and thought. Rationality is pitted against emotionality and a focus on satisfying one's immediate desires. Society's task, often accomplished with the help of religion and education, is to suppress these "primitive" urges by replacing them with more lofty principles and rules of conduct.

A third view of irrationality comes from modern cognitive and social psychologists. From their perspective, erroneous judgments are the result of the misapplication or overextension of normal, rational processes. They suggest that the failures of human intuition and the achievements of human thought are cut from the same rich fabric of cognitive processes. Let's consider this third notion of ordinary irrationality in more detail.

COGNITIVE BIASES

The mental strategies or shortcuts we use can result in a **cognitive bias,** or a systematic error in the inferences we draw from evidence, the judgments we base on our inferences, and the decisions we make using these judgments. At times, these biases are not errors but differences in emphasis or perspective that we bring to a situation we are trying to understand. The fact that the processes we use yield biased conclusions does not necessarily mean the processes are incorrect in themselves but rather that we do not adequately discriminate between appropriate and inappropriate conditions for their use.

Personal experience teaches many useful lessons and obviously aids in making sense of the world. Under many circumstances, however, conclusions based solely on personal *intuition* have been shown to be inferior to those based on *statistical evidence* compiled objectively from many such similar cases—the *base rate* of average responding (Dawes et al., 1989; Dawes, 1979; Meehl, 1954). Nevertheless, we often maintain confidence in the validity of our intuitions in these situations and, as a result, sometimes ignore or discard better objective evidence that is less susceptible to subjective error.

Researchers have identified a number of different biases in judgment. For example, we tend to perceive random events as nonrandom, correlated events as causally related, and people as causal agents instead of situational variables. Psychologists use their observations of such biases to understand the cognitive processes and strategies people use to make judgments in complex situations.

We have noted that heuristics are mental shortcuts useful in solving a problem by means of a direct procedure that reduces the range of possible solutions. A heuristic for psychology multiple-choice tests might be "Select the longest answer," because psychological findings tend to be qualified rather than simple. How can a heuristic that helps in one set of circumstances, such as test taking, be harmful in another? Sometimes, using a mental shortcut causes you to overlook important information that would suggest a different conclusion. People's reliance on heuristics—the *availability heuristic* and the *representativeness heuristic* (see Tversky & Kahneman, 1973, 1980)—can lead to systematic biases in their judgments.

Anchors Aweigh!

Try this interesting experiment with a group of friends or family members. First, divide your subjects arbitrarily into two groups. Then, once they are separated from each other, give members of the first group five seconds to estimate the following mathematical product:

$$1 \times 2 \times 3 \times 4 \times 5 \times 6 \times 7 \times 8$$

Then, give members of the second group the same amount of time to estimate the answer to the same equation but in reverse order:

$$8 \times 7 \times 6 \times 5 \times 4 \times 3 \times 2 \times 1$$

After you have collected everyone's estimates, compute the median estimate for each group—that is, the number above and below which half of the estimates fall.

If your results are similar to those found by **Amos Tversky** and **Daniel Kahneman** (1973), two pioneering researchers in the area of judgment and decision

Amos Tversky and Daniel Kahneman (*Discovering Psychology,* 1990, Program 11)

making, you will find that members of the first group give lower estimates than do members of the second group. In their original experiment, these researchers reported a median estimate of a low 512 for members of the first group and a high 2250 for members of the second group (neither of which, incidentally, bore any resemblance to the correct answer of 40,320!). The researchers explained these findings in terms of an **anchoring bias,** the insufficient adjustment—up or down—from an original starting value when judging the probable value of some event or outcome. Because members of the first group began to evaluate the product with low digits, their estimates were anchored to low numbers. In contrast, members of the second group began with the higher digits and were, therefore, anchored to relatively high numbers.

Anchoring is not restricted to numerical domains. For example, randomly assigned anchors can affect opinions about the SALT-II arms reduction treaty (Quattrone et al., 1984). Anchors can change estimates of personal efficacy which, in turn, affect how persistent we are in performing various tasks (Cervone & Peake, 1986).

The effects of anchoring do not disappear even when subjects *know* that the initial estimate serving as the anchor was determined randomly.

In one experiment, a group of subjects was asked to estimate a series of quantities, such as the percentage of African nations that were members of the United Nations. A roulette wheel was spun in the subjects' presence, and they were asked before they gave their own estimates to indicate whether the quantity in question was higher or lower than the number selected on the wheel. Their estimates were strongly influenced by the anchor provided by the roulette wheel—estimates were higher when a high number appeared on the wheel (Tversky & Kahneman, 1973).

Surprisingly, the effects of anchoring also do not disappear with outrageously extreme anchors. In another experiment, subjects were asked whether the number of Beatles records that had made the Top Ten fell above or below 100,025; whether the average price of a college textbook was more or less than $7128.53; and whether the average temperature in San Francisco was greater or less than 558°F. After the subjects responded, the researchers asked them to estimate the precise number of Top-Ten Beatles hits, the average price of a textbook, and the average temperature in San Francisco. What these researchers found was that, instead of disregarding the unreasonably high anchor values, subjects were affected as much as when more plausible anchors were provided in the opening round of questions (Quattrone et al., 1984). The influence of anchoring grows with the *discrepancy* between the anchor and the "preanchor estimate" (the average estimate subjects make without explicit anchors) until the effect reaches a plateau.

> In a recent study of more than 1000 students, anchoring greatly influenced estimates of both the likelihood of nuclear war and the effectiveness of strategic defenses. Students who were initially asked whether the probability of nuclear war was greater or less than 1 percent subsequently set the odds at 10 percent, whereas respondents who were first asked whether the probability of nuclear war was greater or less than 90 percent gave estimates averaging 26 percent. Similarly, students who were provided with a low anchor in a survey about strategic defenses estimated that, under the best of conditions, nearly one fourth (24 percent) of Soviet missiles would penetrate American strategic defenses, while students who were provided with a high anchor estimated that the majority (57 percent) of all missiles would reach their targets (Plous, 1989).

These results pose intriguing questions for future research. In particular, they raise the possibility that current or initial positions can have a large effect on later ones, inducing a "status quo bias" (Samuelson & Zeckhauser, 1988) in which the current course of action is more likely to be continued than changed. For example, do initial arms control positions unwittingly anchor later ones? By understanding the way anchoring influences other people's decisions, our own decisions may be better informed.

Availability Heuristic

Are there more words in the English language that begin with the letter *k* or more words that have *k* as their third letter? If you are like the subjects in the study by Tversky and Kahneman (1973), then you probably judged that *k* is found more often at the beginning of words. In fact, the letter *k* appears about twice as often in the third position.

How do the number of deaths from tornadoes annually in the United States compare with those from asthma, and how do accidental deaths compare with deaths from disease? When asked to estimate the frequency of deaths from all causes, subjects overestimated those that were rare but dramatic and sensational, and underestimated those that were more frequent but occurred in private, ordinary circumstances (Slovic, 1984). Asthma causes about 20 times more deaths than tornadoes, and diseases kill 16 times as many people as do accidents. Nonetheless, the subjects judged accidents and disease to be equally lethal, and tornadoes to be three times more deadly than asthma.

When we use the **availability heuristic,** we estimate the likelihood of an outcome based on how easily similar or identical outcomes can be brought to mind or imagined. This heuristic causes us to judge as more frequent or probable those events that are more readily imagined or retrieved from memory. It is easier, for example, to recall words beginning with the letter *k* than it is to think of words with *k* in the third position; so, words beginning with a *k* seem more numerous. The ease with which we can recall or imagine some event is *usually* a good cue for making frequency and probability judgments. However, rare events that are dramatized and sensationalized are more memorable and so we tend to mistakenly believe they are also more frequent.

Soviet dictator Joseph Stalin is reputed to have said, "A single death of a Russian soldier is a tragedy; a million deaths is a statistic." Journalists typically focus on the vivid, dramatic, individual case at the expense of the more informative large scale data base. Often that narrow focus is more motivating for readers than a more comprehensive focus. For example, a *New Yorker* article profiling the problems of a single, supposedly "typical" welfare case had more impact in changing readers' attitudes toward welfare than did a presentation of essentially the same relevant data in summary form (Hamill et al., 1980).

Representativeness Heuristic

Another judgmental heuristic that simplifies the complex task of social judgment under conditions of uncertainty is the **representativeness heuristic.** It is based on the presumption that belonging to a particular category implies having the characteristics considered typical of members of that category. When estimating the likelihood that a specific instance is a member of a given category (Did this pizza come from Domino's? Is it likely that Phil is an Aries?), we look to see whether the instance has the features found in a typical category member. This process should remind you of *prototype theory,* which was discussed earlier in this chapter. Such an approach seems reasonable; we're more likely to believe that Phil is an Aries, for example, if he has some of the characteristics we expect the typical Aries person to have. The representativeness heuristic can lead us astray, however, when factors other than typicality should enter into our judgments.

Consider the following question: I have a friend who is a college professor. He is an excellent gardener, reads poetry, is shy, and is slight of build. Would you judge that he is probably in (a) Japanese studies or (b) psychology?

If you decided that my friend was in Japanese studies, you were matching the description of him with your stereotypes of people in the two fields. You probably did not take into consideration the fact that a much larger number of professors teach psychology and, thus, the greater statistical probability that the friend is a psychologist. Neither did you consider the probability that, as a psychologist, I would be likely to have more friends in my own area of study (Nisbett & Ross, 1980). Actually, the friend just described is a psychology professor.

Relying on representativeness and neglecting the relevant *base rate information*—the statistical probability of a given outcome or an accumulated body of data—can lead people to be particularly confident even when making particularly unlikely predictions. For example, subjects presented with a description of a person that fits the stereotype of an engineer were equally confident that the person was an engineer whether they were told the description was drawn at random from a list containing 70 percent engineers or from a list containing only 30 percent engineers (Kahneman & Tversky, 1973). They should have been less confident the person was an engineer if there was only a three in ten chance rather than a seven in ten chance, but they were deceived by the representativeness heuristic.

Consider the following pairs of scenarios: (1a) a massive flood somewhere in North America in the next year in which more than 1000 people drown; (1b) an earthquake in California sometime in the next year causing a flood in which more than 1000 people drown; (2a) a complete suspension of diplomatic relations between the United States and the Soviet Union sometime in the next year; and (2b) a Russian invasion of Poland and a complete suspension of diplomatic relations be-

tween the United States and the Soviet Union sometime in the next year. Although in each pair scenario (a) includes the possibility of scenario (b) and therefore must be more likely, subjects in a study by Tversky and Kahneman (1983) rated (b) as more likely, because the added detail made the scenario seem more probable. Reliance on representativeness, then, can lead to judgments that violate basic rules of probability. This effect is not limited to novices, either—the subjects evaluating scenarios (2a) and (2b) were professional political analysts attending a forecasting conference!

Availability and representativeness are just two of many heuristics that we use in making judgments about the world every day. The biased judgments resulting from these and other rules of thumb can distort our views of reality, and remain compelling even when we know the true state of affairs. We employ these heuristics because they allow us to make quick, acceptable judgments that work well enough most of the time. Often they are the best we can do, given the constraints and uncertainties of the situation.

THE PSYCHOLOGY OF DECISION MAKING

Classic economic theory, which is based on a "rational actor" model, starts with the assumption that people act to maximize gain, minimize loss, and allocate their resources efficiently. It provides a *normative model* of the way reasonable people *ought* to behave in an ideal world. It assumes that people do the best they can with available information and that most people have the same set of information and act as if they understand and can apply the laws of probability properly. However, a *descriptive analysis* of *actual* human choice and decision making by cognitive psychologists shows that the assumptions of economic theory often do not hold (Simon, 1955; Tversky & Kahneman, 1986). People do not always understand and correctly apply the laws of probability, and they are often required to make decisions under *conditions of uncertainty* in which the relevant probabilities are not known anyway.

Once we understand the way people actually behave, it comes as less of a surprise that people often don't follow normative rules. Two criticisms of the rational choice model come from (a) demonstrations that alternative descriptions of the same decision problem can result in different choices and (b) analyses of risk preferences.

Decision Frames

In decision making, preferences between options should be consistent, regardless of the way the decision is presented to them. This *invariance principle* is an essential aspect of normative models of choice. However, decisions *are* influenced by the way in which a decision problem is presented or framed, even when the alternatives are formally equivalent or technically the same. Consider, for example, the choice between surgery and radiation for treatment of lung cancer. Statistical information about the results of each treatment for previous patients can be presented either in terms of survival rates or mortality rates. First read the survival frame for the problem and choose your preferred treatment; then read the mortality frame and see if you feel like changing your preference.

Survival Frame

Surgery: Of 100 people having surgery, 90 live through the postoperative period, 68 are alive at the end of the first year, and 34 are alive at the end of five years.

Radiation Therapy: Of 100 people having radiation therapy, all live through the treatment, 77 are alive at the end of one year, and 22 are alive at the end of five years.

What do you choose: surgery or radiation?

Mortality Frame

Surgery: Of 100 people having surgery, 10 die during surgery or the postoperative period, 32 die by the end of one year, and 66 die by the end of five years.

Radiation Therapy: Of 100 people having radiation therapy, none die during treatment, 23 die by the end of one year, and 78 die by the end of five years.

What do you choose: surgery or radiation?

Note that the data are objectively the same in both frames. When this decision was presented to subjects, however, results indicated that the decision frame had a marked effect on choice of treatment. Radiation therapy was chosen by only 18 percent of the subjects given the survival frame, but by 44 percent of those given the mortality frame. This framing effect held equally for a group of clinic patients, statistically sophisticated business students, and experienced physicians (McNeil et al., 1982).

Risk Strategies

People have attitudes toward risks that they bring into most decision situations. These attitudes influence whether they will make risk-seeking or risk-averse (conservative) choices, sometimes in apparent contradiction with the expected value of the options. Consider the following examples.

1. Which of the following do you choose?
   a. You have an 85 percent chance to win $100.
   b. You have a sure gain of $80.

2. Which of the following do you choose?
   a. You have an 85 percent chance to lose $100.
   b. You have a sure loss of $80.

Most people choose 1b over 1a, a *risk-averse preference* for a sure gain over a probable large gain. They also choose 2a over 2b, a *risk-seeking strategy* in which a gamble is preferred over a sure loss (Tversky & Kahneman, 1986).

The perception of potential risks is also influenced by other psychological factors—whether the risks are perceived as controllable, voluntary, possibly catastrophic, shared by others, delayed in time, or unfamiliar. Experts who assess the degree of risk from various hazards (such as asbestos, terrorism, nuclear power, medical X rays, or motor vehicles) stick close to the actuarial statistics of the known estimates of deaths and injuries from each type of risk. Those statistical outcomes define the severity of a risk. Based on statistical evidence, experts find that X rays are riskier than nuclear power. However, when knowledgeable but nonexpert subjects judge risk potentials of 30 possible hazards, they rank nuclear power as the most risky and X rays among the least risky (Slovic, 1984). People also judge unfamiliar or potentially catastrophic risks as

"WE'LL ONLY DO 72% OF IT, SINCE IT'S BEEN REPORTED THAT 28% OF ALL SURGERY IS UNNECESSARY."

more serious than risks with well-known or delayed effects. Experts do not make these psychological differentiations (Slovic, 1984). This difference in the risk perception of experts and laypeople creates problems when experts in government or business want to persuade the public that some action is necessary in order to avoid a serious risk. The statistical evidence is not psychologically compelling to the public, and the experts ignore the psychological reality of the nonstatistical risk estimate (Vaughan, 1986).

Researchers have recently discovered that an **optimistic bias** operates when people estimate personal risks. When asked about their own chances of suffering as the result of a risk, most people claim they are less likely to be affected than their peers. This optimistic bias shows up when random samples of adults are asked to estimate whether they are above or below average in their chance of experiencing a variety of specific hazards such as asthma, food poisoning, drug addiction, pneumonia, and lung cancer. On 25 of 32 such hazards, a significant optimistic bias was found (Weinstein, 1991). This bias exists for life threatening hazards as well as minor illnesses. It even occurs among those who are clearly in a high-risk group. Optimistic biases are cognitive errors that may benefit some people by promoting a general sense of optimism, which has many positive benefits (Seligman, 1991). On the negative side, however, such mistaken personal risk perceptions may seriously hinder efforts to promote risk-reducing behaviors such as practicing safe sex.

Other Factors in Decision Making

When we are faced with complicated judgments and decisions, we rely on heuristics to help us simplify the problem. However, when these strategies distort our perception of the information leading to the best course of action, we sometimes make faulty decisions. We may also make faulty decisions even when people do not fall prey to cognitive biases. For example, we can be influenced by nonrational psychological factors, such as "wishful thinking." If we want something very much we may underestimate the likelihood of negative outcomes and overestimate the likelihood of positive ones. This misjudgment of the probabilities may play a role in cases where teenagers become pregnant. Their decision not to use contraception is based, in part, on an underestimate of the risk despite what they "know" (Luker, 1975).

Groups can make the same kind of mistake, even at the highest levels of political decision making. The disastrous Bay of Pigs invasion of Cuba in 1960 was approved by President Kennedy after Cabinet meetings in which contrary information was minimized or suppressed by those advisors to the president who were

Kennedy approved the disastrous Bay of Pigs invasion of Cuba in 1960 after cabinet meetings in which contrary information was minimized or suppressed by those who were eager to undertake the mission.

eager to undertake the invasion. **Irving Janis** (1982) has coined the term **group think** for the tendency of a decision-making group to erect mind guards that filter out undesirable input so that a consensus may be reached, especially if it is in line with the leader's viewpoint.

New views of negotiation recast it as a judgmental process in which expert negotiators sometimes use heuristics that are inappropriate for the given situation, have difficulties interpreting the ambiguous feedback available, and frequently fail to give adequate consideration to the other side's perspective. The success of negotiators may be improved by training them to understand the effect that decisional heuristics have on the choices they make and to recognize that similar processes operate to determine the strategy taken by the other side (Neale & Bazerman, 1985; Raiffa, 1982). In the field of management sciences, negotiation is conceptualized by leading researchers such as **Max Bazerman** (1990) as a multiparty decision-making activity that rests on the individual cognitions of each party and the dynamics of the social interactions among the parties. It follows then that, to negotiate most effectively, negotiators need to know how to make more rational decisions. "Making such decisions requires that negotiators understand and reduce the cognitive errors that permeate their decision processes" (Neale & Bazerman, 1991, p. 1).

ECOLOGICAL DECISION MAKING

Fifty years ago, geneticist Russ Hoelzel would not have applied for a permit to do biopsy darting on orcas (killer whales). No agency regulated whale research, and no one cared about killer whales anyway. However, in the 1980s, Hoelzel's proposal to collect tissue samples sparked an ongoing international controversy. Conservationists faced off against researchers (many of whom are themselves conservationists) in a struggle over the values of science and the rights of animals in the wild.

Decision making is hard enough when all the facts are on the table, but in this and other ecological issues, decisions are negotiated on the basis of probabilities about uncertain future events; many facts simply are not available. Since Hoelzel first applied for his research permit in 1985, organizations ranging from Greenpeace to the National Marine Fisheries Service have adopted official positions on the subject. To formulate these positions, they negotiated among themselves, calling upon fragments of data, assumptions, beliefs, and values that seemed relevant to their decisions.

The information available to these organizations is summarized below. After weighing the pros and cons of each argument, reach your *own* conclusion about this issue. Would you grant the permit to Hoelzel? Why or why not?

Background: Hoelzel applied for permission to collect tissue samples from 45 orcas in Puget Sound. He planned to follow the animals in a boat, and, when a target orca was within range, he would shoot it with a specially designed arrow from his longbow. The arrow's sterilized tip was hollow to 1 inch and would be kept from penetrating further by a rubber stopper. "After the arrow impacts the whale, it bounces out with the biopsy sample in its core and it is then reeled in using fishing line attached to the end of the arrow" (Osborne, 1987).

Arguments for: This technique has been used with several species of whales and dolphins. Although short-term startle and avoidance effects have been observed in the whales and dolphins, no long-term effects are known. Orcas in the Puget Sound region are part of an ongoing longitudinal study in which every animal's identity and reproductive history is known. With data from biopsies, the precise genetic relationships among these orcas could be determined. In addition, levels of environmental contaminants in the animals could be measured. Biologist John Calambokidis maintains that "knowing the contaminant levels of these individuals is a unique opportunity for correlating reproduction with contaminants" (Calambokidis, 1986).

Arguments against: Paul Spong is a physiological psychologist whose experiments with captive orcas transformed him from a "tank researcher" to an ardent advocate of whale rights. He contends that Hoelzel's proposal "is insulting and insensitive to the orcas" (Spong, 1988). After more than two decades of observing orcas in the wild, Spong believes that their patterns of swimming and eating could be severely disrupted by the darting program and fears they might leave the area—a long-term effect that might be irreversible. Residents of the islands around which the whales forage (for salmon and marine mammals) share Spong's concerns. Environmental groups argue that data from tissue samples should not make any difference in the formulation of environmentally sound policies. Spong agrees: "Do we really need more proof before taking action against the industrial wastes that are poisoning Puget Sound?" (Spong, 1988).

Based on this limited amount of information, would you support or oppose Hoelzel's plan? Reflect on your decision-making process. What *inferences* did you make? Did you make any *judgments* about the motives of the people supporting either point of view? What are the rational aspects of your decision, and what might be some emotional, or value-laden, influences that could bias your final decision?

Analysis of decision making has traditionally split the topic into a probability component and a value (or utility) component. In short, when we make a decision, we consider the likelihood of various possible outcomes and how much we value each one. Most of the research on decision making has focused mainly on people's probability estimates and related concepts. This work assumes that errors in decision making arise mainly from inaccurate estimates of probability not value. Recently, however, psychologists have turned their attention to the value component and have raised some fascinating questions.

One area of particular interest is our ability to predict how much we will like something at a later time or after repeated exposure. Tastes change—later we might not enjoy something that we do now, and we might not like something as much after being exposed to it every day. Anticipation of such changes should be taken into account when making decisions. For instance, you should be more willing to risk a bad haircut if you think you would soon become used to it anyway. You should be less willing to buy an entire box of some food item you sampled in the grocery store if you think you would quickly become tired of it. Recent evidence suggests that people are not always accurate predictors of changes in their tastes (Kahneman & Snell, 1990), and that their theories of how tastes change lead them to decisions they later regret. For instance, you might decide to buy a house near a highway because you believe you will adapt to the noise, when, in fact, such adaptation is unlikely (Weinstein, 1982).

We can avoid many common pitfalls in decision making by becoming better information processors. Awareness of the biasing effects of beliefs and theories, oversensitivity to vivid cases, failure to take into account base-rate information, misuse of heuristics, and decision frames and personal attitudes toward risk can help improve decision making.

Studying Thinking

The study of cognitive psychology includes looking at the mental processes and structures that enable us to think, reason, make inferences and decisions, solve problems, and use language. Cognitive psychologists generally use an information-processing approach to analyze information into its components which are then processed in stages or sequences. Cognitive psychology has replaced behaviorism as the core area of research in American psychology. Cognitive science pools the efforts of psychologists, researchers in the brain sciences, and computer scientists to study how the brain and mind represent and use knowledge. Cognitive neuroscience is a promising new area that attempts to bridge the gap in our understanding between the molecular level of neurons and the macro level of behavioral functioning.

Mental Structures for Thinking

Thinking is a higher order mental process that forms new abstract representations by transforming available information. Concepts are the building blocks of thinking; they are formed by identifying properties that are common to a class of objects or ideas. We store well defined concepts as definitions and fuzzy concepts as prototypes. Concepts are often arranged in hierarchies, ranging from general to specific. Other mental structures that guide thinking include schemas and scripts. We also rely on visual imagery such as mental maps.

Reasoning and Problem Solving

Deductive reasoning involves drawing conclusions from premises on the basis of rules of logic. Inductive reasoning involves inferring a conclusion from evidence on the basis of its likelihood or probability. Forming and testing scientific hypotheses typically involve inductive reasoning. In solving problems, we must define initial state, goal state, and the operations that get us from the initial to the goal state. Heuristics are mental shortcuts that can help us reach solutions quickly. Metacognitive knowledge provides a mental picture of the task at hand and the skills and background necessary to solve it. Evolutionary psychology shows us that it is more useful to explore the possible adaptive functions served by cognitive processes than it is to label them irrational.

Judging and Deciding

Decision making is always subjective and prone to error. Awareness of mental traps is the first step in avoiding them. Inferential strategies normally serve us well, but occasionally we misapply these strategies to new data; we may not consider that new data inconsistent with prior knowledge could indicate a need to revise a particular theory. We continue to hold certain beliefs and theories or to persist in certain ways of doing things because we assimilate data or new experiences in a biased way. Scientists have advanced three explanations for such lapses into irrationality: mob psychology, passions, and biases. Cognitive biases are now assumed to generate most apparently irrational decisions. Anchoring bias occurs when there is insufficient adjustment up or down from an original starting value. The availability heuristic leads us to estimate an outcome according to how easily similar or identical outcomes can be imagined. The representative heuristic is based on the presumption that belonging to a category implies having the characteristics considered typical of all members of that category. The psychology of decision making shows that people often do not follow normative behavioral rules. Decisions are influenced by the way a problem is framed, even when alternatives are technically the same. People also have attitudes toward risk that influence decision making. Finally, an optimistic bias can influence decisions.

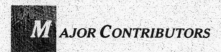 KEY TERMS

algorithm, 406

anchoring bias, 413

artificial intelligence (AI), 383

autistic thinking, 401

availability heuristic, 414

basic level, 395

belief-bias effect, 401

biased assimilation, 411

cognition, 380

cognitive bias, 412

cognitive economy, 392

cognitive model, 382

cognitive neuroscience, 383

cognitive psychology, 381

cognitive science, 382

concept, 392

concept formation, 392

critical feature, 392

Darwinian algorithm, 407

decision making, 410

deductive reasoning, 401

evoked potential, 387

functional fixedness, 404

group think, 417

heuristic, 406

inductive reasoning, 402

inference, 411

information-processing model, 382

judgment, 410

mental map, 398

mental set, 404

metacognitive knowledge, 406

optimistic bias, 417

parallel distributed processing model (PDP), 383

problem solving, 402

prototype, 392

pseudomemory, 394

reaction time, 386

realistic thinking, 401

reasoning, 401

representativeness heuristic, 414

schema, 395

script, 397

selective exposure, 412

spreading activation theory, 387

syllogism, 401

think-aloud protocol, 384

thinking, 391

MAJOR CONTRIBUTORS

Bazerman, Max, 417

Chomsky, Noam, 381

Cosmides, Leda, 409

DeLoache, Judy, 385

Flavell, John, 406

Janis, Irving, 417

John, E. R., 388

Kahneman, Daniel, 413

Newell, Allen, 381

Piaget, Jean, 381

Posner, Michael, 390

Rumelhart, David, 383

Shepard, Roger, 397

Simon, Herbert, 381

Tolman, Edward, 398

Tulving, Endel, 390

Tversky, Amos, 413

Von Neumann, John, 381

Chapter 12

Motivation

UNDERSTANDING MOTIVATION   424
   FUNCTIONS OF MOTIVATIONAL CONCEPTS
   MOTIVATIONAL CONCEPTS IN RESEARCH

   ■ INTERIM SUMMARY

THEORETICAL PERSPECTIVES   428
   CONCEPTUAL OVERVIEW
   INSTINCT THEORY
   DRIVE THEORY AND LEARNING
   AROUSAL THEORY
   HUMANISTIC THEORY OF GROWTH MOTIVATION
   SOCIAL-COGNITIVE MOTIVATIONAL THEORIES

   ■ INTERIM SUMMARY

HUNGER AND EATING   436
   WHAT REGULATES HUMAN FEEDING PATTERNS?
   OBESITY AND DIETING

   ■ INTERIM SUMMARY

SEXUAL MOTIVATION   439
   NONHUMAN SEXUAL AROUSAL
   HUMAN SEXUALITY
   THE MATING GAME: SEXUAL INVESTMENT
      STRATEGIES
   CLOSE-UP: SEXUAL ADDICTION

   ■ INTERIM SUMMARY

ACHIEVEMENT AND WORK MOTIVATION   449
   NEED FOR ACHIEVEMENT
   INDIVIDUALIST VERSUS COLLECTIVIST CULTURES
   ATTRIBUTIONS FOR SUCCESS AND FAILURE
   ATTRIBUTIONAL STYLES: OPTIMISM VERSUS
      PESSIMISM
   INTRINSIC VERSUS EXTRINSIC MOTIVATION
   WORK AND ORGANIZATIONAL PSYCHOLOGY

RECAPPING MAIN POINTS   456

KEY TERMS   457

MAJOR CONTRIBUTORS   457

"Mike, let's do El Capitán!"

Many climbers dream of scaling the majestic, domed cliff that rises 3200 feet from California's Yosemite Valley, but only a few succeed. Mark Wellman had more than the normal number of obstacles to overcome. In 1982, a fall from another Yosemite peak had paralyzed both his legs. However, seven years later, Mark announced that he would climb El Capitán.

For six months, 29-year-old Mark strengthened the muscles of his upper body with daily weight training and with many practice climbs, climbing only with his arms. Finally, he was ready to do what most others thought was impossible. In July of 1989, Mark looked up the sheer rock face at its distant summit. His friend Mike Corbett preceded him, placing the ropes that would be Mark's handholds on the arduous ascent. Mark grabbed the first rope and pulled himself up—six inches closer to his ultimate goal. He grasped the next one: another pullup; another six inches. For a week, Mike placed ropes and Mark did pullups—hundreds of pullups a day, six inches at a time.

On some afternoons, the temperature topped 100°F. The heat, however, was never as bad as the wind, which gusted fiercely between 11 A.M. and 8 P.M. every day. At times the wind pushed the men ten feet out from the cliff face, but they still persevered (*The New York Times*, 1989).

On the eighth night of their adventure, Mark and Mike tied themselves into their sleeping bags and bivouacked on a narrow ledge. The next morning they would begin their final ascent: 300 feet for Mike; 600 pullups for Mark. After a total of more than 7000 pullups, Mark's body ached in places he didn't even know existed; but the next day his pain gave way to euphoria as he pulled himself up those last inches—he had made it to the top of the mountain, the crest of El Capitán. He had achieved the impossible.

How did he feel about it? "It's great; it's fantastic. It was a really great, beautiful climb and a really wonderful experience" (*The New York Times*, 1989).

A reporter asked Mike Corbett about his scariest moment. There had been many: the wind had pushed him away from a crucial foothold; one morning he had opened his eyes to see a 3000-foot drop only centimeters from his sleeping bag; once his sweaty palms had caused him to lose his grip on a rock, on the rope, and on his friend (*Los Angeles Times*, 1989).

What motivates someone to try what others deem impossible? Having already become paralyzed from one fall, why did he choose to risk another? What distinguishes him from those of us who, with all limbs functioning, can barely roll out of bed in the morning to hit the snooze button on the alarm clock? What about Mike? What made him take on this major responsibility of helping his friend?

Centuries ago, the gallant Sir Walter Raleigh, in the company of Queen Elizabeth, wrote on a fogged windowpane, "Fain would I climb, yet fear I to fall." The Queen responded, "If thy heart fails thee, climb not at all" (Fuller, 1952).

The saga of Mark and Mike raises some of the fundamental questions about human motives that we will tackle in this chapter. What makes people act as they do? How are passive creatures energized into action? What makes us persist to attain some goals despite the high effort, pain, and financial costs involved? Why do we procrastinate too long before starting to work on some tasks or give in and quit too soon on others?

We often use the term *motivation* to represent very complex psychosocial concepts: "I didn't do well on that test because I didn't like the teacher; he just never got me motivated enough." We hear sports announcers proclaim, "They won because they wanted the win more than their overconfident, undermotivated opponents." As we read detective stories, we try to figure out the hidden motive for the crime, which will provide a clue to the culprit's identity. Millions of faithful soap opera fans glue themselves to their televisions day after day to peer into the cauldrons of seething motives—greed, power, and lust—bathed in passion-filled emotions of love, hate, jealousy, and envy.

Contemporary psychologists recognize that human actions are motivated by a variety of needs—from fundamental physiological needs to psychological needs for love, achievement, and spirituality. Even simple biological drives such as hunger may be related to needs for personal control and social acceptance that can become distorted into eating disorders. The first part of this chapter deals with the nature of motivation. First, we will explore theories, research, and applications. In the second part of the chapter, we will look in depth at three types of motivation, each important in a different way and each varying in the extent to which biological and psychological factors operate. These three are hunger, sex, and achievement and work.

Soap operas focus on basic human motivation which accounts for their popularity.

UNDERSTANDING MOTIVATION

Motivation is the general term for all the processes involved in starting, directing, and maintaining physical and psychological activities. It is a broad concept that embraces the host of internal mechanisms involved in (a) *preferences* for one activity over another; (b) *vigor*, or strength of responses; and (c) *persistence* of organized patterns of action toward relevant goals. The highly motivated person seeks out certain activities over others; practices behaviors and perfects skills required to attain the objective; and focuses energy on reaching the goal despite frustrations.

The word *motivation* comes from the Latin *movere* which means *to move*. *Action* is the fundamental property of living systems. All organisms approach some stimuli and avoid others as dictated by their appetites and aversions. Evolution favors organisms that can move toward and obtain what they need for survival and move away from or oppose what threatens them. Some appetites escalate into manias and *addictions*, dominating all other motivational systems. Some aversions become pathological fears and freeze our behavioral options. Between the extremes of frenzied action and immobility lie the motivational currents that shape the flow of our daily lives.

Dynamic psychology is the term for all psychological theories that try to understand behavior in terms of motivation. Motivation is an abstract concept and can't be seen directly. Behavior, on the other hand, is observable. To explain the behavioral changes that we can observe, we must make inferences about the underlying psychological and physiological variables that influenced those changes. These inferences about an individual's *goals, needs, wants, intentions,* and *purposes* are formalized in the concept of motivation.

Two terms that researchers frequently use are *drive* and *motive*. Psychologists usually use the label **drive** to refer to motivation that is assumed to be primarily biological, such as hunger. **Motive** refers to psychologically and socially based needs which are generally assumed to be learned through personal experience. Motives can be either *conscious* or *unconscious*, but it is not always easy to distinguish them—how do we figure out whether Mark's pain-filled push to reach the summit was a consciously competitive motive or an unconscious compensation for inadequacies his disability had created in other areas of his life?

Psychologists don't always agree on how motivational terms should be used. Some psychologists, for example, prefer to use the term *need* only in connection with biological demands (the body's need for water or oxygen). Others think *need* is also appropriate in discussing psychological requirements (as in needs for self-actualization or power). Another distinction that often surfaces among psychologists is whether the source of motivation is *person-centered* or *situation-centered*. Does it come from within the individual—from biological factors or internalized early learning—or from without—from culture, social interactions, and currently perceived stimuli?

FUNCTIONS OF MOTIVATIONAL CONCEPTS

Psychologists have used the concept of motivation for five basic purposes:

- *To account for behavioral variability.* Why might you do well on a task one day and poorly on the same task another day? Why does one child do much better at a competitive task than another child with roughly the same ability and knowledge? We use motivational explanations when the *variations* in people's performance in a constant situation cannot be traced to differences in ability, skill, practice, reinforcement history, or chance. If behavior never varied, there would be no need for motivational concepts—or, for that matter, psychology!
- *To relate biology to behavior.* The concept of motivation reminds us that we are biological organisms with complex internal mechanisms automatically regulating our bodily functioning, permitting us to survive. Deprivation states trigger these mechanisms which then motivate us through the sensations of hunger, thirst, or cold to take action to restore the body's balance.
- *To infer private states from public acts.* There are two ways to respond to someone's behavior. We can take it at face value, or we can see it as a significant symptom of an underlying emotional or motivational state. Put differently, we can respond to the *surface* or to the *latent meaning* of behavior. Sigmund Freud's belief that hidden motives instigate much of our behavior has had a profound effect on psychologists' study of motivation. Researchers in cognitive and social psychology are investigating the inferences that people make about inner and outer determinants of behavior. How do we account for our own actions and the actions of others?
- *To assign responsibility for actions.* The concept of personal responsibility is basic in law, religion, and ethics. Personal responsibility presupposes inner motivation and the ability to control one's actions. People are judged less responsible for their actions when (a) they did not intend negative consequences to occur; (b) external forces were powerful enough to provoke the behaviors; or (c) the actions were influenced by drugs, alcohol, intense emotion, or other internal influences. The concept of personal responsibility dissolves without the concept of consciously directed motivation.
- *To explain perseverance despite adversity.* Finally, motivational constructs also help us to understand why organisms can continue to perform consistently despite marked variations in stimulus conditions. Motivation gets you to work or class on time even when you're exhausted. Mark's intense desire to prove to himself and others that he could still perform the daring act of scaling a mountain wall was the result of strong motivational forces. Motivation helps you persist in playing the game to the best of your ability even when you are losing and realize that you can't possibly win.

In the 1984 Olympic Games marathon, the world watched, stunned, as the last runner staggered into the stadium long after the winner had crossed the finish line. Somehow, she was propelled forward on wobbly legs toward the finish line. Her face contorted in pain, her body bent and twisted, she doggedly pushed onward, refusing offers of help, until she had completed her mission to finish the race.

"I just hate to give up," she later told reporters. During interviews she expressed her regret that the heat had not overcome her out-

After completing the Olympic Marathon, Gabriella Anderson-Schiess staggered to the marathon finish, nearly fell, and was assisted from the track by medics, but only after she successfully completed her goal of finishing the Olympic Marathon.

side the stadium so she would have been spared the shame of her awkward, tension-filled laps in the stadium (*Los Angeles Times, 1984*).

MOTIVATIONAL CONCEPTS IN RESEARCH

Because motivation is invisible, it is a slippery concept and, if we are not careful, a *circular* one. For example, we cannot say, "He ate because he was hungry" and then offer as evidence, "He must have been hungry because he ate." To be scientifically useful, the concept of motivation must be tied both to external behavioral indicators (dependent variables) that can be measured on the output side and to observable operations (independent variables) that a researcher can perform or assess on the input side.

In his classic text, *Purposive Behavior in Animals and Men* (1932), learning theorist **Edward Tolman** was the first to describe motivation as a process that intervened between stimulus input and response output occurring inside the organism. He insisted that researchers "anchor" motivational concepts to specific manipulations and measurements. So, instead of trying to link each separate aspect of some behavior to particular stimulus input, motivational psychologists postulate an overall *intervening variable*, such as hunger, sex, or achievement, that interrelates antecedents and consequences. In addition, researchers sometimes begin with a motivational construct based on their theories

and then search for valid ways to manipulate and measure it. **Figure 12.1** outlines how motivation as an intervening variable links stimulus input and response output.

Behavioral Indicators of Motivation

Many different behaviors have been used as indicators of motivation and its strength. Among them are (a) activity level; (b) rate of learning (with practice held constant); (c) final level of performance reached; (d) response's resistance to extinction; (e) interference with ongoing activities (the disruptive effect of high levels of motivation); (f) choices of tasks, goals, rewards; and (g) consummatory behavior (for example, amount eaten).

A Shocking Tale In the late 1920s, Columbia University psychologist C. J. Warden assessed the relative strengths of various drives by means of an *obstruction box*. This apparatus used an electrified grid to separate a deprived rat from incentives it could see on the other side of the grid. The incentives included food, water, a sexually responsive mate, and the rat's offspring. The behavioral index of drive strength was the number of times the animal would cross the hot grid in a given period of time. (Another appropriate index could have been the highest level of shock intensity the rat would tolerate to reach the goal.) **Figure 12.2** shows the typical data obtained with this method.

FIGURE 12.1 MOTIVATION AS AN INTERVENING VARIABLE

Any particular motivation, such as hunger, is assumed to be the result of a number of physiological and/or psychological variables. Motivation may lead to one or more of the kinds of response output shown. The intervening variable links the input conditions to the output consequences that are observable, manipulable, or measurable.

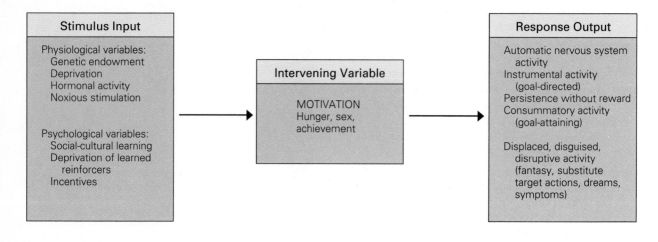

FIGURE 12.2

BEHAVIORAL ASSESSMENT OF THE RELATIVE STRENGTHS OF PRIMARY DRIVES

In reaction to various incentives on the other side, rats crossed an electrified grid in the Columbia obstruction box. Their deprivation level was manipulated by time. For thirst and hunger performance reached a peak and then declined as the animals became debilitated. Sexual motivation peaked soon and remained steady throughout the study. Mothers separated from their offspring showed the highest level of motivation by enduring the most electric shocks to reach their offspring after only a brief period of deprivation.

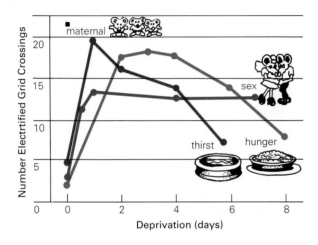

The motivating effects of thirst (and hunger) were greatest after a short period of deprivation but then declined when water or food deprivation became extreme. This function was not found in two cases, however. With a little sex as a reward, sex-deprived rats kept running at a constant rate (after the first few hours). Child-deprived mother rats endured the most suffering, running most often across the hot grid even with a minimal period of social deprivation. This was interpreted as evidence for the existence of a powerful maternal drive.

Self-reports and Projective Tests   Human motivation can be assessed with self-reports and projective tests. Researchers may ask participants to fill out questionnaires evaluating their own needs, desires, and anxieties and use the scores as indicators of strength of motivation. These scores can then be correlated with behavioral measures. In other research, subjects create stories about ambiguous pictures, and researchers use content analysis of these themes to reveal different types of needs.

In a study correlating self-reports and behavior, **Janet Taylor** (1951) measured students' levels of anxi-

ety on a standardized questionnaire and then exposed them to an eyelid conditioning situation in which the stimulus was an air puff to the eye. Subjects who were high in anxiety as measured by the questionnaire acquired the conditioned eyelid response faster than those whose anxiety was low. The investigator reasoned that high anxiety increased the intensity and, hence, the aversive motivational value of the unconditioned stimulus. This caused the high-anxiety subjects to respond more strongly than the low-anxiety subjects (see **Figure 12.3**).

Manipulating Drives and Motives

This study, which related existing individual differences in self-reported anxiety to speed of conditioning, was a *correlational study*. Often researchers studying motivation want to see the way *changes* in motivation cause changes in behavior. To do so, they must use an *experimental design,* in which conditions are manipulated to induce the motivational state or make it stronger or weaker. The three general procedures used to induce or change drive states are *lesioning, deprivation,* and *stimulation*.

Lesioning is an operation that destroys selected brain tissue assumed to be responsible for some aspect of motivation. For example, in studies of animal hunger mechanisms, lesioning one part of the hypothalamus led satiated rats to overeat, while lesions to a nearby part caused them to refuse food when extremely deprived.

FIGURE 12.3

THE EFFECT OF ANXIETY ON CONDITIONING

Anxious subjects conditioned more rapidly than subjects whose pre-measured anxiety level was low on an aversive eyelid conditioning task.

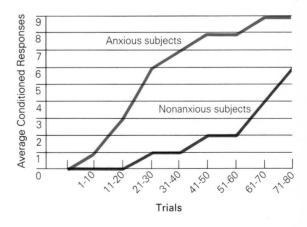

Deprivation for animal subjects may involve denial of food, water, sex, or specific substances such as salt or calcium. The variety of drives tested in the Columbia obstruction box were induced by deprivation. For human subjects, deprivation may involve withholding desired psychological conditions. For instance, social deprivation is assumed to be an aversive state that will motivate people to do something to end it (Schachter, 1957).

Stimulation to trigger motivation may involve giving aversive stimuli, such as shocks, noise, heat, or cold, which lead to responses of avoidance, escape, or disruption of ongoing task performance. Motivation may also be triggered by direct electrical or chemical stimulation to specific regions of the brain. (In studies of hunger, stimulation to selected areas of the hypothalamus had the *opposite* effect of lesioning.) Stimuli leading to affectively positive states may also be investigated—for example, exposure to erotic visual stimuli arouses the sex drive. Barriers, unsolvable tasks, and competition are other stimulus conditions that researchers have used in studies of human motivation.

Incentive Motivation

External stimuli can motivate us independently of our inner states. The sight of a refrigerator, a beverage ad on TV, a beautiful person, or the smell of certain foods can arouse us to take appropriate actions even when we are not impelled from within by thirst, sex, or hunger drives. External stimuli such as these, which make us anticipate rewards, are called **incentives.**

Incentive motivation refers to the activating and energizing effect that stimuli, by promising a reward, can have on us. Although in animal research incentives always involve external stimuli, with humans incentive motivation may be self-induced by mental imagery. For climbers Mark and Mike, the incentive motivation was, in part, the perception that the distance between them and the summit was decreasing. Incentive motivation can also be induced by *negative incentives,* such as not wanting to get punished for doing drugs, being ashamed to drop out of the marathon, or being ashamed to stagger through the last lap of the marathon.

SUMMING UP

Motivation is a general, dynamic concept explaining the processes involved in starting, directing, sustaining, and stopping behavior. It includes mechanisms that affect preferences for goals and activities, vigor of responses, and persistence of organized patterns of action toward relevant goals. Motivational analysis in psychology serves various purposes, such as relating biological and behavioral

processes and helping to explain why people persevere despite obstacles and adversity.

When used in research, motivation acts as an intervening variable that links a host of measurable, manipulatable independent variables with observable responses from dependent variables. The strength of motivation is measured through index variables, such as activity level, rate, and amount of learning, resistance of a response to extinction, preferences, and consummatory behavior. With humans, self reports and projective tests assess different types and degrees of motivation. Motivation has been manipulated in research by lesioning, stimulation, and deprivation procedures. Incentive motivation is at work when the organism is aroused by external stimuli of desired goal objects or by aversive stimuli.

THEORETICAL PERSPECTIVES

Psychologists have sought to explain the source of animal and human behavior with a host of different theories. After a brief historical overview of the way these theories were developed and the reason some ended up on the cutting room floor, we will look in more detail at some of the most influential motivational theories (Cofer, 1988).

CONCEPTUAL OVERVIEW

For centuries, philosophers made a distinction between humans who were guided in their actions by reason and free will and nonhumans whose actions were determined by "brute appetites." Darwin's theory of evolution challenged this dichotomy, paving the way for a theory in which instincts stimulated human as well as animal behavior. The theory of evolution had a lasting effect on the study of the psychology of motivation: it inspired psychologists to look at the *adaptation* or *adjustment* of all creatures to their environment as a motivational factor. This view was embraced by *functional psychologists,* who introduced the concept of motivation into psychology. These psychologists were concerned with the way the mind functions in the interests of the organism's well-being—namely, in its adaptiveness.

The *instinct theory* of functional psychologists fell into disfavor for a number of reasons and was replaced in the 1930s and 1940s by *drive theory.* According to drive theory, a passive organism seeking homeostatic balance is impelled to action by drives. Animals and humans learn new responses when their actions reduce the intensity of drives that motivate them. However, drive theory was discarded because it failed to explain actions that increased arousal instead of reducing drives.

Acknowledging nonhomeostatic drives, such as seeking stimulation or curiosity, led to the concept of *optimal arousal level* and to *arousal theory,* in which variations in individual arousal level are the source of motivation. Arousal theory had weaknesses that limited its utility, but it contributed important ideas to the development of subsequent theories.

Social psychologists of the Gestalt tradition, such as Kurt Lewin, proposed an analysis of motivation as *tension systems* arising from the discrepancy between the person's current place in his or her life space and perceived distant goals. Fritz Heider, another social psychologist, contributed to motivational theory through his concern for the way laypersons make *attributions of causality* for their behavior and that of others. The cognitively oriented psychologists such as Julian Rotter expanded motivational theory by considering the effects of different perceptions of external versus internal *locus of control.*

While many of these motivational theories centered on deficiencies and tensions in passive human actors, humanistic theories of self-actualization emphasized *growth motivation.* Humanist Abraham Maslow's descriptive analysis of the hierarchy of human needs gave human nature an inner imperative for developing to its full potential once basic needs were satisfied.

With this background sketch in mind, let's take a closer look at these five general theoretical perspectives on motivation: instinct theory, drive theory, arousal theory, humanist growth theory, and social-cognitive theory.

INSTINCT THEORY

According to instinct theory, organisms are born with certain preprogrammed tendencies that are essential for the survival of their species. Some instinct theorists have seen this biological force as *mechanistic*. According to them, behavior is determined without purpose and beyond individual control, similar to a complex reflex. Others believe that instincts allow an organism some choice among different courses of action.

Animals engage in regular cycles of activity that enable their species to survive. Salmon swim thousands of miles back to the exact stream where they were spawned, leaping up waterfalls until they come to the right spot, where the surviving males and females engage in ritualized courtship and mating. Fertilized eggs are deposited, the parents die, and, in time, their young swim downstream to live in the ocean until, a few years later, it is time for them to return to complete their part in this continuing drama. Similarly remarkable activities can be reported for most species of animals. Bees communicate the location of food to other bees, army ants go on highly synchronized hunting expeditions,

Salmon swim thousands of miles back to the exact stream where they were spawned.

birds build nests, and spiders spin complex webs—exactly as their parents and ancestors did.

Originally, instinct theorists were content to describe instincts in terms of mysterious inner forces that impelled certain activities to emerge. Today, instincts in animals are usually studied as **fixed-action patterns.** Ethologists study in detail the eliciting stimuli, environmental conditions, developmental stages, and specific response sequences in different animal species in their natural habitat.

However, to study the internal mechanisms underlying certain survival behaviors, researchers must turn to experimental situations where critical variables may be controlled and quantified. For example, to survive, primates must detect danger quickly and activate appropriate defensive behaviors. These behaviors appear to originate from genetic programming and are similar in infant rhesus monkeys and human infants. Both show a fearfulness of strangers at a given age (2–4 months for the rhesus; 7–9 months for the babies). Through experience, both refine their understanding of danger, responding more selectively.

A laboratory experiment of defensive behaviors in infant rhesus monkeys found three behavioral patterns, each controlled by a different neurotransmitter substance. When separated from their mothers, the infants made loud *cooing* sounds, a signal to help their mothers locate them. When faced with the threat of a silent, human intruder who did not make eye contact, the infants *froze*. This reaction reduces danger in the natural environment where movement is a stimulus for predatory attack. When the human stared at the separated infant, it *barked* at him in an aggressive display that often discourages attackers. Administration of various drugs that manipulated different neurotransmitters selectively blocked each of these defensive behaviors (Kalin & Shelton, 1989).

Experiments such as this lead researchers to better understand how neurochemical brain mechanisms work with environmental cues to orchestrate patterns of behavior necessary for animal and human survival. Three functional psychologists—William James, William McDougall, and Sigmund Freud—explored these patterns of behavior.

William James, writing in 1890, stated his belief that humans rely on even more instincts than lower animals do to guide their behavior. In addition to the biological instincts they share with animals, a host of human social instincts, such as sympathy, modesty, sociability, and love, come into play. For James, both human and animal instincts were *purposive*—they served important purposes in the organism's adaptation to its environment.

This view of the vital role of human instincts was extended by psychologist **William McDougall.** McDougall (1908) defined instincts as inherited dispositions that had three components: a general *energizing* aspect, an *action* aspect, and *goal directedness*. However, he viewed human nature as basically immoral and egoistic; "moralization" by society was required to bring base individual nature under social control.

Sigmund Freud (1915) had a somewhat different view of instinct, though hardly more flattering to humanity. Freud thought instincts—life instincts (including sexuality) and death instincts (including aggression)—had neither conscious purpose nor predetermined direction, and that organisms could learn many different means of satisfying them. He believed that instinctive urges exist to satisfy bodily needs, and that they create a *psychic energy*. This tension drives us toward activities or objects that will reduce the tension. Although Freud assumed that instincts operated largely below the level of consciousness, he also knew that they affected our conscious thoughts and feelings as well as our actions, and that, frequently, they put us in conflict with society's demands. Indeed, the Freudian individual is seemingly always in some state of intrapsychic

conflict, which is one reason for considering Freudian theory the most dynamic of all motivational theories.

By the 1920s, lists of over 10,000 human instincts were being compiled by psychologists (Bernard, 1924). Humans were soon seen as superior to animals, because they had more instincts and the power to reason. At this same time, however, the notion of instincts as universal explanations for human behavior was beginning to stagger under the weight of critical attacks. Researchers were pointing out that instincts were not really explanations at all, were not really universal, and did not provide a useful explanation of behavior because they overemphasized fixed, inborn mechanisms although much behavior was clearly modifiable by learning. While instincts were being postulated to explain every action, instinct theorists named every action but explained nothing (Beach, 1955).

Meanwhile crosscultural anthropologists, such as Ruth Benedict (1959) and Margaret Mead (1939), had found enormous behavioral variation between cultures. This finding contradicted the instinct theories that considered only the universals of inborn instincts. Most damaging to the early instinct notions, however, were behaviorist empirical demonstrations that important behaviors and emotions were learned rather than inborn. All but Freud's instinct theory died on the vine. (Freud's instinct doctrine fared better because it was part of his psychoanalytic theory, which many psychologists, using psychoanalysis to treat mental disorders, embraced uncritically.)

DRIVE THEORY AND LEARNING

The concept of motivation as an *inner* drive that determines behavior was introduced into psychology by **Robert Woodworth** (1918), another functionalist who had studied with James. Woodworth defined *drive* in biological terms as energy released from an organism's store; it was *nonspecific energy,* blind to direction. *Drive* was the fuel of action, called forth by initiating stimuli and made available for goal-directed activities. Other mechanisms, such as perceptual and learning processes, guided action in appropriate directions.

Drive theory was most fully developed by Yale University theorist **Clark Hull** (1943, 1952). Hull believed that motivation was necessary for learning to occur, and learning was essential for successful adaptation to the environment. Similar to Freud, Hull emphasized the role of *tension* in motivation; he believed that *tension reduction* was reinforcing. In his view, primary drives were biologically based, aroused when the organism was deprived. These drives activated the organism; when they were satisfied, or reduced, the organism ceased acting. This homeostatic, drive-reduction theory

Humans and animals often participate in activities to increase stimulation.

of motivation and learning was influential until the mid-1950s when it was challenged by new data that it couldn't handle. This data showed that humans and animals often do things in the absence of any apparent deprivation, homeostatic drives, or their reduction to increase stimulation—they play and exhibit exploratory and manipulative behaviors.

Recall the rats in the Columbia Obstruction Box. Without deprivation of any kind, the animals still crossed the hot grid a few times. They crossed the painful barrier even when there was nothing on the other side—except a novel environment. In later research on curiosity motivation, rats deprived of food or water that were placed in a novel environment with plenty of opportunities everywhere to eat or drink, chose to explore instead. Only after they had first satisfied their curiosity, did they begin to satisfy their hunger and thirst (Zimbardo & Montgomery, 1957; Berlyne, 1960; Fowler, 1965). A similar type of motivation, considered to be a *manipulation drive,* was reported in a series of studies in which young monkeys spent much time and energy manipulating gadgets and new objects in their environment, apparently for the sheer pleasure of "monkeying around," without any extrinsic rewards (Harlow et al., 1950).

AROUSAL THEORY

Arousal is a measure of the general responsiveness of an organism to activation of the brainstem's *reticular system.* Arousal theory emerged from several converging sources. One source was the concept of emergency reactions to stress situations. Physiological psychologist Walter Cannon postulated that certain emotions, such as fear and rage, prepare us for or motivate us to action when we are faced with danger. A set of bodily changes that can be measured accompanies these arousal reactions. A second source of arousal theory was research on brain mechanisms along with the widespread use of EEG recordings of sleep, which encouraged psychologists to focus on the ways arousal of the brain prepares individuals to respond to stimuli. The third source were the results of a series of studies relating performance to level of motivation. For the hungry and thirsty subjects in the Columbia Obstruction Box, as motivation increased, the curve of performance first rose and then later declined. This pattern, an *inverted U-shaped function,* suggests that too little or too much motivation may impair performance. It also implies that there is an *optimal arousal level* for best performance.

The concept of **optimal arousal** has been used in several ways. First, it has been used to identify the way motivational intensity and performance vary with tasks of different difficulty. Second, it has been used to account for the fact that some people (and animals) will sometimes work to *increase* their arousal, seeking stimulation rather than trying to reduce it.

Some tasks are best approached with high levels of motivation and others with more moderate levels. On some tasks, performance is highest when motivation is relatively low. The key to the level of motivation is *task difficulty.* With difficult or complex tasks, the optimal level of arousal for success is on the low end of the motivation continuum. As the difficulty decreases and the task becomes simpler, the optimal level of motivation—the level required to perform most effectively—is greater. This relationship has been formalized in the **Yerkes-Dodson law,** which says that performance of difficult tasks decreases as arousal increases, while performance of easy tasks increases as arousal increases (Yerkes & Dodson, 1908). See **Figure 12.4** for an illustration of this principle.

There are *individual differences* in optimal arousal level—variations in how much arousal different people feel or need in order to function most effectively. Some people seem to need high levels of stimulation and work best in tension-filled settings that would make most people ineffective. They may even put pressure on themselves to increase the arousal level, knowing that greater arousal will help them succeed. Football quarterback Joe Montana, of the winning San Francisco Forty-Niners, exemplifies the ability to maintain a cool composure in the final minutes of dozens of tense games, rallying his team to come from behind and win. Some individuals are more sensation-seeking than others (Zuckerman et al., 1980). Individuals who like a higher level of stimulation relish risky activities such as skydiving or motorcycle racing and may use drugs to intensify sensations. However, these individuals are likely to be vulnerable for addiction to substances and to destructive behaviors that give them high intensity reactions.

Experience affects our response to stimulation. As experience makes us jaded, what used to arouse us may

Cool Joe Montana

FIGURE 12.4   *THE YERKES-DODSON LAW*

Performance varies with motivation level and task difficulty. For easy or simple tasks, a higher level of motivation increases performance effectiveness. However, for difficult or complex tasks, a lower level of motivation is optimal. A moderate level of motivation is generally best for tasks of moderate difficulty. These inverted u-shaped functions show that performance is worst at both low and high extremes of motivation.

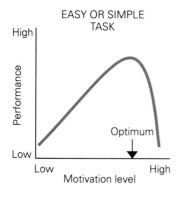

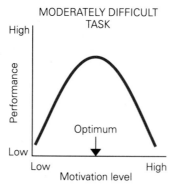

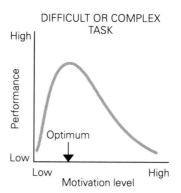

leave us indifferent or bored. Over time, most events become less stimulating, motivating us to seek a greater arousal level in more exciting stimuli (Zuckerman, 1979). On the other hand, when arousal is too high, we act to reduce the amount of stimulation (Maddi, 1980). There is some optimal level of arousal for each organism—below it, stimulation is sought and above it, stimulation is avoided.

Arousal theory generated these new research perspectives, but it didn't hold up as a general theory because different measures of physiological arousal did not correlate well with each other. In addition, REM sleep was found to be filled with intense brain activity even though it was believed to be the anchor of the low end of the arousal continuum.

HUMANISTIC THEORY OF GROWTH MOTIVATION

Humanist psychologist **Abraham Maslow** (1970) formulated a theory of human motivation that explains both tension-reducing and tension-increasing actions. Maslow contrasted **deficiency motivation,** in which individuals seek to restore physical or psychological equilibrium, and **growth motivation,** in which individuals do more than reduce deficits as they seek to realize their fullest potential. Growth-motivated people may welcome uncertainty, an increase in tension, and even pain if they see it as a route toward greater fulfillment of their potential and as a way to achieve their goals. Thus, for example, a person who voluntarily suffers for a religious or political cause may accept pain or humiliation as a necessary part of changing prevailing attitudes and institutions. He or she suffers to achieve meaningful goals that fit with personal values.

Maslow's theory holds that our basic needs form a **needs hierarchy,** as illustrated in **Figure 12.5.** Our inborn needs are arranged in a sequence of stages from primitive to advanced. At the bottom of this hierarchy are the basic *biological needs,* such as hunger and thirst. They must be satisfied before any other needs can begin to operate. When biological needs are pressing, other needs are put on hold and are unlikely to influence our actions; but when they are reasonably well satisfied, the needs at the next level—*safety needs*—motivate us. When we are no longer concerned about danger, we become motivated by *attachment needs*—needs to belong, to affiliate with others, to love, and to be loved. If we are well fed and safe and if we feel a sense of social belonging, we move up to *esteem needs*. These include the needs to like oneself, to see oneself as competent and effective, and to do what is necessary to earn the esteem of others.

Humans are thinking beings, with complex brains

FIGURE 12.5   MASLOW'S HIERARCHY OF NEEDS

According to Maslow, needs at the lower level of the hierarchy dominate an individual's motivation as long as they are unsatisfied. Once these are adequately satisfied, the higher needs occupy the individual's attention.

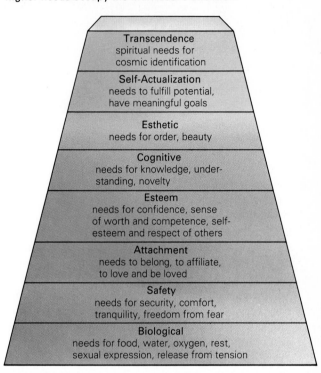

that demand the stimulation of thought. We are motivated by strong *cognitive needs* to know our past, to comprehend the puzzles of current existence, and to predict the future. It is the force of these needs that enables scholars and scientists to spend their lives in the quest of discovering new knowledge. At the next level of Maslow's hierarchy, comes the human desire for beauty and order, in the form of *esthetic needs* that give rise to the creative side of humanity. At the top of the hierarchy, are people who are nourished, safe, loved and loving, secure, thinking, and creating. These people have moved beyond basic human needs in the quest for fullest development of their potentials, or *self-actualization*. A self-actualizing person is self-aware, self-accepting, socially responsive, creative, spontaneous, and open to novelty and challenge, among other positive attributes. Maslow's hierarchy includes a step beyond the total fulfillment of individual potential. *Needs for transcendence* may lead to higher states of consciousness and a cosmic vision of one's part in the universe. Very few people develop the desire to move beyond the self to achieve union with spiritual forces.

Abraham Maslow (*Discovering Psychology,* 1990, Program 12)

Maslow argues that at each level the need is inborn, although family values and culture affect the way it is elicited and expressed. *Pathology* may result when needs at any level are frustrated. Frustrated love needs, for example, can lead to hostility and perversions of sexuality, while frustrated esteem needs can result in painful shyness or self-destructive behavior patterns.

Maslow's theory has had more influence on therapy and education than on psychological research. For Maslow, as for his fellow humanistic psychologist Carl Rogers (1959), the central motivational force for humans is the innate need to grow and actualize one's highest potentials. Other psychologists have suggested that self-actualization motivation is essentially the motivation to be open to new experiences, ideas, and feelings and to explore one's external and mental environments. Because anxiety and guilt inhibit this positive growth motivation, freedom from deficiency motivation is essential for personal competence and fulfillment to occur.

Such an upbeat approach was welcomed by many psychologists who had fed on the earlier diet of negative motivational views. Accentuating the positive fit a new orientation toward helping normal people achieve their potential, rather than just making disturbed people less able to do so.

Harvard psychologists **Henry Murray** and **David McClelland** used a special projective technique called the **thematic apperception test** (TAT) to identify a limited number of human motives that are central in people's lives. Subjects were asked to generate stories in response to a series of ambiguous drawings. Inferences from these resulting projections, or themes of personal needs, uncovered many positive human motives similar to the ones Maslow described. However, mingled with these positive needs were needs that could demean human nature, such as those for abasement, self-blame, and humiliation. Many of the story themes centered on needs for power, dominance, and aggression. This was hardly the stuff of Maslow's higher levels of human potential.

SOCIAL-COGNITIVE MOTIVATIONAL THEORIES

Consider the *Wizard of Oz* as a psychological study of motivation. Dorothy and her three friends work hard to get to the Emerald City, overcoming barriers, persisting against all adversaries. They do so because they expect the Wizard to give them what they are missing; but the wise Wizard makes them aware that they, not he, always had the power to change their deficiencies to fulfill wishes. For Dorothy, *home* is not a place but a feeling of security, of comfort with people she loves, wherever her heart is. The courage the Lion wants, the intelligence the Scarecrow longs for, and the emotions the Tin Man dreams of, are attributes they already possess; they need only to think about them differently—not as internal conditions but as positive ways they are already relating to others. After all, did they not demonstrate those qualities on the journey to Oz, a journey motivated by little more than an *expectation,* an idea about the future likelihood of getting something they wanted? The Wizard of Oz was clearly the first cognitive psychologist.

Cognitive approaches are currently being used by many psychologists to account for what motivates a variety of personal and social behaviors. They all share the Wizard's point of view: the concept that significant human motivation comes not from objective realities but from our *subjective interpretation* of them. The reinforcing effect of a reward is lost if we don't *perceive* that our actions obtained it. What we do now is often controlled by what we *think* was responsible for our past successes and failures, by what we *believe* is possible for us to do, and by what we *anticipate* the outcome of an action will be. Cognitive approaches to motivation put higher mental processes such as these in charge of the acting self—rather than physiological arousal, biological mechanisms, or physical stimulus features. These approaches explain why human beings are often more motivated by imagined future events than by stimulus factors in the immediate environment.

German social psychologist **Kurt Lewin** (1936) introduced the notion that perceiving a *discrepancy* between one's current position and another condition—such as a task to be completed, a desired goal, or a group standard—can have motivating effects. Lewin believed that such perceived discrepancies create intrapersonal tension states that motivate behavior to reduce the discrepancy by completing the task, attaining the goal, or conforming with the group norm.

The Wizard of Oz can be viewed as a psychological study of motivation.

Lewin's student, **Leon Festinger,** carried the motivating effect of discrepancy into his theory of *cognitive dissonance* (1957). According to his theory, discrepancy between beliefs, attitudes, and behavior gives rise to a motivational state of dissonance which we then attempt to reduce by changing one or more of the discrepant elements.

The importance of *expectations* in motivating behavior was developed by **Julian Rotter** in his *social-learning theory* (1954). For Rotter, the probability that we will engage in a given behavior (studying for an exam instead of partying) is determined by our *expectation* of attaining a goal (getting a good grade) that follows the activity and by the *personal value* of that goal. Expectation of a future happening is based on our past reinforcement history which, in turn, has helped us develop a personal sense of locus of control. A **locus of control orientation** is a belief that the outcomes of our actions are contingent on what we do *(internal control orientation)* or on events outside our personal control *(external control orientation).*

Fritz Heider (1958) postulated that the outcome of our behavior (a poor grade, for example) can be attributed to *dispositional forces,* such as lack of effort or insufficient intelligence, or to *situational forces,* such as an unfair test or a biased teacher. These attributions influence the way we will behave; we are likely to try harder next time if we see our poor grade as a result of our lack of effort, but we may give up if we see it resulting from injustice or lack of ability (Dweck, 1975). These ideas have been developed at length in *attribution theory* (presented in Chapter 16).

We have sampled general theories of motivation. In the next section, we will take a closer look at three very different motives that influence our lives: hunger, sexual motivation, and work and achievement motivation.

SUMMING UP

Psychologists have advanced many different theoretical views to understand the nature of motivated behavior, but none have been completely satisfactory. The Darwinian revolution inspired instinct theory which sought to account for complex response patterns of both lower animals and humans. According to instinct theory, motivation is inborn, mechanistic, and mindless.

Under a critical barrage from all sides, instinct theory gave way to drive theory, which was popular during the behaviorist era when the study of animal learning was fashionable. The central idea of drive theory was that tension from primary or acquired drives led to new responses. Responses that lead to tension reduction are learned and retained. This homeostatic theory could not account for behavior motivated by arousal-seeking and nonhomeostatic actions in curiosity and play. Arousal theory dealt with the notion that humans and animals apparently prefer some optimal level of arousal. The Yerkes-Dodson law states that arousal and performance are related in a curvilinear fashion.

Humanistic approaches to motivation, such as that of Abraham Maslow, postulate a hierarchy of needs arranged from the most basic survival needs to those that are more human, such as social, cognitive, and esthetic needs. As individuals seek to grow in their humanness and reach their fullest potential, other needs come into play, such as those for esteem, actualization, and transcendence. Social and cognitive psychologists have influenced psychological thinking about motives by emphasizing individual perception of the situation and the subjective interpretation of the causes of behavior. These causal attributions can motivate or depress responding, at times even more so than the actual stimulus-based, causal source.

 ## HUNGER AND EATING

The primary drives, such as hunger and thirst, represent the body's way of keeping its long-running show on the road even when there isn't time for everyone to learn their roles. Of the body's many homeostatic mechanisms for maintaining optimal internal conditions, those involved in hunger motivation are among the more complex. Biological regulation by certain brain areas, neurotransmitters, hormones, and bodily organs works in tandem with mental, behavioral, and social processes to control the organism's motivation to start and to stop eating.

WHAT REGULATES HUMAN FEEDING PATTERNS?

To regulate food intake effectively, organisms must be equipped with mechanisms that accomplish four tasks: (a) detect internal food need; (b) initiate and organize eating behavior; (c) monitor the quantity and quality of the food eaten; and (d) detect when enough food has been consumed and stop eating. Researchers have tried to understand these processes by relating them either to *peripheral* mechanisms in different parts of the body, such as stomach contractions, or to *central* brain mechanisms, such as the functioning of the hypothalamus. Although hunger is probably the most studied drive, our understanding of it—especially in humans—is still incomplete. What do we know about the motivational dynamics of hunger?

Peripheral Cues: Hunger Pangs

Where do sensations of hunger come from? Does your stomach rumble and send out distress signals—pangs and cramps? A pioneering physiologist, **Walter Cannon** (1934), believed that localized sensations of hunger from gastric activity in an empty stomach were the sole basis for hunger. He believed that an empty stomach created disagreeable stimulation, or cramps, that triggered activity directed toward filling the stomach and turning off these disagreeable stimuli.

Cannon tested his *peripheral cues hypothesis* in an interesting demonstration on his student, A. L. Washburn. Washburn trained himself to swallow an uninflated balloon attached to a rubber tube. The other end of the tube was attached to a device that recorded changes in air pressure. Cannon then inflated the balloon in Washburn's stomach; as the student's stomach contracted, air was expelled from the balloon and deflected the recording pen. Reports of Washburn's hunger pangs were correlated with periods when his stomach was severely contracted but not when it was distended. Cannon thought he had proved that stomach cramps were responsible for hunger (Cannon & Washburn, 1912). He went further, arguing that *local stimulation* was the basis of all biological drives. Cannon advocated looking to the body's peripheral mechanisms to understand the nature of hunger, thirst, sex, and other basic drives.

Cannon had only established a *correlation,* not a *causal* connection. Although hunger pangs accompanied stomach contractions, maybe something else was causing both of those responses. Sure enough, later research showed that stomach contractions are not even a necessary condition for hunger. Injections of sugar into the bloodstream will stop the stomach contractions but not the hunger of an animal with an empty stomach. Human patients who have had their stomachs entirely removed still experience hunger pangs (Janowitz & Grossman, 1950), and rats without stomachs still learn mazes when rewarded with food (Penick et al., 1963). So, although sensations originating in the stomach may play a role in the way we usually experience hunger, they do not explain how the body detects its need for food and is motivated to eat.

A Multiple-system Approach

For many years researchers used models of central regulation, trying to identify "brain hunger centers" that were responsible for the arousal and cessation of hunger and eating mechanisms. However, that view also proved too limited. The current view of hunger and eating uses a complex biological and psychological model. This *multiple-system approach* begins by specifying that the brain works in association with many other systems, both biological and psychological, to gather information about an organism's energy requirements, nutritional state, acquired hungers, and food preferences, as well as information about social-cultural demands on the person. The brain sends signals to neural, hormonal, organ, and muscle systems to start or stop food seeking and eating.

The brain region primarily involved in the control of eating is the *lateral hypothalamus,* while a separate brain area nearby, the *ventromedial hypothalamus,* controls cessation or inhibition of eating. This *dual-hypothalamic mechanism,* together with many inputs and related processes, starts and stops our eating.

Table 12.1 summarizes many of the factors believed to be involved in the complex regulation of hunger detection, feeding, and satiation. In general, the biological systems are responsive to an organism's energy needs and nutritional state. The psychological systems account for acquired food preferences and are responsive to social, emotional, and environmental stimuli that make eating, in general, and specific foods, in particular, either desirable or aversive. We can only touch briefly on the features of each factor.

Sugar (in the form of glucose in the blood) and fat are the energy sources for metabolism. Evidently, the two basic signals that initiate eating come from receptors that monitor the levels of sugar and fat in the blood. When blood glucose is low or unavailable for metabo-

lism, signals from liver cell receptors are sent to the *lateral hypothalamus* where certain neurons acting as glucose detectors change their activity in response to this information. When blood glucose levels fall there is an immediate effect on reported hunger in healthy adults. Other hypothalamic neurons may detect changes in free fatty acids and insulin levels in the blood. Together, these neurons appear to activate appetitive systems in the lateral zone of the hypothalamus and initiate eating behavior (Thompson & Campbell, 1977).

With free access to food, adult animals and humans will maintain a stable body weight over their lifetime at a level consistent for them. Most organisms have a tightly and efficiently controlled process of balancing nutritive intake with energy expenditures. An internal biological scale weighs the fat in the body and keeps the central nervous system informed. Whenever fats stored in specialized fat cells fall below a certain level, termed

TABLE 12.1 MULTIPLE-SYSTEM MODEL SUMMARIZING FACTORS CONTROLLING HUNGER AND FEEDING

Mechanisms Controlling Eating (integrated by lateral hypothalamus)	Mechanisms Controlling Not Eating (integrated by ventromedial hypothalamus)*

Factors of Biological Origin
Nutritional deficiencies
  Low levels of blood glucose (sugar)
  High levels of fatty acids in the blood
    —both stimulate lateral hypothalamus
Set point (level) of stored fats
    —when below critical set point, food
      seeking initiated
	Factors of Biological Origin
	Metabolic signals
	  High levels of blood glucose
	  Low levels of fatty acids
	Peripheral signals
	  Full stomach, monitored by pressure
	    detectors, stimulates ventromedial
	    hypothalamus
	  Taste cues from unpalatable foods induce
	    rejection reflex
	Set point signals
	  Level of stored body fat reaches critical set
	    point of satiety, stimulating
	    ventromedial hypothalamus

Factors of Psychological Origin
Specific hunger
    —learned preference for diets containing
      substances (salt, calcium, etc.) they lack
Stress-induced eating
Socially stimulated eating
    —family and cultural eating rituals;
      symbolically significant food
	Factors of Psychological Origin
	Fear
	Conditioned food aversions
	Conditioned satiety
	Cultural pressures toward slimness, dieting
	Mental disorders, such as anorexia

Factors of Mixed Origin
Sensory clues
    —sensory input to central nervous system
      elicits reflexes activating autonomic
      nervous system, preparing for digestion,
      metabolism, storage
    —palatability of food *maintains* eating by
      eliciting reflexes in brain that stimulate
      the lateral hypothalamus
Anticipatory activities
    —eating that prevents depletion
	*Includes short-term (stop eating) controls and long-term (suppression between meals) controls

the **critical set point,** eat signals are sent out (Keesey & Powley, 1975). This internal set point exerts a major influence on the amount people eat and on their weight.

Besides eating to *satisfy* hunger, we eat to *prevent* it. Observations of free-ranging animals in their native habitat suggest that they do what you probably do: eat *before* hunger sets in. Predators invest enormous energy in hunting for prey before hunger weakens them. Similarly, many species gather, store, and hoard food. These strategies *prevent depletion* instead of making up for a deficiency already present (Collier et al., 1972). Many of the mechanisms that stop eating are similar to those that start it, but they work through the *ventromedial hypothalamus* and rely on an opposite set of cues. *Short-term inhibitors* terminate ongoing feeding and *long-term inhibitors* suppress eating activities between meals.

High glucose levels and low levels of free fatty acids in the blood are signals that the set point has been reached; but even before this nutritional information is processed by the brain, several peripheral cues are signaling stop. Pressure detectors in the stomach signal distension, while unpleasant taste cues can induce a *rejection reflex* (including vomiting).

Similar to eating, inhibition of eating is influenced by a host of emotional and learned psychological processes, some occurring during a meal and some between meals. For example, humans and animals do not eat when they are fearful. In addition, animals do not eat much of a new food; they'll sample a bit, then wait for several hours before eating more if no illness has developed. This protective reaction is known as *bait-shyness*. Just as some cultural influences encourage eating as an important social ritual, others discourage it—in this culture, ultrathin fashion models remind women how they are supposed to look, an ideal that becomes distorted in two self-destructive eating syndromes: *anorexia* and *bulimia*. These serious disorders, so prevalent among female college students, involve issues of personal control of one's body and are often linked to self-image and sexual attitudes.

OBESITY AND DIETING

People programmed to be obese have more *fat cells* (adipose tissue) than people of normal weight as a result of either genetic factors or overfeeding at critical periods in infancy (Brownell, 1982; Sjørstrøm, 1980). Beyond infancy, dieting or overeating changes the *size* of the fat cells, but not their *number*. The number of fat cells a person has remains constant throughout life. Consequently, someone with a large number of fat cells who diets will lose weight and may become skinny. However, the person will still have the same critical set point and so will be a hungry, latent fat person (Nisbett,

1972). Their bodies are programmed to be fat and rebel against extreme interventions that try to make them slim.

When obese people diet and reach their new reduced weight, their body chemistry is severely affected; it becomes disorganized. Fat cells shrink, menstruation may stop, and thyroid hormone levels and white blood cell counts drop as do blood pressure and pulse rate. These formerly obese individuals complain of intolerance to the cold, and they are obsessed with thoughts about food.

Sadly, it tends to be the rule that weight loss from dieting programs is short-term; gradually the body's own weight regulators take over and restore its weight equilibrium (Kolata, 1985). To be effective, any dieting program must include regular exercise, daily monitoring of food intake, systematic record keeping of caloric intake and weight change, techniques for avoiding severe stress, and social (especially family) support. For the obese, dieting is not a question of "mind over matter"; instead, it is a question of biology asserting itself over psychology.

People and animals overeat for many reasons. Stressful stimulation leads to overeating in both human and animal subjects (Antelman et al., 1976; Schachter et al., 1968). In the case of humans, social and cultural factors determine when, how much, how fast, and what people eat. (My Italian mother would respond to protests of "No more food, please! I'm not hungry!" with, "Anyone can eat when he's *hungry*—animals do that. Eating my food when you're not hungry shows that you love me.") Humans also may overeat (or fast) for the symbolic value of food, for example, during religious holidays.

SUMMING UP

Hunger is the most studied of all drives, but our understanding of all the mechanisms involved in initiating and stopping eating is still incomplete. While earlier researchers, such as Walter Cannon, mistakenly believed hunger to be caused by peripheral stimulation of stomach contractions, later researchers also erred in thinking that hunger and eating can be entirely understood by central processes in the brain. A new multiple-system approach to the study of hunger takes account of the complex interactions of brain, hormonal system, local stimulation, and psychological factors. Food seeking and eating are affected by the activities of the lateral hypothalamus, while their opposites—cessation or inhibition of eating—is influenced by the ventromedial hypothalamus.

Food intake and body weight are regulated according to a "set point," a measure of the fat stored in specialized fat cells. People who are obese have a greater number of fat cells in their body than do the nonobese, due to genetics or overeating at critical times early in life. Because the number of fat cells is constant throughout life, dieting only shrinks them, creating latent fat people who happen to be slim. For this reason, it is difficult for people who were obese to maintain weight loss even after extreme dieting. To do so requires a systematic program of exercise, weight monitoring, social support, and other cognitive measures.

SEXUAL MOTIVATION

While eating is essential to individual survival, sex is not. Some animals and humans remain celibate for a lifetime without apparent detriment to their daily functioning. But to evolution, reproduction is even more important than survival: many animals have evolved to breed fast and die young. Evolution does not look kindly upon celibacy and tends to eliminate it very quickly. In general, genes for celibacy die out, while genes for lust proliferate.

Sex is altruistic in the sense that it benefits a breed or a species. Nature makes sexual stimulation intensely pleasurable. A climactic orgasm serves as the ultimate reinforcer for all the costs expended in mating.

There are a number of ways in which *sexual drive* is a unique source of motivation:

- It is not essential to individual survival, but it is essential to the survival of the genes that individuals carry and to the survival of the species.
- It motivates an unusually wide variety of behaviors and psychological processes.
- It may operate independently of sexual deprivation.
- It may be accompanied by other motivations—arousal may release tension as well as provide pleasure; any stimulus associated with sexual arousal can become an acquired motivator, while any stimulus associated with sexual release can become a conditioned reinforcer.
- It can be aroused by almost any stimulus—from touch to fantasies to sexual objects—that represents (however indirectly) a real or imagined opportunity for mating.

Much of what is known about the physiology of sexual arousal and behavior comes from research on nonhuman animals, partly because of the long-standing taboo against studying sex in humans. Though Freud called attention to the importance of sexual motivation, research psychologists did not follow up on his ideas. Sex did not fit well into the then-prevalent, tension-reduction theory of motivation. Fear and anxiety fit the model better and so received more research attention (Brown, 1961). Theoretical reasons aside, psychologists have ignored systematic study of this powerful human motive primarily because of cultural proscriptions against dealing with sexuality openly.

In this section, we will first consider some of what is known about the sex drive and mating behavior in lower animals. Then we will turn our attention to selected issues in human sexuality, among them the sexual response cycle, gender differences in the mating game, the power of touch and fantasy, sexual scripts, date rape, sexual addiction, and homosexuality. Our general perspective will be largely that perspective advanced by evolutionary psychologists supplemented by social-psychological views on human aspects of sexual encounters.

NONHUMAN SEXUAL AROUSAL

In nonhuman species, sexual arousal is determined primarily by physiological processes. Animals become receptive to mating largely in response to the flow of hormones controlled by the pituitary gland and secreted from the *gonads,* the sex organs. In males, these hormones are known as *androgens,* and they are continuously present in sufficient supply so that males are hormonally ready for mating at almost any time; but in the females of many species, the sex hormone, *estrogen,* is released according to regular time cycles of days or months or according to seasonal changes. Thus, the female is not always hormonally receptive to mating.

These hormones act on both the brain and genital tissue and often lead to a pattern of predictable, *stereotyped sexual behavior* for all members of a species. If you've seen one pair of rats in their mating sequence, you've seen them all. The receptive female rat darts about the male until she gets his attention. Then he chases her as she runs away. She stops suddenly and raises her rear, and he enters her briefly, thrusts, and pulls out. She briefly escapes him, the chase continues—interrupted by 10 to 20 intromissions before he ejaculates, rests a while, and starts the sex chase again. Apes also copulate only briefly (for about 15 seconds), but for sables, copulation is slow and long, lasting for as long as eight hours. Predators, such as lions, can afford to indulge in long, slow copulatory rituals. Their prey, however, such as antelope, copulate for only a few seconds, often on the run (Ford & Beach, 1951).

Even in animals, sexual arousal is not determined only by inner states and hormonal influences. Peripheral stimuli can sensitize or activate innate response patterns. In many species, the sight and sound of ritualized display patterns by potential partners is a *necessary* condition for sexual response. Touch, taste, and smell can also serve as stimulants for sexual arousal. Some species, for example, secrete chemical signals, called **pheromones,** that attract suitors, sometimes from great distances. In many species, pheromones are emitted by the female when her fertility is optimal (and hormone level and sexual interest are peaking). These secretions are unconditioned stimuli for arousal and attraction in the male of the species—they inherit the tendency to be aroused by the stimuli. When captive male rhesus monkeys smell the odor of a sexually receptive female in an adjacent cage, they respond with a variety of sex-related physiological changes, including an increase in the size of their testes. In humans, though, reactions to sex-related odors are quite variable, determined more by *who* is giving off the smell than by any unlearned, irresistible, olfactory properties of the chemical communication (Hopson, 1979).

Sexual Reproduction

From a biological perspective, sexual behavior is the set of responses that results in sexual reproduction. A psychological perspective, however, is focused less on reproduction and more on individual feelings associated with sexual activities. **Sexual reproduction** refers to the production of progeny by sexual means. Some species of fish, lizards, and other animals reproduce by nonsexual means, but, in doing so, they produce offspring fit to survive only in highly stable environments. Sexual reproduction confers the advantage of *genetic variability,* enabling some of the offspring to be genetically prepared to survive in a changing world.

Sexual Synchrony

Once sexual reproduction has been set up as an evolutionary scheme, two new biological problems must be solved: *sexual differentiation* and *sexual synchrony*. First, sexual reproduction requires at least two sexual types: males and females. The female must have large gametes (eggs)—the energy store for the embryo to begin its growth—and the male must produce gametes (sperm) that are specialized for motility (to move into the eggs). This basic sex cell differentiation gets amplified as males and females diverge in physical structure, physiological functions, and behavior.

This differentiation creates a second problem to be solved: the two sexes must synchronize their activity so that gametes meet under the appropriate conditions, resulting in production of viable young. There are at least

four forms of synchronization as detailed by **Norman Adler** (1978):

- Finding a *proper* mate: finding one who is of the same species, is reproductively mature (past puberty), and has an optimal type with the greatest genetic potential for the offspring's well-being. Many male displays of strength or other attributes are judged by females when selecting a mate.
- Finding the right place and time: using biological clocks to time the breeding season so that offspring will be produced when the environment can supply enough food and sunlight; setting the circadian clock to ovulate and mate at the correct time of day.
- Behaviorally adapting to each other: getting the female "in the mood" through courtship rituals and foreplay so that reflexes then orient the position of the sex organs in the right way to accomplish fertilization.
- Altering the female's physiological and behavioral state away from sexual receptiveness to pregnancy readiness (in mammals).

Research shows that copulation alters the physiological status of the female rat in two ways. First, it causes secretion of *progesterone,* the hormone necessary for pregnancy. Second, the male's copulatory stimulation primes the female so that, at ejaculation, she is positioned to allow transport of the sperm from the vagina to the uterus. In this way, there is some *behavioral control* of reproduction (Adler & Toner, 1986).

Hormonal activity, so important in regulating sexual behavior among female mammals in other animal species, has no known effect on sexual receptiveness or gratification in women. In men, the sex hormone testosterone (one of the androgens) is necessary for sexual arousal and performance. Testosterone levels become high enough only after *puberty* when hypothalamic neurons secrete a special hormone (gonadotropin-releasing hormone) that plays a critical role in establishing and maintaining normal reproductive activities. Sexual stimulation and orgasm raise the level of this hormone, but so do hostile or anxious mood states. Perhaps this similar effect of sexual stimulation and hostility contributes to many men's association of sex with aggression. Testosterone levels may also affect sexual drive in females, with sexual interest often peaking before and after menstruation. Low estrogen levels can interfere with sexual satisfaction by causing vaginal dryness.

HUMAN SEXUALITY

In humans, sexuality is far more dependent on psychological factors than it is in animals. As a result, it is also more variable in humans than in other species.

Human sexuality can be described as including an evolved motivational core focused on mating for reproduction and pleasure from sexual behavior, along with the societal constraints on and inducements toward sexual activities. **Sexual arousal** in humans is the motivational state of excitement and tension brought about by physiological and cognitive reactions to erotic stimuli. *Erotic stimuli,* which may be physical or psychological, give rise to sexual excitement or feelings of passion. Sexual arousal induced by erotic stimuli is reduced by sexual activities that are perceived by the individual as satisfying, especially by achieving orgasm.

Scientific investigation of normal human sexual behavior was given the first important impetus by the work of **Alfred Kinsey** and his colleagues beginning in the 1940s (1948, 1953). They interviewed some 17,000 Americans about their sexual behavior and revealed—to a generally shocked public—that certain behaviors, previously considered rare and even abnormal, were actually quite widespread—or at least reported to be. However, it was **William Masters** and **Virginia Johnson** (1966, 1970, 1979) who really broke down the traditional sexual taboo. They legitimized the study of human sexuality by directly observing and recording under laboratory conditions the physiological patterns involved in ongoing human sexual performance. By doing so, they studied not what people said about sex (with obvious problems of response bias) but how they actually reacted—during intercourse and masturbation.

Sexual Response Cycle

To study directly the human response to sexual stimulation, Masters and Johnson conducted controlled laboratory observations of thousands of volunteer males and females during tens of thousands of sexual response cycles of intercourse and masturbation. Their pioneering research on sexual arousal dispelled a number of myths and provided a useful model of the phases of human sexual response. However, it is important to note that Masters and Johnson studied arousal and response only. They did *not* study the psychologically significant initial phase of sexual responding—that of *sexual desire,* the motivation to seek out a sexual partner or to make oneself available for sexual experience.

Four of the most significant conclusions drawn from this research on human sexuality are that (a) men and women have similar patterns of sexual responding, regardless of the source of arousal; (b) although the sequence of phases of the sexual response cycle is similar in the two sexes, women are more variable, tending to respond more slowly but often remaining aroused longer; (c) many women can have multiple orgasms, while men rarely do in a comparable time period; and (d) penis size is generally unrelated to any aspect of sexual performance (except in the male's attitude toward having a large penis).

Four phases were found in the human sexual response cycle: excitement, plateau, orgasm, and resolution (see **Figure 12.6**).

- In the *excitement phase* (lasting from a few minutes to more than an hour), there are *vascular* (blood vessel) changes in the pelvic region. The penis becomes erect and the clitoris swells; blood and other fluids become congested in the testicles and vagina; a reddening of the body, or *sex flush,* occurs.
- During the *plateau phase,* a maximum (though varying) level of arousal is reached. There is rapidly increased heartbeat, respiration, and blood pressure, increased glandular secretions, and both voluntary and involuntary muscle tension throughout the body. Vaginal lubrication increases and the breasts swell.
- During the *orgasm phase,* males and females experience a very intense, pleasurable sense of release from the sexual tension that has been building. Orgasm is characterized by rhythmic contractions which occur approximately every eight-tenths of a second in the genital areas. Respiration and blood pressure reach very high levels in both men and women, and heart rate may double. In men, throbbing contractions lead to ejaculation, an "explosion" of semen. In women,

---

FIGURE 12.6   *PHASES OF HUMAN SEXUAL RESPONSE*

The phases of sexual response in males and females have similar patterns. The primary differences are in the time it takes for males and females to reach each phase and in the greater likelihood that females will achieve multiple orgasms.

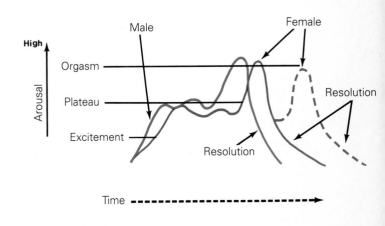

orgasm may be of two different types, achieved from effective stimulation of either the clitoris or the vagina.

- During the *resolution phase,* the body gradually returns to its normal pre-excitement state, with both blood pressure and heartbeat slowing down. After one orgasm, most men enter a refractory period, lasting anywhere from a few minutes to several hours, during which no further orgasm is possible. With sustained arousal, women are capable of multiple orgasms in fairly rapid succession.

THE MATING GAME: SEXUAL INVESTMENT STRATEGIES

Sexual arousal can lead to sexual intercourse and, thus, to offspring (under nonrestrictive conditions). What sorts of sexual passion will evolve for different species and different sexes? If males had adapted to a very different social-sexual environment than females did, we would expect them to have very different sexual passions and motivations. It can be argued that indeed men and women did evolve in different social-sexual environments, even though we are all in the same species.

For females, the reproductive environment consists of the behavioral tendencies and abilities of males and of competing females; for males, the reverse holds. The difference comes down to gametes. Males could reproduce hundreds of times a year if they could find enough willing mates. To produce a child, all they need to invest is a teaspoon of sperm and a few minutes of intercourse. Women can reproduce at most about once a year, and each child reproduced then requires, at minimum, a huge investment of time and energy. (Incidentally, the world record for the number of times a woman has given birth falls short of 50, but men can father many more children. A Moroccan despot, King Ismail the Bloodthirsty, had over 700 children, and the first Emperor of China is said to have fathered over 3000; both had large harems.) Although the average number of offspring produced by men and women is necessarily equal, males of every species have greater variance in their reproductive performance with some having no children and some having very many.

Thus, eggs are the limited resource, and males compete for opportunities to fertilize them. The basic problem facing male animals is to maximize the number of offspring produced by mating with the largest number of females possible. But the basic problem facing female animals is to find a high-quality male to insure the best, healthiest offspring from her limited store of eggs. Throughout nature, males strive for *quantity* and females for *quality.* So each sex evolves the emotions

and motivations that best solve their respective investment strategy problems.

For some animals, such as primates and humans, offspring take so long to mature and are so helpless while growing that substantial **parental investment** is required (Trivers, 1972). Mothers and fathers must spend time and energy raising the children—unlike fish or spiders which simply lay eggs and depart. Females then have the problem of selecting not just the biggest, strongest, smartest, highest-status, most thrilling male but the most loyal, committed male who will help raise their children.

One evolutionary psychologist, **David Buss** (1989), has suggested that men and women evolved different strategies, emotions, and motivations for *short-term mating* versus *long-term mating.* The male strategy of seducing and abandoning—giving signs of loyalty and commitment and then leaving—is a short-term strategy. The male strategy of staying committed to the female and investing in the offspring is a long-term strategy. The female strategy of attracting a loyal male who will stay to help raise her children is a long-term strategy. There is some controversy about whether women have evolved short-term mating strategies. Some argue that indiscriminate sex never pays for women—they can get pregnant without assurance of male investment later. Women do seem much less interested in casual sex than men. Others argue that short-term mating with many men—especially older, rich men—in exchange for immediate rewards may pay off genetically.

As far as reproduction goes, women should be more future-oriented and men more present oriented; the reverse might be true for economic achievement where future orientation is essential for success in commerce and industrial enterprise. All of these arguments depend on the social-sexual environment that existed when humans were evolving. Yet women and men show exactly the patterns predicted by evolutionary psychology across all cultures, even when the modern environment changes the risks and rewards of different mating strategies. Everywhere in the world, sex is considered something that women give away to men, either in exchange for immediate material reward (short-term mating, such as prostitution) or in exchange for long-term commitment and support (marriage). In general, men show a greater desire for a variety of sexual partners and are less discriminating about their mates. This is true even though modern contraception eliminates many of the dangers of short-term mating strategies for women and even though modern economies may allow both men and women to raise children alone. If humans were simply responding rationally to the social-sexual environment, or if social and sexual emotions were learned to fit the current environment, we would expect their emotions and motivations to keep up with technological and social developments. Instead, our evolved mating strategies seem resistant to change.

The human mating game no longer consists of trying to figure out what men and women really want. Men evolved to exploit the reproductive capabilities of women, and women evolved to exploit the reproductive capabilities of men. Although this mutual exploitation evolved for the purposes of reproducing genes, it can give rise to many powerful sexual emotions and experiences. This effect testifies not to our having overcome our biological past but to evolution's ability to construct male and female minds capable of attracting, seducing, and enjoying each other.

Touch, Fantasy, and Association

Although Masters's and Johnson's research focused on the *physiology* of sexual responding, perhaps their most important discovery was the central significance of *psychological* processes in both arousal and satisfaction. They demonstrated conclusively that problems in sexual response often have psychological, rather than physiological, origins and can be changed through therapy. Of particular concern, is the inability to complete the response cycle and achieve gratification. This inability is called *impotence* in men and *frigidity* in women. Often the source of the inability is a preoccupation with personal problems, fear of the consequences of sexual activity, or anxiety about a partner's evaluation of one's sexual performance. However, poor nutrition, fatigue, stress, and excessive use of alcohol or drugs can also diminish sexual drive and performance.

The sequence of sexual activities that may culminate in orgasm can be started by only one unconditioned stimulus and by an endless variety of conditioned stimuli. The unconditioned stimulus is touch. *Touch,* in the form of genital caresses, is a universal component of sexual foreplay (Ford & Beach, 1951). However, virtually any stimuli that become associated with genital touch and orgasm can become conditioned motivators, whether the stimuli are in the external environment or in one's memory or fantasy. Even a picture of a shoe can lead to sexual arousal in this way (Rachman, 1966). A nonsexual object that becomes capable of producing sexual arousal through conditioning is called a **fetish.** A fetish becomes a psychological problem only when it is *necessary* for arousal and/or it is objectionable to one's mate.

It has been suggested that sensations and fantasy during masturbation provide the primal setting for associating virtually any stimulus with pleasurable arousal (Storms, 1980, 1981). Inanimate objects, textures, sounds, visual images, odors—any tangible or imagined stimulus event—can come to elicit arousal through this conditioned association. Through conditioning, some of us learn culturally acceptable sexual orientations, while others learn sexual deviations. Some people learn to become aroused *only* by conditioned stimuli such as the sight of high-heel shoes, young children, or even pain.

In humans, sexuality can be less concerned with meeting physiological need than with satisfying cognitive desires. For most humans, the goal of sexual activity is "the attainment of a cognitive state: the conscious perception of sexual satisfaction. This state depends on a combination of experiences originating in the experiencer's body and in that of the sexual partner" (Davidson, 1980, p. 227). Interpretations of experiences, the meaning of specific sexual events, sexual beliefs and values, and imagination and expectation all play a part in human sexual behavior and satisfaction (Byrne, 1981). Even the subjective experience of orgasm, which has been compared by some to a profound altered state of consciousness (Davidson, 1980), usually depends not only on physical stimulation but on interpersonal factors, such as being in a close, trusting relationship.

We find that differences between males and females match the risks and rewards of their different mating strategies. With a short-term male strategy, orgasm is a ready and frequent, but indiscriminate, reward for any behavior that delivers sperm to a receptive female. With a long-term female strategy, orgasm is a rarer, discriminate reward for mating with the right male in the right circumstances. We see the same differences in male and female patterns of sexual behavior.

Sexual Scripts

Generalized sexual arousal can be channeled into different specific behaviors, depending on how the individual has learned to respond and think about sexual matters. **Sexual scripts** are socially learned programs of sexual responsiveness that include prescriptions, usually unspoken, of what to do, when, where, and how to do it, with whom, or with what to do it, and why it should be done (Gagnon, 1977). Different aspects of these scripts are assembled through social interaction over one's lifetime. The attitudes and values embodied in one's sexual script define one's general orientation to sexuality.

Scripts are combinations of prescriptions generated by social norms (what is proper and accepted), individual expectations, and preferred sequences of behavior from past learning. Your sexual scripts include scenarios of not only what you think is appropriate on your part but also of your expectations for a sexual partner. Differing scripts can create problems of adjustment between partners when they are not discussed or synchronized. For example, there is evidence that touch has different meanings for men and women.

Researchers questioned 40 male and 40 female undergraduates about the meaning they attach to touch, when applied to different parts of the anatomy by a friend. Quite different meanings were found between the sexes. For females, the more a touch was associated with sexual desire, the less it was considered to imply warmth, pleasantness, or friendliness. When a close male friend touches a woman in an area of her body that communicates sexual desire to her, then that is its only meaning to her. For males, the same touch is interpreted as having a cluster of meanings: pleasantness, warmth, love, and sexual desire. Misunderstandings can arise when one person's "friendly touch" is perceived by the other as a "sexual advance" (Nguyen et al., 1975).

This study suggests that, from the female perspective, male touch without the rituals of courtship and the preliminaries of respect and commitment is interpreted as a sexual advance—for "easy," short-term mating. For males, female touch is interpreted as pleasant in most situations since it is assumed to suggest a willingness to mate.

Sexual scripts include similar stage directions for most sexual actors within a given culture, socioeconomic class, gender, and educational level. However, there are unique features in each individual's personal script, learned through his or her own history of sexual experience. Because erotic stimuli can be intensely pleasurable while also often strongly prohibited by society and religion, we learn many different ways of responding to the variety of erotic stimuli we experience in this society. Here's where we really see the power of conditioned associations. Because any stimulus that has been associated with sexual arousal can become a potent elicitor of later arousal, there are enormous variations in the forms our human sexuality takes.

Even the apparent biologically based differences between men and women in the physiological pattern of sexual response, as catalogued by Masters and Johnson, may be influenced by social learning. Females are socialized to repress their sexuality, to act as passive sexual partners, to appear alluring yet sexually innocent, and to be responsible if "anything goes wrong." Female coyness and passivity, within the traditional feminine script, are tactics for attracting those long-term investor males. Males, by contrast, are socialized to play the field, to think of sexual intercourse as validation of their masculine identity, as a performance and as the prelude to orgasm. Their greater anxiety about sexual evaluation may stem from their role conflict: being a low-down, short-term seducer who is trying to give the impression of being that good-guy, long-term investor.

Date Rape

Research into the sexual experience of college students has revealed an area where male and female sexual scripts come into devastating conflict: date rape. In one sample of college women, 57 percent reported having experienced what they thought of as rape (Koss, 1985). The accuracy of this staggering figure is confirmed by surveys of male students. One in every three college men said he would rape a woman if he were sure he would not get caught (Malamuth, 1984). When questioned about their actual experiences, over half the men in another survey admitted to forcing a date to perform some sexual act, and 25 percent admitted to forcing intercourse (Koss & Oros, 1982).

When researchers of a recent study asked college women about their experiences with unwanted sex, they found that, again, over half reported that they had experienced it (Murnen et al., 1989). Next, the researchers asked those women how they had been coerced and how they had coped with the incident at the time. The most common female responses were ignoring or giving in to the attack. Many of the women continued to see the men on subsequent occasions, though they often did not continue sexual relations.

The authors of this study suggest that women may perceive that their role is to give in eventually to male

Dist. by L.A. Times Synd.
©1983 Punch Publs. Ltd.

"Now, tell me. What's it like being a sex symbol?"

insistence and coercion. They may feel that male sexual desire is uncontrollable and that, after the rape, the proper female role is to mend the relationship by forgiving the man. Women in the study tended to blame themselves for getting into dangerous situations (even though most attacks came from men who were their friends or whom they knew moderately well) and even to feel guilty about denying sex to their dates.

If the female script is to give in, what is the male script? Chris O'Sullivan, a social psychologist at Bucknell University, suggests that "groups of men on campus (and in other segments of society) have set up the sexual humiliation of women as a positive value, rewarding it with approval" (*The New York Times,* 12/15/90). Once the rape has occurred, another script begins to operate: "It is common for alleged perpetrators of sexual assault to be regarded as victims within their community. . . . In most cases, those who view alleged perpetrators as victims target the woman as the victimizer (for reporting their behavior), even when the men admit to some form of reprehensible group sexual exploitation" (*The New York Times,* 12/15/90).

A second study of over 500 college women and men casts some more light on how date rape occurs and on how male and female sexual scripts differ (Muehlenhard & Cook, 1988). Over 90 percent of all students surveyed—both men and women—had experienced unwanted intercourse. A factor analysis revealed a variety of reasons these students had engaged in unwanted sex, including verbal and physical coercion by a date, peer pressure, alcohol or drugs, concerns about one's sex role, and concerns about the other person's feelings. Many of the reasons that men had unwanted sex related to their fears about their own sexuality and macho image. They were especially vulnerable to peer pressure to have sex—to the expectation that men are supposed to be experienced—and they were more likely than women to report having unwanted sex while drunk or high. Men were also likely to say that they had been enticed by women into unwanted sex and were unable to refuse any sexual advance for fear of being labeled as inadequate (Muehlenhard & Cook, 1988).

This study also examined the relationship between sexual attitudes and the incidence of unwanted sex. Researchers found that, for both men and women, unwanted sex was related to seeing male-female relations as *adversarial.* Specifically, it was correlated with the male script that women offer token resistance to avoid seeming promiscuous. When men believe they are supposed to disregard a woman's objections, date rape may be the result.

Statistics about date rape, similar to statistics about most negative events, are just abstract data until they have some personal connection. I was alarmed recently to discover that date rape at my university is a common experience. A random survey of 2400 students at Stanford University revealed that one in three women had "full sexual activity when she did not want to." Among men, one in eight said he had a similar experience of having been forced into sex, in most cases by another man he knew. In 98 percent of these cases, the victims knew the persons who assaulted them. Only 2 percent of the incidents were reported to authorities, and few of the victims sought counseling. A university task force urged tougher rules for investigating and prosecuting cases of "sexual aggression," and called for consciousness raising about what constitutes unacceptable sexual conduct in dating situations (*Stanford Observer,* Jan.–Feb. 1991, p. 15). More research is needed to sort out the complex set of motivations and scripts operating when dates turn into rapes.

Homosexuality

Since Alfred Kinsey's early reports, we have known that human sexual orientation is a complex business. Kinsey found that a large percentage of men in his sample had had at least some homosexual experience, and that about 4 percent were exclusively homosexual (percentages for women were somewhat smaller). Since then; psychologists have become gradually more interested in this important, but long neglected aspect of human sexual motivation.

In 1973, the American Psychological Association voted to remove homosexuality from the list of psychological disorders. Spurring this action were research reports suggesting that, in fact, most gays and lesbians are happy, productive human beings who would not change their sexual orientation even if a "magic pill" enabled them to do so (Siegelman, 1972; Bell & Weinberg, 1978).

Crosscultural and historical studies have revealed enormous variation across cultures in sexual customs and in attitudes about homosexuality (Werner, 1979). In some cultures, homosexuality is strongly suppressed, in some it is acceptable before heterosexual marriage but discouraged after, and, in a very few, it is even favored over heterosexuality.

How prevalent is homosexuality? Survey data collected in 1970 and 1988 about same-gender male sexual contact yields the following conclusions about the prevalence and patterns of homosexual experience among adult American males (Fay et al., 1989). About one-fifth of the men surveyed had had at least one homosexual experience (where one partner reached orgasm). Roughly 3 percent had had male sexual contacts during adulthood either "fairly often" or "occasionally." Homosexual contact increased in frequency with educational level, being highest among single, male college graduates, 30 and over. Finally, the survey found that about 8 percent of currently married men report having homosexual experiences occasionally or fairly often. This statistic is especially important because the homosexual experiences of married men are one way that married, monogamous women are contracting AIDS.

Theories about the nature and development of homosexuality reflect the full range of psychological disciplines. Some theories seek to explain the physiological or genetic variations that might produce homosexuality. Others focus on the individual's family life or on early learning experiences that might affect one's sexual orientation.

Psychoanalytic theory suggested that male homosexuality represented an arrested sexual development that occurred because the child did not successfully resolve the Oedipus conflict. This failure to resolve the conflict was brought on by a mother who was dominant in the family and sexually seductive toward the child and a father who was absent or hostile and thus did not provide a male role model (Bieber et al., 1962). However, evidence that parents cause homosexuality in this way has been inconclusive (Bell et al., 1981).

How can a gene for nonreproductive sexual behavior survive? One possibility is that homosexuals reproduce through *kin selection;* in other words, if a gay person's parent, brother, or sister reproduces, some of his or her genes, which are shared by biological relatives, will be passed on. Evidence for this theory depends partly on the observation that, in many societies, homosexuals enjoy high social status, which might in turn benefit their families, increasing the chances that members of those families will reproduce (Wilson, 1975). Homosexuality may also be related to qualities or skills (IQ and acting ability have been suggested) that help a person gain wealth or influence; and wealth or influence could benefit the gay person's family, increasing its member's chances for survival (Ruse, 1981). Critics of this theory wonder why homosexuality seems to continue at a steady rate even in societies where it is stigmatized and disadvantageous to the family.

Attempts to identify physiological causes of homosexuality have been inconclusive. Most of this research has sprung from findings suggesting that rats exposed prenatally to hormones of the other sex develop sexual behaviors of the other sex. It is clear, however, that homosexuality is not due to deficient levels of testosterone in adult gay males nor to too much testosterone in adult lesbians (Meyer-Bahlburg, 1977).

Finally, a cognitive-behaviorist theory suggests that it is early erotic experience that determines sexual orientation (Storms, 1981). Most young children have friendships exclusively with the same sex. If a child begins to masturbate and fantasize relatively early, before having a chance to associate closely with the opposite sex, perhaps sexual pleasure will become associated only with same-sex peers.

Researchers have begun to explore the ways that individual gays and lesbians come to define themselves. Four stages in their self-definition have been outlined (Troiden, 1989):

1. Up through the age of about 12, boys and girls report defining themselves as different from their peers, not in sexual feelings but in their activities. Lesbians feel they are less feminine and more interested in sports than other girls, while gay men tend to avoid typical masculine activities, preferring solitary activities such as art or reading.
2. In adolescence, they start to recognize that they are different from their peers in terms of their sexual feelings, which forces them to consider the possibility that they are not heterosexual. A variety of coping strategies come into play at this time: denial of their feelings, forcing themselves to engage in heterosexual activities in the hopes that they will change, redefining actual homosexual experiences ("This is just a phase I'm going through").
3. An attempt to integrate homosexuality into self-identity comes in later adolescence and early adulthood. Crucial at this time are positive or negative experiences with other gays and lesbians. The person desires to reveal his or her homosexuality, so dealing with stigma becomes more important.
4. The final stage is a fusion of sexual and emotional feelings, allowing the person to see homosexuality as natural and normal for the self. Not all individuals reach this stage, and all may lose confidence from time to time, depending on the amount of pressure or support they are experiencing from family, friends, and society.

These theories are still very much in the early stages of development. In all probability, human sexual orientation does not have any one cause. Some people may be born gay or lesbian, but that does not preclude others from choosing to have homosexual experiences. Cultural variation also reminds us how difficult it is to generalize about homosexuality. We tend to be very flexible in finding solutions to some questions, such as how to reproduce ourselves. We are capable of passing our inheritance on to our children through language and culture as well as through our genes. Choices of sexual partners may be just that—choices.

SEXUAL ADDICTION

Addiction

Are you unable to stop engaging in self-destructive sexual behavior? Do you feel that some aspects of your sexual behavior must be kept secret? Does normal sexual behavior such as masturbation make you feel guilty or empty? Tulane University psychiatrist Mark Schwartz uses questions such as these to diagnose cases of a condition known as *sexual addiction* (Adler et al., 1978).

In meeting rooms and church basements around the country, women and men who have trouble controlling their sexual behavior are getting together to discuss their problems. Many of these groups operate under the rubric of the 12-step program outlined by Alcoholics Anonymous. Even their names—Sexaholics Anonymous, Sex Addicts Anonymous, Sexual Compulsives Anonymous—reflect an underlying philosophical connection that emphasizes addicts' feelings of powerlessness and their desire for moral betterment. Those who have recovered from the despair and chaos caused by this obsessive focus on sex report that their recovery came from approaching their suffering with a new spiritual understanding.

What exactly is sexual addiction? According to therapist **Patrick Carnes** (1991), a leading authority on the subject, sex addicts have allowed sex to assume such a prominent role in their lives that they have difficulty functioning in their jobs and in nonsexual relationships. From his survey of nearly 1000 sex addicts, supplemented by in-depth interviews with more than 100 of them, emerges the following profile of

sexual addiction: A pattern of out-of-control behavior; severe consequences due to sexual behavior; inability to stop despite adverse consequences; persistent pursuit of self-destructive or high-risk behavior; ongoing desire or effort to limit sexual behavior; sexual obsession and fantasy as a primary coping strategy; and a need for ever-increasing levels of sexual experience; severe mood changes caused by sexual activity; excessive time and energy spent in sexual activities of all kinds; neglect of important aspects of life in favor of sexual behavior.

While Carnes estimates that about 6 percent of Americans are afflicted by sexual addiction, Edward Armstrong, Executive Director of the National Association on Sexual Addiction Problems, puts the figure at 10 percent, and others in the field give estimates that run as high as 25 percent (Peele, 1989). Yet, there is controversy about whether sexual addiction is a valid construct and many researchers challenge whether such a disorder even exists.

Those who argue that sexual addiction is a valid psychological disorder compare sex addicts to people addicted to drugs and alcohol because they "are willing to sacrifice what they cherish most in order to preserve their unhealthy behavior and receive the 'high' they seek" (*The Addiction Letter,* 1989). In the recent Carnes's research project, sex addicts not only resembled other types of addicts but often suffered from additional addictions and came from families where addictions flourished, including alcoholism, compulsive

eating, and compulsive gambling. Although many of the addicts grapple with other addictions, they find sex addiction the most difficult to stop. Interestingly, most of those who shared their stories with researchers in the Carnes's project reported being abused as children—sexually, physically, and/or emotionally.

Others believe that obsessive sexual behavior should *not* be classified as an addiction. In 1987, the American Psychiatric Association's Committee on Psychosexual Disorders declined to list sexual addiction with more widely agreed-upon disorders such as premature ejaculation, sexual sadism, and pedophilia.

Psychologist Michael Siever (1990) opposes the notion of sexual addiction: "There's a lot of controversy about whether an addiction model is appropriate to this area. Adherents to that model are putting forth some fairly puritanical ideas about sexuality. They view anything other than a heterosexually monogamous relationship as problematic, if not pathological." Others support this position. In reviewing the concepts of sexual addiction and compulsion, sociologists Martin Levine and Richard Troiden make the point that "sexual expression is condoned when it occurs in social contexts that affirm the traditional sexual order, but medicalized as an 'addiction' when it falls outside existing norms" (Levine & Troiden, 1988, p. 357).

Stanton Peele, author of *Love and Addiction* and *Diseasing of America,* is concerned that commercial drug treatment corporations are capitalizing on the widespread practice of labeling any disruptive, obsessive behavior as an addiction. As popularly described, sexual addiction "has all the traits that characterize the dis-

TABLE 12.2 SEXUAL PREFERENCES AND BEHAVIORS OF ADULT AMERICANS, 1989

Random Survey Sample N = 1401

Category	%/#
I. Sexual Preference	
A. Exclusively heterosexual (since age 18)	91.0%
B. Homosexual or bisexual (since age 18)	6.0
C. Not sexually experienced	3.0
II. Sexual behavior reported	
A. Frequency of intercourse (mean)	
1. All adults	57 times/year
2. Men	66
3. Women	51
4. Married	67
5. Separated	66
6. Widowed	8
7. Under age 40	78
8. Under age 50	67
9. Under age 60	46
10. Under age 70	23
11. Over age 70	8
B. Number of sexual partners (mean)	
1. Men (since age 18)	12 partners/year
2. Women (since age 18)	3
3. People with postgraduate education	13
4. People with college education	8
5. People with less than high-school education	5
C. Abstinence	
1. Overall	22.0%
2. Men	14.0
3. Women	28.0
D. Marital infidelity	1.5
III. AIDS Risk	
A. High risk (5 or more sexual partners, casual partners, male homosexual or bisexual partners)	5.5%
B. Multiple high risk (2 or more of above conditions)	1.3

eases popularized by the alcoholism movement and the addiction treatment industry—loss of control that often serves as an excuse for misbehavior; . . . the inherited, possibly biological nature of the malady; the ever-deepening addictive progression that can only be interrupted by treatment" (Peele, 1989).

Clearly, the scientific community has not yet resolved the issue of whether an addiction model can be applied appropriately to sexual behavior. That controversy is of little comfort for those who define their own out-of-control sexual behavior as an addictive disorder. While some seek to recover through 12-step programs, others, wary of the addiction label, prefer a cognitive-behavioral approach (presented in Chapter 18). Regardless of whether sex is a source of problems or pleasures, it remains an inescapable source of motivation in many aspects of our daily lives. Plots of novels, plays, films, and soap operas revolve around sexual themes. Prostitution, pornography, the sale of birth-control products, and sexual advertising are major multibillion dollar industries in many countries.

However, a recent survey shows that the Protestant work ethic overshadows sex as a motivator, at least in middle-class United States. A survey of nearly 2500 adults indicated that many women thought more about money than about sex (51 percent vs. 12 percent). For men, sex barely edged out money (32 percent vs. 27 percent). When it comes to enjoyment, however, men *reported* enjoying sex much more than money (47 percent vs. 16 percent), while money slightly beat out sex as more enjoyable for women (Lieberman Research, 1985).

A new survey confirms the fact that, for many American adults, sexual passions are decidedly lukewarm. A 1990 survey of 1500 people nationwide, conducted by The National Opinion Research Center at the University of Chicago, revealed that married and unmarried adults had intercourse only about once a week (men reported having intercourse 66 times a year and women about 51 times—a curious discrepancy). **Table 12.2** shows additional highlights of this sex study survey.

SUMMING UP

From an evolutionary perspective, sex is merely an effective way for male and female gametes to find each other and produce progeny that have genetic variability. In this view, orgasms and other pleasures associated with sexual activity are nature's way of rewarding us for engaging in reproductive behaviors.

In animals, sex drive is largely controlled by hormonal activity and follows stereotyped, genetically determined patterns designed to optimize reproductive efficiency. However, to mate effectively, a series of processes and outcomes must be synchronized, such as finding the right partner in the right place and at the right time.

In humans, sexual arousal, sexual behavior, and sexual satisfaction are quite variable and subject to learning and cultural values. Nevertheless, evolutionary pressures are still at work, subtly arranging behind-the-scenes negotiations and compromises between the female's strategies of long-term mating and of major investment in her potential offspring and the male's strategies of short-term mating and minimal investment.

Though only touch is an unconditioned stimulus for sexual arousal, anything associated with sexual arousal can become a conditioned stimulus for arousal. Kinsey's pioneering surveys of American sexual behavior brought the study of sex into the open, and the investigations of Masters and Johnson into the physiology and psychology of intercourse and masturbation provided the first hard data on sexual response cycles of men and women.

We learn sexual scripts through a variety of personal and societal experiences that guide our sexual images, sexual behavior, and expectations of the sexuality of others. Discrepancies in sexual scripts can lead to misunderstandings in communication and serious problems for both men and women.

There are many theories attempting to account for the origin of homosexuality, from the genetic to the psychoanalytic, but none seems entirely satisfactory. Of prime importance is recognition of the stages of awareness and coping experienced by the individual with preference for same-gender sexual contact.

The evidence that sexual addiction fits a model based on drug addiction is equivocal, despite the reports of many people that their sexuality is out of control and that they are driven to have sexual encounters as often as possible.

ACHIEVEMENT AND WORK MOTIVATION

The desire to achieve one's goals, whether they involve getting an A in psychology or climbing to the top of a steep mountain, is a pervasive psychological motive that empowers a wide variety of human actions. Achievement motives are usually satisfied by the knowledge of personal effectiveness on any activity that is significant for the individual. These motives link specific goals, the path to attaining them, planning and effort, and feelings of self-worth. However, in some cases, achievement motives can become so extreme that they lead to limitless aspirations—the desire for perfection, being the best and being "number one" at everything. Another feature of achievement motives is their *future orientation*. The future-oriented person uses cognitive strategies that rely on long-term instrumental steps toward subgoals and distant goals rather than focusing on the hedonistic value of more readily available, ultimately less valuable, present stimuli (DeCharmes & Muir, 1978; Nuttin, 1985).

In an ideal world, these achievement motives are expressed through one's chosen career. They become a central reason for spending a lifetime perfecting some skill, performing some service, and creating some product. Why do we work? *To make money* is the most obvious motivational answer. However, we often take lower paying jobs that fulfill personal values. The motivation to work is complex, influenced by a variety of needs and values.

NEED FOR ACHIEVEMENT

As early as 1938, Henry Murray had postulated a "need to achieve" which varied in strength in different people and influenced their tendency to approach success and evaluate their own performances. *David McClelland* and his colleagues (1953) devised a way to measure the strength of this need and then looked for relationships between strength of achievement motivation in different societies, conditions that had fostered it, and its results in the work world. To measure the strength of the need for achievement, McClelland used his subjects' fantasies.

Subjects shown TAT pictures were asked to make up stories about them—saying what was happening in the picture and probable outcomes. Presumably, they projected into the scene reflections of their own values, interests, and motives. According to McClelland: "If you want to find out what's on a person's mind, don't ask him, because he can't always tell you accurately. Study his fantasies and dreams. If you do this over a period of time, you will discover the themes to which his mind returns again and again. And these themes can be used to explain his actions . . ." (1971, p. 5).

From subject responses to a series of these TAT pictures, McClelland worked out measures of several human needs. The **need for achievement** was designated as *n Ach*. It reflected individual differences in the importance of planning and working toward attaining one's goals. A great many studies in both laboratory and real-life settings have validated the usefulness of this measure. For example, persistence in working on an impossible task was greater for those with high *n Ach* when the task was announced as difficult rather than easy. Low *n Ach* subjects gave up sooner when they were led to believe the task was difficult, but they persisted for the supposedly easy (actually impossible)

task. In other research, high-scoring *n Ach* people were found to be more upwardly mobile than those with low scores; and sons who had high *n Ach* scores were more likely than sons with low *n Ach* measures to advance above their fathers' occupational status (McClelland et al., 1976). **Figure 12.7** shows an example of how a high *n Ach* individual and low *n Ach* individual might interpret a TAT picture.

The need to achieve clearly energizes and directs behavior. It also influences perceptions of many situations and interpretations of our own and others' behavior. Even the economic growth of a society can be related to its encouragement of achievement motivation. McClelland (1955, 1961) found that, in general, Protestant countries (in which achievement and independence tend to be encouraged) were more economically advanced than Catholic countries. He found that men in these "achieving societies" were more often trained to be self-supporting earlier in life and thus, to value an autonomous success-seeking style.

| **FIGURE 12.7** | *ALTERNATIVE INTERPRETATIONS OF A TAT PICTURE* |

Story Showing High *n Ach*
The boy has just finished his violin lesson. He's happy at the progress he is making and is beginning to believe that all his progress is making the sacrifices worthwhile. To become a concert violinist he will have to give up much of his social life and practice for many hours each day. Although he knows he could make more money by going into his father's business, he is more interested in being a great violinist and giving people joy with his music. He renews his personal commitment to do all it takes to make it.

Story Showing Low *n Ach*
The boy is holding his brother's violin and wishes he could play it. But he knows it isn't worth the time, energy, and money for lessons. He feels sorry for his brother who has given up all the fun things in life to practice, practice, practice. It would be great to wake up one day and be a top-notch musician but it doesn't happen that way. The reality is boring practice, no fun, and a big possibility of becoming nothing better than just another guy playing a musical instrument in a small town band.

INDIVIDUALIST VERSUS COLLECTIVIST CULTURES

The cardinal virtues of self-reliance, independence, and personal achievement run deeply in many Western cultures. However, emphasis on *individualism,* with its focus on personal needs and goals, is at odds with the values emphasized in the majority of cultures in Africa, Asia, South America, the Middle East, and Central America. *Individualism* in a society generally guarantees economic success. Cultures based on *collectivism,* which put group loyalty (to family, tribe, or community) above personal goals, do not fare as well economically. Nevertheless, individualism comes with a high price tag.

In reviewing more than 100 scientific studies on the topic, crosscultural psychologist **Harry Triandis** (1990) believes the distinction between individualist and collectivist cultures is the key to understanding many cultural contrasts. The lower economic productivity of collectivist cultures is offset by evidence of a healthier quality of life. These societies, which comprise 70 percent of the world's population, have among the lowest rates of homicide, suicide, juvenile delinquency, divorce, child abuse, and alcoholism. Whereas individualists look for immediate personal rewards, freedom, equality, personal enjoyment, and a varied, exciting life, collectivists put high value on self-discipline, accepting one's position in life, honoring parents and elders, preserving one's image, and working toward long-term goals that benefit the group as a whole.

These deep-rooted cultural differences clearly play vital roles in the motivational psychology of the individual and the group. Asian-American children, for example, have an extensive support system that inspires confidence; their parents have a lifelong sense of purpose and security. "Education is pushed for family reasons, not simply as a means of achieving personal ambition. The idea is that the children will always care for the parents, so anything that serves the younger generation well is a family affair. That can come into direct conflict with American individualism" (F. Lee, quoted by Vivano, 1990). Despite the effect of culture on the psychology of the individual, virtually all the data from modern psychology comes from the most individualistic cultures. The study of the need for achievement is centered on the personal ambitions of the individual; it ignores the need to achieve group goals.

ATTRIBUTIONS FOR SUCCESS AND FAILURE

Motivation for achievement is further complicated by individual attributions, interpretations, and beliefs about the reasons events turn out the way they do. Earlier, we mentioned the *locus of control* orientation—our interpretation that the outcomes of our actions are the result of what *we* do (*internal control orientation*) as opposed to the result of *factors in the environment* (*external control orientation*). In addition to this difference in internal-external control attributions, several other factors influence our interpretations of success and failure: perception of stability-instability, global-specific, and controllable-uncontrollable.

To what extent is a situation or result over time seen as stable and consistent or unstable and varying? When the dimension of attributions of *stability* is crossed with the dimension of locus of control, four possible interpretations about the causes of outcomes follow, as shown in **Figure 12.8.**

Your exam grade in this course may be interpreted as the result of internal factors, such as ability (a stable personality characteristic) or effort (a varying personal quality). Or it may be viewed as caused primarily by external factors such as the difficulty of the task, the actions of others (a stable situational problem), or luck (an unstable external feature). Depending on the nature of the attribution you make for this success or failure, you are likely to experience one of the emotional affects depicted in **Table 12.3.** What is important here is that the basis for your personal interpretation will influence your emotions and subsequent achievement motivation—regardless of the true reason for the success or failure.

FIGURE 12.8 *ATTRIBUTIONS REGARDING CAUSES FOR BEHAVIORAL OUTCOMES*

Four possible outcomes are generated with just two sources of attributions about behavior, the locus of control and the situation in which the behavior occurs. Ability attributions are made for the internal-stable combination; effort for the internal but unstable combination; luck for the unstable-external combination; and a difficult task (test) when external-stable forces are assumed to be operating.

	Locus of Control	
	internal	external
stable	ability	task difficulty
unstable	effort	luck

Stability

TABLE 12.3 ATTRIBUTION-DEPENDENT AFFECTS

Our affective reaction to success and failure depends on the kinds of attributions made regarding the cause of those outcomes. For example, we take pride in success when it is attributed to our ability, but are depressed when lack of ability is perceived to cause our failure. Or, gratitude follows success attributed to the actions of others, but anger when they are seen as contributing to our failure.

	Affects	
Attribution	Success	Failure
Ability	Competence	Incompetence
	Confidence	Resignation
	Pride	Depression
Effort	Relief	Guilt
	Contentment	Shame
	Relaxation	Fear
Action of others	Gratitude	Anger
	Thankfulness	Fury
Luck	Surprise	Surprise
	Guilt	Astonishment

Two other dimensions of achievement attributions add to the complexity of our interpretations of success and failure. Is the effect a highly *specific* one, limited to a particular task or situation, or is it *global,* applying widely across a variety of settings? We would like to believe our failures are specific and our successes global. We often experience psychological trouble when we come to believe the reverse. The other attributional dimension is the degree to which a cause is perceived to be *controllable* and *intentional* or *uncontrollable* and *unintentional.* This theoretical dimension has not yet been integrated into the research, however, due to the difficulty of determining whether a specific action is intentional (Weiner, 1985).

Is it better to succeed because of your ability or because of your effort? Research by Martin Covington (1984) and others suggests that we seek to attribute success to *ability,* which is both internal and stable and which is valued in our culture even over hard work. These researchers see effort as a double-edged sword for students. If you try hard and succeed you may be perceived as smart and motivated. However, if you try hard and fail, your ability will be perceived as low. Some students may prefer not to try at all; that way, if

they fail, the blame will fall on their lack of motivation rather than on their lack of skill.

Beliefs about *why* we have succeeded or failed, then, are important because they lead to (a) different interpretations of past performance and general worth; (b) different emotions, goals, and effort in the present situation; and (c) different motivation in the future—in turn, making future successes more likely or less so. When we attribute a failure to low ability and difficult tasks, we are likely to give up sooner, select simpler tasks, and lower our goals. When we attribute failure to bad luck or lack of effort, we are likely to have higher motivation to try again for success (Fontaine, 1974; Rosenbaum, 1972; Valle & Frieze, 1976).

It is interesting to note that children seem to start out with a sense that intelligence and effort are equivalent. Young children see "smart" kids as those who work hardest, and young children believe they can make themselves smarter by trying hard. Unfortunately, around junior high school students start to shift over to the prevailing view of American society—that some people are more gifted than others (Nicholls, 1984). People with a high sense of self-efficacy, then, seem to retain a childlike faith in their ability to improve themselves (Schunk & Cox, 1986).

ATTRIBUTIONAL STYLES: OPTIMISM VERSUS PESSIMISM

The way we explain the events in our lives—from winning at cards to being turned down for a date—can become lifelong attributional styles that affect the way we view ourselves (Trotter, 1987). The way we account to ourselves for our successes and failures, wins and losses, and freedom and constraints, influences our motivation, mood, and even ability to perform appropriately. University of Pennsylvania researcher **Martin Seligman** has been studying the ways in which people's *explanatory style*—their degree of optimism or pessimism—affects activity and passivity, persisting and giving up, taking risks, and playing it safe (Seligman, 1987, 1991).

Understanding how explanatory style works leads to new perspectives on a range of behaviors where motivation, emotion, and beliefs play important roles. Explanatory style has been shown to influence depression, school failures, success in business, poor health, and the results of presidential elections. A critical attributional dichotomy—between those vulnerable and those invulnerable to threatening, stressful, and failure situations—emerges from several decades of research.

Surprisingly, this dichotomy emerged in early research on *learned helplessness* in dogs and, later, in

Martin Seligman (*Discovering Psychology,* 1990, Program 12)

humans (see Chapter 9). Recall that animals exposed to inescapable, noncontingent shocks became helpless. This failure experience made them passive, retarding their learning in new situations. When human subjects were put in comparable experimental situations where they faced insolvable problems that inevitably led to failure, they behaved much like the animals that had developed this learned helplessness syndrome. Their motivational level plummeted as did their general activity, learning, and self-esteem. Finally, they became sad. When their brain chemistry was analyzed, the patterns found resembled those seen in clinically depressed mental patients.

These effects reliably appeared in a host of studies from many laboratories—for the majority of subjects. Faced with inescapable shock or noise or unsolvable problems, about two thirds became helpless. However, there is another side to the evidence which was ignored initially because it was not as dramatic as the learned-helplessness effects. One third of the subjects turned out to be *invulnerables,* resisting any attempts to make them helpless. They did not give up, kept trying, and did not let the negative experience produce the symptoms that plagued the others who were vulnerable to failure. What accounts for this difference in subjects?

Seligman's research team has been working on the problem of what accounts for one person's ability and another's inability to resist failure. The secret ingredient has turned out to be familiar and seemingly simple: *optimism versus pessimism.* Remarkably, these two divergent ways of looking at the world influence motivation, mood, and behavior. They represent opposite ways of explaining the causes for one's success and failure. Once formed, these *attributional styles* (or *explanatory styles*) operate swiftly, pervasively, and without much

thought. The methods used to assess these styles are an explanatory style self-report questionnaire and analysis of causal statements made in natural speech (found in newspapers, press conferences, and therapy transcripts) to reconstruct people's beliefs. Each statement about the causes of some important life event is then coded by judges who rate the extent to which it is internal-external, stable-unstable, and global-specific. A profile is generated of the kinds of causal statements a person uses in his or her natural speech, indexing him or her as pessimist, optimist, or other.

The *pessimistic attributional style* focuses on the causes of *failure* as internally generated. Furthermore, the bad situation and one's role in causing it are seen as stable and global—"It won't ever change and it will affect everything." The *optimistic attributional style* attributes failure to external causes—"The test was unfair"— and to events that are unstable or modifiable and specific—"If I put in more effort next time, I'll do better, and this won't affect how I perform any other task that is important to me."

These causal explanations are reversed when it comes to the question of *success.* Optimists take full, personal internal-stable-global credit for success. However pessimists attribute their success to external-unstable-global or specific factors.

Trends of optimism or pessimism seem to affect all areas of life. Pessimists appear to be at risk for depression; for low achievement in school and career; and for poor health. Pessimistic women with breast cancer are more likely to die sooner than optimistic women. Optimists, on the other hand, make about half as many visits to doctors as pessimists and have half the number of infectious diseases according to one study. The underlying basis of the link between explanatory style and health is that optimism improves the functioning of the immune system while pessimism impairs it. The effects are enduring. Those who are optimistic early in life (based on diary records and other available verbal reports of their causal explanations) remain so when they are elderly (Seligman, 1991).

Pessimism lowers achievement by driving those with that explanatory style to perform worse than expected according to objective measures of their talent. In the U.S. workplace, how well you survive in jobs that involve challenge, rejection, and failure depends in part on your level of pessimism or optimism. It was possible to predict 18 out of the 22 last presidential elections based on the extent to which the candidates were optimistic and action-oriented or pessimistic and ruminative in their convention acceptance speeches. Americans apparently prefer an optimistic-action leader.

It seems that optimists can't lose and pessimists can't win, regardless of whether they succeed or fail in life's challenges. The practical advice that stems from research on attributional styles is that your chances for success, good health, and long life increase if you think optimistic, positive thoughts. However, at times, a mild degree of realistic pessimism helps to put the brakes on dreams and visions of boundless optimism. Wisdom is this balance performed by the executive function of the mind.

INTRINSIC VERSUS EXTRINSIC MOTIVATION

Motivation to engage in an activity for its own sake, in the absence of external reward, is called **intrinsic motivation.** Things that we do because we simply enjoy doing them—such as playing video games, singing in the shower, doing crossword puzzles, or keeping a secret diary—are intrinsically motivated. Work, too, can be intrinsically motivated when an individual is deeply interested in the job to be done.

Extrinsic motivation is motivation to engage in an activity for some external consequence. In extrinsic motivation, behavior is instrumental to obtaining something else, while in intrinsic motivation, behavior is carried out without a purpose beyond the immediate rewards of doing it. Taking vitamins is extrinsically motivated; eating cream puffs is intrinsically motivated.

What do you predict happens when children are given extrinsic rewards for behavior that they were already motivated intrinsically to produce? Play becomes work when fun activities are given superfluous rewards, as shown in a series of classroom experiments by **Mark Lepper** and his colleagues (Lepper et al., 1973). When an extrinsic reward is given, the motivation becomes extrinsic and the task itself is enjoyed less. When the extrinsic rewards are withdrawn, the activity loses its material value (Deci, 1975; Lepper, 1981; Lepper & Greene, 1978). The moral is: *A reward a day makes work out of play.*

Extrinsic constraints on people, such as evaluation pressure or close surveillance during an activity, seem to have effects on motivation similar to those of rewards. Typically, students in courses where grades are heavily emphasized might find that their motivation, even for their favorite subjects, dwindles after the final exam—they were working only for the grade. Gold stars, grades, and penalties for failure or misbehavior are testament to the (false) belief that schoolchildren are extrinsically motivated and must be given external consequences to learn.

Intrinsically motivating activities have been described as producing a special state of mind called **flow** (Csikszentmihalyi, 1990). Flow experiences are char-acterized by a pleasurable loss of self-awareness and of any sense of the passage of time, along with a deep concentration on the task and not its outcome. *Flow* is inherent in the creative process, produced by the motivation of ultimate involvement in the activity and not by its possible outcomes. Going with the flow is the reward for intrinsic motivation. Although some people turn to drugs or alcohol to experience the flow feeling, researchers have found that work produces more of these optimal flow experiences than do leisure-time activities.

WORK AND ORGANIZATIONAL PSYCHOLOGY

Recognizing that work settings are complex social systems, **organizational psychologists** study various aspects of human relations, such as communication among employees, socialization or enculturation of workers, leadership, attitudes and commitment toward a job and/or an organization, job satisfaction, stress and burnout, and overall quality of life at work. As consultants to businesses, organizational psychologists may assist in recruitment, selection, and training of employees. In some cases, they may recommend against searching for an ideal job candidate and suggest instead that efforts be directed toward job redesign or toward tailoring a job to fit the person. Finally, new theories of management, organizational design, decision making, development, and change are emerging, providing breadth and a scholarly foundation to practical applications (O'Reilly, 1991; Porras & Silvers, 1991).

Organizational psychologists have proposed many theories of work motivation, two of which are *need theories,* which focus on what energizes individual workers, and *cognitive theories,* which describe the way motivation occurs.

Need Theories of Work

Need theories are based on Maslow's theoretical approach. One of these, known as **ERG theory,** specifies only three sets of needs—**E**xistence needs, **R**elatedness needs, and **G**rowth needs (Alderfer, 1972). Existence needs include the need for food, shelter, pay, and safe working conditions. Relatedness needs are social in nature, emphasizing the need for clear and available interpersonal communication. Growth needs encourage development of one's true potential and correspond to Maslow's self-actualization and esteem needs. In contrast to Maslow's theory, ERG theory assumes that higher-level needs can become activated *before* lower-level needs are completely satisfied. Research is generally more supportive of ERG theory than of Maslow's needs hierarchy (Betz, 1982; Wahba & Bridwell, 1976).

Cognitive Theories of Work

Cognitive theories of work motivation, such as *equity theory* and *expectancy theory,* go beyond the individual need level to include social and organizational factors. These theories attempt to explain and predict how people will respond under different working conditions. They assume that workers engage in certain cognitive activities, such as assessing fairness via processes of social comparison with other workers, or estimating expected rewards associated with their performance.

Equity theory proposes that workers are motivated to maintain fair or equitable relationships with other relevant persons (Adams, 1965). Workers take note of their inputs (investments or contributions they make to their jobs) and their outcomes (what they receive from their jobs), and then they compare these with the inputs and outcomes of other workers. When the ratio of outcomes to inputs for Worker A is equal to the ratio for Worker B (outcome A ÷ input A = outcome B ÷ input B) then Worker A will feel satisfied. Dissatisfaction will result when these ratios are *not* equal. When Worker A's ratio is less than that of other workers (perceived underpayment), A will feel angry; but when Worker A's ratio is greater than others (perceived overpayment), A will feel guilty.

Since feeling this inequity is aversive, workers will be motivated to restore equity by changing the relevant inputs and outcomes. These changes could be *behavioral* (for example, reducing input by working less, increasing outcome by asking for a raise). Or, they could be *psychological* (for example, reinterpreting the value of the inputs—"My work isn't really that good").

Research has supported the predictions of equity theory, particularly with regard to perceived underpayment (Carrel & Dittrich, 1978). One study showed that underpaid clerical workers were less productive, and overpaid workers more productive, than equitably paid workers (Pritchard et al., 1972). Similarly, college students who were given additional responsibilities and a high-status job title maintained high levels of performance, whereas students who were given additional responsibilities but no title (underpayment inequity) dramatically reduced their performance, presumably in order to restore equity (Greenberg & Ornstein, 1983).

Expectancy theory proposes that workers are motivated when they expect that their effort and performance on the job will result in desired outcomes (Porter & Lawler, 1968; Vroom, 1964). In other words, people will engage in work they find attractive (leads to favorable consequences) and achievable. Expectancy theory emphasizes three components. *Instrumentality* refers to the perception that one's performance will be rewarded. *Valence* refers to the perceived attractiveness of particular outcomes. *Expectancy* refers to the perceived likelihood that a worker's efforts will result in successful performance. According to expectancy theory, workers rationally and logically assess the probabilities of these three components and combine them by multiplying their individual values, rather than merely summing them additively. Highest levels of motivation, therefore, result when all three components have high probabilities, whereas lowest levels result when any single component is zero.

One of the strengths of expectancy theory is that it distinguishes between motivation and performance, indicating that factors such as skill, ability, and job opportunities can influence performance, in addition to motivation. In other words, poor performance does not necessarily result from low motivation. Research has been supportive of expectancy theory, demonstrating proposed relationships between expectancy, instrumentality, and motivation (Garland, 1984; Mitchell, 1974).

Before concluding, the following cautionary note seems in order for those readers who are high need achievers, work-focused, future-oriented optimists. Despite the probability of being financially successful, there is some evidence that you may come to regret the personal and social sacrifices paid for that success. A 1989 study of over 4000 successful business executives revealed widespread dissatisfaction with the corporate experience. Nearly half of all middle managers said that their lives seemed "empty and meaningless" despite years spent striving to achieve their personal goals. A majority of senior executives reported that they felt they've wasted much of their lives struggling for corporate success, with the consequence that family and personal life was sacrificed. If they could start all over again, they believe they would rearrange their priorities (Tuller, 1989). But do you think they really would?

We have come a long way from rats running across a hot grid, to corporate executives caught up in the rat race. In between, we have considered the biology and psychology of hunger and eating, and the evolutionary and social dimensions of sex, reproduction, and human sexuality. These are but a few of the topics studied by psychologists who seek to understand some basic whys of animal and human nature. The dynamic aspects of motivation are being investigated at many different levels, from the genetic and biological to the behavioral, cognitive, social, and cultural. Throughout we see the intricate interplay of nature and nurture, of biology and behavior, of mind and body. We are the sum total of those continual interactions—and something more.

Our next chapter elaborates several themes previewed here, the significant role that emotions play in our lives, and the consequences of negative emotions and stress on our performance and well-being. You will also be introduced to one of the most important new areas of psychology, that of Health Psychology.

RECAPPING MAIN POINTS

Understanding Motivation

Motivation is a dynamic concept used to describe the processes directing behavior. Motivational analysis helps explain how biological and behavioral processes are related and why people pursue goals despite obstacles and adversity. Researchers use motivation as an intervening variable to link independent variables with observable responses on the dependent variable side. Lesioning, stimulation, and deprivation are three procedures used to manipulate motivation in animal research. External stimuli arouse incentive motivation.

Theoretical Perspectives

No one theory has been able to explain motivation completely. Instinct theory developed out of the Darwinian revolution. Drive theory and arousal theory followed. Humanistic approaches to motivation postulate a hierarchy of needs leading toward self-actualizing action. Social and cognitive psychologists emphasize individual perception and interpretation of a situation.

Hunger and Eating

Hunger is the most studied of all human drives. Early researchers mistakenly sought to explain hunger as the result of peripheral stimulation of stomach contractions. Hunger cannot be entirely explained by central processes in the brain. Complex interactions of the brain, hormonal system, local stimulation, and psychological factors motivate hunger. Food intake and body weight are regulated according to a "set point" which is measured by fat stored in specialized fat cells.

Sexual Motivation

From an evolutionary perspective, sex is the mechanism for producing offspring with genetic variability. In animals, the sex-drive is largely controlled by hormones. In humans, sexual activity is subject to learning and cultural values. Kinsey's surveys of American sexual behavior brought the study of sex into the open. The work of Masters and Johnson provided the first hard data on the sexual response cycles of men and women. Discrepancies in sexual scripts can lead to serious misunderstanding and even date rape. Many theories attempt to account for homosexuality but neither genetic nor psychoanalytic explanations are entirely satisfactory.

Achievement and Work Motivation

Achievement motives are future oriented and drive a wide variety of human activity. People have varying needs for achievement. Societies that emphasize individualism tend to have greater economic success. Societies that place greater emphasis on collectivism do not achieve high economic status but have fewer social problems. Our motivation for achievement is influenced by how we interpret success and failure. Two attributional styles, optimism and pessimism, lead to different attitudes toward achievement and influence both motivation and health. In the absence of external reward, intrinsic motivation directs our activities. Extrinsic motivation leads us to engage in an activity for an external, environmental consequence and may diminish intrinsic motivation for a task. Organizational psychologists study human motivation in work settings. Two important kinds of theories of work motivation are need theories and cognitive theories.

KEY TERMS

critical set point, 438
deficiency motivation, 433
drive, 424
dynamic psychology, 424
equity theory, 455
ERG theory, 454
expectancy theory, 455
extrinsic motivation, 454
fetish, 443
fixed-action pattern, 429
flow, 454
growth motivation, 433
human sexuality, 441
incentive motivation, 428
incentives, 428

intrinsic motivation, 454
locus of control orientation, 435
motivation, 424
motive, 424
need for achievement, 450
needs hierarchy, 433
optimal arousal, 431
organizational psychologists, 454
parental investment, 442
pheromones, 440
sexual arousal, 441
sexual reproduction, 440
sexual scripts, 443
thematic apperception test (TAT), 434
Yerkes-Dodson law, 432

MAJOR CONTRIBUTORS

Adler, Norman, 440
Buss, David, 442
Cannon, Walter, 436
Carnes, Patrick, 447
Festinger, Leon, 435
Freud, Sigmund, 430
Heider, Fritz, 435
Hull, Clark, 430
James, William, 430
Johnson, Virginia, 441
Kinsey, Alfred, 441
Lepper, Mark, 454

Lewin, Kurt, 434
McClelland, David, 434
McDougall, William, 430
Maslow, Abraham, 433
Masters, William, 441
Murray, Henry, 434
Rotter, Julian, 435
Seligman, Martin, 452
Taylor, Janet, 427
Tolman, Edward, 426
Triandis, Harry, 451
Woodworth, Robert, 430

Chapter 13

Emotion, Stress, and Health Psychology

EMOTIONS   460
   EXPERIENCING EMOTION
   FUNCTIONS OF EMOTION
   THEORIES OF EMOTION
   ARE EMOTIONAL EXPRESSIONS UNIVERSAL?

MOOD AND INFORMATION PROCESSING   470

   ▪ INTERIM SUMMARY

STRESS OF LIVING   472
   SOURCES OF STRESS
   STRESS MODERATOR VARIABLES
   CLOSE-UP: PASSIVE SMOKING
   PHYSIOLOGICAL STRESS REACTIONS
   PSYCHOLOGICAL STRESS REACTIONS

   ▪ INTERIM SUMMARY

COPING WITH STRESS   487
   COPING STRATEGIES
   MODIFYING COGNITIVE STRATEGIES
   SUPPORTIVENESS OF THE ENVIRONMENT
   STRUCTURING THE PHYSICAL ENVIRONMENT

   ▪ INTERIM SUMMARY

HEALTH PSYCHOLOGY   492
   THE BIOPSYCHOSOCIAL MODEL OF HEALTH
   THE YIN AND YANG OF HEALTH AND ILLNESS
   HEALTH PROMOTION AND MAINTENANCE
   TREATMENT AND PREVENTION OF ILLNESS
   HEALTHY AGAIN
   CAUSES AND CORRELATES OF HEALTH, ILLNESS,
     AND DYSFUNCTION
   HEALTH CARE SYSTEM AND HEALTH POLICY
     FORMATION
   A TOAST TO YOUR HEALTH

RECAPPING MAIN POINTS   504

KEY TERMS   505

MAJOR CONTRIBUTORS   505

L ucy went to the hospital to visit Emma, a neighbor who had broken her hip. The first thing Lucy saw when the elevator door opened at the third floor was a clown with an enormous orange nose dancing down the hall, pushing a colorfully decorated cart. The clown stopped in front of Lucy, bowed, and then somersaulted to the nurses' station. A cluster of patients cheered. Most of them were in wheelchairs or on crutches. Upon asking for directions, Lucy learned that Emma was in the "humor room," where *Blazing Saddles* was about to start.

Since writer **Norman Cousins's** widely publicized recovery from a debilitating and usually incurable disease of the connective tissue, humor has gained new respectability in hospital wards around the country. Cousins, the long-time editor of the *Saturday Review*, with the cooperation of his physician, supplemented his regular medical therapy with a steady diet of Marx Brothers movies and "Candid Camera" film clips. Although he never claimed that laughter alone effected his cure, Cousins is best remembered for his passionate support of the notion that, if negative emotions can cause distress, then humor and positive emotions can enhance the healing process (Cousins, 1979, 1989).

The idea caught on even before it had much empirical support. Today, hospitals in Houston, Los Angeles, and Honolulu provide patients with videotapes of funny films. "Laugh wagons" carrying humorous books and tapes roll through the halls of health centers across the country. At a Catholic hospital in Texas, the nuns are expected to tell at least one joke a day (Cousins, 1989). Nurse Patty Wooten travels the United States in a clown suit, with bedpan and enema bags strapped to her belt, teaching nurses the importance of using humor to cope with the stresses of health care (*Wellness New Mexico*, 1987). Allen Funt, creator of "Candid Camera," has set up a foundation to distribute his funny videos free of charge to researchers, hospitals, and individual patients in the hope of applying humor therapy for distress and illness and investigating the effects of such therapy.

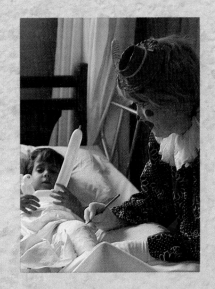

What are the medical benefits of humor? Cousins's doctor found that his sedimentation rate (a measure of inflammation) decreased after only a few moments of robust laughter. This decrease in inflammation was also reflected in Cousins's ability to enjoy two hours of pain-free sleep after ten minutes of hardy laughing (Cousins, 1989). Stanford psychiatric researcher William Fry, Jr., compares laughter to "stationary jogging." Increases in respiration, heart rate, and blood circulation created by laughing brings oxygen to the blood at a rate as much as six times greater than during ordinary speech (Fry, 1986). Some biochemical changes, including reductions in the stress hormone *cortisol*, have also been detected (Berk, 1989). Salivary immunoglobulin A, which is thought to protect the body against certain viruses, increased significantly in people who viewed funny tapes for 30 minutes. In addition, people who said they used humor to deal with difficult situations in everyday life had the highest baseline levels of this protective substance (Dillon & Totten, 1989).

Cousins significantly enhanced the public's awareness of the relatively new field of psychoneuroimmunology, the study of healing interactions between brain, body, emotions, and the immune system. Researchers hope that advances in this area will help explain the physiological underpinnings of laughter's tonic effect.

Emotions, stress, illness, and health are all entwined in this humor approach to treating physical ailments. Emotions are the touchstones of human experience; they give richness to our interactions with people and our contacts with nature, joy to our existence, significance to our memories, and hope to our expectations. In this chapter, we will explore the ways emotion helps motivate our adaptations to situational demands. We will look at the evolutionary significance of emotion and at the many faces human emotion wears. If the demands on our biological and psychological functioning are excessive, we may become overwhelmed and unable to deal with the stressors in our daily lives. This chapter will also examine how stress affects us and how we can combat it.

Finally, we will combine all of these concerns as we look at psychology's most important new area: *health psychology*. Health psychologists investigate the ways in which environmental, social, and psychological processes contribute to the development of illness and the ways they can be utilized to treat and prevent illness.

EMOTIONS

Emotions are elicited by experiences that are important for our survival and general well-being. Reacting emotionally focuses attention on these experiences by marking them as special in some way, by recording them more indelibly in memory, and by rousing us to take action. Because emotions involve so many aspects of human functioning, the study of emotions has emerged recently as a central issue in research and theory for a host of psychologists from different backgrounds (Bower, 1981; Frijda et al., 1989; Hoffman, 1986; Lazarus, 1982; Leventhal, 1980; Plutchik, 1980; Zajonc, 1982).

The general consensus among contemporary psychologists defines **emotion** as a complex pattern of bodily and mental changes including physiological arousal, feelings, cognitive processes, and behavioral reactions made in response to a situation perceived as personally significant (Kleinginna & Kleinginna, 1981). The physiological arousal includes neural, hormonal, visceral, and muscular changes (some of which were described in Chapter 3). The feelings include both a general affective state (good-bad, positive-negative) and a specific feeling tone, such as joy or disgust. The cognitive processes include interpretations, memories, and expectations. The overt behavioral reactions can be expressive (crying, smiling) and/or action oriented (screaming for help). Finally, we may perceive the situation as significant either consciously or nonconsciously.

Humans are unique in the array of events that can trigger emotions (Hebb, 1980). However, emotions are

Overt behavioral reactions can be expressive, such as smiling or yelling, or action oriented, such as calling for help.

surprisingly similar among people throughout the world and some emotions can even be expressed in similar ways among other animals. As we ascend the evolutionary scale from simple organisms to humans, we observe both increasing differentiation of the facial muscles used to express emotion and an increasing diversity of emotional behavior. Humans have not evolved *away* from nonrational, primitive emotions but *toward* a combination of intellect and emotion (Scherer, 1984). How do we experience emotion? What functions do emotions serve? Which emotions are universal?

EXPERIENCING EMOTION

Just imagine what your life would be like if you could think and act but not feel. Would you trade the capacity to experience fear at the expense of not feeling the passion of a lover's kiss? Surely this would be a bad bargain, soon regretted. Society views among its most dangerous enemies those cold-blooded murderers who kill without remorse or any normal human emotion. Of course, there are times when intense emotions burst forth involuntarily, getting in the way of calm, rational thinking. At such times, we wish we could keep our emotions under control to maintain our composure. Emotional reactions involve physiological arousal, brain processes, cognitive interpretations of our physical reactions, experiencing feeling states, and expressing what we feel in facial muscle changes and bodily signals that communicate our feelings to others. Let's begin on the inside with the roles of body and brain functions and then move outward to see how emotions help each of us make the human connection.

Neurophysiology of Emotion

Physiological systems provide the machinery of response to internal and external stimuli by sending signals that activate or inhibit emotional responding. These reactions begin with the arousal of the brain as a whole by the *reticular activating system* through which incoming sensory messages pass on their way to the brain (Lindsley, 1951; Zanchetti, 1967). As we saw in Chapter 3, this system functions as a nonspecific, general alarm system for the rest of the brain. Strong emotional arousal stimulates physical arousal just as sexual arousal stimulates genital arousal. Your heart races, respiration goes up, your mouth dries, your muscles tense, and maybe you even shake. In addition to these changes that you notice, many others occur beneath the surface. They are all designed to mobilize the body for action.

The *autonomic nervous system* (ANS) prepares the body for emotional responses through the action of both its divisions; the balance between the divisions depends on the quality and intensity of the arousing stimulation.

With mild, *unpleasant* stimulation, the *sympathetic* division is more active; with mild, *pleasant* stimulation, the *parasympathetic* division is more active. With more intense stimulation of either kind, both divisions are increasingly involved. Physiologically, strong emotions such as fear or anger *activate* the body's *emergency reaction system* which swiftly and silently prepares the body for potential danger. The sympathetic nervous system takes charge by directing the release of hormones (epinephrine and norepinephrine) from the adrenal glands which in turn lead the internal organs to release blood sugar, raise blood pressure, and increase sweating and salivation. To calm us after the emergency has passed, the parasympathetic nervous system takes over by inhibiting the release of the activating hormones. We may remain aroused for a while after an experience of strong emotional activation because some of the hormones continue to circulate in the bloodstream.

The influence of *hormones* on emotion has been shown in several kinds of studies. Changes in emotional response occur when hormones are administered and in diseases affecting the endocrine glands. Hormone levels in the blood and urine rise during emotional states. Research has also shown that perception of emotional stimuli is accompanied by release of hormones such as epinephrine and norepinephrine. *Steroid hormones* act on many different kinds of body tissue, including nerve cells, by causing them to change their excitability rapidly and directly. They can produce euphoria in short-term low doses but depression in long-term high doses (Majewska et al., 1986). Many of the mood changes associated with stress, pregnancy, and the menstrual cycle may be related to the effects that steroid hormones have on brain cells.

Integration of both the hormonal and the neural aspects of arousal is controlled by the *hypothalamus* and the *limbic system,* old-brain control systems for emotions and for patterns of attack, defense, and flight. Either lesioning or stimulation in various parts of the limbic system produces dramatic changes in emotional responding. Tame animals may become killers; usual prey and predators may become peaceful companions (Delgado, 1969).

Recent neuroanatomy research has focused on the **amygdala** as the part of the limbic system that acts as a gateway for emotion and as a filter for memory by attaching significance to the information it receives from the senses. When the amygdala is damaged in accidents or by surgery, a human patient shows no reaction in situations that normally evoke strong emotional responses. Monkeys whose amygdalae have been surgically removed are completely unresponsive to emotional stimuli in their environment and become socially withdrawn.

Neuroscientist **Joseph LeDoux** (1990) has discovered an anatomical pathway in rats that allows sensory information to go directly to the amygdala before the same information reaches the cortex. The amygdala acts on this raw data to trigger an emotional response *before* the cortex can provide an interpretation of the stimulus event. In most people, if the emotional response proves unnecessary, it is quickly overridden by signals from the cortex to "cool it." However, LeDoux speculates that some people may be overly emotional because their amygdala's response is stronger than the cortex's ability to control it with rational interpretations. The frequent, uncontrollable emotional outbursts of infants may be due to the fact that the parts of the cortex that control emotional responding are not fully developed until sometime between 18 and 36 months, long after the amygdala and other emotional centers in the brain are active. In addition, the amygdala seems to record emotional messages in a permanent way; it does not appear to have a "memory eraser." Rather, its responsivity is inhibited only by cortical control. When the cortex is surgically prevented from influencing the amygdala in rats, their strong conditioned fear responses are maintained permanently despite experimental extinction training. Although not yet proven, similar anatomical pathways are assumed to function in the human brain.

In all complex emotions, the *cortex* is involved through its internal neural networks and its connections with other parts of the body. The cortex provides the associations, memories, and meanings that integrate psychological experience and biological responses. Research is pointing to different emotional centers in the cortex for processing positive and negative emotions. The left hemisphere seems to involve positive emotions, such as happiness, while right hemisphere activity influences negative emotions, such as anger (Davidson 1984). This **lateralization of emotion** in the human brain has been found through EEG analysis of emotional reactions in normal subjects and through research relating emotional facial expression to brain damage of the right or left hemisphere in adult patients (Ahern & Schwartz, 1985; Borod et al., 1988).

The biochemical responses involved in emotional reactions may differ according to the *meaning* we attach to the situations in which they are experienced. Although tears are associated with sorrow, we cry in response to many types of emotional arousal—for example, when we're angry or when we're filled with joy and ecstasy. Tears also flow from eye-irritating stimuli. When researchers compared the biochemistry of emotional tears and irritant tears, they found that emotional tears (generated when subjects watched a sad movie) differ significantly from irritant tears (generated

when subjects inhaled the vapor of freshly grated onions). Under emotional conditions, the lacrimal glands secrete a greater volume of tears and also tears with a higher concentration of protein (Frey & Langseth, 1985). There are no differences between the sexes on either of these measures, but an analysis of *reported* emotional crying over a one-month period shows that more women cried for emotional reasons more frequently than did men (Frey et al., 1983). See **Figure 13.1** for a summary of this analysis.

Interpreting and Labeling Emotions

Shortly after beginning a lecture to psychologists at a midwestern university in January, I noticed that I was perspiring heavily. Everyone else seemed comfortable, so it couldn't be a physical reaction to a hot room. My breathing was also a bit labored and then I noticed that my heart rate seemed to be speeding up. Why was I feeling so *anxious?* I searched for the answer as I continued lecturing. Maybe I was boring the audience; should I pick up the pace and get to the more interesting stuff? Or maybe I just hadn't prepared well enough.

FIGURE 13.1 EPISODES OF EMOTIONAL CRYING IN A MONTH

In the first formal investigation of adult crying behavior, 45 male and 286 female subjects judged to be psychiatrically normal kept records of their emotional crying behavior during a month. Duration of episodes for both groups was about six minutes, and the most frequent stimuli for crying involved interpersonal relations and media presentations. A high proportion of both groups said they felt better after crying.

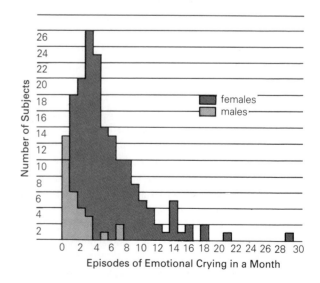

Is she crying because she lost the race? No—she just set a new high-school record.

means in the particular setting in which it is being experienced.

Misattributing Arousal

Typically, the external situation determines your definition of the emotional arousal being experienced, without much need for elaborate interpretation. We can also experience physical arousal from nonemotional sources, such as caffeine, exercise, certain drugs, or intense heat. When we are aware of these sources as the causal stimuli, there is no emotional interpretation. However, what happens when we do not recognize their direct physiological impact?

As in my lecture example, we sometimes *misattribute* physically based arousal as emotionally based arousal, mislabelling our physical symptoms as part of a psychological state. Being overheated can become being anxious, being physically aroused from exercise can be misinterpreted as being sexually aroused. Psychological researchers have contrived experimental demonstrations such as the following that illustrate this emotional misattribution in interesting ways.

> A female researcher interviewed male subjects who had just crossed one of two bridges in Vancouver, Canada. One bridge was a safe, sturdy bridge; the other was a wobbly, precarious bridge. The researcher pretended to be interested in the effects of scenery on creativity and asked the men to write brief stories about an ambiguous picture that included a woman. She also invited them to call her if they wanted more information about the research. Those men who had just crossed the dangerous bridge wrote stories with more sexual imagery, and four times as many of those men called the female researcher than did those who had crossed the safe bridge. To show that arousal was the independent variable influencing the emotional misinterpretation, the researchers also arranged for another group of men to be interviewed 10 minutes or more after crossing the dangerous bridge, enough time for their physical arousal symptoms to be reduced. These nonaroused men did not show the signs of sexual arousal that the aroused men did (Dutton & Aron, 1974).

Just then, someone bolted out of the lecture hall: validation for my hypothesis that I was anxious because I realized I was giving a lousy lecture! However, as I frantically tried to alter my presentation to salvage it, I wiped perspiration from my collar and my hand rubbed across the top of the heavy woolen undershirt I had decided to wear in anticipation of the cold weather so alien to Californians. The undershirt was the source of the perspiration and my symptoms of physical arousal! "What a great lecture that guy is missing by leaving for the bathroom," I thought with relief.

Because arousal symptoms and internal states for many different emotions are similar, it is possible to confuse them at times when they are experienced in ambiguous or novel situations, such as my sweaty lecture. This case study reveals an important feature of emotion: the cognitive processes involved in going beyond the purely physiological activation to *interpret* what we are feeling. We *appraise* our physiological arousal in an effort to discover what we are feeling, what emotional label best fits, and what our reaction

Basic Emotions

Some investigators believe that, despite the complexity of emotional experience, there is a set of basic emotions that is biologically and experientially distinct. The **emotion wheel** of **Robert Plutchik** (1980, 1984) proposes a set of innate emotions. As **Figure 13.2** shows, the model depicts eight basic emotions, made up of four pairs of opposites: joy-sadness, fear-anger, surprise-anticipation, and acceptance-disgust. All other

FIGURE 13.2   *THE EMOTION WHEEL*

Plutchik's model arranges eight basic emotions within a circle of opposites. Pairs of these adjacent primary emotions combine to form more complex emotions noted on the outside of the circle. Secondary emotions emerge from basic emotions more remotely associated on the wheel.

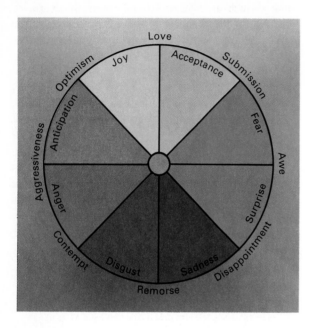

emotions are assumed to be variations, or *blends,* of these basic eight. Complex emotions, shown on the outside of the emotional wheel, result from combinations of two adjacent primary emotions. For example, love is a combination of joy and acceptance; remorse combines sadness and disgust. Plutchik proposes that emotions are most clearly differentiated when they are at high intensities, such as loathing and grief, and least different when they are low in intensity, such as disgust and sadness. He also believes that each primary emotion is associated with an adaptive evolutionary response. Disgust is considered an evolutionary outgrowth of rejecting distasteful foods from the mouth, while joy is associated with reproductive capacities.

Carroll Izard (1977) proposes a slightly different set of basic emotions. His model specifies ten emotions—joy, surprise, anger, disgust, contempt, fear, shame, guilt, interest, and excitement—with combinations of them resulting in other emotional blends (joy + interest/excitement = love).

As we saw in earlier chapters, a child's ability to think and to use language follows a genetically set time-table of development. It appears the same is generally true with emotional development, if appropriate stimulation is available. Some of the developments in emotional response may be linked to specific anatomical changes in the brain (Konner, 1977). For example, smiling emerges in infants of all cultures when the necessary nerve pathways acquire their myelin sheaths one or two months after birth. Similarly, a fairly universal occurrence in infants of fear of separation from their parents and stranger anxiety coincides with the development of neural tracts within the limbic system around the eighth month of life.

Izard contends that a newborn is capable of feeling only a generalized positive state, a generalized negative state, and the emotions of interest and sadness (Izard, 1982). A few months later, joy and anger develop. By the time the infant is nine months old, shame and fear appear—these are emotions requiring a degree of self-awareness that a younger child is believed not to have. Emotional responses may continue to change throughout life, reflecting changes in both physiological and cognitive processes (Mandler, 1984). Many complex emotions involve the ability to empathize with someone else's feelings, an ability that young children must learn from social experience. As memory and expectation develop, emotions can be triggered by thoughts as well as by a wider range of sensory stimuli.

FUNCTIONS OF EMOTION

Why do we have emotions? What functions do emotions serve for us? Different theorists point to different functions as central to the role of emotions in human life (Fridja, 1989). Emotions do many things for us. They serve a motivational function by *arousing* us to move and to take action with regard to some experienced or imagined event. Emotions then *direct* and *sustain* our actions toward specific goals that benefit us, such as energizing behavior toward helpful stimulation and away from the harmful. For the sake of love of another person, we may do all in our power to attract, be near, possess, or change our life-styles. For the love of principle or of country, we may sacrifice our lives. Positive emotions stem from acting in ways that are consistent with our motives (gaining a preferred, rewarding goal), while negative emotions are motive-inconsistent (moving away from preferred goals or toward aversive goals). We feel frustrated when we are unable to act in ways that get us what we want and angry when we are forced to confront a punishing situation (Roseman, 1984). Emotions help to *organize* our experiences by influencing what we attend to, the way we perceive ourselves and others, and the way we interpret and remember various features of life situations (Bower, 1981).

In addition to these functions, by *amplifying* or intensifying selected life experiences, emotions signal that a response is especially significant or that an event has *self-relevance* (Tompkins, 1981). Emotions can give us an *awareness of inner conflicts* when we observe how they can make us react irrationally or inappropriately to a given situation (Jung, 1971).

On a social level, emotions regulate relationships with others, promote prosocial behaviors, and are part of our nonverbal communication system. Emotions serve the broad function of *regulating social interactions;* as a positive social glue, they bind us to some people; as a negative social repellant, they distance us from others (Averill, 1980). Some psychologists go further in arguing that most emotions emerge from and are central to fully experiencing human relationships (DeRivera, 1984).

This social function is illustrated by the account of a woman I knew well who developed hysterical amnesia following a series of traumatic events that caused her to be unable to identify people she had known well. However, she responded unerringly with the emotional reaction appropriate to each of them. She reported feeling good and joyful when with those she had liked previously and feeling bad and distressed when interacting with those whom she had disliked previously—even though nothing about their current behavior gave me a clue of any differences between them.

An ample amount of research points to the impact of emotion on *stimulating prosocial behavior* (Isen, 1984; Hoffman, 1986). When individuals are made to feel good, they are more likely to engage in a variety of helping behaviors. Similarly, when research subjects were made to feel guilty about a misdeed in a current situation, they were more likely to volunteer aid in a future situation, presumably to reduce their guilt (Carlsmith & Gross, 1969).

The *communication* function of emotion reveals our attempts to conceal from others what we are feeling and intending. We back off when someone is bristling with anger and approach when another person signals receptivity with a smile, dilated pupils, and a "come hither" glance. Strong, negatively felt emotions are often suppressed out of respect for another person's status or out of concern that they will reveal information being concealed. Much human communication is carried on in the silent language of nonverbal bodily messages (Buck, 1984; Mehrabian, 1971).

This mandrill monkey is displaying aggression. Notice the bared teeth and clenched jaws that signal others to flee, submit, or fight.

THEORIES OF EMOTION

Theories of emotion attempt to explain what causes emotions, what are the necessary conditions for emotion, and what sequence best captures the way emotions are built up from the complex interaction of the factors we have discussed. We will review briefly four key theories: the James-Lange theory of body reaction, the Cannon-Bard theory of central neural processes, the Lazarus-Schachter theory of cognitive-arousal, and Darwin's evolutionary theory of emotions.

James-Lange Theory of Body Reaction

It is reasonable to assume that when we perceive an emotional stimulus that induces an emotional feeling, it, in turn, creates a chain of bodily reactions—physiological, expressive, and behavioral. The sight of a beautiful person induces feelings of desire. This physically arouses us, which in turn motivates approach reactions and appropriate displays of passion. This explanation of emotion seems reasonable, but is it the true sequence? A hundred years ago, **William James** argued, as Aristotle had much earlier, that the sequence was reversed— we feel *after* our body reacts. As James put it, "We feel sorry because we cry, angry because we strike, afraid because we tremble" (James, 1890/1950, p. 450). Although contrary to common sense, this view that emotion stems from *bodily feedback* was taken seriously by many psychologists and became known as the **James-Lange theory of emotion** (Carl Lange was a Danish scientist who presented similar ideas the same year as James). According to this theory, perceiving a stimulus causes autonomic arousal and other bodily actions that lead to the experience of a specific emotion (see **Figure 13.3**). The James-Lange theory is considered a *peripheralist* organic theory because it assigns the most prominent role in the emotion chain to visceral reactions, from the actions of the autonomic nervous system that are peripheral to the central nervous system.

Cannon-Bard Theory of Central Neural Processes

Physiologist **Walter Cannon** (1927, 1929) rejected the peripheralist view of emotion and the James-Lange theory in favor of a *centralist* focus on the action of the central nervous system. Cannon fired a salvo of criticism against the James-Lange theory based on experimental evidence and logical analysis (Leventhal, 1980). He (and other critics) raised four major objections. First, visceral activity was irrelevant for emotional experience—experimental animals continued to respond emotionally even after their viscera were separated surgically from the CNS. Second, visceral reactions are similar across different arousal situations—the same heart palpitations accompany aerobic exercise, love-making, and fleeing danger—but the reactions do not lead to the same emotion from perceiving feedback on how one is responding. Third, many emotions cannot be distinguished from each other simply by their physiological components; therefore, a person cannot experience different emotions solely by "reading" visceral reactions that are not well differentiated. Finally, ANS responses are typically too slow to be the source of split-second elicited emotions.

According to Cannon, emotion requires that the brain intercede between the input and output of stimulation and response; it especially requires the involvement of the thalamus and the cortex. Signals from the thalamus get routed to one area of the cortex to produce emotional feeling and to another for emotional expressiveness. Another physiologist, Philip Bard, also concluded that visceral reactions were not primary in the emotion sequence. Instead, an emotion-arousing stimulus has two simultaneous effects, causing both bodily arousal via the sympathetic nervous system and the subjective experience of emotion via the cortex. The views of these physiologists were combined in the **Cannon-Bard theory of emotion.** An emotion stimulus produces two concurrent reactions, arousal and experience of emotion, which do not cause each other (see Figure 13.3).

Strong evidence against the Cannon-Bard theory comes from a recent study of people with spinal cord injuries (Chawlisz et al., 1988). Although their injuries prevented them from perceiving any autonomic arousal, they still reported strong emotions, some even stronger than before their injuries. Clearly, autonomic arousal cannot be a necessary condition for emotion.

Lazarus-Schachter Theory of Cognitive Arousal

Many contemporary theories of emotion suggest that cognitive processes direct optimally adaptive emotional responses (Lazarus, 1987; Leventhal, 1980; Roseman, 1984; Smith & Ellsworth, 1985). Sensory experiences lead to emotion only when the stimuli are cognitively appraised as having personal significance. As we noted earlier, the particular emotion that is felt depends on the way a situation is interpreted and the meaning attributed to it by the individual.

Richard Lazarus, a leading proponent of the cognitive appraisal view, maintains that, "Emotional experience cannot be understood solely in terms of what happens in the person or in the brain, but grows out of ongoing transactions with the environment that are evaluated" (1984, p. 124). Lazarus's view plays a central role in the understanding of stress and the way one copes with it.

According to **Stanley Schachter** (1971), the experience of emotion is the joint effect of physiological arousal and cognitive appraisal, with both parts necessary for an emotion to occur. All arousal is assumed to be general and undifferentiated, and it comes first in the emotion sequence. Cognition serves to determine how this ambiguous inner state will be labeled. This position has become known as the *two-factor theory of emotion* or the **Lazarus-Schachter theory of emotion** (Mandler, 1984; Schachter & Singer, 1962). Organic, visceral factors *interact* with mental factors to produce an emotion. Thus, when there is sympathetic arousal *without* a known, specified source, a person will search the environment for relevant, salient cognitions that can be used to label the arousal and give it emotional meaning (see Figure 13.3).

This new view of emotion and the ingenious research used to demonstrate it (Schachter & Singer, 1962) drew attention to the role of cognitive interpretations in emotional experience. Also, it showed that independent components of emotion—arousal states and situational cues—could be manipulated experimentally and studied in a laboratory setting. However, some of the specific aspects of the two-factor theory have been challenged. Awareness of one's physiological arousal is *not* a necessary condition for emotional experience. When experimental subjects are exposed to emotion-

FIGURE 13.3 *COMPARING THREE EMOTION THEORIES*

These classic theories of emotion propose different components of emotion. They also propose different process sequences by which a stimulus event results in the experience of emotion. In body reaction theory (James-Lange), events trigger both autonomic arousal and behavioral action, which are perceived and then result in a specific emotional experience. In central neural theory (Cannon-Bard), events are first processed at various centers in the brain, which then direct three simultaneous reactions of arousal, behavioral action, and emotional experience. In cognitive arousal theory (Lazarus-Schachter), both stimulus events and physiological arousal are cognitively appraised at the same time according to situational cues and context factors, with the emotional experience resulting from the interaction of level of arousal and the nature of the appraisal.

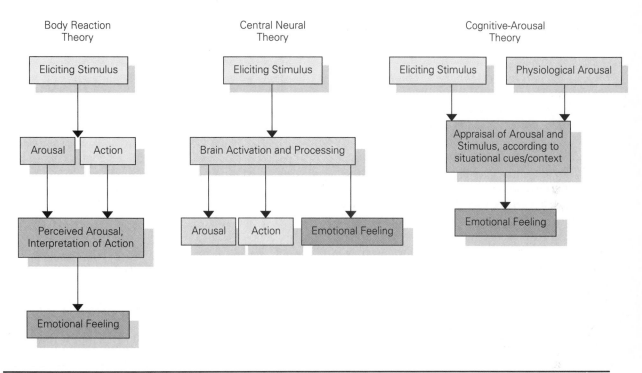

inducing stimuli after receiving beta-blockers that reduce heart rate, they still experience anxiety or anger even though they have minimal physical feelings (Reizenstein, 1983). In addition, experiencing strong arousal without any obvious cause does *not* lead to a neutral, undifferentiated state, as the two-factor theory assumes. *Unexplained* physical arousal is generally interpreted as *negative*, diagnosing that something is wrong, and the search for an explanation tends to be *biased* toward finding stimuli that will explain or justify this negative interpretation (Marshall & Zimbardo, 1979; Maslach, 1979).

We intuitively believe that feelings and preferences follow cognitions and inferences. An alternate view is that feelings and preferences are *not* necessarily derived from thoughts, but may be immediate reactions to stimuli, independent of cognitive analysis. We enjoy chocolate and hate liver and we are attracted to smiling faces and repulsed by frowns; such immediate "gut reactions" can occur independently of our reasoning about them.

Sylvan Tompkins (1962, 1981) was one of the first psychologists to emphasize the pervasive role of immediate, unlearned affective reactions. He points out that infants respond to loud sounds with fear or with difficulties in breathing without cognitive appraisal or prior learning. They seem "prewired" to respond to certain stimuli with an emotional response general enough to fit a wide range of circumstances. Tompkins sees emotions as the primary motivating force for human actions that endow any activity with a sense of importance and transform indifference to desire. In this view, without emotion nothing matters; with emotion, anything can matter.

Another critique of the cognitive appraisal theory of emotion comes from researcher **Robert Zajonc** (pronounced Zy-Onts) who demonstrates conditions under which it is possible to have preferences without inferences and to feel without knowing why. In an extensive series of experiments on the *mere exposure effect,* subjects were presented with a variety of stimuli, such as foreign words, Japanese characters, sets of numbers, and strange faces, that were flashed so briefly the items could not be recognized. Subjects were still able to express a *preference* without knowing why they liked some more than others. Those stimuli that were repeated most often produced the strongest liking; yet this increased liking was shown to occur independently of conscious recognition (Zajonc, 1980).

Darwin's Evolutionary Theory of Emotion

In order to develop a better way of categorizing emotions and investigating how they work, an evolutionary perspective encourages looking at the situations emotions are designed to handle. Evolutionary psychologists, following in Darwin's path, consider the *adaptive* functions of emotions, not as vague, unpredictable, personal states that color how we see the world, but as highly specific, coordinated modes of operation of the human brain. Emotions are viewed as inherited, specialized mental states designed to deal with a certain class of *recurring situations* in the world. Many of the situations that affect an individual's survival and reproduction are not isolated flukes but are part of a repeating pattern or series.

Over the history of our species, humans have been attacked by predators, fallen in love, given birth to children, fought each other, confronted their mates' sexual infidelity, and witnessed the death of loved ones—innumerable times. Any special mode of operation that could be turned on specifically to help humans deal better with these recurring life situations would tend to be passed on to offspring and proliferate through the species. It would become part of the human emotional repertoire. For example, *sexual jealousy* can be seen as a special mode that turns on to deal with the situation of mate infidelity. Physical arousal increases to prepare for possible violent conflict, motivations to deter or injure the rival and to punish or desert the mate emerge, memories are selectively activated to reanalyze the past relationship, and other reactions also emerge to cope with the distressing situation. Evolving humans who had different, less adaptive emotional responses to important life situations did not leave many offspring, so their nonadaptive responding was not passed on.

If emotions evolved as coordinated systems to deal with specific types of situations, we might expect the features of particular emotions to match the threats and opportunities characteristic of the situations with which they were designed to cope. Emotions evolve to control whatever biological or psychological processes are relevant to dealing with their target situation.

This way of thinking can help us understand some aspects of emotion that had been puzzling for a long time. Rather than asking whether every emotion has an opposite (i.e., happy vs. sad), we can ask whether the *situation* corresponding to an emotion has an opposite. Perhaps happiness and sadness are opposite because they are both moods designed to regulate energy expenditure in opposite directions, depending on whether the *environment* is propitious, or favorable (Nesse, 1990). Happiness results when we sense that the environment is rewarding our efforts in situations indicating increased survival or reproductive success. When happy, we generally show more optimism, exuberance, energy, and activity, which is appropriate when these qualities are rewarded with increased species fitness. However, in situations when the environment is not propitious, when it does not reward us no matter what we do, we conserve energy by becoming more passive, and our mood is one of sadness. We wait for the situation to change but do not take direct action to change it because those actions will not be reinforced. The moods of happiness and sadness may be complementary regulatory processes that match our level of activity to the propitiousness of the environment.

ARE EMOTIONAL EXPRESSIONS UNIVERSAL?

If one function of emotion is to prepare and motivate a person to respond adaptively to the demands of living, then two abilities are essential to coordinate social behavior. We must be able to communicate effectively to others our emotional feelings, and we need to decode the way others are feeling. If, for instance, we can signal that we are angry at someone and are likely to become aggressive, we can often get the person to stop doing whatever is annoying us without resorting to overt aggression. Alternatively, if we can communicate to others that we feel sad and helpless, we increase our chances of soliciting their aid. Similarly, by reading the emotional displays of others, we can predict more accurately when to approach and when to avoid them and when to respond with tenderness or toughness.

Emotional facial expression is one of the most effective modes of emotional communication. *Ethologists* have provided evidence that nonhuman primates use facial expressions to establish and maintain dominance hierarchies, and psychologists have shown that facial expression is an important channel of communication for humans in a variety of social situations.

Other researchers have found that the facial expressions displayed by newscasters while talking on TV about politicians seem to influence our attitudes and even our votes (Mullin et al., 1986). Analyses of the facial expressions of leading television network anchors revealed a positive smile bias by Peter Jennings of ABC TV that favored Ronald Reagan. Jennings smiled more when talking about Reagan during the presidential campaign than about other candidates or news items. The effect of the "Jennings smile" was to increase the likelihood that his viewers would vote for Reagan in the election. A separate study of the informational content of the news on all three networks indicates that the stories run by ABC were, in fact, less pro-Reagan than those run on either CBS or NBC (Clancey & Robinson, 1985; Robinson, 1985). This study leads to the conclusion that the Jennings smile and not a network news bias was a contributing factor to the pro-Reagan reactions of his viewers.

According to **Paul Ekman,** the leading researcher on the nature of facial expressions, all people speak and understand the same "facial language" (Ekman, 1984; Ekman, 1982; Ekman & Friesen, 1975). Ekman and his

Jennings smiled more when he talked about Ronald Reagan than he did when reporting on other presidential candidates or news items. His smiling influenced viewers to vote for Reagan.

associates have demonstrated what Darwin first proposed—that the same set of emotional expressions is *universal* to the human species, presumably because they are innate components of our evolutionary heritage. What about the influence of culture on emotion? Culture does play a role in *emotional displays* by establishing social rules for *when* to show certain emotions and for the social *appropriateness* of certain types of emotional displays by given types of people in particular settings. However, people all over the world, regardless of cultural differences, race, sex, or education, express basic emotions in the same way and are able to identify the emotions others are experiencing by reading their facial expressions.

Take the facial emotion identification test in **Figure 13.4** to see how well you can identify these seven universally recognized facial expressions of emotion (Ekman & Friesen, 1986). There is considerable evidence that these seven expressions are recognized and produced worldwide in response to the emotions of happiness, surprise, anger, disgust, fear, sadness, and contempt.

Cross-cultural researchers ask people from a variety of cultures to identify the emotions associated with a variety of expressions in standardized photographs. They are generally able to identify the expressions associated with the seven listed emotions. Children after age 5 can detect the emotion depicted in stimulus displays about as accurately as college students.

In one of Ekman's studies, members of a preliterate culture in New Guinea (the Fore culture), who had almost no exposure to Westerners or to Western culture prior to this experiment, accurately identified the emotions expressed in the Caucasian faces shown in Figure 13.4. They did so by referring to *situations* in which they experienced the same emotion. For example, photo 5 (fear) suggested being chased by a wild boar when you didn't have your spear, and photo 6 (sadness) suggested your child had died. Their only confusion came in distinguishing surprise from fear, perhaps because these people are most fearful when taken by surprise.

Next, researchers asked other members of the culture (who had not participated in the first study) to model the expressions that they used to communicate six of the emotions (excluding contempt). When U.S. college students viewed videotapes of the facial expressions of the Fore people, they were able to identify their emotions accurately—with two exceptions. Not surprisingly, the Americans had difficulty distinguishing between the Fore poses of fear and surprise, the same

FIGURE 13.4   FACIAL EMOTION EXPRESSIONS

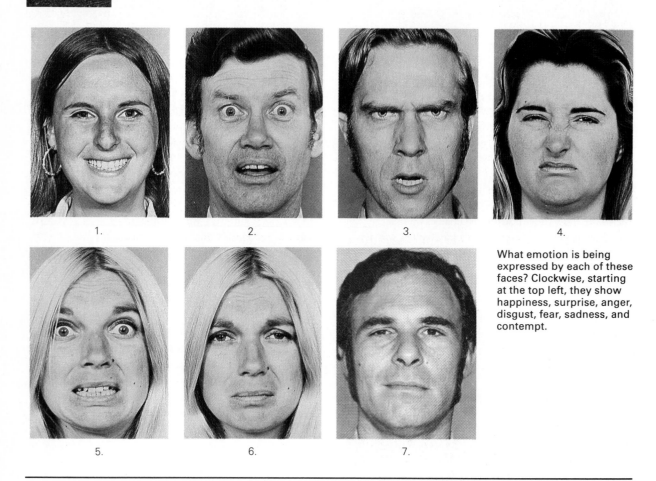

1.   2.   3.   4.

5.   6.   7.

What emotion is being expressed by each of these faces? Clockwise, starting at the top left, they show happiness, surprise, anger, disgust, fear, sadness, and contempt.

emotions that the Fore had confused in the Western poses.

Emotion researchers generally agree about which specific *facial muscle movements* are associated with each of the basic emotions (Smith, 1986). Studies that record facial muscle movements while subjects imagine various mood settings show specific patterns of muscle groups that are different for happy, sad, and angry thoughts (Schwartz, 1975). For example, the expression of happiness consists of raised mouth corners (a smile) and tightened lower eyelids; the expression of surprise consists of raised eyebrows, raised upper eyelids that widen the eyes, and an open mouth; and the expression of fear is very similar to the expression of surprise, except that, in addition to being raised, the eyebrows are pulled together and lowered back down slightly into an eyebrow frown. (The similarity between the two expressions might explain why subjects had such trouble discriminating between them.)

MOOD AND INFORMATION PROCESSING

Cognitive psychologists are showing that emotional states can affect learning, memory, social judgments, categorization, and creativity. **Gordon Bower** (1981) and his students have experimentally demonstrated the ways a person's mood can influence the way information is processed. The two effects they have uncovered are mood-dependent retrieval and mood-congruent processing. When a person experiences a given emotion in a particular situation, that emotion is assumed to be stored in memory along with the ongoing events, as part of the same context.

Mood-dependent retrieval refers to recall of an emotional event experienced earlier that occurs when the person is in the same mood as during the event. People remember more events that were originally sad when they are feeling sad. Happy people are more likely

Facial expressions convey a universal message. Although their culture is very different, it is probably not hard for you to tell how these people from New Guinea are feeling.

to retrieve happy events from their past. A similar *retrieval bias* arises when psychiatrically depressed patients are asked to recall events from their past; their negative mood leads them to recall more negative memories (Blaney, 1986).

Mood-congruent processing occurs when people are selectively sensitized to take in information that agrees with their current mood state. Material that is congruent with one's prevailing mood is more likely to be attended to, noticed, and processed more deeply with greater elaborative associations. This type of processing causes people to learn better information that is congruent with their mood (Gilligan & Bower, 1984).

In more recent studies, Bower (1991) shows that mood states also influence people's attraction and interest in activities, other people, stories, movies, and music that are congruent with their current moods. Mood can also influence how people evaluate their health status. When feeling sad, students reported more past illnesses and complaints than when they were in an emotionally neutral state (Salovey and Hancock, 1987). Students who had the flu or a bad cold rated the severity of the aches and discomfort according to the mood induced by the researchers having them recall happy, sad, or neutral episodes from their lives. Compared to neutral controls, those who were temporarily sad rated their cold symptoms as significantly worse than happy subjects (Salovey & Birnbaum, 1989). The power of moods on cognition is also shown in research that finds happy people offer more creative solutions on standard tests of creativity than do those who are affectively neutral or made to experience a negative mood (Isen et al., 1987).

 ## SUMMING UP

An emotion is a complex pattern of changes including physiological arousal, brain mechanisms, experienced feelings, and cognitive appraisal, as well as behavioral and expressive reactions. These changes occur in response to situations perceived as personally significant. The amygdala in the limbic system processes emotional signals in a direct, immediate fashion, while the cortex is involved in interpreting the meaning of the emotional stimulus and providing the big picture. Although we usually define emotions readily by the nature of the external stimulus situation, when it is ambiguous or novel it is possible to misattribute arousal to situational cues that are salient but not true causal elements. Some theorists maintain that there are a limited set of innate, basic emotions. Plutchik posits eight basic emotions in his color wheel model that can be combined and blended to yield other complex, secondary emotions. Emotions serve many vital functions, such as arousing, directing, and sustaining actions; organizing experience; aiding social communication and social interaction; and motivating prosocial behavior.

Four classic theories of emotion give varying emphasis to peripheral arousal or central brain processing, the sequence by which an external stimulus creates an emotional response, and the involvement of cognitive appraisal and adaption to recurring situations. The James-Lange peripheralist theory makes visceral arousal feedback the important component in emotion. The Cannon-Bard theory is a centralist model in which brain processing causes both arousal and emotional feelings. Lazarus-Schachter's combined view is a cognitive model that highlights the role in experiencing emotion of interpretation of arousal and social cues in the stimulus situation. Darwinian evolutionary theory proposes that emotions are inherited response systems that are adaptive in selectively reacting to recurring life situations relevant for reproduction and survival.

Cross-cultural research supports Darwin's hypothesis that the facial expression of emotion is universal, similar between humans and nonhuman primates and across peoples of different cultures, races, ages and sexes. Cultures vary in the display rules that specify the social appropriateness of showing certain emotions, but seven emotional expressions are universally recognized across cultures, according to Ekman's research.

New research is establishing the many ways emotion influences cognition. Experimental research by Bower and others demonstrates that moods can affect memory, learning, attention, social judgments, creativity, and perception of health.

STRESS OF LIVING

Stress is a unique type of emotional experience that has gained much attention by psychologists and other scientists. Within the broad area of basic and applied research on stress, three general questions are of major concern to psychologists: How does stress affect us physically and psychologically? How do common stressors in our society affect our health? How can we cope with stress more effectively?

Our modern industrialized society sets a rapid, hectic pace for our lives. We often are living in overcrowded conditions, have too many demands placed on our time, are worried about our uncertain future, are holding a frustrating job, or are unemployed, and have little time for family and fun. Would we be better off without stress? A stress-free life would offer no challenge—no difficulties to surmount, no new fields to conquer, and no reason to sharpen our wits or improve our abilities. Stress is an unavoidable part of living. Every organism faces challenges from its external environment and from its personal needs; these challenges are life's problems that the organism must solve to survive and thrive.

Stress is the pattern of specific and nonspecific (general) *responses* an organism makes to stimulus events that disturb its equilibrium and tax or exceed its ability to cope. The stimulus events include a large variety of external and internal conditions that collectively are called stressors. A **stressor** is a *stimulus* event that places a demand on an organism for some kind of adaptive response. The organism's reaction to external stressors is known as **strain.** An individual's response to the need for change is made up of a diverse combination of reactions taking place on several levels, including physiological, behavioral, emotional, and cognitive levels. How can such a complex stress response be studied? In an attempt to better understand the concept of stress, researchers have tried to identify its specific components and their interactions.

Have you ever wondered why some people experience stressful events and seem to suffer little or no

Modern society creates a stressful environment whether we are working or playing.

negative effects, while others are seriously upset by even minor hassles? This difference exists because the effect of most stressors is not controlled only by the objective features of the stressor. Stress is a personal matter. How much stress we experience is determined by the quality and intensity of a combination of variables: the dimensions of the stressor, the way we interpret the meaning of the stressor, the resources we have available to deal with the stressor, and the amount and nature of the total strain placed on the individual. **Figure 13.5** diagrams the elements of the stress process: stressors, stress, cognitive appraisal, resources, and stress responses.

SOURCES OF STRESS

Stress, similar to taxes, is a recurring problem everyone faces. Naturally occurring stressful changes are an unavoidable part of our lives. People close to us get sick, move away, and die. We get new jobs, get fired or laid off, leave home, start college, succeed, fail, begin ro-

mances, get married, and break up. In addition to the big life changes, there are also routine frustrations: traffic jams, snoring roommates, and missed appointments. Unpredictable, catastrophic events, such as earthquakes or major accidents, will affect some of us, and chronic societal problems, such as pollution and crime, will pose important sources of stress for others.

Major Life Stressors

Sudden *changes* in our life situations are at the root of stress for many of us. Although change puts spice in our lives, too much change can ruin our health. Even events that we welcome, such as winning the lottery or getting promoted, may require major changes in our routines and adaptation to new requirements. Recent studies reveal that one of the most sought changes in a married couple's life, the birth of their first child, is also a source of major stress, contributing to reduced marital satisfaction (Cowan & Cowan, 1988). On the other hand, a review of research on the psychological responses to abortion reveals that distress is generally

FIGURE 13.5 *A MODEL OF STRESS*

Cognitive appraisal of the stress situation interacts with the stressor and the physical, social, and personal resources available for dealing with the stressor. Individuals respond to threats on various levels—physiological, behavioral, emotional, and cognitive. Some responses are adaptive and others maladaptive or even lethal.

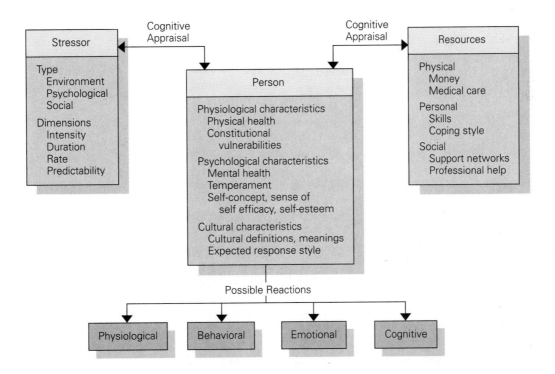

greatest before the abortion. Severe distress is low for women following the abortion of an unwanted pregnancy or a first-trimester abortion, especially if they have had social support for their decision (Adler et al., 1991).

Some researchers have viewed stress as resulting from exposure to major *life changes* or *life events* (Dohrenwend & Dohrenwend, 1974; Dohrenwend & Shrout, 1985; Holmes & Rahe, 1967). Ask social workers about the stresses of their clients, any one of whom may be unemployed, just divorced, or living on the streets or who may have a child selling drugs or an abusive spouse. Sometimes a person can absorb an enormous amount of stress and keep functioning. The reaction depends on individual resources and on the social and interpersonal contexts of the environmental events. (For example, I felt happy once after being robbed of a small amount of cash because I had just spent most of my money buying a new suit—as in telling a good joke, timing made all the difference.)

The influence of major life changes on subsequent mental and physical health has been a target source of considerable research. It started with the development of the *Social Readjustment Rating Scale* (SRRS), a simple scale for rating the degree of adjustment required by the various life changes, both pleasant and unpleasant, that many people experience. The scale was developed from the responses of adults from all walks of life who were asked to identify from a list those life changes that applied to them. These adults rated the amount of readjustment required for each change by comparing each to marriage, which was arbitrarily assigned a value of 50 life change units. Researchers then calculated the total number of **life-change units** (LCU) an individual had undergone during that period, using the units as a measure of the amount of stress the individual had experienced (Holmes & Rahe, 1967). A modification of this scale for college students is shown in **Table 13.1.** What is your LCU rating?

Also, compare the relative severity of hassles in your life with those of the four groups outlined in **Table 13.2** (students, mothers, general community members, and elders).

Early studies examined the hypothesis that the greater the life change intensity, as measured by the SRRS, the greater the risk for subsequent illness. Preliminary studies found support for a relationship between medical problems and the amount of readjustment in life. Patients with heart disease, for example, had higher LCU scores than healthy subjects. Other studies reported that life stress increases a person's overall susceptibility to illness (Holmes & Masuda, 1974), and LCU values are also high for some time after an illness (Rahe & Arthur, 1978).

A modification in measuring the effects of life events is provided in the *Life Experiences Survey* (LES), which has two special features. First, it provides scores for both increases and decreases in change rather than increases only, as in the original scale. Second, its scores reflect individual assessments of the events and their desirability. For example, the death of an estranged spouse who left a big inheritance might be rated as quite desirable. Thus this scale goes beyond a mere count of the number of remembered life changes to measure the personal significance of each change (Sarason et al., 1978).

One interpretive problem with studies relating stressful life events to illness is that they tend to be *retrospective*. That is, both the stress measures and the illness measures are obtained by having subjects recall prior events. This characteristic presents an opportunity for memory distortion to bias the results. For example, subjects who are sick are more likely to remember past negative stressors than subjects who are well. More recently, *prospective* (looking ahead) studies have followed healthy individuals over a period of years; they find significant correlations between the development of medical problems and earlier accumulation of life stress units (Brown & Harris, 1989; Johnson & Sarason, 1979). Despite such support, the bulk of the current research evidence points to a *weak* association between major life events and disease (Brett et al., 1990).

Life's Little Hassles

One current view of stress holds that an accumulation of small frustrations leads to stress more than infrequent big jolts of change do (Weinberger et al., 1987). Life is almost always bubbling with low-level frustrations. To what extent do these minor irritations pile up to become stressors that affect your health? If you interpret these *hassles* as salient and harmful or threatening to your well-being, they affect you more than you might imagine (Lazarus, 1984).

A psychiatrist distributed 100 questionnaires to people waiting for the 7:12 A.M. train from Long Island to Manhattan. From the 40 completed questionnaires returned, it was determined that these average commuters had just gulped down their breakfast in less than 11 minutes, were prepared to spend 3 hours each day in transit, and, in 10 years, had logged about 7500 hours of rail time. Two thirds of the commuters believed their family relations were impaired by their commuting. Fifty-nine percent experienced fatigue, 47 percent were filled with conscious anger, 28 percent were anxious, and others reported headaches, muscle pains, indigestion, and other symptoms of the long-term consequences of beating the rat race in

TABLE 13.1 **STUDENT STRESS SCALE**

The Student Stress Scale represents an adaptation of Holmes and Rahe's Social Readjustment Rating Scale. Each event is given a score that represents the amount of readjustment a person has to make in life as a result of the change. People with scores of 300 and higher have a high health risk. People scoring between 150 and 300 points have about a 50–50 chance of serious health change within two years. People scoring below 150 have a 1 in 3 chance of serious health change. Calculate your total Life Change Score (LCU) each month of this year and then correlate those scores with any changes in your health status.

Event	Life Change Unit
Death of a Close Family Member	100
Death of a Close Friend	73
Divorce Between Parents	65
Jail Term	63
Major Personal Injury or Illness	63
Marriage	58
Being Fired from Job	50
Failing an Important Course	47
Change in Health of Family Member	45
Pregnancy	45
Sex Problems	44
Serious Argument with Close Friend	40
Change in Financial Status	39
Change of Major	39
Trouble with Parents	39
New Girl- or Boyfriend	38
Increased Workload at School	37
Outstanding Personal Achievement	36
First Quarter/Semester in College	35
Change in Living Conditions	31
Serious Argument with Instructor	30
Lower Grades than Expected	29
Change in Sleeping Habits	29
Change in Social Activities	29
Change in Eating Habits	28
Chronic Car Trouble	26
Change in Number of Family Get-togethers	26
Too Many Missed Classes	25
Change of College	24
Dropping of More than One Class	23
Minor Traffic Violations	20

My 1st Total ☐ (date: ____) My 2nd Total ☐ (date: ____) My 3rd Total ☐ (date: ____)

the city by living in the country (F. Charaton, personal communication, 1973).

In a diary study, a group of white, middle-class, middle-aged men and women kept track of their daily hassles over a one-year period (along with a record of major life changes and physical symptoms). A clear relationship emerged between hassles and health problems: the more frequent and intense the hassles people reported, the poorer was their health, both physical and mental (Lazarus, 1981; 1984). As daily hassles go down, well-being goes up (Chamberlain & Zika, 1990). Although daily stressors have been shown to affect one's mood immediately, people habituate to them so

TABLE 13.2   SEVERITY OF HASSLES AS PERCEIVED IN FOUR GROUPS

In these New Zealand samples, each hassle type differed significantly in severity among the four groups. The ranked perceived severity was almost reversed for student and elderly groups with time pressures most important and neighborhood and health pressures least important for students, while the latter were the most important sources of hassles and time pressures were the least for the elderly. Note the hassle priorities for these mothers who had one or more young children at home and no household help.

Hassle type	Students (N = 161)	Mothers (N = 194)	Community (N = 120)	Elderly (N = 150)
Time pressure	1	2	3	4
Future security	2	4	1	3
Finances	3	1	2	4
Household	3	1	2	4
Neighborhood	4	3	2	1
Health	4	3	2	1

that the negative effects do not carry over to the next day. The exception is cases of interpersonal conflicts (Bolger et al., 1989).

Catastrophic Events

When an event is negative, uncontrollable, unpredictable, or ambiguous, the experience is more stressful (Glass, 1977). These conditions hold especially true in the case of *catastrophic events*.

The 1989 World Series was about to begin at San Francisco's Candlestick Park. As my three children and I settled into our seats, the band started playing. Suddenly, the entire stadium started shaking violently, the lights went out, and the scoreboard turned black. Sixty-thousand fans became completely silent.

We had just experienced a major earthquake. The person sitting next to us had a portable TV that showed fires breaking out in the city, a fallen bridge, crushed highways, and numerous deaths.

Shortly after the quake, a team of research psychologists began to study how people coped with the catastrophe.

For the study, nearly 800 people were chosen randomly from the San Francisco area and from several comparison cities some distance away. They were interviewed at either 1, 2, 3, 6, 8, 16, 28, or 50 weeks after the quake. The subjects completed a ten-minute phone survey about their thoughts, social behavior, and health. Three distinct phases of stress reactions were found among the subjects who were San Francisco residents. In the emergency phase (first three to four weeks), social contact, anxiety, and obsessive thoughts about the quake increased. The inhibition phase (three to

eight weeks) was characterized by a sudden decline in talking and thinking about the quake, but indirect, stress-related reactions increased, such as arguments and earthquake dreams. In the adaptation phase (from two months on), the psychological effects of the catastrophe were over for most people. However, as many as 20 percent of the San Francisco area residents remained distressed about the quake even one year later (Pennebaker & Harber, 1991).

A great deal of research on the physical and psychological effects of catastrophic events has been conducted (Baum, 1990). However, these *opportunistic studies*

When an event is unpredictable, such as the 1989 San Francisco earthquake, it tends to be more stressful.

have followed a research tradition that differs from studies of personal stressors, and there is no scale assessing the relative impact of different kinds of natural disasters.

Researchers have found that response to disasters tends to occur in five stages. Typically, there is a period of shock, confusion, and even *psychic numbness,* during which people cannot fully comprehend what has happened. In the next phase, called *automatic action,* people try to respond to the disaster and may behave adaptively but with little awareness of their actions and poor later memory of the experience. In the third stage, people often feel great accomplishment and even a positive sense of communal effort toward a shared purpose. Also in this phase, people feel weary and are aware that they are using up their reserves of energy. During the next phase, they experience a letdown; their energy is depleted and the impact of the tragedy is finally comprehended and felt emotionally. An extended final period of recovery follows, as people adapt to the changes brought about by the disaster (Cohen & Ahearn, 1980).

Knowledge of these typical reaction stages provides a model that is helpful in predicting people's reactions when disaster strikes, enabling rescue workers to anticipate and help victims deal with the problems that arise. Responses to events such as floods, tornadoes, airplane crashes, and factory explosions have all been shown to fit this model of disaster reactions.

Chronic Societal Stressors

What cumulative effect do overpopulation, crime, economic recession, pollution, AIDS, and the threat of nuclear war have on us? How do these and other environmental stressors affect our mental well-being?

Surveys of the attitudes of students throughout the United States have uncovered a general disquiet and uneasiness about the future (Beardslee & Mack, 1983). Studies since 1983 have shown a significant increase in junior high and senior high school students' expression of fear, helplessness, and anger toward the adult generation. Many young people are questioning whether it is worthwhile to work hard to prepare for a future they do not expect to have if there is nuclear war (Hanna, 1984; Yudkin, 1984).

Adults, too, are worried about potential nuclear disasters, but they are also affected by the more immediate concerns of employment and economic security. Many stress-related problems increase when the economy is in a downswing; admission to mental hospitals, infant mortality, suicide, and deaths from alcohol-related diseases and cardiovascular problems all increase (Brenner, 1976).

Psychologists have found that unemployed men report more symptoms, such as depression, anxiety, and worries about health, than do those who are employed. Because these symptoms disappear when the men are subsequently reemployed, researchers have argued that the symptoms are the results of being unemployed rather than indicators of more disturbed workers who are particularly likely to lose their jobs (Liem & Rayman, 1982). According to a recent investigation, high blood pressure among African Americans (long thought to be primarily genetic) appears to be a consequence of chronic stress caused by low status jobs, limited education, fruitless job seeking, and low socioeconomic status (Klag et al., 1991). Hypertension results from frustrations in efforts to achieve basic life goals; it is not linked to genetic factors.

Even pollution creates psychological stress in addition to the severe physical health problems it generates. For example, the release of radioactive steam at the Three Mile Island nuclear power plant in 1979 and the 1986 explosion of the Soviet nuclear power factory in Chernobyl were dramatic examples of environmental stressors. People living in the area experienced considerable stressful fear about immediate and long-term health consequences. In addition, people all over the world experienced stress as they wondered how these accidents might affect them and as they worried about other possible nuclear accidents. After Three Mile Island, the U.S. Court of Appeals declared that psychological stress had to be included in the environmental impact survey required before the plant could be reopened. One form of chronic societal stress comes from passive exposure to cigarette smoke (as described in the Ecology Close-Up on the next page).

STRESS MODERATOR VARIABLES

Variables that change the impact of a stressor on a given type of stress reaction are known as **stress moderator variables.** Moderator variables filter or modify the usual effects of stressors on the individual's reactions. Before a stress response begins, a demand on the organism (stressor) must be recognized at some level and evaluated. For example, your level of fatigue and general health status are moderator variables influencing your reaction to a given psychological or physical stressor. When you're in good shape, you can deal with a stressor better than when you aren't.

The cognitive interpretation and evaluation of a stressor is a major moderator variable. **Cognitive appraisal** plays a central role in defining the situation— what the demand is, how big a threat it is, what resources one has for meeting it, and what strategies are appropriate. Some stressors, such as bodily injury or finding one's house on fire, are experienced as threats

PASSIVE SMOKING

Before cigarette advertising on television was banned, the ruggedly handsome Marlboro Man enjoyed his favorite brand before a campfire. Sexy men and women pursued high adventure with toothy smiles, inhaling smoke as a voice-over counseled viewers: "You only go around once—grab all the good life you can get."

However, since the ban on those commercials went into effect, cigarette companies have still managed to get their message across. A study by the National Coalition on Television Violence showed that in 1990, 85 percent of all Hollywood movies showed characters lighting up. Although cigarette consumption has declined in recent years, the association of smoking with sex, adventure, and sophistication (as communicated through advertisements and film) has helped create an environment in which 30 percent of adults smoke. More than half a trillion cigarettes are consumed in the U.S. each year, an average of 1.5 packs per day per smoker (*Occupational Hazards*, 1990). The figures are even greater in many other countries that do not have anti-smoking campaigns.

Even nonsmokers do not completely avoid exposure to cigarette smoke. **Passive smoking** is inhaling smoke from the cigarettes that other people are smoking. It is especially harmful to children—exposure to tobacco smoke in childhood and, especially, in infancy is associated with increased incidence of respiratory infections, middle ear disease, and growth deficiencies (Chilmonczyk et al., 1990; *Occupational Hazards*, 1990; Rubin, 1990).

A recent study examined the long-term effects of childhood exposure to secondhand smoke (Janerich et al., 1990). The researchers compared the histories of 191 lung cancer patients and a control group of 191 people who did not have lung cancer; none of the subjects had ever smoked. Lifetime

exposure to smoke in the home was calculated by multiplying the number of smokers in the household by the number of years the subject had lived there. Exposure to 25 or more "smoker-years" in childhood and adolescence doubled these nonsmokers' risk of developing lung cancer. The researchers estimated that 17 percent of nonsmoker lung cancers was caused by "passive" smoking in childhood.

Another new study found that nonsmoking spouses of cigarette smokers are 30 percent more likely to die of heart disease than nonsmokers who do not live with smokers (Glantz & Parmely,

1991). Passive smoking kills more than 50,000 nonsmoking Americans annually, making it the third leading cause of preventable death (after active smoking and alcohol abuse).

Even *prenatal* exposure to cigarette smoke is dangerous. A mother who smokes during pregnancy increases the probability of miscarriage, birth complications, low birth weight, and crib death (Schelkun, 1990). Attention deficits reflecting impulsivity and high activity levels have been found in 4 to 7 year olds whose mothers smoked while pregnant. These results held up even when the effects of postnatal exposure to secondhand smoke were taken into account (Kristjansson, 1989).

New laws prohibiting smoking in many public places are aimed at curbing passive smoke health problems. However, you can't legislate what smokers do in the privacy of their own homes. Modifying private behavior requires new psychological efforts aimed at changing the consciousness, attitudes, and behavior of smokers and nonsmokers. Psychologists and health advocates must persuade smokers that, if they continue to smoke, they need to recognize the rights of others whose health they are actively damaging with passive smoke in their shared environment.

by almost everyone. However, many other stressors can be defined in various ways, depending on the personal life situation, the relation of a particular demand to the individual's central goals, competence for dealing with the demand, and self-assessment of that competence. The situation that causes acute distress for one person may be all in a day's work for another.

Your appraisal of a stressor and of your resources for meeting it can be as important as the actual stressor. For example, if you believe a stressor is too much for you to deal with, you might create a negative *self-fulfilling prophecy*. In that case, you are likely to fail even when you are objectively capable of dealing adequately with the stressor. Cognitive appraisal may define a stressor as an interesting new challenge to test yourself against instead of as a threat. The emotional experience may be one of exhilaration, being "psyched up," anticipated achievement, and increased self-esteem. The most successful athletes get a positive high when thinking about upcoming competition, while others get nervous planning for the same event, creating a handicap even before the meet begins. Appraisal of a stressor helps determine your conscious experience of it and how successful you are in meeting its demands.

Richard Lazarus, a pioneer in stress research and emotion research, has distinguished two stages in our cognitive appraisal of demands. He uses the term **primary appraisal** for the initial evaluation of the seriousness of a demand. This evaluation starts with the questions "What's happening?" and "Is this thing good for me, stressful, or irrelevant?" If the answer to the second question is *stressful,* an individual appraises the potential impact of the stressor by determining whether harm has occurred or is likely to and whether action is required (see **Table 13.3**). Once a person decides something must be done, **secondary appraisal** begins. The person evaluates the personal and social resources that are available to deal with the stressful circumstance and considers the action options that are needed (Lazarus, 1976). Appraisal continues as coping responses are tried; if the first ones don't work and the stress persists, new responses are initiated, and their effectiveness is evaluated (Lazarus, 1991).

While cognitive appraisals and good health can moderate the effects of stressors, psychologist **Suzanne Kobasa** believes a special personality type is even more important in diffusing stress. She identified two groups of subjects from a pool of managers working for a big public utility in a large city; the members of one group experienced high levels of stress but seldom were ill, while the members of the second group had high stress and frequently experienced illness (Kobasa et al., 1979). The stress survivors possessed the characteristics of hardiness. **Hardiness** involves welcoming change as a *challenge* and not as a threat, having focused *commitment* to purposeful activities, and having a sense of internal *control* over one's actions. These three C's of health—challenge, commitment, and control—are adaptive interpretations of stressful events (Kobasa, 1984).

When students who differed in their degree of hardiness (as measured by a questionnaire) were presented with a threat, they also differed in terms of their reactions to the threat.

TABLE 13.3	STAGES IN STABLE DECISION MAKING/COGNITIVE APPRAISAL
Stage	**Key Questions**
1. Appraising the challenge	Are the risks serious if I don't change?
2. Surveying alternatives	Is this alternative an acceptable means for dealing with the challenge? Have I sufficiently surveyed the available alternatives?
3. Weighing alternatives	Which alternative is best? Could the best alternative meet the essential requirements?
4. Deliberating about commitment	Shall I implement the best alternative and allow others to know?
5. Adhering despite negative feedback	Are the risks serious if I *don't* change? Are the risks serious if I *do* change?

The 60 men and 60 women who had the top third and bottom third scores were selected from over 800 students who completed the hardiness scale. The stressor was an experimental task in which subjects were expected to be videotaped repeating a lecture they had heard and then to be evaluated and questioned by psychology professors. The researcher manipulated the perceived threat and the challenge of the task along with several other hardiness-related variables. She found that the high-hardiness subjects differed from the low-hardiness subjects in showing higher frustration tolerance and appraising the task as less threatening. In addition, hardiness influenced heart rate responding among the men (but not the women); high-hardiness men had a lower level of physiological arousal (Wiebe, 1991).

While the *hardy personality* has received much attention as a moderator variable in reducing the negative effects of distress, other personality characteristics have also been associated with the concept of stress. Are you a daredevil, mountain climber, or hot dog skier? Does your temperament drive you to a life of risk taking, stimulation, and excitement seeking? If this description fits you, you have a **Type-T personality** where the *T* stands for *thrills*. Psychologist **Frank Farley** (1990, p. 29) issues the challenge:

"You may not have heard of this personality, but I will wager that you know some people who show the pattern of characteristics I have listed above." He adds, "I believe Type T is at the basis of both the most positive and constructive forces in our nation (T+ creativity) and the most negative and destructive forces (T− delinquency, vandalism, crime, drug and alcohol abuse, drinking and driving, etc.)."

Most people fall between the high risk, thrill and stimulation-seeking types and those who actively avoid any risk or thrill. The Type-T personality and its related Type-T behaviors are examples of moderator variables that affect the psychology of stress.

PHYSIOLOGICAL STRESS REACTIONS

We are a nation on the move; most of us will move a number of times; often considerable distances from our families, friends, and hometowns. Moving involves a host of stressors that function at all levels: loss of the familiar, fear of the unknown, the physical work of packing and moving, and the mental distraction of coping with unpacking and putting your belongings in new places. Getting used to a new environment or new roommates also creates stress.

These transient states of arousal, with typically clear onset and offset patterns, are examples of **acute stress. Chronic stress** is a state of enduring arousal,

People who engage in risky behavior, such as skydiving, have Type-T personalities.

continuing over time, in which demands are perceived as greater than the inner and outer resources available for dealing with them (Powell & Eagleston, 1983). An example of chronic stress might be a continuous frustration with the lack of control you have to change your roommate's annoying habit of monopolizing the phone line. These acute or chronic states of arousal are expressed on several levels as physiological aspects of the stress response and also as psychological stress reactions.

In Chapter 3, we learned that the brain developed originally as a center for more efficient coordination of action. *Efficiency* is flexible responding to changing environmental requirements and also quick, often automatic responding. One set of brain-controlled physiological stress responses occurs when an external threat is perceived (a predator or a menacing loud noise in the night, for example). Instant action and extra strength may be needed if the organism is to survive; a whole constellation of automatic mechanisms has evolved to meet this need. Another set of physiological stress reactions occurs when the danger is internal, and the stability and integrity of the organism are threatened by invading microbes or other disease agents that upset the normal physiological processes.

Emergency Reactions to External Threats

In the 1920s, Walter Cannon, a Harvard University physiologist, outlined the first scientific description of the way animals and humans respond to external danger. He found that a sequence of activity is triggered in the nerves and glands to prepare the body for combat and struggle—or for running away to safety. Cannon called this dual-stress response the **fight-or-flight syndrome.**

At the center of this primitive stress response is the *hypothalamus,* which is involved in a variety of emotional responses. The hypothalamus has sometimes been referred to as the *stress center* because of its twin functions in emergencies: (a) it controls the autonomic nervous system and (b) it activates the pituitary gland.

The ANS regulates the activities of the body's organs. In stressful conditions, breathing becomes faster and deeper, heart rate increases, blood vessels constrict, and blood pressure rises. In addition to these internal changes, muscles open the passages of the throat and nose to allow more air into the lungs while also producing facial expressions of strong emotion. Messages go to smooth muscles to stop certain bodily functions, such as digestion, which are irrelevant to preparing for the emergency at hand.

Another function of the autonomic nervous system during stress is to get adrenaline flowing. It signals the inner part of the adrenal glands, the *adrenal medulla,*

to release two hormones, *epinephrine* and *norepinephrine,* which, in turn, signal a number of other organs to perform their specialized functions. The spleen releases more red blood corpuscles (to aid in clotting if there is an injury), while the bone marrow is stimulated to make more white corpuscles (to combat possible infection). The liver is stimulated to produce more sugar, building up body energy.

The *pituitary gland* responds to signals from the hypothalamus by secreting two hormones vital to the stress reaction. The *thyrotrophic hormone* (TTH) stimulates the *thyroid gland,* which makes more energy available to the body. The *adrenocorticotrophic hormone* (ACTH), known as the "stress hormone," stimulates the outer part of the adrenal glands, the *adrenal cortex,* resulting in the release of a group of hormones called **steroids,** which are important in metabolic processes and in the release of sugar from the liver into the blood. ACTH also signals various organs of the body to release about 30 other hormones, each of which plays a role in the body's adjustment to this call to arms. However, ACTH also plays a negative role. Its action reduces the ability of natural killer cells to destroy cancer cells and other life-threatening infections. When the body is stressed chronically, the increased production of "stress hormones" compromises the integrity of the immune system. A summary of this physiological stress response is shown in **Figure 13.6.**

It is obvious, then, that many bodily processes are activated during the physiological stress response to danger signals. Let's consider their adaptive significance in two different stressful situations.

When a call comes into a firehouse, the fire fighters respond with the physiological components of the stress response. Muscles tense, breathing speeds up, heart rate increases, adrenaline flows, extra energy becomes available, and the fire fighters become less sensitive to pain. They will need these responses in order to endure the physical strain of battling a fire. The built-in capacity to deal with *physical stressors* by mobilizing the body's active response systems has been valuable to our species for ages. In studies of African baboon colonies, stress hormone levels are highest when there is least social control and predictability but lowest among dominant males whose behavioral traits reflect high degrees of social skillfulness, outlets for frustration, social affiliation (with infants and females), predictability, and control (Sapolsky, 1990).

Now consider people working on a crisis hot line, taking calls from potentially suicidal strangers. These workers undergo the same physiological stress responses as the fire fighters as a result of the *psychological stressors* they face. However, in contrast to the fire fighters, their physiological responses, except for the

FIGURE 13.6   THE BODY'S REACTION TO STRESS

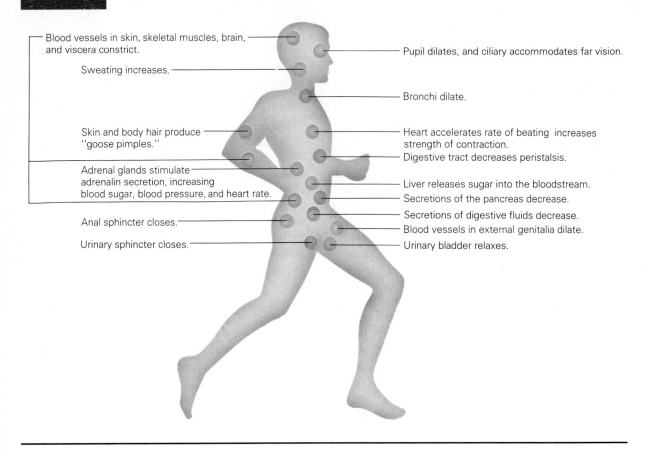

Blood vessels in skin, skeletal muscles, brain, and viscera constrict.

Pupil dilates, and ciliary accommodates far vision.

Sweating increases.

Bronchi dilate.

Skin and body hair produce "goose pimples."

Heart accelerates rate of beating increases strength of contraction.

Digestive tract decreases peristalsis.

Adrenal glands stimulate adrenalin secretion, increasing blood sugar, blood pressure, and heart rate.

Liver releases sugar into the bloodstream.

Secretions of the pancreas decrease.

Anal sphincter closes.

Secretions of digestive fluids decrease.

Blood vessels in external genitalia dilate.

Urinary sphincter closes.

Urinary bladder relaxes.

heightened attentiveness, are not adaptive. The hot line volunteer can't run away from the stressor or fight with the caller; the unconditioned fight-or-flight syndrome is out of place. They must, instead, try to stay calm, concentrate on listening, and make thoughtful decisions. Unfortunately, these interpersonal skills are not enhanced by the stress response. So what has developed in the species as an adaptive preparation for dealing with external danger is counterproductive for dealing with many modern-day sources of stress. Rather than relying on avoidance (flight) or hostility (fight), we must learn new adaptive stress responses.

The General Adaptation Syndrome (GAS)

The first modern researcher to investigate the effects of continued severe stress on the body was **Hans Selye,** a Canadian endocrinologist. Beginning in the late 1930s, Selye reported on the complex response of laboratory animals to damaging agents such as bacterial infections, toxins, trauma or forced restraint, heat, cold, etc. According to Selye's theory of stress, there are many kinds of stress-producing agents (stressors) that can trigger the same systematic reaction or general bodily response. All stressors call for *adaptation;* an organism must maintain or regain its integrity and well-being by restoring equilibrium, or homeostasis. The theory conceptualizes stress as a state within the organism. **Psychosomatic disorders** are problems in organic functioning of the body, such as asthma and peptic ulcers, caused by mental and emotional conditions. They are called diseases of adaptation because they are rooted in the organism's attempts to adapt physiologically to situational stressors.

The general adaptive response to such nonspecific agents was described by Selye as the **general adaptation syndrome** (GAS). It includes three stages: an alarm reaction, a stage of resistance, and a stage of exhaustion (Selye, 1956). The GAS is adaptive because, during the stage of resistance, the organism can endure and *resist* further debilitating effects. This stimulated defense against the stressor develops and maintains an intermediate stage of *restoration*. The three stages are diagrammed in **Figure 13.7** and **Table 13.4.**

FIGURE 13.7 THE GENERAL ADAPTATION SYNDROME

Following exposure to a stressor, the body's resistance is diminished until the physiological changes of the corresponding alarm reaction bring it back up to the normal level. If the stressor continues, the bodily signs characteristic of the alarm reaction virtually disappear; resistance to the particular stressor rises above normal but drops for other stressors. This adaptive resistance returns the body to its normal level of functioning. Following prolonged exposure to the stressor, adaptation breaks down; signs of alarm reaction reappear, the stressor effects are irreversible, and the individual becomes ill and may die.

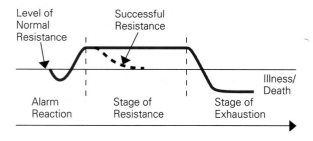

The concept of the general adaptation syndrome has proven valuable to explain disorders that had baffled physicians who had never considered stress as a cause for illness and disease. Within this framework, many disorders can be viewed as the result of the physiological processes involved in the body's long-continued attempts to adapt to a perceived dangerous stressor.

On the other hand, because Selye was a physician and because his research focused on reactions to physical stressors among experimental animals, his theory has had little to say about the importance of *psychological* aspects of stress in the case of human beings. In particular, Selye's critics believe he overstated the role of *nonspecific, systemic* factors in the production of stress-induced illness. (*Systemic* refers to the whole body as a system.) In work on animals, of course, there was no place for recognizing the importance of cognitive appraisal (Mason, 1975).

Psychoneuroimmunology

A relatively new research area that investigates the effects of stress on the physiological and biological functions of the body is **psychoneuroimmunology** (PNI) which is the scientific field that investigates the mind-body link, particularly the interaction between stress and the immune system. Our opening case featured the role of humor in enhancing health by altering immune functions. Researchers have consistently found

TABLE 13.4 GENERAL ADAPTATION SYNDROME

Stage I: Alarm Reaction (continuously repeated throughout life)

- Enlargement of adrenal cortex
- Enlargement of lymphatic system
- Increase in hormone levels
- Response to specific stressor
- Epinephrine release associated with high levels of physiological arousal and negative affect
- Greater susceptibility to increased intensity of stressor
- Heightened susceptibility to illness

(If prolonged, the slower components of the GAS are set into motion, beginning with Stage II.)

Stage II: Resistance (continuously repeated throughout life)

- Shrinkage of adrenal cortex
- Return of lymph nodes to normal size
- Sustaining of hormone levels
- High physiological arousal
- Counteraction of parasympathetic branch of ANS
- Enduring of stressor; resistance to further debilitating effects
- Heightened sensitivity to stress

(If stress continues at intense levels, hormonal reserves are depleted, fatigue sets in, and individual enters Stage III.)

Stage III: Exhaustion

- Enlargement/dysfunction of lymphatic structures
- Increase in hormone levels
- Depletion of adaptive hormones
- Decreased ability to resist either original or extraneous stressors
- Affective experience—often depression

a link between stress and declines in indicators of immune activity. For example, a causal link was shown between being exposed to uncontrollable stress and the increase in cancer among susceptible animals (Laudenslager et al., 1983). Recall the research in Chapter 9 on conditioning of rats' immune systems to respond to a sweet tasting solution by suppressing immune reactions, leading to their untimely deaths (Ader & Cohen, 1981). Also recall the new research on laughter therapy for immune system disfunction described in the opening case.

Unique white blood cells, **T-lymphocytes,** have a number of subgroups with important functions. Two of these groups are *helper* and *suppressor* T-lymphocytes which act by stimulating or shutting off the immunological response to an invading organism. Along with *natural killer cells* they provide an important defense against virus-infected cells and cancer cells. The brain can influence the immune system in two ways: through the nerve connections between brain regions and organs in the immune system and through connections of the endocrine system and immune system. The brain triggers the endocrine system to release hormones; receptors for various hormones are located on lymphocyte cells in the immune system, making the immune system responsive to the action of the endocrine system.

A number of studies with humans have shown that the quality of interpersonal relationships and their disruption or absence have strong effects on the immune system (Cohen & Syme, 1985; Kiecolt-Glaser & Glaser, 1988). Bereavement and depression also produce immunosuppression. Men with wives dying of breast cancer (Schleifer et al., 1983) and recently widowed women (Irwin et al., 1987) are less able to fight disease and face an increased risk of illness and premature death. As expected, the immune functioning of a group of chronically stressed individuals living near the damaged Three Mile Island nuclear power plant lowered more than that of a demographically comparable control group (McKinnon et al., 1989).

Health psychologist **Judith Rodin** of Yale University has been studying the immune system mechanisms by which psychological variables affect the immune system. She is investigating how giving people, especially the elderly, an increased sense of personal control improves their health through intermediary changes generated in the immune system. In addition, Rodin is exploring how stress factors may explain why 80 percent of the women undergoing a precise medical procedure to implant a fertilized egg reject it. In part, the rejection may be due to the stress surrounding the procedure itself (Rodin, 1990; *Discovering Psychology,* Program 23).

PSYCHOLOGICAL STRESS REACTIONS

Our physiological stress reactions are automatic, predictable, built-in responses over which we normally have no conscious control. However, our psychological reactions are learned; they depend on our perceptions

Judith Rodin (*Discovering Psychology,* 1990, Program 23)

and interpretations of the world and on our capacity to deal with stress. Psychological stress reactions are behavioral, emotional, and cognitive.

Behavioral Patterns

The behavior observed as a reaction to a stressor is a key dependent measure in most psychological studies of stress. Certain stress-related behaviors, such as muscle tension or spasms, can be observed. Similarly, nonconscious reactions, such as grinding one's teeth during sleep (known as *bruxism*) can be used as indexes of stress. However, almost any behavior can be part of a stress response. To create a base rate of responding against which to compare stress-related reactions, it is important to have an understanding of the frequency of the behavior prior to the advent of a stressor. For example, eating sweet desserts can be a behavioral stress response if the person never ate sweets before being diagnosed as a diabetic.

The behavior of a person who has been confronted with a stressor depends in part on the *level of stress* experienced. Very different reaction patterns have been associated with mild, moderate, and severe levels of stress.

Mild stress activates and intensifies biologically significant behaviors, such as eating, aggression, and sexual behavior. Mild stress makes an organism more alert—energies are focused and performance may improve. It may lead to positive behavioral adjustments, such as becoming better informed, becoming vigilant to sources of threat, seeking protection and support from others, and learning better attitudes and coping skills. Continued *unresolved mild stressors* can cause maladaptive behavioral reactions such as increased irritability, poor concentration, lessened productivity, and chronic impatience. However, they pose no problem when they occur only occasionally or are perceived as within one's control capacity.

Moderate stress typically disrupts behavior, especially behavior that requires skilled coordination. Giving a speech or playing in a recital are familiar examples of moderate stress situations. For some people, overeating is a typical behavioral response to moderate levels of stress. Overt aggressive behavior can also occur, especially in response to frustration. Moderate stress may also produce repetitive, stereotyped actions, such as pacing in circles or rocking back and forth. These repetitive responses have mixed effects. They are *adaptive* by reducing a high level of stressor stimulation and lessening an individual's sensitivity to the environment. At the same time, they are *nonadaptive* by being rigid and inflexible, and in persisting even when the environmental situation makes other responses more appropriate.

Severe stress inhibits and suppresses behavior and may lead to total immobility. We noted such effects in the case of the dogs and humans that experienced *learned helplessness* when they were shocked electrically, regardless of their actions (Seligman, 1975). It has been argued that immobility under severe stress may be a defensive reaction, representing "an attempt by the organism to reduce or eliminate the deleterious effects of stress . . . a form of self-therapy" (Antelman & Caggiula, 1980).

Emotional Aspects

Most stress is acutely uncomfortable, producing only negative emotions and efforts to lessen the discomfort in direct or indirect ways. Stressful life changes involving loss or separation from friends and loved ones are frequent forerunners of depression. Being left behind is more likely to result in depression than a separation caused by one's own action (Paykel, 1973). Experiencing a cluster of stressful events is another predictor of emotional depression.

Rape and incest victims, survivors of plane and serious automobile crashes, combat veterans, and others who have experienced traumatic events may react emotionally with a **posttraumatic stress disorder** (PTSD). PTSD is a delayed stress reaction that recurs repeatedly, even long after the traumatic experience. In addition, victims experience an emotional numbing in relation to everyday events and feelings of alienation from other people. Finally, the emotional pain of this reaction can result in an increase of various symptoms, such as sleep

problems, guilt about surviving, difficulty in concentrating, and an exaggerated startle response. The clinical symptoms of PTSD are described as *conditioned responses* learned in the context of a powerful life-threatening stimulus situation (Keane et al., 1985).

The following excerpt of a discussion about the aftershock of being raped reveals the powerful and enduring emotional dimension of stress.

Alice: I was in shock for a pretty long time. I could talk about the fact that I was a rape victim, but the emotions didn't start surfacing until a month later.

Beth: During the first two weeks there were people I had chosen to tell who were very, very supportive; but after two weeks, it was like, "Okay, she's over it, we can go on now." But the farther along you get, the more support you need, because, as time passes, you become aware of your emotions and the need to deal with them.

Alice: There is a point where you deny it happened. You just completely bury it.

Beth: It's so unreal that you don't want to believe that it actually happened or that it can happen. Then you go through a long period of fear and anger.

Alice: I'm terrified of going jogging. [Alice had been jogging when she was raped.] I completely stopped any kind of physical activity after I was raped. I started it again this quarter, but every time I go jogging I have a perpetual fear. My pulse doubles. Of course I don't go jogging alone any more, but still the fear is there constantly.

Beth: There's also a feeling of having all your friends betray you. I had a dream in which I was being assaulted outside my dorm. In the dream, everyone was looking out their windows—the faces were so clear—every one of my friends lined up against the windows watching, and there were even people two feet away from me. They all saw what was happening and none of them did anything. I woke up and had a feeling of extreme loneliness.

(*The Stanford Daily,* 2/2/82, with permission. For a systematic analysis of psychological and social issues involved in rape, see Cann et al., 1981; Baron & Straus, 1985.)

The emotional responses of posttraumatic stress can occur in an acute form immediately following a disaster and can subside over a period of several months. These responses can also persist, becoming a chronic syndrome called the **residual stress pattern** (Silver & Wortman, 1980). They can also be delayed

Delayed posttraumatic stress syndrome has been a special problem for Vietnam Veterans. Feeling rejected by the American public seemed to heighten their difficulty in adjusting to civilian life. For some, stress was increased by the contrast between that rejection and the welcome received by soldiers returning from the Persian Gulf War.

for months or even years. Clinicians are still discovering veterans of World War II and the Korean War who are displaying residual or delayed posttraumatic stress disorders (Dickman & Zeiss, 1982).

Cognitive Effects

Once a stressor has been interpreted as threatening to one's well-being or self-esteem, a variety of intellectual functions may be adversely affected, as when admittedly irrational thoughts create generalizations from any element of the stress situation to remotely similar current stimulus events. In general, the greater the stress, the greater the reduction in cognitive efficiency and the more interference with flexible thinking. Because attention is a limited resource, when we focus on the threatening aspects of a situation and on our arousal, we reduce the amount of attention available for effective coping with other tasks at hand. Memory is affected too, because short-term memory is limited by the amount of attention given to new input, and retrieval of past relevant memories depends on smooth operation of the use of appropriate retrieval cues. Similarly, stress may interfere with problem solving, judging, and deci-

sion making by narrowing perceptions of alternatives and by substituting stereotyped, rigid thinking for more creative responding (Janis, 1982a). Finally, there is evidence that a high level of stress impairs children's intellectual development.

To test the hypothesis that stress affects competence and intelligence, researchers developed a stress index based on such variables as family problems and physical disorders. Stress indexes were calculated for over 4000 7-year-old children, and each child's intelligence was tested. The higher the stress index, the lower was the child's IQ. This was particularly true for children with eye problems and for African-American children from poor families. Greater intellectual deficits showed up also in those who had been held back a year or assigned to special education classes. The stress variables combined to influence the performance measured by the IQ test both in the immediate testing situation and also more generally, through interacting with other personal and social factors (Brown & Rosenbaum, 1983).

SUMMING UP

Stress is the pattern of reactions an organism makes in response to stressors, stimulus events that tax its ability to cope. Stress can be negative (distress) or positive (eustress). Change and the need to adapt to biological, social, physical, and environmental demands are basic causes of stress. The accumulation of life change units and especially of chronic hassles of everyday existence become stressors that affect functioning and health. Survey studies of natural disasters and catastrophes find evidence for a sequence of stages or phases that marks changing patterns of coping over time. Chronic stressors of society, such as pollution of the environment, passive smoking, and our fears of anticipated nuclear disasters, crime, and economic failure strain us biologically and mentally.

We do not react directly to the objective qualities of stressors but, instead, in the form of cognitive appraisal, to our perceptions and interpretations of them. Appraisal is one of the primary stress moderator variables, filtering and changing the effect of stressors on our experience of stress. Other moderator variables are our inner and outer resources for dealing with a stressor, certain personality types such as the hardy personality, and coping patterns. Cognitive appraisal defines the demand; primary appraisal determines whether the demand is stressful; secondary appraisal evaluates the available personal and social resources and the appropriate action.

Physiological stress reactions are automatic mechanisms facilitating swift emergency action. They are regulated by the hypothalamus and include many emergency body changes, carried out through the action of the autonomic nervous system and the pituitary gland. They lessen sensitivity to pain and provide extra energy for fight or flight. They are useful for combatting physical stressors, but they can be maladaptive in response to psychological stressors, especially when stress is severe or chronic. The general adaptation syndrome is a three-stage pattern of physiological defenses against continuing stressors that threaten internal well-being. A resistance stage follows the alarm reaction; psychological defenses are activated until adaptive resources fail in the stage of exhaustion. The interaction between body, mind, and environmental stimulation is central to the study of psychoneuroimmunology, which focuses on the impact of psychosocial variables on the immune system.

Psychological stress reactions include behavioral, emotional, and cognitive elements. Mild stress can enhance performance and even be experienced as pleasant and challenging. Moderate stress disrupts behavior and may lead to repetitive, stereotyped actions. Severe stress suppresses behavior and typically causes dysfunctional reactions. Emotional stress reactions include irritation, anger, and depression. Posttraumatic stress disorders are delayed emotional stress reactions that prolong the negative consequences of acutely stressful experiences. Cognitive stress reactions include a narrowing of attention, rigidity of thought, and interference with judgment, problem solving, and memory.

COPING WITH STRESS

If living is inevitably stressful, and if chronic distress can disrupt our lives and even kill us, we need to learn how to manage stress in order to live better. **Coping** refers to the process of dealing with internal or external demands that are perceived as straining or exceeding an individual's resources (Lazarus & Folkman, 1984). Coping may consist of behavioral, emotional, or motivational responses and thoughts. It can also precede a potentially stressful event in the form of **anticipatory coping** (Folkman, 1984). For example, how do you tell your parents that you are dropping out of school or your lover that you are no longer in love? The anticipation of stressful situations leads to many thoughts and feelings

which themselves may be stress inducing, as in the cases of tests, interviews, speeches, or blind dates.

Psychologists have made great advances in conceptualizing and measuring coping (Carver et al., 1989; Folkman et al., 1987; Holahan & Moose, 1987). Measures of coping that are targeted for particular groups, such as adolescents experiencing similar stressors, may be more useful than more general coping measures designed for the so-called average person (Wills, 1986).

Human beings have a tremendous potential for adapting not only biologically over generations but psychologically, within a lifetime—even within a short period of time if they decide they want to change. In this section, we will look at a variety of strategies that people use to alter or reduce the harmful effects of stress.

COPING STRATEGIES

The two main types of ways we can categorize coping strategies are determined by whether the goal is to confront the problem directly—*problem-solving focus*—or lessen the discomfort associated with the stress—*emotion-regulation focus* (Billings & Moos, 1982; Lazarus & Folkman, 1984). Several subcategories of these two basic approaches are shown in **Table 13.5.**

"Taking the bull by the horns" is how we usually characterize the strategy of facing up to a problem situation. This approach includes all strategies designed to deal *directly* with the stressor, whether through overt action or through realistic problem-solving activities. We face up to a bully or run away; we try to win him or her over with bribes or other incentives. Taking martial arts training or notifying the "proper authorities" are other approaches that may prevent a bully from continuing to be a threat. In all these strategies, our focus is on the problem to be dealt with and on the agent that has induced the stress. We acknowledge the call to action, we appraise the situation and our resources for dealing with it, and we undertake a response that is appropriate for removing or lessening the threat. Such problem-solving efforts are useful for managing *controllable stressors*.

The second approach is useful for managing the impact of more *uncontrollable stressors*. We do not look for ways of changing the external stressful situation; instead, we try to change our feelings and thoughts about it. This strategy that regulates emotions is a *remedial coping strategy*.

Ego defense mechanisms, such as repression, denial of reality, and rationalization, are emotion-regulating approaches to personal stress that we often utilize without conscious awareness. The goal of these defense mechanisms is to protect us from anxieties by enabling us to appraise situations in less self-threatening ways. They lead to coping strategies that are essentially aimed at self-protection rather than at solving problems. At times, however, they cause us to distort reality and, when overused, can lead to maladaptive coping.

What is *your* typical coping style? Coping is a situation where more is definitely better (Taylor & Clark, 1986). For coping to be successful, our resources need to match the perceived demand. So, successful coping depends on a match of coping strategies to the features

---

TABLE 13.5   *TAXONOMY OF COPING STRATEGIES*

Problem-focused Coping Change stressor or one's relationship to it through direct actions and/or problem-solving activities	Fight (destroy, remove, or weaken the threat) Flight (distance oneself from the threat) Seek options to fight or flight (negotiating, bargaining, compromising) Prevent future stress (act to increase one's resistance or decrease strength of anticipated stress)
Emotion-focused Coping Change self through activities that make one feel better but do not change the stressor	Somatically focused activities (use of drugs, relaxation, biofeedback) Cognitively focused activities (planned distractions, fantasies, thoughts about oneself) Unconscious processes that distort reality and may result in intrapsychic stress

of the stressful event. The availability of multiple coping strategies would then be most adaptive because we are more likely to achieve a match and manage the stressful event. When we know that we possess a large repertoire of coping strategies, that metacognition increases our confidence in meeting environmental demands (Bandura, 1986). That self-confidence in turn can insulate us from experiencing the full impact of many stressors because believing we have the coping resources readily available immediately short-circuits the stressful chaotic response to "What am I going to do?"

MODIFYING COGNITIVE STRATEGIES

A powerful way to handle stress more adaptively is to change our evaluations of stressors and our self-defeating cognitions about the way we are dealing with them. We need to find a different way to think about a given situation, our role in it, and the causal attributions we make to explain the undesirable outcome. Two ways of mentally coping with stress are reappraising the nature of the stressors themselves and restructuring our cognitions about our stress reactions.

Reappraising Stressors

Learning to think differently about certain stressors, to relabel them, or to imagine them in a less-threatening (perhaps even funny) context are forms of cognitive reappraisal that can reduce stress. Worried about giving a speech to a large, forbidding audience? One stressor reappraisal technique is to imagine your potential critics sitting there in the nude—this surely takes away a great deal of their fearsome power. Anxious about being shy at a party you must attend? Think about finding someone who is more shy than you and reducing his or her social anxiety by initiating a conversation.

Restructuring Cognitions

A summary of the literature on stress and performance points to an individual's *uncertainty* about impending events and *sense of control* over them as the main factors in perceived stress (Swets & Bjork, 1990). Effective coping strategies must counter by providing the person in a stressful setting with some or all of four types of control: *information control* (knowing what to expect); *cognitive control* (thinking about the event differently and more constructively); *decision control* (being able to decide on alternative actions); and *behavioral control* (taking actions to reduce the aversiveness of the event).

We can manage stress better by changing what we tell ourselves about it and by changing our handling of it. These strategies can lead to *cognitive restructuring*

and more effective coping. For example, depressed or insecure people often tell themselves that they are no good, that they'll do poorly, and—if something goes well—that it was a fluke or just random luck.

Cognitive-behavior therapist **Donald Meichenbaum** (1977) has proposed a three-phase process to intentionally change this self-fulfilling cycle. In Phase I, people work to develop a greater awareness of their actual behavior, what instigates it, and what its results are. One of the best ways of doing this is to keep daily logs. By helping people redefine their problems in terms of their causes and results, logs can increase their feelings of control. In Phase 2, they begin to identify new behaviors that negate the maladaptive, self-defeating behaviors—perhaps smiling at someone, offering a compliment, or acting assertively. In Phase 3, after adaptive behaviors are being emitted, individuals appraise their consequences, avoiding the former internal dialogue of put-downs. Instead of telling themselves, "I was lucky the professor called on me when I happened to have read the text," they say, "I'm glad I was prepared for the professor's question. It feels great to be able to respond intelligently in that class."

This three-phase approach means initiating responses and self-statements that are incompatible with previous defeatist cognitions. Once started on this path, people realize that they are changing and taking full credit for it which promotes further successes. **Table 13.6** gives examples of the new kinds of self-statements that help in dealing with stressful situations.

One of the major variables that promotes positive adjustments is **perceived control** over the stressor, a belief that you have the ability to make a difference in the course or the consequences of some event or experience. If you believe that you can affect the course of the illness or the daily symptoms of the disease, you are probably adjusting well to the disorder (Affleck et al., 1987). However, if you believe the source of the stress is another person whose behavior you cannot influence or a situation that you cannot change, chances increase for a poor psychological adjustment to your chronic condition (Bulman & Wortman, 1977).

In a classic study by Ellen Langer and Judith Rodin (1976), two simple elements of perceived control were introduced into a nursing home environment. Each resident was given a plant to take care of (behavioral control) and asked to choose when to see movies (decision control). Comparison subjects on another floor of the institution had neither sense of control; they were given plants that nurses took care of and they saw movies at prearranged times. On delayed measures several weeks later and a full year later, those elderly

TABLE 13.6   EXAMPLES OF COPING SELF-STATEMENTS

Preparation
I can develop a plan to deal with it.
Just think about what I can do about it. That's better than getting anxious.
No negative self-statements, just think rationally.

Confrontation
One step at a time; I can handle this situation.
This anxiety is what the doctor said I would feel; it's a reminder to use my coping exercises.
Relax; I'm in control. Take a slow deep breath.

Coping
When fear comes, just pause.
Keep focus on the present; what is it I have to do?
Don't try to eliminate fear totally; just keep it manageable.
It's not the worst thing that can happen.
Just think about something else.

Self-reinforcement
It worked, I was able to do it.
It wasn't as bad as I expected.
I'm really pleased with the progress I'm making.

patients who had been given some control over the events in this bleak institutional setting were more active, had more positive moods, and were psychologically and physically healthier than the no-control patients. Most amazing is the finding that, one year later, fewer of those in the perceived control situation had died than those on the comparison floor (Rodin & Langer, 1977; Rodin, 1983). Such research findings have important implications for policies and programs in institutional settings (Rodin, 1986).

The social and psychological dimensions of the environment can also be critically important in increasing or decreasing stress. For example, the perceived freedom of choice to either enter or not enter a particular environment may determine whether a person will adapt successfully to it. One study determined that elderly women who chose to enter a retirement home lived longer, as a group, than those with an initially comparable health status who entered feeling they had no choice (Ferrare, 1962).

SUPPORTIVENESS OF THE ENVIRONMENT

We all cope with stress as individuals, but, for a lifetime of effective coping and for the continued success of our species, it is necessary for us to form alliances with others. Isolation can lead to inadequate coping and can itself be the cause of stress. Contemporary research shows that being part of a social support network and living and working in a healthy environment leads to an improvement in coping.

Social Support Networks

Social support refers to the resources others provide, giving the message that one is loved, cared for, esteemed, and connected to other people in a network of communication and mutual obligation (Cobb, 1976; Cohen & Syme, 1985). In addition to these forms of *socioemotional support,* other people may provide *tangible support* (money, transportation, housing) and *informational support* (advice, personal feedback, information). Anyone with whom you have a significant social relationship—such as family members, friends, coworkers, and neighbors—can be part of your social support network in time of need.

Much research points to the power of social support in moderating the vulnerability to stress (Cohen & McKay, 1983). When people have other people they can turn to, they are better able to handle job stressors, unemployment, marital disruption, serious illness, and other catastrophes, as well as their everyday problems of living (Gottlieb, 1981; Pilisuk & Parks, 1986). The positive effects of social support go beyond aiding psy-

Perceived control over the stressor promotes positive adjustments. Nursing-home residents given plants to care for and the choice of when to see movies are more active and have more positive moods.

for particular stressors—for example, help from a spouse might be ideal for a working woman with a newborn (Lieberman, 1982).

Researchers are also trying to determine when sources of support actually increase anxiety. For example, if your mother insisted on accompanying you to a doctor's appointment or to a college interview when you preferred to go alone, you might experience additional anxiety about the situation (Coyne et al., 1988). Too much or too intensive social support may become intrusive and not helpful in the long run; having one close friend may be as beneficial as having many. Research shows that depression symptoms are more likely to increase for a married person who is unable to communicate well with his or her spouse than for a control subject without a spouse (Weissman, 1987).

Leading health psychologist **Shelley Taylor** and her colleagues at UCLA studied the effectiveness of the different types of social support given to cancer patients (Taylor, 1986; Dakof & Taylor, 1990). Patients varied in their assessments of the helpfulness of kinds of support. They thought it was helpful to them for spouses but not for physicians or nurses to "just be there." On the other hand, it was important to the patients to receive information or advice from other cancer patients or from physicians but not from family and friends. Regardless of the source—whether doctors or family or friends—patients did not find forced cheerfulness or attempts to minimize the impact of their disease helpful.

Other research focuses on the problems *caregivers* experience as they attempt to provide social support. These problems including giving support that is intense, long term, unappreciated, or rejected (Coyne, et al., 1988; Kiecolt-Glaser et al., 1987; Schulz et al., 1987).

STRUCTURING THE PHYSICAL ENVIRONMENT

Psychological researchers in NASA's space program have found that they can help astronauts cope with the stress of long duration space travel by designing the space capsule in ways that make it more relaxing. The capsule is painted in colors found to be most psychologically pleasing—the walls are darker at the bottom to create an illusion of more height and space. Nature pictures of Earth's rivers, waterfalls, and mountains are found to be the most effective types of posters for combating the sense of separation and isolation space travellers experience (*Discovering Psychology,* 1990, Program 24).

Psychologists now realize that, in addition to changing behavior patterns and cognitive styles, stress management should involve restructuring our physical environments to reduce their unhealthy or stress-inducing features.

chological adjustment to stressful events; they can improve recovery from diagnosed illness and reduce the risk of death from specific diseases (House et al., 1988; Kulik & Mahler, 1989). Research shows that lack of a social support system clearly increases one's vulnerability to disease and death (Berkman & Syme, 1979). Decreases in social support in family and work environments are related to increases in psychological maladjustment. This negative relationship was found even when the researchers looked at groups who had the same initial levels of support, maladjustment, and life change (Holohan & Moos, 1981). Prospective studies, which control for initial health status, consistently show an increased risk of death among people whose social relationships are low in quantity and quality (House et al., 1988).

Researchers are trying to identify which types of support are most helpful for specific events (Cohen, 1988; Dakof & Taylor, 1990; Dunkell-Schelter et al., 1987). Different sources of support seem to work best

Payload specialist and scientist-astronaut Millie Hughes-Fulford is one of NASA's psychological researchers who has studied ways to help astronauts cope with the stress of long duration space travel (*Discovering Psychology,* 1990, Program 24).

SUMMING UP

Coping strategies are means of dealing with the perceived threat of various types of stressors. Two primary coping categories proposed by Lazarus are problem-focused coping, or taking direct actions, and emotion-regulation coping, which is often indirect or avoidant. We can learn to manage stress better through reappraising the nature of the stressors and by restructuring our relevant cognitions. A significant stress moderator is social support. Health is promoted by developing and being an active member of a social support network. However, the quality and nature of the source of social support are important components that affect people's evaluations of the sources. While social isolation is a reliable predictor of psychological, social, and medical pathologies, appropriate kinds of social networks are health promoting. At times the best coping strategy entails taking action to restructure the physical and/or social environments in which we live, study, and work.

HEALTH PSYCHOLOGY

The acknowledgment of the importance of psychological and social factors in health has spurred the growth of a new field, *health psychology*. **Health psychology** is devoted to understanding the way people stay healthy, the reasons they become ill, and the way they respond when they do get ill (Taylor, 1986, 1990). Among the many areas of concern for health psychologists are health promotion and maintenance; prevention and treatment of illness; causes and correlates of health, illness, and dysfunction; and improvement of the health care system and health policy information (Matarazzo, 1980).

THE BIOPSYCHOSOCIAL MODEL OF HEALTH

Psychological principles have been applied in the treatment of illness and the pursuit of health for all of recorded time. Many ancient cultures understood the importance of communal health and relaxation rituals in the enhancement of the quality of life. Among the Navajo, for example, disease, illness, and well-being have been attributed to social harmony and mind-body interactions. The Navajo concept of **hozho** (pronounced whoa-zo) means harmony, peace of mind, goodness, ideal family relationships, beauty in arts and crafts, and health of body and spirit. Illness is seen as the outcome of any *disharmony,* being caused by evil introduced through violation of taboos, witchcraft, overindulgence, or bad dreams. Tribal healing ceremonies seek to banish illness and restore health, not only through the medicine of the shaman, but also through the combined efforts of all family members who work together with the ill person to reachieve a state of hozho. The illness of any member of a tribe is seen not as his or her individual responsibility (and fault) but rather as a sign of broader disharmony that must be repaired by communal healing ceremonies. This cultural orientation guarantees a powerful social support network that automatically comes to the aid of the sufferer.

Similarly, among the *Nyakusa* of Tanzania, Africa, any sign of disharmony or deviation from the expected "norm" generates a swift communal intervention to set the situation right. Thus, strong anger, the birth of twins, the sudden death of a young person, and illness are all signs of an anomaly because they are unusual events for this tribe. Special tribal rituals are quickly enacted around the person or family in which the discord occurs. One feature of these rituals is evidence of the social acceptance of the person(s) afflicted. The concept of medicine among the Nyakusa differs from the western view that it is solely a biological or pharmacological intervention. For the Nyakusa, medicine is more often given to change the habits, dispositions, and desires of people—for psychological cures. Chiefs get medicine to make them wise and dignified; a bride gets medicine to make her patient and polite as well as fertile. Anger in husbands, employers, and police is controlled by a special medicine; other medicine cures thieves of criminal habits and makes men and women more attractive and more persuasive as lovers and leaders (Wilson, 1959).

Modern western scientific thinking has relied exclusively on a *biomedical model* that has a dualistic conception of body and mind. According to this model, medicine treats the physical body as separate from the psyche; the mind is important only for emotions and beliefs and it has little to do with the reality of the soma. However, research has begun to look at links between the nervous system, the immune system, behavioral styles, cognitive processing, and environmental factors which, in combination, can put us at risk for illness or increase our resistance to stress, trauma, and disease. This new view is embodied in the **biopsychosocial model** of health and illness (Engle, 1976).

THE YIN AND YANG OF HEALTH AND ILLNESS

Health refers to the general condition of the body and mind in terms of their soundness and vigor. It is not simply the absence of illness or injury but is more a matter of how well all the body's component parts are working. "To be healthy is to have the ability, despite an occasional bout of illness, to live with full use of your faculties and to be vigorous, alert, and happy to be alive, even in old age" (Insel & Roth, 1985, p. xvii).

Your physical health is linked to the state of mind and the world around you. Health psychologists view health as a dynamic, multidimensional experience. Optimal health, or **wellness,** incorporates in the physical, intellectual, emotional, spiritual, social, and environmental domains of health the ability to function fully. When you undertake any activity for the purpose of preventing disease or detecting it in the asymptomatic stage, you are exhibiting *health behavior* (Kasl & Cobb, 1966). A *healthy habit,* or behavioral pattern, is one that operates automatically without extrinsic reinforcement or incentives and that contributes directly to your overall health (Hunt et al., 1979).

Is there a difference between illness and illness behavior? **Illness** involves documented pathology, such as biological or physiological damage, cell pathology, and blood chemistry. However, if you ever missed a class you didn't really want to go to because of a stomach ache, you were exhibiting *illness behavior*. Regardless of whether you were really ill, illness behavior (saying "ouch," seeing a doctor, or taking medicine, for example) does not necessarily implicate underlying pathology (Taylor, 1990). A growing number of biopsychosocial researchers are calling for the application of behavioral indicators of illness or behavioral outcomes as dependent measures in scientific studies.

HEALTH PROMOTION AND MAINTENANCE

The role of behavioral factors in disease processes and the maintenance of health are increasingly clear: we need to evaluate our beliefs, change dysfunctional lifestyles, and begin to take the extra behavioral step toward wellness. Health psychologists believe that four elements determine the likelihood of someone engaging in a healthy habit or in changing a faulty one. The person must believe that (a) the threat to health is severe; (b) the perceived personal vulnerability and/or the likelihood of developing the disorder is high; (c) he or she is able to perform the response that will reduce the threat (self-efficacy); and (d) the response is effective in overcoming the threat (Bandura, 1986; Janz & Becker, 1984; Rogers, 1984).

Modifying health behaviors is not a simple matter. For example, in adolescence, faulty health habits have been associated with peer group influence and issues of personal identity (Botvin & Eng, 1982). Even when health habits change for the better, there is always the threat of **relapse.** New health habits need to be practiced regularly to become automatic. However, it is difficult to put new resolve and new actions into a standard regime when you remain in the *behavior setting* that reinforced the unhealthy behavior patterns. Without changing their environment, ex-convicts, recovered drug addicts, and weight clinic clients often relapse into former ways of behaving even when they have learned new, more appropriate, healthy behaviors.

A series of studies by Israeli psychologists shows that *health-oriented individuals* have a cognitive orientation related to physical health and absence of symptoms (Kreitler & Kreitler, 1990). This cognitive-motivational factor, which seems to be characteristic of the whole personality, reflects an emphasis on a positive internal atmosphere (feelings of love, joy, contentment), positive daydreams and inhibition of negative emotions; an active sense of personal control and efficacy; repression of daily threats to keep anxiety low; deemphasis on body concerns; and a matter-of-fact problem-solving focus (Kreitler & Kreitler, 1991).

The promotion of health and wellness requires national and international efforts that go beyond focusing on the psychology of individuals to systemwide involvement. A general model for health promotion developed by the Canadian government outlines three basic health challenges, mechanisms to promote health, and strategies for implementing changes designed to achieve health for all. Similarly, the U.S. Department of Health and Human Services has outlined national public health goals and objectives for the 1990s in a recently released report, *Healthy People 2000*. The three broad national goals for public health over the next decade are (a) to increase the span of healthy life; (b) to reduce the disparities in health status among different populations, such as the poor, minorities, and children; and (c) to provide access to preventive health-care services for all people. To meet these general goals, nearly 300 specific objectives have been identified in 22 priority areas outlined in **Table 13.7**. A comparable earlier agenda for national health has met with reasonably good success, achieving nearly half of the goals set for 1990; but a quarter of them were not met and another quarter could not be evaluated because of inadequate data (McGinnis, 1991).

TABLE 13.7 **HEALTH OBJECTIVES FOR THE YEAR 2000**

Priority Area	
Health Promotion	**Preventive Services**
1. Physical Activity and Fitness	14. Maternal and Infant Health
2. Nutrition	15. Heart Disease and Stroke
3. Tobacco	16. Cancer
4. Alcohol and Other Drugs	17. Diabetes and Chronic Disabling Conditions
5. Family Planning	18. HIV Infection
6. Mental Health and Mental Disorders	19. Sexually Transmitted Diseases
7. Violent and Abusive Behavior	20. Immunization and Infectious Diseases
8. Educational and Community-Based Programs	21. Clinical Preventive Services
Health Protection	**Surveillance**
9. Unintentional Injuries	22. Surveillance and Data Systems
10. Occupational Safety and Health	
11. Environmental Health	
12. Food and Drug Safety	
13. Oral Health	

TREATMENT AND PREVENTION OF ILLNESS

The scientific evidence for the benefits of psychological treatments for diagnosed pathology or illness has also grown with a biopsychosocial model of health. Many investigators now believe that psychological strategies can improve the emotional well-being of individuals. A recent study conducted by **David Spiegel,** a research psychiatrist at Stanford University School of Medicine, and his team of researchers demonstrates the impact of psychosocial treatment on the course of disease.

> Routine medical care was provided to 86 patients with metastatic breast cancer, while an experimental subgroup of 50 also participated in weekly supportive group therapy for one year. These patients met to discuss their personal experiences in coping with the various aspects of having cancer, and they had the opportunity to reveal openly in an accepting environment their fears and other strong emotions.
>
> Although at the 10-year follow-up all but three of the total sample had died, there was a significant difference in the survival times between those given the psychological treatment and those given only medical treatment. Those patients who participated in group therapy survived for an average of 36.6 months, compared to the 18.9 months for the control group. This finding in a well-controlled study indicates that psychological treatments can affect the course of disease, the length of one's life, and the quality of life (Spiegel et al., 1989).

A negative reaction to this encouraging exploratory research on psychological factors in the treatment of disease was sounded by a physician fearful that medicine was incorporating a biopsychosocial model: "What I am fearful of is that the 'alternative' field will go crazy with this and say, 'Aha, we told you all along, psychotherapy cures cancer, so stop your radiation therapy' " (Dr. Jimmie Holland, quoted in Baranaga, 1989, p. 246). To the contrary, many health psychologists want medical treatments to be more flexible and expand to include practices in addition to traditional radiation and chemotherapy for the treatment of metastatic cancer.

Illness prevention means developing general strategies and specific tactics to eliminate or reduce the risk that people will get sick. The prevention of illness in the 1990s poses a much different challenge than it did at the turn of the century, according to pioneering health psychologist **Joseph Matarazzo** (1984). He notes that, in 1900, the primary cause of death was infectious disease. Health practitioners at that time launched the first revolution in American public health.

Through the use of research, public education, the development of vaccines, and changes in public health standards (such as waste control and sewage), they were able to reduce substantially the deaths associated with such diseases as influenza, tuberculosis, polio, measles, and smallpox.

If we are to continue to pursue advances in the quality of life, we must attempt to decrease those deaths associated with life-style factors (see **Table 13.8**). Smoking, being overweight, eating foods high in fat and cholesterol, drinking too much alcohol, driving without seat belts, and leading stressful lives all play a role in heart disease, cancer, strokes, cirrhosis, accidents, and suicide. Changing the behaviors associated with these *diseases of civilization* will prevent much illness and unnecessary premature deaths. **Figure 13.8** shows the estimated percent of deaths that could be prevented by changes in behavior, early detection, and prevention strategies.

Another aspect of prevention involves developing a global consciousness in which disease prevention and health promotion are seen within a worldwide framework and not just from a U.S. or Eurocentric focus. Because most of the world's talent and expertise in behavioral science and preventive medicine/public health exists in the developed world, reaching developing world settings requires support for scholars, researchers, and practitioners in those regions and culturally

relevant models of health and behavior change. A model prevention program for the Asia-Pacific region is being developed at the University of Hawaii (Raymond et al., 1991).

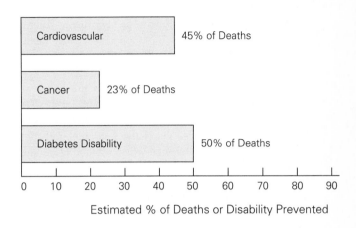

FIGURE 13.8 PREVENTION OF DEATH

Changes in behavior, early detection of problems, and intervention could prevent death in many cases.

Cardiovascular — 45% of Deaths

Cancer — 23% of Deaths

Diabetes Disability — 50% of Deaths

Estimated % of Deaths or Disability Prevented

TABLE 13.8 LEADING CAUSES OF DEATH, UNITED STATES, 1989

Rank	% of Deaths	Cause of Death	Contributors to Cause of Death (D—diet; S—smoking; A—alcohol)
1.	34.1	Heart disease	DS
2.	23.1	Cancers	DS
3.	6.8	Strokes	DS
4.	2.3	Accidents: motor vehicles	A
	2.1	Accidents: all others	
5.	3.9	Chronic obstructive lung diseases	S
6.	3.5	Pneumonia and influenza	S
7.	1.8	Diabetes	D
8.	1.4	Suicide	A
9.	1.2	Chronic liver diseases	A
10.	1.1	Homicide	A
11.	1.0	AIDS, HIV disease	

Staying Healthy

What are prevention strategies in the "war on life-cycle"? One approach is to change or eliminate poor health habits. Examples of this strategy are programs to help people become or stay healthy, quit smoking, exercise, lose excess weight, and be aware of sexually transmitted diseases and how to prevent them. You are more likely to stay well if you practice good health habits such as those listed in **Table 13.9.**

Heart Disease A major study to prevent heart disease was conducted in three towns in California. The goals of the study were to persuade people to reduce their cardiovascular risk via changes in smoking, diet, and exercise and to determine which method of persuasion was more effective.

In one town, a two-year campaign was conducted through the mass media, including television, radio, newspapers, billboards, and mailed leaflets. A second town received the same two-year media campaign plus a personal instruction program on modifying health habits for high-risk individuals. The third town served as a control group and received no persuasive campaign. How successful were the campaigns in modifying life-style? The results showed that the townspeople who had gotten only the mass-media campaign were more knowledgeable about the links between life-style and heart disease, but they showed only modest changes in their own behaviors and health status as seen in **Figure 13.9.** In the town where the media campaign was supplemented with personal instruction, people showed more substantial and long-lasting changes in their health habits, partic-

TABLE 13.9 TEN STEPS TO PERSONAL WELLNESS

1. Exercise regularly
2. Eat nutritious, balanced meals (high in vegetables, fruits, and grains, low in fat and cholesterol)
3. Maintain proper weight
4. Sleep 7–8 hours nightly; rest/relax daily
5. Wear seatbelts and bike helmets
6. Do not smoke or use drugs
7. Use alcohol in moderation, if at all
8. Engage only in protected, safe sex
9. Get regular medical/dental checkups; adhere to medical regimens
10. Develop an optimistic perspective and friendships

ularly in reduced smoking (Farquhar et al., 1984; Maccoby et al., 1977). Follow-ups reveal that the overall risk of mortality decreased 15 percent and coronary heart disease decreased 16 percent, which translates into nearly 560 needless deaths that could be prevented in the next decade if the behavior changes continue (Perlman, 1990).

The good news is that life-style factors can be modified. The bad news is that (a) it is difficult and expensive to do so and (b) mass media campaigns are not as effective in changing some health behaviors, such as obesity, as had been hoped. The campaigns may, however, contribute to long-term changes in social attitudes that support life-style changes.

Smoking We are now paying the burden for past smoking habits; the annual U.S. deaths related to smoking climbed to over 400,000 in 1988 from the estimated 188,000 in 1965 and 390,000 in 1985 (National Center for Disease Control report, 1991). Despite the steady trend toward reduced smoking, especially among the middle aged, 29 percent of Americans continue to smoke. Among the estimated 50 million American pack-a-day smokers, male smokers are 22 times more likely than nonsmokers to die of lung cancer, and the risk of death from lung cancer is 12 times higher for women smokers than for women nonsmokers. Among African Americans, the death rate attributable to smoking is 12 percent higher than for whites. Only 10 percent of smokers initiate this deadly habit after the age of 21. Imagine the results to the long-term health of the society if the 3000 children who start smoking each and every day of the year could be prevented from lighting that first cigarette. The popular national campaign to "Say No to Drugs" would save more lives if it were focused on tobacco.

The health benefits of becoming a nonsmoker are immediate and substantial for men and women of all ages. Even heavy smokers who kick the nicotine habit can improve their chances of avoiding disease and premature death due to smoking. The best health policy appears to be to never start smoking or join the ranks of the estimated 35 million other Americans who have quit. The Surgeon General's 1990 report stated that 90 percent of those that have quit have done so on their own, without professional treatment programs. Because smoking often starts in adolescence, some psychologists have tried to tackle the problem by studying ways to keep teenagers from smoking. The programs that seem to be most successful provide antismoking information in formats that appeal to adolescents, portray a positive image of the nonsmoker as independent and self-reliant, and use peer group techniques—popular peers serve as

FIGURE 13.9 **RESPONSE TO MEDIA HEALTH MESSAGES AND HANDS-ON WORKSHOPS**

Knowledge of cardiovascular disease risk factors was greater among residents of Town B, who were exposed to a 2-year mass media health campaign, than among residents of Town A, who were not exposed to a campaign. Knowledge gain was greater still when residents of Town C participated in intense workshops and instruction sessions for several months during the media blitz. As knowledge increased, bad health habits (risk behaviors) and signs (indicators) decreased, with Town C leading the way, followed by Town B.

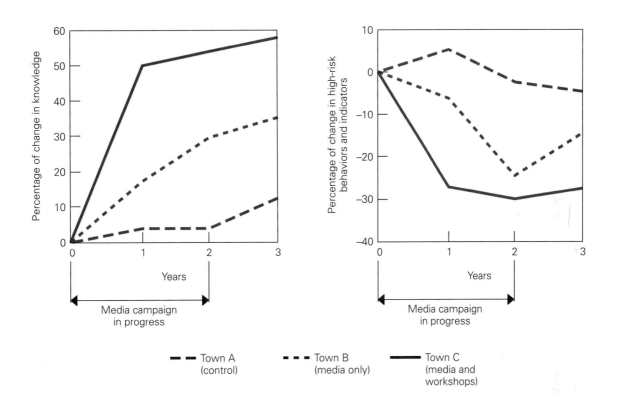

nonsmoking role models—and instruction in ways to help teens resist peer pressure (Evans et al., 1978). The principles developed from campaigns to teach people to "Just say no" can be used to prevent the onset of drug use and other addictive behaviors.

Exercise   Regular exercise has been established as an important factor in promoting and maintaining health. In particular, major improvements in health are gained from such exercises as bicycling, swimming, running, or even fast walking. These aerobic exercises are characterized by high intensity, long duration, and high endurance. They lead to increased fitness of the

heart and respiratory systems, improvement of muscle tone and strength, and many other health benefits. However, most people do not engage in such exercise consistently. Researchers are now exploring the questions of who exercises regularly and why and trying to determine what programs or strategies are most effective in getting people to start and continue exercising (Dishman, 1982). One clear finding is that people are more likely to exercise regularly if it is easy and convenient to do so. This is one reason that many companies are now providing exercise equipment, aerobics classes, or jogging tracks for their employees to use during their work breaks.

TABLE 13.10	AIDS INCIDENCE AND MORTALITY, JUNE 1991	
	Cumulative from June 1981 to June 1991	
	Total Cases	**Total Deaths**
U.S.	182,834	115,984
World (estimate)	1,300,000	500,000
World Health Organization (report)	345,533	—

Sexually Transmitted Diseases The need for a shift toward the values and priorities of a health ethic and the enactment of healthy behaviors is most pronounced in the battle against preventable diseases. A deadly virus is the cause of one of today's most frightening diseases—AIDS. Unheard of until a few years ago, it is now a worldwide epidemic growing in frightening proportions in many countries (see **Table 13.10**).

AIDS is an acronym for *Acquired Immune Deficiency Syndrome*. While hundreds of thousands are dying from this virulent disease, many more people are living with HIV infection. **HIV** (*Human Immunodeficiency Virus*) is a virus that attacks the white blood cells (T-Lymphocytes) in human blood, thus damaging the immune system and weakening the ability to fight other diseases. The individual then becomes vulnerable to infection by a host of other viruses and bacteria that can cause such life-threatening illnesses as cancer, meningitis, and pneumonia. The HIV virus is not airborne; it requires direct access to the bloodstream to produce an infection. The period of time from initial infection with the virus until symptoms occur (incubation period) can be as long as five years. Frequently, the symptoms are opportunistic infections such as yeast infections, rashes, and warts. At the moment, the diagnosis of AIDS or ARC (AIDS-Related Complex) requires a severe deterioration of the immune system and an episode of a life-threatening infection. Although most of the estimated millions of those infected with the HIV virus do not have AIDS (a medical diagnosis), they must live with the continual stress that this life-threatening disease might suddenly emerge.

At the present time, there is neither a cure for AIDS nor a vaccine to prevent its spread. However, there are proven treatments that will improve the quality and length of life of those who are afflicted with the disease. The drug AZT slows the progression of the HIV virus, and there are new treatments that can more effectively manage the opportunistic infections, especially pneumonia. Aerobic exercise and other behavioral interventions at an early stage can arrest HIV disease by improving immune functioning (Antoni et al., 1990). More and more, people are living with HIV and AIDS because of advances in the treatment of the various components of the disease, in addition to the adoption of healthier life styles. However, many people are also dying needlessly because of their inability to access available treatments or the lack of availability of possible treatments.

The HIV virus is generally passed from one person to another in one of two ways: (a) the exchange of semen or blood during sexual contact (especially anal intercourse) and (b) the sharing of intravenous needles and syringes used for injecting drugs. The virus has also been passed through blood transfusions and medical procedures in which infected blood or organs are unwittingly given to healthy people. Many children suffering from hemophilia have gotten AIDS in this way.

Who is at risk? Potentially everyone. Although the initial discovery of AIDS in the United States was in the male homosexual community, the disease has spread widely. AIDS is being found among heterosexuals and homosexuals of both sexes. It is predicted that AIDS will increase and spread throughout the general population, in just the same way as other sexually transmitted diseases such as syphilis and gonorrhea, which have also been on the rise in recent years. According to the National Center for Disease Control Report (Nov., 1990), as many as 35,000 college students, or one in 500, are estimated to be HIV positive. Given the escalating number of AIDS cases, the anticipated additional burden on the health care system and community health budgets will be unprecedented.

The only way to protect oneself from being infected with AIDS is to change those life-style factors that put one at risk. This means making permanent changes in patterns of *sexual behavior* and in use of drug paraphernalia. Health psychologist **Thomas Coates** is part of a multidisciplinary research team that is utilizing an array of psychological principles in a concerted effort to prevent the further spread of AIDS (Coates, 1990; Ekstrand & Coates, 1990; Catania et al., 1990). The team is involved in many aspects of applied psychology, such as assessing psychosocial risk factors, developing behavioral interventions, training community leaders to be most effective in educating their members toward healthier patterns of sexual and drug behavior, assisting with the design of media advertisements and community information campaigns, and systematically evaluating changes in relevant attitudes, values, and behaviors.

Thomas Coates (*Discovering Psychology,* 1990, Program 23)

The safest approach is either to abstain from sexual activity or to have a monogamous relationship with a noninfected partner. However, when engaging in risky behavior, the only way to prevent infection by the AIDS

Educating young people about the risk of AIDS is an important step in eliminating the spread of this fatal disease.

virus is to practice safer sex (use condoms during sexual contact and withdraw prior to ejaculation), use sterile needles, and know your HIV status. There is great potential for the media to show young people how to practice AIDS prevention behaviors while developing new healthful social norms and correcting inaccurate perceptions of social norms (Flora, 1991). Special programs are being developed to reach minorities who are at risk for AIDS but are not easily accessed by traditional educational and standard media efforts. For example, a recent ad designed with the assistance of African-American women addressed in a more sensitive way than previously the problem of selling sex in return for the drug crack.

For further information about AIDS, see Coates et al., 1984; Nungesser, 1986; and Temoshok et al., 1987. You can also call the toll-free National AIDS Hotline (English: 1-800-HIV-INFO; Spanish: 1-800-344-7432; TTY/TDD for Hearing Impaired: 1-800-243-7889).

HEALTHY AGAIN

Unlike prevention, treatment focuses on helping people adjust to their illnesses and recover from them. For example, pain is an enduring aspect of many illnesses and injuries, and there are many psychological techniques of pain control, such as biofeedback, hypnosis, relaxation, and visual imagery for distraction. However, knowledge about one's treatment is also a critical factor in recovery; it is better to know what to expect than to leave it to the doctor. Researchers have found that patients who show the best recovery from surgery are those who received complete information before their operations (Janis, 1958; Johnson, 1983). However, other types of communication between doctor and patient often do not work as planned.

Patient Adherence Patients are often given a *treatment regimen*. This regimen might include medications, dietary changes, prescribed periods of bed rest and exercise, and follow-up procedures such as return check-ups, rehabilitation training, and chemotherapy. Failing to adhere to treatment regimens is one of the most serious problems in health care (Rodin & Janis, 1982). The rate of **patient nonadherence** is estimated to be as high as 50 percent. The culprit seems to be the nature of the communication process between doctor and patient.

Research has shown that health care professionals can take steps to improve patient adherence. Patients are more satisfied with their health care when they trust that the efficacy of the treatment outweighs its costs and when practitioners communicate clearly, make sure that their patients understand what has been said, act courteously, and convey a sense of caring and supportiveness. In addition, health professionals must recognize the role of cultural and social norms in the treatment process and involve family and friends where necessary. Some physicians critical of their profession argue that doctors must be taught to care in order to cure (Siegel, 1988). Compliance-gaining strategies developed by social psychologists are also being used to help overcome the lack of cooperation between patients and practitioners (Zimbardo & Leippe, 1991).

Altering Bodily Reactions   Many people react to stress with tension, resulting in tight muscles, high blood pressure, constricted blood vessels in the brain, and chronic oversecretion of hormones. Fortunately, many of these tension responses can be controlled by a variety of techniques. Relaxation through meditation has ancient roots in many parts of the world. In Eastern cultures, ways to calm the mind and still the body's tensions have been practiced for centuries. Today, Zen discipline and Yoga exercises from Japan and India are part of daily life for many people both there and, increasingly, in the West. In our own culture, a growing number of people have been attracted to therapy in and workshops on relaxation and to various forms of meditation.

Just as stress is the nonspecific response of the body to any demand made on it, there is growing evidence that complete relaxation is a potent antistress response. The **relaxation response** is a condition in which muscle tension, cortical activity, heart rate, and blood pressure all decrease and breathing slows. There is reduced electrical activity in the brain, and input to the central nervous system from the outside environment is lowered. In this low level of arousal, recuperation from stress can take place. Four conditions are regarded as necessary to produce the relaxation response: (a) a quiet environment, (b) closed eyes, (c) a comfortable position, and (d) a repetitive mental device. The first three lower input to the nervous system while the fourth lowers its internal stimulation (Benson, 1975).

Biofeedback (described in Chapter 9) is a self-regulatory technique used for a variety of special applications, such as control of blood pressure, relaxation of forehead muscles (involved in tension headaches), and even overcoming extreme blushing. Paradoxically, although individuals do not know how they do it, concentrating on the desired result in the presence of this signal produces change in the desired direction. While biofeedback can achieve general relaxation and reductions in muscle tension, it does not reduce general levels of

Confiding in others is beneficial for health and happiness.

stress (Birbaumer & Kimmel, 1979; Swets & Bjork, 1990).

Healing Power of Disclosure   Have you ever had a secret too shameful to tell anyone? If so, tell someone now. That is the conclusion from a large body of research by health psychologist **James Pennebaker** (1991) who has shown that suppressing thoughts and feelings associated with personal traumas, failures, and guilty or shameful experiences takes a devastating toll on mental and physical health. Such inhibition is psychologically hard work and, over time, it undermines the body's defenses against illness. Confiding in others neutralizes the negative effects of inhibition; there are immediate changes in brain wave patterns and skin conductance levels, drops in blood pressure, and improvements in immune functions. This experience of *letting go* often is followed by improved physical and psychological health weeks and months later.

Positive Illusions and Well-being   A surprising result emerging from a considerable body of research is the mental health advantage of maintaining a *distorted* perception of the self, the world, and the future in the form of *positive illusions* (Taylor & Brown, 1988). When an individual is receiving negative feedback or being threatened in other ways, apparently adaptive behavior is to filter such incoming information through self-perceptions that are overly positive, unrealistically optimistic, and exaggerated. These characteristics of human thought promote other criteria of mental health such as the abilities to care about others, be happy and content, and engage in productive and creative work.

CAUSES AND CORRELATES OF HEALTH, ILLNESS, AND DYSFUNCTION

Health psychologists are also interested in the causes (etiology) of illness and injury. While poor health habits are important contributors, personality or individual behavioral styles may also play a causal role (H. S. Friedman, 1990).

The two models relating personality traits to disease are (a) the *general personality model* (individual differences related to a host of diseases) and (b) the *specific trait model* (particular personality traits related to specific diseases). Research has asked if there is a general negative affective style or a disease-prone personality characterized by depression, anxiety, and, to a lesser extent, hostility. These negative emotional states affect coronary disease, asthma, headache, ulcers, and arthritis (H. S. Friedman & Booth-Kewley, 1987). Longitudinal studies have also supported the validity of the link between negative emotional states and illness. Chronic negative emotional states tend to produce pathogenic physiological changes, lead people to practice faulty health behaviors, produce illness behavior and result in poor interpersonal relationships (Matthews, 1988).

A great deal of research attention has focused on a particular behavioral style called the **Type-A behavior syndrome** (Strube, 1990). The Type-A syndrome is a complex pattern of behavior and emotions that includes being excessively competitive, aggressive, impatient, time-urgent, and hostile. Type-A people are often dissatisfied with some central aspect of their lives, are highly competitive and ambitious, and often are loners. Some of these Type-A characteristics are valued in our society, but, in general, the behavioral style is very dysfunctional. Type-A businessmen, for example, are

stricken with coronary heart disease more than twice as often as men in the general population (Friedman & Rosenman, 1974; Jenkins, 1976). In fact, many studies have shown that people manifesting the Type-A behavior syndrome are at significantly greater risk for all forms of cardiovascular disease (Dembroski et al., 1978; Haynes & Feinleib, 1980). Unfortunately, Type-A behavior patterns are now being seen among college and high-school students and even among children in grade school (Thoresen & Eagelston, 1983). New research is relating Type-A behavior to many subsequent illnesses in addition to heart disease (Suls & Marco, 1990). The current focus is on identifying the specific dimensions of the Type-A behavior syndrome, particularly hostility, as the personality factor influencing coronary heart disease (Dembroski & Costa, 1987).

A long-term research program by **Martin Seligman** (1991) and his associates at the University of Pennsylvania points the healthy finger at another aspect of personality: *optimism* (detailed in Chapter 12). Optimistic people have fewer physical symptoms of illness, are faster at recovering from certain illnesses, are generally healthier, and live longer (Peterson et al., 1988).

There is more good news about the application of these findings. Interventions to reduce Type-A behavior have been successful in most cases (M. Friedman et al., 1986). While the effect is small, both negative affect associated with being Type A and pessimistic explanatory style have demonstrated the possibility for successful intervention (H. S. Friedman & Booth-Kewley, 1988; Peterson et al., 1988).

> A large-scale intervention program with more than 1000 volunteer survivors of a first-time heart attack has found that a behavioral treatment that alters typical Type-A reaction patterns deters a second heart attack and reduces death from other causes as well (Thoresen et al., 1990). Those who had substantially lowered their Type-A behavior had almost a 50 percent lower mortality rate over an eight year follow-up period than those who did not change substantially.

HEALTH CARE SYSTEM AND HEALTH POLICY FORMATION

A final focus of health psychology is the delivery of health care that includes health institutions, the health professionals who staff them, and health policies.

Providing health care can be an enormously challenging and rewarding career. However, the daily routine of nurses, social workers, emergency room personnel, hospice workers, and other trained specialists includes dealing with pain, illness, poverty, and

Type-A people are often in a hurry, unable to relax, striving intensely for achievement, and prone to hostility.

death. Even the most enthusiastic health care workers run up against the emotional stresses of working intensely with many people suffering from a variety of personal, physical, and social problems. The special type of emotional stress experienced by these professional health and welfare practitioners has been termed *burnout* by **Christina Maslach,** a leading researcher on this widespread problem. **Job burnout** is a syndrome of emotional exhaustion, depersonalization, and reduced personal accomplishment that is often experienced by workers in professions that demand high intensity interpersonal contact with patients, clients, or the public. Health practitioners begin to lose their caring and concern for patients and may come to treat them in detached and even dehumanized ways. They begin to feel bad about themselves and worry that they are failures. Burnout is correlated with greater absenteeism and turnover, impaired job performance, poor relations with coworkers, family problems, and poor personal health (Leiter & Maslach, 1988; Maslach, 1982; Maslach & Florian, 1988).

Several social and situational factors affect the occurrence and level of burnout and, by implication, suggest ways of preventing or minimizing it. For example, the quality of the patient-practitioner interaction is greatly affected by the number of patients for whom a practitioner is providing care—the greater the number, the greater the cognitive, sensory, and emotional overload. Another factor in the quality of that interaction is the amount of direct contact with patients. Longer work hours in continuous direct contact with patients or clients are correlated with greater burnout, especially when the nature of the contact is very difficult and upsetting, such as contact with patients who are dying or who are verbally abusive. The emotional strain of such prolonged contact can be eased by a work schedule that provides chances for a practitioner to withdraw temporarily from such high-stress situations by restructuring the type of contact to use team rather than only individual contact and by arranging for opportunities to get some positive feedback for one's efforts.

▓▓▓▓▓▓▓▓▓▓▓▓▓▓▓▓▓▓▓▓▓▓▓ *A TOAST TO YOUR HEALTH*

Without trying to induce an excessive amount of guilt, I am sure you are aware of making many choices that contribute to your distress and lack of optimal health—choices to eat poorly, not to exercise regularly, to commute long distances, to be overly competitive, to work too much, to relax too little, and not to take time to cultivate friendships. What choices are you making? Are they producing stress that is damaging to your health and well-being?

Instead of waiting for stress or illness to come and then reacting to it, we need to set goals and structure our lives and life-styles in ways that are most likely to forge a healthy foundation. The following ten steps to greater happiness and better mental health are presented as guidelines to encourage you to take a more active role in your own life and to create a more positive psychological environment for yourself and others. Think of the steps as *Year-round Resolutions*.

1. Utilize situational and not just dispositional attributions when searching for the causes of your behavior in the current situation or in its relation to past situations. Understand the context of your behavior.
2. Never say bad things about yourself. Look for sources of your unhappiness in elements that can be modified by future actions. Give yourself and others only *constructive criticism*— what can be done differently next time to get what you want?
3. Compare your reactions, thoughts, and feelings to those of comparable individuals in your current life so that you can gauge the appropriateness and relevance of your responses against a suitable social norm.
4. Have several close friends with whom you can share feelings, joys, and worries. Work at developing, maintaining, and expanding your social support networks.
5. Seek to develop a sense of *balanced time perspective* in which you can flexibly focus on the demands of the task, the situation, and your needs; be future oriented when there is work to be done, present oriented when the goal is achieved and pleasure is at hand, and past oriented to keep you in touch with your roots.
6. Always take full credit for your successes and happiness (and share your positive feeling with other people). Keep an inventory of all the qualities that make you special and unique—those qualities you have to offer others. For example, a shy person can offer a talkative person the gift of attentive listening. Know your sources of personal strength and available coping resources.
7. When you feel you are losing control over your emotions, distance yourself from the situation by physically leaving it, role-playing the position of another person in the situation or conflict, projecting your imagination into the future to gain perspective on what seems an overwhelming problem now, and talking to a sympathetic listener. Feel and express your emotions.
8. Remember that failure and disappointment are sometimes blessings in disguise. They may

tell you that your goals are not right for you or save you from bigger letdowns later on. Learn from every failure. Acknowledge it by saying, "I made a mistake" and move on. Every accident, misfortune, or violation of your expectations is potentially a wonderful opportunity in disguise.

9. If you discover you cannot help yourself or another person in distress, seek the counsel of a trained specialist in your student health department or community. In some cases, a problem that appears to be psychological may really be physical, and vice versa. Check out your student mental health services before you need them, and use them without any concern about being stigmatized.

10. Cultivate healthy pleasures that give you permission to take time out to relax, to meditate, to get a massage, to fly a kite, and to enjoy hobbies and activities that you can do alone and by means of which you can get in touch with and better appreciate yourself.

As a postscript, to end where we began this chapter, take time to laugh at yourself, with others, and even at the occasional absurdity of life itself. Use your imagination to discover the weird, invent the bizarre, and fully appreciate the mundane in all matters. Play with life at times as if it were all part of your Candid Camera scenario, which requires that, in the end, you smile because living well is the best revenge.

RECAPPING MAIN POINTS

Emotions

Emotions are complex patterns of changes made up of physiological arousal, brain mechanisms, experienced feelings, cognitive appraisal, and behavioral and expressive reactions. We usually define emotions by the nature of an external stimulus, but it is possible to misattribute emotional arousal to situational factors that are more obvious than the causal element. Emotions serve many vital functions. Classic theories emphasize different parts of emotional response, such as peripheral bodily reactions or central neural processes. While facial expressions of emotion seem to be universal, cultures vary in their rules of appropriateness for displaying emotions.

The Stress of Living

Stress can be negative or positive. Stress is studied using a variety of models. At the root of most stress is change and the need to adapt to environmental, biological, physical, and social demands. Cognitive appraisal is a primary moderator variable of stress. Physiological stress reactions are regulated by the hypothalamus and a complex interaction of the hormonal and nervous systems. Psychoneuroimmunology is the study of how psychosocial variables affect the immune system. Depending on its severity, stress can be a mild disruption or lead to dysfunctional reactions.

Coping with Stress

Coping strategies either focus on problems (taking direct actions) or attempt to regulate emotions (indirect or avoidant). Social support is a significant stress moderator. At times, the best coping strategy is to restructure one's work or home environment.

Health Psychology

Health psychology is a new field that is devoted to treatment and prevention of illness. The biopsychosocial model of health and illness looks at the connections among physical, emotional, and environmental factors in illness. Health promotion and maintenance are not just individual matters— they represent an important area where community and government policy can help improve everyone's quality of living. Psychosocial treatment of illness adds another dimension to patient treatment. Studies show that the functioning of the immune system improves with this approach to treatment. Illness prevention in the 1990s will focus on lifestyle factors such as weight, nutrition, and risky behavior. AIDS is one of the most threatening illnesses we face today and can be combatted by reducing risky behavior and continuing community education.

KEY TERMS

acute stress, 480

AIDS, 498

amygdala, 461

anticipatory coping, 487

biofeedback, 500

biopsychosocial model, 493

Cannon-Bard theory of emotion, 466

chronic stress, 480

cognitive appraisal, 477

coping, 487

emotion, 460

emotion wheel, 463

fight-or-flight syndrome, 481

general adaptation syndrome (GAS), 482

hardiness, 479

health, 493

health psychology, 492

HIV, 498

hozho, 492

illness, 493

illness prevention, 494

James-Lange theory of emotion, 466

job burnout, 502

lateralization of emotion, 462

Lazarus-Schachter theory of emotion, 466

life-change units (LCU), 474

mood-congruent processing, 471

mood-dependent retrieval, 470

passive smoking, 478

patient nonadherence, 499

perceived control, 489

posttraumatic stress disorder (PTSD), 485

primary appraisal, 479

psychoneuroimmunology (PNI), 483

psychosomatic disorders, 482

relapse, 493

relaxation response, 500

residual stress pattern, 485

secondary appraisal, 479

social support, 490

steroids, 481

strain, 472

stress, 472

stress moderator variables, 477

stressor, 472

T-lymphocytes, 484

Type-A behavior syndrome, 501

Type-T personality, 480

wellness, 493

MAJOR CONTRIBUTORS

Bower, Gordon, 470

Cannon, Walter, 466

Coates, Thomas, 498

Cousins, Norman, 459

Ekman, Paul, 469

Farley, Frank, 480

Izard, Carroll, 464

James, William, 465

Kobasa, Suzanne, 479

Lazarus, Richard, 466

LeDoux, Joseph, 462

Maslach, Christina, 502

Matarazzo, Joseph, 494

Meichenbaum, Donald, 489

Pennebaker, James, 500

Plutchik, Robert, 463

Rodin, Judith, 484

Schachter, Stanley, 466

Seligman, Martin, 501

Selye, Hans, 482

Spiegel, David, 494

Taylor, Shelley, 491

Tompkins, Sylvan, 467

Zajonc, Robert, 467

Chapter 14

Understanding Human Personality

THE PSYCHOLOGY OF THE PERSON 509
STRATEGIES FOR STUDYING PERSONALITY
THEORIES ABOUT PERSONALITY

INTERIM SUMMARY

TYPE AND TRAIT PERSONALITY THEORIES 511
CATEGORIZING BY TYPES
DESCRIBING WITH TRAITS
ALLPORT'S TRAIT APPROACH
COMBINING TYPES AND TRAITS
TRAITS AND HERITABILITY
THE BIG FIVE
THE CONSISTENCY PARADOX
A FRESH LOOK AT TRAITS
CRITICISMS OF TYPE AND TRAIT THEORIES

INTERIM SUMMARY

PSYCHODYNAMIC THEORIES 519
FREUDIAN PSYCHOANALYSIS
POST-FREUDIAN THEORIES

INTERIM SUMMARY

HUMANISTIC THEORIES 525
ROGERS'S PERSON-CENTERED APPROACH
CRITICISMS OF HUMANISTIC THEORIES

INTERIM SUMMARY

SOCIAL-LEARNING AND COGNITIVE THEORIES 527
KELLY'S PERSONAL CONSTRUCT THEORY
COGNITIVE SOCIAL-LEARNING THEORY: MISCHEL
COGNITIVE SOCIAL-LEARNING THEORY: BANDURA
CRITICAL EVALUATION OF LEARNING AND
    COGNITIVE THEORIES

INTERIM SUMMARY

SELF THEORIES 532
SELF AS KNOWER VERSUS KNOWN
DYNAMIC ASPECTS OF SELF-CONCEPTS
CRITICAL EVALUATION OF SELF THEORIES

INTERIM SUMMARY

COMPARING PERSONALITY THEORIES 534
CLOSE-UP: THE ALCOHOLIC PERSONALITY

RECAPPING MAIN POINTS 536

KEY TERMS 537

MAJOR CONTRIBUTORS 537

In 1923, personal tragedy completely transformed the life of an 18-year-old Texan named Howard. This overprotected college freshman had never made a major decision for himself. When a heart attack killed his father, only two years after the death of his

mother, Howard suddenly inherited three fourths of the interest in the family's lucrative tool company. His uncle and grandparents, who owned the rest of the business, urged Howard to return to school. Despite his reputation as a shy and obedient boy, Howard refused. Within four months, he bought out his relatives' share in the company. By the time Howard was 19, a judge had granted him adult status, giving him full legal control of the million-dollar company (Barlett & Steele, 1979). However, he had no interest in running the family business. Instead, he wanted to become the world's top aviator and most famous motion picture producer. "Then," he told his accountant, "I want you to make me the richest man in the world" (Dietrich & Thomas, 1972, p. 73).

By the time he was 38, Howard Hughes was an American legend. He founded the Hughes Aircraft Company, manufacturer of the first spacecraft to land on the moon. He transformed Trans World Airlines into a $500 million empire. He designed and built airplanes for racing, military, and commercial uses. As a pilot, he broke many aviation records, capping his triumphs with a 1938 round-the-world flight. Ticker-tape parades in New York, Chicago, Los Angeles, and Houston honored his achievement (Drosnin, 1985). But long before that, when he was only 20 years old, he had already reaped national honors producing several films, among them an Academy Award winner. As head of the RKO film studio, Hughes used his power to fuel the 1950s anti-communist purge in Hollywood. Eventually, Howard Hughes realized his ambition—he became the world's richest man.

Despite his incredible public success, Howard Hughes was a deeply disturbed individual. As his empire expanded, he became increasingly disorganized. He began to focus so excessively on trivial details that he accomplished less and less. He became a recluse, sometimes vanishing for months at a time.

Hughes's mishaps as a pilot and driver caused three deaths. On several occasions Hughes suffered serious head, face, and, perhaps, brain injuries; one near-fatal plane crash resulted in what became a lifetime addiction to codeine (Fowler, 1986). His risk taking extended to the world of finance as well, where he lost over $100 million of taxpayers', stockholders', and his own money (Dietrich & Thomas, 1972).

As he grew older, Howard Hughes became obsessed with germs. Upon hearing a rumor that an actress he once dated had a venereal disease, he burned all his clothes, towels, and rugs. Eventually, the only people allowed to see him were members of his "Mormon guard," an elite cadre of men who never questioned his often bizarre orders. Those orders included instructions to "wash four distinct and separate times, using lots of lather each time from individual bars of soap" (Drosnin, 1985, p. 167). Anything their employer might touch they wrapped in 50-tissue swaths of Kleenex; each box opened with a clean, unused knife.

Paradoxically, Hughes lived in squalor. He rarely wore clothes or washed, never brushed his teeth, and used an unsterilized needle to inject himself with large doses of codeine. He stayed in bed for days at a time. The richest man in the world slowly starved his 6-foot, 4-inch frame to an emaciated 120 pounds.

Looking to Howard Hughes's childhood for clues to the paradox of his personality reveals many possible links between his early experiences and their later transformation. Similar to his father, Hughes loved mechanical gadgets. At age 3, he started taking pictures with a box camera. He tinkered in his father's workshop, creating objects out of bits of wire and metal. He was allowed to play in the workshop—as long as he kept it spotless.

Hughes's parents fussed excessively about his health. His quiet, dignified mother devoted herself full-time to him, taking him to the doctor at the slightest provocation.

At 14, his parents sent him to a boarding school in Massachusetts. A developing hearing loss isolated him from friendships. The highlight of his stay in the East was a ride with his father in a seaplane that "fired his fascination with airplanes and marked the beginning of a lifelong love affair with aviation, his most enduring passion."

Later, when he went to a California school, Hughes spent much of his time alone, riding his horse in the hills and visiting his Hollywood screenwriter uncle. At his uncle's Sunday brunches, Hughes met many stars and movie moguls, as did his father, who had an eye for beautiful women. Hughes began to perceive people as objects to be avoided or collected. He would bring teenaged aspiring starlets to Hollywood, put them up in apartments, and, as they waited for stardom, forget all about them (Fowler, 1986).

A few years before Hughes's death, his former barber reflected on the eccentric billionaire's personality, "I know he has his problems: don't we all? He just operates a little different from the rest of us. Who's to say who's wrong?" (Keats, 1966, p. x).

From this brief glimpse at the complex life of Howard Hughes, what impressions have you drawn about his personality? What type of person was he? What childhood experiences carried over to shape his adult traits and behavior patterns? Can you identify the significant influences that fueled his ambitions and fed into his destructive life-style? A person such as this fascinates us because understanding what made him "tick" is such a challenge. We are moved to wonder what, if anything, might have made his life story come out with a different, happier ending.

Our *psychological autopsy* of Howard Hughes begins with a search for *continuities* between the personality and reaction patterns of the child and the adult. Obviously, we can find the antecedents of his eventual excessive fear of germs in his parents' excessive concern about his health. Through illness, he received lavish attention from his parents and later in life, through self-induced illness, he regained that kind of attention from the people surrounding him. His mechanical inclinations were strongly reinforced by his father, and his early passion for flying was sustained throughout his life. Hughes was isolated from peers as a child and so he never learned to form any close human bonds. We can also see evidence of an identification with his father in his interest in similar hobbies as well as indirect rebellion against him in his squalid living conditions which contrasted so sharply with his father's compulsion about hygiene. Finally, we note the potential adverse effects on his personality development of his early hearing disorder, later brain injury, stressful deaths of his parents, national publicity for his achievements, and untold wealth that got him almost anything he wanted from almost anyone who wanted access to his power or money.

If psychologists studied you, what portrait of your personality would they draw? What early experiences might they identify as contributing to how you now act and think? What conditions in your current life exert strong influences on your moods and choices? To what extent does your genetic makeup influence your intelligence, personality, and decisions? What makes you different from other individuals who are functioning in many of the same situations as you?

THE PSYCHOLOGY OF THE PERSON

Psychologists define personality in many different ways, but common to all of the ways are two basic concepts: *uniqueness* and *characteristic patterns of behavior*. We will define **personality** as the complex set of unique psychological qualities that influence an individual's characteristic patterns of behavior across different situations and over time. Investigators in the field of personality psychology seek to discover how individuals differ. In addition, they study the extent to which personality traits and behavior patterns are consistent, and thus predictable, from one situation to another. Similar to many of their colleagues in the field of developmental psychology, personality psychologists are interested in continuities in behavioral functioning over time.

Up to this point in our journey, we have seen how scientific investigations focus on specific processes that are similar in all of us. These processes include neural transmission, perception, conditioning, and decision making. We have also been aware that the goal in much of this research is to discover general laws of behavior that explain why different individuals in the same stimulus situation react alike. In this chapter we will examine the individual as the sum of those separate processes of feelings, thoughts, and actions. It is not just that people look different or respond differently to the same stimulus in a common situation. There also seems to be a subjective, private aspect to personality that gives coherence and order to behavior—a core aspect of each of us that we call our *self*.

We will begin by examining the major issues and strategies in the study of personality. Then we will survey the major theories of personality, each of which focuses on slightly different aspects of human individuality. Your task will be to reflect on how each of these different theories of personality could make sense of the personality of someone similar to Howard Hughes or you.

The field of *personality psychology* attempts to integrate all aspects of an individual's functioning. This integration requires the psychologist to build on the accumulated knowledge of all the areas of psychology we have already studied and social psychology, which studies interpersonal and group processes. Personality psychology also goes beyond an interest in the normally functioning individual; it provides the research and theoretical foundation for understanding personal problems and pathologies of body, mind, and behavior (Chapters 13 and 17) as well as a basis for therapeutic approaches to change personality (Chapter 18).

STRATEGIES FOR STUDYING PERSONALITY

Let's begin by examining your personality theory. Think of someone you really trust. Now think of someone you know personally who is a role model for you. Imagine the qualities of a person with whom you would like to spend the rest of your life and then of someone you can't stand to be around at all. In each case, what springs to mind immediately are personal attributes, such as honesty, reliability, sense of humor, generosity, outgoing attitude, aggressiveness, moodiness, and pessimism. Even as a child, you probably developed and put to use your own system for appraising personality. You tried to determine who in your new class would be friend or foe; you worked out techniques for dealing with your parents or teachers in terms of the way you read their personalities. You probably have spent a great deal of time trying to get a handle on who you are, on the distinguishing features of your personality, on the personal traits you would like to change, and on those traits you would like to develop. In all these cases, your judgments were, in fact, naive personality assessments, your *implicit personality theory.* They were based largely on intuition and limited, uncontrolled, nonsystematic observations. Such naive judgments can often be accurate, but they are also open to many sources of error. For example, think of some of the people whose personalities you feel you understand. Now consider the narrow range of situations in which you have observed them. Chances are good that those behavior settings provided limited options for behavioral variation. We tend to have one-dimensional impressions of many people because we see them in only one or a few kinds of situations, and, often, their behavior is strongly influenced by features of those situations. In addition, you may elicit certain types of reactions from them that they do not typically make around other people. You should be aware that your impressions of others may be *biased* by these and other factors, leading you to an interpretation of their personality that may not agree with the way they perceive themselves or the way others see them.

Personality researchers are interested in many different aspects of personality. Their data come from five different sources: (a) *self-report data* are what people say about their own behavior, attitudes, and traits, often in a personality test or inventory; (b) *observer-report data* reveal what friends, parents, co-workers, and other raters or evaluators say about an individual; (c) *specific behavioral data* is systematically recorded information about what a person says or does in a particular situation; (d) *Life-events data* are biographical facts (level of education, marriage status, or having parents who divorced); and (e) *physiological data* include information about heart rate, skin conductance, biochemistry of hormones, and neurotransmitter functioning.

These types of data can be *interpreted* using either of two basic approaches to the study of personality: the *idiographic* approach and the *nomothetic* approach. The **idiographic approach** is *person-centered,* focusing on the way unique aspects of an individual's personality form an integrated whole. It assumes that traits and events take on different meanings in different people's lives. The primary research methodologies of the idiographic approach are the *case study* and the *aggregate case study.* A **case study** uses many data sources to form a psychological biography of a single individual; this chapter's opening case is a short case study of Howard Hughes. The **aggregated case study** is a comparison of idiographic information about many individuals. For example, a summary of the reports on many women with multiple personality disorders, each of whom was studied individually by a given researcher-therapist, is an aggregate case study.

The **nomothetic approach** is *variable-centered,* assuming that the same traits or dimensions of personality apply to everyone in the same way—people simply differ in the *degree* to which they possess each characteristic. Nomothetic research looks for relationships between different personality traits in the general population. The *correlational method* is used to determine the extent to which two traits or types of data tend to show up together in people. The focus of this method is on discovering lawful patterns of relationships among traits, and among the traits and behavior of most people. In nomothetic research, the richness and uniqueness of the individual case is sacrificed for broader knowledge about dimensions of personality that are valid for people in general. When many traits and types of information are studied at once, a special mathematical technique, known as **factor analysis,** is used to analyze these multiple data sources; it enables the researcher to uncover the meaningful dimensions (factors) that they have in common.

When psychologists wish to study how *personality changes over time,* they use either cross-sectional or longitudinal research designs. In a *cross-sectional design,* several groups of subjects, each one representing

Children develop their own styles of assessing the personalities of others.

a different age level, are studied at the same time. However, personality *development* can be better understood through a *longitudinal design,* in which the same group of individuals is studied many times at different ages. Some longitudinal studies span entire lifetimes. These studies are time-consuming and expensive, but they provide very valuable information on personality psychology.

THEORIES ABOUT PERSONALITY

Theories of personality are hypothetical statements about the structure and functioning of individual personalities. They help us achieve two of the major goals of psychology: (a) *understanding* the structure, origins, and correlates of personality and (b) *predicting* behavior and life events based on what we know about personality. Different theories make different predictions about the way people will respond and adapt to certain conditions.

Before we examine some of the major theoretical approaches, we should ask why there are so many different (often competing) theories. Theorists differ in their approaches to personality by varying their starting points and sources of data and by trying to explain different types of phenomena. Some are interested in the structure of individual personality and others in how that personality developed and will continue to grow. Some are interested in what people do, either in terms of specific behaviors or important life events, while others study how people feel about their lives. Finally, some theories try to explain the personalities of people with psychological problems, while others focus on healthy individuals. Thus, each theory can teach us something about personality, and together they can teach us even more about human nature.

Theoretical approaches to understanding personality can be grouped into five categories: type and trait, psychodynamic, humanistic, learning, and cognitive.

SUMMING UP
The implicit theories we use to understand and predict people's behavior may be biased because they are based on unsystematic observations—often we make judgments about people after seeing them in only one type of situation. Personality psychologists draw their theories from systematic observations of individuals in many situations. They combine data from self reports, observer reports, specific behavior observations, life events, and physiological measures to obtain a well-rounded picture of human personality. The personality theories we will examine in this chapter are based on different types of data and aim to explain different types of phenomena, such as relations between traits in the general population, or case studies of individuals, such as the eccentric millionaire Howard Hughes.

TYPE AND TRAIT PERSONALITY THEORIES

Labeling and classifying the many personality characteristics we observe can help us organize human behavior. However, this is no simple task. In fact, a dictionary search by psychologists Gordon Allport and H. S. Odbert (1936) found over 18,000 adjectives in the English language to describe individual differences!

Two of the oldest approaches to describing personality involve classifying people into a limited number of *distinct types* and scaling the degree to which they can be described by *different traits*. What does each concept contribute to our understanding of personality?

CATEGORIZING BY TYPES

We are always classifying people according to some distinguishing feature into a small number of categories. These may include college class, academic major, sex, race, honesty, and shyness. Some personality theorists also group people according to their **personality types,** distinct patterns of personality characteristics used to assign people to categories. These categories do not overlap: if a person is assigned to one category, he or she is not in any other category within that system. Personality types are all-or-none phenomena and not matters of degree.

Early personality typologies were designed to specify a concordance between a simple, highly visible or easily determined characteristic and some behaviors that can be expected from people of that type. If fat, then jolly; if an engineer, then conservative; if female, then sympathetic. You can appreciate why such systems have traditionally had much popular appeal and still do in the mass media—they simplify a very complicated process of understanding the nature of personality.

One of the earliest type theories was proposed in the fifth century B.C. by **Hippocrates,** the Greek physician who gave medicine the Hippocratic oath. He theorized that the body contained four basic fluids or *humors,* each associated with a particular *temperament.* An individual's personality depended on which humor was predominant in his or her body. Hippocrates paired body humors with personality temperaments according to the following scheme:

Clockwise: melancholy patient suffers from an excess of black bile; blood impassions sanguine lutist to play; a maiden, dominated by phlegm, is slow to respond to her lover; choler, too much yellow bile, makes an angry master.

- Blood—sanguine temperament: cheerful and active
- Phlegm—phlegmatic temperament: apathetic and sluggish
- Black bile—melancholy temperament: sad and brooding
- Yellow bile—choleric temperament: irritable and excitable

Another interesting type theory of personality was advanced by **William Sheldon** (1942), a U.S. physician who related physique to temperament. He assigned people to three categories based on their **somatotypes,** or body builds: *endomorphic* (fat, soft, round), *mesomorphic* (muscular, rectangular, strong), or *ectomorphic* (thin, long, fragile). The typology specified relationships between each physique and particular personality traits, activities, and preferences.

What would you expect people with each of these body builds to be like? Sheldon believed that endomorphs are relaxed, fond of eating, and sociable. Mesomorphs are physical people, filled with energy, courage, and assertive tendencies. Ectomorphs are brainy, artistic, and introverted; they would think about life, rather than consuming it or acting upon it. Sheldon's theory of personality and body types is intriguing, but not substantiated. It has proven to be of little value in predicting an individual's behavior (Tyler, 1965). In addi-

tion, people come in many different shapes, and they cannot be assigned readily to one of Sheldon's three somatotypes.

A popular typology is derived from *Carl Jung's* theory of personality types (1933). Using the *Myers-Briggs Type Indicator* (MBTI), people's self-reported preferences are used to measure four dimensions: extraversion-introversion (E-I), sensing-intuition (S-N), thinking-feeling (T-F) and judgment-perception (J-P). If you took this test, you would be assigned to only one side of each dimension, and the combination of dimensions would determine which of the 16 possible types best describes you. For example, people of type ENFP, for Extraverted-Intuitive-Feeling-Perceiving, are said to be "enthusiastic innovators" who are "skillful in handling people" but "hate uninspired routine." This is a type system because the categories are distinct or discontinuous, and people of one type are supposed to be very much like each other in ways that distinguish them from other types (Myers, 1987).

The MBTI typology is widely used because people who take the test find the types easy to understand. However, opponents of the system believe that the four dimensions are informative, but that people should be described according to their actual scores on each dimension instead of being collapsed into types.

DESCRIBING WITH TRAITS

Type theories presume that there are separate, *discontinuous categories* into which people fit. By contrast, trait theories propose hypothetical, *continuous dimensions,* such as intelligence or warmth, that vary in quality and degree. **Traits** are generalized action tendencies that people possess in varying degrees; they lend coherence to a person's behavior in different situations and over time. For example, you may demonstrate honesty on one day by returning a lost wallet and on another day by not cheating on a test. Some trait theorists think of traits as *predispositions that cause behavior,* but more conservative theorists use traits only as *descriptive dimensions* that simply summarize patterns of observed behavior.

ALLPORT'S TRAIT APPROACH

Gordon Allport (1937, 1961, 1966) was one of the most influential personality theorists. He viewed traits as the building blocks of personality and the source of individuality. According to Allport, traits produce coherence in behavior because they are enduring attributes and are general in scope. Traits connect and unify a person's reactions to a variety of stimuli, as shown in **Figure 14.1.**

William Sheldon related physique to temperament by assigning people to categories based on their somatotypes. Endomorphic people are fat, soft, and round. Mesomorphic people are muscular, rectangular, and strong. Ectomorphic people are thin, long, and fragile.

Traits may act as *intervening variables*, relating sets of stimuli and responses that might seem, at first glance, to have little to do with each other. Allport identified three kinds of traits. **Cardinal traits** are traits around which a person organizes his or her life. Howard Hughes organized his life around power and achievement. For Mother Theresa, a cardinal trait might be self-sacrifice for the good of others. Not all people develop cardinal traits, however. **Central traits** are traits that represent major characteristics of a person, such as honesty or optimism. **Secondary traits** are specific, personal features that help us predict the individual's behavior, but are less useful for understanding an individual's personality. Food or dress preferences are examples of secondary traits.

According to Allport, these three kinds of traits form the structure of the personality—which, in turn, determines an individual's behavior. Allport saw *personality structures*, rather than *environmental conditions*, as the critical determiners of individual behavior. *"The same fire that melts the butter hardens the egg,"* was a phrase he used to show that the same stimuli can have different effects on different individuals. Although he recognized *common traits* that individuals in a given culture share, Allport was most interested in discovering the *unique traits* that make each person a singular entity.

> We must acknowledge the roughness and inadequacy of our universal dimensions. Thereby shall we enhance our own ability to understand, predict and control. By learning to handle the individuality of motives and the uniqueness of personality, we shall become better scientists, not worse (Allport, 1960, p. 148).

Allport is the best known of the *idiographic trait* theorists, theorists who believe that each person has some unique characteristics, as well as some common ones, that together form a unique combination of traits. He championed the use of case studies to examine these unique traits.

> In one famous case, he studied in depth 301 letters written by a woman named *Jenny* over an 11-year period. He used factor analysis to examine the way she typically combined key words into units of meaning and found evidence for seven cardinal traits that described the way she expressed herself in the letters. In a separate phase of the experiment, eight cardinal traits—such as *aggressive,*

FIGURE 14.1   SHYNESS AS A TRAIT

Traits may act as intervening variables, relating sets of stimuli and responses that might seem, at first glance, to have little to do with each other.

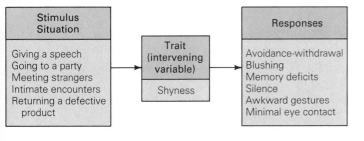

Stimulus Situation	Trait (intervening variable)	Responses
Giving a speech Going to a party Meeting strangers Intimate encounters Returning a defective product	Shyness	Avoidance-withdrawal Blushing Memory deficits Silence Awkward gestures Minimal eye contact

sentimental, possessive—were derived from the impressions of 36 judges who read the letters. The two independently-derived sets of traits were very similar, demonstrating that personality could be reconstructed from other sources when traditional personality tests were unavailable (Allport, 1965, 1966).

COMBINING TYPES AND TRAITS

One of the most important trait theorists is **Hans Eysenck** (1947, 1990) who has proposed a model that links types, traits, and behavior into a hierarchical system. At the lowest level of the hierarchy are *single responses,* such as acts or cognitions. When they occur regularly, they combine to form sets of *habitual responses* at the next level. Correlated habitual responses, in turn, form *traits* at the third level. Correlations among traits form *types* at the top level.

Eysenck derived three broad dimensions from personality test data, *extraversion, neuroticism,* and *psychoticism.* He used these dimensions to define the types at the top level of his hierarchy. However, Eysenck does *not* use these three dimensions to define discrete categories such as those in classical type theories. Instead he discusses general differences, for example, between introverts and extraverts, without claiming that the categories are really discontinuous.

He believes that personality differences on his three basic dimensions are caused by genetic and biological differences between people. He also believes that his hierarchy can be used in combination with other trait models to provide new insights into personality. For example, he has related extraversion-introversion and neuroticism (stability-instability) to the physiological-personality types of Hippocrates, as shown in **Figure 14.2.** Because Eysenck's theory is not a strict typology, people can fall anywhere around the circle, ranging from very introverted to very extraverted and from very unstable (neurotic) to very stable. The traits listed around the circle describe people with each combination of scores. For example, a person who is very extraverted and somewhat unstable is likely to be impulsive.

The extraversion and neuroticism dimensions have been linked to many physiological differences among people, such as arousal, body types, and even blood types. For example, introverts react more strongly to sensory stimulation and have lower levels of the brain chemical dopamine than do extraverts. Introverts also tend to be more ectomorphic than extraverts, particularly if they are both introverted and neurotic. Neuroticism appears to be somewhat more frequent among

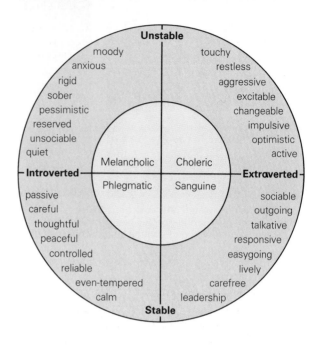

FIGURE 14.2 THE FOUR QUADRANTS OF EYSENCK'S PERSONALITY CIRCLE

people with blood type B than blood type A. The physiological evidence for psychoticism, however, is complex and not well understood (Eysenck, 1982, 1990).

Eysenck has also used standard behavioral tests to study how extraverts, as a group, differ from introverts. One finding shows that introverts have lower thresholds for pain than extraverts. Introverts also learn faster than extraverts when unconditioned stimuli are weak or reinforcement is partial rather than continuous. Generally, memory for associations learned under conditions of low arousal is better than for those learned with high arousal. In contrast, extraverts perform better when more aroused, and need more external arousal to maintain their performance, than do the self-stimulating introverts (Howarth & Eysenck, 1968).

TRAITS AND HERITABILITY

You've probably heard people say things such as "Jim's artistic, like his mother" or "Mary's as stubborn as her grandfather." Or maybe you've felt frustrated because the characteristics that you find irritating in your siblings are those you would like to change in yourself. Where do family resemblances in personality come from? Are they inherited, such as the color of your eyes, or learned, such as speech mannerisms? By now, the *nature-nurture controversy* has become a familiar part of our study of psychology.

Recall that *behavioral genetics* is the study of the degree to which personality traits and behavior patterns are inherited genetically. To determine the effect of genetics on personality, researchers study the personality traits of family members who share different proportions of genes and who have grown up in the same or different households. For example, if a personality characteristic such as *sociability* is passed on genetically, then *sociability* should correlate more highly between identical twins (who share 100 percent of their genes) than among fraternal twins (who share only half of their genes) or among other siblings (who share, on the average, only 25 percent of their genes). However, twins and other siblings are usually raised together, and sharing the same family environment might cause their personalities to be correlated, too. Thus, **adoption studies** are used to examine the degree to which children's personalities correlate with their biological parents as compared to their adoptive parents. One very effective way to differentiate genetic and environmental effects on personality is to find many pairs of twins, some of whom were raised together in the same family and some of whom were raised apart. For each personality trait, researchers compare the size of correlations between identical twins reared together, identical twins reared apart, fraternal twins reared together, and fraternal twins reared apart. The correlations are compared according to mathematical models to determine the percentage of the trait that is inherited and the percentage that can be attributed to environmental influences.

Several large studies of this type are under way, such as the *Minnesota Study of Twins Reared Apart* and the *Swedish Adoption/Twin Study on Aging* as well as many nontwin studies such as the *Texas Adoption Project*. The people who have been studied come from different countries and from different socioeconomic backgrounds. Their ages span from childhood to late adulthood, and their personalities have been assessed using many different inventories and techniques.

Heritability studies show that *almost all personality traits are influenced by genetic factors*. The findings are the same with many different measurement techniques, whether they measure broad traits, such as extraversion and neuroticism, or specific traits, such as self-control or sociability. Estimates of what percentage of the influence on personality traits is genetic range from a low of 20 percent to a high of 60 percent. Although experts still disagree on the exact degree of heritability of personality, they agree that the characteristics your parents

pass on to you genetically have a powerful impact on the person you become (Plomin et al., 1990).

But what about learning and the environment? Are people stuck with the personality traits they inherit? Not at all. Current research indicates the environment has a powerful impact on personality, too, but not in the way that you might think. Behavior geneticists divide environmental influence into two groups: the *common familial environment,* experienced by all children in a family, and the *unshared environment,* experienced uniquely by each child.

Traditionally, psychologists have believed that features of the common familial environment, such as the income and education of the parents and their general style of childrearing, cause the children in one family to be more similar to each other than they would have been if raised by different parents. However, twin and adoption studies show that the influence of common familial factors on personality is very small. For most personality traits, identical twins reared *together* are no more similar than identical twins reared *apart!* Instead, the portion of personality that is not related to genetic factors (at least half) must be attributed to the unshared environment—the idiosyncratic experiences of each child, such as the parent-child relationship, the particular relationships with siblings, and the experiences outside the home (Bouchard & McGue, 1990).

THE BIG FIVE

One hazard of trait psychology is that different researchers study many different traits, design many different ways to measure them, and sometimes create their own idiosyncratic names for the dimensions they measure. This free enterprise system creates a difficult climate for scientific progress. Comparing the constructs and measures derived from two competing theories often resembles comparing apples and computers. More importantly, the confusion over terminology can make it difficult to know whether the empirical results of different studies even agree. For example, criminal behavior in adolescence can be predicted from either high Psychoticism scores, as measured by Eysenck's scale (1982), or from low Socialization scores, as measured by the California Psychological Inventory (Gough, 1968). Paradoxically, the more research we consult, the more confusing the picture seems.

This problem of confusion led to a search for common dimensions of meaning that would link together the wealth of information accumulating—under different names—in personality psychology. The goal of the search was to develop a common language or descriptive system that all personality psychologists could use to compare and contrast their measures and results. Ideally, such a system should be (a) comprehensive, (b) easy to understand, (c) independent of any particular theory, and (d) flexible enough to allow for different levels of analysis.

The search for basic dimensions of personality began with trait terms found in natural language, in the hope that, over time, people would have developed words to describe the important dimensions they perceived in themselves and others. Several research efforts began with a list of all the traits in the English language that Allport and Odbert (1936) had extracted from the dictionary. The traits were boiled down into about 200 synonym clusters which were used to form bipolar trait dimensions, such as responsible-irresponsible. Next, people were asked to rate themselves and others on the bipolar dimensions, and the ratings were factor analyzed to determine how the synonym clusters were interrelated. Using this method, several independent research teams came to the same startling conclusion: that there are only *five basic dimensions* underlying the traits people use to describe themselves and others (Norman, 1967; Tupes & Cristal, 1961).

The five dimensions are very broad, because each brings into one large category many traits that have unique connotations but a common theme. These five dimensions of personality are known as **The Big Five.** Each is summarized below. You'll notice that each dimension is *bipolar*—terms that are similar in meaning to the name of the dimension describe the high pole, and terms that are opposite in meaning describe the low pole.

- *Extraversion:* talkative, energetic, and assertive vs. quiet, reserved, and shy.
- *Agreeableness:* sympathetic, kind, and affectionate vs. cold, quarrelsome, and cruel.
- *Conscientiousness:* organized, responsible, and cautious vs. careless, frivolous, and irresponsible.
- *Emotional Stability:* stable, calm, and contented vs. anxious, unstable, and temperamental.
- *Openness to Experience:* creative, intellectual, and open-minded vs. simple, shallow, and unintelligent.

The Big Five were discovered from rating data in the 1960s, using several different sets of adjectives, and many different subject samples and rating tasks. Since then, very similar dimensions have also been found in personality questionnaires, interviewer checklists, and other data. The five-factor structure has already been replicated in studies of German and Dutch traits, and there is preliminary evidence for some or all of the factors in non-Western languages as well (John, 1990).

The Big Five are not meant to replace the many specific trait terms that carry their own nuances and shades of meaning. Rather, they outline a taxonomy that demonstrates the relationships between trait words, and between sophisticated theoretical concepts and the personality scales psychologists use. For example, the low Socialization and high Psychoticism scores that predict criminality have both been shown in factor analyses to be related to the low poles of Agreeableness and Conscientiousness. On the other hand, risk factors for violent crimes all seem to be related to the low pole of Emotional Stability (Lewis, 1986). Thus, we can understand that—in plain English—boys who are likely to become criminals are typically cold, quarrelsome, and irresponsible, while those who go on to commit violent crimes are likely to be anxious, temperamental, and unstable as well.

As a descriptive system, The Big Five is comprehensive—almost any trait imaginable can be related to one or a few of the dimensions. The dimensions are theory-free and easy to understand because they were derived from natural language. They are very flexible and can accommodate many scientific approaches because they outline a taxonomy for many concepts, both broad and specific. Most importantly, the five dimensions have been replicated with many different subject samples, many different types of data, and several languages.

The Big Five are not universally accepted by all personality psychologists, and research continues to determine how each of the dimensions should be precisely interpreted and named. For example, the Extraversion dimension is sometimes called Surgency, and the Emotional Stability dimension is sometimes called Neuroticism and scored for its other pole. Nonetheless, many researchers accept The Big Five as the broad dimensions of a common descriptive system, and agree in general—if not precisely—upon their meanings.

THE CONSISTENCY PARADOX

Both trait theory and type theory presume that personality characteristics influence behavior across different types of *situations*. However, in the 1920s several researchers set out to observe trait-related behaviors in different situations and were surprised to find little evidence that behavior was cross-situationally consistent at all. For example, two behaviors presumably related to the trait of honesty—lying and cheating on a test—were only weakly correlated among school children (Hartshorne & May, 1928). Similar results were found by other researchers who examined the cross-situational consistency for other traits such as introversion or punctuality (Dudycha, 1936; Newcomb, 1929).

If trait-related behaviors are not cross-situationally consistent—that is, if people's behavior changes in different situations, how is it that we perceive our own and others' personalities to be relatively stable? Even more puzzling, the personality ratings of observers who know an individual from one situation correlate with the ratings of observers who know the individual from another situation. The observation that personality ratings across time and among different observers *are consistent,* while behavior ratings across situations *are not consistent* came to be called the **consistency paradox** (Mischel, 1968).

One proposed explanation for the consistency paradox is that personality is socially constructed on the basis of (a) stereotypes about how physical appearance is related to certain traits, (b) implicit personality theories about what additional traits we can infer from knowledge about a few traits, and (c) cognitive bias to perceive behavior as consistent even when it is not. For example, people who have been only briefly introduced to an individual make similar guesses about that individual's personality. Ratings made under these circumstances might be attributed to first impressions and stereotypes the raters share. However, the finding that agreement between observers *improves* as the raters observe more and more of the person's behavior cannot be explained away so easily (Norman & Goldberg, 1966). Implicit theories of personality and cognitive biases may contribute to, but cannot entirely explain, our stable and consensual perceptions of personality.

In looking for clues, some researchers have turned to idiographic trait theorists such as Allport (1937) who suggested that the same traits don't apply to all people, or at least not in the same way. Bem and Allen (1974) demonstrated that greater trait-related behavioral consistency was observed for subjects who said that the trait in question applied to them. Magnusson and Endler (1977) found that traits predicted cross-situational behaviors better when the *interaction* between traits and particular situations was also assessed. However, these findings were difficult to replicate and, in any case, provided only a partial solution to the paradox that raters typically agree on ratings of most traits for most people but behavior is often inconsistent across situations.

Another approach is to measure behavior more carefully. Many factors may influence your behavior at any one time and in any one situation. Thus, cross-situational consistency should be examined, not by correlating one behavior in one situation with one behavior in another situation but by correlating *aggregated behaviors,* observed many times in each situation (Epstein, 1979). This technique did lead to evidence for the *temporal stability* of the same behavior in the same sit-

uation over time, showing high correlations of 0.65. Nevertheless, on average, aggregated behavior in one situation correlated with trait-related aggregated behavior in another situation only very weakly—the coefficient was a low 0.13 (Mischel & Peake, 1982).

So what is causing the consistency paradox? How is it that trait psychology had a long and successful history before anyone ever discovered that behavior is not cross-situationally consistent? It turns out that behavioral inconsistency is a problem only for very specific behaviors. The paradox was not about consistency, but about *levels of analysis*—the use of *specific* vs. *summary* types of data.

The consistency debate was led primarily by *social learning theorists* who wanted to isolate very *specific* behaviors and to identify the situational cues that elicit them. With that information they hoped to encourage adaptive behaviors and modify problem behaviors. They found that specific behavioral measures are fine tuned to predict the same behavior in a very similar situation with a high degree of accuracy, but they do not generalize well to different situations.

On the other hand, trait theorists find meaningful relationships between self-reported traits, observer-reported traits, life events, and *general* patterns of behavior because all of these types of data operate at a *broad* level of analysis in which many different types of events and experiences occurring over a period of time are *summarized* into a single score. Broad summary measures are multipurpose instruments that can predict a very wide range of phenomena, but they do so somewhat less accurately than fine-tuned specific measures. For example, suppose you wanted to learn about aggressive behavior in children so you could intervene to reduce its frequency. In a study of boys with behavior problems at a summer camp, Jack Wright and Walter Mischel (1987) found that aggregated measures of specific aggressive behaviors, such as threatening other children, correlated only 0.35 across different types of situations but correlated more highly, 0.60, across similar situations. A general trait measure of aggressiveness, based on counselors' ratings, correlated well, about 0.50, with specific aggressive behaviors, regardless of the situation.

Which measure would you find most useful? If you wanted to predict which children would threaten other children in a particular type of situation, your best bet is a previous observation of the same behavior in the same type of situation (correlation of 0.60). However, if you didn't know what type of situation the children would encounter, and you wanted to predict threats in many situations, the trait measure would be a better predictor than previous threats in any particular situation (0.50 vs. 0.35). In addition, the trait measure might have a few bonus predictions in store: medium-sized correlations with future life events, such as going to prison or becoming a top business executive.

A FRESH LOOK AT TRAITS

Although trait theorists had not originally been interested in specific behaviors, the consistency debate forced them to reconceptualize traits in a more precise way—to outline precisely what classes of behavior *should* be related to personality traits and under what conditions. It seems now that personality is not a matter of *behavioral consistency* at all. Instead, personality produces patterns of *behavioral coherence*. A trait may be expressed through different behaviors in different situations and at different ages, but as long as the theory of a trait *predicts* the range of behavioral expressions, the pattern is coherent. For example, one study found that boys who were very shy as children later seemed reluctant to take on new social roles; they lagged 3 to 4 years behind their nonshy peers in getting married, having children, and entering stable careers (Caspi et al., 1988).

Situations are also important in the expression of personality. In one sense, details of the situation influence what you will do at any given time. However, research shows that *situations* differ in the extent to which personality is likely to be expressed in behavior. Personality traits are likely to influence behavior when situations are (a) novel, (b) ill-defined (offering many behavioral alternatives but no clear guidelines regarding what is proper), and (c) stressful or challenging (Caspi & Bem, 1990).

On the other hand, your personality influences the situations you're likely to get into in the first place. Sometimes you deliberately select certain types of situations, for example, going to many campus parties or never raising your hand to answer a question you know in order to avoid speaking in front of your entire psychology class. Other times, your personality influences the nature of a situation because you evoke particular responses from others. For example, if you typically talk a great deal and in a very loud voice, then other people might contribute less to a conversation with you than they usually do with others.

In the aftermath of the consistency paradox, it is easy to see why personality traits—even though they may be broadly defined and imperfectly measured—have so many important consequences in people's lives.

CRITICISMS OF TYPE AND TRAIT THEORIES

Type and trait theories have been criticized for not being real theories because they do not *explain* how behavior is caused, or how personality develops; they merely identify and describe characteristics that are simply correlated with behavior. Longitudinal studies can bring trait theories one step closer to personality development, but the findings are often interpreted *post hoc* (instead of being predicted in advance), are usually based on relatively small samples, and are difficult to replicate because different measures have been used in different longitudinal studies. Trait theories typically portray a *static*, or at least stabilized, view of personality structure as it currently exists. By contrast, dynamic theories of personality emphasize conflicting forces within the individual and the fast-paced challenges of the environment which together lead to continuous change and development within the individual. Let's see such a theory in action.

SUMMING UP

Type theories, such as those of Sheldon and Jung, use personal characteristics to sort people into discrete groups or types (for example, extraverts or introverts) and attempt to predict behavior on the basis of a person's type. Trait theories describe people according to continuous dimensions of personality (individuals can be very low on the dimension, very high on the dimension, or anywhere in between) and predict behavior from the degree to which a person possesses certain traits. Eysenck combines types, traits, habits, and behaviors into a hierarchy. In the hierarchy, specific behaviors are correlated into groups, correlated groups of behaviors form habits, correlated habits form traits, and correlated traits form types.

Hundreds of traits have been shown to predict behaviors, physiological responses, and life events. In addition, twin and adoption studies have shown that many personality traits are, in part, genetically inherited. Fortunately, we can simplify our knowledge about all these traits by what they have in common. The Big Five dimensions of personality—Extraversion, Agreeableness, Conscientiousness, Emotional Stability, and Openness to Experience—are the common themes or dimensions that underlay the various traits researchers have studied. Nearly all traits can be translated into a common language by specifying their relation to one or a few of The Big Five.

The observation that personality ratings are consistent across time and across observers while specific behaviors are usually not *consistent across situations, came to be called the consistency paradox. In time, researchers realized that specific behaviors are influenced by features of the situation rather than by personality traits. Personality traits, because they are summary measures, are better for predicting general patterns of behavior in unknown situations. They are especially good predictors of life events because personality traits influence the types of situations people are likely to get into, the choices they are confronted with, and the decisions they make that shape their lives.*

PSYCHODYNAMIC THEORIES

By the end of the nineteenth century, Charles Darwin had made the world aware of the common bonds between human beings and animals. Psychologists were quick to borrow Darwin's concept of instinct and transform it from its original use—accounting for patterns of animal behavior—to account for virtually all human actions. If a person went around hitting other people, for example, that person could have been described as having an inborn instinct of aggression. A miserly person might have been perceived as having a hoarding instinct. If psychologists had a new kind of behavior they wanted to explain, they had only to postulate a new instinct. However, *identifying* something is not the same as *explaining* it. Psychologists had developed a new term—*instinct*—not a better understanding of the psychological processes it was meant to describe. Clearly, they needed a more fruitful approach to understanding behavior.

Sigmund Freud provided the new approach. He gave new meaning to the concept of human instinct and, in doing so, revolutionized the very concept of human personality. To Ernest Jones, Freud's biographer, Freud was "the Darwin of the mind" (1953). Common to all **psychodynamic personality theories,** which are based on Freud's work, is the assumption that personality is shaped and behavior is motivated by powerful inner forces.

FREUDIAN PSYCHOANALYSIS

Freud's theory of personality boldly attempts to explain the origins and course of personality development, the nature of mind, the abnormal aspects of personality, and the way personality can be changed by therapy. Here we will focus only on normal personality; Freud's other views will be treated at length in Chapters 18 and 19.

According to psychoanalytic theory, at the core of personality are events within a person's mind (*intrapsychic events*) that motivate behavior. Often we are aware of these motivations, however, some motivation also operates at an unconscious level. The *psycho-dynamic* nature of this approach comes from its emphasis on these inner wellsprings of behavior. For Freud, *all behavior was motivated*. No chance or accidental happenings cause behavior; all acts are *determined* by motives. Every human action has a cause and a purpose that can be discovered through psychoanalysis of thought associations, dreams, errors, and other behavioral clues to inner passions.

The wish is parent to the deed; our actions emerge from what we really desire—even when we don't know what it is that we want. Prominent among our desires, according to Freud, are *sexual* and *aggressive wishes*. Through both conscious and unconscious processes, these wishes affect our thoughts and behaviors.

The primary data for Freud's hypotheses about personality came from clinical observations and in-depth case studies of individual patients in therapy. Curiously, he developed a theory of normal personality from his intense study of those with mental disorders. Although this *idiographic approach* yields a rich harvest of ideas from which to formulate a complex theory, Freud's theoretical ground is too soft for the heavy methodological equipment necessary to test a hypothesis scientifically. We shall return to the problem of validating Freud's ideas after we consider some of his fundamental concepts, his original ideas on the way personality is structured, and the roles of repression and psychological defenses.

Four Fundamental Concepts

The core of the psychodynamic approach is based upon four concepts: psychic determinism, early experience, drives and instincts, and unconscious processes. Together they provide a conceptually rich perspective on the development and functioning of personality.

Psychic Determinism In the late 1800s, many cases of hysteria were recorded in Europe for which no adequate physical explanation could be found. The afflicted (who were mostly women) would experience impaired bodily functioning—paralysis or blindness, for example—and yet they would have intact nervous systems and no obvious organic damage to their muscles or eyes. As a young physician, Freud became interested in treating the bizarre symptoms of this disorder. Along with his colleague, Joseph Breuer, Freud observed that the particular physical symptom often seemed related to an earlier forgotten event in a patient's life. For instance, under hypnosis, a "blind" patient might recall witnessing her parents having intercourse when she was a small child. As an adult, her anticipation of her first sexual encounter might then have aroused powerful feelings associated with this earlier, disturbing episode.

Her blindness might represent an attempt on her part to undo seeing the original event and perhaps also to deny sexual feelings in herself. So the symptoms might also have a *secondary function* that is reinforcing to the patient. For example, by making her helpless and dependent, blindness would bring her attention, comfort, and sympathy from others.

Psychic determinism is the assumption that all mental and behavioral reactions (symptoms) are determined by earlier experiences. Freud believed that symptoms, rather than being arbitrary, were related in a meaningful way to significant life events.

Early Experience   Freud assumed a continuity of personality development from "the womb to the tomb." He believed that experiences in infancy and early childhood—especially during the early stages of psychosexual development—had the most profound impact on personality formation and adult behavior patterns. However, Freud never studied children—only the adult recollections of their childhood experiences. Nonetheless, his emphasis on early experience helped to make the scientific study of infant and child behavior respectable.

Drives and Instincts   Freud's medical training as a neurologist led him to postulate a common biological basis for the mental abnormalities he observed in his patients. He ascribed the source of motivation for human actions to *psychic energy* found within each individual. How this energy was exchanged, transformed, and expressed was a central concern of psychoanalysis. Each person was assumed to have inborn instincts or drives that were *tension systems* created by the organs of the body. These energy sources, when activated, could be expressed in many different ways. One of Freud's contributions was in showing the way a drive, such as the sex drive, could be expressed directly through sexual activity as well as indirectly through jokes or creative art, for example.

Freud originally postulated two basic drives. One he saw as involved with the *ego,* or *self-preservation* (meeting the needs of hunger and thirst). The other he called **Eros,** the driving force related to sexual urges and preservation of the species. Of the two drives, Freud was more interested in the sexual urges, although some of his followers have given the ego drive an important place in personality, as we will see later. Freud greatly expanded the notion of human sexual desires to include, not only the urge for sexual union, but also all other attempts to seek pleasure or to make physical contact with others. He used the term **libido** to identify the source of energy for sexual urges—a psychic energy that drives us toward sensual pleasures of all types.

Freud suggested that the primitive urge, Thanatos, drives people toward aggressive and destructive behaviors.

Sexual urges demand immediate satisfaction, whether through direct actions or through indirect means such as fantasies and dreams.

According to Freud, Eros, as a broadly defined sexual drive, does not suddenly appear at puberty but operates from birth. Eros is evident, he argued, in the pleasure infants derive from physical stimulation of the genitals and other sensitive areas, or *erogenous zones,* such as the mouth and the anus. Infantile sexuality was a radical concept in Victorian times when even adult sexuality was not discussed in proper society. This aspect of Freud's theory was widely criticized and rarely accepted. Of course, that kind of reaction is exactly what Freud would expect from people who could not accept their own repressed infantile sexuality.

Clinical observation of patients who had suffered traumatic experiences during the First World War led Freud to add the concept of **Thanatos,** or death instinct, to his collection of drives and instincts. Thanatos was a negative force that drove people toward aggressive and destructive behaviors. These patients continued to relive their wartime traumas in nightmares and hallucinations, phenomena that Freud could not work into his self-preservation or sexual drive theory. He suggested that this primitive urge was part of the tendency for all living things to follow the law of entropy and return to an inorganic state.

Unconscious Processes   Public opposition to the notion of infantile sexuality was strong, but reaction to another of Freud's novel ideas—the **unconscious**—was even stronger. Other writers had pointed to such a process, but Freud put the concept of the unconscious determinants of human thought, feeling, and action at center stage in the human drama. According to Freud's belief in the unconscious determinants of behavior, behavior can be motivated by drives of which we are not aware. We may act without knowing why or without direct access to the true cause of our actions. There is a *manifest* content to our behavior—what we say, do, and perceive—of which we are fully aware, but there is also a *latent* content that is concealed from us by unconscious processes. The meaning of neurotic (anxiety-based) symptoms, dreams, and slips of the pen and tongue are found at the unconscious level of thinking and information processing. Many psychologists today consider this concept of the unconscious to be Freud's most important contribution to the science of psychology.

According to Freud, impulses within us that we find unacceptable still strive for expression. A *Freudian slip* occurs when an unconscious desire is betrayed by our speech or behavior. For example, a host says to an unwanted guest, "I'm so sorry to see you—I mean so *happy* to see you." Being consistently late for a date with a particular person is no accident—it is an expression of the way you really feel.

Experimental research has provided validation for the theory that hidden thoughts compete with intended verbal statements to create Freudian slips.

> Two groups of men saw word pairs such as *sham dock* or *past fashion* flashed on a screen at one-second intervals. The men read the word pairs silently unless a buzzer signaled. Then they would read the words aloud. In the *fear condition,* the subjects anticipated receiving an electric shock, while in the *sexual arousal condition,* the task was performed in the presence of a sexually provoca-

tive female experimenter. The word lists contained an equal number of words that could result in slips related to shocks or sexy women.

> The kinds of errors made by the men who had been randomly assigned to the two conditions were quite different. Those expecting to be shocked were more likely to say *damn shock* for *sham dock* and *cursed wattage* for *worst cottage.* When in the presence of the sexy female, more men read *past fashion* as *fast passion* and *brood nests* as *nude breasts* (Motley, 1987).

Research indicates that most slips of the tongue are the result of mental competition between two or more words—some from hidden thoughts but others from simple linguistic alternatives not unconsciously motivated (*chee canes* instead of *key chains*).

The concept of unconscious motivation adds a new dimension to personality by allowing for greater complexity of mental functioning. The notion of an unconscious mind threatens those who want to believe they are in full command of their mental state's ship as it travels along life's tributaries.

The Structure of Personality

In this theory, personality differences arise from the different ways in which people deal with their fundamental drives. To explain these differences, Freud pictured a continuing battle between two antagonistic parts of the personality—the *id* and the *superego*—moderated by a third aspect of the self, the *ego.*

The **id** is conceived of as the primitive, unconscious part of the personality—the storehouse of the fundamental drives. It operates irrationally, acting on impulse and pushing for expression and immediate gratification without considering whether what is desired is realistically possible, socially desirable, or morally acceptable. The id is governed by the *pleasure principle,* the unregulated search for gratification—especially sexual, physical, and emotional pleasures—to be experienced here and now without concern for consequences.

The **superego** is the storehouse of an individual's values, including moral attitudes learned from society. The superego corresponds roughly to our common notion of *conscience.* It develops as a child comes to accept as his or her own values the prohibitions of parents and other adults against socially undesirable actions. It is the inner voice of *oughts* and *should nots.* The superego also includes the *ego ideal,* an individual's view of the kind of person he or she should strive to become. Thus the superego is often in conflict with the id. The id wants to do what feels good, while the superego, operating on the *morality principle,* insists on doing what is right.

"All right, deep down it's a cry for psychiatric help—but at one level it's a stick-up."

The **ego** is the reality-based aspect of the self that arbitrates the conflict between id impulses and superego demands. The ego represents an individual's personal view of physical and social reality—his or her conscious beliefs about the causes and consequences of behavior. Part of the ego's job is to choose actions that will gratify id impulses without undesirable consequences. The ego is governed by the *reality principle,* which puts reasonable choices before pleasurable demands. Thus, the ego would block an impulse to cheat on an exam because of concerns for the consequences of getting caught, and it would substitute the resolution to study harder the next time or solicit the teacher's sympathy. When the id and the superego are in conflict, the ego arranges a compromise that at least partially satisfies both. However, as id and superego pressures intensify, it becomes more difficult for the ego to work out optimal compromises.

Repression and Ego Defense

Sometimes this compromise between id and superego involves "putting a lid on the id." Extreme desires are pushed out of conscious awareness into the privacy of the unconscious. **Repression** is the psychological process that functions to protect an individual from experiencing extreme anxiety or guilt about having impulses, ideas, or memories that are unacceptable and/or dangerous to express. The ego remains unaware of both the mental content that is censored and the process by which repression keeps information out of consciousness. Repression is considered to be the most basic of the various ways in which the ego defends against being overwhelmed by threatening impulses and ideas.

Ego defense mechanisms are mental strategies the ego uses to defend itself in the daily conflict between id impulses that seek expression and the superego's demand to deny them. In psychoanalytic theory, these mechanisms are considered vital to an individual's psychological coping with powerful inner conflicts. By using them, a person is able to maintain a favorable self-image and to sustain an acceptable social image. For example, if a child has strong feelings of hatred toward her father—which, if acted out, would be dangerous—repression may take over. The hostile impulse is then no longer consciously pressing for satisfaction or even recognized as existing. However, although it is not seen or heard, it is not gone; these feelings continue to play a role in personality functioning. For example, by developing a strong *identification* with his father, the child may increase his sense of self-worth and reduce his unconscious fear of being discovered as a hostile agent. Given strong sexual desires that are frustrated, the ego defense of *sublimation* may allow someone to engage in activities that are indirectly sexual but so-cially approved—such as producing sexy movies. Do you see these defenses at work in the personality of Howard Hughes? For a summary of some of the major ego defenses, see **Table 14.1.**

In Freudian theory, **anxiety** is an intense emotional response triggered when a repressed conflict is about to emerge into consciousness. Anxiety is a danger signal: Repression is not working! Red alert! More defenses needed! This is the time for a second line of defense, one or more additional ego-defense mechanisms that will relieve the anxiety and send the distressing impulses back down into the unconscious. For example, a mother who does not like her son and does not want to care for him might use *reaction formation* which transforms her unacceptable impulse into its *opposite:* "I don't hate my child" becomes "I love my child. See how I smother the dear little thing with love?" Such defenses serve important coping functions.

> From a psychoanalytic point of view, ego mechanisms of defense are mental processes that attempt to resolve conflicts among drive states, attacks, and external reality. . . . They moderate levels of emotion produced by stress, they help keep awareness of certain drives at a minimal level, they provide time to help an individual deal with life traumas, and they help deal with unresolvable loss (Plutchik et al., 1979, p. 229).

Useful as they are, ego mechanisms of defense are ultimately self-deceptive. When overused, they create more problems than they solve. It is psychologically unhealthy to spend a great deal of time and psychic energy deflecting, disguising, and rechanneling unacceptable urges in order to reduce anxiety. Doing so leaves little energy for productive living or satisfying human relationships. Some forms of mental illness result from excessive reliance on defense mechanisms to cope with anxiety, as we shall see in a later chapter on mental disorders.

Criticisms of Freudian Theory

We have devoted a great deal of space to outlining the essentials of psychoanalytic theory because Freud's ideas have had an enormous impact on the way many psychologists think about normal and abnormal aspects of personality. However, there probably are more psychologists who criticize Freudian concepts than support them. What is the basis of some of their criticisms?

First, psychoanalytic concepts are vague and not operationally defined; thus much of the theory is difficult to evaluate scientifically. Because some of its central hypotheses cannot be disproved even in principle, Freud's theory remains questionable. How can the concepts of libido, the structure of personality, and repres-

TABLE 14.1 MAJOR EGO DEFENSE MECHANISMS

Denial of Reality	Protecting self from unpleasant reality by refusing to perceive it
Displacement	Discharging pent-up feelings, usually of hostility, on objects less dangerous than those that initially aroused the emotion
Fantasy	Gratifying frustrated desires in imaginary achievements ("daydreaming" is a common form)
Identification	Increasing feelings of worth by identifying self with another person or institution, often of illustrious standing
Isolation	Cutting off emotional charge from hurtful situations or separating incompatible attitudes into logic-tight compartments (holding conflicting attitudes that are never thought of simultaneously or in relation to each other); also called *compartmentalization*
Projection	Placing blame for one's difficulties upon others or attributing one's own "forbidden" desires to others
Rationalization	Attempting to prove that one's behavior is "rational" and justifiable and thus worthy of the approval of self and others
Reaction Formation	Preventing dangerous desires from being expressed by endorsing opposing attitudes and types of behavior and using them as "barriers"
Regression	Retreating to earlier developmental levels involving more childish responses and usually a lower level of aspiration
Repression	Pushing painful or dangerous thoughts out of consciousness, keeping them unconscious; this is considered to be *the most basic of the defense mechanisms*
Sublimation	Gratifying or working off frustrated sexual desires in substitutive nonsexual activities socially accepted by one's culture

sion of infantile sexual impulses be studied in any direct fashion? How is it possible to predict whether an overly anxious person will use projection, denial, or reaction formation to defend a threatened ego?

A second, related criticism is that Freudian theory is good history but bad science. It does not reliably *predict* what will occur; it is applied *retrospectively*— after events have occurred. Using psychoanalytic theory to understand personality typically involves *historical reconstruction* not scientific construction of probable actions and predictable outcomes. In addition, by overemphasizing historical origins of current behavior the theory misdirects attention away from current stimuli that may be inducing and maintaining the behavior.

Research that has attempted to isolate predictor variables derived from the theory is beset by problems of validity of the dependent measures of psychoanalytic constructs (Silverman, 1976). For example, one researcher predicted that women would hoard more pencils than men, because pencils are phallic symbols and

women allegedly have penis envy. He did, in fact, find more hoarding among female subjects (Johnson, 1966). Do you have a viable alternative explanation? Perhaps females hoard more pencils because they are more likely than men to be asked if they have a pencil that can be borrowed or because they carry handbags that can hold them, or maybe women also hoard more things, in general, than do men.

Freud's theory was developed from speculation based on clinical experience with patients in therapy, almost all of them women with similar symptoms. Thus, another criticism is that the theory has little to say about healthy life-styles, which are not primarily defensive or defective. Instead, it offers the pessimistic view that human nature develops out of conflicts, traumas, and anxieties. As such, it does not fully acknowledge the positive side of our existence nor offer any information about healthy personalities striving for happiness and realization of their full potential.

Three other criticisms of Freudian theory are that it is a developmental theory that never included observations or studies of children, that it minimizes traumatic experiences (such as child abuse) by reinterpreting memories of them as fantasies (based on a child's desire for sexual contact with a parent), and that it has an *androcentric bias* because it uses a male model as the norm without trying to determine how females might be different. To end on a more positive note, a recent critical evaluation of Freud's ideas has validated many of his theories about the *developmental* aspects of personality and psychopathology (Fisher & Greenberg, 1985). Whether or not you accept many of Freud's theories, you must agree that Freud changed forever the way we think about the human mind and its complex possibilities and variations.

POST-FREUDIAN THEORIES

Some of those who came after Freud retained his basic representation of personality as a battleground on which unconscious primal urges fight with social values; but many of Freud's intellectual descendants were also dissidents who made major adjustments in the psychoanalytic view of personality. In general, these post-Freudians have made the following changes: (a) they put greater emphasis on ego functions, including ego defenses, development of the self, conscious thought processes, and personal mastery; (b) they view social variables (culture, family, and peers) as playing a greater role in shaping personality; (c) they put less emphasis on the importance of general sexual urges, or libidinal energy; and (d) they have extended personality development beyond childhood to include the entire life span. Among Freud's many celebrated followers, two of the most important were also severe critics, Alfred Adler and Carl Jung.

Alfred Adler (1929) accepted the notion that personality was directed by unrecognized wishes: "Man knows more than he understands." However, he rejected the significance of Eros and the pleasure principle. Adler believed that as helpless, dependent, small children we all experience feelings of inferiority. He argued that our lives become dominated by the search for ways to overcome those feelings. We compensate to achieve feelings of adequacy or, more often, overcompensate for inferiority feelings in an attempt to become superior. Personality is structured around this underlying striving; people develop life-styles based on particular ways of overcoming their basic, pervasive feelings of inferiority. Personality conflict arises from incompatibility between external environmental pressures and internal strivings for adequacy, rather than from competing urges within the person.

Carl Jung (1959) greatly expanded the conception of the unconscious. For him, the unconscious was not limited to an individual's unique life experiences but was filled with fundamental psychological truths shared by the whole human race. The concept of **collective unconscious** predisposes us all to react to certain stimuli in the same way. It is responsible for our intuitive understanding of primitive myths, art forms, and symbols—which are the universal archetypes of existence. An **archetype** is a primitive symbolic representation of a particular experience or object. Each archetype is associated with an instinctive tendency to feel and think about it or experience it in a special way. Jung postulated many archetypes from history and mythology: the sun god, the hero, the earth mother. *Animus* was the male archetype, while *anima* was the female archetype, and all men and women experienced both archetypes in varying degrees. In reacting to someone of the opposite sex, then, we react to *their* particular characteristics as well as to *our own* male or female archetype. The archetype of the self is the *mandala* or magic circle; it symbolizes striving for unity and wholeness (Jung, 1973).

Jung saw the healthy, integrated personality as balancing opposing forces, such as masculine aggressiveness and feminine sensitivity. This view of personality as a constellation of compensating internal forces in dynamic balance was called **analytic psychology.** Jung, although chosen by Freud as the crown-prince of the psychoanalytic movement, led a palace revolt by rejecting the primary importance of libido, so central to Freudian sexual theory. To the basic urges of sex and aggression Jung added two equally powerful uncon-

Jungian mandala

scious instincts: the need to create and the need to self-actualize. Jung's views became central to the emergence of humanistic psychology in America (Jung, 1965).

SUMMING UP

Freud's psychodynamic theory of personality identifies unconscious motives and conflicts as important determinants of behavior. He believed that conflicts occur between three parts of the personality: the id (ruled by the pleasure principle), the superego (ruled by the morality principle), and the ego (ruled by the reality principle). To solve these conflicts and maintain a favorable self-image, the ego often resorts to defense mechanisms. For example, the ego may use repression to keep unacceptable id impulses out of awareness and sublimation to divert the id's sexual energy into socially acceptable activities. Freud's most controversial contribution was his theory of psychosexual stages in which sexual desires and conflicts in infancy and early childhood form the cornerstone of adult personality.

Psychodynamic theories that came after Freud generally put greater emphasis on ego functions and social variables and less emphasis on sexual urges; these later theories reconceptualized personality development as a process that continues throughout adult life. Adler argued that the ego's attempt to compensate for feelings of inferiority played a central role in personality development; Jung deemphasized the sexual drive and incorporated the drives to create and to self-actualize. Jung also expanded the unconscious to include the collective unconscious, a storehouse of archetypes or symbolic representations of common human experiences.

HUMANISTIC THEORIES

Humanistic approaches to understanding personality are characterized by a concern for the integrity of an individual's personal and conscious experience and growth potential. Humanistic personality theorists, such as Carl Rogers and Abraham Maslow, believe that a basic drive toward self-actualization is the organizer of all the diverse forces whose interplay continually creates what a person is.

In the humanistic view, the motivation for behavior comes from a person's unique biological and learned tendencies to develop and change in positive directions toward the goal of *self-actualization*. **Self-actualization** is described as a constant striving to realize one's inherent potential—to fully develop one's capacities and talents. Experiences that are perceived to maintain or enhance the self are evaluated positively and sought out. Those experiences that oppose the positive growth of the person are evaluated negatively and avoided. This innate striving toward self-fulfillment and the realization of one's unique potential is a constructive, guiding force that moves each person toward generally positive behaviors and enhancement of the self. Humanistic theories have been described as being holistic, dispositional, phenomenological, and existential; and they are definitely optimistic about human nature.

Humanistic theories are *holistic* because they explain people's separate acts always in terms of their entire personalities; people are not seen as the sum of discrete traits that each influence behavior in different ways. Maslow believed that people are intrinsically motivated toward the upper levels of the hierarchy of needs (discussed in Chapter 12), unless deficiencies at the lower levels weigh them down.

Humanistic theories are *dispositional* because they focus on the innate qualities within a person that exert a major influence over the direction behavior will take. Situational inputs are more often seen as constraints and barriers, similar to strings that tie down balloons. Once freed from negative situational conditions, the actualizing tendency should actively guide people to choose life-enhancing situations. Humanistic theories are not dispositional in the same way as trait theories or psychodynamic theories. In those views, personal dispositions are recurrent themes played out in behavior again and again. Humanistic dispositions are oriented specifically toward creativity and growth. Each time a humanistic disposition is exercised, the person changes a little so that the disposition is never expressed in the same way twice. Over time, humanistic dispositions guide the individual toward self-actualization, the purest expression of these motives.

Humanistic theories are *phenomenological* because they emphasize an individual's frame of reference and subjective view of reality—not the objective perspective of an observer, or therapist. This view is also a present view; past influences are important only to the extent that they have brought the person to the present situation; the future represents goals to achieve.

Finally, humanistic theories have been described by theorists such as Rollo May (1975) as having an *existential perspective*. They focus on higher mental processes that interpret current experiences and enable us to meet or be overwhelmed by the everyday challenges of existence. A unique aspect of these theories is the focus on *freedom*, which separates them from the more deterministic behaviorists and psychoanalysts.

ROGERS'S PERSON-CENTERED APPROACH

Carl Rogers (1947, 1951, 1977) developed the practice of *client-centered therapy,* in which it was up to the *client* to determine the therapeutic goals and the direction the therapy should take to achieve those goals. Later, Rogers called his therapy *person-centered* because it was an approach for dealing with people in general and with clients as people. Rogers's advice was to listen to what people said about themselves—to their concepts and to the significance they attach to their experiences. As we have noted, at the core of this theoretical approach is the concept of self-actualization.

The drive for self-actualization at times comes into conflict with the need for approval from the self and others, especially when the person feels that certain obligations or conditions must be met in order to gain approval. Thus, Rogers stressed the importance of *unconditional positive regard* in raising children. By this he meant that children should feel they will always be loved and approved of, in spite of any of their mistakes and misbehavior—that they do not have to earn their parents' love. He recommended that, when a child misbehaves, parents should emphasize that it is the *behavior* they disapprove of, not the child. Unconditional positive regard is important in adulthood, too, because worrying about seeking approval interferes with self-actualization. As adults, we need to give and receive unconditional positive regard from those to whom we are close. Most importantly, we need to feel unconditional positive *self-regard,* or acceptance of ourselves, in spite of the weaknesses we might be trying to change. In recent years, Rogers expanded upon these concepts to create healthy psychological climates that facilitate personal growth in education and interracial and intercultural harmony.

Such an upbeat view of personality was a welcome treat for many therapists who had been brought up on a diet of bitter-tasting Freudian medicine. Humanistic approaches focus directly on improvement—on making life more palatable, rather than dredging up painful memories that are sometimes better left repressed. Client-centered therapies encourage the clients to write their own recipes for improvement, deciding what aspects of their lives they would like to change.

CRITICISMS OF HUMANISTIC THEORIES

It is difficult to criticize theories that encourage us and appreciate us, even for our faults. Who could possibly object to an emphasis on growth, self-concept, and fulfilling one's human potential? Behaviorists could and they do. Behaviorists criticize humanistic concepts for being fuzzy. They ask, What exactly is self-actualization? Is it an inborn tendency or is it created by the cultural context? Behaviorists also have difficulty understanding how humanistic theories account for the particular characteristics of individuals, judging them to be theories about human nature and about qualities we all share more than about any individual personality or the basis of differences among people. Experimental psychologists contend that too many of the concepts in humanistic psychology are so unclear that they defy testing in controlled research. Although this contention is true for some of the more general humanistic concepts, considerable research has evaluated many of the more specific concepts in humanistic theories of personality (Roberts, 1973). Other psychologists note that, by emphasizing the role of the self as a source of experience and action, humanistic psychologists neglect the important environmental variables that also influence behavior.

Psychoanalytic theorists criticize the humanistic emphasis on present conscious experience. They argue that this approach does not recognize the power of the unconscious. Subjects who have unconscious conflicts and use defensive strategies for dealing with their conflicts cannot accurately describe themselves with simple introspection. Other criticisms of this general theory of personality include the following: (a) it ignores individual history and influences from the past as well as the developmental aspects of personality; (b) it oversimplifies the complexity of personality by reducing it to the "given" of a self-actualizing tendency; (c) it fails to predict how a specific individual will respond in a given situation; and (d) it makes the self unaccountable to skeptical researchers—as some hostile critics conclude, "In the last analysis, explaining personality on the basis of hypothesized self-tendencies is reassuring doubletalk, not explanation" (Liebert & Spiegler, 1982, p. 411).

SUMMING UP

Humanistic theories emphasize self-actualization, a basic tendency for humans to develop their potential for creativity and growth. These theories are holistic, dispositional, phenomenological, and existential in that they try to understand the whole personality, including the innate qualities, subjective experiences, and coping with the challenges of existence that together direct behavior. Carl Rogers's person-centered therapy permits the client to decide what needs to be changed and in what direction the therapy should proceed. One ingredient that is necessary for self-actualization, Rogers says, is unconditional positive regard from the self and from significant others such as parents, friends, or a ther-

apist. Humanistic theories have been criticized because they deal with conscious experiences while ignoring the role of unconscious motives and environmental stimuli. In addition, fundamental concepts such as self-actualization are vaguely defined and difficult to observe.

SOCIAL-LEARNING AND COGNITIVE THEORIES

Common to all the theories we have reviewed is an emphasis on hypothesized inner mechanisms—traits, instincts, impulses, tendencies toward self-actualization—that propel behavior and form the basis of a functioning personality. Psychologists with a learning theory orientation, however, have quite a different focus. They look for environmental contingencies—reinforcing circumstances—that control behavior. From this perspective, behavior and personality are shaped primarily by the outside environment. Personality, then, is seen as the sum of overt and covert responses that are reliably elicited by an individual's *reinforcement history;* people are different because they have had different histories of reinforcement. In this view, personality has no active role; it does not cause behavior—it is defined by behavior.

This narrow, and rather sterile, behaviorist conception of personality was first developed by a team of Yale University psychologists headed by John Dollard and Neal Miller (1950). It was considerably expanded by Albert Bandura and Walter Mischel into a meaningful integration of core ideas from the learning-behavioral tradition and the newly emerging ideas from social and cognitive psychology.

Dollard and Miller liberalized the strict behaviorist view of personality by introducing concepts such as learned drives, inhibition of responses, and learned habit patterns. Similar to Freud, they emphasized the roles of the motivating force of tension and the reinforcing (pleasurable) consequences of *tension reduction.* Organisms act to reduce tension produced by unsatisfied drives. Behavior that successfully reduces such tensions is repeated, eventually becoming a learned habit that is reinforced by repeated tension reduction. Dollard and Miller also showed that one could learn by *social imitation*—by observing the behavior of others without having to actually perform the response first. This idea broadened the ways psychologists perceived that effective and destructive habits are learned. Personality emerges as the sum of these learned habits.

Bandura and Mischel agreed that it was vital for personality approaches to recognize the powerful influences that current, specific environmental stimuli exert and to downplay the role of vague, poorly operationalized mechanisms and processes, such as traits and instincts. They also emphasized the importance of learned behavioral patterns based on *social learning*—observation of others and social reinforcement from others. They went one critical step further to emphasize the importance of cognitive processes as well as behavioral ones, returning a thinking mind to the acting body.

Those who have proposed cognitive theories of personality point out that there are important individual differences in the way people think about and define any external situation. Cognitive theories stress the mental processes through which people turn their sensations and perceptions into organized impressions of reality. Similar to humanistic theories, they emphasize that individuals participate in creating their own personalities. People actively *choose* their own environments to a great extent; so, even if the environment has an important impact on us, we are not just passive reactors. We weigh alternatives and select the settings in which we act and are acted upon—we choose to enter those situations which are expected to be reinforcing and to avoid those that are unsatisfying and uncertain.

The relationship between situational variables (social and environmental stimuli) and cognitive variables in regulating behavior is found in a number of personality theories. In this section of our presentation of conceptual approaches to the study of human personality, we will review the personal construct theory of George Kelly and then examine in greater depth the cognitive social-learning theories of Walter Mischel and Albert Bandura.

KELLY'S PERSONAL CONSTRUCT THEORY

George Kelly (1955) developed a theory of personality that places primary emphasis on each person's active, cognitive construction of his or her world. He argued strongly that no one is ever a victim of either past history or the present environment. Although events cannot be changed, all events are open to alternative interpretations; people can always reconstruct their past or define their present difficulties in different ways.

Kelly used science as a metaphor for this process of cognitive construction. Scientists develop theories to *understand* the natural world and to make *predictions* about what will occur in the future under particular conditions. The test of a scientific theory is its utility—how well it explains and predicts. If a theory isn't working well or if it is extended outside the set of events where it does work well, then a new, more useful theory can and should be developed. Kelly argued that all people function as scientists. We want to be able to predict and explain the world around us—especially our interpersonal world. We build theories about the world from units called *personal constructs*. Kelly defined a **personal construct** as a person's belief about what two objects or events have in common and what sets them apart from a third object or event. For example, I might say that my uncle and my brother are alike because they are highly competitive. My sister is different from them because she likes to take a back seat to others. I seem to be using a construct of competitiveness versus giving in to others to organize my perceptions of people around me. By applying that construct to many people I know, I might arrange them into categories, or along a scale that ranges from the most competitive people I know to those who are most likely to give in to others.

You have many different personal constructs that you can apply to understanding any person or situation. Although many people share some of the constructs you use, some of your constructs are uniquely yours. All of your constructs are put together into an integrated belief system that influences the way you interpret, respond to, and feel about each situation you encounter. Chronically accessible constructs are those that you use frequently and automatically. They influence the way you evaluate information and form impressions of others. They are likely to be relatively stable over long periods of time (Lau, 1989; Higgins, 1990). We can think of them as *schema*—types of knowledge clusters that guide the way one processes information (as we discussed in Chapter 11). Adapting to new situations requires that your construct system be open to change; when you have trouble understanding or predicting the course of events, it is helpful to find new ways to interpret them. Kelly believed that people differ in their readiness to change constructs, and that they can run into trouble either by rigidly refusing to change their old, ineffective constructs or by nervously changing their constructs every time the wind turns.

Kelly emphasized the idiographic nature of each person's system of personal constructs, discussing systems, structures, and processes only in general terms and saying little about the content of personal constructs. Recently, Higgins (1990) has elaborated Kelly's theory by outlining different types of constructs, such as *facts, guides,* and *possibilities,* that deal with aspects of self, others, and social contexts; each type of construct is expected to influence behavior in particular ways.

COGNITIVE SOCIAL-LEARNING
THEORY: MISCHEL

Walter Mischel questioned the utility of describing personality according to traits. As an alternative, he has proposed a cognitive theory of personality that also draws heavily on principles from social-learning theory. Similar to other social-learning theorists, Mischel places a great deal of emphasis on the influence of environmental variables on behavior. In his view, much of what we do and many of our beliefs and values are *not* best thought of as emerging properties of the self. He sees them instead as responses developed, maintained, or changed by our observation of influential models and by specific stimulus-response pairings in our own experience.

Dimensions of Individual Difference

Mischel also emphasizes that people actively participate in the cognitive organization of their interactions with the environment (Mischel & Peake, 1982). (It is interesting to note that Mischel was a student of Kelly.) According to Mischel, how you respond to a specific environmental input depends on any or all of the following variables or processes:

- *Competencies*—what you know, what you can do, and your ability to generate certain cognitive and behavioral outcomes
- *Encoding strategies*—the way you process incoming information, selectively attending, categorizing, and making associations to it
- *Expectancies*—your anticipation of likely outcomes for given actions in particular situations
- *Personal values*—the importance you attach to stimuli, events, people, and activities
- *Self-regulatory systems and plans*—the rules you have developed for guiding your performance, setting goals, and evaluating your effectiveness

What determines the nature of these variables for an individual? According to Mischel, they result from an individual's observations and interactions with other people and with inanimate aspects of the physical environment. People respond differently to the same environmental input because of differences in these person-based variables based in part on previous environmental input (Mischel, 1973).

Person Versus Situational Variables

Mischel's approach highlights the *adaptive flexibility* of human behavior. Although the person variables previously listed are a continuing influence on our behavior, we are also able to adapt and change in response to the new demands of our environment. Mischel tried to sort out this consistency paradox, arguing that, because people are so sensitive to situational cues, features of situations are as important as features of people in our attempts to understand behaviors. He hypothesized that person variables will have their greatest impact on behavior when cues in the situation are *weak* or *ambiguous*. When situations are strong and clear, there will be less individual variation in response. For example, in an elevator, most of us tend to behave pretty much the same in response to the strong, silent situational demands. At a party, however, where many behaviors are appropriate, person variables will lead to large differences in behavior. There is extensive evidence in support of this view (Mischel, 1979; Wright & Mischel, 1987; Caspi & Bem, 1990).

COGNITIVE SOCIAL-LEARNING THEORY: BANDURA

Through his theoretical writing and extensive research with children and adults, **Albert Bandura** (1986) of Stanford University has been an eloquent champion of a social-learning approach to understanding personality. This approach combines principles of learning with an emphasis on human interactions in social settings. From a social-learning perspective, human beings are neither driven by inner forces nor are they helpless pawns of environmental influence.

A social-learning approach stresses the uniquely human cognitive processes that are involved in acquiring and maintaining patterns of behavior and, thus, personality. Because we can manipulate symbols and think about external events, we can foresee the possible consequences of our actions without having to actually experience them. In addition to learning from our own experience, we learn *vicariously* through observation of other people. However, we do not passively absorb this knowledge; we make fine distinctions in the stimulus conditions that lead to a given behavior and the consequences that follow it. So, when observed behavior is punished, we still learn the behavior but do not perform it as we might if we saw it being positively rewarded.

We can also evaluate our own behavior according to personal standards and provide ourselves with reinforcements, such as self-approval or self-reproach. Thus we are capable of self-regulation; we are able to control our own actions, rather than being automatically controlled by external forces. However, we often gauge our own behavior according to imposed standards. Someone who accepts an external standard as a behavioral guide will react differently than someone who has developed his or her own personal standard.

Bandura's theory points to a complex interaction of individual factors, behavior, and environmental stimuli. Each can influence or change the others, and the direction of change is rarely one-way—it is *reciprocal*. Your behavior can be influenced by your attitudes, beliefs, or prior history of reinforcement as well as by stimuli available in the environment. What you do can have an effect on the environment, and important aspects of your personality can be affected by the environment or by feedback from your behavior. In this important

concept of social-learning theory called **reciprocal determinism** (Bandura, 1981a), it is necessary to examine all components if you want to completely understand human behavior, personality, and social ecology (see **Figure 14.3**). So, if I am overweight, I do not choose to be active in track and field events, but if I live near a pool, I may spend time swimming. If I am outgoing, I'll talk to others sitting around the pool and thereby create a more sociable atmosphere, which in turn, makes it a more enjoyable environment. This is one instance of reciprocal determinism between person, place, and behavior.

Observational Learning

Perhaps the most important contribution of Bandura's theory is its focus on **observational learning** as the process by which a person changes his behavior based on observations of another person's behavior. In Chapter 9 we saw that this approach challenged traditional behavioristic theory because it states that a person can learn without overt behavior. Through observational learning, children and adults acquire an enormous range of information about their social environment—what is appropriate and gets rewarded and what gets punished or ignored. Skills, attitudes, and beliefs may be acquired simply by watching what others do and the consequences that follow. This means, for example, that a child can develop a greater identity

FIGURE 14.3   RECIPROCAL DETERMINISM

In reciprocal determinism, the individual, the individual's behavior, and the environment all interact.

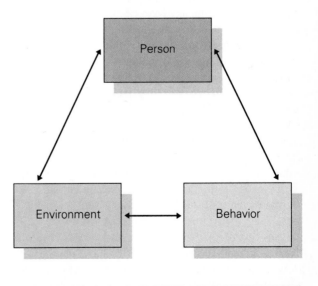

Children can develop greater identity by observing how men and women behave in their culture.

by observing how men and women behave in their culture and how the culture responds differently to each (S. Bem, 1984). Children may also learn personality traits such as altruism (Straub, 1974) or the ability to delay gratification by observing models that are with them personally or seen indirectly in books, in movies, and on TV.

Self-efficacy

Bandura has recently elaborated the concept of self-efficacy as a central part of social-learning theory (1986). As described briefly in Chapter 12, **self-efficacy** is a belief that one can perform adequately in a particular situation. A person's sense of self-efficacy influences his or her perceptions, motivation, and performance in many ways. We don't even try to do things or take chances when we expect to be ineffectual. We avoid situations when we don't feel adequate. Even when we do, in fact, have the ability—and the desire— we may not take the required action or persist to complete the task successfully, if we *think* we lack what it takes.

Self-efficacy is not the same as an overall sense of self-confidence. Bandura believes that perceptions of one's abilities are best thought of as a host of *specific evaluations*. This view cautions that we should be careful to avoid oversimplifying people's complex self-knowledge and self-evaluations into a simplistic single label such as *self-esteem*. However, a sense of self-efficacy can affect behavior in situations that differ from those in which it was generated, because, once established, positive expectations about one's efficacy can generalize to new situations (Bandura, 1977b).

Beyond our actual accomplishments—often referred to as *enactive attainment*—there are three other sources of efficacy expectations: (a) vicarious experience or our observations of the performance of others; (b) social and self-persuasion (others may convince us that we can do something, or we may convince ourselves); and (c) self-monitoring of our emotional arousal as we think about or approach a task. For example, anxiety suggests low expectations of efficacy; excitement suggests expectations of success.

Besides influencing our choices of activities, tasks, situations, and companions, our self-efficacy judgments also influence how much effort we expend and how long we persist when faced with difficulty. How vigorously and persistently a student pursues academic tasks depends more on his or her sense of self-efficacy than on actual ability. Expectations of success or failure can be influenced by feedback from performance, but they are more likely to create the *predicted* feedback and, thus, to become self-fulfilling prophecies. (In Chapter 18, we will review ways of inducing each of these four types of efficacy expectations through therapy.)

Expectations of failure—and a corresponding decision to stop trying—may, of course, be based on the perception that a situation is unresponsive, punishing, or unsupportive instead of on a perception of one's own inadequacy. Such expectations are called *outcome-based expectancies*. Perception of one's own inadequacy are called *efficacy-based expectancies*. (See **Figure 14.4.**) The person who believes that responding is useless because of low self-efficacy must develop competencies that will boost self-perception of efficacy. On the other

Albert Bandura (*Discovering Psychology*, 1990 Program 15)

FIGURE 14.4   BANDURA'S SELF-EFFICACY
MODEL

The model positions efficacy expectations between the
person and his or her behavior; outcome expectations are
positioned between behavior and its anticipated
outcomes.

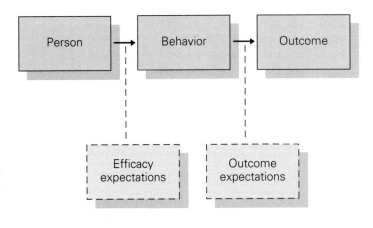

hand, when a person believes that responding is useless
because of outcome expectancies, the environment, and
not the person, may need to be changed so that reinforcements will, in fact, follow competent responding.

Can a teacher's self-efficacy affect student achievement? The results of a classroom field study strongly
support the association between personality and performance variables.

> Forty-eight teachers in four high schools with
> large numbers of "culturally deprived" students
> participated in this study. The researchers mea-
> sured the teachers' sense of teaching efficacy on
> self-report scales, made classroom observations of
> "climate and atmosphere," and assessed student
> achievement on standardized tests. Correlations
> between these and a number of other measures
> reveal that teachers with a greater sense of self-
> efficacy tend to maintain a positive emotional cli-
> mate in their classes, avoiding the harsh modes of
> behavior control that tend to characterize low-
> efficacy teachers. In addition, student achieve-
> ment on the mathematics test was significantly
> correlated with the teachers' self-efficacy; stu-
> dents scored higher as teacher self-efficacy was
> higher. However, this effect was specific to the
> teaching of mathematics. It did not hold for read-
> ing achievement test performance—perhaps be-
> cause the basic skills language classes the teachers
> taught did not teach reading (Ashton & Webb,
> 1986).

CRITICAL EVALUATION OF LEARNING AND COGNITIVE THEORIES

Critics hold that behavioristic approaches to personality
have thrown out the baby's vibrant personality and kept
the cold bath water; by searching so much for environmental stimuli, they have lost contact with the person.
Is personality all about stimulus variables or living people? If personality is built upon the learned repetition
of previously reinforced responses, where is the origin
of new behavior—creative achievements, innovative
ideas, inventions, and works of art? Critics also argue
that much of the learning that behaviorists observe is
highly specific responding that is reinforced because an
organism is in a state of deficiency motivation (tension
states), and because other kinds of action and reinforcements are not available. Also, because the focus is on
the learning *process,* what gets obscured is the *content*
of the unique characteristics that form each distinct human personality.

One set of criticisms leveled against cognitive theories is that they generally overlook *emotion* as an important component of personality. They emphasize
rational, information-processing variables, such as constructs and encoding strategies. Emotions are perceived
merely as by-products of thoughts and behavior or just
included with other types of thoughts, rather than being
assigned independent importance. For those who feel
that emotions are central to the functioning of human
personality, this is a serious flaw. A great deal of research has demonstrated that emotions have an important effect on cognitive processes such as memory,
reaction time, and decision making (Bower, 1981;
Zajonc, 1980). Feelings may themselves be important
determinants of cognitive content and structure, rather
than just "cognitive coatings." Cognitive theories are
also attacked for not fully recognizing the impact of
unconscious motivation on behavior and affect.

A second set of criticisms focuses on the vagueness
of explanations about the way personal constructs and
competencies are created. Cognitive theorists have little
to say about the developmental origins of adult personality; their focus on the individual's perception of the
current behavior setting obscures the individual's history. This criticism is leveled particularly at Kelly's
theory, which has been described as more of a conceptual system than a theory because it focuses on structure
and processes but says little about the content of personal constructs.

Despite these criticisms, cognitive personality theories have made major contributions to current thinking. Kelly's theory has influenced a large number of
cognitive therapists. Bandura's ideas have improved the
way we educate our children and help them to achieve.
Mischel's awareness of situation has brought about a

better understanding of the complexity and significance of the interaction between what the person brings to a behavior setting and what that setting brings out of the person.

SUMMING UP

Learning theorists view behavior as caused, not by internal mechanisms such as traits, but by a combination of environmental stimuli and prior reinforcements. Personality is the sum of the responses that can be reliably elicited from an individual as a function of past learning history. Learning theorists Dollard and Miller added learned drives, inhibition of responses, and learned habits to Freudian concepts, such as tension reduction, in an effort to form hypotheses about personality that could be tested in the laboratory. Bandura additionally emphasized that social and cognitive factors—especially observational learning, reciprocal determinism, and perceptions of self-efficacy—influence behavior in important ways.

Kelly suggested that personal constructs influence the way individuals process information about people, the environment, and the behavioral alternatives that are open to them. Chronically accessible constructs are those that people rely on frequently and in a wide range of situations. Mischel has combined social learning theory with a cognitive approach similar to Kelly's. He emphasizes that people adapt flexibly to very subtle changes in environmental conditions or reinforcements. People respond differently to the same situation because they have different competencies, encoding strategies, expectancies, personal values, and self-regulatory systems and plans. Social learning and cognitive theories have been criticized because they focus on rational information processing and tend to overlook emotions and unconscious motives as important determinants of behavior.

SELF THEORIES

When cognitive social-learning theories reopened the black box of internal experiences that behaviorists had refused to examine, they found a store of treasures and tribulations. Although the cognitive approach to the self was new, a foundation of self theory had already been laid by philosophers, sociologists, analytic and humanistic psychologists.

The concern for analysis of the self found its strongest advocate in **William James** (1890). James identified three components of self-experience: the *material me* (the bodily self, along with surrounding physical objects); the *social me* (one's awareness of his or her reputation in the eyes of others); and the *spiritual me* (the self that monitors private thoughts and feelings). James believed everything that one associated with one's identity became, in some sense, a part of self. People react defensively when their friends or family members are insulted because a part of the self has been attacked. Some theorists assert that the pride we take in our cars and our attachment to old record albums and memorabilia are evidence of an extended self that also includes possessions (Belk, 1988).

Knowledge is a central concept in theories of the self. Self-insight was an important part of the psychoanalytic cure in Freud's theory, and Jung stressed that to fully develop the self, one must integrate and accept all aspects of one's conscious and unconscious life.

SELF AS KNOWER VERSUS KNOWN

Some self theorists make a distinction between *the knower* and *the known*. The *knower* refers to the part of you that experiences thoughts, feelings, and perceptions—the part that guides behavior. The *known* refers to what Carl Rogers and others have called the **self-concept;** that is, all the conscious or potentially conscious thoughts, ideas, and evaluations you have of yourself.

Many psychologists criticized the concept of self as knower because it suggests that there is a little person in the head who integrates experience and directs behavior. On the other hand, the concept of self as known involves material that is consciously accessible to an individual (Berkowitz, 1988). Thus, we can measure various aspects of the self-concept through self-report—by asking people about their self-beliefs. The self-concept includes many components. Among them are your self-referent memories; beliefs about your traits, motives, values, and abilities; the ideal self that you would most like to become, the possible selves that you contemplate enacting; positive or negative evaluations of yourself (self-esteem); and beliefs about what others think of you (McGuire & McGuire, 1988).

DYNAMIC ASPECTS OF SELF-CONCEPTS

The self-concept is a dynamic mental structure that motivates, interprets, organizes, mediates, and regulates intrapersonal and interpersonal behaviors and processes. The content and structure of your self-concept influence the way you process information about yourself, and research indicates that the self-schemas, or concepts you frequently use to interpret your *own* behavior, influence the way you process information about other people as well (Markus & Smith, 1981; Cantor & Kihlstrom, 1987). The salient aspects of self-concept show developmental changes: very young children think of themselves in terms of physical characteristics, gradually incorporate moods and preferences, and finally focus on their interpersonal traits, morals, and life philosophies (Damon & Hart, 1988; Livesley & Bromley, 1973). Many aspects of the self-concept are reflected in behavior. We have already seen from Bandura's work how perceived self-efficacy influences whether and how hard people try to achieve particular goals (Markus & Nurius, 1986; Markus et al., 1990).

A person's **self-esteem** is a *generalized* evaluative attitude toward the self, which can strongly influence our thoughts, moods, and behavior. Interestingly, belief in the impact of self-esteem on performance has generated a congressional appropriation in California (1987) to establish a Self-Esteem Commission. The commission's task is to discover ways in which self-esteem can be enhanced to benefit both individuals and society.

Evidence suggests that most people go out of their way to maintain self-esteem and to sustain the integrity of their self concept (Steele, 1988). For example, when experiencing self-doubt about their ability to perform a task, people sometimes engage in **self-handicapping** behavior. They deliberately sabotage their performance! The purpose of this strategy is to have a ready-made excuse for failure that does not implicate *lack of ability* (Jones & Berglas, 1978). Thus, if you are afraid to find out whether you have what it takes to be premed, you might party with friends instead of studying for an important exam. That way, if you fail, you can blame it on low effort without finding out whether you really had the *ability* to make it. Research shows that, most of the time, people do engage in *self-verification,* trying to know themselves better. However, it seems that sometimes, when confronted by self-doubt, people prefer to remain in the dark about personal problems and engage in *self-enhancement* processes, trying to be adored rather than known. In self-enhancement, people deny or distort information to sustain a desired self-image (Swann, 1990).

When you deliberately manipulate your public self, trying to create a particular impression on another person, you are engaging in *impression management.* Sometimes you may try to manage your public self without even realizing it, in order to maintain an impression that agrees with the way you see yourself. In this process, known as **behavioral confirmation,** your beliefs about the self control your behavior (source) in the presence of particular others (target) (Snyder, 1984). Target people are then more likely to react according to the behavioral context established and confirm the original belief about what kind of person you

really are. In this way, beliefs create reality. People who are extraverted solicit extraverted behaviors in others (Fong & Markus, 1982); those who are anxious cause anxiety in others (Riggs & Cantor, 1981); and those who are feeling depressed provoke depressed, hostile feelings in others (Strack & Coyne, 1983).

Although separating the self-concept from the self as knower has generated a great deal of research and advanced our understanding of certain types of behavior, some theorists believe we must ultimately return to an integrated, or unified, conception of self. These theorists promote a conception of the *interpersonal self,* in which behavior is directed not by an invisible *homunculus* (little man) from within the person but by the social context within which the person lives (Rosenberg, 1988). **Hazel Markus** believes that the self is a dynamic construct, deriving its meaning only in interpersonal contexts; without others there can be no self (Markus & Cross, 1990). There are no clean dichotomies between public and private aspects of the self or between what we think of ourselves and what we think others think of us. All of our interpersonal behavior becomes incorporated into the self. In addition, much of our behavior is scripted by the social roles we play, and the behaviors we characteristically display in different roles become worked into the self as well.

CRITICAL EVALUATION OF SELF THEORIES

Critics of self theory approaches argue against its limitless boundaries. Some argue that *self* is not useful as a theoretical construct, because it simply passes the buck, explaining behavior by attributing it to an invisible persona that is not accountable to evaluation or research. Paradoxically, other critics argue that the more easily measured self-concept is an empty set of schemas that cannot direct behavior in the absence of a self as knower.

SUMMING UP

William James was one of the first psychologists to theorize about the self-concept and its different material, social, and spiritual aspects. A distinction is made between the knowing self that is the experiencing agent and the self that is known by the process of self-reflection. New views make the self-concept a dynamic mental structure that not only is involved in interpreting experience and regulating personal and social behavior but that motivates action as well. Modern researchers are investigating many facets of the self-concept and self-processes, among them self-esteem, self-handicapping, self-verification and self-enhancement.

COMPARING PERSONALITY THEORIES

There is no unified theory of personality that a majority of psychologists can endorse. Several differences in basic assumptions have come up repeatedly in our survey of the various theories. It may be helpful to recap five of the most important differences in assumptions about personality and the approaches that advance each assumption.

1. *Heredity versus environment.* This difference is also referred to as *nature vs. nurture.* What is more important: genetic and biological factors or influences from the environment? Trait theories have been split on this issue: Freudian theory depends heavily on heredity; humanistic, learning, cognitive and self theories all emphasize either environment as a determinant of behavior or interaction with the environment as a source of personality development and differences.

2. *Learning processes versus innate laws of behavior.* Should emphasis be placed on *modifiability* or on the view that personality development follows an internal timetable? Again, trait theories have been divided. Freudian theory has favored the inner determinant view—a pessimistic one—while humanists postulate an optimistic view that people change as a result of their experiences. Learning, cognitive, and self theories clearly support the idea that behavior and personality change as a result of learned experiences.

3. *Emphasis on past, present, or future.* Trait theories emphasize past causes, whether innate or learned; Freudian theory stresses past events in early childhood; learning theories focus on past reinforcements and present contingencies; humanistic theories emphasize present phenomenal reality or future goals; and cognitive and self theories emphasize past and present (and the future if goal-setting is involved).

4. *Consciousness versus unconsciousness.* Freudian theory emphasizes unconscious processes; humanistic, learning, and cognitive theories emphasize conscious processes. Trait theories pay little attention to either consciousness or unconsciousness; self theories are unclear on this score.

5. *Inner disposition versus outer situation.* Learning theories emphasize situational factors; traits play up dispositional factors; and the others allow for an interaction between person-based and situation-based variables.

Each type of theory makes different contributions to our understanding of human personality. Trait theories provide a catalog that describes parts and structures. Psychodynamic theories add a powerful engine and the fuel to get the vehicle moving. Learning theories supply the steering wheel, directional signals, and other regulation equipment. Humanistic theories put a person in the driver's seat. Cognitive theories add reminders that the way the trip is planned, organized, and remembered will be affected by the mental map the driver chooses for the journey. Self theories remind the driver to consider the image his or her driving ability is projecting to back-seat drivers and pedestrians.

THE ALCOHOLIC PERSONALITY

Is there evidence for an *alcoholic personality*? In trying to identify individuals who are especially susceptible to problems with alcohol abuse, theorists have tried to define the *alcoholic personality*. Alcoholism has been linked to a large number of personality traits, including impulsivity, poor self-image, inability to delay gratification, poor ego strength, lack of self-control, depression, antisocial tendencies, and contradictory behavior (Miller, 1990; Butcher, 1988; Donovan, 1986). Research on children of alcoholics has suggested that certain characteristics of temperament—high activity, low persistence, emotional lability, disinhibition, and agitation after stress—may predict increased risk of alcohol abuse in adulthood (Tarter et al., 1985).

Unfortunately, the personality characteristics implicated by these studies are so common that a large segment of the population could be classified as *at risk* for alcoholism. However, some psychologists claim that a large at risk population is a realistic situation. Therapist Anne

Wilson Schaef believes we live in an *addictive society*. She maintains that everyone, even the Pope, is addicted to something (1987). Although it is egalitarian, Schaef's approach has not clarified the relationship between personality and addiction. While some people skip from one addiction to another, researchers have been unable to validate the existence of an *addictive personality* (Butcher, 1988).

One theory, proposed by psychiatrist Robert Cloninger (1987), recognizes two genetically different subtypes of alcoholism and provides a neurophysiological explanation for the personality characteristics associated with each type. He maintains that alcoholism type can be predicted on the basis of three personality dimensions: novelty seeking, reward dependence, and harm avoidance. In addition, he suggests that variations in these personality dimensions reflect differences in neurological functioning—specific neurotransmitter systems are involved in each dimension: dopamine in novelty seeking; serotonin in harm avoidance; and norepinephrine in reward dependence. According to Cloninger, individual differences in alcohol-related behavior are intimately tied to these biological variables.

Cloninger's *Type I alcoholics* are likely to be binge drinkers who lose control once they begin to drink but can abstain for periods of time. They usually do not start having problems with alcohol until after age 25. On a personality test, they would score low on measures of novelty-seeking and high on measures of harm avoidance and reward dependence. In general, Type I alcoholics are worriers. They look to others for approval and feel guilty about their loss of control and dependence on alcohol. Most female alcoholics—and their male alcoholic relatives—fall into this category.

Type II alcoholics reveal a dramatically different personality profile. High on novelty seeking and low on harm avoidance and reward dependence, these impulsive risk-takers are spontaneous alcohol seekers who find it difficult to abstain from alcohol. Drinking gets them into trouble at an early age. They care little about the judgments of others and are often classified as "antisocial personalities." Alcoholics in this group are almost all male.

Cloninger argues that each type of alcoholism is linked to a different sort of genetic predisposition. While the genetic predisposition alone is usually enough to launch Type II alcoholism, exposure to environments conducive to alcohol abuse is needed to develop a Type I. In order to test his theory,

Cloninger and his colleagues developed a 100-item true-false questionnaire, the Tridimensional Personality Questionnaire (TPQ), which generates scores on each of the three alcoholism-relevant dimensions of personality. After administering the TPQ to 267 patients in chemical dependency treatment units, researchers found that alcoholics did *not* fall into the classifications predicted by the theory (Nixon & Parsons, 1990). Contrary to Cloninger's prediction, the majority of female alcoholics did not show the Type I pattern

(low novelty seeking/high harm avoidance), and the majority of male alcoholics did not show the Type II pattern (high novelty seeking/low harm avoidance). In another study, only 6 percent of 360 alcoholics could be classified by Cloninger's system (Penick et al., 1990). Other researchers have also failed to confirm the proposed alcoholism personality types (Gallant, 1990; Shuckit & Irwin, 1989; Shuckit, Irwin, & Mahler, 1990). Although some of the model's predictions may be valid, further testing makes little sense until alcoholics can be reliably assigned to each type.

This kind of research poses many problems for researchers. While it is hypothesized that neurophysiological and personality differences underlie patterns of alcohol abuse, severe alcohol abuse could *cause* such differences. For this reason, it is important to do *prospective* studies in which people thought to be at risk for alcoholism are assessed before any problems develop. It is also possible that personality, while not causal, functions as a mediating variable that affects the ways biological predispositions and life experiences interact in alcoholism.

Finally, researchers and clinicians should beware of the prejudice that can result from labeling. In one study, mental health and medical professionals were asked to evaluate videotaped interviews of teenage actors, some of whom were falsely described as children of alcoholics (COAs). The actors thought to be COAs were judged more psychopathological and were rated more likely to be dysfunctional than were the controls (Burk & Sher, 1990). So, for now, there is no evidence for a reliably measured alcoholic personality, but there is clear evidence for stereotypes and stigma regarding alcoholism.

The Psychology of the Person

Personality is what characterizes an individual—what is characteristic and unique about a person across different situations and over time. Personality theorists study the whole person as the sum of the separate processes of feelings, thoughts, and actions.

The five sources of data used in personality research are self reports, observer reports, specific behaviors, life events, and physiological measures. The focus of the idiographic approach is the organization of the unique person. The nomothetic approach attempts to understand all people in terms of individual differences along common dimensions.

Type and Trait Personality Theories

Some theorists categorize people by all-or-none types, assumed to be related to particular characteristic behaviors. Others view traits as the building blocks of personality. Allport, an idiographic theorist, differentiated cardinal, central, and secondary traits, while Eysenck combined the type and trait approaches and has explored the relationship between personality and physiological characteristics.

Twin and adoption studies reveal that personality traits are partially inherited. The environment is important, but the common familial environment is less important than the unshared environment that is experienced differently by each sibling.

The Big Five is a comprehensive, theory-free, descriptive personality system that maps out the relationships between common trait words, theoretical concepts, and personality scales.

Specific behaviors are not consistent across different situations, although they do show temporal stability when the same behavior is measured in the same situation. However, the consistency paradox is resolved by showing that, although trait measures do not show cross-situational behavioral consistency, they do predict life events and behavioral coherence.

Psychodynamic Theories

Freud's psychodynamic theory accepted Darwin's emphasis on instinctive biological energies as sources of all human motivation. Basic concepts of Freudian theory include psychic determinism; early experiences as key determinants of lifelong personality; psychic energy as powering and directing behavior; and powerful unconscious processes. Personality structure consists of the id (guided by the pleasure principle), the superego (guided by learned social and moral restrictions), and the reconciling ego (guided by the reality principle). Unacceptable impulses are repressed and ego-defense mechanisms are developed to lessen anxiety and bolster self-esteem.

Post-Freudians have put greater emphasis on ego functioning and social variables and less on sexual urges. They see personality development as a lifelong process. Adler thought each person developed a consistent life-style aimed at compensating or overcompensating for feelings of inferiority. Jung emphasized the notion of a collective unconscious, including archetypes (symbols of universal significance); he saw the needs to create and self-actualize as powerful unconscious instincts in all people.

Humanistic Theories

Humanistic theories focus on the growth potential of the individual. These theories are holistic, dispositional, phenomenological, existential, and optimistic. At the core of Rogers's person-centered personality theory is the concept of self-actualization, a constant striving to realize one's potential and to develop one's talents.

Social-learning Theories

Social-learning theorists focus on understanding individual differences in behavior and personality as a consequence of different histories of reinforcement. They have added new ideas about the social dimension of learning to traditional behavioral analysis. Cognitive theorists emphasize individual differences in perception and subjective interpretation of the environment. Bandura's cognitive social-learning theory combines principles of learning with an emphasis on social interactions. Reciprocal determinism, observational learning, and self-efficacy are concepts that are critical in the analysis of person-behavior-situation interactions.

Self Theories

Self theories, which developed primarily from the humanistic tradition, focus on the importance of the self-concept for a full understanding of human personality. The self-concept is a dynamic mental structure that motivates, interprets, organizes, mediates, and regulates intrapersonal and interpersonal behaviors and processes.

The many different personality theories vary in their assumptions about many fundamental aspects of human nature, including its structure, influences, and processes.

Predictions from a comprehensive theory about the alcoholic personality do not actually support the theory.

KEY TERMS

adoption studies, 515
aggregated case study, 510
analytic psychology, 524
anxiety, 522
archetype, 524
behavioral confirmation, 533
The Big Five, 516
cardinal trait, 513
case study, 510
central trait, 513
collective unconscious, 524
consistency paradox, 517
ego, 522
ego defense mechanisms, 522
Eros, 520

factor analysis, 510
id, 521
idiographic approach, 510
libido, 520
nomothetic approach, 510
observational learning, 529
personal construct, 528
personality, 509
personality types, 511
psychic determinism, 520
psychodynamic personality
    theories, 519
reciprocal determinism, 529

repression, 522
secondary trait, 513
self-actualization, 525
self-concept, 532
self-efficacy, 530
self-esteem, 533
self-handicapping, 533
somatotypes, 512
superego, 521
Thanatos, 520
trait, 512
unconscious, 520

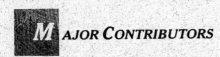

MAJOR CONTRIBUTORS

Adler, Alfred, 524
Allport, Gordon, 512
Bandura, Albert, 529
Eysenck, Hans, 514
Freud, Sigmund, 519

Hippocrates, 511
James, William, 532
Jung, Carl, 524
Kelly, George, 527
Markus, Hazel, 533

Mischel, Walter, 528
Rogers, Carl, 526
Sheldon, William, 512

Chapter 15

Assessing Individual Differences

WHAT IS ASSESSMENT?   540
  HISTORY OF ASSESSMENT
  PURPOSES OF ASSESSMENT

  ■ INTERIM SUMMARY

METHODS OF ASSESSMENT   542
  BASIC FEATURES OF FORMAL ASSESSMENT
  SOURCES OF INFORMATION
  *CLOSE-UP: ALL DRINKERS ARE NOT CREATED
    EQUAL*

  ■ INTERIM SUMMARY

ASSESSING INTELLIGENCE   548
  HISTORICAL CONTEXT
  IQ TESTS
  THE USE AND MISUSE OF IQ

  ■ INTERIM SUMMARY

ASSESSING PERSONALITY   562
  OBJECTIVE TESTS
  PROJECTIVE TESTS

  ■ INTERIM SUMMARY

ASSESSMENT AND YOU   568
  VOCATIONAL INTERESTS AND APTITUDES
  POLITICAL AND ETHICAL ISSUES

RECAPPING MAIN POINTS   571

KEY TERMS   573

MAJOR CONTRIBUTORS   573

At the age of 37, *Esquire* columnist Bob Greene started to suspect that he "was dumber than [he] had been in high school" (Greene, 1985). At 17 he had been able to add, subtract, and multiply without using a calculator. Twenty years later, those skills seemed to have disappeared completely. To see if he could still make the grade, Greene decided to retake the Scholastic Aptitude Test (SAT), the three-hour examination of verbal and mathematical abilities that many colleges use to select students for admission. Greene sent in his $11, and on the designated Saturday morning, he showed up at his local high school with six sharpened no. 2 pencils in his pocket. After one hour, "all of us looked dazed, unhappy, and disoriented, although I believe that I was the only student to go to the water fountain and take an Inderal for his blood pressure" (Greene, 1985).

The SAT was designed as a standardized measure of high-school students' academic performance—admissions officers had difficulty interpreting grade-point averages from thousands of high schools with different standards and grading policies. Although the tests were designed as objective evaluations, they have been accused of bias, and, despite many revisions over the years, it has been difficult to quell those accusations. Across all ethnic groups, average SAT scores increase as family income goes up. Whites and Asian Americans consistently outperform Mexican Americans, Puerto Ricans, and African Americans (Hacker, 1986). Men, on the average, score higher than women (Gordon, 1990).

However, the SAT is changing. Consider the question of calculators. When the SAT was introduced in 1941, pocket calculators did not exist. When Greene took the test for the second time, the proctor instructed that "Calculators or wristwatches with calculator functions may not be used." In 1994, students will be permitted to use calculators for the first time and 20 percent of the math questions will require students to produce their own response rather than select from a set of multiple-choice alternatives. Test-takers will have to come up with their own answers for questions such as "If the population of a certain country is increasing at the rate of one person every 12 seconds, by how many persons does it increase every half hour?" (Educational Testing Service, 1990).

When Greene's test results finally arrived in the mail, his hands were shaking. He felt ridiculous. After all, he already had a college degree and a successful career. Nevertheless, he nervously ripped open the envelope. Not surprisingly for a writer, Greene's verbal score had gone up 56 points. In math, over the two decades, his score had nose-dived by 200 points! Just as it is difficult to know why some groups perform better than others on the SAT, it is impossible to know for sure why Bob Greene's math score plummeted. Wasn't the test supposed to measure his basic aptitude for math—what he understood and not just what he had learned? Had his math aptitude decreased because in his work he doesn't often use the math skills that he once practiced regularly in high school? Would he have improved his score if he had signed up for a course that prepared him in advance for the test? Had he just been watching too much TV and the only numbers he had needed to know in the past few years were the channels of his favorite stations?

The use of psychological tests to assess differences between individuals' mental abilities is considered by some to be "one of psychology's unquestioned success stories" (Tyler, 1988). That "success" is determined in several ways. Psychological tests allow people to be compared on various dimensions of intelligence and specific aptitudes according to objective standards that are not open to the biases of subjective interpreters. They are supposed to be fair comparisons of the mental capacities of all individuals taking the same test under the same conditions. These tests have been perceived as "tools of democracy," enabling selection of individuals for education and employment to be based on what the individuals know and can show, rather than on *who* they know and what their family can show (Sokol, 1987).

Test results, such as those from the SAT, are generally good predictors of later academic grades, just as tests for personnel selection predict some types of job performance. Any test can be said to work if it accurately predicts performance in future situations. When a person's aptitudes, interests, attitudes, and personality are all taken into account, the chances of improving the fit of person to school or job are greatly increased—to the benefit of all concerned.

There are more than 2500 commercially published psychological tests now available designed to measure mental abilities of all sorts, school achievement, vocational interests, and aspects of personality and mental disorders. In the 30-year period between 1938 and 1965, a book that analyzes tests of mental measurements increased the number of pages devoted to reviews of all the tests in current use from 167 to 1319 (*Buros Mental Measurements Yearbook*). Many psychologists spend most of their time on the construction, evaluation, administration, and interpretation of psychological tests. Psychological testing is big business. It is a multimillion dollar industry—thousands of children and adults regularly take some form of the thousands of tests distributed by the more than 40 major U.S. test publishers. Virtually everyone in our society who has attended school, gone to work, joined the military services, or registered in a mental health clinic has undergone some kind of psychological testing.

Despite the widespread use of standardized psychological tests, some psychologists believe that such testing is psychology's worst embarrassment. They argue that many of the tests are not objective measures of native ability and basic capacity. The tests may overcome the biases of teacher and employer evaluations, but they are themselves biased in more fundamental ways because they are based, in part, on specific learning experiences even though such experiences vary with social class, cultural background, and personal experiences.

Writer Bob Greene's SAT scores show that people improve at the tasks they practice and worsen at the tasks they neglect. Similarly, practicing test-taking actually can improve performance. The *Educational Testing Service,* which designs and distributes the SAT, markets courses for high schools and how-to-succeed books for the general public. Because scores can be improved with practice, schools have been accused of "teaching the test" rather than mastering the material on which students will be tested.

The most damning criticism of psychological tests comes from those who believe that testing mental ability contributes to elitism—these tests play up the importance of *differences* between people while most of the rest of psychology focuses on similarities. Some people use test scores as evidence of innate mental abilities, evidence that they then use to justify discrimination against the disadvantaged poor, women, minorities, and immigrants in educational and career opportunities and in formulating public policy (Gould, 1981; Hirsch et al., 1990; Kamin, 1974).

In this chapter, we will examine the foundations and applications of psychological assessment. We will review the contributions psychologists have made to our understanding of individual differences in three broad areas: intelligence, personality, and vocational ability. Our focus will be on what makes any test useful, how tests work, and why they may not always be doing the job they were intended to do. Finally, we will conclude on a personal note by considering the role of psychological assessment in your life and mine.

WHAT IS ASSESSMENT?

Psychological assessment is the use of specified testing procedures to evaluate the abilities, behaviors, and personal qualities of people. Assessment contributes to our understanding of an individual so that she can make more informed decisions about current problems or future choices (Maloney & Ward, 1976). Psychological assessment is often referred to as the measurement of *individual differences,* since the majority of assessments specify how an individual is different from or similar to other people on a given dimension.

The use of objective assessment procedures to estimate a person's abilities and skills eliminates the effect of arbitrary, subjective, and unconsciously biased evaluations of authorities, such as employers and admissions officers. Assessment is especially valuable in helping clinical psychologists detect problems that may require special counseling or treatment. Before we examine in detail the purposes of psychological testing, let's outline some milestones in the history of assessment.

HISTORY OF ASSESSMENT

The development of formal tests and procedures for assessment is a relatively new enterprise in psychology, coming into wide use only in the early 1900's. It is surprising to discover that long before Western psychology began to devise tests to evaluate people, assessment techniques were commonplace in ancient China. In fact, China employed a sophisticated program of civil service testing over 4000 years ago—officials were required to demonstrate their competence every third year at an oral examination. Two thousand years later, during the Han Dynasty, written civil service tests were used to assess competence in the areas of law, the military, agriculture, and geography. During the Ming Dynasty (1368–1644 A.D.), public officials were chosen on the basis of their performance at three stages of an objective selection procedure. During the first stage, examinations were given at the local level. The 4 percent who passed these tests had to endure the second stage: nine days and nights of essay examinations on the classics. The 5 percent who passed the essay exams were allowed to complete a final stage of tests conducted at the nation's capital.

China's selection procedures were observed and described by British diplomats and missionaries in the early 1800s. Modified versions of China's system were soon adopted by the British and later by the Americans for the selection of civil service personnel (Wiggins, 1973).

The key figure in the era of modern intelligence testing was an upper-class Englishman, **Sir Francis Galton.** His book *Hereditary Genius,* published in 1869, greatly influenced subsequent thinking on the methods, theories, and practices of testing. Galton, a half-cousin to Charles Darwin, attempted to apply Darwinian evolutionary theory to the study of human abilities. He was interested in how and why people differ in their abilities. He wondered why some people were gifted and successful while many others were not.

Galton was the first to postulate that (a) differences in intelligence were *quantifiable* in terms of degrees of intelligence; (b) these differences formed a *bell-shaped curve* or *normal distribution* (where most people clustered in the middle and fewer were found toward the genius extreme or the mental deficiency extreme); (c) intelligence, or mental ability, could be measured by objective tests; and (d) the precise extent to which two sets of test scores were related could be determined by a statistical procedure he called *co-relations,* now known as *correlations*. These ideas proved to be of lasting value.

Unfortunately, Galton also believed that genius was inherited; talent, or eminence, ran in families; nurture had only a minimal effect on intelligence; and intelli-

Sir Francis Galton

gence was related to Darwinian species fitness and, somehow, to moral worth. Galton attempted to base public policy on the concept of genetically superior and inferior people. He started the **eugenics** movement, which advocated improving the human species by applying evolutionary theory to encouraging biologically superior people to interbreed while discouraging biologically inferior people from having offspring. Galton wrote, "There exists a sentiment, for the most part quite unreasonable, against the gradual extinction of an inferior race" (Galton, 1983, p. 200).

These controversial ideas were endorsed and extended later by many who argued forcefully that the intellectually superior race should propagate at the expense of those with inferior minds. Among the proponents of these ideas were American psychologists Goddard and Terman and, of course, Nazi dictator Adolf Hitler.

PURPOSES OF ASSESSMENT

While early assessment techniques were used only for job placement, they now are used for many different purposes and take place in a multitude of settings. Among the types of ability and aptitude assessment we use today are tests to determine how well people do in school, what their interests are, what job-related skills they have, and how well they function in different settings.

The goals of formal assessment are not very different from your own concerns when you size up another person. You may want to know how smart, trustworthy, creative, responsible, or dangerous a new acquaintance is, and you may attempt to evaluate these qualities with whatever evidence you can gather informally.

Error in such predictions, of course, can go in either of two directions. It is possible for a test to predict failure when a student would have been effective. This incorrect prediction is known as a *Type-One Error* (a false negative). Predicting success for a student who eventually flunks out is known as a *Type-Two Error* (a false positive). Similarly, of course, there are two kinds of accurate predictions: those that predict success that is eventually achieved and those that predict failure that is eventually observed. Good tests reduce both kinds of error and increase both kinds of accurate prediction.

Scientific psychology attempts to formalize the procedures by which predictions about individual behavior can be made accurately. Assessment begins with the measurement of a limited number of individual attributes and samples of behavior. From this narrow body of information about a person in a testing situation—which can be collected conveniently and inexpensively—predictions are made about his likely reactions at some future time in some other real-life situation that is not identical to the test situation.

Psychologists use assessment techniques to understand individuals and to make sense of the ways people differ. The science of assessment aspires to describe and provide a formal measurement of diverse individual behavior and experiences. By testing and classifying individuals who share similar traits, psychologists correlate behavioral differences with personality or cognitive differences. In this way, they can test empirically the predictive value of different theories of personality or different conceptions of intelligence.

While a clinical psychologist uses testing to make predictions about a *particular* client, a research psychologist tries to discover the regularities in personality that translate in *general* to behavior patterns or life events. For example, a research psychologist might test to see if there are certain ages at which children acquire a certain skill.

When certain questions arise about the behavioral or mental functioning of an individual, she is referred to a psychologist who is trained to make an assessment that might provide some answers. A judge may want to know if a confessed murderer is capable of understanding the consequences of her actions, or a teacher may want to know why a child has difficulty learning. A mental health worker may want to know the extent to which a patient's problems result from psychological disorders or from physical, organic disorders. When the psychologist's judgment may have a profound impact on a person's life, a *complete* assessment must involve more than just psychological testing. Tests may be very helpful but results should be interpreted in light of *all* available information about a person, including medical history, family life, previous difficulties, or noteworthy achievements (Matarazzo, 1990).

SUMMING UP

Assessment is the controlled measurement of individual differences which is used to understand and predict the behavior of individuals. The tradition of assessment for job placement can be traced back 4000 years to civil service exams in China. Galton proposed important early ideas about the measurement of intelligence but extended his theory to make social-political recommendations. Modern-day assessments are used for a variety of research and applied purposes, and they measure attributes such as general knowledge, cognitive capabilities, attitudes and interests, particular skills, and personality traits. The basic applied goal of assessment is to use samples of behavior to predict future behavior. The scientific goal of assessment is to use information gathered from systematic assessment of a large number of people to improve understanding of the reasons why people differ on certain attributes and traits that are of theoretical interest to researchers.

METHODS OF ASSESSMENT

Clearly, there are similarities between our own *informal* assessments of self and others and the *formal* assessments of professionals; but there are important differences, too. The methods of assessment psychologists use are developed more systematically, applied in a more organized way, and used for carefully specified purposes.

The way people differ in their abilities, personality, and behavior has long been of interest to philosophers, theologians, dramatists, and novelists. It is psychologists, however, who have taken as their special province the objective *measurement* of these differences. *Psychometrics* is the measurement of psychological functioning. This field achieves its objectives with statistical analysis and test construction as well as an understanding of mental processes.

We will first consider some of the characteristics that make professional assessments *formal*. We will then examine some of the techniques and sources of information psychologists use to make assessments. While some techniques are derived from particular *theoretical* perspectives, others are based on purely *empirical* grounds. Empirically constructed techniques are guided only by the data; they are built to make specific predictions and, therefore, utilize the items or questions that do the job regardless of whether or not they make theoretical sense. For example, students might be asked to indicate their views on a series of psychology issues.

If males consistently differ from females in their scores on this measure, then it could be used as one test of gender differences—even without offering any theory about why the two groups differ.

BASIC FEATURES OF FORMAL ASSESSMENT

To be useful for classifying individuals or for selecting those with particular qualities, an assessment procedure should meet three requirements. The assessment instrument should be (a) *reliable,* (b) *valid,* and (c) *standardized.* If it fails to meet these requirements, we cannot be sure whether the conclusions of the assessment can be trusted.

Reliability

A test is *reliable* if it measures something consistently. **Reliability** is the extent to which an assessment instrument can be trusted to give consistent scores, either on retests or when different raters judge the same performance. If your bathroom scale gives you a different reading each time you step on it (even though you haven't eaten or changed your clothing and little time has passed between testings), it is not doing its job. You would call it *unreliable* because you could not count on it to give consistent results.

One straightforward way to find out if a test is reliable is to calculate its **test-retest reliability.** This is a measure of the correlation between the scores of the same people on the same test given on two different occasions. A perfectly reliable test will yield a correlation coefficient of +1.00. This means that the same exact pattern of scores emerges both times; the same people who got the highest and lowest scores the first time do so again. A totally unreliable test results in a 0.00 correlation coefficient. That means there is no relationship between the first set of scores and the second set; someone who got the top score initially gets a completely different score the second time. As the correlation coefficient moves higher (toward the ideal of +1.00), the test is increasingly reliable.

There are two other ways to assess reliability. One is to administer alternate, **parallel forms** of a test instead of giving exactly the same test twice. Doing so reduces the effects of direct practice of the test questions, memory of the test questions, and the desire of an individual to appear consistent from one test to the next. Reliable tests yield comparable scores on parallel forms of the test. The other measure of reliability is the **internal consistency** of responses on a single test. For example, we can compare a person's score on the odd-numbered items of a test to the score on the even-numbered items. A reliable test yields the same score for each of its halves. It is then said to have high internal consistency on this measure of *split-half reliability*.

The best psychological tests have coefficients of reliability above 0.70. By comparison, achievement tests constructed by classroom teachers generally range in reliability from lows of 0.30 to highs of only about 0.60. These estimates apply to objective, true-false, and multiple-choice tests; you probably already know from personal experience about the greater unreliability of essay test scores.

Although a reliable test tends to give the same test scores when it is repeated, obtaining different test scores does not necessarily mean that a test is unreliable. Sometimes the variable being measured actually changes from one testing to the next. For example, if you took a test on theories of personality before and after reading Chapter 14, you would (I hope!) do better the second time—because you would then actually know more. In addition, many variables other than the one of primary interest may affect test scores; you may have different scores on different occasions because of changes in your mood, fatigue, and level of effort. Unless a test is designed to measure mood, fatigue, or motivation, these extraneous variables will alter the desired test performance, giving a false picture of your ability. Similarly, a teacher may grade an essay differently if he is fatigued (or bored) after reading many student essays. In such a case, the test itself would not be unreliable, but the scoring procedure would be. (What procedures should teachers follow to improve the reliability of their scoring process?)

Validity

The **validity** of a test is the degree to which it measures what an assessor intends it to measure. A valid test of intelligence measures a person's intelligence and predicts performance in situations where intelligence is important. Scores on a valid measure of creativity reflect actual creativity not drawing ability or moods. In general, then, validity is not a property of the test itself, but a feature of its use in making accurate predictions about outcomes.

To assess the **criterion validity** of a test, we compare a person's score on the test to his or her score on some other standard, or *criterion,* theoretically associated with what was measured by the test. Ideally, scores on the criterion directly reflect a personal characteristic or behavior that is related to, but not the same as, that assessed by the test. For example, if an aptitude test is designed to predict success in college, then college grades would be an appropriate criterion. If the test scores correlate highly with college grades, then the test has criterion validity. A major task of test developers is finding appropriate, measurable criteria.

For many personal qualities of interest to psychologists, no ideal criterion exists. No single behavior or objective measure of performance can tell us, for example, how anxious, depressed, or aggressive a person is overall. Psychologists have theories or *constructs* about these abstract qualities. Constructs are ideas about what affects personal qualities, the way they show up in behavior, and the way they relate to other variables. Although there may be no perfect, direct measure of a construct, there might be several tests or criteria that tap into a part of the construct. For example, we want to know if test items actually tap into constructs of intelligence.

Construct validation is the process of combining what we know about a large set of related measures, such as different tests, judges' ratings, and observed behaviors, to determine whether a theoretical construct is useful for understanding the data. Once we have determined that a construct is a good working model that explains a large body of data, we can examine separately each of the measures of the construct. The **construct validity** of a particular test is the degree to which it correlates positively with all the other data that represent valid measures of the construct (Loevinger, 1957). The initial stages of test construction are concerned with construct validity—with discovering the set of evidence about the traits and qualities that underlie the broader construct of interest, such as intelligence or creativity. Construct validity is not a quantitative or static measure of validity but a subjective evaluation of the appropriateness of the available evidence for measuring a given construct.

In the real world, tests with high construct validity correlate with many, but not all, of the other measures to which they are theoretically related. Sometimes the pattern of *which* criteria a test does and does not correlate with reveals something new about the measures, the construct, or the complexity of human behavior. The conditions under which a test is valid may be very specific, so it is always important to ask about a test, "For what purpose is it valid?"

For example, suppose you design a test to measure the ability of medical students to cope with stress, and you find that scores on it correlate well with students' ability to cope with classroom stress. You presume your test will also correlate with students' ability to deal with stressful hospital emergencies, but you discover it does not. Since you have demonstrated some validity, the important question is not *whether* the test is valid, but *when* it is valid, and *for what purpose*.

Validity has something in common with reliability. While reliability is measured by the degree to which a test correlates with itself (administered at different times or using different items), validity is measured by the degree to which the test correlates with something external to it (another test, a behavioral criterion, or judges' ratings). Usually, a test that is not reliable is also not valid, because a test that cannot predict *itself* will be unable to predict *anything else*. For example, if your class took a test of aggressiveness today, and scores were uncorrelated with scores from a parallel form of the test tomorrow (demonstrating unreliability), it is unlikely that the scores from either day would predict which students had fought or argued most frequently over a week's time—the two sets of test scores would not even make the same prediction!

A third type of validity is based on the *content*, rather than the correlates, of a test. When test items appear to be directly related to the construct or attribute of interest, the test has **face validity.** Face valid tests are very straightforward—they simply ask what the test maker needs to know, without any trick questions that a psychologist might interpret differently than the person taking the test. The person taking the test is simply trusted to answer accurately and honestly.

Of course, face validity is never enough of a reliability measure. In order to be useful, a face valid test must also have criterion or construct validity (to demonstrate that it does *in fact* measure what the items appear to measure). When it does, face validity can be very helpful because it allows the test makers to understand *why* a test works as it does. When people taking the test are not motivated to lie about themselves, face valid tests can have excellent criterion and construct validity. Often they can uncover information that no one else would know. However, face validity is problematic when people are motivated to misrepresent themselves. One interesting instance of the problem with face validity was found in the case of institutionalized mental patients who did *not* want to be released from their familiar, structured environment.

> These long-term schizophrenic patients were interviewed by the staff about how disturbed they were. When they were given an interview to assess if they were well enough to be moved to an open ward, these patients gave generally positive self-references. However, when the purpose of the interview was to assess their suitability for *discharge,* the patients gave more negative self-references because they did not want to be discharged. Psychiatrists who rated the interview data, without awareness of this experimental variation in the purpose of the interview, judged those who gave more negative self-references as more severely disturbed and recommended against their discharge. So the patients achieved the

assessment outcome that they had wanted. The psychiatrists' assessment may also have been influenced by their perspective that anyone who wanted to stay in a mental hospital must be very disturbed (Braginsky & Braginsky, 1967).

Time out for a *critical thinking exercise*. Can you think of an instance when a test might be highly reliable but not valid at all? A popular cult group currently is using a bogus test as a recruitment gimmick. Expensive courses offered by the cult promise to remedy the alleged defects in personality that have been uncovered by their test.

The responses on this test appear to be scored by a computer that generates an impressive looking graph of summary scores on a series of traits, such as *irresponsible, unstable,* and *inhibited.* The test is highly reliable—it gives about the same pattern of scores each time. Those scores invariably reveal the unstable character of the test taker.

The test is highly reliable because the scores are preprogrammed into the computer and have nothing to do with the individual's answers to the test items. Recently, I conducted a class exercise to expose students to this false use of psychological testing. On different trials, I asked students to fill out the test randomly, to answer the questions honestly, and to answer them consistently but in opposite ways. Regardless of the way the students completed the test, the results were always the same. According to an evaluator's standard instruction sheet (which had been attached mistakenly to one of the test analysis sheets that I have seen), everyone is told that the test shows they are "undependable," "have little self-confidence," "have an unstable character," and "are irresponsible" in their "lives and work." Beware of sophisticated hucksters with a test in one hand and a contract for repairing your personality—or your roof—in the other.

Standardization and Norms

To be most useful, a measuring device should be standardized. **Standardization** is the administration of a testing device to all persons in the same way under the same conditions. Through this method, we can establish **norms,** or statistical standards for a test that allow each individual's score to be compared with the scores of others in a defined group.

Suppose you get a score of 18 on a test designed to reveal how depressed you are. What does that mean? Are you a little depressed, not at all depressed, or about averagely depressed? You would want to compare your individual score to typical scores of other students. You would check the test norms to see what the usual range of scores is and what the average is for students of your age and sex. You probably encountered test norms when you received your scores on aptitude tests such as the SAT. The norms let you know how your scores compared to those of other students and helped you interpret how well you had done relative to that *normative population.*

Group norms are most useful for interpreting individual scores when the standardization group shares important qualities with the individuals tested (such as age, social class, and experience). When this is the case, the group norms are a useful measure against which an individual's score can be interpreted. So whenever you are given the results of any psychological test, the first question you should ask is, "*Compared to what?*" What norms were used to interpret *relative* performance?

For norms to be meaningful, everyone must take the same test. That sounds obvious, but it may not always occur in practice. Some people may be allowed more time than others, given clearer or more detailed instructions, permitted to ask questions, or motivated by a tester to perform better.

> As a graduate student at Yale, I administered a scale to assess children's degree of test anxiety in grade-school classes. Before starting, one teacher told her class, "We're going to have some fun with this new kind of question game this nice man will play with you." A teacher in another classroom prepared her class for the same assessment by cautioning, "This psychologist from Yale University is going to give you a test to see what you are thinking; I hope you will do well and show how good our class is!" (Zimbardo, 1958).

Could I directly compare the scores of the children in these two classes on this "same" test? The answer is no, because the test was not administered in a standardized way. In this case, the scores of the children in the second class were higher on test anxiety. If my interest was in class atmosphere and anxiety, the test results would have provided very useful information; however, in this case, I wanted to know about individual children's usual levels of test anxiety. When procedures do not include explicit instructions about the way to administer the test or the way to score the results, it is difficult to interpret what a given test score means or how it relates to any comparison group.

SOURCES OF INFORMATION

Psychological assessment methods can be organized according to four techniques used to gather information about a person: interviews, life history or archival data, tests, and situational observations. They can also be

A psychologist may administer a battery of tests to determine whether there is an emotional problem.

classified according to the person who is supplying the information: the person being assessed or other people reporting on the person being assessed. When the person being assessed is providing the information, the methods are called *self reports;* when others are supplying the data, the methods are called *observer reports*.

Which technique you use and who you ask to supply information depends on the nature of data you need and the purpose of the assessment. A complete assessment should use as many different techniques and sources of information as are available.

Four Assessment Techniques

An **interview** is a very direct approach to learning about someone. The interview content and style may be casual and unstructured, tailored to fit the person being interviewed. On the other hand, interviews may be highly structured or standardized, asking very specific questions in a very specific way. Counselors find unstructured interviews useful in planning individualized treatment programs. Structured interviews are preferred for job interviews and psychological research, when it is important that many people be assessed accurately, completely, consistently, and without bias.

A well-trained interviewer must have five important skills. These abilities are putting the respondent at ease, knowing how to elicit the desired information, maintaining control of the direction and pace of the

interview, establishing and maintaining feelings of rapport between interviewer and respondent, and finally, bringing the interview to a satisfactory conclusion.

Interview data may be supplemented with **life history** or **archival data,** information about a person's life taken from different types of available records, especially those of different time periods and in relation to other people. These records may include school or military performances, written work (stories and drawings), personal journals, medical data, photographs, and videotapes.

A **psychological test** can measure virtually all aspects of human functioning, including intelligence, personality, and creativity. A major advantage of tests over interviews is that they provide *quantitative* characterizations of an individual by using normative comparisons with others.

Tests are economical, easy to use, and provide important normative data in quantitative form, but they are not always useful for finding out what a person actually *does,* especially when a person cannot objectively judge or report his or her own behavior. Psychologists use **situational behavior observations** to assess behavior objectively in laboratory or real-life settings. An observer watches an individual's behavioral patterns in one or more situations, such as at home, at work, or in school. The goal of these observations is to discover the determinants and consequences of various responses and habits of the individual. This approach came out of the traditions of experimental psychology and social-learning theory. Direct situational observations are especially useful for (a) finding out the conditions in which problem behaviors occur in order to plan and evaluate behavior-modification therapy; (b) observing job applicants' behavior in a joblike situation; and (c) determining whether what people say corresponds to what they do in order to validate test and interview data.

Self-report Methods

Self-report methods require respondents to answer questions or give information about themselves. This information may be gathered from an interview, a test, or a personal journal. One very easily administered self-report is the *inventory,* a standardized, written test with a multiple choice, true-false, or rating format. An inventory might require about your personality, your health, or your life experiences. For example, you might be asked how frequently you have headaches, how assertive you think you are, or how stressful you find your job to be. Such measures are valuable because they tap into an individual's personal experiences and feelings. They are convenient because they do not require trained interviewers and they are generally easy to score. The greatest shortcoming of self-report measures is that

ALL DRINKERS ARE NOT CREATED EQUAL

When she started college, Marcy had no experience with alcohol. Her parents neither smoked nor drank, and throughout high school Marcy respected their wishes that she abstain. In her freshman year of college, however, after some friendly prodding by dorm mates, she decided it was time she learned how to drink. At first, Marcy limited herself to mixed drinks, such as whiskey sours and rum and cokes, but soon she broadened her repertoire. She prided herself on being able to "keep up with the boys" and believed her increased tolerance to alcohol would prove an asset when she entered the business world, where drinks and deals often keep close company. What Marcy did not know is that women are physiologically more susceptible to the effects of alcohol than men. The alcohol industry targets women in many of their ads, expecting that, by 1994, American women will spend $30 billion a year on alcohol, a 50 percent boost in only a decade. These ads present an intoxicating mix of glamour and power and fail to mention biological differences that enhance the risk that females will suffer alcohol-related problems (*University of California, Berkeley, Wellness Letter*, 1989).

Several studies in the 1970s and 1980s established that women were more susceptible than men to alcohol-related liver disease (Norton et al., 1987). Women were also found to have higher blood-alcohol levels than men after drinking equivalent amounts (Jones &

Jones, 1976), but, until recently, this difference was unexplained.

Although most alcohol is not metabolized until it reaches the liver, some is broken down by an

enzyme called *alcohol dehydrogenase* while still in the stomach. The amount of alcohol that reaches the blood stream is decreased when the activity level of this enzyme is high (Frezza et al., 1990). In 1990, a team of American and Italian researchers discovered that alcohol dehydrogenase is significantly weaker in women than men. The researchers studied 20 men and 23 women; six in each group were alcoholics. Measurements of blood alcohol levels and stomach enzyme activity indicated that women metabolized alcohol much less efficiently than men. Even after controlling for differences in body weight, researchers discovered that significantly more alcohol circulated in the women's blood-streams than the men's. For alcoholics, the results were especially striking. Male alcoholics metabolized alcohol less efficiently than non-alcoholics, but female alcoholics showed almost no evidence of *any* stomach enzyme activity; it was as though the alcohol had been injected directly into their veins (Frezza et al., 1990).

What is the message for college women such as Marcy? Because all drinkers are *not* created equal, moderate drinking does not mean the same thing for males and females. Females are unlikely to drink a male "under the table." Rather, it is more likely that their drinking will result in a greater loss of control.

sometimes people are not really in touch with their feelings or can't objectively report their own behavior. However, depending on the purpose of the assessment, sometimes a person's subjective experience is actually of more interest to the tester than the objective reality. For example, your *perceived* competence may be more important than your actual skills in determining whether you enter a challenging and exciting career.

Observer-report Methods

In psychological assessment, **observer-report methods** involve a systematic evaluation of some aspect of a person's behavior by another person, a rater, or judge. Observer reports may consist of very specific situational behavior observations or more generalized ratings. For example, teacher's aides may observe a preschool class and record the number of times each child performs particular behaviors, such as shoving, hitting, or sharing a toy, during a particular observation period. Alternately, teachers, parents, and anyone else who knows them well might be asked to rate the children on the way they play with others and on how shy they are around strangers.

While situational behavior observations are typically made *on-line,* at the time the behavior is performed, ratings are typically made *after* an observation period. Sometimes judges are asked to first record specific behaviors and then make overall ratings based on them. Often, ratings are made according to detailed guidelines provided by the developers of an assessment technique. At other times, the guidelines are less precise, allowing spontaneous reactions and informal impressions to play a greater role.

What drawbacks could result from such ratings? One is that ratings may tell more about the *judge,* or about the judge's relationship with the person, than about the true characteristics of the person being rated. For example, if you like someone, you may tend to judge him or her favorably on nearly every dimension. This type of rating bias—in which an overall positive or negative feeling about the person is extended to the specific dimensions being evaluated—is referred to as a **halo effect.** A different type of bias occurs when a rater thinks most people in a certain category (for example, Republicans, Arabs, antiwar protesters, the unemployed) have certain qualities. The rater may "see" those qualities in any individual who happens to be in that category. This type of bias is called a **stereotype effect.**

Rating biases can be reduced by (a) phrasing rating items in ways that do not reflect connotations, such as "keeps to him/herself" in place of "withdrawn"; (b) making specific rules for each rating level, such as "if the person does X, give a rating of 10"; and (c) using several raters so that the bias introduced by each judge's unique point of view is canceled out by the other judges.

Whenever you have more than one observer, you can calculate the **interjudge reliability,** which is the degree to which the different observers make similar ratings or agree about what each subject did during an observation period. Typically, interjudge reliability will be highest when judges record the specific behaviors observed in a specific situation rather than general impressions of behavior. Therefore, people who see you in *different* situations will agree more about what you are like (general ratings) than about the precise behaviors that you exhibit.

Before turning to examine the specifics of mental and personality testing, let's consider one final general point about assessment. In our everyday lives, we often

make inferences about people's characteristics and traits from our observations of their behavior in particular settings. However, in trying to understand the causes of these individual differences, we frequently fail to take into consideration cohort effects, group membership, or cultural differences that play a dominant role in the behavior of individuals. For example, if one child is more impulsive than another, it may be because of an age difference or cultural difference. What might you conclude about a woman who drinks only a moderate amount at a party but gets drunk very fast and loses control? This chapter's Close-Up feature provides an example of why, in some cases, we have to interpret individual performance according to norms that are appropriate for a specific subgroup.

Summing Up

We have seen that the information used in assessments can come from many sources. Self-report or observer-report information may be gathered through interviews, compilation of life history data, and psychological tests. Observer reports can also be gathered through situational behavior observations. A comprehensive assessment should include data from as many different sources as possible.

The most important features for any method of assessment is that it should be reliable, valid, and standardized. Reliability means that a technique gives consistent scores on different occasions (test-retest reliability), on different test items (parallel forms and split-half reliability), and with different observers (interjudge reliability). Validity means that a technique measures what it is supposed to measure, as shown by its correlation with a related technique (criterion validity) or with a large body of relevant data (construct validity). Finally, standardization means that a test is always administered and scored in the same way, so that a person's score may be compared to the norms of other people of the same age and sex who took the same test. Gender differences in alcohol tolerance, controlling for weight differences, put women at risk for quicker loss of control when they drink the same amount of alcohol as men.

Assessing Intelligence

How should we define intelligence? Scientists have yet to agree on a single definition, but most would include in their measure of intelligence at least three types of skills: (a) adapting to new situations and changing task demands; (b) learning or profiting optimally from experience or training; and (c) thinking abstractly using symbols and concepts (Phares, 1984).

More specific ways of defining intelligence are linked to various theories of human adaptation and intellectual functioning. These theories have emerged from all walks of psychology, including neurological-biology, learning theory, and human development.

We will define **intelligence** as the capacity to profit from experience—to go beyond what is perceived to imagine symbolic possibilities. It is a hypothetical construct, usually equated with higher-level abstract thought processes. Not directly observable, intelligence is verified only by the operations (tests) used to measure it and by how it functions in criterion situations that are developed to validate it.

Through intellectual development, humans have been able to transcend their physical limitations and gain dominance over more physically powerful or numerous animals. Intelligence enables us to respond flexibly and imaginatively to environmental challenges; it is the reason our species has survived and prospered.

The way we think about intelligence and mental functioning influences the way we try to assess it. Some psychologists believe that human intelligence can be quantified and reduced to a single score. Others argue that assessment should depend on a schema of the way the different components of a person's intelligence work together (Hunt, 1984; Sternberg, 1985).

Is intelligence a unitary attribute (such as height) meaning that people can be assessed in terms of how smart they are? Is intelligence instead a collection of mental competencies (analogous to athletic abilities) meaning that people's intelligence for different kinds of tasks can be assessed? In this section, we will consider alternative views about the best way to define and understand intelligence. We will also tackle the question of why intelligence should be measured. We mentioned earlier that, while some people believe that assessment of intellectual abilities is one of psychology's most significant contributions to society, others maintain that it is a systematic attempt by elitists to weed out undesirables (Gould, 1981). We will examine some of the evidence for such conflicting claims, but, first, we need a bit more history to set the stage of these claims.

HISTORICAL CONTEXT

A brief look at the history of intelligence testing will reveal how practical social and political concerns, measurement issues, and theory were entwined in the development of intelligence tests for children and adults. The movement to measure intelligence began in France as an attempt to identify children who were unable to learn in school. Soon, however, intelligence testing became an all-American enterprise.

Binet's First Intelligence Test

The year 1905 marked the first published account of a workable intelligence test. **Alfred Binet** had responded to the call of the French Minister of Public Instruction for the development of a way to more effectively teach developmentally disabled children in the public schools. Binet and his colleague, Theophile Simon, believed that measuring a child's intellectual ability was necessary for planning an instructional program. Their radical proposal was that education be fit to the child's level of competence and not that the child be fit to a fixed curriculum.

Binet attempted to devise an objective test of intellectual performance that could be used to classify and separate developmentally disabled from normal schoolchildren. He hoped that such a test would reduce the school's reliance on the more subjective, and perhaps biased, evaluations of teachers.

There are four important features of Binet's approach. First, he interpreted scores on his test as an estimate of *current performance* and *not* as a measure of *innate intelligence*. Second, he wanted the test scores to be used to identify children who needed special help and not to stigmatize them. Third, he emphasized that training and opportunity could affect intelligence and he wanted to identify areas of performance in which special education could help these children. Finally, he constructed his test empirically, rather than tying it to a particular theory of intelligence.

To *quantify* intellectual performance, Binet designed age-appropriate problems or test items on which many children's responses could be compared. The problems on the test were chosen so that they could be scored objectively, could vary in content, were not heavily influenced by differences in children's environments, and tested judgment and reasoning rather than rote memory (Binet, 1911).

Children of various ages were tested, and the average score for normal children at each age was computed. Then, each individual child's performance was compared to the average for other children of his or her age. Test results were expressed in terms of the average age at which normal children achieved a particular score. This measure was called the **mental age** (MA). When a child's scores on various items of the test added up to the average score of a group of 5 year olds, the child was said to have a *mental age* of 5, regardless of his or her actual **chronological age** (CA). *Retardation* was then defined operationally by Binet as being two mental-age years behind chronological age.

As more children were tested longitudinally, Binet found that those assessed as developmentally disabled at one age fell further behind the mental age of their birth cohorts as they grew older. A child of 5 who performed at the level of 3 year olds might, at the age of 10, perform at the level of 6 year olds. Although the *ratio* of mental age to chronological age would be constant (3/5 and 6/10), the total number of mental-age years of retardation would have increased from two to four.

Binet's successful development of an intelligence test had great impact in the United States. A unique combination of historical events and social-political forces had prepared the United States for an explosion of interest in assessing mental ability. Since the early decades of this century, the interest of psychologists in intellectual assessment has flourished into a mental-measurement industry.

Mental Measurement in the United States

At the beginning of the twentieth century, the United States was a nation in turmoil. Global economic, social, and political conditions resulted in millions of immigrants entering the country. New universal education laws flooded schools with students. When World War I began, millions of volunteers marched into recruiting stations. These events—world conditions, new education laws, and World War I—all resulted in large numbers of people needing to be identified, documented, and classified. Some form of assessment was needed to facilitate these tasks (Chapman, 1988). At the time, "Intelligence test results were used not only to differentiate [among] children experiencing academic problems, but also as a measuring stick to organize an entire society" (Hale, 1983, p. 373). Assessment was seen as a way to inject order into a chaotic society and as an inexpensive, democratic way to separate those who could benefit from education or military leadership training from those who could not.

In 1917, when the United States declared war on Germany, it was necessary to establish quickly a military force led by competent leaders. Recruiters needed to determine who of the many people who had been drafted had the ability to learn quickly and benefit from special leadership training. New nonverbal, group-administered tests of mental ability were used to evaluate over 1.7 million recruits. Incidentally, a group of famous psychologists, including Lewis Terman, Edward Thorndike, and Robert Yerkes, designed these new tests in only one month's time (Lennon, 1985).

One consequence of this large-scale testing program was that the American public came to accept the idea that intelligence tests could differentiate people in terms of leadership ability and other socially important characteristics. This acceptance led to the widespread use of tests in schools and industry. Another, more unfortunate, consequence was that the tests reinforced prevailing prejudices, because the army reports indicated that differences in test scores were linked to race and country of origin (Yerkes, 1921). Of course, the same statistics *could* have been used to demonstrate that environmental disadvantages limit the full development of people's intellectual abilities. Instead, they simply fueled racist ideology.

IQ TESTS

Although Binet began the standardized assessment of intellectual ability, statistically-minded U.S. psychologists took the ball from him and ran. U.S. psychologists modified Binet's scoring procedure, improved the reliability of the tests, and studied the scores of enormous normative samples of people who took the new tests. They also developed the IQ, or *intelligence quotient*. The IQ was a numerical, standardized measure of intelligence, obtained from an individual's score on an intelligence test. Two families of individually administered IQ tests are used widely today: the Stanford-Binet scales and the Wechsler scales.

The Stanford-Binet Intelligence Scale

Stanford University's **Lewis Terman,** a former public school administrator, realized that Binet's method for assessing intelligence was important. He adapted Binet's test questions for U.S. schoolchildren, standardized administration of the test, and developed age-level norms by giving the test to thousands of children. In 1916 he published the Stanford Revision of the Binet Tests, commonly referred to as the *Stanford-Binet Intelligence Scale* (Terman, 1916).

With his new test, Terman provided a base for the concept of the **intelligence quotient,** or IQ (coined by Stern, 1914). The IQ was the ratio of mental age to chronological age (multiplied by 100 to eliminate decimals):

$$IQ = MA \div CA \times 100$$

A child with a CA of 8 whose test scores revealed an MA of 10 had an IQ of 125 *(10 ÷ 8 × 100 = 125),* while a child of that same chronological age who performed at the level of 6 year olds had an IQ of 75 *(6 ÷ 8 × 100 = 75).* Individuals who performed at the mental age equivalent to their chronological age had IQs of 100, which was considered to be the average or normal IQ.

The new Stanford-Binet test soon became a standard instrument in clinical psychology, psychiatry, and educational counseling. At the same time, Terman's

A psychologist administers an intelligence test to a 4-year-old child. The performance part of this test includes a block design task, an object completion task, and a shape identification task.

make up intelligence. His implicit message was that IQ reflected something essential and unchanging about human intelligence.

Terman was influenced in his beliefs by the leading assessment theorist of the 1920s, **Charles Spearman** of England. Spearman had concluded that all mental tests were a combination of an innate general intellectual ability, the **g-factor,** and some specific abilities as well (Spearman, 1927). "It was almost universally assumed by psychologists and by the general public in these early years that individual differences in intelligence were innately determined. One's intellectual level was a characteristic one must accept rather than try to change" (Tyler, 1988, p. 128).

The Stanford-Binet contains a series of subtests, each tailored for a particular mental age. A series of minor revisions were made on these subtests in 1937, 1960, and 1972, to achieve three goals: (a) to extend the range of the test to measure the IQ of very young children and very intelligent adults; (b) to update vocabulary items that had changed in difficulty with changes in society, and (c) to update the norms, or age-appropriate average scores (Terman & Merrill, 1937, 1960, 1972).

IQ scores are no longer derived by dividing mental age by chronological age. If you took the test today, your score would be added up and directly compared to the scores of other people your age. An IQ of 100 would indicate that 50 percent of those your age earned lower scores. Scores between 90 and 110 are now labeled normal, above 120 are superior, and below 70 are evidence of developmental disability (see **Figure 15.1**).

The Stanford-Binet scales were criticized because the subtests used to measure IQ at different ages focused on different types of skills. For example, 2 to 4 year olds were tested on their ability to manipulate objects, whereas adults were tested almost exclusively on verbal

adoption of the IQ concept contributed to the development of a new conceptualization of the purpose and meaning of intelligence testing. Unlike Binet, Terman believed that intelligence was an inner quality, that it was largely hereditary, and that IQ tests could measure this inner quality throughout the range of abilities that

FIGURE 15.1 *DISTRIBUTION OF IQ SCORES AMONG A LARGE SAMPLE*

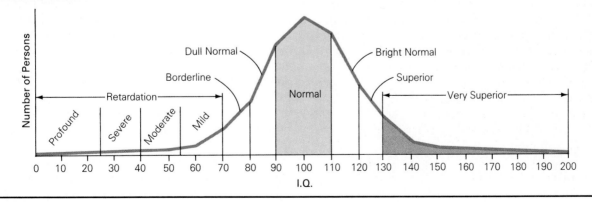

items. As the scientific understanding of intelligence increased, psychologists found it increasingly important to measure *several* intellectual abilities at *all* age levels. A recent revision of the Stanford-Binet now provides different scores for several mental skills, but it has not been widely accepted (Vernon, 1987).

The Wechsler Intelligence Scales

David Wechsler of Bellevue Hospital in New York set out to correct the dependence on verbal items in the assessment of adult intelligence. In 1939, he published the Wechsler-Bellevue Intelligence Scale, which combined verbal subtests with nonverbal or performance subtests. Thus, in addition to an overall IQ score, subjects were given separate estimates of verbal IQ and nonverbal IQ. After a few changes, the test was retitled the *Wechsler Adult Intelligence Scale*—the WAIS in 1955, and the revised WAIS-R today (Wechsler, 1981).

There are six *verbal* subtests of the WAIS-R: Information, Vocabulary, Comprehension, Arithmetic, Similarities (stating how two things are alike), and Digit Span (repeating a series of digits after the examiner). These tests are both written and oral. The five *performance* subtests involve manipulation of materials and have little or no verbal content. In the Block Design test, for example, a subject tries to reproduce designs shown on cards by fitting together blocks with colored sides. The Digit Symbol test provides a key that matches 9 symbols to 9 numeric digits, and the task is to write the appropriate digits under the symbols on another page. Other performance tests involve Picture Arrangement, Picture Completion, and Object Assembly. If you

One of the tests adults can take is the WAIS-R.

were to take the WAIS-R, you would perform all 11 subtests, and receive 3 scores: a Verbal IQ, a Performance IQ, and an overall or Full-scale IQ.

The WAIS-R is designed for people 18 years or older, but similar tests have been developed for children. The *Wechsler Intelligence Scale for Children—Revised* (WISC-R, 1974) is suited for children ages 6 to 17, and the *Wechsler Preschool and Primary Scale of Intelligence* (WPPSI) for children ages 4 to 6 1/2 years. Some subtests were specially created for use with children, but most have a direct counterpart in the WAIS-R. For example, the WAIS-R Digit Symbol test is very similar to the WISC-R Coding test and the WPPSI Animal House test. Digit Symbol and Coding involve matching symbols to numeric digits, while Animal House requires preschoolers to match pictures of animals with houses of different colors.

The WAIS-R, the WISC-R, and the WPPSI form a family of intelligence tests that yield a Verbal IQ, a Performance IQ, and a Full-Scale IQ at all age levels. In addition, they provide comparable subtest scores that allow researchers to track the development of even more specific intellectual abilities. For this reason, the Wechsler scales are particularly valuable when the same individual is to be tested at different ages—for example, when a child's progress in response to different educational programs is monitored.

Group Tests of Intelligence

In addition to the individually given Stanford-Binet and Wechsler scales, there are many other tests that are given to groups of individuals. If you went through a U.S. school system, chances are you took several of these—some students take as many as 20 standardized group tests before graduating from high school (Seligman, 1988). These tests are restricted to written items that can be scored easily, so they measure a narrowly-defined type of intellectual functioning, often called *school ability* or *scholastic aptitude*.

Two of the most popular group tests of intelligence are the *Cognitive Abilities Test* (CAT; Thorndike and Hagen, 1978), and the *School and College Ability Tests* (SCAT, Series III; Educational Testing Service, 1980). They provide separate verbal and quantitative (math) scores, and the CAT also provides a nonverbal score. They are valid predictors of school achievement, and are as reliable as the Stanford-Binet and the Wechsler tests.

The primary benefits of group tests are that they require no special training to administer, they can be administered to a large group in less time than a Stanford-Binet or Wechsler test can be given to one person, and they are quickly and accurately scored by computer. These tests are ideal when a large number of

In these examples from the WAIS-R for children, subjects are asked to put the frames in order so they make a story.

people must be tested in an economical way. However, individualized tests provide some rich, clinical detail that group tests cannot. For example, a psychologist providing counseling or planning a treatment may wish to observe firsthand how a person deals with a frustrating test problem or note the tasks a person most enjoyed (Lennon, 1985).

In addition, there are many reasons that people's *scores* on an intelligence test can be lower than their actual ability. One person may be distracted by unusual surroundings or by extreme test anxiety. Another may misunderstand the instructions because of visual or hearing impairments or difficulty with the English language. These effects contaminate test performance and can invalidate an individual's score on any test. However, the problem is more likely to be noticed (and corrected) when an intelligence test is administered individually than in an anonymous mass testing.

It is important to remember that IQ scores, by themselves, do not tell how much children know or what they can do. A high-school student with an IQ of 100 has knowledge and skills that a fourth-grader with a higher IQ of 120 does not have. In addition, people labeled developmentally disabled on the basis of their IQ scores vary considerably in what they are able to do and in how much they can learn through instruction. Similarly, elderly subjects whose response speed has slowed down perform more poorly than the young on test items where speed is important, but they still have greater *wisdom* in many measurable domains (Baltes, 1990). Thus, an operational definition such as "intelligence *is* what intelligence tests *measure*," does not

cover all that we mean by the concept of human intelligence.

Psychometric Theories of Intelligence

Psychometrics is the field of psychology that specializes in mental testing in any of its facets, including personality assessment, intelligence evaluation, and aptitude measurement. Psychometric approaches to intelligence study the *statistical relationships* between different measures, such as the 11 subtests of the WAIS-R, and then make inferences about the nature of human intelligence on the basis of those relationships. One common approach uses a technique called *factor analysis,* a statistical procedure that locates a smaller number of dimensions, clusters, or factors from a larger set of independent variables or items on a test. The goal of factor analysis is to identify a small number of factors that represent the basic psychological dimensions being investigated. Factors are not traits, they are statistical regularities in the data base. However, traits are inferred from the factor; researchers can analyze the nature of the items or information that makes up each factor.

Raymond Cattell (1963), using more advanced factor analytic techniques, determined that general intelligence can be broken down into two relatively independent components he called *crystallized* and *fluid* intelligence. **Crystallized intelligence** involves the knowledge a person has already acquired and the ability to access that knowledge; it is measured by tests of vocabulary, arithmetic, and general information. **Fluid intelligence** is the ability to see complex relationships and solve problems; it is measured by tests of block designs and spatial visualization in which the background information needed to solve a problem is included or readily apparent.

Recent investigations indicate that both crystallized and fluid intelligence are partly inherited and partly learned. In addition, some psychometricians believe there may be no such thing as general intelligence. Instead, there may be four or five relatively independent characteristics of people which influence their performance on different intellectual tasks. Likely candidates for these characteristics are fluid, crystallized, verbal, and auditory intelligence as well as speediness (Horn, 1985).

Guilford's Structure of Intellect

J. P. Guilford, another psychometrician, used factor analysis to examine the demands of many intelligence-related tasks. His Structure of Intellect model specifies three features of intellectual tasks: the *content,* or type of information; the *product,* or form in which information is represented; and the *operation,* or type of mental activity performed.

As shown in **Figure 15.2,** in the Structure of Intellect model, there are five kinds of content—visual, auditory, symbolic, semantic, and behavioral; six kinds of

products—units, classes, relations, systems, transformations, and implications; and five kinds of operations—evaluation, convergent production, divergent production, memory, and cognition. Each task performed by the intellect can be identified according to the particular types of content, products, and operations involved. Further, Guilford believes that each content-product-operation combination (each small cube in the model) represents a distinct mental ability.

There are 150 possible combinations of contents, products, and operations; that is, any of the five types of content may take the form of any of the six products *(5 × 6 = 30),* and on these 30 resulting kinds of information, any of the five types of operations may be performed *(30 × 5 = 150).* For example, a test of vocabulary would assess your ability for *cognition* of *units* with *semantic content,* while learning a dance routine requires *memory* for *behavioral systems.*

This theoretical model is analogous to a chemist's periodic table of elements. By means of such a systematic framework, intellectual factors, similar to chemical elements, may be postulated before they are discovered. In 1961, when Guilford proposed his model, nearly 40 intellectual abilities had been identified. Researchers have since accounted for over 100 (Guilford, 1985).

Cognitive Science Approaches

Since Guilford, many psychologists have broadened their conceptions of intelligence to include much more than performance on traditional IQ tests. However, while Guilford denied mental abilities in terms of the features of the *tasks* we confront, cognitive scientists focus on the different *cognitive processes,* or mental activities, we use when we learn new things or find a novel solution to a problem.

Hunt's Problem-solving Intelligence One proponent of the cognitive processes view, **Earl Hunt** (1983), believes that the interesting individual differences in people's intelligence are not to be found in test scores but in the way different individuals go about solving a problem. He identifies three ways cognitive processes may differ in individuals: (a) choice about the way to internally (mentally) represent a problem; (b) strategies for manipulating mental representations; and (c) the abilities necessary to execute whatever basic information-processing steps a strategy requires.

Hunt encourages cognitive scientists to do something they have largely avoided: study *individual differences* instead of only the averaged reactions of many people to the same experimental stimuli. Using Hunt's model, special tasks can be designed to allow scientists to observe individual differences in the way people represent problems (using images or verbalization, for ex-

---

FIGURE 15.2   *THE STRUCTURE OF INTELLECT*

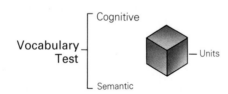

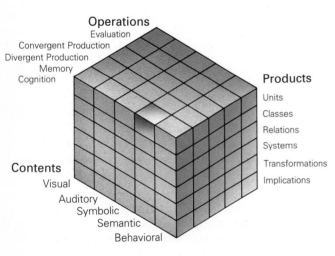

---

ample), the way they encode material, and the way information is transferred in their working memories. This approach encourages scientists to see the flexibility and adaptiveness of human thinking. Second, it promotes a different view of classification and selection. Rather than categorizing people by their IQ level, this view supports *diagnostic assessment* with the goal of making the best use of each person's cognitive abilities and skills (Hunt, 1984).

Sternberg's Componential Analysis **Robert Sternberg** (1986) also stresses the importance of cognitive processes in problem solving. For tasks such as those on traditional IQ tests that involve general information, vocabulary, arithmetic, insight, or analytic reasoning, Sternberg recommends *componential analysis* of the processes used to solve them. He identifies three types of *components* that are central to his model of information processing: (a) knowledge acquisition components, for learning new facts; (b) performance components, for problem-solving strategies and techniques; and (c) metacognitive components, for selecting a strategy and monitoring progress toward success.

However, these components tell only part of the story. In addition to this *componential intelligence*, which is reflected in IQ scores and college grades, Sternberg identifies two other important types of intelligence: experiential and contextual.

Experiential intelligence is reflected in creative accomplishments. It involves the ability to picture the external world using alternate types of internal (mental) representations and the ability to combine very different experiences in unique and original ways. It is easy to see how artists, such as Pablo Picasso, William Shakespeare, and Twyla Tharp, captivate audiences by representing commonplace things in unusual ways. Others, such as Albert Einstein and Sigmund Freud, have used their experiential intelligence to develop provocative scientific theories.

Contextual intelligence is reflected in the practical management of day-to-day affairs. It involves your ability to adapt to new and different contexts, make the most of your available resources, and effectively shape your environment to suit your needs. Contextual intelligence is what people sometimes call *street smarts* or *business sense*. Keep in mind that contextual and experiential intelligence would be overlooked if we examined only IQ scores.

Sternberg's method of breaking down traditional IQ into its components of knowledge acquisition, performance, and metacognitive control, has been useful for identifying specific problems and designing interventions to help people who are developmentally disabled or who have suffered a decline in their cognitive

Robert Sternberg (*Discovering Psychology,* 1990, Program 16)

skills due to trauma or disease. In addition, his idea of three distinct intelligences that are important in different areas of life is useful in assessing people's special strengths and in helping them to make the most of the skills the have.

> In one study, adults who had been diagnosed as developmentally disabled in childhood were studied 40 years later. Those who had been in a stable, supportive environment had developed good contextual intelligence that helped them to hold jobs and lead satisfying lives in spite of their deficit in componential intelligence (R. Ross et al., 1986).

Gardner's Seven Intelligences Another new and different theory of intelligence has been proposed by **Howard Gardner** (1983). He identifies intelligence in terms of numerous abilities, each of which is equally important. The value of any of the abilities is culturally determined, according to what is needed by, useful to, and prized by a given society. There are seven intelligences:

1. linguistic ability
2. logical-mathematical ability
3. spatial ability (navigating in space, forming, transforming, and using mental images)
4. musical ability (perceiving and creating pitch patterns)
5. bodily-kinesthetic ability (skills of motor movement, coordination)
6. interpersonal ability (understanding others)
7. intrapersonal ability (understanding oneself, developing a sense of identity)

One of Gardner's seven intelligences is bodily kinesthetic ability, shown here in the grace and coordination of the dancers.

Gardner argues that Western society promotes the first two intelligences, while other societies value others. For example, in the Caroline Island of Micronesia, sailors must be able to navigate long distances without maps, using only their spatial intelligence and bodily-kinesthetic intelligence. Such abilities count more in that society than the ability to write a term paper. In Bali, where artistic performance is part of everyday life, musical intelligence and talents involved in coordinating intricate dance steps are highly valued. Interpersonal intelligence is more central to collectivist societies where collective action and communal life are emphasized than it is in individualistic societies such as our own (Triandis, 1990).

Assessing these kinds of intelligence demands more than paper-and-pencil tests and simple quantified

Howard Gardner (*Discovering Psychology,* 1990, Program 16)

measures. Gardner's tests of intelligence require that the subject be observed and assessed in a variety of life situations as well as in the artificial samples of life depicted in traditional intelligence tests. The theory is sound, but the way to operationally verify it through valid, reliable tests is still in the process of being developed.

THE USE AND MISUSE OF IQ

What purposes do IQ test scores serve? How should an IQ score be interpreted? What damage might be done if an IQ score is used inappropriately? These questions have been the source of many emotionally charged debates because the use of tests has an extensive impact on industry, society, and individual lives. We will first outline the issues in this debate and then examine the evidence for each side.

The Debate over IQ Testing

In the early 1900s, psychologist **Henry Goddard** endorsed the IQ scale as a fixed measure of the mind. He advocated mental testing of all immigrants and the *selective exclusion* of those who were found to be "mentally defective." Indeed, with some encouragement from assessment-minded psychologists, Congress passed the 1924 Immigration Restriction Act designed to bar immigrants supposedly proven to be inferior on the basis of their low IQ test score. Thus it became national policy to administer intelligence tests to immigrants as they arrived at Ellis Island in New York harbor. Vast numbers of Jewish, Italian, and Russian immigrants were classified as "morons" on the basis of IQ tests. Some psychologists interpreted these statistical findings as evidence that immigrants from southern and eastern Europe were genetically inferior to those from the hardy northern and western European stock. However, these groups were also least familiar with the dominant language and culture because they had immigrated most recently. (Within a few decades, these group differences completely disappeared from IQ tests; but the theory of racially inherited differences in intelligence did not.)

Goddard (1917) and others then went beyond merely associating low IQ with hereditary racial and ethnic origins—they added moral worthlessness, mental deficiency, and immoral social behavior to the mix of negatives related to low IQ. Evidence for their view came from case studies of two infamous families: the **Juke Family** and the **Kallikak Family.** These families allegedly were traced for many generations to show that bad seeds planted in family genes yield defective human offspring.

Over 2000 members of a New York state family with "Juke's blood" were reported to have been traced (by 1875) because the family had such a notorious record of developmental disability, delinquency, and crime. Of these family members, 458 were found to be developmentally disabled in their school performance, 171 classified as criminals, and hundreds of their kin were labeled as "paupers, intemperates, and harlots." The conclusion reached was that heredity was a dominant factor in the disreputable development of members of this family (and presumably others similar to it).

Goddard drew the same conclusion from his case study of the Kallikaks, a family with one "good seed" side and one "bad seed" side to its family tree (In his study, Goddard renamed the family Kallikak, which means *good-bad* in Greek). Martin Kallikak was a revolutionary war soldier who had an illegitimate son with a woman described as developmentally disabled. Their union eventually produced 480 descendants. Goddard classified 143 of them as "defective," and only 46 as normal. He found crime, alcoholism, mental disorders, and illegitimacy common among the rest of the family members. By contrast, when Martin later married a "good woman," their union produced 496 descendants, only three of whom were classified as "defective."

Henry Goddard studied the alleged genetic transfer of mental deficiency and worked on the training of exceptional children.

Goddard also found that many offspring from this quality union had become "eminent" (Goddard, 1912).

Goddard came to believe that heredity determined intelligence, genius, and eminence on the positive side and delinquency, alcoholism, sexual immorality, developmental disability, and maybe even poverty on the negative side (McPherson, 1985).

Time out for a *critical thinking exercise*. If Goddard's argument were valid, what detailed public policy recommendations would you make for dealing with the social problems created by such people? How can you determine the argument's validity? List all the possible methodological artifacts (sources of error, biases) in the case studies of the Jukes and the Kallikaks that lead you to challenge the conclusions drawn.

Goddard's genetic superiority argument was further reinforced by the fact that on the World War I Army Intelligence tests, African Americans and other racial minorities scored lower than the white majority. Louis Terman responded to the intelligence test data he had helped collect on U.S. racial minorities:

> Their dullness seems to be racial. . . . There seems no possibility at present of convincing society that they should not be allowed to reproduce, although from a eugenics point of view, they constitute a grave problem because of their unusually prolific breeding (Terman, 1916, pp. 91–92).

The names have changed, but the problem remains the same. In the United States today, African Americans and Latinos score, on the average, lower than Asian Americans and whites on standardized intelligence tests. Of course, there are individuals in all groups who score at the highest (and the lowest) extremes of the IQ scale. How should we interpret IQ scores, and what is the source of these group differences? There are three common explanations—genetics, environment, and test bias—and each leads to important social consequences.

The genetic position claims that IQ tests measure inherent intellectual ability, and that some racial or cultural groups score lower because they are genetically inferior. Group differences are used to justify racist views which, in the extreme, support eugenics programs to limit "breeding" by undesirable groups, laws restricting the immigration of certain groups, and legal inequality that favors the group in power. The "moderate" consequences of this position are that it feeds intergroup conflict, encourages school segregation and discriminatory hiring practices, and argues against funding for intervention programs that help minorities. This position was supported by William Shockley, Nobel prizewinner in physics (for co-inventing the transistor). He alleged that the lower IQ test scores of African Americans and Latinos in the United States are "hereditary and racially genetic in origin and thus not remedial to a major degree by practical improvements in environment" (Shockley, 1986, p. 67). However, in our pluralistic culture, it is difficult to determine how much of the variation in intellectual performance on any standard test can be assigned to hereditary factors and what proportion is attributable to environmental influences, or, indeed, why there is so much variation.

The environmental position interprets IQ scores as a measure of current functioning and alleges that low scores often reflect social factors. Group differences in IQ scores are believed to be a symptom of larger social problems. In the United States the minority groups with the lowest average IQ scores are those for whom poverty, illiteracy, and hopelessness are most widespread. People who support the environmental position believe that it was racism and discrimination that landed many minorities in the ghettos in the first place and that work to keep them there even today. The consequences of this view include equal opportunity legislation, better schools, and intervention programs, such as *Head Start*, which helps disadvantaged children build self-confidence and learn the skills necessary to succeed in school.

Proponents of the third view are also interested in protecting the civil rights of minority group members. They believe that group differences in IQ scores are caused by systematic bias in the tests questions, making them invalid and unfair for minorities. There are significant dialect differences between whites and blacks, for example, that could affect an African-American person's verbal scores on a standardized test with a bias toward standard English. Proponents of this view also believe that remedial classes do more harm than good for minority children who are incorrectly assigned to them on the basis of unfair IQ tests; these classes stigmatize them and encourage their distaste for the school experience.

There have been several suggestions made in response to the test bias position. One is that test makers try to improve their tests to make them *culture fair*. Another is that courts restrict the use of IQ tests so that they can no longer be used to assign minority children to special classes. This second suggestion has been carried out in some states. Another consequence of this view is that when test bias is seen as the sole cause for group differences, it may become a convenient excuse for legislators to pretend that racial injustice in the larger society is not a serious problem, thereby reducing incentives for supporting remedial action programs.

Heredity vs. Environment

There is no question that heredity *influences* those elusive mental qualities that we call intelligence. Many different lines of research have shown there is a strong genetic basis to a variety of human attributes. Research used to assess the genetic contribution of a given type of functioning compares identical twins (*monozygotic, MZ*) with same-sex fraternal twins (*dizygotic, DZ*) and sometimes with siblings. Significant genetic effects have been found on attributes as diverse as heart functioning (Brown, 1990); personality traits (Tellegen et al., 1988); and hypnotizability (Morgan et al., 1970). So it is reasonable to believe that there is also a genetic basis to intellectual functioning. The question is how much basis is there. In researching the contributions of environment, psychologists have also compared performances of MZ and DZ twins and siblings who have been reared together or apart. **Table 15.1** compares IQ scores of individuals on the basis of their degree of genetic relationship. The greater the genetic similarity the greater the IQ similarity. The correlation between IQ scores increases as we move up in degree of heredity from cousins to siblings to fraternal twins to identical twins. It is also greater between parent and child than between foster parent and adopted child. Environment also reveals its contribution in the greater IQ similarities among those who have been reared together.

A recent large-scale study comparing twins has stirred up controversy by claiming that heredity makes a much more important contribution to intelligence than

TABLE 15.1 *IQ AND GENETIC RELATIONSHIP*

	Correlation
Identical twins	
Reared together	0.86
Reared apart	0.72
Fraternal twins	
Reared together	0.60
Siblings	
Reared together	0.47
Reared apart	0.24
Parent/child	0.40
Foster parent/child	0.31
Cousins	0.15

environmental factors. It reports that even when identical twins are raised in different families, as much as 70 percent of the variance in their IQ scores is due to genetic makeup (Bouchard et al., 1990). This figure is being debated, but most psychologists agree that heredity plays an important part in variance of IQ scores. It is difficult to determine the relative roles of genetics and environment in the development of intelligence or other aspects of mental functioning (Plomin, 1989; Scarr, 1988; Stevenson et al., 1989). Children who live in the same family setting do not necessarily share the same critical, psychological environment. You probably are aware of this fact if you have siblings with interests and lifestyles that differ from yours.

Another problem arises when we use comparisons of IQ scores to make inferences about group differences, using measures of the genetic basis of IQ. A **heritability estimate** of a particular trait, such as intelligence, is based on the proportion of the *variability* in test scores on that trait that can be traced to inherited factors. The estimate is found by computing the variation in all the test scores for a given population (college students or mental patients, for example) and then identifying what portion of the total variance is due to genetic or inherited factors (by comparing twins and others whose genetic similarity differ). As more of the total variance is due to heredity, knowing the degree of genetic similarity allows a better prediction of the similarity in test scores within this population. There are two key points regarding heritability estimates. First, the estimates have no implications for individual cases; they pertain only to the average in a given population of individuals. Thus, we cannot determine how much of your height, which has a high heritability estimate, is due to genetic influences. Second, heritability is based on an estimate *within* a given group and cannot be used to interpret differences *between* groups, no matter how large those differences are on an objective test. The fact that on an IQ test one racial or ethnic group scores lower than another group does not mean that the difference *between* these groups is genetic in origin, even if the heritability estimate for IQ scores is high as assessed *within* a group. Despite a high heritability estimate in intelligence, education and other advantages can improve performance on IQ tests, while malnutrition, lead poisoning, and poor schooling can lower performance (environmental influences). If one group is more environmentally advantaged, it will do better on tests that are responsive to such influences. Those who focus on genetic explanations typically ignore the environmental, situational determinants of mental and behavioral functioning. Those who are stigmatized by genetic inferiority theories suffer by believing they cannot improve their fated genetic destiny.

Another reason that genetic makeup does not appear to be responsible for group differences in IQ has to do with the relative sizes of the differences. For example, even though some studies show that the group average for African Americans is as much as 10 to 15 IQ points below the group average for U.S. whites, there is much overlapping of scores, and the difference *between* groups is small compared to the differences among the scores of individuals *within* each group (Loehlin et al, 1975). In fact, geneticist **Stephen Jay Gould** (1981) argues that for human characteristics in general, the differences between the gene pools of different racial groups are minute compared to the genetic differences among individual members of the same group (see also Zuckerman, 1990).

A third argument against the genetic interpretation of group differences is that many other variables are *confounded* with race, each of which can influence IQ scores (see **Figure 15.3**). For example, in a large-scale, longitudinal study of more than 26,000 children, the best predictors of a child's IQ at age 4, for both black and white children, were the family's socioeconomic status and the level of the mother's education (Broman et al., 1975).

There is ample evidence that environments influence intellectual development. Poverty can affect intellectual functioning in many ways. Poor health during pregnancy and low birth weight are solid predictors of

FIGURE 15.3 *THE RELATIONSHIP BETWEEN HEREDITY, ENVIRONMENT, AND IQ*

This chart shows evidence for the contribution of heredity and environment to IQ scores. We see similar IQs for fathers and sons (influence of heredity), but the IQs of both fathers and sons are related to social class (influence of environment).

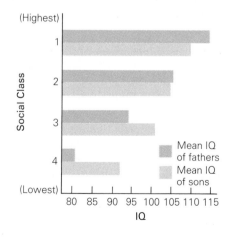

a child's lowered mental ability. So too, poor nutrition, a lack of books and other materials for verbal stimulation, and a survival orientation that leaves parents little time or energy to play with and intellectually stimulate their children can be detrimental to performance on tasks such as those on standard IQ tests. We know that a significant proportion of children with low IQs were adversely affected by "environmental insults," such as lead-based paint chips peeling from walls (Needleman et al., 1990).

> When underprivileged black children were adopted by middle-class white families, they developed IQs significantly above the average of 100. Those who were adopted into these transracial families within the first year of life had much higher IQ scores than those adopted later. Thus, when given access to an intellectually stimulating environment, black children perform as well as their white peers (see **Figure 15.4;** Scarr & Weinberg, 1976).

More evidence for the importance of the environment comes from the success of intervention programs. For example, Head Start programs, in which disadvantaged children are given extra skills and encouragement to succeed in school, have impressive results; they do not change IQ scores directly, but they enhance school performance which then may have a positive impact on many other areas of the child's life (Jordan et al., 1985). Preschoolers in Head Start programs achieve more in school than their peers and are more likely to graduate from high school (Schweinhart & Weikart, 1990). In fact, environmental factors, such as the cognitive complexity and intellectual demands of one's job, can influence IQ throughout adulthood (Dixon et al., 1985). Most adult IQs are stable over many years simply because they remain in environments that provide a stable amount of intellectual stimulation. Recall that columnist Bob Greene's verbal SAT scores increased while his math SAT scores plummeted—in part due to his use of verbal skills and his disuse of math skills.

Perhaps the best way to summarize these and other relevant findings is to say that *both* heredity and environment affect intelligence. Heredity plays a big role in differences between individuals but not in differences among groups. Environmental factors play important roles in creating differences between individuals and between groups. Although heredity may make learning easier for some people than for others, genetic makeup alone does not determine level of intellectual achievement. Intervention programs and enriched learning environments can help overcome the disadvantages of poverty and discrimination.

Validity and Test Bias in IQ Tests

Because group differences do exist in IQ scores, many people are concerned about the appropriateness of using these scores in education and industry. Are they valid predictors of success? Are they equally valid for different racial and cultural groups?

Extensive research shows that IQ scores are valid predictors of school grades from elementary school through college, of job status, and of performance in certain jobs (Brody & Brody, 1976; Gottfredson, 1986; Lennon, 1985). However, because some groups score lower on IQ and achievement tests than the white middle-class majority on whom these tests are normed, many people are concerned that test scores should not be used to make decisions about the lives of minority school children and job applicants.

How could the tests themselves be biased? One culprit is language differences. Because minority group children may have learned a different language at home, or a nonstandard dialect of English, the instructions and item content of IQ tests may use words and phrases that are unfamiliar to them. Nonverbal items may be suspect as well. Some critics believe that the abstract nature of these items may be totally foreign to the practical, survival-oriented experience of economically disadvantaged children. As a result of criticisms such as these, many test companies removed biased items from their tests and tried to make tests more *culture fair,* or equally challenging for people of different cultures.

Unfortunately, decades of attempts have demonstrated that it is impossible to make a test that is both

FIGURE 15.4 *IQ SCORES OF AFRICAN-AMERICAN CHILDREN ADOPTED BY WHITE FAMILIES*

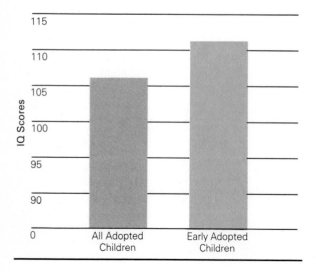

The environmental contrasts are sharp in these two photos. At left is an allegedly "separate but equal" Tennessee schoolroom in the 1950s where African-American children are receiving little personal attention. At right are African-American parents deeply involved in their children's learning.

valid and free of any cultural bias—at least, it is impossible to prove that a test is completely culture fair. Even the best IQ and achievement tests show group differences in terms of average scores. How do we know whether those differences are due to test bias or to real group differences in intellectual functioning (Haney, 1982)?

There have been many court battles involving the use of intelligence and ability tests in business and education. In conjunction with affirmative action legislation, the movement to ensure fair testing practices seeks to remove discriminatory practices in our society. Unfortunately, sometimes when standardized tests are forbidden, educators and employers must revert to more expensive, less valid, and perhaps *more* discriminatory assessment procedures—such as interviews or the subjective impressions of teachers or supervisors. The rights and interests of many people must be considered and sometimes poor decisions are made that can have negative consequences for school or business as well as for the student or job applicant involved. The decision to use a test should always be based on the validity and fairness of the test as compared to other selection methods.

SUMMING UP

Our coverage of intelligence testing has shown that the construct of intelligence has been defined and measured in many ways. Today, the most popular individually administered tests of intelligence are the Stanford-Binet and the Wechsler scales (the WAIS-R, the WISC-R, and the WPPSI). Group tests of intelligence, though more convenient and inexpensive, offer somewhat more narrow results because they are restricted to written items.

Psychometric analyses of IQ, which are based on statistical relationships between mental measurements, suggest that there are several types of abilities that contribute to IQ scores, such as separate fluid and crystallized types of intelligence. Cognitive science approaches, which study mental processes, encourage us to conceive of and measure intelligence very broadly by assessing the skills and insights people use to solve all the types of problems they encounter. Cognitive scientists claim that IQ tells only a small part of the story; a fuller scenario must include many different components of intellectual functioning.

Because some racial and cultural groups score lower on IQ tests on the average than other groups, some critics believe that IQ doesn't—or shouldn't—tell any story at all. Although IQ differences between groups are sometimes blamed on genetic differences between groups, the evidence suggests that group differences reflect both environmental disadvantages and cultural bias in the tests themselves. However, IQ tests have proven to be equally valid predictors of school grades and success in certain jobs for members of both groups, suggesting that test bias may be less of a problem than environmental disadvantages that impair intellectual functioning. Group differences in IQ can be reduced, and in time probably eliminated, by improving public education for minority groups and through very early special intervention programs aimed at giving disadvantaged children an advantaged intellectual foundation.

ASSESSING PERSONALITY

There is much more to understanding people than knowing how intelligent they are. Think of all the other ways in which you differ from your best friend or sibling. Psychologists wonder about the nonintellectual attributes that characterize an individual, set one person apart from others, or distinguish people in one group from those in another (for example, shy people from nonshy or paranoid individuals from normal). Personality assessment is the traditional approach to such questions.

Two assumptions are basic to these attempts to understand and describe human personality: first, there are personal characteristics of individuals that give coherence to behavior and, second, those characteristics can be assessed or measured. In order to describe and study personality, psychologists use tests designed to reveal important personal traits and the way those traits fit together in particular individuals. This information may be used in psychological research, individual therapy, career counseling, or personnel selection and training. The many different types of personality tests can be classified as being either objective or projective.

OBJECTIVE TESTS

Objective tests of personality are those in which the scoring and the administration is relatively simple and follows objective rules. Some tests may be scored, and even interpreted, by computer programs. The final score is usually a number scaled along a single dimension (such as adjustment to maladjustment) or a set of scores on different traits (such as masculinity, dependency, or extroversion) reported relative to some normative sample.

A *self-report inventory* is an objective test in which individuals answer a series of questions about their thoughts, feelings, and actions. One of the first self-report inventories focused on adjustment problems. The *Woodworth Personal Data Sheet* (written in 1917) asked questions such as "Are you often frightened in the middle of the night?" (see DuBois, 1970). Today, a person taking a **personality inventory** reads a series of statements and indicates whether each one is true for himself or herself. On some inventories the person is asked to assess how frequently each statement is true or how well each describes her typically experienced behavior, thoughts, or feelings.

The most famous test of this type is the *Minnesota Multiphasic Personality Inventory,* or MMPI (Dahlstrom et al., 1975). It is used in many clinical settings to aid in the diagnosis of patients and to act as a guide in their treatment. After reviewing its features and applications,

we will briefly discuss three personality inventories that are used widely with nonpatient populations: the *California Psychological Inventory* (CPI), the *NEO Personality Inventory* (NEO-PI), and the *Myers-Briggs Type Inventory*.

The MMPI

The MMPI was developed at the University of Minnesota during the 1930s by psychologist Starke Hathaway and psychiatrist J. R. McKinley. It was first published in the 1940s (Hathaway & McKinley, 1940, 1943). Its basic purpose is to diagnose individuals according to a set of psychiatric labels. The first test consisted of 550 items which the subject determined to be either true or false for himself or to which he responded, "Cannot say." From that item pool, scales were developed that were relevant to the kinds of problems patients showed in psychiatric settings. Norms were established for both psychiatric patients and normal subjects (visitors to the University of Minnesota hospital).

The MMPI scales were unlike other existing personality tests of the time because they were developed using an *empirical* strategy known as *criterion keying,* rather than the usual intuitive approach. Items were included on a scale only if they clearly distinguished between two groups, for example, schizophrenic patients and a normal comparison group. Each item had to demonstrate its validity by being answered similarly by members within each group, but differently between the two groups. Thus the items were not selected on a rational basis (what the content seemed to mean to experts) but on an empirical basis.

The MMPI has 10 *clinical scales,* each constructed to differentiate a special clinical group (such as schizophrenics or paranoids) from a normal control group. The test is scored by adding up the number of items on a particular scale that a person answered in the same way as the clinical group; the higher the score, the more the person is like the clinical group and the less like the normal group.

The test includes *validity scales* that detect suspicious response patterns, such as blatant dishonesty, carelessness, defensiveness, and evasiveness. When an MMPI is interpreted, the tester first checks the validity scales to be sure the test is valid and then looks at the rest of the scores. The pattern of the scores—which are highest, how they differ—forms the "MMPI profile" (see **Figure 15.5**). Individual profiles are compared to those common for particular groups, such as paranoids, felons, and gamblers.

Recently, the MMPI has undergone a major revision, and it is now called the *MMPI-2* (Dahlstrom et al, 1989). Some items have been dropped, others added,

FIGURE 15.5   A COMPUTERIZED PRINTOUT OF AN MMPI PROFILE

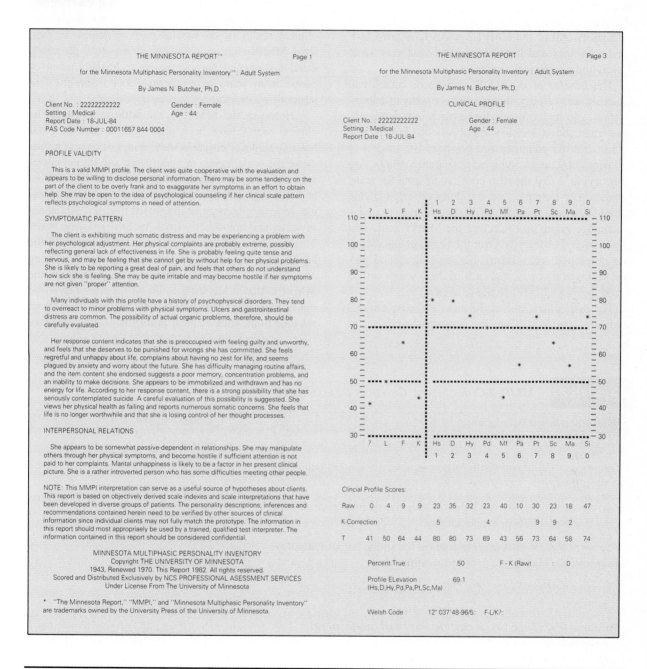

THE MINNESOTA REPORT™   Page 1

for the Minnesota Multiphasic Personality Inventory™: Adult System

By James N. Butcher, Ph.D.

Client No. : 22222222222   Gender : Female
Setting : Medical   Age : 44
Report Date : 18-JUL-84
PAS Code Number : 00011657 844 0004

PROFILE VALIDITY

This is a valid MMPI profile. The client was quite cooperative with the evaluation and appears to be willing to disclose personal information. There may be some tendency on the part of the client to be overly frank and to exaggerate her symptoms in an effort to obtain help. She may be open to the idea of psychological counseling if her clinical scale pattern reflects psychological symptoms in need of attention.

SYMPTOMATIC PATTERN

The client is exhibiting much somatic distress and may be experiencing a problem with her psychological adjustment. Her physical complaints are probably extreme, possibly reflecting general lack of effectiveness in life. She is probably feeling quite tense and nervous, and may be feeling that she cannot get by without help for her physical problems. She is likely to be reporting a great deal of pain, and feels that others do not understand how sick she is feeling. She may be quite irritable and may become hostile if her symptoms are not given "proper" attention.

Many individuals with this profile have a history of psychophysical disorders. They tend to overreact to minor problems with physical symptoms. Ulcers and gastrointestinal distress are common. The possibility of actual organic problems, therefore, should be carefully evaluated.

Her response content indicates that she is preoccupied with feeling guilty and unworthy, and feels that she deserves to be punished for wrongs she has committed. She feels regretful and unhappy about life, complains about having no zest for life, and seems plagued by anxiety and worry about the future. She has difficulty managing routine affairs, and the item content she endorsed suggests a poor memory, concentration problems, and an inability to make decisions. She appears to be immobilized and withdrawn and has no energy for life. According to her response content, there is a strong possibility that she has seriously contemplated suicide. A careful evaluation of this possibility is suggested. She views her physical health as failing and reports numerous somatic concerns. She feels that life is no longer worthwhile and that she is losing control of her thought processes.

INTERPERSONAL RELATIONS

She appears to be somewhat passive-dependent in relationships. She may manipulate others through her physical symptoms, and become hostile if sufficient attention is not paid to her complaints. Marital unhappiness is likely to be a factor in her present clinical picture. She is a rather introverted person who has some difficulties meeting other people.

NOTE: This MMPI interpretation can serve as a useful source of hypotheses about clients. This report is based on objectively derived scale indexes and scale interpretations that have been developed in diverse groups of patients. The personality descriptions, inferences and recommendations contained herein need to be verified by other sources of clinical information since individual clients may not fully match the prototype. The information in this report should most appropriately be used by a trained, qualified test interpreter. The information contained in this report should be considered confidential.

THE MINNESOTA REPORT   Page 3

for the Minnesota Multiphasic Personality Inventory : Adult System

By James N. Butcher, Ph.D.

CLINICAL PROFILE

Client No. : 22222222222   Gender : Female
Setting : Medical   Age : 44
Report Date : 18-JUL-84

Clincial Profile Scores:

	?	L	F	K	Hs	D	Hy	Pd	Mf	Pa	Pt	Sc	Ma	Si
Raw	0	4	9	9	23	35	32	23	40	10	30	23	18	47
K-Correction					5			4			9	9	2	
T	41	50	64	44	80	80	73	69	43	56	73	64	58	74

Percent True :   50   F - K (Raw)   :   0

Profile ELevation :   69.1
(Hs,D,Hy,Pd,Pa,Pt,Sc,Ma)

Welsh Code :   12" 037'48-96/5:   F-L/K?:

---

and others rewritten to remove sexist language and themes that are no longer culturally relevant. Much of the item pool is unchanged, so the original clinical scales are still scored in the MMPI-2 but the revision uses an improved scoring procedure. The validity scales have changed slightly, and the MMPI-2 has seven validity scales, rather than four. The most dramatic change is the addition of 15 new *content scales* that were derived using a rational method instead of criterion keying. For each of 15 clinically relevant topics (such as anxiety or family problems), items were selected on two bases: if they seemed theoretically related to the topic area and if they statistically formed a *homogeneous scale,* meaning that each scale measures a single, unified concept. The MMPI-2s clinical and content scales are given in **Table 15.2.** You'll notice that most of the clinical scales measure several related concepts and that the names of the content scales are simple and self-explanatory. All of the MMPI-2 scales have good test-retest reliability and have been normed on very large clinical and nonclinical samples.

The *benefits* of the MMPI include its established reliability and validity, its ease and economy of administration, and its usefulness for research in psychopathology and making decisions about patients. In fact, it is used in over 65 countries and has been the subject of well over 8000 books and articles (Butcher, 1989). Another benefit is that the item pool can be used for many purposes. For example, you could use criterion-keying to build a creativity scale by finding a creative and a noncreative group and selecting the MMPI items that they answered differently. Over the years, psychologists have developed and validated hundreds of special purpose scales in this way, and each of these scales can be scored from *any* MMPI response sheet.

For researchers, one of the most attractive characteristics of the MMPI are the enormous archives, or data banks, of MMPIs collected from different types of people all over the world. Because all of these people have been tested on the same items in a standardized way, they can be compared either on the traditional clinical scales or on special purpose scales. In fact, these MMPI archives allow researchers to apply newly developed special purpose scales to MMPIs taken by people many years earlier, perhaps long before the construct being measured was even conceived.

However, the MMPI is not without its faults. Its clinical scales have been criticized because they are heterogeneous (measure several things at once) and because the scale names are confusing and do not correspond to what they measure. Complicated clinical lore is required to interpret a profile correctly—schizophrenia, for example, must be diagnosed from a combination of scales and not directly from the *Schizophrenia* scale. This problem still exists for the clinical scales of the MMPI-2, but its new content scales are less confusing and easier to interpret. Another shortcoming of the MMPI is that it has little to do with personality—the items, including those for the new content scales, were selected to measure clinical problems, so the inventory

---

TABLE 15.2	*MMPI-2 CLINICAL AND CONTENT SCALES (1989)*

Clinical Scales and Descriptions	Content Scales
Hypochondriasis (Hs): Abnormal concern with bodily functions	*Anxiety*
Depression (D): Pessimism; hopelessness; slowing of action and thought	*Fears*
	Obsessiveness
Conversion Hysteria (Hy): Unconscious use of mental problems to avoid conflicts or responsibility	*Depression*
Psychopathic Deviate (Pd): Disregard for social custom; shallow emotions; inability to profit from experience	*Health Concerns*
	Bizarre Mentation
Masculinity-Femininity (Mf): Differences between men and women	*Anger*
	Cynicism
Paranoia (Pa): Suspiciousness; delusions of grandeur or persecution	*Antisocial Practices*
Psychasthenia (Pt): Obsessions; compulsions; fears; guilt; indecisiveness	*Type A* (workaholic)
	Low Self-Esteem
Schizophrenia (Sc): Bizarre, unusual thoughts or behavior; withdrawal; hallucinations; delusions	*Social Discomfort*
	Family Problems
Hypomania (Ma): Emotional excitement; flight of ideas; overactivity	*Work Interference*
Social introversion (Si): Shyness; disinterest in others; insecurity	*Negative Treatment Indicators* (negative attitudes about doctors and treatment)

is not well-suited to measure personality in nonpatient populations.

The CPI

Harrison Gough (1957) created the California Psychological Inventory (CPI), an MMPI-type instrument that measures individual differences in personality among people who are more or less normal and well-adjusted. Its personality scales measure *folk concepts* that lay persons can easily understand, such as Dominance, Self-Control, Tolerance, and Intellectual Efficiency. Validity scales are included in the test to detect invalid response sheets. All the scales are presented on a profile sheet that shows how a person scored on each scale relative to same-sex norms.

The most recent version of the CPI contains 20 folk scales. Over the years, the CPI has been administered to thousands of people all over the world and has been the subject of many research studies, generating valuable archives of data.

The CPI has been used to study personality structure in healthy adults and to evaluate characteristic personality structures of various groups, such as people in different occupations. Longitudinal studies employing the CPI have helped psychologists understand how personality develops and how personality traits in young adulthood are related to life events as much as 40 years later. In addition, many special purpose scales have been created and validated for research and applied purposes, such as selecting police officers for special training programs and predicting job performance for dentists, student teachers, and many other groups (Gough, 1989; Gynter & Gynter, 1976).

Similar to the MMPI, the CPI has been criticized because many of its scales are heterogeneous and because certain scales correlate highly with other scales (in part because some items are included on more than one scale). However, unlike the MMPI, the CPI scales are easy to understand, because, as research accumulates, the names have been changed to reflect what the scales measure. In addition, today's profiles include scores for three special scales that are nonoverlapping and uncorrelated with each other. They measure broad dimensions having to do with one's overall interpersonal style, acceptance of rules or norms, and psychological adjustment (Gough, 1987).

The NEO-PI

The NEO Personality Inventory (NEO-PI) was also designed to assess personality characteristics in non-clinical adult populations. It measures the five factor model of personality, sometimes called *The Big Five,* which we discussed in the previous chapter. If you took the NEO-PI, you would receive a profile sheet that showed your standardized scores relative to a large normative sample on each of the five major dimensions: Neuroticism (N), Extraversion (E), Openness (O), Agreeableness (A), and Conscientiousness (C). Also included on your profile would be your standardized scores on *facet scales,* or specific subscales that measure different aspects of each dimension. For example, the N (Neuroticism) dimension is broken down into six facet scales: Anxiety, Hostility, Depression, Self-Consciousness, Impulsiveness, and Vulnerability. There are likewise six facets each for E and O, and new facet scales are planned for the A and C dimensions in the next revision (Costa & McCrae, 1985). Much research has demonstrated that the NEO dimensions are homogeneous, highly reliable, and show good criterion and construct validity (McCrae & Costa, 1987, 1989).

The NEO is being used to study personality stability and change across the life-span as well as the relationship of personality characteristics to physical health and various life events, such as career success or early retirement. In applied settings, a therapist might want to administer both the MMPI-2 and the NEO-PI in order to plan a treatment program that is well-suited to a patient's personality as well as to his or her psychiatric needs. The NEO may also be useful in career counseling—to help people select jobs that are right for them. However, it has never been validated (or recommended) for making decisions about hiring or promoting employees.

The Myers-Briggs Type Indicator

This popular personality test, based on Carl Jung's typology theory (1923, 1971), assigns people to one of sixteen categories or types. As developed by Peter Myers and Isabel Briggs, the test attempts to find "an orderly reason for personality differences" in the ways people perceive their world and make judgments about it (Myers, 1962, 1976, 1980).

Basic differences in perception and judgment are assumed to result in corresponding differences in behavior. Both perception and judgment are subdivided into dual ways of perceiving—by direct sensing (S) and unconscious intuition (I)—and judging—by thinking (T) and feeling (F). The third factor added to the Myers-Briggs test—preferences for extraversion (E) or introversion (I)—is based on Jung's idea that people focus on either their inner or outer worlds. Sixteen types emerge from the combination of these preferences, such as extraverts who show thinking with intuition or intraverts who show sensing with feeling. "A person's type is the product of conscious orientation to life: habitual, purposeful ways of using one's mind—habitual because they seem good and interesting and trustworthy" (Briggs, 1980, p. 85). A major use of the Myers-

Briggs test is relating type to occupation—showing that certain preferences for perceiving, thinking, and extraversion or intraversion influence occupational choice and job satisfaction (McCaulley, 1978). Its appeal lies in its ability to categorize people into a small number of types that simplify the enormous complexity of personality differences between individuals.

PROJECTIVE TESTS

Have you ever looked at a cloud and seen a face or the shape of an animal? If you asked your friends to look too, they may have seen a reclining nude or a dragon. Psychologists rely on a similar phenomenon in their use of projective tests for personality assessment.

In a **projective test,** a person is given a series of stimuli that are purposely ambiguous, such as abstract patterns, incomplete pictures, and drawings that can be interpreted in many ways. The person may be asked to describe the patterns, finish the pictures, or tell stories about the drawings. Because the stimuli are vague, responses to them are determined partly by what the person brings to the situation—namely, inner feelings, personal motives, and conflicts from prior life experiences. These idiosyncratic aspects, which are projected onto the stimuli, permit the personality assessor to make various interpretations.

Projective tests were first used by psychoanalysts who hoped that such tests would reveal their patients' unconscious personality dynamics. For example, to uncover emotionally charged thoughts and fears, Carl Jung studied subjects' **word associations** with common words ("What is the first thing brought to mind by the word *house?*").

In addition to this technique of *associating* a verbal, auditory, or visual stimulus with its personal meaning, four other projective techniques have been used to assess personality (Lindzey, 1961): (a) *construction,* such as making up a story; (b) *completion,* such as finishing a sequence of events in a story; (c) *ordering,* or arranging materials or pictures in some order; and (d) *expression,* such as acting or performing some role or expressing the self through art. Two of the most common projective tests are the Rorschach test and the Thematic Apperception Test (TAT).

The Rorschach

In the Rorschach test, developed by Swiss psychiatrist **Hermann Rorschach** in 1921, the ambiguous stimuli are symmetrical inkblots (Rorschach, 1942). Some are black and white and some are colored (see **Figure 15.6**). During the test, a respondent is shown an inkblot and asked, "Tell me what you see, what it might be to you. There are no right or wrong answers."

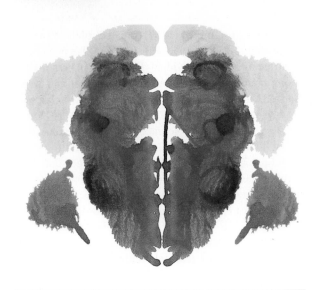

FIGURE 15.6 *A SAMPLE RORSCHACH INKBLOT*

The tester records verbatim what the subject says, how much time she takes to respond, the total time she takes per inkblot, and the way she handles the inkblot card. Then, in a second phase called an *inquiry,* the respondent is reminded of the previous responses and asked to elaborate on them.

The responses are scored on three major features: (a) the *location* or part of the card mentioned in the response—whether the respondent refers to the whole stimulus or to part of it and the size of the details mentioned; (b) the *content* of the response—the nature of the object and activities seen; and (c) the *determinants*—which aspects of the card (such as its color or shading) prompted the response. Some scorers also note whether responses are original and unique or popular and conforming.

Interpreting a person's scores into a coherent portrait of personality dynamics is a complex, highly subjective process that relies on clinical expertise and skilled intuition. Ideally, a tester uses these data as a source of hypotheses about a person that are then evaluated through other assessment procedures. Although the Rorschach has questionable reliability and validity, it is recommended as an indirect way to identify sources of information, such as sexual interests or aggressive fantasies, that people may resent being questioned about or lie about on objective tests (Levy & Orr, 1959). It is gaining renewed popularity among clinicians interested in using it along with other forms of personality assessment.

The TAT

In the Thematic Apperception Test (developed by U.S. psychologist **Henry Murray** in 1938), respondents are shown pictures of ambiguous scenes and asked to generate stories about them, describing what the people in the scenes are doing and thinking, what led up to each event, and how each situation will end (see **Figure 15.7**). The person administering the TAT evaluates the structure and content of the stories as well as the behavior of the individual telling them, in an attempt to discover some of the respondent's major concerns, motivations, and personality characteristics. For example, an examiner might evaluate a person as *conscientious* if his stories concerned people who lived up to their obligations and if he told them in a serious, orderly way. The test can be used with clinical patients to reveal emotional problems or with normal individuals to reveal dominant needs, such as needs for power, affiliation, and achievement (McClelland, 1961). (Recall that in Chapter 12 we described in some detail the use of the TAT for assessing individual differences in these needs.)

Statistical Versus Clinical Prediction

Which is better: prediction based on subjective expert judgments of clinical psychologists or cold-blooded objective prediction generated by computer analysis of test scores? Psychologist **Paul Meehl** (1954) answered this irreverent question by comparing computerized predictions about various aspects of the lives of people tested with predictions made by clinical judges. The results surprised many psychologists. The statistical approach was equal or superior to the clinical approach in many instances. Based on probability formulas and actuarial tables of reactions of large numbers of people, the statistical approach was good at predicting specific outcomes (Meehl, 1965; Sawyer, 1966). The judgment of a sensitive, skilled clinician has proven best, however, when no good tests are available, for individual cases studied over time, and to predict the behavior of rare, atypical cases (Phares, 1984). In practice, then, the best predictions are made when the strengths of each approach are utilized (Holt, 1970).

Personology

Some critics argue that these many different ways of assessing personality use the wrong approach to understanding the richness and uniqueness of personality. Their focus on individual differences and normative comparisons serve us well in ability testing but do us a disservice when extended to personality testing (Rorer & Widiger, 1983). These critics call for an emphasis on understanding what is characteristic and special about individual persons. **Personology** is the study of personality structure, dynamics, and development in the *individual*. The data for this formidable task come from diaries, biographies, literature, case studies, letters, and general observations and *not* from psychometric tests.

FIGURE 15.7	A SAMPLE CARD FROM THE TAT TEST

SUMMING UP

Objective tests such as the MMPI-2, the CPI, and the NEO-PI are very reliable and valid for specific purposes. All three are valuable research tools, in part because of the enormous archives of data available about them. In applied settings, the MMPI-2 is good for making rough clinical diagnoses and forming hypotheses about clients. The CPI and NEO-PI are good for finding out about a person's preferences, values, interpersonal style, and level of functioning. They can be used to plan treatment programs or aid in self-understanding. In addition, the CPI measures various cognitive and social skills, which makes it especially useful for career counseling and (in special cases) for hiring employees and planning training programs. Similarly, the Myers-Briggs test, which identifies 16 different types of people, has been useful in vocational and career counseling.

> *On the other hand, projective techniques such as the Rorschach and the TAT depend heavily on the clinician's subjective judgment and are not as reliable or valid for revealing personality dynamics. These tests are best used as therapeutic icebreakers and as sources of preliminary clinical hypotheses to be confirmed by more objective techniques. Even the most carefully standardized and validated personality inventories are not infallible. In applied settings, when a diagnosis or decision is being made that could influence an individual's life, test data should always be used in combination with other relevant information, such as interviews, situational observations, medical history, or prior job experience. The personology orientation rejects traditional psychometric testing and individual differences approaches; it proposes that the proper study of personality focuses on the personal uniqueness of each individual.*

ASSESSMENT AND YOU

Thus far we have presented some of the major features of assessment techniques and have discussed in detail certain approaches used to assess intelligence, personality, and creativity. As a college student, you may be struggling with decisions about the kind of job you would like to have when you finish school. In our final section, we will first discuss the role of assessment in vocational counseling. Then we will address some of the political and ethical issues posed by the widespread use of formal assessment procedures in our society today.

VOCATIONAL INTERESTS AND APTITUDES

Have you already determined a career path? Are you still undecided or perhaps thinking of leaving a job you already have? Many assessment instruments have been developed to help people learn what vocations best fit their personalities, values, interests, and skills—or, in some cases, to show them before it's too late that the career they have chosen may not be the wisest choice.

Assessing Interests

Even if you do not yet know what jobs you might like best, you would like to have a job that suits your interests and serves goals that you consider worthwhile. However, you may be unsure about what your major interests and abilities are. Furthermore, you may have little idea of what people in many occupations actually

do, and you may not really know how their job activities relate to your personal situation. A number of tests have been designed to help people identify major interests, abilities, and appropriate career directions.

The most widely used test for measuring vocational interests is the *Strong-Campbell Interest Inventory*, which was constructed in 1927 by psychologist **Edward Strong.** The test is based on an empirical approach similar to that used later for the MMPI. First, groups of men in different occupations answered items about activities they liked or disliked. Then the answers of those who were successful in particular occupations were compared with the answers of men in general to create a scale. Subsequent versions of the test have added scales relevant to women and to newer occupations. If you took this test, a vocational counselor could tell you what types of jobs are typically held by people with interests such as yours, since these are the jobs that are likely to appeal to you.

Assessing Abilities

Even if a job appeals to you and it suits your personality and fits your values and interests, you are unlikely to be satisfied with it unless you can do it well. Your employer is also unlikely to be satisfied with you if you are unable to do the job for which you were hired.

In order to recommend a career path for you, therefore, a vocational counselor will want to assess your abilities as well as your interests. Ability has two components: aptitude and achievement. An **aptitude test** measures your potential for acquiring various skills—not necessarily how well you can perform tasks now but how well you will be able to in the future, presumably with adequate training. An **achievement test,** on the other hand, measures your current level of competence. A test of how well you can speak a foreign language or program a computer would be an example of an achievement test.

Tests have been developed to assess aptitude and achievement in many domains. With knowledge of not only what you like to do but also what you can do well, a counselor is in a good position to predict your suitability for different jobs (Anastasia, 1975; Sundberg & Matarazzo, 1979; Tyler, 1974).

Tests of ability are also used by companies seeking new employees. If you apply for a specific job, you may be asked to take tests involving the abilities and skills required for that job. If a job involves typing, you may be given a timed typing test; if it involves hard physical labor, you may be given a test of strength. If managing other people will be an important part of the job, your tolerance for interpersonal stress and ability to assert yourself may be assessed. The goal of such tests is to match people with the jobs for which they are best

Career counselors help individuals match their abilities with potential careers.

suited, thereby increasing the satisfaction of both employees and their employers.

Assessing Jobs

Organizations often invest substantial time and money in personnel selection. They rely not only on an assessment of an applicant's characteristics but also on a careful identification and analysis of the requirements of the job. In a **job analysis,** a specific job is carefully examined to determine the nature and degree of *skill* required, the amount of *effort* demanded, and the extent to which an individual is *responsible* for decisions that affect company resources or personnel and to identify any other types of *stress* the job may entail (Tenopyr & Oeltjen, 1982). The results of job analyses are used not only in selecting personnel but also in determining the pay scale for different jobs.

Job assessment is performed in many ways. Workers, supervisors, and specially trained job analysts are asked to provide information about the abilities required for particular jobs. Subject-matter experts may rate the relevance of various kinds of knowledge, skills, and abilities. An inventory of requirements, including the tasks and duties a worker must perform, can then be prepared for each occupation. One such inventory that has been developed—the *Occupational Analysis Inventory*—provides information about a wide spectrum of occupations and can be very helpful to a job seeker (Pass & Cunningham, 1978).

Some companies supplement other assessment methods with *realistic job previews*. They show applicants what will be expected of them on the job through films, tapes, employee checklists of most- and least-liked aspects of a job, and simulations of critical incidents likely to arise (Wanous, 1980). These previews give applicants a clearer picture of what will be expected of them if they take a job and help them decide how well the job fits their abilities and interests.

In one study, 11 different assessment methods used in hiring were compared according to how well they predicted an applicant's later job success. The top ranked method was an ability composite based on several psychological tests. Surprisingly, the factors that were not significant in predicting on-the-job success were experience, interview ratings, and academic achievement (Hunter & Hunter, 1984).

How one person does at a job often depends on more than knowledge and hard work. Among the other variables affecting job performance might be assertiveness, social skills, appearance, and general congruence or fit with a company's picture of its ideal supervisor, manager, or executive. When these types of characteristics are important, personality tests such as the CPI can be used in employee selection—but *only* for those jobs for which a test has been specifically validated.

POLITICAL AND ETHICAL ISSUES

The primary goal of psychological assessment is to reduce errors of judgment that bias accurate assessments of people. This goal is achieved by replacing subjective judgments of teachers, physicians, employers, and other evaluators with more objective measures that have been carefully constructed and are open to critical evaluation. This is the goal that motivated Alfred Binet in his pioneering work. Binet and others hoped that testing would help democratize society and minimize decisions based on arbitrary criteria of sex, race, nationality, or physical appearance. However, despite these lofty goals, there is no area of psychology more controversial than assessment. Three unresolved issues that are central to the controversy are the fairness of test-based decisions, the utility of tests for evaluating education, and the implications of using test scores as labels.

Critics concerned with the fairness of testing practices argue that the costs or negative consequences may be higher for some test-takers than for others. The costs are quite high, for example, when tests on which minority groups receive low scores are used to keep them out of certain jobs—in some cities, applicants for civil service janitor jobs must pass a verbal test, rather than a more appropriate test of janitorial manual skills. According to researcher William Banks, this is a strategy unions use to keep minorities from access to jobs (1990). Sometimes, minority group members test poorly because their scores are evaluated relative to inappropriate norms. In addition, arbitrary cutoff scores that favor applicants from one group may be used to make selection decisions, when, in reality, a lower cutoff score that is more fair would produce just as many correct hiring decisions.

Even when tests are valid predictors of job performance, they should not be used as an excuse to ignore the special needs of some specific groups in society. For example, some allegedly valid employment tests predict performance in training sessions but *not* performance on the job. People with less education or experience who have difficulty in training may, with a few extra training sessions, learn to perform a job as proficiently as people who already had the necessary skills when they were hired (Haney, 1982). In addition, reliance on testing may make personnel selection too often an automatic attempt to fit people into available jobs. Instead, sometimes we might benefit more by changing job descriptions to fit the needs and abilities of people.

Testing not only helps evaluate students; it also plays an indirect role in education. The quality of school systems and the effectiveness of teachers are frequently judged on the basis of how well their students score on standardized achievement tests. Local support of the schools through tax levies and even individual teacher salaries may ride on test scores.

These test scores may not accurately reflect what students really know, however. The same tests are used for several years between revisions, so that teachers come to know what is on the test and prepare their students for those items. Scores improve, but the norms are not updated, so students in each district *appear* to be doing better and better each year until a revision

comes out that makes them look inept in comparison to the previous year's students with their inflated scores. Some teachers resort to asking students who they believe will not test well to stay home on test days and some even change students' answers after the tests are over. Many students are made to feel overly anxious about their performance by teachers who spend more time teaching them to be "testwise" than teaching them to think for themselves (Leslie & Wingert, 1990).

We are a nation of test-takers and we sometimes forget that our test scores are, at best, statistical measures of our current functioning. Instead, we imbue them with an absolute significance that is not limited to appropriate normative comparisons. People too often think of themselves as *being* an IQ of 110 or a B student as if the scores were labels stamped on their foreheads. Such labels may become barriers to advancement as people come to believe that their mental and personal qualities are fixed and unchangeable—that they cannot improve their lot in life. For those who are negatively assessed, the scores can become self-imposed motivational limits that lower their sense of self-efficacy and restrict the challenges they are willing to tackle.

This tendency to give test scores a sacred status has societal as well as personal implications. When test scores become labels that identify traits, states, maladjustment, conflict, and pathology *within* an individual, people begin to think about the "abnormality" of individual children rather than about educational systems that need to modify programs to accommodate all learners. Labels put the spotlight on deviant personalities rather than on problems in the environment. Human assessors need to recognize that what people are now is a product of where they've been, where they think they are headed, and what situation is currently influencing their behavior. Such a view can help to unite different assessment approaches and theoretical camps as well as lead to more humane treatment of those who do not fit the norm.

I'd like to conclude on a personal note, one that may have some inspirational value to some students who do not do well on objective tests. Although I have gone on to have a successful career as a professional psychologist, the relevant tests I took many years ago would have predicted otherwise. Despite being an Honors undergraduate student, I got my only C grade in Introductory Psychology, where grades were based solely on multiple-choice exams. I was initially rejected for graduate training at Yale University; then I became an alternate, and finally, I was accepted reluctantly, in part because my GRE math scores were below the criterion cut-off level in the psychology department. As was the case with Bob Greene, the writer whose story opened this chapter, successful performance in a career and in life requires something more than the ability recognized by standardized tests. While the best tests perform the valuable function of predicting how well people will do on the average, there is always room for error when desire, ambition, imagination, self-esteem, and personal pride get in the way, for better or worse. Perhaps it is vital to know when you should believe more in yourself than in the results of a test.

RECAPPING MAIN POINTS

What Is Assessment?

The purpose of psychological assessment is to describe or classify individuals in ways that will be useful for prediction or treatment. A wide variety of personal characteristics may be assessed, including intelligence, personality traits, attitudes, interests, skills, and behaviors.

A useful assessment tool must be reliable, valid, and standardized. A reliable measure gives consistent results on different testings; reliability is an index of the degree to which a test correlates with itself across occasions or across different test forms or items. A valid measure assesses the attributes for which the test was designed; validity is the degree to which a test correlates with one or more related criterion measures. A standardized test is always administered and scored in the same way; norms allow a person's score to be compared to the averages of others of the same age and sex.

Methods of Assessment

Formal assessment is carried out through interviews, review of life history data, tests, and situational observations. These important sources of assessment information may come from self-report or observer-report methods. Self-report measures require subjects to answer questions or supply information about themselves; for better or worse, they are tied to subjective reports. Observer-report measures require persons who know or have observed a subject person to provide the information. They may be biased due to halo and stereotype effects, so their reliability should be enhanced by the reports of several independent observers.

Assessing Intelligence

Binet began the tradition of objective, intelligence testing in France in the early 1900s. His test was designed to separate developmentally disabled from normal schoolchildren in order to plan special training programs. Scores were given in terms of mental ages and were meant to represent children's current level of functioning.

Terman created the Stanford-Binet Intelligence Scale and the concept of IQ. He supported the idea that intelligence was an inner, largely inherited capacity. Wechsler designed special intelligence tests for adults, children, and preschoolers; each test consists of 11 different subtests and gives separate verbal, nonverbal, and full-scale IQs at each age level. Highly efficient group tests of intelligence, which measure a narrower conception of intelligence (often called school ability), are widely used in education and business.

Psychometric analyses of IQ suggest that several basic abilities, such as fluid and crystallized aspects of intelligence, contribute to IQ scores. Cognitive science approaches, which study mental processes, conceive of and measure intelligence very broadly by considering the skills and insights people use to solve all the types of problems they encounter. For example, Sternberg differentiates componential, experiential, and contextual aspects of intelligence.

IQ tests are controversial because, on the average, some racial and cultural groups score lower on the tests than other groups. Instead of genetic differences, environmental disadvantages and test bias seem to be responsible for the lower scores of certain groups. Research shows that these group differences can be corrected through educational interventions. No test is entirely culture free, but the best IQ tests are valid predictors of school grades and success in certain jobs for *both* majority and minority groups, although no test is entirely culture free.

Assessing Personality

Personality characteristics are assessed by both objective and projective tests. The MMPI-2 is used to diagnose clinical problems. It contains 10 criterion-keyed clinical scales, 7 validity scales, and 15 homogeneous content scales. The CPI is a similar inventory that measures 20 folk concepts of personality, such as Dominance and Self-Control. It is intended for use with normal (nonclinical) populations. The NEO-PI is a newer personality test that measures five major dimensions of personality: Neuroticism, Extraversion, Openness, Agreeableness, and Conscientiousness. The Myers-Briggs Type Indicator identifies 16 personality types based on Jung's type theory, organized around preferences for sensing, feeling, thinking, intuiting, extraversion, and intraversion.

All four inventories have been used in longitudinal studies of personality structure and development. The MMPI and CPI are especially popular for research because there are extensive archives of MMPIs and CPIs taken by many types of people over many years. Hundreds of special-purpose scales have been constructed from the original item pools and validated in archival data banks. In applied settings, the CPI and the NEO can be used in informal career counseling or planning therapy in conjunction with an MMPI. The CPI has been validated for screening job applicants for certain jobs.

Projective tests of personality are less reliable and valid than objective tests. They are used primarily as a source of clinical hypotheses that must be evaluated through other assessment techniques. Two popular projective tests are the Rorschach test and Murray's TAT.

Statistical predictions from computerized test score results are superior to those made by clinical judges for specific predictions, but a combination of the two is preferred for more global, complex predictions. A personology orientation rejects psychometric testing, individual differences, and normative comparisons in favor of studying a broad range of idiographic information about the uniqueness of each person.

Assessment and You

Vocational assessment includes assessment of an individual's interests, aptitudes, and current level of achievement. The Strong-Campbell Interest Inventory compares an individual's interests with those of people who are successful in various occupations. The Occupations Analysis Inventory provides information about the requirements of various jobs.

Assessment is prevalent in many areas of our lives, but it also has become highly controversial. Though often useful for prediction and as an indication of current performance, test results should not be used to limit an individual's opportunities for development and change. When the results of an assessment will touch an individual's life, it is important to be sure that the techniques used are reliable and valid for that individual and for the purpose in question, and that the assessment is as thorough as possible, using all available sources of information.

KEY TERMS

achievement test, 568

aptitude test, 568

archival data, 546

chronological age (CA), 549

construct validity, 544

criterion validity, 543

crystallized intelligence, 553

eugenics, 541

face validity, 544

fluid intelligence, 553

g-factor, 551

halo effect, 548

heritability estimate, 559

intelligence, 549

intelligence quotient (IQ), 550

interjudge reliability, 548

internal consistency, 543

interview, 546

job analysis, 569

Juke Family, 556

Kallikak Family, 556

life history, 546

mental age (MA), 549

norms, 545

observer-report methods, 547

parallel forms, 543

personality inventory, 562

personology, 567

projective test, 566

psychological assessment, 540

psychological test, 546

psychometrics, 553

reliability, 543

self-report methods, 546

situational behavior observations, 546

standardization, 545

stereotype effect, 548

test-retest reliability, 543

validity, 543

word associations, 566

MAJOR CONTRIBUTORS

Binet, Alfred, 549

Cattell, Raymond, 553

Galton, Sir Francis, 541

Gardner, Howard, 555

Goddard, Henry, 556

Gough, Harrison, 565

Gould, Stephen Jay, 559

Guilford, J. P., 554

Hunt, Earl, 554

Meehl, Paul, 567

Murray, Henry, 567

Rorschach, Hermann, 566

Spearman, Charles, 551

Sternberg, Robert, 555

Strong, Edward, 568

Terman, Lewis, 550

Wechsler, David, 552

Chapter 16

Social Psychology

THE POWER OF THE SITUATION   577
   SOCIAL FACILITATION
   SOCIAL ROLES AND RULES
   SOCIAL NORMS
   CONFORMITY VERSUS INDEPENDENCE
   AUTHORITY INFLUENCE
   BYSTANDER INTERVENTION

   ■ INTERIM SUMMARY

CONSTRUCTING SOCIAL REALITY   595
   GUIDING BELIEFS AND EXPECTATIONS
   COGNITIVE FRAMEWORKS
   SOCIAL RELEVANCE OF SOCIAL PSYCHOLOGY'S
     DUAL LESSONS

   ■ INTERIM SUMMARY

SOLVING SOCIAL PROBLEMS   608
   ENVIRONMENTAL PSYCHOLOGY
   PEACE PSYCHOLOGY
   CLOSE-UP: CHANGING CONSERVATION ATTITUDES
     AND BEHAVIORS

RECAPPING MAIN POINTS   614

KEY TERMS   615

MAJOR CONTRIBUTORS   615

On a summer Sunday in California, a siren shattered the serenity of college student Tommy Whitlow's morning. A police car screeched to a halt in front of his home. Within minutes, Tommy was charged with a felony, informed of his constitutional rights, frisked, and handcuffed. After he was booked and fingerprinted, Tommy was blindfolded and transported to the Stanford County Prison, where he was stripped, sprayed with disinfectant, and issued a smock-type uniform with an I. D. number on the front and back. Tommy became Prisoner 647. Nine other college students were also arrested and assigned numbers.

The prison guards were not identified by name, and their anonymity was enhanced by khaki uniforms and reflector sunglasses—Prisoner 647 never saw their eyes. He referred to each of his jailers as "Mr. Correctional Officer, Sir"; to them, he was only number 647.

The guards insisted that prisoners obey all rules without question or hesitation. Failure to do so led to the loss of a privilege. At first, privileges included opportunities to read, write, or talk to other inmates. Later on, the slightest protest resulted in the loss of the "privileges" of eating, sleeping, and washing. Failure to obey rules also resulted in menial, mindless work such as cleaning toilets with bare hands, doing push-ups while a guard stepped on the prisoner's back, and spending hours in solitary confinement. The guards were always devising new strategies to make the prisoners feel worthless. Every guard Prisoner 647 encountered engaged in abusive, authoritarian behavior at some point during his incarceration. The main difference among the guards was in the frequency and regularity of their hostility toward the prisoners.

Less than 36 hours after the mass arrest, prisoner 8412, one of the ringleaders of an aborted prisoner rebellion that morning, began to cry uncontrollably. He experienced fits of rage, disorganized thinking, and severe depression. On successive days, three more prisoners developed similar stress-related symptoms. A fifth prisoner developed a psychosomatic rash all over his body when the Parole Board rejected his appeal.

At night, Prisoner 647 tried to remember what Tommy had been like before he became a prisoner. He also tried to imagine his tormentors before they became guards. He reminded himself that he was a college student who had answered a newspaper ad and agreed to be a subject in a two-week experiment on prison life. He had thought it would be fun to do something unusual, and he could always use some extra money.

Everyone in the prison, guard and prisoner alike, had been selected from a large pool of student volunteers who, on the basis of extensive psychological tests and interviews, had been judged as law-abiding, emotionally stable, physically healthy, and "normal-average." In this mock prison experiment, assignment of participants to "guard" or "prisoner" had been *randomly determined* by the flip of a coin. The prisoners lived in the jail around the clock, the guards worked standard eight-hour shifts.

In guard roles, college students who had been pacifists and "nice guys" behaved aggressively—sometimes even sadistically. As prisoners, psychologically stable students soon behaved pathologically, passively resigning themselves to their unexpected fate of learned helplessness. The power of the simulated prison situation had created a new *social reality*—a real prison—in the minds of the jailers and their captives.

Because of the dramatic and unexpectedly extreme emotional and behavioral effects observed, those prisoners with extreme stress reactions were released early from their pretrial detention in this unusual prison, and the psychologists were forced to terminate their two-week study after only six days.

Although Tommy Whitlow said he wouldn't want to go through it again, he valued the personal experience because he learned so much about himself and about human nature. Fortunately, he and the other students were basically healthy, and they readily bounced back from that highly charged situation. Follow-ups over many years revealed no lasting negative effects. The participants had all learned an important lesson: Never underestimate the power of a bad situation to overwhelm the personalities and good upbringing of even the best and brightest among us (Haney & Zimbardo, 1977; Zimbardo, 1975; replicated in Australia by Lovibond et al., 1979).

Suppose YOU had been a subject in the Stanford Prison Experiment. What kind of guard would you have been? As a prisoner, would you have blindly obeyed the authorities, become depressed from feeling so helpless, or resisted the situational pressures and acted heroically? We'd all like to believe we would be good guards and heroic prisoners, but the best predictor for the way you might react in this setting is the way a typical student, someone resembling you, actually behaved. The results of this study indicate that, despite optimistic beliefs, most of us would fall on the negative side of the good-bad, hero-victim dichotomy. The results do not offer an upbeat, positive message. However, it is a message that social psychologists, such as myself, feel obliged to pass along in the hope that such knowledge may be an antidote to mindless submission to the powerful forces that operate subtly and pervasively in many social situations to shape human behavior.

Welcome to the study of *social psychology,* that area of psychology that investigates the ways in which individuals affect each other. **Social psychology** is the study of the ways thoughts, feelings, perceptions, motives, and behavior are influenced by interactions and transactions between people. Social psychologists try to understand behavior within its *social context.* This social context is the vibrant canvas on which we paint the movements, strengths, and vulnerabilities of the social animal. Defined broadly, the **social context** includes (a) the real, imagined, or symbolic presence of other people; (b) the activities and interactions that take place between people; (c) the features of the settings in which behavior occurs; and (d) the expectations and norms that govern behavior in a given setting (C. Sherif, 1981).

The prison experiment in our Opening Case is not typical of research conducted in social psychology, but it underscores one of the main themes that has emerged from much innovative research social psychologists have conducted over the past 50 years: the *power of social situations* to control human behavior. In the first part of this chapter, we will explore this theme in a general context and its personal relevance for you. In doing so, we will consider a large body of research that shows the surprising extent to which small features of social settings can have a significant impact on what we think and how we act.

A second vital theme of social psychology is that situations matter not so much in their objective features but in their *subjective* nature, in the way that people perceive, interpret, and find meaning in them. We will study this second lesson of social psychology, *construction of social reality,* by investigating how people go about creating social realities for themselves and others.

Finally, we will look at a third issue of social psychology: determining how to solve *social problems* by applying the information generated by basic research on social processes. Social psychologists are making significant contributions to the improvement of the human condition by taking leading roles in applied fields such as health psychology, environmental psychology, psychology and law, and peace psychology. On this dimension of *social relevance,* abstract theory meets the stern test of practicality: does the theory make a difference in the lives of people and society?

THE POWER OF THE SITUATION

Throughout our study of psychology, we have seen that psychologists strive to understand the causes of behavior. However, depending on their orientation, they tend to look in different places for their answers. Some look to genetic factors, others to biochemical and brain processes, while still others focus on the causal influence of physical stimuli. We have seen that developmental researchers primarily consider childhood experiences, critical periods, and changes in age and stages. Personality psychologists study individual personality traits.

Social psychologists believe that the primary determinant of individual behavior is the nature of the social situation in which that behavior occurs. They argue that social situations exert significant control over individual behavior, often dominating personality and a person's past history of learning, values, and beliefs. Situational aspects that appear trivial to most observers—words, labels, signs, rules, social roles, the mere presence or number of other people, a group norm—can powerfully influence how we behave. Often, subtle situational variables affect us without our awareness. In this section, we will review some classic research and recent experiments that explore **situationism,** or the effect of these subtle situational variables on people.

SOCIAL FACILITATION

The earliest demonstration that the *mere presence* of other people has a measurable impact on individual behavior was conducted by **Norman Triplett** in 1897. The researcher, an avid cyclist, had noticed that bicycle racers had faster times when they were racing with other people than when they were racing against a clock. To determine whether this effect held true for other activities, he had children perform the task of winding fishing reels. Sure enough, the children performed faster when another child was present in the room than when they were alone.

This finding was not simply the result of *competition;* later studies found that it occurred also when an individual performed in front of an audience. It was also found in a *coacting group*—a group of people engaged in the same behavior but not interacting with each other, such as when several people play separate carnival games side-by-side. This improvement of individual performance brought about by the presence of other people is called **social facilitation.**

The social facilitation effect turned out to be more complicated than it seemed at first, however. Subsequent researchers found that sometimes the presence of others *interferes* with performance. Standing up before an audience, for example, may cause stage fright. One explanation for these apparently contradictory findings is that the presence of other people has the general effect of increasing an individual's level of arousal, or drive. This high drive will facilitate performance when a person is engaging in behavior that is well-learned. However, as we discussed in Chapter 12, if the responses are relatively new and not well-learned, then the increased drive can be disruptive. An individual will become tense and the drive will interfere with optimal performance (Zajonc, 1976).

Can you think of a time when you were in a group setting when you were less productive on a task than when you performed it alone? Aren't there times when working with other people seems to encourage goofing off? This phenomenon occurs often enough to be viewed as the flip side of social facilitation. **Social loafing** is defined as the unconscious tendency to slack off when performing in a group, regardless of whether the task is interesting and meaningful (Latané, 1981). The negative effects of social loafing are that people not only work less, but they take less responsibility for what they are doing.

Social loafing by any one person becomes greater as the size of the group increases. This group effect is attributed to the person's reduced self-attention as he or she must process more external inputs from other group members. When self-attention diminishes, so do the usual self-imposed controls of surveillance on behavior. When that happens, people become less concerned about matching their own behavior to standards of behavior that are salient in the situation or reflected in their past history of performance. They tend to go with the slower flow of the group (Carter & Scheier, 1981; Mullen & Baumeister, 1987). It is interesting to note that social loafing occurs more often in male than in female work groups (Hunt, 1985).

The social facilitation, interference, and loafing effects demonstrate the power of even the simplest social situation—the mere presence of other people. Most groups, however, involve more dynamic and direct interactions among their members.

SOCIAL ROLES AND RULES

The situations in which you live and function determine the roles available to you. Being a college student diminishes the likelihood that you will become a warrior, drug pusher, shaman, or prisoner, for example. Because you have college experience, numerous other roles, such as manager, teacher, and politician, are available to you.

Situations also help define the social meaning that each role will have for the people who have assumed it. A single action can be interpreted in many different ways, depending on the meaning different people assign to it. For example, defying authority can be interpreted as admirable and heroic, foolish and troublemaking, or dangerous and deviant. A **social role** is a socially defined pattern of behavior that is expected of a person when functioning in a given setting or group. People play many different social roles in the various situations in which they usually operate.

In order to promote social interaction and to achieve the desired outcomes of those in the majority or in power, situations also are characterized by the operation of **rules,** behavioral guidelines for certain settings. Some rules are explicitly stated in signs (*Don't Smoke, No Eating in Class*) or in socialization practices (Respect the elderly, Never take candy from a stranger). Other rules are implicit—they are learned through transactions with others in particular settings. How loud you can play your stereo, how close you can stand to another person, when you can call your teacher or boss by a first name, and what is the way to react to a compliment or a gift all depend on the situation. For example, the Japanese do not open a gift in the presence of the gift giver for fear of not showing sufficient appreciation; foreigners not aware of this unwritten rule will misinterpret the behavior as rude instead of sensitive.

Generic Prisoner-Guard Roles

At the conclusion of the **Stanford Prison Experiment,** guards and prisoners differed from one another in virtually every observable way; yet, just a week before, their role identities had been interchangeable. Chance, in the form of random assignment, had decided their roles, and these roles created status and power differences that were validated in the prison situation. The social context induced a host of differences in the way those in each group thought, felt, and acted (see **Figure 16.1**).

No one taught the participants to play their roles. We have to assume that each of the students had the

FIGURE 16.1   GUARD AND PRISONER BEHAVIOR

This interaction profile shows categories and frequencies of guard and prisoner behavior across 25 observation periods over six days in the Stanford Prison Experiment. Note the dramatic difference between the dominating, controlling, hostile behavior of the guards and the passive-resistance behavior of the prisoners.

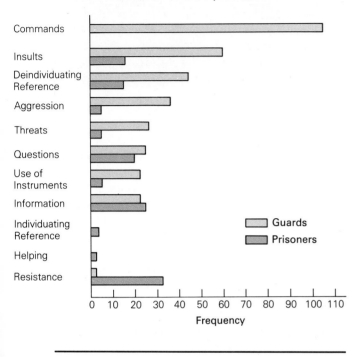

capacity to become either a prisoner or a guard by calling upon stored structures of knowledge about those roles. Without ever visiting a real prison, we have all learned from other personal experiences something about the interaction between the powerful and the powerless (Banuazizi & Movahedi, 1975). In our schemas and scripts, a guard-type is someone who limits the freedom of prisoner-types to manage their behavior and make them behave more predictably. This task is aided by the use of *coercive rules,* which include explicit punishment for violation. Prisoners can only *react* to the social structure of a prisonlike setting created by those with power. Rebellion or compliance are the primary options of the prisoners; the first option results in punishment, while the second results in a loss of a sense of autonomy and dignity. Some prisoners even go beyond strategic compliance and resign themselves to helplessness; they passively wait until the situation changes.

The student participants had already experienced such power differences in many of their previous social interactions: parent-child; teacher-student; doctor-patient; boss-worker; male-female. They merely refined and intensified their improvised scripts for this particular setting. Each student could have played either role. Many students in the guard role reported being surprised at how easy it was for them to enjoy controlling other people and how putting on the uniform was enough to transform them from college student research subjects into prison guards who had to manage inmates (*Discovering Psychology,* Program 18).

SOCIAL NORMS

In addition to the expectations regarding role behaviors, groups develop many expectations for the ways their members *should act.* The specific expectations for socially appropriate attitudes and behaviors that are embodied in the stated or implicit rules of a group are called **social norms.** Social norms can be broad guidelines; if you are member of Democrats for Social Action, you may be expected to hold liberal political beliefs. Social norms can also embody specific standards of conduct; if you are a spy, you may be expected to resist any attempt to extract secret information from you, including torture, imprisonment, and death. Norms can guide conversation; faculty do not talk about their work during meals at high table in Cambridge University. Norms can define rigid dress codes for members of groups; business people, gang members, and students are all expected to dress in certain ways.

Adjustment to a group typically involves discovering the set of social norms that regulates desired behavior in the group setting. This adjustment occurs in two ways: by noticing the *uniformities* in certain behaviors of all or most members and by observing the *negative consequences* when someone behaves in a nonnormative way, violating a social norm.

Norms serve several important functions. Awareness of the norms operating in a given group situation helps orient members and regulate their social interaction. Each participant can anticipate the way others will enter the situation, the way they will dress, what they are likely to say and do, as well as what type of behavior will be expected of them and gain approval. Some *tolerance for deviating* from the standard is also part of the norm—wide in some cases, narrow in others. Members are usually able to estimate how far they can go before experiencing the coercive power of the group in the form of the three painful R's: *ridicule, reeducation,* and *rejection.*

Adhering to the norms of a group is the first step in establishing *identification* with the group. Such identification allows an individual to have the feeling of

Social norms can define rigid dress codes for group members.

sharing in whatever prestige and power the group possesses. The social control imposed by group norms influences us almost from birth as part of the socialization process discussed in Chapter 5.

Norms emerge in a new group through two processes: *diffusion* and *crystallization*. When people first enter a group, they bring with them their own expectations, previously acquired through other group memberships and life experiences. These various expectations are diffused and spread throughout the group as the members communicate with each other. As people talk and carry out activities together, their expectations begin to converge or crystallize into a common perspective.

Sherif's Autokinetic Effect

The classic experiment that demonstrated **norm crystallization** was conducted by social psychologist **Muzafer Sherif** (1935). Subjects were asked to judge the amount of movement of a spot of light that was actually stationary but appeared to move when viewed in total darkness with no reference points, a perceptual illusion known as the **autokinetic effect.** Originally, individual judgments varied widely. However, when the subjects were brought together in a group and stated their judgments aloud, their estimates began to converge. They began to see the light move in the same direction and in similar amounts. Even more interesting was the final part of Sherif's study—when alone in the darkened room after the group viewing, these subjects continued to follow the group norm that had emerged when they were together.

Once norms are established in a group, they tend to perpetuate themselves. In later research, these autokinetic group norms persisted even when tested a year later and without peers witnessing the judgments (Roh-

rer et al., 1954). Other research shows that current group members exert social pressure on incoming members to adhere to the norms, and they, in turn, put direct or indirect pressure on successive newcomers to conform to the norms. Norms can be transmitted from one generation of group members to the next and can continue to influence people's behavior long after the original group that created the norm no longer exists (Insko et al., 1980). In autokinetic effect studies, researchers replaced one group member with a new one after each set of autokinetic trials until all the members of the group were new to the situation. The group's autokinetic norm remained true to that which had been handed down to them across several successive generations (Jacobs & Campbell, 1961). In natural groups, group *rituals* often serve the purpose of transmitting symbols, history, and values important to the group from old to new members.

Gordon Allport (1937; 1985), a major contributor to both personality theory and social psychology, has argued that two profound questions face social psychological researchers: How does one generation impose its culture and thought forms on the next and what happens to the mental life of the individual when he or she enters into association with others? The first question is addressed by studies such as those conducted on norm crystallization and by the research of cultural anthropologists and sociologists. The second question is studied in depth by analyzing group processes and the nature of social influence.

Group norms have a strong impact on an individual's behavior as long as the individual values the group. If the person comes to value and identify with a new group, then he or she will change to follow the norms of the new group. **Reference group** is the term for a formal or informal group from which an individual derives attitudes and standards of acceptable and appropriate behavior and to which the individual refers for information, direction, and support for a given lifestyle.

Bennington's Liberal Norms

Often, the process of being influenced by group norms is so gradual and so subtle that an individual does not perceive what is happening. Some insights into this process are provided by a classic study conducted, not in a laboratory, but in a small New England college for women in the late 1930s. Researcher **Theodore Newcomb** studied the shifts in political and social attitudes experienced by these students during their four years at Bennington College and then followed up the observed effects 20 years later to determine if they were enduring.

> The prevailing norm at Bennington College was one of political and economic liberalism, as encouraged by its young, dynamic, politically committed, and liberal faculty. On the other hand, most of the students had come from privileged, conservative homes and brought conservative attitudes with them. The study examined the impact of the college's liberal atmosphere on the attitudes of individual students. Among first-year Bennington students, over 60 percent supported the Republican presidential candidate, and fewer than 30 percent supported Franklin Roosevelt, the Democratic incumbent. Second-year students, however, were equally divided in their support for the two candidates. This liberal shift continued among the juniors and seniors—only 15 percent favored the Republican candidate, while 54 percent supported the Democratic candidate and more than 30 percent advocated support for the Socialist or Communist candidates! The conservatism of the new students steadily declined as they progressed through college, so that, by their senior year, most had been converted to a clearly liberal position.
>
> Newcomb accounted for this change in terms of several features of this unique situation and the powerful reference group norms that were operating. The girls were in a close-knit social community, self-sufficient and physically isolated from the outside world. The strong sense of school spirit included activist concerns and support for the norm of liberalism. Politically active liberal students were most likely to be chosen for positions of leadership, recognition, and for friendship. Pressures toward uniformity of attitudes and political actions were enforced by greater social acceptance and implied threats of rejection. These values became *internalized*, accepted as one's

own, by students for whom Bennington students had become the primary reference group.

> The students who *resisted* this pervasive norm and retained their conservatism fell into two categories: some were part of a small, close-knit, isolated group who were unaware of the conflict between their conservatism and the prevailing campus attitudes; others maintained strong ties with their conservative families, conforming to family standards rather than the school's (Newcomb, 1943).

Twenty years later, the marks of the Bennington experience were still evident. Most women who had left as liberals were still liberals (about 65 percent); those who had resisted had remained conservatives (about 16 percent); the rest were "middle of the roaders." Most had married men with values similar to their own, thus creating a supportive home environment. Of those who left college as liberals but married conservative men, a high proportion had returned to their first-year student conservatism (Newcomb, 1963). However, in the 1960 election, the Bennington allegiance showed through as about 60 percent of the 1935–1939 graduates voted for John F. Kennedy as compared to less than 30 percent support for Kennedy among comparable college graduates (Newcomb et al., 1976).

These substantial changes in important social and political attitudes were brought about by the combination of variables in the situation and the pressures of the reference-group norms. The more people rely on social rewards from a group for their primary sense of self-work and legitimacy, the greater will be the social influence that the group can bring to bear on them to be the kind of person the group values. Because social situations include the operation of roles, rules, and norms, they can be powerful agents of change, affecting people in socially prescribed ways or inhibiting and restraining them from changing in ways that are not deemed socially appropriate or situationally acceptable. In this way, people become not only liberals and conservatives, but supporters of apartheid if they are white South Africans, revolutionary nationalists if they are citizens of a former communist-bloc country, or radicals willing to bomb abortion clinics if they belong to pro-life groups. Finally, social norms assume greater force according to the extent that group members are in a **total situation,** one in which they are isolated from contrary points of view and in which sources of information, social rewards, and punishments are all highly controlled by group leaders. The thought reform that Chinese communists imposed on Chinese citizens, the "brainwashing" of prisoners of war, and the alleged coercive persuasion of cult members all have in common this element of intense indoctrination of new beliefs and values within the social isolation of a total situation (Lifton, 1969; Osherow, 1981).

"Candid Camera" Revelations

Social psychologists have attempted to demonstrate the power of situational forces by devising experiments that reveal the ease with which smart, independent, rational, good people can be led into behaving in ways that are dumb, compliant, irrational, and even evil. Although social psychologists have shown the *serious* consequences of situational power, it is equally possible to demonstrate this principle with *humor*. Indeed, "Candid Camera" scenarios, created by intuitive social psychologist **Allen Funt,** have been doing so for over 40 years. Funt showed how human nature follows a situational script to the letter. Millions in his TV audiences laughed when a diner stopped eating a hamburger whenever a "Don't Eat" counter light flashed; when pedestrians stopped and waited at a red street light above the *sidewalk* on which they were walking; when highway drivers turned back when seeing a road sign that read "Delaware is Closed"; and when customers jumped from one white tile to another in response to a store sign that instructed them not to walk on black tiles, for no good reason. One of the best "Candid Camera" illustrations of the subtle power of implicit situational rules to control behavior is the "elevator caper." A person riding a rigged elevator first obeyed the usual silent rule to face the front, but when a group of other passengers all faced the rear, the hapless victim followed the new *emerging group norm* and faced the rear as well.

We see in these slice-of-life episodes the minimal situational conditions needed to elicit unusual behaviors in ordinary people. We laugh because people who appear similar to us behave so foolishly and act so irrationally in response to small modifications in their commonplace situations. We implicitly distance ourselves from them by assuming we would not act that way. The lesson of much social psychological research is that, more than likely, you *would* behave exactly as others have if you were placed in the same situation. Poet John Donne reminds us that "No man is an island, entire of itself; every man is a piece of the continent." We are all interconnected by the situations and norms and rules we share. The wise reply to someone asking how you would have acted if you were in a situation in which people behaved in evil, foolish, or irrational ways is, "I don't know; it depends on how powerful the situation is." We can predict your behavior best by knowing the base rate or extent of compliance of those in the situation and making the conservative assumption that you would probably behave as the majority did. It is the

In this 1960s "Candid Camera" scenario, the woman with three legs asks the man if he would like to go dancing.

heroes among us who are able to do otherwise—to resist and overcome situational forces—and there are fewer heroes than followers in everyday life.

CONFORMITY VERSUS INDEPENDENCE

In the Bennington Study, conformity to the group norm had clear adaptive significance for the students; they were more likely to be accepted, approved, and recognized for various social rewards if they adopted the liberal norm. However, in the autokinetic situation, the subjects were not part of a reference group that controlled such vital social reinforcements and punishments. Their conformity to the crystallized norm of a transient group was not based on *normative pressures* but rather on other needs, such as the need for cognitive clarity about one's world. When uncertain, we typically turn to others in the situation to satisfy *information needs* that will help us understand what is happening (Deutsch & Gerard, 1955). Two of the reasons that account for why people conform to group pressures and comply with pressures from individuals are **normative influence** processes—wanting to be liked, accepted, and approved of by others—and **informational influence** processes—wanting to be correct and right and to understand how best to act in a given situation (Insko et al., 1985).

The Asch Effect: Yielding to Lying Lines

Although Sherif demonstrated that perceptions could be socially conditioned, his paradigm was not very relevant to important life situations because the subjects were judging a very ambiguous stimulus situation where any reaction by others might seem to clarify it. What would happen if individuals were making judgments under conditions where the physical reality was absolutely clear but the rest of the group saw the world differently? That is the situation created by one of the most important social psychologists, **Solomon Asch** (1940; 1956). Asch believed that physical reality constraints on perception would be stronger than the power of the social context to distort individual judgments. He was wrong, and his studies produced the **Asch effect,** which describes the influence of a unanimous group majority on the judgments of individuals even under unambiguous conditions. The Asch effect has become the classic illustration of **conformity,** the tendency for people to adopt the behavior and opinions presented by other group members.

Groups of seven to nine male college students were led to believe they were in a study of simple visual perception. They were shown cards with three lines of differing lengths and asked to indicate which of the three lines was the same length as the standard line (see **Figure 16.2**). The lines were different enough so that mistakes were rare,

CONFORMITY IN THE ASCH EXPERIMENTS

Faced with a unanimous majority giving an erroneous judgment, the concern of naive subject #6 is evident in the photo from Asch's study. A sample of stimulus materials is shown above on the left. The graph illustrates conformity across 12 critical trials when solitary individuals were with a unanimous majority and also their greater independence when paired with a dissenting partner.

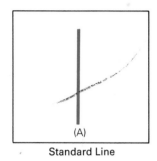
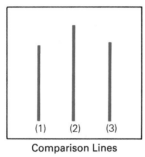

Standard Line (A)

Comparison Lines (1) (2) (3)

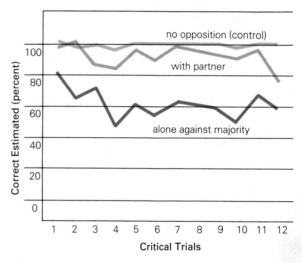

and their relative sizes changed on each series of trials.

On the first three trials, everyone agreed on the correct comparison. However, the first person to respond on the fourth trial reported seeing as equal two lines that were obviously different. So did the next person and so on, until all members of the group but one unanimously agreed on a judgment that conflicted with the perception of the final student. That student had to decide if he should go along with everyone else's view of the situation and conform or if he remain independent, standing by what he clearly saw. That dilemma was repeated on 12 of the 18 trials. Unknown to this last subject, the others were all experimental confederates who were following a prearranged script, which also included no communication other than calling out the perceptual judgment. The subject showed signs of disbelief and obvious discomfort when faced with a majority who saw the world so differently than he did. What did he and others in his position do?

Only one fourth of the subjects remained completely *independent*. Between 50 and 80 percent of the subjects (in different studies in the research program) *conformed* with the false majority estimate at least once, while a third of the subjects yielded to the majority's wrong judgments on half or more of the critical trials. Asch describes some subjects who yielded to the majority most of the time as "disoriented" and "doubt-ridden," and they "experienced a powerful impulse not to appear different from the majority" (1952, p. 396).

In other studies, Asch varied three factors: the size of the unanimous majority, the presence of a partner who dissented from the majority, and the size of the discrepancy between the correct physical stimulus comparison and the majority's position. He found that strong conformity effects were elicited with a unanimous majority of only three or four people, but that no effects were elicited with just one confederate. Giving the naive subject one ally who dissented from the majority opinion sharply reduced conformity, as can be seen in Figure 16.2. With a partner, the subject was usually able to resist the pressures to conform to the majority. As you might expect, independence also increased with the magnitude of the contradiction between one's perception and the group's erroneous judgment. Remarkably, a certain proportion of individuals continued to yield to the group even under the most extreme stimulus circumstances. All who yielded underestimated

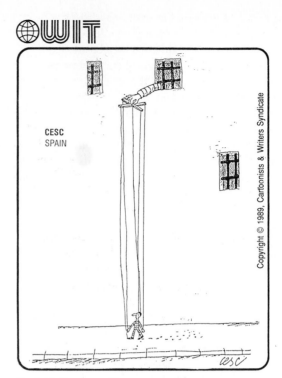

Social influence without awareness

the influence of the social pressure and the frequency of their conformity; some even claimed that they really had *seen* the lines as the same (Asch, 1955, 1956).

Numerous studies of conformity have confirmed these results. They hold across a wide range of different types of judgments, with many types of stimuli and even in the absence of an actual face-to-face group when the individual subject only sees the alleged group judgments displayed on a "conformity machine" (Crutchfield, 1955). The power of the group majority depends on its unanimity. Once it is broken—in any way—the rate of conformity drops dramatically. A person is also more likely to conform when (a) a judgment task is difficult or ambiguous; (b) a group is highly cohesive and the individual feels attracted to it; (c) the group members are perceived as competent and the person feels relatively incompetent on the task; and (d) a person's responses are made public to others in the group. In many cases, people conform and are influenced without awareness that they have been affected, maintaining an *illusion* of freedom and independence that is unwarranted by their actions.

Minority Influence and Nonconformity

Given the power of the majority to control resources and reinforcements, the extent of conformity that exists at all levels of our society is not surprising. How can anyone escape group domination and how can anything new (counternormative) ever come about? How do revolutions against the status quo emerge? Are there any conditions under which a small minority can turn the majority around and create new norms? While researchers in the United States have concentrated their studies on conformity, in part because conformity is intertwined with the democratic process which is based on the concept of strength in numbers, some European social psychologists have instead focused on the power of the few to change the majority. **Serge Moscovici** of France has pioneered the study of minority influence.

> In one study where subjects were given color naming tasks, the majority correctly identified the color patches, but two of the experimenter's confederates consistently identified a green color as *blue*. Their consistent minority opposition had no immediate effect on the majority but, when later tested alone, some of the subjects shifted their judgments by moving the boundary between blue and green toward the blue side of the color continuum (Moscovici, 1976; Moscovici & Faucheux, 1972).

Researchers have also studied minority influence in the context of *simulated jury deliberations,* where a disagreeing minority prevents the unanimous acceptance of the majority point of view. The minority group was never well liked, and its persuasiveness, when it occurred, only worked over time (Nemeth, 1979). The vocal minority was most influential when it had four qualities: it persisted in affirming a *consistent* position, appeared *confident,* avoided seeming rigid and dogmatic, and was skilled in social influence. Eventually, the power of the many may be undercut by the conviction of the dedicated few (Moscovici, 1980).

What makes a minority have influence over the deliberations of the majority? Majority decisions tend to be made without engaging *systematic thought* and *critical thinking skills* of the individuals in the group. They are often taken at face value, given the force of the group's normative power to shape the opinions of the followers who conform without thinking things through. The persistent minority forces the others to process the relevant information more *mindfully* (Langer, 1989). Research shows that the decisions of the group as a whole are more *thoughtful* and *creative* when there has been minority dissent than in its absence (Nemeth, 1986). The group also *better recalls* the information after having been exposed to a consistent minority view than to only the majority or inconsistent minority view (Nemeth et al., 1990).

Another demonstration of the power of situational variables comes from research on the way individuals affect jury deliberations. To have the most influence on a jury, you must get elected foreperson, which can be accomplished quite simply by speaking first in the group, volunteering for the job, or sitting in the "power seat" at the head of a rectangular table, if there is one. Jurors seated at the ends of a table both initiate and receive the most communication in the group, which makes them more influential (Strodtbeck & Hook, 1961).

In society, the majority tends to be the defender of the *status quo,* while the force for innovation and change comes from the minority members or individuals either dissatisfied with the current system or able to visualize new options and creative alternative ways of dealing with current problems. The conflict between the entrenched majority view and the dissident minority perspective is an essential precondition of innovations that can lead to positive social change. An individual is constantly engaged in a two-way exchange with society—adapting to its norms, roles, and status prescriptions but also acting upon society to reshape those norms (Moscovici, 1985). Perhaps the greatest challenge for social psychologists is to understand the dynamics of the interplay of group forces that influence an individual's behavioral and mental processes and those individual factors that maintain or change group functioning.

AUTHORITY INFLUENCE

We have been considering how groups influence individuals, but there are certain individuals—leaders and authorities—who exert considerable power on group behavior and on other people. The ultimate demonstration of this effect was seen in the 1930s with the emergence of Adolf Hitler in Germany and Benito Mussolini in Italy. These leaders were able to transform rational individuals into mindless masses with unquestioning loyalty to a fascist ideology bent on world conquest. Their authoritarian regimes threatened democracies and freedom everywhere. Curiously, modern social psychology developed out of this crucible of fear, war, and prejudice. Its early concerns were focused on understanding the nature of the *authoritarian personality* behind the fascist mentality (Adorno et al., 1950), the effects of propaganda and persuasive communications (Hovland et al., 1949), and the impact of group atmosphere and leadership styles on group members. Later research by Stanley Milgram added a concern for understanding how individuals could become so blindly obedient to the commands of authorities.

Lewin's Group Dynamics

The pioneering figure in social psychology was **Kurt Lewin,** a German refugee who escaped Nazi oppression. Lewin could not help but wonder how his nation could succumb so totally to the tyranny of a dictator. He witnessed the spectacle of rallies of tens of thousands of people shouting allegiance to their führer, frightening testimony to the dynamic power of groups to transform the minds and actions of individuals and the power of an individual to affect the masses. Lewin investigated the ways in which leaders directly influenced their followers and how group processes changed the behavior of individuals. His approach was dynamic and motivational, based on the principle that behavior changed when motivations were aroused, channeled in specific directions, and satisfied by a given action or behavior pattern. Lewin started the study of **group dynamics,** investigating how group processes changed individual functioning. His students at MIT and later at the University of Michigan studied group-level variables such as group cohesiveness, social power, cooperation and competition, and conflict resolution. However, his most important contribution was in demonstrating that it was possible to pose socially significant questions that could be translated into hypotheses and tested in ingenious experiments in field studies.

In 1939, Lewin and his colleagues Ron Lippitt and Ralph White designed an experiment to investigate the effects of group atmosphere and different leadership styles. They wanted to find out if people are happier or more productive under autocratic or democratic leadership. To those who had witnessed both the rise of Hitler's fascism and the initially confused, ineffectual response of the Western democracies, answers to the question these researchers posed were crucial.

Kurt Lewin (*Discovering Psychology,* 1990, Program 19)

To assess the effects of different leadership styles, the researchers created three experimental groups, gave them different types of leaders, and observed the groups in action. The subjects were four small groups of 10 year-old boys, meeting after school. The group leaders were men who were trained to play each of the three leadership styles. When they acted as *autocratic leaders,* the men were to make all decisions and work assignments but not participate in the group activity. As *democratic leaders,* they were to encourage and assist group decision-making and planning. Finally, when they acted as *laissez-faire leaders,* their job was to allow complete freedom with little leader participation. At the end of each six-week period, the leaders took over a different group and also changed their leadership style according to the researchers' prearranged script. Thus, all groups experienced each of the three leadership styles under a different person, so that the leadership style was largely *independent* of the leader's personality.

The results of this field experiment suggested a number of generalizations. First, *autocratic* leaders produced a mixed bag of effects on their followers—some positive and some quite negative. At times, the boys worked very hard but typically only when the leader—acting as boss—was watching them, and they rarely did so when on their own. However, there was little originality in what they produced. What most characterized the boys in the autocratic groups was their high level of aggression. These boys showed up to *30 times more hostility* when under autocratic leaders than they did under the other types of leaders. They demanded more attention, were more likely to destroy their own property, and showed more **scapegoating** behavior—using weaker individuals as displaced targets for their frustration and anger. Coupled with this greater aggressiveness was more dependence on and submission to the leader's authority—they behaved similar to fascists.

As for the *laissez-faire groups,* not much good resulted. They were the most inefficient of all, doing the least amount of work and of the poorest quality. In the absence of any social structure, they simply goofed off. However, when the same groups were *democratically run,* members worked the most steadily and they were most efficient. The boys showed the highest levels of interest, motivation, and originality under democratic leadership. When discontent arose, it was likely to be openly expressed. Almost all the boys

These photos from Lewin's classic study show the three leadership styles in action. The autocratic leader directs work, the democratic leader works with the boys, and the laissez-faire leader remains aloof.

preferred the democratic group to the others. Democracy promoted more group loyalty and friendliness. There was more mutual praise, more friendly remarks, more sharing, and, overall, more playfulness (Lewin et al., 1939).

Democracy proved superior psychologically to the other forms of group atmosphere, and democratic leaders generated the most healthy reactions from group members, while autocratic-leader groups generated the most destructive individual reactions. Another psychological lesson emerged form this pioneering experiment: general leadership style was proven more important than the specific personality of individual leaders. No matter what a leader's personality traits, his impact on the group depended entirely on the leadership style he enacted. Because *leadership style* was a core part of the social situation the boys faced, this study was one of the first to show that aspects of social situations significantly control individual behavior.

Milgram's Obedience to Authority

When you think of the long and gloomy history of man, you will find more hideous crimes have been committed in the name of obedience than have been committed in the name of rebellion (C. P. Snow, 1961, p. 3).

What made Adolf Eichmann and other Nazis willing to send millions of Jews to the gas chambers? Did a character defect lead them to carry out orders blindly, even if the orders violated their own values and moral principles? How can we explain the 1978 mass suicide-murders of the members of the Peoples Temple? Over 900 American citizens belonging to the cult willingly gave cyanide poison to their children and to themselves because their leader, Reverend Jim Jones, told them to commit "revolutionary suicide."

Let's get personal. How about YOU? Would you electrocute a stranger if Hitler or Eichmann asked you? Are there any conditions under which you would blindly obey an order from your religious leader to poison others and then commit suicide? Could you imagine being part of the American massacre of hundreds of innocent citizens of the Vietnamese village of My Lai (Hersh, 1971; Opton, 1970, 1973)?

Your answer—as mine used to be—is most likely, "No! What kind of person do you think I am?" After reading this next section, you may be more willing to answer, "Maybe. I don't know for sure." Depending on the power of the social forces operating on your moral judgment and weakening your will to resist, you might do what other human beings have done in those situations, however horrible and alien their actions may seem outside that setting.

In 1978, over 900 members of the Peoples Temple either committed mass suicide or were murdered at the command of their leader, Reverend Jim Jones.

The most convincing demonstration of situational power over individual behavior was created by **Stanley Milgram,** a student of Solomon Asch. Milgram's research (1965, 1974) showed that the blind obedience of Nazis was less a product of dispositional characteristics (their unusual personality or German national character) than it was the outcome of situational forces that could engulf anyone—even you and me. How did he demonstrate this "banality of evil," that evil deeds could be engaged in by good people for what they felt were noble purposes (Hannah Arendt, 1963, 1971)? Milgram's obedience research is one of the most controversial in psychology both because of the ethical issues it raises and its significant implications for real world phenomena (Miller, 1986; Ross & Nisbett, 1991).

The Obedience Paradigm To separate the variables of personality and situation, which are always entangled in natural settings, Milgram used a series of controlled laboratory experiments involving more than 1000 subjects. Milgram's first experiments were conducted at Yale University with Yale college students and then male residents of New Haven who received payment for their participation. In later variations, Milgram took his obedience laboratory to the community. He set up a storefront research unit in Bridgeport, Connecticut, recruiting through newspaper ads a broad cross section of the population, varying widely in age, occupation, and education and of both sexes. Volunteers thought they were participating in a scientific study of memory and learning.

The basic experimental paradigm involved individual subjects delivering a series of what they thought were extremely painful electric shocks to another person. They did so not because they were sadistic but because they were participating in a worthwhile cause—or so they believed. They were led to believe that the purpose of the study was to discover how *punishment* affects memory so that learning and memory could be improved through the proper balance of reward and punishment. In their *social roles* as *teachers,* the subjects were to punish each error made by someone playing the role as *learner.* The major *rule* they were told to follow was to increase the level of shock by a fixed amount each time the learner made an error until the learning was errorless. The white-coated experimenter acted as the *legitimate authority* figure—he presented the rules, arranged for the assignment of roles (by a rigged drawing of lots), and ordered the *teachers* to do their jobs whenever they hesitated or dissented.

The *dependent variable* was the final level of shock—on a shock machine that went up to 435 volts in 15 volt steps—that a "teacher" gave before refusing to continue to obey the authority. The initial study was

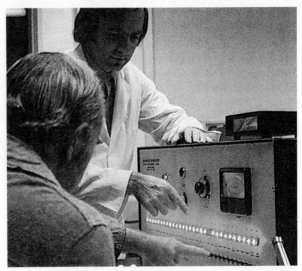

An experimenter shows the "teacher" how to use the shock generator. How would you behave in this situation?

simply a demonstration of the phenomenon of obedience; there was no manipulation of an independent variable. Later versions did study the effect of varying many situational factors, such as the physical distance between the *teacher* and the *authority* and the *learner.* Milgram did not use a formal no-treatment control or comparison group, as was also true of the Stanford Prison Study. In both these demonstrations, the comparison group was implicit: typical readers of the research who had beliefs about the way they would have behaved under such circumstances—you and other ordinary people.

The Test Situation The study was staged to make a subject think that, by following orders, he or she was causing pain and suffering and perhaps even killing an innocent person. Each *teacher* had been given a sample shock of about 75 volts to feel the amount of pain it caused. The *learner* was a pleasant, mild-mannered man, about 50 years old, who mentioned something about a heart condition but was willing to go along with the procedure. He was strapped into an "electric chair" in the next room and communicated with the *teacher* via an intercom. His task was to memorize pairs of words, giving the second word in a pair when he heard the first one. The *learner* soon ran into difficulty and began making errors, and the *teacher* began shocking the learner. The protests of the victim rose with the shock level. At 75 volts, he began to moan and grunt; at 150 volts he demanded to be released from the experiment; at 180 volts he cried out that he could not stand the pain any longer. At 300 volts he insisted that he would no longer take part in the experiment and must be freed. He yelled out about his heart condition and screamed. If a *teacher* hesitated or protested delivering the next shock, the experimenter said, "Teacher, you have no other choice; you must go on! Your job is to punish the learner's mistakes." As you might imagine, the situation was stressful for the subjects. Most subjects complained and protested, repeatedly insisting they could not continue. That the experimental situation produced considerable conflict in the subjects is readily apparent from their protests:

- 180 volts delivered: "He can't stand it! I'm not going to kill that man in there! You hear him hollering? He's hollering. He can't stand it. What if something happens to him? . . . I mean, who is going to take the responsibility if anything happens to that gentleman?" [The experimenter accepts responsibility.] "All right."
- 195 volts delivered: "You see he's hollering. Hear that. Gee, I don't know." [The experimenter says, "The experiment requires that you go on."] "I know it does, sir, but I mean—huh—he don't know what he's in for. He's up to 195 volts."
- 240 volts delivered: "Aw, no. You mean I've got to keep going up with that scale? No sir, I'm not going to kill that man! I'm not going to give him 450 volts!" (1965, p. 67).

When the *learner* stopped responding, some subjects called out to him to respond, urging him to get the answer right so they would not have to continue shocking him. All the while they protested loudly to the experimenter, but the experimenter insisted that the *teacher* continue. "Rules are rules!" Even when there was only silence from the *learner's* room, the *teacher* was ordered to keep shocking him more and more strongly, all the way up to the button that was marked "Danger: Severe Shock XXX (450 volts)."

Did they obey? Would YOU? How far do you think the average subject in Milgram's experiment actually went in administering the shocks? (Your estimate: _____ volts). What percentage do you estimate went all the way up to the end of the shock scale in blindly obeying authority? (Your estimate: _____ percent). Suppose for a moment that you were the subject-teacher. How far up the scale would you go? Which of the levels of shock would be the absolute limit beyond which you would refuse to continue? (Your estimate: _____ volts).

To Shock or Not to Shock? When 40 psychiatrists were asked to predict the performance of subjects in this experiment, they estimated that most would not go beyond 150 volts. In their professional opinions, fewer than four percent of the subjects would still be

obedient at 300 volts and only about 0.1 percent would continue to 450 volts. The psychiatrists presumed that only those few individuals who were *abnormal* in some way, the sadists, would blindly obey orders to harm another person in an experiment. How close are your predictions to theirs? Do your estimates agree with these experts?

If so, you are both wrong! The psychiatrists based their evaluations on presumed *dispositional* qualities of people who would engage in such abnormal behavior; they were overlooking the power of this special situation to influence the thinking and actions of most people caught up in its social context. *The majority of subjects obeyed the authority fully!* Nearly two thirds delivered the maximum 450 volts to the learner. The average subject did not quit until about 300 volts. No subject who got within five switches of the end ever refused to go all the way. By then, their resistance was broken; they had resolved their own conflict—and just tried to get it over with as quickly as possible. It is important to note that most people *dissented* verbally, but the majority did not *disobey* behaviorally. From the point of view of the victim that's a critical difference.

Why Do We Obey Authority? From the many variations of situational stimuli that Milgram conducted, we can conclude that the obedience effect is strongest under the following conditions, as shown in **Figure 16.3:** (a) with the social influence of a peer who first models obedience; (b) when there is great remoteness of victim from subject; (c) when there is direct surveillance of the subject by the authority; (d) when a subject acts as an *intermediary bystander* assisting another person who actually delivers the shock; and (e) when the relative status of the authority figure to the subject is greater. This last finding comes from a replication of the study with high-school students tested by a Princeton University experimenter—a study in which obedience reached 80 percent (Rosenhan, 1969). Evidence that the obedience effect is due to situational variables and not personality variables is demonstrated by increasing the effect through manipulating the above conditions, and by knocking out the effect through varying other stimulus conditions (experiments 11, 12, 14, 15, and 17 in Figure 16.3). For example, subjects don't obey authority when the *learner* demands to be shocked, when two authorities give contradictory commands, or when the authority figure is the victim. We can rule out the role of personality effects with the finding that personality tests administered to the subjects did *not* reveal any traits that differentiated those who obeyed from those who refused or any psychological disturbance or abnormality in the obedient punishers.

FIGURE 16.3 OBEDIENCE IN 18 EXPERIMENTS

The graph shows a profile of weak to strong obedience effects across Milgram's 19 (one experiment has two variations) experimental variations.

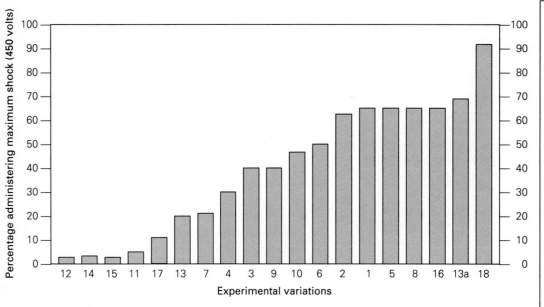

1. Remote victim
2. Voice feedback
3. Proximity
4. Touch proximity
5. New baseline
6. Change of personnel
7. Remote authority
8. Women as subjects
9. The victim's limited contract
10. Institutional context
11. Subjects free to choose shock level
12. Learner demands to be shocked
13. An ordinary man gives orders
13a. The subject as bystander
14. Authority as victim—an ordinary man commanding
15. Two authorities—contradictory commands
16. Two authorities—one as victim
17. Two peers rebel
18. A peer administers shock

So why did they do it? One possibility is that the subjects did not really believe the "cover story" of the experiment, knowing that the victim was not really getting hurt. This alternative was ruled out by an independent replication that made the effects of being obedient vivid, immediate, and direct for the subjects.

College students were asked to train a puppy on a discrimination task by punishing it with increasing levels of shock whenever it made an error. They could see it jumping around on an electrified grid when they pressed a switch. Actually, the puppy received only a low level of shock—just enough to make it squeal but not hurt it. The students dissented and complained and got upset, and some even cried. At a given point, an odorless, colorless anesthetic was secretly released into the puppy's enclosed chamber. The dog wobbled and finally fell asleep. The subjects thought they had killed the puppy, but the experimenter reminded them of the *situational rule;* failure to respond is a punishable error; they must continue to give shocks.

Three fourths of all students delivered the maximum shock possible. Every one of the female subjects proved to be totally obedient despite their dissent (Sheridan & King, 1972).

Another alternative explanation for subjects' behavior is that the effect is limited to the **demand characteristics** of the experimental situation. Sometimes cues in the experimental setting influence subjects' perceptions of what is expected of them and systematically influence their behavior. Is blind obedience to authority in Milgram's study merely a response to the demands of the unusual experimental setting? Can it be shown that the same effect would occur in a real-life situation in which obeying authority could harm someone?

A team of psychiatrists and nurses performed the following field study to test the power of obedience in the natural setting of a hospital. A nurse (the subject) received a call from a staff doctor whom she had not met. He told her to administer some medication to a patient so that it could take effect by the time he arrived. He would sign the drug order after he got to the ward. The doctor ordered a dose of 20 milligrams of a drug called *Astroten*. The label on the container of Astroten stated that 5 milligrams was the usual dose and warned that the maximum dose was 10 milligrams.

Would a nurse actually administer an excessive dose of a drug on the basis of a telephone call from an unfamiliar person when doing so was contrary to standard medical practice? When this dilemma was *described* to 12 nurses, 10 *said* they would disobey. However what nurses did was another, by now, familiar story. When another group of them were actually in the situation, almost every nurse obeyed! Twenty-one of 22 had started to pour the medication (actually a harmless substance) before a physician researcher stopped them (Hofling et al., 1966).

Two reasons people obey authority in these situations can be traced to the effects of *normative* and *informational* sources of influence, which we discussed earlier. People want to be liked and they want to be right. They tend to do what others are doing or requesting (normative peer influence and normative authority influence) in order to be socially acceptable and approved. In addition, when in an ambiguous, novel situation, people rely on others for cues as to what is the appropriate and correct way to behave. They are more likely to do so when experts or credible communicators tell them what to do. A third factor in the Milgram paradigm is that subjects were probably confused about *how to disobey;* nothing they said in dissent satisfied the authority. If they had a simple, direct way out of the situation, for example, by pressing a "quit" button, it is likely more would have disobeyed (Ross, 1988). Finally, obedience to authority in this experimental situation is part of an *ingrained habit* that is learned by children in many different settings—obey authority without question (Brown, 1986). This heuristic usually serves us and our society well when authorities are legitimate and deserving of our obedience. The problem is that *the rule gets overapplied,* just as when children first learn the grammatical rules for past tense they add *ed* to all verbs even when it is wrong to do so. Similarly, blind obedience to authority means obeying any and all authority figures simply because of their ascribed status, regardless of whether they are unjust or just in their requests and commands.

What is the personal significance to you of this obedience research? Recall the image of a lone man standing before tanks in Tiannamen Square during the rebellion of Chinese students in June 1989. We must ask ourselves if we would do the same. What choices will you make when faced with moral dilemmas throughout your life? Many of the scandals at the highest level of government, military, and business involve authorities expecting their subordinates to behave in unethical and illegal ways.

Even our nation's leaders are subject to the pressures applied to those who disobey the wishes of their leaders and the other "team players." It was discovered in 1986 that high-level government officials were involved in a complex, illegal deal that sold arms to Iran in return for the release of American hostages. These officials then diverted the profits from those arms sales to aid the right-wing Contra rebels in Nicaragua. The former director of the National Security Council, Robert McFarlane, testified before a Congressional investigating committee that he was part of the attempt by the White House to deceive Congress about this Iran-Contra affair. He said he "didn't have the guts" to tell President Reagan that he thought the method for achieving their goal was wrong. Why not? "To tell you the truth, probably the reason I didn't is because if I'd done that, Bill Casey [former CIA Director], Jeanne Kirkpatrick [former U. N. ambassador], and Cap Weinberger [Defense Secretary] would have said I was some kind of Commie, you know" (*Newsweek,* May 25, 1987).

Resisting such situational forces requires being aware of and accepting the fact that they can be powerful enough to affect almost anyone, even you. Then you

Would you have the courage to stand up to authority?

need to analyze the situation mindfully and critically for the details that don't fit, for flaws in the "cover story," or the rationales that don't make sense upon careful analysis. For example, why did the Milgram experimenter need to hire naive subjects to shock other people when he could have better used a trained research assistant or had the shocking done automatically by an electronic apparatus? Most important in resisting all compliance-gaining situations, is leaving the situation, taking a "time out" to think things over, never signing on the dotted line the first time, and being willing to appear to make a mistake and to appear as a poor team player.

As in the case of the Stanford prison study, this obedience research challenges the myth that evil lurks in the minds of evil people—the bad *they* who are different dispositionally from the good *us* who would never do such things. The purpose in recounting these findings is not to debase human nature but to make clear that even normal, well-meaning individuals are subject to the human potential for frailty in the face of strong situational and social forces.

▬▬▬▬▬▬▬▬ Time out for a *critical thinking exercise*. In August 1991, the world shuddered as a group of Soviet leaders attempted to overthrow the government of Mikhail Gorbachev. These high-ranking politicians, military men, and KGB police leaders were political hardliners bent on turning the Soviet Union away from its recent democratic reforms and new policies that were weakening the Communist Party and its central control over the Soviet Republics. The coup failed for many reasons. Try to explain some of the social psychological reasons it may have failed by using the principles outlined in the previous sections on the effectiveness of minority influence and the ineffectiveness of obedience to authority.

Interestingly, Russian President Boris Yeltsin praised the *disobedience* of an elite group of KGB commandos who were ordered by the plotters to capture or kill Yeltsin and take over Parliament. Despite threats of court-martial and even death, these commandos refused to obey illegitimate authority, a heroic action that contributed to the failure of the coup (*San Francisco Chronicle,* 8/26/91). ▬▬▬▬▬

BYSTANDER INTERVENTION

Consider a different perspective on the obedience situation of Milgram's experiments: If you were a *bystander,* would you intervene to help one of the distressed *teachers* disobey the authority and exit from the situation? Would you be more likely to intervene if you were the only bystander or if you were part of a group of observers? Before answering, you might want to reflect on what social psychologists have discovered about the nature of **bystander intervention** and the way it reflects another aspect of situational forces.

For more than half an hour, 38 respectable, law-abiding citizens in Queens, New York, watched a killer stalk and stab a woman in three separate attacks. Two times the sound of the bystanders' voices and the sudden glow of their bedroom lights interrupted the assailant and frightened him. Each time, however, he returned and stabbed her again. Not a single person telephoned the police during the assault; only one witness called the police after the woman was dead (*The New York Times,* March 13, 1964). This newspaper account of the murder of *Kitty Genovese* shocked a nation that could not accept the idea of such apathy on the part of its responsible citizenry. In a similar case, an 18-year-old secretary was beaten, choked, stripped, and raped in her office. She finally broke away from her assailant and, naked and bleeding, she ran down the stairs of the building to the doorway screaming, "Help me! Help me! He raped me!" A crowd of 40 persons gathered on the busy street and watched passively as the rapist dragged her back upstairs. Only the chance passing of the police put an end to further abuse and possibly murder (*The New York Times,* May 6, 1964).

Would you have called the police to help Kitty Genovese or intervened in some way to help the woman being raped? The temptation is to say, "Yes, of course." However, we must be careful to resist overconfidence about the way we would react in an unfamiliar situation. Why don't bystanders help in cases such as these? What would make them more likely to do so? A classic series of studies of the bystander intervention problem was carried out soon after the Kitty Genovese murder by social psychologists **Bibb Latané** and **John Darley** (1968). They ingeniously created in the laboratory an experimental analogue of the bystander-intervention situation. A college student, placed in a room by himself with an intercom, was led to believe that he was communicating with one or more students in an adjacent room. During the course of a discussion about personal problems, he heard what sounded like one of the other students having an epileptic seizure and gasping for help.

During the "seizure" it was impossible for the subject to talk to the other students or to find out what, if anything, they were doing about the emergency. The dependent variable was the speed with which he reported the emergency to the experimenter. The major independent variable was the number of people he thought were in the discussion group with him.

It turned out that the likelihood of intervention depended on the number of bystanders he thought were present. The more there were, the slower he was in reporting the seizure, if he did so at all. As you can see in **Figure 16.4,** everyone in a two-person situation intervened within 160 seconds, but nearly 40 percent of those who believed they were part of a larger group never bothered to inform the experimenter that another student was seriously ill. Personality tests showed no significant relationship between particular personality characteristics and speed or likelihood of intervening. The best predictor of bystander intervention is the situational variable of size of the group present. The likelihood of intervention decreases as the group increases in size, probably because each person makes the assumption that others will help, so he or she does not have to make that commitment.

When similar studies of bystander intervention are carried out in *field situations* rather than in the labora-

tory, a victim's chances of getting help increase considerably.

A man on a moving New York subway train suddenly collapsed and fell to the floor. A number of bystanders witnessed this event. The experimenters manipulated the situation by varying the characteristics of the "victim"—an invalid with a cane, a drunk smelling of liquor, or, in a companion study, a disabled person apparently bleeding (or not bleeding) from the mouth. The researchers unobtrusively recorded the bystander responses to these emergency situations. One or more persons responded directly in most cases (81 out of 103) with little hesitation. Help was slower when the apparent *cost* of intervening was higher (that is,

---

FIGURE 16.4   *Bystander Intervention in an Emergency*

The likelihood of bystanders intervening in an emergency decreases as the number of other people present increases. Bystanders act most quickly in two-person groups

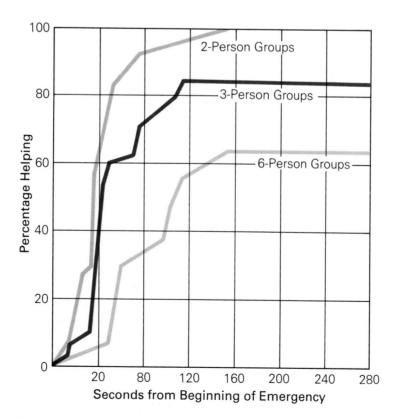

slower for a bloody victim who might require a greater degree of involvement than a victim who simply collapsed), but it usually still came (Pilia-van & Piliavan, 1972; Piliavan et al., 1969).

What accounts for the fact that students do not help as much in a laboratory situation as citizens in a natural setting? Intervention in the laboratory setting is likely to be inhibited for any or all of the following reasons: (a) the college student subjects have already adopted the *passive* role of "subject"; (b) they assume that the experimenter in charge is ultimately responsible for everything that occurs during an experimental session; (c) they often do not actually see the victim-in-distress; and (d) they are severely restricted by obedience to an unstated rule of the laboratory setting—"Stay in your seat; stay put and follow instructions until told you can get up." (Where do you think they learned that heuristic?) In unstructured, informal settings, none of these conditions hold, and the decision to intervene is based more on an observer's weighing of the personal costs of intervention against the consequences of not doing so.

Despite the higher rate of help in field studies, however, the fact remains that many people do *not* help and that some settings render help less likely than others. For example, when an experimental accomplice on crutches pretended to collapse in an airport, the percentage of those who helped was much lower than in the subway—41 percent as compared with 83 percent. The important factor seemed to be familiarity with the environment; the subway riders felt more at home on the subway and thus were more likely to deal with the trouble that arose (Latané & Darley, 1970).

The Time-bind of the Good Samaritan

The presence or absence of other people is one situational factor that apparently affects bystander intervention. In addition, if a bystander is in a hurry to do something else, he or she is less likely to offer help. In the biblical tale of the Good Samaritan, several important people are too busy to help a stranger in distress. He is finally assisted by a man who has plenty of time on his hands. Could the failure of the important people to help really be due to time pressures rather than their personal dispositions? A research team recreated in a study the story of the Good Samaritan.

Students at the Princeton Theological Seminary were the subjects of an experiment that they thought involved evaluation of their sermons, one of which was to be about the parable of the Good Samaritan. Before they left the briefing room to have their sermons recorded in a nearby building, they were each told something about the time they

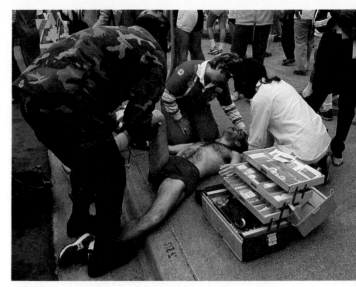

A victim has a better chance of being helped if the bystanders see the situation as a clear emergency and if they are familiar with the environment.

had available to get to the studio. Some were randomly assigned to a *late condition,* in which they had to hurry to make the next session; others to an *on-time condition,* in which they would make the next session just on time, and a third group to an *early condition,* in which they had a few spare minutes before they would be recorded.

When each seminarian walked down an alley between the two buildings, he came upon a man slumped in a doorway, in obvious need of help. On their way to deliver a sermon about the Good Samaritan, these seminary students now had the chance to practice what they were about to preach. Did they? Of those who were in a hurry, only 10 percent helped. If they were on time, 45 percent helped the stranger. Most bystander intervention came from those who were not in a time bind— 63 percent of these seminarians acted as Good Samaritans (Darley & Batson, 1973).

The situational manipulation of time had a marked effect on the altruism of these young men, increasing it sixfold between the late and early conditions, when all else was held constant. We can hardly attribute the lack of intervention of those in the late condition to their callousness or other dispositions since they were randomly assigned to that condition and had chosen a career based on helping others. It is likely that, while fulfilling their obligation to the researcher to hurry and not be late for their appointment, their single-minded purpose blinded them to "irrelevant events" that might interfere with that obligation. Some of those who did not help may not have noticed the man in distress, others might have misinterpreted what they saw as a man merely resting.

Need Help? Just Ask!

To demonstrate the positive effects of situational power, social psychologist **Tom Moriarity** (1975) arranged two fascinating experiments. In the first study, New Yorkers watched as a thief snatched a women's suitcase in a restaurant when she left her table. In the second, they watched as a thief snatched a portable radio from a beach blanket when the owner left it for a few minutes. What did these onlookers do? Some did nothing, they let the thief go on his merry way. What were the conditions under which some *did* help and others *did not*?

> In each experiment, the would-be theft victim (the experimenter's accomplice) asked the soon-to-be observer of the crime either "Do you have the time?" or "Will you please keep an eye on my bag (radio) while I'm gone?" The first interaction elicited no personal responsibility, and the bystander simply stood by idly as the theft unfolded. However, of those who agreed to watch the victim's property, almost every bystander intervened. They called for help, and some even tackled the runaway thief on the beach.

The encouraging message is that we can convert apathy to action and transform callousness to kindness just by asking for it. The act of requesting a favor forges a special human bond that involves other people in ways that materially change the situation. It makes them responsible to you and, thereby, responsible for what happens in your shared social context.

SUMMING UP

Throughout this section, we have explored the basic theme of social psychology—the power of situational variables to influence individual behavior. A wide body of controlled laboratory experiments and field studies strongly supports the generalization that human thought and action are affected by situational influences to a far greater extent than we realize and would predict. This first lesson of social psychology was illustrated by a number of classic studies in which apparently minor or even trivial situational stimuli altered behavioral outcomes. The mere presence of others can serve to facilitate and intensify reactions under some circumstances. Being assigned to play social roles, even in artificial settings such as a mock prison, can modify individual reactions dramatically in ways contrary to one's personal values, beliefs, and dispositions. Other influential situational variables include behavioral rules, signs, symbols, and uniforms.

Social norms function within groups to direct and shape members' behavior. Informational influence processes lead to conformity and compliance when the situation is ambiguous and the person wants to be right and act correctly. Studies of the autokinetic effect revealed how a crystallized norm could influence individual judgments even long after the group was no longer present. The Bennington studies pointed to the power of social norms in a total living situation to affect students' basic attitudes and values, sometimes for a lifetime. Even in highly structured situations, perceptions can be influenced by conformity pressures, as demonstrated in the Asch situation. Members of a minority can be effective in changing majority opinion if their efforts are consistent, unanimous, and non-rigid. Lewin showed that socially significant questions could be tested experimentally, as in his study of the effects of different leadership styles and group atmosphere on the productivity and emotional reactions of schoolchildren. One of the most powerful and controversial demonstrations of situational power was Milgram's series of studies on obedience to authority, in which many good people typically behaved in evil ways with the best of motives. The final proof of the significance of situational forces came from studies in which bystander intervention decreased as the number of observing bystanders increased and as bystanders' sense of time urgency increased. The positive effects of situational power showed up in research that indicates we can induce altruism in others by simply asking for it. By changing a small aspect of the social context, it is possible to generate prosocial behavior in strangers.

CONSTRUCTING SOCIAL REALITY

An unusual experience I had some years ago involved people subjectively interpreting and constructing social reality.

> I was riding with other faculty members to our downtown campus when, suddenly, the university's limousine crashed head-on into another car. There were screams, moans, blood, and silence. As I waited to be x-rayed, I was almost embarrassed by my head injury which seemed insignificant compared to the injuries suffered by the driver and other passengers. Then I passed out. I

awakened from what was obviously a serious concussion to find myself in the trauma ward of a local charitable hospital, strapped to the bed, stuck full of I.V. tubes.

As my vision sharpened, I saw what appeared to be the set for a prison movie. Paint was peeling off the walls and the windows were thick with grime. I observed my fellow patients: a rheumy-eyed alcoholic who had stumbled into an open manhole; a derelict who was beaten for his last quarter; an old man so thin and frail that he looked like the Ghost of Christmas Past. These were the down-and-outers whose eyes I always tried to avoid when I walked through the sleazy part of town. They all wore grubby green pajamas. The only thing that set me apart from them was my red shirt. "Say, Red," summoned the nurse. "You're sure lucky. That other Italian, the driver, he didn't make it. But don't doze off! That's dangerous for someone with a concussion. Stay awake. Talk to the other guys."

Talk to the other guys? What did we have in common? I didn't belong with the people in green. I was the man in the red shirt. No one talked to the red shirt. No one asked the red shirt to pass along the newspaper or to share the sugar. The other patients wanted nothing to do with me. My red shirt was a visual barrier that separated the likes of me from the likes of them. I was glad my shirt functioned as a stop light.

After a few days, though, I decided it was silly to keep wearing a dirty old red shirt. I never liked it much anyway. So I took it off and donned a pair of green pajamas. Within minutes, the invisible shield around my bed had shattered. One patient handed me his newspaper; another came by to tell a joke. They crowded around, expressing concern about my condition and asking questions about the fatal accident. We played poker and joked about the staff and the food. It felt good to laugh again. It felt even better to hear one patient exclaim, "I knew you wuz one of da bunch—a regular guy after all."

"Thanks, I'm glad we're gonna be buddies," I replied, proud of having won their friendship, proud to be accepted into their group—*our* group. The trauma ward was no longer traumatic for me; it was not as bad as it might have looked to an outsider, such as that fellow in the red shirt.

What accounted for the changes in the behavior of the men on the trauma ward? You could attribute the behavior change to the situational change that occurred when I exchanged my unique red shirt for the standard green uniform, thereby eliminating my symbolic distinctiveness. However, before that stimulus change took place, there was a change in how I perceived my status—I went from feeling unique, special, and different to lonely, deviant, and without social support. My new perception and interpretation of the situation led me to initiate a change in my appearance which, in turn, triggered a cascade of responsive social actions on the part of the others in the ward.

To understand *how* the situation matters, we need to discover how the behavioral setting is *perceived* and *interpreted* by those people in it and what *meanings* they attribute to its various components. This second lesson of social psychology thus emphasizes the nature of *social reality* that individuals construct from its objective features. The way actors view their situation can engage psychological processes that change the situation so that it comes to be assimilated into their egocentric perception, values, and attitudes. It is not so much the physical, objective features of a situation that control individual and group behavior; it is the *mental representations of the person in the situation* that matter most.

For the social psychologist then, an adequate account of any behavior includes three basic components: the features of the current situation, the specific *content* and *context* of the observed behavior, and the actor's subjective interpretations of the important elements in the behavioral setting. What complicates this type of behavior analysis is that different people often interpret shared events in different ways. When we acknowledge the unique **phenomenological perspective** that each person brings to her or his personal interpretation and understanding of a given situation, we minimize the focus on objective, physical reality as the determinant of social phenomena. When members of a group—whether a small group of friends, a community, or a culture—reach a common interpretation of an event, activity, or person, their shared phenomenological perspective is known as *social reality*. **Social reality** is the consensus of perceptions and beliefs about a situation generated by the social comparisons made by members of a social group.

In this section, we will see the power of situations in a slightly different light, as it is filtered through a person's mind. After reviewing a body of field and laboratory studies that illustrates the ways in which our subjective constructions of reality operate, we will outline several theoretical approaches that social psychologists have taken to help them make sense of the ways people think about and perceive their social world. It will become apparent that, at the core of much social psychology, is a strong cognitive orientation.

GUIDING BELIEFS AND EXPECTATIONS

Have you ever disagreed with a friend about what *really* took place at some event you both experienced? People's beliefs can lead them to view the same situation from different vantage points and to make contrary conclusions about what "really happened." One example of these contrary conclusions comes from a study of a famous football game that took place some years ago between two Ivy League teams.

> The undefeated Princeton team played Dartmouth in the final game of the season. The game had been given much publicity because it was the last game for Princeton's All-American star player. The game was rough, filled with penalties and serious injuries to both sides.
>
> The Princeton star suffered a broken nose and mild concussion. After the game, the newspapers of the two schools offered very different accounts of what had happened. A team of social psychologists, intrigued by the different perceptions, surveyed students at both schools, showed them a film of the game, and recorded their judgments about the number of infractions committed by each of the teams.
>
> Nearly all Princeton students judged the game as "rough and dirty," none saw it as "clean and fair," and most believed that Dartmouth players started the dirty play. In contrast, the majority of Dartmouth students thought both sides were equally to blame for the rough game, and many thought it was "rough, clean, and fair." These beliefs, stimulated by the differing media articles, showed up in contrasting judgments of game pen-

Not all the people who watched this game would perceive it the same way.

alties. When the Princeton students viewed the game film, they "saw" the Dartmouth team commit twice as many penalties as their own team. When viewing the same film, Dartmouth students "saw" both sides commit the same number of penalties (Hastorf & Cantril, 1954).

This study makes clear that a complex social occurrence, such as a football game, cannot be observed in an objective fashion. Social situations become *experiential events* only when they are given significance by observers who *selectively encode* what is happening in terms of what they expect to see and want to see. In the case of this football game, people *looked* at the same activity, but they *saw* two different games.

Fulfilling Prophecies

Can beliefs and expectations go beyond coloring the way we interpret experiences to actually shape social reality? Much research suggests that the very nature of some situations can be modified significantly by the beliefs and expectations people have about them. Such *social expectancy effects* are similar to *placebo effects* in which belief that a medical treatment will work makes it work for about a third of all people. For example, ordinary students or underachievers can be transformed into high achievers if their teachers believe they are "special," or if the students are led to think so.

In George Bernard Shaw's *Pygmalion* (popularized as the musical *My Fair Lady*), a street waif is transformed into a proper society lady under the intense training of her teacher, Professor Henry Higgins. The effect of social expectancy, or the *pygmalion effect,* was re-created in an experiment by psychologist **Robert Rosenthal** (in conjunction with school principal Leonore Jacobson).

> Some elementary school teachers in Boston were informed by researchers that their testing had revealed that some of their students were "academic spurters." The teachers were led to believe that these particular students were "intellectual bloomers who will show unusual gains during the academic year." In fact, there was no objective basis for that prediction; the names of these late bloomers were chosen *randomly*. By the end of that school year, 30 percent of the children arbitrarily named as spurters had gained an average of 22 IQ points. Almost all of them had gained at least 10 IQ points. Their gain in intellectual performance, as measured by a standard test of intelligence, was significantly greater than that of their control group classmates. In absolute terms, their improvement is remarkably significant for any known kind of enriched education program over

such a short time, and these were students in ordinary classes (Rosenthal & Jacobson, 1968a, 1968b).

How did the false expectations of the teachers get translated into such positive student performance? In some way, the teachers must have used influence strategies that motivated the targeted students to work harder and more efficiently. These strategies were probably communicated in many nonverbal ways, perhaps even nonconsciously, through the teachers' facial expressions and body language. Rosenthal points to at least four processes that were activated by the teachers' expectations. First, they acted warmer and more friendly, creating a climate of social approval and acceptance. Second, they put greater demands—involving both quality and level of difficulty of material to be learned—on those for whom there were high hopes. Next, they gave more immediate and differentiated feedback (praise and criticism) about the selected students' performance. Finally, the teachers created more opportunities for the special students to respond in class, show their stuff, and be reinforced, thus giving them hard evidence that they were good. We could add a fifth factor, the halo effect, in which anything a presumably good student does is interpreted in a positive light or given the benefit of a doubt. This *attributional charity* is rarely extended to the ordinary students and never to the "bad" kids (Rosenthal, 1990, *Discovering Psychology,* Program 20).

In one sense, this research put some students on the fast track. The opposite happens when students are assigned to slow learner or learning disability tracks; they often become slower when they have been identified in this way. Negative teacher expectations may be responsible for poorer performance of females and some minority students in science and mathematics courses even at the college level. If this is true, could the performance of college students in something as objective as mathematics be improved by changing the social reality of the situation? Yes, according to new research by **Urie Treisman,** a mathematician who studied the poor mathematics grades of African-American students at the University of California, Berkeley.

First, Treisman observed the study habits of students in college mathematics. Asian-American students, who usually did best, studied in groups, while African-American students tended to study alone. Group study has many advantages, such as the possibility of learning effective strategies that work for others, social support, public commitment to study and practice, and discovering that other people have difficulty with some math problems too.

Studying in a group can significantly enhance performance.

The researcher-educator then persuaded a group of entering African-American college students to enroll in a special honors program in mathematics that included required group study. He also monitored their progress and provided encouragement. Changing these few features of the situation, as well as enhancing the students' beliefs about their ability had dramatic effects. The many African-American students in this ongoing program have consistently performed at the same high level as the other students in the course, and their dropout rate has decreased markedly (U. Treisman, 1989).

Self-fulfilling prophecies (Merton, 1957) are predictions made about some future behavior or event that modify its outcome so as to produce what is expected. Social reality can be changed in several ways by the operation of such prophecies. A shy student has the expectation that he won't have a good time at an upcoming dance. An extraverted student predicts the same dance will be fun and enjoyable. At the dance, both students experience what they expected.

In earlier chapters, we noted the positive effects on health and well-being of an optimistic outlook on life (Seligman, 1991). Optimism is a general system of beliefs that gets translated into actions that affect someone's health and well-being. Mediating between those general beliefs and specific actions is social perception. Research has shown that our wishes and hopes for how life will turn out can actually have some influence on the way it does. The ways we frame future options motivate the ways we reason about paths to attaining them.

This motivated reasoning comes to determine the kind of evidence we focus on in making our self-predictions, the methods we use to make those predictions, the confidence we invest in our predictions, and our insensitivity to contrary evidence that might disconfirm our predictions (Kunda, 1990). Optimists assume setbacks are temporary and persevere in the face of adversity until they reach their goals.

Confirming Expectations

Mark Snyder (1984) uses the term **behavioral confirmation** for the process by which someone's expectations about another person actually influence that person to behave in ways that confirm the original hypothesis.

> In a series of studies, students were led to expect that they would interact with another person who was described in particular ways (not necessarily true) such as *introvert, extravert, depressed,* or *intelligent.* After interacting with the target person, the subject rated the person on a variety of dimensions. Typically, the target person was more likely to act in whatever way the subject expected him or her to behave. The subjects and the observers (who did not know what the expectation was) agreed that those hypothesized to be outgoing were indeed very sociable, that the introvert target people behaved unsociably, and so forth (Kulik, 1983; Snyder & Swann, 1978).

The expectations were turned into behavioral confirmations by the selective verbal and nonverbal behaviors of the subject relating to the target person. The extraverted target person was likely to be asked how she would liven up a party, while the shy target person was asked about what makes it hard to open up to others. These different questions elicited different responses that guided the evaluation without the evaluator being aware that the question had a strong role in creating and distorting social reality.

A recent incident shows how expectations can lead to false conclusions and regrettable actions. Two California police officers beat a blind man with their batons while he was standing at a bus stop. Why? They mistakenly thought that the folding cane in his pocket was an illegal martial arts weapon and they "demanded that he hand over the contents of his pockets." The man believed he was being robbed because the police officers, assuming he could see their uniforms, did not identify themselves. When he tried to defend himself from being mugged by reaching for his cane, the police felt his behavior confirmed their suspicions and they began to hit him (*The New York Times*, 5/17/89).

Creating and Reversing Prejudices

Of all human weaknesses, none is more destructive of the dignity of the individual and the social bonds of humanity than prejudice. Social psychology has always put the study of prejudice high on its agenda in an effort to understand its complexity and persistence and to develop strategies to change prejudiced attitudes and discriminatory behavior. The Supreme Court's 1954 decision to outlaw segregated public education was, in part, based on research, presented in Federal Court by social psychologist **Kenneth Clark,** which showed the negative impact on black children of their separate and unequal education (Clark & Clark, 1948).

Prejudice is the prime example of social reality gone awry—a situation created in the minds of people that can demean and destroy the lives of others. **Prejudice** is defined as a learned attitude toward a target object, involving negative affect (dislike or fear), negative beliefs (stereotypes) that justify the attitude, and a behavioral intention to avoid, control, dominate, or eliminate those in the target group. Because prejudices are often formed on the basis of limited or false information, they are typically unwarranted and irrational. A false belief qualifies as prejudiced when it resists change even in face of appropriate evidence of its falseness. Prejudiced attitudes serve as biasing filters that influence the way individuals are perceived and treated once they are categorized as members of a target group. Once formed, prejudice exerts a powerful force on the way pertinent information is selectively processed, organized, and remembered. Although there are many origins of prejudice and a variety of needs that prejudice serves (Allport, 1954; Pettigrew, 1985; Sar-

Prejudice is a learned attitude that is usually formed on the basis of limited or false information.

noff & Katz; 1954), one of its most basic purposes is satisfying the cognitive goal of simplifying a complex environment and increasing future predictability by categorizing individuals in certain ways.

The simplest and most pervasive form of categorizing consists of an individual determining whether people are like him or her. This categorization develops from a "me versus not me" orientation to an "us versus them" orientation. These cognitive distinctions result in an in-group bias, a evaluation of one's own group as better than others (Brewer, 1979). Surprisingly, the most minimal of distinctive cues is sufficient to trigger the formation of this bias and, with it, the formation of prejudice.

> In a series of experiments in Holland, subjects were randomly divided into two groups: a blue group and a green group. According to the subjects' group membership, they were given either blue or green pens and asked to write on either blue or green paper. The experimenter addressed subjects in terms of their group color. Even though these color categories had no intrinsic psychological significance and assignment to the groups was completely arbitrary, subjects gave a more positive evaluation of their own group than of the other. Furthermore, this in-group bias, based solely on color identification, appeared even before the group members began to work together on an experimental task (Rabbie, 1981).

Social categorization is the process by which people organize their social environment by categorizing themselves and others into groups (Wilder, 1986). This categorization has been shown to have the following consequences: perception of similarity of those within one's group and dissimilarity of those in the out-group; failure to distinguish among individuals in the out-group; reduced influence of out-group members on the in-group; hostile attitudes toward and beliefs in the inferiority of the out-group (Tajfel, 1982; Tajfel & Billig, 1974). These consequences developed regardless of limited exposure to the out-groups and despite the contrary experience of their individual members with any other out-group category (Park & Rothbart, 1982; Quattrone, 1985).

Does there need to be a kernel of truth in the basis for categorization that leads to prejudiced attitudes and discriminatory actions? No—all that is necessary is any salient cue on which individuals can be sorted into exclusive categories. A third-grade teacher, **Jane Elliott,** wanted her pupils from an all-white, rural Iowa farm community to experience how prejudice and discrimination felt to those in minority groups. She devised an activity to provide her students with that experience.

Her demonstration clearly illustrates the arbitrariness of the categorization involved in prejudice.

> One day she arbitrarily designated brown-eyed children as "superior" to the "inferior" blue-eyed children. The superior, allegedly more intelligent, brown-eyes were given special privileges, while the inferior blue-eyes had to obey rules that enforced their second-class status. Within a day, the blue-eyed children began to do more poorly in their schoolwork and became depressed, sullen, and angry. They described themselves as "sad," "bad," "stupid," and "mean."
>
> Of the brown-eyed superiors, the teacher reported, "What had been marvelously cooperative, thoughtful, children became nasty, vicious, discriminating little third-graders. . . . It was ghastly." They mistreated their former friends, called them "blue-eyes," refused to play with them, got into fights with them, and worried that school officials should be notified that the blue-eyes might steal things.
>
> The second day of the activity, Elliott told the class that she had been wrong. It was really the blue-eyed children who were superior and the brown-eyed ones who were inferior. The brown-eyes now switched from their previously "happy," "good," "sweet," and "nice" self labels to derogatory labels similar to those used the day before by the blue-eyes. Their academic performance deteriorated, while that of the new ruling class improved. Old friendship patterns between children temporarily dissolved and were replaced with hostility until the experiment was ended (Elliott, 1977).

The experience of being in a disadvantaged out-group can have the positive effect of enabling people to develop greater empathy for members of groups that are discriminated against in society. In a replication of Elliott's study, psychologists found that, weeks later, the children who had participated held less prejudicial beliefs than did a comparison group without this experience (Weiner & Wright, 1973). The paradigm of categorizing people by arbitrary cues of differentness—eye color—was equally effective with the adult groups that Elliott instructed. The effects were also long lasting. A ten-year follow-up of her original grade-school students revealed that, as young adults, they were tolerant of group differences and were *actively* opposed to prejudice (Elliott, 1990, *Discovering Psychology,* Program 20).

Sadly, in many school rooms throughout the country, students are made to feel inferior through their negative interactions with other pupils or their teachers.

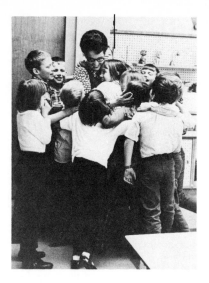

Jane Elliott's experiment measured overt changes in prejudicial behavior among children and changes in their schoolwork. She obtained measures of their feelings toward each other by asking the children to draw pictures of the way they felt. The picture on the left was drawn by a child who felt "on top," confident, and capable because he had the superior eye color.

These students often begin to act in ways to confirm this prejudiced belief and come to internalize this sense of academic inadequacy. When competing for the scarce resource of teacher's attention and affection, the more verbal, advantaged students take charge; the others back off, fearing failure and further rejection. This system fosters a situation characterized by envy, competitiveness, suspicion, self-derogation, and disidentification with school and academics by those in the out-group.

Social psychologist **Elliot Aronson** (1978) and his colleagues found a simple way to change the negative dynamics of such classrooms.

The research team created conditions in which fifth-grade students had to depend on one another rather than compete against one another to learn required material. In a technique known as *jigsawing,* each pupil was given part of the total material to master and then share with other group members. Performance was evaluated on the basis of the overall group presentation. Thus, every member's contribution was essential and valued. Pupils were made to feel they were team workers rather than competitors, and those in desegregated settings discovered the advantages of sharing knowledge (and friendship) with "equal and interdependent" peers—regardless of race, creed, or sex.

Interracial conflict has decreased in classes where jigsawing has united formerly hostile white, Latino, and African-American students in a common fate team (Aronson & Gonzalez, 1988; Gonzales, 1983). When Carlos, who had been ignored because his primary language was not English, was assigned the vital part of the team assignment on the life of Joseph Pulitzer, the other teammates

had to listen to him. They had to figure out how to get him to share the information he was responsible for providing. Carlos got his teammates' attention, felt needed, develop affection for the group members who helped him do the team assignment, and also discovered that learning was fun. Both his self-esteem and his grades increased (Aronson & Gonzalez, 1990, *Discovering Psychology,* Program 20).

COGNITIVE FRAMEWORKS

Having seen that the way situations are interpreted can influence behavioral outcomes in a variety of ways, we are ready for the next big question: How do people go

Jigsawing promotes cooperation and teamwork.

about constructing their views of other people and understanding their transactions with them within a shared social context? They do so by observing the ways that they and others behave in various settings and over time. To this observation, they add what they have learned about the kinds of stimulus events that cause certain behaviors. Such information helps them form a personal theory, or mental representation, of what other people are like, what they themselves are like, and what causes human actions and reactions. The general process by which we come to perceive and know the personal attributes of ourselves and others is called **social perception.**

A major task of everyday social perception in guiding our behavior involves solving problems in social inference, figuring out what behavior "means," forming accurate impressions, and making reliable predictions about what we and others are likely to do under certain circumstances. We are constantly trying to make sense of our world by applying old knowledge and beliefs to new events, assimilating the new to the familiar, and, at times, accommodating the old to the novel. To make social inferences and judgments, we rely on a host of cognitive structures such as schemas, scripts, heuristics (described in chapters 11 and 14), and personal theories.

Social psychology can be said to be cognitively oriented because it has always found in its analysis of human behavior a prominent place for the role of subjective perceptions, symbolic causal stimuli and imagined results, and, above all, a thinking organism that tries rationally to make sense of the workings of the social world and physical environment. Before examining several of the most important cognitive theories that have guided research in social psychology, we should identify some different conceptions of the human being as social thinker.

Four Types of Social Thinkers

The roles that cognition and motivation have played in social psychological theories cast the social thinker into one of four types: consistency seeker, naive scientist, cognitive miser, and motivated tactician (Fiske & Taylor, 1991). These views about different types of social thinkers reflect different approaches taken in the study of social cognition.

Consistency-seeking thinkers are disturbed by a perceived inconsistency between their thoughts, feelings, and actions. This subjective inconsistency motivates them to reduce the cognitive inconsistency. People change their attitudes and their behavior in response to the need to make their mental worlds cognitively comfortable (Festinger, 1957; Heider, 1958; Abelson et al., 1968). How do you bring into line, for example, the cognitions that you are on a diet and that you just ate an entire pizza?

For the *naive-scientist* thinkers, motivation recedes into the background as rational analysis takes over. Thoughts and perceptions of inconsistencies do not motivate these thinkers' actions; they are assumed to be able to tolerate cognitive inconsistencies. They should act as scientists in the pursuit of truth, their logical conclusions based on reasoned inferences from carefully collected data about the social environment. The shortcomings of this normative approach became apparent when researchers examined the way people actually went about solving problems of social influence (Ross, 1977). They weren't very rational or thoughtful much of the time. Instead, researchers found the alleged naive scientist to be cognitively lazy, avoiding mental effort, sustained attention, and careful analysis even when it is necessary, and cognitively naive, blindly trusting personal theories, overly confident in personal predictions, and overly impressed by vivid, exceptional instances at the cost of utilizing substantial base-rate data (Nisbett & Ross, 1980). The tendency for human information processing to be susceptible to many types of errors in thinking makes the naive scientist more naive than scientific (Markus & Zajonc, 1985).

When researchers examined what thinking people actually did rather than the way they were supposed to think, the normative model was replaced by a descriptive cognitive model (Kahneman et al., 1982). *Cognitive-miser* thinkers are limited in how well they can come up with accurate solutions to problems in social inference because of inherent limitations in cognitive capacity (Taylor, 1981). They seek to simplify complexity by overusing categorical thinking and stereotypes. They search for quick and easy answers rather than slow and carefully arrived at solutions. When the goal of efficiency dominates that of accuracy, errors and cognitive biases slip in because of inherent features of cognitive systems (as we noted in chapters 10 and 11).

While the cognitive-miser and naive-scientist views had no use for motivation, the currently accepted approach in social cognition once again finds a place for motivation and emotion in directing cognitive processes (Showers & Cantor, 1985; Langer, 1989). *Motivated-tactician* thinkers blend interests in wise, accurate, adaptable solutions with situational demands for efficiency, personal needs for self-esteem, and defensive motives. They want to look good, be liked and approved, get what they want, and still get it right. A tall order, but that is what the complex social thinker is all about—using the best tactics to achieve personal goals.

Dissonance Theory: Self-justification

The version of consistency theories that has been most influential within the field of social psychology is the theory of **cognitive dissonance,** as developed by **Leon Festinger** (1957), a student of Kurt Lewin. Cognitive dissonance is the state of conflict someone experiences after making a decision, taking an action, or being exposed to information that is contrary to prior beliefs, feelings, or values. It is assumed that when cognitions about one's behavior and relevant attitudes are dissonant—they do not follow psychologically—an aversive state arises that people are motivated to reduce. Dissonance-reducing activities modify this unpleasant state and achieve consonance among one's cognitions. The motivation to reduce dissonance increases with the magnitude of dissonance created by the cognitive inconsistency. When dissonance arises between something we've done and something we believe or value, the magnitude of dissonance becomes greater as the relevant cognitions are more important; the decision to take the dissonant action is perceived as freely chosen and there is minimal justification for having done so (there are barely sufficient incentives).

For example, suppose the two dissonant cognitions are some self-knowledge ("I smoke") and a belief about smoking ("Smoking causes lung cancer"). To reduce the dissonance involved, you could take one of several different actions: change your belief ("The evidence that smoking causes lung cancer is not very convincing"); change your behavior (stop smoking); reevaluate the behavior ("I don't smoke very much"); or add new cognitions ("I smoke low-tar cigarettes") that make the inconsistency less serious.

Cognitive dissonance produces a motivation to make discrepant behavior seem more rational, as if it followed naturally from personal beliefs and attitudes. If you can't deny that you took an action, you might change your attitudes to make them fit your action. The attitude change is then internalized to make acceptable what otherwise appears to be "irrational behavior." You did something you didn't believe in when you had the choice to do otherwise and did so in the absence of sufficient external force to justify why you took the discrepant action. Hundreds of experiments and field studies have shown the power of cognitive dissonance to change attitudes and behavior (Wicklund & Brehm, 1976).

In the classic dissonance experiment, college students told a lie to other students and came to believe in their lie when they got a small, rather than a large, reward for doing so. The nonobvious prediction that behavior is more affected by a smaller reward contradicted behavior theory.

Subjects participated in a very dull task and were then asked (as a favor to the experimenter because his assistant hadn't shown up) to lie to another subject by saying that the task had been fun and interesting. Half the subjects were paid $20 to tell the lie, while the others were paid only $1 (and asked to be on call for future assistance). The $20 payment was sufficient external justification for lying, but the $1 payment was an inadequate justification for lying. The people who were paid $1 were left with two dissonant cognitions: "The task was dull" and "I chose to tell another student it was fun and interesting without a good reason for doing so."

To reduce their dissonance, these $1 subjects changed their evaluations of the task. They later expressed the belief that "It really was fun and interesting—I might like to do it again." In comparison, the subjects who lied for $20 did not change their evaluations—the task was still a bore, they had only lied "for the money" (Festinger & Carlsmith, 1959; Festinger, 1990, *Discovering Psychology,* Program 11).

According to dissonance theory, under conditions of high dissonance, an individual acts to justify his or her behavior after-the-fact, engages in self-persuasion, and often becomes a most convincing communicator and convinced target audience. This analysis says that the way to change attitudes is to first change behavior (eliciting attitude-inconsistent behavior under a condition of high choice and low justification). Biblical scholars knew this principle: they urged rabbis not to insist that people believe before praying but to get them to pray first and then they would come to believe.

Self-perception Theory

People observe how others act and make inferences about the causes of their actions. They also observe themselves in order to figure out the reasons they act as they do. This notion is at the heart of **self-perception theory,** developed by **Daryl Bem** (1972). People infer what their internal states (beliefs, attitudes, motives, and feelings) are or should be by perceiving how they are acting and recalling how they have acted in the past in a given situation. They use that self-knowledge to reason backward to the most likely causes or determinants of their behavior. The self-perceiver responds to the question, "Do you like psychology?" by saying, "Sure, I am taking the basic course and it is not required, I do all the readings, I pay attention during lectures, and I'm getting a good grade in the course." A question of personal preferences is answered by a behavioral description of relevant actions and situational factors. This process should remind you of William James's theory of emotion (Chapter 12) which proposed that we notice our behavior (running away or laughing) and infer the relevant emotion of fear or happiness.

Self-perception theory is all cognitive, with no motivational component that energizes reactions. By the time we get to be adults, we do have a great deal of self-knowledge without having to infer what it is by perceiving how we just behaved. Self-perception processes occur mainly when we are in ambiguous situations and dealing with unfamiliar events, where we have a "need for structure regarding some novel attitude object" (Fazio, 1987). One flaw in the process of gaining self-knowledge through self-perception is that people are often insensitive about the extent to which their behavior is influenced by situational forces. Thus, for example, they may err in inferring their strengths and weaknesses by observing their successes and failures without adequately taking into account the contributions made by the social context. It is remarkable how much we can fail to recognize obvious constraints and supports for our behavior in external settings, such as social roles that are situationally determined.

Student research subjects were asked to play a "College Bowl" type of quiz game in which one contestant was arbitrarily chosen to ask the other challenging questions for which he or she knew the answers. At the end of the session, the questioner, the contestant, and observers rated the general knowledge of both questioner and contestant. Although they had only this limited, biased sample of evidence on which to base their inferences, all involved rated the questioner as far more knowledgeable than the contestant or the "average" university student. The contestant's self-perception was of not being able to answer all the questions that the questioner asked, thus inferring less "smarts." However, the contestant's situational analysis failed to include awareness of the role advantage the questioner had been given in selecting to ask about known esoteric areas of information (Ross et al., 1977).

Attribution Theory: Causal Inferences

One of the most important inferential tasks facing all social perceivers is determining the causes for events. We want to know the why's of life. Why did my girlfriend break off the relationship? Why did he get the job and not I? Why did my parents divorce after so many years of marriage? All such why's lead to an analysis of possible causal determinants for some action, event, or outcome. **Attribution theory** is a general

approach to describing the ways the social perceiver uses information to generate causal explanations for events. It has come to play an important role not only in social psychological thinking but in many other areas of psychology, because it focuses on a basic aspect of human functioning—the way individuals make causal attributions for achievement (Weiner, 1986), depression (Abramson et al., 1978), and other life domains.

The Intuitive Psychologist

The origin of attribution theory came from the writings of **Fritz Heider** (1958). Heider argued that people continually make causal analyses as part of their attempts at general comprehension of the social world. Such causal understanding serves the basic functions of predicting future events and trying to control them. If you know what makes your roommate get upset, then you may be able to reduce or induce that reaction by manipulating those causal conditions. Two general questions that Heider believed are part of most attributional analyses are whether the cause for the behavior is found in the person (internal causality) or in the situation (external causality), and who is responsible for the outcomes. A woman kills her husband; her defense is that he had been battering her for years and she was fearful of her life and her children's when he was drunk, which was becoming ever more frequent. The case rests largely on the determination of the causality for her admitted crime, given the mitigating circumstances.

Heider suggested that instead of developing theories about how people are supposed to think and act, psychologists should discover the personal theories—belief systems—that ordinary people themselves use to make sense of the causes and effects of behavior. After all, he argued, aren't we all **intuitive psychologists** who try to figure out what people are like and what causes their behavior, just as professional psychologists do for a living? Heider used a simple film to demonstrate the tendency for people to leap from observing actions to making causal inferences and attributing motives to what they see. The film involved three geometric figures that moved around an object without any prearranged plan. Research subjects, however, always make up scripts that animated the action, turning the figures into actors and attributing personality traits and motives to their causal actions (see **Figure 16.5**).

The Covariation Principle

Attribution theory was given a boost by the contributions of **Harold Kelley** (1967) who focused on the issue that often we have to make causal attributions for events under conditions of uncertainty. We may not have sufficient information, the information we have may be poor or vague, our self-confidence may be low, or our

FIGURE 16.5 *HEIDER'S DEMONSTRATION OF THE NATURAL TENDENCY TO MAKE CAUSAL ATTRIBUTIONS*

These geometric figures were stimuli in a convincing demonstration of the fact that we infer rather than observe personal characteristics and causes. When subjects were shown a film in which the geometrical forms simply moved in and out of the large rectangle at different speeds and in different patterns, they attributed underlying "motivations" to the "characters." They often "saw" the triangles as two males fighting over a female (the circle). The large triangle was "seen" as being aggressive, the small triangle as being heroic, and the circle as being timid. In the sequence shown here, most observers reported seeing T chase t and c into the house and close the door.

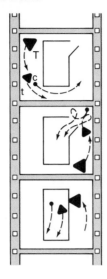

capacities may be limited to solving the inferential problem at hand. We then seek out additional information and are susceptible to social influence from peers and experts. In cases where we have access to information about multiple events, we tend to employ the **covariation principle** to infer the causes of events—by observing co-occurrences of two events. People will attribute a behavior to a causal factor if that factor was present whenever the behavior occurred but was absent whenever it didn't occur. For example, in trying to figure out why you had insomnia one night, you would analyze what events and activities were associated with this experience that are absent on nights you sleep well. Caffeine becomes a likely causal candidate if you had late night coffee and you usually don't drink it. However, many potential causes are lurking in the analytical woods. Suppose you also had a new mattress, you were upset about failing a test, you were excited about a big competition the next morning, and there was a noisy party next door. To assess which cause or set of causes were responsible requires a more complex attributional process in which you consider multiple events.

Kelley formalized Heider's line of thinking by specifying the variables that people use to make their attributions. People assess covariation information across three dimensions relevant to the person whose acts they are trying to explain: *distinctiveness, consistency,* and *consensus. Distinctiveness* refers to whether the entity or event is unique—whether the effect occurs only when it is present. *Consistency* refers to whether

the effect occurs each time and across different situations when the entity is present. *Consensus,* or normativeness, refers to whether other people also experience the same effect with respect to the entity. We use these three sources of information to determine if some experience or effect is due to a cause in another person or in ourselves (a dispositional attribution) or comes from something external (a situational attribution).

In the insomnia example, you want to know if it's you (your psychological arousal) or an external variable (coffee, mattress, noise) that caused the insomnia in order to better deal with the problem in the future. People are likely to make dispositional attributions, locating the cause in the qualities of other people, under three conditions (when the behavior is high in all three factors). An attractive person pays you a great compliment, and, after you say "Thanks, I need that," you wonder what really caused that effect (complimenting behavior). First, if the behavior is distinctive (no one else ever compliments you), you might attribute it to the kind of person he or she is, such as a mindless flatterer or a hustler. Second, if the person always compliments you over many situations, his or her consistency tells you about the person and not about the object of the compliment (you). Third, if the person acts this way with others, the high consensus of the behavior means you make a dispositional attribution about the person and not about the situation that you hoped motivated the compliment—your appearance or behavior.

Thousands of studies have been conducted to refine and extend attribution theory (Fiske & Taylor, 1991). These studies reveal the conditions under which the search for causal explanations proceeds rationally with a systematic search of available information and also when the social thinker is more rationalizing than rational. You can probably imagine wanting to believe that something special about you elicited a compliment. If so, you might not want to find out if the attractive person's reaction to you was common. You could end up with the conclusion you desire by distorting the attributional search through selective questioning or by limiting observations. When personal goals, motives, and strongly held attitudes get in the way of systematic analysis of causes, the attributional process is biased. One class of attributional biases is known as the **self-serving bias,** in which people tend to take credit for their successes while denying responsibility for their failures. Self-serving biases are quite robust, occurring in many situations for most people and even across cultures (Fletcher & Ward, 1988). We tend to make dispositional attributions for success and situational attributions for failure—"I got the prize because of my ability, and I lost the competition because it was rigged." This is an instance of the motivated tactician at work to protect the self-esteem of the social thinker.

Dispositional Dominance: The Fundamental Attribution Error

One of the most pervasive attributional biases is the tendency for social perceivers to identify dispositional variables as the causes of most behaviors. Laypersons too readily identify personal traits of the actor—generous, honest, shy, hysterical—as the causes of his or her observed behavior. One explanation for this dispositional dominance comes from cultural socialization that emphasizes the "cult of the ego," focused on individual initiative and personal responsibility for achievement, sin, legal liability, and madness.

However, if we are focused too much on dispositions, what are we overlooking? Situational attributions and contextual factors tend to get slighted by the dominating influence of dispositions. Observers take behavior at "face value," as reflecting something stable about the disposition of the actor, often disregarding powerful situational stimuli that are causing the behavior. **Lee Ross** (1977) has termed this dual tendency to *overestimate* dispositional causes of behavior and to *underestimate* situational ones the **fundamental attribution error** (FAE). Evidence abounds that people infer dispositions from behavior even when it is clearly situationally produced, as when they know the person had no choice, was arbitrarily assigned to engage in the behavior (as the role-playing in the College Bowl study), or was in an unusual setting that made most people behave similarly (as in the Milgram study). They do more, they overlook important situational context factors that control behavioral reactions, and they make overly confident predictions when they have only a small amount of trait information (Ross & Nisbett, 1991). See **Table 16.1** for a list of reasons that the fundamental attribution error is so deeply ingrained.

We are all guilty of making the fundamental attribution error at times. On a societal level, the fundamental attribution error can be seen in the tendency to blame the victim (Ryan, 1976). People tend to hold the victims of poverty and racial discrimination personally responsible for their plights. Unemployment among minorities leads to the attribution "They're lazy," squalid living conditions to "They're filthy," and high rates of crime to "They're bad." Somehow, the external societal variables that foster these conditions are largely overlooked, and, instead, the consequences of poverty are blamed on the personal deficits of the poor. Similarly, people often blame rape on its victims—as if the unfortunate person invited the assault. This failure of "attributional charity," eliminating possible situational

TABLE 16.1	REASONS FOR THE FUNDAMENTAL ATTRIBUTION ERROR

Information: Social realities in the situation (norms, power relationships) may be unknown to the observer.

Ideology: People tend to accept the doctrine of personal responsibility for their actions.

Perception: To observers, actors are figures that stand out against the background of the situation.

Language: Western languages have many more terms for describing personality than for describing situations.

causes of negative effects, can become part of a more general political philosophy that has action implications. This ingrained way of thinking about the causes of behavior is revealed in a recent article by a conservative attorney Mona Charen, who was a speech writer for President Reagan. In writing about the crack epidemic in U.S. inner cities, she described political conservatives:

> Conservatives see people destroying their lives by ingesting drugs and conclude that the problem lies not with the society but the lack of self-control on the part of the individuals involved (Charen, 1990, p. 3).

When people see evidence of poverty, they infer negative individual dispositions instead of perceiving connections between urban society and urban problems.

Social Relevance of Social Psychology's Dual Lessons

We have seen that the two main lessons that emerge from the social psychological tradition are the power of the situation and the construction of social reality by the person as a social perceiver in a behavior setting. When these two fundamental principles are taken together, they lead to a significant conclusion with important action implications. People are basically similar in their basic biological and psychological processes. Whenever this principle is violated—someone seems or acts different from us—we should base our subsequent actions on the awareness of two possibilities: first, that their situation is different from ours or has changed in some way we don't notice and second, that their perception of the situation we are sharing is different in some important way that we may not recognize.

The source of much human misunderstanding and social conflict between groups and nations, is the belief that we, as reasonable people, perceive the world or some vital part of it accurately—the only rational way it could be seen—while they, the other side who sees it differently, are wrong. These differences go beyond merely point-of-view variations when we attribute to ourselves personal characteristics that justify this difference—our wisdom, goodness, or righteousness—and to them characteristics such as stupidity, foolishness, and inadequacies. Obviously, however, *we* are *they* to them. Each group or nation attributes negative dispositions to other groups and nations and positive ones to itself, all the while ignoring the situational determinants of the differences that, if changed, can reverse its perceptions and actions.

The error that individuals and societies make by overemphasizing such personal or dispositional determinants of behavior while simultaneously underestimating the situational or contextual factors that are operating can have serious consequences. This fundamental attribution error often leads to policy decisions to deal with social problems by changing those who are "different" through re-education, therapy, conversion, segregation, imprisonment, sterilization, or execution. Social psychological wisdom does not excuse evil deeds by demonstrating their situational determinants; rather, it shows that the best way to change problem behaviors is to change problem situations. For example, it does not appear that the nation's so-called "war on crime" can ever by won by identifying criminals (dispositional finger pointing), sentencing them to long prison terms, and building ever more prisons to hold them without identifying and trying to change the root conditions in society (situational determinants) that make so many citizens turn to lives of crime.

Summing Up

To understand the way situations can exert powerful influences on behavior, social psychologists analyze the way people perceive, interpret, and give meaning to the features of behavior. In doing so, each person constructs a version of social reality. This is the second lesson, or principle, of social psychology. Research evidence from laboratory and field studies illustrates the way beliefs and expectations can come to guide actions and shape aspects of the behavioral setting. Predictions can become self-fulfilling prophesies that lead to desirable outcomes, such as improved student achievement, by changing the way the relevant behavioral actors view the situation. Our expectancies can be confirmed by our verbal and nonverbal actions which induce in others the actions we expect them to show, without anyone's awareness of the process involved. The cognitive tendency to simplify complex information processing by categorizing individuals can contribute to prejudiced attitudes and discriminatory behavior against those categorized as different and inferior. Minimal cue differences are sufficient to make extreme categorizations, as in the case of the blue-eyed and brown-eyed schoolchildren. Some effects of prejudice can be reversed by changing aspects of situations that foster new conceptions of the people in them, as demonstrated in the jigsaw classroom research.

Many social psychologists have long endorsed the use of cognitive frameworks in understanding social phenomena. They have been interested in issues of social perception and social cognition, in learning how people go about constructing mental representations of their world. Cognitive theories abound to explain the ways social thinkers make sense of the stimuli and responses they experience and create. Some theoretical approaches emphasize motivation, while others are coolly cognitive. Dissonance theory accounts for the self-justification that people engage in when they have behaved in ways that are discrepant from their internal states. The tension that is created by cognitive dissonance is reduced by changing some aspect of the situation or of oneself. Self-perception theory suggests that we infer our internal states, attitudes, beliefs, and emotions from perceptions of our behavior in its social context. Attribution theory is a general attempt to describe the ways in which people find the causes for the behavior they observe in others and themselves. Some attributional rules lead to explanations that are based on the traits of the actor and others on the nature of the situation. However, there is a biased tendency to make the fun-

damental attribution error by overusing dispositional explanations and underutilizing situational ones, even when the evidence is manifestly tilted toward the situational dimension. Important social and political implications follow the tendency to blame people for their failures and negative life outcomes rather than to examine their life situations.

SOLVING SOCIAL PROBLEMS

Many social psychologists are motivated by psychology's fifth goal: to improve the human condition. This concern is expressed in two major ways. First, studies by social psychologists are often carried out in natural field settings as well as in laboratory analogies of those natural settings—in housing projects, at dances, in nursing homes, in factories, or wherever the action is (Rodin, 1985). Efforts are made to include elements of mundane realism in the experimental situation and to capture the conceptual essence of the vital phenomena in simulations of real-world settings. Second, the knowledge obtained from basic research and theories is used to explain social phenomena and systematic attempts are made to apply that knowledge to remedy a range of social problems (Deutsch & Hornstein, 1975). A major organization of social psychologists, the Society for the Psychological Study of Social Issues, is, in fact, dedicated to just that principle.

Kurt Lewin, the founder of modern social psychology, believed that for psychology to make its greatest contribution, theory and research must be integrated with practical application. "No action without research, no research without action" was his dictum (1948). He practiced what he preached by conducting research designed to solve social problems, while yielding significant information about the underlying social processes involved. A good example is his study of the way to get housewives during the Second World War to serve food that their families did not like to eat but that was plentiful, nutritious, and cheap.

Ordinary meats were scarce and rationed; highly nutritional visceral meats, such as liver and kidneys, were plentiful but unpopular. Lewin's objective was to find an effective way to change the purchasing and cooking habits of U.S. housewives. Some women in his group of housewives heard a persuasive lecture on the positive effects of serving these glandular meats to their families—the usual type of education recommended to influence the public. Other women met in small groups to discuss the issue and consider ways to make the undesirable meats appealing to their families. These women then made a public commitment to follow through and buy the visceral meats. The results were clear: the lecture had little effect on the women's attitudes or behavior; however, the democratically run discussion groups worked to make many of the women far more likely to take the socially beneficial action of buying and preparing visceral meats for their families (Lewin, 1947).

The key idea in this research was the effectiveness of involving people in the decision-making process—"participatory management"—and of making public commitments to other members of one's group. Later research by Lewin, his students, and group dynamics colleagues showed that workers who were given an active role in decisions about production performed far better on the job than did passive workers who were told what to do and got paid for doing only what they were ordered to do. The active decision makers surpassed the passive laborers on measures of productivity, efficiency, morale, and satisfaction (Coch & French, 1948; Pelz, 1955, 1965). Although these results were brought to the attention of many American executives, few decided to implement the recommended procedures because they objected to the idea of the group as a unit of democratic decision making and behavior. This recommended approach did not conform to the American ethic of individualism and it bore a superficial resemblance to communism. However, these recommendations were put to productive use in another part of the world. In Japan, where societal norms favor group-based behavior and where psychologists recognized the value of Lewinian group dynamics, this approach was put to good use; it was a costly missed opportunity for American business. There is another message here: Researchers can only make policy recommendations based on their best available knowledge. Policy makers in government, business, and other agencies have the power to accept or reject that input—often on the basis of political expediency or personal prejudices about attempts to change the *status quo*.

The focus on solving social problems moves us a long way from the traditional view of psychology as the study of individual actions and mental processes. We become aware of the person as only one level in a complex system that includes social groups, institutions, cultural values, historical circumstances, political and economic realities, and specific situational forces. Modern social psychologists have expanded the domain of their inquiry to include this broader network of interacting elements. Many new areas of application have opened up to both the curious investigator and the psychologist as social change agent (Fisher, 1982).

Psychological knowledge is applied in many different areas with the potential to enrich all concerned. In addition, this expansion of psychology's relevance to life problems provides great opportunities and challenges to psychologists just beginning their professional careers. Among the exciting liaisons that are encouraged by social psychology and infused with its research paradigms and perspectives are psychology and law; psychology and education; psychology and health care; political psychology (international relations, terrorism, conflict, public policy); psychology and the consumer; psychology and business, environmental or ecological psychology; and a field of importance to everyone on the planet, peace psychology (see Oskamp, 1984, and Rodin, 1985, for more applications of social psychology to everyday life). We dealt at length with health psychology in Chapter 13. Here we will look at environmental psychology and peace psychology.

ENVIRONMENTAL PSYCHOLOGY

Systematic study of the effects of the larger environment (in contrast to specific stimuli) on behavior began in the 1950s with studies of behavior in psychiatric wards, where different physical arrangements seemed to produce different patient behavior. Such studies have led to the new field of **environmental psychology** (Proshansky, 1976; Altman & Christensen, 1990).

Environmental psychologists study the relationships between psychological processes and physical environments, both natural and human-made (Darley & Gilbert, 1985). Environmental psychologists use an ecological approach to study the way people and environments affect each other. The ecological approach emphasizes the reciprocity and mutual influence in an organism-environment relationship. Organism and environment influence each other, and both keep changing as a result. We see a circular pattern—we change the natural environment and create physical and social structures that in turn, confine, direct, and change us, encouraging certain behaviors and discouraging or preventing others, often in unanticipated ways.

Environmental psychology is oriented not so much toward past determinants of behavior as toward the future that is being created. This orientation means that environmental psychologists have to be concerned with values. Some environments are more nourishing for us than others, and some uses of the environment are destructive. This new psychology is concerned with identifying what makes environments supportive and what human behaviors are involved in creating and maintaining those environments, while not trespassing on the health of the ecosystem that makes life possible in the first place (Russell & Ward, 1982).

There is ample evidence of the influence of physical design on psychological activities and processes. Different physical arrangements have been studied in hospital settings, workplaces, homes, and entire cities. Different moods, self-images, and overt behaviors are consistently found to be related to these physical differences. The way space is partitioned can help bring people together or isolate them. The type of windows in an apartment building can encourage residents to look out at activities on their streets and keep an eye on the neighborhood or can discourage such people watching. An architect can design space to appeal to snobbery, to invite informality, or to induce confusion (Altman, 1976).

Can we make our cities more livable? What features of the environment encourage vandalism and crime? Does crowding cause physical and social pathology? What is the impact of uncontrollable levels of noise in the work place or the home? Can psychological knowledge contribute to energy conservation programs? These are among the intriguing questions being studied by environmental psychologists. By reformulating massive social issues into smaller, less overwhelming prob-

Environmental psychologists use an ecological approach to make cities more livable.

lems, social psychologists are beginning to obtain small victories that can add up to big victories (Weick, 1984).

Recognition that natural energy is a limited resource throughout the world is leading social psychologists with interests in environmental psychology to develop strategies for aiding people in conserving energy and water in drought-sensitive areas and in reducing reliance on petroleum. The Close-Up on page 612 shows one approach to energy conservation involving the use of social psychological principles.

PEACE PSYCHOLOGY

Psychologists for Social Responsibility is an organization of psychologists who not only study various aspects of the complex issues involved in war and peace but conduct educational programs on these topics for professionals, schoolchildren, and the lay public. In addition, they try to have input in relevant political decision-making policies at the state and national levels. This organization is just one example of the dual roles that many psychologists have chosen to play as dedicated, objective scientists and, at other times, as committed, impassioned advocates of social-political action based on knowledge and personal values.

How to help resolve the dilemmas of superpower competition—or, for that matter, many of the domestic and international problems that we now face—poses challenges that psychology is uniquely equipped to study. **Peace psychology** represents an interdisciplinary approach to prevention of nuclear war and maintenance of peace (Plous, 1987). Psychologists committed to contributing their talents and energies to this area so vital to our future draw upon this work of investigators in many areas. Among them are political scientists, economists, physicists, mathematicians, computer scientists, anthropologists, climatologists, and physicians.

Some of these psychologists are conducting research that examines the basis for false beliefs, misperceptions, and erroneous attributions on issues germane to nuclear arms, military strength, risk, and national security. They study the fears of children and the anxieties of adults about nuclear war. Exploring some of the individual and cultural forces that create war and promote peace involves studies of propaganda and images of the enemy through content and fantasy analysis of violence and war themes in the media. Although most cultures oppose individual aggression as a crime, nations train millions of soldiers to kill. Part of this mass social influence involves dehumanizing the soldiers of the other side into "the enemy"—nonhuman objects to be hated and destroyed. This dehumanization is accomplished through political rhetoric and through the media, especially cartoonists, in their vivid depic-

tions of the enemy. Sketches of the enemy can arouse fear and unconscious anxieties and stimulate the hostile imagination. A variety of dehumanizing faces is superimposed over the enemy to allow him to be killed without guilt. The problem of military psychology is to convert the act of murder into patriotism (Keen, 1986, p. 12). According to army veterans, a soldier's most important weapon in war is not a gun but this internalized view of the hated enemy (see **Figure 16.6**).

Let's examine a few of the directions being taken by some peace psychologists. For quite some time, social scientists have been investigating arms negotiations, international crisis management, and conflict resolution strategies. They have been developing experimental gaming studies to test the utility of different models of the nuclear arms race. These studies use the beliefs and strategies of individual protagonists as the behavioral data that might ultimately motivate the political decisions of national leaders. Personality analyses of these people suggest that their drive for power may be the impetus for the nuclear arms race.

Arms negotiations or international crises are simulated to resemble historical situations. Participants are divided into bilateral or multilateral teams, often with internal decision hierarchies and domestic constraints on their bargaining positions (Guetzkow et al., 1963). By varying factors, such as the opening position, the presence or absence of an intermediary, or the amount of emphasis on verification, parallel negotiations can be compared according to the patterns of cooperation or competition they produce. These simulations also generate new negotiating strategies and techniques for crisis management (Bazerman, 1990).

A similar approach has been to analyze the historical record of actual negotiations and crises. One such project, which was directed by psychologist **Irving Janis** and political scientist Richard Ned Lebow, has led to some interesting preliminary results. Janis and Lebow categorized the quality of decision making in 19 major international crises since World War II. Characterizing these decisions along seven independent dimensions, the researchers found a strong relationship between the way decisions were made and whether or not international conflict intensified. The researchers also found that "defective decision making" predominated in more than a third of the crises, and they suggested various safeguards to ensure better decision making in future crises (Fisher, 1985).

Some psychologists believe that to affect policy making toward nuclear war, it is necessary to study the way those in authority have handled nuclear crises, the most feared events that are least understood by those in charge of nuclear weapons. By learning how decision makers have made sense of events that could have led to

FIGURE 16.6 *FACES OF THE ENEMY*

Notice how the cartoonists have dehumanized the "enemy" in each case.

This is the Enemy

THIS IS THE ENEMY

nuclear war, psychologists may be in a position to offer more fully formed decision rules that minimize the cognitive and motivational biases of policy makers. The goal of their work is to prevent future crises through an understanding of past and current crisis management (Blight, 1987).

From a psychodynamic perspective, the impetus for the nuclear arms race is the drive for personal power among national leaders (Frank, 1987). Some of their errors of judgment are seen as deriving from the constellation of personality traits that characterize most superpower leaders—toughness, persuasiveness, suspiciousness, optimism, and competitiveness. Faced with the difficulty of changing the very traits that make the leaders successful in many aspects of their jobs, psychologists stress the need to promote awareness of

CHANGING CONSERVATION ATTITUDES AND BEHAVIORS

U.S. citizens do not seem to understand that unchecked consumption of petroleum products is linked to air pollution, oil spills, and even war. Drivers stopped for speeding on a Massachusetts freeway were asked what they thought about slowing down to save oil. Some of their responses included "I never really thought about it," "There's a lot of oil around the country," and "We have enough in Texas and other places to keep us going" (Stipp, 1991).

These views persist despite apparent changes in attitudes toward conservation. A 1989 *New York Times*/CBS News poll reported that 80 percent of U.S. citizens believed that "protecting the environment is so important that requirements and standards cannot be too high, and continuing environmental improvements must be made regardless of cost" (Hayes, 1991).

However committed Americans may feel to the principle of preserving the earth, their actual behavior is another matter. How do you get people to act differently? An experiment by social psychologist Elliot Aronson (1990) suggests that *modeling* the desired behavior is much more effective than simply telling people what they should be doing. Administrators at the University of California at Santa Cruz wanted students to conserve energy and water. Because students at UC Santa Cruz claimed to be ardent environmentalists, the bureaucrats believed that displaying a conservation message on signs would lead to significant changes in behavior.

A sign on the wall of the men's shower room at the field house en-

couraged water conservation by urging users to "(1) Wet down. (2) Turn water off. (3) Soap up. (4) Rinse off." Over a period of five days, only six percent of the men taking showers followed the suggested routine. When the sign was placed on a tripod and moved to a more prominent spot at the shower room entrance, compliance went up to 19 percent. However, the overall effectiveness of the sign was probably negligible, as some

users, resenting the sign, knocked it over and took extra long showers.

Finally, all signs were removed, and a student modeled appropriate shower-taking behavior: "Our stooge entered the shower room when it was momentarily empty, turned on the tap, and waited with his back turned to the entrance. As soon as he heard someone enter, he followed the admonition of the sign: He turned off the water, soaped up, rinsed off, and left." Compliance under this approach jumped to 49 percent. When two models were used, 67

percent of those who observed them followed their lead. Aronson concluded that modeling works better than signs because it "provides a checkpoint from similar people of what is reasonable behavior in a given situation" (Aronson, 1990).

If the government really wants people to conserve energy, perhaps our president should (a) drive a Honda Civic; (b) give up his speedboat; and (c) shower with a friend. More realistically, recycling of disposable waste products, such as paper, glass, and metal, can be vastly expanded by having door-to-door weekly pickups arranged through city contracts with local sanitation or scavenger companies. Any efforts at energy conservation must involve minimal human energy consumption; since most people are not going to go to distant recycling centers, the services have to come to them. Once the service is established, several psychological factors come into play. Seeing neighbors using their brightly colored recycling bins every Monday morning creates social pressure for others to conform to this new neighborhood standard. Periodic feedback from the pickup agency or the city about the extent of success of the recycling program through the media or in flyers sent with the utility bills will help sustain individual efforts. Another social modeling tactic is to distribute signs to regular recyclers to put in their windows or in front yards— *We recycle to save energy. Won't you help also?*

Another area of behavior change important for reducing nondegradable waste involves the use of disposable baby diapers. In response to the media advertising blitz for the past few generations, many families have come to use and discard plastic disposable diapers in hugh quantities. Rented cloth diapers are less convenient, but they do not pollute the environment. Efforts at motivating people to return to using cloth diapers have to rely on social pressures and not just individual antipollution attitudes. Having day-care services actively promote or sponsor diaper services is one step in this direction. They could convey to parents directly the reasons for using cloth instead of plastic diapers (informational influence). They could also list the names of families who have signed up for this service under a banner: *Families who have made the diaper switch. Our babies are helping to improve their future environment and getting cuddled by softer cloth as their reward* (normative influence). The point is that we have to be more imaginative in using social psychological principles to design strategies and tactics that transform general ecological concerns into specific action programs that will work to achieve prosocial goals.

▓▓▓▓▓▓▓▓▓▓▓▓ Would YOU like to become more involved in protecting the resources of your environment? If so, consider the following recommendations:

• Read *The Student Environmental Action Guide: 25 Simple Things We Can Do,* Harper-Collins Publishers and the Earth Works Group, 1991 ($4.95). This book is written for students by students. It addresses campus environmental issues and is filled with a combination of facts, success stories about the environmental actions taken by student groups, and prescriptions for actions that you and your fellow students can take.

• Join SEAC, the Student Environmental Action Coalition, P. O. Box 1168, Chapel Hill, N. C. 27514-1168, (919) 967-4600, FAX (919) 967-4648. SEAC provides information about all student environmental organizations, listings of valuable resources for people concerned about the environment, and a subscription to *Threshold,* a national student environmental magazine distributed eight times a year (for $15 or whatever you can afford). ▓▓▓▓▓

superordinate goals upon which leaders can agree. Also, there is a need to provide effective alternatives for violence as the ultimate expression of power. Many researchers are focusing their attention on the socio-psychological effects of nuclear war—the way people perceive and respond to its threat and the reason citizens who are fearful of nuclear destruction do not get involved in activities to promote peace (Allen, 1985; Fiske, 1987).

Psychologists have a new role in the revolution that is sweeping away entire political systems and economic orders throughout the world. The transition of hundreds of millions of people from a totalitarian to a democratic mentality and from a central collectivist society to a free-market economy is a change of unprecedented proportions. Generations of communist citizens have never experienced the freedoms and responsibilities of democratic ideas and practices. Democracy is more than a political system; it is a unique way of thinking about the significance of the individual and the role of oneself in shaping shared societal goals. Those who have lived with some sense of security in government-controlled economy and state-run industries must learn to cope with the risks and uncertainties of competitive market economies. Additionally, individuals and whole communities need help to deal with decades of abuses by totalitarian regimes—exiles, imprisonments, forced labor, displacement, and ecological catastrophes. This psychological help involves education, research, therapy, and social policy planning. The Center for the Psychology of Democracy is a newly formed organization of psychologists committed to assisting people and societies in reshaping their lives and country within the framework of democratic principles and practices (Balakrishnan, 1991).

This psychology peace sampler barely touches on the many new directions that researchers and social change agents are taking to reduce the threat of war and increase the prospects for peace. (See *Discovering Psychology,* Program 24 for other illustrations of peace psychology in action.) However, it does suggest how the basic research and theories we have been discussing can be applied to solve some of the urgent problems facing us. The goal is to improve the quality of life for individuals, societies, and the planet.

RECAPPING MAIN POINTS

The Power of the Situation

Human thought and action are affected by situational influences. Being assigned to play a social role, even in artificial settings, can cause individuals to act contrary to their beliefs, values, and dispositions. Social norms shape the behavior of group members, as demonstrated by the Asch experiments and the Bennington study. Lewin tested the effect of leadership styles on schoolchildren, demonstrating that socially significant questions could be explored experimentally. Milgram's studies on obedience are a powerful testimony to the influence of situational factors. Bystander intervention studies show that, when among a large group of people or when in a hurry, individuals are less likely to aid a person in distress. Directly asking for help is an effective way of promoting altruism.

Constructing Social Reality

Each person constructs his or her own social reality that is shared by their social group. Beliefs and expectations can guide actions and shape outcomes in any behavioral setting. Prejudice develops as an outcome of the desire to simplify complex information through categorization. Even minimal cue differences, such as eye color, are enough basis for extreme categorizations. Social psychologists often use cognitive frameworks to understand social phenomena. They vary in their use of motivational or purely cognitive factors. Theories using cognitive frameworks include dissonance theory, self-perception theory, and attribution theory.

Solving Social Problems

Many social psychologists strive to improve the human condition by applying psychological principles to various social problems. In the field of environmental psychology, researchers look at the way people and environments affect each other. The ecological approach emphasizes reciprocity and mutual influence in an organism-environment relationship. Environmental psychologists look for ways that human behavior can make environments supportive without trespassing on the health of ecosystems. Peace psychologists look for ways to help resolve superpower competition and hostilities among nations. They conduct research that examines the basis for false beliefs, misperceptions, and erroneous attributions in areas related to national security and nuclear arms. They also study fears about war among children and adults. Social psychology aims to be both practical and theoretical.

KEY TERMS

Asch effect, 583
attribution theory, 604
autokinetic effect, 580
behavioral confirmation, 599
bystander intervention, 592
cognitive dissonance, 603
conformity, 583
covariation principle, 605
demand characteristics, 590
environmental psychology, 609
fundamental attribution error (FAE), 606
group dynamics, 586
informational influence, 582
intuitive psychologists, 604
norm crystallization, 580
normative influence, 582
peace psychology, 610
phenomenological perspective, 596
prejudice, 599

reference group, 580
rules, 578
scapegoating, 586
self-fulfilling prophesy, 598
self-perception theory, 603
self-serving bias, 605
situationism, 577
social categorization, 600
social context, 577
social facilitation, 578
social loafing, 578
social norms, 579
social perception, 602
social psychology, 577
social reality, 596
social role, 578
Stanford Prison Experiment, 578
total situation, 581

MAJOR CONTRIBUTORS

Allport, Gordon, 580
Aronson, Elliot, 601
Asch, Solomon, 583
Bem, Daryl, 603
Clark, Kenneth, 599
Darley, John, 592
Elliott, Jane, 600
Festinger, Leon, 603
Funt, Allen, 582
Heider, Fritz, 604
Kelley, Harold, 604
Janis, Irving, 610

Latané, Bibb, 592
Lewin, Kurt, 586
Milgram, Stanley, 588
Moriarity, Tom, 595
Moscovici, Serge, 585
Newcomb, Theodore, 581
Rosenthal, Robert, 597
Ross, Lee, 606
Sherif, Muzafer, 580
Snyder, Mark, 599
Treisman, Urie, 598
Triplett, Norman, 577

Chapter 17

Abnormal Psychology

THE NATURE OF PSYCHOLOGICAL DISORDERS 618
  DECIDING WHAT IS ABNORMAL
  HISTORICAL PERSPECTIVES
  THE ETIOLOGY OF PSYCHOPATHOLOGY
  ALTERNATIVE VIEWS

  INTERIM SUMMARY

CLASSIFYING PSYCHOLOGICAL DISORDERS 625
  GOALS OF CLASSIFICATION
  DSM-III-R

  INTERIM SUMMARY

MAJOR TYPES OF PSYCHOLOGICAL DISORDERS 628
  PERSONALITY DISORDERS
  DISSOCIATIVE DISORDERS
  ANXIETY DISORDERS: TYPES
  ANXIETY DISORDERS: CAUSES
  CLOSE-UP: ADDICTED TO GAMBLING
  AFFECTIVE DISORDERS: TYPES
  AFFECTIVE DISORDERS: CAUSES
  SEX DIFFERENCES IN DEPRESSION

  INTERIM SUMMARY

SCHIZOPHRENIC DISORDERS 645
  MAJOR TYPES OF SCHIZOPHRENIA
  CAUSES OF SCHIZOPHRENIA
  IS SCHIZOPHRENIA UNIVERSAL?

  INTERIM SUMMARY

JUDGING PEOPLE AS ABNORMAL 653
  THE PROBLEM OF OBJECTIVITY
  THE PROBLEM OF STIGMA

RECAPPING MAIN POINTS 658

KEY TERMS 659

MAJOR CONTRIBUTORS 659

Another incidence of psychopathology is found in the case of Jim Backus, whom you might remember as the funny voice of Mr. Magoo and the eccentric millionaire in "Gilligan's Island."

> Backus was a sociable humorist, a comic actor, a writer, and a good golfer. In his later years, however, he became a recluse; when a reporter visited him, he learned that Backus refused to see old friends and feared going into restaurants or working in front of a camera. He even stopped writing and playing golf. The reporter noted: "The other day Backus sat in a chair in his home, a frightened, insecure man, contrasting tragically with the raucous extroverted Backus of old, needing reassurance that he wasn't, indeed, in the clutches of a life-threatening disease."

> Backus suffered from an extreme case of *hypochondria*, believing he was afflicted with Parkinson's disease. Despite medical reassurances, his panic, depression, and fears got steadily worse. He told the interviewer, "I haven't been out of this house in almost six years. I was terrified when the doorbell rang. I'd run and hide. I'm trying to get over the acute panic right now as we talk. . . . Your mind can do this to you. You know it's doing it to you, but you're powerless to stop it." With the help of his wife, Backus wrote and published the story of this living nightmare in *Backus Strikes Back* (D. M. Scott, 1990, p. 58).

DECIDING WHAT IS ABNORMAL

What is a psychological disorder? Experts in the field of abnormal psychology do not agree completely about what behaviors constitute psychological disorders. As we shall see, there is a great deal of social judgment involved in labeling behaviors as abnormal or psychopathological and in classifying mental health problems. The judgment that someone has a mental disorder is typically based on the evaluation of the individual's *behavioral* functioning by people with some special authority or power. The terms used to describe these phenomena—*mental disorder, mental illness,* or *abnormality*—depend on the particular perspective, training, and cultural background of the speaker; the situation; and the status of the person being judged. For example, in some cases, judgments of abnormality are confused with evaluations of morality—it is "bad" to have hallucinations in our culture because they are taken as signs of mental disturbance, but it is "good" in cultures where hallucinations are interpreted as mystical visions from spirit forces.

We have already cited a few statistics about how common psychological problems are, but we have offered only vague definitions of these problems. The first step in classifying someone as having a psychological disorder is making a judgment that some aspect of the person's functioning is *abnormal*. A **psychological diagnosis** is the identification made by classifying and categorizing the observed behavior pattern into an approved diagnostic system that a disorder, syndrome, or condition exists. Such a diagnosis is in many ways more difficult to make than a medical diagnosis and is subject to greater interpretation. In the medical context, a doctor can rely on physical evidence, such as X rays, blood tests, and biopsies, to inform a diagnostic decision. In the case of psychological disorders, the evidence for diagnosis comes from interpretations of a person's actions. What does it mean to say someone is *abnormal* or *suffering from a psychological disorder*? How do psychologists decide what is abnormal? Is it always clear when behavior moves from the normal to the abnormal category? Judgments about abnormality are far from being clear cut; mental disorder is best thought of as a *continuum*, as shown in **Figure 17.1.** Because the definition of *abnormality* is not very precise, there are no fail-safe rules we can use to identify abnormality.

What follows are six indicators of possible abnormality (Rosenhan & Seligman, 1989):

- *Distress:* experiencing personal distress or intense anxiety.
- *Maladaptiveness:* acting in ways that hinder goals, do not contribute to personal well-being, and interfere strongly with the goals and needs of society. Someone who is drinking so heavily that she cannot hold down a job or who is endangering others through her intoxication is displaying maladaptive behavior.
- *Irrationality:* acting or talking in ways that are irrational or incomprehensible to others. A man who responds to voices that do not exist in objective reality is behaving irrationally.
- *Unpredictability:* behaving unpredictably or erratically from situation to situation, as if experiencing a loss of control. A child who smashes his fist through a wall for no apparent reason displays unpredictability.
- *Unconventionality and Statistical Rarity:* behaving in ways that are statistically rare and violate social standards of what is morally acceptable or desirable. Just being statistically unusual, however, does not lead to a psychological judgment of abnormality. For example, possessing genius-level intelligence is extremely rare, but it is also considered desirable. On the other hand, having an

FIGURE 17.1   MENTAL DISORDER CONTINUUM

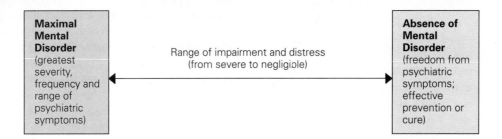

Maximal Mental Disorder (greatest severity, frequency and range of psychiatric symptoms) ← Range of impairment and distress (from severe to negligible) → Absence of Mental Disorder (freedom from psychiatric symptoms; effective prevention or cure)

extremely low intelligence is also rare but is considered undesirable; thus, it has often been labeled abnormal.

• *Observer Discomfort:* creating discomfort in others by making them feel threatened or distressed in some way. A woman walking down the middle of the street, having a vivid conversation with herself, creates observer discomfort in the drivers of cars trying to drive around her.

Most of these indicators of abnormality are not immediately apparent to all observers—in other words, they involve a large degree of judgment. At the end of this chapter we will consider the negative consequences and dangers associated with such judgments.

We are more confident in labeling behavior as "abnormal" when more than just one of the six indicators are present and valid. The more extreme and prevalent the indicators are, the more confident we can be that they indicate an abnormal condition.

None of these six criteria is a *necessary* condition shared by all cases of abnormality. For example, during his murder trial, a Stanford University graduate student who had killed his math professor with a hammer and then taped to his office door a note that read, "No office hours today," reported feeling neither guilt nor remorse. Despite the absence of personal suffering, we would not hesitate to label his overall behavior as abnormal. It is also true that none, by itself, is a *sufficient* condition that distinguishes all cases of abnormal behavior from normal variations in behavior. The distinction between normal and abnormal is not so much a difference between two independent types of behaviors as it is a matter of the *degree* to which a person's actions resemble a set of agreed-upon criteria of abnormality. When making judgments on normality, it is important to operate from a perspective on *mental health* as well

as from a perspective on *mental illness*, as shown in **Figure 17.2.**

FIGURE 17.2   MENTAL HEALTH CONTINUUM

Optimal Mental Health

Individual, group and environmental factors work together effectively, ensuring

• subjective well-being;
• optimal development and use of mental abilities;
• achievement of goals consistent with justice; and
• conditions of fundamental equality.

Minimal Mental Health

Individual, group and environmental factors conflict, producing

• subjective distress;
• impairment or underdevelopment of mental abilities;
• failure to achieve goals;
• destructive behaviors; and
• entrenchment of inequities.

Before we consider specific examples of abnormality that are classified as psychological disorders, we will explore the approaches and models that psychologists and psychiatrists use to explain how abnormal behavior develops. Let's begin by looking briefly at the way psychological problems have been viewed throughout history and the way these perspectives have contributed to the understanding of psychological disorders.

HISTORICAL PERSPECTIVES

Throughout history, humans have feared psychological disorders, often associating them with evil. Because of this fear, people have reacted aggressively and decisively to any behaviors they perceived as bizarre or abnormal. Not until very recently have people begun to accept the notion that psychological disorders are a form of illness that is very often treatable.

Attitudes about the link between mental illness and evil may be as old as human history. Archaeologists have found prehistoric skulls with holes drilled in them. These discoveries might indicate that our ancestors believed such holes would allow the demons that had possessed a loved one to escape.

The following tenth-century invocation was intended to alleviate **hysteria,** an affliction characterized by a cluster of symptoms that included paralysis or pains, dizziness, lameness, and blindness. Hysteria was originally thought to affect only women and it was believed to be caused by a wandering uterus under the devil's control. Notice how the invocation illustrates the role demonic forces were believed to play in psychological disorders.

> O womb, womb, womb, cylindrical womb, red womb, white womb, fleshy womb, bleeding womb, large womb, neufredic womb, bloated womb, O demoniacal one! . . . I conjure thee, O womb, in the name of the Holy Trinity to come back to the place from which thou shouldst neither move nor turn away . . . and to return, without anger, to the place where the Lord has put thee originally (Zilboorg and Henry, 1941, quoted in Neitzel et al., 1991, p. 19).

During the Renaissance (about 1350–1630 A.D.), intellectual and artistic enlightenment flourished. Oddly enough, amid this intellectual fervor, fear of the devil and evil peaked as the Catholic Church launched a campaign of trials and torture to weed out evil and all nonbelievers. This *Inquisition* led to the torture and execution of thousands.

In 1692, in the Massachusetts colony of Salem, numerous young women began experiencing convulsions, nausea, and weakness. They reported sensations of being pinched, pricked, or bitten. Many became temporarily blind or deaf; others reported visions and sensations of flying through the air. Such strange symptoms sparked a frantic search for an explanation. Many people theorized that the symptoms were the work of the devil who, through the efforts of earthbound witches, had taken over the minds and bodies of the young women. These theories led to a witchcraft panic and to the execution of over 20 women believed to be witches. A recent analysis strongly suggests that the "bewitched" Salem women may have been suffering from ergot poisoning—*ergot,* a fungus that grows on rye, is a source of LSD (Caporeal, 1976; Matossian, 1982).

Until the end of the eighteenth century, the mentally ill in Western societies were perceived as mindless beasts who could be controlled only with chains and physical discipline. They were not cared for in hospitals but were incarcerated with criminals.

In 1905, a group of young artists gathered in Paris to open an exhibition of work that broke entirely from traditional realistic art. These artists had painted their personal impressions of reality. The public reacted to the exhibition with outrage, accused the artists of being wild beasts—fauvists—and suggested that they be committed to institutions for the insane. Among the artists were several whose work is now honored and highly valued, including Henri Matisse.

Salem witchcraft trials, Salem, Massachusetts, 1692

"L'Estaque" by André Derain, one of the fauvists

Emergence of the Medical Model

In the latter part of the eighteenth century, a new perspective about the origins of abnormal behavior emerged—people began to perceive those with psychological problems as *sick,* suffering from illness, rather than as *possessed* or *immoral.* A number of reforms were gradually implemented in the facilities for the insane. **Phillipe Pinel** (1745–1826) was one of the first clinicians to use these ideas to attempt to develop a classification system for psychological difficulties based on the ideas that disorders of thought, mood, and behavior are similar in many ways to the physical, organic symptoms of illness and that each disorder is seen as having a group of characteristic symptoms that distinguishes it from other disorders and from healthy functioning. Disorders are classified according to the patterns of observed symptoms, the circumstances surrounding the onset of the disturbance, the natural course of the disorder, and its response to treatment. Such classification systems are modeled after the biological classification systems naturalists use and are intended to help clinicians identify common disorders more easily.

In 1896, **Emil Kraepelin** (1855–1926), a German psychiatrist, was responsible for creating the first truly comprehensive *classification system* of psychological disorders. Strongly motivated by a belief that there was a physical basis to psychological problems, he gave the process of psychological diagnosis and classification the flavor of medical diagnosis, a flavor that still remains today (Rosenhan & Seligman, 1989). His perspective is most readily seen in the terminology used by psychiatrists. They speak of *mental illness,* and *treat* mental *patients* in the hope of *curing* their *diseased* brains. The medical model also tends to be based on **organic pathology,** the perspective that mental illness is caused by deficits in structure or neurobiological functioning.

Emergence of Psychological Models

An alternative perspective to the medical approach focuses on the psychological causes and treatment of abnormal behavior. This perspective began to emerge most clearly at the end of the eighteenth century. It was helped along by the dramatic work of **Franz Mesmer** (1734–1815) whose legacy remains with us today in the concepts of *animal magnetism* and *mesmerism.* Mesmer believed that many disorders, including hysteria, were caused by disruptions in the flow of a mysterious force that he called *animal magnetism.* He unveiled several new techniques to study animal magnetism, including one that eventually became known as *hypnotism* but was originally referred to as *mesmerism* in his honor. While his general theory of animal magnetism was discredited by a scientific advisory commission, his hypnotic techniques were adopted by many researchers, including a prominent French neurologist, **Jean Charcot** (1825–1893). Charcot found that some of the symptoms of hysteria, such as paralysis of a limb, could be eliminated when a patient was under hypnosis. Hypnosis even had the power to *induce* the symptoms of hysteria in healthy individuals, dramatically illustrating the potential of *psychological factors* to cause problems that were believed to have an exclusively physical basis.

One of Charcot's students, Sigmund Freud, continued to experiment with hypnosis. Freud used his experiments to elaborate his psychodynamic theories of personality and abnormality that continue to exert tremendous influence on current theories of the nature and causes of psychopathology. (He later abandoned hypnotherapy for psychoanalysis as the treatment for psychological disorders.)

There are many different *psychological models* used to account for the onset and progress of various mental disorders, some of which we will review. All psychological models share the assumption that the origins of mental disorders and the sources that maintain abnormal behavior are not biological but psychological. Psychological models are based on **functional pathology,** the perspective that there is no known organic disorder responsible for the symptoms of mental illness. These models identify learning, reinforcement, motivation, cognitions, cultural factors, family systems, and other psychological processes as contributing to mental disorders.

THE ETIOLOGY OF PSYCHOPATHOLOGY

Etiology refers to the factors that cause or contribute to the development of psychological and medical problems. Knowing why the disorder occurs, what its origins are, and the way it affects thought and emotional and behavioral processes may lead to new ways of treating and, ideally, preventing it. Approaches to understanding the causal factors in psychopathology can be grouped into two major categories: biological and psychological.

Biological Approaches

Building on the heritage of the medical model, modern biological approaches assume that psychological disturbances are directly attributable to underlying biological factors, most often linked to the brain or nervous system. Biological researchers and clinicians most often investigate structural abnormalities in the brain, biochemical processes, and genetic influences (Gottesman, 1991; Meltzer, 1987; Snyder, 1976).

The brain is a complex organ whose interrelated elements are held in delicate balance. Subtle alterations in its chemical messengers—the neurotransmitters—or in its tissue can have significant effects. Genetic factors, brain injury, and infection are a few of the causes of these alterations. We have seen in earlier chapters that technological advances in scanning techniques, such as PET scans and brain imaging techniques, allow mental health professionals to view the structure of the brain and specific biochemical processes in living individuals without surgery. Using these techniques, biologically oriented researchers are discovering new links between psychological disorders and specific abnormalities in the brain. For example, the brains of some patients with schizophrenic disorders have a larger ventricular area filled with fluid than normal brains do. Also, extreme violence has been linked to brain tumors located in the area of the brain associated with aggressive behavior. Biochemical approaches to psychopathology have been affirmed by studies showing the ways drugs can alter the normal reality of the mind and by the proven success of drug therapies in alleviating certain symptoms of psychological disorders (Bowers, 1980; Papolos & Papolos, 1987). Continuing advances in the field of behavioral genetics have improved researchers' abilities to identify the links between specific genes and the presence of psychological disorders (Joyce, 1989; Tsuang & Vandermey, 1981). However, despite the promise of these approaches, there are still many unknowns about the connections between biology, genes, and psychopathology.

Psychological Approaches

Psychological approaches focus on the causal role of psychological or social factors in the development of psychopathology. These approaches perceive personal experiences, traumas, conflicts, and environmental factors as the roots of psychological disorders. We will outline three dominant psychological models of abnormality: the psychodynamic, the behaviorist, and the cognitive.

Psychodynamic Like the biological approach, the psychodynamic model holds that the causes of psychopathology are located inside the person. However, according to **Sigmund Freud,** who developed this model, the internal causal factors are psychological rather than biological. As we noted in earlier chapters, Freud developed psychoanalytic theory to explain apparently irrational and senseless behavior in a rational way. His ideas profoundly changed our basic concept of human nature and our approach to abnormal behavior. He believed that many psychological disorders were simply an extension of "normal" processes of psychic conflict and ego defense that we all experience. In the psychodynamic model, early childhood experiences and personal development shape both normal and abnormal behavior in life.

Behavior is motivated by drives and wishes of which we are often unaware. Symptoms of psychopathology have their roots in *unconscious conflict* and thoughts. If the unconscious is conflicted and tension filled, a person will be plagued by anxiety and other disorders. Much of this psychic conflict arises from struggles between the irrational, pleasure-seeking impulses of the *id* and the internalized social constraints imposed by the *superego*. The *ego* is normally the arbiter of this struggle; however, its ability to perform its function can be weakened by abnormal development in childhood. Individuals attempt to avoid the pain caused by conflicting motives and anxiety with *defense mechanisms,* such as repression or denial. Defenses can become overused, distorting reality or leading to self-defeating behaviors. When psychic energy is bound up in attempts to defend against the emergence of repression-bound anxiety, little is left for a productive and satisfying life (Table 14.1 on page 523 summarizes defense mechanisms).

Behavioral Freudian notions gained ready acceptance among American clinical psychologists and psychiatrists as well as among their European colleagues. However, you will recall that American research psychology from the 1930s to the early 1970s was dominated by a behavioristic orientation. Those who insisted that observable responses are the only acceptable psychological data had no use for hypothetical psychodynamic processes.

Behavioral theorists argue that abnormal behaviors are acquired in the same fashion as healthy behaviors—

through learning and reinforcement. They do not focus on internal psychological phenomena or early childhood experiences. Instead, they focus on the *current* behavior and the *current* conditions or reinforcements that sustain the behavior, even if it is not the most adaptive or appropriate response to a situation. The symptoms of psychological disorders arise because an individual has learned self-defeating or ineffective ways of behaving. By discovering the environmental contingencies that maintain any undesirable, abnormal behavior, an investigator or clinician can then recommend treatment to change those contingencies and extinguish the unwanted behavior (Emmelkamp, 1986). Behaviorists rely on both classical and operant conditioning models to understand the processes that can result in maladaptive behavior.

Cognitive The cognitive perspective of human nature that has evolved over the last several decades is often used to supplement behavioristic views. The cognitive perspective suggests that we should *not* expect to discover the origins of psychological disorders in the *objective reality* of stimulus environments, reinforcers, and overt responses. Rather, we must look at how we *perceive* or *think* about ourselves and about our relations with other people and our environment. Among the cognitive variables that can guide—or misguide—adaptive responses are our perceived degree of control over important reinforcers, beliefs in our own efficacy to cope with threatening events, the ways in which we attribute the causes of our behavior to situational or personal factors, and other mental strategies we use to make sense of our problems, successes, failures, and unusual experiences (Bandura, 1986).

The cognitive approach assumes that emotional upsets are not caused by the mediating processes of perceiving and interpreting events. Psychological problems are the result of distortions in the reality of a situation or of ourselves, faulty reasoning, or poor problem solving. Sometimes our personal constructions help us and sometimes they harm us; either way, they are our own personal way of dealing with the complexities and uncertainties of everyday life (Ellis & Grieger, 1986).

Today researchers are increasingly taking an **interactionist perspective** on psychopathology, seeing it as the product of a complex interaction between a number of biological and psychological factors (Cowan, 1988). For example, genetic predispositions may make a person vulnerable to a psychological disorder by affecting neurotransmitter levels or hormone levels, but psychological or social stresses or certain learned behaviors may be required for the disorder to develop fully.

ALTERNATIVE VIEWS

In many cultures, folk beliefs about the causes of mental illness are part of a more general view of unexpected personal disasters—sudden illness, infertility, crop failure, and premature deaths of loved ones. Such disasters are often attributed to "evil magic." In the witchcraft theories of West Africa, in beliefs about sorcery among Cree Indians of Canada, in the voodoo practices of Haitians, and in the "evil eye" beliefs still common among many Mediterranean cultures, a person can call upon supernatural, evil power to inflict some disaster or mental affliction on an enemy.

In many cultures, notably those of some African groups and of the southwestern American Indians, psychological disorders are not perceived as *intrapsychic,* occurring within the mind. Instead they are viewed as *intrapopulation,* occurring among the people of the community. Thus, they suggest *disharmony* in the relationship of tribal members to their earthly environment and spiritual reality. Treatment in this view consists of communal rituals that renew the vitality of the bonds among afflicted individuals, their society, and the natural habitat in which they live (Nobles, 1972).

SUMMING UP

We have considered how psychologists conceptualize psychological disorders; they classify behavior as psychopathological by making a judgment about whether the behavior is abnormal. Abnormality is judged by the degree to which a person's actions resemble a set of indicators including distress, maladaptiveness, irrationality, unpredictability, unconventionality, and observer discomfort. Throughout history, people have tried to explain the origins of psychopathology. Early views regarded psychopathology as the product of evil spirits or weak character. In the latter part of the eighteenth century, emerging modern perspectives considered psychopathological functioning to be a result of psychological factors or underlying bodily disturbances.

Today, biological approaches to the etiology of mental illness concentrate on structural abnormalities in the brain, biochemical processes, and genetic influences. Psychological approaches include the psychodynamic, behavioral, and cognitive models. In the psychodynamic model, early childhood experiences, unconscious conflicts, and defenses play a key role. The behavioral perspective focuses on overt behavioral reactions and the environmental conditions that help create and maintain them. In the cognitive model, distortions in an individual's beliefs and per-

ceptions of self and the world are at the heart of psychological disorders. Interactionist approaches combine these psychological and biological views.

CLASSIFYING PSYCHOLOGICAL DISORDERS

Why is it helpful to have a diagnostic and classification system for psychological disorders? What advantages are gained by moving beyond a global assessment that abnormality exists to distinguishing among different types of abnormality? Does the conceptual approach to the etiology of abnormality affect the classification of psychopathology?

Given the impreciseness of discussions about abnormality and the existence of a number of distinctly different approaches for explaining psychological disorders, it should not surprise you that the diagnosis of a disturbed person often has as much to do with the theoretical orientation of the clinician as it does with the actual symptoms presented (Franklin, 1987). In order to create greater consistency among clinicians and coherence in their diagnostic evaluations, psychologists have helped to develop a system of diagnosis and classification that provides precise descriptions of symptoms and other criteria to help clinicians decide whether a person's behavior is evidence of a particular disorder.

GOALS OF CLASSIFICATION

To be most useful, a diagnostic system should provide the following benefits:

• *Common shorthand language.* To facilitate quick and clear understanding among clinicians or researchers working in the field of psychopathology, it is helpful to have a common set of terms with agreed-upon meanings. A diagnostic category, such as *depression*, summarizes a large and complex collection of information, including characteristic symptoms and the typical course of a disorder. In clinical settings, a diagnostic system allows mental health professionals to communicate more effectively about the people they are helping. Researchers studying different aspects of psychopathology or evaluating treatment programs must agree on the disorder they are observing. With a good classification scheme, individuals can be diagnosed reliably and researchers can design studies to determine the causes of and treatments for different kinds of problems.

• *Understanding etiology.* Ideally, a diagnosis of a specific disorder should suggest the causes of the

symptoms. Unfortunately, because there is substantial disagreement or lack of knowledge about the etiology of many psychological disorders, this goal is difficult to meet.

• *Plan treatment.* A diagnosis should also suggest what types of treatment to consider for particular disorders. Researchers and clinicians have found that certain treatments or therapies work most effectively for specific kinds of psychological disorders. For example, drugs that are quite effective in treating schizophrenia do not help and may even hurt people with depression. Further advances in our knowledge of the effectiveness and specificity of treatments will make fast and reliable diagnosis even more important.

DSM-III-R

In the United States, the most widely accepted classification scheme is one developed by the American Psychiatric Association. It is called the *Diagnostic and Statistical Manual of Mental Disorders*. A revision of the third edition of the manual, which was published in 1987, is known by clinicians and researchers as *DSM-III-R*. It classifies, defines, and describes over 200 mental disorders.

In *DSM-III-R*, each of the mental disorders described is seen as a behavioral or psychological syndrome occurring *within* the person and associated with present distress (a painful symptom), the risk of future distress, impairment in one or more important areas of functioning, or with an important loss of freedom (*DSM-III-R*, 1987).

To reduce the diagnostic difficulties generated by variability in approaches to psychological disorders, *DSM-III-R* emphasizes the *description* of patterns of symptoms and courses of disorders rather than etiological theories or treatment strategies. The purely descriptive terms allow clinicians and researchers to use a common language to describe problems, while leaving opportunity for disagreement and continued research about which models best explain the problems.

The first version of *DSM*, which appeared in 1952 (*DSM-I*), listed several dozen mental illnesses. *DSM-II*, introduced in 1968, revised the diagnostic system to make it more compatible with another popular system, the World Health Organization's *International Classification of Diseases* (*ICD*). A committee is currently hard at work on a fourth edition of *DSM* that is scheduled to be introduced after 1992, at about the same time as the tenth version of the *ICD*.

To encourage clinicians to consider the psychological, social, and physical factors that may be associated with a psychological disorder, *DSM-III-R* uses *dimensions* or *axes* that portray information about all of these factors (see **Table 17.1**). Most of the principal psychological disorders are contained on Axis I. Axis II lists disorders that generally begin in childhood or adolescence and continue into adulthood. These include developmental difficulties, such as language disabilities, and personality traits or disorders that may accompany Axis I disorders. Axis III incorporates information about physical disorders, such as diabetes, that may be relevant to understanding or treating an Axis I or II disorder. Axes IV and V provide supplemental information that can be useful when planning an individual's treatment or assessing the *prognosis* (predictions of future change). For example, when there is an external stressor, such as job loss associated with the onset of the mental disorder, a positive outcome is predicted. In addition, return to standard level of functioning is likely to be speedier than when the stressor is internal. A clinician can assess the severity of psychological

TABLE 17.1	THE FIVE AXES OF DSM-III-R	
Axis	**Classes of Information**	**Description**
Axis I	Clinical Syndromes	These mental disorders present symptoms or patterns of behavioral or psychological problems that typically are painful or impair an area of functioning (for example, being able to do schoolwork).
Axis II	a) Personality Disorders	These are the dysfunctional strategies of perceiving and responding to the world. Personality characteristics or traits can also be noted on this axis when *no* personality disorder exists.
	b) Developmental Disorders	These disorders affect such specific skills as reading, language, and articulation.
Axis III	Physical Disorders and Conditions	These disorders include physical problems relevant to understanding or managing an individual's mental problems.
Axis IV	Severity of Psychosocial Stressors	On this axis, the clinician rates the amount and degree of stressors contributing to the current disorder. The coding of the stressors varies from none or minimal to extreme or catastrophic. This judgment takes into account the sociocultural values and responsiveness of an average person.
Axis V	Global Assessment of Functioning	This axis shows the highest level of functioning achieved in three life areas (social, work, and leisure) during the past year. Usually, the present level can be compared with the previous as an indication of recovery from the presenting problem.

stressors on Axis IV and the highest level of adaptive functioning in the past year on Axis V. A full diagnosis in the *DSM-III-R* system would involve consideration of each of the axes. Individuals also may receive multiple diagnoses on each of the axes of disorders.

Evolution of Diagnostic Categories

The diagnostic categories and the methods used to organize and present them have shifted with each of the editions of *DSM*. These shifts reflect changes in the opinions of a majority of mental health experts about exactly what constitutes a psychological disorder and where the lines between different types of disorders should be drawn. They also reflect changing perspectives among the public about what constitutes *abnormality*.

The revisions for *DSM-III-R* were based on the judgments of over 200 mental health experts who worked on advisory panels in specific areas of psychopathology. In the revision process of each *DSM*, some diagnostic categories were dropped and others were added. For example, with the introduction of *DSM-III* in 1980, the traditional distinction between *neurotic* and *psychotic* disorders were eliminated. **Neurotic disorders,** or *neuroses,* were originally conceived of as relatively common psychological problems in which a person did not have signs of brain abnormalities, did not display grossly irrational thinking, and did not violate basic norms; but he or she did experience subjective distress or a pattern of self-defeating or inadequate coping strategies. **Psychotic disorders,** or *psychoses,* were thought to differ in both quality and severity from neurotic problems. It was believed that psychotic behavior deviated significantly from social norms and was accompanied by a profound disturbance in rational thinking and general emotional and thought processes. The *DSM-III-R* advisory committees felt that the terms *neurotic disorders* and *psychotic disorders* had become too general in their meaning to have much usefulness as diagnostic categories (they continue to be used by many psychiatrists and psychologists to characterize the general level of disturbance in a person).

A new diagnostic category was proposed for inclusion on Axis II in *DSM-III-R: masochistic personality disorder* (Franklin, 1987). **Masochism** is currently diagnosed as one of the psychosexual disorders in which sexual gratification requires being hurt or humiliated. Clinicians on one of the advisory panels recommended it be included as a more pervasive personality disorder in which a person seeks failure on the job, at home, and in relationships; rejects opportunities for pleasure; and engages in excessive self-sacrifice. Feminist therapists and researchers argued that the diagnosis was biased against women and perpetuated the myth of women's masochism (Caplan, 1985). After a year-long debate, the label was changed to *self-defeating personality disorder* and put in the appendix of the revised manual under the heading, "Proposed Diagnostic Categories Needing Further Study." This example shows the political and ideological implications of diagnosing certain behavior patterns as mental disorders.

Is DSM-III-R Effective?

In order for a diagnostic system to become a shorthand language for communicating, its users have to be able to agree reliably on what the criteria and symptoms are for each disorder and what the diagnoses would be in specific cases. *Reliability* has improved substantially with the introduction of the more descriptive and precise *DSM-III-R* (Klerman, 1986), although it is still far from complete, especially for certain categories of disorders. Improved reliability has helped facilitate research efforts to improve understanding of psychopathology and its treatment.

Concerns about the *validity* of *DSM-III-R* have been raised. Validity in descriptions and diagnoses of mental disorders is a complex concept. It involves, in part, fulfilling the second and third goals of classification systems: identifying etiology and identifying treatments. One such concern is whether disorders that are regarded as unrelated might be better regarded as similar. This distinction has implications for etiology and treatment. For example, are all the subtypes of schizophrenia in *DSM-III-R* best thought of as variants of one basic kind of problem, or are there very different kinds of schizophrenia that have different causes and require different treatments?

Some critics argue that, by emphasizing theoretically *neutral* descriptions of disorders, *DSM-III-R* does not include information on important psychological dimensions, such as impulsiveness, perceptual style, or prominent defenses, that may be helpful for treatment decisions and for understanding the causes of a disorder (Frances & Cooper, 1981; Persons, 1986). Even though it has its critics, *DSM-III-R* is the most widely used classification system in clinical practice and is frequently employed in the training of new clinicians.

SUMMING UP

There are several goals that any diagnostic and classification system of psychological disorders should seek to fulfill. They include (a) providing a common shorthand language for communicating about types of psychopathology and particular cases in order to facilitate clinical and research work and (b) offering information about etiology and about pre-

ferred modes of treatment. Disagreement over approaches to etiology and treatment and the lack of knowledge in these areas place limits on how well these goals can be met.

DSM-III-R is the most widely accepted diagnostic and classification system used by psychologists and psychiatrists. DSM-III-R emphasizes description of symptom patterns rather than identifying etiology or treatments, and it utilizes a multidimensional system of five axes that encourages mental health professionals to consider psychological, physical, and social factors that might be relevant to psychological disorders. The continually evolving diagnostic categories of the DSM system reflect the shifting views of mental health experts and the public about what is or is not abnormal and about how best to describe particular categories of abnormality.

The reliability of diagnosis of psychological disorders has improved substantially with the more descriptive and precise DSM-III-R. However, some critics have raised concerns about the limited usefulness of DSM-III-R for making treatment decisions or helping people understand the causes of psychological disorders.

MAJOR TYPES OF PSYCHOLOGICAL DISORDERS

We now turn to a detailed analysis of several prominent categories of psychological disorders: anxiety, depression, and schizophrenia. For each category, we will begin by describing what sufferers experience and how they appear to observers. Then we will consider how each of the major biological and psychological approaches to etiology explains the development of these disorders. We will selectively highlight widely used explanations and those that have been investigated through research.

There are many other categories of psychopathology that we will not be able to examine, simply because of space limitations. However, what follows is a capsule summary of some of the most important:

- *Sexual disorders* involve problems with sexual inhibition or dysfunction and deviant sexual practices.
- *Organic mental disorders* are psychological or behavioral abnormalities associated with temporary or permanent brain damage or malfunction. They may be a product of aging of the brain, disease, accidents, or excessive ingestion of substances, such as alcohol, lead, and many types of phar-

macological agents, including barbiturates, amphetamines, and opiates.
- *Substance-use disorders* include both dependence on and abuse of alcohol and drugs. We discussed many of these issues of substance abuse in the broader context of states of consciousness and in our addiction Close-Ups.
- *Somatoform disorders* involve physical (soma) symptoms, such as paralysis or pains in a limb, that arise without a physical cause. This category includes the symptoms of what used to be called *hysteria.*
- *Disorders that typically arise in infancy or childhood* include retardation, stuttering, or behavior problems. Also within this group is a subset referred to as *eating disorders,* such as anorexia and bulimia, which typically occur in adolescence or young adulthood.

As you read about the symptoms and experiences that are typical of the various psychological disturbances, you may begin to feel that some of the characteristics seem to apply to you—at least part of the time—or to someone you know. Some of the disorders that we will consider are not uncommon, so it would be surprising if they sounded completely alien. Many of us have some human frailties that appear on the list of criteria for a particular psychological disorder. Recognition of this familiarity can be a useful way of furthering your understanding of abnormal psychology, but it is important to remember that a diagnosis for any disorder depends on a number of criteria and requires the judgment of a trained mental health professional. Please resist the temptation to use this new knowledge to diagnose friends and family members as pathological. On the other hand, being sensitive to others' needs for counsel and social support in times of personal trouble is always appropriate.

Before exploring anxiety, depression, and schizophrenia in depth, we will briefly consider examples of disorders from two additional classification categories: personality disorders and dissociative disorders. Once again, because of space limitations, our treatment of these disorders will be brief.

PERSONALITY DISORDERS

A **personality disorder** is long-standing (chronic), inflexible, maladaptive pattern of perceiving, thinking, or behaving. These patterns can seriously impair an individual's ability to function in social or work settings and can cause significant distress. They are usually recognizable by the time a person reaches adolescence. There are many types of personality disorders (*DSM-III-R* recognizes 12 types); we will discuss two of the better known forms: *narcissistic personality disorder* and *antisocial personality disorder*.

People with a **narcissistic personality disorder** have a grandiose sense of self-importance, a preoccupation with fantasies of success or power, and a need for constant attention or admiration. These people often respond inappropriately to criticism or minor defeat, either by displaying an apparent indifference to criticism or by markedly overreacting. Finally, they have problems in interpersonal relationships; they tend to feel entitled to special favors with no reciprocal obligations, exploit others for their own indulgence and have difficulty recognizing and experiencing how others feel. For example, an individual with narcissistic personality disorder may express annoyance and no empathy when a friend has to cancel a date because of a death in the family.

Antisocial personality disorder is marked by a longstanding pattern of irresponsible behavior that has negative consequences for others and is typically carried out without guilt. Lying, stealing, and fighting are common symptoms. People with antisocial personality disorder often do not experience shame or intense emotion of any kind; thus, they can "keep their cool" in situations that would make other people emotionally aroused and upset. Violations of social norms begin early in their lives—disrupting class, getting into fights, and running away from home. Their actions are marked by indifference to the rights of others. Although they can be found among street criminals and con artists, they are well represented among successful politicians and business people who put career, money, and power above everything and everyone. Two to three percent of the population in the United States is believed to have antisocial personality disorder. Men are four times more likely to be diagnosed than women (Regier et al., 1988).

Personality disorders as a group are among the *least reliably* judged of all the psychological disorders and are the most controversial. Psychologists even disagree about whether personality disorders can be said truly to exist. There is also controversy about evaluating lifelong behavior patterns independent of the *contexts* in which they developed. Economic, social, family, and cultural factors may provide better explanations of the observed symptoms of a given patient than do diagnoses of personality disorders by themselves.

DISSOCIATIVE DISORDERS

A **dissociative disorder** is a disturbance in the integration of identity, memory, or consciousness. It is important for us to see ourselves as being in control of our behavior—including our emotions, thoughts, and ac-

The term *narcissistic personality disorder* is derived from the mythological character Narcissus who was enchanted with his own reflection.

tions. Essential to this perception of self-control is the sense of selfhood—the consistency of different aspects of the self and the continuity of our identity over time and place. Psychologists believe that, in dissociated states, individuals escape from their conflicts by giving up this precious consistency and continuity—in a sense, disowning part of themselves. Not being able to recall details of a traumatic event—*amnesia*—even though neurological damage is not present, is one example of dissociation. Psychologists have only recently begun to appreciate the degree to which such memory dissociation accompanies instances of sexual and physical childhood abuse. The forgetting of important personal experiences caused by psychological factors in the absence of any organic dysfunction is termed **psychogenic amnesia** or *functional amnesia*.

Multiple personality disorder (MPD) is a relatively rare dissociative mental disorder in which two or more distinct personalities exist within the same individual. At any particular time, one of these personalities is dominant in directing the individual's behavior. Multiple personality disorders have been popularized in books and movies, such as *The Three Faces of Eve* (Thigpen & Cleckley, 1957) and *Sybil* (Schreiber, 1973). Multiple personality disorder is popularly known as *split personality,* and sometimes mistakenly de-

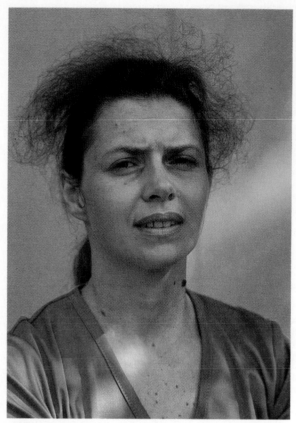

When found in a park in Florida, this woman (dubbed "Jane Doe" by authorities) was emaciated, incoherent, and near death. She was suffering from a rare form of psychogenic amnesia in which she had lost the memory of her name and her past and the ability to read and write.

scribed as *schizophrenia,* a disorder in which personality often is impaired but is not split into multiple versions. In MPD, although the original personality is unaware of the other personalities, *they* are conscious of *it* and often of each other. Each of the emerging personalities contrasts in some significant way with the original self—they might be outgoing if the person is shy, tough if the original personality is weak, and sexually assertive if the other is fearful and sexually naive. Each personality has a unique identity, name, behavior pattern, and even characteristic brain wave activity. In some cases, dozens of different characters emerge to help the person deal with a difficult life situation. The emergence of these alternate personalities, each with its own consciousness, is sudden and typically precipitated by stress.

Patients experiencing MPD typically respond best to treatment that centers on *hypnotherapy.* The alternate selves come out under hypnosis and a therapist can assist the patient in eliminating some of them while integrating others into a more effective single self. We now believe that the reason hypnotherapy is the best treat-

ment with many cases of MPD is because patients apparently used a form of self-hypnosis to develop the characters in the first place, to defend themselves from the hostile environment in which they were forced to live.

During a therapy session in which the therapist was using hypnosis to uncover the source of a client's chronic problems with dizziness, fainting, nausea, unexplained terrors, and suicidal episodes, a strange voice emerged from her. It spoke in a contemptuous voice, reporting that it "began with the existence of evil." The alien voice of the client identified itself as "a demon." The therapist's hypothesis was that this demonic aspect of the client's personality probably developed from repeated beatings by her mother and years of sexual abuse by her stepfather during her childhood. However, this adult woman had no conscious contact with this other personality nor conscious awareness of her earlier abuse until this hypnotherapy session—when her inner demon was released (Kierulff, 1987).

Typically, MPD victims are women who were severely abused physically or sexually by parents, relatives, or close friends for extended periods during childhood. One study obtained questionnaire data from 448 clinicians who had treated cases of multiple personality disorders and major depressions (used for comparative purposes). As shown in **Table 17.2,** the dominant features of the 355 cases of multiple personality disorder (MPD) are an almost universal incidence among mostly female patients of being abused at a very early age, starting around 3 years old and continuing for more than a decade. Although many of the 255 comparison patients with depression disorder also had a high incidence of abuse, it was significantly less than that experienced by those with MPD (Schultz et al., 1989).

MPD victims may have been beaten, locked up, or abandoned by those who were supposed to love them—those on whom they were so dependent that they could not fight them, leave them, or even hate them. Instead, they have fled their terror symbolically through dissociation. Psychologists believe that multiple personalities develop to serve a vital survival function. Individuals in horrifying situations may protect their egos by creating stronger internal characters to help cope with the ongoing traumatic situation and also to provide relief from their pain by numbing the dominant personality to the abuse. **F. W. Putnam** (1989), a leading researcher in the study of multiple personality disorder, has found

These two paintings by Sybil, a multiple personality disorder victim, illustrate differences between the personalities. The painting on the left was done by Peggy, Sybil's angry, fearful personality. The painting on the right was done by Mary, a home-loving personality.

that, in the typical case, there are many different alter egos, of different ages and even of both sexes, within the mind of the troubled person.

Until recently, information on multiple personality disorders has come from single cases treated by one therapist over an extended period of time. However, newer research being conducted with the collaboration of many investigators at the National Institute of Mental Health and elsewhere is enabling clinicians to get a more complete picture of this remarkable disorder that puts on stage too many actors for any one director to manage (Putnam, 1984).

TABLE 17.2 *RESPONSES TO INQUIRIES REGARDING ABUSE: COMPARING MULTIPLE PERSONALITY DISORDER AND DEPRESSION*

Questionnaire Item	MPD (N = 355) %		Major Depression (N = 235) %		Significance
Abuse Incidence	98		54		p<.0001
Type(s)					
Physical	82		24		p<.0001
Sexual	86		25		p<.0001
Psychological	86		42		p<.0001
Neglect	54		21		p<.0001
All of above	47		6		p<.0001
Physical and sexual	74		14		p<.0001
	Mean	S.D.	Mean	S.D.	
Beginning age of abuse	3.3	2.6	7.5	8.7	p<.0001
Ending age of abuse	17.3	7.5	22.6	15.6	p<.001
Gender					
Female	90.0		73.0		p<.001
Male	10.0		27.0		

ANXIETY DISORDERS: TYPES

Everyone experiences anxiety or fear in certain life situations. The feelings of uneasiness that characterize anxiety and fear are often accompanied by physical reactions, such as a sweaty brow or clammy palms, and may include a sense of impending harm. For some people, anxiety becomes problematic enough to interfere with their ability to function effectively or enjoy everyday life. It has been estimated that 15 percent of the general population has, at some time, experienced the symptoms that are characteristic of the various anxiety disorders recognized in *DSM-III-R* (Regier et al., 1988). While anxiety plays a key role in each of these disorders, they differ in the extent to which anxiety is experienced, the severity of the anxiety, and the situations that trigger the anxiety. We will review four major categories of anxiety: generalized anxiety disorder, panic disorder, phobic disorder, and obsessive-compulsive disorder. We have talked already about a fifth kind of anxiety disorder, posttraumatic stress disorder, in Chapter 13.

Generalized Anxiety Disorder

When a person feels anxious or worried most of the time for at least six months, when not threatened by any specific danger or object, a **generalized anxiety disorder** is diagnosed. The anxiety might be focused on specific life circumstances, such as unrealistic concerns about finances or the well-being of a loved one, or it just might consist of a general apprehensiveness about impending harm. The way the anxiety is expressed—the specific symptoms—varies from person to person. The common symptoms can be grouped into three categories:

- *Body tension;* jitters, trembling, tension, aches, fatigue, twitches, or restlessness
- *Physical arousal:* heart pounding or racing, shortness of breath, sweating, cold clammy hands, dizziness, upset stomach, diarrhea, smothering sensations, flushes, or chills
- *Vigilance:* hyperattentiveness to external events and to one's own internal reactions, poor concentration, edginess, sleep difficulties, or irritability

In spite of these symptoms, a chronically anxious person may continue to function with only mild impairment in his or her social life or job. The constant physical and psychological drain, however, takes a toll that may show up as greater susceptibility to many common ailments, such as colds, headaches, and infections.

Panic Disorder

In contrast to the chronic presence of anxiety in generalized anxiety disorder, sufferers of **panic disorder** experience unexpected (at least initially) but severe attacks of anxiety that may last only minutes. These attacks occur at least several times a month and typically begin with a feeling of intense apprehension, fear, or terror. Accompanying these feelings are physical symptoms of anxiety including autonomic hyperactivity (such as rapid heart rate), dizziness, faintness, or sensations of choking or smothering.

The following comments made during a panic attack will help you appreciate the degree of panic that is commonly experienced by someone with panic disorder:

> Uh, I'm not going to make it. I can't get help, I can't get anyone to understand the feeling. It's like a feeling that sweeps over from the top of my head to the tip of my toes. And I detest the feeling. I'm very frightened.
>
> It feels, I just get all, like hot through me, and shaky, and my heart just feels like it's pounding and breathing really quick. . . . It feels like I'm going to die or something (Muskin & Fyer, 1981, p. 81).

Because of the unexpected nature of these "hit and run" attacks, *anticipatory anxiety* often develops as an added complication in panic disorders. The dread of the next attack and of being helpless and suddenly out of control can lead a person to avoid public places yet fear being left alone. Ellen is a 28-year-old woman who is suffering from panic disorder:

> Ellen has worked very hard to create a niche for herself in a highly competitive company. She lives in Los Angeles, far from her family and most of her friends. Ellen doesn't have time to make new friends, and, besides, she's not sure if she can really trust any of the people that she meets through her work. Ellen is ambitious and she's doing well, but, at least once a week, she experiences intense anxiety. Her heart pounds fast, she has trouble breathing, and she feels dizzy and unsteady. At the same time, she feels unreal, as if this couldn't really be happening. At these times, Ellen is terrified that she might be going crazy and worries about whether she might do something bizarre and uncontrollable during an attack. The attacks usually occur on weekends, when she is alone and has no plans. Lately she worries a great deal about what would happen if she ever had an attack at work. What would people think? What would happen to her hard-won career?

Phobic Disorders

Fear is a rational reaction to an objectively identified external danger (such as a fire in one's home or being mugged) that may induce a person to flee or attack in self-defense. In contrast, a person with a **phobic disorder,** or *phobia,* suffers from a persistent and irrational fear of a specific object, activity, or situation that creates a compelling desire to avoid it.

Many of us have irrational fears of spiders or snakes (or even multiple-choice tests). Such fears become phobic disorders only when they interfere with our adjustment, cause significant distress, or inhibit necessary action toward goals.

Edith is afraid of writing her name in public. When placed in a situation where she might be asked to sign her name, Edith is terrified, and she experiences the common anxiety symptoms: muscle tension, rapid heart rate, and apprehension.

This phobia has far-reaching effects on her life. She can't use checks or credit cards to shop or to eat in a restaurant. She no longer can play golf because she can't sign the golf register. She can't go to the bank unless all transactions are prepared ahead of time in her home. She can't sign any papers that require approval of a notary public, and she can't vote because she can't sign the voting register.

Even a very specific, apparently limited phobia can have a great impact on one's whole life. Phobias are a relatively common psychological problem. Recent studies suggest that 12.5 percent of Americans suffer some form of phobia at some point in their lives (Regier et al., 1988). Almost any stimulus can come to generate a phobic avoidance reaction (see **Table 17.3**), although some phobias are much more common than others. We shall discuss two of the most common: *agoraphobia* and *social phobia.*

TABLE 17.3 **THE COMMON PHOBIAS**

	Approximate Percent of All Phobias	Sex Difference	Typical Age of Onset
Agoraphobias (fear of places of assembly, crowds, open spaces)	10–50	Large majority are women	Early adulthood
Social Phobias (fear of being observed doing something humiliating)	10	Majority are women	Adolescence
The Specific Phobias *Animals* Cats (allurophobia) Dogs (cynophobia) Insects (insectophobia) Spiders (arachnophobia) Birds (avisophobia) Horses (equinophobia) Snakes (ophidiophobia) Rodents (rodentophobia)	5–15	Vast majority are women	Childhood
Inanimate Objects or Situations Dirt (mysophobia) Storms (brontophobia) Heights (acrophobia) Darkness (nyctophobia) Closed spaces (claustrophobia)	20	None	Any age
Illness-Injury (nosophobia) Death (thanatophobia) Cancer (cancerophobia) Venereal disease (venerophobia)	15–25	None	Middle age

Agoraphobia   **Agoraphobia** is an extreme fear of being in public places or open spaces from which escape may be difficult or embarrassing. Individuals with agoraphobia fear places such as crowded rooms, malls, buses, and freeways. They are often afraid that, if they experience some kind of difficulty outside the home, such as a loss of bladder control or panic attack symptoms, that help might not be available or the situation will be embarrassing to them. These fears deprive individuals of their freedom, and, in extreme cases, they become prisoners in their own homes. They cannot hold a job or carry on normal daily activities because their fears restrict contact with the outside world.

Agoraphobia is the most commonly cited phobia among people who seek psychiatric or psychological treatment. As many as 50 percent of all those with phobias who are being treated in clinics suffer from this disorder. Between 2.7 percent and 5.8 percent of American adults are estimated to suffer from agoraphobia (NIMH, 1986). Most of them are women for whom the phobia begins in early adulthood, often with an extreme

This crowded scene would cause many agoraphobics to panic.

anxiety attack. Besides their fear of going out into public places, agoraphobics have other psychological problems, such as anxiety, depression, and obsessive-compulsive symptoms, more so than do other phobic individuals. Similar to others with extreme anxiety, they may abuse alcohol and drugs in an effort to suppress emotional arousal.

Social Phobia   **Social phobia** is a persistent, irrational fear that arises in anticipation of a public situation in which one can be observed by others. Similar to Edith, who was afraid of writing her name in public, a person with a social phobia fears that he or she will act in ways that could be embarrassing. The person recognizes that the fear is excessive and unreasonable yet feels compelled by the fear to avoid situations in which public scrutiny is possible. Examples of typical social phobias are the fear of choking on food when eating in front of others and the fear of trembling embarrassingly when speaking in public. Sometimes the phobia is more general and may include fears about acting foolishly in social situations.

Social phobia often involves self-fulfilling prophecy. A person may be so fearful of the scrutiny and rejection of others that enough anxiety is created to actually impair performance. Brilliant students with social phobias have been known to drop out of law school, for example, when they discovered that public oral performance was regularly expected of them.

Obsessive-Compulsive Disorders

Only a year or so ago, 17-year-old Jim seemed to be a normal adolescent with many talents and interests. Then, almost overnight, he was transformed into a lonely outsider, excluded from social life by his psychological disabilities. Specifically, he developed an obsession with washing. Haunted by the notion that he was dirty—in spite of what his senses told him—he began to spend more of his time cleansing himself of imaginary dirt. At first, his ritual ablutions were confined to weekends and evenings, but soon they began to consume all his time, forcing him to drop out of school (Rapoport, 1989).

Jim is suffering from a condition known as **obsessive-compulsive disorder** that is estimated to affect 2.5 percent of Americans at some point during their lives (Regier et al., 1988). *Obsessions* are thoughts, images, or impulses (such as Jim's belief that he is unclean) that recur or persist despite a person's efforts to suppress them. Obsessions are experienced as an unwanted invasion of consciousness, seem to be senseless or repugnant, and are unacceptable to the person experiencing them. Frequently, the individual avoids the situations that relate to the content of the obsessions. For

THE FAR SIDE

By GARY LARSON

© 1991 Universal Press Syndicate

example, a person with an obsessive fear about germs may avoid using bathrooms outside his or her home or refuse to shake hands with strangers.

You probably have had some sort of mild obsessional experience, such as the intrusion of petty worries—"Did I really lock the door?"; "Did I turn off the oven?"—or the persistence of a haunting melody you simply could not stop from running through your mind. The obsessive thoughts of people with this obsessive-compulsive disorder are much more compelling, cause much more distress, and may interfere with their social or role functioning.

Obsessive thoughts, images, or impulses often focus around characteristic themes. A content analysis of the obsessions of 82 people with obsessive-compulsive disorder yielded five broad categories, in the following order of frequency: (1) dirt and contamination, (2) aggression, (3) the orderliness of inanimate objects, (4) sex, and (5) religion (Akhtar et al., 1975).

Compulsions are repetitive, purposeful acts (such as Jim's washing) performed according to certain rules or in a ritualized manner in response to an obsession. Compulsive behavior is intended to reduce or prevent the discomfort associated with some dreaded situation, but it is either unreasonable or clearly excessive. Typical compulsions include irresistible urges to clean, to check

that lights or appliances have been turned off, and to count objects or possessions.

At least initially, people with obsessive-compulsive disorder resist carrying out their compulsions. When they are calm, they view their compulsion as senseless. When anxiety rises, however, the power of the compulsive behavior ritual to relieve tension seems irresistible—and must be performed. Part of the pain experienced by people with this mental problem is created by their frustration at recognizing the irrationality or excessive nature of their obsessions without being able to eliminate them.

ANXIETY DISORDERS: CAUSES

How do psychologists explain the development of anxiety disorders? Each of the four etiological approaches that we have outlined (psychodynamic, behavioral, cognitive, and biological) emphasizes different factors. Let's analyze how they each add something unique to our understanding of anxiety disorders.

Psychodynamic

The psychodynamic model begins with the assumption that the symptoms of anxiety disorders and obsessions and compulsions come from underlying psychic conflicts or fears. The symptoms are attempts to protect the individual from psychological pain.

In anxiety disorders, intense pain attacks and phobias are the result of unconscious conflicts bursting into consciousness. The unconscious conflicts are seen as having their roots in early childhood experiences. For example, a child's older sibling may receive a scholarship to a prestigious school. He may see how his older sister receives a great deal of praise for her success but must then move out of the house and out of state to attend college. He may then develop a strong desire to be recognized for individual achievement and, at the same time, an intense fear that success will separate him from the comfort and guidance of his parents. He may thus develop unconscious conflicting feelings about achievement and recognition. In later life, a phobia may be activated by an object or situation that symbolizes the conflict. In our same example, a bridge might come to symbolize the path that the child must traverse from the comforting world of home and family to the world of work, achievement, and potential failure and rejection. The sight of a bridge would then force the unconscious conflict into awareness, bringing with it the fear and anxiety common to phobias. So, the individual would develop a fear of bridges—a fear that they might collapse. Avoiding bridges would be his symbolic attempt to stay clear of achievement situations and the anxiety that accompanies them.

ADDICTED TO GAMBLING

You ask me why I gamble and I tell you, it's the thrill. I know the game is crooked and that I haven't got a chance, but when I put my money on a horse and hear its name on the speaker, my heart stands still. I know I'm alive (Newman, 1972, p. 206).

In the United States, gambling is a major source of revenue for states, churches, and charitable organizations; 80 to 90 percent of Americans gamble. However, when we are playing bingo, buying a lottery ticket, or signaling the dealer for another card, few of us think about how our losses will enhance the public good. Instead, we fantasize about buying a new car or a beach house or quitting our jobs.

Three to five percent of Americans feel they cannot control their gambling behavior (Shaffer, 1989). These people are classified as compulsive gamblers. According to the American Psychiatric Association, compulsive gambling is a "chronic and progressive failure to resist impulses to gambling, and gambling behavior that compromises, disrupts, or damages personal, family, or vocational pursuits" (Breo, 1989).

The compulsive gambler typically has been portrayed as an upper- or middle-class white man in his 40s or 50s who is employed and who enjoyed a fairly stable family life until his gambling problems escalated. However, this profile, based on people who sought treatment or joined Gamblers Anony-

mous, is biased. Recent population surveys conducted in English and Spanish found that women, young people, and ethnic minorities have all been under-represented in demographic studies of compulsive gamblers. The surveys also reveal that people who are unemployed, have not graduated from high school, or make less than $25,000 per year are at higher than average risk for becoming compulsive gamblers (Volberg, 1989).

I have recollections of gambling as a kid—whether it was flipping baseball cards, pitching pennies against the wall, or playing strip poker. . . . I was there first and stayed there longer. . . . For four-and-a-half years of college I did every form of gambling. . . . I remember my parents said they stopped spanking me when I was about seven or eight years old because I would not cry. I would not laugh. I would not tell jokes. I was a loner. Me and my gambling (Carone et al., 1982).

Although gambling is not legally permitted for those under age 18, as many as 7 million high school students gambled for money in 1988. More than a million feel they cannot stop and use their lunch money, steal, or shoplift to keep themselves in "action" (Gilman, 1989). The heavy emphasis on antidrug campaigns for teenagers, coupled with society's generally accepting attitudes toward gambling, may help explain why compulsive gambling often remains undetected in young people.

The phenomenon of compulsive gambling forces psychologists to look at addiction as a *behavior* rather than a problem caused by a *substance* that has been ingested, injected, or inhaled. Researchers hope that investigations of this behavior will let them "study the struggle against human impulses without the confounding effects of uncontrolled biochemical interference" (Schaffer et al., 1989).

In obsessive-compulsive disorders, the obsessive behavior is an attempt to displace anxiety created by a related but far more feared desire or conflict. By substituting an obsession that symbolically captures the forbidden impulse, a person gains some relief. For example, the obsessive fears of dirt experienced by Jim, the adolescent we described earlier, may have their roots in the conflict between his desire to become sexually active and his fear of "dirtying" his reputation. Compulsive preoccupation with carrying out a minor ritualistic task also allows the individual to avoid the issue creating unconscious conflict. In some cases, a compulsive act, such as repetitive handwashing, seems intended to undo feelings of guilt over real or imagined sins.

Behavioral

Behavioral explanations of anxiety focus on the way symptoms of anxiety disorders are reinforced or conditioned. They do not search for underlying unconscious conflicts or early childhood experiences because these are phenomena that can't be measured objectively or observed directly. Behavioral theories are often used to explain the development of phobias, which are seen as classically conditioned fears. A previously neutral object or situation becomes a stimulus for a phobia by being paired with a frightening experience. For example, a man who calls his home from a shopping mall only to receive the painful information that a loved one has suddenly died may develop a phobia of shopping malls. After this experience, upon approaching a shopping mall he may experience a wave of fear and gloom that cannot be relieved. Phobias continue to be maintained by the reduction in anxiety that occurs when a person withdraws from the feared situation.

Cognitive

Cognitive perspectives on anxiety concentrate on the perceptual processes or attitudes that may distort a person's estimation of the danger that he or she is facing. A person may either overestimate the nature or reality of a threat or underestimate his or her ability to cope with the threat effectively. Faulty thinking processes, such as a tendency to *catastrophize* (to focus selectively on the worst possible outcomes in a situation) are at the heart of anxiety disorders. In the case of panic attacks, for example, a person may attribute undue significance to minor physical sensations or distress, such as shortness of breath after some physical exertion. A vicious cycle is initiated when a person mistakenly interprets the distress as being a sign of impending physical disaster, which leads to an increase

in anxiety that may exacerbate the physical sensations and confirm the person's fears (Beck & Emery, 1985).

Before delivering a speech to a large group, a person with a social phobia may feed his or her anxiety by a chain of catastrophizing conditions:

> What if I forget what I was going to say? I will look foolish in front of all these people. Then I will get even more nervous and start to perspire, and my voice will shake, and I'll look even sillier. Whenever people will see me from now on they will remember me as the foolish person who tried to give a speech.

With each new thought, the anxiety of the speaker escalates. Researchers have indeed found that anxious patients may contribute to the *maintenance* of their anxiety by employing cognitive biases that highlight threatening stimuli.

> Clinically anxious (but not depressed) subjects were compared to normal controls on a task that measured attention to a visual display of 48 threat-related or neutral words (such as *injury, agony, failure,* and *lonely*). The words were presented in pairs for a brief duration; the pairs consisted of either a neutral word and a threat word or two neutral words. On a random one-third of the 288 trials, a dot of light (a probe) appeared in the area where one of the two words had just been flashed. The subjects pressed a button as quickly as possible when this probe appeared. The dependent variable was the speed with which the probe was detected when it replaced neutral versus threat-related words.
>
> The highly anxious subjects were faster than the controls in detecting the presence of the probe when it appeared in the vicinity of threat words. These subjects had shifted their attention toward threatening stimuli, while normal control subjects had shifted attention away from such material. The study suggested that anxious patients may use an encoding bias mechanism that makes them more susceptible to noticing threatening stimuli (MacLeod et al., 1986).

Biological

Various investigators have suggested that anxiety disorders have biological origins. One theory attempts to explain why certain phobias, such as of spiders or heights, are more common than phobias of other dangers, such as electricity. Because many fears are shared across cultures, it has been proposed that, at one time in the evolutionary past, certain fears enhanced our ancestors' chances of survival. Perhaps humans are born with a predisposition to fear whatever is related to sources of serious danger in the distant past. Because electricity is a modern discovery, an evolutionary tendency to fear it has not had time to develop. This *preparedness hypothesis* suggests we carry around an evolutionary tendency to respond quickly and "thoughtlessly" to once-feared stimuli (Seligman, 1971). However, this hypothesis has difficulty explaining the hundreds of "exotic" brands of phobia that have little apparent survival value, among them autophobia, fear of oneself; hypergiaphobia, fear of responsibility; tropophobia, fear of moving or making changes; and triskaidekaphobia, fear of the number 13 (a problem for some readers of this 13th edition of *Psychology and Life*).

The ability of certain drugs to relieve and of others to produce symptoms of anxiety offers evidence of a biological role in anxiety disorders. When a panic attack sufferer is given an infusion of sodium lactate, the patient "usually complains first of palpitations, difficulty catching his or her breath, dizziness, lightheadedness, . . . and sweating. Some normal control subjects may complain of these symptoms as well, but only the patient quickly develops overwhelming dread and fear that disastrous physical consequences are imminent" (Gorman et al., 1989, p. 150). Studies suggest that abnormalities in sites within the brainstem might be linked to panic attacks. Researchers studying CAT and PET scans of obsessive-compulsive disorder patients have found some evidence that links the disorder and abnormalities in the basal ganglia and frontal lobe of the brain (Rapoport, 1989). Currently, work is under way to investigate how these abnormalities may influence the obsessive-compulsive symptoms.

Each of the major approaches to anxiety disorders may explain part of the etiological puzzle. Continued research of each approach is needed to further our understanding of the factors that are most important to the etiology of the disturbances that comprise the anxiety disorders.

AFFECTIVE DISORDERS: TYPES

An **affective disorder** is a mood disturbance, such as excessive depression or depression alternating with mania. A person experiencing a period of mania, which is referred to as a **manic episode,** generally acts and feels unusually elated and expansive. However, sometimes the individual's predominant mood is irritability rather than elation, especially if the person feels thwarted in some way. Other symptoms accompany these highly charged mood states which typically last from a few days to months. During a manic episode, a person often experiences an inflated sense of self-esteem or an unrealistic belief that he or she possesses special abilities or powers. The person may feel a dramatically decreased need to sleep and may engage excessively in work or in social or other pleasurable activities. The individual may speak faster, louder, or more often than usual and his or her mind may be racing with thoughts. Caught up in this manic mood, the person shows unwarranted optimism, takes unnecessary risks, promises anything, and may give away everything. Sam was a 20-year-old college student experiencing the symptoms of a manic episode:

Lately Sam has been feeling fantastic. He has so much energy that he almost never needs to sleep, and he is completely confident that he is the top student at his school. He is bothered that everyone else seems so slow; they don't seem to understand the brilliance of his monologues, and no one seems able to keep up with his pace. Sam has some exciting financial ideas and can't figure out why his friends aren't writing checks to get in on his schemes.

Sam has been having problems lately with his bank, which is foolishly insisting that he not overdraw his account. It lacks the visionary wisdom, he is sure, to comprehend his financial wizardry, but its nervous concerns shouldn't be allowed to hold him back. Sam's other problem is that he is failing several of his courses, but he knows that is only because his professors are too dull to appreciate his brilliant contributions and too rigid about certain deadlines. Sam knows that he is just fine; his euphoria is not dimmed at all by his withdrawing friends, his sinking credit rating, and his failure in school.

Bipolar Disorder

It is not unusual for people in manic episodes to spend their life savings on extravagant purchases and to engage promiscuously in a number of sexual liaisons or other potentially high-risk actions. When the mania begins to diminish, people such as Sam are left trying to deal with the damage and predicaments they created during their frenetic period. Those who have manic episodes will almost always also experience periods of severe depression. This condition is called **bipolar disorder,** or manic-depressive disorder, to signify the experience of both types of mood disturbances. The duration and frequency of the mood disturbances in bipolar disorder vary from person to person. Some people experience long periods of normal functioning punctuated by occasional, short manic or depressive episodes. A small percentage of unfortunate individuals go right from manic episodes to clinical depression and back again in continuous, unending cycles that are devastating to them, their families, their friends, and their co-workers. While manic, they may gamble away life savings or give lavish gifts to strangers, which later adds to guilt feelings when they are in the depressed phase.

Unipolar Depression

Depression has been characterized as the "common cold of psychopathology" because it occurs so frequently and almost everyone has experienced elements of the full scale disorder at some time in life. We have all, at one time or another, experienced grief after the loss of a loved one or felt sad or upset when failing to achieve a desired goal. These sad feelings, which most of us experience in our lives, are only one symptom experienced by people suffering from a clinical **unipolar depression** (see **Table 17.4**). As opposed to victims of bipolar depression, those who suffer from unipolar depression do not also experience manic highs.

Novelist William Styron (1990) wrote a moving story about his experience with severe depression. The pain he endured convinced him that clinical depression is much more than a bad mood; it is best characterized as "a daily presence, blowing over me in cold gusts" and "a veritable howling tempest in the brain" that can

Almost everyone has experienced elements of depression; in some people, however, it becomes a full scale disorder.

begin with a "gray drizzle of horror" and result in "death" (*Darkness Visible,* Random House, 1990).

People diagnosed with unipolar depression differ in terms of the severity and duration of their depressive symptoms. While many individuals only struggle with clinical depression for several weeks at one point in their lives, others experience depression episodically or chronically for many years. Estimates of the prevalence of affective disorders reveal that about 20 percent of females and 10 percent of males suffer a major unipolar depression at some time in their lives. Bipolar disorder is much rarer, occurring in about 1 percent of adults and distributed equally between males and females.

Unipolar and bipolar disorders take an enormous toll on those afflicted, their families, and society. One European study found that those with recurrent depression spend a fifth of their entire adult lives hospitalized, while 20 percent of sufferers are totally disabled by their symptoms and do not ever work again (Holder, 1986). In the United States, depression accounts for the majority of all mental hospital admissions, but it is still believed to be underdiagnosed and undertreated (Bielski & Friedel, 1977). According to a 1983 NIMH survey, 80 percent of those suffering from clinical depression never receive treatment.

AFFECTIVE DISORDERS: CAUSES

What factors are involved in the development of affective disorders? Because of its prevalence, unipolar

| TABLE 17.4 | CHARACTERISTICS OF CLINICAL DEPRESSION |

Characteristic	Example
Dysphoric Mood	Sad, blue, hopeless; loss of interest or pleasure in almost all usual activities
Appetite	Poor appetite; significant weight loss
Sleep	Insomnia or hypersomnia (sleeping too much)
Motor Activity	Markedly slowed down (motor retardation) or agitated
Guilt	Feelings of worthlessness; self-reproach
Concentration	Diminished ability to think or concentrate; forgetfulness
Suicide	Recurrent thoughts of death; suicidal ideas or attempts

depression has been studied more extensively than bipolar depression. We will look at it from the cognitive, psychodynamic, behavioral, and biological approaches.

Cognitive

At the center of the cognitive approach to unipolar depression are two theories. One theory suggests that **negative cognitive sets** lead people to take a negative view of events in their lives for which they feel responsible. The **learned helplessness** model proposes that depression arises from the belief that one has little or no personal control over significant life events. **Aaron Beck** (1983; 1985; 1988), a leading researcher on depression, has argued that depressed people have three types of negative cognitions which he calls the *cognitive triad* of depression: negative views of themselves, negative views of ongoing experiences, and negative views of the future. Depressed people have a tendency to view themselves as inadequate or defective in some way, to interpret ongoing experiences in a negative way, and to believe that the future will continue to bring suffering and difficulties. This pattern of negative thinking clouds all experiences and produces the other characteristic signs of depression; an individual who always anticipates a negative outcome is not likely to be motivated to pursue any goal, leading to the *paralysis of will* that is prominent in depression.

In the learned helplessness view, developed by **Martin Seligman** (see Chapter 12), individuals learn, correct or not, that they cannot control future outcomes that are important to them. This conclusion creates feelings of helplessness, that lead to depression (Abramson et al., 1970; Peterson & Seligman, 1984; Seligman, 1975). Suppose that Maria has just received a poor grade on a psychology exam. Maria attributes the negative outcome on the exam to an *internal* factor ("I'm stupid"), which makes her feel sad, rather than an *external* one ("The exam was really hard"), which would have made her angry. Maria could have chosen a less *stable* internal quality than intelligence to explain her performance ("I was tired that day"). Rather than attributing her performance to an internal, stable factor that has *global* or far-reaching influence (stupidity), Maria could even have limited her explanation to the psychology exam or course ("I'm not good at psychology courses"). The learned helplessness theory suggests that individuals such as Maria who attribute failure to internal, stable, and global causes are vulnerable to depression.

> A study of college students supports the notion that depressed people have a negative type of attribution style. Depressed students attributed failure on an achievement test to an internal, stable factor—their lack of ability—while attributing

successes to luck. In comparison, on an achievement test, nondepressed students took more credit for successes and less blame for failures than they were due, blaming failures on an external factor—bad luck (Barthe & Hammen, 1981).

While this and other studies have demonstrated the common presence of negative attribution styles and thoughts in depressed people, there is considerable debate over the key proposition of the cognitive model of depression—that cognitive factors play a *causal* role in the development of depression. Despite the appeal of the model and its successful application in therapies for depression (as we will discuss in the following chapter), it remains plausible that the negative cognitive patterns are, in fact, a *consequence* rather than a *cause* of depression.

Research has confirmed what many people already believed about depression—that major changes in one's life, especially those that involve a loss of some sort such as the death of a loved one, divorce, or loss of a job, often precede the onset of depression. Loss events are seen as important precipitators of depression in both behavioral and psychodynamic approaches but in very distinct ways.

Psychodynamic

In the psychodynamic approach, unconscious conflicts and hostile feelings that originate in early childhood are seen to play key roles in the development of depression. Freud was struck by the degree of self-criticism and guilt that depressed people displayed. He believed that the source of this self-reproach was anger, originally directed at someone else, that had been turned inward against the self. The anger was believed to be tied to an especially intense and dependent childhood relationship, such as a parent-child relationship, in which the person's needs or expectations were not met. Losses, real or symbolic, in adulthood trigger hostile feelings that were originally experienced in childhood. A part of the person who was the object of these conflicting feelings of love and anger (the parent) becomes incorporated into the ego of depressed people. The anger that is reactivated by a later loss is now directed toward the person's own ego, creating the self-reproach and guilt that is characteristic of depression.

Behavioral

Rather than searching for the roots of depression in past relationships or for the unconscious meaning of a recent loss experience, one behavioral approach focuses on the effects of the amount of positive reinforcement and punishments a person receives (Lewinsohn, 1975). In this view, depressed feelings result from a lack of sufficient positive reinforcements and from experiencing many punishments in the environment following a loss or other major change in one's life. These life changes may lead a person to spend less time in activities that had previously provided gratification. Without sufficient positive reinforcement from the environment, a person begins to feel sad and withdraws further. This state of sadness and withdrawal is initially reinforced by increased attention and sympathy from others. Typically, however, friends, who at first respond with support, grow tired of the depressed person's negative moods and attitudes and begin to avoid him or her. This reaction eliminates another source of positive reinforcement, plunging the person further into depression. This cycle of reduced reinforcement can also be initiated when a person is unskilled in obtaining social reinforcements (has difficulty making friendships or gaining support from others) or moving to a new environment. Research shows that depressed people give themselves fewer rewards and more punishment than others, and that they underestimate their levels of reward while overestimating their levels of punishment (Rehm, 1977; Nelson & Craighead, 1977).

Biological

The ability of certain drugs such as lithium (a salt compound) to relieve depressive symptoms has provided support for a biological view of unipolar depression. Reduced levels of two chemical messengers in the brain, serotonin and norepinephrine, have been linked with depression, and drugs that are known to increase the levels of these neurotransmitters are commonly used to treat depression. However, the exact biochemical mechanisms of depression have not yet been discovered. Researchers have used PET scans to show differences in the way the brain metabolizes *cerebral glucose* (a type of sugar utilized to produce energy) during manic and depressive phases (see **Figure 17.3**), but such differences may be the consequence rather than the cause of the two mood states.

While our overall understanding of the cause of bipolar disorder remains limited, there is some growing evidence that it is influenced by genetic factors. Because family members usually share the same environment, similarities among family members do not prove that the cause of a psychological disorder is hereditary. To separate the influence of heredity from environmental or learned components in psychopathology, researchers study twins and adopted children.

Studies of identical twins (twins who have the same genetic material) show that, when one twin is afflicted by bipolar disorder, there is an 80 percent chance that the second twin will have the disorder. (The rate at which twin pairs share a trait is called the *concordance*

FIGURE 17.3 *PET SCANS OF BIPOLAR DEPRESSION*

PET scans indicate a higher level of cerebral glucose metabolism during manic phases than during depressive phases. The top and bottom rows show the patient during a depressive phase. The middle row shows the manic phase. The color bar on the right indicates the glucose metabolism rates.

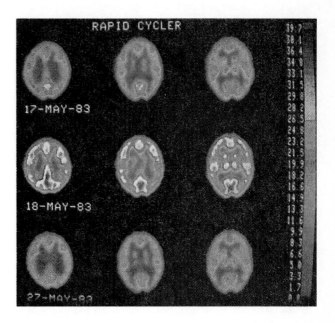

rate.) Adoption studies demonstrate that the concordance rates of bipolar disorder among adopted children is stronger with their biological parents than with their adoptive parents. While these studies suggest that genetic factors play some role in bipolar disorder, more direct evidence of this role seemed to come from a 1987 study that linked bipolar disorder to a specific gene in a unique population of people. In this study, the pattern of transmission of bipolar disorder was traced among the Amish community in Pennsylvania (Egeland et al., 1987).

The Amish are ideal subjects for such research because they have large families, keep detailed genealogical records, are genetically isolated, and display few behavioral factors, such as alcoholism or violence, that could confuse the findings. All 15,000 members of the religious sect are descended from just 30 couples who migrated from Europe in the early eighteenth century. Although their incidence of manic depression is the same as that of the rest of the population, there is a genetic tendency for the associated extreme mood

Research on the Amish in Pennsylvania has investigated a proposed link between a particular gene and bipolar disorder.

swings to run in some but not other Amish families. Researchers isolated a piece of DNA that was common in all bipolar members of one extended Amish family. The defective gene was passed on to children half of the time, and of those who received it, 80 percent had at least one manic episode in their lives. Not all who had the genetic vulnerability developed the symptoms of bipolar disorder, suggesting that other biological or psychological variables, which have not yet been identified, may also play an important role in etiology. The implicated gene was localized at the tip of chromosome 11.

This result was hailed as a real breakthrough—until the predictions made from this genetic analysis to other Amish relatives failed to be supported. When a team of independent researchers checked out the procedures and evaluated the predictions of Dr. Egeland's team, they were forced to blow the whistle and declare there was no convincing proof (Kelso et al., 1989). At present, there are two possibilities being pursued: either the gene for manic depression is not on chromosome 11, or the Amish have two such genes, only one of which may be in that chromosome location (Barinaga, 1989).

A dramatic example of a biological approach to understanding one type of psychological disorder comes from an experiment that sheds new light on an unusual form of depression. Some people regularly become depressed during the winter months, especially in the long Scandinavian winters (see **Figure 17.4**). This disturbance in mood has been appropriately named *seasonal affective disorder* or *SAD*. An internal body rhythm involving the hormone melatonin, which is secreted by the pineal gland into the blood, has been linked to SAD. In most species, including humans, the level of melatonin rises after dusk and falls at or before dawn. Melatonin is implicated in sleep processes as well as circadian (24-hour) rhythms that set the body's biological clock.

> When depressed patients and normal control subjects were exposed to bright light in the morning, the melatonin cycle was changed. Bright morning light reduced the symptoms of depression in those patients who regularly suffered from recurring winter depression. While it is not clear that disrupted melatonin cycles are responsible for *causing* the depressive symptoms of SAD, it does appear that a biological intervention that "resets" their abnormal circadian rhythm is an effective treatment (Lewy et al., 1987).

FIGURE 17.4	SEASONAL AFFECTIVE DISORDER

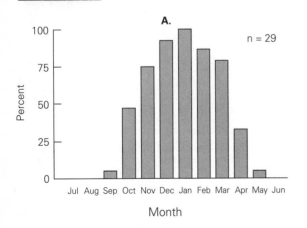

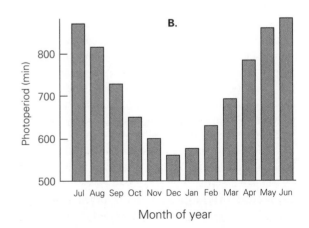

SEX DIFFERENCES IN DEPRESSION

The finding that women are twice as likely to experience unipolar depression as men has challenged psychologists to account for this difference (Boyd & Weissman, 1981). One recent proposal by **Susan Nolen-Hoeksema** (1987) points to the response styles of men and women once they begin to experience negative moods. According to this view, when women experience sadness, they tend to think about the possible causes and implications of their feelings. In contrast, men attempt actively to distract themselves from depressed feelings, either by focusing on something else or by engaging in a physical activity that will take their minds off their current mood state. This model suggests that it is the more *ruminative* response style of women, the tendency to obsessively focus on their problems, that increases women's vulnerability to depression. From a cognitive approach, paying attention to one's negative moods can increase thoughts of negative events which eventually increase the quantity and/or the intensity of negative feelings.

The response styles of both men and women can be seen as a product of socialization. In the United States and many other cultures, the female schema includes being passive, paying attention to feelings, and experiencing emotions fully as well as sharing them with others. In contrast, the male schema is focused on being tough, physical, and nonemotional and on not displaying signs of weakness by talking about bad moods.

The response styles of men may have certain advantages in terms of reduced vulnerability to depression, but they create other problems. Some researchers have pointed to the maladaptive tendency of men to distract themselves by acting out their depressed feelings in excessive drinking and drug use or in violent behavior. They cite statistics that indicate that twice as many men as women are alcoholic and suggest that alcoholism is often a mask for depression (Williams & Spitzer, 1983).

A task force of the American Psychological Association has recently reviewed research on the origins of sex differences in rates of unipolar depression (McGrath et al., 1990). Their report suggests that women's higher risk for depression can only be understood as the product of an interaction between a number of psychological, social, economic, and biological factors. Many of these factors relate to the experience of being female in many cultures, such as a greater likelihood for women of experiencing physical or sexual abuse or of living in poverty while being the primary caregiver for children and elderly parents. Such a finding indicates that the causes of depression may be a complex combination of factors and that there are multiple paths from "normal" behavior to depression.

Depression and Suicide

"The will to survive and succeed had been crushed and defeated. . . . There comes a time when all things cease to shine, when the rays of hope are lost" (Shneidman, 1987, p. 57). This sad statement by a young suicidal man reflects the most extreme consequence of any psychological disorder—suicide. While most depressed people do not commit suicide, most suicides are attempted by those who are suffering from depression (Shneidman, 1985). Depressed people commit suicide at a rate 25 times higher than nondepressed people in comparison groups (Flood & Seager, 1968). In the general population, the number of suicidal deaths is estimated to run as high as 100,000 per year, with attempted suicides estimated to reach up to half a million yearly in the United States alone. Based on data compiled by the National Center for Health Statistics (1989), the following patterns hold for suicide:

- It is the eighth leading cause of death in the United States, the third among the young, and the second among college students.
- An average of one person commits suicide every 17 minutes.
- Five million living Americans have attempted to kill themselves.
- For every completed suicide there are 8 to 20 suicide attempts.
- A suicide usually affects at least 6 other people intimately, putting the number of survivors of suicides in the United States at over 3.5 million (between 1970 and 1992).

The most typical suicide is committed by an older white male who is unemployed, living alone, in poor health, and divorced. The breakdown of suicides in the United States by sex, age, and race is shown in **Table 17.5.** Despite these high numbers, suicide is underre-

TABLE 17.5 **SUICIDE IN THE UNITED STATES, 1987**

Day and rate data are rounded. Rate is the number of suicides by group divided by the population size of the group and multiplied by 100,000.

	Number	Per Day	Rate
Nation	30,796	84	13
Males	24,272	66	20
Females	6,524	18	5
Whites	28,217	77	14
Nonwhites	2,579	7	7
Blacks	1,963	5	7
Elderly (65 +)	6,464	18	22
Young (15–24)	4,924	14	13

ported since single-car fatal accidents and other deaths that may be suicidal are not listed as such without the evidence of a suicide note, and because the potential stigma leads family members to deny suicide when it occurs.

Because depression occurs more frequently in women, it is not surprising that women *attempt* suicide about three times more often than men do; attempts by men, however, are more successful. This difference is largely because men use guns more often, and women tend to use less lethal means, such as sleeping pills (Perlin, 1975).

One of the most alarming social problems in recent decades is the rise of youth suicide. Every nine minutes, a teenager attempts suicide, and every 90 minutes, a teenager succeeds. In one week, 1000 teenagers will try suicide and 125 will succeed in killing themselves. In the last two decades, the suicide rate among American teenagers has jumped by 300 percent (Coleman, 1987).

What life-style patterns are most commonly found to be associated with youth suicides? Among males, the majority of suicides are found in those who abuse drugs and are seen as aggressive and unruly. The next most common pattern is the hard-driving male perfectionist who is socially inhibited and overly anxious about many social or academic challenges. Among females, depression ranks as the primary predictor of youth suicide. The symptoms of depression reflect serious emotional disorders that often go unrecognized or not treated.

In addition to long-standing psychological problems of maladjustment, there are several precipitating factors that can trigger suicidal actions. The breakup of a close relationship is the leading traumatic incident for both sexes. Other significant incidents that create shame and guilt that can overwhelm immature egos and lead to suicide attempts include being assaulted, beaten, raped, or arrested for the first time. Suicide is an extreme reaction to these acute stressors that occurs especially when adolescents feel unable to cry out to others for help.

Youth suicide is not a spur-of-the-moment impulsive act, but, typically, it occurs as the final stage of a period of inner turmoil and outer distress. The majority of young suicide victims have talked to others about their intentions or have written about them. Thus, talk of suicide should always be taken seriously (Shafii et al., 1985). Because girls are more often part of a social support network than are boys, they are more able to confide in others about their distress (Holden, 1986a, 1986b). Recognizing the signs of suicidal thinking and the experiences that can start or intensify such destructive thoughts is a first step toward prevention. **Edwin Shneidman,** a psychologist who, for almost 40 years, has studied and treated people with suicidal tendencies,

concludes that "Suicide is the desperate act of a perturbed and constricted mind, in seemingly unbearable and unresolvable pain. . . . The fact is that we can relieve the pain, redress the thwarted needs, and reduce the constriction of suicidal thinking" (1987, p. 58). Being sensitive to signs of suicidal intentions and caring enough to intervene are essential for saving lives of youthful and mature people who have come to see no exit for their troubles except total self-destruction.

Although suicide rates are generally lower for non-whites than whites, there is one startling exception: among Native American youth, suicide is five times greater than among youth of the general population. Suicide is one of several forms of self-destructive behavior seen as part of the ongoing destruction of Indian communities in the United States. **Teresa La Framboise,** a Native American psychologist who has been studying the problem and developing prevention and treatment strategies, identifies the social causes of youth suicide among her people. With poverty rampant and unemployment high in depressed Indian communities, suicide rates are boosted by "family disruption, pervasive hardship, a severe number of losses (whether through death, desertion, or divorce), substance abuse, the increased mobilities of families, and the incarceration of a significant caretaker" (La Framboise, 1988, p. 9). In addition, the Native American belief that the living continuously interact with their ancestors in the spiritual world, means that death holds little fear.

Teresa La Framboise (*Discovering Psychology,* 1990, Program 21)

SCHIZOPHRENIC DISORDERS

Everyone knows what it is like to feel depressed or anxious, even though most of us never experience these feelings to the degree of severity that constitutes a disorder. Schizophrenia, however, is a disorder that represents a qualitatively different experience from normal functioning (Bellak, 1979). A **schizophrenic disorder** is a severe form of psychopathology in which personality seems to disintegrate, perception is distorted, emotions are blunted, thoughts are bizarre, and language is strange. The person with a schizophrenic disorder is the one we conjure up when we think about madness, psychosis, or insanity.

Those with schizophrenia do not necessarily first develop other types of mental disorders nor do very disturbed "neurotic" individuals eventually become schizophrenic. For many of the millions of people afflicted with this disorder, it is a life sentence without possibility of parole, endured in the solitary confinement of a mind that must live life apart. Between two and three million living Americans at one time or another have suffered from this most mysterious and tragic mental disorder (Regier et al., 1988). Half of the beds in this nation's mental institutions are currently occupied by schizophrenic patients. For as yet unknown reasons, the first occurrence of schizophrenia typically occurs for men before they are 25 and for women between 25 and 45 years of age (Lewine et al., 1981).

Mark Vonnegut, son of novelist Kurt Vonnegut, was in his early 20s when he began to experience symptoms of schizophrenia. In *Eden Express* (1975), he tells the story of his break with reality and his eventual recovery after being hospitalized twice for acute schizophrenia. Once, while pruning some fruit trees, he hallucinated—he distorted reality, creating a different reality:

> I began to wonder if I was hurting the trees and found myself apologizing. Each tree began to take on personality. I began to wonder if any of them

liked me. I became completely absorbed in looking at each tree and began to notice that they were ever so slightly luminescent, shining with a soft inner light that played around the branches. And from out of nowhere came an incredibly wrinkled, iridescent face. Starting as a small point infinitely distant, it rushed forward, becoming infinitely huge. I could see nothing else. My heart had stopped. The moment stretched forever. I tried to make the face go away but it mocked me. . . . I was holding my life in my hands and was powerless to stop it from dripping through my fingers. I tried to look the face in the eyes and realized I had left all familiar ground (1975, p. 96).

During the weeks after the pruning experience, young Vonnegut's behavior went out of control more often and more extremely. He would cry without reason. His terror would evaporate into periods of ecstasy, with no corresponding change in his life situation. "There were times when I was scared, shaking, convulsing in excruciating pain and bottomless despair." For 12 days he ate nothing and slept not at all. One day, while visiting friends in a small town, he stripped off his clothes and ran naked down the street. Suicidal despair nearly ended his young, once promising life.

In the world of schizophrenia, *thinking* becomes illogical; associations among ideas are remote or without apparent pattern. *Language* may become incoherent—a "word salad" of unrelated or made-up words— or an individual may become mute. *Emotions* may be flat, with no visible expression, or they may be inappropriate to the situation. *Psychomotor behavior* may be disorganized (grimaces, strange mannerisms), or posture may become rigid. Even when only some of these symptoms are present, deteriorated functioning in work, social relations, and self-care is likely. *Interpersonal relationships* are often difficult as individuals withdraw socially or become emotionally detached.

Hallucination often occurs, involving imagined sensory perceptions—sights, smells, or most commonly, sounds (usually voices)—that are assumed to be real. A person may hear a voice that provides a running commentary on his or her behavior or may hear several voices in conversation.

Delusion is also common in schizophrenia; these are false or irrational beliefs maintained in spite of clear contrary evidence. Delusions are often patently absurd, such as the belief that one's thoughts are being broadcast, controlled, or taken away by aliens. In other cases, delusions may not seem as outlandish, but they are still not realistic or true. For example, a person may experience delusional jealousy, believing that one's sexual partner is not being faithful or believing that he or she is being persecuted.

Psychologists divide these symptoms between a positive category and a negative category. During *acute* or *active phases* of schizophrenia, the positive symptoms—hallucinations, delusions, incoherence, and disorganized behavior—are prominent. At other times, the negative symptoms—social withdrawal and flattened emotions—become more apparent. Some individuals, such as Mark Vonnegut, just experience one or a couple of acute phases of schizophrenia and recover to live normal lives. Others, often described as chronic sufferers, experience either repeated acute phases with short periods of negative symptoms or occasional acute phases with extended periods marked by the presence of negative symptoms. The manifestations of schizophrenia are characterized more by variability than by constancy over time (Liberman, 1982). Even the most seriously disturbed are not acutely delusional all the time.

MAJOR TYPES OF SCHIZOPHRENIA

Because of the wide variety of symptoms that can characterize schizophrenia, investigators consider it not a single disorder but rather a constellation of separate types. The four most commonly recognized subtypes are outlined in **Table 17.6.**

Disorganized Type

In this subtype of schizophrenia, a person displays incoherent patterns of thinking and grossly bizarre and disorganized behavior. Emotions are flattened or inap-

TABLE 17.6   *TYPES OF SCHIZOPHRENIC DISORDERS*

Type of Schizophrenia	Major Symptoms
Disorganized	Inappropriate behavior and emotions; incoherent language
Catatonic	Frozen, rigid, or excitable motor behavior
Paranoid	Delusions of persecution or grandeur with hallucinations
Undifferentiated	Mixed set of symptoms with thought disorders and features from other types

propriate to the situation. Often, a person acts in a silly or childish manner, such as giggling for no apparent reason. Language can become so incoherent, full of unusual words and incomplete sentences, that communication with others breaks down. Delusions or hallucinations are common, but are not organized around a coherent theme.

> Mr. F. B. was a hospitalized mental patient in his late 20s. When asked his name, he said he was trying to forget it because it made him cry whenever he heard it. He then proceeded to cry vigorously for several minutes. Then, when asked about something serious and sad, Mr. F. B. giggled or laughed. More striking was his disorganized speech production, evidenced in his answers to interview questions, sentence completions, and proverb interpretations, a few examples of which follow:
> Q: "What sort of *mood* have you been in for the past few days?"
> A: "If the world *moved,* the world moved."
> Q: "What is the meaning of the proverb 'When the cat's away the mice will play'?"
> A: "Takes less place. Cat didn't know what mouse did and mouse didn't know what cat did. Cat represented more on the suspicious side than the mouse. Dumbo was a good guy. He saw what the cat did, put himself with the cat so people wouldn't look at them as comedians."

Mr. F. B.'s mannerisms, depersonalized, incoherent speech, and delusions are the hallmarks of the *disorganized* type of schizophrenia.

Catatonic Type

The catatonic person seems frozen in a stupor. For long periods of time, the individual can remain motionless, often in a bizarre position, showing little or no reaction to anything in the environment. When the individual is moved, he or she freezes in a new position, assuming the waxy flexibility of a soft plastic toy.

Catatonic negativity sometimes involves motionless resistance to instructions. Sometimes it involves doing the opposite of what is requested—sitting when told to stand, for example.

For the catatonic person, stupor sometimes alternates with excitement. During the excited phase, motor activity is agitated, apparently without purpose, and not influenced by external stimuli.

Paranoid Type

Individuals suffering from this form of schizophrenia experience complex and systematized delusions focused around specific themes. What follows are the four common types of delusions:

- *Delusions of Persecution.* Individuals feel that they are being constantly spied on and plotted against and that they are in mortal danger.
- *Delusions of Grandeur.* Individuals believe that they are important or exalted beings—millionaires, great inventors, or religious figures such as Jesus Christ. Delusions of persecution may accompany delusions of grandeur—an individual is a great person but is continually opposed by evil forces.
- *Delusional Jealousy.* Individuals become convinced—without due cause—that their mates are unfaithful. They contrive data to fit the theory and "prove" the truth of the delusion.
- *Delusions of Reference.* Individuals misconstrue chance happenings as being directed at them. A paranoid individual who sees two people in earnest conversation immediately concludes that they are talking about him or her. Even lyrics in popular songs or words spoken by radio or TV actors are perceived as having some special message for the individual, often exposing some personal secret. The individual may even hallucinate voices or images of people organized around themes of persecution or grandiosity.

The onset of symptoms in paranoid schizophrenic individuals tends to occur later in life than it does in other schizophrenic types. Paranoid schizophrenic individuals rarely display obviously disorganized behavior. Instead, it is more likely that their behavior will be intense and quite formal.

Undifferentiated Type

This is the grab bag category describing a person who exhibits prominent delusions, hallucinations, incoherent speech, or grossly disorganized behavior that fit the criteria of more than one type or of no clear type. The hodgepodge of symptoms experienced by these individuals does not clearly differentiate among various schizophrenic reactions.

CAUSES OF SCHIZOPHRENIA

Different etiological models point to very different initial causes of schizophrenia, different pathways along which it develops, and different avenues for treatment. Let's look at the contributions several of these models can make to our understanding of the way a person may develop a schizophrenic disorder.

Genetic Approaches

It has long been known that schizophrenia tends to run in families (Bleuler, 1978; Kallmann, 1946). Thus, the possibility of genetic transmission of some predisposition for schizophrenia is a likely causal candidate. Three independent lines of research—family studies, twin studies, and adoption studies—point to a common conclusion: persons related genetically to someone who has been schizophrenic are more likely to become affected than those who are not (Kessler, 1980).

When both parents are schizophrenic, the schizophrenia risk for their offspring is about 40 percent, as compared to one percent in the general population. When either parent is not schizophrenic, the risk for the offspring drops sharply to about 14 percent. The risk is greater for first-degree relatives (siblings and children), greater in families with many affected relatives, and greater where schizophrenic reactions are severe (Hanson et al., 1977). In fact, for all close relatives of a diagnosed *index case* of schizophrenia, the risk factor may be as great as 46 times higher than for the general population (see **Figure 17.5**).

Twin studies show that, when one member of a pair of twins is schizophrenic, the chances that the other will also be affected are four to five times greater for identical twins than for pairs of fraternal twins, even though, in both cases, the twins usually have shared the same general environments. Environmental factors also play a role, as shown by the fact that the concordance rates among identical twins are far from perfect—there are many cases in which one member of the pair develops schizophrenia and the other one never does.

The most compelling evidence for the role of genetic factors in the etiology of schizophrenia comes from adoption studies. When the offspring of a schizophrenic parent are reared by a normal parent in a foster home, they are as likely to develop the disorder as if they had been brought up by the biological parent (Heston, 1970; Rosenthal et al., 1975). In addition, adoptees who are schizophrenic have significantly more biological relatives with schizophrenic disorders than adoptive relatives with the disorder (Kety et al., 1975).

A summary of the risks of being affected with schizophrenia for the various kinds of relatives of a schizophrenic is shown in **Figure 17.6.** Leading schizophrenia researcher **Irving Gottesman** (1991) pooled these data from about 40 reliable studies conducted in Western Europe between 1920 and 1987; he dropped the poorest data sets. As you can see, the data are arranged according to degree of genetic relatedness which correlates highly with the degree of risk. Examine the data carefully to determine the limits you want to place on the conclusion that there is a genetic basis for schizophrenia. While there is certainly a strong relationship

---

FIGURE 17.5   GENETIC RISK FOR SCHIZOPHRENIC DISORDER

Out of a sample of 100 children of schizophrenic parents, from 10 to 50 percent will have the genetic structure that can lead to schizophrenia. Of these, about 5 percent will develop schizophrenia early and 5 percent later in life. It is important to note that as many as 40 percent of the high-risk subjects will not become schizophrenic.

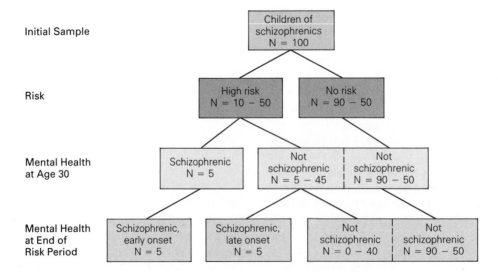

FIGURE 17.6   GENETIC RISK OF DEVELOPING SCHIZOPHRENIA

The graph shows average risks for developing schizophrenia. Data were compiled from family and twin studies conducted in European populations between 1920 and 1987; the degree of risk correlates highly with the degree of genetic relatedness.

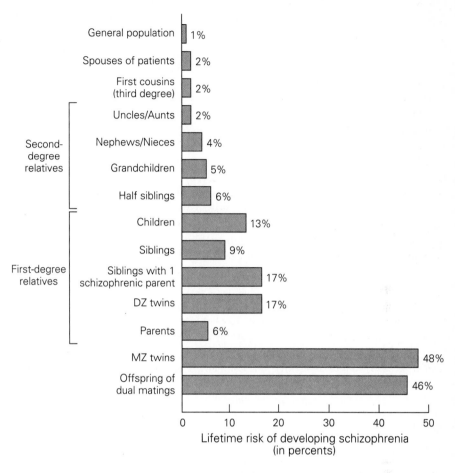

between genetic similarity and schizophrenia risk, even in the groups with the greatest genetic similarity, the risk factor is less than 50 percent. This indicates that, although genes play some role, schizophrenia is a complex disorder with other contributing factors also involved.

The genetics of schizophrenia is still undetermined. While one team of researchers claims to have found evidence of a genetic defect on chromosome 5 in seven families with a dominant gene for schizophrenia, another did not replicate this finding with a different family in which one third of 104 relatives was diagnosed as schizophrenic (Barnes, 1988). Critics of the genetic hypothesis of schizophrenia argue that the available evidence is weak for all types of schizophrenia except for *chronic* forms of the disorder. They point to the fact that 90 percent of the relatives of schizophrenics do not have

schizophrenia (Barnes, 1987). Taken as a whole, the research on genetic influences suggests that genetic factors may contribute to schizophrenia but may not by themselves be sufficient for the development of schizophrenia (Nicol & Gottesman, 1983). This line of research has not revealed anything about the way in which genes may exert their influence on schizophrenia.

One problem with the current research may be the nature of the diagnosis of schizophrenia; if there is error and variability in that diagnosis, then the relationship with genetic factors may be mixed in different studies. A new line of research uses a biological marker for schizophrenia in place of the traditional diagnosis. A schizophrenia **biological marker** is a biological variable that can be used to index or mark the presence of schizophrenic disorder in the absence of a complex, *DSM-III-R* diagnosis. For example, persons with schizophrenia are more likely than normal people to have an eye movement dysfunction when they scan the visual field. This biological marker can be quantified in individuals and is shown to be related to the manifestation of schizophrenia in families (Clementz & Sweeney, 1990).

A widely accepted hypothesis for the cause of schizophrenia is the **diathesis-stress hypothesis.** It suggests that genetic factors place the individual at risk, but environmental stress factors must impinge in order for the potential risk to be manifested as a schizophrenic disorder.

Neurochemicals and Brain Structure

Are the brains of individuals who are genetically at risk for schizophrenia unusual in some way? Current research is using brain scanning techniques to study the way genetic factors might be linked with specific biochemical processes in the brain that previously have been associated with schizophrenia.

Particular neurotransmitters and processes in the brain have been associated with the production and reduction of schizophrenic reactions. The biochemical approach to schizophrenia gained support in the 1950s with the development of a new group of drugs, the *phenothiazines,* that dramatically relieved many schizophrenic symptoms. The success of drug therapy led medical researchers to search for the natural biochemical processes that influence the development or remission of schizophrenia. The most promising biochemical research focuses on the influence of a specific neurotransmitter, dopamine, and its receptor sites in the brain. Dopamine may be responsible for both the abnormalities in movement found in Parkinson's

disease and at least some of the symptoms seen in schizophrenia.

The **dopamine hypothesis** holds that schizophrenia is associated with a relative excess of the chemical dopamine at specific receptor sites in the central nervous system (Carlsson, 1978). Schizophrenic symptoms may be the result of an increase in the activity of nerve cells that use dopamine as their neurotransmitter. Support for the dopamine hypothesis has been drawn from research on the effects of the phenothiazines. Phenothiazines, which seem to be most effective in relieving the positive symptoms of schizophrenia (hallucinations, delusions, and disorganized behavior), are also known to *block* the brain's receptors for dopamine. Recent research conducted by medical laboratories has used PET scan technology to look at the density of dopamine receptors in the brains of schizophrenic individuals. These studies, along with examinations of the brain tissue of schizophrenic individuals after death, suggest that in the brains of schizophrenics there may be an increased number of receptors for dopamine rather than increased levels of the neurotransmitter itself (Snyder, 1976). Although impressive evidence has been accumulated for the dopamine hypothesis, we still must be cautious. It is possible that dopamine availability may be one factor in the sequence of development of schizophrenia but not the original cause.

Another area of interest in the biology of schizophrenia is the association of subtle brain abnormalities, such as reduced brain volume in specific areas of the brain or enlarged ventricles (fluid-filled chambers in the brain), with schizophrenic symptoms. Further research comparing structure and functions of the brains of twins who are *discordant* for schizophrenia (one has the dis-

These four genetically identical women each experience a schizophrenic disorder which suggests that heredity plays a role in the development of schizophrenia. For each of the Genain quadruplets, the disorder differed in severity, duration, and outcome.

E. Fuller Torrey (*Discovering Psychology,* 1990, Program 21)

order, the other does not) and normal control twins is being conducted by an interdisciplinary research team headed by Irving Gottesman and **Fuller Torrey** using magnetic resonance imaging and biological and psychological assessment (*Discovering Psychology,* 1989, Program 21).

It is unlikely that one biological silver bullet will ever be found to explain the origins of the wide range of schizophrenic symptoms. There is no question, however, that increasingly refined methodology will clarify our understanding of the genetic factors, biochemical processes, and structural brain factors at work in schizophrenia.

Psychodynamics and Family Interaction

If it is difficult to prove that a highly specific biological factor is a *sufficient* cause of schizophrenia, it is equally hard to prove that a vague general psychological one is a *necessary* condition. Sociologists, family therapists, and psychologists have all studied the influence of family role relationships and communication patterns in the development of schizophrenia. Their studies were originally conceptualized as extensions of psychodynamic theory. From a psychodynamic view, schizophrenia is a regression to an infantile stage of functioning and is marked by a fragile ego that has difficulty distinguishing between the self and the outside world and by immature defenses that further distort reality. One psychodynamic model developed by **Margaret Mahler** (1979) traces a schizophrenic individual's difficulty in differentiating between self and external world to an early, intense *symbiotic attachment* between mother and child. She believes the two failed to differentiate themselves from each other, were highly dependent on one another, intruded on each other's lives, and had difficulty separating.

Research on this type of parent-child relationship and other unusual patterns in role relationships between mothers and fathers and parents and children has not offered consistent evidence in support of the belief that they are linked to schizophrenia. Researchers have provided some evidence for theories that emphasize the influence on the development of schizophrenia of deviations in parental communication (Liem, 1980). These deviations include a family's inability to share a common focus of attention and parents' difficulties in taking the perspective of other family members or in communicating clearly and accurately. Studies suggest that the speech patterns of families with a schizophrenic member show less responsiveness and less interpersonal sensitivity than those of normal families.

Deviant communication in families may contribute to the child's distortion of reality by concealing or denying the true meaning of an event or by injecting a substitute meaning that is confusing (Wynne et al., 1979). Anthropologist **Gregory Bateson** used the term **double bind** to describe a situation in which a child receives from a parent multiple messages that are contradictory and cannot all be met. A mother may complain that a son is not affectionate and yet reject his attempts to touch her because he is so dirty. Torn between these different verbal and nonverbal meanings, between demands and feelings, a child's grip on reality may begin to slip. The result may be that the child will see his or her feelings, perceptions, and self-knowledge as unreliable indicators of the way things really are (Bateson et al., 1956).

Uncertainty still remains over whether the deviant family patterns are a cause of schizophrenia or a reaction to a child's developing symptoms of schizophrenia. To help answer this question, studies of family interactions *before* schizophrenia appears in the offspring are needed. One such prospective study focused on a pattern of harsh criticism or intrusiveness expressed by a parent toward a teenage child. It revealed that this negative communication pattern is likely to predate the development of disorders similar to, but not quite as severe as, schizophrenia (Goldstein & Strachan, 1987).

This evidence is not sufficient to rally confidence in the hypothesis that family factors play a causal role in the *development* of schizophrenia. However, there is reliable evidence that family factors do play a role in influencing the functioning of an individual *after* the first symptoms appear. When parents reduce their criticism, hostility, and intrusiveness toward a schizophrenic offspring, the recurrence of acute schizophrenic symptoms and the need for rehospitalization is also reduced (Doane et al., 1985).

Cognitive Processes

Among the hallmarks of schizophrenia are abnormalities in attention, thought, memory, and language. Some cognitive psychologists argue that, instead of being consequences of schizophrenia, these abnormalities may play a role in causing the disorder. One view focuses on the role of attentional difficulties. "The crucial behavior, from which other indicators of schizophrenia may be deduced, lies in the extinction of attention to social stimuli to which 'normal' people respond" (Ullmann & Krasner, 1975, p. 375).

Attentional deficits may involve ignoring important environmental or cultural cues that most people use to socially regulate or "normalize" their behavior. They may lead a person to notice remote, irrelevant thought or word associations while thinking or talking, thereby confusing these distracting peripheral ideas and stimuli with the main points or central themes of the conversation or thoughts.

The speech of some schizophrenic individuals seems to be under the control of immediate stimuli in the situation. Distracted from complete expression of a simple train of thought by constantly changing sensory input and vivid inner reality, a schizophrenic speaker may make little sense to a listener. The incoherence of schizophrenic speech is due, in part, to bizarre *intrusions* by thoughts that are not directly relevant to the statement being uttered—intrusions that the person cannot suppress. Normal speaking requires that a speaker remember what has just been said (past), monitor where he or she is (present), and direct the spoken sentence toward some final goal (future). This coherence between past, present, and future may be difficult for some schizophrenic individuals, accounting for their inability to maintain long strings of interconnected words. What comes out is often termed "word salad," wildly tossed semantic confusion.

A cognitive approach taken by psychologist **Brendan Maher** (1968) focuses more directly on disturbances in language processes. The bizarre speech of schizophrenic individuals may be a result of deviant processing whenever a person comes to a "vulnerable" word—one that has multiple meanings to him or her. At that point, a personally relevant, but semantically inappropriate, word is used. For example, a patient may say, "Doctor, I have pains in my chest and hope and wonder if my box is broken and heart is beaten." *Chest* is a vulnerable word; it can mean a *respiratory cage* or a *container* such as a *hope* chest. *Wonder* could mean *Wonder Bread* that is kept in a bread *box*. Hearts *beat* and are *broken*.

Reality testing is also impaired in schizophrenia; while most of us evaluate the reality of our inner worlds against criteria in the external world, individuals with schizophrenic disorders typically *reverse* this usual reality-testing procedure. Their inner experiences are the criteria against which they test the validity of outer experience (Meyer & Ekstein, 1970). Theirs is a world in which thinking it makes it so—as in the fantasy world of children or the dream world of adults. Thus, it may be that what appears to us as bizarre, inappropriate, and irrational behavior follows from the creation of a closed system that is self-validating and internally consistent. By carefully listening to schizophrenic speech, it is often possible for a clinician to decode the sense in what appears at first to be pure nonsense (Forest, 1976).

The number of explanations of schizophrenia that we have reviewed and the questions that remain despite a significant amount of research suggest how much we have to learn about this powerful psychological disorder. Complicating our understanding is the likelihood that the phenomena we call schizophrenia are probably best thought of as a group of disorders, each with potentially distinct causes (Meltzer, 1982). Genetic predispositions, neurochemical processes and brain structure, family structure and communication, and cognitive processes have all been identified as participants in at least some cases of schizophrenia. However, no *one* of them explains schizophrenia in every case. We do not yet know the exact ways in which they may combine to cause schizophrenia. Much of the mystery of schizophrenia waits for creative researchers and clinicians to solve.

Is Schizophrenia Universal?

All cultures establish certain rules, or norms, to be followed and roles to be enacted if people are to be considered normal and acceptable members. As we have noted, each culture also maintains more general belief systems about the forces that determine life and death, health and sickness, and success and failure. In other words, there is some *cultural relativity* in what is judged as "mad" or abnormal in different societies; what one culture sees as abnormal, another may see as appropriate (such as wearing your mother's skull around your neck to ward off evil spirits). Also, some styles of psychological disorder are more likely than others to be seen in a particular society (Triandis & Draguns, 1980).

Our view of the origins and manifestations of psychopathology is broadened by a *cross-cultural perspective* (Mezzich & Berganza, 1984). What can we learn about schizophrenia from looking at its manifestations in different cultures? All known cultures consider people abnormal if they exhibit unpredictable behavior and/

What are perceived as symptoms of psychological disorders, such as schizophrenia, in some cultures are judged to be perfectly normal behaviors in others.

subtypes—disorganized, catatonic, paranoid, and undifferentiated.

Evidence for the cause of schizophrenia has been found in genetic factors, biochemical and brain abnormalities, family structure and communication, and faulty cognitive processes. Investigators with a medical model perspective argue that schizophrenia is a disease, not just a matter of faulty mental and behavioral functioning due to stress, trauma, or conflict. Despite widely differing views of psychological disorders across the world, the symptoms of schizophrenia seem to be experienced in all cultures. This crosscultural commonality leads to the conclusion that schizophrenia is a universal human phenomena.

As with the differing explanations of the etiology of anxiety and affective disorders, each of the systematic attempts to make sense of the origins of schizophrenia offers only a partial explanation, because the development of most cases of psychopathology is likely to be influenced by a number of interacting complex factors.

or do not communicate with others. These symptoms of psychological disorders appear to be *universal* manifestations of affliction and are regarded as pathological in all known cultural settings. From such distinctly contrasting groups as the Inuit of northwest Alaska and the Yoruba of rural tropical Nigeria, we hear descriptions of a disorder in which beliefs, feelings, and actions are thought to come from a person's mind over which he or she has lost control. This pattern resembles what is diagnosed as schizophrenia in the United States (Murphy, 1976). The incidence of schizophrenia across diverse cultures is a relatively standard 1 percent. Biologically oriented psychologists often point to these findings as further evidence of the biological roots of schizophrenia.

JUDGING PEOPLE AS ABNORMAL

Although diagnosis and classification yield benefits for research and clinical purposes, these same processes can also have negative consequences. The task of actually assigning a person with the label "psychologically or mentally disordered" remains a matter of human judgment—thus open to bias and error. The labels of mental illness, insanity, or psychological disorder can be acquired in a number of ways other than by the diagnosis of a trained clinician. When psychologically untrained people are in the position to judge the mental health of others, their decisions are often vulnerable to biases based on expectations, status, gender, prejudice, and context. Too often those identified as psychologically disordered suffer stigma, as we saw in the letter from Cherish at the beginning of the chapter.

THE PROBLEM OF OBJECTIVITY

The label "mentally ill" is typically assigned on the basis of the following evidence: (a) the person is under some form of psychological or psychiatric care; (b) influential members of the community (teachers, judges, parents, spouses, priests) agree that the person's behavior represents a dangerous degree of maladjustment; (c) the person's scores on psychological inventories, school achievement tests, or intelligence tests deviate by

SUMMING UP

Schizophrenia is a severe form of psychopathology affecting about one percent of the population. It is different in kind as well as in degree from the other mental disorders we have considered. Someone with a schizophrenic disorder experiences extreme distortions in perception, thinking, emotion, behavior, and language. Hallucinations and delusions are common, and there may be a disintegration of the coherent functioning of personality. Because of the range of symptoms that can characterize schizophrenia, psychologists have identified four a specified extent from scores of individuals designated as normal; (d) the person declares himself or herself to be "mentally sick" by applying this term directly or by expressing feelings, such as unhappiness, anxiety, depression, hostility, or inadequacy, that are extreme enough to be associated with emotional disturbance; (e) the person behaves publicly in ways dangerous to himself or herself (by making suicidal threats or gestures, by showing problems with self-care) or to others (by demonstrating aggressive or homicidal impulses or gestures).

The criteria psychologists and psychiatrists use to make diagnostic decisions also influence judgments of the legal system and of the insurance and health care businesses. The legal determination of **insanity** carries with it serious implications regarding a defendant's competence to stand trial and to be held responsible for criminal indictments. It also can deprive a defendant of the right to administer his or her own estate, and it can be the basis for an involuntary commitment to a mental hospital for further evaluation or court-ordered care. *Insanity* is a legal concept that may be informed by psychology but is determined by judges and juries. Payments and reimbursements by health insurance and medical plans for psychological disability and its treatment typically require that the disorder be diagnosed and labeled by a mental health specialist. *DSM-III-R* is the standard diagnostic guide for this purpose.

The decision to declare someone psychologically disordered or insane is always a *judgment* about behavior. It is a judgment made by one or more people about another individual, often someone of lesser political power or socioeconomic status. In the Soviet Union, it has been customary to diagnose political dissidents as mentally disordered for their unacceptably deviant ideology and to sentence them to long terms in remote mental hospitals. For example, the artist who painted the cover of *Psychology and Life,* Mihail Chemiakin, was declared insane and exiled for refusing to paint in the government-approved tradition of Soviet socialist realism.

Research has shown that clinicians in the United States use a double standard to assess the maladjustment of men and women. In one study, both male and female clinicians ascribed more positive characteristics to males and less desirable characteristics to normal, healthy females (Broverman et al., 1972). Other research shows that clinicians tend to judge females as maladjusted when they show behaviors that are incongruent with their gender role. When women act "like men"—use foul language, drink excessively, or exhibit uncontrollable temper—they are seen as neurotic or self-destructive. Moreover, clinicians reflect the biases of their society in regarding masculinity as more important than femininity. Male behavior that was incongruent with the male gender role was rated as a more serious violation than was female gender-role incongruity (Page, 1987).

We have seen throughout our study of psychology that the meaning of behavior is jointly determined by its *content* and by its *context*. The same act in different settings conveys very different meanings. A man kisses another man; it may signify a gay relationship in the United States, a ritual greeting in France, and a Mafia "kiss of death" in Sicily. Unfortunately, the diagnosis of a behavior as abnormal can depend on where the behavior occurs—even professionals' judgments may be influenced by context. Is it possible to be judged as sane if you are "a patient" in an insane place? This question was addressed in a classic study by **David Rosenhan** (1973, 1975).

Rosenhan and seven other sane people gained admission to different psychiatric hospitals by pretending to have a single symptom: hallucinations. All eight of these *pseudopatients* were diagnosed on admission as either paranoid schizophrenic or manic-depressive. Once admitted, they behaved normally in every way. When a sane person is in an insane place, he or she is likely to be judged insane, and any behavior is likely to be reinterpreted to fit the context. If the pseudopatients discussed their situation in a rational way with the staff, they were reported to be using "intellectualization" defenses, while their notes of their observations were evidence of "writing behavior." The pseudopatients remained on the wards for almost three weeks, on the average, and not one was identified by the staff as sane. When they were finally released—only with the help of spouses or colleagues—their discharge diagnosis was still "schizophrenia" but "in remission"; that is, their symptoms were not active (Fleischman, 1973; Lieberman, 1973).

David Rosenhan

Rosenhan's research challenged the former system of classifying mental disorders, but it also raised basic issues about the validity of judgments of abnormality in other people, about how dependent such judgments may be on factors other than behavior itself, and about how difficult psychological labels are to remove once they are "stuck" on a person. In the view of radical psychiatrist **Thomas Szasz,** mental illness does not even exist—it is a "myth" (1961, 1977). Szasz argues that the symptoms used as evidence of mental illness are merely medical labels that sanction professional intervention into what are social problems—deviant people violating social norms. Once labeled, these people can be treated either benignly or harshly for their problem "of being different," with no threat of disturbing the existing status quo. British psychiatrist **R. D. Laing** (1967) goes further yet, proposing that labeling people as mad often suppresses the creative, unique probing of reality by individuals who are questioning their social context. Laing believes that by regarding the novel and unusual as *mad* rather than as *creative genius,* mental diagnosis may hurt both the person and the society (1965; 1970).

Few clinicians would go this far, but there is a movement of psychologists who advocate a *contextual* or *ecological model* in lieu of the classic medical model (Levine & Perkins, 1987). In an ecological model, abnormality is viewed not as the result of a disease within a person but as a product of an interaction between individuals and society. Abnormality is seen as a *mismatch* between a person's abilities and the needs and norms of society. For example, schools typically demand that children sit quietly for hours at desks and work independently in an orderly fashion. Some children are not able to do this and are often labeled "hyperactive." The abilities of these children do not conform to the needs of most school settings and they quickly come to the attention of school authorities. However, if these same children were in an alternative school setting where they were free to roam around the classroom and talk to others as part of their work, the mismatch would not exist and these children would not be labeled.

In some cases, prevailing *stereotypes* can influence the judgments of those with the power to label others. An outrageous example of the *medicalization of deviance* in the United States is found in an 1851 report in a medical journal on "The Diseases and Physical Peculiarities of the Negro Race." Its author, Doctor Samuel Cartwright, had been appointed by the Louisiana Medical Association to chair a committee to investigate the "strange" practices of African-American slaves. "Incontrovertible scientific evidence" was amassed to justify the accepted practice of slavery. In the course of

doing so, several "diseases" previously unknown to the white race were discovered. One finding was that blacks allegedly suffered from a sensory disease that made them insensitive "to pain when being punished" (thus no need to spare the whip).

The committee also invented the disease **drapetomania,** a mania to seek freedom—a mental illness that caused certain slaves to run away from their masters. Runaway slaves needed to be caught so that their illness could be properly treated (Chorover, 1981)!

THE PROBLEM OF STIGMA

From a sociological point of view, people with psychological disorders are *deviant*. However, *deviance* and *abnormality* are rarely used in a value-free statistical sense. The fact that it has been estimated that 32 percent of Americans have struggled with some kind of psychopathology is, at least statistically, relatively normal (Regier et al., 1988). In practice, being *deviant* connotes moral inferiority and brings social rejection. In addition, the term *deviant* implies that the whole person "is different in kind from ordinary people and that there are no areas of his personality that are not afflicted by his 'problems' " (Scott, 1972, p. 14).

It has been proposed that each society defines itself negatively by pointing out what is *not* rather than what *is* appropriate, thereby setting boundaries on what is socially acceptable. Deviants, since they clarify these boundaries, serve to make the rest of the society feel more normal, healthy, moral, and law abiding (Ericksen, 1966). In any case, there is little doubt that in our society to be *mentally disordered* is to be publicly degraded and personally devalued. Society extracts costly penalties from those who deviate from its norms (see **Figure 17.7**).

People who are psychologically disordered are stigmatized in ways that most physically ill people are not. A **stigma** is a mark or brand of disgrace; in the psychological context it is a set of negative attitudes about a person that sets him or her apart as unacceptable (Clausen, 1981). Negative attitudes toward the psychologically disturbed come from many sources. Prominent among these sources are mass media portrayals of psychiatric patients as prone to violent crime, "jokes," family denial of the mental distress of one of its members, an individual's fear of loss of employment if others discover his or her distress or former mental health care, and legal terminology that stresses mental incompetence (Rabkin et al., 1980). The stigmatizing process discredits a person as "flawed" (Jones et al., 1984).

A recovered patient wrote, "For me, the stigma of mental illness was as devastating as the experience of

FIGURE 17.7 "LET THE PUNISHMENT FIT THE CRIME"

This figure illustrates a continuum of behaviors that are deemed increasingly unacceptable and are responded to with increasing severity. Basically, each reaction is a punishment for deviance, so behavior toward those who act neurotically or psychotically can be seen to resemble behavior toward criminals and other deviants.

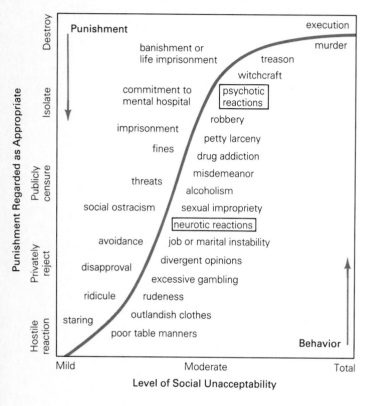

awkwardness of others around me, and my own discomfort and self-consciousness propelled me into solitary confinement.

My recovery from mental illness and its aftermath involved a struggle—against my own body, which seemed without energy and stamina, and against a society that seemed reluctant to embrace me. It seemed that my greatest needs—to be wanted, needed, valued—were the very needs which others could not fulfill (Houghton, 1980, pp. 7–8).

At a 1986 congressional hearing, the director of the National Institute of Mental Health reported on several aspects of the national neglect of schizophrenia. Although in 1986 one in every 100 Americans were diagnosed as a sufferer of this insidious disease, only $17 in federal funds per year and per schizophrenic victim were being spent on research. In comparison, $300 were being spent for each cancer victim. Nearly 60 percent of all schizophrenia sufferers received no treatment.

Our negative attitudes toward the psychologically disturbed bias our perceptions of and actions toward them and also influence their behavior toward us. A series of experiments conducted in laboratory and naturalistic settings demonstrates the unfavorable influences of the social situation on both the behavior of a person perceived to be a mental patient (even when not so) and the behavior of the person making that judgment.

hospitalization itself." She went on to describe her personal experience in vivid terms:

Prior to being hospitalized for mental illness, I lived an enviable existence. Rewards, awards, and invitations filled my scrapbook. My diary tells of many occasions worth remembering. . . . The crises of mental illness appeared as a nuclear explosion in my life. All that I had known and enjoyed previously was suddenly transformed, like some strange reverse process of nature, from a butterfly's beauty into a pupa's cocoon. There was a binding, confining quality to my life, in part chosen, in part imposed. Repeated rejections, the

Although 1 in every 100 Americans is diagnosed as schizophrenic, 60 percent receive no treatment. Federal funds for research amount to only $17 per patient per year.

When one member of a pair of male college students was (falsely) led to believe the other had been a mental patient, he perceived the pseudo expatient to be inadequate, incompetent, and not likable. By making one of a pair of interacting males falsely believe he was perceived by the other as stigmatized, he behaved in ways that actually caused the other naive subject to reject him (Farina, 1980; Farina et al., 1971).

Our growing understanding of psychopathology does more than enable society to reclaim its "familiar strangers," such as the young woman whose personal account of schizophrenia opened this chapter. In making sense of psychopathology, we are forced to come to grips with basic conceptions of normality, reality, and social values. A mind "loosed from its stable moorings" does not just go on its solitary way; it bumps into other minds, sometimes challenging their stability. In discovering how to understand, treat, and, ideally, to prevent psychological disorders, we not only help those who are suffering and losing out on the joys of living, but we also expand the basic understanding of our own human nature. How do psychologists and psychiatrists intervene to right minds gone wrong and to modify behavior that doesn't work? We shall see in the next chapter.

RECAPPING MAIN POINTS

The Nature of Psychological Disorders

Abnormality is judged by the degree to which a person's actions resemble a set of indicators that include distress, maladaptiveness, irrationality, unpredictability, unconventionality, and observer discomfort. In the past, psychopathology was considered to be the result of evil spirits or weak character. Today, there are a number of approaches to studying etiology. The biological approach concentrates on abnormalities in the brain, biochemical processes, and genetic influences. The psychological approach includes the psychodynamic, behavioral, and cognitive models. The interactionist approach combines these views.

Classifying Psychological Disorders

Classification systems for psychological disorders should provide a common shorthand for communicating about general types of psychopathology and specific cases. The most widely accepted diagnostic and classification system is *DSM-III-R*. It emphasizes descriptions of symptom patterns and uses a multidimensional system of five axes that encourages mental health professionals to consider psychological, physical, and social factors that might be relevant to a specific disorder. While the *DSM* system has been updated over the years to reflect evolving views of psychological disorders, critics contend that it is limited in its ability to add to understanding of etiology or to make treatment decisions.

Major Types of Psychological Disorders

Personality disorders are patterns of perception, thinking, or behavior that are long-standing and inflexible and that impair an individual's functioning. Dissociative disorders involve a disruption of the integrated functioning of memory, consciousness, or personal identity. The four major types of anxiety disorders are generalized, panic, phobic, and obsessive-compulsive. Biological and psychological explanations of anxiety disorders account for different facets of the etiology of anxiety. Affective disorders involve disturbances of mood. Unipolar depression is the most common affective disorder while bipolar disorder is much rarer. Suicides are most frequent among people suffering from depression.

Schizophrenic Disorders

Schizophrenia is a severe form of psychopathology. It is characterized by extreme distortions in perception, thinking, emotion, behavior, and language. The four subtypes of schizophrenia are disorganized, catatonic, paranoid, and undifferentiated. Evidence for the cause of schizophrenia has been found in a variety of factors including genetics, biochemical and brain abnormalities, family environment and communication, and faulty cognitive processes. Schizophrenia seems to be a universal human phenomenon.

Judging People as Abnormal

The task of labeling someone psychologically or mentally disordered is ultimately a matter of human judgment. Even professional judgments can be influenced by context and biased by gender, race, and other prejudices. Those with psychological disorders are often stigmatized in ways that most physically ill people are not. Understanding psychopathology enables us to help those who are suffering from mental illness and to improve our understanding of human nature.

KEY TERMS

affective disorder, 638

agoraphobia, 634

antisocial personality disorder, 629

biological marker, 649

bipolar disorder, 638

delusion, 646

diathesis-stress hypothesis, 650

dissociative disorder, 629

dopamine hypothesis, 650

double bind, 651

drapetomania, 655

DSM-III-R, 625

etiology, 622

fear, 633

functional pathology, 622

generalized anxiety disorder, 632

hallucination, 646

hysteria, 621

insanity, 654

interactionist perspective, 624

learned helplessness, 640

manic episode, 638

masochism, 627

multiple personality disorder (MPD), 629

narcissistic personality disorder, 629

negative cognitive sets, 640

neurotic disorder, 627

obsessive-compulsive disorder, 634

organic pathology, 622

panic disorder, 632

personality disorder, 628

phobic disorder, 633

psychogenic amnesia, 629

psychological diagnosis, 619

psychopathological functioning, 618

psychotic disorder, 627

schizophrenic disorder, 645

social phobia, 634

stigma, 655

unipolar depression, 639

MAJOR CONTRIBUTORS

Bateson, Gregory, 651

Beck, Aaron, 640

Charcot, Jean, 622

Freud, Sigmund, 623

Gottesman, Irving, 648

Kraepelin, Emil, 622

La Framboise, Teresa, 644

Laing, R. D., 655

Maher, Brendan, 652

Mahler, Margaret, 651

Mesmer, Franz, 622

Nolen-Hoeksema, Susan, 643

Pinel, Phillipe, 622

Putnam, F. W., 630

Rosenhan, David, 654

Seligman, Martin, 640

Shneidman, Edwin, 644

Szasz, Thomas, 655

Torrey, Fuller, 651

Chapter 18

Therapies for Personal Change

THE THERAPEUTIC CONTEXT 662
- OVERVIEW OF MAJOR THERAPIES
- ENTERING THERAPY
- GOALS AND SETTINGS
- HEALERS AND THERAPISTS
- HISTORICAL AND CULTURAL CONTEXTS

   ■ INTERIM SUMMARY

PSYCHODYNAMIC THERAPIES 668
- FREUDIAN PSYCHOANALYSIS
- POST-FREUDIAN THERAPIES

   ■ INTERIM SUMMARY

BEHAVIOR THERAPIES 673
- COUNTERCONDITIONING
- AVERSION THERAPY
- CONTINGENCY MANAGEMENT
- SOCIAL-LEARNING THERAPY
- GENERALIZATION TECHNIQUES

   ■ INTERIM SUMMARY

COGNITIVE THERAPIES 682
- COGNITIVE BEHAVIOR MODIFICATION
- CHANGING FALSE BELIEFS

   ■ INTERIM SUMMARY

EXISTENTIAL-HUMANIST THERAPIES 684
- PERSON-CENTERED THERAPY
- HUMAN-POTENTIAL MOVEMENT
- GROUP THERAPIES
- MARITAL AND FAMILY THERAPY

   ■ INTERIM SUMMARY

BIOMEDICAL THERAPIES 689
- PSYCHOSURGERY AND ELECTROCONVULSIVE THERAPY
- CHEMOTHERAPY

   ■ INTERIM SUMMARY

DOES THERAPY WORK? 694
- EVALUATING THERAPEUTIC EFFECTIVENESS
- CLOSE-UP: THERAPY FOR DRINKING PROBLEMS: WHAT WORKS?
- PREVENTION STRATEGIES
- CLOSE-UP: THE SYSTEM VERSUS THE SCHOOL BULLIES

A PERSONAL ENDNOTE 701

RECAPPING MAIN POINTS 702

KEY TERMS 703

MAJOR CONTRIBUTORS 703

S haron felt overwhelmed by a sense of impending doom. Nothing in her childhood or her current life circumstances explained her anxiety. Her therapist, Dr. José Stevens, suggested that Sharon focus her attention inward to discover what part of her body was most affected by these feelings. After Sharon identified the area just above her solar plexus, Dr. Stevens asked her to breathe deeply into that place, allowing her body to move spontaneously, expressing any images that came to her. This is how Dr. Stevens described Sharon's experience:

"As she began to stir, I accompanied her movements with soft drumbeats. She began to curl up, then abruptly she straightened and circled the room in a gliding movement that ended with some low guttural sounds. The dance continued with many flying gestures, sounds, and much emotional intensity, coming to a resolution and completion after some time. She was quite out of breath, but her eyes were clear and bright; her face was flushed with excitement. . . .

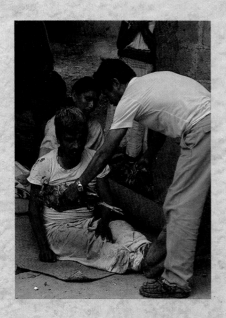

"She explained she had begun with an image of a dark cave deep in her body at the place where she had focused. This cave felt familiar but filled her with dread. She cried for help and a bird appeared who lifted her on his back and circled out above a strange landscape. There she could look down and see a double of herself hurriedly leading a group of others toward the cave. Before the group could make it, they were overtaken by an avalanche, and all were buried except her double who lay dying, pinned under a tree. The bird swooped with her down to where the people lay; she climbed off and rushed to the side of her dying double. She was able to comfort her, explaining to her double that the avalanche was not her fault, but an act of nature, and that her life and the lives of the others had come to an end in the natural course of events. With this done, the bird swept her up and returned her to the cave which now felt bright and homelike, without the former feeling of dread. The bird then told her a number of things that were to be kept in absolute confidence until many days later. The dance ended there" (Stevens, 1986, p. 48).

After this therapy session, Sharon's vague sense of dread disappeared. She felt more powerful and decisive, and she started using her leadership skills, taking responsibility without feeling guilty if things didn't work out. "Her previous, limiting feelings were literally worked out of her system in the concentrated and intense healing dance with her guardian spirit" (Stevens, 1986).

When traditional western "talk therapy" did not help Sharon, Dr. Stevens turned to **shamanism,** an ancient and powerful spiritual tradition that has been practiced for close to 30,000 years. *Shamanism* originally referred to the religion of the Ural-Altaic peoples of Siberia. It was characterized by belief in demons, gods, and ancestral spirits. According to Native American psychologist Leslie Gray, in the shamanistic tradition "all forms of suffering and disease are diagnosed as powerlessness. The remedy is to regain power for the patient by restoring a vital soul, retrieving a guardian spirit, or instructing in ceremonial practices that return power" (Gray, 1989). Drumming, chanting, and other rituals are used to inspire awe and induce altered states of consciousness that facilitate the quest for knowledge and empowerment (Walsh, 1990).

Recently, the medical, psychiatric, and psychological professions have begun to work with shamans in an effort to integrate Western psychotherapies that involve self-analysis with the therapies of collectivist societies that view the individual within the current communal context. These attempts at integration will make therapies more culturally appropriate to a wider range of clients (Kraut, 1990). [For an excellent analysis of shamanism, I recommend Mircea Eliade's *Shamanism: Archaic Techniques of Ecstasy,* 1964.]

How has the treatment of psychological disorders been influenced by historical, cultural, and social forces? What is the relationship between theory, research, and practice? What can be done to influence a mind ungoverned by ordinary reason to modify uncontrolled behavior, to alter unchecked emotions, and to correct abnormalities of the brain and even genes themselves? These are some of the formidable questions that we will address in this final chapter of our journey through *Psychology and Life.*

This chapter surveys the major types of treatments currently used by health care providers: psychoanalysis, behavior modification, cognitive alteration, humanistic therapies, and drug therapies. We will examine the way these treatments work. We will also evaluate the validity of claims about the success of any therapy.

"OF COURSE I'VE BECOME MORE MATURE SINCE YOU STARTED TREATING ME. YOU'VE BEEN AT IT SINCE I WAS 14 YEARS OLD."

THE THERAPEUTIC CONTEXT

There are different types of therapy for mental disorders and there are many reasons someone seeks help (and others who need it do not). Even the purposes or goals of therapy, the settings in which therapy occurs, and the kinds of therapeutic helpers are varied. Despite any differences between therapies, however, all are *interventions* into a person's life, designed to change that person's functioning in some way.

Treatment of physical illness and mental illness is determined by the severity of illness. Some illnesses, such as cancer or schizophrenia, are so serious that they require long-term, intensive treatment by highly trained professionals in special institutional settings. On the other hand, relatively minor problems, such as a noticeable wart or a mild phobia of escalators, do not usually require treatment. In between these two extremes are a range of problems that may be intense but not long lasting; mild but disturbingly repetitive; and varying in the degree of discomfort they cause and in the degree of their interference with daily living.

OVERVIEW OF MAJOR THERAPIES

If we think of the brain as a computer, we can say that mental problems may occur either in the brain's hardware or the software that programs its actions. The two main kinds of therapy for mental disorders focus on either the hardware or the software.

Biomedical therapies focus on changing the hardware: the mechanisms that run the central nervous system, endocrine system, and the metabolism. These therapies try to alter brain functioning with chemical or physical interventions, including surgery, electric shock, and drugs that act directly on the brain-body connection. Only psychiatrists and specialists with M.D. degrees can administer biomedical therapies.

Psychological therapies, which are collectively called **psychotherapy,** focus on changing the software—the faulty behaviors we have learned and the words, thoughts, interpretations, and feedback that direct our daily strategies for living. These therapies are practiced by clinical psychologists as well as by psychiatrists. There are four major types of psychotherapy: psychodynamic, behavioral, cognitive, and existential-humanistic.

The *psychodynamic approach,* commonly known as the *psychoanalytic approach,* views adult neurotic suffering as the outer symptom of inner, unresolved childhood traumas and conflicts. *Psychoanalysis* treats mental disorder with words. It is a "talking cure" in which a therapist helps a person develop insights about the relation between the overt symptoms and the unresolved hidden conflicts that presumably caused them.

Behavior therapy treats the behaviors themselves as disturbances that must be modified. Disorders are viewed as learned behavior patterns rather than as the symptoms of mental disease. Behavior therapists believe that changing the problem behavior corrects the disorder. This transformation is accomplished in many ways including changing reinforcement contingencies for desirable and undesirable responding, extinguishing conditioned fear responses, and providing models of effective problem solving.

Cognitive therapy tries to restructure the way a person thinks by altering the often distorted self-statements a person makes about the causes of a problem. Restructuring cognitions changes the way a person defines and explains difficulties, often enabling the person to cope with the difficulties.

Therapies that have emerged from the *existential-humanistic tradition* emphasize the *values* of patients. Existential-humanistic therapies are directed toward self-actualization, psychological growth, the development of more meaningful interpersonal relationships, and the enhancement of freedom of choice. They tend to focus more on improving the functioning of essentially healthy people than on correcting the symptoms of seriously disturbed individuals. These therapies have given rise to encounter group and personal growth types of therapy.

Before we examine the conceptual rationale for and methods of each of these types of therapeutic intervention, let's start at the beginning of the process.

ENTERING THERAPY

Why does anyone go into therapy? As in the case of physical illness, it is not easy to specify the reasons people decide to seek professional help for their psychological problems. Most often, people will enter therapy when their everyday functioning violates societal criteria of normality and/or their own sense of adequate adjustment. They may seek therapy on their own initiative after trying ineffectively to cope with their problems, or they may be advised to do so by family, friends, doctors, or co-workers. In some cases, psychological problems associated with long-term medical problems that drastically affect the person's life can be helped by psychotherapy. Sudden life changes due to unemployment, death of a loved one, or divorce may trigger or worsen one's psychological problems, necessitating outside support. Students often seek therapy in their college mental health facilities because of difficulties in interpersonal relationships and concerns about academic performance. Some people are in treatment because they are legally required by the court to do so in connection with a criminal offense or insanity hearing. Those whose behavior is judged dangerous to self or others can be involuntarily committed by a state court to a mental institution for a limited period of time for treatment, testing, and/or observation.

Many people who might benefit from therapy do not seek professional help. Sometimes it is inconvenient for them to do so, but there are many other possible reasons. These reasons include lack of accessible mental health facilities in the community, ignorance of available resources, lack of money, older age, language difficulties, fear of stigmatization, and value systems that devalue seeking help from a psychologist.

One's ability to get help can be affected even by the psychological problems themselves. The person with agoraphobia finds it hard, even impossible, to leave home to seek therapy; a paranoid person will not trust mental health professionals. Extremely shy people cannot call for an appointment or go to an initial diagnostic interview precisely because of the problem for which they desire help. In many communities, it is still much easier to get help from a medical doctor for physical health problems than it is to find a qualified mental health worker who has time to provide needed, affordable psychological help.

People who do enter therapy are usually referred to as either *patients* or *clients*. The term **patient** is used by professionals who take a biomedical approach to the treatment of psychological problems. The term **client** is used by professionals who think of psychological disorders as "problems in living" and not as mental illnesses (Rogers, 1951; Szasz, 1961). We will try to use the preferred term for each approach: *patient* for biomedical and psychoanalytic therapies and *client* for other therapies.

GOALS AND SETTINGS

The therapeutic process can involve four primary tasks or goals: (a) reaching a *diagnosis* about what is

Cathy □ Cathy Guisewite

wrong, possibly determining an appropriate psychiatric (*DSM-R*) label for the presenting problem, and classifying the disorder; (b) proposing a probable *etiology* (cause of the problem), identifying the probable origins of the disorder and the functions being served by the symptoms; (c) making a *prognosis,* or estimate, of the course the problem will take with and without any treatment; and, finally, (d) prescribing and carrying out some form of *treatment,* a therapy designed to minimize or eliminate the troublesome symptoms and, perhaps, also their sources.

There are many settings in which therapy is conducted: hospitals, clinics, schools, and private offices. Some humanistic therapists prefer to conduct group sessions in their homes in order to work within a more natural environment. Newer community-based therapies that aim to take the treatment to the client may operate out of local store fronts or church facilities. Finally, therapists who practice **in vivo therapy** work with clients in the life setting that is associated with their problem. For example, they work in airplanes with pilots or flight attendants who suffer from flying phobias or in shopping malls with people who have social phobias.

HEALERS AND THERAPISTS

A *cross-cultural perspective* shows that communally oriented societies—for example, Native Americans and many African tribes—treat cases of behavior pathology within a social group context. By contrast, societies with more individualistic values such as ours have therapies that generally reflect those dominant values. Most treatment for mental and behavioral problems in our society is typically conducted in an environment alien to the patient, in a one-on-one interaction with an expert-stranger who is paid to try to improve a client's well-being or alleviate a patient's suffering.

When psychological problems arise, most of us initially seek out informal counselors who operate in more familiar settings. Many people turn to family members, close friends, personal physicians, lawyers, or favorite teachers for support, guidance, and counsel. Those with religious affiliations may seek that help from a religious leader. Others get advice and a chance to talk by opening up to neighborhood bartenders, beauticians, cab drivers, or other people willing to listen. In our society, these informal therapists carry the bulk of the daily burden of relieving pent-up frustration and conflict.

Although more people seek out therapy now than in the past, people usually turn to trained mental health professionals only when their psychological problems become severe or persist for extended periods of time. When they do, they usually turn to one of six main types of therapists: counseling psychologists, psychiatric social workers, pastoral counselors, clinical psychologists, psychiatrists, and psychoanalysts.

The term **counseling psychologist** describes a member of the general category of professional psychologists who specializes in providing guidance in areas such as vocation selection, school problems, drug abuse, and marital conflict. Typically, these counselors work in community settings related to the problem areas—within a business, a school, a prison, the military service, or a neighborhood clinic—and use interviews, tests, guidance, and advising to help individuals solve specific problems and make decisions about future options.

A **psychiatric social worker** is a mental health professional whose specialized training in a school of social work prepares him or her to work in collaboration with psychiatrists and clinical psychologists. Unlike psychiatrists and psychologists, these counselors are trained to consider the social contexts of people's problems, so they may also involve other family members in the therapy or at least become acquainted with clients' homes or work settings.

A **pastoral counselor** is a member of a religious order who specializes in the treatment of psychological disorders. Often these counselors combine spiritual and practical problem-solving directions.

A **clinical psychologist** is required to have concentrated his or her graduate school training in the assessment and treatment of psychological problems, completed a supervised internship in a clinical setting, and earned a Ph.D. These psychologists tend to have a broader background in psychology, assessment, and research than do psychiatrists.

A **psychiatrist** must have completed all medical school training for an M.D. degree and also have completed some postdoctoral specialty training in dealing with mental and emotional disorders. Psychiatrists' training lies more in the biomedical base of psychological problems, and they are the only therapists who can prescribe medications or physically based therapy.

A **psychoanalyst** is a therapist with either an M.D. or Ph.D degree. Psychoanalysts must have completed specialized postgraduate training in the Freudian approach to understanding and treating mental disorders.

Before looking at the various modern approaches in more detail, we will first consider the historical contexts in which treatment of the mentally ill was delivered and then broaden the Western perspective with a look at the healing practices of other cultures.

HISTORICAL AND CULTURAL CONTEXTS

What kind of treatment might you have received in past centuries if you were suffering from psychological problems? If you lived in Europe or the United States, chances are the treatment would not have helped and could even have been harmful. In other cultures, treatment of psychological disorders has usually been seen within a broader perspective that includes religious and

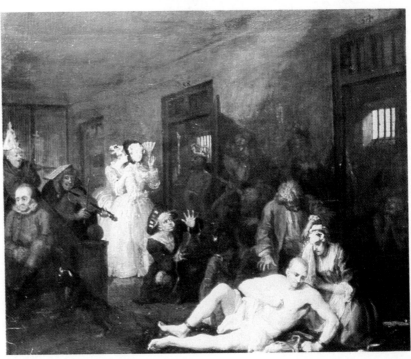

The engraving at right depicts the conditions that existed in the 1730s at Bethlehem. Above is patient William Norris in his cell.

social values which often have been associated with kinder treatment of those with aberrant behavior.

Western History of Treatment

Population increases and migration to big cities in fourteenth-century Western Europe created unemployment, poverty, and social alienation. These conditions led to poverty, crime, and psychological problems. Special institutions were soon created to warehouse society's three emerging categories of misfits: the poor, criminals, and the mentally disturbed.

In 1403, a London hospital—St. Mary of Bethlehem—admitted its first patient with psychological problems. For the next 300 years, mental patients of the hospital were chained, tortured, and exhibited to an admission-paying public. Over time, a mispronunciation of *Bethlehem—bedlam*—came to mean *chaos* because of the horrible confusion reigning in the hospital and the dehumanized treatment of patients there (Foucault, 1975).

In fifteenth-century Germany, the mad were assumed to be possessed by the Devil who had deprived them of reason. As the Inquisition's persecutory mania spread throughout Europe, mental disturbances were "cured" by painful death. See *The Malleus Malificarum* of 1486 (Summers, ed., 1971) to find out about the case made by German clerics against witches.

It wasn't until the late eighteenth century that the perception of psychological problems as *mental illness* emerged in Europe. The French physician **Philippe Pinel** wrote in 1801, "The mentally ill, far from being guilty people deserving of punishment, are sick people whose miserable state deserves all the consideration that is due to suffering humanity. One should try with the most simple methods to restore their reason" (Zilboorg & Henry, 1941, pp. 323–24).

In the United States, psychologically disturbed citizens were confined for their own protection and for the safety of the community, but they were given no treatment. However, by the mid-1800s, when psychology as a field of study was gaining some credibility and respectability, "a cult of curability" emerged throughout the country. Insanity was then thought to be related to the environmental stresses brought on by the turmoil of newly developing cities. Eventually, madness came to be viewed as a social problem to be cured through mental hygiene, just as contagious physical diseases were being treated by physical hygiene.

One of the founders of modern psychiatry, German psychiatrist **J. C. Heinroth,** helped provide the conceptual and moral justification for the disease model of mental illness. In 1818, Heinroth wrote that madness is a complete loss of inner freedom or reason depriving those afflicted of any ability to control their lives. Others who "know best" what is good for the patient must be in charge of care. Heinroth maintained that it was the duty of the state to cure mentally ill patients of diseases that forced them to burden society (Szasz, 1979).

From Heinroth's time to the present, "In this alliance between psychology and state, the state's protective power to confine the mentally ill has been transformed into a power of the state to treat, through its agent the mental health profession, the mental disorder thought to be the basis of the problem" (White & White, 1981, p. 954). Heinroth and, later in the 1900s,

Philippe Pinel frees the insane.

Clifford Beers spurred on the mental hygiene movement. Eventually, the confinement of the mentally ill assumed a new *rehabilitative* goal. The *asylum* then became the central fixture of this social-political movement. The disturbed were, thus, confined to asylums in rural areas, far from the stress of the city, not only for protection but also to be treated (Rothman, 1971). Unfortunately, many of the asylums that were built became overcrowded. Then the humane goal of rehabilitation was replaced with the pragmatic goal of *containing* strange people in remote places.

Cultural Symbols and Rituals of Curing

Our review of these historical trends in the treatment of psychological disorders has been limited to Western views and practices which emphasize the uniqueness of the individual, competition, independence, survival of the fittest, a mastery over nature, and personal responsibility for success and failure. Both demonology and the disease model are consistent with this emphasis, regarding mental disorder as something that happens *inside* a person and as an individual's failure.

This view is not shared by many other cultures (Triandis, 1990). For example, in the African world view the emphasis is on groupness, commonality, cooperation, interdependence, tribal survival, unity with nature, and collective responsibility (Nobles, 1976). It is *contrary* to the thinking of many non-European cultures to treat mentally ill individuals by *removing* them from society. Among the Navajo and African cultures, for example, healing is a matter that always takes place in a social context, involving a distressed person's beliefs, family, work, and life environment. The African use of group support in therapy has been expanded into a procedure called "network therapy," where a patient's entire network of relatives, co-workers, and friends becomes involved in the treatment (Lambo, 1978).

The research of *cultural anthropologists* has broadened the conception of madness in all its forms by providing analyses of the explanations and treatments for psychological disorders across different cultures (Bourguignon, 1979; Evans-Pritchard, 1937; Kluckhorn, 1944; Marsella, 1979). In many cultures, the treatment of mental and physical disease is bound up with religion and witchcraft; certain human beings are given special mystical powers to help in the transformation of their distressed fellow beings. Belief systems often *personalize* the vague forces of fate or chance that intervene in one's life to create problems. This personalization permits direct action to be taken against presumed evildoers and direct help to be sought from assumed divine healers (Middleton, 1967). Often, the pathological state that is seen as a result of the spirit possession of the afflicted person is transformed by therapeutic intervention of shaman healers into a positive ritualized possession that enables him or her to join the cult of the shamans.

Common to all folk healing ceremonies are the important roles of symbols, myths, and ritual (Levi-Strauss, 1963). **Ritual healing** ceremonies infuse special emotional intensity and meaning into the healing process. They heighten patients' suggestibility and sense of importance, and, combined with the use of symbols, they connect the individual sufferer, the shaman, and the society to supernatural forces to be won over in the battle against madness (Devereux, 1981; Wallace, 1966).

One therapeutic practice used in a number of healing ceremonies is *dissociation of consciousness,* which is induced in either a distressed person or a faith healer. While in Western views dissociation is itself a symptom of mental disorder to be prevented or corrected, in other cultures, as consciousness is altered, good spirits are communicated with and evil spirits are exorcised. The use of ceremonial alteration of consciousness can be seen today among the cult of Puerto Rican *Espiritistas* in New York City, whose healing ceremonies involve communication with good spirits that are believed to exist outside a person's skin (Garrison, 1977). Some of these non-Western views have begun to work their way into Western practices. The influence of the social-interactive concept and the focus on the *family context* and *supportive community* are evident in newer therapeutic approaches that emphasize social support networks and family therapy.

SUMMING UP

People enter therapy for help with mental or emotional problems that are causing suffering, dysfunctional behavior, or social problems. Biomedical therapies affect physiological processes; psychological therapies try to change thoughts, feelings, or behaviors. There are four major types of psychotherapy: the psychodynamic approach focuses on gaining insight into how conflicts from the person's past influences present behavior; behavior therapy modifies the behaviors themselves by using conditioning principles; cognitive therapy deals with a person's thoughts; existential-humanist therapies emphasize ways to help a patient fulfill values and achieve personal growth goals.

The therapeutic process involves four tasks: diagnosing what is wrong; figuring out the etiology, or source, of the problem; making a prognosis about probable outcomes with or without treatment; and carrying out a specific kind of treatment. There are various kinds of professionals who work in the therapeutic mold; among them are counseling psychologists, psychiatric social workers, pastoral counselors, clinical psychologists, psychiatrists, and psychoanalysts.

A historical perspective on the treatment of mental disorders shows how conceptions of disease and deviant behavior were influenced by religious, social, and political agendas of different countries in different eras. Emerging conceptions of the afflicted person as mentally ill led to more humane treatment and hospitalization in mental institutions. Programs in mental asylums for rehabilitation of mentally ill patients eventually became custodial warehouses for social misfits.

Cultural anthropologists extend the boundaries of Western psychological views of mental disorder and therapy by revealing a broader social-religious context. Folk healing typically involves a blend of magic and witchcraft practiced by a healer, or shaman. The key ingredients of folk healing are the manipulation of symbols, myths, and ritual ceremonies and the patient's total belief in that culturally prescribed system of cure.

PSYCHODYNAMIC THERAPIES

Psychodynamic therapies assume that a patient's problems have been caused by the psychological tension between unconscious impulses and the constraints of his or her life situation. These therapies locate the core of the disturbance inside the disturbed person, accepting a general model of a *disease core* that shows up in overt symptoms.

FREUDIAN PSYCHOANALYSIS

Psychoanalytic therapy, as developed by **Sigmund Freud,** is the premier psychodynamic therapy. It is an intensive and prolonged technique for exploring unconscious motivations and conflicts in neurotic, anxiety-ridden individuals. The major goal of psychoanalysis is "to reveal the unconscious." A former president of the American Psychoanalytic Institute explained the premise of psychoanalysis:

> We believe an unconscious exists in all humans and that it dictates much of our behavior. If it is a relatively healthy unconscious, then our behavior will be healthy, too. Many who are plagued by symptoms from phobias, depression, anxiety, or

panic may have deposits of unconscious material that are fostering their torment. Only the psychoanalyst is qualified to probe the unconscious . . . (Theodore Rubin, quoted in Rockmore, 1985, p. 71).

As we saw in earlier chapters, Freudian theory views anxiety (or neurotic) disorders as inabilities to resolve adequately the inner conflicts between the unconscious, irrational impulses of the *id* and the internalized social constraints imposed by the *superego*. As an individual progresses through the biologically determined stages from infancy to adulthood, according to Freudian theory his or her particular psychological experiences at each stage determine whether there will be a fixation at an immature stage or progress to a more mature level of development. The goal of psychoanalysis is to establish intrapsychic harmony that expands one's awareness of the forces of the *id*, reduces overcompliance with the demands of the *superego*, and strengthens the role of the *ego*.

Of central importance to a therapist is understanding the way a patient uses the process of *repression* to handle conflicts. Symptoms are considered to be messages from the unconscious that something is wrong. A psychoanalyst's task is to help a patient bring repressed thoughts to consciousness and to gain *insight* into the relation between the current symptoms and the repressed conflicts from years gone by. In this psychodynamic view, therapy works and patients recover when they are "released from repression" established in early childhood (Munroe, 1955). Because a central goal of a therapist is to guide a patient toward discovering insights between present symptoms and past origins, psychodynamic therapy is often called **insight therapy.**

The goals of psychoanalysis are ambitious. They involve not just the elimination of the symptoms of psychopathology but a total personality reorganization. When psychoanalysis overcomes barriers to self-awareness and to freedom of thought and communication, a person can achieve more intimate human associations as well as more intellectual creativity. Because traditional psychoanalysis is an attempt to reconstruct long-standing repressed memories and then work through painful feelings to an effective resolution, it is a therapy that takes a long time (several years at least, with as many as five sessions a week). It also requires introspective patients who are verbally fluent, highly motivated to remain in therapy, and willing and able to undergo considerable expense. Some of the newer forms of psychodynamic therapy try to make therapy briefer in total duration. In *time-limited psychotherapy*, the therapist and patient contract for a specific number of

Sigmund Freud's office with his well-known couch

sessions or time period for the treatment. Short-term therapy may be for only a few weeks, perhaps 10 sessions, while an intermediate form of therapy gaining popularity with many therapists lasts months or up to a year but is shorter than formal psychoanalysis.

> A recent review related improvement in therapy as a function of the number of therapy sessions. This meta-analysis of 2431 patients in reported studies for over the past 30 years indicates that, by the 8th session, approximately half the patients are measurably improved and that 75 percent of the patients are measurably improved by six months with weekly sessions (Howard et al., 1986).

Psychoanalysts use several techniques to bring repressed conflicts to consciousness and to help a patient resolve them (Langs, 1981; Lewis, 1981). These techniques include free association, analysis of resistance, dream analysis, and analysis of transference and countertransference.

Catharsis and the Talking Cure

Modern psychotherapy began in 1880 with the case of Fraulein Anna O. and her famous physician **Joseph Breuer.** This bright, personable, 21-year-old Viennese woman became incapacitated and developed a severe cough while nursing her ill father. When the physician began to treat her "nervous cough," he became aware of many more symptoms that seemed to have a psychological origin. Anna squinted, had double vision, and experienced paralysis, muscle contractions, and anesthesias (loss of sensitivity to pain stimuli).

Breuer told a young physician named Sigmund Freud about this unusual patient. Together they coined the term *hysterical conversion* for the transformation of Anna O.'s blocked emotional impulses into physical symptoms (Breuer & Freud, 1895; 1955). The case of Anna O. is the first detailed description of physical symptoms resulting from *psychogenic* causes—a hysterical illness. It was Anna O. herself who devised her own treatment, with Breuer acting as therapist. She referred to the procedures as a "talking cure" and jokingly, as "chimney sweeping."

In the context of hypnosis, Anna O. talked freely, giving full reign to her imagination (free associations). Once she was able to express herself in an open and direct fashion to her therapist, she no longer needed to use the indirect and disguised communication of physical symptoms. According to Breuer, her "complexes were disposed of by being given verbal expression during hypnosis."

Breuer and Freud analyzed Anna O.'s disorder in terms of internal psychodynamic forces (instincts and impulses). What they failed to acknowledge fully were the external social obstacles of the time that limited the ambitions and aspirations of all women. In addition, they didn't recognize that Anna O.'s intellectual and emotional involvement with her therapist helped break the monotony of her existence.

Anna O. went on to become a pioneer of social work, a leader in the struggle for women's rights, a playwright, and a housemother of an orphanage. Her true name was **Bertha Pappenheim** (Rosenbaum & Muroff, 1984). Although this case played an extremely important role in the development of modern psychotherapy, a provocative new view of Anna O.'s illness casts doubt on the original diagnosis. A reasonably good alternative diagnosis is that her symptoms were those associated with *tuberculous meningitis,* which she might have contracted from her father who probably was dying from a form of tuberculosis himself (Thornton, 1984). After Anna O. had terminated her treatment with Breuer, she entered a sanatorium from which she was later discharged, relatively recovered from her illness. It is likely that many of her "hysterical conversion" reactions were of organic not psychological origin, but she may have experienced considerable suppressed rage and guilt from nursing her father for so long and been frustrated by the lack of opportunities for women of her social class.

Free Association

The principal procedure used in psychoanalysis to probe the unconscious and release repressed material is called **free association.** A patient sitting comfortably in a chair or lying in a relaxed position on a couch, lets his or her mind wander freely and gives a running account of thoughts, wishes, physical sensations, and mental images as they occur. The patient is encouraged to reveal every thought or feeling, no matter how personal, painful, or seemingly unimportant.

Freud maintained that free associations are *predetermined,* not random. The task of an analyst is to track the associations to their source and identify the significant patterns that lie beneath the surface of what are apparently just words. The patient is encouraged to express strong feelings, usually toward authority figures, that have been repressed for fear of punishment or retaliation. Any such emotional release, by this or other processes, is termed **catharsis.**

Among many Native American tribes, confession is part of the therapy when a person's disease is believed to be due to the violation of a social rule or taboo. Confession to a ritual healer works as cathartic therapy (La Barre, 1964) and so does the interpretation and acting out of dreams as "wishes of the soul" (Hollowell, 1963).

Resistance

At some time during the process of free association, a patient will show **resistance**—an inability or unwillingness to discuss certain ideas, desires, or experiences. Resistances prevent repressed material from returning to consciousness. This material is often related to an individual's sexual life (which includes all things pleasurable) or to hostile, resentful feelings toward parents. Sometimes a patient shows resistance by coming late to therapy or "forgetting" a session altogether. When the repressed material is finally brought into the open, a patient generally claims that it is unimportant, absurd, irrelevant, or too unpleasant to discuss. The therapist is sensitized to the likelihood of the opposite; it's pay dirt.

A psychoanalyst, thus, attaches particular importance to subjects that a patient does *not* wish to discuss. Such resistances are conceived of as *barriers* between the unconscious and the conscious. The aim of psychoanalysis is to break down resistances and enable the patient to face these painful ideas, desires, and experiences. Breaking down resistances is a long and difficult process that is essential if the underlying problem is to be brought to consciousness where it can be resolved.

Dream Analysis

Psychoanalysts believe that dreams are an important source of information about a patient's unconscious motivations. When a person is asleep, the superego is presumably less on guard against the unacceptable impulses originating in the id, so a motive that cannot be expressed in waking life may find expression in a dream. Some motives are so unacceptable to the conscious self that they cannot be revealed openly, even in dreams, but must be expressed in disguised or symbolic form. In analysis, dreams are assumed to have two kinds of content: *manifest* (openly visible) content that we remember upon awakening and *latent* (hidden) content—the actual motives that are seeking expression but are so painful or unacceptable to us that we do not want to recognize them. Therapists attempt to uncover these hidden motives by using **dream analysis,** a therapeutic technique that examines the content of a person's dreams to discover the underlying or disguised motivations and symbolic meanings of significant life experiences and desires.

Transference and Countertransference

During the course of the intensive therapy of psychoanalysis, a patient usually develops an emotional reaction toward the therapist. Often the therapist is identified with a person who has been at the center of an emotional conflict in the past—most often a parent or a lover. This emotional reaction is called **transference.** The transference is called *positive transference* when the feelings attached to the therapist are those of love or admiration and *negative transference* when the feelings consist of hostility or envy. Often a patient's attitude is *ambivalent,* including a mixture of positive and negative feelings.

An analyst's task in handling transference is a difficult and potentially dangerous one because of the patient's emotional vulnerability; however, it is a crucial part of treatment. A therapist helps a patient to interpret the present transferred feelings by understanding their original source in earlier experiences and attitudes (Langs, 1981).

Personal feelings are also at work in a therapist's reactions to a patient. **Countertransference** refers to what happens when a therapist comes to like or dislike a patient because the patient is perceived as similar to significant people in the therapist's life. In working through countertransference, a therapist may discover some unconscious dynamics of his or her own. The therapist becomes a "living mirror" for the patient and the patient, in turn, for the therapist. If the therapist fails to recognize the operation of countertransference, the therapy may not be as effective (Little, 1981). Because of the emotional intensity of this type of therapeutic relationship and the vulnerability of the patient, therapists must be on guard about the ease of crossing the boundary between professional caring and personal involvement with their patients.

POST-FREUDIAN THERAPIES

Some of Freud's followers have retained many of his basic ideas but modified certain of his principles and practices. In general, these neo-Freudians place more emphasis than Freud did on (a) a patient's *current* social environment (less focus on the past); (b) the continuing influence of life experiences (not just infantile fixations); (c) the role of social motivation and interpersonal relations of love (rather than of biological instincts and selfish concerns); (d) the significance of ego functioning and development of the self-concept (less on the conflict between id and superego); (g) the extension of psychotherapy to schizophrenic patients; and (f) shorter, time-limited therapy.

In Chapter 17, we noted two other prominent Freudians, Carl Jung and Alfred Adler. To get a flavor of the more contemporary psychodynamic approaches of the neo-Freudians, here we will look at the work of Harry Stack Sullivan, Margaret Mahler, Karen Horney, and Heinz Kohut (see Ruitenbeek, 1973, for a look at other members of the Freudian circle).

Harry Stack Sullivan (1953) emphasized the social dimension of a patient's life and its role in creating mental problems. He felt that Freudian theory and therapy did not recognize the importance of social relationships or a patient's needs for acceptance, respect, and love. Mental disorders, he insisted, involve not only traumatic intrapsychic processes but troubled interpersonal relationships and even strong societal pressures. A young child needs to feel secure and to be treated by others with caring and tenderness. Anxiety and other mental ills arise out of insecurities in relations with parents and significant others. In Sullivan's view, a self-system is built up to hold anxiety down to a tolerable level. This self-system is derived from a child's interpersonal experiences and is organized around conceptions of the self as the *good-me* (associated with the mother's tenderness), the *bad-me* (associated with the mother's tensions), and the *not-me* (a dissociated self that is unacceptable to the rest of the self).

Therapy based on this interpersonal view involves observing a *patient's feelings* about the *therapist's attitudes.* The therapeutic interview is seen as a social setting in which each party's feelings and attitudes are influenced by the other's. The patient is gently provoked to state his or her assumptions about the therapist's attitudes and other assumptions as well. Above all, the therapeutic situation, for Sullivan, was one where the therapist learned and taught lovingly (Wallach & Wallach, 1983).

Margaret Mahler (1979) was one of the first psychoanalysts to recognize and treat childhood schizophrenia. She traced a child's fragmentation of ego and retreat from reality to sources of disharmony in the mother-child relationship. The normal development of an independent ego requires a process of gradual sepa-

Margaret Mahler
(1897–1985)

Karen Horney
(1885–1952)

ration of the mother and child, along with an emerging sense of *individuation*—a unique, stable identity. A child's development can be skewed toward mental disorder by the pathology of the mother, a need on her part not to separate from her child, or re-engulfing of the separated child into an infantile dependency. Mahler also saw a mother's lack of "emotional availability" as a contributor to abnormal development. A therapist must treat the disturbed parent-child relationship as well as the disturbed child, being sensitive to the conflict over separation-individuation and to the process by which the "dual unity" of mother and child needs to be differentiated into distinct selves. The therapy works through the phases of this process toward the goal of forming a stable sense of personal identity in the patient (Karon & Vandenbos, 1981).

Karen Horney (1937, 1945, 1950) expanded the boundaries of Freudian theory in many ways. She stressed the importance of environmental and cultural contexts in which neurotic behavior is expressed. She also took a more flexible view of personality as involving rational coping and continual development that deals with current fears and impulses rather than being determined solely by early childhood experiences and instincts. Horney was one of the first neo-Freudians to question the extent to which Freud's theory was applicable to women. She rejected Freud's *phallocentric* emphasis on the importance of the penis (male concern for castration by the father and penis envy by females), hypothesizing that *male envy* of pregnancy, motherhood, breasts, and suckling is a dynamic force in the unconscious of boys and men (1926). This alternative emphasis is *gynocentric*, centered on the female womb. Males' intense desires for material achievement and creative products thus were seen as unconscious means of

overcompensating for feelings of inferiority in the creative area of reproduction.

Psychodynamic therapies continue to evolve with a varying emphasis on Freud's constructs. One of the most important new directions for these is the modern concern for the *self* in all its senses, notably the ways one's self-concept emerges, is experienced by the person, and, at times, becomes embattled and requires defending. According to **Heinz Kohut** (1977), a leading proponent of this emphasis on the self and founder of the *object relations* school of psychoanalysis, the various aspects of self require *selfobjects*, supportive people and significant things that each of us needs in order to maintain optimal personality functioning.

Although psychoanalytic therapy and Freud's theories have been widely criticized (Fisher & Greenberg, 1985), there are still many enthusiastic supporters, especially in many Western European countries and in large urban centers in the United States.

SUMMING UP

Sigmund Freud's psychoanalytic therapy is the main form of psychodynamic therapy. One of Freud's main contributions was postulating the dynamic role of unconscious processes in normal and pathological reactions. He argued that behavior is affected by hidden conflicts and drives between the hedonistic impulses of the id and the controlling forces of the superego. The goal of this kind of therapy is to reconcile these conflicts into a stronger ego that mediates these drives. Important concepts in psychodynamic therapy include repression of unacceptable impulses, free association that allows repressed material to surface in undirected speech, resistance of a patient to discuss significant feelings and experiences, and dream analysis to reveal latent meaning in manifest content. Freud's other major contribution involved the notion of transference, the patient's identification of the therapist with significant others, and countertransference, the therapist's strong emotional reaction to the patient.

Neo-Freudians Harry Stack Sullivan, Margaret Mahler, Karen Horney, and Heinz Kohut differ from classic Freudian psychoanalysts in their emphasis on the patient's current social situation, interpersonal relationships, self-concept, differing motivations and sources of mental disorder between women and men, and the use of psychoanalysis to treat severe disorders such as schizophrenia.

BEHAVIOR THERAPIES

While psychodynamic therapies focus on presumed inner causes, behavior therapies focus on observable outer behaviors. Behavior therapies apply the principles of conditioning and reinforcement to modify undesirable behavior patterns associated with mental disorders. This orientation rejects the medical model along with all assumptions about patients suffering from mental illness that is cured by therapy.

Behavior therapists argue that abnormal behaviors are acquired in the same way as normal behaviors—through a learning process that follows the basic principles of conditioning and learning. They assert that all pathological behavior, except where there is established organic causation, can be best understood and modified by focusing on the behavior itself rather than by attempting to alter any underlying "disease core." The term *behavior* is used to describe all reactions that are influenced by learning variables—thoughts and feelings as well as overt actions.

The therapies that have emerged from the theories of conditioning and learning are grounded in a pragmatic, empirical research tradition. The central task of all living organisms is to learn how to adapt to the demands of the current social and physical environment. When organisms do not learn how to cope effectively, their maladaptive reactions can be overcome by therapy based on principles of learning (or relearning). The target behavior is *not* assumed to be a symptom of any underlying process. The symptom is the problem itself. Behaviorists believe that if the problem behavior is changed, the problem is solved.

Behavior modification is defined as "the attempt to apply learning and other experimentally derived psychological principles to problem behavior" (Bootzin, 1975). The terms *behavior therapy* and *behavior modification* are often used interchangeably. Both refer to the systematic use of principles of learning to increase the frequency of desired behaviors and/or decrease that of problem behaviors. The range of deviant behaviors and personal problems that typically are treated by behavior therapy is extensive and includes fears, compulsions, depression, addictions, aggression, and delinquent behaviors. In general, behavior therapy works best with specific rather than general types of personal problems; with a phobia better than with an inadequate personality. Psychodynamic therapists predicted that treating only the outer behavior without confronting the true, inner problem would result in **symptom substitution,** the appearance of a new physical or psychological problem. However, research has shown that when pathological behaviors are eliminated by behavior therapy, new

Mary Cover Jones
(1896–1987)

symptoms are *not* substituted (Kazdin, 1982). "On the contrary, patients whose target symptoms improved often reported improvement in other, less important symptoms as well" (Sloane et al., 1975, p. 219).

The earliest recorded use of behavior therapy was carried out by **Mary Cover Jones** in 1924. She showed how fears learned through conditioning could be unlearned. You may remember the case of Little Albert from Chapter 9. In a sense, Cover Jones followed up on Watson's demonstration.

> Her subject was Peter, a 3-year-old boy who, for some unknown reason, was afraid of rabbits. The therapy involved feeding Peter at one end of a room while the rabbit was brought in at the other end. Over a series of sessions, the rabbit was gradually brought closer until, finally, all fear disappeared and Peter played freely with the rabbit.

Behavior therapies today are more sophisticated, but they still are based on classical conditioning, operant conditioning, or a combination of the two. The development of irrational fears and other undesirable *emotional* reactions is assumed to follow the paradigm of classical conditioning. Therapy to change these negative responses uses principles of **counterconditioning,** substituting a new response for the inadequate one. Operant conditioning principles are applied when the therapeutic task is to increase the frequency of desired actions or decrease undesired habits. **Contingency management** refers to the general treatment strategy of changing behavior by modifying its consequences. Special adaptations also have been developed for *social learning;* **generalization techniques** have been developed to make connections between new responses learned in the therapy setting and the client's life situations. Our presentation of behavior therapy will be organized around these four basic aspects of conditioning and learning approaches to changing behavior patterns.

COUNTERCONDITIONING

Why does someone become anxious when faced with a harmless stimulus, such as a fly, a nonpoisonous snake, an open space, or a social contact? Is the anxiety due to simple conditioning principles we reviewed earlier? We know that *any* neutral stimulus may acquire the power to elicit strong conditioned reactions on the basis of prior association with an unconditioned stimulus. However, not everyone who is exposed to situations that are alarming, dangerous, or traumatic develop long-lasting conditioned fears that become *phobias* that lead to avoidance of those situations. In fact, it is surprising that relatively few people do develop such fears. In one survey of 8000 British schoolchildren exposed to bombing attacks, only 4 percent developed anxiety symptoms attributable to the air raids, 96 percent were unaffected (Agras, 1985).

Although conditioning can be rapidly developed, it is another matter for it to persist. A variety of experimental and observational studies of humans and animals reveals a new understanding of the conditions under which phobias develop and, thus, provide clues as to how to counteract their negative effects with behavior therapy. According to **Stewart Agras** (1985), a prominent theorist and behavior therapist for phobias and panic attacks, there are five factors that must be considered in phobic conditioning. First, phobias develop primarily to certain classes of *objects* that appear to have *evolutionary significance* because they are dangerous, such as animals, and also of primal threat situations, such as heights and social separation from caretakers. Second, only certain types of *fear-evoking conditioned stimuli* can be coupled with these objects to produce phobias. They seem to be stimuli that have a relevant *sensory association* with the feared object, such as tactile stimuli, but not loud sounds for animal phobias (possibly because animals bite the skin). Third, phobias can be learned through *social transmission* of fear from other individuals. Fourth, emotionally intense fears *persist* partly because of other people. Significant people may repeatedly show fear of the phobic situation and prevent children and others from exploring it, depriving them of the chance to extinguish fears through experience. Fifth, it appears that certain individuals are born with a *predisposition* to learn avoidance behavior more quickly and more persistently than others.

Strong emotional reactions that disrupt a person's life "for no good reason" are often conditioned responses that the person does not recognize as having been learned previously. To weaken the strength of negative learned associations, behavior therapists use the techniques of systematic desensitization, implosion, exposure, and aversive learning.

Systematic Desensitization

The nervous system cannot be relaxed and agitated or anxious at the same time because different incompatible processes can't be activated simultaneously. This simple notion was central to a new *theory of reciprocal inhibition* developed by South African psychiatrist **Joseph Wolpe** (1958, 1973) who used it to treat fears and phobias. First, he showed that strong fears in experimental cats could be overcome. He would relax the cats by feeding them in rooms that were initially different from the one in which they had developed their fear and then in rooms increasingly similar to the original learned fear setting. Finally, the cats were able to eat in the feared room, and, as they did, their fear diminished.

On the basis of this simple animal analogue, Wolpe applied this method to cases of human phobias. He taught his patients to *relax* their muscles, and then to *imagine* visually their feared situation. They did so in gradual steps that moved from initially remote associations to direct images of it. Psychologically confronting the feared stimulus while being relaxed and doing so in a *graduated* sequence is the therapeutic technique known as **systematic desensitization.**

| TABLE 18.1 | HIERARCHY OF ANXIETY-PRODUCING STIMULI FOR A TEST-ANXIOUS COLLEGE STUDENT |

1. On the way to the university on the day of an examination.

2. In the process of answering an examination paper.

3. Before the unopened doors of the examination room.

4. Awaiting the distribution of examination papers.

5. The examination paper face down.

6. The night before an examination.

7. One day before an examination.

8. Two days before an examination.

9. Three days before an examination.

10. Four days before an examination.

11. Five days before an examination.

12. A week before an examination.

13. Two weeks before an examination.

14. A month before an examination.

Desensitization therapy involves three major steps. The client identifies the stimuli that provoke anxiety and arranges them in a *hierarchy* ranked from weakest to strongest. For example, a student suffering from severe test anxiety constructed the hierarchy in **Table 18.1.** Note that she rated immediate anticipation of an examination as more stressful than taking the exam itself. Then, the client is trained in a system of progressive deep-muscle relaxation. Relaxation training requires several sessions in which the client learns to distinguish between sensations of tension and relaxation and to let go of tension in order to achieve a state of physical and mental relaxation. Finally, the actual process of desensitization begins: the relaxed client vividly imagines the *weakest* anxiety stimulus on the list. If it can be visualized without discomfort, the client goes on to the next stronger one. After a number of sessions, the most distressing situations on the list can be imagined without anxiety—even situations that could not be faced originally (Lang & Lazovik, 1963). A number of evaluation studies have shown that this behavior therapy works remarkably well with most phobic patients and better than any other form of therapy (Smith & Glass, 1977). Desensitization has also been successfully applied to a diversity of human problems, including such generalized fears as test anxiety, stage fright, impotence, and frigidity (Kazdin & Wilcoxin, 1976).

Implosion and Flooding

Implosion therapy uses an approach that is opposite systematic desensitization. If the latter is a kind of back-door approach, implosion is a fear-in-the-face form of therapy. Instead of experiencing a gradual, step-by-step progression, a client is exposed at the start to the most frightening stimuli at the top of the anxiety hierarchy but in a safe setting. The idea behind this procedure is that the client is not allowed to deny, avoid, or otherwise escape from experiencing the anxiety-arousing stimulus situations. He or she must discover that contact with the stimulus does not actually have the anticipated negative effects (Stampfl & Levis, 1967).

One way to extinguish an irrational fear is to force a client to experience a full-blown anxiety reaction. The therapeutic situation is arranged so that the client cannot run away from the frightening stimulus. The therapist *describes* an extremely frightening situation relating to the client's fear, such as snakes crawling all over his or her body and urges the client to *imagine* it fully, experiencing it through all the senses as intensely as possible. Such imagining is assumed to cause an explosion of panic. Because this explosion is an inner one, the process is called *implosion;* hence the term *implosion therapy*. As the situation happens again and again,

the stimulus loses its power to elicit anxiety. When anxiety no longer occurs, the maladaptive behavior previously used to avoid it disappears.

Flooding is similar to implosion except that it involves clients, with their permission, actually being put into the phobic situation. A claustrophobic is made to sit in a dark closet and a child with a fear of water is put into a pool. Flooding through stimulating the imagination may involve listening to a tape that describes the most terrifying version of the phobic fear in great detail for an hour or two. Once the terror subsides, the client is then taken to the feared situation, which, of course, is not nearly as frightening as just imagined. Flooding is more effective than systematic desensitization in the treatment of some behavior problems such as agoraphobia, and treatment gains are shown to be enduring for most clients (Emmelkamp & Kuipers, 1979).

Time out for some *critical thinking*. What is the ingredient common to systematic desensitization, implosion, and flooding therapies? The critical causal ingredient in modifying phobic behavior patterns is *exposure*. Therapy that employs a strategy for approaching the feared situation, forcing the client to confront the fear, and that reinforces a successful approach is known as **exposure therapy.** This approach works most quickly for specific phobias, such as fear of spiders, but can take longer for fear of flying (Serling, 1986), for example, and as many as 50 hours for complex phobias, such as agoraphobia, that involve many

A behavior therapist uses exposure therapy to help a client overcome fear of flying.

elements. Curiously, research comparing these different treatments for phobia showed that clients least preferred exposure therapy but found it to be the most effective treatment.

A reversed form of exposure therapy is used to counteract obsessive-compulsive disorders. Three-and-a-half million adult Americans and more than 300,000 children are unable to think clearly or to work because they suffer from recurring thoughts that steal into their minds and repetitive behaviors they can't control. One woman obsessed with dirt compulsively washed her hands over and over until they cracked and bled. She even thought of killing herself because this disorder totally prevented her from leading a normal life. Under the supervision of a behavior therapist, she confronted the things she feared most—dirt and trash—and eventually even touched them. She gave up washing and bathing her hands and face for 5 days. "The first time I washed my hands normally it was like a miracle to me," she reported (Londer, 1988). While the majority of those treated by exposure therapy for their obsessions improve, for those who do not, the antidepressant drug *clomipramine* has been extremely effective. █████████

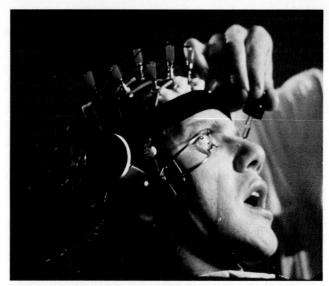

A Clockwork Orange

AVERSION THERAPY

These forms of exposure therapy help clients deal directly with stimuli that are not really harmful, but what can be done to help those who are *attracted* to stimuli that *are* harmful or illegal? Drug addiction, sexual perversions, and uncontrollable violence are human problems in which deviant behavior is elicited by tempting stimuli. **Aversion therapy** uses counterconditioning procedures of aversive learning to pair these stimuli with strong noxious stimuli (such as electric shocks or nausea-producing drugs). In time, through conditioning, the same negative reactions are elicited by the conditional tempting stimuli, and the person develops an aversion for them that replaces his or her former desire.

Aversion therapy for a client who is a *pedophile* (sexually attracted to children) might begin by having him watch slides of children and adults. When he gets aroused to the children's images, he gets an electric shock; when he sees adult slides or is told to imagine socially acceptable fantasies, the shock is extinguished. However, it is difficult for any form of therapy to modify long-standing sexual perversions that have vivid fantasy components that have been repeatedly reinforced with masturbation to orgasm (McConaghy, 1969).

In the extreme, aversion therapy resembles torture, so why would anyone submit voluntarily to it? Usually people do so only because they realize that the long-term consequences of continuing their behavior pattern will destroy their health or ruin their careers or family lives. They may also be coerced to do so by institutional pressures, as has happened in some prison treatment programs. Many critics are concerned that the painful procedures in aversion therapy give too much power to a therapist, can be more punitive than therapeutic, and are most likely to be used in situations where people have the least freedom of choice about what is done to them. The movie *A Clockwork Orange,* based on Anthony Burgess's novel, depicted aversion therapy as an extreme form of mind control in a police state. In recent years, use of aversion therapy in institutional rehabilitation programs has become more regulated by state laws and ethical guidelines for clinical treatment. The hope is that, under these restrictions, it will be a therapy of choice rather than coercion.

CONTINGENCY MANAGEMENT

The operant conditioning approach of **B. F. Skinner** to developing desirable behavior is simple: find the reinforcer that will maintain a desired response, apply that reinforcer (contingent upon the appropriate response), and evaluate its effectiveness. This positive approach has been used to modify behavior in the classroom, in mental hospitals, and in homes for the aged. The two major techniques of contingency management in behavior therapy are *positive reinforcement strategies* and specific *extinction strategies*.

Positive Reinforcement Strategies

When a response is followed immediately by a reward, the response will tend to be repeated and will increase in frequency over time. This central principle of operant learning becomes a therapeutic strategy when it is used to modify the frequency of emission of a desirable response in place of an undesirable one. Dramatic success has been obtained from the application of positive reinforcement procedures to the behavior problems of children with psychiatric disorders. Two examples were cited in Chapter 9: the case of shaping the behavior of the little boy who would not wear his glasses and the Premack principle of using running and screaming in a preschool as reinforcement for sitting still.

Positive reinforcement procedures have been extended to many other settings and problems. We described exposure therapy under counterconditioning procedures because it emerged out of systematic desensitization which clearly involves conditioning incompatible responses. However, what is the learning process that makes exposure therapy work? It is the positive reinforcement that comes from the praise of the therapist or the self-praise of the client upon making the desired response. Exposure therapy is clearly a form of contingency management.

Critics of contingency management therapies that use material rewards argue that they work best with those who are underprivileged in some way. Behavior therapists have generally agreed with this criticism, but they have wanted to maintain the obvious benefits of positive reinforcement systems. One resolution to the problem has been to involve individuals directly in their own contingency management. A **behavioral contract** is an explicit agreement (often in writing) that states the consequences of specific behaviors. Such contracts are often required by behavior therapists working with clients on obesity or smoking problems. The contract may specify what the client is expected to do (client's obligations) and what, in turn, the client can expect from the therapist (therapist's obligations).

Behavioral contracting facilitates therapy by making both parties responsible for achieving the agreed-upon changes in behavior. Treatment goals are spelled out as are the specific rewards corresponding to meeting planned responsibilities and reaching desired subgoals. The therapeutic situation becomes more structured in terms of what each party can reasonably expect as appropriate content and acceptable interpersonal behavior. The person with less status and power (patient or child, for example) benefits if a condition for third-party arbitration of alleged contract violation is included (Nelson & Mowrey, 1976). Some parents have found that contracts with their teenagers have generated acceptable behavior while greatly improving the emotional climate of the home. Reinforcements often include more reasonable parental behaviors (Stuart, 1971).

Extinction Strategies

Why do people continue to do something that causes pain and distress when they are capable of doing otherwise? The answer is that many forms of behavior have multiple consequences—some are negative and some are positive. Often, subtle positive reinforcements keep a behavior going despite its obvious negative consequences. For example, children who are punished for misbehaving may continue to misbehave if punishment is the only form of attention they seem to be able to earn.

Extinction is useful in therapy when dysfunctional behaviors have been maintained by unrecognized reinforcing circumstances. Those reinforcers can be identified through a careful situational analysis and then a program can be arranged to withhold them in the presence of the undesirable response. When this approach is possible, and everyone in the situation who might inadvertently reinforce the person's behavior cooperates, extinction procedures work to diminish the frequency of the behavior and eventually to eliminate the behavior completely.

Even psychotic behavior can be maintained and encouraged by unintentional reinforcement. It is standard procedure in many mental hospitals for the staff to ask patients frequently, as a form of social communication, how they are feeling. Patients often misinterpret this question as a request for diagnostic information, and they respond by thinking and talking about their feelings, unusual symptoms, and hallucinations. Such responding is likely to be counterproductive since it leads staff to conclude that the patients are self-absorbed and not behaving normally. In fact, the more bizarre the symptoms and verbalizations, the more attention the staff members may show to the patient, which reinforces continued expression of bizarre symptoms.

Just as positive reinforcement can increase the incidence of a behavior, *lack* of desirable consequences can decrease its incidence. Dramatic decreases in psychotic behavior sometimes have been observed when hospital staff members were simply instructed to ignore the psychotic behavior and to give attention to the patients only when they were behaving normally (Ayllon & Michael, 1959). With a *time-out from reinforcement,* the target behavior stops being followed by its usual consequence and should begin to extinguish.

SOCIAL-LEARNING THERAPY

The focus of behavior therapies has been expanded by social learning theorists who point out that humans learn—for better or worse—by observing the behavior of other people. Often we learn and apply rules to new experiences, not just through direct participation, but also through symbolic means, such as watching other people's experiences in life, in a movie, or on TV. **Social-learning therapy** is designed to modify problematic behavior patterns by arranging conditions in which the client will observe models being reinforced for the desirable form of responding. This vicarious learning process has been of special value in overcoming phobias and building social skills. We have noted in earlier chapters that this social learning approach was largely developed by the pioneering theorizing and empirical research of **Albert Bandura** (1977, 1986). We will only mention two aspects of his approach: imitation of models and social skills training.

Imitation of Models

When discussing phobias, we noted that one way such fears could be learned was through vicarious conditioning—through the transmission of fear displayed by others, such as from mother to child. An interesting series of studies with monkeys illustrates this imitation of modeled behavior.

> Young monkeys reared in the laboratory, where they never saw a snake, observed their parents, who had been raised in the wild, react fearfully to real snakes and toy snakes. In less than ten minutes, the young monkeys showed a strong fear of snakes, and, by the sixth modeling session, their fear was as intense as that of their parents. The more disturbed the parents were at the sight of the snakes, the greater the fear in their offspring (Mineka et al., 1984).
>
> In a follow-up study, young, laboratory-raised rhesus monkeys observed the fearful reactions of adult monkeys who were strangers to them. As can be seen in **Figure 18.1,** the young monkeys showed little fear initially in the pretest, but, after observing models reacting fearfully, they did also, both to the real and toy snakes. This fear persisted in intensity when measured three months later. However, the fear was less strong and showed more variation than that of the other young monkeys who had observed their own parents' fearful reactions (Cook et al., 1985).

Before desired responses can be reinforced, they must occur. Many new responses, especially complex

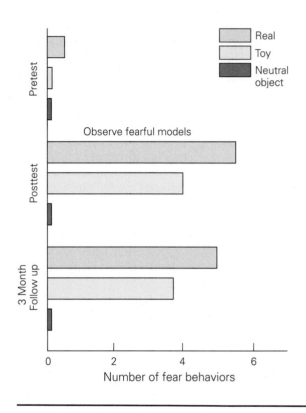

FIGURE 18.1 FEAR REACTIONS IN MONKEYS

After young laboratory-raised monkeys observe adult stranger monkeys showing a strong fear of snakes, they are vicariously conditioned to fear snakes with an intensity that persists over time.

ones, can be acquired more readily if a person can observe and imitate another person performing the desired behavior and be reinforced for doing so. If snake fears can be learned by observing such reactions, then it should be possible for people with snake phobias to unlearn them through imitation of models.

In treating a phobia of snakes, a therapist will first demonstrate fearless approach behavior at a relatively minor level, perhaps approaching a snake's cage or touching a snake. The client is aided, through demonstration and supportive encouragement, to imitate the modeled behavior. Gradually the approach behaviors are shaped so that the client can pick the snake up and let it crawl freely over him or her. At no time is the client forced to perform any behavior. Resistance at any level is overcome by having the client return to a previously successful, less threatening approach behavior.

The power of this form of **participant modeling** can be seen in research comparing the participant modeling technique just described with symbolic modeling, desensitization, and a control condition (see **Figure 18.2**). In *symbolic modeling therapy,* subjects who had been trained in relaxation techniques watched a film in which several models fearlessly handled snakes; the subjects could stop the film and relax themselves whenever a scene made them feel anxious. In the control condition, no therapeutic intervention was used. Participant modeling was clearly the most successful of these techniques. Snake phobia was eliminated in 11 of the 12 subjects in the participant modeling group (Bandura, 1970).

Social-skills Training

A major therapeutic innovation encouraged by social learning therapists involves training people with inadequate social skills to be more effective (Hersen & Bellack, 1976). Many difficulties arise for someone with a mental disorder, or even just an everyday problem, if he or she is socially inhibited, inept, or unassertive. *Social skills* are sets of responses that enable people to effectively achieve their social goals when approaching or interacting with others. These skills include knowing *what* (content) to say and do in given situations in order to elicit a desired response (consequences), *how* (style) to say and do it, and *when* (timing) to say and do it. One of the most common social

---

| FIGURE 18.2 | PARTICIPANT MODELING THERAPY |

The subject shown in the photo first watched a model make a graduated series of snake-approach responses and then repeated them herself. She eventually was able to pick up the snake and let it crawl about on her. The graph compares the number of approach responses subjects made before and after receiving participant modeling therapy with the behavior of those exposed to two other therapeutic techniques and a control group.

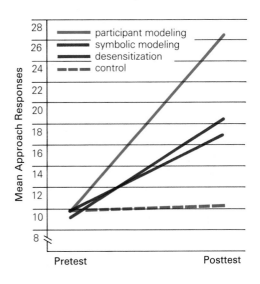

skill problems is lack of assertiveness—inability to state one's own thoughts or wishes in a clear, direct, non-aggressive manner (Bower & Bower, 1991). To help people overcome such a problem, many social learning therapists recommend **behavioral rehearsal**—visualizing how one should behave in a given situation and the desired positive consequences. Rehearsal can be used to establish and strengthen any basic skill, from personal hygiene to work habits to social interactions. Behavioral rehearsal procedures are being widely used in social skills training programs with many different populations (Yates, 1985).

Adult pathology has often been preceded by deficits in social skills in childhood (Oden & Asher, 1977). A considerable amount of research and therapy is currently directed at building competence in shy and withdrawn disturbed children (Conger & Keane, 1981; Zimbardo & Radl, 1981). One study demonstrated that preschool-age children diagnosed as *social isolates* could be helped to become sociable in a short training period.

Twenty-four subjects were randomly assigned to one of three play conditions: with a same-age peer, with a peer 1 to 1½ years younger, or with no partner (control condition). The pairs were brought together for ten play sessions, each only 20 minutes long, over a period of about a month. Their classroom behavior before and after this treatment was recorded, and it revealed that the intervention had a strong effect. The opportunity to play with a younger playmate doubled the frequency with which the former social isolates interacted later on with other classmates—bringing them up to the average level of the other children. Playing with a same-age peer also increased children's sociability, but not nearly so much. The researchers concluded that the one-on-one play situation had offered the shy children safe opportunities to be socially assertive. They were allowed to practice leadership skills that were likely to be approved by the nonthreatening, younger playmates (Furman et al., 1979).

In another study, social skills training with a group of hospitalized emotionally disturbed children changed both verbal and nonverbal components of their behavior in social settings. The children were taught to give appropriate verbal responses in various social situations (giving help or compliments, making requests). They were also taught to display appropriate affect (for example, to smile while giving a compliment) and to make eye contact and use proper body posture (face the person being talked to). These improved social skills were generalized to "untreated" situations outside of training. The children also put them into practice on their own when on the ward. These positive effects continued even months later (Matson et al., 1980).

GENERALIZATION TECHNIQUES

An ongoing issue of concern for behavior therapists is whether new behavior patterns generated in a therapeutic setting will actually be used in the everyday situations faced by their clients. This question is important for all therapies because any measure of treatment effectiveness must include maintenance of long-term changes that go beyond a therapist's couch, clinic, or laboratory.

When essential aspects of a client's real-life setting are absent from the therapy program, behaviors that have been modified by therapy can be expected to deteriorate over time after therapy terminates. To prevent this gradual loss, it is becoming common practice to build generalization techniques into the therapeutic procedure itself. These techniques attempt to *increase* the similarity of target behaviors, reinforcers, models, and stimulus demands between therapy and real-life settings. For example, behaviors are taught that are likely to be reinforced naturally in a person's environment, such as showing courtesy or consideration. Rewards are given on a partial reinforcement schedule to ensure that their effect will be maintained when rewards are not always forthcoming in the real world. Expectation of tangible extrinsic rewards is gradually *faded out* while social approval and more naturally occurring consequences, including reinforcing self-statements, are incorporated. Opportunities are provided for patients to practice new behaviors under the supportive guidance of staff members during field trips. Halfway houses also help to transfer new behaviors from the institution to the community setting (Fairweather et al., 1969; Orlando, 1981). Careful attention to ways of increasing the generalizability of treatment effects clearly enhances the long-term success of behavior therapy (Marks, 1981).

Before turning to cognitive therapies, take a few minutes to review the major differences between the two dominant psychotherapies outlined thus far—the psychoanalytic and the behavioral—as summarized in **Table 18.2.**

Issue	Psychoanalysis	Behavior Therapy
Basic human nature	Biological instincts, primarily sexual and aggressive, press for immediate release, bringing people into conflict with social reality.	Similar to other animals, people are born only with the capacity for learning, which follows similar principles in all species.
Normal human development	Growth occurs through resolution of conflicts during successive stages. Through identification and internalization, mature ego controls and character structures emerge.	Adaptive behaviors are learned through reinforcement and imitation.
Nature of psychopathology	Pathology reflects inadequate conflict resolutions and fixations in earlier development, which leave overly strong impulses and/or weak controls. Symptoms are defensive responses to anxiety.	Problematic behavior derives from faulty learning of maladaptive behaviors. The *symptom* is the problem; there is no *underlying disease*.
Goal of therapy	Psychosexual maturity, strengthened ego functions, and reduced control by unconscious and repressed impulses are attained.	Symptomatic behavior is eliminated and replaced with adaptive behaviors.
Psychological realm emphasized	Motives, feelings, fantasies, and cognitions are experienced.	Therapy involves behavior and observable feelings and actions.
Time orientation	The orientation is discovering and interpreting past conflicts and repressed feelings in light of the present.	There is little or no concern with early history or etiology. Present behavior is examined and treated.
Role of unconscious material	This is primary in classical psychoanalysis and somewhat less emphasized by neo-Freudians.	There is no concern with unconscious processes or with subjective experience even in the conscious realm.
Role of insight	Insight is central; it emerges in "corrective emotional experiences."	Insight is irrelevant and/or unnecessary.
Role of therapist	The therapist functions as a *detective,* searching basic root conflicts and resistances; detached and neutral, to facilitate transference reactions.	The therapist functions as a *trainer,* helping patients unlearn old behaviors and/or learn new ones. Control of reinforcement is important; interpersonal relationship is minor.

SUMMING UP

Behavior therapy rejects the medical model and views abnormal behavior as a set of learned responses that can be modified with principles of reinforcement and conditioning. Behavior modification attempts to apply these learning principles to problem behaviors in a systematic way. Counterconditioning includes systematic desensitization, implosion, flooding, exposure, and aversive learning. Systematic desensitization, developed by Wolpe, uses relaxation and graduated exposure to a feared stimuli to reduce phobic responses. Implosion and flooding are the opposite of systematic desensitization; they require the client to voluntarily confront the fearful stimulus as it is imagined or in the actual phobic setting. All these phobia modification therapies have in common the key element of exposure therapy, encouraging the client to seek exposure to the feared stimulus. Aversion therapy pairs tempting but destructive stimuli with negative unconditioned stimuli to weaken their attraction.

Contingency management uses operant conditioning to modify behavior. This conditioning primarily involves the introduction of positive reinforcement strategies and extinction strategies. Positive reinforcement increases the frequency of specific desirable responses, often with an explicit behavioral contract that outlines the goals, commitments, and responsibilities of client and therapist. Extinction strategies identify and eliminate rewards that perpetuate undesirable behavior.

Social learning therapy, developed by Bandura, uses imitation of models and social skills training to make individuals feel more confident about their abilities.

In all these therapies, generalization techniques are used to increase the carryover of therapeutic gains to clients' real-life settings. These techniques build into the therapy setting elements that will have similarity to the natural features of daily life.

COGNITIVE THERAPIES

Cognitive therapy attempts to change problem feelings and behaviors by changing the way a client thinks about significant life experiences. The underlying assumption of such therapy is that abnormal behavior patterns and emotional distress start with problems in *what* we think (cognitive content) and *how* we think (cognitive process). As cognitive psychology has become more prominent in all areas of psychology, therapies based on cognitive principles have proliferated. These therapies focus on different types of cognitive processes and different methods of cognitive restructuring. We discussed some of these approaches in Chapter 13 as ways to cope with stress and improve health. The two major forms of cognitive therapy involve cognitive behavior modification (including self-efficacy), and alteration of false belief systems (including rational-emotive therapy and cognitive therapy for depression).

COGNITIVE BEHAVIOR MODIFICATION

We are what we tell ourselves we can be, and we are guided by what we believe we ought to do. This is a starting assumption of **cognitive behavior modification.** This therapeutic approach combines the cognitive emphasis on the role of thoughts and attitudes in influencing motivation and response with the behaviorism focus on reinforcement contingencies in the modification of performance. Unacceptable behavior patterns are modified by changing a person's negative *self-statements* into constructive coping statements (as we saw in Chapter 13).

A critical part of this therapeutic approach is the discovery by therapist and client of the way the client thinks about and expresses the problem for which therapy is sought. Once both therapist and client understand the kind of thinking that is leading to unproductive or dysfunctional behaviors, they develop new self-statements that are constructive and minimize the use of self-defeating ones that elicit anxiety or reduce self-esteem (Meichenbaum, 1977). For example, they might substitute the negative self-statement "I was really boring at that party; they'll never ask me back" with constructive criticism: "Next time, if I want to appear interesting, I will plan some provocative opening lines, practice telling a good joke, and be responsive to the host's stories." Instead of dwelling on negatives in past situations that are unchangeable and part of past history, the client is taught to focus on positives in the future that can be realized.

Building *expectations of being effective* increases the likelihood of behaving effectively. It is through setting attainable goals, developing realistic strategies for attaining them, and evaluating feedback realistically that people develop a sense of mastery and *self-efficacy* (Bandura, 1986). **Figure 18.3** outlines the four major sources of efficacy expectations and the specific modes by which each of them is induced. For example, different types of modeling influence different efficacy sources, just as different types of desensitization do.

FIGURE 18.3   EFFICACY EXPECTATIONS

According to Bandura (1989), each of the four major sources of efficacy information that an individual can utilize has a specific mode of treatment that operates to induce it.

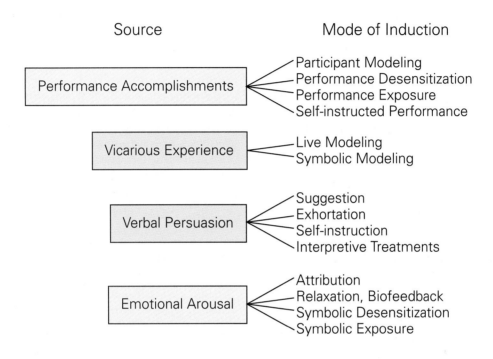

Source   Mode of Induction

Performance Accomplishments
- Participant Modeling
- Performance Desensitization
- Performance Exposure
- Self-instructed Performance

Vicarious Experience
- Live Modeling
- Symbolic Modeling

Verbal Persuasion
- Suggestion
- Exhortation
- Self-instruction
- Interpretive Treatments

Emotional Arousal
- Attribution
- Relaxation, Biofeedback
- Symbolic Desensitization
- Symbolic Exposure

CHANGING FALSE BELIEFS

Some cognitive behavior therapists emphasize the important role of thoughts but still maintain many behavioral assumptions—such as the rewarding or punishing function of thoughts. Other cognitive therapists put less emphasis on behavioral processes. Their primary targets for change are beliefs, attitudes, and habitual thought patterns, or schemas. These cognitive therapists argue that many psychological problems arise because of the way we think about ourselves in relation to other people and the events we face. Faulty thinking can be based on (a) unreasonable attitudes ("Being perfect is the most important trait for a student to have"), (b) false premises ("If I do everything they want me to, then I'll be popular"), and (c) rigid rules that put behavior on automatic pilot so that prior patterns are repeated even

when they have not worked ("I must obey authorities"). Emotional distress is believed to be caused by misunderstandings and by failure to distinguish between current reality and one's imagination (or expectations).

Cognitive Therapy for Depression

A cognitive therapist induces a patient to correct faulty patterns of thinking by applying more effective problem-solving techniques. **Aaron Beck** has successfully pioneered cognitive therapy for the problem of depression. He states the formula for treatment in simple form: "The therapist helps the patient to identify his warped thinking and to learn more realistic ways to formulate his experiences" (1976, p. 20). For example, depressed individuals may be instructed to write down negative thoughts about themselves, figure out why these self-criticisms are unjustified, and come up with more realistic (and less destructive) self-cognitions.

Beck believes that depression is maintained because depressed patients are unaware of the negative automatic thoughts that they habitually say to themselves, such as "I will never be as good as my brother"; "Nobody would like me if they really knew me"; and "I'm not smart enough to make it in this competitive school." A therapist then uses four tactics to change the cognitive foundation that supports the depression: (a) evaluating the evidence the patient has for and against these automatic thoughts; (b) reattributing blame to situational factors rather than to the patient's incompetence; (c) openly discussing alternative solutions to the problem; and (d) challenging basic assumptions (Beck et al., 1979). This therapy is similar to behavior therapies in that it centers on the present state of the client.

One of the worst side-effects of being depressed is having to live with all the negative feelings and lethargy associated with depression. One aspect of new therapeutic approaches deals with depression's downward spiral by directing the client in ways not to become further depressed about depression itself (Teasdale, 1985). Becoming obsessed with thoughts about one's negative mood cues memories of all the bad times in life, which further worsens the depressive feelings. By filtering all input through a darkly colored lens of depression, depressed people see criticism where there is none and hear sarcasm when they listen to praise—further "reasons" for being depressed (Diamond, 1989).

Rational-Emotive Therapy

One of the earliest forms of cognitive therapy was the **rational-emotive therapy** (RET) developed by **Albert Ellis** (1962, 1977). RET is a comprehensive system of personality change based on transforming irrational beliefs that are causing undesirable, highly charged emotional reactions, such as severe anxiety. Clients may have core values *demanding* that they succeed and be approved, *insisting* that they be treated fairly, and *dictating* that the universe be more pleasant. A therapist teaches clients how to recognize the "shoulds," "oughts," and "musts" that are controlling their actions and preventing them from choosing the lives they want.

A therapist attempts to break through a client's closed-mindedness by showing that an emotional reaction that follows some event is really the effect of unrecognized beliefs about the event. For example, failure to achieve orgasm during intercourse (event) is followed by an emotional reaction of depression and self-derogation. The belief that is causing the emotional reaction is likely to be "I am sexually inadequate and may be impotent or frigid because I failed to perform as expected." This belief (and others) is openly disputed through rational confrontation and examination of alternative reasons for the event, such as fatigue, too much alcohol, false notions of sexual performance, or not wanting to engage in intercourse at that time, or with that particular partner. This technique is followed by a variety of others—those used in behavior modification, humor, and role-playing to replace dogmatic, irrational thinking with rational, situationally appropriate ideas.

Rational-emotive therapy aims to increase an individual's sense of self-worth and the potential to be self-actualized by getting rid of the system of faulty beliefs that block personal growth. As such, it shares much with humanistic therapies, which we consider next.

SUMMING UP

Cognitive therapy seeks to change a person's behavior by affecting nonproductive, negative, or irrational thought patterns about oneself and social relationships. The principles of cognitive behavior modification involve discovering how the client thinks about a problem, learning more constructive thought patterns, and applying these new techniques to other situations. In many cases, the goal is to change false beliefs that a client has internalized about him- or herself or about how the world operates.

Two popular types of cognitive therapy have been devised by Aaron Beck and Albert Ellis. Beck uses his therapy to treat depression by getting the client to reality test, reattribute blame appropriately, discuss alternative solutions, and challenge false assumptions. Ellis uses rational-emotive therapy to help clients recognize their irrational beliefs that prevent them from living the lives they want.

EXISTENTIAL-HUMANIST THERAPIES

Among the primary symptoms for which many college students seek therapy are general dissatisfaction, feelings of alienation, and failure to achieve all they feel they should. Problems in everyday living, the lack of meaningful human relationships, and the absence of significant goals to strive for are common *existential crises* according to proponents of humanist and existentialist perspectives on human nature. These orientations have been combined to form a general type of therapy addressing the basic problems of existence common to all human beings.

The *humanistic movement* has been called a "third force in psychology" because it grew out of a reaction to the two dominant forces with a pessimistic view of human nature: early psychoanalytic theory and the mechanistic view offered by early radical behaviorism. At the time the humanistic movement was forming in the United States, similar viewpoints, which came to be known collectively as *existentialism,* had already gained acceptance in Europe. One of the first American therapists to embrace existentialism was **Rollo May** (1950; 1969; 1972) whose popular books and therapy are designed to combat feelings of emptiness, anomie, and cynicism by emphasizing basic human values, such as love, creativity, and free will.

At the core of both humanistic and existential therapies is the concept of a whole person in the continual process of changing and of becoming. Although environment and heredity place certain restrictions on the process of becoming, we always remain free to choose what we will become by creating our own values and committing ourselves to them through our decisions. Along with this *freedom to choose,* however, comes the burden of responsibility. Since we are never fully aware of all the implications of our actions, we experience anxiety and despair. We also suffer from guilt over lost opportunities to achieve our full potential.

Psychotherapies that apply the principles of this general theory of human nature attempt to help clients define their own freedom, value their experiencing selves and the richness of the present moment, cultivate their individuality, and discover ways of realizing their fullest potential (self-actualization). Of importance in the existential perspective is the current life situation as experienced by the person—the *phenomenological view.*

PERSON-CENTERED THERAPY

As developed by **Carl Rogers** (1951; 1977), *person-centered therapy* has had a significant impact on the way many different kinds of therapists define their relationships to their clients. The primary goal of **person-centered therapy** is promoting the healthy psychological growth of the individual.

The approach begins with the assumption that all people share the basic tendency to self-actualize; that is, to realize one's potential. Rogers believed that "It is the inherent tendency of the organism to develop all its capacities in ways which seem to maintain or enhance the organism" (1959, p. 196). Healthy development is hindered by faulty learning patterns in which

Carl Rogers (*Discovering Psychology,* 1990, Program 15)

a person accepts the evaluation of others in place of those provided by his or her own mind and body. A conflict between one's naturally positive self-image and negative external criticisms creates anxiety and unhappiness. This conflict, or *incongruence,* may function outside of one's awareness so that a person experiences feelings of unhappiness and low self-worth without knowing why.

The task of Rogerian therapy is to create a therapeutic environment that allows a client to learn how to behave in order to achieve self-enhancement and self-actualization. Because people are assumed to be basically good, the therapist's task is mainly to help remove barriers that limit the expression of this natural positive tendency. The basic therapeutic strategy is to recognize, accept, and clarify a client's feelings. This is accomplished within an atmosphere of *unconditional positive regard*—nonjudgmental acceptance and respect for the client, with no strings attached and no performance evaluations. The therapist allows his or her own feelings and thoughts to be transparent to the client. In addition to maintaining this *genuineness,* the therapist tries to experience the client's feelings. Such total empathy requires that the therapist care for the client as a worthy, competent individual—not to be judged or evaluated but to be assisted in discovering his or her individuality (Meador & Rogers, 1979).

The emotional style and attitude of the therapist is instrumental in *empowering* the client to attend once again to the true sources of personal conflict and to begin to remove the distracting influences that suppress self-actualization. Unlike practitioners of other therapies who interpret, give answers, or instruct, the client-centered therapist is a supportive listener who reflects and, at times, restates the client's evaluative statements and feelings. Person-centered therapy strives to be *nondirective* by having the therapist merely facilitate the patient's search for self-awareness and self-acceptance and never to direct it.

Rogers believes that, once freed to relate to others openly and to accept themselves, individuals have the potential to lead themselves back to psychological health. This optimistic view and the humane relationship between therapist-as-caring-expert and client-as-person has influenced many practitioners (Smith, 1982).

HUMAN-POTENTIAL MOVEMENT

The **human-potential movement,** which emerged in the United States in the late 1960s, encompasses practices and methods that release the potential of the average human being for greater levels of performance and greater richness of experience. The seeds of the movement were sown in the general perspective of the existential-humanist therapies. Therapy for growth, personal enrichment, increased interpersonal sensitivity, and greater joy in sex is the modern offspring of existential and humanistic views of human nature.

Through this movement, therapy originally intended for the mentally disturbed has been extended to normal people who want to be more effective, more productive, and happier human beings. Therapy has also spilled out of the confines of therapists' offices into the popular culture through large group activities in which hundreds of people are brought together for intensive weekend encounter sessions. Although these brief, relatively impersonal sessions can help many people, they must be viewed with caution since they involve no systematic follow-up through which facilitators can learn about and deal with any adverse reactions of individual participants.

GROUP THERAPIES

All the treatment approaches outlined thus far are primarily designed as one-on-one relationships between a patient or client and a therapist. There are, however, many reasons that therapy in groups has begun to flourish and may even be more effective that individual therapy in some cases (Rosenbaum & Berger, 1975). The advantages of group therapy are that it (a) is less expensive to participants; (b) helps to make limited mental health personnel available more widely; (c) is a less-threatening power situation for many people who have problems with solo dealings with authority; (d) allows powerful group processes to be used to influence individual maladaptive behavior; and (e) provides opportunity to observe and practice interpersonal skills within the therapy session.

The use of group processes as a medium for personal change is common to an extraordinarily diverse range of groups with varied goals and philosophies. Some estimates put the number of Americans who have participated in some form of encounter group for personal growth at over five million. Untold others participate in self-help groups, such as those for weight reduction, alcoholism, and consciousness raising about male violence or homosexuality. Many people are involved in more formal varieties of group psychotherapy that share some of the basic views of the humanist and existentialist approaches (Lieberman, 1977).

Some of the basic premises of group therapies differ from those of individual therapy. The social setting of group therapies provides an opportunity to learn how one comes across to others; how the self-image that is projected differs from the one that is intended or personally experienced. In addition, the group provides confirmation that one's symptoms, problems, and "deviant" reactions are not unique but often are quite common. Because we tend to conceal from others the negatives about ourselves, it is possible for many people with the same problem to believe "It's only me." The shared group experience can help to dispel this pluralistic ignorance in which many share the same false belief about their unique failings. In addition, the group of peers can provide social support outside of the therapy setting, as the members of Alcoholics Anonymous do in virtually any city an individual member visits.

What variables seem to account for the curative value of group therapy? Some of the general variables

Group therapy can be designed to accommodate a variety of goals.

are feelings of belonging and acceptance; opportunities to observe, imitate, and be socially rewarded; the chance to experience the universality of human problems, weaknesses, and strengths; and the experience of recreating analogues of the primary family group, which enables corrective emotional experiences to take place (Klein, 1983).

Gestalt Therapy

Gestalt therapy focuses on ways to unite mind and body to make a person whole (recall the Gestalt school of perception described in Chapter 8). Its goal of self-awareness is reached by helping participants express pent-up feelings in a group and to recognize unfinished business from past conflicts that is carried into new relationships and must be finished for growth to proceed. **Fritz Perls** (1969), the originator of Gestalt therapy, asked participants to act out fantasies concerning conflicts and strong feelings and also to recreate their dreams, which were seen as repressed parts of personality. Perls said, "We have to *re-own* these projected, fragmented parts of our personality, and re-own the hidden potential that appears in the dream" (1967, p. 67). In Gestalt therapy workshops, therapists borrow from Zen teachings a temporal focus so that the client is aware of emerging feelings, attitudes, and actions. Also, similar to some Eastern philosophies, Gestalt therapy uses paradox to instruct: "Change is possible only when we accept who we are at the moment, and awareness is itself the cure" (Thompson, 1988).

Community Support Groups

The most dramatic development in therapy has been the surge of interest and participation in self-help groups. It is estimated that there are 500,000 such groups, which are attended by 15 million Americans every week (Leerhessen, 1990). These support group sessions are typically free, especially when they are not directed by a health care professional, and they give people a chance to meet others with the same problems who are surviving and sometimes thriving. The self-help concept applied to community group settings was pioneered by Alcoholics Anonymous, but it was the women's consciousness-raising movement of the 1960s that helped to extend self-help beyond the arena of alcoholism. Now, support groups deal with four basic categories of problems: addictive behavior problems, physical and mental disorders, life transition or other crises, and the traumas of friends or relatives of those with specific types of problems. Virtually every community now has a self-help clearinghouse you can phone to find out where and when a local group that addresses a given problem meets (the National Self-Help Clearinghouse number is 212-642-2944).

A valuable development in group therapy is the application of psychological group therapy techniques to the situations of terminally ill patients. The goals of such therapy are to help patients and their families live lives as fulfilling as possible during their illnesses; to cope realistically with impending death; and to adjust to the terminal illness (Adams, 1979; Yalom & Greaves,

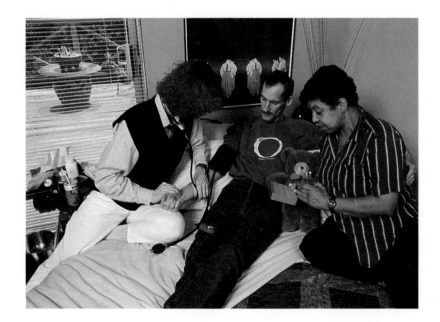

Home care and outpatient programs must absorb the caseload of people with AIDS. Hospice workers visit patients at home, giving them physical and emotional support. Many hospitals and clinics now offer group therapy for these patients.

It is estimated that in the United States there are 500,000 self-help groups attended by 15 million people every week (Leerhessen, 1990).

1977). One general focus of such support groups for the terminally ill is helping them learn "how to live fully until you say goodbye" (Nungessor, 1990).

Objective evidence for the psychological benefit of supportive group intervention for terminally ill patients was demonstrated in a controlled experiment by David Spiegel and his associates (1981) with women who had metastatic (spreading) cancer of the breast.

A large group of women patients with breast cancer were randomly assigned to a control or year-long treatment program of weekly supportive group meetings. The groups focused on facing the problems of terminal illness; improving relationships with family, friends, and staff; and living as fully as possible in the face of death. Evaluations conducted at four-month intervals revealed that the treatment group members were less anxious, confused, fatigued, and fearful than the controls. Their moods were significantly less distressed, and they showed fewer maladaptive coping responses. Later follow-ups showed that the women who were part of the group therapy program lived significantly longer than those in the control group (Spiegel et al., 1989).

MARITAL AND FAMILY THERAPY

Much group therapy consists of strangers coming together periodically to form temporary associations from which they may benefit. However, some people having problems with spouses or family members need to ad-dress the issues directly with them. Therapy for couples and for families is expanding in scope and influence throughout the United States.

Couples counseling for marital problems seeks to clarify the typical communication patterns of the partners and then to improve the quality of their interaction. By seeing a couple together, and often videotaping and playing back their interactions, a therapist can help them appreciate the verbal and nonverbal styles they use to dominate, control, or confuse each other. Each party is taught how to reinforce desirable responding in the other and withdraw reinforcement for undesirable reactions; they are also taught nondirective listening skills to help the other person clarify and express feelings and ideas. Couples therapy is more effective in resolving marital problems than is individual therapy for only one partner, and it has been shown to reduce marital crises and keep marriages intact (Cookerly, 1980; Gurman & Kniskern, 1978).

In *family therapy,* the client is a whole nuclear family, and each family member is treated as a member of a *system* of relationships. A family therapist works with troubled family members to help them perceive what is creating problems for one or more of them. The focus is on altering the *psychological spaces* between people and the interpersonal dynamics of people acting as a unit, rather than on changing processes within maladjusted individuals (Foley, 1979). This therapy considers the *synergy,* or power, of the group as its members interact and stimulate each other, which is absent in solitary individuals.

Family therapy can reduce tensions within a family and improve the functioning of individual members by helping clients recognize the positives as well as the negatives in their relationships. **Virginia Satir** (1967), one of the innovative developers of family therapy approaches, notes that the family therapist plays many roles, acting as an interpreter and clarifier of the interactions that are taking place in the therapy session and as influence agent, mediator, and referee. Most family therapists assume that the problems brought into therapy represent *situational* difficulties between people or problems of social interaction rather than *dispositional* aspects of an individual. These difficulties may develop over time as members are forced into or accept unsatisfying roles. Nonproductive communication patterns may be set up in response to natural transitions in a family situation—loss of a job, a child's going to school, dating, getting married, or having a baby.

In a *structured family therapy* approach, the family is seen as the system that is creating disturbances in the individuals rather than the other way around (Minuchin, 1974). The therapist focuses on the way the family interacts in the present in order to understand its organizational structure, power hierarchy, channels of communication, and who gives and gets blame for what goes wrong. Similar to a consultant to an organization, a family therapist actively (but not always directly) tries to help the family reorganize its structure and function better to meet the needs of its members and the demands imposed on it. Family therapists are also concerned with aiding in the harmonious role relationships between generations within a family, as in the case of grandparents and their grandchildren whose parents have divorced (see Nichols, 1984).

SUMMING UP

Existential-humanist therapies focus on the process of becoming more fully self-actualized. Client-centered therapy, developed by Carl Rogers, emphasizes the therapists' unconditional positive regard for the client. The therapist strives to be genuine and nondirective in helping the client to establish congruence between naturally positive self-image and external criticisms. The third force of humanist therapy began in the United States in the 1960s as a reaction against the negative view of human nature of early psychoanalytic and behaviorist therapies. The human potential movement includes group therapies that use the social setting to practice interpersonal skills. A revolution in group therapy is occurring with the explosion of community self-help groups. Group therapy can also be used as on-line social support, for example, with terminally ill patients. Gestalt therapy, developed by Fritz Perls, attempts to combine body and mind to make a person be more whole and able to experience the present moment. In marital and family therapy the unit of analysis is no longer the individual but a distressed couple or an entire nuclear family. These therapies focus on situational difficulties and interpersonal dynamics that the couple or group can work to change or minimize instead of directing treatment efforts toward problematic dispositional tendencies of the individuals in the couple or group.

BIOMEDICAL THERAPIES

The ecology of the mind is held in delicate balance. It can be upset by mishaps in the workings of our genes, hormones, enzymes, and metabolism. Behavior, thinking, and affect (emotional tone) are end-products of brain mechanisms. When something goes wrong with the brain, we see the consequences in abnormal patterns of behavior and peculiar cognitive and emotional reactions. Similarly, environmental, social, or behavioral disturbances, such as certain kinds of pollution, drugs, and violence, can alter brain chemistry.

One approach to correcting these wrongs has been to change the functioning of the brains of disturbed people. This change has been accomplished by means of surgically destroying specific areas in the brain or by administering electroshock of sufficient intensity to cause a temporary coma and, presumably, disruption of the brain's own electrical activity.

Newer interventions have been guided by research discoveries from many fields of neuroscience. The most dramatic modern therapeutic approach emerging from this research is *chemotherapy*—the use of drugs that alter mood and mental states—for a range of mental disorders. In addition, a growing awareness of the genetic involvement in certain kinds of mental disorders is likely to encourage applications of genetic engineering to making direct alterations in genes identified as causally linked to particular mental disorders.

Biomedical therapies treat mental disorders as "hardware problems" in the brain and in the nervous, hormonal, and endocrine systems. They emerge from a medical model of abnormal mental functioning that assumes an organic basis for mental illnesses and treats schizophrenia as a disease.

In medieval times, those suffering from madness might have been treated by cutting "the stone of folly" from their brains.

PSYCHOSURGERY AND ELECTROCONVULSIVE THERAPY

The headline in the *Los Angeles Times* read, "Bullet in the Brain Cures Man's Mental Problem" (2/23/1988). The article revealed that a 19-year-old man suffering from severe obsessive-compulsive disorder had shot a .22 caliber bullet through the front of his brain in a suicide attempt. Remarkably, he survived, his pathological symptoms were cured, and his intellectual capacity was not affected, although some of the underlying causes of his problems remained.

This case illustrates the potential effects of one of the most direct biomedical therapies: intervention in the brain. Such intervention involves lesioning connections between parts of the brain, removing small sections of the brain, and subjecting the whole brain to intensive electrical stimulation. These therapies are often considered methods of last resort to treat psychopathologies that have proven intractable to other, less extreme forms of therapy. There is an ongoing, heated controversy about their usefulness and their side-effects.

Psychosurgery is the general term for surgical procedures performed on brain tissue to alleviate psychological disorders. In medieval times, psychosurgery involved "cutting the stone of folly" from the brains of those suffering from madness, as shown vividly in many engravings and paintings from that era.

Modern psychosurgical procedures include severing the fibers of the corpus callosum to reduce violent seizures of epilepsy, as we saw in Chapter 4; severing pathways that mediate limbic system activity (amygdalotomy); and prefrontal lobotomy. The best-known, and most frequently used, form of psychosurgery is the **prefrontal lobotomy,** an operation that severs the white-matter nerve fibers connecting the frontal lobes of the brain with the diencephalon, especially those fibers of the thalamic and hypothalamic areas. The procedure was developed by neurologist **Egas Moniz** who, in 1949, won a Nobel Prize for this treatment which seemed to transform the functioning of mental patients.

The ideal candidates for lobotomy were agitated schizophrenic patients and patients who were compulsive and anxiety ridden. The effects of this psychosurgery were dramatic: a new personality without intense emotional arousal and, thus, without overwhelming anxiety, guilt, or anger emerged. In part, this positive effect occurred because the operation disconnected present functioning from memory for past traumas and conflicts and also from future concerns. However, the operation permanently destroyed basic aspects of human nature. Lobotomized patients lost something special: their unique personality. Specifically, the lobotomy resulted in inability to plan ahead, indifference to the opinions of others, childlike actions, and the intellectual and emotional flatness of a person without a coherent sense of self. (One of Moniz's own patients was so distressed by these unexpected consequences that she shot him, partially paralyzing him.) Because the effects of psychosurgery are permanent, its negative effects severe and common, and its positive results less certain, its continued use is limited to special cases (Valenstein, 1980).

Electroconvulsive therapy (ECT) is the use of electroconvulsive shock for certain psychiatric disorders. It is designed to produce a temporary upheaval in the central nervous system, scrambling the brain's own electrical circuits. The technique consists of applying weak electric current (20–30 milliamps) to a patient's temples for a fraction of a second until a *grand mal seizure* occurs (loss of consciousness and strong bodily convulsions, followed by a brief comalike sleep). Patients are prepared for this traumatic intervention by sedation with a short-acting barbiturate and muscle relaxant which minimize the violent physical reactions (Malitz & Sackheim, 1984).

ECT produces temporary disorientation and a variety of memory deficits, most of which are permanent. After a typical series of ECT treatments (every other day), some patients are calmer and more susceptible to psychotherapy when it is available. Today, ECT is often administered to only one side of the brain—the nondominant hemisphere—so as to reduce the possibility of speech impairment. Such unilateral ECT is reported to be an effective antidepressant (Scovern & Kilmann, 1980).

The effects of ECT were initially hailed as unparalleled in the history of psychiatry. ECT has been especially effective in cases of severe depression; but no one knows exactly why it works. It may increase available norepinephrine and other neurotransmitters, or induce a strong psychological reaction, such as determination to avoid another treatment or feeling sufficiently punished to get rid of guilt over an imagined wrong (Fink, 1979). Because the technique involves so many physical reactions, it is unlikely that a single key ingredient can be isolated (Squire, 1986).

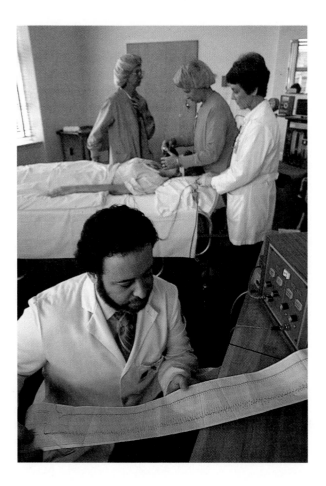

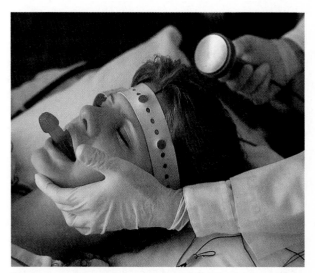

Electroconvulsive therapy has been effective in cases of severe depression. However, there is considerable controversy about its therapeutic value.

In 1985, a National Institutes of Health panel concluded that ECT "is demonstrably effective for a narrow range of severe psychiatric disorders" that include depression, mania, and some schizophrenias. ECT is often used as emergency treatment for suicidal or severely malnourished, depressed patients and for depressed patients who do not respond to antidepressant drugs or can't tolerate their side effects. It is effective with patients who have had a recent onset of symptoms; but, while it reduces some of the bizarre symptoms of schizophrenia such as catatonic posturing, it does not change the problems of cognitive processing that seem central to schizophrenic pathology (Salzman, 1980).

There are many critics of this extreme form of biomedical therapy, especially of its uncontrolled and unwarranted use in many large, understaffed mental institutions where it may be used simply to make patients docile and manageable or as a punishment (Breggin, 1979). The side effects may include impaired language and memory functioning in some patients as well as loss of self-esteem from not being able to recall important personal information or perform routine tasks. With extensive ECT treatments, signs of personality deterioration may appear. Even today, the debate continues between those who argue it is dramatically effective and opponents who claim its many faults outweigh its limited utility (Diamond, 1989).

In 1982, the citizens of Berkeley, California, voted to ban the use of electroconvulsive shock in any of their community mental health facilities. Though the action was later overturned on legal grounds, it exemplifies the public's ability to organize an effective protest against an established form of treatment for mental disorders. In part, this opposition by patients'-rights advocates underscored a theme in Ken Kesey's *One Flew Over the Cuckoo's Nest* (1962): be wary of any "therapy" that might be a disguised form of institutional suppression of dissent. Critics worry that ECT may again become overly and capriciously prescribed because it is such a cost-effective procedure for mental hospitals (Frank, 1978; Squire, 1988).

CHEMOTHERAPY

In the history of the treatment of mental disorder, nothing has ever rivaled the revolution created by the discovery of drugs that could calm anxious patients, restore contact with reality in withdrawn patients, and suppress hallucinations in psychotic patients. This new therapeutic era began in 1953 with the introduction of tranquilizing drugs, notably *chlorpromazine* (the U.S. brand name is *Thorazine*), into mental hospital treatment programs.

Chemotherapy is any form of therapy that treats mental and behavioral disorders with drugs and chemicals. The scientific field of psychopharmacology gained almost instant recognition and status as an effective therapy for transforming patient behavior. With chemotherapy, unruly, assaultive patients became cooperative, calm, and sociable. People absorbed in their delusions and hallucinations began to be responsive to the physical and social environment around them. No longer did mental hospital staff have to act as guards, putting patients in seclusion or straitjackets; staff morale improved as rehabilitation replaced mere custodial care of the mentally ill (Swazey, 1974).

Another profound effect of the chemotherapy revolution was its impact on the nation's mental hospital population. Over half a million Americans were living in mental institutions in 1955, staying an average of several years. The introduction of chlorpromazine and other drugs reversed the steadily increasing numbers of patients. By the early 1970s, it was estimated that less than half the country's mental patients actually resided in mental hospitals; those who did were institutionalized for an average of only a few months.

Those who benefited most from psychopharmacology were younger patients suffering from acute, rather than chronic, psychoses and who had recent, few, and short periods of institutionalization. Older, chronic patients who had been hospitalized for more than five years were not affected as much by chemotherapy, but it still reduced their hallucinations and delusions.

Three major categories of drugs are used today in chemotherapy programs: *antipsychotic, antidepressant,* and *antianxiety* compounds. As their names suggest, these drugs chemically alter specific brain functions that are responsible for psychotic symptoms, depression, and extreme anxiety, respectively.

Antipsychotic Drugs

Antipsychotic drugs alter the psychotic symptoms of delusions, hallucinations, social withdrawal, and occasional agitation. Chlorpromazine, derived from the compound *phenothiazine,* is an antipsychotic drug. Patients treated with such drugs become calm and tranquil but remain alert. Many of these patients are then able for the first time to be treated with psychotherapy.

There are several negative side effects of long-term administration of antipsychotic drugs. *Tardive dyskinesia* is an unusual disturbance of motor control, especially of the facial muscles, caused by antipsychotic drugs. *Agranulocytosis,* a rare blood disease, develops in two percent of patients treated with *Clopazine,* an antipsychotic drug that, in some cases, controls the negative symptoms of schizophrenia.

Antidepressant Drugs

The two basic antidepressants are the *tricyclics,* such as *Tofranil* and *Elavil,* and the *monoamine oxidase (MAO) inhibitors.* A third generation, which consists mostly of tetracyclics but appears to have fewer side effects than earlier variations, is now being used.

One of these third generation antidepressants is *Prozac,* touted as the new miracle drug whose therapeutic effects are more potent than its competitors. With an estimated 15 million Americans suffering from clinical depression and physicians writing or renewing 650,000 Prozac prescriptions every month, sales of this drug alone exceed $500 million and are expected to top $1 billion by 1995 (Cowley, 1990).

Another remarkable chemical is *Lithium salt,* the extract of a rock, which can influence the uniquely subtle property of mind that regulates mood. It has proven effective in the treatment of manic disorders. People who experience uncontrollable periods of hyperexcitement, when their energy seems limitless and their behavior extravagant and flamboyant, are brought down from their state of manic excess by doses of lithium. Up to eight of every ten manic patients treated with lithium have a good chance of recovery even when other treatments have previously failed (NIMH, 1977). Furthermore, regular maintenance doses of lithium can help break the cycle of recurring episodes of mania and/or depression. Lithium also allows a person to be alert and creative (Ehrlich & Diamond, 1980).

Antianxiety Drugs

To cope with everyday hassles, untold millions of Americans take pills to reduce tension and suppress anxiety. In general, these antianxiety drugs work by sedating the user.

There are three classes of such antianxiety compounds: *barbiturates, propanediols,* and *benzodiazepines.* Barbiturates have a general relaxing effect, but they can be dangerous if taken in excess or in combination with alcohol. Propanediol drugs, such as *Miltown* and *Equanil,* reduce the tension that accompanies agitated anxiety. Benzodiazepine drugs, such as *Valium* and *Librium,* are effective in reducing generalized fears and anxiety without affecting a person's ability to pay attention or process information. A new class of antianxiety drugs, such as *busparin,* appears to have fewer negative side effects than other antianxiety drugs.

Caution: Your Brain on "Good" Drugs

Because these tranquilizers work so well, it is easy to become psychologically dependent on them or physically addicted to them. Many people are coping chemically with conflicts or sources of emotional distress rather than confronting their problems, trying to solve them, or accepting pain and grief as part of the human experience.

Since 1975, when Valium was the most frequently prescribed drug in the United States, its sales have fallen somewhat, but the eight to nine million Americans who still take doses of Valium every day make it the nation's most popular tranquilizer. Valium has a high *abuse potential* and is being overly relied upon to handle the emotional chores of modern life. Critics point to it as the symbol of the "pill-for-anything-that-ails-you" mentality that is actively promoted by drug companies who make billions of dollars in profit from sales. These critics argue that it is self-defeating for people to believe that pills control their stress rather than their own actions. Unfortunately, drug therapy is often given in place of, and not as an adjunct to, the psychotherapy a person may need to learn how to cope effectively with life's recurring hassles.

Here are some *cautions* about tranquilizers, the drugs that students are most likely to take: Benzodiazepines should not be taken to relieve anxieties that are part of the ordinary stresses of everyday life. When used for extreme anxiety, they should not be taken for more than four months at a time, and their dosage should be gradually reduced by a physician. Abrupt cessation can lead to *withdrawal symptoms,* such as convulsions, tremors, and abdominal and muscle cramps. Because these drugs depress the central nervous system, they can impair driving, operating machinery, and tasks that require alertness (such as studying or taking exams). In combination with alcohol (also a central nervous system depressant) or with sleeping pills, benzodiazepines can lead to unconsciousness and even death (Hecht, 1986).

SUMMING UP

Biomedical therapies try to change directly the physiological aspects of mental illness. These therapies now rely primarily on a range of psychoactive drugs to alleviate the pathological symptoms of behavioral and mental disorders. However, they do not cure the disorder. Psychosurgery, such as the prefrontal lobotomy, once a popular medical treatment, is used infrequently because of the irreversible nature of its negative side effects. Electroconvulsive therapy is undergoing a resurgence of use for severely depressed patients; current techniques are neither as aversive nor have the same kinds of negative consequences as earlier forms. However, both psychosurgery and electroconvulsive therapy are still controversial, extreme treatments for a select class of disorders.

Chemotherapy includes antipsychotic medication for schizophrenics. Antidepressants, such as tricyclics and MAO inhibitors, are used to chemically control depression. Lithium is used to treat bipolar mental disorders. Antianxiety medication is used to reduce tension and sometimes to promote sleep. Antianxiety drugs include barbiturates, propanediols, and benzodiazepines. Such medication is particularly susceptible to abuse because it is readily prescribed, is self-administered, and has calming, reinforcing effects for millions of normal people suffering from the ordinary stress of living.

 ## DOES THERAPY WORK?

Do these therapies work? The answer is not easily discerned, and the methodological issues involved in evaluating therapeutic success are complex and not fully agreed upon by researchers and clinicians.

Time out for a *critical thinking exercise:* Imagine you were hired to collect data to answer the question, "Does college education work?" Where would you begin, how many different ways are there to reframe your task, and how might you be criticized for collecting the wrong data? Now consider your exercise in light of the question, "Do these therapies work?"

Many conceptual and practical issues and problems plague attempts to assess whether any given therapy is effective or is more effective than other forms of treatment. For example, if we restrict the evaluation of therapy to just one of the hundreds of types of mental disorders, say depression, it still is complex. One expert notes that "there may be a dozen kinds of depression . . . it's not one disorder, like measles . . . and it's carried within the person's personality or within their character. The treatment for depression for one person may look quite different from the effective treatment of depression with another. So it depends on the person as well as the disorder that they're suffering from" (Coyne, 1990; *Discovering Psychology,* Program 22). Certain general factors seem related to the success of therapy, however; some of these are listed in **Table 18.3.**

TABLE 18.3	FACTORS AFFECTING THE SUCCESS OF PSYCHOTHERAPY	
Factors*	**Conditions leading to success**	**Conditions making success less likely**
Disorder	Neurotic, especially anxiety	Schizophrenic; paranoid
Pathology	Short duration; not severe	Serious chronic disturbance
Ego strength	Strong; good	Weak; poor
Anxiety	Not high	High
Defenses	Adequate	Lacking
Patient's attitudes	Motivated to change	Indifferent
	Realistic expectations for therapeutic change	Unrealistic or no expectations for change
Patient's role in therapy	Active; collaborative; involved; responsible for problem solving	Passive; detached; makes therapist responsible
Therapeutic relationship	Mutual liking and attraction	Unreciprocated attraction
Therapeutic characteristics	Personally well adjusted; experienced	Poorly adjusted

*No differences in outcome and no inconsistencies were found for these factors: age, sex, social class, and race.
Source: Adapted with permission from the *Annual Review of Psychology,* vol. 29, copyright © 1978 by Annual Reviews, Inc.

EVALUATING THERAPEUTIC EFFECTIVENESS

British psychologist **Hans Eysenck** (1952) created a furor some years ago by declaring that psychotherapy does not work at all. He reviewed available publications that reported the effects of various therapies and found that patients who received no therapy had just as high a recovery rate as those receiving psychoanalysis or other forms of insight therapy. His claim was that roughly two thirds of all people with neurotic problems will recover spontaneously within two years of the onset of the problem.

For a variety of reasons, some percentage of mental patients and clients in psychotherapy *do* improve without any professional intervention. This **spontaneous-remission effect** is one *baseline* criterion against which the effectiveness of therapies must be assessed. Simply put, doing something must be shown to lead to a significantly greater percentage of improved cases than doing nothing.

Placebo therapy must also be distinguished from substantive therapeutic effects if we are to determine whether client improvement results from specific clinical procedures or just from being in any therapy situation. Many psychologists and psychiatrists believe that the key placebo ingredients in the success of any therapy are a patient's *belief* that therapy will help and a therapist's social influence in conveying this suggestion (Fish, 1973). Psychiatrist **Jerome Frank** (1961) has compared the processes that take place in modern psychotherapy, religious revivalism, native healing ceremonies, and Communist thought-reform programs. He argues that "belief is really crucial to all the healing processes of any sort because without the belief the person does not participate in any real way. . . . Nothing happens unless they really believe that this could help them" (Frank, 1990; *Discovering Psychology,* Program 2).

While most psychotherapy researchers agree with Eysenck that it is important to show that psychotherapy is more effective than spontaneous recovery or client expectations, they criticize his findings because of many methodological problems in the studies he reviewed. A later evaluation of nearly a hundred therapy-outcome studies found that psychotherapy *did* lead to greater improvement than spontaneous recovery in 80 percent of the cases (Meltzoff & Kornreich, 1970). Thus, we begin to feel a little more confident that the therapeutic experience itself is a useful one for many people much of the time.

A general model of the way theory, clinical observation, and research all play a role in the development and evaluation of any form of treatment (for mental and physical disorders) is diagrammed in the flowchart in Figure 18.4. It shows that systematic research is needed to help clinicians discover if their therapies are making the differences that their theories predict.

One well-controlled study compared patients who had undergone psychoanalytic or behavior therapy with patients who had simply been on a waiting list for therapy. Both types of therapy turned out to be beneficial, with behavior therapy leading to the greatest overall improvement. The researchers also concluded that the improvement of patients in therapy was "not entirely due either to spontaneous recovery or to the placebo effect of the nonspecific aspects of therapy, such as arousal of hope, expectation of help, and an initial cathartic interview" (Sloane et al., 1975, p. 224). Because of such findings, current researchers are less concerned about asking *whether* psychotherapy works and

FIGURE 18.4

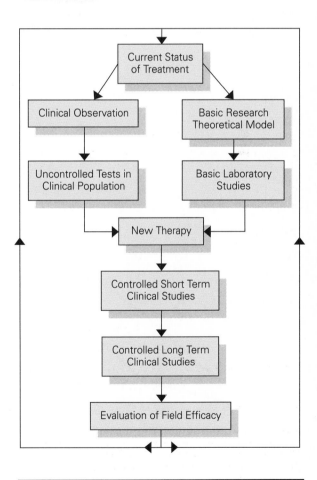

more concerned about asking *why* it works and whether any one treatment is most effective for any particular problem and for certain types of patients (Goldfried et al., 1990).

Some of the confounding variables encountered by using data from various studies to compare the effectiveness of different types of therapy (in a meta-analysis across hundreds of studies) are differences in therapist experience, duration of therapy, accuracy of the initial diagnosis, type of the disorder, differences in the severity and types of patient difficulties, the kinds of outcome measures used, the fit between a patient's expectations and the type of therapy offered, and length of follow-up times, to name but a handful (Kazdin, 1986; Kazdin & Wilson, 1980; Smith et al., 1980; Smith & Glass, 1977).

We might also wonder whether a combination of therapies is better than a single one for some kinds of disorders. According to research with acutely depressed patients, the answer is *yes* (see **Figure 18.5**).

NIMH Depression Treatment Evaluation

The first collaborative research program to assess the outcome of psychotherapy in treating a specific mental disorder—depression—has been completed recently. The long-term evaluation study was coordinated and funded by the National Institutes for Mental Health (NIMH). Its special features include (a) comparisons of the effectiveness of two different forms of brief psychotherapy—a tricyclic drug treatment and placebo control; (b) careful definition and standardization of the treatments accomplished by training 28 therapists in each of the four treatment conditions, with each treatment delivered at three different institutions in different cities; (c) random assignment of 240 outpatients who met standard diagnostic criteria for definite major depressive disorder; (d) standardized assessment procedures to monitor both the process of the therapy (by analysis of therapy-session videotapes, for example) as well as a battery of outcome measures administered before treatment began, during the 16-week treatment period, at termination, and 18 months later; and (e) independent assessment of the results at an institution separate from any involved in the training or treatment phases of the study (Elkin et al., 1989).

The psychotherapies evaluated were two that had been developed, or modified, especially for the treatment of depression in people outside a hospital setting. The methods were also sufficiently standardized to be transmitted to other clinicians in training manuals. Cognitive behavior therapy and interpersonal psychotherapy, which is a psychodynamically oriented therapy that focuses on a patient's current life and interpersonal relationships, were compared (Klerman et al., 1979). *Imipramine,* a tricyclic antidepressant, and a placebo control were administered in a double-blind procedure. For ethical reasons, the placebo patients received more than just an inert pill. They were seen weekly by a psychiatrist who provided minimal supportive therapy along with the placebo.

One set of results from this model program of therapy outcome is presented in **Figure 18.6.** The graph shows that each of the treatments for severely depressed patients had an effect beyond that of the placebo control, with the antidepressant drug being most effective and the psychodynamic and cognitive therapies having an intermediate level of effectiveness. Other results of note were that (a) the placebo treatment did help reduce depressive symptoms in patients who were only *moder-*

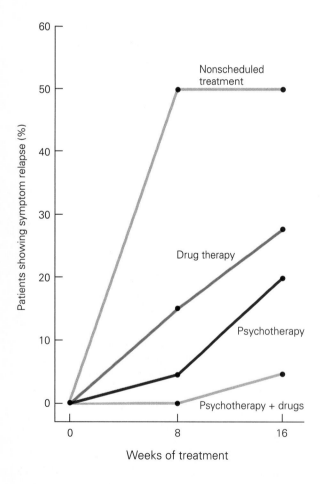

FIGURE 18.5

ately depressed, but many of them dropped out of the study before it was completed; (b) the positive effects of the drug therapy appeared sooner in treatment than did the psychotherapies and were more consistent across the different institutions; (c) improvement was found across many areas of patient functioning; and (d) patient characteristics, such as marital status, expectation of improvement, and daily functioning, also contributed to the success of the two psychotherapy treatments.

The complex analysis of treatments is one of the important contributions of this innovative evaluative research. It serves as a model for the way scientifically sound research can be conducted to evaluate the claims of other therapeutic approaches. While various therapists disagree with certain aspects of this clinical comparison study, the program of rigorous, systematic evaluations of the specific treatments is definitely welcome. Not only can such collaborative research compare the effectiveness of different therapies, it can do a much more valuable service by giving us a new understanding of the complex interaction between therapist, treatment, symptoms, patient, and the process of change.

However, some critics argue persuasively that this standardized comparative approach that separates treatment from assessment does not recognize the power of individualized treatments. Instead, it is proposed that assessment be formulated in terms of the therapist's own theory-driven procedure for evaluating therapy outcomes against the goals set for each individual patient (Persons, 1991).

FIGURE 18.6   DEPRESSION THERAPIES

For treating severely depressed patients, drugs used in combination with psychotherapy and cognitive therapy are very effective.

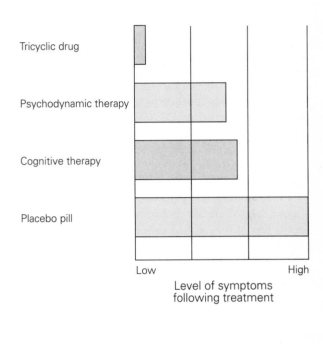

Level of symptoms following treatment

THERAPY FOR DRINKING PROBLEMS: WHAT WORKS?

Addiction

Celebrity testimonials and advertising claims may suggest that the path to sobriety starts with 10 to 30 days of intensive therapy at a residential treatment center such as the one founded by former First Lady Betty Ford. Recent research, however, does not support that con-

clusion. When psychologists Reid Hester and William Miller reviewed two dozen studies comparing long-term versus short-term treatment, residential versus non-residential programs, and high-intensity versus low-intensity programs, they found that "without a single exception, the studies failed to show any advantage for the more intensive, longer, or residential approaches over less intensive and less expensive alternatives" (Hester & Miller, 1989, p. xii).

For the best outcome, treatment for alcohol and other drug problems should be carefully matched to the needs of the person seeking help. Socially stable people who are not severely addicted to alcohol tend to do better with *less* intensive treatments. Depending on an individual's personality, health, social support system, and previous history, a variety of levels of treatment intensity could be appropriate.

However, more fundamental than the issue of intensity and duration of alcohol treatment programs are two interrelated questions: Is alcoholism an inherited disease or a maladaptive life style habit? Can alcoholism best be treated by the total *abstinence approach* popularlized by Alcoholics Anonymous (AA) or by *controlled drinking* within a program of individual behavior therapy? An intense debate raging over these issues pits medicine against psychology, genetic views against behavioral views, religious leaders against researchers, and scientists against scientists (Marlatt, 1983; Peele, 1984).

Conventional wisdom suggests that alcoholism is a disease that is largely genetically determined and thus out of the jurisdiction of voluntary control. The only way to change it is by never drinking a drop of alcohol. The total abstinence treatment approach that adheres to this disease model is put into practice by the 12-step program of Alcoholics Anonymous. This program involves acknowledging one's powerlessness over the disease and turning to a "higher being" for needed help. This medical disease model is also embraced by the American Medical Association and the National Institute on Alcohol Abuse and Alcoholism.

Conventional wisdom may be wrong. A large, steadily growing body of literature shows that the genetic contribution to alcoholism is limited, and that the genetic factor always interacts with "behavioral, psychodynamic, existential and social-group factors in all

kinds of drinking problems . . . " (Peele, 1986). Also, "controlled-drinking training seems to be most effective with individuals who have been defined as *problem drinkers*" (Marlatt, 1983). Scholarly reviews of this literature indicate that moderate drinking by alcoholics does not create problem drinking outcomes even when it is done secretly by patients in abstinence-oriented treatment programs (Heather & Robertson, 1981). When moderate drinking is part of a therapy program that teaches controlled-drinking skills, virtually all studies show successful, lasting outcomes (Miller, 1983). In contrast, conventional abstinence treatments, including that practiced by AA, have little demonstrated effectiveness for alcohol problems (Edwards, 1980; Miller & Hester, 1980; Valliant, 1983).

"That 12-step groups (and the related disease-model of addiction) should have such apparent popularity and renown coupled with a lack of empirical support and actual attendance, is a fascinating phenomenon . . ." (Horvath, 1991, p. 13). The Institute of Medicine has estimated that only 20 percent of those with alcohol problems who are referred to AA ever attend meetings regularly. The 1990 report to Congress by the Secretary of Health and Human Services concludes that "the effectiveness of AA has not been scientifically documented and methodological problems make such an evaluation difficult."

The **controlled-drinking controversy** was triggered by the 1962 report by British physician D. L. Davies that challenged the traditional emphasis on total abstinence by showing that the vast majority of alcoholics participating in controlled drinking maintained moderate, non-problematic drinking over many years. The controversy was revived some 20 years later with the publication of a detailed, large-scale study by Mark and Linda Sobell, a team of behavioral psychologists (1973). Their individualized behavior therapy for alcoholics included many of the behavioral strategies we outlined earlier in the chapter but used them in conjunction with controlled amounts of alcohol drinking. The success of their therapy was challenged by other researchers (Pendery et al., 1982), ridiculed on the popular TV program "60 Minutes" (3/6/83), and led to several independent investigations of their scientific integrity and evaluation of their data. They were completely vindicated by these investigations (Marlatt, 1983; Sobell & Sobell, 1984).

What works? Controlled-drinking therapy is best for younger problem drinkers who have no signs of physical dependence, while abstinence may be called for only with older chronic alcoholics who show evidence of organic consequences of alcohol dependence. Alcoholism is the disease that results from excessive, long-term drinking rather than the cause of such drinking. In opposing the disease-abstinence-sin model of alcoholism, psychological researchers and therapists are taking an unpopular path, but one that needs to be traveled.

PREVENTION STRATEGIES

Two friends were walking on a riverbank. Suddenly, a child swept downstream in the current. One of the friends jumped in the river and rescued the child. Then the two friends resumed their stroll. Suddenly, another child appeared in the water. The rescuer jumped in and again pulled the victim to safety. Soon, a third drowning child swept by. The still-dry friend began to trot up the riverbank. The rescuer yelled, "Hey, where are you going?" The dry one replied, "I'm going to get the bastard that's throwing them in" (Wolman, 1975, p. 3).

The moral of this story is clear: *preventing* a problem is the best solution. All traditional therapies we have examined here share the focus of changing a person who is already distressed or disabled. They begin to do their work *after* the problem behaviors show up and *after* the suffering starts. By the time someone elects to go into therapy or is required to, it is often too *long* after the time when the psychological disorder has "settled in" and had its disruptive effects on the person's daily functioning, social life, job, or career.

The goal of *preventing* psychological problems is being put into practice by a number of community mental health centers under the general direction of the National Association for Mental Health (as we noted in Chapter 13). The first step toward this goal is the recognition that systematic efforts toward combatting psychological problems can take place at any of three levels by reducing the *severity* of existing disorders (using traditional therapies); the *duration* of disorders by means of new programs for early identification and prompt treatment; and the *incidence* of new cases among the unaffected, normal population that is potentially at risk for a particular disorder (Klein & Goldston, 1977).

The development of this three-stage model has signaled major shifts in the focus and in the basic paradigms of mental health care. The most important of these paradigm shifts are (a) supplementing treatment with prevention; (b) going beyond a medical disease model to a public health model; (c) focusing on *situations* and ecologies that put people at risk and away from "at-risk people"; (d) looking for current precipitating factors in life settings rather than long-standing predisposing factors in people; and (e) not just preventing problems but promoting positive mental health (Albee & Joffe, 1977; Price et al., 1980).

Although the medical model is concerned with treating people who are afflicted, a public health model includes identifying and eliminating the sources of disease and illness that exist in the environment. In this approach, an affected individual is seen as the host or carrier—the end-product of an existing process of disease. Change the conditions that breed illness and there will be no need to change people later with expensive, extensive treatments. The dramatic reduction of many contagious and infectious diseases, such as tuberculosis, smallpox, and malaria, has come about through this approach. With psychopathology, too, many sources of environmental or organizational stress can be identified; plans can then be made to alleviate them, thus reducing the number of people who will be exposed to them. The new field of **clinical ecology** expands the boundaries of biomedical therapies by relating disorders, such as anxiety and depression, to environmental irritants, such as chemical solvents, noise pollution, seasonal changes, and radiation (Bell, 1981).

These newer mental health approaches are directing attention toward *precipitating* factors in a person's current environment and focusing on practical ways to change *what is* rather than reinterpreting *what was*. In recognizing that certain situations are likely to foster psychopathology—when people are made to feel anonymous, rejected, isolated, or abused—new approaches instruct people in ways to avoid or modify these noxious life situations individually or through community action.

Preventing mental disorders is a complex and difficult task. It involves not only understanding the relevant causal factors but overcoming individual, institutional, and governmental resistance to change. A major reeducation effort is necessary to demonstrate the long-range utility of prevention and the community mental health approach to psychopathology in order to justify the necessary expense in the face of the many other pressing problems demanding immediate solutions.

Our final Ecology Close-Up reports on a unique treatment program developed by a psychologist who gained the support of concerned individuals at many levels—students, teachers, school administrators, and government officials—to combat a widespread social-psychological problem caused by *school bullies*. The goal was both to reduce and prevent the incidence of abusive confrontation among school children. The methodology used was not the traditional one of giving individual therapy to the bullies but of changing many features of the system and the environment in which bullying occurs.

THE SYSTEM VERSUS THE SCHOOL BULLIES

Most of us remember either being bullied or watching someone else being bullied by one of the tough kids in our grade schools or high schools. Sometimes the bullies did it for spare change or lunch money, but often it seemed that they were abusive just to show that they had power. They could make life miserable especially for those kids who, for some unknown reason, were targeted as their favorite victims.

School becomes an aversive environment for the children who get picked on, robbed, beaten up, or verbally humiliated with clocklike regularity by bullies. Afraid to report the offender to teachers and embarrassed to tell their parents, these children may create excuses to stay away from school and even develop psychosomatic illnesses that justify staying home whenever possible. In any event, for these oppressed youngsters, what should be a joy-filled time of youth becomes a nightmare.

Psychologist **Dan Olweus** (1991) of the University of Bergen, Norway, has found that bullying is a serious and persistent problem in the schools of Sweden and Norway. His research has shown that nine percent of school-aged children are the victims of bullying classmates and nearly one in seven school children engage in some sort of bullying behavior. Surprisingly, this is true for girls as well as boys. His research has also shown that most parents and teachers are unaware of the extent of the problem or the involvement of their children in the problem. It doesn't seem to matter if the school is rural or urban, large or small; bullying seems to be prevalent in all schools.

Contrary to expectation, Olweus found that bullying does not seem to be a result of the bullies' frustration with their poor school performance. The major distinction between the bullies and their victims is simply physical strength. Bullies are stronger and pick on others that are obviously weaker physically. Bullies typically are aggressive not only toward their victims but also toward their teachers, siblings, and parents. They have a

need to dominate and they tend to be impulsive, acting out whatever they feel. They have little empathy for their victims but are not generally anxious or insecure.

Surveys and interviews reveal a sad portrait of the victims of bullying. They tend to be anxious, insecure, cautious, sensitive, and quiet. They react to bullying most typically with tears and social withdrawal. These children view themselves as stupid, ashamed, and unattractive. They are usually lonely and physically weak, and they feel abandoned. While they do nothing in the way of directly provoking the bullying, the combination of their physical and psychological characteristics marks them as "victim bait" for the school bully.

Do bullies have any negative effect beyond the grief they cause their weaker classmates? Olweus believes they do. He has found that bullying is part of a behavioral pattern that is linked to later delinquency and adult criminality. He has shown that more than 35 percent of young bullies have three or more court convictions by the time they are 24 years old. They create serious problems for themselves and their families, neighborhoods, and society.

How can this serious problem be remedied? Traditional approaches might involve treating the individual bullies with psychotherapy designed to give them insight into their problem or to restructure their cognitions about physical dominance. Dan Olweus decided on a different option: to modify the social and physical ecology in which bullying occurs. To combat the bully problem, Olweus developed and tested an intervention program based on three principles. The first principle is to create a warm, positive, and involved school faculty that also applies firm limits on what is and what is not acceptable behavior. The second principle is that rule violators should be met with nonhostile and nonphysical but consistent reactions from all concerned persons. The third principle is that adults must be willing to be *authoritative* in interacting with the children; to be caring but within the context of structured guidelines that they enforce. Olweus and his colleagues applied these principles as part of a nationwide program at the school, class, and individual levels. The two goals of the intervention were to reduce as much as possible existing bully/victim problems and to prevent the development of new problems. The program emphasized education of both school personnel and parents by means of information booklets, folders, and videos about the nature and extent of the problem and by means of activities to counteract bullying. Schools were encouraged to provide better supervision of recess time, so that recess was no longer an opportunity for bullies to abuse their targets. The school administration also helped to create parent/ teacher discussion groups. Clear rules and sanctions against bullying were put in place. Role-plays of bullying incidents and a series of positive group activities were encouraged. Bullies or victims had serious talks with school authorities and parents.

Did the program work? Evaluation of the outcome of the intervention was made at several time periods up to two years after it was begun. Outcome data were collected from about 2500 students in 112 grade schools and 42 primary and junior-high schools, with different age-grade cohorts assessed separately. Evaluation showed that the intervention was very successful and resulted in a marked reduction of bullying of both boys and girls across all class levels over the 20-month period of the study. Bullies said that they bullied less and schools reported a general reduction in a variety of antisocial behaviors (such as truancy, vandalism, and theft). Not only was bullying reduced in school, it declined as well on the way to and from school. Importantly, most students reported more fun and pleasure during recess.

This unique intervention into a problem of aggression merits our attention because it was conducted nationwide with governmental support, was based on sound psychological principles, and adopted an ecological systems approach to analyzing and combatting a complex problem. We should note also that the program did not operate as a vague "war on bullies" campaign as we have seen in the United States in the case of government-sponsored programs against drugs, poverty, and other national problems. This ecologically sound intervention shows the effectiveness of a sensitive analysis of the components of a social-psychological problem, education of all those involved, and system-wide changes.

A PERSONAL ENDNOTE

After this case study of the successful application of psychological principles to a specific problem, we come to the end of our long journey through *Psychology and Life*. Upon reflection, and, ideally, when you take your final examination, you will realize just how much you have learned on the way. Yet, we have barely scratched the surface of the excitement and challenges that await the student of psychology, those curious people watchers who choose to continue onto the next phase of the journey into more advanced realms of psychology. I hope you will be among them, and that you may even go on to contribute to this dynamic enterprise as a scientific researcher or a clinical practitioner or by applying what is known in psychology to the solution of social and personal problems.

One last point before you exit, if I may. Playwright Tom Stoppard reminds us that "Every exit is an entry somewhere else." I'd like to believe that the entry into the next phase of your life will be facilitated by what you have learned from *Psychology and Life* and from your introductory psychology course. In that next journey may you infuse new life into the psychology of human nature, while strengthening the human connection between all people you encounter. Ciao,

Phil Zimbardo

The Therapeutic Context

The four major types of psychotherapy are psycho-dynamic, behavior, cognitive, and existential-humanist; a fifth type of therapy is biomedical. The therapeutic tasks involves diagnosing the problem, finding the source of the problem, making a prognosis about probable outcomes with and without treatment, and carrying out treatment. A variety of professionals work under this model. In earlier times, treatment for those with mental problems were usually harsh and dehumanizing. It has only been fairly recently in history that people with emotional problems have been treated as individuals with illnesses to be cured. This way of viewing mental illness has led to more humane treatment of patients. Cultural anthropology shows us that many cultures have their own way of understanding and treating mental disorders.

Psychodynamic Therapies

Psychodynamic therapies grew out of Sigmund Freud's psychoanalytic theory. One of Freud's main contributions to psychodynamic therapy was his postulating of the role of the unconscious in mental processes. Psychodynamic therapy seeks to reconcile conflicts of the id (desires that often remain unconscious) and the superego. Free association, repression, resistance, and dream analysis are all important components of this therapy. Neo-Freudians place more emphasis on the patient's current social situation, interpersonal relationships, and self-concept and on differences in the psychology of men and women.

Behavior Therapies

Behavior therapy attempts to apply the principles of learning and reinforcement to problem behaviors. Counterconditioning and systematic desensitization are two categories of techniques commonly employed. Exposure therapy is the common element in phobia-modification therapies. Contingency management uses operant conditioning to modify behavior, primarily through positive reinforcement and extinction strategies. Social learning therapy involves the use of models and social skills training to help individuals gain confidence about their abilities.

Cognitive Therapies

Cognitive therapy concentrates on changing negative or irrational thought patterns about oneself and social relationships. Cognitive behavior modification calls for the client to learn more constructive thought patterns in reference to a problem and to apply the new technique to other situations. Cognitive therapy has been used to treat depression. Rational-emotive therapy helps clients recognize that their irrational beliefs about themselves interfere with life and learn how to change those thought patterns.

Existential-Humanist Therapies

Existential-humanist therapies focus on individuals becoming more fully self-actualized. Therapists strive to be nondirective in helping their clients establish a positive self-image that can deal with external criticisms. Group therapy has grown out of the human potential movement. It has many applications including community self-help groups and support groups for the terminally ill. Gestalt therapy focuses on the whole person—body, mind, and life setting. Family and marital therapy concentrate on situational difficulties and interpersonal dynamics of the couple or family group as a system in need of improvement.

Biomedical Therapies

Biomedical therapies concentrate on changing the physiological aspects of mental illness. These therapies rely on a range of drugs that alleviate the pathological symptoms but do not cure the disorder. Psychosurgery has lost popularity in recent years because of its radical, irreversible side-effects. Electroconvulsive therapy is undergoing a resurgence of use with depressed patients, but it remains controversial. Chemotherapy includes antipsychotic medicine for schizophrenics as well as anti-depression and antianxiety drugs. Antianxiety medication is particularly susceptible to abuse and should not be used by people suffering from the ordinary stress of living.

Does Therapy Really Work?

Some researchers have argued that therapy for mental illness does not work any better than the passage of time or nonspecific placebo treatment. Research shows that behavior therapy and psychotherapy are effective for specific types of disorders, but the reasons for this are not clear. Innovative evaluation projects, such as the NIMH study of depression therapies, are helping to answer the question of what makes therapy effective. Prevention strategies have become especially important in the new public health model.

KEY TERMS

aversion therapy, 676
behavior modification, 673
behavioral contract, 677
behavioral rehearsal, 680
biomedical therapy, 662
catharsis, 670
chemotherapy, 692
client, 663
clinical ecology, 699
clinical psychologist, 665
cognitive behavior modification, 682
cognitive therapy, 682
contingency management, 673
controlled-drinking controversy, 698
counseling psychologist, 664
counterconditioning, 673

countertransference, 671
dream analysis, 671
electroconvulsive therapy (ECT), 691
exposure therapy, 675
flooding, 675
free association, 670
Gestalt therapy, 687
generalization techniques, 673
human-potential movement, 686
implosion therapy, 675
insight therapy, 668
in vivo therapy, 664
participant modeling, 679
pastoral counselor, 665
patient, 663
person-centered therapy, 685
placebo therapy, 695

prefrontal lobotomy, 690
psychiatric social worker, 664
psychiatrist, 665
psychoanalyst, 665
psychoanalytic therapy, 668
psychosurgery, 690
psychotherapy, 662
rational-emotive therapy (RET), 684
resistance, 670
ritual healing, 667
shamanism, 661
social-learning therapy, 678
spontaneous-remission effect, 695
symptom substitution, 673
systematic desensitization, 674
transference, 671

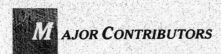

MAJOR CONTRIBUTORS

Agras, Stewart, 674
Bandura, Albert, 678
Beck, Aaron, 683
Beers, Clifford, 667
Breuer, Joseph, 669
Cover Jones, Mary, 673
Ellis, Albert, 684
Eysenck, Hans, 695
Frank, Jerome, 695

Freud, Sigmund, 668
Heinroth, J. C., 666
Horney, Karen, 672
Kohut, Heinz, 672
Mahler, Margaret, 671
May, Rollo, 685
Moniz, Egas, 690
Olweus, Dan, 700
Pappenheim, Bertha, 670

Perls, Fritz, 687
Pinel, Phillipe, 666
Rogers, Carl, 685
Satir, Virginia, 689
Skinner, B. F., 676
Sullivan, Harry Stack, 671
Wolpe, Joseph, 674

APPENDIX

UNDERSTANDING STATISTICS: ANALYZING DATA INTO CONCLUSIONS

ANALYZING THE DATA   APPENDIX–3
   Descriptive Statistics
   Inferential Statistics

HOW TO MISLEAD WITH STATISTICS   APPENDIX–9

All research data is analyzed statistically to help make sense of what was observed and measured and to discover if the findings are "real." Knowing something about statistics can, therefore, help you appreciate the process by which psychological knowledge is developed. On a more personal level, having a basic understanding of statistics will help you make better decisions.

Most students perceive statistics as a dry, uninteresting topic. However, statistics have many vital applications to our lives. Consider the following items taken from the front pages of your newspaper. They show how statistics help answer some crucial questions about human behavior.

Fred Cowan was described by relatives, co-workers, and acquaintances as a "nice, quiet man," a "gentle man who loved children," and a "real pussycat." The principal of the parochial school Cowan had attended as a child reported that his former student had received *A* grades in courtesy, cooperation, and religion. According to a co-worker, Cowan "never talked to anybody and was someone you could push around." Cowan, however, surprised everyone who knew him when, one Valentine's Day, he strolled into work toting a semiautomatic rifle and shot and killed four co-workers, a police officer, and, finally, himself.

To friends and neighbors, Patrolman Stephen Richard Smith seemed a polite, shy man with a taste for classical music and a habit of feeding stray cats. One day, this 31-year-old police officer was shot to death by his best friend, who was his former patrol partner. Authorities alleged that Smith's former partner had been forced to shoot his friend in the line of duty—Smith was suspected of being a brutal vigilante who had beaten and murdered several people (Reinhold, 1986).

Stories such as these lead all of us—lay people and research psychologists alike—to wonder about the meaning and causes of human behavior. How could people who were perceived by everyone who knew them as "gentle" and "shy" commit such atrocities? These stories also make us wonder how well we *really* know anyone.

Both stories have a common plot: A shy, quiet person suddenly becomes violent, shocking everyone who knows him. What do Fred Cowan and Stephen Smith have in common with other people who were suddenly transformed from gentle and caring into violent and ruthless? What personal attributes might distinguish them from us?

I had a hunch that there might be a link between shyness and other personal characteristics and violent behavior. Along with several colleagues, I began to collect some data that might reveal such a connection.

First, we reasoned that people who become sudden murderers are probably typically shy, nonaggressive people who keep their passions in check and their impulses under tight control. For most of their lives, they suffer many silent injuries. Seldom, if ever, do they express anger, regardless of how angry they really feel. On the outside, they appear unbothered, but on the inside they may be fighting to control furious rages. So, they give the impression that they are nice, quiet, passive, responsible children, and, when they grow up, the same kind of adults. Since they are shy, they probably do not let others get close to them so no one knows how they really feel. Then, suddenly, something explodes. At the slightest provocation—one more small insult, one more little rejection, one more bit of social pressure to comply with a request they did not want to honor—the fuse is lit and they release the suppressed violence that has been building up for so long. Because they did not learn to deal with interpersonal conflicts by discussion and verbal negotiation, these sudden murderers act out their anger physically.

Our mini-theory led us to the hypothesis that shyness would be more characteristic of people who had engaged in homicide—without any prior history of violence or antisocial behavior—than it would of those who had committed homicide but had had a previous record of violent criminal behavior. In addition, sudden murderers should have higher levels of control over their impulses than habitually violent people. Their passivity and dependence would be manifested in more feminine and androgynous characteristics than those of habitual criminals.

To test these hypotheses, we had to collect three kinds of data from two types of subjects: shyness scores, impulse control scores, and sex-role identification scores from people who had recently committed murder, with and without previous criminal records. This type of research, in which the behavior of interest—the dependent variable—has already occurred before the study begins, uses what is called an ***ex post facto* experimental design.** The task of the researcher is the detective work of figuring out what kinds of independent variables could have influenced the known outcomes. A second form of *ex post facto* design is one in which subjects are matched *after* the independent variable has already been administered. Here the research task is finding out the consequences of this existing difference between subjects. Subjects are not randomly assigned to conditions; instead, they are categorized according to already existing characteristics—specifically, by something they did or

some personal attribute. Because alternative explanations cannot be ruled out, this design does not permit causal conclusions from the data. However, it does allow for the discovery of variables that may help to explain some existing phenomenon that may then lead to controlled experiments assessing the causal connections.

To test our ideas about sudden murderers, we obtained permission to administer psychological questionnaires to a group of inmates serving time in California prisons for murder. Nineteen inmates (all male) agreed to participate in the study. Prior to committing murder, some had committed a series of crimes, while the other part of our sample had had no criminal record. All participants filled out three different questionnaires. Each questionnaire required a different type of information from the subject.

The first was the Stanford Shyness Survey (Zimbardo, 1990). The most important item on this questionnaire asked if the subject were shy; the answer could be either a simple *yes* or *no.* Other items on the scale tapped degree and kinds of shyness and a variety of dimensions related to origins and triggers of shyness.

The second questionnaire was the Bem Sex-role Inventory (BSRI), which presented a list of adjectives, such as *aggressive* and *affectionate,* and asked how well each adjective described the subject (Bem, 1974, 1981). Some adjectives were typically associated with being "feminine," and the total score of these adjectives was a subject's femininity score. Other adjectives were considered "masculine," and the total score of those adjectives was a subject's masculinity score. The final sex-role score, which reflected the difference between a subject's femininity and masculinity, was calculated by subtracting the masculinity score from the femininity score. A combination of the masculinity and femininity scores shows up as a subject's androgyny score.

The third questionnaire was the Minnesota Multiphasic Personality Inventory (MMPI), which was designed to measure many different aspects of personality (see Chapter 18). We used only the "Ego-overcontrol" scale, which measures the degree to which a person acts out or controls impulses. The higher the subject's score on this scale, the more ego-overcontrol the subject exhibits.

We predicted that, compared to murderers with a prior criminal record, sudden murderers would (a) more often describe themselves as shy on the shyness survey; (b) select more feminine traits than masculine ones on the sex-role scale; and (c) score higher in ego-overcontrol. What did we discover?

Before you find out, it is essential that you learn some of the basic procedures that were used to analyze these data. The actual sets of data we collected will be used as the source material to teach you about some of the different types of statistical analyses and also about the kinds of conclusions they make possible.

ANALYZING THE DATA

Whatever the research design and whatever the measures used, the outcome of a research study is always the same: a set of data. For most researchers in psychology, analyzing the data is an exciting step. They can find out if their results will contribute to a better understanding of a particular aspect of behavior or if they have to go back to the drawing board and redesign their research. In short, they can discover if their studies have worked.

Data analysis can involve many different procedures, some of them surprisingly simple and straightforward. In this section, we will work step-by-step through an analysis of some of the data from the Sudden Murderers Study. If you have looked ahead and are turned off at the sight of numbers and equations, your phobia is understandable. Many psychological researchers began their careers as dyed-in-the-wool math-haters. However, you do not need to be good in math to be able to understand the concepts we will be discussing. You just need the courage to see mathematical symbols for what they are—a shorthand for representing ideas and operations.

The raw data—the actual scores or other measures obtained—from the 19 inmates in the Sudden Murderers Study are listed in **Table A.1.** As you can see, there were ten inmates in the *Sudden Murderers* group and nine in the *Habitual Criminal Murderers* group. When first glancing at these data, any researcher would feel what you probably feel: confusion. What do all these scores mean? Do the two groups of murderers differ from one another on these various personality measures? It is difficult to know just by examining this disorganized array of numbers.

Psychologists rely on a mathematical tool called *statistics* to help make sense of and draw meaningful conclusions from the data they collect. There are two types of statistics: descriptive and inferential. **Descriptive statistics** use mathematical procedures in an objective, uniform way to describe different aspects of numerical data. If you have ever computed your grade-point average, you already have used descriptive statistics. **Inferential statistics** use probability theory to make sound decisions about which results might have occurred simply through chance variation.

DESCRIPTIVE STATISTICS

Descriptive statistics provide a summary picture of patterns in the data. They are used to describe sets of scores collected from one subject or, more often, from different groups of subjects and to describe relationships among variables. Thus, instead of trying to keep in mind all the scores obtained by each of the subjects, researchers get special indexes of the scores that are most *typical* for each group. They also get measures of the way those scores are typical—whether the scores are spread out or clustered closely together. Measures of frequency and central tendency help researchers analyze patterns of scores.

Frequency Distributions

The shyness data are easy to summarize. Of the 19 scores, there are 9 *yes* and 10 *no* responses, and almost all the *yes* responses are in group 1 and almost all the *no* responses are in group 2. On the overcontrol scale, the scores range from 6 to 19; it is harder to get a sense from just looking at the scale of how the groups compare. We'll need a way to reorganize those scores.

Now let's examine the sex-role scores. The highest score is +61 (most feminine) and the lowest is −33 (most masculine). Of the 19 scores, 9 are positive and 10 negative—this means that 9 of the murderers described themselves as more feminine and 10 as more masculine.

To get a clearer picture of how these scores are distributed, we can draw up a **frequency distribution**—a summary of how frequently each of the

TABLE A.1 RAW DATA FROM THE SUDDEN MURDERERS STUDY

	Inmate	Shyness	BSRI Femininity – Masculinity	MMPI Ego-overcontrol
Group 1: Sudden Murderers	1	yes	+5	17
	2	no	−1	17
	3	yes	+4	13
	4	yes	+61	17
	5	yes	+19	13
	6	yes	+41	19
	7	no	−29	14
	8	yes	+23	9
	9	yes	−13	11
	10	yes	+5	14
Group 2: Habitual Criminal Murderers	11	no	−12	15
	12	no	−14	11
	13	yes	−33	14
	14	no	−8	10
	15	no	−7	16
	16	no	+3	11
	17	no	−17	6
	18	no	+6	9
	19	no	−10	12

TABLE A.2 RANK ORDERING OF SEX-ROLE DIFFERENCE SCORES

Highest	+61	
	+41	−7
	+23	−8
	+19	−10
	+6	−12
	+5	−13
	+5	−14
	+4	−17
	+3	−29
	−1	−33 Lowest

Note: + scores are more feminine; − scores are more masculine.

various scores occurs. The first step in preparing a frequency distribution for a set of numerical data is to *rank order* the scores from highest to lowest. The rank ordering for the sex-role scores is shown in **Table A.2.** The second step is to group these rank-ordered scores into a smaller number of categories called *intervals.* In this study, 10 categories were used, with each category covering 10 possible scores. The third step is to construct a frequency distribution table, listing the intervals from highest to lowest and noting the *frequencies*—the number of scores within each interval. Our frequency distribution shows us that the sex-role scores are largely between −20 and +9 (see **Table A.3**). The majority of the inmates' scores did not deviate much from zero, that is, they were neither strongly positive nor strongly negative.

We can now make some preliminary conclusions about the data. By examining frequency distributions for our variables, we can already see that each of our three predictions is accurate. Forty percent of the American people describe themselves as shy. By

TABLE A.3 FREQUENCY DISTRIBUTION OF SEX-ROLE DIFFERENCE SCORES

Category	Frequency
+60 to +69	1
+50 to +59	0
+40 to +49	1
+30 to +39	0
+20 to +29	1
+10 to +19	1
+0 to +9	5
−10 to −1	4
−20 to −11	4
−30 to −21	1
−40 to −41	1

comparison, eight out of ten of the sudden murderers (80 percent) described themselves as shy, while only one of nine of the habitual criminal murderers (11 percent) did so. On the sex-role scale, 70 percent of the sudden murderers chose adjectives that were more feminine than masculine, while only 22 percent of the habitual criminals said that the feminine adjectives described them more accurately than did the masculine ones. Sudden murderers scored higher in overcontrolling their impulses than habitual criminal murderers did (Lee, Zimbardo, & Bertholf, 1977). In addition, there was a noticeable difference in the circumstances that precipitated the murders committed by the shy men. In virtually every case, the precipitating incidents were minor for the sudden murderers relative to the incidents that triggered the violence of the habitual murderers.

Although summaries of data such as this are very compelling, there are a number of other analyses we must look at before we can state our conclusions with any certainty.

Graphs

Distributions are often easier to understand when they are displayed in graphs. The simplest type of graph is a *bar graph.* We can use a bar graph to illustrate how many more sudden murderers than habitual criminal murderers described themselves as shy (see **Figure A.1**). Bar graphs allow you to see patterns in the data.

For more complex data, such as the sex-role scores, we can use a *histogram,* which is similar to a bar graph except that the histogram's bars touch each

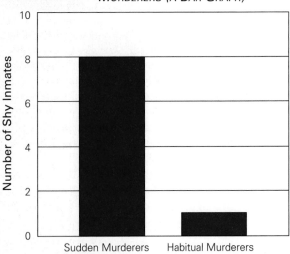

FIGURE A.1 SHYNESS FOR TWO GROUPS OF MURDERERS (A BAR GRAPH)

SEX-ROLE SCORES (A HISTOGRAM)

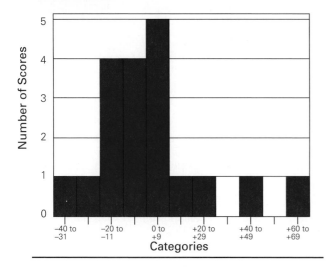

other and its categories are *intervals*—number categories instead of the name categories used in the bar graph. A histogram gives a visual picture of the number of scores in a distribution that are in each interval. It is easier to see from the sex-role scores shown in the histogram (in **Figure A.2**) than from the frequency distribution that most scores cluster between −20 and +9 and that there are only a few extremely positive scores.

Central Tendency

So far, we have formed a general picture of how the scores are *distributed.* Tables and graphs increase our general understanding of research results, but we want to know more—for example, the one score that is most typical of the group as a whole. This score becomes particularly useful when we want to compare two or more groups; it is much easier to compare the typical scores of two groups than it is their entire distributions. A single, *representative* score that can be used as an index of the most typical score obtained by a group of subjects is called a **measure of central tendency.** (It is located in the center of the distribution, and other scores tend to cluster around it.) Actually, psychologists use three different measures of central tendency: the *mode,* the *median,* and the *mean.*

The **mode** is the score that occurs more often than any other. For the measure of shyness, the modal response of the sudden murderers was *yes*—eight out of ten said they were shy. Among habitual criminal murderers, the modal response was *no.* The sex-role scores for the sudden murderers had a mode of +5. Can you figure out what the mode of their ego-overcontrol scores is?

The mode is the easiest index of central tendency to determine, but it is often the least useful. You can see one reason for this relative lack of usefulness if you notice that only one overcontrol score lies above the mode of 17, while six lie below it. Although 17 is the score obtained most often, it may not fit your idea of "typical" or "central."

The **median** is more clearly a central score; it separates the upper half of the scores in a distribution from the lower half. The number of scores larger than the median is the same as the number that are smaller. If you rank-order the sex-role scores of only the sudden murderers on a separate piece of paper, you will see that the median score is +5 (in this case, the same as the mode, although this is not always true). Four scores are higher than +5 and four scores are lower. Similarly, the median overcontrol score for these subjects is 15, with four scores below it and four above it. The median is quite simply the score in the middle of the distribution.

The median is not affected by extreme scores. For example, even if the highest sex-role score had been +129 instead of +61, the median value would still have been +5. That score would still separate the upper half of the data from the lower half.

The **mean** is what most people think of when they hear the word *average.* It is also the statistic most often used to describe a set of data. To calculate the mean, you simply add up all of the scores in a distribution and divide by the total number of scores. The operation is summarized by the following formula:

$$M = \Sigma X \div N$$

In this formula, M is the mean, X is each individual score, Σ (the Greek letter *sigma*) is the summation of what immediately follows it, and N is the total number of scores. Since the summation of all the scores (ΣX) is 115 and the total number of scores (N) is 10, the mean (M) of the sex-role scores of the sudden murderers would be calculated as follows:

$$M = 115 \div 10 = 11.5.$$

Try to calculate their mean overcontrol scores yourself. You should come up with a mean of 14.4.

Unlike the median, the mean *is* affected by the precise values of all scores in the distribution. Changing the value of an extreme score *does* change the value of the mean. For example, if the sex-role score of inmate 4 were +101 instead of +61, the mean for the whole group would increase from 11.5 to 15.5.

Variability

In addition to knowing which score is most representative of the distribution as a whole, it is useful to know how representative that measure of central tendency really is. Are most of the other scores fairly close to it or widely spread out? **Measures of variability** are statistics about the proximity of the scores in a distribution.

Can you see why measures of variability are important? An example may help. Suppose you are a grade school teacher. It is the beginning of the school year, and you will be teaching reading to a group of 30 second graders. Knowing that the average child in the class can now read a first-grade reading book will help you to plan your lessons. You could plan better, however, if you knew how *similar* or how *divergent* the reading abilities of the 30 children were. Are they all at about the same level (low variability)? If so, then you can plan a fairly standard second-grade lesson. What if several can read advanced material and others can barely read at all (high variability)? Now the mean level is not so representative of the entire class, and you will have to plan a variety of lessons to meet the children's varied needs.

The simplest measure of variability is the **range,** the difference between the highest and the lowest values in a frequency distribution. For the sudden murderers' sex-role scores, the range is 90: (+61)–(–29). The range of their overcontrol scores is 10: (+19)–(+9). To compute the range, you need to know only two of the scores: the highest and the lowest. The range is simple to compute, but psychologists often prefer measures of variability that are more sensitive and take into account *all* the scores in a distribution, not just the extremes. One widely used measure is the **standard deviation** (SD), a measure of variability that indicates the *average* difference between the scores and their mean. To figure out the standard deviation of a distribution, you need to know the mean of the distribution and the individual scores. Although the arithmetic involved in calculating the standard deviation is very easy, the formula is a bit more complicated than the one used to calculate the mean and, therefore, will not be presented here. The general procedure, however, involves subtracting the value of each individual score from the mean and then determining the average of those mean deviations.

The standard deviation tells us how variable a set of scores is. The larger the standard deviation, the more spread out the scores are. The standard deviation of the sex-role scores for the sudden murderers is 24.6, but it is only 10.7 for the habitual criminals. This shows that there was less variability in the habitual criminals group. Their scores clustered more closely about their mean than did those of the sudden murderers. When the standard deviation is small, the mean is a good representative index of the entire distribution. When the standard deviation is large, more individual scores are different from the mean, and the mean is less typical of the whole group.

Correlation

Another useful tool in interpreting psychological data is the *correlation coefficient,* which indicates the degree of relationship between two variables (such as height and weight or sex-role score and overcontrol score). It tells us the extent to which scores on one measure are associated with scores on the other. A more formal definition says that the **correlation coefficient** is a measure of the strength and direction of the straight-line association between two quantitative variables. If people with high scores on one variable tend to have high scores on the other variable too, then the correlation coefficient will be positive (greater than 0). If, however, most people with high scores on one variable tend to have *low* scores on the other variable, then the correlation will be negative (less than 0). If there is *no* consistent relationship between the scores, the correlation will be close to 0.

Correlation coefficients range from +1 (perfect positive correlation) through 0 to –1 (perfect negative correlation). The further a coefficient is from 0 in *either* direction, the more closely related the two variables are, positively or negatively. Higher coefficients permit better predictions of one variable, given knowledge of the other.

In the Sudden Murderers Study, the correlation coefficient (symbolized as r) between the sex-role scores and the overcontrol scores turns out to be +0.35. The sex-role scores and the overcontrol scores are, thus, positively correlated—in general, subjects seeing themselves as more feminine also tend to be higher in overcontrol. However, the correlation is modest, compared to the highest possible value, +1.00. So, we know that there are many exceptions to this relationship. If we had also measured the self-esteem of these inmates and found a correlation of –0.68 between sex-role scores and self-esteem, it would mean that there was a negative correlation. If this were the case, we could say that the male subjects who saw themselves as more feminine tended to be lower in self-esteem. It would still be a stronger relationship than the relationship between the sex-role scores and the overcontrol scores because –0.68 is farther from 0, the point of no relationship, than is +0.35.

INFERENTIAL STATISTICS

We have used a number of descriptive statistics to characterize the data from the Sudden Murderers Study, and now we have an idea of the pattern of results. However, some basic questions remain unanswered. Recall that the research team hypothesized that sudden murderers would be shyer, more overcontrolled, and more feminine than habitual criminal murderers. Descriptive statistics let us compare average responses

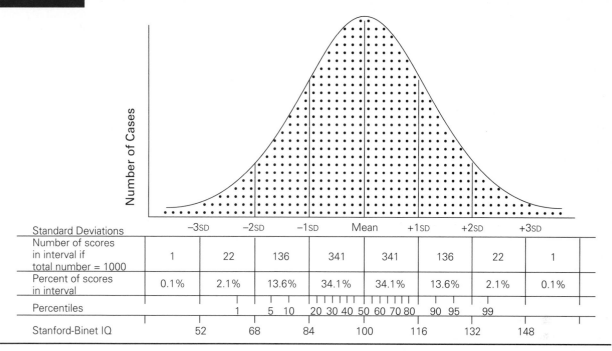

Standard Deviations		–3SD	–2SD	–1SD	Mean	+1SD	+2SD	+3SD	
Number of scores in interval if total number = 1000	1		22	136	341	341	136	22	1
Percent of scores in interval	0.1%		2.1%	13.6%	34.1%	34.1%	13.6%	2.1%	0.1%
Percentiles			1	5 10	20 30 40 50 60 70 80		90 95	99	
Stanford-Binet IQ		52	68	84	100	116	132	148	

The figure represents a normal curve, or normal distribution. It shows the distribution of scores that would be expected if 1000 randomly selected persons were measured on IQ or some other continuously variable trait. Each dot represents an individual's score. The baseline, or horizontal axis, shows the amounts of whatever is being measured. The vertical axis shows how many individuals have each amount of the trait, as represented by their scores. Usually only the resulting curve at the top is shown, since this indicates the frequency with which each measure has occurred. Actual data-based curves only approximate this hypothetical one but come remarkably close to it with very large samples.

The normal distribution is very useful to psychologists because they know that in a large, randomly selected group a consistent percentage of the cases will fall in a given segment of the distribution. For example, if the trait is one that is distributed normally, about 68 percent will fall in the middle third of the range of scores, between one standard deviation below and one standard deviation above the mean. Most of the scores in a distribution fall within three standard deviations above the mean and three standard deviations below it (but usually a few scores in an actual distribution will be lower and a few higher).

The distance of the standard deviation from the mean can be indicated along the baseline of the curve, as is done here. Since the standard deviations are equally spaced along the distributions, they are convenient dividing points for classification. Percentiles indicate the percentage of all scores that fall below a given value. On the IQ scores noted here, a score of 100 is at the 50th percentile, indicating that half of all scores are less than 100.

and variability in the two groups, and it appears that there are some differences between the groups; but how do we know if the differences are large enough to be meaningful? Are they reliable? If we did this study again with other sudden murderers and other habitual criminal murderers, would we expect to find the same pattern of results or could these results have been an outcome of chance? If we could somehow measure the entire population of sudden murderers and habitual criminal murderers, would the means and standard deviations be the same as those we found for these small samples?

Inferential statistics are used to answer these kinds of questions. They tell us which inferences we *can* make from our samples and which conclusions we can legitimately draw from our data. Inferential statistics use probability theory to determine the likelihood that a set of data occurred simply by chance variation.

The Normal Curve

In order to understand how inferential statistics work, we must look first at the special properties of a distribution called the *normal curve*. When data on a variable (height, IQ, or femininity, for example) are collected from a large number of subjects, the numbers obtained often fit a curve roughly similar to that shown in **Figure A.3.** Notice that the curve is symmetrical (the left half is a mirror image of the right) and bell-shaped—high in the middle, where most scores are, and lower the farther you get from the mean. This type of curve is called a **normal curve,** or *normal distribution.* (A *skewed distribution* is one in which scores cluster toward one end instead of around the middle.)

In a normal curve, the median, mode, and mean

values are the same. A specific percentage of the scores can be predicted to fall under different sections of the curve. Figure A.3 shows IQ scores on the Stanford-Binet Intelligence Test. These scores have a mean of 100 and a standard deviation of 16. If you indicate standard deviations as distances from the mean along the baseline, you find that a little over 68 percent of all the scores are between the mean of 100 and one standard deviation above and below—between IQs of 84 and 116. Roughly another 27 percent of the scores are found between the first and second standard deviations below the mean (IQ scores between 68 and 84) and above the mean (IQ scores between 116 and 132). Less than 5 percent of the scores fall in the third standard deviation above and below the mean, and *very* few scores fall beyond—only about a quarter of one percent.

Inferential statistics indicate the probability that the particular sample of scores obtained are actually related to whatever you are attempting to measure or whether they could have occurred by chance. For example, it is more likely that someone would have an IQ of 105 than an IQ of 140, but an IQ of 140 is more probable than one of 35.

A normal curve is also obtained by collecting a series of measurements whose differences are due only to chance. If you flip a coin 10 times in a row and record the number of heads and tails, you will probably get 5 of each—most of the time. If you keep flipping the coin for 100 sets of 10 tosses, you probably will get a few sets with all heads or no heads, more sets where the number is between these extremes, and, most typically, more sets where the number is about half each way. If you made a graph of your 1000 tosses, you would get one that closely fits a normal curve, such as the one in the figure.

Statistical Significance

When a researcher finds a difference between the mean scores for two samples, she must ask if it is a *real* difference, or if it occurred simply because of chance. Because chance differences have a normal distribution, a researcher can use the normal curve to answer this question.

A simple example will help to illustrate the point. Suppose your psychology professor wants to see if the gender of a person proctoring a test makes a difference in the test scores obtained from male and female students. For this purpose, the professor randomly assigns half of the students to a male and half to a female proctor. The professor then compares the mean score of each group. The two mean scores would probably be fairly similar; any slight difference would most likely be due to chance. Why? Because if only chance is operating and both groups are from the same

population (no difference), then the means of male proctor and female proctor samples should be fairly close most of the time. From the percentages of scores found in different parts of the normal distribution, you know that less than a third of the scores in the male proctor condition should be greater than one standard deviation above or below the female proctor mean. The chances of getting a male mean score more than three standard deviations above or below most of your female proctor means would be very small. If the professor *did* get a difference that great, then he or she would feel fairly confident that the difference is a real one and is somehow related to the gender of the test proctor. The next question would be *how* that variable influences test scores.

If male and female students were randomly assigned to each type of proctor it would be possible to analyze whether an overall difference found between the proctors were consistent across both student groups or were limited to only one sex. For example, male proctors grade female students higher than do female proctors, but they do not differ in grading males. Psychologists use a statistical inference procedure to estimate the probability that an observed difference could have occurred by chance. This computation is based on the size of the difference and the spread of the scores. By common agreement, psychologists accept a difference as "real" when the probability that it might be due to chance is less than 5 in 100 (indicated by the notation $p < 0.05$). A **significant difference** is one that meets this criterion. However, in some cases, even stricter probability levels are demanded, such as $p < 0.01$ (less than 1 in 100) and $p < 0.001$ (less than 1 in 1000). Such levels would be demanded when the decision based on the research evidence is of such importance that one wants to have a high level of confidence in the data, for example, when predicting suicide attempts on the basis of certain psychological traits.

With a statistically significant difference, a researcher can draw a conclusion about the behavior that was under investigation. There are many different types of tests for estimating the statistical significance of sets of data. The type of test chosen for a particular case will depend upon the design of the study, the form of the data, and the size of the groups. We will only mention one of the most common tests, the *t-test*, which may be used when an investigator wants to know if the difference between the means of two small groups is statistically significant.

We can use a *t*-test to see if the mean sex-role score of the sudden murderers is significantly different from that of the habitual criminal murderers. If we carry out the appropriate calculations, we find that there is a very slim chance, less than 5 in 100 (*p < 0.05*) of obtaining such a large *t* value if no true difference exists. The difference is, therefore, statistically significant, and we can feel more confident that there is a real difference between the two groups. The sudden murderers *did* rate themselves as more feminine than did the habitual criminal murderers. On the other hand, the difference between the two groups of murderers in overcontrol scores turns out *not* to be statistically significant ($p < 0.10$), so we must be more cautious in talking about this difference. There is a *trend* in the predicted direction—the difference is one that would occur by chance only 10 times in 100. However, the difference is not within the standard 5-in-100 range. (The difference in shyness, analyzed using another statistical test for frequency of scores, *is* highly significant.)

So, by using inferential statistics, we are able to answer some of the basic questions with which we began and we are closer to understanding the psychology of people who suddenly change from mild-mannered, shy individuals into mass murderers. Any conclusion, however, is only a statement of the *probable* relationship between the events that were investigated; it is never one of certainty. Truth in science is provisional, always open to revision by later data from better studies, developed from better hypotheses.

HOW TO MISLEAD WITH STATISTICS

Now that we have considered what statistics are, how they are used, and what they mean, we should talk about how they can be misused. Many people accept unsupported "facts" that are bolstered by the air of authority of a statistic. Others choose to believe or disbelieve what the statistics say without having any idea of how to question the numbers that are presented in support of a product, politician, or proposal.

Although it is possible to fabricate statistics or conclusions supported by no evidence, there are many more devious ways to give a very misleading impression using statistics. Almost all stages of research, from who the subjects are to how the study is designed and to what statistics are selected and how they are used, can have a profound effect on the conclusions that can be drawn from the data.

The group of subjects can make a large difference that can easily remain undetected when the results are reported. For example, a survey of views on abortion rights will yield very different results if conducted in a small Fundamentalist community in the South as opposed to a university in New York City. Likewise, a pro-life group surveying the opinions of its membership will very likely arrive at conclusions that differ from those obtained by the same survey conducted by a pro-choice group.

Even if the subjects are randomly selected and not biased by the methodology, the statistics that are used can produce very misleading results if the assumptions of the statistics are violated. For example, if 20 people take an IQ test on which 19 of them receive scores of 90–110 and one receives a score of 220, the mean of the group will be strongly elevated by that one outlying high score. With this sort of a data set, it would be much more accurate to present the median or the mode, which would accurately report the group's generally average intelligence, rather than the mean, which would make it look as if the average member of this group were very smart. This sort of bias is especially powerful in a small sample. If, on the other hand, the number of people in this group were 2000 instead of 20, the one extreme outlier would make virtually no difference and the mean would be a legitimate summary of the group's intelligence.

One good way to avoid falling for this sort of deception is to check on the size of the sample—large samples are less likely to be misleading than small ones (although in the *very* large samples, very small average differences between sets of data can attain statistical significance because the variability is likely to be low). Another check is to look at the median or the mode as well as the mean—the results can be interpreted with more confidence if they are similar than if they are different.

One way to guard against being misled by the misuse of statistics is to closely examine the methodology and results of the research reported. Check to see if the experimenters report their sample size, significance levels, and error margins. Try to find out if the methods they used measure accurately and consistently whatever they claim to be investigating.

No test is 100 percent accurate all the time, but it is possible to calculate a range within which the "true" score probably lies. Responsible statisticians report this

| TABLE A.4 | BELIEF IN THE SUPERNATURAL: GALLUP POLL RESULTS, 1990 |

Beliefs in	People Who Believe	People Who Are Not Sure
The devil	55%	8%
ESP	49%	22%
Devil possession	49%	16%
Psychic healing	46%	20%
Telepathy	36%	25%
Extraterrestrials	27%	32%
Astrology	25%	21%

N = 1225 U.S. adults, margin of error ±4 percent

range as the *margin of error.*

For example, examine the data in **Table A.4,** which summarizes the results from a recent survey asking Americans about their beliefs in the supernatural. Nearly half of the respondents indicated that they believed that the devil could possess humans. Notice in the small print at the bottom of the chart that there is a margin of error of plus or minus 4 percent. In other words, 49 percent may not be a truly accurate representation of the population at large. However, it is highly probable that somewhere between 45 percent and 53 percent of the population really does believe in devil possession. Since the survey was conducted using representative sampling techniques with 1225 American adults, it is likely that the sample is fairly representative of the population as a whole. (The conclusion of this survey is distressing to educators and scientists, as is the rest of the data on the widespread belief in supernatural phenomena. We wonder if the results of the survey are an effect of the spate of recent movies and TV shows that give credence to such irrational beliefs.)

Before drawing your own conclusions from the results presented, it is always a good idea to check such things as sample size and margin of error. Paying attention to the fine print and applying what you have learned in this book should make you less likely to be taken in by statistical misdirection and make you a much wiser consumer of psychological research.

Statistics is the backbone of psychological research. It is used to understand observations and to determine whether the findings are, in fact, correct. Through the methods described, psychologists can prepare a frequency distribution of data and find the central tendencies and variability of the scores. The strength and direction of the association between sets of scores can be determined by the correlation coefficient. Finally, psychological investigators can then find out how representative the observations are and whether they are significantly different from the general population. Statistics, however, can be used poorly or

deceptively, misleading those who do not understand them. Therefore, it is very important to keep in mind the many possible factors that can bias evidence—intentionally or unintentionally—when you are drawing conclusions from psychological research.

 KEY TERMS

correlation coefficient, 6

descriptive statistics, 3

ex post facto experimental design, 2

frequency distribution, 3

inferential statistics, 3

mean, 5

measure of central tendency, 5

median, 5

mode, 5

normal curve, 7

range, 6

significant difference, 8

standard deviation, 6

measure of variability, 6

GLOSSARY

The key terms from every chapter are defined here with page references.
Additional terms of psychological significance are also defined for your reference.

A

A-B-A design. Experimental design in which subjects first experience the baseline condition (A), then experience the experimental treatment (B), and then return to the baseline (A) (p. 43).

Absolute threshold. Minimum amount of physical energy needed to reliably produce a sensory experience (p. 217).

Accommodation. Process of restructuring or modifying cognitive structures so that new information can fit into them more easily (concept developed by Jean Piaget—used with assimilation); also the process by which the ciliary muscles change the thickness of the lens to permit variable focusing on near and distant objects (pp. 161, 224).

Achievement test. Standardized test designed to measure an individual's current level of competence in a given area (p. 568).

Acquired drive. Learned motivational state.

Acquisition. Classical conditioning experiment stage during which the conditional response is first elicited by the conditional stimulus (p. 308).

Action potential. Nerve impulse activated in an axon when the graded potential is above a certain threshold (p. 86).

Acute stress. Transient states of arousal with typically clear onset and offset patterns (p. 480).

Addiction. Physical state in which withdrawal symptoms occur if a certain drug is not present in the body (pp. 21, 128).

Adolescence. Stage of life commonly defined as beginning at the onset of puberty when sexual maturity or the ability to reproduce is attained (p. 185).

Adoption studies. Heritability-assessment studies that examine the degree to which adopted children's traits and behavioral patterns (such as IQ and personality) correlate with their biological parents and their adoptive parents (p. 515).

Adrenocorticotrophic hormone (ACTH). Pituitary hormone that stimulates the adrenal cortex to release hormones important in metabolic processes and in physiological reactions to prolonged stress.

Affect. Emotion or mood state.

Affective disorder. Disorder in which the primary symptoms are associated with mood disturbances, such as excessive depression, excessive elation, or both (p. 638).

Afferent systems. Systems that process information coming into the brain; sensory systems (p. 216).

Afterimage. Visual sensation occurring after a stimulus has ended.

Age regression. Technique used in which a hypnotized individual receives suggestions that he or she is "returning" to an earlier period in life.

Ageism. Prejudice against older people, similar to racism and sexism in its negative stereotypes (p. 200).

Aggregated case study. Research technique used to compare and contrast information about many individuals by combining and summarizing the results of a number of individual case studies (p. 510).

Aggression. Physical or verbal behavior with the intent to injure or destroy.

Agoraphobia. Extreme fear of being in public places or away from familiar surroundings (p. 634).

AI approach. Artificial-intelligence approach used to study cognitive processes; in the study of perception, it utilizes three levels of analysis: a) neurophysiological mechanisms; b) algorithms for operation that specify the processes of perception; and c) analysis of the physical properties of the world that allow humans to perceive (p. 268).

AIDS. Acronym for Acquired Immune Deficiency Syndrome, lethal syndrome caused by a virus that damages the immune system and weakens the body's ability to fight bacteria (p. 498).

Algorithm. Rote problem-solving procedure in which every possible solution is tried; guaranteed to lead to a correct solution eventually if there is one (p. 406).

All-or-none law. Property of axon firing in which a uniform action potential is generated when a threshold has been reached, and no nerve impulse is generated when it has not been reached (p. 86).

Alternative explanation. Interpretation or explanation of a behavioral effect that differs from that proposed in the hypothesis being tested (p. 35).

Altruism. Putting the welfare, interests, and survival of others above one's own.

Alzheimer's disease. Chronic organic brain syndrome characterized by gradual loss of memory, decline in intellectual ability, and deterioration of personality; the most common form of dementia in the elderly (pp. 208, 373).

Ambiguity. Property of perceptual situations when critical information is missing, elements are in unexpected relationships, and usual patterns are not apparent or vague; a condition in which illusions occur (p. 262).

American Sign Language (ASL). Language of the hearing-impaired community of the United States; it is a true language with its own system of symbols and grammar (p. 154).

Amoral. Lacking in understanding of people's responsibilities to each other; neither moral nor immoral.

Amplitude. Physical property of the strength of a sound wave as measured by its peak-to-valley height.

Amygdala. Portion of the limbic system; brain center for aggression and some forms of memory (pp. 72, 461).

Anal stage. Second of Freud's psychosexual developmental stages; during this stage (approximately 2 years of age), gratification comes primarily from the elimination process.

Analytic psychology. View of psychology as a constellation of compensatory internal forces in a dynamic balance, as proposed by Carl Jung (p. 524).

Anchoring bias. Insufficient adjustment up or down from an original starting value when judging the probable value of some event or outcome (p. 413).

Anterograde amnesia. Type of amnesia in which there is a loss of the ability to form memories for newly presented information (p. 341).

Anticipatory coping. Efforts made, in advance of a potentially stressful event, to overcome, reduce, or tolerate the imbalance between perceived demands and available resources (p. 487).

Antisocial personality disorder. Personality disorder in which the symptoms include an absence of conscience and a lack of sense of responsibility to others (p. 629).

Anxiety. Intense emotional response caused by the preconscious recognition that a repressed conflict is about to emerge into consciousness (p. 522).

Anxiety disorder. Mental disorder marked by physiological arousal and feelings of tension, tremor, shaking, and intense apprehension without reason.

Anxiety states. Neurotic disorders in which anxiety occurs in the absence of specific phobias.

Apparent motion. Movement illusion in which one or more stationary lights going on and off in succession are perceived as a single moving light; also called the *phi phenomenon* (p. 283).

Appetitive conditioning. Classical conditioning procedures in which the unconditional stimulus is of positive value to the organism.

Applied research. Research undertaken with the explicit goal of finding solutions to practical problems.

Aptitude test. Test designed to measure an individual's potential for acquiring various skills (p. 568).

Archetype. In Jungian personality theory, a universal, inherited, primitive, and symbolic representation of a particular experience or object; part of the collective unconscious (p. 524).

Archival data. Previously published findings or data already existing in documents, books, or cultural artifacts (p. 546).

Artificial intelligence (AI). Computer programs that can make the kinds of judgments and problem solving decisions that humans make (p. 383).

Asch effect. Phenomenon illustrating the influence of a unanimous majority on the judgments of individuals, even under unambiguous conditions; classic illustration of conformity developed by Solomon Asch (p. 583).

Assimilation. Process whereby new cognitive elements are fit in with old elements or modified to fit more easily; concept developed by Jean Piaget—used with accommodation (p. 161).

Association cortex. Area of the brain where processes such as planning and decision-making are believed to occur (p. 75).

Association psychology. View identified with John Locke and other seventeenth-century British philosophers that emphasizes the role of experience in mental growth by suggesting that most knowledge and abilities are determined by experience.

Associationism. View developed by the British empirical philosophers that ideas arise from sensory experiences and that thought and memory are composed of chains of these ideas.

Attachment. Close emotional relationship between a child and the regular caregiver; inferred from behaviors that elicit and maintain nearness between the two (p. 168).

Attention. State of focused awareness accompanied by sensory clearness and a central nervous system readiness to respond.

Attitude. Learned, relatively stable tendency to respond to people, concepts, and events in an evaluative way.

Attribution theory. Social-cognitive approach that is influential in explaining the individual and social causes of behavior (p. 604).

Audition. Sensation of hearing.

Auditory cortex. Area of the temporal lobes of the cerebral hemisphere that receives and processes auditory signals (pp. 75, 243).

Auditory nerve. Nerve that carries impulses from the cochlea to the cochlear nucleus of the brain (p. 243).

Autistic thinking. Personal, idiosyncratic process involving fantasy, daydreaming, unconscious reactions, and ideas that are not testable by external reality criteria (p. 401).

Autohypnosis. Practice of inducing a hypnotic state in oneself.

Autokinetic effect. Visual illusion in which a stationary point of light in a dark room appears to move slowly from its initial position (p. 580).

Automaticity. In information processing, an apparently effortless, involuntary process triggered without a person's supporting intention (p. 277).

Autonomic nervous system (ANS). Part of the peripheral nervous system that governs activities not normally under voluntary control, such as processes of bodily maintenance (p. 79).

Availability heuristic. Heuristic for estimating probabilities, based on dependence on one's personal experience (p. 414).

Aversion therapy. Type of behavioral therapy used to treat individuals attracted to harmful stimuli in which procedures of aversive learning pair a presently attractive substance with noxious stimuli in order to elicit a negative reaction to the target substance (p. 676).

Aversive conditioning. Classical conditioning procedures in which an unconditional stimulus is of negative value to an organism.

Axon. Extended fiber of a neuron in which nerve impulses occur; transmits signals from the soma to the terminal buttons (p. 83).

B

Backward conditioning. Temporal pattern in classical conditioning in which a conditional stimulus comes on after an unconditional stimulus.

Backward masking. Phenomenon in which a sensory stimulus presented within a certain time after another similar stimulus erases or masks the perception or processing of the first stimulus (p. 351).

Barbiturates. Drugs classified as depressants and used in low doses to reduce anxiety and in higher doses to induce sleep.

Base rate. Statistic that identifies the normally occurring frequency of a given event (p. 6).

Basic level. Optimal level of categorization for thinking about an object; level that can be accessed from memory most quickly and used most efficiently (p. 395).

Basic research. Research undertaken to study a phenomenon or processes for accurate and comprehensive knowledge, initially without regard to later practical applications.

Basilar membrane. Membrane in the cochlea that, when set into motion, stimulates hair cells that produce the neural effects of auditory stimulation (p. 242).

Behavior. Actions by which organisms adjust to their environments (p. 3).

Behavior analysis. Using systematic variation of stimulus conditions to determine all the ways that various kinds of environmental conditions affect the probability that a given response will occur (p. 305).

Behavior assessment. Method of personality assessment in which specific, current, and observable behaviors are identified and rated by judges in a personality profile.

Behavior genetics. Field of research that attempts to identify genetic components of behavioral traits.

Behavior modification. Behavioral psychotherapeutic approach that involves the use of operant and classical-conditioning procedures to eliminate unwanted responses and reinforce desired ones (p. 673).

Behavioral confirmation. Process in which people behave in ways that elicit from others specific reactions that they expect and then use those reactions to confirm their beliefs about themselves (pp. 533, 599).

Behavioral contingency. Conditioning approach using systematic variation of stimulus conditions to determine all the ways that various kinds of experience affect the probability of responses; developed by B. F. Skinner.

Behavioral contract. Explicit agreement (often in writing) about the consequences of specific behaviors; often developed prior to the start of therapy to specify terms of agreement between therapist and client (p. 677).

Behavioral data. Factual information about the behavior of organisms and the conditions under which the behavior occurs or changes (p. 4).

Behavioral ecology. Study of the interaction between the environment and the behavior of the organisms in it; analysis of the ecological settings characteristic of certain behaviors (p. 21).

Behavior genetics. Field of research that attempts to identify genetic components in behavioral traits; study of human behavior genetics by psychologists has greatly increased in recent years (p. 62).

Behavioral gerontology. Study of all the psychological issues of aging and of the elderly (p. 200).

Behavioral measure. Overt action and reaction that is observed and recorded, exclusive of self-reported behavior (p. 37).

Behavioral rehearsal. All the procedures used to establish and strengthen any basic skills; often used in social skills training programs; require client to rehearse mentally a desirable behavior sequence (p. 680).

Behaviorism. Scientific approach formulated by John B. Watson that limits the study of psychology to measurable or observable behavior (p. 17).

Behavioristic approach. Psychological model that is primarily concerned with observable behavior and its relationships to environmental stimulation; behaviorally oriented investigators attempt to understand the ways particular environmental stimuli control certain kinds of behavior (p. 16).

Belief-bias effect. Situation that occurs when a person's prior knowledge, attitudes, or values distort the reasoning process by influencing the person to accept invalid arguments (p. 401).

Bias. Unwanted, systematic source of error in scientific results and conclusions generated by factors not related to the variables being studied or measured.

Biased assimilation. Process in which data consistent with one's beliefs, because they are expected, are given little attention before they are filed mentally as evidence supporting already held views; any ambiguity in data resolved in terms of existing beliefs (p. 411).

Binocular disparity. Displacement between the horizontal positions of corresponding images projected on the retina of each eye.

Biofeedback training. Procedure by which an individual acquires voluntary control over nonconscious biological processes by receiving information about successful changes in those processes; identified through the early work of Neal Miller (pp. 327, 500).

Biological approach. Approach to identifying the causes of behavior that focuses on the functioning of genes, the brain, the nervous system, and the endocrine system (p. 16).

Biological constraint on learning. Any limitation on an organism's capacity to learn that is caused by the inherited sensory, response, or cognitive capabilities of members of a given species (p. 330).

Biological marker. Reliable, biological index of some process or phenomenon of interest (such as depression or schizophrenia) (p. 649).

Biological senescing. Process of becoming biologically older over time (p. 182).

Biomedical therapy. Therapy used to treat psychological disorders by associating the disorders with changing biological or physical mechanisms (p. 662).

Biopsychosocial model. Model of health and illness that suggests that links between the nervous system, the immune system, behavioral styles, cognitive processing, and environmental factors can put people at risk for illness (p. 493).

Bipedalism. Ability to walk upright; an important development in human evolution (p. 59).

Bipolar cell. Nerve cell that combines impulses from many receptors and sends the results to ganglion cells (p. 226).

Bipolar disorder. Mood disturbance characterized by alternating periods of mania and depression (p. 638).

Blind spot. Region of the retina that contains no photoreceptor cells; place where the optic nerve leaves the eye.

Blindsight. Accurate visually guided behavior that occurs nonconsciously in individuals whose visual cortex has been removed (p. 228).

Blocking. Phenomenon in which the ability of a new stimulus to signal an unconditional stimulus is not learned when it is presented simultaneously with a stimulus that is already effective as a signal (p. 316).

Blood-brain barrier. Semipermeable membrane that keeps foreign substances in the bloodstream from flowing into the brain.

Body image. Subjective experience of the appearance of one's body; may include image of the ideal body (p. 188).

Bottom-up process. Process in which incoming stimulus information is perceived as coming from sensory data and is sent upward to the brain for extraction and analysis of relevant information (p. 260).

Brain stem. Hindbrain structure in front of the cerebellum that contains the reticular activating system (RAS) and structures involved in the control of basic life processes.

Brightness. Dimension of color space that captures the intensity of light (p. 230).

Burnout. Syndrome in which an individual loses concern and emotional feeling as a result of continuing emotional arousal and stress; emotional exhaustion; often appears in conjunction with service or health jobs that involve close contact with people in need of help; identified through the research of Christina Maslach (p. 502).

Bystander intervention. Act of assisting a person in need of help;

research shows that the more people who are present when help is needed, the less likely it is that any one of them will provide assistance (p. 592).

C

Cannon-Bard theory of emotion. Central, neural process theory stating that an emotion stimulus produces two co-occurring reactions—arousal and experience of emotion—that do not cause each other; developed independently by Walter Cannon and Philip Bard (p. 466).

Cardinal trait. Trait around which a person organizes his or her life; concept developed by Gordon Allport (p. 513).

Case study. Extensive biography of selected individual used in idiographic personality study (p. 510).

Catch trial. Trial on which no stimulus is presented in order to determine whether response biases are operating in sensory detection tasks.

Catharsis. Process and beneficial effect of expressing strongly felt, but usually inhibited, emotions (p. 670).

Causal theory. Belief about which factors can bring about a particular outcome and which factors cannot.

Cell assembly. Group of neurons acting together as a consequence of particular, repeated stimulation; theory proposed by Donald Hebb.

Central core. Area of the brain containing structures involved primarily in autonomic processes such as heart rate, breathing, swallowing, and digestion (p. 71).

Central nervous system (CNS). Part of the nervous system consisting of the brain and spinal cord (p. 79).

Central sulcus. Vertical groove that divides the cerebral hemispheres into lobes.

Central trait. Major characteristic assumed to yield understanding of an individual (p. 513).

Centration. Thought pattern common during the beginning of the preoperational stage of cognitive development; characterized by the inability of a child to take more than one perceptual factor into account at the same time (p. 163).

Cerebellum. Structure under the back of the cerebrum that controls balance and motor coordination (p. 71).

Cerebral cortex. See *cerebrum* (p. 73).

Cerebral dominance. Tendency for one cerebral hemisphere to play a more dominant role than the other in controlling particular functions (p. 94).

Cerebral hemispheres. Two halves of the cerebrum, connected by the corpus callosum (p. 73).

Cerebrum. Upper part of the brain covered by the cerebral cortex.

Chaining. Operant procedure in which many different responses in a sequence are reinforced until an effective chain of behaviors has been learned (p. 325).

Chemotherapy. Use of drugs to treat mental and behavioral disorders (p. 692).

Chromosome. Large molecule consisting of double strands of DNA and proteins which contain the genes responsible for hereditary traits; every human cell contains 46 chromosomes except the germ cells, which contain only 23 (p. 137).

Chronic stress. Continuous state of arousal in which an individual perceives demands as greater than the inner and outer resources available for dealing with them (p. 480).

Chronological age (CA). Number of months or years since birth (pp. 136, 549).

Chunk. Meaningful unit of information (p. 353).

Chunking. Process of taking single items of information and recoding them on the basis of similarity or some other organizing principle (p. 353).

Ciliary muscle. Structure attached to the edge of the lens that controls its shape.

Circadian rhythm. Consistent pattern of cyclical body activities that lasts approximately 24 hours and is determined by an internal "biological clock" (p. 113).

Classical conditioning. Form of learning in which behavior (conditional response) comes to be elicited by a stimulus (conditional stimulus) that has acquired its power through an association with a biologically significant stimulus (unconditional stimulus); also called *Pavlovian* or *respondent conditioning* (p. 306).

Classification. Processes that group perceptual objects into meaningful categories.

Client. People who enter therapy conducted by professionals who think of psychological disorders as problems in living and not as mental illnesses (p. 663).

Clinical ecology. Field that relates disorders, such as anxiety and depression, to environmental irritants and sources of trauma (p. 699).

Clinical psychologist. Individual who has earned a doctorate in psychology and whose training is in the assessment and treatment of psychological problems; unlike a psychiatrist, a psychologist cannot prescribe medications or physical treatments (pp. 8, 665).

Clinical psychology. Field of psychology specializing in the psychological treatment of individuals with mental and behavioral disorders.

Closure. Perceptual organizing process that leads individuals to see incomplete figures as complete (p. 280).

Cochlea. Primary organ of hearing; it is fluid filled and located in the inner ear (p. 242).

Cognition. Processes of knowing, including attending, remembering, and reasoning; also the content of these processes, such as concepts and memories (p. 380).

Cognitive appraisal. Recognition and evaluation of a stressor to assesses the demand, the size of the threat, the resources available for dealing with it, and the strategies that are appropriate (p. 477).

Cognitive approach. Approach to psychology stressing human thought and all the processes of knowing, such as attending, thinking, remembering, expecting, solving problems, fantasizing, and consciousness (p. 17).

Cognitive behavior modification. Therapeutic approach that combines the cognitive emphasis on the role of thoughts and attitudes in influencing motivation and response with the behavioral emphasis on changing performance through modification of reinforcement contingencies (p. 682).

Cognitive bias. Systematic way of thinking that generally works but may result in faulty inferences, decisions, or judgments when an individual fails to discriminate between appropriate and inappropriate conditions for its use (p. 412).

Cognitive development. Development of processes of knowing, including imagining, perceiving, reasoning, and problem solving (p. 161).

Cognitive dissonance. Theory that the tension-producing effects of discrepant or incongruous cognitions motivate individuals to reduce such tension; developed by Leon Festinger (p. 603).

Cognitive economy. Minimization of the amount of time and effort required to process information (p. 392).

Cognitive map. Mental representation of physical space (p. 334).

Cognitive model. Psychological model of the mental processes intervening between stimulus input and overt responses (p. 382).

Cognitive neuroscience. Field of study combining analysis of the brain's use of neuronal signals to represent and process information with analysis of the mind's cognitive symbol processing (p. 383).

Cognitive psychology. Study of higher mental processes and structures (p. 381).

Cognitive science. Interdisciplinary field of study of the approach to systems and processes that manipulate information (p. 382).

Cognitive therapy. Psychotherapeutic treatment that attempts to change problem feelings and behaviors by changing the way a client thinks about or perceives significant life experiences (p. 682).

Cohort. Group of individuals defined as similar in some way (a birth cohort, for example, consists of individuals born the same year).

Collective unconscious. In Jungian personality theory, that part of an individual's unconscious that is inherited, evolutionarily developed, and common to all members of the species (p. 524).

Color blindness. Inability to distinguish between some or all of the colors in the color solid.

Color space. Three-dimensional model for describing color experience in terms of hue, saturation, and brightness.

Complementary colors. Colors opposite each other on the color circle (p. 230).

Compliance. Conforming one's outward behavior to that of others in order to avoid punishment or rejection by members of a valued group.

Compulsion. Undesired repetitive act carried out in stereotypic, ritualistic fashion by an individual who feels compelled to do so.

Compulsive personality disorder. Personality disorder marked by an excessive concern with rules, roles, trivia, and work and an inability to express warm and tender emotions.

Concept. Mental representation of kinds or categories of items or ideas; formed through experience with the world (p. 392).

Concept formation. Identification of the properties of stimuli that are common to a class of objects or ideas (p. 392).

Concordance rate. Extent to which both members of a set of twins share a particular characteristic or trait; used in assessing heritability, typically of intelligence or mental disorders.

Concrete operational stage. Third of Piaget's cognitive developmental stages (from 7 to 11 years); characterized by understanding of conservation and readiness for other mental operations involving concrete objects.

Conditional response (CR). In classical conditioning, a response elicited by some previously neutral stimulus; occurs as a result of pairing the neutral stimulus with an unconditional stimulus (p. 307).

Conditional stimulus (CS). In classical conditioning, a previously neutral stimulus that comes to elicit a conditional response (p. 307).

Conditioned reinforcer. In instrumental conditioning, a formerly neutral stimulus that has become a reinforcer.

Conditioning trial. In classical conditioning, each pairing of a neutral stimulus with an unconditional stimulus.

Cone. Photoreceptor concentrated in the center of the retina that is responsible for visual experience under normal viewing conditions and for all experiences of color (p. 225).

Conformity. Tendency for people to adopt the behaviors, attitudes, and values of other members of a reference group (p. 583).

Confounding variable. Stimulus other than the variable an experimenter explicitly introduces into a research setting that changes a subject's behavior (p. 35).

Connectionism. Originally, a model of learning in which the hypothetical unit that is learned is an association, habit, or stimulus response bond; in contemporary psychology, a model of mental processes that is based on an analogy with the neuron with connections being developed between a series of nodes; see *parallel distributed processing models* (p. 335).

Consciousness. State of awareness of internal events and of the external environment (p. 107).

Consensual validation. Mutual affirmation of views of reality (p. 108).

Consensus criterion. Criterion used to decide whether an action should be attributed to situational or dispositional factors; involves deciding whether most people would have behaved in a similar or dissimilar fashion in the same situation.

Conservation. Understanding that physical properties do not change when nothing is added or taken away, even though appearances may change; also, the principle that many aspects of biological mechanisms are similar across species which permits studies of systems in lower animals to be valid and informative for understanding human functioning (p. 164).

Consistency criterion. Criterion used to decide whether an action should be attributed to situational or dispositional factors; involves deciding whether an action is a reliable one for a particular person.

Consistency paradox. Observation that personality ratings across time and among different observers are consistent, while behavior ratings across situations are not consistent (p. 517).

Consolidation. Process by which learned information is gradually transformed from a fragile, short-term memory code to a more durable, long-term memory code (p. 373).

Constitutional factor. Basic physical or psychological characteristic shaped by genetic and early environmental influences and remaining fairly consistent throughout a person's life (p. 141).

Construct validity. Degree to which scores on a test based on the defined variable correlate with scores of other tests, judges' ratings, or experimental results already considered valid indicators of the characteristic being measured (p. 544).

Contact comfort. Comfort derived from physical contact with the mother; important in physical and emotional development; developed by Harry Harlow (p. 170).

Context dependence. Principle that material learned when in a particular context will be recalled best when one is exposed to that same context (p. 360).

Context of discovery. Initial phase of research in which observations, beliefs, information, and general knowledge lead to a new idea or a different way of thinking about some phenomenon (p. 28).

Contingency management. General treatment strategy involving changing behavior by modifying its consequences (p. 673).

Continuity. Theoretical view in developmental psychology that development is essentially continuous and occurs through the accumulation of quantitative changes in behaviors.

Control condition. Group of subjects in a controlled experiment that shares all of the characteristics and procedures of the experimental group except exposure to the independent variable being studied (p. 42).

Controlled-drinking controversy. Dispute triggered by the 1962 report of British physician D.L. Davies which challenged the notion that alcoholic recovery could only come about with total abstinence by showing that the vast majority of alcoholics participating in controlled drinking maintained moderate, nonproblematic drinking over many years (p. 698).

Controlled experiment. Research method in which observations of specific behaviors are conducted under systematically varied conditions to which subjects are randomly assigned (p. 42).

Controlled procedures. Consistent procedures for giving instructions, scoring responses, and holding all other variables constant except those being systematically varied.

Convergence. Binocular depth cue in which the two eyes turn inward toward the nose as they fixate on a object that is relatively close.

Convergent thinking. Aspect of creativity involving the use of knowledge and logic to eliminate possibilities and identify the best solution to a problem.

Conversion disorder. Type of psychological disorder in which, in the absence of any psychological or organic cause, there is a loss of a specific sensory or motor function.

Coping. Means of dealing with a situation perceived to be threatening (p. 487).

Cornea. Transparent bulge at the front of the eye filled with a clear liquid called the *aqueous humor.*

Corpus callosum. Bundle of myelinated axons that connects the two cerebral hemispheres (p. 73).

Correlation. Measure of the degree to which two variables are related or covary systematically.

Correlation coefficient. Statistic that indicates the degree of relationship between two variables (p. 41).

Correlational study. Research design that assesses the degree of relationship between variables; does not allow for causal conclusions.

Cortex. See *neocortex.*

Counseling psychologist. Professional psychologist who specializes in providing guidance in areas such as vocational selection, school problems, drug abuse, and marital conflict (p. 664).

Counterconditioning. Technique used in therapy to substitute a new response for an inadequate one by means of conditioning procedures (p. 673).

Countertransference. Process through which a psychoanalyst develops personal feelings about a client because of perceived similarity of the client to significant people in the therapist's life (p. 671).

Covariation principle. Postulated social judgment rule regarding the way attributions about the cause of an event are made in relation to the conditions that vary systematically with the event; developed by Harold Kelley (p. 605).

Covert behaviors. Unseen psychological processes such as thoughts, images, feelings, and physiological reactions that cannot be directly observed.

Creativity. Uninhibited, imaginative thought processes involved in the act of creating; occurrence of uncommon or unusual, but appropriate, responses to situations.

Criterion validity. Degree to which test scores indicate a result on a specific measure that is consistent with some other criterion of the characteristic being assessed (p. 543).

Critical feature. Attribute that is a necessary and sufficient condition for a concept to be included in a category (p. 392).

Critical period. Sensitive time during development when an organism is optimally ready to acquire a particular behavior if the proper stimuli and experiences occur; also, the period of most rapid biochemical change for a given structure of the brain and nervous system (p. 152).

Critical set point. Level on an internal biological "scale" that alerts the central nervous system about the fat in the body; whenever fats stored in specialized fat cells fall below this certain level, signals to eat are sent out; exerts a major influence on the amount eaten and on weight (p. 438).

Cross-cultural research. Research designed to discover whether some behavior found in one culture also occurs in other cultures (p. 42).

Cross-sectional design. Research method in which groups of subjects of different chronological ages are observed and compared at a given time (p. 150).

Crystallized intelligence. Facet of intelligence involving the knowledge a person has already acquired and the ability to access that knowledge; measured by vocabulary, arithmetic, and general information tests; developed by Raymond Cattell (p. 553).

CT (computer tomography) scanner. Device that passes X rays through the brain to scan for abnormalities in brain tissue; allows researchers to link brain structure to the psychological symptoms exhibited by an individual; also known as *CAT Scan* (p. 68).

Cutaneous sense. Skin sense that produces sensations of pressure, warmth, and cold (p. 248).

Cytoplasm. Substance in which most of a cell's biochemical reactions take place and metabolism occurs.

D

Dark adaptation. Process through which the eyes become more sensitive to light under conditions of low illumination.

Darwinian algorithm. Mental shortcut in problem solving that is related to specific aspects of survival or reproduction; first used by Leda Cosmides (p. 407).

Data. Reports of observations; factual evidence.

Daydreaming. Mild form of consciousness alteration in which attention is temporarily shifted away from a response to external stimulation toward an internal stimulus (p. 111).

Debriefing. Procedure, conducted at the end of an experiment, in which the researcher provides the subject with as much information about the study as possible and makes sure that no one leaves feeling confused, upset, or embarrassed (p. 47).

Decentration. Ability to take into account two or more physical dimensions at the same time.

Decibel (db). Unit used to describe physical intensities of sound (p. 240).

Decision making. Process of choosing between alternatives; selecting or rejecting available options (p. 410).

Declarative memory. Memory of explicit information; also known as *fact memory* (p. 344).

Deductive reasoning. Form of thinking in which one draws a conclusion that is intended to follow logically from two or more statements, or premises (p. 401).

Deficiency motivation. Motivation to restore physical or psychological equilibrium (p. 433).

Dehumanization. Defense mechanism in which the human qualities and values of other people are psychologically erased or cancelled.

Delayed forward conditioning. Temporal pattern in classical conditioning in which the conditional stimulus stays on (is delayed) until the unconditional stimulus comes on.

Delta sleep. Stage during the sleep cycle in which electrical brain activity is characterized by large, slow waves.

Delusion. False belief maintained despite contrary evidence and lack of social support; may arise from unconscious sources and appear to serve personal needs, such as relieving guilt or bolstering self-esteem (pp. 262, 646).

Demand characteristic. Cue in an experimental setting that influences the subjects' perception of what is expected of them and systematically influences their behavior within that setting; provides alternative explanations of hypothesized causal effects of given independent variables (p. 590).

Dementia. Disorder in which memory, reasoning, judgment, and other higher mental processes are lost or can no longer be carried out (p. 203).

Dendrite. Branched fiber of a neuron that receives incoming signals (p. 82).

Dependence. Process in which the body or mind becomes adjusted to and dependent on the ingestion of a certain substance.

Dependent variable. Response whose form or amount is expected to vary with changes in the independent variable (p. 7).

Depressant. Drug that slows down mental and physical activities by reducing or inhibiting the transmission of nerve impulses in the central nervous system; examples include alcohol, barbiturates, and opiates.

Depressive episodes. Recurrent periods characterized by a loss of interest or pleasure in most activities and by feelings of sadness, discouragement, dissatisfaction, worthlessness, guilt, and decreased energy.

Descriptive statistics. Collections of data that are used to describe sets of scores collected from different groups of subjects and to describe relationships among variables in terms of averages, variability, and correlation (p. 45).

Determinism. Doctrine that all events—physical, behavioral, and mental—are determined by specific causal factors that are potentially knowable (pp. 12, 32).

Developmental age. Chronological age at which most children show a particular level of physical or mental development (p. 136).

Developmental disability. Significant handicap appearing in childhood or early adolescence, such as dyslexia, that continues for the life of the individual unless treated (p. 62).

Developmental dyslexia. Reading disability that often involves transposition of letters and/or numbers and difficulty knowing right from left and up from down; now thought to involve a brain disorder (p. 145).

Developmental psychology. Branch of psychology concerned with interaction between physical and psychological processes and with stages of growth from conception on (p. 136).

Developmental stage. Period during which physical, mental, or behavioral functioning differs from the functioning before or after (p. 151).

Diathesis-stress disorder. Predisposition to develop a particular disorder as a consequence of pressure to adjust; interactional effect between stressful demands and personal predispositions (p. 650).

Dichotic listening. Experimental technique in which a different auditory stimulus is simultaneously sent to each ear (pp. 110, 273).

Diencephalon. Lower part of the forebrain.

Difference threshold. Smallest physical difference between two stimuli that will be recognized as a difference; also known as the *just noticeable difference* (p. 220).

Direct observation. Observation that can be made with the naked eye and easily recorded in writing or on videotape.

Discontinuity. Theoretical view in developmental psychology that development is discontinuous; describes qualitatively different behaviors at different life periods.

Discounting principle. Tendency for people to consider certain causes as less likely explanations of behavior to the extent that other plausible causes are present.

Discriminative stimulus. Stimulus that acts as a predictor of reinforcement, signaling when a particular behavior will result in positive reinforcement (p. 322).

Diseases of adaptation. Diseases that have their roots in attempts to adapt to stressors.

Dishabituation. Recovery from habituation; occurs when novel stimuli are presented (p. 150).

Display rule. Social norm governing the public expression or display of emotions.

Dispositional theory. Personality theory that focuses on innate qualities as the main influences on behavior.

Dispositional variable. Factor that operates within the individual, such as genetic makeup, motivation, intelligence level, and self-esteem (p. 7).

Dissociation. Functioning of consciousness at different levels without awareness of relevant information at other levels (p. 125).

Dissociative disorder. Psychological reaction in which an individual experiences a sudden, temporary alteration of consciousness in the form of a severe memory loss or loss of personal identity (p. 629).

Distal stimulus. Object in the environment that is the source of external stimulation, as contrasted with the *proximal stimulus,* which is the source of internal stimulation (p. 259).

Distinctiveness criterion. Criterion used to decide if an action should be attributed to situational or dispositional factors; involves determining whether an action is unusual and atypical for a particular person.

Distraction. Inability to focus perceptual processing on the sights and sounds that are relevant to some task in the current situation because of interference from competing thoughts, images, and irrelevant sensory stimuli (p. 269).

Distress. Negative or debilitating reactions to events resulting when the stress response exceeds the individual's controllable limits.

Divergent thinking. Aspect of creativity characterized by an ability to produce unusual, but appropriate, responses to standard questions.

Dominant gene. Gene that is expressed in an individual's development.

Dopamine hypothesis. Theory proposing a relationship between many of the symptoms associated with schizophrenia and a relative excess of the neurotransmitter dopamine at specific receptor sites in the central nervous system (p. 650).

Double bind. Situation in which a child receives from a parent multiple, contradictory messages; hypothesized to contribute to schizophrenic reactions (p. 651).

Double-blind control. Experimental technique in which biased expectations of experimenters can be eliminated by keeping both subjects and experimental assistants unaware of which subjects get which treatment (p. 35).

Drapetomania. Fictitious mental illness believed to cause slaves to run away from their masters; an example of the misuse of the medical model of psychopathology (p. 655).

Dream analysis. Psychoanalytic interpretation of dreams in order to gain insight into a person's unconscious motives or conflicts (p. 671).

Dream work. Process in which the censor transforms the latent content of a dream into manifest content that appears to the dreamer; proposed by Sigmund Freud (p. 120).

Drive. Motivation that is biologically instigated (p. 424).

DSM-III-R. Current diagnostic and statistical manual of the American Psychiatric Association which classifies, defines, and describes over 200 mental disorders (p. 625).

Dual-code model of memory. Theory about the nature of the memory coding system that proposes that both visual *and* verbal codes are used to store information in memory (p. 361).

Dual hypothalamic theory of hunger. Theory that the lateral hypothalamus and ventromedial hypothalamus control the starting and stopping of feeding.

Dualism. Belief that the mechanistic body and brain act independently of the spiritual soul and ephemeral mind (p. 105).

Duplex theory of memory. Theory about the structure of the memory system that postulates qualitatively different systems for short- and long-term memory (p. 363).

Dynamic psychology. Psychological theories that make motivation the most important focus in the effort to understand human nature (p. 424).

E

Echo. Auditory memory lasting several seconds (p. 349).

Ecological optics. Theory of perception that emphasizes the richness of the stimulus information and views the perceiver as an active explorer of the environment; developed by James Gibson (p. 267).

Ecology. Study of the relationship between organisms and their environments (p. 21).

Ectomorph. Somatotype characterized by a body build that is thin, long, and fragile in appearance.

EEG. See *electroencephalogram.*

Efferent system. System that processes information going from the brain to muscles and glands; motor system (p. 216).

Ego. In Freudian theory, that aspect of the personality involved in self-preservation activities and in directing instinctual drives and urges into appropriate channels (p. 522).

Ego defense mechanism. Freudian concept referring to a mental strategy (conscious or unconscious) used by the ego to defend itself from the conflicts experienced in the normal course of life (p. 522).

Ego ideal. In Freudian theory, an individual's view of the kind of person he or she should strive to become.

Egocentrism. Aspect of centrism that refers to a preoperational child's difficulty in imagining a scene from someone else's perspective (p. 163).

Eidetic imagery. Uncommon memory phenomenon in which individuals seem to be able to store detailed, whole images of scenes or complex patterns for a relatively long period of time (p. 361).

Einstellung effect. Mental set, or readiness to respond to new problems, using the same procedures, rules, or formulas that have worked in the past.

Elaboration. Act of relating new input to other information one already has or to goals or purposes for which the new input might later prove relevant; tends to increase retention of learned material (p. 346).

Elaborative rehearsal. Repetition of incoming information permitting new information to be analyzed and related to already stored knowledge; enhances memory retrieval (p. 354).

Electroconvulsive therapy (ECT). "Shock" treatment in which electric current is applied to a patient's temples for a fraction of a second in order to produce upheaval in the central nervous system; used with severely depressed mental patients (p. 691).

Electrode. Thin wire through which small amounts of electric current can pass; used in recording electrical activity in the brain (p. 67).

Electroencephalogram (EEG). Recording of electrical activity of the brain at the scalp (p. 68).

Electromagnetic spectrum. Energy spectrum that includes X rays, microwaves, radio waves, TV waves, and visible light waves.

Emergent-interaction theory. Perspective on the mind-body problem based on five main hypotheses: (a) brain activities give rise to mental states, but these mental states are different from and not wholly reducible to brain states; (b) the mind and conscious experience are interpreted as emergent properties of brain activity; (c) the phenomenon of "inner experience" is a high-order emergent property of the brain which is organized into a hierarchy of increasing degrees of control and regulation of higher levels over lower levels; (d) brain and mind interact; and (e) the conscious mind exerts top-level causal influence over the brain in directing and controlling behavior (p. 107).

Emotion. Complex pattern of changes, including physiological arousal, feelings, cognitive processes, and behavioral reactions, made in response to a situation perceived to be personally significant (p. 460).

Emotion wheel. Model of emotion consisting of a set of innate emotions depicting eight basic emotions made up of four pairs of opposites: joy-sadness, fear-anger, surprise-anticipation, and acceptance-disgust; developed by Robert Plutchik (p. 463).

Empathy. Feeling someone else's emotion; may represent part of the foundation for a child's future system of moral behavior (p. 199).

Empirical investigation. Careful observation of perceivable events or phenomena; a bottom-up type of research based on data collection (p. 28).

Encephalization. Increase in brain size; important development in human evolution (p. 59).

Encoding. Conversion of information into a code capable of being conveyed in a communication channel (p. 346).

Encoding specificity principle. Assumption that subsequent retrieval of information is enhanced if cues received at the time of recall are consistent with those present at the time of encoding (p. 360).

Endocrine system. Glandular system transferring information between cells in different parts of the body by way of hormonal messengers (p. 76).

Endomorph. Somatotype characterized by a body build that is full, round, or soft in appearance.

Endorphin. Neurotransmitter involved in many reactions to pleasure and pain (p. 89).

Engram. Coding of information acquired in the brain; also called *memory trace* (p. 371).

Environmental psychology. Study of the relationships between psychological processes and physical environments, both natural and human-made, emphasizing the reciprocity and mutual influence in an organism-environment relationship (p. 609).

Environmental variable. External influence on behavior (p. 7).

Episodic memory. Component of long-term memory that stores autobiographical information in conjunction with some type of coding designating a time frame for past occurrences (p. 344).

Equity theory. Cognitive theory of work motivation that proposes that workers are motivated to maintain fair and equitable relationships with other relevant persons; also, model that postulates that equitable relationships are those in which the participants' outcomes are proportional to their inputs (p. 455).

ERG theory. Need theory of work motivation that proposes that workers are motivated by three sets of needs—existence needs, relatedness needs, and growth needs; also assumes that higher-level needs can become activated before lower-level needs are met (p. 454).

Erogenous zone. Area of the skin surface that is especially sensitive to stimulation and that gives rise to erotic or sexual sensations (p. 249).

Eros. Life instinct that provides energy for growth and survival; concept of Freudian theory (p. 520).

Estrogen. Female hormone triggering the release of eggs from the ovaries (p. 78).

Ethology. Observational study of animal behavior patterns in the natural environment.

Etiology. Causes of or factors related to the development of a disorder (p. 622).

Eugenics. Movement that advocated improving the human species by encouraging biologically superior people to interbreed while discouraging biologically inferior types from having offspring (p. 541).

Eustress. Positive reaction to a stressor; stressor is defined as a challenge rather than a threat.

Evaluation research. Research that evaluates whether a particular social program or type of therapy achieves previously specified goals and whether it is cost effective.

Evoked potential. Pattern of brain activity caused by specific stimulus (p. 387).

Evolution. Theory that, over time, organisms originate and become adapted to their unique environments through the interaction of biological and environmental variables (p. 57).

Evolutionary approach. Approach to psychology that stresses the importance of behavioral and mental adaptiveness; based on the assumption that human mental abilities, similar to physical abilities, evolved over millions of years to serve particular adaptive purposes (p. 18).

Evolutionary psychology. Branch of psychology that focuses on understanding the evolutionary function served by various aspects of mental and behavioral functioning (p. 14).

Evolutionism. Scientific account of how species have survived and are related through natural selection processes; as proposed by Charles Darwin (p. 13).

Excitation. Stimulation that increases the activity or "firing rate" of a nerve cell.

Existentialism. Philosophy that emphasizes an individual's responsibility and potential for existence fully through choice; in psychology, it is the view that the essential problem of existence is to find oneself, be oneself, and actualize one's potential.

Expectancy bias. Bias that occurs when a researcher or observer subtly communicates to subjects just what kind of behavior he or she expects to find, thereby creating that very reaction in them (p. 29).

Expectancy theory. Cognitive theory of work motivation that proposes that workers are motivated when they expect their effort and job performance to result in desired outcomes (p. 455).

Experience-sampling method. Experimental method in which subjects wear electronic pagers and are asked to record what they are feeling and thinking whenever the pager signals (p. 110).

Experimental analysis of behavior. Skinnerian approach to operant conditioning that systematically varies stimulus conditions in order to discover the ways that various kinds of experience affect the probability of responses; makes no inferences about inner states or nonobservable bases for behavioral relationships demonstrated in the laboratory (p. 318).

Experimental condition. In a controlled experiment, the subject for whom the independent variables or treatment variables are systematically altered (p. 42).

Exposure therapy. Therapy that employs strategies for approaching a feared situation, forcing the client to confront the fear and to be reinforced for successfully approaching it (p. 675).

Extinction. In conditioning, the weakening of a conditioned association in the absence of a reinforcer or unconditional stimulus (p. 309).

Extrinsic motivation. Motivation to engage in an activity to achieve some external consequence (p. 454).

F

Face validity. Degree to which test takers can figure out what a test is supposed to measure (p. 544).

Factor analysis. Mathematical technique used to analyze multiple data sources; enables the researcher to understand how all the data are interrelated by uncovering the meaningful dimensions (factors) that they have in common (p. 510).

Faculty psychology. Rationalistic view associated with Immanuel Kant that assumed that the mind had built-in structures for its development that did not depend on experience.

Fear. Rational emotional reaction to an objectively identified external danger that may induce a person to flee or attack in self-defense (p. 633).

Feature-detection cell. Cell in the visual cortex that responds when specific patterns are present in its receptive field (p. 236).

Feature-detection model. Theory that cells at different levels in the visual system detect different features of a stimulus (p. 236).

Fechner's law. Assertion that the strength of a sensation is proportional to the logarithm of physical stimulus intensity (p. 222).

Fetal brain transplant. Approach to counteracting memory impairment in the aged by transplanting neuron-rich, developing tissue from the brains of aborted fetuses directly into the brains of the elderly (p. 206).

Fetish. Nonsexual object that, through conditioning, becomes capable of producing sexual arousal (p. 443).

Fetishism. Paraphilia in which sexual excitement is achieved with the aid of nonliving objects.

Fetus. Developing embryo, eight weeks after conception until birth.

Field dependence. Proposed personality dimension that reflects a person's preference for external versus internal sources of information in perceptual and social situations (p. 290).

Fight-or-flight syndrome. Sequence of internal activities triggered when an organism is faced with a threat; prepares the body for combat and struggle or for running away to safety (p. 481).

Figural goodness. Perceptual organizational process in which a figure is seen according to its perceived simplicity, symmetry, and regularity; Gestalt principle of perception (p. 281).

Figure. Objectlike regions of the visual field that are distinguished from background (p. 279).

Fixation. According to Freudian theory, arrested psychosexual development because of excessive frustration or overgratification during the current stage.

Fixed-action pattern. Unlearned set of responses stimulated in a given species by a specific environmental event or object (p. 429).

Fixed-interval schedule (FI). In operant conditioning, a procedure in which reinforcement is delivered for the first response made after a fixed amount of time has elapsed.

Fixed-ratio schedule (FR). In operant conditioning, a procedure in which reinforcement is delivered only after a fixed number of responses.

Flooding. Therapy for phobias in which clients are exposed, with their permission, to the stimuli most frightening to them to force them to test reality (p. 675).

Flow. State of near ecstasy that develops when one is totally focused on an activity in the present moment, increasing the likelihood of creative outputs (p. 454).

Fluid intelligence. Ability to see complex relationships and solve problems; measured by tests involving block designs and spatial visualization; developed by Raymond Cattell (p. 553).

Formal operational stage. Fourth of Piaget's cognitive developmental stages; characterized by abstract thinking and conceptualization.

Forward conditioning. Temporal pattern in classical conditioning in which the conditional stimulus comes on before the unconditional stimulus.

Fovea. Area of the retina that contains densely packed cones and forms the point of sharpest vision (p. 226).

Free association. Principal psychoanalytic procedure in which a patient gives a running account of thoughts, wishes, physical sensations, and mental images as they occur (p. 670).

Free-floating anxiety. Anxiety not focused on any particular agent or not associated with any known cause.

Frequency. Number of cycles a wave completes in a given amount of time.

Frequency distribution. Array of individual scores arranged in order from highest to lowest.

Frequency theory. Theory that neural firing rate is determined by a tone's frequency (p. 243).

Frustration. State assumed to exist when goal-directed activity is blocked in some manner.

Function words. Words, such as *the, and,* and *of* that help express relationships between other words.

Functional fixedness. Inhibition in perceiving a new use for an object previously associated with some other purpose; adversely affects problem solving and creativity (p. 404).

Functional pathology. Psychotic disorders, not attributable to brain damage or organic factors, that include affective disorders, paranoid states, and the schizophrenias (p. 622).

Functionalism. Perspective on mind and behavior that focused on examination of the intact organism's interactions with the environment; study of the contents of consciousness (p. 13).

Fundamental attribution error (FAE). Dual tendency of observers to underestimate the impact of situational factors and to overestimate the influence of dispositional factors on an actor's behavior (p. 606).

G

G-factor. General intelligence factor, assumed to be the inherited basic intelligence to which are added specific kinds of additional intelligences, or S-factors (p. 551).

Ganglion cell. Cell that integrates impulses from many bipolar cells into a single firing rate (p. 226).

Gate-control theory. Theory about pain modulation that proposes that certain cells in the spinal cord act as gates to interrupt and block some pain signals while sending others on to the brain (p. 250).

Gender. Psychological phenomenon that refers to learned sex-related behaviors and attitudes of males and females (p.172).

Gender identity. One's sense of "maleness" or "femaleness"; usually includes awareness and acceptance of one's biological sex (p. 172).

Gender role. Set of behaviors and attitudes associated by society with being male or female and expressed publicly by the individual (p. 172).

Gene. Ultramicroscopic area of DNA within a chromosome; basic unit of hereditary transmission (pp. 61, 137).

General adaptation syndrome (GAS). Pattern of nonspecific adaptational physiological mechanisms that occurs in response to continuing threat by almost any serious stressor (p. 482).

Generalization techniques. Techniques that attempt to increase the similarity between therapy and real-life settings of target behaviors, reinforcers, models, and stimulus demands (p. 673).

Generalized anxiety disorder. Disorder in which an individual experiences anxiety that persists for at least one month and is not focused on a specific object or situation (p. 632).

Genetics. Study of the inheritance of physical and psychological traits from ancestors (p. 61).

Genital development. Development of genital tissue.

Genital stage. Fifth and final stage of psychosexual development proposed by Freud (from puberty throughout adulthood); during this period, an individual moves from autoeroticism to gaining sexual gratification from others and also learns socially appropriate channels for the expression of sexual impulses.

Genotype. Genetic constitution of an organism; many genes are not expressed in an individual's development, and those that are show up in phenotypes (p. 58).

Germ cell. In humans, the spermatozoid in the male and the ovum in the female; cell that carries and transmits the genetic information of parents to offspring (p. 137).

Gestalt. German word, meaning *whole configuration,* from which is derived *Gestaltism,* the theoretical approach to perception that emphasizes whole configurations and emergent properties.

Gestalt psychology. School of psychology founded in Germany that maintains that psychological phenomena can be understood only when viewed as organized, structured wholes and not when broken down into primitive perceptual elements (p. 267).

Gestalt therapy. Therapy that focuses on ways to unite mind and body to make a person whole (p. 687).

Glial cells (glia). Cells that hold neurons close together and facilitate neural transmission by forming a sheath that insulates the axons of some neurons, thereby speeding conduction of electrochemical impulses; also function in removal of damaged and dead neurons and prevent poisonous substances in the blood from reaching the brain by forming the blood-brain barrier (p. 84).

Goal setting. Intention to work toward an explicit goal, a primary motivating force in work behavior as goals direct and focus attention, mobilize effort, and increase persistence.

Graded potential. Spreading activity along a dendrite or cell body membrane produced by stimulation from another neuron (p. 85).

Ground. Background areas of the visual field against which figures stand out (p. 279).

Group. Two or more persons who are engaged in interaction so that each influences and is influenced by the other(s).

Group dynamics. Study of how group processes change individual functioning (p. 586).

Group think. Tendency of a decision-making group to filter out undesirable input so that a consensus may be reached, especially if it is line with the leader's viewpoint; developed by Irving Janis (p. 417).

Grouping. Perceptual organizing process through which one tends to group independent items; such grouping follows the laws of proximity, common fate, and similarity.

Growth motivation. Motivation to develop oneself beyond what one has been and done in the past; central to humanistic theories of personality (p. 433).

Gustation. Sensation of taste.

H

Habituation. Decrease in strength of responding when a stimulus is presented repeatedly (p. 150).

Hallucination. False sensory perception produced by a variety of conditions such as mental disorders, brain diseases, and intoxication from various drugs (pp. 126, 260, 646).

Hallucinogen. Psychoactive drug that is capable of producing altered states of awareness in which visual, auditory, and other sensory hallucinations occur.

Halo effect. Bias in which an observer judges a liked person favorably on most or all dimensions (p. 548).

Hardiness. Quality of personal health resulting from the three C's of health: challenge (welcoming change as a tonic not a threat), commitment (developing focused involvement in purposeful activities), and control (maintaining sense of internal control to guide actions) (p. 479).

Hawthorne effect. Bias in which the psychological effect of knowing one is participating in an experiment affects the variables being manipulated and measured.

Health. General condition of the body and mind in terms of their soundness and vigor; not simply the absence of illness or injury (p. 493).

Health psychology. Field of psychology devoted to understanding the ways people stay healthy, the reasons they become ill, and the ways they respond when they become ill (p. 492).

Heredity. Biological transmission of traits from parent to offspring (p. 57).

Heritability estimate. Statistical estimate of the degree of inheritance of a given trait or behavior, assessed by the degree of similarity between individuals who vary in their extent of genetic similarity (p. 559).

Hertz (Hz). Unit of sound frequency expressed in cycles per second (p. 240).

Heuristic. Cognitive strategy, or "rule of thumb," often used as a shortcut in solving a complex inferential task (p. 406).

Hidden observer. Part of the self that maintains an intellectual awareness of, and contact with, reality, even under altered states of awareness, such as hypnosis; concept developed by Ernest Hilgard.

Hippocampus. Part of the limbic system involved in memory (p. 72).

Historical approach. Research design, used in the study of development, in which time is the primary independent variable (p. 183).

HIV. Human immunodeficiency disease, a virus that attacks white blood cells (T-lymphocytes) in human blood, thereby weakening the functioning of the immune system; in many cases, HIV develops into AIDS (p. 498).

Holistic approach. Theoretical approach that explains separate actions in terms of a person's entire personality.

Homeostasis. Constancy or equilibrium of the internal conditions of the body; tendency of organisms to maintain equilibrium and resist change (p. 73).

Hormone. Substance secreted into the bloodstream from specialized cells located in various glands; is carried in the blood until it attaches to the surface of a target tissue (p. 76).

Hospice approach. Approach to serving the needs of the chronically ill in a homelike atmosphere rather than a hospital; intended to make the process of dying more humane than it can be in institutional settings (p. 208).

Hozho. Navajo concept referring to harmony, peace of mind, goodness, ideal family relationships, beauty in arts and crafts, and health of body and spirit (p. 492).

Hue. Dimension of color space that corresponds to the light's wavelength (p. 230).

Human-potential movement. Therapy movement that encompasses all those practices and methods that release the potential of the average human being for greater levels of performance and greater richness of experience (p. 686).

Human sexuality. Combination of the physical characteristics and capacities for specific sex behaviors; psychosexual learning, values, norms, and attitudes about sexual behaviors (p. 441).

Humanistic approach. Psychological model that emphasizes an individual's phenomenal world and inherent capacity for making rational choices and developing to maximum potential (p. 18).

Hypnosis. Altered state of awareness induced by a variety of techniques and characterized by deep relaxation, susceptibility to suggestions, and changes in perception, memory, motivation, and self-control (p. 123).

Hypnotic induction. Preliminary set of activities that prepares a participant for the altered awareness state of hypnosis.

Hypnotizability. Degree to which an individual is responsive to standardized hypnotic suggestions (p. 123).

Hypochondriasis. Pathological condition characterized by a preoccupation that certain bodily sensations are possible signs of serious disease, despite medical reassurance.

Hypothalamus. Structure below the thalamus that regulates eating, drinking, body temperature, hormonal activity, and other processes (p. 72).

Hypothesis. Tentative and testable explanation of the relationship between two (or more) events or variables; often stated as a prediction that a certain outcome will result from specific conditions (p. 32).

Hysteria. Mental illness, characterized by a cluster of symptoms that includes paralysis or pains in different parts of the body, dizziness, lameness, and blindness, all without clear physical cause; no longer used diagnostically (p. 621).

I

Icon. Visual memory lasting about half a second (p. 349).

Id. In Freudian theory, the primitive, unconscious part of the personality that operates irrationally and acts on impulse (p. 521).

Identification and recognition. Two ways of attaching meaning to percepts; top-down process of perception (p. 258).

Identity. Sense of self; includes the perception of oneself as being distinct from other people and the perception of others as being related to oneself or alien to oneself.

Idiographic approach. Methodological approach to the study of personality processes in which emphasis is placed on understanding the unique aspects of each individual's personality rather than on common dimensions across which all individuals can be measured (p. 510).

Illness. Documented pathology, such as biological or physiological damage, cell pathology, and blood chemistry (p. 493).

Illness prevention. General strategies and specific tactics to eliminate or reduce the risk that people will get sick (p. 494).

Illusion. Experience of a stimulus pattern in a manner that is demonstrably incorrect but shared by others in the same perceptual environment (p. 260).

Illusory conjunctions. Perceptual errors that occur when the primitive features of objects, such as their colors and shapes, are not combined correctly by the visual system (p. 271).

Immediate memory span. Limited, brief (between five and nine chunks of information) storage capacity of short-term memory (p. 353).

Implicit memory. Nonconscious form of memory marked by the facilitation or improvement in performance of a task when a learner has recently had some experience relevant to the task but is not conscious of that experience (p. 345).

Implosion therapy. Behavioral, therapeutic technique that exposes a client to stimuli, previously rated by the client as most anxiety-provoking, in an attempt to extinguish the anxiety associated with the stimuli (p. 675).

Impression formation. Process of knowing other people and of determining their traits, abilities, and attitudes.

Imprinting. Primitive form of learning in which some infant animals physically follow and form an attachment to the first moving object they see and/or hear (p. 169).

In-group. Term used by members for their own group when one group of people is differentiated from another.

In-group bias. Tendency for a person to evaluate more positively his or her own group.

In vivo therapy. Therapy approach in which therapists work with their clients in the settings associated with the clients' problems, such as in airplanes for those who suffer from flying phobias and must fly for their jobs (p. 664).

Incentive. External stimulus that arouses motives in the laboratory or in everyday settings (p. 428).

Incentive motivation. Motivation aroused by external stimuli (p. 428).

Independent variable. In a controlled experiment, the stimulus that, when varied, is expected to change some behavior (the dependent variable) (p. 7).

Index variable. Variable that is itself not causal but is a manifest sign of an underlying causal variable.

Induced motion. Illusion in which a stationary point of light within a moving reference frame is seen as moving and the reference frame is perceived as stationary (p. 283).

Inductive reasoning. Form of reasoning in which a conclusion is made about the probability of some state of affairs, given the available evidence (p. 402).

Infancy period. In humans, the period from birth to 18 months; from the Latin word for _incapable of speech_.

Inference. Logical assumption made on the basis of some evidence, other than direct observation, about something that is happening inside an organism; the reasoning process of drawing a conclusion on the basis of a sample of evidence or on the basis of prior beliefs and theories (p. 411).

Inferential statistics. Measures that allow researchers to know what conclusions can legitimately be drawn from data.

Information-processing model. Common approach to studying cognitive processes that proposes that all forms of cognition (such as memory, perception, and the structure of knowledge) can be understood by analyzing them into component parts; operations are performed on incoming information that goes through a series of stages arranged in a processing hierarchy that moves from simpler to more complex (p. 382).

Informational influence. Reason that people conform to group pressures; desire to be correct and right, to understand how best to act in a given situation (p. 582).

Inhibition. Stimulation that decreases activity or the "firing rate" of a nerve cell.

Initiation rite. Ritual in many nonindustrial societies that takes place around puberty and serves as public acknowledgment of the passage from childhood to adulthood; also called _rite of passage_ (p. 185).

Insanity. Legal designation for the state of an individual judged to be legally irresponsible or incompetent (p. 654).

Insight. Phenomenon in problem-solving tasks in which learning results from an understanding of relationships (often sudden) rather than from blind trial and error (p. 335).

Insight therapy. Technique by which the therapist guides a patient toward discovering insights between present symptoms and past origins; also known as _psychodynamic therapy_ (p. 668).

Insomnia. Chronic inability to sleep normally; shown by difficulties in falling asleep, frequent wakings, and inability to return to sleep; often cause by anxiety or pain (p. 117).

Instinct. Unlearned behavior pattern that appears in the same form in every member of a species at a certain point in the species' development.

Instinctual drift. Tendency for learned behavior to drift toward instinctual behavior over time (p. 330).

Instrumental conditioning. Learning about the relationship between a response and its consequences; see also _operant conditioning_.

Intelligence. Global capacity to profit from experience and to go beyond given information about the environment (p. 549).

Intelligence quotient (IQ). Index derived from standardized tests of intelligence; originally obtained by dividing an individual's mental age by chronological age and then multiplying by 100; now directly computed as an IQ test score (p. 550).

Interaction. Joint effect of two independent variables on a behavior that could not have been predicted from the separate effect of each on the dependent measure.

Interactionist perspective. View that psychopathology is the product of a complex interaction between a number of biological and psychological factors (p. 624).

Interjudge reliability. Degree to which different observers make similar ratings of or agree about what a subject did during an observation period (p. 548).

Internal consistency. Measure of reliability; the degree to which a test yields similar scores across its different parts, on odd vs. even items, and on split halves (p. 543).

Interneuron. Neuron providing communication between other neurons; make up the bulk of nerve cells in the brain (p. 83).

Interposition. Depth cue present when one object blocks the view of part of another object; also known as *occlusion* (p. 285).

Intervening variable. Condition or event whose existence is inferred in order to explain a link between some observable input and a measurable response output (p. 5).

Interview. Face-to-face conversation between a researcher and a respondent for the purpose of gathering detailed information about the respondent (p. 546).

Intimacy. Capacity to make a full commitment—sexual, emotional, and moral—to another person (p. 192).

Intrinsic motivation. Motivation to engage in an activity for its own sake (p. 454).

Introspection. Method of gathering data in which trained subjects report their current conscious experiences as accurately as possible.

Introversion-extraversion. Personality dimension that describes people by the degree to which they need other people as sources of rewards and as providers of cues to appropriate behaviors.

Intuitive psychologist. Layperson with naive, or untrained, theories about the nature of personality, motivation, and the causes of human behavior (p. 604).

Invariant. Entity in the environment that does not change its identity even though it does change its appearance.

Invulnerable. Describes children who can withstand extreme stress, deprivation, or disadvantage and emerge relatively unscathed, showing normal personality functioning and good adjustment.

Ion. Electrically charged particle that flows through the membrane of a cell, changing its polarity and thereby its capacity to conduct electrochemical signals.

Ion channel. Excitable membrane molecule that produces and transduces signals in living cells (p. 87).

Iris. Muscular disk that surrounds the pupil and expands and contracts to control the amount of light entering the eye.

J

James-Lange theory of emotion. Peripheral-feedback theory of emotion stating that an eliciting stimulus triggers a behavioral response that sends different sensory and motor feedback to the brain and creates the feeling of a specific emotion; developed independently by William James and Carl Lange (p. 466).

Job analysis. Study of a specific job focusing on the nature and degree of skill required, the amount of effort demanded, the extent to which an individual in that job is responsible for decisions that affect company resources or personnel, and any other types of stress the job may entail (p. 569).

Job design. Research design of which the goals are to identify the characteristics of work that make it enjoyable and motivating and then to use this information in designing or redesigning jobs.

Judgment. Process by which we form opinions, reach conclusions, and make critical evaluations of events and people based on available material; also, the product of that mental activity (p. 410).

Juke Family. Family allegedly studied for many generations in an attempt to show that "bad seeds" planted in family genes yield defective human offspring; used as an example of the need for sterilization and extreme remedial treatments for those who are mentally and morally incompetent; see *Kallikak Family* (p. 556).

Just noticeable difference (JND). See *difference threshold* (p. 220).

K

Kallikak Family. Family allegedly studied for many generations to show that "bad seeds" planted in family genes yield defective human offspring; father sired two lines—a "bad" one from mating with a "defective" woman and a "good" one from mating with a supposedly "normal" woman; see *Juke Family* (p. 556).

Kinesthetic sense. Sense concerned with bodily position and movement of the body parts relative to each other (p. 246).

L

Language acquisition device (LAD). Proposed biologically based mental structure that many theorists believe plays a major role in children's language learning, facilitating the comprehension and production of speech; concept of Noam Chomsky (p. 156).

Latency stage. Fourth of Freud's psychosexual developmental stages (from age 6 to puberty); during this stage satisfaction is gained primarily through exploration of the environment and development of skills and interests.

Latent content. In Freudian dream analysis, the hidden, actual content of a dream (p. 120).

Latent learning. Associations learned from experience and observation during which there is no change in overt behavior.

Lateral geniculate nucleus. Relay point in the thalamus through which impulses pass when going from the eye to the occipital cortex (p. 227).

Lateral inhibition. Tendency for a receptor excited by an intense amount of light to suppress neighboring receptors receiving less intense light (p. 235).

Lateral sulcus. Deep horizontal groove that serves to divide the cerebral hemispheres into lobes.

Lateralization of emotion. Different influence of the two brain hemispheres on various emotions; the left hemisphere seems to influence positive emotions, such as happiness, while negative emotions, such as anger, are more influenced by the right hemisphere (p. 462).

Law of association. Doctrine that holds that we acquire knowledge through associating ideas, or mental events that originate in sensory information from the environment.

Law of common fate. Law of grouping that states that elements moving in the same direction at the same rate are grouped together (p. 281).

Law of effect. Basic law of learning that states that the power of a stimulus to evoke a response is strengthened when the response is followed by a reward and weakened when it is not followed by a reward (p. 317).

Law of forward conduction. Principle stating that neurons transmit information in only one direction—from the axon of one neuron to the dendrites or soma of the next (p. 83).

Law of pragnanz. In Gestalt psychology, the general principle that the simplest organization requiring the least cognitive effort will emerge in our perceptions (p. 281).

Law of proximity. Law of grouping that states that the nearest, or "most proximal," elements are grouped together (p. 280).

Law of similarity. Law of grouping that states that the most similar elements are grouped together (p. 281).

Law of specific nerve energy. Principle that all nerve impulses are virtually identical and that the quality of sensory experience is determined by the type of receptor stimulated.

Lazarus-Schachter theory of emotion. Theory stating that the experience of emotion is the joint effect of physiological arousal and cognitive appraisal, which serves to determine how an ambiguous inner state of arousal will be labeled; aspects developed independently by Richard Lazarus and Stanley Schachter (p. 466).

Learned helplessness. General pattern of nonresponding in the presence of noxious stimuli that often follows after an organism has previously experienced noncontingent, inescapable aversive stimuli; concept of Martin Seligman (pp. 328, 640).

Learning. Process based on experience that results in a relatively permanent change in behavior or behavioral potential (p. 303).

Learning-performance distinction. Difference between what has been learned and what is expressed in overt behavior that the organism performs (p. 303).

Lens. Structure behind the iris through which light travels before reaching the central chamber of the eye.

Lesion. Careful destruction of a particular brain area by surgical removal, the cutting of connections, or the destruction of brain tissue (p. 67).

Levels-of-processing theory. Theory that there is a single system of memory in which the only differentiation is in the levels of processing applied to incoming information (p. 364).

Libido. In Freudian theory, the psychic energy that drives individuals toward sensual pleasures of all types, including sexual ones (p. 520).

Life-change unit. In stress research, the measure of the stress levels of different types of change experienced during a given period; used to predict subsequent illness—as LCU increase above a certain level, the likelihood of illness also increases (p. 474).

Life history data. Information about a person's life taken from different types of available records, such as school or military records, written productions, personal journals, and medical data (p. 546).

Life-span development. Study of the continuities, stabilities, and changes in physical and psychological processes that characterize human functioning from conception through the final phases of life (p. 180).

Life-span developmental psychology. Study of personality, mental functioning, and other vital aspects of human nature as they continue to develop and change throughout the entire life cycle (p. 181).

Limbic system. Area at the upper end of the old brain that contains centers for emotional behavior and basic motivational urges (p. 71).

Linear perspective. Depth cue based on the illusion that parallel lines converge to a point on the horizon as they recede into distance.

Locus of control orientation. Generalized belief about whether outcomes of our actions are caused by what we do or by events outside our control (p. 435).

Loneliness. Perception of being unable to achieve the level of affiliation that a person desires.

Long-term memory (LTM). Memory processes associated with the preservation of information for retrieval at any later time; theoretically having unlimited capacity (p. 357).

Long-term potentiation. High-frequency stimulation of inputs to the hippocampus, which has been found to increase memory strength for new learning by causing changes in the shape of synapses, leading to the formation of new synaptic contacts on nerve cells (p. 374).

Longitudinal design. Research design in which the same subjects are observed repeatedly, sometimes over many years (p. 150).

Longitudinal study. Method of scientific investigation in which selected measurements and observations of the same individuals are taken repeatedly over time.

Loudness. Perceptual dimension influenced by the amplitude of a sound wave; sound waves with large amplitudes are experienced as loud and those with small amplitudes as soft (p. 240).

Lucid dreaming. Being consciously aware while you are still sleeping that you are dreaming (p. 122).

M

Magnetic resonance imaging (MRI). Technique for exploring the living brain; uses magnetic fields and radio waves to generate pulses of energy within the brain (p. 68).

Magnitude estimation. Method of constructing psychophysical scales by having observers scale their sensations directly into numbers; developed by S. S. Stevens (p. 222).

Main effect. In a 2 x 2 research design, the effect that one independent variable has on the dependent variable, regardless of the other independent variable or their interaction.

Maintenance rehearsal. Active repetition of information in order to enhance subsequent access to it (p. 354).

Manic episode. Psychotic reaction characterized by recurring periods of extreme elation, unbounded euphoria without sufficient reason, and grandiose thoughts or feelings about personal abilities (p. 638).

Manifest content. In Freudian dream analysis, the surface content of a dream that is remembered; assumed to mask the real meaning of a dream (p. 120).

Masochism. Psychosexual disorder in which sexual excitement is derived from the experience of personal suffering (p. 627).

Materialism. See *monism.*

Maturation. Continuing influence of heredity during development and later life; age-related physical and behavioral changes characteristic of a species (p. 139).

Mean. Most commonly used measure of the central tendency of a distribution; the average value for a group of scores (p. 45).

Mechanistic approach. Belief that complex behavior can be reduced to its underlying physical basis.

Median. Measure of the central tendency of a distribution; the score within a group of observations of which half have lower scores and half have greater scores (p. 45).

Mediated observation. Observation that requires the use of special equipment or instrumentation.

Medical model. Paradigm that defines and studies psychological abnormality in a way analogous to that used to study and treat physical illness.

Meditation. Form of consciousness alteration designed to enhance self-knowledge and well-being by losing self-awareness through special rituals and exercises (p. 125).

Medulla. Area of the brain stem responsible for controlling repetitive processes such as breathing and heartbeat (p. 71).

Memory. Mental capacity to store and later recognize or recall events that were previously experienced (p. 343).

Memory code. Representation of information in some encoded form in storage (p. 352).

Memory trace. See *engram* (p. 371).

Menarche. Onset of menstruation (p. 188).

Mental age (MA). In Binet's measure of intelligence, the age at which a child is performing intellectually, expressed in terms of the average age at which normal children achieve a particular score (p. 549).

Mental disorder. Clinically significant behavioral or psychological syndrome or pattern that occurs in an individual and that is typically associated with either a distressing symptom or impairment in one or more important areas of functioning.

Mental map. Cognitive representation of physical space (p. 398).

Mental operation. Mental manipulation of information; depends on concepts of objects rather than direct perceptual information.

Mental set. Tendency to respond to a new problem in the manner used to respond to a previous problem (p. 404).

Mere exposure effect. Ability of repeated exposures to the same stimulus to produce greater attraction toward that stimulus; preference that can develop without awareness of the cognitions involved.

Mesomorph. Somatotype characterized by a body build that is muscular, rectangular, and strong.

Metabolism. Breakdown of nutrients into body energy.

Metacognition. Thinking about thinking.

Metacognitive knowledge. Awareness of what you know and how well you are comprehending a situation (p. 406).

Mnemonics. Special strategies or devices that use already familiar items during the encoding of new information to enhance subsequent access to the information in memory (p. 359).

Mode. Measure of the central tendency of a distribution; score occurring most frequently among the observations (p. 45).

Model. Conceptual framework that provides a simplified way of thinking about the basic components of a field of knowledge (p. 14).

Moderator variable. Condition in a situation or in an individual's functioning that can change the effect of a stressor.

Molar level of analysis. Level of analysis that focuses on the behavior of the whole functioning organism in a complex environment; also known as *macro level.*

Molecular level of analysis. Level of analysis that focuses on precisely defined units of behavior that are somewhat larger than those at the micro level but smaller than those at the molar level.

Monism. View that mind and brain are aspects of a single reality; also called *materialism* (p. 105).

Mood-congruent processing. Processing of material that is congruent with one's prevailing mood; it is more likely to be attended to, noticed, and processed more deeply with greater elaborative associations; developed by Gordon Bower (p. 471).

Mood-dependent retrieval. Better recall of events experienced earlier that had an emotional component when the person doing the recall is in that same mood; concept developed by Gordon Bower (p. 470).

Morality. System of beliefs and values that ensures that individuals will keep their obligations to others in society and will behave in ways that do not interfere with the rights and interests of others (p. 197).

Motherese. Special form of speech with an exaggerated and high-pitched intonation that adults use to speak to infants and young children; concept developed by Anne Fernald (p. 157).

Motivation. Process of starting, directing, and maintaining physical and psychological activities; includes mechanisms involved in preferences for one activity over another and the vigor and persistence of responses (p. 424).

Motive. Psychologically and socially instigated motivation, assumed to be, at least in part, learned (p. 424).

Motor cortex. Area of the cerebral cortex along the front of the central sulcus; devoted to sending messages to the muscles; also known as the *motor projection area* (p. 74).

Motor neuron. Neuron that carries messages from the central nervous system to the muscles or glands (p. 83).

Motor projection area. See *motor cortex.*

Multiple personality disorder (MPD). Dissociative disorder in which different aspects of a personality function independently of one another creating the appearance of two or more distinct personalities within the same individual (p. 629).

Myelin sheath. Covering made up of glial cells that insulates some axons, speeding the conduction of nerve impulses.

N

Narcissistic personality disorder. Personality disorder marked by a grandiose sense of self-importance, preoccupation with fantasies of success and power, and a need for constant attention or admiration (p. 629).

Narcolepsy. Sleep disorder characterized by an irresistible urge to sleep during the daytime (p. 117).

Natural selection. Darwin's idea that favorable adaptations to features of the environment allow some members of a species to produce more offspring than others (p. 58).

Naturalistic observation. Observation of naturally occurring behaviors with no attempt to change or interfere with them; data collection without laboratory controls or the manipulation of variables.

Nature. In the nature-nurture debate, hereditary influences on behavior (p. 14).

Nature-nurture controversy. Debate in psychology concerning the relative importance of heredity (nature) and learning or experience (nurture) in determining development and behavior (p. 143).

Need for achievement. Assumed basic human need to strive toward achievement of goals that motivates a wide range of behavior and thinking; concept developed by Henry Murray and David McClelland using TAT projective assessment (p. 450).

Needs hierarchy. Sequence from the most primitive level of basic needs to higher levels of needs that are attended to only after lower ones are satisfied; model developed by Abraham Maslow (p. 433).

Negative cognitive sets. Idea that people take a negative view of events in their lives for which they feel responsible (p. 640).

Negative reinforcement. Following a response, the condition of not receiving or escaping an aversive stimulus that increases the probability of the response.

Negative reinforcer. Stimulus not received (terminated or avoided)

after a response that increases the probability of that response (p. 320).

Neocortex. Outer layer of the cerebrum necessary for precise perception and conscious thought; also known as the *cortex.*

Neonate. Newborn infant; human between birth and one month of age.

Neural network. Circuits or systems of neurons functioning together to perform tasks that individual cells cannot carry out alone (p. 92).

Neural substrate. Basis of thoughts, feelings, and actions in the activity of the brain and nervous system; sought by neuropsychologists.

Neuromodulator. Substance that modifies or modulates the activities of a postsynaptic neuron (p. 89).

Neuron. Nerve cell specialized to provide rapid communication within and between adjacent cells (p. 82).

Neuron doctrine. Theory advanced by Ramon y Cajál that states that all parts of the brain are composed of specialized cells called *neurons.*

Neuropathic pain. Pain caused by abnormal functioning or overactivity of nerves (p. 249).

Neuropsychology. Branch of physiological psychology that studies behavior and mental processes as functions of the activities of the brain and nervous system.

Neuroscience. Branch of the life sciences that deals with the anatomy, physiology, and biochemistry of the brain and nervous system.

Neurosis. Mental disorder in which there are one or more symptoms related to ineffective attempts to deal with anxiety; no longer used as diagnostic category in *DSM-III.*

Neurotic disorder. Mental disorder in which a person does not have signs of brain abnormalities and does not display grossly irrational thinking or violate basic norms but does experience subjective distress, especially anxiety (p. 627).

Neurotransmitter. Chemical messenger released from neurons that crosses the synapse and interacts with receptors on the postsynaptic cell membrane (p. 87).

Nociceptive pain. Pain resulting from signals sent from specialized nerve endings in the skin, through the spinal cord, and into the brain (p. 249).

Nomothetic approach. Methodological approach to the study of personality processes in which emphasis is placed on identifying universal trait dimensions or lawful relationships between different aspects of personality functioning (p. 510).

Non-REM sleep (NREM). Period when a sleeper is not showing REM (rapid eye movements); characterized by less dream activity than REM sleep (p. 113).

Nonconscious processes. Processes involving information that is not represented in either consciousness or memory, such as the organization of incoming stimuli into figure and ground (p. 108).

Norm. Standard based on measurements of a large group of people; used for comparing the score of an individual with those of others within a well-defined group; in social psychology, the group standard of approved behavior (p. 545).

Norm crystallization. Convergence of the expectations of a group of individuals into a common perspective as they talk and carry out activities together (p. 580).

Normal curve. Symmetrical distribution of scores where, in the ideal case, the mean, median, and mode have the same value.

Normative influence. Effect of a group on an individual striving to be liked, accepted, and approved of by others (p. 582).

Normative investigation. Research effort designed to describe what is characteristic of a specific age or developmental stage (p. 149).

Nucleus. Area of the cell that contains DNA and directs activities in the cytoplasm through the production of nucleic acids.

Nurture. In the nature-nurture debate, environmental influences on behavior (p. 14).

Nymphomania. Exaggerated sexual desire in females.

O

Object permanence. Recognition that objects exist independently of an individual's action or awareness (p. 163).

Observational learning. Process of learning new responses by watching the behavior of another (pp. 332, 529).

Observer bias. Distortion of perceptual evidence due to the personal motives and expectations of the viewer (p. 29).

Observer-report method. In psychological assessment, the evaluation of some aspect of a person's behavior by another person (p. 547).

Obsession. Persistent and unwanted thought, image, or impulse.

Obsessive-compulsive disorder. Mental disorder characterized by obsessions and compulsions (p. 634).

Occlusion. See *Interposition*.

Olfaction. Sensation of smell.

Olfactory bulb. Center where odor-sensitive receptors send their signals, located just below the frontal lobes of the cortex (p. 246).

Operant. Organism behavior that can be characterized in terms of the observable effects it has on the environment (p. 318).

Operant conditioning. Learning in which the probability or ratio of a response is changed by a change in its consequences; see also *instrumental conditioning*.

Operant extinction. Withholding delivery of a positive reinforcer in order to extinguish an operant behavior (p. 320).

Operational definition. Definition of a variable or condition in terms of the specific operations an investigator uses to determine its presence (p. 34).

Opiate. Drug derived from the opium poppy; classified as a depressant.

Opponent-process theory. Theory that all color experiences arise from three systems, each of which include two "opponent" elements (red vs. green, blue vs. yellow, and black vs. white) (p. 233).

Optic chiasma. Region of the brain where messages from the inner half of each retina cross over to the opposite hemisphere.

Optic nerve. Axons of the ganglion cells that carry information from the eye back toward the brain (p. 227).

Optimal arousal. Level of arousal at which people best perform tasks of different levels of difficulty (p. 431).

Optimistic bias. Cognitive bias in which people claim that they are less likely than their peers to be affected by hazards; promotes a general sense of optimism (p. 417).

Oral stage. First and most primitive of Freud's psychosexual developmental stages, during which the mouth region is the primary source of gratification—from nourishment, stimulation, and contact with the environment.

Organic pathology. Pathology that is caused by a known organic condition (p. 622).

Organismic variable. Dispositional factors such as traits, states, status characteristics, and time; term used by those who study only human behavior (p. 7).

Organizational psychologist. Psychologist who studies various aspects of human relations, such as communication among employees, socialization or enculturation of workers, leadership, job satisfaction, stress and burnout, and overall quality of life in work environments (p. 454).

Orientation constancy. Ability to perceive the actual orientation of objects in the world despite their varying orientation in the retinal image.

Orienting reaction. Physiological and behavioral response that maximizes sensitivity to environmental input and prepares the body for emergency action.

Orienting response. General response of attention to a source of novel stimulation.

Out-group. Term used by members of one group to describe another group when one group of persons is differentiated from another that is the in-group.

Oval window. Structure at the base of the cochlea against which the footplate of the stirrup vibrates.

Overregularization. Grammatical error, usually appearing during early language development, in which rules of the language are applied too widely, resulting in incorrect linguistic forms (notably in forming past tense and plurals) (p. 160).

Overt behavior. Response that is visible to an observer.

P

Pain. Body's response to noxious stimuli that are intense enough to cause, or threaten to cause, tissue damage (p. 249).

Panic disorder. Anxiety disorder in which an individual experiences recurrent episodes of intense anxiety and feelings of unpredictability and symptoms of autonomic hyperactivity that usually last for a few minutes (p. 632).

Paradigm. Symbolic model in research that represents the essential features of a process being investigated (p. 32).

Parallel distributed processing model (PDP). Model of the mind in which information is processed in a massively distributed, interactive, parallel system that can carry out various activities simultaneously through exciting or inhibiting the connections between processing units; also known as *connectionism* (p. 383).

Parallel forms. Different forms of a test used to assess test reliability; the variance of forms reduces effects of direct practice, memory, or the desire of an individual to appear consistent on the same items (p. 543).

Paranoid disorders. A group of psychotic disorders characterized by well-developed, systematized, intricate delusions.

Paraphilia. Psychosexual disorder in which sexual excitement necessarily and involuntarily demands the presence of nonconventional sexual objects, practices, or circumstances.

Parasympathetic division. Division of the autonomic nervous system that deals with internal monitoring and regulation of various bodily functions (p. 80).

Parental investment. Time and energy parents must spend raising their offspring (p. 442).

Partial reinforcement effect. Behavioral principle that responses acquired under intermittent reinforcement are more difficult to extinguish than those acquired with continuous reinforcement (p. 326).

Partial-report procedure. Experimental technique used in memory studies in which subjects presented with a pattern containing several individual stimuli are subsequently asked to recall a portion of the pattern instead of all the information presented (p. 350).

Participant modeling. Therapeutic technique in which a therapist demonstrates the desired behavior and a client is aided, through supportive encouragement, to imitate the modeled behavior (p. 679).

Passive smoking. Inhaling the cigarette smoke of others which is in the atmosphere of one's living or working environment (p. 478).

Pastoral counselor. Member of a religious order who specializes in the treatment of psychological disorders, often by combining spiritual direction with practical problem-solving direction (p. 665).

Patient. Those hospitalized with mental problems; term used by professionals who take a biomedical approach to the treatment of psychological problems to describe those being treated (p. 663).

Patient nonadherence. Failure of patients to adhere to medical regimens or to follow physicians' recommendations (p. 499).

Patterns of reinforcement. In operant conditioning, the patterns of delivering or withholding reinforcement that determine the timing and spacing of consequences.

Payoff matrix. Matrix for estimating gains and losses in a detection trial.

Peace psychology. Interdisciplinary approach to the prevention of nuclear war and the maintenance of peace (p. 610).

Pedophilia. Paraphilia that involves an adult's sexual activity or fantasy about sexual activity with young children.

Perceived control. Belief that one has the ability to make a difference in the course or the consequences of some event or experience; often helpful in dealing with stressors (p. 489).

Percept. What a perceiver experiences (p. 256).

Perception. Processes that organize information in the sensory image and interpret it as having been produced by properties of objects in the external, three-dimensional world (pp. 215, 257).

Perceptual constancy. Ability to retain an unchanging percept of an object despite variations in the retinal image (p. 287).

Perceptual defense. Hypothesized perceptual process that protects a person from identifying stimuli that are unpleasant or anxiety provoking.

Perceptual grouping. Ways we perceive a number of individual elements in terms of groups; based on a number of principles described by Gestalt psychologists (p. 280).

Perceptual organization. Processes that put sensory information together to give the perception of a coherent scene over the whole visual field (p. 278).

Perceptual set. Readiness to detect a particular stimulus in a given context.

Performance. External behavior that indicates learning has taken place; however, performance does not reveal everything that has been learned (p. 303).

Peripheral nervous system (PNS). Part of the nervous system outside of the central nervous system; links sensory receptors to CNS and from CNS to muscles and glands (p. 79).

Permissive parenting. Parenting characterized by little parental structure.

Person-centered therapy. Humanistic approach to treating people with problems that emphasizes the healthy psychological growth of the individual; based on the assumption that all people share the basic tendency of human nature toward self-actualization; developed by Carl Rogers (p. 685).

Personal bias. Error in estimating or evaluating some experience or phenomenon due to the operation of subjective factors (p. 29).

Personal construct. In George Kelly's theory, a person's interpretation of reality, or beliefs about the way two things are similar to each other and different from a third (p. 528).

Personality. Unique psychological qualities of an individual that influence a variety of characteristic behavior patterns (both overt and covert) across different situations and over time (p. 509).

Personality disorder. Chronic, inflexible, maladaptive pattern of perceiving, thinking, and behaving that seriously impairs an individual's ability to function in social or other settings (p. 628).

Personality inventory. Self-report questionnaire used for personality assessment that includes a series of items about personal thoughts, feelings, and behaviors (p. 562).

Personality psychology. Field of psychology that uses an integrative approach to study all aspects of an individual's normal and abnormal functioning.

Personality type. Distinct pattern of personality characteristics used to assign people to categories; qualitative difference, rather than difference in degree, used to discriminate between people (p. 511).

Personology. Study of personality structure, dynamics, and development in the individual involving data from diaries, biographies, literature, case studies, letters, and general observations, but not psychometric test results (p. 567).

Persuasion. Systematic attempts to influence another person's thoughts, feelings, or actions by means of communicative arguments.

PET scanner. *See* Positron emission typography.

Phallic stage. Third of Freud's psychosexual developmental stages (from 3 to 5 years) during which satisfaction is gained primarily through genital manipulation and exploration; according to Freud, a strong attraction develops for the opposite-sex parent during this stage.

Phantom limb phenomenon. As experienced by amputees, extreme or chronic pain in the limb that is no longer there (p. 251).

Phenomenological approach. Approach in personality psychology that attempts to understand a person by understanding his or her view of reality.

Phenomenological perspective. Person's subjective view and interpretation of a situation or environment (p. 596).

Phenomenon. Any event singled out for notice or investigation; plural is *phenomena*.

Phenotype. Observable set of organism characteristics resulting from the interaction of genotype and the environment (p. 58).

Pheromone. Chemical signal released by organisms to communicate with other members of the species; often a sexual attractor at a distance (pp. 246, 440).

Phi phenomenon. See *apparent motion* (p. 283).

Phobia. Maladaptive avoidance response of objectively harmless stimulus that interferes with normal functioning.

Phobic disorder. Neurotic pattern of behavior in which anxiety is associated with some specific external environmental object or situation (p. 633).

Phoneme. Minimal unit of speech in any given language that makes a difference in speech production and reception by a fluent speaker of that language; *r* and *l* are two distinct phonemes in English but variations of one in Korean (p. 155).

Photon. Single, indivisible unit of electromagnetic energy.

Photoreceptor. Receptor cell in the retina that is sensitive to light (p. 225).

Physiological dependence. Process in which the body becomes adjusted to and dependent on a drug, in part because of depletion of neurotransmitters by the frequent presence of the drug (p. 128).

Physiological psychology. Branch of psychology that studies the physical and chemical factors involved in behavior and mental processes.

Physiological zero. Intermediate temperature point at which one feels neither warmth nor cold.

Pitch. Sound quality of "highness" or "lowness"; primarily dependent upon the frequency of the sound wave (p. 240).

Pituitary gland. Gland located in the brain that secretes a variety of hormones that influence growth and the secretion of other hormones by other glands (p. 78).

Place theory. Theory that different frequencies produce maximum activation at different locations along the basilar membrane, with the result that pitch can be coded by the place where activation occurs (p. 243).

Placebo control. Experimental control procedure used in cases where placebo effects might occur (p. 35).

Placebo effect. Clinically significant response to a stimulus or treatment that occurs independently of its physiological effect (p. 31).

Placebo therapy. Therapy independent of specific clinical procedures that results in client improvement (p. 695).

Polarity. Electrical state (positive or negative) of the membrane of a cell.

Polygenic. Human characteristic dependent on a combination of several genes (p. 137).

Pons. Areas of the brain stem involved in dreaming and waking from sleep (p. 71).

Positive reinforcement. Condition of receiving a stimulus, following a response, that increases the rate or probability of the response.

Positive reinforcer. Stimulus, received after a response, that increases the probability of that response (p. 320).

Positron emission tomography (PET). Technique for obtaining detailed pictures of activity in the living brain that involves injecting a radioactive substance that is taken up by the active neurons.

Postformal thought. Type of adult thinking that is suited to solving real-world problems because it is less abstract and absolute than formal thought, is more adaptive to life's inconsistencies, and is more integrative by combining contradictory elements into a meaningful whole (p. 197).

Postsynaptic membrane. Membrane of the dendrite on the receiving side of the synapse.

Posttraumatic stress disorder (PTSD). Reaction in which an individual involuntarily reexperiences the emotional, cognitive, and behavioral aspects of past trauma (p. 485).

Power function. In psychophysics, a mathematical equation (S = kIb) that expresses the relationship between the magnitude of a physical stimulus and the intensity of the sensory experience it evokes.

Preattentive processing. Processing that operates on sensory inputs as they first come into the brain from the sensory receptors, before we attend to them (p. 269).

Preconscious memory. Memory accessible to consciousness only after something calls one's attention to it (p. 109).

Prefrontal lobotomy. Operation that severs the nerve fibers connecting the frontal lobes of the brain with the diencephalon, especially those of the thalamic and hypothalamic areas (p. 690).

Prejudice. Learned attitude toward a target object, with negative affect (dislike or fear), negative beliefs (stereotypes) that justify the attitude, and a behavioral intention to avoid, control, dominate, or eliminate the target object (p. 599).

Premack principle. Principle, developed by David Premack, that a more preferred activity can be used to reinforce a less preferred one (p. 324).

Prenatal. Period of development prior to birth.

Preoperational stage. Second of Piaget's stages of cognitive development (from 2 to 7 years); characterized by centrism, discovery of qualitative identity, increasing use of symbols, and continued dependence on appearances.

Presynaptic membrane. Membrane of the axon on the sending side of a synapse.

Primacy effect. Tendency for the first information people learn about others to have greater impact than later information.

Primary appraisal. In stress research, the first stage in the cognitive appraisal of a potentially stressful situation, in which an individual evaluates the situation or the seriousness of a demand (p. 479).

Primary drive. Motivational state induced by biological needs and not dependent on learning.

Priming effect. Triggering of specific memories by a particular cue; typical example of implicit memory (p. 345).

Proactive interference. Memory phenomenon in which previously stored information interferes with the learning of new but similar information (p. 370).

Problem solving. Thinking that is directed toward solving specific problems and that moves from an initial state to a goal state by means of a set of mental operations (p. 402).

Procedural memory. Component of long-term memory that stores the way we remember how things get done and the way perceptual, cognitive, and motor skills are acquired, retained, and utilized (p. 343).

Progressive relaxation. Technique that teaches people alternately to tense and relax their muscles, in order to learn the experience of relaxation and discover how to extend it to each specific muscle.

Projective test. Method of personality assessment in which an individual is presented with a standardized set of ambiguous, abstract stimuli and asked to interpret the meaning of the stimuli; the individual's responses are assumed to reveal inner feelings, motives, and conflicts (p. 566).

Proposition. Abstract unit of meaning that expresses a relationship between concepts, objects, or events (p. 360).

Prototype. Most representative example of a category (p. 392).

Proximal stimulus. Image on the retina; as contrasted with *distal stimulus* (p. 259).

Pseudomemory. Form of memory in which one confidently believes a new stimulus was experienced previously because a number of its attributes have been stored in memory (p. 394).

Psychiatric social worker. Mental health professional who has received specialized training in a school of social work and whose training emphasizes the importance of the social context of people's problems (p. 664).

Psychiatrist. Individual who has completed all medical school training for the M.D. degree and also has completed some postdoctoral specialty training in mental and emotional disorders; a psychiatrist may prescribe medications for the treatment of psychological disorders (pp. 8, 665).

Psychic determinism. Assumption that all mental and behavioral reactions are determined by earlier experiences (p. 520).

Psychoactive drug. Chemical that affects mental processes and behavior by changing conscious awareness of reality (p. 128).

Psychoanalyst. Individual who has earned either a Ph.D. or an M.D. and has completed postgraduate training in the Freudian approach to understanding and treating mental disorders (pp. 8, 665).

Psychoanalytic therapy. Psychodynamic therapy developed by Freud; an intensive and prolonged technique for exploring unconscious motivations and conflicts in neurotic, anxiety-ridden individuals (p. 668).

Psychodynamic approach. Psychological model in which behavior is explained in terms of past experiences and motivational forces; actions are viewed as stemming from inherited instincts, biological drives, and attempts to resolve conflicts between personal needs and social requirements (p. 15).

Psychodynamic personality theories. Theories of personality that share the assumption that personality is shaped by, and behavior is motivated by, powerful inner forces (p. 519).

Psychogenic amnesia. Amnesia not caused by any physical damage or neurological disorder but precipitated by psychological distress; involves a sudden inability to recall important personal information (p. 629).

Psychogenic fugue. Amnesic state during which an individual travels to a new place and assumes a new identity and life-style.

Psychological adolescing. Process of growing up to full adulthood, realizing the full potential of our humanity; one part of the aging process that develops along with biological senescing, or growing older biologically (p. 182).

Psychological assessment. Use of specified procedures to evaluate the abilities, behaviors, and personal qualities of people (p. 540).

Psychological dependence. Pervasive psychological drive to obtain and use a drug; not based on a physiological need for continued doses in order to maintain normal functioning (p. 128).

Psychological diagnosis. Several aspects of the process of diagnosing mental disorders, including diagnosis made by a clinical psychologist, diagnosis made using psychological test evidence, and diagnosis of a psychological, functional basis for a disorder (p. 619).

Psychological models. Theories of mental disorders that share the assumption that the causes of abnormal behavior are psychological in nature not biological; also general models or conceptions of mental and behavioral functioning.

Psychological test. Instrument used to assess an individual's standing relative to others on some mental or behavioral characteristic (p. 546).

Psychology. Scientific study of the behavior and mental processes of organisms.

Psychometric function. Graph that plots the percentage of detections of a stimulus (on the vertical axis) for each stimulus intensity (on the horizontal axis) (p. 217).

Psychometrics. Field of psychology that specializes in mental testing (p. 553).

Psychoneuroimmunology (PNI). Research area that investigates the effects of stress on the physiological and biological functions of the body, particularly the effects on the immune system (p. 483).

Psychopathological functioning. Psychological abnormalities (p. 618).

Psychophysics. Study of the correspondence between psychological experience and physical stimulation (p. 217).

Psychophysiological approach. Paradigm based on the assumption that the functioning of an organism is best explained in terms of the biological or physical structures and processes that make it work.

Psychosexual disorder. Psychological disorder centering on sexual inhibitions, dysfunctions, and deviations.

Psychosexual stages. Freud's stages of sexual development in children involving stimulation of different areas of the body (the mouth, anus, and genitals) to satisfy instinctual biological urges.

Psychosocial dwarfism. Syndrome in which children's normal development is inhibited by traumatic living conditions; growth may be stunted when young children are stressed by circumstances of a traumatic family life or by being abandoned by a caregiver (p. 170).

Psychosocial stages. Successive developmental stages, proposed by Erik Erikson, that focus on an individual's orientation toward the self and others; these stages incorporate both sexual and social aspects of a person's development and social conflicts that arise from the interaction between an individual and the social environment (p. 173).

Psychosomatic disorder. Physical disorder aggravated by, or primarily attributable to, prolonged emotional stress or other psychological causes (p. 482).

Psychosurgery. Surgical procedures performed on brain tissue to alleviate psychological disorders (p. 690).

Psychotherapy. Group of therapies used to treat psychological disorders that focus on changing faulty behaviors, thoughts, perceptions, and emotions that may be associated with specific disorders (p. 662).

Psychotic disorder. Severe mental disorder in which a person experiences impairments in reality-testing manifested through thought, emotional, or perceptual difficulties; no longer used as diagnostic category in *DSM-III* (p. 627).

Puberty. Attainment of sexual maturity; indicated for girls by menarche and for boys by the production of live sperm and the ability to ejaculate (p. 188).

Pubescent growth spurt. Physical growth spurt that is the first concrete indicator of the end of childhood.

Punisher. Aversive stimulus that decreases the probability of the preceding response (p. 321).

Pupil. Opening in the iris that allows light to enter the eye.

Pure tone. Sound produced by a single sine wave.

Q

Questionnaire. Written set of questions used to elicit individual reactions.

R

Randomization. Assignment of subjects to either the experimental or control groups by a chance procedure so that each subject has an equal chance of being placed in either group (p. 43).

Range. Difference between the highest and the lowest scores in a frequency distribution; the simplest measure of variability (p. 45).

Rapid eye movement (REM). Reliable behavioral sign that a sleeper's mental activity is centered around dreaming (p. 113).

Rational-emotive therapy (RET). Comprehensive system of personality change based on changing irrational beliefs causing undesirable, highly charged emotional reactions, such as severe anxiety; developed by Albert Ellis (p. 684).

Rationalism. View, associated with Plato and René Descartes, that the human mind came prepared with certain basic ideas that ordered all sensory experience.

Reaction time. Elapsed time between a stimulus presentation and a designated response; used as a measure of the time required for mental processes (p. 386).

Realistic thinking. Thinking based on fitting one's ideas to the reality of situational demands, time constraints, and operational rules, and based on accurate evaluation of one's personal resources (in contrast to autistic thinking) (p. 401).

Reasoning. Process of realistic thinking in which conclusions are drawn from a set of facts; thinking directed toward a given goal or objective (p. 401).

Recall. Method of retrieval in which an individual is required to reproduce the information previously presented; compared to *recognition* (p. 347).

Receptive field. Visual area from which a given ganglion cell receives messages (p. 235).

Recessive gene. Gene that is expressed in an individual's development only when paired with similar genes.

Reciprocal determinism. Concept of Albert Bandura's social learning theory that refers to the notion that a complex reciprocal interaction exists between factors of an individual, behavior, and environmental stimuli, and that each of these components affects the others (p. 529).

Recognition. Method of retrieval in which an individual is required to identify present stimuli as having been experienced before; compared to *recall* (p. 347).

Reductionism. Belief that observable phenomena at one level of analysis can be accounted for by more fundamental laws at a lower or more basic level.

Redundancy. Duplication in a cellular system that provides a "margin of safety" to guarantee that a specific job will get done even if some cells are damaged.

Reference frame. Spatial or temporal context for a stimulus (p.

281).

Reference group. Formal or informal group from which a person derives attitudes and standards of acceptability and appropriateness and to which a person refers for information, direction, and support for life-style (p. 580).

Reflex. Reaction in which an external stimulus leads to a physical response; also, an unlearned response elicited by specific stimuli that have biological relevance for an organism (p. 306).

Reflex arc. Neural circuit including nerve pathways carrying incoming sensory information and pathways carrying outgoing motor signals.

Refractory period. Period of rest during which a nerve impulse cannot be activated (p. 86).

Reinforcement contingency. Consistent relationship between a response and the changes in the environment that it produces (p. 319).

Reinforcer. Stimulus occurring after a response that changes its rate or probability of recurring.

Relapse. Reverting to former behavior patterns that have been changed; for instance, smoking again after quitting for some period; usually occurs when person returns to original environment where addictive behavior was maintained (p. 493).

Relative motion parallax. Source of information about depth in which the relative distances of objects from a viewer determine the amount and direction of their relative motion in the retinal image (p. 285).

Relaxation response. Condition in which muscle tension, cortical activity, heart rate, and blood pressure all decrease and breathing slows (p. 500).

Releaser. Environmental cue that evokes a specific response pattern in members of a species.

Reliability. Degree to which individuals earn the same relative scores each time they are measured; index of stability or consistency (pp. 35, 543).

REM sleep. Stage during the sleep cycle in which electrical brain activity is characterized by erratic, low-voltage patterns similar to those observed during the waking state and during which there are bursts of rapid eye movements; also known as *paradoxical sleep.*

Remembering. Retaining or recalling experiences (p. 343).

Replication. Repetition of an experiment under similar conditions in order to see if the same results will be obtained; usually conducted by an independent investigator.

Representativeness heuristic. Cognitive strategy that assigns something to a category on the basis of a few characteristics regarded as representative of the category (p. 414).

Repression. In Freudian theory, the most basic defense mechanism by which painful or guilt-producing thoughts, feelings, or memories are excluded from conscious awareness (pp. 371, 522).

Research design. Special conditions under which an investigator observes and measures behavior.

Residual stress pattern. Chronic syndrome in which the emotional responses of posttraumatic stress persist over time (p. 485).

Resiliency. Special ability to deal effectively with stressful, traumatic situations and bounce back from their usually debilitating effects; also used to describe children who are termed *invulnerables* because they cope effectively with harsh, abusive environments (p. 180).

Resistance. Inability or unwillingness of a patient in psychoanalysis to discuss certain ideas, desires, or experiences (p. 670).

Resistance to extinction. Persistence of the conditional response in the absence of the unconditional stimulus (p. 308).

Response. Behavior of organisms in reaction to a stimulus.

Response bias. Systematic tendency, as a result of nonsensory factors, for an observer to favor responding in a particular way (p. 218).

Reticular formation. Long structure in the middle of the brain stem through which sensory messages pass on their way to higher centers of the brain (p. 71).

Retina. Layer at the back of the eye that contains photoreceptors (p. 225).

Retrieval. Recovery of stored information from memory at a later time (p. 346).

Retrieval cues. Internally or externally generated stimuli available to help with the retrieval of a memory (p. 362).

Retroactive interference. Memory phenomenon in which the learning of new information interferes with the memory of a previously stored similar item (p. 370).

Retrograde amnesia. Amnesia in which there is loss of memory for events experienced prior to the event that precipitated the amnesia (p. 341).

Rite of passage. See *initiation rite.*

Ritual healing. Ceremonies that infuse special emotional intensity and meaning into the healing process; heightens patients' suggestibility and sense of importance; often directed by a shaman and including family members of the afflicted person (p. 667).

Rod. Photoreceptor concentrated in the periphery of the retina that is most active for seeing in dim illumination; rods do not produce sensations of color (p. 225).

Role. Socially defined pattern of behavior that is expected of a person who has a certain function within a group or setting.

Rorschach test. Projective test used for clinical diagnosis in which the ambiguous symmetrical stimuli are inkblots; developed by Hermann Rorschach.

Round window. Structure that absorbs wave motion circulating through the cochlea.

Rule. Behavioral guideline for acting in a certain way in certain situations (p. 578).

Rule learning. Recognition of the behavioral implications of rules and the contexts in which they are relevant and perception of reinforcing contingencies for obeying or violating rules (p. 333).

S

Sadism. Psychosexual disorder involving sexual excitement derived from inflicting pain, suffering, or humiliation on others.

Saturation. Dimension of color space that captures the purity and vividness of color sensations (p. 230).

Satyriasis. Exaggerated sexual desire in males.

Savings. Phenomenon in which a conditional response that has been extinguished gains strength more rapidly with further acquisition training than it did initially (p. 309).

Savings method. Method of measuring memory originally used by Hermann Ebbinghaus; involves measuring memory by the savings in the amount of time it takes to relearn original material (p. 345).

Scapegoating. Process of displacing aggression on a target other than the original source of frustration (p. 586).

Schedule of punishment. In operant conditioning, the pattern of delivering punishment.

Schedule of reinforcement. In operant conditioning, the pattern of delivering and withholding reinforcement (p. 325).

Schema. Integrated cluster of knowledge organized around a topic; includes expectations (pp. 294, 366, 395).

Scheme. Piaget's term for cognitive structures that develop as infants and young children learn to adopt specific behaviors, sensorimotor sequences, to environmental conditions (p. 161).

Schizophrenic disorder. Psychotic disorder characterized by the breakdown of integrated personality functioning, withdrawal from reality, emotional distortions, and disturbed thought processes (p. 645).

Schwann cell. Specialized glial cell that wraps itself around the axons forming the myelin sheath and promotes more rapid nerve signal transmission.

Scientific method. Set of attitudes and procedures for gathering and interpreting objective information in a way that minimizes sources of error and yields dependable generalizations (pp. 3, 33).

Script. Cluster of knowledge about a sequence of interrelated specific events and actions that are expected to occur in a certain way in particular settings (p. 397).

Second messenger. Chemical substance released by the sensor portion of an ion channel in a neuron when it detects a sensory stimulus.

Second-order conditioning. Classical conditioning procedure in which a neutral stimulus is paired with a conditional stimulus rather than an unconditional stimulus; also called *higher-order conditioning.*

Secondary appraisal. In stress research, the second stage in the cognitive appraisal of a potentially stressful situation; the individual evaluates the personal and social resources available to deal with the stressful circumstance and determines the needed action (p. 479).

Secondary trait. Characteristic that is not crucial to an understanding of an individual but nevertheless provides some information about enduring qualities of the person (p. 513).

Selective attention. The ability to be aware of only part of the available sensory input (p. 351).

Selective exposure. The way we expose ourselves to information that tends to agree with what we want to believe; we notice and process more data that support our beliefs than that disconfirm them (p. 412).

Selective optimization. Strategy for successful aging in which one makes the most of gains while minimizing the impact of losses that accompany normal aging; doing fewer things that one does well and doing them better (p. 201).

Self. In humanistic psychology, the irreducible unit out of which the coherence and stability of a personality emerge.

Self-actualization. Concept in personality psychology referring to a person's constant striving to realize his or her potential and to develop inherent talents and capabilities; many humanistic psychologists see the need for self-actualization as the most basic human need; concept developed by Carl Rogers and Abraham Maslow and earlier by Carl Jung (p. 525).

Self-awareness. Process of becoming aware of the autobiographical character of personally experienced events (p. 108).

Self-concept. Individual's awareness of his or her continuing identity as a person (p. 532).

Self-construct. Set of beliefs and values that a person holds about his or her personal functioning; also, the psychological notion of a self with distinctive characteristics that affect thought, feeling, and action.

Self-deception. Mind's tendency to filter out information that is threatening to a person's self-esteem (p. 262).

Self-efficacy. Set of beliefs that one can perform adequately in a particular situation; concept developed by Albert Bandura (p. 530).

Self-esteem. Generalized evaluative attitude toward the self that influences both moods and behavior and that exerts a powerful effect on a range of personal and social behaviors (p. 533).

Self-fulfilling prophesy. Notion that a hypothesis or expectation about the way someone will act exerts a subtle influence on the person to act in the expected way or on the perceiver to "see" what is expected (p. 598).

Self-handicapping. Process of developing, in anticipation of failure, behavioral reactions and explanations that minimize ability deficits as possible causes for the failure (p. 533).

Self-perception theory. Idea that people observe themselves in order to figure out the reasons that they act as they do; people infer what their internal states are by perceiving how they are acting in a given situation; concept developed by Daryl Bem (p. 603).

Self-report measure. The self-behavior that is identified through a subject's own observations and reports (p. 37).

Self-report method. Often-used research technique in which a personality assessment is achieved through respondents' answers to a series of questions (p. 546).

Self-serving bias. Class of attributional biases in which people tend to take credit for their successes and yet deny responsibility for their failures (p. 605).

Semantic memory. Aspect of long-term memory that stores the basic meaning of words and concepts (p. 344).

Semicircular canal. Fluid-filled canal in the inner ear that provides vestibular sense information.

Sensation. Processes that analyze physical energy in the world (for example, light and sound waves) and convert it into neural activity that codes simple information about the way the receptor organs are being stimulated (pp. 215, 257).

Sensorimotor stage. First of Piaget's stages of cognitive development (from about 0 to 2 years); characterized by improvement and coordination of sensorimotor sequences, object permanence, and the beginning of internal symbolic representation.

Sensory adaptation. Phenomenon in which visual receptor cells lose their power to respond after a period of unchanged stimulation (p. 223).

Sensory coding. Way in which intensity of a sensory stimulus is coded in terms of the rate of firing of neural impulses in a sensory system (p. 223).

Sensory gating. Brain-directed process in which information in one sensory channel may be enhanced while information in another is suppressed or disregarded (p. 350).

Sensory memory. Initial memory processes involved in the momentary preservation of fleeting impressions of sensory stimuli; also called *sensory register* (p. 349).

Sensory modalities. General term covering all the separate sensory systems that take in information (p. 214).

Sensory neuron. Neuron that carries messages from the cells in the periphery toward the central nervous system (p. 83).

Sensory physiology. Study of the way biological mechanisms convert physical events into neural events (p. 216).

Sensory preconditioning. Learning of an association between two paired stimuli prior to any pairing of either one with an unconditional stimulus.

Sensory processes. Processes associated with the sense organs and peripheral aspects of the nervous system that put us in direct contact with sources of stimulation (p. 214).

Sensory register. See *sensory memory* (p. 349).

Sensuality. State or quality of fondness for pleasures of bodily sensations (p. 214).

Sequential design. Research approach in which a group of subjects spanning a small age range are grouped according to year of birth and are observed repeatedly over several years; design combines some features of both the cross-sectional and longitudinal approaches (p. 150).

Serial position effect. Characteristic of retrieval in which the recall of beginning and end items on a list is better than memory for items appearing in the middle (p. 364).

Set. Temporary readiness to perceive or react to a stimulus in a particular way (p. 294).

Sex. Biologically based characteristics that distinguish males from females (p. 172).

Sex chromosome. Chromosome that contains genes that code for the development of male or female physical characteristics (p. 61).

Sexual arousal. Motivational state of excitement and tension brought about by physiological and cognitive reactions to erotic stimuli (p. 441).

Sexual reproduction. Production of progeny by sexual means; it confers the advantage of genetic variability (p. 440).

Sexual script. Socially learned program of sexual responsiveness (p. 443).

Shamanism. Ancient and powerful spiritual tradition that has been practiced by Native American cultures for nearly 30,000 years; involves both healing and gaining contact with the spirit world (p. 661).

Shape constancy. Ability to perceive the true shape of an object despite variations in the size of the retinal image (p. 289).

Shaping. Operant learning technique in which a new behavior is produced by reinforcing successive approximations of the final behavior desired; developed by B. F. Skinner (p. 325).

Short-term memory (STM). Memory processes associated with the preservation of events or experiences recently perceived; short-term memory is of limited capacity and stores information for only a short length of time without rehearsal (p. 352).

Significant difference. Statistical inference measure that shows that the difference between groups or conditions is probably not caused by chance; $p<.05$ is the agreed upon minimally acceptable difference in psychology for a result to be termed statistically significant.

Simultaneous conditioning. Temporal pattern in classical conditioning in which a conditional stimulus and an unconditional stimulus are presented at the same time.

Situational behavior observations. Observations of an individual's behavioral patterns in one or more situations, such as work or in school (p. 546).

Situational variable. External influence on behavior; also known as *environmental variable* (p. 7).

Situationism. View that, much more than we realize, our actions are determined by forces and constraints in behavior settings rather than by personal qualities (p. 577).

Size constancy. Ability to perceive the true size of an object despite variations in the size of its retinal image (p. 287).

Sleep apnea. Upper respiratory sleep disorder in which the person stops breathing while asleep (p. 117).

Social categorization. The process by which people organize their social environment by categorizing themselves and others into groups (p. 600).

Social context. Part of the total environment that includes other people, both real and imagined, interactions, the setting in which the interactions take place, and unwritten rules and expectations that govern the way people relate to each other (p. 577).

Social facilitation. The facilitating effect that the presence of other people sometimes has on individual performance (p. 578).

Social-learning theory. Learning theory that stresses the role of observation and the imitating of behaviors observed in others; developed by Albert Bandura and Walter Mischel.

Social loafing. The unconscious tendency to slack off when performing in a group (p. 578).

Social norm. Expectation that a group has for its members regarding acceptable and appropriate attitudes and behaviors (p. 579).

Social perception. Process by which a person comes to know or perceive the personal attributes of him- or herself and other people (p. 602).

Social phobia. Phobia in which an individual experiences an irrational fear of speaking, writing, performing artistically, or eating in public; extreme form of shyness (p. 634).

Social psychology. Branch of psychology that studies the effect of social variables on individual behavior, attitudes, perceptions, and motives; it also studies group and intergroup phenomena (p. 577).

Social reality. The consensus of perceptions and beliefs about a situation that is derived by making social comparisons among members of a social group (p. 596).

Social referencing. Process of searching for emotional information from others' reactions as a behavioral regulator.

Social role. Socially defined pattern of behavior that is expected of a person when functioning in a given setting or group (p. 578).

Social stereotype. Beliefs people have about the personality traits and abilities commonly found among individual members of a particular social group.

Social support. Resources, including material aid, socioemotional support, and informational aid, provided by others to help a person cope with stress (p. 490).

Socialization. Lifelong process whereby an individual's behavioral patterns, values, standards, skills, attitudes, and motives are shaped to conform to those regarded as desirable in a particular society (p. 168).

Sodium and potassium pump. Transport mechanism that pushes sodium out of a cell and potassium back into it, thus returning it to resting potential.

Soma. Cell body of a neuron; contains the nucleus and cytoplasm of the cell (p. 83).

Somatic nervous system. Part of the peripheral nervous system that controls the skeletal muscles of the body (p. 79).

Somatoform disorders. A group of disorders characterized by bodily (somatic) complaints in the absence of any known organic problems that is assumed to reflect psychological conflicts.

Somatosensory cortex. Area of the parietal lobes that receives sensory input from various body areas (p. 75).

Somatotype. Descriptive category that classifies a person on the basis of a few salient physical characteristics with the hope of relating these to personality characteristics (p. 512).

Sound spectrum. Graph of all the frequencies, with their amplitudes, present in a sound.

Spatial frequency. Number of dark-light cycles in a pattern over a given distance of visual space.

Spatial-frequency model. Theory that the visual system analyzes complex stimuli into spatial frequencies; challenges feature-detection model of stimulus analysis (p. 237).

Spinal cord. The nerve tract in the spinal column between the brain and the peripheral nervous system.

Split-span task. Experimental task requiring recall of simultaneous input to the two ears.

Spontaneous recovery. Reappearance of an extinguished conditional response after a rest period (p. 309).

Spontaneous-remission effect. Improvement of some mental patients and clients in psychotherapy without any professional intervention; a baseline criterion against which the effectiveness of therapies must be assessed (p. 695).

Spreading activation theory. Cognitive model that describes a person's mental dictionary as organized into a network of interconnected words and concepts in which activation of any part vibrates and spreads to related ones (p. 387).

Standard deviation. Measure of the variability of scores in a distribution, which will indicate the average difference between scores and their mean (p. 45).

Standardization. Uniform procedures for treating each participant or for recording data; in test construction, includes giving the test to a large number of representative individuals to establish norms (pp. 34, 545).

Standardized measuring device. Measuring device that has been administered to a large group of subjects who are representative of the group for which the device is intended, thus yielding statistical standards or norms to be used for comparisons.

Stanford-Binet Intelligence Test. Most widely used children's intelligence test; version of the Binet written intelligence test, using age-level subtests, in which subjects are tested individually.

Stanford Prison Experiment. Study demonstrating the surprising power of social and environmental factors on behavior; subjects were randomly assigned to be guards or prisoners in a mock prison environment and the randomly assigned roles created status and power differences that were validated in the prison situation; developed by Philip Zimbardo (p. 578).

State-dependent learning. Characteristic of the memory system in which retrieval is better if the psychological or physical state present at the time of learning is similar to that present at the time of retrieval (p. 360).

Statistics. Mathematical tool used by researchers to describe their findings in an objective, uniform way; provides a sound standard for inferring whether the results are real or chance occurrences.

Stereochemical theory. Theory of smell which suggests that receptor sites in odor-sensitive cells have distinctive sizes and shapes. corresponding to those of the chemical molecules which stimulate them.

Stereotype effect. Bias sometimes occurring in ratings or observations in which judges' beliefs about the qualities of most people who belong to a certain category influence the perception of an observed individual who belongs to that particular category (p. 548).

Steroids. Group of hormones that are important in metabolic processes and in the release of sugar from the liver into the blood (p. 481).

Stigma. Negative reaction of people to an individual or group because of some assumed inferiority or source of difference that is degraded; also, what is experienced by the target of stigmatization (p. 655).

Stimulant. Drug that increases the transmission of impulses in the central nervous system and tends to speed up mental and physical activity.

Stimulus. Environmental condition or energy source that elicits a response from an organism.

Stimulus control. Control of the occurrence of a response by means of a dependable signal (a discriminative stimulus) to indicate a reinforcer is available.

Stimulus discrimination. Conditioning process in which an organism learns to respond differently to stimuli that differ from the conditional stimulus on some dimension (p. 310).

Stimulus generalization. Automatic extension of conditioned responding to similar stimuli that have never been paired with the unconditional stimulus (p. 309).

Storage. Retention of encoded material over time, involving neurophysiological changes in certain synapses (p. 346).

Strain. Organism's reaction to external stressors (p. 472).

Stress. Pattern of specific and nonspecific responses an organism makes to stimulus events that disturb its equilibrium and tax or exceed its ability to cope (p. 472).

Stress moderator variables. Variables that change the impact of a stressor on a given type of stress reaction (p. 477).

Stressor. Internal or external event or stimulus that induces stress (p. 472).

Structuralism. View, associated with Wilhelm Wundt and Edward Titchener, that all human mental experience can be understood as the combination of simple events or elements and that the underlying structure of the human mind can be revealed by analyzing all the basic elements of sensation and other experience that forms an individual's mental life; the study of the how and why of experience (p. 12).

Subconscious awareness. Mental processes involving material not currently in consciousness but retrievable by special recall procedures (p. 109).

Subject. Participant in an experiment whose behavior is being observed.

Subjective construal. Meanings supplied by the social perceiver of events and experiences.

Subjective contours. Perceived contours that do not exist in the distal stimulus but only in subjective experience (p. 280).

Subliminal perception. Phenomenon in which people behave as though they have perceived something even when their detection performance has indicated a stimulus below the sensory threshold (p. 217).

Superego. In Freudian theory, that aspect of personality representing the internalization of society's values, standards, and morals; the inner conscious (p. 521).

Superior colliculus. Cluster of nerve cell bodies in the midbrain region of the brain stem involved in the integration of sensory input of different types; assumed to mediate primitive form of sensory perception (p. 227).

Survey. Method of gathering information from a large number of people; self-report information is gathered in response to a list of questions that follow a fixed format.

Syllogism. Form of deductive reasoning that has a major premise, a minor premise, and a conclusion that follows from the premises (p. 401).

Sympathetic division. Division of the autonomic nervous system that deals with emergency responding (p. 80).

Symptom substitution. Appearance of a new physical or psychological problem after a problem behavior has been changed (p. 673).

Synapse. Gap between one neuron and the next; it is filled with a fluid that does not permit electrical activity to pass across (p. 87).

Synaptic transmission. Relaying of information from one neuron to another (p. 87).

Synaptic vesicles. Tiny sacs in the terminal button of the axon that release precisely measured amounts of transmitter chemicals into the synaptic gap.

Systematic desensitization. Behavioral therapy technique in which a client is taught to prevent the arousal of anxiety by relaxing (p. 674).

T

T-lymphocyte. White blood cell that stimulates or shuts off the immunological response to an invading organism (p. 484).

Tabula rasa. Idea associated with the philosophical view of John Locke that individuals are born with a "blank slate" and that all knowledge comes from experience.

Taste-aversion learning. Biological constraint on learning in which an organism learns in one trial to avoid a food whose ingestion is followed by illness; first studied by John Garcia (p. 331).

Taste buds. Receptors for taste, located primarily on the upper side of the tongue (p. 247).

Telegraphic speech. Speech pattern of a normal child 2 to 3 years of age consisting of short, simple sentences with many nouns and verbs but lacking tense endings, plurals, and function words.

Teleology. View that an immaterial, purposeful mind gives behavior its direction by acting on a passive, mechanistic brain.

Temporal contiguity. Principle stating that sensations, movements, or ideas occurring closely in time become associated with one another.

Tension reduction. Reinforcing state that follows from the reduction of unpleasant sensations that occur as a result of unsatisfied drives.

Terminal button. Bulblike structure at the branched endings of axons that transmits impulses to the next neuron in the chain (p. 83).

Territoriality. Drive to gain and defend property or space.

Test-retest reliability. Measure of the correlation between the scores of the same people on the same test given on two different occasions (p. 543).

Testosterone. Male hormone secreted by the testes; responsible for sex-linked characteristics such as facial hair and deep voice (p. 78).

Texture gradient. Change in apparent texture when a uniform textured surface is slanted away from an observer.

Thalamus. Structure below the corpus callosum that serves as a relay station for all incoming sensory information (p. 71).

Thanatos. In Freudian theory, the death instinct, assumed to drive people toward aggressive and destructive behavior (p. 520).

The Big Five. Comprehensive, theory-free, descriptive personality system that maps out the relationships among common trait words, theoretical concepts, and personality scales (p. 516).

Thematic apperception test (TAT). Projective test in which pictures of ambiguous scenes are presented to an individual who is encouraged to generate stories about the stimuli (p. 434).

Theory. In psychology, a body of interrelated concepts and principles used to explain or predict some psychological phenomenon or to explain how some aspect of brain, mind, behavior, or environment functions (p. 32).

Theory of signal detection (TSD). Theory that all perceptual judgments combine sensory and decision-making processes, the relative contributions of which can be determined (p. 219).

Think-aloud protocol. Report of mental processes and strategies made by experimental subject while working on a task (pp. 110, 384).

Thinking. Complex mental process of forming a new mental representation by transforming available information (p. 391).

Three-term contingency. Means by which organisms learn that, in the presence of some stimuli but not others, their behavior is likely to have a particular effect on the environment; also known as antecedent-behavior-consequence (p. 322).

Threshold. Minimum stimulus energy sufficient to excite a neuron and nerve impulse.

Thyrotrophic hormone (TTH). Hormone released from the pituitary gland that stimulates the thyroid gland to make more energy available to the body during a stress reaction.

Timbre. Dimension of auditory sensation that reflects the complexity of a sound wave (p. 241).

Time perspective. Partitioning the flow of perceived events and experiences into the mental frames of past, present, and future.

Token economy. Technique of positive reinforcement in which individuals are rewarded for socially constructive behaviors with tokens that may later be exchanged for privileges.

Tolerance. Lessened effect of a drug following continued use (p. 128).

Top-down processing. Perceptual processes in which information from an individual's past experience, knowledge, expectations, motivations, and background influence the way a perceived object is interpreted and classified (p. 260).

Total situation. Situation in which people are isolated from contrary points of view; and sources of information, social rewards, and punishments are all highly controlled by group leaders (p. 581).

Trace forward conditioning. Temporal pattern in classical conditioning in which a conditional stimulus goes off before the onset of an unconditional stimulus; presumably, however, some form of memory trace bridges the gap between the offset of the conditional stimulus and the onset of the unconditional stimulus.

Trait. Enduring and continuous quality or attribute that influences behavior because it acts as a generalized action tendency (p. 512).

Trance logic. In hypnosis, the nonrational system that may be used by a hypnotized person to explain unusual perceptions or reactions caused by hypnotic suggestions.

Transactional perception. Theory of "perception as hypothesis" that stresses the importance of transactions with the environment as the basis for developing hypotheses (p. 267).

Transduction. Transformation of one form of energy into another; for example, chemical energy is transformed into physical energy and light into neural impulses (p. 215).

Transference. Process by which a person in psychoanalysis attaches to a therapist feelings formerly held toward some significant person who figured in a past emotional conflict (p. 671).

Trichromatic theory. Theory that there are three types of color receptors producing the psychologically "primary" color sensations—red, green, and blue (p. 232).

Two-factor theory of emotion. Theory that emotion is the joint effect of two central processes—physiological arousal and cognitive appraisal.

Tympanic membrane. Thin membrane in the ear set into motion by the pressure variations of sound waves; also known as the *eardrum.*

Type. Distinct pattern of personality characteristics.

Type-A behavior syndrome. Competitive, compulsive, and hostile behavior characteristic of a particular style of coping with stress; assumed to increase the risk of coronary heart disease (p. 501).

Type-T personality. Personality characterized by the desire to take risks and seek out thrills, stimulation, and excitement (p. 480).

U

Unconditional response (UCR). In classical conditioning, the response elicited by an unconditional stimulus without prior training or learning (p. 307).

Unconditional stimulus (UCS). In classical conditioning, the stimulus that elicits and reinforces an unconditional response (p. 307).

Unconscious. In psychoanalytic theory, the domain of the psyche that stores repressed urges and primitive impulses (pp. 109, 520).

Unconscious inference. Helmholtz' term for *perception,* which occurs outside the conscious awareness (p. 267).

Unconscious process. In Freudian theory, mental process that is not directly observable or subject to verification by self-report but whose existence is inferred from effects on observable behaviors (p. 520).

Unipolar depression. *DSM-III-R* category for those who suffer from intense feelings of depression over an extended time without the manic high phase of bipolar depression; also called *clinical depression* (p. 639).

V

Validity. Extent to which a test measures what it was intended to measure (pp. 36, 543).

Variable. Factor that varies in amount or kind (p. 32).

Variable interval schedule (VI). In operant conditioning, a schedule in which reinforcement is delivered after differing lengths of time, regardless of the number of correct responses that have occurred.

Variable ratio schedule (VR). In operant conditioning, a schedule in which reinforcement is given after a changing number of responses.

Verbal report. Measurement technique in which subjects provide answers to questions.

Vestibular sense. Sense that tells us how our bodies are oriented in the world with respect to gravity (p. 245).

Violence. Expression of hostility and rage against people or property.

Visual cortex. Area at the back of the brain in the occipital lobes where visual information is processed (pp. 75, 227).

Volley principle. Extension of frequency theory that proposes that, when peaks in a sound wave come too frequently for a single neuron to fire at each peak, several neurons as a group fire at the frequency of the stimulus tone (p. 243).

Voyeurism. Paraphilia in which the preferred means of sexual arousal is observation of others—who are unaware of being observed—disrobing or engaging in sexual activity.

W

Wavelength. Physical property of waves measured in units of distance along the wavelike propagation; wavelength is the only property that distinguishes one photon from another.

Weber's law. Assertion that the size of a difference threshold is proportional to the intensity of the standard stimulus (p. 220).

Wellness. Optimal health, incorporating the ability to function fully and actively over the physical, intellectual, emotional, spiritual, social, and environmental domains of health (p. 493).

Whole-report procedure. Experimental technique, used in memory studies, in which subjects presented with a pattern containing several stimuli are subsequently asked to recall as many of the individual stimuli as possible (p. 350).

Wisdom. Expertise in the fundamental pragmatics of life; often reached in late adulthood (p. 204).

Withdrawal symptom. Painful physical symptom experienced when the level of a drug to which physical addiction has occurred is decreased or when the drug is eliminated (p. 128).

Word association. Technique of personality assessment using an individual's responses to a list of common words to identify unconscious personality dynamics (p. 566).

Working memory. Short-term memory; material transferred to it from either sensory or long-term memory can be worked over and organized (p. 352).

Y

Yerkes-Dodson law. Correlation between task difficulty and optimal level of motivation; performance of difficult tasks decreases as arousal increases, while performance of easy tasks increases as arousal increases to form an inverted-U function (p. 431).

Z

Zeigarnik effect. Motivational effect induced by uncompleted tasks that create "task tensions" sometimes leading to better recall of uncompleted than completed tasks; Lewinian concept first demonstrated by Bluma Zeigarnik.

REFERENCES

A

Abelin, T., Muller, P., Buehler, A., Vesanen, K., & Imhof, P. R. (1989, January 7). Controlled trial of transdermal nicotine patch in tobacco withdrawal. *The Lancet*, pp. 7–10.

Abelson, R. P. (1981). Psychological status of the script concept. *American Psychologist, 36*, 715–729.

Abelson, R. P., Aronson, E., McGuire, W. J., Newcomb, T. J., Rosenberg, M. J., & Tannenbaum, P. H. (Eds.). (1968). *Theories of cognitive consistency: A sourcebook.* Chicago: Rand McNally.

Abramson, L. Y., Garber, J., Edwards, N., & Seligman, M. E. P. (1978). Expectancy changes in depression and schizophrenia. *Journal of Abnormal Psychology, 87*, 102–109.

Abramson, L. Y., Seligman, M. E. P., & Teasdale, J. D. (1978). Learned helplessness in humans: Critique and reformulation. *Journal of Abnormal Psychology, 87*, 32–48, 49–74.

Ackerman, D. (1990). *A natural history of the senses.* New York: Random House.

Adams, J. (1979). Mutual-help groups: Enhancing the coping ability of oncology clients. *Cancer Nursing, 2*, 95–98.

Adams, J. A. (1987). Historical review and appraisal of research on the learning, retention, and transfer of human motor skills. *Psychological Bulletin, 101*, 41–74.

Adams, J. L. (1979). *Conceptual blockbusting* (2nd ed.). New York: Norton.

Adams, J. L. (1986). *Conceptual blockbusting* (3rd ed.). New York: Norton.

Adams, J. S. (1965). Inequity in social exchange. In L. Berkowitz (Ed.), *Advances in experimental social psychology* (Vol. 2, pp. 267–299). New York: Academic Press.

Ader, R. (1981). A historical account of conditioned immunobiologic responses. In R. Ader (Ed.), *Psychoneuroimmunology.* New York: Academic Press.

Ader, R. (1990). In *Discovering Psychology*, Program 8 [PBS video series]. Washington, DC: Annenberg/CPB Project.

Ader, R., & Cohen, N. (1981). Conditioned immunopharmacological responses. In R. Ader (Ed.), *Psychoneuroimmunology* (pp. 281–319). New York: Academic Press.

Adler, A. (1929). *The practice and theory of individual psychology.* New York: Harcourt, Brace & World.

Adler, J., Huck, J., McKillop, P., & Calonius, E. (1987, July 20). Taking life one night at a time. *Newsweek*, pp. 48–49.

Adler, N. (1990). In *Discovering Psychology*, Program 12 [PBS video series]. Washington, DC: Annenberg/CPB Project.

Adler, N. E., David, H. P., Major, B. N., Roth, S. H., Russo, N. F., & Wyatt, G. E. (1990). Psychological responses after abortion. *Science, 248*, 41–44.

Adler, N. T. (1978). On the mechanisms of sexual behaviour and their evolutionary constraints. In J. B. Hutchison (Ed.), *Biological determinants of sexual behavior* (pp. 657–694). New York: Wiley.

Adler, N. T., & Toner, J. P. (1986). The effects of copulatory behavior on sperm transport and fertility in rats. *Annals of the New York Academy of Sciences, reproduction: A behavioral and neuroendocrine perspective, 474*, 2–32.

Adorno, T. W., Frenkel-Brunswick, E., Levinson, D. J., & Sanford, R. N. (1950). *The authoritarian personality.* New York: Harper.

Affleck, G., Tennen, H., Pfeiffer, C., & Fifield, J. (1987). Appraisals of control and predictability in adapting to a chronic disease. *Journal of Personality and Social Psychology, 53*, 273–279.

Agras, S. (1985). *Panic: Facing fears, phobias, and anxiety.* New York: Freeman.

Agras, W. S., Taylor, C. B., Kraemer, H. C., Allen, R. A., & Schneider, J. A. (1980). Relaxation training: Twenty-four-hour blood pressure changes. *Archives of General Psychiatry, 37*, 859–863.

Ahern, G. L., & Schwartz, G. E. (1985). Differential lateralization for positive and negative emotion in the human brain: EEG spectral analysis. *Neuropsychologia, 23*, 744–755.

Ainsworth, M. D. S. (1973). The development of infant-mother attachment. In B. M. Caldwell & H. N. Ricciuti (Eds.), *Review of child development research* (Vol. 3). Chicago: University of Chicago Press.

Ainsworth, M. D. S. (1989). Attachments beyond infancy. *American Psychologist, 44*, 709–716.

Ainsworth, M. D. S., Blehar, M., Waters, E., & Wall, S. (1978). *Patterns of attachment.* Hillsdale, NJ: Erlbaum.

Ajzen, I., & Fishbein, M. (1977). Attitude-behavior relations: A theoretical analysis and review of empirical research. *Psychological Bulletin, 84*, 888–918.

Akhtar, S., Wig, N. H., Verma, V. K., Pershod, D., & Verma, S. K. (1975). A phenomenological analysis of symptoms in obsessive-compulsive neurosis. *British Journal of Psychiatry, 127*, 342–348.

Akil, H. (1978). Endorphins, beta-LPH and ACTH: Biochemical pharmacological and anatomical studies. *Advances in Biochemical Psychopharmacology, 18*, 125–139.

Alba, J. W., & Hasher, L. (1983). Is memory schematic? *Psychological Bulletin, 93*, 203–231.

Albee, G. W., & Joffe, J. M. (Eds.). (1977). *Primary prevention of psychopathology: Vol. 1. Issues.* Hanover, NH: University Press of New England.

Albuquerque, E. X., Aguayo, L. G., Warnick, R. K., Ickowicz, R. K., & Blaustein, M. P. (1983, June). Interactions of phencyclidine with ion channels of nerve and muscle: Behavioral implications. *Federation Proceedings, 42*(9), 2584–2589.

Alden, L. E. (1988). Behavioral self-management controlled-drinking strategies in a context of secondary prevention. *Journal of Consulting and Clinical Psychology, 56*, 280–286.

Alderfer, C. (1972). *Existence, relatedness, and growth.* New York: Free Press.

Alker, H., & Poppen, P. J. (1973). Ideology in university students. *Journal of Personality, 41*, 653–671.

Allen, B. P. (1985). After the missiles: Sociopsychological effects of nuclear war. *American Psychologist, 40*, 927–937.

Allen, V. L., & Wilder, D. A. (1975). Categorization, belief, similarity, and intergroup competition. *Journal of Personality and Social Psychology, 32*, 971–977.

Allison, T., & Cicchetti, D. (1976). Sleep in mammals: Ecological and constitutional correlates. *Science, 194*, 732–734.

Alloy, L. B., & Abramson, L. Y. (1979). Judgment of contingency in depressed and nondepressed students: Sadder but wiser? *Journal of Experimental Psychology: General, 108*, 441–485.

Alloy, L. B., & Abramson, L. Y. (1980). The cognitive component of human helplessness and depression. In J. Garber & M. E. P. Seligman (Eds.), *Human helplessness: Theory and applications.* New York: Academic Press.

Allport, D. A., Tipper, S. P., & Chmiel, N. R. J. (1985). Perceptual integration and post categorical filtering. In M. T. Posner & O. S. M. Marin (Eds.), *Attention and performance XI* (pp. 107–132). Hillsdale, NJ: Erlbaum.

Allport, G. W. (1937). *Personality: A psychological interpretation.* New York: Holt, Rinehart & Winston.

Allport, G. W. (1954). *The nature of prejudice.* Cambridge, MA: Addison-Wesley.

Allport, G. W. (1960). *Personality and social encounter.* Berkeley,

CA: Beacon Press.

Allport, G. W. (1961). *Pattern and growth in personality.* New York: Holt, Rinehart & Winston.

Allport, G. W. (1965). *Letters from Jenny.* New York: Harcourt, Brace & World.

Allport, G. W. (1966). Traits revisited. *American Psychologist, 21,* 1–10.

Allport, G. W. (1968). The historical background of modern social psychology. In G. Lindzey & E. Aronson (Eds.), *The handbook of social psychology* (2nd ed.). Reading, MA: Addison-Wesley.

Allport, G. W., & Odbert, H. S. (1936). Trait-names, a psycho-lexical study. *Psychological Monographs, 47* (1, Whole No. 211).

Allport, G. W., & Postman, L. J. (1947). *The psychology of rumor.* New York: Holt, Rinehart & Winston.

Almli, C. R. (1978). The ontogeny of feeding and drinking behavior: Effects of early brain damage. *Neuroscience and Behavioral Reviews, 2,* 281–300.

Altman, I., & Christensen, K. (Eds.). (1990). *Environment and behavior studies: Emergence of intellectual traditions.* New York: Plenum.

Altman, I. A. (1976). Environmental psychology and social psychology. *Personality and Social Psychology Bulletin, 2,* 96–113.

Amabile, T. M. (1987). The motivation to be creative. In S. Isaksen (Ed.), *Frontiers in creativity: Beyond the basics* (pp. 223–254). Buffalo, NY: Bearly.

American Psychological Association. (1982). *Guidelines and ethical standards for researchers.*

American Psychological Association. (1989). *1989 APA directory.* Office of demographic, employment, and educational research.

Ames, A. (1951). Visual perception and rotating trapezoidal window. *Psychological Monographs, 324.*

Amnesty International. (1983). *Chile: Evidence of torture.* London: Amnesty International Publications.

Amoore, J. E. (1965). Psychophysics of odor. *Cold Spring Harbor symposia in quantitative biology, 30,* 623–637.

Anastasi, A. (1982). *Psychological testing* (5th ed.). New York: Macmillan.

Andersen, A. (1985). *Practical and comprehensive treatment of anorexia nervosa and bulimia.* Baltimore: Johns Hopkins University Press.

Andersen, S. M., & Zimbardo, P. G. (1980, November). Resisting mind control. *U.S.A. Today,* pp. 44–47.

Anderson, J. R. (1976). *Language, memory, and thought.* Hillsdale, NJ: Erlbaum.

Anderson, J. R. (1978). Arguments concerning representations for mental imagery. *Psychological Review, 85,* 249–277.

Anderson, J. R. (1980). *Cognitive psychology and its implications.* San Francisco: Freeman.

Anderson, J. R. (Ed.). (1981). *Cognitive skills and their acquisition.* Hillsdale, NJ: Erlbaum.

Anderson, J. R. (1982). Acquisition of cognitive skill. *Psychological Review, 89,* 369–406.

Anderson, J. R., & Bower, G. H. (1973). *Human associative memory.* Washington, DC: Winston & Sons.

Anderson, W. F. (1984). Prospects for human gene therapy. *Science, 226,* 401–409.

Andersson, T., & Magnusson, D. (1990). Biological maturation in adolescence and the development of drinking habits and alcohol abuse among young males: A prospective longitudinal study. *Journal of Youth and Adolescence, 19,* 33–41.

Andreason, N. C. (1988). Brain imaging: Applications in psychiatry. *Science, 239,* 1381–1388.

Andrews, E. L. (1990, April 29). A nicotine drug patch to end smoking. *The New York Times Index* (Vol. 139, Section 1, Col. 1, p. 27, June 3, 1990).

Angier, R. P. (1927). The conflict theory of emotion. *American Journal of Psychology, 39,* 390–401.

Antelman, S. M., & Caggiula, A. R. (1980). Stress-induced behavior: Chemotherapy without drugs. In J. M. Davidson & R. J. Davidson (Eds.), *The psychobiology of consciousness* (pp. 65–104). New York: Plenum.

Antelman, S. M., Rowland, N. E., & Fisher, A. E. (1976).

Stimulation bound ingestive behavior: A view from the tail. *Physiology and Behavior, 17,* 743–748.

Antoni, M. H., Schniederman, N., Fletcher, M. A., Goldstein, D. A., Ironson, G., & Laperriere, A. (1990). Psychoneuroimmunolgy and HIV-1. *Journal of Consulting and Clinical Psychology, 58,* 38–49.

Antrobus, J. (1991). Dreaming: Cognitive processes during cortical activation and high afferent thresholds. *Psychological Review, 98,* 96–121.

Ardrey, R. (1966). *The territorial imperative.* New York: Atheneum.

Arendt, H. (1963). *Eichmann in Jerusalem: A report on the banality of evil.* New York: Viking Press.

Arendt, H. (1971). Organized guilt and universal responsibility. In R. W. Smith (Ed.), *Guilt: Man and society.* Garden City, NY: Doubleday Anchor Books.

Arkin, R. M. (Ed.). (1990). Centennial celebration of the principles of psychology. *Personality and Social Psychology Bulletin, 16(4).*

Arkin, R. M., & Baumgardner, A. H. (1985). Self-handicapping. In J. H. Harvey & G. Weary (Eds.), *Attribution: Basic issues and applications* (pp. 169–202). New York: Academic Press.

Armstrong, D. M. (1968). *A materialist theory of the mind.* London: Routledge & K. Paul.

Arnold, M. B. (1970). Perennial problems in the field of emotion. In M. B. Arnold (Ed.), *Feelings and emotions: The Loyola Symposium* (pp. 169–185). New York: Academic Press.

Aronson, E. (1990). Applying social psychology to desegregation and energy conservation. *Personality and Social Psychology Bulletin, 16,* 118–132.

Aronson, E. (1990). In *Discovering Psychology,* Program 20 [PBS video series]. Washington, DC: Annenberg/CPB Program.

Aronson, E., Blaney, N., Stephan, C., Sikes, J., & Snapp, M. (1978). *The jigsaw classroom.* Beverly Hills, CA: Sage.

Aronson, E., & Gonzalez, A. (1988). Desegregation, jigsaw, and the Mexican-American experience. In P. A. Katz & D. Taylor (Eds.), *Towards the elimination of racism: Profiles in controversy.* New York: Plenum.

Aronson, E., Turner, J. A., & Carlsmith, J. M. (1963). Communicator credibility and communication discrepancy as determinants of opinion change. *Journal of Abnormal and Social Psychology, 67,* 31–36.

Asarnow, R. F., Cromwell, R. L., & Rennick, P. M. (1978). Cognitive and evoked response measures of information processing in schizophrenics with and without a family history of schizophrenia. *The Journal of Nervous and Mental Disease, 166,* 719–730.

Asch, S. (1990). In *Discovering Psychology,* Program 19 [PBS video series]. Washington, DC: Annenberg/CPB Program.

Asch, S. E. (1940). Studies in the principles of judgments and attitudes: 11. Determination of judgments by group and by ego standards. *Journal of Social Psychology, 12,* 433–465.

Asch, S. E. (1955). Opinions and social pressure. *Scientific American, 193(5),* 31–35.

Asch, S. E. (1956). Studies of independence and conformity: A minority of one against a unanimous majority. *Psychological Monographs, 70* (9, Whole No. 416).

Aserinsky, E., & Kleitman, N. (1953). Regularly occurring periods of eye mobility and concomitant phenomena during sleep. *Science, 118,* 273–274.

Ashley, W. R., Harper, R. S., & Runyon, D. L. (1951). The perceived size of coins in normal and hypnotically induced economic states. *American Journal of Psychology, 64,* 564–572.

Ashton, P. T., & Webb, R. B. (1986). *Making a difference: A teacher's sense of efficacy and student achievement.* New York: Longman.

Aspinwall, L. G., Kemeny, M. E., Taylor, S. E., Schneider, S. G., & Dudley, J. P. (in press). Psychosocial predictors of gay men's AIDS risk-reduction behavior. *Health Psychology.*

Associated Press. (1991, April 8). New study on suicide by older people.

Atkinson, J. W., & Birch, D. (1970). *The dynamics of action.* New York: Wiley.

Atkinson, R. C., & Shiffrin, R. M. (1968). Human memory: A proposed system and its control processes. In K. W. Spence & J.

T. Spence (Eds.), *The psychology of learning and motivation: Advances in research and theory* (Vol. 2). New York: Academic Press.

Atkinson, R. L., Atkinson, R. C., Smith, E. E., & Bem, D. J. (1990). *Introduction to psychology (10th ed.)*. San Diego, CA: Harcourt Brace Jovanovich.

Averbach, I., & Coriell, A. S. (1961). Short-term memory in vision. *Bell System Technical Journal, 40*, 309–328.

Averill, J. R. (1969). Autonomic response patterns during sadness and mirth. *Psychophysiology, 5*, 399–414.

Averill, J. R. (1976). Emotion and anxiety: Sociocultural, biological, and psychological determinants. In M. Zuckerman & C. O. Spielberger (Eds.), *Emotion and anxiety: New concepts, methods and applications* (pp. 87–130). Hillsdale, NJ: Erlbaum.

Ayllon, T., & Azrin, N. H. (1965). The measurement and reinforcement of behavior of psychotics. *Journal of Experimental Analysis of Behavior, 8*, 357–383.

Ayllon, T., & Azrin, N. H. (1968). *The token economy: A motivational system for therapy and rehabilitation.* New York: Appleton-Century-Crofts.

Ayllon, T., & Michael, J. (1959). The psychiatric nurse as a behavioral engineer. *Journal of the Experimental Analysis of Behavior, 2*, 323–334.

Azrin, N. H., & Fox, R. M. (1976). *Toilet training in less than a day.* New York: Pocket Books.

Azrin, N. H., & Holz, W. C. (1966). Punishment. In N. K. Honig (Ed.), *Operant behavior* (pp. 380–447). New York: Appleton-Century-Crofts.

B

Bachman, J. G., O'Malley, P. M., & Johnston, J. (1979). *Adolescence to adulthood: Change and stability in the lives of young men.* Ann Arbor, MI: Institute for Social Research.

Backus, J., & Backus, H. (1984). *Backus strikes back.* Briarcliff Manor: Stein and Day.

Baddeley, A., & Salame, P. (1986). The unattended speech effect: Perception or memory? *Journal of Experimental Psychology: Learning, Memory & Cognition, 12*, 525–529.

Baddeley, A. D. (1982). *Your memory, a user's guide.* New York: Macmillan.

Baddeley, A. D. (1986). *Working memory.* New York: Oxford University Press.

Baddeley, A. D., & Hitch, G. (1974). Working memory. In G. H. Bower (Ed.), *The psychology of learning and motivation* (Vol. 8). New York: Academic Press.

Baer, J. S., Kivlahan, D. R., Fromme, K., & Marlatt, G. A. (1991). Secondary prevention of alcohol abuse with college student populations: A skills-training approach. In N. Heather, W. R. Miller, & J. Greeley (Eds.), *Self control and the addictive behaviors* (pp. 339–356). Sydney: Maxwell MacMillan.

Bahrick, H. P., Bahrick, P. O., & Wittlinger, R. P. (1975). Fifty years of memory for names and faces: A cross-sectional approach. *Journal of Experimental Psychology: General, 104*, 54–75.

Baillargeon, R. (1986). Representing the existence and the location of hidden objects: Object permanence in 6- and 8-month-old infants. *Cognition, 23*, 21–42.

Baillargeon, R. (1990). In *Discovering Psychology*, Program 5 [PBS video series]. Washington, DC: Annenberg/CPB Project.

Baillargeon, R., Spelke, E. S., & Wasseman, S. (1985). Object permanence in five-month-old infants. *Cognition, 20*, 191–208.

Baker, A. A., & Thorpe, J. G. (1957). Placebo response. *AMA Archives of Neurology and Psychiatry, 78*, 57–60.

Balakrishnan, S. (1991). Psychology of democracy. *The California Psychologist, 24*, pp. 16, 21.

Baldwin, A. L., & Baldwin, C. P. (1973). Study of mother–child interaction. *American Scientist, 61*, 714–721.

Bales, R. F. (1958). Task roles and social roles in problem-solving groups. In E. E. Maccoby, T. M. Newcomb, & E. L. Hartley (Eds.), *Readings in social psychology* (3rd ed.). New York: Holt, Rinehart & Winston.

Balsam, P. D., & Tomie, A. (Eds.). (1985). *Context and learning.*

Hillsdale, NJ: Erlbaum.

Baltes, M. M. (1986, November). *Selective optimization with compensation: The dynamics between independence and dependence.* Paper presented at the meeting of the Gerontological Society of America, Chicago.

Baltes, P. B. (1987). Theoretical propositions on life-span developmental psychology: On the dynamics between growth and decline. *Developmental Psychology, 23*, 611–626.

Baltes, P. B. (1990, November). *Toward a psychology of wisdom.* Invited address presented at the annual convention of the Gerontological Society of America, Boston, MA.

Baltes, P. B., Reese, H. W., & Lipsitt, L. P. (1980). Life-span developmental psychology. In M. Rosenzweig & L. Porter (Eds.), *Annual review of psychology.* Palo Alto, CA: Annual Reviews Press.

Bandura, A. (1965). Influence of models' reinforcement contingencies on the acquisition of imitative responses. *Journal of Personality and Social Psychology, 1*, 589–595.

Bandura, A. (1970). Modeling therapy. In W. S. Sahakian (Ed.), *Psychopathology today: Experimentation, theory and research.* Itasca, IL: Peacock.

Bandura, A. (1973). *Aggression: A social learning analysis.* Englewood Cliffs, NJ: Prentice-Hall.

Bandura, A. (1977a). *Social learning theory.* Englewood Cliffs, NJ: Prentice-Hall.

Bandura, A. (1977b). Self-efficacy. *Psychological Review, 84*, 191–215.

Bandura, A. (1981a). In search of pure unidirectional determinants. *Behavior Therapy, 12*, 30–40.

Bandura, A. (1981b). Self-referent thought: A developmental analysis of self-efficacy. In J. H. Flavell & L. Ross (Eds.), *Social cognitive development: Frontiers and possible futures.* Cambridge: Cambridge University Press.

Bandura, A. (1982a). The psychology of chance encounters and life paths. *American Psychologist, 37*, 747–755.

Bandura, A. (1982b). Self-efficacy mechanism in human agency. *American Psychologist, 37*, 122–147.

Bandura, A. (1986). *Social foundations of thought and action: A social cognitive theory.* Englewood Cliffs, NJ: Prentice-Hall.

Bandura, A. (1988). Self-regulation of motivation and action through goal systems. In V. Hamilton, G. H. Bower, & N. H. Frijda (Eds.), *Cognition perspectives on emotion and motivation* (pp. 37–61). Dordrecht: Kluwer Academic Publishers.

Bandura, A. (1990). In *Discovering Psychology*, Program 15 [PBS video series]. Washington, DC: Annenberg/CPB Program.

Bandura, A. (1990). Mechanisms of moral disengagement. In W. Reich (Ed.), *Origins of terrorism: Psychologies, ideologies, theologies, states of mind* (pp. 161–191). New York: Cambridge University Press.

Bandura, A., Adams, N. E., Hardy, A. B., & Howells, G. N. (1980). Tests of the generality of self-efficacy theory. *Cognitive Therapy and Research, 4*, 39–66.

Bandura, A., & Mischel, W. (1965). Modification of self-imposed delay of reward through exposure to live and symbolic models. *Journal of Personality and Social Psychology, 2*, 698–705.

Bandura, A., Ross, D., & Ross, S. A. (1963). Imitation of film-mediated aggressive models. *Journal of Abnormal and Social Psychology, 66*, 3–11.

Bandura, A., Underwood, B., & Fromson, M. E. (1975). Disinhibition of aggression through diffusion of responsibility and dehumanization of victims. *Journal of Research in Personality, 9*, 253–269.

Bane, M. J., & Ellwood, D. T. (1989). One fifth of the nation's children: Why are they poor? *Science, 245*, 1047–1053.

Banks, M. S., & Bennet, P. J. (1988). Optical and photoreceptor immaturities limit the spatial and chromatic vision of human neonates. *Journal of the Optical Society of America, 5*, 2059–2079.

Banks, W. C. (1990). In *Discovering Psychology*, Program 16 [PBS video series]. Washington, DC: Annenberg/CPB Program.

Banks, W. P., & Krajicek, D. (1991). Perception. *Annual Review of Psychology, 42*, 305–331.

Banuazizi, A., & Movahedi, S. (1975). Interpersonal dynamics in a simulated prison: A methodological analysis. *American Psychologist, 30,* 152–160.

Banyai, E. I., & Hilgard, E. R. (1976). Comparison of active-alert hypnotic induction with traditional relaxation induction. *Journal of Abnormal Psychology, 85,* 218–224.

Barber, T. X. (1976). *Hypnosis: A scientific approach.* New York: Psychological Dimensions.

Barchas, J. D., Ciaranello, R. D., Kessler, S., & Hamburg, D. A. (1975). Genetic aspects of catecholamine synthesis. In R. R. F. Eve, D. Rosenthal, & H. Brill (Eds.), *Genetic research in psychiatry* (pp. 27–62). Baltimore: Johns Hopkins University Press.

Baribeau-Braun, J., Dicton, T. W., & Gosselin, J. Y. (1983). Schizophrenia: A neurophysiological evaluation of abnormal information processing. *Science, 219,* 874–876.

Barinaga, M. (1989). Can psychotherapy delay cancer deaths? *Science, 46,* 246, 249.

Barinaga, M. (1989). Manic depression gene put in limbo. *Science, 246,* 886–887.

Barinaga, M. (1990). Technical advances power neuroscience. *Science, 250,* 908–909.

Barker, L. M., Best, M. R., & Domjan, M. (Eds.). (1978). *Learning mechanisms in food selection.* Houston: Baylor University Press.

Barland, G., & Raskin, D. C. (1976). *Validity and reliability of polygraph examinations of criminal suspects* (Report No. 76-1, Contract 75-NI-99-0001). Washington, DC: U.S. Department of Justice.

Barlett, D. L., & Steele, J. B. (1979). *Empire: The life, legend, and madness of Howard Hughes.* New York: Norton.

Barlow, H. B., Hill, R. M., & Levick, W. R. (1964). Retinal ganglion cells responding selectively to direction and speed of image motion in the rabbit. *Journal of Physiology (London), 173,* 377–407.

Barnes, D. (1987). Defect in Alzheimer's is on Chromosome 21. *Science, 235,* 846–847.

Barnes, D. M. (1987). Biological issues in schizophrenia. *Science, 235,* 430–433.

Barnes, D. M. (1988). Schizophrenia genetics a mixed bag. *Science, 242,* 1009.

Barnett, S. A. (1967). Attack and defense in animal societies. In C. D. Clemente & D. B. Lindsley (Eds.), *Aggression and defense.* Los Angeles: University of California Press.

Baron, A., Perone, M., & Galizio, M. (1991, in press). Analyzing the reinforcement process at the human level: Can application and behavioristic interpretation replace laboratory research? *The Behavior Analyst, 14.*

Baron, L., & Straus, M. A. (1989). *Four theories of rape in American society.* New Haven, CT: Yale University Press.

Baron, L., & Straus, M. A. (1989). *Four theories of rape in American society: A state-level analysis.* New Haven, CT: Yale University Press.

Barrios, B. A., & Shigetomi, C. C. (1980). Coping skills training: Potential for prevention of fears and anxieties. *Behavior Therapy, 11,* 431–439.

Barron, F., & Harrington, D. M. (1981). Creativity, intelligence, and personality. *Annual Review of Psychology, 32,* 439–476.

Barron, F. X. (1963). *Creativity and psychological growth: Origins of personal vitality and creative freedom.* Princeton, NJ: Van Nostrand.

Barrow, H. G., & Tenenbaum, J. M. (1986). Computational Approaches to Vision. In K. Boff, L. Kaufman, & J. Thomas (Eds.), *Handbook of perception and human performance* (Vol. 2, pp. 38–70). New York: Wiley.

Bar-Tal, D., & Saxe, L. (Eds.). (1978). *Social psychology of education: Theory and research.* Washington, DC: Hemisphere.

Barthe, D. G., & Hammen, C. L. (1981). The attributional model of depression: A naturalistic extension. *Personality & Social Psychology Bulletin, 7*(1), 53–58.

Bartlett, F. C. (1932). *Remembering: A study in experimental and social psychology.* Cambridge: Cambridge University Press.

Bartoshuk, L. (1990, August/September). Psychophysiological insights on taste. *Science Agenda,* 12–13.

Basseches, M. (1984). *Dialectical thinking and adult development.* Norwood, NJ: Ablex.

Bateson, G., Jackson, D. D., Haley, J., & Weakland, J. H. (1956). Toward a theory of schizophrenia. *Behavioral Science, 1,* 251–264.

Baum, A. (1990). Stress, intrusive imagery, and chronic distress. *Health Psychology, 9,* 653–675.

Baum, A., Calesnick, L. E., Davis, G. E., & Gatchel, R. J. (1982). Individual differences in coping with crowding: Stimulus screening and social overload. *Journal of Personality and Social Psychology, 43,* 821–830.

Baum, A., & Valins, S. (1979). Architectural mediation of residential density and control: Crowding and the regulation of social contact. In L. Berkowitz (Ed.), *Advances in experimental social psychology* (Vol. 12). New York: Academic Press.

Baumann, L. J., & Leventhal, H. (1985). I can tell when my blood pressure is up, can't I? *Health Psychology, 4,* 203–218.

Baumrind, D. (1967). Child care practices anteceding three patterns of preschool behavior. *Genetic Psychology Monographs, 75,* 43–88.

Baumrind, D. (1973). The development of instrumental competence through socialization. In A. Pick (Ed.), *Minnesota Symposium in Child Development* (Vol. 7). Minneapolis: University of Minnesota Press, 1973.

Baumrind, D. (1985). Research using intentional deception: Ethical issues revisited. *American Psychologist, 40,* 165–174.

Baumrind, D. (1986). Sex differences in moral reasoning: Response to Walker's (1984. conclusion that there are none. *Child Development, 57,* 511–521.

Bavelas, A., Hastorf, A. H., Gross, A. E., & Kite, W. R. (1965). Experiments on the alteration of group structure. *Journal of Experimental and Social Psychology, 1,* 55–70.

Bayley, N. (1956). Individual patterns of development. *Child Development, 27,* 45–74.

Bayley, N. (1969). *Bayley Scales of Infant Development.* New York: The Psychological Corporation.

Baylor, D. (1987). Photoreceptor signals and vision. *Investigative Opthalmology and Visual Science, 28,* 34–49.

Bazerman, M. (1990). In *Discovering Psychology,* programs 11 and 24 [PBS video series]. Washington, DC: Annenberg/CPB Project.

Bazerman, M. H. (1990). *Judgment in managerial decision making* (2nd ed.). New York: Wiley.

Beach, F. A. (1955). The descent of instinct. *Psychological Review, 62,* 401–410.

Beardslee, W. R., & Mack, J. E. (1983). Adolescents and the threat of nuclear war: The evolution of a perspective. *Yale Journal of Biological Medicine, 56*(2), 79–91.

Beck, A. T. (1967). *Depression: Clinical, experimental, and theoretical aspects.* New York: Harper & Row.

Beck, A. T. (1976). *Cognitive therapy and emotional disorders.* New York: International Universities Press.

Beck, A. T. (1983). Cognitive theory of depression: New perspectives. In P. J. Clayton, & J. E. Barrett (Eds.), *Treatment of depression: Old controversies and new approaches* (pp. 265–290). New York: Raven Press.

Beck, A. T. (1985). Cognitive therapy. In H. I. Kaplan & J. Sandock (Eds.), *Comprehensive textbook of psychiatry* (4th ed.). Baltimore: Williams & Wilkins.

Beck, A. T. (1988). Cognitive approaches to panic disorders: Theory and therapy. In S. Rachman & J. D. Maser (Eds.), *Panic: Psychological perspectives.* New York: Guilford Press.

Beck, A. T., & Emery, G. (1985). *Anxiety disorders and phobias: A cognitive perspective.* New York: Basic Books.

Beck, A. T., Rush, A. J., Shaw, B. F., & Emery, G. (1979). *Cognitive therapy of depression.* New York: Guilford Press.

Beck, J. (1966). Effects of orientation and of shape similarity on perceptual grouping. *Perception and Psychophysics, 1,* 300–302.

Beck, J. (1972). Similarity groupings and peripheral discriminability under uncertainty. *American Journal of Psychology, 85,* 1–20.

Beck, J. (Ed.). (1982). *Organization and representation in perception.* Hillsdale, NJ: Erlbaum.

Beck, M., & Crowley, G. (1990, March 26). Beyond lobotomies: Psychosurgery is safer—but still a rarity. *Newsweek,* p. 44.

Becker, G. (1978). *The mad genius controversy: A study in the sociology of deviance.* Beverly Hills, CA: Sage.

Beecher, E. (1972). *Licit and illicit drugs.* Boston: Little, Brown.

Beecher, H. K. (1956). Relationship of significance of wound to the pain experienced. *Journal of the American Medical Association, 161,* 1609–1613.

Beecher, H. K. (1959). *Measurement of subjective responses.* New York: Oxford University Press.

Begg, I., & Paivio, A. V. (1969). Concreteness and imagery in sentence meaning. *Journal of Verbal Learning and Behavior, 8,* 821–827.

Begley, S. (1989, May 14). The stuff that dreams are made of. *Newsweek,* pp. 41–44.

Bekerian, D. A., & Bowers, J. M. (1983). Eyewitness testimony: Were we misled? *Journal of Experimental Psychology: Learning, Memory, and Cognition, 9,* 139–145.

Belk, R. W. (1988). Possessions and the extended self. *Journal of Consumer Research, 15,* 139–168.

Bell, A. P., & Weinberg, M. S. (1978). *Homosexualities: A study of diversity among men and women.* New York: Simon & Schuster.

Bell, A. P., Weinberg, M. S., & Hammersmith, S. K. (1981). *Sexual preference.* Bloomington: Indiana University Press.

Bell, I. R. (1982). *Clinical ecology.* Bolinas, CA: Common Knowledge Press.

Bell, L. V. (1980). *Treating the mentally ill: From colonial times to the present.* New York: Praeger.

Bell, R. R. (1974). Female sexual satisfaction as related to levels of education. In L. Gross (Ed.), *Sexual behavior* (pp. 3–11). Flushing, NY: Spectrum.

Bellak, L. (Ed.). (1979). *Disorders of the schizophrenic syndrome.* New York: Basic Books.

Belloc, N. B. (1973). Relationship of health practices and mortality. *Preventive Medicine, 2,* 67–81.

Belloc, N. B., & Breslow, L. (1972). Relationship of physical health status and family practices. *Preventive Medicine, 1,* 409–421.

Bellugi, U., Klima, E. S., & Siple, P. A. (1975). Remembering in signs. *Cognition, 3,* 93–125.

Bem, D. J. (1970). *Beliefs, attitudes, and human affairs.* Belmont, CA: Brooks/Cole.

Bem, D. J. (1972). Self-perception theory. In L. Berkowitz (Ed.), *Advances in experimental social psychology* (Vol. 6, pp. 1–62). New York: Academic Press.

Bem, D. J., & Allen, A. (1974). On predicting some of the people some of the time: The search for cross-situational consistencies in behavior. *Psychological Review, 81*(6), 506–520.

Bem, S. L. (1974). The measurement of psychological androgyny. *Journal of Consulting and Clinical Psychology, 42,* 155–162.

Bem, S. L. (1981a). *The Bem Sex Role Inventory: Professional manual.* Palo Alto, CA: Consulting Psychology Press.

Bem, S. L. (1981b). Gender schema theory: A cognitive account of sex typing. *Psychological Review, 88,* 354–364.

Bem, S. L. (1984). Androgyny and gender schema theory: A conceptual and empirical integration. In T. B. Sonderegger (Ed.), Nebraska Symposium on Motivation, 1984: *The psychology of gender.* Lincoln, NE: University of Nebraska Press.

Benbow, C. P., & Stanley, J. C. (1987). Sex differences in mathematical reasoning ability. *Science, 222,* 1029–1031.

Benedict, R. (1938). Continuities and discontinuities in cultural conditioning. *Psychiatry, 1,* 161–167.

Benedict, R. (1959). *Patterns of culture.* Boston: Houghton Mifflin.

Beninger, J. R. (1986). *The control revolution: Technological and economic origins of the information society.* Cambridge, MA: Harvard University Press.

Bennett, B. M., Hoffman, D. D., & Prakash, C. (1989). *Observer mechanics: A formal theory of perception.* NY: Academic Press.

Bennett, H. L. (1983). Remembering drink orders: The memory skills of cocktail waitresses. *Human Learning, 2,* 157–169.

Benson, H. (1975). *The relaxation response.* New York: Morrow.

Berglas, S., & Jones, E. E. (1978). Drug choice as a self-handicapping strategy in response to noncontingent success. *Journal of Personality and Social Psychology, 36,* 405–417.

Berk, L. S., Ian, S. A., Fry, W. F., Napier, B. J., Lee, J. W., Hubbard, R. W., Lewis, J. E., & Eby, W. C. (1989). Neuroendocrine and stress hormone changes during mirthful laughter. *American Journal of Medical Science, 298,* 390–396.

Berkman, L. F., & Syme, S. L. (1979). Social networks, host resistance, and mortality: A nine-year follow-up study of Alameda County residents. *American Journal of Epidemiology, 109,* 186–204.

Berkowitz, L. (1982). Aversive conditions as stimuli to aggression. *Advances in Experimental Social Psychology, 15,* 249–288.

Berkowitz, L. (1988). Introduction to social psychological studies of the self: Perspectives and programs. In L. Berkowitz (Ed.), *Advances in experimental social psychology* (Vol. 21, pp. 57–95). New York: Academic Press.

Berlyne, D. E. (1950). Stimulus intensity and attention in relation to learning theory. *Quarterly Journal of Experimental Psychology, 2,* 71–75.

Berlyne, D. E. (1951). Attention to change. *British Journal of Psychology, 42,* 269–278.

Berlyne, D. E. (1958). The influence of complexity and novelty in visual figures on orienting responses. *Journal of Experimental Psychology, 55,* 289–296.

Berlyne, D. E. (1960). *Conflict, arousal, and curiosity.* New York: McGraw-Hill.

Berlyne, D. E. (1967). Reinforcement and arousal. In O. Levine (Ed.), *Nebraska Symposium on Motivation, 1966.* Lincoln: University of Nebraska Press.

Bernard, C. (1878). *La science experimentale.* Paris: J. B. Baille'ere & Fils.

Bernard, L. L. (1924). *Instinct.* New York: Holt, Rinehart & Winston.

Berndt, T. J. (1979). Developmental changes in conformity to peers and parents. *Developmental Psychology, 15,* 608–616.

Bernstein, I. L. (1988). What does learning have to do with weight loss and cancer? *Proceedings of the Science and Public Policy Seminar of the Federation of Behavioral, Psychological and Cognitive Sciences.* Washington, DC.

Bernstein, I. L. (1990). Salt preference and development. *Developmental Psychology, 26,* 552–554.

Berry, J. W. (1967). Independence and conformity in subsistence level societies. *Journal of Personality and Social Psychology, 7,* 415–418.

Berscheid, E., & Walster, E. H. (1978). *Interpersonal attraction* (2nd ed.). Reading, MA: Addison-Wesley.

Bettleheim, B. (1962). *Symbolic wounds, puberty rites and the envious male.* New York: Collier.

Betz, E. L. (1982). Need fulfillment in the career development of women. *Journal of Vocational Behavior, 20,* 53–66.

Biaggio, M. K., & Bittner, E. (1990). Psychology and optometry: Interaction and collaboration. *American Psychologist, 45,* 1313–1315.

Bieber, I., Dain, H. J., Dince, P. R., Drellich, M. G., Grand, H. G., Bundlach, R. H., Dremer, M. W., Rifkin, A. H., Wilbur, C. B., & Bieber, T. B. (1962). *Homosexuality.* New York: Vintage Books.

Biederman, I. (1985). Recognition by components: A theory of object recognition. *Computer Vision Graphics and Image Processing, 32,* 29–73.

Biederman, I. (1987). Recognition by components. *Psychological Review, 94,* 173–211.

Biederman, I. (1989). Higher-level vision. In D. N. Osherson, H. Sasnik, S. Kosslyn, K. Hollerbach, E. Smith, & N. Block (Eds.), *An invitation to cognitive science.* Cambridge, MA: MIT Press.

Bielski, R. J., & Friedel, R. O. (1977). Subtypes of depression, diagnosis and medical management. *Western Journal of Medicine, 126,* 347–352.

Bigelow, H. J. (1850). Dr. Harlow's case of recovery from the passage of an iron bar through the head. *American Journal of Medical Science, 20,* 13–22.

Billings, A. G., & Moos, R. H. (1982). Family environments and adaptation: A clinically applicable typology. *American Journal of Family Therapy, 10,* 26–38.

Binet, A. (1894). *Psychologie des grandes calculateurs et joueurs d'echecs.* Paris: Hachette.

Binet, A. (1911). *Les idées modernes sur les enfants.* Paris:

Flammarion.

Binkley, S. (1979). A timekeeping enzyme in the pineal gland. *Scientific American, 204*(4), 66–71.

Birbaumer, N., & Kimmel, H. (Eds.). (1979). *Biofeedback and self-regulation.* Hillsdale, NJ: Erlbaum.

Bird, O. A. (1974). *Humanities. Encyclopaedia Brittanica (Macropaedia),* Vol. 8, 1179–1183.

Bitner, R. (1983). Awareness during anesthesia. In F. Orkin & L. Cooperman (Eds.), *Complications in anesthesiology* (pp. 349–354). Philadelphia: Lippincott.

Bitterman, M. E. (1975). The comparative analysis of learning. *Science, 188,* 699–709.

Black, I. B., Adler, J. E., Dreyfus, C. F., Friedman, W. F., LaGamma, E. F., & Roach, A. H. (1987). Biochemistry of information storage in the nervous system. *Science, 236,* 1263–1268.

Blake, R., & Hirsch, H. V. B. (1975). Deficits in binocular depth perception in cats after altering monocular deprivation. *Science, 190,* 1114–1116.

Blakemore, C., & Campbell, P. W. (1969). On the existence of neurons in the human visual system selectively sensitive to the orientation and size of retinal images. *Journal of Physiology, 203,* 237–260.

Blaney, P. H. (1986). Affect and memory: A review. *Psychological Bulletin, 99,* 229–246.

Blank, A. A., Jr. (1982). Stresses of war: The example of Vietnam. In L. Goldberger & S. Breznitz (Eds.), *Handbook of stress* (pp. 631–643). New York: Free Press/Macmillan.

Blass, E. M. (1990). Suckling: Determinants, changes, mechanisms, and lasting impressions. *Developmental Psychology, 26,* 520–533.

Blass, E. M., & Teicher, M. H. (1980). Suckling. *Science, 210,* 15–22.

Bleuler, M. (1978). The long-term course of schizophrenic psychoses. In L. C. Wynne, R. L. Cromwell, & S. Mattysse (Eds.), *The nature of schizophrenia: New approaches to research and treatment* (pp. 631–636). New York: Wiley.

Blight, J. G. (1987). Toward a policy-relevant psychology of avoiding nuclear war: Lessons for psychologists from the Cuban missile crisis. *American Psychologist, 42,* 12–19.

Bloch, S., & Reddaway, P. (1977). *Psychiatric terror: How Soviet psychiatry is used to suppress dissent.* New York: Basic Books.

Block, A. (1980). An investigation of the response of the spouse to chronic pain behavior. *Pain, 9,* 243–252.

Block, J. (1990). In *Discovering Psychology,* Program 17 [PBS video series]. Washington, DC: Annenberg/CPB Program.

Block, J. H. (1983). Differential premises arising from differential socialization of the sexes: Some conjectures. *Child Development, 54,* 1335–1354.

Blodgett, R. (1986, May). Lost in the stars: Psychics strike out (again). *People Expression,* 32–35.

Bly, R. (1990). *Iron John.* New York: Addison-Wesley.

Bohman, M., Cloninger, R., Sigvardson, S., & von-Knorring, A. L. (1987). The genetics of alcoholisms and related disorders. *Journal of Psychiatric Research, 21,* 447–452.

Bolger, N., DeLongis, A., Kessler, R. C., & Schilling, E. A. (1989). Effects of daily stress on negative mood. *Journal of Personality and Social Psychology, 57,* 808–818.

Bolles, R. C., & Faneslow, M. S. (1982). Endorphins and behavior. *Annual Review of Psychology, 33,* 87–101.

Bond, C. F., & Brockett, D. R. (1987). A social context-personality index theory of memory for acquaintances. *Journal of personality and social psychology, 52,* 1110–1121.

Bond, L. A. (1988). Teaching developmental psychology. In P. A. Bronstein & K. Quinna (Eds.), *Teaching a psychology of people: Resources for gender and sociocultural awareness* (pp. 45–52). Washington, DC: APA.

Bongiovanni, A. (1977). *A review of research on the effects of punishment in the schools.* Paper presented at the Conference on Child Abuse, Children's Hospital National Medical Center, Washington, DC.

Bootzin, R. R. (1975). *Behavior modification and therapy: An introduction.* Cambridge, MA: Winthrop.

Bootzin, R. R., & Nicasio, P. M. (1978). Behavioral treatments for insomnia. In M. Hersen, R. Eisler, & P. Miller (Eds.), *Progress in behavior modification.* New York: Academic Press.

Boring, E. G. (1950). *A history of experimental psychology* (2nd ed.). New York: Appleton-Century-Crofts.

Boring, E. G., Langfeld, H. S., & Weld, H. P. (1948). *Foundations of Psychology.* New York: Wiley.

Borke, H. (1975). Piaget's mountains revisited: Changes in the egocentric landscape. *Developmental Psychology, 11,* 240–243.

Borkovec, T. D. (1982). Insomnia. *Journal of Consulting and Clinical Psychology, 50,* 880–985.

Bornstein, P. A., & Quinna, K. (Eds.). (1988). *Teaching a psychology of people: Resources for gender and sociocultural awareness.* Washington, DC: American Psychological Association.

Borod, C., Koff, E., Lorch, M. P., Nicholas, M., & Welkowitz, J. (1988). Emotional and non-emotional facial behavior in patients with unilateral brain damage. *Journal of Neurological and Neurosurgical Psychiatry, 5,* 826–832.

Botvin, G. J., & Eng, A. (1982). The efficacy of a multicomponent approach to the prevention of cigarette smoking. *Preventive Medicine, 11,* 199–211.

Botwinick, J. (1977). Intellectual abilities. In J. E. Birren & K. W. Schaie (Eds.), *Handbook of the psychology of aging* (pp. 580–605). New York: Van Nostrand Reingold.

Bouchard, T. J., Jr., Lykken, D. T., McGue, M., Segal, N. L., & Tellegen, A. (1990). Sources of human psychological differences: The Minnesota study of twins reared apart. *Science, 250,* 223–228.

Bouchard, T. J., Jr., & McGue, M. (1981). Familial studies of intelligence: A review. *Science, 212,* 1055–1059.

Bouchard, T. J., Jr., & McGue, M. (1990). Genetic and environmental influences on adult personality: An analysis of adopted twins reared apart. *Journal of Personality, 58,* 263–295.

Bourguignon, E. (1973). Introduction: A framework for the comparative study of altered states of consciousness. In E. Bourguignon (Ed.), *Religion, altered states of consciousness, and social change.* Columbus: Ohio State University Press.

Bourguignon, E. (1979). *Psychological anthropology: An introduction to human nature and cultural differences.* New York: Holt, Rinehart, and Winston.

Bower, G. H. (1972). A selective review of organizational factors in memory. In E. Tulving & W. Donaldson (Eds.), *Organization of memory.* New York: Academic Press.

Bower, G. H. (1981). Mood and memory. *American Psychologist, 36,* 129–148.

Bower, G. H. (1990). In *Discovering Psychology,* Program 9 [PBS video series]. Washington, DC: Annenberg/CPB Project.

Bower, G. H. (1991, April). *Emotions and social perception.* Speech given at Western Psychological Association, San Francisco, CA.

Bower, S. A., & Bower, G. H. (1991). *Asserting yourself: A practical guide for positive change.* Reading, MA: Addison-Wesley. (Original work published 1976)

Bowers, K. S. (1976). *Hypnosis for the seriously curious.* New York: Norton.

Bowers, M. B., Jr. (1980). Biochemical processes in schizophrenia: An update. In S. J. Keith & L. R. Mosher (Eds.), *Special Report: Schizophrenia, 1980.* Washington, DC: U.S. Government Printing Office.

Bowlby, J. (1969). *Attachment and loss, Vol. 1. Attachment.* New York: Basic Books.

Bowlby, J. (1973). *Attachment and loss: Vol. 2. Separation, anxiety and anger.* London: Hogarth.

Boyd, J. H., & Weissman, M. M. (1981). Epidemiology of affective disorders: A reexamination and future directions. *Archives of General Psychiatry, 38,* 1039–1046.

Braginsky, B., & Braginsky, D. (1967). Schizophrenic patients in the psychiatric interview: An experimental study of their effectiveness at manipulation. *Journal of Consulting Psychology, 31,* 543–547.

Braginsky, B., Braginsky, D., & Ring, K. (1969). *Methods of madness: The mental hospital as a last resort.* New York: Holt, Rinehart & Winston.

Braine, M. D. S. (1976). Children's first word combinations. *Monographs of the Society for Research in Child Development, 41* (Serial No. 164).

Bransford, J., Sherwood, R., Vye, N., & Reiser, J. (1986). Teaching, thinking and problem solving. *American Psychologist, 41,* 1078–1089.

Bransford, J. D., & Franks, J. J. (1971). The abstraction of linguistic ideas. *Cognitive Psychology, 2,* 331–350.

Bransford, J. D., & Johnson, M. K. (1972). Contextual prerequisites for understanding: Some investigations of comprehension and recall. *Journal of Verbal Learning and Verbal Behavior, 11,* 17–21.

Bransford, J. D., & Johnson, M. K. (1973). Considerations of some problems of comprehension. In W. G. Chase (Ed.), *Visual information processing.* New York: Academic Press.

Breakey, W. R., & Fischer, P. J. (1990). Homelessness: The extent of the problem. *Journal of Social Issues, 46,* 31–47.

Breggin, P. R. (1979). *Electroshock: Its brain disabling effects.* New York: Springer.

Bregman, A. S. (1981). Asking the "what for" question in auditory perception. In M. Kobovy & J. Pomerantz (Eds.), *Perceptual organization* (pp. 99–118). Hillsdale, NJ: Erlbaum.

Breland, K., & Breland, M. (1951). A field of applied animal psychology. *American Psychologist, 6,* 202–204.

Breland, K., & Breland, M. (1961). A misbehavior of organisms. *American Psychologist, 16,* 681–684.

Brennan, P., Kaba, H., & Keverne, E. B. (1990). Olfactory recognition: A simple memory system. *Science, 250,* 1223–1226.

Brenner, M. H. (1976). *Estimating the social costs of national economic policy: Implications for mental and physical health and criminal violence.* Report prepared for the Joint Economic Committee of Congress, Washington, DC: U.S. Government Printing Office.

Breo, D. L. (1989). In treating the pathological gambler, MDs must overcome the attitude, "why bother?" *Journal of the American Medical Association, 262,* 2599–2603.

Brett, J. F., Brief, A. P., Burke, M. J., George, J. M., & Webster, J. (1990). Negative affectivity and the reporting of stressful life events. *Health Psychology, 9,* 57–68.

Breuer, J., & Freud, S. (1955). Studies on hysteria. In J. Strachey (Ed. and Trans.), *The standard edition of the complete psychological works of Sigmund Freud* (Vol. 2). London: Hogarth Press. (Original work published 1895)

Brewer, M. B. (1979). In-group bias in the minimal intergroup situation: A cognitive-motivational analysis. *Psychological Bulletin, 86,* 307–324.

Briand, K. A., & Klein, R. M. (1988). Conceptual masking in brief visual displays. *Canadian Journal of Psychology, 42,* 496–502.

Bridgeman, B. (1983). Independent evidence for neural systems mediating blindsight. *The Behavioral and Brain Sciences, 6,* 450–451.

Brim, O. G., & Kagan, J. (1980). *Constancy and change in human development.* Cambridge: Harvard University Press.

Brislin, R. W. (1981). *Cross-cultural encounters: Face-to-face encounters.* New York: Pergamon.

Broadbent, D. E. (1954). The role of auditory localization in attention and memory span. *Journal of Experimental Psychology, 47,* 191–196.

Broadbent, D. E. (1958). *Perception and communication.* London: Pergamon Press.

Broadbent, D. E. (1971). *Decision and stress.* New York: Academic Press.

Broadbent, D. E., & Gregory, M. (1967). Perception of emotionally toned words. *Nature, 215,* 581–584.

Brody, E. B., & Brody, N. (1976). *Intelligence: Nature, determinants, and consequences.* New York: Academic Press.

Brody, R. V. (1986). Pain management in terminal disease. *Focus: A Review of AIDS Research, 1,* 1–2.

Broman, S. H., Nichols, P. I., & Kennedy, W. A. (1975). *Preschool IQ: Prenatal and early developmental correlates.* Hillsdale, NJ: Erlbaum.

Bronfenbrenner, U. (1977). Toward an experimental ecology of human development. *American Psychologist, 32,* 513–531.

Broverman, I. K., Vogel, S. R., Broverman, D. M., Clarkson, F. E., & Rosenkrantz, P. S. (1972). Sex-role stereotypes: A current appraisal. *Journal of Social Issues, 28*(2), 59–78.

Brown, A. L., & De Loache, J. L. (1978). Skills, plans, and self-regulation. In R. S. Siegler (Ed.), *Children's thinking: What develops?* (pp. 3–35). Hillsdale, NJ: Erlbaum.

Brown, A. M. (1990). *Human universals.* Unpublished manuscript, University of California, Santa Barbara.

Brown, B., & Rosenbaum, L. (1983, May). *Stress effects on IQ.* Paper presented at the meeting of the American Association for the Advancement of Science, Detroit, MI.

Brown, C. C. (Ed.). (1984). *The many facets of touch.* Skillman, NJ: Johnson & Johnson.

Brown, G. W., & Harris, T. O. (Eds.). (1989). *Life events and illness.* New York: Guilford.

Brown, J. D. (1991). Staying fit and staying well: Physical fitness as a moderator of life stress. *Journal of Personality and Social Psychology, 60,* 555–561.

Brown, J. S. (1961). *The motivation of behavior.* New York: McGraw-Hill.

Brown, L. (Ed.). (1989). *State of the world 1989.* New York: Norton.

Brown, R. (1986). *Social psychology: The second edition.* New York: The Free Press.

Brown, R., & Hanlon, C. (1970). Derivational complexity and order of acquisition. In J. R. Hayes (Ed.), *Cognition and the development of language.* New York: Wiley.

Brown, R. W., & McNeil, D. (1966). The "tip-of-the-tongue" phenomenon. *Journal of Verbal Learning and Verbal Behavior, 5,* 325–337.

Brownell, K. D. (1982). Obesity: Understanding and treating a serious, prevalent, and refractory disorder. *Journal of Clinical and Consulting Psychology, 50,* 820–840.

Brownell, K. D., Marlatt, G. A., Lichtenstein, E., & Wilson, G. T. (1986). Understanding and preventing relapse. *American Psychologist, 41,* 765–782.

Bruner, J. (1986). *Actual minds, possible worlds.* Cambridge, MA: Harvard University Press.

Bruner, J. S. (1973). *Beyond the information given.* New York: Norton.

Bruner, J. S., & Goodman, C. C. (1947). Value and need as organizing factors in perception. *Journal of Abnormal and Social Psychology, 42,* 33–44.

Bruner, J. S., Olver, R. R., & Greenfield, P. M. (1966). *Studies in cognitive growth.* New York: Wiley.

Bryant, D. J. (1990). Implicit associative responses influence encoding in memory. *Memory & Cognition, 18,* 348–358.

Buchsbaum, M. S. (1980). The two brains. In *1981 yearbook of sciences and the future* (pp. 138–153). Chicago: Encyclopaedia Britannica.

Buck, R. (1984). *The communication of emotion.* New York: Guilford.

Buhler, C. (1968). Fulfillment and failure in life. In C. Buhler & F. Massarik (Eds.), *The course of human life.* New York: Springer.

Bullock, M., & Gelman, R. (1979). Preschool children's assumptions about cause and effect: Temporal coding. *Child Development, 50,* 89–96.

Bulman, J. R., & Wortman, C. B. (1977). Attribution of blame and coping in the "real world": Severe accident victims react to their lot. *Journal of Personality and Social Psychology, 35,* 351–363.

Burk, J. P., & Sher, K. J. (1990). Labeling the child of an alcoholic: Negative stereotyping by mental health professionals and peers. *Journal of Studies of Alcohol, 51,* 156–163.

Buros, O. K. (Ed.). (1974). *Tests in print: II.* Highland Park, NJ: Gryphon Press.

Buros, O. K. (Ed.). (1978). *The eighth mental measurements yearbook.* Highland Park, NJ: Gryphon Press.

Burrows, G. D., & Dennerstein, L. (Eds.). (1980). *Handbook of hypnosis and psychosomatic medicine.* New York: Elsevier/North Holland Biomedical Press.

Buss, A. H. (1980). *Self-consciousness and social anxiety.* San Francisco: Freeman.

Buss, D. M. (1991). Evolutionary personality psychology. *Annual Review of Psychology, 42,* 459–492.

Butcher, J. N. (1988). Personality factors in drug addiction. *NIDA Research Monograph, 89,* 87–92.

Butcher, J. N. (1989). Why use the MMPI-2? In J. N. Butcher & J. R. Graham (Eds.), *Topics in MMPI-2 Interpretation.* Minneapolis: MMPI-2 Workshops and Symposia, Department of Psychology, University of Minnesota.

Butcher, J. N., Dahlstrom, W. G., Graham, J. R., Tellegen, A., & Kaemmer, B. (1989). *Manual for the restandardized Minnesota Multiphasic Personality Inventory: MMPI-2. An administrative and interpretive guide.* Minneapolis: University of Minnesota Press.

Butcher, J. N., & Finn, S. (1983). Objective personality assessment in clinical settings. In M. H. Jersen, A. E. Kazdin, & A. S. Bellock (Eds.), *The clinical psychology handbook* (pp. 329–344). New York: Pergamon.

Butler, M. J., & Rice, L. N. (1963). Audience, self-actualization, and drive theory. In J. M. Wepman & R. W. Heine (Eds.), *Concepts of personality* (pp. 79–110). Chicago: Aldine.

Butler, R. A., & Harlow, H. F. (1954). Persistence of visual exploration in monkeys. *Journal of Comparative and Physiological Psychology, 47,* 258–263.

Butler, R. N., & Lewis, M. I. (1982). *Aging and mental health: Positive psychosocial and biomedical approaches* (3rd ed.). St. Louis: Mosby.

Buzan, T. (1976). *Use both sides of your brain.* New York: Dutton.

Bykov, K. M. (1957). *The cerebral cortex and the internal organs.* New York: Academic Press.

Byrne, D. (1971). *The attraction paradigm.* New York: Academic Press.

Byrne, D. (1981, August). *Predicting human sexual behavior.* G. Stanley Hall Lecture presented at the meeting of the American Psychological Association, Los Angeles, CA.

C

Cairns, R. B., & Valsinger, J. (1984). Child psychology. *Annual Review of Psychology, 35,* 553–577.

Calambokidis, J. (1986, October 20). [Letter to Greenpeace].

Calkins, M. P. (1988). *Design for dementia: Planning environments for the elderly and the confused.* Owings Mills, MD: National Health Publishing.

Calkins, M. W. (1893). Statistics of dreams. *American Journal of Psychology, 5,* 311–343.

Cameron, P., Frank, R., Lifter, M., & Morrissey, P. (1968, September). *Cognitive functionings of college students in a general psychology class.* Paper presented at the meeting of the American Psychological Association, San Francisco, CA.

Campbell, F. W., & Robson, J. G. (1968). Application of Fourier analysis to the visibility of gratings. *Journal of Physiology, 197,* 551–566.

Campion, J., Latto, R., & Smith, Y. M. (1983). Is blindsight an effect of scattered light, spared cortex, and near threshold vision? *The Behavioral and Brain Sciences, 6,* 423–486.

Campos, J. J., Barrett, K. C., Lamb, M. E., Goldsmith, H. H., & Stenberg, C. (1983). *Socioemotional development* (Vol. 2). New York: Wiley.

Cann, A., Calhoun, L. G., Selby, J. W., Kin, H. E. (Eds.). (1981). Rape. *Journal of Social Issues, 37* (whole no. 4).

Cannon, W. B. (1927). The James-Lange theory of emotion: A critical examination and an alternative theory. *American Journal of Psychology, 39,* 106–124.

Cannon, W. B. (1929). *Bodily changes in pain, hunger, fear and rage* (2nd ed.). New York: Appleton-Century-Crofts.

Cannon, W. B. (1934). Hunger and thirst. In C. Murchison (Ed.), *A handbook of general experimental psychology.* Worcester, MA: Clark University Press.

Cannon, W. B. (1942). "Voodoo" death. *American Anthropologist, 44,* 169–181.

Cannon, W. B. (1957). "Voodoo" death. *Psychosomatic Medicine, 19,* 182–190.

Cannon, W. B., & Washburn, A. L. (1912). An explanation of hunger. *American Journal of Physiology, 29,* 441–454.

Cantor, N., & Kihlstrom, J. F. (1987). Social intelligence: The cognitive basis of personality. In P. Shaver (Ed.), *Review of personality and social psychology, Vol. 6* (pp. 15–34). Beverly Hills, CA: Sage.

Cantor, N., & Mischel, W. (1979). Traits as prototypes: Effects on recognition memory. *Journal of Personality and Social Psychology, 35,* 38–48.

Caplan, G. (1969, November). A psychiatrist's casebook. *McCall's,* p. 65.

Caplan, P. J. (1984). The myth of women's masochism. *American Psychologist, 39,* 130–139.

Caplow, T. (1982). *Middletown families: Fifty years of change and continuity.* Minneapolis: University of Minnesota Press.

Caporeal, L. R. (1976). Ergotism: The Satan loosed in Salem? *Science, 192,* 21–26.

Carey, S. (1978). The child as word learner. In M. Halle, J. Bresnan, & G. A. Miller (Eds.), *Linguistic theory and psychological reality* (pp. 265–293). Cambridge, MA: MIT Press.

Carlsmith, J. M., & Gross, A. (1969). Some effects of guilt on compliance. *Journal of Personality and Social Psychology, 11,* 232–240.

Carlsmith, J. M., Lepper, M. R., & Landauer, T. K. (1974). Children's obedience to adult requests: Interactive effects of anxiety arousal and apparent punitiveness of adults. *Journal of Personality and Social Psychology, 30,* 822–828.

Carlson, J. G., & Wood, R. D. (1974). *Need the final solution be justified?* Unpublished manuscript, University of Hawaii.

Carlsson, A. (1978). Antipsychotic drugs, neurotransmitters, and schizophrenia. *American Journal of Psychiatry, 135,* 164–173.

Carlton, J. (1990, December 4). When Californians use leaf blowers, life is less mellow. *The Wall Street Journal,* pp. A1, A7.

Carmichael, L. (1926). The development of behavior in vertebrates experimentally removed from the influence of external stimulation. *Psychological Review, 33,* 51–58.

Carmichael, L. (1970). The onset and early development of behavior. In P. H. Mussen (Ed.), *Carmichael's manual of child psychology* (3rd ed., Vol. 1). New York: Wiley.

Carnes, P. (1983). *Out of the shadows: Understanding sexual addiction.* Minneapolis, MN: CompCare Publications.

Carnes, P. (1991). *Don't call it love: Recovery from sexual addiction.* New York: Bantam.

Carone, P. A., Yolles, S. F., Kieffer, S. N., & Krinsky, L. W. (Eds.). (1982). Presentation by three compulsive gamblers. In *Addictive Disorders Update: Alcoholism /Drug Abuse /Gambling.* New York: Human Sciences Press.

Carpenter, G. C. (1973). Differential response to mother and stranger within the first month of life. *Bulletin of the British Psychological Society, 16,* 138.

Carr, T. H. (1979). Orthography and familiarity effects in word processing. *Journal of Experimental Psychology: General, 108,* 389–414.

Carrell, M. R., & Dittrich, J. E. (1978). Equity theory: The recent literature, methodological considerations, and new directions. *Academy of Management Review, 3,* 202–210.

Carskadon, M. A., & Dement, W. C. (1989). Normal human sleep: An overview. In M. Krugger, T. Roth, & W. C. Dement (Eds.), *Principles and practice of sleep medicine* (pp. 3–13). Philadelphia: Saunders.

Carstensen, L. L. (1987). Age-related changes in social activity. In L. L. Carstensen & B. A. Edelstein (Eds.), *Handbook of clinical gerontology* (pp. 222–237). New York: Pergamon Press.

Carstensen, L. L. (in press). Selectivity theory: Social activity in life-span context. In K. W. Schaie (Ed.), *Annual Review of Geriatrics and Gerontology* (Vol. 11). New York: Springer.

Cartwright, R. D. (1978). *A primer on sleep and dreaming.* Reading, MA: Addison-Wesley.

Cartwright, R. D. (1982). The shape of dreams. In *1983 yearbook of science and the future.* Chicago: Encyclopaedia Britannica.

Cartwright, R. D. (1984). Broken dreams: A study of the effects of divorce and depression on dream content. *Psychiatry, 47,* 251–259.

Cartwright, S. (1851, May). The diseases and physical peculiarities of the Negro race. *New Orleans Medical and Surgical Journal.*

Carver, C. S., Scheier, M. F., & Weintraub, J. K. (1989).

Assessing coping strategies: A theoretically based approach. *Journal of Personality and Social Psychology, 56,* 267–283.

Carver, C. S., & Scheier, M. P. (1981). *Attention and self-regulation: A control theory approach to human behavior.* New York: Springer-Verlag.

Case, R. S. (1985). *Intellectual development: A systematic reinterpretation.* New York: Academic Press.

Caspi, A., & Bem, D. J. (1990). Personality continuity and change across the life course. In L. A. Pervin (Ed.), *Handbook of personality theory and research* (pp. 549–575). New York: Guilford Press.

Caspi, A., Elder, G. H., Jr., & Bem, D. J. (1988). Moving away from the world: Life-course patterns of shy children. *Developmental Psychology, 24,* 824–833.

Catania, J. A., Kegeles, S. M., & Coates, T. J. (1990). Towards an understanding of risk behavior: An AIDS risk reduction model (ARRM). *Health Education Quarterly, 17,* 53–72.

Cattell, R. B. (1963). Theory of fluid and crystallized intelligence: A critical experiment. *Journal of Educational Psychology, 54,* 1–22.

Cattell, R. B. (1971). *Abilities: Their structure and growth.* Boston: Houghton Mifflin.

Cattell, R. B. (1972). The 16 PF and basic personality structure: A reply to Eysenck. *Journal of Behavioral Science, 1,* 169–187.

Cattell, R. B. (1982). *The inheritance of personality and ability: Research methods and findings.* New York: Academic Press.

Catterall, W. A. (1984). The molecular basis of neuronal excitability. *Science, 223,* 653–661.

Centers for Disease Control. (1985). *Suicide surveillance report, United States, 1970–1980.* Atlanta: Department of Health and Human Services.

Cermak, L. S., & Craik, F. I. M. (1979). *Levels of processing in human memory.* Hillsdale, NJ: Erlbaum.

Cervone, D., & Peake, P. K. (1986). Anchoring, efficacy, and action: The influence of judgmental heuristics on self-efficacy judgments. *Journal of Personality and Social Psychology, 50,* 492–501.

Chamberlain, K., & Zika, S. (1990). The minor events approach to stress: Support for the use of daily hassles. *British Journal of Psychology, 81,* 469–481.

Chapin, S. F. (1913). *Introduction to the study of social evolution.* New York: Century.

Chapman, P. D. (1988). *Schools as sorters: Lewis M. Terman, applied psychology, and the intelligence testing movement, 1890–1930.* New York: New York University Press.

Chapman, R. M., McCrary, J. W., & Chapman, J. A. (1978). Short-term memory: The "storage" component of human brain responses predicts recall. *Science, 202,* 1211–1213.

Charen, M. (1990, March 11). Say 'no way: Time for good old self-control. *San Francisco Examiner-Chronicle,* This World Section, p. 3.

Chase, W. G., & Ericsson, K. A. (1981). Skilled memory. In J. R. Anderson (Ed.), *Cognitive skills and their acquisition.* Hillsdale, NJ: Erlbaum.

Chase, W. G., & Simon, H. A. (1973). Perception in chess. In W. G. Chase (Ed.), *Visual information processing* (pp. 215–281). New York: Academic Press.

Chasnoff, I. J. (1989). Temporal patterns of cocaine use in pregnancy. *Journal of the American Medical Association, 261,* 24–31.

Chasnoff, I. J., Burns, W. J., Schnoll, S. H., & Burns, K. A. (1985). Cocaine use in pregnancy. *New England Journal of Medicine, 313,* 666–669.

Chasnoff, I. J., Griffith, D. R., MacGregor, S., Dirkes, K., & Burns, K. (1989). Temporal patterns of cocaine use in pregancy: Perinatal outcome. *Journal of the American Medical Association, 261,* 1741–1744.

Chawlisz, K., Diener, E., & Gallagher, D. (1988). Autonomic arousal feedback and emotional experience: Evidence from the spinal cord injured. *Journal of Personality and Social Psychology, 54,* 820–828.

Cheek, D. (1979, November). *Awareness of meaningful sounds under general anesthesia: Consideration and a review of the literature 1959 to 1979.* Paper presented at the annual meeting of the American Society of Clinical Hypnosis.

Cheek, J. (1989). *Conquering shyness: The battle anyone can win.* New York: Putnam.

Cheek, J. M., & Busch, C. M. (1981). The influence of shyness on loneliness in a new situation. *Personality and Social Psychology Bulletin, 7,* 572–577.

Chen, I. (1990, July 13). Quake may have caused baby boom in Bay Area. *The San Francisco Chronicle,* p. A3.

Cheney, D. L., & Seyfarth, R. (1985). Vervet monkey alarm calls: Manipulation through shared information. *Behavior, 4,* 150–166.

Cherfas, J. (1990, August 31). Science responds to terror. *Science,* p. 981.

Cherkin, A., & Harrour, P. (1971). Anesthesia and memory processes. *Anesthesiology, 34,* 469–474.

Cherry, E. C. (1953). Some experiments on the recognition of speech, with one and with two ears. *Journal of the Acoustical Society of America, 25,* 975–979.

Chi, M. T. H., Feltovich, P. J., & Glaser, R. (1981). Categorization and representation of physics problems by experts and novices. *Cognitive Science, 5,* 121–152.

Chi, M. T. H, & Koeske, R. D. (1983). Network representation of a child's dinosaur knowledge. *Developmental Psychology, 19,* 29–39.

Chilman, C. S. (Ed.). (1979). *Adolescent sexuality in a changing American society: Social and psychological perspectives* (Dhew Publications No. 79–1426). Washington, DC: National Institute of Health.

Chilman, C. S. (1983). *Adolescent sexuality in a changing American society* (2nd ed.). New York: Wiley.

Chilmonczyk, B. A., Knight, G. J., Palomaki, G. E., Pulkkinen, A. J., Williams, J., & Haddow, J. E. (1990). Environmental tobacco smoke exposure during infancy. *The American Journal of Public Health, 80,* 1205–1208.

Chomsky, N. (1957). *Syntactic structures.* The Hague: Mouton.

Chomsky, N. (1965). *Aspects of a theory of syntax.* Cambridge, MA: MIT Press.

Chomsky, N. (1975). *Reflections on language.* New York: Pantheon Books.

Chomsky, N. (1984). *Modular approaches to the study of the mind.* San Diego, CA: San Diego University Press.

Chomsky, N. (1986). *Knowledge of language: Its nature, origin, and use.* New York: Praeger.

Chorover, S. (1981, June). *Organizational recruitment in "open" and "closed" social systems: A neuropsychological perspective.* Conference paper presented at the Center for the Study of New Religious Movements, Berkeley, CA.

Christy, P. R., Gelfand, D. M., & Hartman, D. P. (1971). Effects of competition-induced frustration on two classes of modeled behavior. *Developmental Psychology, 5,* 104–111.

Churchland, P. S. (1986). *Toward a unified science of the mind-brain.* Cambridge, MA: MIT Press.

Churchland, P. S., & Sejnowski, T. J. (1988). Perspectives on cognitive neuroscience. *Science, 242,* 741–745.

Cialdini, R. B. (1985). *Influence: Science and practice.* Glenview, IL: Scott, Foresman.

Ciminero, A. R., Calhoun, K. S., & Adams, H. E. (Eds.). (1977). *Handbook of behavioral assessment.* New York: Wiley.

Clancey, M., & Robinson, M. J. (1985). General election coverage: Part 1. *Public Opinion, 7,* 49–54, 59.

Claparede, E. (1928). Feelings and emotions. In M. L. Reymert (Ed.), *Feelings and emotions: The Wittenberg Symposium* (pp. 124–139). Worcester, MA: Clark University Press.

Clark, E. E. (1953). *Indian legends of the Pacific Northwest.* Berkeley, CA: University of California Press.

Clark, E. V. (1928). Feelings and emotions. In M. L. Reymert (Ed.), *Feelings and emotions: The Wittenberg Symposium* (pp. 124–139). Worcester, MA: Clark University Press.

Clark, E. V. (1973). What's in a word? On the child's acquisition of semantics in his first language. In T. E. Moore (Ed.), *Cognitive development and the acquisition of language.* New York: Academic Press.

Clark, H. H., & Clark, E. V. (1977). *Psychology and language: An introduction to psycholinguistics.* New York: Harcourt Brace

Jovanovich.

Clark, K., & Clark, M. (1947). Racial identification and preference in Negro children. In T. M. Newcomb & E. L. Hartley (Eds.), *Readings in social psychology.* New York: Holt.

Clarke-Stewart, K. A. (1978). Recasting the lone stranger. In J. Glick & K. A. Clarke-Stewart (Eds.), *The development of social understanding.* New York: Gardner Press.

Clausen, J. A. (1981). Stigma and mental disorder: Phenomena and mental terminology. *Psychiatry, 44,* 287–296.

Clausen, T. (1968). *Perspectives on childhood socialization.* In J. A. Clausen (Ed.), Socialization and society. Boston: Little, Brown.

Clayman, C. B. (1989). *The American Medical Association Encyclopedia of Medicine.* New York: Random House.

Clearwater, Y. (1990). In *Discovering Psychology,* Program 24 [PBS video series]. Washington, DC: Annenberg/CPB Program.

Cleek, M. B., & Pearson, T. A. (1985). Perceived causes of divorce: An analysis of interrelationships. *Journal of Marriage and the Family, 47,* 179–191.

Clementz, B. A., & Sweeney, J. A. (1990). Is eye movement dysfunction a biological marker for schizophrenia? A methodological review. *Psychological Bulletin, 108,* 77–92.

Cloninger, C. R. (1987). Neurogenetic adaptive mechanisms in alcoholism. *Science, 236,* 410–416.

Coates, T. (1990). In *Discovering Psychology,* Program 23 [PBS video series]. Washington, DC: Annenberg/CPB Program.

Coates, T. (1990). Strategies for modifying sexual behavior for primary and secondary prevention of HIV infection. *Journal of Consulting and Clinical Psychology, 58,* 57–69.

Coates, T. J., Temoshok, L., & Mandel, J. (1984). Psychosocial research is essential to understanding and treating AIDS. *American Psychologist, 39,* 1309–1314.

Cobb, S. (1976). Social support as a moderator of stress. *Psychosomatic Medicine, 35,* 375–389.

Coch, L., & French, J. R. P., Jr. (1948). Overcoming resistance to change. *Human Relations, 1,* 512–532.

Cofer, C. (1988). Motivation. In E. R. Hilgard (Ed.), *Fifty years of psychology: Essays in honor of Floyd Ruch* (pp. 113–125). Glenview, IL: Scott, Foresman.

Cohen, B. S., & Nagel, E. (1934). *An introduction to logic and scientific method.* New York: Harcourt Brace Jovanovich.

Cohen, L. B., & Gelber, E. R. 1975). Infant visual memory. In L. Cohen & P. Salapatek (Eds.), *Infant perception: From sensation to cognition, Vol. 1: Basic visual processes* (pp. 347–403). New York: Academic Press.

Cohen, R. E., & Ahearn, F. L., Jr. (1980). *Handbook for mental health care of disaster victims.* Baltimore: Johns Hopkins University Press.

Cohen, R. Y., Brownell, K. D., & Felix, M. R. J. (1990). Age and sex differences in health habits and beliefs of schoolchildren. *Health Psychology, 9,* 208–224.

Cohen, S. (1988). Psychosocial models of the role of social support in the etiology of physical disease. *Health Psychology, 7,* 269–297.

Cohen, S., & McKay, G. (1983). Social support, stress, and the buffering hypotheses: A theoretical analysis. In A. Baum, S. E. Taylor, & J. Singer (Eds.), *Handbook of psychology and health* (Vol. 4). Hillsdale, NJ: Erlbaum.

Cohen, S., & Syme, S. L. (Eds.). (1985). *Social support and health.* Orlando, FL: Academic Press.

Coleman, J. C. (1980). Friendship and the peer group in adolescence. In J. Adelson (Ed.), *Handbook of adolescent psychology.* New York: Wiley.

Coleman, L. (1987). *Suicide clusters.* Winchester, MA: Faber & Faber.

Coleman, R. M. (1986). *Wide awake at 3: 00 A.M.: By choice or by chance?* New York: Freeman.

Collier, G., Hirsch, E., & Hamlin, P. (1972). The ecological determinants of reinforcement. *Physiology and Behavior, 9,* 705–716.

Conant, J. B. (1958). *On understanding science: An historical approach.* New York: New Amsterdam Library.

Condry, J., & Condry, S. (1976). Sex differences: A study in the eye of the beholder. *Child Development, 47,* 812–819.

Conger, J. C., & Keane, S. P. (1981). Social skills intervention in the treatment of isolated or withdrawn children. *Psychological Bulletin, 90,* 478–495.

Conger, J. J. (1977). *Adolescence and youth: Psychological development* (2nd ed.). New York: Harper & Row.

Conger, J. J. (1991). *Adolescence and youth* (4th ed.). New York: HarperCollins.

Connors, M. M., Harrison, A. A., & Akins, F. R. (1986). Psychology and the resurgent space program. *American Psychologist, 41,* 906–913.

Conrad, R. (1964). Acoustic confusions in immediate memory. *British Journal of Psychology, 55,* 75–84.

Conrad, R. (1972). Short-term memory in the deaf: A test for speech coding. *British Journal of Psychology, 63,* 173–180.

Cook, M., Mineka, S., Woklenstein, B., & Laitsch, K. (1985). Observational conditioning of snake fear in unrelated rhesus monkeys. *Journal of Abnormal Psychology, 94,* 591–610.

Cookerly, J. R. (1980). Does marital therapy do any lasting good? *Journal of Marital and Family Therapy, 6,* 393–397.

Cooper, A. F. (1976). Deafness and psychiatric illness. *British Journal of Psychiatry, 129,* 216–226.

Cooper, L. (1989). Mental models of the structure of visual objects. In B. Shepp & S. Ballisteros. (Eds.), *Object perception* (pp. 91–119). Hillsdale, NJ: Erlbaum.

Cooper, L. A., & Shepard, R. N. (1973). The time required to prepare for a rotated stimulus. *Memory and Cognition, 1,* 246–250.

Coren, S., & Girgus, J. S. (1978). *Seeing is deceiving: The psychology of visual illusions.* Hillsdale, NJ: Erlbaum.

Coren, S., Porac, C., & Ward, L. M. (1978). *Sensation and perception.* New York: Academic Press.

Coren, S., & Ward, L. M. (1989). *Sensation and perception* (3rd ed.). San Diego: Harcourt Brace Jovanovich.

Cornsweet, T. N. (1970). *Visual perception.* New York: Academic Press.

Corsini, R. J. (1977). *Current theories of personality.* Itasca, IL: Peacock.

Cosmides, L. (1989). The logic of social exchange: Has natural selection shaped how humans reason? Studies with the Wason Selection Task. *Cognition, 31,* 187–276.

Cosmides, L., & Tooby, J. (1987). From evolution to behavior: Evolutionary psychology as the missing link. In J. Dupre (Ed.), *The latest on the best: Essays on evolution and optimality* (pp. 277–306). Cambridge, MA: MIT Press.

Costa, P. T., Jr., & McCrae, R. R. (1985). *The NEO personality inventory manual.* Odessa, FL: Psychological Assessment Resources.

Cousins, N. (1979). *The anatomy of an illness as perceived by a patient: Reflections on healing and rejuvenation.* New York: Norton.

Cousins, N. (1983). *The healing heart.* New York: Norton.

Cousins, N. (1989). *Head first: The biology of hope.* New York: Dutton.

Cousins, N. (1990). In *Discovering Psychology,* Program 2 [PBS video series]. Washington, DC: Annenberg/CPB Project.

Covington, M. V. (1984). The motive for self-worth. In R. Ames & C. Ames (Eds.), *Research on motivation in education* (Vol. 1). New York: Academic Press.

Cowan, P., & Cowan, P. A. (1988). Changes in marriage during the transition to parenthood. In G. Y. Michaels & W. A. Goldberg (Eds.), *The transition to parenthood: Current theory and research.* Cambridge: Cambridge University Press.

Cowan, P. A. (1988). Developmental psychopathology: A nine-cell map of the territory. In E. Nannis & P. A. Cowan (Eds.), *Developmental psychopathology and its treatment: New directions for child development* (No. 39, pp. 5–29). San Francisco: Jossey Bass.

Cowan, W. M. (1979). The development of the brain. In *The brain* (pp. 56–69). San Francisco: Freeman.

Cowings, P. (1990). In *Discovering Psychology,* Program 24 [PBS video series]. Washington, DC: Annenberg/CPB Program.

Cowles, J. T. (1937). Food tokens as incentives for learning by chimpanzees. *Comparative Psychology Monographs, 74,* 1–96.

Cowley, G. (1990, March 26). The promise of Prozac. *Newsweek, 115,* p. 38.

Cox, T., & McKay, C. (1978). Stress at work. In T. Cox (Ed.), *Stress.* Baltimore, MD: University Park Press.

Coyne, J. (1990). In *Discovering Psychology,* Program 22 [PBS video series]. Washington, DC: Annenberg/CPB Project.

Coyne, J. C. (1976). Toward an interactional description of depression. *Psychiatry, 39,* 28–40.

Coyne, J. C., Aldwin, C., & Lazarus, R. S. (1981). Depression and coping in stressful episodes. *Journal of Abnormal Psychology, 90,* 439–447.

Coyne, J. C., & Downey, G. (1991). Social factors and psychopathology: Stress, social support, and coping processes. *Annual Review of Psychology, 42,* 401–425.

Coyne, J. C., Wortman, C. B., & Lehman, D. R. (1988). The other side of support: Emotional overinvolvement and miscarried helping. In B. Gottlieb (Ed.), *Marshalling social support* (pp. 305–330). Newbury Park, CA: Sage.

Craik, F. I. M., & Lockhart, R. S. (1972). Levels of processing; A framework for memory research. *Journal of Verbal Learning and Verbal Behavior, 11,* 671–684.

Craik, K. (1943). *The nature of explanation.* Cambridge: Cambridge University Press.

Cranston, M. (1991). *The noble savage: Jean-Jacques Rousseau, 1754–1762.* Chicago: University of Chicago Press.

Crapo, L. (1985). *Hormones: The messengers of life.* Stanford, CA: Stanford Alumni Association Press.

Crick, F., & Mitchison, G. (1983). The function of dream sleep. *Nature, 304,* 111–114.

Crick, F. H. C. (1979, September). Thinking about the brain. *Scientific American, 247,* 219–232.

Critelli, J. W. (1984). The placebo: Conceptual analysis of a construct in transition. *American Psychologist, 39,* 57–61.

Critelli, J. W., & Neuman, K. F. (1984). The placebo: Conceptual analysis of a construct in transition. *American Psychologist, 39,* 32–39.

Cronbach, L. J., & Meehl, P. E. (1955). Construct validity in psychological tests. *Psychological Bulletin, 52,* 281–302.

Crook, J. H. (1973). The nature and function of territorial aggression. In M. F. A. Montague (Ed.), *Man and aggression* (2nd ed.). New York: Oxford University Press.

Crosby, F. J. (1982). *Relative deprivation and working women.* New York: Oxford University Press.

Cross, P. (1977). Not can but will teaching be improved. *New Directions for Higher Education, 17,* 1–15.

Cross, P. G., Cafiell, R. B., & Butcher, H. J. (1967). The personality patterns of creative artists. *British Journal of Educational Psychology, 37,* 292–299.

Crowder, R. G., & Morton, J. (1969). Precategorical acoustic storage (PAS). *Perception and Psychophysics, 8,* 815–820.

Crutchfield, R. A. (1955). Conformity and character. *American Psychologist, 10,* 191–198.

Csikszentmihalyi, M. (1990). *Flow: The psychology of optimal experience.* New York: Harper & Row.

Csikszentmihalyi, M., Larson, R., & Prescott, S. (1977). The ecology of adolescent activity and experience. *Journal of Youth and Adolescence, 6,* 281–294.

Culliton, B. J. (1990). Gene therapy: Into the home stretch. *Science, 249,* 974–976.

Cumming, E., & Henry, W. E. (1961). *Growing old: The process of disengagement.* New York: Basic Books.

Curtiss, S. (1977). *Genie: A psycholinguistic study of a modern-day "wild child."* New York: Academic Press.

Cushing, F. H. (1974). *Zuni fetishes.* Las Vegas, NV: K C Publications (Box 14883).

Cutler, W. B., Preti, G., Krieger, A., Huggins, G. R., Ramon Garcia, C., & Lawley, H. J. (1986). Human axillary secretions influence women's menstrual cycles: The role of donor extract from men. *Hormones and Behavior, 20,* 463–473.

Cutting, J. (1981). Six tenets of event perception. *Cognition, 10,* 71–78.

Cutting, J., & Proffitt, D. (1982). The minimum principle and the perception of absolute, common and relative motions. *Cognitive Psychology, 14,* 211–246.

Cutting, J. E. (1987). Perception and information. *Annual Review of Psychology, 38,* 61–90.

Cynader, M. N., & Chernenko, G. (1976). Abolition of directional sensitivity in the visual cortex of the cat. *Science, 193,* 504–505.

Czeisler, C. A., Allan, J. S., Strogatz, S. H., Ronda, J. M., Sanchez, R., Dios, C. D., Freitag, W. O., Richardson, G. S., & Kronauer, R. E. (1986). Bright light resets the human circadian pacemaker independent of the timing of the sleep-wake cycle. *Science, 233,* 667–670.

D

Dackman, L. (1986). Everyday illusions. *Exploratorium Quarterly, 10,* 5–7.

Dahlstrom, W. G., Welsh, H. G., & Dahlstrom, L. E. (1975). *An MMPI handbook, Vol. 1: Clinical interpretation.* Minnesota: University of Minnesota Press.

Dakof, G. A., & Taylor, S. E. (1990). Victims' perceptions of social support: What is helpful from whom? *Journal of Personality and Social Psychology, 58,* 80–89.

Damon, W., & Hart, D. (1986). Stability and change in children's self-understanding. *Social Cognition, 4,* 102–118.

Darley, J., & Gilbert, D. T. (1985). Social psychological aspects of environmental psychology. In G. Lindzey & E. Aronson (Eds.), *Handbook of social psychology* (2nd ed., Vol. 2, pp. 949–992). New York: Random House.

Darley, J., & Latané, B. (1968). Bystander intervention in emergencies: Diffusion of responsibility. *Journal of Personality and Social Psychology, 8,* 377–383.

Darley, J. M., & Batson, C. D. (1973). From Jerusalem to Jericho: A study of situational and dispositional variables in helping behavior. *Journal of Personality and Social Psychology, 27,* 100–108.

Darley, J. M., & Goethals, G. R. (1980). People's analysis of the causes of ability-linked performances. In L. Berkowitz (Ed.), *Advances in experimental social psychology* (Vol. 13, pp. 1–37). New York: Academic Press.

Darley, J. M., & Gross, P. H. (1983). A hypothesis-confirming bias in labeling effects. *Journal of Personality and Social Psychology, 44,* 20–33.

Darwin, C. (1859). *On the origin of species.* London: John Murray.

Darwin, C. (1965). *The expression of emotions in man and animals.* Chicago: University of Chicago Press. (Originally published 1872)

Darwin, C. J., Turvey, M. T., & Crowder, R. G. (1972). The auditory analogue of the Sperling partial report procedure: Evidence for brief auditory stage. *Cognitive Psychology, 3,* 255–267.

Darwin, F. (Ed.). (1950). *Charles Darwin's autobiography.* New York: Schuman.

Davidson, J. M. (1980). The psychobiology of sexual experience. In J. M. Davidson & R. J. Davidson (Eds.), *The psychobiology of consciousness* (pp. 271–331). New York: Plenum.

Davidson, R. (1984). Hemispheric asymmetry and emotion. In K. Scherer & P. Ekman (Eds.), *Approaches to emotion.* Hillsdale, NJ: Erlbaum.

Davidson, R. J. (1983). Affect, repression, and cerebral asymmetry. In L. Temoshok, C. Van Dyke, & L. S. Zegans (Eds.), *Emotions in health and illness: Theoretical and research foundations* (pp. 123–135). New York: Grune & Stratton.

Davies, D. L. (1962). Normal drinking in recovered alcoholics. *Quarterly Journal of Studies on Alcohol, 23,* 94–104.

Davis, G. C. (1985). Oral history: Accounts of lives and times. In G. Lesnoff-Caravalglia (Ed.), *Values, ethics, and aging* (pp. 172–184). New York: Human Sciences Press.

Davis, I. P. (1985). *Adolescents: Theoretical and helping perspectives.* Boston: Kluwer-Nijhoff Publishing.

Davison, G. C., & Valins, S. (1969). Maintenance of self-attributed and drug-attributed behavior change. *Journal of Personality and Social Behavior, 11,* 25–33.

Daw, N. W., & Wyatt, H. J. (1976). Kittens reared in a unidirectional environment: Evidence for a critical period.

Journal of Physiology, 257, 155–170.

Dawes, R., Faust, D., & Meehl, P. E. (1989). Clinical versus actuarial judgment. *Science, 243,* 1668–1674.

Dawes, R. M. (1979). The robust beauty of improper linear models in decision making. *American Psychologist, 34,* 571–582.

Dawkins, R. (1976). *The selfish gene.* Oxford, UK: Oxford University Press.

D'Azevedo, W. L. (1962). Uses of the past in Gola discourse. *Journal of African History, 3,* 11–34.

Dealing with date rape. (1991, January/February). *Stanford Observer,* p. 15.

Deaux, K. (1985). Sex and gender. *Annual Review of Psychology, 36,* 49–81.

de Bono, F. (1970). *Lateral thinking.* New York: Harper.

DeCasper, A. J., & Fifer, W. P. (1980). Of human bonding: Newborns prefer their mothers' voices. *Science, 208,* pp. 1174–1176.

DeCasper, A. J., & Prescott, P. A. (1983). Human newborns' perception of male voices: Preference, discrimination, and reinforcing value. *Developmental Psychology, 17,* 481–491.

DeCasper, A. J., & Spence, M. J. (1986). Prenatal maternal speech influences newborns' perception of speech sounds. *Infant Behavior and Development, 9,* 133–150.

De Charms, R., & Moeller, G. (1962). Values expressed in American children's readers: 1800–1950. *Journal of Abnormal and Social Psychology, 64,* 136–142.

De Charms, R. C., & Muir, M. S. (1978). Motivation: Social approaches. *Annual Review of Psychology, 29,* 91–113.

Deci, E. L. (1975). *Intrinsic motivation.* New York: Plenum.

De Fries, J. C., & Decker, S. N. (1982). Genetic aspects of reading disability: The Colorado family reading study. In P. G. Aaron & H. Malatesha (Eds.), *Reading disorders: Varieties and treatments* (pp. 255–279). New York: Academic Press.

DeGroot, A. D. (1965). *Thought and choice in chess.* The Hague: Mouton.

Delishi, C. (1988). The human genome project. *American Scientist, 76,* 488–493.

Dellas, M., & Gaier, E. L. (1970). Identification of creativity: The individual. *Psychological Bulletin, 73,* 55–73.

DeLoache, J. (1987). Rapid change in the symbolic functioning of very young children. *Science, 238,* 1556–1557.

DeLoache, J. (1990). In *Discovering Psychology,* Program 5 [PBS video series]. Washington, DC: Annenberg/CPB Project.

Dembroski, T. M., Weiss, S. M., Shields, J. L. et al. (1978). *Coronary-prone behavior.* New York: Springer-Verlag.

Dembrowski, T. M., & Costa, P. T., Jr. (1987). Coronary prone behavior: Components of the Type A pattern and hostility. *Journal of Personality, 55,* 211–235.

Dement, W. C. (1976). *Some watch while some must sleep.* San Francisco: San Francisco Book Co.

Dement, W. C., & Kleitman, N. (1957). Cyclic variations in EEG during sleep and their relations to eye movement, body mobility and dreaming. *Electroencephalography and Clinical Neurophysiology, 9,* 673–690.

Dennett, D. C. (1978). *Brainstorms.* Cambridge, MA: Bradford Books.

Dennett, D. C. (1987). Consciousness. In R. L. Gregory (Ed.), *The Oxford companion to the mind* (pp. 160–164). New York: Oxford University Press.

Depue, R. A., & Monroe, S. M. (1983). Psychopathology research. In M. Hersen, A. E. Kazdin, & A. S. Bellack (Eds.), *The clinical psychology handbook* (pp. 239–264). New York: Pergamon Press.

Deregowski, J. B. (1980). *Illusions, patterns and pictures: A cross-cultural perspective* (pp. 966–977). London: Academic Press.

DeRivera, J. (1984). Development and the full range of emotional experience. In C. Malastesta & C. Izard (Eds.), *Emotion in adult development* (pp. 45–63). Beverly Hills: Sage.

Descartes, R. (1911). Traitées de l'homme. In E. S. Haldane & G. T. Ross (Trans.), *The philosophical works of Descartes.* New York: Dover. (Original work published 1642)

Descartes, R. (1951). The passions of the soul. In E. S. Haldane & G. T. Ross (Trans.), *The philosophical works of Descartes.* New York: Dover. (Original work published 1646)

Deutsch, J. A., & Deutsch, D. (1963). Attention: Some theoretical considerations. *Psychological Review, 70,* 80–90.

Deutsch, M., & Gerard, H. B. (1955). A study of normative and informational social influence. *Journal of Abnormal and Social Psychology, 51,* 629–636.

Deutsch, M., & Hornstein, H. A. (1975). *Applying social psychology.* Hillsdale, NJ: Erlbaum.

De Valois, R. L., & De Valois, K. K. (1980). Spatial vision. *Annual Review of Psychology, 80.*

De Valois, R. L., & Jacobs, G. H. (1968). Primate color vision. *Science, 162,* 533–540.

Devereux, G. (1961). Mohave ethnopsychiatry and suicide: The psychiatric knowledge and psychic disturbances of an Indian tribe. *Bureau of American Ethology* (Bulletin 175). Washington, DC: Smithsonian Institution.

Devine, P. G. (1989). Stereotypes and prejudice: Their automatic and controlled components. *Journal of Personality and Social Psychology, 56,* 5–18.

De Vos, G. A., & Hippler, A. A. (1969). Cultural psychology: Comparative studies of human behavior. In G. Lindzey & E. Aronson (Eds.), *The handbook of social psychology* (2nd ed., pp. 323–417). New York: Random House.

DeVries, R. (1969). Constancy of generic identity in the years three to six. *Society for Research in Child Development Monographs, 34* (3 Serial No. 127).

Dhruvarajan, V. (1990). Religious ideology, Hindu women, and development in India. *Journal of Social Issues, 46,* 57–69.

Diamond, D. (1989, Fall). The unbearable darkness of being. *Stanford Medicine,* pp. 13–16.

Diamond, J. (1987, August). Soft sciences are often harder than hard sciences. *Discover,* pp. 34–39.

Diamond, J. (1990). The great leap forward. *Discover* (Special Issue), pp. 66–77.

Diamond, M. J. (1974). Modification of hypnotizability: A review. *Psychological Bulletin, 81,* 180–198.

Dickinson, A. (1980). *Contemporary animal learning theory.* Cambridge: Cambridge University Press.

Dickman, H., & Zeiss, R. A. (1982). *Incidents and correlates of post-traumatic stress disorder among ex–Prisoners of War of World War II.* Manuscript in progress. Palo Alto, CA.: Veterans Administration.

Diener, E. (1980). Deindividuation: The absence of self-awareness and self-regulation in group members. In P. Paulus (Ed.), *The psychology of group influence* (pp. 209–242). Hillsdale, NJ: Erlbaum.

Diener, E., & Crandall, R. (1978). *Ethics in social and behavioral research.* Chicago: University of Chicago Press.

Dietrich, N., & Thomas, B. (1972). *Howard: The amazing Mr. Hughes.* Greenwich, CT: Fawcett.

Dillon, K. M., & Totten, M. C. (1989). Psychological factors affecting immunocompetence and health of breastfeeding mothers and their infants. *Journal of Genetic Psychology, 150,* 155–162.

DiLollo, V. (1980). Temporal integration in visual memory. *Journal of Experimental Psychology: General, 109,* 75–97.

DiMatteo, M. R., & DiNicola, D. D. (1982). *Achieving patient compliance: The psychology of the medical practitioner's role.* New York: Pergamon.

Dion, K. L., Berscheid, E., & Walster, E. (1972). What is beautiful is good. *Journal of Personality and Social Psychology, 24,* 285–290.

Dishman, R. K. (1982). Compliance/adherence in health-related exercise. *Health Psychology, 1,* 237–267.

Dixon, N. F. (1971). *Subliminal perception: The nature of a controversy.* London: McGraw-Hill.

Dixon, R. A., Kramer, D. A., & Baltes, P. B. (1985). Intelligence: A life-span developmental perspective. In B. B. Wolman (Ed.), *Handbook of intelligence* (pp. 301–352). New York: Wiley.

Doane, J. A., Falloon, I. R. H., Goldstein, M. J., & Mintz, J. (1985). Parental affective style and the treatment of schizophrenia. *Archives of general psychiatry, 42,* 34–42.

Dohrenwend, B. P., & Dohrenwend, B. S. (1974). Social and cultural influences on psychopathology. *Annual Review of Psychology, 25,* 417–452.

Dohrenwend, B. P., & Shrout, P. E. (1985). "Hassles" in the conceptualization and measurement of life stress variables. *American Psychologist, 40*, 780–785.

Dohrenwend, B. S., & Dohrenwend, B. P. (1974). *Stressful life events: Their nature and effects.* New York: Wiley.

Dollard, J., Doob, L. W., Miller, N., Mower, O. H., & Sears, R. R. (1939). *Frustration and aggression.* New Haven, C T: Yale University Press.

Dollard, J., & Miller, N. E. (1950). *Personality and psychotherapy.* New York: McGraw-Hill.

Donchin, E. (1975). On evoked potentials, cognition, and memory. *Science, 790*, 1004–1005.

Donchin, E. (1985). *Can the mind be read in brain waves?* Presentation at a Science and Public Policy Seminar. Washington, DC: Federation of Behavioral, Psychological, and Cognitive Sciences.

Donchin, E. (1990). In *Discovering Psychology*, Program 1 [PBS video series]. Washington, DC: Annenberg/CPB Project.

Donnerstein, E. (1980). Aggressive-erotica and violence against women. *Journal of Personality and Social Psychology, 39,* 269–277.

Donnerstein, E. (1983). Erotica and human aggression. In R. G. Green & E. Donnerstein (Eds.), *Aggression: Theoretical and empirical reviews, Vol. 2: Issues in research.* New York: Academic Press.

Donnerstein, E. I., & Linz, D. G. (1986, December). The question of pornography. *Psychology Today,* 56–59.

Donovan, J. M. (1986). An etiological model of alcoholism. *American Journal of Psychiatry, 143,* 1–11.

Dooling, D. J., & Lachman, R. (1971). Effects of comprehension on retention of prose. *Journal of Experimental Psychology, 88,* 216–222.

Dorfman, D. D. (1965). Esthetic preference as a function of pattern information. *Psychonomic Science, 3,* 85–86.

Dorner, G. (1976). *Hormones and brain differentiation.* Amsterdam: Elsevier.

Dorris, M. (1989). *The broken cord.* New York: Harper & Row.

Dowis, R. T. (1984). The importance of vision in the prevention of learning disabilities and juvenile delinquency. *Journal of Optometric Vision Development, 15,* 20–22.

Drabman, R. S., & Thomas, M. H. (1974). Does media violence increase children's tolerance of real-life aggression? *Developmental Psychology, 10,* 418–421.

Driver, J., & Tipper, S. (1989). On the nonselectivity of "selective" seeing: Contrasts between interference and priming in selective attention. *Journal of Experimental Psychology: Human Perception and Performance, 15,* 304–314.

Driver, P. M., & Humphries, D. A. (1988). *Protean behavior: The biology of unpredictability.* Oxford: Clarendon Press.

Drosnin, M. (1985). *Citizen Hughes.* New York: Holt, Rinehart & Winston.

Drug Policy Foundation. (1989, September/October). The Drug Policy Letter, Vol. I (4).

Dryfoss, J. G. (1990). *Adolescents at risk: Prevalence and prevention.* New York: Oxford University Press.

DSM-III-R. (1987). *Diagnostic and statistical manual of mental disorders.* Washington, DC: American Psychiatric Association.

Duba, R. O., & Shortliffe, E. H. (1983). Expert systems research. *Science, 220,* 261–268.

DuBois, P. H. (1970). *A history of psychological testing.* Boston: Allyn and Bacon.

Dudycha, G. J. (1936). An objective study of punctuality in relation to personality and achievement. *Archives of Psychology, 204,* 1–53.

Dugan, T. F., & Coles, R. (Eds.). (1989). *The child in our times: Studies in the development of resiliency.* New York: Mazel.

Dugdale, R. L. (1912). *The Jukes* (4th ed.). New York: Putnam's Sons.

Dumont, J. P. C., & Robertson, R. M. (1986). Neuronal circuits: An evolutionary perspective. *Science, 233,* 849–853.

Dumont, J. P. C., & Wine, J. J. (1986). The telson flexor neuromuscular system of the crayfish, III. The role of feedforward inhibition in shaping a stereotyped behaviour pattern.

Journal of Experimental Biology, 127, 295–311.

Duncan, B. L. (1976). Differential social perception and attribution of intergroup violence: Testing the lower limits of stereotyping of blacks. *Journal of Personality and Social Psychology, 34,* 590–598.

Duncan, J., & Humphreys, G. W. (1989). Visual search and stimulus similarity. *Psychological Review, 96,* 433–548.

Duncker, K. (1945). On problem solving. *Psychological Monographs, 58* (No. 270).

Dunkel-Schetter, C., Folkman, S., & Lazarus, R. S. (1987). Correlates of social support receipt. *Journal of Personality and Social Psychology, 53,* 71–80.

Dunning, D., Griffin, D. W., Milojkovic, J. D., & Ross, L. (1990). The overconfidence effect in social prediction. *Journal of Personality and Social Psychology, 58,* 568–581.

Dutton, D. G., & Aron, A. P. (1974). Some evidence for heightened sexual attraction under conditions of high anxiety. *Journal of Personality and Social Psychology, 30,* 510–517.

Dweck, C. S. (1975). The role of expectations and attributions in the alleviation of learned helplessness. *Journal of Personality and Social Psychology, 31,* 674–685.

E

Eastwell, H. D. (1984). Death watch in East Arnhem, Australia. *American Anthropologists, 86,* 119–121.

Ebbinghaus, H. (1913). *Memory.* New York: Columbia University. (Original work published 1885, Leipzig: Altenberg)

Ebbinghaus, H. (1973). *Psychology: An elementary text-book.* New York: Arno Press. (Original work published 1908)

Eccles, J. (1964). Quoted in R. L. Gregory (Ed.), *The Oxford companion to the mind* (p. 164). New York: Oxford University Press.

Edmonds, B., Klein, M., Dale, N., & Kandel, E. R. (1990). Contributions of two types of calcium channels to synaptic transmission and plasticity. *Science, 250,* 1142–1147.

Educational Testing Service (1990). *Manual and technical report for the School and College Ability Tests, Series III.* Menlo Park, CA: Addison-Wesley.

Educational Testing Service (1990, October 31). Background on the new SAT-I and SAT-II. Announced at the College Board National Forum.

Edwards, A. E., & Acker, L. E. (1962). A demonstration of the long-term retention of a conditioned galvanic skin response. *Psychosomatic Medicine, 24,* 459–463.

Edwards, D. A. (1971). Neonatal administration of androstenedione, testosterone, or testosterone propionate: Effects on ovulation, sexual receptivity, and aggressive behavior in female mice. *Physiological Behavior, 6,* 223–228.

Edwards, G. (1980). Alcoholism treatment: Between guesswork and certainty. In G. Edwards & M. Grant (Eds.), *Alcoholism treatment in transition.* London: Croon Helm.

Efron, R. (1990). *The decline and fall of hemispheric specialization.* Hillsdale, NJ: Erlbaum.

Egeland, J. A., Gerhard, D. S., Pauls, D. L., Sussex, J. N., Kidd, K. K., Allen, C. R., Hostetter, A. M., & Housman, D. E. (1987). Bipolar affective disorder linked to DNA markers on chromosome 11. *Nature, 325,* 783–787.

Eger, E. E. (1990). Auschwitz at 16, Auschwitz at 61. *California State Psychologist,* pp. 6–9.

Ehrhardt, A. A., & Baker, S. W. (1974). Fetal androgens, human central nervous system differentiation, and behavior sex differences. In R. C. Friedman, R. M. Richart, & R. L. Vande Wiele (Eds.), *Sex differences in behavior.* New York: Wiley.

Ehrlich, B. E., & Diamond, J. M. (1980). Lithium, membranes, and manic-depressive illness. *Journal of Membrane Biology, 52,* 187–200.

Eimas, P., Siqueland, E., Jusczyk, P., Y Vigorito, J. (1971). Speech perception in infants. *Science, 171,* 303–306.

Eisenberg, N., & Mussen, P. H. (1989). *The roots of prosocial behavior in children.* New York: Cambridge University Press.

Ekman, P. (1972). Universal and cultural differences in facial expressions of emotion. In J. Cole (Ed.), *Nebraska Symposium on*

Motivation. Lincoln, NE: University of Nebraska Press.

Ekman, P. (Ed.). (1973). *Darwin and facial expression: A century of research in review*. New York: Academic Press.

Ekman, P. (1983). Cross cultural studies of emotion. In P. Ekman (Ed.), *Darwin and facial expression: A century of research in review* (pp. 169–222). New York: Academic Press.

Ekman, P. (1984). Expression and the nature of emotion. In K. R. Scherer & P. Ekman (Eds.), *Approaches to emotion*. Hillsdale, NJ: Erlbaum.

Ekman, P. (1985). *Telling lies: Clues to deceit in marketplace, politics and marriage*. New York: Norton.

Ekman, P., & Friesen, W. V. (1971). Constants across cultures in the face and emotion. *Journal of Personality and Social Psychology, 17*, 124–129.

Ekman, P., & Friesen, W. V. (1975). *Unmasking the face: A guide to recognizing emotions from facial clues*. Englewood Cliffs, NJ: Prentice-Hall.

Ekman, P., & Friesen, W. V. (1986). A new pan-cultural facial expression of emotion. *Motivation and Emotion, 10*, 159–168.

Ekman, P., Sorenson, E. R., & Friesen, W. V. (1969). Pan-cultural elements in facial displays in emotion. *Science, 764*, 86–88.

Ekstrand, M. L., & Coates, T. J. (1990). Maintenance of safer sexual behaviors and predictors of risky sex: The San Francisco men's health survey. *American Journal of Public Health, 80*, 973–977.

Eliade, M. (1964). *Shamanism: Archaic techniques of ecstasy*. New York: Pantheon.

Elkin, I., Shea, M. T., Watkins, J. T., Imber, S. D., Sotsky, S. M., Collins, J. F., Glass, D. R., Pilkonis, P. A., Leber, W. R., Kocherty, J. P., Fiester, S. J., & Parloff, M. B. (1989). National Institutes of Mental Health treatment of depression collaborative research program: General effectiveness of treatments. *Archives of General Psychiatry, 46*, 971–982.

Elliott, J. (1977). The power and pathology of prejudice. In P. G. Zimbardo & F. L. Ruch, *Psychology and life* (9th ed., Diamond Printing). Glenview, IL: Scott, Foresman.

Elliott, J. (1990). In *Discovering Psychology*, Program 20 [PBS video series]. Washington, DC: Annenberg/CPB Program.

Ellis, A. (1962). *Reason and emotion in psychotherapy*. New York: Lyle Stuart.

Ellis, A. (1977). The treatment of a psychopath with rational therapy. In S. J. Morse & R. I. Watson (Eds.), *Psychotherapies: A comparative casebook*. New York: Holt, Rinehart & Winston.

Ellis, A., & Grieger, R. (1986). *Handbook of rational emotive therapy* (Vol. 2). New York: Springer.

Eme, R., Maisiak, R., & Goodale, W. (1979). Seriousness of adolescent problems. *Adolescence, 14*, 93–99.

Emmelkamp, P. M. (1982). *Phobic and obsessive-compulsive disorders: Theory, research and practice*. New York: Plenum.

Emmelkamp, P. M. (1986). Behavior therapy with adults. In S. L. Garfield & A. E. Bergin (Eds.), *Handbook of psychotherapy and behavior change* (pp. 385–442). New York: Wiley.

Emmelkamp, P. M. G., & Kuipers, A. (1979). Agoraphobia: A follow-up study four years after treatment. *British Journal of Psychology, 134*, 352–355.

Emmons, R. A. (1986). Personal strivings: An approach to personality and its subjective well being. *Journal of Personality and Social Psychology, 51*, 1058–1068.

Endler, N. S. (1983). Interactionism: A personality model, but not yet a theory. In M. M. Page (Ed.), *Nebraska Symposium on Motivation, 1982: Personality—current theory and research* (pp. 155–200). Lincoln, NE: University of Nebraska Press.

Engen, T. (1989). Remembering odors and their names. *American Scientist, 75*, 497–503.

Engle, G. L. (1976). The need for a new medical model: A challenge for biomedicine. *Science, 196*, 129–136.

Epstein, S. (1979). The stability of behavior: 1. On predicting most of the people much of the time. *Journal of Personality and Social Psychology, 37*, 1097–1126.

Epstein, W. (1961). The influence of syntactical structure on learning. *American Journal of Psychology, 74*, 80–85.

Erdelyi, M. H. (1974). A new look at the New Look: Perceptual defense and vigilance. *Psychological Review, 87*, 1–25.

Erdley, C. A., & D'Agostino, P. R. (1988). Cognitive and affective components of automatic priming effects. *Journal of Personality and Social Psychology, 54*, 741–747.

Ericksen, C. W. (1966). Cognitive responses to internally cued anxiety. In C. D. Spielberger (Ed.), *Anxiety and behavior*. New York: Academic Press.

Ericsson, K. A., & Chase, W. G. (1982). Exceptional memory. *American Scientist, 70*, 607–615.

Ericsson, K. A., Chase, W. G., & Falcoon, S. (1980). Acquisition of a memory skill. *Science, 208*, 1181–1183.

Eriksen, C., & Yeh, Y. (1985). Allocation of attention in the visual field. *Journal of Experimental Psychology: Human Perception & Performance, 11*, 583–597.

Erikson, E. (1990). In *Discovering Psychology*, Program 18 [PBS video series]. Washington, DC: Annenberg/CPB Program.

Erikson, E. H. (1963). *Childhood and society* (2nd. ed.). New York: Norton.

Erikson, E. H. (1968). *Identity: Youth and crisis*. New York: Norton.

Eron, L. D., Huesmann, L. R., Lefkowitz, M. M., & Walder, L. O. (1972). Does television violence cause aggression? *American Psychologist, 27*, 253–263.

Estes, W. K. (1991). Cognitive architectures from the standpoint of an experimental psychologist. *Annual Review of Psychology, 42*, 1–28.

Evans, F. J. (1989). The independence of suggestibility, placebo response, and hypnotizability. In V. A. Gheorghiu, P. Netter, H. J. Eysenck, & R. Rosenthal (Eds.), *Suggestion and suggestibility* (pp. 145–154). New York: Springer-Verlag.

Evans, G. W., Palsane, M. N., Lepore, S. J., & Martin, J. (1989). Residential density and psychological health: The mediating effects of social support. *Journal of Personality and Social Psychology, 57*, 994–999.

Evans, J. S. B., Barston, J. L., & Pollard, P. (1983). On the conflict between logic and belief in syllogistic reasoning. *Memory and Cognition, 11*, 295–306.

Evans, R. I., Rozelle, R. M., Mittelmark, M. B., Hansen, W. B., Bane, A. L., & Havis, J. (1978). Deterring the onset of smoking in children: Knowledge of immediate physiological effects and coping with peer pressure, media pressure, and parent modeling. *Journal of Applied Social Psychology, 8*, 126–135.

Evans-Pritchard, E. E. (1937). *Witchcraft, oracles and magic among the Azande*. Oxford: Oxford University Press.

Eysenck, H. (1990). Biological dimensions of personality. In L. A. Pervin (Ed.), *Handbook of personality theory and research* (pp. 244–276). New York: Guilford Press.

Eysenck, H. J. (1952). The effects of psychotherapy: An evaluation. *Journal of Consulting Psychology, 16*, 319–324.

Eysenck, H. J. (1970). *The structure of human personality* (3rd ed.). London: Methuen.

Eysenck, H. J. (1973). *The inequality of man*. London: Temple Smith.

Eysenck, H. J. (1975). *The inequality of man*. San Diego, CA: Educational and Industrial Testing Service.

Eysenck, H. J., & Kamin, L. (1981). *The intelligence controversy: H. J. Eysenck vs. Leon Kamin*. New York: Wiley-Interscience.

F

Fagot, B. I. (1978). The influence of sex of child on parental reactions to toddler children. *Child Development, 49*, 459–465.

Fairweather, G. W., Sanders, D. H., Maynard, R. F., & Cresler, D. L. (1969). *Community life for the mentally ill: Alternative to institutional care*. Chicago: Aldine.

Fanslow, C. A. (1984). Touch and the elderly. In C. Caldwell Brown (Ed.), *The many facets of touch* (pp. 183–189). Skillman, NJ: Johnson & Johnson.

Fantz, R. L. (1963). Pattern vision in newborn infants. *Science, 140*, 296–297.

Farah, M. J. (1984). The neurological basis of mental imagery: A componential analysis. *Cognition, 18*, 245–272.

Farina, A. (1980). Social attitudes and beliefs and their role in mental disorders. In J. G. Rabkin, L. Gelb, & J. B. Lazar (Eds.), *Attitudes toward the mentally ill: Research perspectives* (pp.

35–37). Rockville, Md.: National Institute of Mental Health.

Farina, A., Gliha, D., Boudreau, L. A., Allen, J. G., & Sherman, M. (1971). Mental illness and the impact of believing others know about it. *Journal of Abnormal Psychology, 77,* 1–5.

Farina, A., & Hagalauer, H. D. (1975). Sex and mental illness: The generosity of females. *Journal of Consulting and Clinical Psychology, 43,* 122.

Farley, F. (1986, May). The Big T in personality. *Psychology Today,* pp. 44–52.

Farley, F. (1990, May). The Type T personality, with some implications for practice. *The California Psychologist, 23,* 29.

Farquhar, J. W. (1978). *The American way of life need not be hazardous to your health.* New York: Norton.

Farquhar, J. W., Maccoby, N., & Solomon, D. S. (1984). Community applications of behavioral medicine. In W. D. Gentry (Ed.), *Handbook of behavioral medicine* (pp. 437–478). New York: Guilford Press.

Farr, M. J. (1984). Cognitive psychology. *Naval Research Reviews, 36,* 33–36.

A fascination with rock climbing. (1989, August 5). *Los Angeles Times,* pp. II, 8.

Fass, P. S. (1980). The IQ: A cultural and historical framework. *American Journal of Education, 88,* 431–458.

Fay, R. E., Turner, C. F., Klassen, A. D., & Gagnon, J. H. (1989). Prevalence and patterns of same-gender sexual contact among men. *Science, 243,* 338–348.

Fazio, R. H. (1987). Self-perception theory: A current perspective. In M. P. Zanna, J. M. Olson, & C. P. Herman (Eds.), *Social influence: The Ontario Symposium* (Vol. 5, pp. 129–150). Hillsdale, NJ: Erlbaum.

Fechner, G. T. (1860). *Elemente der psychophysik.* Germany: Breitkopf und Hartel.

Fechner, G. T. (1966). *Elements of psychophysics* (Vol. 1, E. G. Boring & D. H. Howes, Eds. and H. E. Adler, Trans.) New York: Holt, Rinehart & Winston. (Original work published 1860)

Feigenbaum, E. A., & McCorduck, P. (1983). *The fifth generation.* Reading, MA: Addison-Wesley.

Fernald, A. (1985). Four-month-old infants prefer to listen to motherese. *Infant Behavior and Development, 8,* 118–195.

Fernald, A. (1990). In *Discovering Psychology,* Program 6 [PBS video series]. Washington, DC: Annenberg/CPB Project.

Fernald, A., Taeschner, T., Dunn, J., Papousek, M., De Boysson-Bardies, B., & Fukui, I. (1989). A cross-cultural study of prosodic modification in mothers' and fathers' speech to preverbal infants. *Journal of Child Language, 16,* 477–501.

Fernald, D. (1984). *The Hans legacy.* Hillsdale, NJ: Erlbaum.

Fernald, R. (1984). Vision and behavior in an African cichlid fish. *American Scientist, 72,* 58–65.

Fernald, R. (1990). In *Discovering Psychology,* Program 4 [PBS video series]. Washington, DC: Annenberg/CPB Project.

Ferrare, N. A. (1962). *Institutionalization and attitude change in an aged population.* Unpublished doctoral dissertation, Western Reserve University.

Ferster, C. B., Culbertson, S., & Perron Boren, M. C. (1975). *Behavior principles* (2nd ed.). Englewood Cliffs, NJ: Prentice-Hall.

Ferster, C. B., & Skinner, B. F. (1957). *Schedules of reinforcement.* New York: Appleton-Century-Crofts.

Feshbach, S., & White, M. J. (1986). Individual differences in attitudes toward nuclear arms policies: Some psychological and social policy considerations. *Journal of Peace Research, 23,* 129–138.

Festinger, L. (1954). A theory of social comparison processes. *Human Relations, 7,* 117–140.

Festinger, L. (1957). *A theory of cognitive dissonance.* Stanford, CA: Stanford University Press.

Festinger, L. (1990). In *Discovering Psychology,* Program 11 [PBS video series]. Washington, DC: Annenberg/CPB Project.

Festinger, L., & Carlsmith, J. M. (1959). Cognitive consequences of forced compliance. *Journal of Abnormal and Social Psychology, 58,* 203–211.

Feuerstein, M., Labbe, E. E., & Kuczmierczyk, A. R. (1986). *Health psychology: A psychobiological perspective.* New York: Plenum.

Field, T. (1990). In *Discovering Psychology,* Program 4 [PBS video series]. Washington, DC: Annenberg/CPB Project.

Field, T. F., & Schanberg, S. M. (1990). Massage alters growth and catecholamine production in preterm newborns. In N. Gunzenhauser (Ed.), *Advances in touch* (pp. 96–104). Skillman, NJ: Johnson & Johnson Co.

Fields, H. L., & Levine, J. D. (1984). Placebo analgesia: A role for endorphins. *Trends in Neuroscience, 7,* 271–273.

Fink, M. (1979). *Convulsive therapy: Theory and practice.* New York: Raven Press.

Fischer, K. W. (1980). A theory of cognitive development: The control and construction of hierarchies of skills. *Psychological Review, 87,* 477–531.

Fischer, S., & Greenberg, R. P. (1985). *The scientific credibility of Freud's theories and therapy.* New York: Columbia University Press.

Fish, J. M. (1973). *Placebo therapy.* San Francisco: Jossey-Bass.

Fishbein, M., & Ajzen, I. (1975). *Belief, attitude, intention, and behavior: An introduction to theory and research.* Reading, MA: Addison-Wesley.

Fisher, S., & Greenberg, R. P. (1985). *The scientific credibility of Freud's theories and therapy.* New York: Columbia University Press.

Fiske, S. (1987). People's reactions to nuclear war: Implications for psychologists. *American Psychologist, 42,* 207–217.

Fiske, S. T., & Pavelchak, M. A. (1986). Category-based versus piecemeal-based affective response: Developments in schema-triggered affects. In R. M. Sorrentino & E. T. Higgins (Eds.), *The handbook of motivation and cognition: Foundations of social behavior* (pp. 167–203). New York: Guilford Press.

Fiske, S. T., & Taylor, S. E. (1991). *Social cognition.* New York: McGraw-Hill.

Fitts, P. M., & Posner, M. (1967). *Human performance.* Belmont, CA: Brooks/Cole.

Fitzgerald, R., & Ellsworth, P. C. (1984). Due process vs. crime control: Death qualification and jury attitudes. *Law and Human Behavior, 8,* 31–51.

Flavell, J. H. (1977). *Cognitive development.* Englewood Cliffs, NJ: Prentice-Hall.

Flavell, J. H. (1979). Metacognition and cognitive monitoring: A new area of cognitive-developmental inquiry. *American Psychologist, 34,* 906–911.

Flavell, J. H. (1981). Cognitive monitoring. In W. P. Dickson (Ed.), *Children's oral communication skills* (pp. 35–60). New York: Academic Press.

Flavell, J. H. (1985). *Cognitive development* (2nd ed.). Englewood Cliffs, NJ: Prentice-Hall.

Fleischman, P. R. (1973). [Letter to the editor concerning "On being sane in insane places"]. *Science, 180,* 356.

Fletcher, G. J. O., & Ward, C. (1988). Attribution theory and processes: A cross-cultural perspective. In M. H. Bond (Ed.), *The cross-cultural challenge to social psychology* (pp. 230–244). Newbury Park, CA: Sage.

Fletcher, H. (1929). *Speech and hearing.* New York: Van Nostrand.

Floderus-Myrhed, B., Pedersen, N., & Rasmussen, I. (1980). Assessment of heritability for personality, based on a short form of the Eysenck Personality Inventory: A study of 12,898 twin pairs. *Behavior Genetics, 10,* 507–520.

Flood, R. A., & Seager, C. P. (1968). A retrospective examination of psychiatric case records of patients who subsequently committed suicide. *British Journal of Psychiatry, 114,* 433–450.

Flora, J. A. (1991, May). AIDS prevention among young people. *California Psychologist,* pp. 14, 18.

Fodor, J. (1983). *The modularity of mind.* Cambridge, MA: MIT Press.

Fogel, A. (in press). Movement and communication in human infancy: The social dynamics of development. *Journal of Human Movement Studies.*

Foley, V. D. (1979). Family therapy. In R. J. Corsini (Ed.), *Current psychotherapies* (2nd ed., pp. 460–469). Itasca, IL: Peacock.

Folkins, D. H., Lawson, K. D., Opton, E. M., Jr., & Lazarus, R. S. (1968). Desensitization and the experimental reduction of threat.

Journal of Abnormal Psychology, 73, 100–113.

Folkman, S. (1984). Personal control and stress and coping processes: A theoretical analysis. *Journal of Personality and Social Psychology, 46,* 839–852.

Folkman, S., Lazarus, R. S., Dunkel-Schetter, C., DeLongis, A., & Gruen, R. J. (1986). Dynamics of a stressful encounter: Cognitive appraisal, coping, and encounter outcomes. *Journal of Personality and Social Psychology, 50,* 992–1003.

Fong, G. T., & Markus, H. (1982). Self-schemas and judgments about others. *Social Cognition, 1,* 191–204.

Fontaine, G. (1974). Social comparison and some determinants of expected personal control and expected performance in a novel situation. *Journal of Personality and Social Psychology, 29,* 487–496.

Ford, C. S., & Beach, F. A. (1951). *Patterns of sexual behavior.* New York: Harper & Row.

Fordyce, W. E. (1973). An operant conditioning method for managing chronic pain. *Postgraduate Medicine, 53,* 123–128.

Forest, D. V. (1976). Nonsense and sense in schizophrenic language. *Schizophrenia Bulletin, 2,* 286–381.

Forgas, J. P. (1982). Episodic cognition: Internal representation of interaction routines. In L. Berkowitz (Ed.), *Advances in experimental social psychology* (Vol. 5). New York: Academic Press.

Foster, G. M., & Anderson, B. G. (1978). *Medical anthropology.* New York: Wiley.

Foucault, M. (1975). *The birth of the clinic.* New York: Vintage Books.

Fouts, R. S., Bouts, D., & Schoenfeld, D. (1984). Sign language conversational interactions between chimpanzees. *Sign Language Studies, 41,* 1–12.

Fouts, R. S., & Rigby, R. L. (1977). Man-chimpanzee communication. In T. A. Sebeok (Ed.), *How animals communicate.* Bloomington: University of Indiana Press.

Fowler, H. (1965). *Curiosity and exploratory behavior.* New York: Macmillan.

Fowler, R. D. (1986, May). Howard Hughes: A psychological autopsy. *Psychology Today,* pp. 179–185.

Fox, M. W. (1974). *Concepts in ethology: Animal and human behavior.* Minneapolis: University of Minnesota Press.

Foy, D. W., Eisler, R. M., Pinkston, S. (1975). Modeled assertion in a case of explosive rages. *Journal of Behavioral Therapy and Experimental Psychiatry, 6,* 135–137.

Fraisse, P. (1968). Les émotions. In P. Fraisse & J. Piaget (Eds.), *Traité de psychologie expérimentale* (Vol. 5). Paris: Presses Universitaires.

Frances, A., & Cooper, A. M. (1981). Descriptive and dynamic psychiatry: A perspective on DSM-III. *American Journal of Psychiatry, 138,* 1198–1202.

Frank, J. (1987). The drive for power and the nuclear arms race. *American Psychologist, 42,* 337–344.

Frank, J. (1990). In *Discovering Psychology,* Program 2 [PBS video series]. Washington, DC: Annenberg/CPB Project.

Frank, J. D. (1963). *Persuasion and healing.* New York: Schochen Books.

Frank, J. D. (1979). The present status of outcome studies. *Journal of Consulting and Clinical Psychology, 47,* 310–316.

Frank, L. R. (Ed.). (1978). *The history of shock treatment.* (Available from L. R. Frank, San Fransisco, CA).

Franklin, D. (1987, January). The politics of masochism. *Psychology Today,* pp. 52–57.

Franks, C. M., & Barbrack, C. R. (1983). Behavior therapy with adults: An integrative perspective. In M. Hersen, A. E. Kazdin, & A. S. Bellack (Eds.), *The clinical psychology handbook* (pp. 507–523). New York: Pergamon Press.

Franz, C. E., McClelland, D. C., & Weinberger, J. (1991). Childhood antecedents of conventional social accomplishment in midlife adults: A 36-year prospective study. *Journal of Personality and Social Psychology, 60,* 586–595.

Fraser, S. C. (1974). *Deindividuation: Effects of anonymity on aggression in children.* Unpublished mimeograph report, University of Southern California.

Frederiksen, L. W., Jenkins, J. O., Foy, D. W., & Eisler, R. M. (1976). Social-skills training to modify abusive verbal outbursts in adults. *Journal of Applied Behavior Analysis, 9,* 117–125.

Fredrickson, B. L. (1991). Anticipated endings: An explanation for selective social interaction (doctoral dissertation, Stanford University, 1990). *Dissertation Abstracts International, 3,* AAD91–00818.

Fredrickson, B. L., & Carstensen, L. L. (1990). Choosing social partners: How old age and anticipated endings make people more selective. *Psychology and Aging, 5,* 335–347.

Freed, W. J. (1990). Fetal brain grafts and Parkinson's Disease. *Science, 250,* 1434.

Freedman, D. G., & DeBoer, M. M. (1979). Biological and cultural differences in early child development. *Annual Review of Anthropology, 8,* 579–600.

Freedman, J. L. (1984). Effect of television violence on aggressiveness. *Psychological Bulletin, 96,* 227–246.

Freedman, J. L., & Doob, A. N. (1968). *Deviancy: The psychology of being different.* New York: Academic Press.

Freedman, J. L., & Fraser, S. C. (1966). Compliance without pressure: The foot-in-the-door technique. *Journal of Personality and Social Psychology, 4,* 195–202.

Freeman, F. R. (1972). *Sleep research: A critical review.* Springfield, IL: Charles C Thomas.

Freud, A. (1946). *The ego and the mechanisms of defense.* New York: International Universities Press.

Freud, A. (1958). Adolescence. *Psychoanalytic Study of the Child, 13,* 255–278.

Freud, S. (1900). *The interpretation of dreams.* In J. Strachey (Ed. and Trans.), *The standard edition of the complete psychological works of Sigmund Freud* (Vol. 5). London: Hogarth Press.

Freud, S. (1914). *The psychopathology of everyday life.* New York: Macmillan. (Original work published 1904)

Freud, S. (1915). Instincts and their vicissitudes. In S. Freud, *The collected papers.* New York: Collier.

Freud, S. (1923). *Introductory lectures on psycho-analysis* (J. Riviera, Trans.). London: Allen & Unwin.

Freud, S. (1925). The unconscious. In S. Freud, *The collected papers* (Vol. 4). London: Hogarth.

Freud, S. (1949). *A general introduction to psychoanalysis.* New York: Penguin Books.

Freud, S. (1949). *An outline of psycho-analysis.* New York: Norton.

Freud, S. (1960). *Jokes and their relation to the unconscious.* New York: Norton. (Original work published 1905)

Freud, S. (1961). *Civilization and its discontents* (J. Strachey, Trans.). New York: Norton. (Original work published 1930)

Freud, S. (1976). Three essays on the theory of sexuality. In J. Strachey (Ed. and Trans.), *The standard edition of the complete psychological works of Sigmund Freud.* (Vol. 7). London: Hogarth Press. (Original work published 1905)

Freud, S. (1976). Totem and taboo. In J. Strachey (Ed. and Trans.), *The standard edition of the complete psychological works of Sigmund Freud.* (Vol. 13). London: Hogarth Press. (Original work published 1913)

Frey, W. H., & Langseth, M. (1986). *Crying: The mystery of tears.* New York: Winston Press.

Frey, W. H., II, Hoffman-Ahern, C., Johnson, R. A., Lydden, D. T., & Tuason, V. B. (1983). Crying behavior in the human adult. *Integrative Psychiatry, 1,* 94–98.

Frezza, M., di Padova, C., Pozzato, G., Terpin, M., Baraona, E., & Lieber, C. S. (1990). High blood alcohol levels in women: The role of decreased gastric alcohol dehydrogenase activity and first-pass metabolism. *New England Journal of Medicine, 322,* 95–99.

Fridja, N., Kuipers, P., & Peter Schure, E. (1989). Relations among emotion, appraisal, and emotional action readiness. *Journal of Personality and Social Psychology, 57,* 212–228.

Fridlund, A. J. (1990). Evolution and facial action in reflex, social motive, and paralanguage. In P. K. Ackles, J. R. Jennings, & M. G. H. Coles (Eds.), *Advances in psychophysiology.* Greenwich, CT: JAI Press.

Friedman, H. S. (Ed.). (1990). *Personality and Disease.* New York: Wiley.

Friedman, H. S., & Booth-Kewley, S. (1987). The "disease-prone personality": A meta-analytic view of the construct. *American*

Psychologist, 42, 539–555.

Friedman, H. S., & Booth-Kewley, S. (1988). Validity of the Type A construct: A reprise. *Psychological Bulletin, 104*, 381–384.

Friedman, M., & Rosenman, R. F. (1974). *Type A behavior and your heart.* New York: Knopf.

Friedman, M., Thoresen, C. E., Gill, J. J., Powell, L. H., Ulmer, D., Thompson, L., Price, V. A., Rabin, D. D., Breall, W. S., Dixon, T., Levy, R., & Bourg, E. (1984). Alteration of Type A behavior and reduction in cardiac recurrences in postmyocardial infarction patients. *American Heart Journal, 108*, 237–248.

Friedman, M., Thoresen, C. E., Gill, J. J., Ulmer, D., Powell, L. H., Price, V. A., Brown, B., Thompson, L., Rabin, D. D., Breall, W. S., Bourg, E., Levy, R., & Dixon, T. (1986). Alteration of Type A behavior and its effect on cardiac recurrences in post-myocardial infarction patients: Summary results of the Recurrent Coronary Prevention Project. *American Heart Journal, 11*, 653–665.

Frisby, J. P. (1979). *Seeing: Illusion, brain and mind.* Oxford: Oxford University Press.

Frisby, J. P. (1980). *Seeing.* Oxford: Oxford University Press.

Fromkin, V. A. (Ed.). (1980). *Errors in linguistic performance: Slips of the tongue, pen, and hand.* New York: Academic Press.

Fromm, E. (1947). *Man for himself.* New York: Holt, Rinehart & Winston.

Fromm, E., & Shor, R. E. (Eds.). (1979). *Hypnosis: Developments in research and new perspectives* (2nd ed.). Hawthorne, NY: Aldine.

Frumkin, B., & Anisfeld, M. (1977). Semantic and surface codes in the memory of deaf children. *Cognitive Psychology, 9*, 475–493.

Fry, W. F., & Allen, M. (1975). Make 'em laugh. Palo Alto, CA: *Science and Behavior Books.*

Fry, W. F., Jr. (1986). Humor, physiology, and the aging process. In L. Nahemow, K. A. McCluskey-Fawcett, & P. E. McGhee (Eds.), *Humor and aging* (pp. 81–98). Orlando: Academic Press.

Fuller, J. L. (1982). Psychology and genetics: A happy marriage? *Canadian Psychology, 23*, 11–21.

Fuller, T. (1952). *Worthies of England.* London: Allen & Unwin.

Funder, D. (1991). Global traits: A neo-Allportian approach to personality. *Psychological Science, 2*, 31–44.

Furman, W., Rahe, D., & Hartup, W. W. (1979). Rehabilitation of socially withdrawn preschool children through mixed-aged and same-sex socialization. *Child Development, 50*, 915–922.

Furstenberg, F., Jr. (1985). Sociological ventures in child development. *Child Development, 56*, 281–288.

G

Gage, F. (1990). In *Discovering Psychology*, Program 3 [PBS video series]. Washington, DC: Annenberg/CPB Project.

Gagnon, J. H. (1977). *Human sexualities.* Glenview, IL: Scott, Foresman.

Galaburda, A. M., LeMay, M., Kemper, T. L., & Geschwind, N. (1978). Right-left asymmetries in the brain. *Science, 199*, 852–856.

Gallagher, J. M., & Reid, D. K. (1981). *The learning theory of Piaget and Inhelder.* Monterey, CA: Brooks/Cole.

Gallant, D. M. (1990). The type 2 primary alcoholic? *Alcoholism, Clinical and Experimental Research, 14*, 631.

Gallup, G., Jr., & Newport, F. (1990, August 6). One in 4 Americans believes in ghosts: Poll shows strong belief in paranormal. *The San Francisco Chronicle*, pp. B1, B5.

Galluscio, E. H. (1990). *Biological psychology.* New York: Macmillan.

Galton, F. (1869). *Hereditary genius.* London: Macmillan.

Galton, F. (1884). Measurement of character. *Fortnightly Review, 42*, 179–185.

Galton, F. (1907). *Inquiries into human faculty and its development.* London: Dent Publishers. (Original work published 1883)

Garcia, J. (1990). Learning without memory. *Journal of Cognitive Neuroscience, 2*, 287–305.

Garcia, J., & Garcia y Robertson, R. (1985). Evolution of learning mechanisms. In B. L. Hammonds (Ed.), *Psychology and learning: 1984 Master Lecturers* (pp. 187–243). Washington,

DC: American Psychological Association.

Garcia, J., & Koelling, R. A. (1966). The relation of cue to consequence in avoidance learning. *Psychonomic Science, 4*, 123–124.

Gardner, H. (1983). *Frames of mind.* New York: Basic Books.

Gardner, H. (1985). *The mind's new science: A history of the cognitive revolution.* New York: Basic Books.

Gardner, H. (1990). In *Discovering Psychology*, programs 10 and 16 [PBS video series]. Washington, DC: Annenberg/CPB Project.

Gardner, L. I. (1972). Deprivation dwarfism. *Scientific American, 227*(7), 76–82.

Garfield, P. (1975). Psychological concomitants of the lucid dream state. *Sleep Research, 4*, 184.

Garland, H. (1984). Relation of effort-performance expectancy to performance in goal setting experiments. *Journal of Applied Psychology, 69*, 79–84.

Garmezy, N. (1976). Vulnerable and invulnerable children: Theory, research, and intervention. *Journal Abstract Supplement Service. Catalog of Selected Documents in Psychology, 6*, 96.

Garmezy, N. (1977). The psychology and psychopathology of Allen Head. *Schizophrenia Bulletin, 3*, 360–369.

Garmezy, N., & Mattysse, S. (Eds.). (1977). Special issue on the psychology and psychopathology of attention. *Schizophrenic Bulletin, 3*(3).

Garner, W. R. (1974). *The processing of information and structure.* Potomac, MD: Lawrence Erlbaum Associates.

Garrison, V. (1977). The "Puerto Rican syndrome" in psychiatry and Espiritismo. In V. Crapanzano & V. Garrison (Eds.), *Case studies in spirit possession.* New York: Wiley Interscience.

Gawin, F. H. (1991). Cocaine addiction: Psychology and neurophysiology. *Science, 251*, 1580–1586.

Gay, P. (1988). *Freud: A life for our time.* New York: Norton.

Gayle, H. D., Keeling, R. P., Garcia-Tunon, M., Kilbourne, B. W., Narkunas, J. P., Ingram, F. R., Rogers, M. F., & Curran, J. W. (1990). Prevalence of Human Immunodeficiency Virus among university students. *New England Journal of Medicine, 323*, 1538–1541.

Gazzaniga, M. (1970). *The bisected brain.* New York: Appleton-Century-Crofts.

Gazzaniga, M. (1980). *Psychology.* New York: Harper & Row.

Gazzaniga, M. (1990). In *Discovering Psychology*, Program 14 [PBS video series]. Washington, DC: Annenberg/CPB Program.

Gazzaniga, M. S. (1985). *The social brain.* New York: Basic Books.

Geen, R. G. (1991). Social motivation. *Annual Review of Psychology, 42*, 377–400.

Geer, J. H., Davidson, G. C., & Gatchel, R. I. (1970). Reduction of stress in humans through nonveridical perceived control of aversive stimulation. *Journal of Personality and Social Psychology, 16*, 731–738.

Geldard, F. A. (1972). *The human senses* (2nd ed.). New York: Wiley.

Gelman, R. (1979). Preschool thought. *American Psychologists, 34*, 900–905.

Gelman, R., & Baillargeon, R. (1983). A review of Piagetian concepts. In J. Flavell & E. Markman (Eds.), *Handbook of child psychology* (Vol. 3, pp. 167–230). New York: Wiley.

Gerbner, G., Gross, L., Signorielli, N., & Morgan, M. (1986, September). *Television's mean world: Violence profile no. 14–15.* Philadelphia: University of Pennsylvania, The Annenberg School of Communication.

Gergen, K. J., Gergen, M. M., & Barton, W. (1973, October). Deviance in the dark. *Psychology Today*, pp. 129–130.

Geschwind, N. (1979). Specializations of the human brain. *Scientific American, 241*(3), 180–199.

Gevins, A. S., Morgan, N. H., Bressler, S. L., Cutillo, B. A., White, R. M., Illes, J., Greer, D. S., Doyle, J. C., & Zeitlin, G. M. (1987). Human neuroelectric patterns predict performance accuracy. *Science, 235*, 580–585.

Gevins, A. S., Shaffer, R. E., Doyle, J. C., Cutillo, B. A., Tannehill, R. S., & Bressler, S. L. (1983). Shadows of thought: Shifting lateralization of human brain electrical potential patterns during brief visuo-motor task. *Science, 220*, 97–99.

Gibbs, J. C. (1977). Kohlberg's stages of moral judgment: A constructive critique. *Harvard Educational Review, 47,* 43–61.

Gibbs, J. C., Arnold, K. D., & Burkhart, J. E. (1984). Sex differences in the expression of moral judgment. *Child Development, 55,* 1040–1043.

Gibson, F. (1990, Fall). When drinking kills: The tragic story of Ted McGuire. *The Student Body,* pp. 1, 8.

Gibson, J. J. (1950). *The perception of the visual world.* New York: Houghton-Mifflin.

Gibson, J. J. (1966). *The senses considered as perceptual systems.* New York: Houghton-Mifflin.

Gibson, J. J. (1979). *An ecological approach to visual perception.* New York: Houghton-Mifflin.

Gibson, J. T., & Haritos-Fatouros, M. (1986, November). The education of a torturer. *Psychology Today,* pp. 50–58.

Gieringer, D. (1990). How many crack babies? *The Drug Policy Letter, 2:2,* pp. 4–6.

Gilliam, H. (1986, July 6). Fencing out world prosperity. *San Francisco Chronicle,* p. 18.

Gillig, P. M., & Greenwald, A. G. (1974). Is it time to lay the sleeper effect to rest? *Journal of Personality and Social Psychology, 29,* 132–139.

Gilligan, C. (1982). *In a different voice: Psychological theory and women's development.* Cambridge, MA: Harvard University Press.

Gilligan, S., & Bower, G. H. (1984). Cognitive consequences of emotional arousal. In C. Izard, J. Kagan, & R. Zajonc (Eds.), *Emotions, cognitions, and behavior* (pp. 547–588). Cambridge: Cambridge University Press.

Gilman, L. (1989, July/August). Teens take to gambling: lifelong addiction can start with a lottery ticket. *American Health: Fitness of Body and Mind, 8,* p. 113.

Gist, R., & Stolz, S. B. (1982). Mental health promotion and the media: Community response to the Kansas City hotel disaster. *American Psychologist, 37,* 1136–1139.

Givens, A. (1989a). Dynamic functional topography of cognitive tasks. *Brain Topography, 2,* 37–56.

Givens, A. (1989b). Signs of model making by the human brain. In E. Basar & T. H. Bullock (Eds.), *Brain dynamics 2* (pp. 408–419). Berlin: Springer-Verlag.

Glantz, S., & Parmley, W. W. (1991, January). Passive smoking and heart disease: Epidemiology, physiology, and biochemistry. *Circulation, 83,* 1–12.

Glanzer, M., & Cunitz, A. R. (1966). Two storage mechanisms in free recall. *Journal of Verbal Learning and Verbal Behavior, 5,* 351–360.

Glaser, R. (1984). Education and thinking: The role of knowledge. *American Psychologist, 39,* 93–104.

Glass, A. L., Holyoak, K. J., & Santa, J. L. (1979). *Cognition.* Reading, MA: Addison-Wesley.

Glass, D. C. (1977). *Behavior patterns, stress, and coronary disease.* Hillsdale, NJ: Erlbaum.

Glassman, A. H., Jackson, W. K., Walsh, B. T., & Roose, S. P. (1984). Cigarette craving, smoking withdrawal, and clondine. *Science, 226,* 864–866.

Glassman, R. B. (1983). Free will has a neural substrate: Critique of Joseph F. Rychlak's *Discovering free will and personal responsibility. Zygon, 18,* 67–82.

Glucksberg, S., & Danks, J. H. (1975). *Experimental psycholinguistics.* Hillsdale, NJ: Erlbaum.

Goddard, H. H. (1914). *The Kallikak family. A study of the heredity of feeble-mindedness.* New York: Macmillan.

Goddard, H. H. (1917). Mental tests and immigrants. *Journal of Delinquency, 2,* 243–277.

Goffman, E. (1959). *The presentation of self in everyday life.* New York: Doubleday.

Goffman, E. (1963). *Stigma.* Englewood Cliffs, NJ: Prentice-Hall.

Gold, P. E. (1984). Memory modulation: Neurobiological contexts. In G. Lynch, J. L. McGaugh, & N. M. Weinberger (Eds.), *Neurobiology of learning and memory* (pp. 374–382). New York: Guilford Press.

Gold, P. E. (1987). Sweet memories. *American Scientist, 75,* 151–155.

Goldfried, M. R., Greenberg, L., & Marmar, C. (1990). Individual psychotherapy: Process and outcome. *Annual Review of Psychology, 41,* 659–688.

Golding, S. L. (1977). The problem of construal styles in the analysis of person-situation interactions. In D. Magnusson & N. E. Endler (Eds.), *Personality at the crossroads* (pp. 401–408). Hillsdale, NJ: Erlbaum.

Goldstein, E. B. (1980). *Sensation and perception.* Belmont, CA: Wadsworth.

Goldstein, M., & Rodnick, E. H. (1975). The family's contribution to the etiology of schizophrenia: Current status. *Schizophrenia Bulletin, 14,* 48–63.

Goldstein, M. J., & Strachan, A. M. (1987). The family and schizophrenia. In T. Jacob (Ed.), *Family interaction and psychopathology: Theories, methods and findings* (pp. 481–507). New York: Plenum.

Goleman, D. (1987). Who are you kidding? *Psychology Today,* pp. 24–30.

Gomes-Schwartz, B., Hadley, S. W., & Strupp, H. H. (1978). Individual psychotherapy and behavior therapy. *Annual Review of Psychology, 29,* 435–471.

Gonzalez, A. (1990). In *Discovering Psychology,* Program 20 [PBS video series]. Washington, DC: Annenberg/CPB Program.

Gonzalez, A., & Zimbardo, P. G. (1985, March). Time in perspective. *Psychology Today,* pp. 20–26.

Goodall, J. (1986). *The chimpanzees of Gombe: Patterns of behavior.* Cambridge, MA: Harvard University Press.

Goodkind, M. (1989, Spring). The cigarette habit. *Stanford Medicine,* 10–14.

Goodman, D. A. (1978). Learning from lobotomy. *Human Behavior, 7*(1), 44–49.

Goodman, L. S., & Gilman, A. (1970). *The pharmacological basis of therapeutics* (4th ed.). New York: Macmillan.

Goodstadt, M. S. (1986). Alcohol education research and practice: A logical analysis of the two realities. *Journal of Drug Education, 16,* 349–365.

Gordon, C., & Gergen, K. J. (1968). *The self in social interaction* (Vol. 1). New York: Wiley.

Gordon, L. (1990, September 2). Proposal to overhaul SAT to consider relevance, bias. *The Seattle Times/Post-Intelligencer.*

Gorman, B. S., & Wessman, A. E. (1977). *The personal experience of time.* New York: Plenum.

Gorman, J. M., Liebowitz, M. R., Fyer, A. J., & Stein, J. M. (1989). A neuroanatomical hypothesis for panic disorder. *American Journal of Psychiatry, 146,* 148–161.

Gorney, R. (1976, September). Paper presented at annual meeting of the American Psychiatric Association.

Gottesman, I. (1990). In *Discovering Psychology,* Program 21 [PBS video series]. Washington, DC: Annenberg/CPB Program.

Gottesman, I. I. (1963). Genetic aspects of intelligent behavior. In N. Ellis (Ed.), *Handbook of mental deficiency: Psychological theory and research.* New York: McGraw-Hill.

Gottesman, I. I. (1991). *Schizophrenia genesis: The origins of madness.* New York: Freeman.

Gottesman, I. I., & Shields, J. (1972). *Schizophrenia and genetics: A twin study vantage point.* New York: Academic Press.

Gottesman, I. I., & Shields, J. (1976). A critical review of recent adoption, twin, and family studies of schizophrenia: Behavioral genetics perspective. *Schizophrenia Bulletin, 2,* 360–401.

Gottfredson, L. S. (1986). The g-factor in employment. *Journal of Vocational Behavior, 29,* 293–296.

Gottleib, G. (1983). The psychobiological approach to developmental issues. In M. M. Haith & J. J. Campos (Eds.), *Handbook of child psychology: Infancy and developmental psychobiology* (pp. 1–26). New York: Wiley.

Gottlieb, B. H. (Ed.). (1981). *Social networks and social support.* Beverly Hills, CA: Sage.

Gough, H. G. (1957). *California psychological inventory manual.* Palo Alto, CA: Consulting Psychology Press.

Gough, H. G. (1961). Techniques for identifying the creative research scientist. In *Conference on the creative person.* Berkeley: University of California, Institute of Personality Assessment & Research.

Gough, H. G. (1968). An interpreter's syllabus for the California

Psychological Inventory. In P. McReynolds (Ed.), *Advances in psychological assessment, vol. one* (pp. 55–79). Palo Alto, CA: Science and Behavior Books.

Gough, H. G. (1989). The California Psychological Inventory. In C. S. Newmark (Ed.), *Major psychological assessment inventories* (Vol. 2). Boston: Allyn and Bacon.

Gould, J. L. (1985). How bees remember flower shapes. *Science, 227,* 1492–1494.

Gould, J. L., & Marler, P. (1984). Ethology on the natural history of learning. In P. Marler & H. Terrace (Eds.), *The biology of learning* (pp. 47–74). Berlin: Springer-Verlag.

Gould, S. J. (1981). *The mismeasure of man.* New York: Norton.

Graf, P., Squire, L. R., & Mandler, G. (1984). The information that amnesic patients do not forget. *Journal of Experimental Psychology: Learning, Memory, and Cognition, 10,* 164–178.

Grant, P. R. (1986). *Ecology and evolution of Darwin's finches.* Princeton, NJ: Princeton University Press.

Gray, C. R., & Gummerman, K. (1975). The enigmatic eidetic image: A critical examination of methods, data, and theories. *Psychological Bulletin, 82,* 383–407.

Gray, L. (1989, June). Quoted in M. Knaster, Paths to power. *East West,* pp. 42–50.

Green, D. M., & Swets, J. A. (1966). *Signal detection theory and psychophysics.* New York: Wiley.

Green, W. H., Campbell, M., & David, R. (1984). Psychosocial dwarfism: A critical review of the evidence. *Journal of the American Academy of Child Psychiatry, 23,* 39–48.

Greenberg, J., & Ornstein, S. (1983). High status job title as compensation for underpayment: A test of equity theory. *Journal of Applied Psychology, 68,* 285–297.

Greene, B. (1985). A testing time. In B. Greene, *Cheeseburgers* (pp. 56–61). New York: Ballantine.

Greenfield, P. M., & Smith, J. H. (1976). *The structure of communication in early language development.* New York: Academic Press.

Greening, T. (Ed.). (1984). Special peace issue. *Journal of Humanistic Psychology, 23*(3).

Greeno, C. G., & Maccoby, E. E. (1986). How different is the "different voice"? *Signs, 11,* 310–316.

Greenwald, A. G., Klinger, M. R., & Liu, T. J. (1989). Unconscious processing of dichoptically masked words. *Memory & Cognition, 17,* 35–47.

Greenwald, A. G., Spangenber, E. R., Pratkanis, A. R., & Eskenazi, J. (1991). Double-blind tests of subliminal self-help audiotapes. *Psychological Science, 2,* 119–122.

Griffin, D. R. (1984). Animal thinking. *American Scientist, 72,* 456–464.

Griffin, D. W., & Ross, L. (1991). Subjective construal, social inference, and human misunderstanding. In M. P. Zanna (Ed.), *Advances in Experimental Social Psychology* (pp. 319–359). New York: Academic Press.

Gross, R. T., and Staff. (1990). Enhancing the outcomes of low-birth-weight, premature infants: A multi-site, randomized trial. *Journal of the American Medical Association, 263,* 3035–3042.

Grossman, S. P. (1979). The biology of motivation. *Annual Review of Psychology, 30,* 209–242.

Group for the Advancement of Psychiatry. (1950). *Revised electro-shock therapy report, special volume: Report No. 15,* 1–3.

Guerra, F., & Aldrete, J. (1980). *Emotional and psychological responses to anesthesia and surgery.* New York: Grune & Stratton.

Guetzkow, H., Alger, C. F., Brody, R. A., Noel, R. C., & Snyder, R. C. (1963). *Simulation in international relations.* Englewood Cliffs, NJ: Prentice-Hall.

Guilford, J. P. (1961). *Psychological Review, 68,* 1–20.

Guilford, J. P. (1967). *Crystalized intelligences: The nature of human intelligence.* New York: McGraw-Hill.

Guilford, J. P. (1973). Theories of intelligence. In B. B. Wolman (Ed.), *Handbook of general psychology.* Englewood Cliffs, NJ: Prentice-Hall.

Guilford, J. P. (1985). The Structure-of-Intellect model. In B. B. Wolman (Ed.), *Handbook of intelligence.* New York: Wiley.

Guilleminault, C. (1989). Clinical features and evaluation of obstructive sleep apnea. In M. Kryser, T. Roth, & W. C. Dement (Eds.), *Principles and practice of sleep medicine* (pp. 552–558). New York: Saunders Press.

Guilleminault, C., Dement, W. C., & Passonant, P. (Eds.). (1976). *Narcolepsy.* New York: Spectrum.

Gummerman, K., Gray, C. R., & Wilson, J. M. (1972). An attempt to assess eidetic imagery objectively. *Psychonomic Science, 28,* 115–118.

Gunzenhauser, N. (Ed.). (1990). *Advances in touch: New implications in human development.* Skillman, NJ: Johnson & Johnson Co.

Gur, R. C., & Gur, R. E. (1974). Handedness, sex and eyedness as moderating variables in the relation between hypnotic susceptibility and functional brain asymmetry. *Journal of Abnormal Psychology, 83,* 635–643.

Gynther, M. D. (1981). Is the *MMPI* an appropriate assessment device for blacks? *Journal of Black Psychology, 7,* 67–75.

Gynther, M. D., & Gynther, R. A. (1976). Personality inventories. In I. B. Weiner (Ed.), *Clinical methods in psychology.* New York: Wiley-Interscience.

H

Haas, H., Fink, H., & Hartfelder, G. (1959). *Das placebo-problem. Fortschritte der Arzneimittleforchung, 1,* 279–454. In *Psychopharmacology Service Center Bulletin, 1963, 8* (pp. 1–65). U.S. Department of Health, Education and Welfare, Public Health Service.

Haas, K. (1965). *Understanding ourselves and others.* Englewood Cliffs, NJ: Prentice-Hall.

Habot, T. B., & Libow, L. S. (1980). The interrelationship of mental and physical status and its assessment in the older adult: Mind-body interaction. In J. E. Birren & R. B. Sloane (Eds.), *Handbook of mental health and aging* (pp. 701–716). Englewood Cliffs, NJ: Prentice-Hall.

Hacker, A. (1986, February 13). The decline of higher learning. *The New York Review.*

Hackman, J. R., & Oldham, G. R. (1980). *Work redesign.* Reading, MA: Addison-Wesley.

Haier, R. J. (1980). The diagnosis of schizophrenia: A review of recent developments. In S. J. Keith & L. R. Mosher (Eds.), *Special report: Schizophrenia, 1980* (pp. 2–13). Washington, DC: U.S. Government Printing Office.

Hale, R. L. (1983). Intellectual assessment. In M. Hersen, A. E. Kazdin, & A. S. Bellack (Eds.), *The clinical psychology handbook* (pp. 345–376). New York: Pergamon.

Hall, G. S. (1904). *Adolescence: Its psychology and its relations to physiology, anthropology, sociology, sex, crime, religion and education* (Vols. 1 and 2). New York: D. Appleton.

Hallowell, A. I. (1976). Ojibwa world view and disease. In *Contributions to anthropology: Selected papers of A.I. Hallowell* [Introductions by R. D. Fogelson et al.]. Chicago: University of Chicago Press. (Original work published 1963)

Hamill, R., Wilson, T. D., & Nisbett, R. E. (1980). *Ignoring sample bias: Inferences about populations from atypical cases.* Unpublished manuscript, University of Michigan, Ann Arbor.

Hamilton, D. (1990, September 2). *Los Angeles Times.*

Hamilton, D. L., Katz, L. B., & Leirer, V. O. (1980). Memory for persons. *Journal of Personality and Social Psychology, 39,* 1050–1063.

Hamilton, V. (1980). An information processing analysis of environmental stress and life crisis. In I. G. Sarason & C. D. Spielberger (Eds.), *Stress and anxiety* (Vol. 7). New York: Hemisphere Publishing.

Hammer, D. L., & Padesky, C. A. (1977). Sex differences in the expression of depressive responses on the Beck Depression Inventory. *Journal of Abnormal Psychology, 86,* 609–614.

Haney, C. (1982). Employment tests and employment discrimination: A dissenting psychological opinion. *Industrial Relations Law Journal, 5,* 1–86.

Haney, C. (1984). On the selection of capital juries: The biasing effects of the death-qualification process. *Law and Human Behavior, 8,* 121–132.

Haney, C., & Zimbardo, P. G. (1977). The socialization into criminality: On becoming a prisoner and a guard. In J. L. Tapp & F. L. Levine (Eds.), *Law, justice and the individual in society: Psychological and legal issues* (pp. 198–223). New York: Holt, Rinehart & Winston.

Hanson, D., Gottesman, I., & Meehl, P. (1977). Genetic theories and the validation of psychiatric diagnosis: Implications for the study of children of schizophrenics. *Journal of Abnormal Psychology, 86,* 575–588.

Hareven, T. (1985). Historical changes in the family and the life course: Implications for child development. *Monographs of the Society for Research in Child Development, 50* (Serial No. 211), 8–23.

Harlow, H. F. (1965). Sexual behavior in the rhesus monkey. In F. Beach (Ed.), *Sex and behavior.* New York: Wiley.

Harlow, H. F., & Harlow, M. K. (1966). Learning to love. *American Scientist, 54,* 244–272.

Harlow, H. F., Harlow, M. K, & Meyer, D. R. (1950). Learning motivated by a manipulation drive. *Journal of Experimental Psychology, 40,* 228–234.

Harlow, H. F., & Zimmerman, R. R. (1958). The development of affectional responses in infant monkeys. Proceedings of the *American Philosophical Society, 102,* 501–509.

Harner, M. J. (1973). The sound of rushing water. In M. J. Harner (Ed.), *Hallucinogens and shamanism* (pp. 15–27). Oxford: Oxford University Press.

Harper Atlas of World History. (1986). New York: Harper & Row.

Harris, B. (1979). Whatever happened to Little Albert? *American Psychologist, 34,* 151–160.

Harris, G., Thomas, A., & Booth, D. A. (1990). Development of salt taste in infancy. *Developmental Psychology, 26,* 534–538.

Harris, P. (1989). The prevalence of visual conditions in a population of juvenile delinquents. *Journal of the American Optometric Association, 37,* 461–468.

Harris, P. R. (1980). *Promoting health—preventing disease: Objectives for the nation.* Washington, DC: U.S. Government Printing Office.

Harrison, J. (1978). Male sex role and health. *Journal of Social Issues, 34*(1), 65–86.

Harshman, R. A., Crawford, H. J., & Hecht, E. (1976). Marijuana, cognitive style, and lateralized hemispheric functions. In S. Cohen & R. C. Stillman (Eds.), *The therapeutic potential of marijuana* (pp. 205–254). New York: Plenum.

Hart, R. A., & Moore, G. I. (1973). The development of spatial cognition: A review. In R. M. Downs & D. Stea (Eds.), *Image and environment.* Chicago: Aldine.

Hart, S. N. (1991). From property to person status: Historical perspective on children's rights. *American Psychologist, 46,* 53–59.

Hartmann, D. P., Roper, B. L., & Bradford, D. (1979). Some relationships between behavioral and traditional assessment. *Journal of Behavioral Assessment, 1,* 3–21.

Hartmann, E. (1989). Boundaries of dreams, boundaries of dreamers: Thin and thick boundaries as a new personality measure. *Psychiatric Journal of the University of Ottawa, 14,* 557–560.

Hartmann, E. (1990). In *Discovering Psychology*, Program 13 [PBS video series]. Washington, DC: Annenberg/CPB Program.

Hartshorne, H., & May, M. A. (1928). *Studies in the nature of character, Vol. 1: Studies in deceit.* New York: Macmillan.

Hartshorne, H., & May, M. A. (1929). *Studies in the nature of character, Vol. 2: Studies in service and self-control.* New York: Macmillan.

Hartup, W. W. (1989). Social relationships and their developmental significance. *American Psychologist, 44,* 120–126.

Harvey, O. J., & Consalvi, C. (1960). Status and conformity in informal groups. *Journal of Abnormal and Social Psychology, 60,* 182–187.

Harvey, P. H., & Krebs, J. R. (1990). Comparing brains. *Science, 249,* 140–146.

Hasenfus, N., & Magaro, P. (1976). Creativity and schizophrenia: An equality of empirical constructs. *British Journal of Psychiatry, 129,* 346–349.

Hass, A. (1979). *Teenage sexuality: A survey of teenage sexual behavior.* New York: Macmillan.

Hastorf, A. H., & Cantril, H. (1954). They saw a game: A case study. *Journal of Abnormal and Social Psychology, 49,* 129–134.

Hatfield, E., & Sprecher, S. (1986). *Mirror, mirror. The importance of looks in everyday life.* New York: State University of New York Press.

Hauri, P. (1977). *The sleep disorders.* Kalamazoo, MI: Upjohn.

Hayes, D. (1991). Harnessing market forces to protect the earth. *Issues in Science and Technology, 7,* 46–51.

Hayes-Roth, B., & Hayes-Roth, F. (1979). A cognitive model of planning. *Cognitive Science, 3,* 275–310.

Haygood, R. C., & Bourne, L. E., Jr. (1965). Attribute and rule-learned aspects of conceptual behavior. *Psychological Review, 72,* 175–195.

Haynes, S. G., & Feinleib, M. (1980). Women, work, and coronary heart disease: Prospective findings from the Framingham Heart Study. *American Journal of Public Health, 70,* 133–141.

Haynes, S. N. (1983). Behavioral assessment. In M. Hersen, A. E. Kazdin, & A. S. Bellack. (Eds.), *The clinical psychology handbook* (pp. 397–425). New York: Pergamon.

Haynes, S. N., & Wilson, C. C. (1979). *Behavioral assessment: Recent advances in methods and concepts.* San Francisco: Jossey-Bass.

Hazan, C., & Shaver, P. (1987). Romantic love conceptualized as an attachment process. *Journal of Personality and Social Psychology, 52,* 511–524.

Heath, A. C., Jardine, R., & Martin, N. G. (1989). Interactive effects of genotype and social environment on alcohol consumption in female twins. *Journal of Studies of Alcohol, 50,* 38–48.

Heather, N., & Robertson, I. (1983). *Controlled drinking* (2nd ed.). New York: Methuen.

Hebb, D. (1974). What is psychology about? *American Psychologist, 29,* 71–79.

Hebb, D. O. (1949). *The organization of behavior: A neuropsychological theory.* New York: Wiley.

Hebb, D. O. (1955). Drives and the CNS (conceptual nervous system). *Psychological Review, 62,* 243–254.

Hebb, D. O. (1966). *A textbook of psychology* (2nd ed.). Philadelphia: Saunders.

Hebb, D. O. (1980). *Essay on mind.* Hillsdale, NJ: Erlbaum.

Heber, R. (1976, June). *Sociocultural mental retardation: A longitudinal study.* Paper presented at the Vermont Conference on the Primary Prevention of Psychopathology.

Hecht, A. (1986, April). A guide to the proper use of tranquilizers. *Healthline Newsletter,* pp. 5–6.

Hedlund, J. L. (1977). MMPI clinical scale correlated. *Journal of Consulting and Clinical Psychology, 45,* 739–750.

Heider, F. (1958). *The psychology of interpersonal relationships.* New York: Wiley.

Heider, F., & Simmel, M. (1944). An experimental study of apparent behavior. *American Journal of Psychology, 57,* 243–259.

Heider, R. (1944). Social perception and phenomenal causality. *Psychological Review, 51,* 358–374.

Helson, R. (1971). Women mathematicians and the creative personality. *Journal of Consulting and Clinical Psychology, 36,* 210–220.

Henderson, N. D. (1980). Effects of early experience upon the behavior of animals: The second twenty-five years of research. In E. C. Simmel (Ed.), *Early experiences and early behavior: Implications for social development* (pp. 39–77). New York: Academic Press.

Hensel, H. (1968). Electrophysiology of cutaneous thermoreceptors. In D. R. Kenshalo (Ed.), *The skin senses* (pp. 384–399). Springfield, IL: Charles C Thomas.

Heppenheimer, T. A. (1990). How von Neuman showed the way. *Invention and Technology, Fall,* 7–16.

Hering, E. (1861–1864). *Beitrage zur physiologie.* Leipzig: W. Engelmann.

Herman, M. (1972). The poor: Their medical needs and the health services available to them. *Annals of the American Academy of*

Political and Social Science, 399, 12–21.

Herrnstein, R. J., & Wilson, J. Q. (1985). *Crime and human nature.* New York: Simon & Schuster.

Herrnstein, R. J., Nickerson, R. S., de Sanchez, M., & Swets, J. A. (1986). Teaching thinking skills. *American Psychologist, 41,* 1279–1289.

Hersen, M., & Bellack, A. J. (1976). Assessment of social skills. In A. R. Ciminero, K. R. Calhoun, & H. E. Adams (Eds.), *Handbook of behavioral assessment* (pp. 509–554). New York: Wiley.

Hersh, S. M. (1971). *My Lai 4: A report on the massacre and its aftermath.* New York: Random House.

Hess, E. H. (1972). Pupillometrics: A method of studying mental, emotional, and sensory processes. In N. E. Greenfield & R. A. Steinbach (Eds.), *Handbook of psychophysiology.* New York: Holt, Rinehart & Winston.

Hess, W., & Akert, K. (1955). Experimental data on the role of hypothalamus in the mechanism of emotional behavior. *Archives of Neurological Psychiatry, 73,* 127–129.

Hester, R. K., & Miller, W. R. (Eds.). (1989). *Handbook of alcoholism treatment approaches: Effective alternatives.* New York: Pergamon.

Hetherington, E. M., & Parke, R. D. (1975). *Child psychology: A contemporary viewpoint.* New York: McGraw-Hill.

Higgins, E. T. (1989). Continuities and discontinuities in self-regulatory and self-evaluative processes: A developmental theory relating self and affect. *Journal of Personality, 57,* 407–444.

Hilgard, E. (1965). *Hypnotic susceptibility.* New York: Harcourt Brace Jovanovich.

Hilgard, E. R. (1968). *The experience of hypnosis.* New York: Harcourt Brace Jovanovich.

Hilgard, E. R. (1973). The domain of hypnosis with some comments on alternative paradigms. *American Psychologist, 28,* 972–982.

Hilgard, E. R. (1977). *Divided consciousness: Multiple controls in human thought and action.* New York: Wiley.

Hilgard, E. R. (1979). The Stanford hypnotic arm levitation induction and test (SHALIT): A six minute hypnotic induction and measurement scale. *International Journal of Clinical and Experimental Hypnosis, 27,* 111–124.

Hilgard, E. R. (1980). Consciousness in contemporary psychology. *Annual Review of Psychology, 31,* 1–26.

Hilgard, E. R. (1986). *Psychology in America: A historical survey.* San Diego, CA: Harcourt Brace Jovanovich.

Hilgard, E. R., & Hilgard, J. R. (1974, Spring-Summer). Hypnosis in the control of pain. *The Stanford Magazine,* 58–62.

Hilgard, J. R. (1970). *Personality and hypnosis: A study of the imaginative involvement.* Chicago: University of Chicago Press.

Hilgard, J. R. (1974). Imaginative involvement: Some characteristics of the highly hypnotizable and the non-hypnotizable. *International Journal of Clinical and Experimental Hypnosis, 22,* 281–298.

Hilgard, J. R. (1979). *Personality and hypnosis: A study of imaginative involvement* (2nd ed.). Chicago: University of Chicago Press.

Hille, B. (1984). *Ionic channels of excitable membranes.* Sunderland, MA: Sinauer Associates.

Hillis, W. D. (1985). *The connection machine.* Cambridge, MA: MIT Press.

Hinton, G. F., & Anderson, J. A. (1981). *Parallel models of associative memory.* Hillsdale, NJ: Erlbaum.

Hirsch, H. V. B., & Spinelli, D. N. (1970). Visual experience modifies distribution of horizontally and vertically oriented receptive fields in cats. *Science, 168,* 869–871.

Hirsch, J., Harrington, G., & Mehler, B. (1990). An irresponsible farewell gloss. *Educational Theory, 40,* 501-508.

Hirschfield, R. M. A., & Cross, C. K. (1982). Epidemiology of affective disorders: Psychosocial risk factors. *Archives of General Psychiatry, 39,* 35–46.

Hirst, W., Spelke, E. S., Reaves, C. C., Charack, G., & Neisser, U. (1980). Dividing attention without alternation of automaticity. *Journal of Experimental Psychology: General, 109,* 98–117.

Hite, S. (1987). *Hite report: Women and love: A cultural revolution in progress.* New York: Knopf.

Hitler, A. (1933). *Mein Kampf.* Cambridge, MA: Riverside.

Hobson, J. A. (1988). *The dreaming brain.* New York: Basic Books.

Hobson, J. A., & McCarley, R. W. (1977). The brain as a dream state generator: An activation-synthesis hypothesis of the dream process. *American Journal of Psychiatry, 134,* 1335–1348.

Hochberg, J. (1988). Perception of objects in space. In E. R. Hilgard (Ed.), *Fifty years of psychology* (pp. 57–74). Glenview, IL: Scott, Foresman.

Hockett, C. F. (1960). The origin of speech. *Scientific American, 203,* 89–96.

Hofer, M. (1981). *The roots of human behavior: An introduction to the psychobiology of early development.* San Francisco: Freeman.

Hoffman, M. (1986). Affect, cognition, and motivation. In R. Sorrentino & E. Higgins (Eds.), *Handbook of motivation and cognition: Foundations of social behavior* (pp. 244–280). New York: Guilford.

Hoffman, M. L. (1987). The contribution of empathy to justice and moral judgment. In N. Eisenberg & J. Strayer (Eds.), *Empathy and its development* (pp. 47–80). New York: Cambridge University Press.

Hofling, C. K., Brotzman, E., Dalrymple, S., Graves, N., & Pierce, C. M. (1966). An experimental study in nurse-physician relationships. *Journal of Nervous and Mental Disease, 143*(2), 171–180.

Hofstede, G. (1980). *Culture's consequences: International differences in work-related values.* Beverly Hills, CA: Sage.

Holahan, C. J., & Moos, R. (1981). Social support and psychological distress: A longitudinal analysis. *Journal of Abnormal Psychology, 90,* 365–370.

Holahan, C. J., & Moos, R. H. (1987). Personal and contextual determinants of coping strategies. *Journal of Personality and Social Psychology, 52,* 946–955.

Holden, C. (1978). Patuxent: Controversial prison clings to belief in rehabilitation. *Science, 199,* 665–668.

Holden, C. (1986a). Depression research advances, treatment lags. *Science, 233,* 723–725.

Holden, C. (1986b). Youth suicide: New research focuses on a growing social problem. *Science, 233,* 839–841.

Holen, M. C., & Oaster, T. R. (1976). Serial position and isolation effects in a classroom lecture simulation. *Journal of Educational Psychology, 68,* 293–296.

Holland, P. C., & Rescorla, R. A. (1975). Second-order conditioning with food unconditioned stimulus. *Journal of Comparative and Physiological Psychology, 88,* 459–467.

Hollender, M. H. (1980). The case of Anna O.: A reformulation. *American Journal of Psychiatry, 137,* 797–800.

Holloway, M. (1990, October). Profile: Vive la différence. *Scientific American,* pp. 40–42.

Holmes, D. S. (1984). Meditation and somatic arousal: A review of the experimental evidence. *American Psychologist, 39,* 1–10.

Holmes, J. A., & Stevenson, C. A. Z. (1990). Differential effects of avoidant and attentional coping strategies on adaptation to chronic and recent-onset pain. *Health Psychology, 9,* 577–584.

Holmes, T. H., & Masuda, M. (1974). Life change and stress susceptibility. In B. S. Dohrenwend & B. P. Dohrenwend, (Eds.), *Stressful life events: Their nature and effects* (pp. 45–72). New York: Wiley.

Holmes, T. H., & Rahe, R. H. (1967). The social readjustment rating scale. *Journal of Psychosomatic Research, 11*(2), 213–218.

Holt, P. (1990, September 4). Coming to terms with depression [Review of *Darkness visible: A memoir of madness*]. *San Francisco Chronicle.*

Holt, R. R. (1970). Yet another look at clinical and statistical prediction: Or is clinical psychology worthwhile? *American Psychologist, 25,* 337–349.

Homme, L. E., de Baca, P. C., Devine, J. V., Steinhorst, R., & Rickert, E. J. (1963). Use of the Premack principle in controlling the behavior of nursery school children. *Journal of the Experimental Analysis of Behavior, 6,* 544.

Honzik, M. P. (1984). Life-span development. *Annual Review of Psychology, 35,* 309–331.

Hooper, J., & Teresi, D. (1986). *The three-pound universe.* New York: Macmillan.

Hopson, J. L. (1979). *Scent signals: The silent language of sex.* New

York: Morrow.

Hopson, J. L. (1988, July/August). A pleasurable chemistry. *Psychology Today*, pp. 29–33.

Horn, J. L. (1985). Remodeling old models of intelligence. In B. B. Wolman (Ed.), *Handbook of intelligence* (pp. 267–300). New York: Wiley.

Horne, J. A. (1988). *Why we sleep: The functions of sleep in humans and other mammals*. Oxford: Oxford University Press.

Horney, K. (1937). *The neurotic personality of our time*. New York: Norton.

Horney, K. (1939). *New ways in psychoanalyses*. New York: Norton.

Horney, K. (1945). *Our inner conflicts: A constructive theory of neurosis*. New York: Norton.

Horney, K. (1950). *Neurosis and human growth*. New York: Norton.

Horowitz, R. M. (1984). Children's rights: A look backward and a glance ahead. In R. M. Horowitz & H. A. Davidson (Eds.), *Legal rights of children* (pp. 1–9). New York: McGraw-Hill.

Horton, L. E. (1970). Generalization of aggressive behavior in adolescent delinquent boys. *Journal of Applied Behavior Analysis, 3,* 205–211.

Horvath, A. T. (1991). Beyond AA. *The California Psychologist, 24,* 13, 26.

Horvath, F. S. (1977). The effects of selected variables on the interpretation of polygraph records. *Journal of Applied Psychology, 62,* 127–136.

Hosobuchi, Y., Rossier, J., Bloom, F. E., & Guillemin, R. (1979). Stimulation of human periaqueductal gray for pain relief increases immunoreactive B-endorphin in ventricular fluid. *Science, 203,* 279–281.

Houghton, J. (1980). One personal experience: Before and after mental illness. In J. G. Rabkin, L. Gelb, & J. B. Lazar (Eds.), *Attitudes toward the mentally ill: Research perspectives* (pp. 7–14). Rockville, MD: National Institute of Mental Health.

House, J. S., Landis, K. R., & Umberson, D. (1988). Social relationships and health. *Science, 241,* 540–545.

Hovland, C. I., Janis, I. L., & Kelley, H. H. (1953). *Communication and persuasion*. New Haven, CT: Yale University Press.

Hovland, C. I., Lumsdaine, A. A., & Sheffield, F. D. (1949). *Experiments on mass communication*. Princeton, NJ: Princeton University Press.

Hovland, C. I., Lumsdaine, A. A., & Sheffield, F. D. (1949). *Studies in social psychology in World War II—Vol. 3, Experiments in mass communication*. Princeton, NJ: Princeton University Press.

Howard, A., Pion, G. M., Gottfredson, G. O., Flattau, P. E., Oskamp, S., Pfafflin, S. M., Bray, D. W., & Burstein, A. G. (1986). The changing face of American psychology: A report from the committee of employment and human resources. *American Psychologist, 41,* 1311–1327.

Howard, D. T. (1928). A functional theory of emotions. In M. L. Reymert (Ed.), *Feelings and emotions: The Wittenberg Symposium* (pp. 140–149). Worcester, MA: Clark University Press.

Howard, K. I., Kopta, S. M., Krause, M. S., & Korlinsky, P. E. (1986). The dose-effect relationship in psychotherapy. *American Psychologist, 41,* 159–164.

Howarth, E., & Eysenck, H. J. (1968). Extroversion, arousal, and paired associate recall. *Journal of Experimental Research in Personality, 3,* 114–116.

Hrubec, Z., & Omenn, G. S. (1981). Evidence of genetic predisposition to alcoholic cirrhosis and psychosis: Twin concordance for alcoholism and its end points by zygosity among male veterans. *Alcoholism (NY), 5,* 207–215.

Hubel, D. (1990). In *Discovering Psychology*, Program 7 [PBS video series]. Washington, DC: Annenberg/CPB Project.

Hubel, D. H. (1979). The brain. *Scientific American, 241*(9), 45–53.

Hubel, D. H., & Wiesel, T. N. (1959). Receptive fields of single neurons in the cat's striate cortex. *Journal of Physiology (London), 148,* 574–591.

Hubel, D. H., & Wiesel, T. N. (1962). Receptive fields, binocular interaction, and functional architecture in the cat's visual cortex. *Journal of Physiology (London), 160,* 106–154.

Hubel, D. H., & Wiesel, T. N. (1979). Brain mechanisms of vision.

Scientific American, 241(9), 150–168.

Huesmann, L. R., & Malamuth, N. M. (Eds.). (1986). Media violence and antisocial behavior. *Journal of Social Issues, 42* (Whole issue).

Hughes, D., Johnson, K., Rosenbaum, S., Butler, E., & Simons, J. (1988). *The health of America's children: Maternal and child health data book*. Washington, DC: Children's Defense Fund.

Hughes, J., Smith, T. W., Kosterlitz, H. W., Fotergill, L. A., Morgan, B. A., & Morris, H. R. (1975). Identification of two related pentapeptides from the brain with potent opiate antagonist activity. *Nature, 258,* 577–579.

Hull, C. L. (1943). *Principles of behavior: An introduction to behavior theory*. New York: Appleton-Century-Crofts.

Hull, C. L. (1952). *A behavior system: An introduction to behavior theory concerning the individual organism*. New Haven, CT: Yale University Press.

Hultsch, D. F., & Dixon, R. A. (1984). Memory for text materials in adulthood. In P. Baltes & O. Brim (Eds.), *Life-span development and behavior* (Vol. 6, pp. 77–108). New York: Academic Press.

Hume, D. (1951). In L. A. Selby-Bigge (Ed.), *Inquiries concerning the human understanding and concerning the principles of morals*. London: Oxford University Press. (Original work published 1748)

Humphrey, N. K. (1976). The social function of intellect. In P. P. G. Bateson & R. A. Hinde (Eds.), *Growing points in ethology* (pp. 303–317). Cambridge, MA: Cambridge University Press.

Humphrey, T. (1970). The development of human fetal activity and its relation to postnatal behavior. In H. W. Reese & L. P. Lipsitt (Eds.), *Advance in child development and behavior* (Vol. 5). New York: Academic Press.

Hunt, E. (1983). On the nature of intelligence. *Science, 219,* 141–146.

Hunt, E. (1984). Intelligence and mental competence. *Naval Research Reviews, 36,* 37–42.

Hunt, M. (1985). *Profiles of social research: The scientific study of human interactions*. New York: Russell Sage Foundation.

Hunt, W. A., Matarazzo, J. D., Weiss, S. M., & Gentry, W. D. (1979). Associative learning, habit, and health behavior. *Journal of Behavioral Medicine, 2,* 111–123.

Hunter, F., & Youniss, J. (1982). Changes in functions of three relations during adolescence. *Developmental Psychology, 18,* 806–811.

Hunter, J. E., & Hunter, R. F. (1984). Validity and utility of alternative predictors of job performance. *Psychological Bulletin, 96,* 72–98.

Hurlburt, R. T. (1979). Random sampling of cognitions and behavior. *Journal of Research in Personality, 13,* 103–111.

Hurvich, L. M., & Jameson, D. (1957). An opponent process theory of color vision. *Psychological Review, 64,* 384–404.

Hutchins, D. (1961). The value of suggestion given under anesthesia. *American Journal of Clinical Hypnosis, 4,* 106–114.

Hyman, I. A., McDowell, E., & Raines, B. (1977). Corporal punishment and alternatives in the schools: An overview of theoretical and practical issues. In J. H. Wise (Ed.), *Proceedings: Conference on corporal punishment in the schools* (pp. 1–18). Washington, DC: National Institute of Education.

I

Ickes, W., Layden, M. A., & Barnes, R. D. (1978). Objective self-awareness and individuation: An empirical link. *Journal of Personality, 46,* 146–161.

Inglis, J., & Lawson, J. S. (1981). Sex differences in the effects of unilateral brain damage on intelligence. *Science, 212,* 693–695.

Insel, P. L., & Roth, W. T. (1985). *Core concepts in health*. Palo Alto, CA: Mayfield.

Insko, C. A., Smith, R. A., Alicke, M. D., Wade, J., & Taylor, S. (1985). Conformity and group size: The concern with being right and the concern with being liked. *Personality and Social Psychology Bulletin, 11,* 41–50.

Insko, C. A., Thibaut, J. W., Moehle, D., Wilson, M., Diamond, W. D., Gilmore, R., Solomon, M. R., & Lipsitz, A. (1980). Social evolution and the emergence of leadership. *Journal of*

Personality and Social Psychology, 39, 431–448.

Institute of Medicine, Division of Mental Health and Behavioral Medicine. (1989). *Prevention and treatment of alcohol problems: Research opportunities.* Washington, DC: National Academy Press.

Irwin, M., Daniels, M., Smith, T. L., Bloom, E., & Weiner, H. (1987). Impaired natural killer cell activity during bereavement. *Brain Behavior Immunology, 1,* 98–104.

Isen, A. (1984). Toward understanding the role of affect in cognition. In R. Wyer & T. Srull (Eds.), *Handbook of social cognition* (pp. 174–236). Hillsdale, NJ: Erlbaum.

Isen, A. M., Daubman, K. A., & Nowicki, G. P. (1987). Positive affect facilitates creative problem solving. *Journal of Personality and Social Psychology, 52,* 1122–1131.

Isen, A. M., Horn, N., & Rosenhan, D. L. (1973). Effects of success and failure on children's generosity. *Journal of Personality and Social Psychology, 27,* 239–247.

Itani, J. (1961). The society of Japanese monkeys. *Japan Quarterly, 8*(4), 421–430.

Itard, J. M. G. (1962). *The wild boy of Aveyron* (G. & M. Humphrey, Trans.). New York: Appleton-Century-Crofts.

Iversen, L. L. (1979). The chemistry of the brain. *Scientific American, 241*(9), 134–149.

Izard, C. (1971). *The face of emotion.* New York: Appleton-Century-Crofts.

Izard, C. E. (Ed.). (1982). *Measuring emotions in infants and children.* New York: Cambridge University Press.

Izard, C. E. (1990). The substrates and functions of emotion feelings: William James and current emotion theory. *Personality and Social Psychology Bulletin, 16,* 626–635.

J

Jacob, F. (1977). Evolution and tinkering. *Science, 196,* 161–166.

Jacobs, B. L. (1987). How hallucinogenic drugs work. *American Scientist, 75,* 386–392.

Jacobs, B. L., & Trulson, M. E. (1979). Mechanisms of action of L. S. D. *American Scientist, 67,* 396–404.

Jacobs, R. C., & Campbell, D. T. (1961). The perpetuation of an arbitrary tradition through several generations of a laboratory microculture. *Journal of Abnormal and Social Psychology, 62,* 649–658.

Jacobson, E. (1970). *Modern treatment of tense patients.* Springfield, IL: Charles C Thomas.

Jacoby, L. L., Baker, J. G., & Brooks, L. R. (1989). Episodic effects of picture identification: Implications for theories of learning and theories of memory. *Journal of Experimental Psychology: Learning, Memory & Cognition, 15,* 275–281.

James, J. (1953). The origin of guardian spirits of sweat lodge. As told to V. F. Ray in E. E. Clark, *Indian legends of the Pacific Northwest* (p. 183). Berkeley, CA: University of California Press.

James, W. (1884). What is an emotion? *Mind, 9,* 188–205.

James, W. (1890). *The principles of psychology* (2 vols.). New York: Holt, Rinehart & Winston.

Janerich, D. T., Thompson, W. D., Varela, L. R., Greenwald, P., Chorost, S., Tucci, C., Zaman, M. B., Melamed, M. R., Kiely, M., & McKneally, M. F. (1990). Lung cancer and exposure to tobacco smoke in the household. *The New England Journal of Medicine, 323,* 632–636.

Janis, I. (1990). In *Discovering Psychology,* Program 11 [PBS video series]. Washington, DC: Annenberg/CPB Project.

Janis, I. L. (1958). *Psychological stress.* New York: Wiley.

Janis, I. L. (1982a). Decisionmaking under stress. In L. Goldberger & S. Breznitz (Eds.), *Handbook of stress* (pp. 69–87). New York: Free Press.

Janis, I. L. (1982b). *Groupthink: Psychological studies of policy decisions and fiascoes* (2nd ed.). Boston: Houghton Mifflin.

Janis, I. L. (1985). International crisis management in the nuclear age. *Applied Social Psychology Annual, 6,* 63–86.

Janis, I. L., & Frick, F. (1943). The relationship between attitudes toward conclusions and errors in judging logical validity of syllogisms. *Journal of Experimental Psychology, 33,* 73–77.

Janowitz, H. D., & Grossman, M. I. (1950). Hunger and appetite:

Some definitions and concepts. *Journal of the Mount Sinai Hospital, 16,* 231–240.

Janz, N. K., & Becker, M. H. (1984). The health belief model: A decade later. *Health Education Quarterly, 11,* 1–47.

Jemmott, J. B., III, Croyle, R. T., & Ditto, P. H. (1988). Common sense epidemiology: Self-based judgments from lay persons and physicians. *Health Psychology, 7,* 55–73.

Jenkins, C. D. (1976). Recent evidence supporting psychologic and social risk factors for coronary disease. *New England Journal of Medicine, 294,* 987–994, 1033–1038.

Jenkins, J. G., & Dallenbach, K. M. (1924). Oblivescence during sleep and waking. *The American Journal of Psychology, 35,* 605–612.

Jenkins, J. J. (1979). Four points to remember: A tetrahedral model of memory experiments. In L. S. Cermak & F. I. M. Craik (Eds.), *Levels of processing in human memory* (pp. 429–446). Hillsdale, NJ: Erlbaum.

Jenni, D. A., & Jenni, M. A. (1976). Carrying behavior in humans: Analysis of sex differences: *Science, 194,* 859–860.

Jensen, A. R. (1962). Spelling errors and the serial position effect. *Journal of Educational Psychology, 53,* 105–109.

Jensen, A. R. (1973). *Educability and group differences.* New York: Harper & Row.

Jervis, R., Lebow, R. N., & Stein, J. G. (1985). *Psychology and deterrence.* Baltimore: Johns Hopkins University Press.

Jessor, R. (1982, May). Problem behavior and developmental transition in adolescence. *Journal of School Health,* pp. 295–300.

Johanson, C., & Fischman, M. (1989). The pharmacology of cocaine related to its abuse. *Pharmacological Reviews, 41,* 3–52.

John, E. R. (1990). In *Discovering Psychology,* Program 3 [PBS video series]. Washington, DC: Annenberg/CPB Project.

John, E. R., Prichep, L. S., Fridman, J., & Easton, P. (1988). Neurometrics: Computer-assisted differential diagnosis of brain dysfunction. *Science, 239,* 162–169.

John, O. P. (1990). The "Big Five" factor taxonomy: Dimensions of personality in the natural language and in questionnaires. In L. A. Pervin (Ed.), *Handbook of personality theory and research* (pp. 67–100). New York: Guilford Press.

Johnson, G. B. (1966). Penis envy or pencil hoarding? *Psychological Reports, 19,* 758.

Johnson, J. E. (1983). Psychological interventions and coping with surgery. In A. Baum, S. E. Taylor, & J. E. Singer (Eds.), *Handbook of psychology and health* (Vol. 4). Hillsdale, NJ: Erlbaum.

Johnson, J. H., & Sarason, I. B. (1979). Recent developments in research on life stress. In V. Hamilton & D. M. Warburton (Eds.), *Human stress and cognition: An information processing approach* (pp. 205–233). Chichester, England: Wiley.

Johnson, T. D., & Gottlieb, G. (1981). Visual preferences of imprinted ducklings are altered by the maternal call. *Journal of Comparative and Physiological Psychology, 95*(5), 665–675.

Johnson-Laird, P. (1983). *Mental models.* Cambridge, England: Cambridge University Press.

Johnson-Laird, P. N., & Byrne, R. M. J. (1989). Only reasoning. *Journal of Memory and Language, 28,* 313–330.

Johnston, J., & Dark, V. (1986). Selective Attention. *Annual Review of Psychology, 37,* 43–75.

Johnston, L. D., Bachman, J. G., & O'Malley, P. M. (1982). *Student drug use, attitudes and beliefs: National trends 1975–1982.* Rockville, MD: National Institute on Drug Abuse.

Johnston, L. D., O'Malley, P. M., & Bachman, J. G. (1989). *Drug use, drinking, and smoking: National survey results from high school, college, and young adult populations, 1975–1988.* Rockville, MD: U.S. Department of Health and Human Services.

Jones, B. M., & Jones, M. K. (1976). Male and female intoxication levels for three alcohol doses or do women really get higher than men? *Alcoholism Technical Report, 5,* 11–14.

Jones, E. (1953). *The life and works of Sigmund Freud.* New York: Basic Books.

Jones, E. (1990). In *Discovering Psychology,* Program 22 [PBS video series]. Washington, DC: Annenberg/CPB Program.

Jones, E. E. (1985). Major developments in social psychology during the last five decades. In G. Lindzey & E. Aronson (Eds.), *The* *handbook of social psychology* (Vol. 1, pp. 47–107). New York: Random House.

Jones, E. E., & Berglas, S. (1978). Control of attributions about the self through self-handicapping strategies: The appeal of alcohol and the role of underachievement. *Personality and Social Psychology Bulletin, 4,* 200–206.

Jones, E. E., & Davis, K. E. (1965). From acts to dispositions: The attribution process in person perception. In L. Berkowitz (Ed.), *Advances in experimental social psychology* (Vol. 2). New York: Academic Press.

Jones, E. E., & Nisbett, R. E. (1972). The actor and the observer: Divergent perceptions on the causes of behavior. In E. E. Jones et al. (Eds.), *Attribution: Perceiving the causes of behavior.* Morristown, NJ: General Learning Press.

Jones, E. E., & Pittman, T. (1982). Toward a general theory of strategic self-presentation. In J. Suls (Ed.), *Psychological perspectives on the self* (pp. 231–262). Hillsdale, NJ: Erlbaum.

Jones, E. E., Farina, A., Hastod, A. H., Markus, H., Miller, D. T., & Scott, R. A. (1984). *Social stigma: The psychology of marked relationships.* New York: Freeman.

Jones, M. C. (1924). A laboratory study of fear: The case of Peter. *Pedagogical Seminary and Journal of Genetic Psychology, 31,* 308–315.

Jones, R. (1978). The third wave. In A. Pines & C. Maslach (Eds.), *Experiencing social psychology.* New York: Knopf.

Jones, S. S., Collins, K., & Hong, H. W. (1991). An audience effect on smile production in 10-month-old infants. *Psychological Science, 2,* 45–49.

Jones, W., Cheek, J. M., & Briggs, S. R. (1986). *Shyness: Perspectives on research and treatment.* New York: Plenum.

Jordan, T. G., Grallo, R., Deutsch, M., & Deutsch, C. P. (1985). Long-term effects of enrichment: A 20-year perspective on persistence and change. *American Journal of Community Psychology, 13,* 393–414.

Joyce, L. (1989, Fall). Good genes, bad genes. *Stanford Medicine,* pp. 18–23.

Joyce, L. (1990, Fall). Losing the connection. *Stanford Medicine,* pp. 19–21.

Joyce, L. (1990, Winter). Fast Asleep. *Stanford Medicine,* pp. 28–31.

Julesz, B. (1981). Figure and ground perception in briefly presented isodipole textures. In M. Kubovy & J. R. Pomerantz (Eds.), *Perceptual organization* (pp. 27–54). Hillsdale, NJ: Erlbaum.

Julesz, B. (1981). Textons, the elements of texture perception and their interaction. *Nature, 290,* 91–97.

Jung, C. G. (1953). *Collected works.* New York: Bollingen Series/Pantheon.

Jung, C. G. (1959). The concept of the collective unconscious. In *The archetypes and the collective unconscious, collected works* (Vol. 9, Part 1, pp. 54–74). Princeton, NJ: Princeton University Press. (Original work published 1936)

Jung, C. G. (1965). *Memories, dreams, reflections.* New York: Random House.

Jung, C. G. (1971). Psychological types [Bollingen Series XX]. *The collected works of C. G. Jung* (Vol. 6). Princeton: Princeton University Press. (Original work published 1923)

Jung, C. G. (1973). *Memories, dreams, reflections* (Rev. ed., A. Jaffe, Ed.). New York: Pantheon Books.

Just, H. A., & Carpenter, P. A. (1981). Cognitive processes in reading: Models based on reader's eye fixations. In C. A. Prefetti & A. M. Lesgold (Eds.), *Interactive processes and reading.* Hillsdale, NJ: Erlbaum.

K

Kagan, J. (1990). In *Discovering Psychology,* Program 5 [PBS video series]. Washington, DC: Annenberg/CPB Project.

Kagan, J., & Klein, R. E. (1973). Cross-cultural perspectives on early development. *American Psychologist, 28,* 947–961.

Kagan, J., & Snidman, N. (1991). Infant predictors of inhibited and uninhibited profiles. *Psychological Science, 2,* 40–44.

Kagan, J., Reznick, J. S., & Snidman, N. (1986). Temperamental inhibition in early childhood. In R. Plomin & J. Dunn (Eds.), *The study of temperament: Changes, continuites, and challenges.*

Hillsdale, NJ: Erlbaum.

Kahn, M. (1966). The physiology of catharsis. *Journal of Personality and Social Psychology, 3,* 278–286.

Kahneman, D. (1973). *Attention and effort.* Englewood Cliffs, NJ: Prentice-Hall.

Kahneman, D. (1990). In *Discovering Psychology,* Program 11 [PBS video series]. Washington, DC: Annenberg/CPB Project.

Kahneman, D., & Snell, J. (1990). Predicting utility. In R. Hogarth (Ed.), *Insights in decision making.* Chicago: University of Chicago Press.

Kahneman, D., & Treisman, A. (1984). Changing views of attention and automaticity. In R. Parasuraman, D. R. Davies, & J. Beatty (Eds.), *Varieties of attention* (pp. 29–61). New York: Academic Press.

Kahneman, D., & Tversky, A. (1973). On the psychology of prediction. *Psychological Review, 80,* 237–251.

Kahneman, D., Slovic, P., & Tversky, A. (Eds.). (1982). *Judgment under uncertainty: Heuristics and biases.* Cambridge, MA: Cambridge University Press.

Kaij, L. (1960). *Alcoholism in twins. Studies on the etiology and sequelae of abuse of alcohol.* Stockholm, Sweden: Alonquist & Winkell Publishers.

Kalat, J. W. (1974). Taste salience depends on novelty, not concentration in taste-aversion learning in the rat. *Journal of Comparative and Physiological Psychology, 86,* 47–50.

Kalat, J. W. (1984). *Biological psychology.* (2nd ed.). Belmont, CA: Wadsworth.

Kalin, N. H., & Shelton, S. E. (1989). Defensive behaviors in infant rhesus monkeys: Environmental cues and neurochemical regulation. *Science, 243,* 1718–1721.

Kalish, R. A. (1985). The social context of death and dying. In R. H. Binstock & E. Shanas (Eds.), *Handbook of aging and the social sciences* (pp. 149–172). New York: Van Nostrand Reingold.

Kallmann, F. J. (1946). The genetic theory of schizophrenia: An analysis of 691 schizophrenic index families. *American Journal of Psychiatry, 103,* 309–322.

Kamin, L. J. (1969). Predictability, surprise, attention, and conditioning. In B. A. Campbell & R. M. Church (Eds.), *Classical conditioning: A symposium.* New York: Appleton-Century-Crofts.

Kamin, L. J. (1974). *The science and politics of IQ.* Potomac, MD: Erlbaum.

Kandel, D. (1973). Adolescent marijuana use: Role of parents and peers. *Science, 181,* 1067–1070.

Kandel, E. R. (1976). *The cellular basis of behavior.* San Francisco: Freeman.

Kandel, E. R. (1979). Cellular insights into behavior and learning. *The Harvey Lectures,* Series 73, 29–92.

Kanigel, R. (1981). Storing yesterday. *Johns Hopkins Magazine, 32,* 27–34.

Kanizsa, G. (1979). *Organization in vision.* New York: Praeger.

Kaplan, J. (1983). *The hardest drug: Heroin and public policy.* Chicago: University of Chicago Press.

Kaplan, J. (1988). The use of animals in research. *Science, 242,* 839–840.

Kaplan, R. M. (1985). The controversy related to the use of psychological tests. In B. B. Wolman (Ed.), *Handbook of intelligence* (pp. 465–504). New York: Wiley.

Kaplan, R. M. (1990). Behavior as the central outcome in health care. *American Psychologist, 45,* 1211–1220.

Karlsson, J. L. (1978). *Inheritance of creative intelligence.* Chicago: Nelson-Hall.

Karon, B. P., & Vandenbos, G. R. (1981). *Psychotherapy of schizophrenia: The treatment of choice.* New York: Jason Aronson.

Kasl, S. V., & Cobb, S. (1966). Health behavior and illness behavior: I. Health and illness behavior. *Archives of Environmental Health, 12,* 246–266.

Kastenbaum, R. (1986). *Death, society, and the human experience.* Columbus, OH: Merrill.

Kaufman, L., & Rock, I. (1962). The moon illusion. *Scientific American, 207*(7), 120–130.

Kaufmann, Y. (1984). Analytical psychotherapy. In R. J. Corsini &

Contributors (Eds.), *Current psychotherapies* (3rd ed., pp. 108–126). Itasca, IL: Peacock.

Kaushall, P. I., Zetin, M., & Squire, L. R. (1981). A psychological study of chronic, circumscribed amnesia: Detailed report of a noted case. *Journal of Nervous and Mental Disorders, 169,* 383–389.

Kay, D. W. K., & Bergman, K. (1982). Epidemiology of mental disorders among the aged in the community. In J. E. Birren & R. B. Sloane (Eds.), *Handbook of mental health and aging* (pp. 34–56). Englewood Cliffs, NJ: Prentice-Hall.

Kazdin, A. E. (1980). *Behavior modification in applied settings* (2nd ed.). Homewood, IL: Dorsey.

Kazdin, A. E. (1982). The token economy: A decade later. *Journal of Applied Behavior Analysis, 15,* 431–445.

Kazdin, A. E. (1986). Comparative outcome studies of psychotherapy: Methodological issues and strategies. *Journal of Consulting and Clinical Psychology, 54,* 95–105.

Kazdin, A. E., & Wilcoxin, L. A. (1976). Systematic desensitization and nonspecific treatment effects: A methodological evaluation. *Psychological Bulletin, 83,* 729–758.

Kazdin, A. E., & Wilson, G. T. (1980). *Evaluation of behavior therapy: Issues, evidence, and research strategies.* Lincoln: University of Nebraska Press.

Keane, T. M., Zimering, R. T., & Caddell, J. M. (1985). A behavioral approach to assessing and treating post-traumatic stress disorder in Vietnam veterans. In C. R. Figley (Ed.), *Trauma and its wake.* New York: Bruner/Mazel.

Keats, J. (1966). *Howard Hughes.* New York: Random House.

Keen, S. (1986). *Faces of the enemy: Reflections of the hostile imagination.* New York: Harper & Row.

Keesey, R. E., & Powley, T. L. (1975). Hypothalamic regulation of body weight. *American Scientist, 63,* 558–565.

Keller, H. (1902). *The Story of My Life.* New York: Doubleday, 1954.

Keller, H. (1990). In D. Ackerman, *A Natural History of the Senses.* New York: Random House.

Kelley, H. H. (1967). Attribution theory in social psychology. In D. Levine (Ed.), *Nebraska Symposium on Motivation* (Vol. 15). Lincoln, NE: University of Nebraska Press.

Kelley, H. H. (1971a). *Attribution: Perceiving the causes of behavior.* New York: General Learning Press.

Kelley, H. H. (1971b). Attribution in social interaction. In E. E. Jones, D. E. Kanouse, H. H. Kelley, R. E. Nisbett, S. Valins, & B. Weiner (Eds.), *Attribution: Perceiving the causes of behavior.* New York: General Learning Press.

Kelley, H. H., & Thibaut, J. W. (1978). *Interpersonal relations: A theory of interdependence.* New York: Wiley-Interscience.

Kellman, P. J., & Spelke, E. S. (1983). Perception of partly occluded objects in infancy. *Cognitive Psychology, 15,* 483–524.

Kelly, G. A. (1955). *A theory of personality: The psychology of personal constructs* (2 vols.). New York: Norton.

Kelman, H. C., & Hamilton, L. (1989). *Crimes of obedience: Toward a social psychology of authority and responsibility.* New Haven, CT: Yale University Press.

Kelsoe, J. R., Ginns, E. I., Egeland, J. A., Gerhard, D. S., Goldstein, A. M., Bale, S. J., Pauls, D. L., Long, R. T., Kidd, K. K., Conte, G., Housman, D. E., & Paul, S. M. (1989). Re-evaluation of the linkage relationship between chromosome 11p loci and the gene for bipolar affective disorder in the Old Order Amish. *Nature, 342,* 238–243.

Kemp, M. (1990). *The science of art: Optical themes in Western art from Brunelleschi to Seurat.* New Haven: Yale University Press.

Kennedy, G. C. (1953). The role of depot fat in the hypothalamic control of food intake in the rat. *Proceedings of the Royal Society, 140* (Series B), 578–592.

Kennedy, S., Kiecolt-Glaser, J. K., & Glaser, R. (1988). Immunological consequences of acute and chronic stressors: The mediating role of interpersonal relationships. *British Journal of Medical Psychology, 61,* 77.

Kesey, K. (1962). *One flew over the cuckoo's nest.* New York: Viking Press.

Kessen, S., & Cahan, E. D. (1986). A century of psychology: From subject to object to agent. *American Scientist, 74,* 640–649.

Kessler, S. (1980). The genetics of schizophrenia: A review. In S. J. Keith & L. R. Mosher (Eds.), *Special report: Schizophrenia, 1980* (pp. 14–26). Washington, DC: U.S. Government Printing Office.

Kett, J. F. (1977). *Rites of passage: Adolescence in America, 1790 to present.* New York: Basic Books.

Kety, S. S., Rosenthal, D., Wender, P. H., Schulsinger, F., & Jacobsen, B. (1975). Mental illness in the biological and adoptive families of adopted individuals who have become schizophrenic: A preliminary report based on psychiatric interviews. In R. R. Fieve, D. Rosenthal, & H. Brill (Eds.), Genetic research in psychiatry (pp. 147–165). Baltimore: Johns Hopkins University Press.

Kiecolt-Glaser, J. K., Glaser, R., Shuttleworth, E. C., Dyer, C. S., Ogrocki, P., & Speicher, C. E. (1987). Chronic stress and immunity in family caregivers of Alzheimer's disease victims. *Psychosomatic Medicine, 49,* 523–535.

Kierulff, S. (1989, March). *Conversation with a demon.* Symposium conducted at the meeting of the California State Psychological Association, San Francisco, CA.

Kiester, E., Jr. (1980, May). Images of the night: The physiologial roots of dreaming. Sleep research. In A. L. Hammond & P. G. Zimbardo (Eds.), *Readings in human behavior: The best of Science 80–86* (pp. 8–15). Glenview, IL: Scott, Foresman.

Kihlstrom, J. F. (1985). The cognitive unconscious. *Science, 237,* 1445–1452.

Kihlstrom, J. F., & Harackiewicz, J. M. (1982). The earliest recollection: A new survey. *Journal of Personality, 50,* 134–148.

Kihlstrom, J. F., Schacter, D. L., Cork, R. C., Hurt, C. A., & Behr, S. E. (1990). Implicit and explicit memory following surgical anesthesia. *Psychological Science, 1,* 303–306.

Kimmel, D. C., & Weiner, I. B. (1985). *Adolescence: A developmental transition.* Hillsdale, NJ: Erlbaum.

Kimura, D. (1985, November). Male brain, female brain: The hidden difference. *Psychology Today,* pp. 50–58.

King, R. J. (1986). Motivational diversity and mesolimbic dopamine: A hypothesis concerning temperaments. In R. Plutchik & H. Kellerman (Eds.), *Emotion: Theory, research, and experience: Biological foundations of emotions* (Vol. 3, pp. 363–380). Orlando, FL: Academic Press.

King, R. J., Mefford, I. N., Wang, C., Murchison, A., Caligari, E. J., & Berger, P. A. (1986). CSF dopamine levels correlate with extraversion in depressed patients. *Psychiatry Research, 19,* 305–310.

Kinsey, A. C., Martin, C. E., & Pomeroy, W. B. (1948). *Sexual behavior in the human male.* Philadelphia: Saunders.

Kinsey, A. C., Pomeroy, W. B., Martin, C. E., & Gebhard, R. H. (1953). *Sexual behavior in the human female.* Philadelphia: Saunders.

Kintsch, W. (1974). *The representation of meaning in memory.* Hillsdale, NJ: Erlbaum.

Kintsch, W. (1981). Semantic memory: A tutorial. In R. S. Nickerson (Ed.), *Attention and performance* (Vol. 8). Hillsdale, NJ: Erlbaum.

Kipnis, D. (1991). The technological perspective. *Psychological Science, 2,* 62–69.

Klag, M. J., Whelton, P. K., Grim, C. E., & Kuller, L. H. (1991). The association of skin color with blood pressure in U.S. blacks with low socioeconomic status. *Journal of the American Medical Association, 265,* 599–602.

Klatzky, R. (1980). *Human memory: Structures and processes* (2nd ed.). San Francisco: Freeman.

Klaus, M., & Kennel, J. (1976). *Maternal-infant bonding.* St. Louis, MO: Mosby.

Klein, D. C., & Goldston, S. E. (Eds.). (1977). *Primary prevention: An idea whose time has come.* Washington, DC: U.S. Government Printing Office.

Klein, G. (1970). *Perception, motives, and personality.* New York: Knopf.

Klein, G. S., & Schlesinger, H. J. (1949). Where is the perceiver in perceptual theory? *Journal of Personality, 18,* 32–47.

Klein, R. H. (1983). Group treatment approaches. In M. Hersen, A. E. Kazdin, & A. S. Bellack (Eds.), *The clinical psychology handbook.* New York: Pergamon Press.

Kleinginna, P. R., & Kleinginna, A. M. (1981). A categorized list of motivation definitions with a suggestion for a consensual definition. *Motivation and Emotion, 5,* 263–291.

Kleinke, C. L. (1986). Gaze and eye contact: A research review. *Psychological Bulletin, 100,* 78–100.

Kleinmuntz, B., & Szucko, J. J. (1984). Lie detection in ancient and modern times: A call for contemporary scientific study. *American Psychologist, 39,* 766–776.

Klerman, G. L. (1986). Historical perspectives on contemporary schools of psychopathology. In T. Millon & G. L. Klerman (Eds.), *Contemporary directions in psychopathology: Toward the DSM-IV* (pp. 3–28). New York: Guilford Press.

Klerman, G. L., Weissman, M. M., & Rounsaville, E. S. (1984). *Interpersonal psychotherapy of depression.* New York: Basic.

Klinger, E. (1987, May). The power of daydreams. *Psychology Today,* pp. 37–44.

Klinnert, M. D., Campos, J. J., Sorce, J. F., Emde, R. N., & Svejda, M. (1983). Emotions as behavioral regulators: Social referencing in infancy. In R. Plutchik & H. Kellerman (Eds.), *Emotion: Theory, research, and experience* (Vol. 2, pp. 57–86). New York: Academic Press.

Kluckhorn, C. (1944). Navaho Witchcraft. *Papers of the Yale University Peabody Museum* (Vol. 24, No. 2). New Haven, CT: Yale University.

Knox, V. J., Morgan, A. H., & Hilgard, E. R. (1974). Pain and suffering in ischemia: The paradox of hypnotically suggested anesthesia as contradicted by reports from the "hidden observer." *Archives of General Psychiatry, 30,* 840–847.

Kobasa, S. O. (1984). How much stress can you survive? *American Health, 3,* 64–77.

Kobasa, S. O., Hilker, R. R., & Maddi, S. R. (1979). Who stays healthy under stress? *Journal of Occupational Medicine, 21,* 595–598.

Kobre, K. R., & Lipsitt, L. P. (1972). A negative contrast effect in newborns. *Journal of Experimental Child Psychology, 2,* 81–91.

Koch, R., Graliker, B., Fishler, K., & Ragsdale, N. (1963). Clinical aspects of phenylketonuria. In *First Inter-American Conference on Congenital Defects.* Philadelphia: Lippincott.

Koch, S., & Leary, D. E. (1985). *A century of psychology as science.* New York: McGraw-Hill.

Koestler, A. (1964). *The act of creation.* London: Hutchinson.

Koffka, K. (1935). *Principles of Gestalt psychology.* New York: Harcourt Brace.

Koh, S. O., & Peterson, R. A. (1974). A perceptual memory for numerousness in "nonpsychotic schizophrenics." *Journal of Abnormal Psychology, 83,* 215–226.

Kohlberg, L. (1964). Development of moral character and moral ideology. In M. L. Hoffman & L. W. Hoffman (Eds.), *Review of child development research* (Vol. 1). New York: Russell Sage Foundation.

Kohlberg, L. (1966). A cognitive-developmental analysis of children's sex-role concepts and attitudes. In E. E. Maccoby (Ed.), *The development of sex differences.* Stanford, CA: Stanford University Press.

Kohlberg, L. (1967). Moral and religious education and the public schools: A developmental view. In T. Sizer (Ed.), *Religion and public education.* Boston: Houghton Mifflin.

Kohlberg, L. (1969). Stage and sequence: The cognitive-developmental approach to socialization. In D. A. Goslin (Ed.), *Handbook of socialization theory and research.* Chicago: Rand McNally.

Kohlberg, L. (1981). *The philosophy of moral development.* New York: Harper & Row.

Köhler, W. (1925). *The mentality of apes.* New York: Harcourt Brace Jovanovich.

Köhler, W. (1947). *Gestalt psychology.* New York: Liveright.

Kohut, H. (1977). *The restoration of the self.* New York: International Universities Press.

Kolata, G. (1985). Why do people get fat? *Science, 227,* 1327–1328.

Kolata, G. (1986). Maleness pinpointed on Y chromosomes. *Science, 234,* 1076–1077.

Kolb, B. (1989). Development, plasticity, and behavior. *American Psychologist, 44,* 1203–1212.

Kolb, L. C. (1973). *Modern clinical psychiatry.* Philadelphia: Saunders.

Kondo, T., Antrobus, J., & Fein, G. (1989). Later REM activation and sleep mentation. *Sleep Research, 18,* 147.

Konecni, V. J., & Ebbesen, E. B. (1984). The mythology of legal decision making. *International Journal of Law and Psychiatry, 7,* 5–18.

Konecni, V. J., & Ebbesen, E. B. (1986). Courtroom testimony by psychologists on eyewitness identification issues: Critical notes and reflections. *Law and Human Behavior, 10,* 117–126.

Konner, M. J. (1977). Research reported in J. Greenberg, The brain and emotions. *Science News, 112,* 74–75.

Korchin, S. J. (1976). *Modern clinical psychology.* New York: Basic Books.

Korn, J. (1987). Judgments of acceptability of deception in psychological research. *Journal of General Psychology, 114,* 205–216.

Korn, J. W. (1985). Psychology as a humanity. *Teaching of Psychology, 12,* 188–193.

Kosecoff, J. B., & Fink, A. (1982). *Evaluation basics: A practitioner's manual.* Beverly Hills, CA: Sage Publications.

Koslow, S. H. (1984). Preface. In *The neuroscience of mental health: A report on neuroscience research* (DHHS Publication No. ADM 84–1363). Rockville, MD: National Institute of Mental Health.

Koss, M. P. (1985). The hidden rape victim: Personality, attitudinal, and situational characteristics. *Psychology of Women Quarterly, 9,* 193–212.

Koss, M. P., & Oros, C. J. (1982). Sexual experiences survey: A research instrument investigating sexual aggression and victimization. *Journal of Consulting and Clinical Psychology, 50,* 455–457.

Kosslyn, S. M. (1980). *Image and mind.* Cambridge, MA: Harvard University Press.

Kosslyn, S. M. (1983). *Ghosts in the mind's machine: Creating and using images in the brain.* New York: Norton.

Kosslyn, S. M. (1985). Computational neuropsychology: A new perspective on mental imagery. *Naval Research Reviews, 37,* 30–50.

Kosslyn, S. M., Holtzman, J. D., Farah, M. J., & Gazzaniga, M. S. (1985). A computational analysis of mental image generation: Evidence from functional dissociations in split-brain patients. *Journal of Experimental Psychology: General, 114,* 311–341.

Kraft, C. L. (1978). A psychophysical contribution to air safety: Simulator studies of visual illusions in night visual approaches. In H. Pick, H. W. Leibowitz, J. R. Singer, A. Steinschneider, & H. W. Stevenson (Eds.), *Psychology from research to practice* (pp. 363–385). New York: Plenum.

Kraft, D. P. (1984). A comprehensive prevention program for college students. In P. M. Miller & T. D. Nirenberg (Eds.), *Prevention of Alcohol Abuse.* New York: Plenum.

Krajick, K. (1990, July 30). Sound too good to be true? Behind the boom in subliminal tapes. *Newsweek,* p. 61.

Krasner, L. (1985). Applications of learning theory in the environment. In B. L. Hammonds (Ed.), *Psychology and learning: 1984 master lecturers* (pp. 51–93). Washington, DC: American Psychological Association.

Kraus, S. (1990). The power of pain. *Stanford Medicine, 8,* pp. 5–8.

Kraut, A. M. (1990). Healers and strangers: Immigrant attitudes toward the physician in America —A relationship in historical perspective. *Journal of the American Medical Association, 263,* 1807–1811.

Kreitler, S., & Kreitler, H. (1990a). Cognitive orientation and sexual dysfunctions in women. *Annals of Sex Research, 3,* 75–104.

Kreitler, S., & Kreitler, H. (1990b). Repression and the anxiety-defensiveness factor: Psychological correlates and manifestations. *Personality and Individual Differences, 11,* 559–570.

Kreitler, S., & Kreitler, H. (1990c). *The cognitive orientation of health and susceptibility to illness in college students.* Unpublished manuscript, Psychology Department, University of Tel Aviv, Tel Aviv.

Kreitler, S., & Kreitler, H. (1991). The psychological profile of the health-oriented individual. *European Journal of Personality, 5,*

35–60.

Krieger, L., & Garrison, J. (1991, August 4). Hospitals praised for AIDS care. *San Francisco Examiner*, p. B-2.

Krieger, L. M. (1990, October 12). Huh? I can't hear you. *San Francisco Examiner*, pp. D16–D17.

Kristjansson, E. A., Fried, P. A., & Watkinson, B. (1989). Maternal smoking during pregnancy affects children's vigilance performance. *Drug and Alcohol Dependence, 24,* 11–19.

Kubler-Ross, E. (1969). *On death and dying.* Toronto: Macmillan.

Kubler-Ross, E. (1975). *Death: The final stage of growth.* Englewood Cliffs, NJ: Prentice-Hall.

Kubovy, M., & Pomerantz, J. R. (Eds.). (1981). *Perceptual Organization.* Hillsdale, NJ: Erlbaum.

Kuffler, S. W., Nicholls, J. G., & Martin, A. R. (1984). *From neuron to brain: A cellular approach to the function of the nervous system* (2nd ed.). Sunderland, MA: Sinauer Associates.

Kuhn, T. S. (1970). *The structure of scientific revolutions* (2nd ed.). Chicago: University of Chicago Press.

Kuklick, H. (1987). The testing movement and its founders. *Science, 237,* 1358–1359.

Kulik, J. A. (1983). Confirmatory attribution and the perpetuation of social beliefs. *Journal of Personality and Social Psychology, 44,* 1171–1181.

Kulik, J. A., & Mahler, H. I. M. (1989). Social support and recovery from surgery. *Health Psychology, 8,* 221–238.

Kunda, Z. (1990). The case for motivated reasoning. *Psychological Bulletin, 108,* 480–498.

Kupfermann, I. et al. (1974). Local, reflex, and central commands controlling gill and siphon movements in Aplysia. *Journal of Neurophysiology, 37,* 996–1019.

Kurtines, W., & Greif, E. B. (1974). The development of moral thought: Review and evaluation of Kohlberg's approach. *Psychological Bulletin, 8,* 453–470.

Kutas, M., & Hillyard, S. A. (1980). Reading senseless sentences: Brain potentials reflect semantic incongruity. *Science, 207,* 203–205.

L

LaBarre, W. (1964). Confessions as psychotherapy in American Indian tribes. In A. Kiev (Ed.), *Magic, faith and healing.* New York: Free Press.

LaBerge, S. (1986). *Lucid dreaming.* New York: Valentine Books.

LaBerge, S. (1990). In *Discovering Psychology*, Program 13 [PBS video series]. Washington, DC: Annenberg/CPB Program.

LaBerge, S., & Rheingold, H. (1990). *Exploring the world of lucid dreaming.* New York: Ballantine.

LaBerge, S. P., Nagel, L. E., Dement, W. C., & Zarcone, V. P., Jr. (1981). Evidence for lucid dreaming during REM sleep. *Sleep Research, 10,* 148.

Labouvie-Vief, G. (1985). Intelligence and cognition. In J. E. Birren, & K. W. Schaie (Eds.), *Handbook of the psychology of aging* (2nd ed., pp. 500–530). New York: Van Nostrand Reingold.

Lachman, R., & Naus, M. (1984). The episodic/semantic continuum in an evolved machine. *Behavioral and Brain Sciences, 7,* 244–246.

Lachman, R., Lachman, J. L., & Butterfield, E. C. (1979). *Cognitive psychology and information processing: An introduction.* Hillsdale, NJ: Erlbaum.

Lachman, S. (1983). The concept of learning: Connecting and selecting. *Academic Psychology Bulletin, 5,* 155–166.

Lachman, S. J. (1983). A physiological interpretation of voodoo illness and voodoo death. *Omega, 13*(4), 345–360.

Lackner, J. R., & Garrett, M. (1973). Resolving ambiguity: Effects of biasing context in the unattended ear. *Cognition, 1,* 359–372.

LaFramboise, T. (1988, March 30). Suicide prevention. In *Campus Report* (p. 9). Stanford, CA: Stanford University.

LaFramboise, T. (1990). In *Discovering Psychology*, Program 21 [PBS video series]. Washington, DC: Annenberg/CPB Program.

Laing, R. D. (1965). *The divided self.* Baltimore: Penguin.

Laing, R. D. (1967). *The politics of experience.* New York: Pantheon.

Laing, R. D. (1967, February 3). Schizophrenic split. *Time*, p. 56.

Laing, R. D. (1970). *Knots.* New York: Pantheon.

Laird, J. D., & Bresler, C. (1990). William James and the mechanisms of emotional experience. *Personality and Social Psychology Bulletin, 16,* 636–651.

Lambert, A. J. (1985). Selectivity and stages of processing: An enduring controversy in attentional theory: A review. *Current Psychological Research and Reviews, 4,* 239–256.

Lambert, N. M. (1981). Psychological evidence in Larry P. versus Wilson Riles. *American Psychologist, 36,* 937–952.

Lambo, T. A. (1978). Psychotherapy in Africa. *Human Nature, 1*(3), 32–39.

Lane, H. (1976). *The wild boy of Aveyron.* Cambridge, MA: Harvard University Press.

Lane, H. (1986). The wild boy of Aveyron and Dr. Jean-Marc Itard. *History of Psychology, 17,* 3–16.

Lang, P. J. (1979). A bio-informational theory of emotional imagery. *Psychophysiology, 16,* 495–512.

Lang, P. J., & Lazovik, D. A. (1963). The experimental desensitization of a phobia. *Journal of Abnormal and Social Psychology, 66,* 519–525.

Langer, E. (1978). Rethinking the role of thought in social interaction. In J. H. Harvey, W. J. Ickes, & R. F. Kidd (Eds.), *New directions in attribution research* (Vol. 2, pp. 35–38). Hillsdale, NJ: Erlbaum.

Langer, E. (1989). *Mindfulness.* Reading, MA: Addison-Wesley.

Langer, E. (1990). In *Discovering Psychology*, Program 19 [PBS video series]. Washington, DC: Annenberg/CPB Program.

Langer, E. J. (1975). The illusion of control. *Journal of Personality and Social Psychology, 32,* 311–328.

Langer, E. J., & Rodin, J. (1976). The effects of choice and enhanced personal responsibility for the aged: A field experiment in an institutional setting. *Journal of Personality and Social Psychology, 34,* 191–198.

Langlois, J. H., & Downs, A. C. (1980). Mothers, fathers and peers as socialization agents of sex-typed play behaviors in young children. *Child Development, 51,* 1237–1247.

Langlois, J. H., & Roggman, L. A. (1991). Attractive faces are only average. *Psychological Science, 1,* 115–121.

Langs, R. (Ed.). (1981). *Classics in psychoanalytic technique.* New York: Jason Aronson.

Lanzetta, J. T., Sullivan, D. G., Masters, R. G., & McHugo, G. J. (1985). Viewers' emotional and cognitive responses to televised images of political leaders. In S. Kraus & R. M. Perloff (Eds.), *Mass media and political thought: An information processing approach* (pp. 50–67). Beverly Hills, CA: Sage.

La Piere, R. (1934). Attitudes versus actions. *Social Forces, 13,* 230–237.

Lashley, K. S. (1929). *Brain mechanisms and intelligence.* Chicago: University of Chicago Press.

Lashley, K. S. (1950). In search of the engram. In *Physiological mechanisms in animal behavior: Symposium of the Society for Experimental Biology.* New York: Academic Press.

Lasswell, H. D. (1948). The structure and function of communication in society. In L. Bryson (Ed.), *Communication of ideas.* New York: Harper.

Latané, B. (1981). The psychology of social impact. *American Psychologist, 36,* 343–356.

Latané, B., & Darley, J. M. (1970). *The unresponsive bystander: Why doesn't he help?* New York: Appleton-Century-Crofts.

Latham, G. P., & Yukl, G. A. (1975). A review of research on the application of goal setting in organizations. *Academic Management Journal, 18,* 824–845.

Lau, R. R. (1989). Construct accessibility and electoral choice. *Political Behavior, 11,* 5–32.

Lau, R. R., Bernard, T. M., & Hartman, K. A. (1989). Further explorations of common sense representations of common illnesses. *Health Psychology, 8,* 195–219.

Laudenslager, M. L., Ryan, S. M., Drugan, R. C., Hyson, R. L., & Maier, S. F. (1983). Coping and immunosuppression: Inescapable but not escapable shock suppresses lymphocyte proliferation. *Science, 231,* 568–570.

Lawton, M. P. (1977). An ecological theory of aging applied to elderly housing. *Journal of Architecture and Education, 31,* 8–10.

Lazarus, R. S. (1966). *Psychological stress and the coping process.* New York: McGraw-Hill.

Lazarus, R. S. (1975). A cognitively oriented psychologist looks at biofeedback. *American Psychologist, 30,* 553–561.

Lazarus, R. S. (1976). *Patterns of adjustment* (3rd ed.). New York: McGraw-Hill.

Lazarus, R. S. (1981, July). Little hassles can be hazardous to your health. *Psychology Today,* pp. 58–62.

Lazarus, R. S. (1982). Thoughts on the relations between emotion and cognition. *American Psychologist, 37,* 1019–1024.

Lazarus, R. S. (1984). On the primacy of cognition. *American Psychologist, 39,* 124–129.

Lazarus, R. S. (1984). Puzzles in the study of daily hassles. *Journal of Behavioral Medicine, 7,* 375–389.

Lazarus, R. S. (1991). Progress on a cognitive-motivational-relational theory of emotion. *American Psychologist, 46,* 819–834.

Lazarus, R. S., & Folkman, S. (1984). *Stress, appraisal, and coping.* New York: Springer.

Leask, J., Haber, R. N., & Haber, R. B. (1969). Eidetic imagery in children: II. Longitudinal and experimental results. *Psychonomic Monograph Supplements, 3* (3, Whole No. 35).

LeBon, G. (1960). *The crowd.* New York: Viking Press. (Original work published 1895)

LeDoux, J. (1989). Cognitive-emotional interactions in the brain. *Cognition and Emotion, 3,* 267–289.

Le Doux, J. E., Wilson, D. H., & Gazzaniga, M. S. (1977). A divided mind: Observations on the conscious properties of the separated hemispheres. *Annals of Neurology, 2,* 417–421.

Lee, M., Zimbardo, P., & Bertholf, M. (1977, November). Shy murderers. *Psychology Today,* pp. 68–70, 76, 148.

Leeper, R. W. (1948). A motivational theory of emotion to replace "emotions as disorganized response." *Psychological Review, 55,* 5–21.

Leerhsen, C. (1990, February 5). Unite and conquer: America's crazy for support groups. *Newsweek,* pp. 50–55.

Leff, H. (1984). *Playful perception: Choosing how to experience your world.* Burlington, VT: Waterfront Books.

Leger, D. (1992). *Biological foundations of behavior: An integrative approach.* New York: HarperCollins.

Leiberman, M. A. (1982). The effects of social supports on responses to stress. In L. Goldberger & L. Bresnitz (Eds.), *Handbook of Stress* (pp. 764–783). New York: Free Press.

Leibowitz, H. W. (1988). The human senses in flight. In E. L. Wiener & D. C. Nagel (Eds.), *Human factors in aviation* (pp. 83–110). New York: Academic Press.

Leiter, M. P., & Maslach, C. (1988). The impact of interpersonal environment on burnout and organizational commitment. *Journal of Organizational Behavior, 9,* 297–308.

Lemert, E. M. (1962). Paranoia and the dynamics of exclusion. *Sociometry, 25,* 2–20.

Lenneberg, E. H. (1962). Understanding language without ability to speak: A case report. *Journal of Abnormal and Social Psychology, 65,* 415–419.

Lenneberg, E. H. (1969). On explaining language. *Science, 164,* 635–643.

Lennon, R. T. (1985). Group tests of intelligence. In B. B. Wolman (Ed.), *Handbook of intelligence* (pp. 825–847). New York: Wiley.

Leowontin, R. C., Rose, S., & Kamin, L. J. (1984). *Not in our genes: Biology, ideology, and human nature.* New York: Pantheon.

Lepper, M. R. (1981). Intrinsic and extrinsic motivation in children: Detrimental effects of superfluous social controls. In U. A. Collins (Ed.), *Aspects of the development of competence: The Minnesota Symposium on Child Psychology* (Vol. 14, pp. 155–214). Hillsdale, NJ: Erlbaum.

Lepper, M. R., & Greene, D. (Eds.). (1978). *The hidden costs of reward.* Hillsdale, NJ: Erlbaum.

Lepper, M. R., Greene, D., & Nisbett, R. E. (1973). Undermining children's intrinsic interest with extrinsic reward: A test of the overjustification hypothesis. *Journal of Personality and Social Psychology, 28*(1), 129–137.

Lerner, R. M., Orlos, J. R., & Knapp, J. (1976). Physical attractiveness, physical effectiveness and self-concept in adolescents. *Adolescence, 11,* 313–326.

Leslie, C., & Wingert, P. (1990, January 8). Not as easy as A, B, or C. *Newsweek,* pp. 56–58.

Lettvin, J. Y., Maturana, H. R., McCulloch, W. S., & Bitts, W. H. (1959). What the frog's eye tells the frog's brain. *Proceedings of the Institute of Radio Engineers, 47,* 1940–1951.

Levenson, R. W., Carstensen, L. L., Friesen, W. V., & Ekman, P. (1991). Emotion, physiology, and expression in old age. *Psychology and Aging, 6,* 28–35.

Leventhal, H. (1970). Findings and theory in the study of fear communications. In L. Berkowitz (Ed.), *Advances in experimental social psychology* (Vol. 5, pp. 120–186). New York: Academic Press.

Leventhal, H. (1980). Toward a comprehensive theory of emotion. In L. Berkowitz (Ed.), *Advances in experimental social psychology* (Vol. 13, pp. 139–207). New York: Academic Press.

Leventhal, H. (1984). A perceptual motor theory of emotion. In K. R. Scherer & P. Ekman (Eds.), *Approaches to emotion* (pp. 271–291). Hillsdale, NJ: Erlbaum.

Leventhal, H., & Cleary, P. D. (1980). The smoking problem: A review of the research and theory in behavioral risk modification. *Psychological Bulletin, 88,* 370–405.

Levi, P. (1985). *A quiet city: Moments of reprieve.* New York: Simon & Schuster.

Levi-Strauss, C. (1963). The effectiveness of symbols. In C. Levi-Strauss (Ed.), *Structural anthropology.* New York: Basic Books.

Levine, M. (1987, April). *Effective problem solving.* Englewood Cliffs, NJ: Prentice-Hall.

Levine, M., & Perkins, D. V. (1987). *Principles of community psychology: Perspectives and applications.* New York: Oxford University.

Levine, M. P., & Troiden, R. R. (1988). The myth of sexual compulsivity. *The Journal of Sex Research, 25,* 347–363.

Levine, M. W., & Shefner, J. M. (1981). *Fundamentals of sensation and perception.* Reading, MA: Addison-Wesley.

Levine, R., Lynch, K., Miyake, K., & Lucia, M. (1989). The Type A city: Coronary heart disease and the pace of life. *Journal of Behavioral Medicine, 12,* 509–524.

Levinson, B. W. (1967). States of awareness during general anesthesia. In J. Lassner (Ed.), *Hypnosis and psychosomatic medicine* (pp. 200–207). New York: Springer-Verlag.

Levinson, D. (1990). In *Discovering Psychology,* Program 18 [PBS video series]. Washington, DC: Annenberg/CPB Program.

Levinson, D. L. (1978). *The seasons of a man's life.* New York: Knopf.

Levinson, D. L. (1986). A conception of adult development. *American Psychologist, 41,* 3–13.

Levy, J., & Trevarthen, C. (1976). Metacontrol of hemispheric function in human split brain patients. *Journal of Experimental Psychology: Human perception and performance, 2,* 299–312.

Lewin, K. (1936). *Principles of topological psychology.* New York: McGraw-Hill.

Lewin, K. (1947). Group decision and social change. In T. N. Newcomb & E. L. Hartley (Eds.), *Readings in social psychology.* New York: Holt, Rinehart & Winston.

Lewin, K. (1948). *Resolving social conflicts.* New York: Harper.

Lewin, K. (1990). In *Discovering Psychology,* Program 19 [PBS video series]. Washington, DC: Annenberg/CPB Program.

Lewin, K., Lippitt, R., & White, R. K. (1939). Patterns of aggressive behavior in experimentally created "social climates." *Journal of Social Psychology, 10,* 271–299.

Lewin, R. (1985). Gregarious grazers eat better. *Science, 228,* 567–568.

Lewin, R. (1987). The origin of the modern human mind. *Science, 236,* 668–670.

Lewine, R. R., Strauss, J. S., & Gift, T. E. (1981). Sex differences in age at first hospital admission for schizophrenia: Fact or artifact? *American Journal of Psychiatry, 138,* 440–444.

Lewinsohn, P. M. (1975). The behavioral study and treatment of depression. In M. Hersen, R. M. Eisler, & P. M. Miller (Eds.), *Progress in behavior modification* (pp. 19–64). New York:

Academic Press.

Lewinsohn, P. M., Mischel, W., Chapline, W., & Barton, R. (1980). Social competence and depression: The role of illusory self-perceptions. *Journal of Abnormal Psychology, 89*, 203–212.

Lewis, C. (1981). The effects of parental firm control: A reinterpretation of findings. *Psychological Bulletin, 90*, 547–563.

Lewis, D. O. (1990, May 11). [Interview]. *San Francisco Chronicle.*

Lewis, H. B. (1981). *Freud and modern psychology—Vol. 1: The emotional basis of mental illness.* New York: Plenum.

Lewis, J. W., Cannon, J. T., & Liebeskind, J. C. (1980). Opiod and nonopiod mechanisms of stress analgesia. *Science, 208*, 623–625.

Lewy, A. J., Sack, R. L., Miller, S., & Hoban, T. M. (1987). Antidepressant and circadian phase-shifting effect of light. *Science, 235*, 352–354.

Leyland, C. M., & Mackintosh, N.J. (1978). Blocking of first and second-order autoshaping in pigeons. *Animal Learning and Behavior, 6*, 391–394.

Li, P. (1975). *Path analysis: A primer.* Pacific Grove, CA: The Boxwood Press.

Liberman, R. P. (1982). What is schizophrenia? *Schizophrenia Bulletin, 8*, 435–437.

Lidz, T., Fleck, S., & Cornelison, A. R. (1965). *Schizophrenia and the family.* New York: International University Press.

Lieberman, L. R. (1973, April 3). [Letter to *Science* concerning "On being sane in insane places"]. *Science, 179.*

Lieberman, M. A. (1977). Problems in integrating traditional group therapies with new forms. *International Journal of Group Psychotherapy, 27*, 19–32.

Lieberman, M. A. (1982). The effects of social support on responses to stress. In L. Goldberger & S. Breznitz (Eds.), *Handbook of stress* (pp. 764–783). New York: Free Press.

Liebert, R. M., & Spiegler, M. D. (1982). *Personality: Strategies and issues.* Homewood, IL: Dorsey Press.

Liem, J. H. (1980). Family studies of schizophrenia: An update and commentary. In S. J. Keith & L. R. Mosher (Eds.), *Special report: Schizophrenia, 1980* (pp. 82–108). Washington, DC: U.S. Government Printing Office.

Liem, R., & Rayman, P. (1982). Health and social costs of unemployment: Research and policy considerations. *American Psychologist, 37*, 1116–1123.

Lifton, R. K. (1969). *Thought reform and the psychology of totalism.* New York: Norton.

Light, L. L. (1991). Memory and aging: Four hypotheses in search of data. *Annual Review of Psychology, 42*, 333–376.

Lillard, A. S., & Flavell, J. H. (1990). Young children's preference for mental-state over behavioral descriptions of human action. *Child Development, 61*, 731–742.

Lindsay, P. H., & Norman, D. A. (1977). *Human information processing* (2nd ed.). New York: Academic Press.

Lindsley, D. B. (1951). Emotion. In S. S. Stevens (Ed.), *Handbook of experimental psychology.* New York: Wiley.

Lindvall, O. et al. (1990). Grafts of fetal dopamine neurons survive and improve motor function in Parkinson's Disease. *Science, 247*, 574–577.

Linn, R. L. (Ed.). (1989). *Intelligence: Measurement, theory and public policy—Proceedings of a symposium in honor of Lloyd G. Humphreys.* Urbana, IL: University of Illinois Press.

Lipsitt, L. P., & Reese, H. W. (1979). *Child development.* Glenview, IL: Scott, Foresman.

Lipsitt, L. P., Reilly, B., Butcher, M. G., & Greenwood, M. M. (1976). The stability and interrelationships of newborn sucking and heart rate. *Developmental Psychobiology, 9*, 305–310.

Little, M. I. (1981). *Transference neurosis and transference psychosis.* New York: Jason Aronson.

Livesley, W. J., & Bromley, D. B. (1973). *Person perception in childhood and adolescence.* London: Wiley.

Livingstone, M., & Hubel, D. (1988). Segregation of form, color, movement, and depth: Anatomy, physiology, and perception. *Science, 240*, 740–749.

Locke, E. A. (1982). *A new look at work motivation: Theory V* (Technical Report GS-12). Arlington, VA: Office of Naval Research.

Locke, E. A., Shaw, K. N., Saari, L. M., & Latham, G. P. (1981).

Goal setting and task performance: 1969–1980. *Psychological Bulletin, 90*, 125–152.

Locke, J. (1975). *An essay concerning human understanding.* Oxford: P. H. Nidditch. (Original work published 1690)

Lockhart, R. S., & Craik, F. I. M. (1990). Levels of processing: A retrospective commentary on a framework for memory research. *Canadian Journal of Psychology, 44*, 87–122.

Loehlin, J. C., Lindzey, G., & Spuhler, J. N. (1975). *Race differences in intelligence.* San Francisco: Freeman.

Loevinger, J. (1957). Objective tests as instruments of psychological theory. *Psychological Reports, 3*, 635–694.

Loftus, E. F. (1979). *Eyewitness testimony.* Cambridge, MA: Harvard University Press.

Loftus, E. F. (1984). The eyewitness on trial. In B. D. Sales & A. Alwork (Eds.), *With liberty and justice for all.* Englewood Cliffs, NJ: Prentice Hall.

Loftus, E. F., & Kaufman, L. (in press). Why do traumatic experiences sometimes produce good memory (flashbulbs) and sometimes no memory (repression)? In E. Winograd & U. Neisser (Eds.), *Affect and accuracy in recall.* New York: Cambridge University Press.

Logan, F. A. (1960). *Incentive.* New Haven, CT: Yale University Press.

Logan, G. (1980). Attention and automaticity in Stroop and priming task: Theory and data. *Cognitive Psychology, 12*, 523–553.

Londer, R. (1988, July 24). When you've just got to do it: Millions of Americans are slaves to their obsessions. *San Francisco Examiner-Chronicle*, This World Section, p. 9.

London, K. A., Mosher, W. D., Pratt, W. F., & Williams, L. B. (1989, March). *Preliminary findings from the National Survey of Family Growth, Cycle IV.* Paper presented at the annual meeting of the Population Association of America, Baltimore, MD.

Loomis, A. L., Harvey, E. N., & Hobart, G. A. (1937). Cerebral states during sleep as studied by human brain potentials. *Journal of Experimental Psychology, 21*, 127–144.

Lorenz, K. (1937). Imprinting. *The AUK, 54*, 245–273.

Lott, B., & Lott, A. J. (1985). Learning theory in contemporary social psychology. In G. Lindzey & E. Aronson (Eds.), *The handbook of social psychology* (3rd ed., Vol. 1, pp. 109–135). Hillsdale, NJ: Erlbaum.

Lovaas, O. I. (1968). Learning theory approach to the treatment of childhood schizophrenia. In *California Mental Health Research Symposium: No. 2. Behavior theory and therapy.* Sacramento, CA: Department of Mental Hygiene.

Lovaas, O. I. (1977). *The autistic child: Language development through behavior modification.* New York: Halsted Press.

Lovibond, S. H., Adams, M., & Adams, W. G. (1979). The effects of three experimental prison environments on the behavior of nonconflict volunteer subjects. *Australian Psychologist, 14*, 273–285.

Luborsky, L., Blinder, B., & Schimek, J. G. (1965). Cooking, recalling and GSR as a function of defense. *Journal of Abnormal Psychology, 70*, 270–280.

Lubow, R. E., Rifkin, B., & Alex, M. (1976). The context effect: The relationship between stimulus preexposure and environmental preexposure determines subsequent learning. *Journal of Experimental Psychology: Animal Behavior Processes, 2*, 38–47.

Luchins, A. S. (1942). Mechanization in problem solving. *Psychological Monographs, 54* (No. 248).

Luchins, A. S. (1957). Primacy-recency in impression formation. In C. I. Hovland (Ed.), *The order of presentation in persuasion* (pp. 34–35). New Haven, CT: Yale University Press.

Ludwig, A. M. (1966). Altered states of consciousness. *Archives of General Psychiatry, 15*, 225–234.

Luker, K. C. (1975). *Taking chances: Abortion and the decision not to contracept.* Berkeley: University of California Press.

Lunde, A. S. (1981). Health in the United States. *Annals of the American Academy of Political and Social Science, 453*, 28–69.

Lykken, D. T. (1979). The detection of deception. *Psychological Bulletin, 86*, 47–53.

Lykken, D. T. (1981). *A tremor in the blood: Uses and abuses of the lie detector.* New York: McGraw-Hill.

Lykken, D. T. (1984). Polygraphic interrogation. *Nature, 307,* 681–684.

Lynch, G. (1986). *Synapses, circuits, and the beginnings of memory.* Cambridge, MA: MIT Press.

Lynch, J. J. (1979). *The broken heart: The medical consequences of loneliness.* New York: Basic Books.

Lyons, N. (1983). Two perspectives: On self, relationships, and morality. *Harvard Educational Review, 53,* 125–146.

M

Maccoby, E. (1990). In *Discovering Psychology,* Program 17 [PBS video series]. Washington, DC: Annenberg/CPB Program.

Maccoby, E. E. (1980). *Social development: Psychological growth and the parent-child relationship.* San Diego, CA: Harcourt Brace Jovanovich.

Maccoby, E. E. (1988). Gender as a social category. *Developmental Psychology, 24,* 755–765.

Maccoby, E. E., & Jacklin, C. N. (1974). *The psychology of sex differences.* Stanford, CA: Stanford University Press.

Maccoby, E. E., & Jacklin, C. N. (1987). Gender segregation in childhood. In H. Reese (Ed.), *Advances in child behavior and development* (Vol. 20). New York: Academic Press.

Maccoby, E. E., & Martin, J. A. (1983). Socialization in the context of the family: Parent-child interaction. In P. H. Mussen (Ed.), *Carmichael's manual of child psychology.* New York: Wiley.

Maccoby, N., Farquhar, J. W., Wood, P. D., & Alexander, J. K. (1977). Reducing the risk of cardiovascular disease: Effects of a community-based campaign on knowledge and behavior. *Journal of Community Health, 3,* 100–114.

Mace, W. M. (1977). James J. Gibson's strategy for perceiving: Ask not what's inside your head, but what your head's inside of. In R. Shaw & J. Bransford (Eds.), *Perceiving, acting, and knowing.* Hillsdale, NJ: Erlbaum.

Machlowitz, M. (1980). *Workaholics: Living with them, working with them.* Reading, MA: Addison-Wesley.

Mack, J. (1990). In *Discovering Psychology,* Program 24 [PBS video series]. Washington, DC: Annenberg/CPB Program.

Mackintosh, N. J. (1975). A theory of attention. *Psychological Review, 82,* 276–298.

MacLean, P. (1977). On the evolution of three mentalities. In S. Arieti & G. Chrzanowki (Eds.), *New directions in psychiatry: A world view* (Vol. 2). New York: Wiley.

MacLeod, C., Mathews, A., & Tata, P. (1986). Attentional bias in emotional disorders. *Journal of Abnormal Psychology, 95,* 15–20.

Maddi, S. (1980). *Personality theories: A comparative analysis.* Homewood, IL: Dorsey.

Magnani, F. (1990). In *Discovering Psychology,* Program 9 [PBS video series]. Washington, DC: Annenberg/CPB Project.

Magnusson, D. (1987). Adult delinquency in the light of conduct and physiology at an early age: A longitudinal study. In D. Magnusson & A. Ohman (Eds.), *Psychopathology* (pp. 221–324). Orlando, FL: Academic Press.

Magnusson, D., & Bergman, L. R. (1990). A pattern approach to the study of pathways from childhood to adulthood. In L. N. Robins & M. Rutter (Eds.), *Straight and devious pathways from childhood to adulthood* (pp. 101–115). Cambridge: Cambridge University Press.

Magnusson, D., & Endler, N. S. (1977). Interactional psychology: Present status and future prospects. In D. Magnusson & N. S. Endler (Eds.), *Personality at the crossroads: Current issues in interactional psychology.* Hillsdale, NJ: Erlbaum.

Maher, B., & Ross, J. S. (1984). Delusions. In H. E. Adams & P. B. Sutker (Eds.), *Comprehensive handbook of psychopathology* (pp. 383–987). New York: Plenum.

Maher, B. A. (1968, November). The shattered language of schizophrenia. *Psychology Today,* pp. 30ff.

Maher, B. A. (1974). Delusional thinking and cognitive disorder. In M. London & R. E. Nisbett (Eds.), *Thought and feeling: Cognitive alteration of feeling states.* Chicago: Aldine.

Mahler, M. S. (1979). *The selected papers of Margaret S. Mahler* (2 vols.). New York: Jason Aronson.

Mahoney, M. J. (1974). *Cognition and behavior modification.*

Cambridge, MA: Ballinger.

Maier, N. R. F. (1931). Reasoning in humans: II. The solution of a problem and its appearance in consciousness. *Journal of Comparative Psychology, 12,* 181–194.

Maier, S. (1984, March). Stress: Depression, disease and the immune system. *Science and public policy seminars.* Washington, DC: Federation of Behavioral, Psychological, and Cognitive Sciences.

Maier, S. F., & Seligman, M. E. P. (1976). Learned helplessness: Theory and evidence. *Journal of Experimental Psychology, 105,* 3–46.

Main, M., & George, C. (1985). Responses of abused and disadvantaged toddlers to distress in agemates: A study in the day care setting. *Developmental Psychology, 21,* 407–412.

Main, M., Kaplan, N., & Cassidy, J. (1985). Security in infancy, childhood, and adulthood: A move to the level of representation. In I. Bretherton & E. Waters (Eds.), *Growing points of attachment theory and research: Monographs of the Society of Research in Child Development, 4* (Serial No. 209, pp. 66–104).

Majewska, M. D., Harrison, N. L., Schwartz, R. D., Barker, J. L., & Paul, S. M. (1986). Steroid hormone metabolites are barbiturate-like modulators of the GABA receptor. *Science, 232,* 1004–1007.

Malamuth, N. E., & Donnerstein, E. (1982). The effects of aggressive-pornographic mass media stimuli. *Advances in Experimental Social Psychology, 15,* 103–136.

Malamuth, N. E., & Donnerstein, E. (1984). *Pornography and sexual aggression.* New York: Academic Press.

Malamuth, N. M. (1984). Aggression against women: Cultural and individual causes. In N. M. Malamuth & E. Donnerstein (Eds.), *Pornography and sexual aggression* (pp. 19–52). Orlando, FL: Academic Press.

Malatesta, C. Z., & Kalnok, M. (1984). Emotional experience in younger and older adults. *Journal of Gerontology, 39,* 301–308.

Malitz, S., & Sackheim, H. A. (1984). Low dosage ECT: Electrode placement and acute physiological and cognitive effects. *American Journal of Social Psychiatry, 4,* 47–53.

Maloney, M. P., & Ward, M. P. (1976). *Psychological assessment: A conceptual approach.* New York: Academic Press.

Mandler, G. (1975). *Mind and emotion.* New York: Wiley.

Mandler, G. (1984). *Mind and body: The psychology of emotion and stress.* New York: Norton.

Manfredi, M., Bini, G., Cruccu, G., Accornero, N., Beradelli, A., & Medolago, L. (1981). Congenital absence of pain. *Archives of Neurology, 38,* 507–511.

Mann, L. (1979). *On the trail of progress: A historical perspective on cognitive processes and their training.* New York: Grune & Stratton.

Manning, C. A., Hall, J. L., & Gold, P. E. (1990). Glucose effects on memory and other neuropsychological tests in elderly humans. *Psychological Science, 1,* 307–311.

Manschreck, T. C. (1989). Delusional (paranoid) disorders. In H. I. Kaplan & B. J. Sadock (Eds.), *Comprehensive textbook of psychiatry* (pp. 816–829). Baltimore: William & Wilkins.

Manuck, S. B., Cohen, S., Rabin, R. S., Muldoon, M. F., & Bachen, E. A. (1991). Individual differences in cellular immune response to stress. *Psychological Science, 2,* 111–115.

Marcel, A. J. (1983). Conscious and unconscious perception: An approach to the relation between phenomenal experience and perceptual processes. *Cognitive Psychology, 15,* 238–300.

Marcus, A.D. (1990, December 3). Mists of memory cloud some legal proceedings. *The Wall Street Journal,* p. B1.

Marek, G. R. (1975). *Toscanini.* London: Vision Press.

Markman, E. M., Cox, B., & Machida, S. (1981). The standard object-sorting task as a measure of conceptual organization. *Developmental Psychology, 17,* 115–117.

Marks, I. (1981). *Cure and care of neuroses: Theory and practice of behavioral psychotherapy.* New York: Wiley.

Marks, R. (1976–1977). Providing for individual differences: A history of the intelligence testing movement in North America. *Interchange, 1,* 3–16.

Markus, H., & Cross, S. (1990). The interpersonal self. In L. A. Pervin (Ed.), *Handbook of personality theory and research* (pp. 576–608). New York: Guilford Press.

Markus, H., & Cross, S., & Wurf, E. (1990). The role of the self-system in competence. In R. J. Sternberg & J. Lollgian, Jr. (Eds.), *Competence considered* (pp. 205–225). New Haven, CT: Yale University Press.

Markus, H., & Nurius, P. (1986). Possible selves. *American Psychologist, 41,* 954–969.

Markus, H., & Smith, J. (1981). The influence of self-schemas on the perception of others. In N. Cantor & J. F. Kihlstrom (Eds.), *Personality, cognition, and social interaction* (pp. 233–262). Hillsdale, NJ: Erlbaum.

Markus, H., & Zajonc, R. B. (1985). The cognitive perspective in social psychology. In G. Lindzey & E. Aronson (Eds.), *The handbook of social psychology: Vol. 1. Theory and methods* (3rd ed., pp. 137–230). New York: Random House.

Marlatt, G. A. (1978). Behavioral assessment of social drinking and alcoholism. In G. A. Marlatt & P. E. Nathan (Eds.), *Behavioral approaches to alcoholism.* New Brunswick, NJ: Rutgers Center for Alcohol Studies.

Marlatt, G. A. (1983). The controlled-drinking controversy: A commentary. *American Psychologist, 38,* 1097–1110.

Marler, P. R., & Hamilton, W. J. (1966). *Mechanisms of animal behavior.* New York: Wiley.

Marquis, J. N. (1970). Orgasmic reconditioning: Changing sexual object choice through controlling masturbation fantasies. *Journal of Behavior Therapy and Experimental Psychiatry, 1,* 263–271.

Marr, D. (1982). *Vision.* San Francisco: Freeman.

Marr, D., & Nishihara, H. K. (1978). Representation and recognition of the spatial organization of three-dimensional shapes. *Proceedings of the Royal Society of London (Series B), 200,* 269–294.

Marsella, A. J. (1979). Cross-cultural studies of mental disorders. In A. J. Marsella, R. G. Sharp, & T. J. Ciborowski (Eds.), *Perspectives on cross-cultural psychology* (pp. 233–262). New York: Academic Press.

Marshall, G. D., & Zimbardo, P. G. (1979). Affective consequences of inadequately explained physiological arousal. *Journal of Personality and Social Psychology, 37,* 970–988.

Marshall, M. (1987). G. T. Fechner: In memorium (1801–1887). *History of Psychology Newsletter, XIX,* 1–9.

Martin, C. L., & Halverson, C. F. (1981). A schematic processing model of sex typing and stereotyping in children. *Child Development, 52,* 1119–1134.

Martin, G., & Pear, J. (1983). *Behavior modification: What it is and how to do it* (2nd ed.). Englewood Cliffs, NJ: Prentice-Hall.

Martin, J. A. (1981). A longitudinal study of the consequences of early mother-infant interaction: A microanalytic approach. *Monographs of the Society for Research in Child Development, 46* (203, Serial No. 190).

Masangkay, Z. S., McCluskey, K. A., McIntyre, C. W., Sims-Knight, J., Vaughn, B., & Flavell, J. H. (1974). The early development of inferences about the visual percepts of others. *Child Development, 45,* 357–366.

Maslach, C. (1974). Social and personal bases of individuation. *Journal of Personality and Social Psychology, 29,* 411–425.

Maslach, C. (1979). Negative emotional biasing of unexplained arousal. *Journal of Personality and Social Psychology, 37,* 953–969.

Maslach, C. (1982). *Burnout: The cost of caring.* Englewood Cliffs, NJ: Prentice-Hall.

Maslach, C., & Florian, V. (1988). Burnout, job setting, and self-evaluation among rehabilitation counselors. *Rehabilitation Psychology, 33,* 135–157.

Maslach, C., Stapp, J., & Santee, R. T. (1985). Individuation: Conceptual analysis and assessment. *Journal of Personality and Social Psychology, 49,* 729–738.

Maslow, A. H. (1970). *Motivation and personality* (Rev. ed.). New York: Harper & Row.

Mason, J. W. (1975). An historical view of the stress field: Parts 1 & 2. *Journal of Human Stress, 1,* 6–12, 22–36.

Mason, W. A., & Kenney, M. D. (1974). Reduction of filial attachments in Rhesus monkeys: Dogs as mother surrogates. *Science, 183,* 1209–1211.

Masters, J. C. (1981). Developmental psychology. *Annual Review of Psychology, 32,* 117–151.

Masters, W. H., & Johnson, V. E. (1966). *Human sexual response.* Boston: Little, Brown.

Masters, W. H., & Johnson, V. E. (1970). *Human sexual inadequacy.* Boston: Little, Brown.

Masters, W. H., & Johnson, V. E. (1979). *Homosexuality in perspective.* Boston: Little, Brown.

Matarazzo, J. D. (1972). *Wechsler's measurement and appraisal of adult intelligence* (5th ed.). Baltimore: Williams & Wilkins.

Matarazzo, J. D. (1980). Behavioral health and behavioral medicine: Frontiers for a new health psychology. *American Psychologist, 35,* 807–817.

Matarazzo, J. D. (1984). Behavioral immunogens and pathogens in health and illness. In B. L. Hammonds & C. J. Scheirer (Eds.), *Psychology and health: The Master Lecture Series, Vol. 3* (pp. 9–43). Washington, DC: American Psychological Association.

Matarazzo, J. D. (1990). Psychological assessment versus psychological testing: Validation from Binet to the school, clinic, and courtroom. *American Psychologist, 45,* 999–1017.

Matas, L., Arend, R. A., & Sroufe, L. A. (1978). Continuity of adaptation in the second year: The relationship between quality of attachment and later competence. *Child Development, 49,* 547–556.

Matossian, M. (1982). Ergot and the Salem witchcraft affair. *American Scientist, 70,* 355–357.

Matson, J. L., Esveldt-Dawson, K., Andrasik, F., Ollendick, T. H., Petti, T., & Hersen, M. (1980). Direct, observational, and generalization effects of social skills training with emotionally disturbed children. *Behavior Therapy, 11,* 522–531.

Matthews, K. A. (1988). Coronary heart disease and Type A behavior: Update on an alternative to the Booth-Kewley and Friedman (1987) quantitative review. *Psychological Bulletin, 104,* 373–380.

Maugh, T. H. (1982). Sleep-promoting factor isolated. *Science, 216,* 1400.

May, R. (1969). *Love and will.* New York: Norton.

May, R. (1972). *Power and innocence: A search for the sources of violence.* New York: Delta.

May, R. (1975). *The courage to create.* New York: Norton.

May, R. (1977). *The meaning of anxiety* (Rev. ed.). New York: Norton. (Original work published 1950)

Mayer, G. R., Butterworth, T., Nafpaktitis, M., & Sulzer-Azaroff, B. (1983). Preventing school vandalism and improving discipline: A three-year study. *Journal of Applied Behavior Analysis, 16,* 355–369.

Mayer, J. (1955). Regulation of energy intake and body weight: The glucostatic theory and lipostatic hypothesis. *Annals of the New York Academy of Sciences, 63,* 15–43.

Mayer, R. E. (1981). *The promise of cognitive psychology.* San Francisco: Freeman.

Mayr, E. (1974). Behavior programs and evolutionary strategies. *American Scientist, 38,* 650–659.

Mazur, J. (1990). *Learning and behavior.* Englewood Cliffs, NJ: Prentice-Hall.

McAdams, D. P., & Vaillant, G. E. (1982). Intimacy motivation and psychosocial adjustment: A longitudinal study. *Journal of Personality Assessment, 46,* 586–593.

McCabe, K. (1990). Beyond cruelty. *The Washingtonian,* pp. 72–77.

McCall, R. B. (1977). Childhood IQs as predictors of adult education and occupational status. *Science, 197,* 483–485.

McCarley, R. (1990). In *Discovering Psychology,* Program 13 [PBS video series]. Washington, DC: Annenberg/CPB Program.

McCarthy, S. J. (1979, September). Why Johnny can't disobey. *The Humanist,* pp. 30–33.

McCaulley, M. H. (1978). *Application of the Myers-Briggs Type Indicator to medicine and health professions* [Monograph 1]. Gainesville, FL: Center for Applications of Psychological Type.

McClelland, D. C. (1955). Some social consequences of achievement motivation. In M. R. Jones (Ed.), *Nebraska Symposium on Motivation* (Vol. 3). Lincoln, NE: University of Nebraska Press.

McClelland, D. C. (1961). *The achieving society.* Princeton, NJ: Van Nostrand.

McClelland, D. C. (1971). *Motivational trends in society.* Morristown, NJ: General Learning Press.

McClelland, D. C., Atkinson, J. W., Clark, R. A., & Lowell, E. L. (1976). *The achievement motive* (2nd ed.). New York: Irvington.

McClelland, J. L., & Rumelhart, D. E. (1988). *Explorations in parallel distributed processing: A handbook of models, programs, and exercises.* Cambridge, MA: MIT Press/Bradford Books.

McClintock, M. K. (1971). Menstrual synchrony and suppression. *Nature, 229,* 244–245.

McCloskey, M., & Egeth, H. E. (1983). Eyewitness identification: What can a psychologist tell a jury? *American Psychologist, 38,* 550–563.

McConaghy, N. (1969). Subjective and penil plesthsmograph response following aversion-relief and apomorphine aversion therapy for homosexual impulses. *British Journal of Psychology, 115,* 723–730.

McCormick, D. A., & Thompson, R. F. (1984). Cerebellum: Essential involvement in the classically conditioned eyelid response. *Science, 223,* 296–299.

McCoy, E. (1988). Childhood through the ages. In K. Finsterbusch (Ed.), *Sociology 88/89* (pp. 44–47). Guilford, CT: Duskin.

McCrae, R. R. (1982). Consensual validation of personality traits: Evidence from self-reports and ratings. *Journal of Personality and Social Psychology, 43,* 293–303.

McCrae, R. R. (1987). Creativity, divergent thinking, and openness to new experience. *Journal of Personality and Social Psychology, 52,* 1258–1265.

McCrae, R. R., & Costa, P. T., Jr. (1987). Validation of the five-factor model of personality across instruments and observers. *Journal of Personality and Social Psychology, 56,* 81–90.

McCrae, R. R., & Costa, P. T., Jr. (1989). Rotation to maximize the construct validity of factors in the NEO Personality Inventory. *Multivariate Behavioral Research, 24,* 107–124.

McCrae, R. R., Costa, P. T., Jr., & Busch, C. M. (1986). Evaluating comprehensiveness in personality systems: The California Q-Set and the five factor model. *Journal of Personality, 54,* 430–446.

McDougall, W. (1908). *An introduction to social psychology.* London: Methuen.

McGaugh, J. L. (1983). Hormonal influences on memory. *Annual Review of Psychology, 34,* 297–323.

McGaugh, J. L., & Herz, M. J. (1972). *Memory consolidation.* San Francisco: Albion.

McGaugh, J. L., Weinberger, N. M., Lynch, G., & Granger, R. H. (1985). Neural mechanisms of learning and memory: Cells, systems and computations. *Naval Research Reviews, 37,* 15–29.

McGhee, P. E. (1979). *Humor: Its origin and development.* San Francisco: Freeman.

McGinnies, E. (1949). Emotionality and perceptual defense. *Psychological Review, 56,* 244–251.

McGinnis, J. M. (1991). Health objectives for the nation. *American Psychologist, 46,* 520–524.

McGlashan, T. H., Evans, F. J., & Orne, M. T. (1978). The nature of hypnotic analgesia and placebo response to experimental pain. *Psychosomatic Medicine, 31,* 227–246.

McGrath, E., Keita, G. P., Strickland, B. R., & Russo, N. F. (1990). *Women and depression: Risk factors and treatment issues.* Hyattsville, MD: American Psychological Association.

McGuire, R. J., Carlise, J. M., & Young, B. G. (1965). Sexual deviations as conditioned behavior: A hypothesis. *Behavioral Research and Theory, 12,* 185–190.

McGuire, W. J., & McGuire, C. V. (1988). Content and process in the experience of self. In L. Berkowitz (Ed.), *Advances in experimental social psychology* (Vol. 21, pp. 97–144). New York: Academic Press.

McGuire, W. J., McGuire, C. V., Child, P., & Fujioka, T. A. (1978). Salience of ethnicity in the spontaneous self-concept as a function of one's ethnic distinctiveness in the social environment. *Journal of Personality and Social Psychology, 36,* 511–520.

McKean, K. (1986, October). Pain. *Discover,* pp. 82–92.

McKinnon, W., Weisse, C. S., Reynolds, C. P., Bowles, C. A., & Baum, A. (1989) Chronic stress, leukocyte subpopulations, and humoral response to latent viruses. *Health Psychology, 8,* 389–402.

McLearn, G. E., & De Fries, J. C. (1973). *Introduction to behavioral genetics.* San Francisco: Freeman.

McNeil, B. J., Pauker, S. G., Sox, H. C., Jr., & Tversky, A. (1982). On the elicitation of preferences for alternative therapies. *New England Journal of Medicine, 306,* 1259–1262.

McPherson, K. S. (1985). On intelligence testing and immigration legislation. *American Psychologist, 40,* 242–243.

Mead, M. (1928). *Coming of age in Samoa.* New York: Morrow.

Mead, M. (1939). *From the South Seas: Studies of adolescence and sex in primitive societies.* New York: Morrow.

Meador, B. D., & Rogers, C. R. (1979). Person-centered therapy. In R. J. Corsini (Ed.), *Current psychotherapies* (2nd ed., pp. 131–184). Itasca, IL: Peacock.

Meaney, M. (1990). In *Discovering Psychology,* Program 17 [PBS video series]. Washington, DC: Annenberg/CPB Program.

Meany, M. J., Aitken, D. H., Van Berkel, C., Bhatnagar, S., & Sapolsky, R. M. (1988). Effect of neonatal handling on age-related impairments associated with the hippocampus. *Science, 239,* 766–768.

Meany, M. J., Stewart, J., & Beatty, W. W. (1985). Sex differences in social play: The socialization of sex roles. *Advances in the Study of Behavior, 15,* 1–58.

Meehl, P. E. (1954). *Clinical versus statistical prediction.* Minneapolis: University of Minnesota Press.

Meehl, P. E. (1965). Seer over sign; The first good example. *Journal of Experimental Research in Personality, 1,* 27–32.

Meeker, M. (1985). Toward a psychology of giftedness: A concept in search of measurement. In B. B. Wolman (Ed.), *Handbook of intelligence* (pp. 787–800). New York: Wiley.

Mehrabian, A. (1971). *Silent messages.* Belmont, CA: Wadsworth.

Meichenbaum, D. (1975). A self-instructional approach to stress management: A proposal for stress innoculating training. In D. C. Spielberger & I. G. Sarason (Eds.), *Stress and anxiety* (Vol. 1, pp. 237–263). New York: Wiley.

Meichenbaum, D. (1977). *Cognitive-behavior modification: An integrative approach.* New York: Plenum.

Meier, R. P. (1991). Language acquisition by deaf children. *American Scientist, 79,* 60–70.

Meisner, W. W. (1978). *The paranoid process.* New York: Jason Aronson.

Meltzer, H. Y. (1982). What is schizophrenia? *Schizophrenia Bulletin, 8,* 433–435.

Meltzer, H. Y. (1987). Biological studies of schizophrenia. *Schizophrenia Bulletin, 13,* 827–838.

Meltzoff, A. N. (1988). Infant imitation and memory: Nine-month-olds in immediate and deferred tests. *Child Development, 59,* 217–225.

Meltzoff, A. N., & Borton, R. W. (1979). Intermodal matching by human neonates. *Nature, 282,* 403–404.

Meltzoff, J., & Kornreich, M. (1970). *Research in psychotherapy.* New York: Atherton.

Melville, J. (1977). *Phobias and obsessions.* New York: Penguin Books.

Melzack, R. (1973). *The puzzle of pain.* New York: Basic Books.

Melzack, R. (1980). Psychological aspects of pain. In J. J. Bonica (Ed.), *Pain.* New York: Raven.

Melzack, R. (1989). Phantom limbs, the self and the brain (the D. O. Hebb Memorial Lecture). *Canadian Psychology, 30,* 1–16.

Menzel, E. M. (1978). Cognitive mapping in chimpanzees. In S. H. Hulse, H. Fowler, & W. K. Honzig (Eds.), *Cognitive processes in animal behavior* (pp. 375–422). Hillsdale, NJ: Erlbaum.

Meredith, M. A., & Stein, B. E. (1985). Descending efferents from the superior colliculus relay integrated multisensory information. *Science, 227,* 657–659.

Merton, R. K. (1957). *Social theory and social structures.* New York: Free Press.

Mervis, C. B., & Rosch, E. (1981). Categorization of natural objects. *Annual Review of Psychology, 32,* 89–115.

Meyer, M. M., & Ekstein, R. (1970). The psychotic pursuit of reality. *Journal of Contemporary Psychotherapy, 3,* 3–12.

Meyer, N. (1974). *The seven percent solution.* New York: Dutton.

Meyer-Bahlburg, H. F. L. (1978). Sex hormones and female

homosexuality: A critical examination. *Archives of Sexual Behavior, 8,* 101–119.

Mezzich, J. E., & Berganza, C. E. (Eds.). (1984). *Culture and psychopathology.* New York: Columbia University Press.

Middleton, J. (Ed.). (1967). *Magic, witchcraft, and curing.* Garden City, NY: The Natural History Press.

Milam, J., & Ketcham, K. (1981). *Under the influence: A guide to the myths and realities of alcoholism.* Seattle: Madrona Publications.

Milgram, S. (1965). Some conditions of obedience and disobedience to authority. *Human Relations, 18,* 56–76.

Milgram, S. (1974). *Obedience to authority.* New York: Harper & Row.

Milgram, S. (1977, October). Subject reaction: The neglected factor in the ethics of experimentation. *Hastings Center Report,* pp. 19–23.

Milgram, S. (1990). In *Discovering Psychology,* Program 19 [PBS video series]. Washington, DC: Annenberg/CPB Program.

Milgram, S., & Jodelet, D. (1976). Psychological maps of Paris. In H. M. Proshansky, W. H. Ittleson, & L. G. Rivlin (Eds.), *Environmental psychology.* New York: Holt, Rinehart & Winston.

Millar, K., & Watkinson, N. (1983). Recognition of words presented during general anesthesia. *Ergonomics, 26,* 585–594.

Miller, A. G. (1986). *The obedience paradigm: A case study in controversy in social science.* New York: Praeger.

Miller, G. A. (1956). The magic number seven plus or minus two: Some limits on our capacity for processing information. *Psychological Review, 63,* 81–97.

Miller, G. A. (1962). Some psychological studies of grammar. *American Psychologist, 17,* 748–762.

Miller, J. D. (1987, Sept. 27). Ignoramus Americanus. *San Francisco Examiner-Chronicle,* This World Section, p. 7.

Miller, L. (1990). Neuropsychodynamics of alcoholism and addiction: Personality, psychopathology, and cognitive style. *Journal of Substance Abuse Treatment, 7,* 31–49.

Miller, N. E. (1941). The frustration-aggression hypothesis. *Psychological Review, 48,* 333–342.

Miller, N. E. (1948). Fear as an acquired drive. *Journal of Experimental Psychology, 38,* 89–101.

Miller, N. E. (1978). Biofeedback and visceral learning. *Annual Review of Psychology, 29,* 373–404.

Miller, N. E. (1983). Behavioral medicine: Symbiosis between laboratory and clinic. *Annual Review of Psychology, 34,* 1–31.

Miller, N. E. (1985). The value of behavioral research on animals. *American Psychologist, 40,* 423–440.

Miller, N. E. (1990). In *Discovering Psychology,* Program 23 [PBS video series]. Washington, DC: Annenberg/CPB Program.

Miller, P. Y., & Simon, W. (1968). The development of sexuality in adolescence. In J. Adelson (Ed.), *Handbook of adolescent psychology* (pp. 383–407). New York: Wiley.

Miller, P. Y., & Simon, W. (1980). The development of sexuality in adolescence. In J. Adelson (Ed.), *Handbook of adolescent psychology.* New York: Wiley.

Miller, W. R. (1983). Controlled drinking: A history and critical review. *Journal of Studies on Alcohol, 44,* 68–83.

Miller, W. R., & Hester, R. K. (1980). Treating the problem drinker: Modern approaches. In W. R. Miller (Ed.), *The addictive behaviors.* Oxford, England: Pergamon Press.

Mills, K. C., & McCarty, D. (1983). A data based alcohol abuse prevention program in a university setting. *Journal of Alcohol and Drug Education, 28,* 15–27.

Millstein, S. G., & Irwin, C. E., Jr. (1987). Concepts of health and illness: Different constructs of variations on a theme? *Health Psychology, 6,* 515–524.

Milner, B. (1966). Amnesia following operation on the temporal lobes. In C. W. Whitty & O. L. Zangwill (Eds.), *Amnesia* (pp. 109–133). London: Butterworth.

Milojkovic, J. D. (1982). Chess imagery in novice and master. *Journal of Mental Imagery, 6,* 125–144.

Mineka, S., Davidson, M., Cook, M., & Keir, R. (1984). Observational conditioning of snake fear in rhesus monkeys. *Journal of Abnormal Psychology, 93,* 355–372.

Minuchin, S. (1974). *Families and family therapy.* Cambridge, MA: Harvard University Press.

Mischel, W. (1968). *Personality and assessment.* New York: Wiley.

Mischel, W. (1973). Toward a cognitive social learning reconceptualization of personality. *Psychological Review, 80,* 252–283.

Mischel, W. (1976). *Introduction to personality* (2nd ed.). New York: Holt, Rinehart & Winston.

Mischel, W. (1979). On the interface of cognition and personality; Beyond the person-situation debate. *American Psychologist, 34,* 740–754.

Mischel, W. (1984). Convergences and challenges in the search for consistency. *American Psychologist, 39,* 351–364.

Mischel, W., & Peake, P. (1982). Beyond déja vu in the search for cross-situational consistency. *Psychological Review, 89*(6), 730–755.

Misgeld, V., Deisz, R. A., Dodt, H. U., & Lux, H. D. (1986). The role of chloride transport in postsynaptic inhibition of hippocampal neurons. *Science, 232,* 1413–1415.

Mishkin, M. (1982). A memory system in the monkey. *Philosophical Transactions of the Royal Society of London, 298,* 85–95.

Mishkin, M., & Appenszeller, G. (1987). The anatomy of memory. *Scientific American, 256,* 80–89.

Mishkin, M., Malamut, B., & Backevalier, J. (1984). Memories and habits: Two neural systems. In G. Lynch, J. L. McGaugh, & N. M. Weinberger (Eds.), *The neurobiology of learning and memory* (pp. 65–77). New York: Guilford Press.

Mishkin, M., & Petri, H. L. (1984). Memories and habits: Some implications for the analysis of learning and retention. In L. R. Squire & N. Butters (Eds.), *Neurophysiology of memory* (pp. 287–296). New York: Guilford Press.

Mitchell, T. R. (1974). Expectancy models of job satisfaction, occupational preference, and effort: A theoretical, methodological, and empirical appraisal. *Psychological Bulletin, 81,* 1053–1077.

Miyake, K., Chen, K., & Campos, J. J. (1985). Infant temperament, mother's mode of interaction, and attachment in Japan: An interim report. In I. Bretherton & E. Waters (Eds.), *Growing points of attachment theory and research. Monographs of the Society for Research in Child Development, 50* (1–2, Serial No. 209), 276–297.

Moar, I. (1980). The nature and acquisition of cognitive maps. In D. Cantor & T. Lee (Eds.), *Proceedings of the international conference on environmental psychology.* London: Architectural Press.

Modern couples say they are happy together: Poll differs with Shere Hite report. (1987, October 27). *Washington Post,* p. WH–8.

Molnar, J. M., Rath, W. R., & Klein, T. P. (1990). Constantly compromised: The impact of homelessness on children. *Journal of Social Issues, 46,* 109–123.

Moncrieff, R. W. (1951). *The chemical senses.* London: Leonard Hill.

Money, J., & Ehrhardt, A. A. (1972). *Man and woman, boy and girl.* Baltimore, MD: Johns Hopkins University Press.

Money, J., Hampson, J. G., & Hampson, J. L. (1957). Imprinting and the establishment of gender role. *AMA Archives of Neurology and Psychiatry, 77,* 333–336.

Moniz, E. (1973). Prefrontal leucotomy in the treatment of mental disorders. *American Journal of Psychiatry, 93,* 1379–1385.

Monroe, S. M. (1983). Major and minor life events as predictors of psychological distress: Further issues and findings. *Journal of Behavioral Medicine, 6,* 189–205.

Monson, T. C., Hesley, J. W., & Chernick, L. (1982). Specifying when personality traits can and cannot predict behavior: An alternative to abandoning the attempt to predict single-act criteria. *Journal of Personality and Social Psychology, 43,* 385–399.

Montague, A. (1986). *Touching: The human significance of the skin.* New York: Harper & Row.

Montague, W. E., Adams, J. A., & Kiess, H. O. (1966). Forgetting and natural language mediation. *Journal of Experimental Psychology, 72,* 829–833.

Montgomery, G. (1990). The mind in motion. [Special issue]. *Discover*, pp. 12–19.

Moore, B. S., Underwood, B., & Rosenhan, D. L. (1973). Affect and altruism. *Developmental Psychology, 9,* 99–104.

Moore, P. (1990). In *Discovering Psychology*, Program 18 [PBS video series]. Washington, DC: Annenberg/CPB Program.

Moore, T. E. (1982). Subliminal advertising: What you see is what you get. *Journal of Marketing, 46,* 38–47.

Moos, R. (1979). *Evaluating educational environments.* San Francisco: Jossey-Bass.

Moos, R., & Lemke, S. (1984). Supportive residential settings for older people. In I. Altman, M. P. Lawton, & J. F. Wohlwill (Eds.), *Elderly people and the environment* (pp. 159–190). New York: Plenum.

Moos, R. H., & Engel, B. T. (1962). Psychophysiological reactions in hypertensive and arthritic patients. *Journal of Psychosomatic Research, 6,* 227–241.

Moran, J., & Desimone, R. (1985). Selective attention gates visual processing in the extrastriate cortex. *Science, 229,* 782–785.

Morehouse, R. E., Farley, F. H., & Youngquist, J. V. (1990). Type T personality and the Jungian classification system. *Journal of Personality Assessment, 54,* 231–235.

Morgan, A. H., Hilgard, E. R., & Davert, E. C. (1970). The heritability of hypnotic susceptibility of twins: A preliminary report. *Behavior Genetics, 1,* 213–224.

Morgan, A. H., Johnson, D. L., & Hilgard, E. R. (1974). The stability of hypnotic susceptibility: A longitudinal study. *International Journal of Clinical and Experimental Hypnosis, 22,* 249–257.

Moriarity, T. (1990). In *Discovering Psychology*, Program 19 [PBS video series]. Washington, DC: Annenberg/CPB Program.

Moriarty, T. (1975). Crime, commitment and the responsive bystander: Two field experiments. *Journal of Personality and Social Psychology, 31,* 370–376.

Morris, C., & Hackman, J. (1969). Behavioral correlates of perceived leadership. *Journal of Personality and Social Psychology, 13,* 350–361.

Morris, J. J., & Clarizio, S. (1977). Improvement in IQ of high risk, disadvantaged preschool children enrolled in a developmental program. *Psychological Reports, 41*(1), 111–114.

Morrison, M. A. (1990, May). Addiction in adolescents. *The Western Journal of Medicine,* p. 543–546.

Moscovici, S. (1976). *Social influence and social change.* New York: Academic Press.

Moscovici, S. (1980). Toward a theory of conversion behavior. In L. Berkowitz (Ed.), *Advances in experimental social psychology* (Vol. 13, pp. 209–239). New York: Academic Press.

Moscovici, S., & Faucheux, C. (1972). Social influence, conformity bias, and the study of active minorities. In L. Berkowitz (Ed.), *Advances in experimental social psychology* (Vol. 6). New York: Academic Press.

Moskowitz, B. A. (1978). The acquisition of language. *Scientific American, 239*(11), 92–108.

Motley, M. T. (1987, February). What I meant to say. *Psychology Today,* pp. 24–28.

Mowrer, O. (1960). *Learning theory and symbolic processes.* New York: Wiley.

Muehlenhard, C. L., & Cook, S. W. (1988). Men's self-reports of unwanted sexual activity. *The Journal of Sex Research, 24,* 58–72.

Mullen, B., & Baumeister, R. F. (1987). Group effects on self-attention and performance: Social loafing, social facilitation, and social impairment. In C. Hendrick (Ed.), *Review of personality and social psychology.* Beverly Hills, CA: Sage.

Mullin, B., Futrell, D., Stairs, D., Tice, D. M., Baumeister, R. F., Dawson, K. E., Riordan, C. A., Radloff, C. E., Goethals, G. R., Kennedy, J. G., & Rosenfeld, P. (1986). Newscasters' facial expressions and voting behavior of viewers: Can a smile elect a president? *Journal of Personality and Social Psychology, 51,* 291–295.

Mullin, P. A., & Egeth, H. E. (1989). Capacity limitations in visual word processing. *Journal of Experimental Psychology: Human Perception and Performance, 15,* 111–123.

Munroe, R. L. (1955). *Schools of psychoanalytic thought.* New York: Dryden.

Munsterberg, H. (1908). *On the witness stand.* New York: McClure.

Munsterberg, H. (1927). *On the witness stand: Essays on psychology and crime.* New York: Clark Boardman. (Original work published 1908)

Murnen, S. K., Perolt, A., & Byrne, D. (1989). Coping with unwanted sexual activity: Normative responses, situational determinants, and individual differences. *The Journal of Sex Research, 26,* 85–106.

Murphy, J. M. (1976). Psychiatric labeling in cross-cultural perspective. *Science, 191,* 1019–1028.

Murray, H. A. (1938). *Explorations in personality.* New York: Oxford University Press.

Murray, J. P., & Kippax, S. (1977). Children's social behavior in three towns with differing television experience. *Journal of Communication, 28,* 19–29.

Muskin, P. R., & Fyer, A. J. (1981). Treatment of panic disorder. *Journal of Clinical Psychopharmacology, 1,* 81–90.

Mussen, P. H., Honzik, M. P., & Eichorn, D. H. (1982). Early adult antecedents of life satisfaction at age 70. *Journal of Gerontology, 37,* 316–322.

Myers, I. B. (1962). *The Myers-Briggs type indicator.* Palo Alto, CA: Consulting Psychologists Press.

Myers, I. B. (1976). *Introduction to type* (2nd ed.). Gainesville, FL: Center for Applications of Psychological Type.

Myers, I. B. (1985). *Gifts differing.* Palo Alto, CA: Consulting Psychologist Press.

Myers, R. E., & Sperry, R. W. (1958). Interhemispheric communication through the corpus callosum: Mnemonic carry-over between the hemispheres. *Archives of Neurology and Psychiatry, 80,* 298–303.

N

Nadi, S. N., Nurnberger, J. I., & Gershon, E. S. (1984). Muscarinic cholinergic receptors on skin fibroblasts in familial affective disorder. *New England Journal of Medicine, 311*(4), 225–230.

Nancy Nurse spoofs the healing profession. (1987, Spring). *Wellness New Mexico,* pp. 19–21.

Nasrallah, H. A., & Weinberger, D. W. (1986). *The neurology of schizophrenia: Handbook of schizophrenia, Vol. 1.* Amsterdam: Elsevier.

Nathans, J., Thomas, D., & Hogness, D. S. (1986). Molecular genetics of human color vision: The genes encoding blue, green, and red pigments. *Science, 232,* 193–202.

National Assessment of Educational Progress. (1983). *The third national mathematics assessment: Results, trends, and issues* (13-MA-01). Denver, CO: Educational Commission of the States.

National Institute on Drug Abuse. (1982). *Student drug use, attitudes, and beliefs: National trends 1975–1982.* Washington, DC: U.S. Government Printing Office.

National Institute on Drug Abuse Capsules. (August 1989).

National Institutes of Mental Health. (1977). *Lithium and the treatment of mood disorders* (DHEW Publication No. ADM 77–73). Washington, DC: U.S. Government Printing Office.

National Institutes of Mental Health. (1982). *Television and behavior: Ten years of scientific evidence and implications for the eighties: Vol. 1. Summary report.* Washington, DC: U.S. Government Printing Office.

National Institutes of Mental Health. (1986). *Useful information on phobias and panic* (DHHS Publication No. ADM 86–1472). Washington, DC: U.S. Government Printing Office.

Natsoulas, T. (1978). Consciousness. *American Psychologist, 33*(10), 906–914.

Natsoulas, T. (1981). Basic problems of consciousness. *Journal of Personality and Social Psychology, 41,* 132–178.

Nauta, W. J. H., & Feirtag, M. (1979). The organization of the brain. *Scientific American, 241*(9), 88–111.

Navon, D., & Gopher, D. (1979). On the economy of the human processing system. *Psychological Review, 86,* 214–255.

Navon, D., & Gopher, D. (1980). The difficulty resources and dual-task performance. In R. S. Nickerson (Ed.), *Attention and performance VIII* (pp. 297–318). Hillsdale, NJ: Erlbaum.

Neale, M. A., & Bazerman, M. H. (1985). Perspectives for understanding negotiation: Viewing negotiation as a judgmental process. *Journal of Conflict Resolution, 29,* 33–55.

Neale, M. A., & Bazerman, M. H. (1991). *Cognition and rationality in negotiation.* New York: Free Press.

Needleman, H., Schell, A., Belinger, D., Leviton, A., & Allred, E. (1990). The long-term effects of exposure to low doses of lead in childhood: An 11-year follow-up report. *New England Journal of Medicine, 322,* 83–88.

Neese, R. M. (1990). Evolutionary explanations of emotions. *Human Nature, 1,* 261–289.

Neisser, U. (1967). *Cognitive psychology.* New York: Appleton-Century-Crofts.

Neisser, U. (1976). *Cognition and reality.* San Francisco, CA: Freeman.

Neligan, G. A., Kolvin, I., Scott, D. M., Garside, R. F. (1976). *Born too soon or born too small: A follow-up study to seven years of age.* Philadelphia, PA: Lippincott.

Nelson, K. E. (1971). Accommodation of visual tracking patterns in human infants to object movement patterns. *Journal of Experimental Child Psychology, 16,* 180–196.

Nelson, R. E., & Craighead, W. E. (1977). Selective recall of positive and negative feedback, self-control behaviors and depression. *Journal of Abnormal Psychology, 86,* 379–388.

Nelson, R. K. (1989, Spring). Hunters and animals in a native land: Ancient ways for the new century. *Orion Nature Quarterly,* pp. 48–53.

Nelson, Z. P., & Mowrey, D. D. (1976). Contracting in crisis intervention. *Community Mental Health Journal, 12,* 37–43.

Nemeth, C. (1979). The role of an active minority in intergroup relations. In W. Austin & S. Worchel (Eds.), *The social psychology of intergroup relations.* Monterey, CA: Brooks/Cole.

Nemeth, C. J. (1986). Differential contributions of majority and minority influence. *Psychological Review, 93,* 23–32.

Nemeth, C. J., Mayseless, O., Sherman, J., & Brown, Y. (1990). Exposure to dissent and recall of information. *Journal of Personality and Social Psychology, 58,* 429–437.

Nesselroade, J. R., & Baltes, P. B. (1974). Adolescent personality development and historical change: 1970–1972. *Monographs of the Society for Research in Child Development, 39.*

Neugarten, B. L. (1976). *The psychology of aging: An overview* [Master lectures on developmental psychology]. Washington, DC: American Psychological Association.

Newcomb, M. D., & Bentler, P. M. (1988). *Consequences of adolescent drug use: Impact on the lives of young adults.* Newbury Park, CA: Sage.

Newcomb, T. M. (1929). *The consistency of certain extrovert-introvert behavior traits in 50 problem boys* (Contributions to Education, No. 382). New York: Columbia University.

Newcomb, T. M. (1943). *Personality and social change.* New York: Holt.

Newcomb, T. M. (1963). Persistence and regression of changed attitudes: Long-range studies. *Journal of Social Issues, 19,* 3–4.

Newcomb, T. M., Koenig, D. E., Flacks, R., & Warwick, D. P. (1967). *Persistence and change: Bennington College and its students after twenty-five years.* New York: Wiley.

Newell, A., Shaw, J. C., & Simon, H. A. (1958). Elements of a theory of human problem solving. *Psychological Review, 65,* 152–166.

Newell, A., & Simon, H. A. (1972). *Human problem solving.* Englewood Cliffs, NJ: Prentice-Hall.

Newman, O. (1972). *Gambling: Hazard and reward.* London: Athlone.

Newport, E. (1990). Maturational constraints on language learning. *Cognitive Science, 14,* 11–28.

Newsome, W. T., & Pare, E. B. (1988). A selective impairment of motion perception following lesions of the middle temporal visual area. *Journal of Neuroscience, 8,* 2201–2211.

Newton, I. (1671–1672). New theory about light and colors. *Philosophical Transactions of the Royal Society of London, 80,* 3075–3087. In D. L. MacAdam (Ed.), *Sources of color science.* Cambridge, MA: MIT Press.

Nguyen, T., Heslin, R., & Nguyen, M. L. (1975). The meanings of touch: Sex differences. *Journal of Communication, 25,* 92–103.

Nhat Hanh, T. (1991). *Peace is every step: The path of mindfulness in everyday life.* New York: Bantam.

NIAAA. (1984). *Report of the 1983 Prevention Planning Panel.* Rockville, MD: NIAAA.

Nichols, M. P. (1984). *Family therapy: Concepts and methods.* New York: Gardner Press.

Nicol, S. E., & Gottesman, I. I. (1983). Clues to the genetics and neurobiology of schizophrenia. *American Scientist, 71,* 398–404.

Nicoll, C., Russell, S., & Katz, L. (1988, May 26). Research on animals must continue. *The San Francisco Chronicle,* p. A25.

Nideffer, R. M. (1976). Altered states of consciousness. In T. X. Barber, *Advances in altered states of consciousness and human potentialities* (Vol. 1, pp. 3–35). New York: Psychological Dimensions.

Nietzel, M. T., Bernstein, D. A., & Milich, R. (1991). *Introduction to clinical psychology.* Englewood Cliffs, NJ: Prentice-Hall.

Nisbett, R. E. (1972). Hunger, obesity and the ventromedial hypothalamus. *Psychological Review, 79,* 433–453.

Nisbett, R. E., & Ross, L. (1980). *Human inference: Strategies and shortcomings of social judgment.* Englewood Cliffs, NJ: Prentice-Hall.

Nisbett, R. E., & Wilson, T. D. (1977). Telling more than we can know: Verbal reports on mental processes. *Psychological Review, 84,* 231–259.

Nissen, M. J., & Bullimer, P. (1987). Attentional requirements of learning: Evidence from performance measures. *Cognitive Psychology, 19,* 1–32.

Nixon, S. J., & Parsons, O. A. (1990). Application of the tridimensional personality questionnaire to a population of alcoholics and other substance abusers. *Alcoholism: Clinical and Experimental Research, 14,* 513–517.

Nobles, W. W. (1972). African psychology: Foundations for black psychology. In R. L. Jones (Ed.), *Black psychology.* New York: Harper & Row.

Nobles, W. W. (1976). Black people in white insanity: An issue for black community mental health. *Journal of Afro-American Issues, 4,* 21–27.

Nolen-Hoeksema, S. (1987). Sex differences in unipolar depression: Evidence and theory. *Psychological Bulletin, 101,* 259–282.

Nolen-Hoeksema, S. (1990). *Sex differences in depression.* Stanford, CA: Stanford University Press.

Norman, D. A. (1981). Categorization of action slips. *Psychological Review, 88,* 1–15.

Norman, D. A. (1983). Design rules based on analyses of human error. *Communications of the Association for Computing Machinery, 26,* 254–258.

Norman, D. A., & Rumelhart, D. E. (1975). *Explorations in cognition.* San Francisco: Freeman.

Norman, W. T., & Goldberg, L. R. (1966). Raters, ratees, and randomness in personality structure. *Journal of Personality and Social Psychology, 4,* 681–691.

Norton, R., Batey, R., Dwyer, T., & MacMahon, S. (1987). Alcohol consumption and the risk of alcohol related cirrhosis in women. *British Medical Journal, 295,* 80–82.

Novick, L. (1990). Representational transfer in problem solving. *Psychological Science, 1,* 128–132.

Nungesser, L. G. (1986). *Epidemic of courage: Facing AIDS in America.* New York: St. Martin's Press.

Nungesser, L. G. (1990). *Axioms for survivors: How to live until you say goodbye.* Santa Monica, CA: IBS Press.

Nuttin, J. (1985). *Future time perspective and motivation: Theory and research method.* Hillsdale, NJ: Erlbaum.

O

Oatley, K., & Bolton, W. (1985). A social-cognitive theory of depression in reaction to life events. *Psychological Review, 92,* 372–388.

Occupational Hazards. (1990). Survey cites passive smoking hazards. *Occupational Hazards, 52,* 19–20.

O'Connor, S., Hesselbrock, V., Tasman, A., & DePalma, N.

(1987). P3 amplitudes in two distinct tasks are decreased in young men with a history of paternal alcoholism. *Alcoholism, 4,* 323–330.

Oden, S., & Asher, S. R. (1977). Coaching children in social skills for friendship making. *Child Development, 48,* 495–506.

Offer, D., & Offer, J. B. (1975). *From teenage to young manhood.* New York: Basic Books.

Offer, D., Ostrov, E., & Howard, K. I. (1981a). *The adolescent: A psychological self-portrait.* New York: Basic Books.

Offer, D., Ostrov, E., & Howard, K. I. (1981b). The mental health professional's concept of the normal adolescent. *AMA Archives of General Psychiatry, 38,* 149–153.

Oldham, D. G. (1978a). Adolescent turmoil: A myth revisited. In S. C. Feinstein & P. L. Giovacchini (Eds.), *Adolescent psychiatry* (Vol. 6). Chicago: University of Chicago Press.

Oldham, D. G. (1978b). Adolescent turmoil and a myth revisited. In A. H. Esman (Ed.), *The psychology of adolescence.* New York: International University Press.

Olds, J. (1973). Commentary on positive reinforcement produced by electrical stimulation of septal areas and other regions of the rat brain. In E. S. Valenstein (Ed.), *Brain stimulation and motivation: Research and commentary.* Glenview, IL: Scott, Foresman.

Olds, J., & Milner, P. (1954). Positive reinforcement produced by electrical stimulation of septal area and other regions of the rat brain. *Journal of Comparative and Physiological Psychology, 47,* 419–427.

Olin, B. R., Hebel, S. K., Connell, S. I., Dombek, C. E., & Kastrup, E. K. (Eds.). (1990). *Drug facts and comparisons.* St. Louis, MO: J. B. Lippincott.

Olton, D. S. (1979). Mazes, mazes, and memory. *American Psychologist, 34,* 583–596.

Olton, D. S., Aaron, A., & Noonberg, R. (1980). *Biofeedback: Clinical applications in behavioral medicine.* Englewood Cliffs, NJ: Prentice-Hall.

Olweus, D. (1991). Bully/victim problems among school children: Basic facts and effects of a school-based intervention program. In K. Rubin & D. Pepler (Eds.), *The development and treatment of childhood aggression.* Toronto, Ontario: Erlbaum.

Olweus, D., Block, J., & Radke-Yarrow, M. (Eds.). (1986). *The development of anti-social and pro-social behavior: Research, theories, and issues.* New York: Academic Press.

Oppel, J. J. (1854–55). Ueber geometrisch-optische Tauschungen. *Jahresbericht des physikalischen Vereins zu Frankfurt a. M.,* 34–47.

Opton, E. M. (1970). Lessons of My Lai. In N. Sanford & C. Comstock (Eds.), *Sanctions for evil.* San Francisco: Jossey-Bass.

Opton, E. M., Jr. (1973). "It never happened and besides they deserved it." In W. E. Henry & N. Sanford (Eds.), *Sanctions for evil* (pp. 49–70). San Francisco: Jossey-Bass.

O'Reilly, C. A. (1991). Organizational behavior: Where we've been, where we're going. *Annual Review of Psychology, 42,* 427–458.

Orlando, N. J. (1981). Mental patient as therapeutic agent—self-change, power, and caring. *Psychotherapy: Theory, Research, and Practice, 7,* 58–62.

Orne, M. T. (1972). On the stimulating subject as a quasi-control group in hypnosis research: What, why, and how? In E. Fromm & R. E. Shor (Eds.), *Hypnosis: Research developments and perspectives* (pp. 399–443). Chicago: Aldine.

Orne, M. T. (1980). Hypnotic control of pain: Toward a clarification of the different psychological processes involved. In J. J. Bonica (Ed.), *Pain* (pp. 155–172). New York: Raven Press.

Ornstein, P. A., & Naus, M. J. (1978). Rehearsal processes in children's memory. In P. A. Ornstein (Ed.), *Memory development in children.* Hillsdale, NJ: Erlbaum.

Ornstein, R., & Sobel, D. (1989). *Healthy pleasures.* Reading, MA: Addison-Wesley.

Ornstein, R. E. (1986a). *Multimind: A new way of looking at human behavior.* Boston: Houghton-Mifflin.

Ornstein, R. E. (1986b). *The psychology of consciousness* (Rev. ed.). New York: Penguin Books.

Osborne, R. (1987, Winter). Whale Museum opposed biopsy research project. *Orca Update,* p. 6.

Osherow, N. (1981). Making sense of the nonsensical: An analysis of Jonestown. In E. Aronson (Ed.), *Readings in the social animal.* San Francisco, CA: Freeman.

Oskamp, S. (1984). *Applied social psychology.* Englewood Cliffs, NJ: Prentice-Hall.

Oskamp, S. (Ed.). (1985). International conflict and national public policy issues. *Applied Social Psychology Annual, 6.*

O'Sullivan, C. (1990, December 15). Quoted in G. Eskenazi, When athletic aggression turns into sexual assault. *The New York Times Index* (Vol. 139, p. 18, March 17, 1990).

Owen, D. (1985). *None of the Above: Behind the Myth of Scholastic Aptitude.* Boston, MA: Houghton Mifflin.

P

Page, S. (1987). On gender roles and perception of maladjustment. *Canadian Psychology, 28,* 53–59.

Paivio, A. (1983). The empirical case for dual coding. In J. C. Yuille (Ed.), *Imagery, memory and cognition* (pp. 307–332). Hillsdale, NJ: Erlbaum.

Paivio, A. (1986). *Mental representations: A dual coding approach.* New York: Oxford University Press.

Palmer, S. (1981). The psychology of perceptual organization. In J. Beck (Ed.), *Organization and representation in perception* (pp. 269–339). Hillsdale, NJ: Erlbaum.

Palmer, S. (1989). Reference frames in the perception of shape and orientation. In B. Shepp & M. Ballisteros (Eds.), *Object Perception* (pp. 121–163). Hillsdale, NJ: Erlbaum.

Palmer, S. E. (1975). The effects of contextual scenes on the identification of objects. *Memory and Cognition, 3,* 519–526.

Palmer, S. E. (1984). The psychology of perceptual organization: A transformational approach. In A. Rosenfeld & J. Beck (Eds.), *Human and machine vision.* New York: Academic Press.

Palys, T. S. (1986). Testing the common wisdom: The social content of video pornography. *Canadian Psychology, 27,* 22–35.

Papolos, D. F., & Papolos, J. (1987). *Overcoming depression.* New York: Harper & Row.

Pappas, A. M. (1983). Introduction. In A. M. Pappas (Ed.), *Law and the status of the child* (pp. xxvii–lv). New York: United Nations Institute for Training and Research.

Paraplegic reaches summit after 9-day mountain climb. (1989, July 27). *The New York Times,* p. A10(N).

Park, B., & Rothbart, M. (1982). Perception of out-group homogeneity and levels of social categorization: Memory for the subordinate attributes of in-group and out-group members. *Journal of Personality and Social Psychology, 42,* 1051–1068.

Park, R. D., & Walters, R. H. (1967). Some factors influencing the efficacy of punishment training for inducing response inhibition. *Monographs of the Society for Research in Child Development, 32* (1, Whole No. 109).

Parke, R. D., & Sawin, D. B. (1976). The father's role in infancy. *Family Coordinator, 25,* 265–371.

Parks, T. (1965). Post-retinal visual storage. *American Journal of Psychology, 78,* 145–147.

Parpal, M., & Maccoby, E. E. (1985). Maternal responsiveness and subsequent child compliance. *Child Development, 56,* 1326–1334.

Parrott, J., & Gleitman, H. (1984, April). *The joy of peekaboo: Appearance or reappearance?* Paper presented at the meeting of the Eastern Psychological Association, Baltimore, MD.

Pass, J. J., & Cunningham, J. W. (1978). Occupational clusters based on systematically derived work dimensions: Final report. *Journal of Supplemental Abstract Service: Catalogue of selected documents: Psychology, 8,* 22–23.

Paul, G. L. (1969). Outcome of systematic desensitization: II, Controlled investigations of individual treatment technique variations, and current status. In C. M. Franks (Ed.), *Behavior therapy: Appraisal and status.* New York: McGraw-Hill.

Paul, S. M., Crawley, J. N., & Skolnick, P. (1986). The neurobiology of anxiety: The role of the GABA/benzodiazepine complex. In P. A. Berger & H. K. H. Brodie (Eds.), *American handbook on psychiatry: Biological psychology* (2nd ed.). New York: Basic Books.

Pavlov, I. (1990). In *Discovering Psychology,* Program 8 [PBS video series]. Washington, DC: Annenberg/CPB Project.

Pavlov, I. P. (1927). *Conditioned reflexes* (G. V. Anrep, Trans.). London: Oxford University Press.

Pavlov, I. P. (1928). *Lectures on conditioned reflexes: Twenty-five years of objective study of higher nervous activity (behavior of animals)* (Vol. 1, W. H. Gantt, Trans.). New York: International Publishers.

Paykel, E. S. (1973). Life events and acute depression. In J. P. Scott & E. C. Senay (Eds.), *Separation and depression* (pp. 215–236). Washington, DC: American Association for the Advancement of Science.

Pear, T. H. (1927). Skill. *Journal of Personnel Research, 5,* 478–489.

Pearce, M. (1988). A memory artist. *The Exploratorium Quarterly, 12,* 13–17.

Pearson, R. E. (1961). Response to suggestions given under general anesthesia. *American Journal of Clinical Hypnosis, 4,* 106–114.

Pedersen, P. E., William, C. L., & Blass, E. M. (1982). Activation and odor conditioning of suckling behavior in 3-day-old albino rats. *Journal of Experimental Psychology: Animal Processes, 8,* 329–341.

Peele, S. (1984). The cultural context of psychological approaches to alcoholism: Can we control the effects of alcohol? *American Psychologist, 39,* 1337–1351.

Peele, S. (1985). The implications and limitations of genetic models of alcoholism and other addictions. *Journal of Studies on Alcohol, 47,* 63–73.

Peele, S. (1989). *Diseasing of America: Addiction treatment out of control.* Lexington, MA: Lexington Books.

Pelletier, K. R., & Peper, E. (1977). Developing a biofeedback model: Alpha EEG feedback as a means for main control. *The International Journal of Clinical and Experimental Hypnosis, 25,* 361–371.

Pelletier, L., & Herold, E. (1983, May). *A study of sexual fantasies among young single females.* Paper presented at the meeting of the World Congress of Sexuality, Washington, DC.

Pelz, E. B. (1965). Some factors in "Group decision." In H. Proshansky & B. Seidenberg (Eds.), *Basic studies in social psychology* (pp. 437–444). New York: Holt, Rinehart & Winston. (Original work published 1955)

Pendery, M. L., Maltzman, I. M., & West, L. J. (1982). Controlled drinking by alcoholics? New finding and a reevaluation of a major affirmative study. *Science, 217,* 169–174.

Penfield, W., & Baldwin, M. (1952). Temporal lobe seizures and the technique of subtotal lobectomy. *Annals of Surgery, 136,* 625–634.

Penfield, W., & Perot, P. (1963). The brain's record of auditory and visual experience. *Brain, 86,* 596–696.

Penick, E. C., Powell, B. J., Nickel, E. J., Read, M. R., Gabrielli, W. F., & Liskow, B. I. (1990). Examination of Cloninger's Type I and Type II alcoholism with a sample of men alcoholics in treatment. *Alcoholism: Clinical and Experimental Research, 14,* 623–629.

Pennebaker, J. W. (1990). *Opening up: The healing power of confiding in others.* New York: Morrow.

Pennebaker, J. W., & Harber, K. D. (1991, April). *Coping after the Loma Prieta earthquake: A preliminary report.* Paper presented at the Western Psychological Association Convention, San Francisco, CA.

Pennebaker, J. W., Kiecolt-Glaser, J. K, & Glaser, R. (1988). Disclosure of traumas and immune function: The health implications for psychotherapy. *Journal of Consulting and Clinical Psychology, 56,* 239.

Pennick, S., Smith, G., Wienske, K., & Hinkle, L. (1963). An experimental evaluation of the relationship between hunger and gastric motility. *American Journal of Physiology, 205,* 421–426.

Penrose, L. S., & Penrose, R. (1958). Impossible objects: A special type of visual illusion. *British Journal of Psychology, 49.*

Perenin, M. T., & Jeannerod, M. (1975). Residual vision in cortically blind hemifields. *Neuropsychologia, 13,* 1–7.

Perlin, S. (Ed.). (1975). *A handbook for the study of suicide.* New York: Oxford University Press.

Perlman, D. (1990, July 18). Heart risk lowered in community

experiment. *San Francisco Chronicle,* pp. 1, A6.

Perlmutter, C. (1989, September). The dance of healing: Psychiatrist Carl Hammerschlag offers healing lessons based on Native American traditions. *Prevention, 41,* 69.

Perlmutter, M., & Hall, E. (1985). *Adult development and aging.* New York: Wiley.

Perls, F. S. (1967). Group vs. individual therapy. *ECT: A Review of General Semantics, 34,* 306–312.

Perls, F. S. (1969). *Gestalt therapy verbatim.* Lafayette, CA: Real People Press.

Persons, J. (1991). Psychotherapy outcome studies do not accurately represent current models of psychotherapy. *American Psychologist, 46,* 99–106.

Persons, J. B. (1986). The advantages of studying psychological phenomena rather than psychiatric diagnoses. *American Psychologist, 41,* 1252–1260.

Pert, C. B., & Snyder, S. H. (1973). Opiate receptor: Demonstration in the nervous tissue. *Science, 179,* 1011–1014.

Peters, T. J., & Waterman, R. H., Jr. (1983). *In search of excellence: Lessons from America's best-run companies.* New York: Warner.

Peterson, C., & Seligman, M. E. P. (1984). Explanatory style and depression: Theory and evidence. *Psychological Review, 91,* 341–374.

Peterson, C., Seligman, M. E. P., & Vaillant, G. E. (1988). Pessimistic explanatory style is a risk factor for physical illness: A thirty-five year longitudinal study. *Journal of Personality and Social Psychology, 55,* 23–27.

Peterson, J. L., & Zill, N. (1981). Television viewing in the United States and children's intellectual, social, and emotional development. *Television and Children, 2,* 21–28.

Peterson, L. R., & Peterson, M. J. (1959). Short-term retention of individual verbal items. *Journal of Experimental Psychology, 58,* 193–198.

Petitto, L. A., & Marentette, P. A. (1991). Babbling in the manual mode: Evidence for the ontogeny of language. *Science, 251,* 1493–1496.

Pettigrew, T. F. (1985). New patterns of racism: The different worlds of 1984 and 1964. *Rutgers Law Review, 37,* 673–706.

Pfaffman, C. (1959). The sense of taste. In J. Field (Ed.), *Handbook of physiology: Section 1. Neurophysiology* (Vol. 1). Washington, DC: American Physiological Society.

Pfefferbaum, A. (1977). Psychotherapy and psychopharmacology. In J. D. Barchas, P. A. Berger, R. D. Ciacanello, & G. R. Elliott (Eds.), *Psychopharmacology: From theory to practice* (pp. 481–492). New York: Oxford University Press.

Pfungst, O. (1911). *Clever Hans (the horse of Mr. Von Osten)* (R. Rosenthal, Trans.). New York: Holt, Rinehart & Winston.

Phares, E. J. (1984). *Clinical psychology: Concepts, methods, and professionals* (Rev. ed.). Homewood, IL: Dorsey.

Phelps, M. E., & Mazziotta, J. C. (1986). Positron emission tomography: Human brain function and biochemistry. *Science, 228,* 799–809.

Phillips, D. P. (1983). The impact of mass media violence on U.S. homicides. *American Sociological Review, 48,* 560–568.

Piaget, J. (1954). *The construction of reality in the child.* New York: Basic Books.

Piaget, J. (1965). *The moral judgment of the child* (M. Gabain, Trans.). New York: Macmillan.

Piaget, J. (1977). *The development of thought: Equilibrium of cognitive structures.* New York: Viking Press.

Piaget, J., & Inhelder, B. (1967). *The child's conception of space.* New York: Norton.

Piccione, C., Hilgard, E. R., & Zimbardo, P. G. (1989). On the degree of stability of measured hypnotizability over a 25-year period. *Journal of Personality and Social Psychology, 56,* 289–295.

Pifer, A., & Bronte, L. (Eds.). (1986). *Our aging society: Paradox and promise.* New York: Norton.

Piliavin, I. M., Rodin, J., & Piliavin, J. A. (1969). Good Samaritanism: An underground phenomenon? *Journal of Personality and Social Psychology, 13,* 289–300.

Piliavin, J. A., & Piliavin, I. M. (1972). Effect of blood on reactions to a victim. *Journal of Personality and Social Psychology, 23,* 353–361.

Pilisuk, M., & Parks, S. H. (1986). *The healing web: Social networks and human survival.* Hanover, NH: University Press of New England.

Pines, M. (1981, October 4). Genie: The "Wild Child" of California. *San Francisco Examiner-Chronicle,* This World Section, pp. 8–14.

Pines, M. (1983, November). Can a rock walk? *Psychology Today,* pp. 46–54.

Pinkerton, J. (Ed.). (1814). *A general collection of the best and most interesting voyages and travels in all parts of the world, 1808–1814.* London: Longman, Hurst, Rees, & Orne.

Pittenger, J. B. (1988). Direct perception of change. *Perception, 17,* 119–133.

Pitts, F. N. (1969). The biochemistry of anxiety. *Scientific American, 220*(2), 69–75.

Place, E. J. S., & Gilmore, G. C. (1980). Perceptual organization in schizophrenia. *Journal of Abnormal Psychology, 89,* 409–418.

Plomin, R. (1989). Environment and genes: Determinants of behavior. *American Psychologist, 44,* 105–111.

Plomin, R., Chipuer, H. M., & Loehlin, J. C. (1990). Behavioral genetics and personality. In L. A. Pervin (Ed.), *Handbook of personality theory and research* (pp. 225–243). New York: Guilford Press.

Plomin, R., & Daniels, D. (1987). Genetics and shyness. In W. W. Jones, J. M. Cheek, & S. R. Briggs (Eds.), *Shyness: Perspectives on research and treatment* (pp. 63–80). New York: Plenum.

Plomin, R., DeFries, J. C., & McClearn, G. E. (1980). *Behavioral genetics: A primer.* San Francisco: Freeman.

Plomin, R., & Rende, R. (1991). Human behavioral genetics. *Annual Review of Psychology, 42,* 161–190.

Plous, S. (1985). Perceptual illusions and military realities: A social-psychological analysis of the nuclear arms race. *Journal of Conflict Resolution, 29,* 363–389.

Plous, S. (1986, February). *The effects of anchoring on subjective probability estimates of an imminent nuclear war.* Paper presented at the meeting of the California State Psychological Association, San Francisco, CA.

Plous, S. (1989). Thinking the unthinkable: The effects of anchoring on likelihood estimates of nuclear war. *Journal of Applied Social Psychology, 19,* 67–91.

Plous, S., & Zimbardo, P. G. (1984, November). The looking glass war. *Psychology Today,* pp. 48–59:

Plutchik, R. (1980). *Emotion: A psychoevolutionary synthesis.* New York: Harper & Row.

Plutchik, R. (1984). Emotions: A general psychoevolutionary theory. In K. Scherer & P. Ekman (Eds.), *Approaches to emotion.* Hillsdale, NJ: Erlbaum.

Plutchik, R., Kellerman, H., & Conte, H. Q. (1979). A structural theory of ego defenses and emotions. In C. Izard (Ed.), *Emotions and psychopathology* (pp. 229–257). New York: Plenum.

Police officers beat blind man. (1989, May 17). *The New York Times,* p. 7.

Pomerantz, J., & Kubovy, M. (1986). Theoretical approaches to perceptual organization. In K. R. Boff, L. Kaufman, & J. P. Thomas (Eds.), *Handbook of perception and human performance* (Vol. 3, pp. 1–46). New York: Wiley.

Poon, L. W. (1985). Differences in human memory with aging: Nature, causes, and clinical implications. In J. E. Birren & W. K. Schaie (Eds.), *Handbook of the psychology of aging* (pp. 427–462). New York: Van Nostrand Reinhold.

Poppel, E. (1977). Midbrain mechanisms in human vision. In E. Poppel, R. Held, & J. E. Downing (Eds.), *Neurosciences research program bulletin: Vol. 15, Neuronal mechanisms in visual perception* (pp. 335–343). Cambridge, MA: MIT Press.

Porras, J. I., & Silvers, R. C. (1991). Organization development and transformation. *Annual Review of Psychology, 42,* 51–78.

Porter, G. (1987). Socioeconomic transformations [Review of *The control revolution*]. *Science, 236,* 970–972.

Posner, J. K. (1982). The development of mathematical knowledge in two West African societies. *Child Development 53,* 200–208.

Posner, M., & Petersen, S. E. (1990). The attentional system of the human brain. *Annual Review of Neuroscience, Vol. 13,* 25–42.

Posner, M. I. (1978). Cumulative development of attentional theory. *American Psychologist, 37,* 168–179.

Posner, M. I. (1982). Cumulative development of attentional theory. *American Psychologist, 37,* 168–179.

Posner, M. I. (1988). Structures and functions of selective attention. In T. Boll & B. Bryant (Eds.), *Master lectures in clinical neuropsychology* (pp. 173–202). Washington, DC: American Psychological Association.

Posner, M. I. (1990). In *Discovering Psychology,* Program 10 [PBS video series]. Washington, DC: Annenberg/CPB Project.

Posner, M. I., & Snyder, C. R. (1975). Facilitation and inhibition in the processing of signals. *Journal of Experimental Psychology: General, 109,* 160–174.

Posner, M. I., & Snyder, C. R. R. (1974). Attention and cognitive control. In R. L. Solso (Ed.), *Information processing and cognition: The Loyola Symposium* (pp. 55–88). Potomac, MD: Erlbaum.

Post, F. (1980). Paranoid, schizophrenic-like, and schizophrenic states in the aged. In J. E. Birren & R. B. Stone (Eds.), *Handbook of mental health and aging* (pp. 591–615). Englewood Cliffs, NJ: Prentice-Hall.

Postman, L., & Phillips, L. (1965). Short-term temporal changes in free recall. *Quarterly Journal of Experimental Psychology, 17,* 132–138.

Pound, E. (1934). *The ABC of reading.* New York: New Directions Publishing Co.

Powell, L. H., & Eagleston, J. R. (1983). The assessment of chronic stress in college students. In E. M. Altmaier (Ed.), *Helping students manage stress—new directions for student services* (Vol. 21, pp. 23–41). San Francisco: Jossey-Bass.

Powley, T. L. (1977). The ventromedial hypothalamic syndrome, satiety, and a cephalic phase hypothesis. *Psychological Review, 84,* 89–126.

Pratkanis, A. R., Greenwald, A. G. (1988). Recent perspective on unconscious processing: Still no marketing applications. *Psychology & Marketing, 5,* 337–353.

Premack, D. (1965). Reinforcement theory. In D. Levine (Ed.), *Nebraska Symposium on Motivation* (pp. 128–180). Lincoln, NE: University of Nebraska Press.

Prentice-Dunn, S., & Rogers, R. W. (1983). Deindividuation in aggression. In R. G. Green & E. I. Donnerstein (Eds.), *Aggression: Theoretical and empirical reviews* (Vol. 2, pp. 155–171). New York: Academic Press.

Prentky, R. A. (1980). *Creativity and psychopathology.* New York: Praeger.

Preti, G., Cutler, W. B., Garcia, G. R., Huggins, & Lawley, J. J. (1986). Human axillary secretions influence women's menstrual cycles: The role of donor extract from females. *Hormones and Behavior.*

Pribram, K. H. (1979). Behaviorism, phenomenology and holism in psychology: A scientific analysis. *Journal of Social and Biological Sciences, 2,* 65–72.

Pribram, K. H., & Gill, M. M. (1976). *Freud's "Project" reassessed.* New York: Basic Books.

Price, R. (1953/1980). *Droodles.* Los Angeles, CA: Price/Stern/Sloan.

Price, R. H., Ketterer, R. F., Bader, B. C., & Monahan, J. (Eds.). (1980). *Prevention in mental health: Research, policy, and practice* (Vol. 1). Beverly Hills, CA: Sage.

Prince, A., & Pinker, S. (1988). On language and connectionism: Analysis of a parallel distributed processing model of language acquisition. *Cognition, 28,* 73–194.

Pritchard, R. D., Dunnette, M. D., & Jorgenson, D. O. (1972). Effects of perceptions of equity and inequity on worker performance and satisfaction. *Journal of Applied Psychology, 56,* 75–94.

Proshansky, H. M. (1976). Environmental psychology and the real world. *American Psychologist, 31,* 303–310.

Putnam, F. W. (1984, March). The psychophysiologic investigation of multiple personality disorder [Symposium on Multiple Personality]. *The Psychiatric Clinics of North America, 7*(1), 31–40.

Putnam, F. W. (1990). In *Discovering Psychology*, Program 14 [PBS video series]. Washington, DC: Annenberg/CPB Program.

Q

Quattrone, G. (1986). On the perception of a group's variability. In S. Worchell & W. Austin (Eds.), *The psychology of intergroup relations* (Vol. 2, pp. 25–48). New York: Nelson-Hall.

Quattrone, G. A. (1982). Overattribution and unit formation: When behavior engulfs the person. *Journal of Personality and Social Psychology, 42,* 593–607.

Quattrone, G. A., Lawrence, C. P., Warren, D. L., Souza-Silva, K., Finkel, S. E., & Andrus, D. E. (1984). *Explorations in anchoring: The effects of prior range, anchor extremity, and suggestive hints.* Unpublished manuscript, Stanford University.

Quindlen, A. (1990, October 7). Hearing the cries of crack. *The New York Times,* Section 4, Col. 1, p. E19.

R

Rabbie, J. M. (1981). The effects of intergroup competition and cooperation on intra- and intergroup relationships. In J. Grzelak & V. Derlega (Eds.), *Living with other people: Theory and research on cooperation and helping.* New York: Academic Press.

Rabbie, J. M., & Wilkens, G. (1971). Intergroup competition and its effect on intragroup and intergroup relations. *European Journal of Psychology, 1,* 215–234.

Rabinowitz, F. M. (1987). An analysis of the maturation/learning controversy. *Canadian Psychology, 28,* 322–337.

Rabkin, J. G., Gelb, L., & Lazar, J. B. (Eds.). (1980). *Attitudes toward the mentally ill: Research perspectives* [Report of an NIMH workshop]. Rockville, MD: National Institutes of Mental Health.

Rachman, S. (1966). Sexual fetishism: An experimental analogue. *Psychological Record, 6,* 293–296.

Rachman, S., & Hodgson, R. (1980). *Obsessions and compulsions.* Englewood Cliffs, NJ: Prentice-Hall.

Radke-Yarrow, M., Zahn-Waxler, C., & Chapman, M. (1983). Children's prosocial dispositions and behavior. In P. H. Mussen (Ed.), *Handbook of child development: Socialization, personality, and social development* (Vol. 4, pp. 469–545). New York: Wiley.

Rahe, R. H., & Arthur, R. J. (1977). Life-change patterns surrounding illness experience. In A. Monat & R. S. Lazarus (Eds.), *Stress and coping* (pp. 36–44). New York: Columbia University Press.

Rahe, R. H., & Arthur, R. J. (1978, March). Life change and illness studies: Past history and future directions. *Journal of Human Stress,* pp. 3–15.

Raiffa, H. (1982). *The art and science of negotiation.* Cambridge, MA: Harvard University Press.

Rakic, P. (1985). Limits of neurogenesis in primates. *Science, 227,* 1054–1057.

Rapoport, J. L. (1989, March). The biology of obsessions and compulsions. *Scientific American,* pp. 83–89.

Rasmussen, G. L., & Windle, W. F. (1960). *Neural mechanisms of the auditory and vestibular systems.* Springfield, IL : Charles C Thomas.

Ray, O., & Ksir, C. (1987). *Drugs, society, and human behavior.* St. Louis: Times Mirror/Mosby.

Ray, W. J., & Cole, H. W. (1985). EEG alpha activity reflects attentional demands, and beta activity reflects emotional and cognitive processes. *Science, 228,* 750–752.

Raymond, J. S., Chung, C. S., & Wood, D. W. (1991). Asia-Pacific prevention research: Challenges, opportunities, and implementation. *American Psychologist, 46,* 528–531.

Reason, J. (1978). Motion sickness: Some theoretical and practical considerations. *Applied Ergonomics, 9,* 163–167.

Regier, D. A., Boyd, J. H, Burke, J. D., Rae, D. S., Myers, J. K., Kramer, M., Robins, L. N., George, L. K., Karno, M., & Locke, B. Z. (1988). One-month prevalence of mental disorders in the United States. *Archives of General Psychiatry, 45,* 977–986.

Rehm, L. P. (1977). A self-control model of depression. *Behavior Therapy, 8,* 787–804.

Reid, T. (1785/1850). *Essays on the intellectual powers of man.* Cambridge: J. Bartlett.

Reinisch, J. M. (1981). Prenatal exposure to synthetic progestions increases potential for aggression in humans. *Science, 211,* 1171–1173.

Reisenzein, R. (1983). The Schachter theory of emotion: Two decades later. *Psychological Bulletin, 94,* 239–264.

Reiser, B. J., Black, J. B., & Abelson, R. P. (1985). Knowledge structures in the organization and retrieval of autobiographical memories. *Cognitive Psychology, 17,* 89–137.

Reisman, J. (1986, January 16). *A content analysis of* Playboy, Penthouse, *and* Hustler *magazines with special attention to the portrayal of children, crime, and violence.* Supplementary testimony given to the United States Attorney General's Commission on Pornography, New York.

Reiterman, T., & Jacobs, J. (1983). *Raven: The untold story of Jim Jones and his people.* New York: Dutton.

Rescorla, R. A. (1966). Predictability and number of pairings in Pavlovian fear conditioning. *Psychonomic Science, 4,* 383–384.

Rescorla, R. A. (1972). Information variables in Pavlovian conditioning. In G. Bower (Ed.), *The psychology of learning and motivation* (Vol. 6). New York: Academic Press.

Rescorla, R. A. (1980). *Pavlovian second-order conditioning: Studies in associative learning.* Hillsdale, NJ: Erlbaum.

Rescorla, R. A. (1988). Pavlovian conditioning: It's not what you think it is. *American Psychologist, 43,* 151–160.

Rescorla, R. A., & Wagner, A. R. (1972). A theory of Pavlovian conditioning: Variations in the effectiveness of reinforcement and nonreinforcement. In A. H. Black & W. F. Prokasy (Eds.), *Classical conditioning, II: Current research and theory* (pp. 64–94). New York: Appleton-Century-Crofts.

Rest, J. R., & Thoma, S. J. (1976). Relation of moral judgment development to formal education. *Developmental Psychology, 21,* 709–714.

Reston, N. J. (1986, December 24). Questions about the President's memory. *The New York Times.*

Restrepo, D., Miyamoto, T., Bryant, B. P., & Teeter, J. H. (1990). Odor stimuli trigger influx of calcium into olfactory neurons of the channel catfish. *Science, 249,* 1166–1168.

Revkin, A. C. (1989, January). Dilutions of grandeur. *Discover, 10,* pp. 74–75.

Reynolds, J. E. (Ed.). (1989). *Martindale: The extra pharmacopoeia.* London: The Pharmaceutical Press.

Rheingold, H. L., & Cook, K. V. (1975). The contents of boys' and girls' rooms as an index of parents' behavior. *Child Development, 46,* 459–463.

Richardson-Klavern, A., & Bjork, R. A. (1988). Primary versus secondary rehearsal in an imaginary voice: Differential effects recognition memory and perceptual identification. *Bulletin of Psychonomic Society, 26,* 187–190.

Richter, C. P. (1957). On the phenomenon of sudden death in animals and man. *Psychosomatic Medicine, 19,* 191–198.

Richter, C. P. (1965). *Biological clocks in medicine and psychiatry.* Springfield, IL: Charles C Thomas.

Riddle, D., & Morin, S. (1977). Removing the stigma from individuals. *American Psychological Association Monitor, 16,* 28.

Riggs, J. M., & Cantor, N. (1981). *Information exchange in social interaction: Anchoring effects of self-concepts and expectancies.* Unpublished manuscript, Gettysburg College.

Rips, L. (1988). Deduction. In R. J. Sternberg & E. E. Smith (Eds.), *The psychology of human thought* (pp. 118–152). Cambridge: Cambridge University Press.

Riskind, J. H. (1984). They stoop to conquer: Guiding and self-regulatory functions of physical posture after success and failure. *Journal of Personality and Social Psychology, 47,* 479–493.

Ritz, M. C., Lamb, R. J., Goldberg, S. R., & Kuhar, M. J. (1987). Cocaine receptors on dopamine transporters are related to self-administration of cocaine. *Science, 237,* 1219–1223.

Robbins, L. C. (1963). The accuracy of parental recall of aspects of child development and of child rearing practices. *Journal of Abnormal and Social Psychology, 66,* 261–270.

Roberts, T. B. (1973). Maslow's human motivation needs hierarchy: A bibliography. *Research in Education* (ERIC Document Reproduction Service No. ED 069 591).

Robins, L. N., Helzer, J. E., Weissman, M. M., Orvaschel, H., Gruenberg, E. Burke, J. D., & Regier, D. A. (1984). Lifetime prevalence of specific psychiatric disorders in three sites. *Archives of General Psychiatry, 41,* 949–958.

Robinson, M. J. (1985). Jesse Helms take stock: Study shows Rather bears no liberal bias. *Washington Journalism Review, 7,* 14–17.

Robles, R., Smith, R., Carver, C. S., & Wellens, A. R. (1987). Influence of subliminal visual images on the experience of anxiety. *Personality and Social Psychology Bulletin, 13,* 399–410.

Rock, I. (1975). *An introduction to perception.* New York: Macmillan.

Rock, I. (1983). *The logic of perception.* Cambridge, MA: Bradford Books/MIT Press.

Rock, I. (1986). The description and analysis of object and event perception. In K. R. Boff, L. Kaufman, & J. P. Thomas (Eds.), *Handbook of perception and human performance* (Vol. 2, pp. 33–71). New York: Wiley.

Rock, I., & Gutman, D. (1981). The effect of inattention on form perception. *Journal of Experimental Psychology: Human Perception and Performance, 7,* 275–285.

Rockmore, M. (1985, March 5). Analyzing analysis. *American Way,* pp. 71–75.

Rodin, J. (1983, April). Behavioral medicine: Beneficial effects of self control training in aging. *International Review of Applied Psychology, 32,* 153–181.

Rodin, J. (1985). The application of social psychology. In G. Lindzey & E. Aronson (Eds.), *Handbook of social psychology* (3rd ed., Vol. 2, pp. 805–882). New York: Random House.

Rodin, J. (1986). Aging and health: Effects of the sense of control. *Science, 233,* 1271–1276.

Rodin, J. (1990). In *Discovering Psychology,* Program 23 [PBS video series]. Washington, DC: Annenberg/CPB Program.

Rodin, J., Bohm, L. C., & Wack, J. T. (1982). Control, coping, and aging: models for research and intervention. In L. Bickman (Ed.), *Applied social psychology annual* (pp. 153–180). London: Sage.

Rodin, J., & Janis, I. J. (1982). The social influence of physicians and other health care practitioners as agents of change. In H. S. Freidman & M. R. DiMatteo, *Interpersonal issues in health care* (pp. 33–49). New York: Academic Press.

Rodin, J., & Salovey, P. (1989). Health psychology. *Annual Review of Psychology, 40,* 533–579.

Roediger, H. L. (1990). Implicit memory. *American Psychologist, 45,* 1043–1056.

Roediger, H. L., & Crowder, R. G. (1976). A serial position effect in recall of United States presidents. *Bulletin of the Psychonomic Society, 8,* 275–278.

Roffwarg, H. P., Munzio, J. N., & Dement, W. C. (1966). Ontogenetic development of the human sleep-dream cycle. *Science, 152,* 604–619.

Rogers, C. R. (1947). Some observations on the organization of personality. *American Psychologist, 2,* 358–368.

Rogers, C. R. (1951). *Client-centered therapy: Its current practice, implications and theory.* Boston: Houghton-Mifflin.

Rogers, C. R. (1959). A theory of therapy, personality, and interpersonal relationships, as developed in the client-centered framework. In S. Koch (Ed.), *Psychology: A study of a science* (Vol. 3). New York: McGraw-Hill.

Rogers, C. R. (1977). *On personal power: Inner strength and its revolutionary impact.* New York: Delacorte.

Rogers, R. W. (1984). Changing health-related attitudes and behavior: The role of preventive health psychology. In J. H. Harver, J. E. Maddux, R. P. McGlynn, & C. D. Stoltenberg (Eds.), *Social perception in clinical and consulting psychology* (Vol. 2, pp. 91–112). Lubbock, TX: Texas Tech University Press.

Rohrer, J. H., Baron, S. H., Hoffman, E. L., & Swinder, D. V. (1954). The stability of autokinetic judgment. *Journal of Abnormal and Social Psychology, 49,* 595–597.

Rook, K. (1984). Promoting social bonding: Strategies for helping the lonely and socially isolated. *American Psychologist, 37,* 1389–1407.

Rorer, L. G., & Widiger, T. A. (1983). Personality structure and assessment. *Annual Review of Psychology, 34,* 431–463.

Rorschach, H. (1942). *Psychodiagnostics: A diagnostic test based on perception.* New York: Grune & Stratton.

Rosch, E. H. (1973). Natural categories. *Cognitive Psychology, 4,* 328–350.

Rosch, E. H. (1978). Principles of categorization. In E. Rosch & B. B. Lloyd (Eds.), *Cognition and categorization* (pp. 27–48). Hillsdale, NJ: Erlbaum.

Rosch, E. H., Mervis, C. B., Gray, W. D., Johnson, D. M., & Boyes-Braem, P. (1976). Basic objects in natural categories. *Cognitive Psychology, 8,* 382–439.

Rose, S. (1973). *The conscious brain.* New York: Knopf.

Roseman, I. J. (1984). Cognitive determinants of emotions: A structural theory. In P. Shaver (Ed.), *Review of personality and social psychology: Vol. 5, Emotions, relationships, and health* (pp. 11–36). Beverly Hills, CA: Sage.

Rosenbaum, M., & Berger, M. M. (Eds.). (1975). *Group psychotherapy and group function* (Rev. ed.). New York: Basic Books.

Rosenbaum, M., & Muroff, M. (Eds.). (1984). *Fourteen contemporary reinterpretations.* New York: Free Press.

Rosenberg, D. (1990, November 19). Bad times at Hangover U.: College parties lead to ER or drunk tank. *Newsweek, 116,* p. 81.

Rosenberg, S. (1988). Self and others: Studies in social personality and autobiography. In L. Berkowitz (Ed.), *Advances in experimental social psychology* (Vol. 21, pp. 57–95). New York: Academic Press.

Rosenhan, D. (1990). In *Discovering Psychology,* Program 21 [PBS video series]. Washington, DC: Annenberg/CPB Program.

Rosenhan, D. L. (1969). Some origins of concern for others. In P. Mussen, J. Langer, & M. Covington (Eds.), *Trends and issues in developmental psychology.* New York: Holt, Rinehart & Winston.

Rosenhan, D. L. (1973). On being sane in insane places. *Science, 179,* 250–258.

Rosenhan, D. L. (1975). The contextual nature of psychiatric diagnoses. *Journal of Abnormal Psychology, 84,* 462–474.

Rosenhan, D. L., & Seligman, M. E. P. (1989). *Abnormal Psychology* (2nd ed.). New York: Norton.

Rosenthal, D. (Ed.). (1963). *The Genain quadruplets.* New York: Basic Books.

Rosenthal, D., Wender, P. H., Kety, S. S., Schulsinger, F., Weiner, J., & Rieder, R. (1975). Parent-child relationships and psychopathological disorder in the child. *Archives of General Psychiatry, 32,* 466–476.

Rosenthal, N. E., Sack, D. A., Gillin, J. C., Lewy, A. J., Goodwin, F. K., Davenport, Y., Mueller, P. S., Newsome, D. A., & Wehr, T. A. (1984). Seasonal affective disorder: A description of the syndrome and preliminary findings with light therapy. *Archives of General Psychiatry, 41,* 72–80.

Rosenthal, R. (1966). *Experimenter effects in behavioral research.* New York: Appleton-Century-Crofts.

Rosenthal, R. (1990). In *Discovering Psychology,* programs 1 and 20 [PBS video series]. Washington, DC: Annenberg/CPB Project.

Rosenthal, R., & Jacobson, L. F. (1968a). *Pygmalion in the classroom.* New York: Holt.

Rosenthal, R., & Jacobson, L. F. (1968b). Teacher expectations for the disadvantaged. *Scientific American, 218*(4), 19–23.

Rosenweig, M., & Leiman, A. L. (1982). *Physiological psychology.* Lexington, MA: D. C. Heath.

Rosenzweig, M. R. (1984a). U.S. psychology and world psychology. *American Psychologist, 39,* 877–884.

Rosenzweig, M. R. (1984b). Experience, memory, and the brain. *American Psychologist, 39,* 365–376.

Ross, L. (1977). The intuitive psychologist and his shortcomings. In L. Berkowitz (Ed.), *Advances in experimental social psychology* (Vol. 10). New York: Academic Press.

Ross, L. (1988). Situational perspectives on the obedience experiments. [Review of The obedience experiments: A case study of controversy in social science]. *Contemporary Psychology, 33,* 101–104.

Ross, L., Amabile, T., & Steinmetz, J. (1977). Social roles, social control and biases in the social perception process. *Journal of Personality and Social Psychology, 37,* 485–494.

Ross, L., & Lepper, M. R. (1980). The perseverance of beliefs: Empirical and normative considerations. In R. A. Shweder & D. Fiske (Eds.), *New directions for methodology of behavioral science: Fallible judgments in behavioral research* (pp. 17–36). San Francisco: Jossey-Bass.

Ross, L., & Nisbett, R. E. (1991). *The person and the situation: Perspectives of social psychology.* New York: McGraw-Hill.

Ross, R. T., Begab, M. J., Dandis, E. M., Giannipiccolo, J. S., Jr., & Meyers, C. E. (1986). *Lives of the mentally retarded.* Stanford, CA: Stanford University Press.

Rossi, A. (1984). Gender and parenthood. *American Sociological Review, 49,* 1–19.

Roth, J. D., Le Roith, D., & Shiloach, J. (1982). The evolutionary origins of hormones, neurotransmitters, and other extracellular chemical messengers. *New England Journal of Medicine, 306,* 523–527.

Roth, T., Roehrs, T., Carskadon, M. A., & Dement, W. C. (1989). Daytime sleepiness and alertness. In M. Kryser, T. Roth, & W. C. Dement (Eds.), *Principles and practice of sleep medicine* (pp. 14–23). New York: Saunders.

Rothman, D. J. (1971). *The discovery of the asylum: Social order and disorder in the new republic.* Boston: Little, Brown.

Rotter, J. B. (1954). *Social learning and clinical psychology.* Englewood Cliffs, NJ: Prentice-Hall.

Rotton, J., & Frey, J. (1984). Psychological costs of air pollution: Atmospheric conditions, seasonal trends, and psychiatric emergencies. *Population and Environment: Behavioral and Social Issues, 7,* 3–16.

Rovee-Collier, C. K., Sullivan, M. W., Enright, M., Lucas, D., & Fagen, J. W. (1980). Reactivation of infant memory. *Science, 208,* 1159–1161.

Rozee, P., & Van Boemel, G. (1989). The psychological effects of war trauma and abuse on older Cambodian refugee women. *Women and Therapy, 8,* 23–50.

Rozin, P. (1976). The evolution of intelligence and access to the cognitive unconscious. In J. M. Sprague & A. A. Epstein (Eds.), *Progress in psychobiology and physiological psychology* (pp. 245–280). New York: Academic Press.

Rozin, P., & Fallon, A. E. (1987). A perspective on disgust. *Psychological Review, 94,* 23–41.

Rozin, P., & Kalat, J. W. (1971). Specific hungers and poison avoidance as adaptive specializations of learning. *Psychological Review, 78,* 459–486.

Rubin, B. K. (1990). Exposure of children with cystic fibrosis to environmental tobacco smoke. *The New England Journal of Medicine, 323,* 782–788.

Rubin, J. Z., Provenzano, F. J., & Luria, Z. (1974). The eye of the beholder: Parents' views on sex of newborns. *American Journal of Orthopsychiatry, 44,* 512–519.

Rubin, L. B. (1976, October). The marriage bed. *Psychology Today,* pp. 44–50, 91–92.

Rubin, Z. (1973). *Liking and loving.* New York: Holt, Rinehart & Winston.

Rudy, J. W., & Wagner, A. R. (1975). Stimulus selection in associative learning. In W. K. Estes (Ed.), *Handbook of learning and cognition* (Vol. 2). Hillsdale, NJ: Erlbaum.

Ruitenbeek, H. M. (1973). *The first Freudians.* New York: Jason Aronson.

Rumelhart, D. E., & McClelland, J. L. (1986). *Parallel distributed processing: Explorations in the microstructure of cognition* (2 vols.). Cambridge, MA: MIT Press.

Runner tells why she tried to kill herself. (1986, December 22). *San Francisco Examiner-Chronicle,* Sports Extra Section, p. 66.

Ruse, M. (1981). Are there gay genes? Sociobiology and homosexuality. *Journal of Homosexuality, 6,* 5–33.

Rushton, J. P., Fulker, D. W., Neale, M. C., Nias, D. K. B., & Eysenck, H. J. (1986). Altruism and aggression: The heritability of individual differences. *Journal of Personality and Social Psychology, 50,* 283–305.

Russell, B. (1948). *Human knowledge, its scope and limits.* New York: Simon & Schuster.

Russell, D., & McAuley, E. (1986). Causal attributions, causal dimensions, and affective reactions to success and failure. *Journal of Personality and Social Psychology, 50,* 1174–1185.

Russell, J. A., & Ward, L. M. (1982). Environmental psychology. *Annual Review of Psychology, 33,* 651–688.

Rutter, M. (1979). Maternal deprivation, 1972–1978: New findings, new concepts, new approaches. *Child Development, 50,* 283–305.

Ryan, W. (1976). *Blaming the victim.* (Rev. ed.). New York: Vintage Books.

Rychlak, J. (1979). *Discovering free will and personal responsibility.* New York: Oxford University Press.

Rylsky, M. (1986, February). A town born of the atom. *Soviet Life,* p. 8.

S

Saarinen, T. F. (1987). *Centering of mental maps of the world: Discussion paper.* Tucson: University of Arizona, Department of Geography and Regional Development.

Sabini, J., & Silver, M. (1982). *Moralities of everyday life.* New York: Oxford University Press.

Sachs, O. (1985). *The man who mistook his wife for a hat and other clinical tales.* New York: Summit.

Sachs, S. (1990, May 28). Romanian children suffer in asylums. *San Francisco Chronicle,* p. A12.

Sacks, O. (1973). *Migraine: Evolution of a common disorder.* Berkeley: University of California Press.

Saegert, S., & Hart, R. (1976). The development of sex differences in the environmental competence of children. In P. Burnett (Ed.), *Women in society.* Chicago: Maarouta.

Saks, M. J. (1977). *Jury verdicts: The role of group size and social decision rule.* Lexington, MA: Lexington Books.

Salmon, D. P., Zola-Morgan, S., & Squire, L. R. (1987). Retrograde amnesia following combined hippocampus-amygdala lesions in monkeys. *Psychobiology, 15,* 37–47.

Salovey, P., & Birnbaum, D. (1989). Influence of mood on health-relevant cognitions. *Journal of Personality and Social Psychology, 57,* 539–551.

Salovey, P., & Hancock, M. E. (1987). *The effects of state mood, trait depression, and cognitive set on personal health appraisal.* Unpublished manuscript, Yale University, New Haven, CT.

Salovey, P., & Rodin, J. (1985). Cognitions about the self: Connecting feeling states and social behavior. In L. Wheeler (Ed.), *Review of Personality and Social Psychology* (Vol. 6, pp. 143–167). Beverly Hills, CA: Sage.

Salzman, C. (1980). The use of ECT in the treatment of schizophrenia. *American Journal of Psychiatry, 137,* 1032–1041.

Salzman, C. D., Britten, K. H., & Newsome, W. T. (1990). Cortical microstimulation influences perceptual judgements of motion direction. *Nature, 346,* 174–177.

Samuelson, W., & Zeckhauser, R. (1988). Status quo bias in decision making. *Journal of Risk and Uncertainty, 1,* 7–59.

Sanchez-Craig, M., Annis, H. M., Bornet, A. R., & MacDonald, K. R. (1984). Random assignment to abstinence and controlled drinking: Evaluation of a cognitive-behavioral program for problem drinkers. *Journal of Consulting & Clinical Psychology, 52,* 390–403.

Sanders, R. S., & Reyhen, J. (1969). Sensory deprivation and the enhancement of hypnotic susceptibility. *Journal of Abnormal Psychology, 74,* 375–381.

Sapolsky, R. (1990). In *Discovering Psychology,* Program 4 [PBS video series]. Washington, DC: Annenberg/CPB Project.

Sapolsky, R. M. (1990). Adrenocortical function, social rank, and personality among wild baboons. *Biological Psychiatry, 28,* pp. 1–17.

Sarason, I. G., Johnson, J. H., & Siegel, J. M. (1978). Assessing the impact of life changes: Development of the Life Experiences Survey. *Journal of Consulting and Clinical Psychology, 46,* 932–946.

Sarbin, T. R., & Coe, W. C. (1972). *Hypnosis: A social psychological analysis of influence communication.* New York: Holt, Rinehart & Winston.

Sarnoff, I., & Corwin, S. M. (1959). Castration anxiety and the fear of death. *Journal of Personality, 27*, 374–385.

Sarnoff, I., & Katz, D. (1954). The motivational basis of attitude change. *Journal of Abnormal and Social Psychology, 49*, 115–124.

Satir, V. (1967). *Conjoint family therapy* (Rev. ed.). Palo Alto, CA: Science and Behavior Books.

Sattler, J. M. (1982). *Assessment of children's intelligence and special abilities*. Boston: Allyn & Bacon.

Savage, C. W. (1970). *The assessment of sensation*. Berkeley: University of California Press.

Sawyer, J. (1966). Measurement and prediction, clinical and statistical. *Psychological Bulletin, 66*, 178–200.

Scammon, R. E. (1930). The measurement of the body in childhood. In J. Harris, C. M. Jackson, D. G. Patterson, & R. E. Scammon (Eds.), *The measurement of man*. Minneapolis: University of Minnesota Press.

Scardamalia, M., & Bereiter, C. (1985). Fostering the development of self-regulation in children's knowledge processing. In S. F. Chapman, J. W. Segall, & R. Glaser (Eds.), *Thinking and learning skills: Research and open questions, Vol. 2* (pp. 563–577). Hillsdale, NJ: Erlbaum.

Scarr, S. (1981). *Race, social class, and individual differences in IQ*. Hillsdale, NJ: Erlbaum.

Scarr, S. (1988a). How genotypes and environments combine: Development and individual differences. In N. Bolger, A. Caspi, G. Downey, & M. Morehouse (Eds.), *Persons in context: Developmental processes*. New York: Cambridge University Press.

Scarr, S. (1988b). Race and gender as psychological variables: Social and ethical issues. *American Psychologist, 43*, 56–59.

Scarr, S., & Weinberg, R. A. (1976). I.Q. test performance of black children adopted by white families. *American Psychologist, 31*, 726–739.

Schachter, S. (1959). *The psychology of affiliation*. Stanford, CA: Stanford University Press.

Schachter, S. (1971). *Emotion, obesity and crime*. New York: Academic Press.

Schachter, S., & Singer, J. (1962). Cognitive, social and physiological determinants of emotional state. *Psychological Review, 69*, 379–399.

Schacter, D. L. (1987). Implicit memory: History and current status. *Journal of Experimental Psychology: Learning, Memory, and Cognition, 13*, 501–518.

Schacter, D. L. (1989). Modality specificity of implicit memory for new associations. *Journal of Experimental Psychology: Learning, Memory, and Cognition, 15*, 3–12.

Schacter, D. L., Kihlstrom, J. F., Kihlstrom, L. C., & Berren, M. B. (1989). Autobiographical memory in a case of multiple personality disorder. *Journal of Abnormal Psychology, 98*, 508–514.

Schaef, A. W. (1987). *When society becomes an addict*. New York: Harper & Row.

Schaffer, H. R. (1984). *The child's entry into a social world*. New York: Academic Press.

Schaie, K. W. (1980). Intelligence and problem solving. In J. E. Birren & R. B. Sloan (Eds.), *Handbook of mental health and aging* (pp. 262–284). Englewood Cliffs, NJ: Prentice-Hall.

Schaie, K. W. (1989). The hazards of cognitive aging. *The Gerontologist, 29*, 484–493.

Schaie, K. W., & Willis, S. L. (1986). Can decline in adult intellectual functioning be reversed? *Developmental Psychology, 22*, 223–232.

Schaie, W. (1990). In *Discovering Psychology*, Program 18 [PBS video series]. Washington, DC: Annenberg/CPB Program.

Schanberg, S. M. (1990). In *Discovering Psychology*, Program 4 [PBS video series]. Washington, DC: Annenberg/CPB Project.

Schanberg, S. M., Kuhn, C. M., Field, T. M., & Barolome, J. V. (1990). Maternal deprivation and growth suppression. In N. Guzenhauser (Ed.), *Advances in touch* (pp. 3–10). Skillman, NJ: Johnson & Johnson Co.

Schank, R. C., & Abelson, R. (1977). *Scripts, plans, goals and understanding: An inquiry into human knowledge and structures*. Hillsdale, NJ: Erlbaum.

Scheier, M. F., Magovern, G. J., Sr., Abbott, R. A., Matthews, K. A., Owens, J. F., Fefebvre, R. C., & Carver, C. S. (1989). *Journal of Personality and Social Psychology, 57*, 1024–1040.

Schelkun, P. H. (1990). Secondhand smoke — more than annoying. *Cooking Light, 4*, 14–17.

Scherer, K. R. (1984). On the nature and function of emotion: A component process approach. In K. R. Scherer & P. Ekman (Eds.), *Approaches to emotion* (pp. 293–317). Hillsdale, NJ: Erlbaum.

Schieffelin, B. B. (1985). The acquisition of Kaluli. In D. I. Slobin (Ed.), *The crosslinguistic study of language acquisition: Vol. 1: The data* (pp. 525–594). Hillsdale, NJ: Erlbaum.

Schleifer, S. J., Keller, S. E., Camerino, M., Thornton, J. C., & Stein, M. (1983). Suppression of lymphocyte stimulation following bereavement. *Journal of the American Medical Association, 250*, 374–377.

Schmidt, W. E. (1987, June 7). Paddling in school: A tradition is under fire. *The New York Times*, pp. A1, A22.

Schneider, D. J. (1991). Social cognition. *Annual Review of Psychology, 42*, 527–561.

Schneider, D. J., Hastorf, A. H., & Ellsworth, P. C. (1979). *Person perception* (2nd ed.). Reading, MA: Addison-Wesley.

Schneider, G. E. (1969). Two visual systems. *Science, 163*, 895–902.

Schneider, W. (1984). Developmental trends in the meta-memory-memory behavior relationship. In D. L. Forrest-Pressley, G. E. Mackinnon, & P. G. Waller (Eds.), *Metacognition, cognition, and human performance*. New York: Academic Press.

Schneider, W., & Shiffrin, R. M. (1977). Controlled and automatic information processing: 1, Detection, search, and attention. *Psychological Review, 84*, 1–66.

Schneidman, E. S. (Ed.). (1976). *Deaths of man*. New York: Quadrangle.

Schrag, P. (1978). *Mind control*. New York: Delta.

Schreiber, F. (1973). *Sybil*. New York: Warner Books.

Schreiner, L., & Kling, A. (1963). Behavioral changes following rhinencephalic injury in the cat. *Journal of Neurophysiology, 16*, 634–659.

Schultz, R., Braun, R. G., & Kluft, R. P. (1989). Multiple personality disorder: Phenomenology of selected variables in comparison to major depression. *Dissociation, 2*, 45–51.

Schulz, R. (1976). Effects of control and predictability on the physical and psychological well-being of the institutionalized aged. *Journal of Personality and Social Psychology, 33*, 563–573.

Schulz, R. (1978). *The psychology of death, dying, and bereavement*. Reading, MA: Addison-Wesley.

Schulz, R., Tompkins, C., Wood, D., & Decker, S. (1987). The social psychology of caregiving: The physical and psychological costs of providing support to the disabled. *Journal of Applied Social Psychology, 17*, 401–428.

Schunk, D. H., & Cox, P. D. (1986). Strategy training and attributional feedback with learning disabled students. *Journal of Educational Psychology, 78*, 201–209.

Schwartz, B. (1984). *Psychology of learning and behavior* (2nd ed.). New York: Norton.

Schwartz, B., & Lacey, H. (1982). *Behaviorism, science, and human nature*. New York: Norton.

Schwartz, G. E. (1975). Biofeedback, self-regulation, and the patterning of physiological processes. *The American Scientist, 63*, 314–324.

Schwartz, G. E., Brown, S. L., & Ahern, G. L. (1980). Facial muscle patterning and subjective experience during affective imagery: Sex differences. *Psychophysiology, 17*, 75–82.

Schwartz, P., & Strom, D. (1978). The social psychology of female sexuality. In J. Sherman & F. L. Denmark (Eds.), *Psychology of women: Future directions of research* (pp. 149–177). New York: Psychological Dimensions.

Schweder, R. A., & Bourne, E. J. (1982). Does the concept of the person vary cross-culturally? In A. J. Marsella & G. M. White (Eds.), *Cultural conceptions of mental health and therapy* (pp. 97–137). London: Reidel.

Schweinhart, L. J., & Weikart, D. P. (1990). Research support for Head Start. *Science, 248*, 1174–1175.

Scott, D. T. (1987). Premature infants in later childhood: Some recent follow-up results. *Seminars in Perinatalology, 11,* 191–199.

Scott, J. P. (1963). The process of primary socialization in canine and human infants. *Monographs of the Society for Research in Child Development 28,* 1–47.

Scott, J. P., Stewart, J. M., & De Ghett, V. J. (1974). Critical periods in the organization of systems. *Developmental Psychobiology, 7,* 489–513.

Scott, R. A. (1972). A proposed framework for analyzing deviance as a property of social order. In R. A. Scott & J. D. Douglas (Eds.), *Theoretical perspectives on deviance.* New York: Basic Books.

Scott, V. (1984, June 13). A six-year nightmare for Jim Backus [United Press]. *San Francisco Chronicle,* p. 58.

Scovern, A. W., & Kilmann, P. R. (1980). Status of electroconvulsive therapy: Review of outcome literature. *Psychological Bulletin, 87,* 260–303.

Sears, P., & Barbee, A. H. (1977). Career and life situations among Terman's gifted women. In J. C. Stanley, W. C. George, & C. H. Solano (Eds.), *The gifted and the creative: A fifty-year perspective* (pp. 28–65). Baltimore: Johns Hopkins University Press.

Sears, R. R. (1961). Relation of early socialization experiences to aggression in middle childhood. *Journal of Abnormal and Social Psychology, 63,* 466–492.

Sears, R. R. (1977). Sources of life satisfactions of the Terman gifted men. *American Psychologist, 32,* 119–128.

Sebeok, T. A., & Rosenthal, R. (1981). The clever Hans phenomenon. *Annals of the New York Academy of Sciences,* Whole Vol. 364.

Secretary of Health and Human Services. (1990). *Alcohol and health.* Alexandria, VA: Editorial Experts.

Selfridge, O. G. (1955). Pattern recognition and modern computers. *Proceedings of the Western Joint Computer Conference.* New York: Institute of Electrical and Electronics Engineers.

Seligman, K. (1988, October 9). Educators are alarmed over testing frenzy. *San Francisco Examiner,* pp. B-1, B-5.

Seligman, M. E. P. (1971). Preparedness and phobias. *Behavior Therapy, 2,* 307–320.

Seligman, M. E. P. (1975). *Helplessness: On depression, development, and death.* San Francisco: Freeman.

Seligman, M. E. P. (1987). *Predicting depression, poor health and presidential elections.* Washington, DC: Federation of Behavioral, Psychological and Cognitive Sciences.

Seligman, M. E. P. (1991). *Learned optimism.* New York: Norton.

Seligman, M. E. P., & Maier, S. F. (1967). Failure to escape traumatic shock. *Journal of Experimental Psychology, 74,* 1–9.

Selman, R. (1980). *The growth of interpersonal understanding.* New York: Academic Press.

Selye, H. (1956). *The stress of life.* New York: McGraw-Hill.

Selye, H. (1974). *Stress without distress.* New York: New American Library.

Selye, H. (1976). *Stress in health and disease.* Reading, MA: Butterworth.

Selye, H. (1978). On the real benefits of eustress. *Psychology Today, 12,* pp. 60–64.

Selye, H. (1980). The stress concept today. In I. L. Kutash & L. B. Schlesinger (Eds.), *Handbook on stress and anxiety* (pp. 127–129). San Francisco: Josey-Bass.

Serling, R. J. (1986). Curing a fear of flying. *USAIR,* pp. 12–19.

Sex addicts: Many are professionals who exhibit varied behaviors. (1989, August 5). *Addiction Letter,* p. 9.

Shaffer, H. J. (1989). Conceptual crises in the addictions: The role of models in the field of compulsive gambling. In H. J. Shaffer, S. A. Stein, B. Gambino, & T. N. Cummings (Eds.), *Compulsive gambling: Theory, research, and practice.* Lexington, MA: D. C. Heath.

Shaffer, H. J., Stein, S. A., Gambino, B., & Cummings, T. N. (Eds.). (1989). *Compulsive gambling: Theory, research, and practice.* Lexington, MA: D. C. Heath.

Shaffer, L. H. (1975). Multiple attention in continuous verbal tasks. In P. M. A. Rabbit & S. Dornic (Eds.), *Attention and performance, Vol. 5.* London: Academic Press.

Shafii, M., Carrigan, S., Whittinghill, J. R., & Derrick, A. (1985). Psychological autopsy of completed suicide in children and adolescents. *American Journal of Psychiatry, 142,* 1061–1064.

Shallice, T. (1978). The dominant action system: An information-processing approach to consciousness. In K. S. Pope & J. L. Singer (Eds.), *The stream of consciousness: Scientific investigations into the flow of human experience* (pp. 117–157). New York: Plenum.

Shapiro, A. K. (1960). A contribution to a history of the placebo effect. *Behavioral Science, 5,* 109–135.

Shapiro, A. K. (1971). Placebo effects in medicine, psychotherapy and psychoanalysis. In A. E. Bergin & S. C. Garfield (Eds.), *Handbook of psychotherapy and behavior change: Empirical analysis.* (pp. 439-473). New York: Wiley.

Shapiro, A. K., & Morris, L. A. (1978). The placebo effect in medical and psychological therapies. In A. E. Bergin & S. C. Garfield (Eds.), *Handbook of psychotherapy and change.* (2nd ed., pp. 369–410). New York: Wiley.

Shapiro, D. H. (1985). Clinical use of meditation as a self-regulation strategy: Comments on Holmes's conclusions and implications. *American Psychologist, 40,* 719–722.

Shapiro, S., Skinner, E. A., Kessler, L. G., Von Korff, M., German, P. S., Tischler, F. L., Leaf, P. J., Benham, L., Cottler, L., & Regier, D. A. (1984). Utilization of health and mental health services. *Archives of General Psychiatry, 41,* 971–978.

Shatz, M., & Gelman, R. (1973). The development of communication skills: Modifications in the speech of young children as a function of listener. *Monographs of the Society for Research in Child Development, 38* (5, Serial No. 152).

Shatz, M., Wellman, H. M., & Silber, S. (1983). The acquisition of mental verbs: A systematic investigation of the first reference to mental state. *Cognition, 14,* 301–321.

Shaw, R., & Turvey, M. T. (1981). Coalitions as models for ecosystems: A realist perspective on perceptual organization. In M. Kubovy & J. R. Pomerantz (Eds.), *Perceptual organization* (pp. 343–346). Hillsdale, NJ: Erlbaum.

Sheehy, G. (1976). *Passages: Predictable crises of adult life.* New York: Dutton.

Sheffield, F. D. (1966). New evidence on the drive-induction theory of reinforcement. In R. N. Haber (Ed.), *Current research in motivation* (pp. ·111–122). New York: Holt.

Sheffield, F. D., & Roby, T. B. (1950). Reward value of a non-nutritive sweet taste. *Journal of Comparative and Physiological Psychology, 43,* 471–481.

Sheingold, K., & Tenney, Y. J. (1982). Memory for a salient childhood event. In U. Neisser (Ed.), *Memory observed.* San Francisco: Freeman.

Sheldon, W. (1942). *The varieties of temperament: A psychology of constitutional differences.* New York: Harper.

Shepard, R. N. (1978). Externalization of mental images and the act of creation. In B. S. Randhawa & W. E. Coffman (Eds.), *Visual learning, thinking, and communicating.* New York: Academic Press.

Shepard, R. N. (1984). Ecological constraints on internal representation: Resonant kinematics of perceiving, imagining, thinking and dreaming. *Psychological Review, 91,* 417–447.

Shepard, R. N. (1990). *Mind sights: Original visual illusions, ambiguities, and other anomalies, with a commentary on the play of mind in perception and art.* New York: Freeman.

Shepard, R. N., & Cooper, L. A. (1982). *Mental images and their transformations.* Cambridge, MA: MIT Press.

Shepard, R. N., & Jordan, D. S. (1984). Auditory illusions demonstrating that tones are assimilated to an internalized musical scale. *Science, 226,* 1333–1334.

Shepp, B., & Ballisteros, M. (Eds.). (1989). Object Perception. Hillsdale, NJ: Erlbaum.

Sheridan, C. L., & King, R. G. (1972). Obedience to authority with an authentic victim. *Proceedings of the 80th Annual Convention, American Psychological Association, Part 1, 7,* 165–166.

Sherif, C. W. (1981, August). *Social and psychological bases of social psychology.* The G. Stanley Hall Lecture on social psychology, presented at the annual convention of the American

Psychological Association, Los Angeles, CA.

Sherif, M. (1935). A study of some social factors in perception. *Archives of Psychology, 27*(187).

Sherif, M., Harvey, O. J., White, B. J., Hood, W. E., & Sherif, C. W. (1961). *Intergroup conflict and cooperation: The Robber's Cave experiment.* Norman, OK: University of Oklahoma Press.

Sherif, M., & Sherif, C. W. (1979). Research on intergroup relations. In W. G. Austin & S. Worchel (Eds.), *The social psychology of intergroup relations* (pp. 7–18). Monterey, CA: Brooks/Cole.

Sherman, J. A. (1963). Reinstatement of verbal behavior in a psychotic by reinforcement methods. *Journal of Speech and Hearing Disorders, 28,* 398–401.

Sherrington, C. S. (1906). *The integrative action of the nervous system.* New York: Scribner.

Sherrod, K., Vietze, P., & Friedman, S. (1978). *Infancy.* Monterey, CA: Brooks/Cole.

Shiffman, S. S., & Erickson, R. P. (1971). A theoretical review: A psychophysical model for gustatory quality. *Physiology and Behavior, 7,* 617–633.

Shiffrin, R. M., & Schneider, W. (1977). Controlled and automatic human information processing: II. Perceptual learning, automatic attending, and a general theory. *Psychological Review, 84,* 127–190.

Shinn, M., & Weitzman, B. C. (1990). Research on homelessness: An introduction. *Journal of Social Issues, 46,* 1–13.

Shirley, M. M. (1931). *The first two years.* Minneapolis: University of Minnesota Press.

Shneidman, E. (1987, March). At the point of no return. *Psychology Today,* pp. 54–59.

Shortliffe, E. H. (1983). Medical consultation systems: Designing for doctors. In M. S. Sime & M. J. Coombs (Eds.), *Designing for human computer communication* (pp. 209–238). London: Academic Press.

Shotter, J. (1984). *Social accountability and selfhood.* Oxford: Blackwell.

Showers, C., & Cantor, N. (1985). Social cognition: A look at motivated strategies. *Annual Review of Psychology, 36,* 275–305.

Shuckit, M. A., & Irwin, M. (1989). An analysis of the clinical relevance of Type 1 and Type 2 alcoholics. *British Journal of Addiction, 84,* 869–876.

Shuckit, M. A., Irwin, M., & Mahler, H. I. M. (1990). Tridimensional personality questionnaire scores of sons of alcoholic and nonalcoholic fathers. *American Journal of Psychiatry, 147,* 481–487.

Siegel, B. (1988). *Love, medicine & miracles.* New York: Harper & Row.

Siegel, J. M. (1990). Stressful life events and use of physician services among the elderly: The moderating role of pet ownership. *Journal of Personality and Social Psychology, 58,* 1081–1086.

Siegel, S. (1977). Morphine tolerance acquisition as an associative process. *Journal of Experimental Psychology: Animal Behavior Processes, 3,* 1–13.

Siegel, S. (1979). The role of conditioning in drug tolerance and addiction. In J. D. Keehn (Ed.), *Psychopathology in animals: Research and clinical applications* (pp. 143–167). New York: Academic Press.

Siegel, S. (1984). Pavlovian conditioning and heroin overdose: Reports by overdose victims. *Bulletin of the Psychonomic Society, 22,* 428–430.

Siegel, S., Hinson, R. E., Krank, M. D., & McCully, J. (1982). Heroin "overdose" death: The contribution of drug-associated environmental cues. *Science, 216,* 436–437.

Siegelman, M. (1972). Adjustment of homosexual and heterosexual women. *British Journal of Psychiatry, 120,* 477–481.

Siegler, R. S. (1983). Information processing approaches to cognitive development. In W. Kessen (Ed.), *Handbook of child psychology: History, theory, and methods* (Vol. 1). New York: Wiley.

Siegman, A. W., & Feldstein, S. (1985). *Multichannel integrations of nonverbal behavior.* Hillsdale, NJ: Erlbaum.

Siever, M. (1990, December). Personal communication regarding sexual addiction.

Silberfeld, M. (1978). Psychological symptoms and social supports. *Social Psychiatry, 13,* 11–17.

Silver, R., & Wortman, E. (1980). Coping with undesirable life events. In J. Garber & M. E. P. Seligman (Eds.), *Human helplessness: Theory and application.* New York: Academic Press.

Silverman, L. H. (1976). Psychoanalytic theory: "The reports of my death are greatly exaggerated." *American Psychologist, 31,* 621–637.

Simmel, E. C. (1980). *Early experiences and early behavior: Implications for social development.* New York: Academic Press.

Simon, H. (1955). A behavioral model of rational choice. *Quarterly Journal of Economics, 69,* 99–118.

Simon, H. (1973). The structure of ill-structured problems. *Artificial Intelligence, 4,* 181–202.

Simon, H. (1985). *Using cognitive science to solve human problems.* Presentation at a Science and Public Policy Seminar, Federation of Behavioral, Psychological, and Cognitive Sciences, Washington, DC.

Simon, H. (1990a). A mechanism for social selection and successful altruism. *Science, 250,* 1665–1668.

Simon, H. (1990b). In *Discovering Psychology,* Program 10 [PBS video series]. Washington, DC: Annenberg/CPB Project.

Simon, H. A., & Gilmartin, K. (1973). A simulation of memory for chess positions. *Cognitive Psychology, 5,* 29–46.

Simon, Herbert. (1990). A mechanism for social selection and successful altruism. *Science, 250,* 1665–1668.

Simpson, E. E. L. (1974). Moral development research: A case study of scientific cultural bias. *Human Development, 17,* 81–106.

Sinclair, J. D. (1983, December). The hardware of the brain. *Psychology Today,* pp. 8, 11, 12.

Singer, C. (1958). *From magic to science: Essays on the scientific twilight.* New York: Dover.

Singer, J. (1990). *Seeing through the visible world: Jung, Gnosis, and chaos.* New York: Harper & Row.

Singer, J. L. (1966). *Daydreaming: An introduction to the experimental study of inner experience.* New York: Random House.

Singer, J. L. (1975). Navigating the stream of consciousness: Research in daydreaming and related inner experience. *American Psychologist, 30,* 727–739.

Singer, J. L. (1976). Fantasy: The foundation of serenity. *Psychology Today, 10,* pp. 32ff.

Singer, J. L. (1978). Experimental studies of daydreaming and the stream of thought. In K. S. Pope & J. L. Singer (Eds.), *The stream of consciousness: Scientific investigations into the flow of human experience* (pp. 187–223). New York: Plenum.

Singer, J. L., & Antrobus, J. S. (1966). *Imaginal processes inventory.* New York: Authors.

Singer, J. L., & McCraven, V. J. (1961). Some characteristics of adult daydreaming. *Journal of Psychology, 51,* 151–164.

Sinnott, J. D. (Ed.). (1989). *Everyday problem solving: Theory and applications.* New York: Praeger.

Sjoberg, B. M., & Hollister, L. F. (1965). The effects of psychotomimetic drugs on primary suggestibility. *Psychopharmacologia, 8,* 251–262.

Sjorstrom, L. (1980). Fat cells and body weight. In A. J. Stunkard (Ed.), *Obesity.* Philadelphia: Saunders.

Skeels, H. M. (1966). Adult status of children with contrasting early life experiences. *Monographs of the Society for Research in Child Development, 31*(3).

Skinner, B. F. (1938). *The behavior of organisms.* New York: Appleton-Century-Crofts.

Skinner, B. F. (1953). *Science and human behavior.* New York: Macmillan.

Skinner, B. F. (1957). *Verbal behavior.* New York: Appleton-Century-Crofts.

Skinner, B. F. (1966). What is the experimental analysis of behavior? *Journal of the Experimental Analysis of Behavior, 9,* 213–218.

Skinner, B. F. (1981). Selection by consequences. *Science, 213,* 501–504.

Skinner, B. F. (1990). Can psychology be a science of mind?

American Psychologist, 45, 1206–1210.

Skinner, B. F. (1990). In *Discovering Psychology,* programs 8 and 18 [PBS video series]. Washington, DC: Annenberg/CPB Project.

Skolnick, A. (1986). Early attachment and personal relationships across the life course. In P. B. Baltes, D. M. Featherman, & R. M. Lerner (Eds.), *Lifespan development and behavior* (Vol. 7, pp. 173–206). Hillsdale, NJ: Erlbaum.

Sladek, J. R, Jr., & Shoulson, I. (1988). Neural transplantation: A call for patience rather than patients. *Science, 240,* 1386–1388.

Sleep disorders can be a nightmare. (1990, September 26). *Associated Press.*

Sloane, R. B., Staples, F. R., Cristol, A. H., Yorkston, N. J., & Whipple, K. (1975). *Psychotherapy versus behavior therapy.* Cambridge, MA: Harvard University Press.

Slobin, D. (1979). *Psycholinguistics* (2nd ed.). Glenview, IL: Scott, Foresman.

Small, G. W., & Nicholi, A. M., Jr. (1982). Mass hysteria among schoolchildren. *Archives of General Psychiatry, 39,* 721–724.

Smart, M. S., & Smart, R. C. (1973). *Adolescents: Development and relationships.* New York: Macmillan.

Smith, C., & Lloyd, B. (1978). Maternal behavior and perceived sex of infant revisited. *Child Development, 49,* 1263–1265.

Smith, C. A. (1989). Dimensions of appraisal and physiological response in emotion. *Journal of Personality and Social Psychology, 56,* 339–353.

Smith, C. A., & Ellsworth, P. C. (1985). Patterns and cognitive appraisal in emotion. *Journal of Personality and Social Psychology, 48,* 813–838.

Smith, C. A., & Ellsworth, P. C. (1987). Patterns of appraisal and emotion related to taking an exam. *Journal of Personality and Social Psychology, 52,* 475–488.

Smith, D. (1982). Trends in counseling and psychotherapy. *American Psychologist, 37,* 802–809.

Smith, D., & Kraft, W. A. (1983). DSM-III: Do psychologists really want an alternative? *American Psychologist, 38,* 777–785.

Smith, E. E., & Medin, D. L. (1981). *Cognitive Science Series: 4. Categories and concepts.* Cambridge, MA: Harvard University Press.

Smith, J., & Baltes, P. B. (1990). Wisdom-related knowledge: Age/cohort differences in response to life-planning problems. *Developmental Psychology, 26,* 494–505.

Smith, M. L., & Glass, G. V. (1977). Meta-analysis of psychotherapy outcome studies. *American Psychologist, 32,* 752–760.

Smith, M. L., Glass, G. V., & Miller, T. I. (1980). *The benefits of psychotherapy.* Baltimore: Johns Hopkins University Press.

Smith, S. M., Brown, H. O., Toman, J. E. P., & Goodman, L. S. (1947). The lack of cerebral effects of d-tubercurarine. *Anesthesiology, 8,* 1–14.

Smith, T. W. (1991, May/June). Adult sexual behavior in 1989: Number of partners, frequency of intercourse and risk of AIDS. *Family Planning Perspectives, 23,* 102–107.

Smuts, A. B., & Hagen, J. W. (1985). History and research in child development. *Monographs of the Society for Research in Child Development, 50* (Serial No. 211), 4–5.

Snow, C. P. (1961, January 7). In the name of obedience. *Nation,* 3.

Snow, R. (1983). The relationship between vision and juvenile delinquency. *Journal of the American Optometric Association, 54,* 509–511.

Snowden, C. T. (1969). Motivation, regulation and the control of meal parameters with oral and intragastric feeding. *Journal of Comparative and Physiological Psychology, 69,* 91–100.

Snyder, C. R., & Fromkin, H. L. (1980). *Uniqueness: The human pursuit of difference.* New York: Plenum.

Snyder, C. R., & Smith, T. (1982). Symptoms as self-handicapping strategies: The virtue of old wine in new bottles. In G. Weary & H. Mirels (Eds.), *Integrations of clinical and social psychology.* New York: Oxford University Press.

Snyder, M. (1984). When beliefs create reality. In L. Berkowitz (Ed.), *Advances in experimental social psychology, Vol. 18* (pp. 247–305). New York: Academic Press.

Snyder, M., & Frankel, A. (1976). Observer bias: A stringent test of behavior engulfing the field. *Journal of Personality and Social Psychology, 34,* 857–864.

Snyder, M., & Jones, E. E. (1974). Attitude attribution when behavior is constrained. *Journal of Experimental Social Psychology, 10,* 585–600.

Snyder, M., & Swann, W. B., Jr. (1978a). Behavioral confirmation in social interaction: From social perception to social reality. *Journal of Experimental Social Psychology, 14,* 148–162.

Snyder, M., & Swann, W. B., Jr. (1978b). Hypothesis-testing processes in social interaction. *Journal of Personality and Social Psychology, 36,* 1202–1212.

Snyder, S. H. (1974). Catecholamines as mediators of drug effects in schizophrenia. In F. O. Schmitt & F. G. Worden (Eds.), *The neurosciences: Third study program* (pp. 721–732). Cambridge, MA: MIT Press.

Snyder, S. H. (1976). The dopamine hypothesis of schizophrenia. *American Journal of Psychiatry, 133,* 197–202.

Snyder, S. H. (1981). Dopamine receptors, neuroleptics and schizophrenia. *American Journal of Psychiatry, 138,* 460–464.

Snyder, S. H., & Childers, S. R. (1979). Opiate receptors and opioid peptides. *Annual Review of Neurosciences, 2,* 35–64.

Snyder, S. H., & Mattysse, S. (1975). *Opiate receptor mechanisms.* Cambridge, MA: MIT Press.

Sobell, M. B., & Sobell, L. C. (1973). Individualized behavior therapy for alcoholics. *Behavior Therapy, 4,* 49–72.

Sobell, M. B., & Sobell, L. C. (1984). The aftermath of heresy: A response to Pendery et al.'s (1982) critique of "individualized behavior therapy for alcoholics." *Behaviour Research and Therapy, 22,* 413–440.

Sokol, M. M. (Ed.). (1987). *Psychological testing and American society, 1890–1930.* New Brunswick, NJ: Rutgers University Press.

Solso, R. L. (1991). *Cognitive psychology* (3rd ed.). Boston: Allyn and Bacon.

Solso, R. L., & McCarthy, J. E. (1981). Prototype formation of faces: A case study of pseudomemory. *British Journal of Psychology, 72,* 499–503.

Solvic, P. (1984). *Facts vs. fears: Understanding perceived risk.* Presentation at a Science and Public Policy Seminar. Federation of Behavioral, Psychological, and Cognitive Sciences, Washington, DC.

Sonnenstein, F. S., Pleck, J. H., & Ku, L. C. (1989). Sexual acting, condom use and AIDS awareness among adolescent males. *Family Planning Perspectives, 21,* 152–158.

Sorce, J. F., Emde, R. N., Campos, J., & Klinnert, M. D. (1985). Maternal emotional signaling: Its effect on the visual cliff behavior of 1-year-olds. *Developmental Psychology, 21,* 195–200.

Sorenson, R. C. (1973). *Adolescent sexuality in contemporary America.* Cleveland: World.

Spanos, N. P., & Gottlieb, J. (1976). Ergotism and the Salem village witch trials. *Science, 194,* 1390–1394.

Spearman, C. (1923). *The nature of "intelligence" and the principles of cognition.* London: Macmillan.

Speisman, J. C., Lazarus, R. S., Mordkoff, A. M., & Davison, L. A. (1964). The experimental reduction of stress based on ego-defense theory. *Journal of Abnormal and Social Psychology, 68,* 367–380.

Spelke, E., Hirst, W., & Neisser, U. (1976). Skills of divided attention. *Cognition, 4,* 215–230.

Spence, D. P. (1967). Subliminal perception and perceptual defense: Two sides of a single problem. *Behavioral Science, 12,* 183–193.

Spence, M. J., & DeCasper, A. J. (1987). Prenatal experience with low-frequency maternal-voice sounds influence neonatal perception of maternal voice samples. *Infant Behavior and Development, 10,* 133–142.

Sperling, G. (1960). The information available in brief visual presentations. *Psychological Monographs, 74,* 1–29.

Sperling, G. (1963). A model for visual memory tasks. *Human Factors, 5,* 19–31.

Sperry, R. W. (1952). Neurology and the mind-brain problem. *American Scientist, 40,* 291–312.

Sperry, R. W. (1968). Mental unity following surgical disconnection of the cerebral hemispheres. *The Harvey Lectures,* Series 62. New

York: Academic Press.

Sperry, R. W. (1976). Changing concepts of consciousness and free will. *Perspectives in Biology and Medicine, 20,* 9–19.

Sperry, R. W. (1987). Consciousness and causality. In R. L. Gregory (Ed.), *The Oxford companion to the mind* (pp. 164–166). New York: Oxford University Press.

Spiegel, D., Bloom, J. R., Kraemer, H. C., & Gottheil, E. (1989, October 14). Effect of psychosocial treatment on survival of patients with metastatic breast cancer. *The Lancet,* pp. 888–891.

Spiegel, D., Bloom, J. R., & Yalom, I. (1981). Group support for patients with metastatic cancer. *Archives of General Psychiatry, 38,* 527–533.

Spiro, R. J. (1977). Remembering information from text: The "state of schema" approach. In R. C. Atkinson, R. J. Spiro, & W. E. Montague (Eds.), *Schooling and the acquisition of knowledge.* Hillsdale, NJ: Erlbaum.

Spitz, R. A., & Wolf, K. (1946). Anaclitic depression. *Psychoanalytic Study of Children, 2,* 313–342.

Spitzer, R. (1981, October). Nonmedical myths and the DSM-III. *APA Monitor.*

Spong, P. (1988, September 17). [Letter to Shari Anderson, President of the Puget Chapter of the American Cetacean Society].

Springer, S. P., & Deutsch, G. (1984). *Left brain, right brain* (2nd ed.). San Francisco: Freeman.

Squire, L. R. (1986). Mechanisms of memory. *Science, 232,* 1612–1619.

Squire, L. R. (1986). Memory functions as affected by electroconvulsive therapy. *Annals of the New York Academy of Sciences, 462,* 307–314.

Squire, L. R., Amaral, D. G., Zola-Morgan, S., Kritchevsky, M., & Press, G. (1989). Description of brain injury in the amnesic patient N. A. based on magnetic resonance imaging. *Experimental Neurology, 105,* 23–35.

Squire, L. R., & Slater, P. C. (1975). Forgetting in very long-term memory as assessed by an improved questionnaire technique. *Journal of Experimental Psychology: Human Learning and Memory, 104,* 50–54.

Squire, S. (1988, January 3). Shock therapy. *San Francisco Examiner-Chronicle,* This World Section, p. 16.

Squires, S. (1985, August 19). It's hard to tell a lie. *San Francisco Chronicle,* This World Section, p. 9.

Staats, A. W., Gross, M. C., Guay, P. F., & Carlson, C. C. (1973). Personality and social systems and attitude-reinforcer-discriminative theory: Interest (attitude) formation, function, and measurement. *Journal of Personality and Social Psychology, 26,* 251–261.

Staats, A. W., Minke, K. A., Martin, C. H., & Higa, W. R. (1972). Deprivation-satiation and strength of attitude conditioning: A test of attitude-reinforcer-discriminative theory. *Journal of Personality and Social Psychology, 24,* 178–185.

Staats, A. W., & Staats, C. K. (1958). Attitudes established by classical conditioning. *Journal of Abnormal and Social Psychology, 57,* 37–40.

Staff. (1989, January). You've come a long way, baby, part II. *University of California, Berkeley, Wellness Letter,* p. 1.

Staff. (1990). *1989 survey results from monitoring the future: A continuing study of the lifestyles and values of youth.* Ann Arbor, MI: University of Michigan, Institute for Social Research.

Staff. (1990, Fall). Changing the image: regulating alcohol advertising. The Student Body (p. 7). Stanford, CA: Stanford University.

Stampfl, T. G., & Levis, D. J. (1967). Essentials of implosive therapy: A learning theory-based psychodynamic behavioral therapy. *Journal of Abnormal Psychology, 72,* 496–503.

Stanford Daily. (1982, February 2, pp. 1, 3, 5).

Stangler, R. S., & Printz, A. M. (1980). DSM–III: Psychiatric diagnosis in a university population. *American Journal of Psychiatry, 137,* 937–940.

Stanley, J. (1976). The study of the very bright. *Science, 192,* 668–669.

Stanovich, K. (1986). *How to think straight about psychology.* Glenview, IL: Scott, Foresman.

Stapp, J., & Fulcher, R. (1981). The employment of APA members.

American Psychologist, 36, 1263–1314.

Stayton, D., Hogan, R., & Ainsworth, M. D. S. (1971). Infant obedience and maternal behavior: The origins of socialization reconsidered. *Child Development, 42,* 1057–1069.

Steele, C. M. (1988). The psychology of self-affirmation: Sustaining the integrity of the self. In L. Berkowitz (Ed.), *Advances in experimental social psychology* (Vol. 21, pp. 261–302). New York: Academic Press.

Steers, R. M., & Porter, L. W. (1974). The role of task-goal attributes in employee performance. *Psychological Bulletin, 81,* 434–452.

Stein, M., Keller, S. E., & Schleifer, S. J. (1985). Stress and immunomodulation: The role of depression and neuroendocrine function. *Journal of Immunology, 135,* 827–833.

Steiner, J. (1980). The SS yesterday and today: A sociopsychological view. In J. E. Dimsdale (Ed.), *Survivors, victims, and perpetrators: Essays on the Nazi holocaust* (pp. 405–456). Washington, DC: Hemisphere Publishing.

Steininger, M., Newell, J. D., & Garcia, L. T. (1984). *Ethical issues in psychology.* Homewood, IL: Dorsey.

Stellar, E. (1954). The physiology of motivation. *Psychological Review, 61,* 5–22.

Steriade, M., & McCarley, R. W. (1990). *Brainstem control of wakefulness and sleep.* New York: Plenum.

Stern, M., & Karraker, K. H. (1989). Sex stereotyping of infants: A review of gender labeling studies. *Sex Roles, 20,* 501–522.

Stern, P., & Aronson, E. (Eds.). (1984). *Energy use: The human dimension.* New York: Freeman.

Stern, R. M., & Ray, W. J. (1977). *Biofeedback.* Chicago: Dow Jones-Irwin.

Stern, W. (1914). The psychological methods of testing intelligence. *Educational Psychology Monographs* (No. 13).

Stern, W. C., & Morgane, P. S. (1974). Theoretical view of REM sleep function: Maintenance of catecholamine systems in the central nervous system. *Behavioral Biology, 11,* 1–32.

Sternbach, R. A., & Tursky, B. (1965). Ethnic differences among housewives in psychophysical and skin potential responses to electric shock. *Psychophysiology, 1,* 241–246.

Sternberg, R. (Ed.). (1982). *Handbook of human intelligence.* Cambridge, MA: Cambridge University Press.

Sternberg, R. (1985). *Beyond IQ.* Cambridge, MA: Cambridge University Press.

Sternberg, R. (1986a). Inside intelligence. *American Scientist, 74,* 137–143.

Sternberg, R. (1986b). *Intelligence applied.* San Diego, CA: Harcourt Brace Jovanovich.

Sternberg, R. (1986c). A triangular theory of love. *Psychological Review, 93,* 119–135.

Sternberg, R. (1990). In *Discovering Psychology,* Program 16 [PBS video series]. Washington, DC: Annenberg/CPB Program.

Sternberg, R. J., Conway, B. E., Ketron, J. L., & Bernstein, M. (1981). People's conceptions of intelligence. *Journal of Personality and Social Psychology, 41,* 37–55.

Sternberg, S. (1966). High-speed scanning in human memory. *Science, 153,* 652–654.

Sternberg, S. (1969). Memory-scanning: Mental processes revealed by reaction time experiments. *American Scientist, 57,* 421–457.

Stevens, C. F. (1979). The neuron. *Scientific American, 241*(9), 54–65.

Stevens, J. (1986, Fall). The dance of the tonal. In *Shaman's Drum* (pp. 47–52).

Stevens, S. S. (1961). To honor Fechner and repeal his law. *Science, 133,* 80–86.

Stevens, S. S. (1962). The surprising simplicity of sensory metrics. *American Psychologist, 17,* 29–39.

Stevens, S. S. (1975). In G. Stevens (Ed.), *Psychophysics: Introduction to its perceptual, neutral, and social prospects.* New York: Wiley.

Stevenson, H. W. (1990). Adapting to school: Children in Beijing and Chicago (pp. 51–67). Palo Alto, CA: Center for Advanced Study in the Behavioral Sciences.

Stevenson, J., Graham, P., Fredman, G., & McLoughlin, V. A. (1987). Twin study of genetic influences on reading and spelling ability and disability. *Journal of Child Psychiatry, 28,* 229–247.

Stipp, D. (1991, January 30). Split personality: Americans are loath to curb energy use despite war concerns. *The Wall Street Journal,* pp. A1, A5.

Stone, C. A., & Church, J. (1957). *Childhood and adolescence: A psychology of the growing person.* New York: Random House.

Storms, M. D. (1980). Theories of sexual orientation. *Journal of Personality and Social Psychology, 38,* 783–792.

Storms, M. D. (1981). A theory of erotic orientation development. *Psychological Review, 88,* 340–353.

Strack, S., & Coyne, J. C. (1983). Social confirmation of dysphoria: Shared and private reactions to depression. *Journal of Personality and Social Psychology, 50,* 149–167.

Straub, E. (1974). Helping a distressed person: Social, personality, and stimulus determinants. In L. Berkowitz (Ed.), *Advances in experimental and social psychology* (Vol. 7). New York: Academic Press.

Strodtbeck, F. L., & Hook, L. H. (1961). The social dimensions of a twelve-man jury table. *Sociometry, 24,* 397–415.

Stroebe, W., Stroebe, M. S., Gergen, K. J., & Gergen, M. (1982). The effects of bereavement on mortality: A social psychological analysis. In J. R. Eiser (Ed.), *Social psychology and behavioral medicine* (pp. 527–560). New York: Wiley.

Stromeyer, D. F., & Psotka, J. (1970). The detailed texture of eidetic images. *Nature, 225,* 346–349.

Strong, E. K. (1927). Differentiation of certified public accountants from other occupational groups. *Journal of Educational Psychology, 18,* 227–238.

Stroop, J. R. (1935). Studies of interference in serial verbal reactions. *Journal of Experimental Psychology, 18,* 643–662.

Strube, M. J. (Ed.). (1990). *Type A behavior.* Corte Madera, CA: Select Press.

Strupp, H. (1990). In *Discovering Psychology,* programs 21 and 22 [PBS video series]. Washington, DC: Annenberg/CPB Program.

Stuart, R. B. (1971). Behavioral contracting with families of delinquents. *Journal of Behavior Therapy and Experimental Psychiatry, 2,* 1–11.

Study finds that deaf babies "babble" in sign language. (1991, March 22). *The New York Times,* p. 1.

Styron, W. (1990). *Darkness visible: A memoir of madness.* New York: Random House.

Suchman, A. L., & Ader, R. (1989). Placebo response in humans can be shaped by prior pharmalogic experience. *Psychosomatic Medicine, 51,* 251.

Suedfeld, P. (1980). *Restricted environmental stimulation: Research and clinical applications.* New York: Wiley.

Sullivan, A. (1908). Letters to Sophia C. Hopkins. In H. Keller, *The Story of My Life.* New York: Doubleday, 1954.

Sullivan, H. S. (1953). *The interpersonal theory of psychiatry.* New York: Norton.

Suls, J., & Fletcher, B. (1985). The relative efficacy of avoidant and nonavoidant coping strategies: A meta-analysis. *Health Psychology, 4,* 249–288.

Suls, J., & Marco, C. A. (1990). Relationship between JAS- and FTAS-Type A behavior and non-CHD illness: A prospective study controlling for negative affectivity. *Health Psychology, 9,* 479–492.

Summers, M. (Ed.). (1971). *The Malleus maleficarum of Heinrich Kramer and James Sprenger.* New York: Dover. (Original work published 1486)

Sundberg, N. D. (1977). *Assessment of persons.* Englewood Cliffs, NJ: Prentice-Hall.

Sundberg, N. D., & Matarazzo, J. D. (1979). Psychological assessment of individuals. In M. E. Meyer (Ed.), *Foundations of contemporary psychology* (pp. 580–617). New York: Oxford University Press.

Suomi, S. (1987). Genetic and maternal contributions to individual differences in rhesus monkey biobehavioral development. In N. A. Krasnegor, E. M. Blass, M. A. Hofer, & W. P. Smotherman (Eds.), *Prenatal development: A psychobiological perspective* (pp. 397–420). New York: Academic Press.

Suomi, S. (1990). In *Discovering Psychology,* Program 5 [PBS video series]. Washington, DC: Annenberg/CPB Project.

Suomi, S., & Harlow, H. F. (1972). Social rehabilitation of isolate-reared monkeys. *Developmental Psychology, 6,* 487–496.

Svenson, O. (1981). Are we all less risky and more skillful than our fellow drivers? *Acta Psychologica, 47,* 143–148.

Swann, W. B., Jr. (1985). The self as architect of social reality. In B. Schlenker (Ed.), *The self and social life* (pp. 100–126). New York: McGraw-Hill.

Swann, W. B., Jr. (1990). To be adored or to be known?: The interplay of self-enhancement and self-verification. In R. M. Sorrentino & E. T. Higgins (Eds.), *Handbook of motivation and cognition* (Vol. 2). New York: Guilford Press.

Swazey, J. P. (1974). *Chlorpromazine in psychiatry: A study of therapeutic innovation.* Cambridge, MA: MIT Press.

Sweet, W. H., Ervin, F., & Mark, V. H. (1969). The relationship of violent behavior to focal cerebral disease. In S. Garattini & E. Sigg (Eds.), *Aggressive behavior.* New York: Wiley.

Swets, J. A., & Bjork, R. A. (1990). Enhancing human performance: An evaluation of "new age" techniques considered by the U.S. Army. *Psychological Science, 1,* 85–96.

Swift, W. J., Andrews, D., & Barklage, N. E. (1986). The relationship between affective disorders and eating disorders: A review of the literature. *American Journal of Psychiatry, 143,* 290–299.

Szasz, T. S. (1961). *The myth of mental illness.* New York: Harper & Row.

Szasz, T. S. (1977). *The manufacture of models.* New York: Dell.

Szasz, T. S. (1979). *The myth of psychotherapy.* Garden City, NY: Doubleday.

T

Tajfel, H. (1970). Experiments in intergroup discrimination. *Scientific American, 223,* 96–102.

Tajfel, H. (Ed.). (1982). *Social identity and intergroup relations.* New York: Cambridge University Press.

Tajfel, H., & Billig, M. (1974). Familiarity and categorization in intergroup behavior. *Journal of Experimental Social Psychology, 10,* 159–170.

Talbot, J. D., Marrett, S., Evans, A. C., Meyer, E., Bushnell, M. C., & Duncan, G. H. (1991). Multiple representations of pain in the human cerebral cortex. *Science, 251,* 1355–1358.

Tanner, J. M. (1962). *Growth at adolescence* (2nd ed.). Oxford: Blackwell Scientific Publications.

Targ, R., & Harary, K. (1984). *The mind race: Understanding and using psychic abilities.* New York: Villard Books.

Tarpy, R. M. (1982). *Principles of animal learning and motivation.* Glenview, IL: Scott, Foresman.

Tart, C. T. (1969). *Altered states of consciousness.* New York: Wiley.

Tart, C. T. (1971). *On being stoned: A psychological investigation of marijuana intoxication.* Palo Alto, CA: Science and Behavior Books.

Tarter, R. E., Alterman, A. I., & Edwards, K. L. (1985). Vulnerability to alcoholism in men: A behavior-genetic perspective. *Journal of Studies on Alcohol, 46,* 329–356.

Taylor, F. W. (1911). *Principles of scientific management.* New York: Harper & Row.

Taylor, J. A. (1951). The relationship of anxiety to the conditioned eyelid response. *Journal of Experimental Psychology, 41,* 81–92.

Taylor, S. E. (1980). The interface of cognitive and social psychology. In J. H. Harvey (Ed.), *Cognition, social behavior, and the environment* (pp. 189–211). Hillsdale, NJ: Erlbaum.

Taylor, S. E. (1981). A categorization approach to stereotyping. In D. L. Hamilton (Ed.), *Cognitive processes in stereotyping and intergroup behavior* (pp. 88–114). Hillsdale, NJ: Erlbaum.

Taylor, S. E. (1982). The availability bias in social perception and interaction. In D. Kahneman, P. Slovic, & A. Tversky (Eds.), *Judgment under uncertainty: Heuristics and biases* (pp. 190–200). Cambridge: Cambridge University Press.

Taylor, S. E. (1986). *Health psychology.* New York: Random House.

Taylor, S. E. (1990). Health psychology: The science and the field. *American Psychologist, 45,* 40–50.

Taylor, S. E., & Brown, J. D. (1988). Illusion and well-being: A social psychological perspective on mental health. *Psychological Bulletin, 103,* 193–210.

Taylor, S. E., & Clark, L. F. (1986). Does information improve adjustment to noxious events? In M. J. Saks & L. Saxe (Eds.), *Advances in applied social psychology* (Vol. 3, pp. 1–28). Hillsdale, NJ: Erlbaum.

Taylor, S. E., Crocker, J., Fiske, S. T., Sprinzen, M., & Winkler, J. D. (1979). The generalizability of salience effects. *Journal of Personality and Social Psychology, 39.*

Taylor, S. P., Vardaris, R. M., Rawtich, A. B., Gammon, C. B., Cranston, J. W., & Lubetkin, A. I. (1976). The effects of alcohol and delta-9-tetrahydrocannabinol on human physical aggression. *Aggressive Behavior, 2,* 153–161.

Taylor, W., Pearson, J., Mair, A., & Burns, W. (1965). Study of noise and hearing in jute weaving. *Journal of the Acoustical Society of America, 38,* 113–120.

Teasdale, J. D. (1985). Psychological treatments for depression: How do they work? *Behavior Research and Therapy, 23,* 157–165.

Teitelbaum, P. (1966). The use of operant methods in the assessment and control of motivational states. In W. K. Honig (Ed.), *Operant behavior.* New York: Appleton-Century-Crofts.

Tellegen, A., & Atkinson, S. (1974). Openness to absorbing and self-altering experiences ("absorption"), a trait related to hypnosis. *Journal of Abnormal Psychology, 83,* 268–277.

Tellegen, A., Lykken, D. T., Bouchard, T. J., Wilcox, K. J., Segal, N. L., & Rich, S. (1988). Personality similarity in twins reared apart and together. *Journal of Personality and Social Psychology, 54,* 1031–1039.

Temoshok, L., Sweet, M. D., & Zick, J. (1987). A three city comparison of the public's knowledge and attitudes about AIDS. *Psychology and Health: An International Journal.*

Tenopyr, M. L., & Oeltjen, P. D. (1982). Personnel selection and classification. *Annual Review of Psychology, 33,* 581–618.

Terman, L. M. (1916). *The measurement of intelligence.* Boston: Houghton-Mifflin.

Terman, L. M. (1925). *Genetic studies of genius: Vol 1, Mental and physical traits of a thousand gifted children.* Stanford, CA: Stanford University Press.

Terman, L. M., & Merrill, M. A. (1937). *Measuring intelligence.* Boston: Houghton-Mifflin.

Terman, L. M., & Merrill, M. A. (1960). *The Stanford-Binet intelligence scale.* Boston: Houghton-Mifflin.

Terman, L. M., & Merrill, M. A. (1972). *Stanford-Binet intelligence scale—manual for the third revision, Form L–M.* Boston: Houghton-Mifflin.

Terman, L. M., & Oden, M. H. (1947). The gifted child grows up. *Genetic studies of genius* (Vol. 4). Stanford, CA: Stanford University Press.

Terman, L. M., & Oden, M. H. (1959). The gifted group at mid-life. *Genetic studies of genius: Vol. 5.* Stanford, CA: Stanford University Press.

Thatcher, R. W., Walker, R. A., & Giudice, S. (1987). Human cerebral hemispheres develop at different rates and ages. *Science, 236,* 1110–1113.

Thienes-Hontos, P., Watson, C. G., & Kucala, T. (1982). Stress-disorder symptoms in Vietnam and Korean War veterans. *Journal of Consulting and Clinical Psychology, 50,* 558–561.

Thigpen, C. H., & Cleckley, H. A. (1957). *Three faces of Eve.* New York: McGraw-Hill.

Thompson, D. A., & Campbell, R. G. (1977). Hunger in humans induced by 2-Deoxy-D-Glucose: Glucoprivic control of taste preference and food intake. *Science, 198,* 1065–1068.

Thompson, J. A. (1985). *Psychological aspects of nuclear war.* Chichester: The British Psychological Society.

Thompson, K. (1988, Oct. 2). Fritz Perls. *San Francisco Examiner-Chronicle,* This World Section, pp. 14–16.

Thompson, M. J., & Harsha, D. W. (1984, January). Our rhythms still follow the African sun. *Psychology Today,* pp. 50–54.

Thompson, P. (1980). Margaret Thatcher: A new illusion. *Perception, 9,* 483–484.

Thompson, R. (1990). In *Discovering Psychology,* Program 9 [PBS video series]. Washington, DC: Annenberg/CPB Project.

Thompson, R. F. (1972). Sensory preconditioning. In R. F. Thompson & J. F. Voss (Eds.), *Topics in learning and performance.* New York: Academic Press.

Thompson, R. F. (1975). *Introduction to physiological psychology.* New York: Harper & Row.

Thompson, R. F. (1984, February 4). Searching for memories: Where and how are they stored in your brain? *Stanford Daily.*

Thompson, R. F. (1986). The neurobiology of learning and memory. *Science, 233,* 941–944.

Thompson, R. F. (1987). The cerebellum and memory storage: A response to Bloedel. *Science, 238,* 1729–1730.

Thoresen, C. (1990, June 29). *Recurrent coronary prevention program: Results after eight and a half years.* Address given to First International Congress of Behavioral Medicine, Uppsala, Sweden.

Thoresen, C. E., & Eagleston, J. R. (1983). Chronic stress in children and adolescents [Special edition: Coping with stress]. *Theory into Practice, 22,* 48–56.

Thorndike, E. L. (1898). Animal intelligence. *Psychological Review Monograph Supplement, 2* (4, Whole No. 8).

Thorndike, R. L., & Hagen, E. (1978). *The cognitive abilities test.* Lombard, IL: Riverside.

Thorndyke, P. W., & Hayes-Roth, B. (1979). *Spatial knowledge acquisition from maps and navigation.* Paper presented at the Psychonomic Society Meeting, San Antonio, TX.

Thorne, B., & Luria, Z. (1986). Sexuality and gender in children's daily worlds. *Social Problems, 33,* 176–190.

Thornton, E. M. (1984). *The Freudian fallacy: An alternative view of Freudian theory.* New York: The Dial Press/Doubleday.

Tillich, P. (1952). *The courage to be.* New Haven, CT: Yale University Press.

Timiras, P. S. (1978). Biological perspectives on aging. *American Scientist, 66,* 605–613.

Tipper, S. P., & Driver, J. (1988). Negative priming between pictures and words in a selective attention task: Evidence for semantic processing of ignored stimuli. *Memory and Cognition, 16,* 64–70.

Titchener, E. B. (1898). The postulates of structural psychology. *Philosophical Review, 7,* 449–453.

Tizzard B., & Hodges, J. (1978). The effect of early institutional rearing on the development of eight-year-old children. *Journal of Child Psychology and Psychiatry, 19,* 99–118.

Tolman, E. C. (1948). Cognitive maps in rats and men. *Psychological Review, 55,* 189–208.

Tolman, E. C., & Honzik, C. H. (1930). "Insight" in rats. *University of California Publications in Psychology, 4,* 215–232.

Tomkins, S. (1962). *Affect, imagery, consciousness* (Vol. 1). New York: Springer.

Tomkins, S. (1981). The quest for primary motives: Biography and autobiography of an idea. *Journal of Personality and Social Psychology, 41,* 306–329.

Tompkins, R. D. (1981). *Before it's too late. . . :The prevention manual on drug abuse for people who care.* Englewood Cliffs, NJ: Family Information Center.

Torrey, E. F. (1990). In *Discovering Psychology,* Program 21 [PBS video series]. Washington, DC: Annenberg/CPB Program.

Tourangeau, R., & Ellsworth, P. C. (1979). The role of facial response in the experience of emotion. *Journal of Personality and Social Psychology, 37,* 1519–1531.

Townsend, J. T. (1972). Some results concerning the identifiability of parallel and serial processes. *British Journal of Mathematical and Statistical Psychology, 25,* 168–199.

Tranel, D., & Damasio, A. R. (1985). Knowledge without awareness: An autonomic index of facial recognition by prosopagnosics. *Science, 228,* 1453–1454.

Treisman, A. (1960). Contextual cues in selective listening. *Quarterly Journal of Experimental Psychology, 12,* 242–248.

Treisman, A. (1986). Properties, parts and objects. In K. Boff, L. Kaufman, & J. Thomas (Eds.), *Handbook of perception and human performance, Vol. 2.* New York: Wiley.

Treisman, A. (1988). Features and objects: The fourteenth Bartlett Memorial Lecture. *The Quarterly Journal of Experimental Psychology, 40,* 201–237.

Treisman, A., & Gelade, G. (1980). A feature integration theory of attention. *Cognitive Psychology, 12*, 97–136.

Treisman, A., & Gormican, S. (1988). Feature analysis in early vision: Evidence from search asymmetries. *Psychological Review, 95*, 15–48.

Treisman, A., & Sato, S. (1990). Conjunction search revisited. *Journal of Experimental Psychology: Human Perception and Performance, 16*, 459–478.

Treisman, A., & Souther, J. (1985). Search asymmetry: A diagnostic for preattentive processing of separable features. *Journal of Experimental Psychology: General, 114*, 285–310.

Treisman, U. (1989). *A study of mathematics performance of black students at the University of California, Berkeley.* Unpublished manuscript, Dana Center, University of California, Berkeley.

Triandis, H. (1990). Cross-cultural studies of individualism and collectivism. In J. Berman (Ed.), *Nebraska Symposium on Motivation, 1989* (pp. 42–133). Lincoln, NE: University of Nebraska Press.

Triandis, H. C., & Draguns, J. G. (Eds.). (1980). *Handbook of cross-culture psychology: Vol. 6, Psychopathology.* Boston: Allyn & Bacon.

Trinder, J. (1988). Subjective insomnia without objective findings: A pseudodiagnostic classification. *Psychological Bulletin, 103*, 87–94.

Triplett, N. (1897). The dynamagenic factors in pacemaking and competition. *American Journal of Psychology, 9*, 507–533.

Trivers, R. L. (1972). Parental investment and sexual selection. In B. Campbell (Ed.), *Sexual selection and the descent of man* (pp. 139–179). Chicago: Aldine.

Trivers, R. L. (1983). The evolution of cooperation. In D. L. Bridgeman (Ed.), *The nature of pro-social behavior.* New York: Academic Press.

Tronick, E., Als, H., & Brazelton, T. B. (1980). Moradic phases: A structural description analysis of infant-mother face to face interaction. *Merrill-Palmer Quarterly, 26*, 3–24.

Trotter, R. J. (1987, February). Stop blaming yourself. *Psychology Today,* pp. 30–39.

Tryon, W. W. (1979). The test-trait fallacy. *American Psychologist, 34*, 402–406.

Tsuang, M. T., & Vandermey, R. (1980). *Genes and the mind: Inheritance of mental illness.* New York: Oxford University Press.

Tucker, O. M. (1981). Lateral brain functions, emotion, and conceptualization. *Psychological Bulletin, 89*, 19–46.

Tuller, D. (1989, March 8). Male businessmen say lives "empty." *San Francisco Chronicle,* p. B3.

Tulving, E. (1972). Episodic and semantic memory. In E. Tulving & W. Donaldson (Eds.), *Organization of memory.* New York: Academic Press.

Tulving, E. (1983). *Elements of episodic memory.* Oxford: Clarendon Press.

Tulving, E. (1985). Memory and consciousness. *Canadian Psychology, 26*, 1–12.

Tulving, E. (1989). Remembering and knowing the past. *American Scientist, 77*, 361–367.

Tulving, E., & Pearlstone, Z. (1966). Availability versus accessibility of information in memory for words. *Journal of Verbal Learning and Verbal Behavior, 5*, 381–391.

Tulving, E., & Schacter, D. L. (1990). Priming and human memory systems. *Science, 247*, 301–306.

Tulving, E., & Thomson, D. M. (1973). Encoding specificity and retrieval processes in episodic memory. *Psychological Review, 80*, 352–373.

Tupes, E. G., & Christal, R. C. (1961). *Recurrent personality factors based on trait ratings* (Tech. Rep. No. ASD-TR-61-97). Lackland Air Force Base, TX: U.S. Air Force.

Turnbull, C. (1962). *The forest people.* New York: Simon & Schuster.

Turner, R. H., & Killian, L. M. (1972). *Collective behavior* (2nd ed.). Englewood Cliffs, NJ: Prentice-Hall.

Tversky, A. (1990). In *Discovering Psychology,* Program 11 [PBS video series]. Washington, DC: Annenberg/CPB Project.

Tversky, A., & Kahneman, D. (1973). Availability: A heuristic for judging frequency and probability. *Cognitive Psychology, 5*, 207–232.

Tversky, A., & Kahneman, D. (1980). Causal schemata in judgments under uncertainty. In M. Fishbein (Ed.), *Progress in social psychology.* Hillsdale, NJ: Erlbaum.

Tversky, A., & Kahneman, D. (1983). Extensional versus intuitive reasoning: The conjunction fallacy in probability judgment. *Psychological Review, 90*, 293–315.

Tversky, A., & Kahneman, D. (1986). Rational choice and the framing of decisions. *Journal of Business, 59*, S251–S278.

Tversky, B. (1981). Distortions in memory for maps. *Cognitive Psychology, 13*, 407–433.

Twain, M. [S. L. Clemens]. (1923). *Mark Twain's speeches.* New York: Harper & Row.

Tyler, L. (1988). Mental testing. In E. R. Hilgard (Ed.), *Fifty years of psychology* (pp. 127–138). Glenview, IL: Scott, Foresman.

Tyler, L. E. (1965). *The psychology of human differences* (3rd ed.). New York: Appleton-Century-Crofts.

Tyler, L. E. (1974). *Individual differences.* Englewood Cliffs, NJ: Prentice-Hall.

Tzeng, O. J. L., & Wang, W. S. Y. (1983). The first two R's. *American Scientist, 71*, 238–243.

U

Ullman, S. (1979). *The interpretation of visual motion.* Cambridge, MA: MIT Press.

Ullmann, L. P., & Krasner, L. (1975). *Psychological approach to abnormal behavior* (2nd ed.). Englewood Cliffs, NJ: Prentice-Hall.

Ultan, R. (1969). Some general characteristics of interrogative systems. *Working Papers in Language Universals, 1*, 41–63.

Underwood, B. J. (1948). Retroactive and proactive inhibition after five and forty-eight hours. *Journal of Experimental Psychology, 38*, 28–38.

Underwood, B. J. (1949). Proactive inhibition as a function of time and degree of prior learning. *Journal of Experimental Psychology, 39*, 24–34.

United Press International. (1984, April 12). *Testimony on child molesting* [Press Release, Senate Judiciary Subcommittee hearings on Child Molesting, Washington, DC].

United Press International. (1990, September 4). In P. Shenon, Crisis of drugs remains top priority, Bush says. *The New York Times,* Section A, col. 4, p. 22, Sept. 6, 1990.

United Press International. (1990, September 5). Lest we forget that drug crisis—small signs of progress, but still lots to do. *Los Angeles Times,* Section B, p. 6.

U.S. Bureau of the Census. (1984). *Educational attainment in the United States: March 1981 and 1980* (Current Population Reports, Series P-20, No. 390). Washington, DC: U.S. Government Printing Office.

U.S. Bureau of the Census. (1985a). *Marital status and living arrangements: March 1984* (Current Population Reports, Series P-20, No. 399). Washington, DC: U.S. Government Printing Office.

U.S. Bureau of the Census. (1985b). *Statistical abstract of the United States: 1986* (106th ed.). Washington, DC: U.S. Government Printing Office.

U.S. Bureau of the Census. (1986a). *Demographic and socioeconomic aspects of aging in the United States* (Current Population Reports, Series P-23, No. 138). Washington, DC: U.S. Government Printing Office.

U.S. Bureau of the Census. (1986b). *Money income and poverty status of families and persons in the United States: 1985* (Current Population Report, Series P-60, No. 154). Washington, DC: U.S. Government Printing Office.

U.S. Department of Health, Education, and Welfare. (1979). *Healthy people: The Surgeon General's report on health promotion and disease prevention* (USPHS Publication No. 79–55071). Washington, DC: U.S. Government Printing Office.

U.S. National Center for Health Statistics. (1984). *Vital statistics of the United States.* Quoted in U.S. Department of Commerce, Bureau of the Census, Statistical Abstract of the United States

(104th ed.). Washington, DC: U.S. Government Printing Office.

U.S. Public Health Service. (1986). *Surgeon General's report on Acquired Immune Deficiency Syndrome.* Washington, DC: U.S. Government Printing Office.

"U.S. Women Today" (1983, Nov. 11–20). *The New York Times* poll, reported in the *International Herald Tribune.*

V

Vaillant, G. E. (1977). *Adaptation to Life.* Boston: Little, Brown.

Valenstein, E. S. (Ed.). (1980). *The psychosurgery debate.* New York: Freeman.

Valle, V. A., & Frieze, I. H. (1976). Stability of causal attributions as a mediator in changing expectations for success. *Journal of Personality and Social Psychology, 33,* 579–587.

Van Wagener, W., & Herren, R. (1940). Surgical division of commissural pathways in the corpus callosum. *Archives of Neurology and Psychiatry, 44,* 740–759.

Vasari, G. (1967). *Lives of the most eminent painters.* New York: Heritage.

Vaughan, E. (1977). Misconceptions about psychology among introductory psychology students. *Teaching of Psychology, 4,* 138–141.

Vernon, P. E. (1987). The demise of the Stanford-Binet Scale. *Canadian Psychology, 28,* 251–258.

Vivano, F. (1989, October 8). When success is a family prize. *San Francisco Examiner-Chronicle,* This World Section, pp. 7–9.

Vogel, F., & Motulsky, A. G. (1982). *Human genetics.* New York: Springer-Verlag.

von Békésy, G. (1960). *Experiments in hearing.* New York: McGraw-Hill.

von Békésy, G. (1961). Concerning the fundamental component of periodic pulse patterns and modulated vibrations observed in the cochlear model with nerve supply. *Journal of the Acoustical Society of America, 33,* 888–896.

von Helmholtz, H. (1962). Treatise on physiological optics (Vol. 3, J. P. Southall, Ed. and Trans.). New York: Dover Press. (Original work published 1866)

von Hofsten, C., & Lindhagen, K. (1979). Observations on the development of reaching for moving objects. *Journal of Child Psychology, 28,* 158–173.

Vonnegut, M. (1975). *The Eden express.* New York: Bantam.

Von Wright, J. M., Anderson, K., & Stenham, U. (1975). Generalization of conditioned GSRs in dichotic listening. In P. M. A. Rabbit & S. Dornic (Eds.), *Attention and performance* (pp. 194–204). New York: Academic Press.

W

Wahba, M. A., & Bridwell, L. G. (1976). Maslow reconsidered: A review of research in the need hierarchy theory. *Organizational Behavior and Human Performance, 15,* 212–240.

Waldron, I. (1976, March). Why do women live longer than men? *Journal of Human Stress,* 2–13.

Waldron, T. P. (1985). *Principles of language and mind: An evolutionary theory of meaning.* Boston: Routledge and Kegan Paul.

Waldrop, M. M. (1984). Artificial intelligence: I, Into the world (research news). *Science, 223,* 802–805.

Waldvogel, S. (1948). The frequency and affective character of childhood memories. *Psychological Monographs, 62* (Whole No. 291).

Walker, B. B., & Sandman, C. A. (1977). Physiological response patterns in ulcer patients: Phasic and tonic components of the electrogastrogram. *Psychophysiology, 14,* 393–400.

Walker, B. B., & Sandman, C. A. (1977). Physiological response patterns in ulcer patients: Phasic and tonic components of the electrogastrogram. *Psychophysiology, 14,* 393–400.

Walker, L. (1984). Sex differences in the development of moral reasoning: A critical review. *Child Development, 55,* 667–691.

Wallach, M. A., & Wallach, L. (1983). *Psychology's sanction for selfishness.* San Francisco: Freeman.

Waller, J. H. (1971). Achievement and social mobility:

Relationships among IQ score, education, and occupation in two generations. *Social Biology, 18,* 252–259.

Wallis, C. (1984, June 11). Unlocking pain's secrets. *Time,* pp. 58–66.

Walsh, R. N. (1990). *The Spirit of Shamanism.* Los Angeles: J. P. Tarcher.

Walsh, R. N., & Vaughan, F. (Eds.). (1980). *Beyond ego: Transpersonal dimensions in psychology.* Los Angeles: Tarcher.

Walters, C. C., & Grusec, J. E. (1977). *Punishment.* San Francisco: Freeman.

Walters, R. G. (1974). *Primers for prudery: Sexual advice to Victorian America.* Englewood Cliffs, NJ: Prentice-Hall.

Walton, R. E. (1977). Successful strategies for diffusing work innovations. *Journal of Contemporary Business, 6,* 1–22.

Wanous, J. P. (1980). *Organizational entry: Recruitment, selection, and socialization of newcomers.* Reading, MA: Addison-Wesley.

Ward, W. C., Kogan, N., & Pankove, E. (1972). Incentive effects in children's creativity. *Child Development, 43*(2), 669–676.

Warden, C. J. (1931). *Animal motivation: Experimental studies on the albino rat.* New York: Columbia University Press.

Warshaw, L. (1979). *Managing stress.* Reading, MA: Addison-Wesley.

Wasser, S. K. (1990). Infertility, abortion, and biotechnology: When it's not nice to fool mother nature. *Human Nature, 1,* 3–24.

Wasser, S. K., & Starling, A. K. (1988). Proximate and ultimate causation of reproductive suppression among female Yellow Baboons at Mikumi National Park, Tanzania. *American Journal of Primatology, 16,* 97–121.

Watkins, L. R., & Mayer, D. J. (1982). Organization of the endogenous opiate and nonopiate pain control systems. *Science, 216,* 1185–1193.

Watson, J. B. (1913). Psychology as the behaviorist views it. *Psychological Review, 20,* 158–177.

Watson, J. B. (1919). *Psychology from the standpoint of a behaviorist.* Philadelphia: Lippincott.

Watson, J. B. (1926). *Behaviorism.* New York: Norton.

Watson, J. B. (1930). *Behaviorism.* New York: Norton.

Watson, J. B., & Rayner, R. (1920). Conditioned emotional reactions. *Journal of Experimental Psychology, 3,* 1–14.

Watterlond, M. (1983). The holy ghost people. Reprinted in A. L. Hammond & P. G. Zimbardo (Eds.), *Readings on human behavior: The best of Science '80–'86* (pp. 48–55). Glenview, IL: Scott, Foresman.

Weakland, J. H., Fish, R., Watzlawick, P., & Bodin, A. M. (1974). Brief therapy: Focused problem resolution. *Family Process, 13,* 141–168.

Webb, W. B. (1974). Sleep as an adaptive response. *Perceptual and Motor Skills, 38,* 1023–1027.

Webb, W. B. (1981). The return of consciousness. In L. T. Benjamin, Jr. (Ed.), *The G. Stanley Hall Lecture Series, 100* (Vol. 1), pp. 133–152. Washington, DC: American Psychological Association.

Weber, E. H. (1834). *De pulsu, resorptione, auditu et tactu: Annotationes anatomical et physiological.* Leipzig: Koehler.

Weber, M. (1958). *The Protestant ethic and the spirit of capitalism* (T. Parsons, Trans.). New York: Scribners. (Original work published 1904–1905)

Wechsler, D. (1974). *Wechsler intelligence scale for children—revised.* New York: Psychological Corp.

Wechsler, D. (1981). *Manual for the Wechsler Adult Intelligence Scale—revised.* New York: Psychological Corp.

Weick, K. E. (1984). Small wins: Redefining the scale of social problems. *American Psychologist, 39,* 40–49.

Weigel, R. H., & Newman, L. S. (1976). Increasing attitude-behavior correspondence by broadening the scope of the behavioral measure. *Journal of Personality and Social Psychology, 33,* 793–802.

Weil, A. T. (1977). The marriage of the sun and the moon. In N. E. Zinberg (Ed.), *Alternate states of consciousness* (pp. 37–52). New York: Free Press.

Weinberger, M., Hiner, S. L, & Tierney, W. M. (1987). In support of hassles as a measure of stress in predicting health outcomes. *Journal of Behavioral Medicine, 10,* 19–31.

Weiner, B. (1980). *Human motivation.* New York: Holt, Rinehart & Winston.

Weiner, B. (1985). An attributional theory of achievement motivation and emotion. *Psychological Review, 92,* 548–573.

Weiner, B. (1986). *An attributional theory of motivation and emotion.* New York: Springer-Verlag.

Weiner, B., Frieze, I., Kukla, A., Reed, L., Rest, S., & Rosenbaum, R. M. (1971). Perceiving the causes of success and failure. In E. E. Jones et al. (Eds.), *Attribution: Perceiving the causes of behavior.* Morristown, NJ: General Learning Press.

Weiner, B., Russell, D., & Lerman, D. (1978). Affective consequences of causal ascriptions. In J. H. Harvey, W. J. Ickes, & R. F. Kidd (Eds.), *New directions in attribution research* (Vol. 2). Hillsdale NJ: Erlbaum.

Weiner, M. J., & Wright, F. E. (1973). Effects of undergoing arbitrary discrimination upon subsequent attitudes toward a minority group. *Journal of Applied Social Psychology, 3,* 94–102.

Weins, A. N., & Matarazzo, J. D. (1983). Diagnostic interviewing. In M. Hersen, A. E. Kazdin, & A. S., Bellack (Eds.), *The clinical psychology handbook* (pp. 309–328). New York: Pergamon.

Weinstein, N. D. (1980). Unrealistic optimism about future life events. *Journal of Personality and Social Psychology, 39,* 806–820.

Weinstein, N. D. (1982). Community noise problems: Evidence against adaptation. *Journal of Environmental Psychology, 2,* 87–97.

Weinstein, N. D. (1990a). Optimistic biases and personal risks. *Science, 246,* 1232–1233.

Weinstein, N. D. (1990b). Determinants of self-protective behavior: Home radon testing. *Journal of Applied Social Psychology, 20,* 783–801.

Weisenberg, M. (1977). Cultural and racial reactions to pain. In M. Weisenberg (Ed.), *The control of pain.* New York: Psychological Dimensions.

Weiskrantz, L. (1990). *Blindsight: A case study and implications.* New York: Oxford University Press.

Weiskrantz, L., Warington, E. K., Sanders, M. D., & Marshall, J. (1974). Visual capacity in the hemianopic field following a restricted occipital ablation. *Brain, 97,* 709–728.

Weiss, B., & Laties, V. G. (1962). Enhancement of human performance by caffeine and amphetamines. *Pharmacological Review, 14,* 1–27.

Weiss, P. (1991, April). The sexual revolution: Sexual politics on campus: A case study. *Harper's Magazine,* pp. 58–72.

Weiss, R. F., Buchanan, W., Alstatt, L., & Lombardo, J. P. (1971). Altruism is rewarding. *Science, 171,* 1262–1263.

Weiss, R. S. (1973). *Loneliness: The experience of emotional and social isolation.* Cambridge, MA: MIT Press.

Weiss, R. S. (1987). Reflections on the present state of loneliness research. *Journal of Behavior and Personality, 2*(2), 1–16.

- Weissman, M. M., Prusoff, B. A., DiMascio, A., Neu, C., Goklaney, M., & Klerman, G. L. (1979). The efficacy of drugs and psychotherapy in the treatment of acute depressive episodes. *American Journal of Psychiatry, 136,* 555–558.

Weissman, W. W. (1987). Advances in psychiatric epidemiology: Rates and risks for depression. *American Journal of Public Health, 77,* 445–451.

Welker, R. L., & Wheatley, K. L. (1977). Differential acquisition of conditioned suppression in rats with increased and decreased luminance levels as CS+S. *Learning and Motivation, 8,* 247–262.

Welner, A., Reish, T., Robbins, I., Fishman, R., & van Doren, T. (1976). Obsessive-compulsive neurosis. *Comprehensive Psychiatry, 17,* 527–539.

Wender, P. H. (1972). Adopted children and their families in the evaluation of nature-nurture interactions in the schizophrenic disorders. *Annual Review of Medicine, 23,* 255–372.

Werner, D. (1979). A cross-cultural perspective on theory and research on male homosexuality. *Journal of Homosexuality, 4,* 345–361.

Werner, E. E., & Smith, R. S. (1982). *Vulnerable but invincible: A longitudinal study of resilient children and youth.* New York: McGraw-Hill.

Wertheimer, M. (1923). Untersuchungen zur lehre von der gestalt, II. *Psychologische Forschung, 4,* 301–350.

Wever, E. G. (1949). *Theory of hearing.* New York: Wiley.

Weyler, J. (1984, September 11). An unforgettable moment: It's one Gabriele wishes she could forget. *Los Angeles Times,* Part III, pp. 1, 10.

Whalen, R., & Simon, N. G. (1984). Biological motivation. *Annual Review of Psychology, 35,* 257–276.

Whitbourne, S. K., & Hulicka, I. M. (1990). Ageism in undergraduate psychology texts. *American Psychologist, 45,* 1127–1136.

White, B. W., Saunders, F. A., Scadden, L., Bach-Y-Rita, P., & Collins, C. C. (1970). Seeing with the skin. *Perception & Psychophysics, 7*(1), 23–27.

White, G. L., Fishbein, S., & Rutstein, J. (1981). Passionate love and the misattribution of arousal. *Journal of Personality and Social Psychology, 41,* 56–62.

White, M. D., & White, C. A. (1981). Involuntarily committed patients' constitutional right to refuse treatment. *American Psychologist, 36,* 953–962.

White, R. K. (1952). *Lives in progress.* New York: Dryden Press.

Whorf, B. L. (1956). *Language, thought, and reality.* Cambridge, MA: MIT Press.

Wicklund, R. A., & Brehm, J. W. (1976). *Perspectives on cognitive dissonance.* Hillsdale, NJ: Erlbaum.

Wiebe, D. J. (1991). Hardiness and stress modification: A test of proposed mechanisms. *Journal of Personality and Social Psychology, 60,* 89–99.

Wiggins, J. S. (1973). *Personality and prediction: Principles of personality assessment.* Reading, MA: Addison-Wesley.

Wilcoxon, H. G., Dragoin, W. B., & Kral, P. A. (1971). Illness-induced aversions in rat and quail: Relative salience of visual and gustatory cues. *Science, 171,* 826–828.

Wilder, D. A. (1986). Social categorization: Implications for creation and reduction of intergroup bias. *Advances in Experimental Social Psychology, 19,* 291–355.

Williams, J. B. W., & Spitzer, R. L. (1983). The issue of sex bias in DSM-III. *American Psychologist, 38,* 793–798.

Williams, J. H. (1983). *The psychology of women* (2nd ed.). New York: Norton.

Williams, T. (1989, Spring). Attitudes toward wildlife in 2049 A.D. *Orion Nature Quarterly,* pp. 28–33.

Wills, T. A. (1986). Stress and coping in early adolescence: Relationships to substance use in urban school samples. *Health Psychology, 5,* 503–529.

Wilson, E. D., Reeves, A., & Culver, C. (1977). Cerebral commissurotomy for control of intractable seizures. *Neurology, 27,* 708–715.

Wilson, E. O. (1973). The natural history of lions. *Science, 179,* 466–467.

Wilson, E. O. (1975). *Sociobiology: The new synthesis.* Cambridge, MA: Harvard University Press.

Wilson, J. P. (1980). Conflict, stress, and growth: The effects of war on the psychosocial development of Vietnam veterans. In C. R. Figley & S. Leventman (Eds.), *Strangers at home: Vietnam veterans since the war* (pp. 123–165). New York: Praeger.

Wilson, M. (1959). *Communal rituals among the Nyakusa.* London: Oxford University Press.

Wilson, T. D., & Lassiter, G. D. (1982). Increasing intrinsic interest with superfluous extrinsic constraints. *Journal of Personality and Social Psychology, 42,* 811–819.

Wing, C. W., & Wallach, M. A. (1971). *College admissions and the psychology of talent.* New York: Holt, Rinehart & Winston.

Wingerson, L. (1990). *Mapping our genes.* New York: Dutton.

Wingfield, A. (1973). Effects of serial position and set size in auditory recognition memory. *Memory and Cognition, 1,* 53–55.

Wingfield, A., & Byrnes, D. L. (1981). *The psychology of human memory.* New York: Academic Press.

Winning through intimidation. (1987, August 31). *U.S. News and World Report.*

Winton, W. M., Putnam, L. E., & Krauss, R. M. (1984). Facial and autonomic manifestations of the dimensional structure of emotions. *Journal of Experimental Social Psychology, 20,* 196–216.

Wintrob, R. M. (1973). The influence of others; Witchcraft and root-work as explanations of behavior disturbances. *Journal of Nervous and Mental Diseases, 156,* 318–326.

Wise, S. P., & Desimone, R. (1988). Behavioral neurophysiology: Insights into seeing and grasping. *Science, 242,* 736–740.

Wispé, L. G., & Drambarean, N. C. (1953). Physiological need, word frequency, and visual duration threshold. *Journal of Experimental Psychology, 46,* 25–31.

Witkin, H. A., Dyk, R. B., Faterson, H. F., Goodenough, D. R., & Karp, S. A. (1962). *Psychological differentiation.* New York: Wiley.

Witkin, H. A., & Goodenough, D. R. (1977). Field dependence and interpersonal behavior. *Psychological Bulletin, 84,* 661–689.

Witkin, H. A., Moore, C. A., Goodenough, D. R., & Cox, P. W. (1977). Field-dependent and field-independent cognitive styles and their educational implications. *Review of Educational Research, 47,* 1–64.

Witkin-Lanoil, G. (1988). *The male stress syndrome: How to recognize and live with it.* New York: Newmarket Press.

Wolf, M., Risley, T., & Mees, H. (1964). Application of operant conditioning procedures to the behavior problems of an autistic child. *Behavior Research and Therapy, 1,* 305–312.

Wolitzky, D. L., & Wachtel, P. L. (1973). Personality and perception. In B. J. Wolman (Ed.), *Handbook of general psychology* (pp. 826–857). Englewood Cliffs, NJ: Prentice-Hall.

Wolman, C. (1975). Therapy and capitalism. *Issues in Radical Therapy, 3*(1).

Wolpe, J. (1958). *Psychotherapy by reciprocal inhibition.* Stanford, CA: Stanford University Press.

Wolpe, J. (1973). *The practice of behavior therapy* (2nd ed.). New York: Pergamon.

Woodruf-Pak, D. S. (1988). *Psychology and aging.* Englewood Cliffs, NJ: Prentice-Hall.

Woodruf-Pak, D. S., & Thompson, R. F. (1988). Cerebeller correlates of classical conditioning across the life span. In P. B. Baltes, D. M. Featherman, & R. M. Learner (Eds.), *Life span development and behavior* (Vol. 9, pp. 1–37). Hillsdale, NJ: Erlbaum.

Woods, D. L., Hillyard, S. A., Courchesne, E., & Galambos, R. (1980). Electrophysiological signs of split-second decision making. *Science, 207,* 655–657.

Woodworth, R. S. (1918). *Dynamic psychology.* New York: Columbia University Press.

Woodworth, R. S., & Schlossberg, H. (1954). *Experimental psychology* (Rev. ed.). New York: Holt.

Woolridge, D. E. (1963). *The machinery of the brain.* New York: McGraw-Hill.

Workman, B. (1990, December 1). Father guilty of killing daughter's friend in '69. *San Francisco Examiner-Chronicle,* pp. 1, 4.

Worthington, E. L., Jr., Martin, G. A., Shumate, M., & Carpenter, J. (1983). The effect of brief Lamaze training and social encouragement on pain endurance in a cold pressor task. *Journal of Applied Social Psychology, 13,* 223–233.

Wortman, C. B., & Dunkel-Schetter, C. (1979). Interpersonal relationships and cancer: A theoretical analysis. *Journal of Social Issues, 35,* 120–155.

Wundt, W. (1907). *Outlines of psychology* (7th ed., C. H. Judd, Trans.). Leipzig: Englemann. (Original work published 1896)

Wurtman, R. J. (1982). Nutrients that modify brain functions. *Scientific American, 246*(4), 50–59.

Wynne, L. C., Roohey, M. L., & Doane, J. (1979). Family studies. In L. Bellak (Ed.), *The schizophrenic syndrome.* New York: Basic Books.

Y

Yalom, I. D., & Greaves, C. (1977). Group therapy with the terminally ill. *American Journal of Psychiatry, 134,* 396–400.

Yantis, S., & Jonides, J. (1984). Abrupt visual onsets and selective attention: Evidence from visual search. *Journal of Experimental Psychology: Human Perception and Performance, 10,* 601–621.

Yantis, S., & Jonides, J. (1990). Abrupt visual onsets and selective attention: Voluntary vs. automatic allocation. *Journal of Experimental Psychology: Human Perception and Performance, 16,* 121–134.

Yarrow, L. (1975). *Infant and environment: Early cognitive and motivational development.* New York: Halsted.

Yates, B. (1985). *Self-management.* Belmont, CA: Wadsworth.

Yates, B. T. (1980). *Improving effectiveness and reducing costs in mental health.* Springfield, IL: Charles C Thomas.

Yeltsin says KGB unit refused plotter's orders to seize him. (1991, August 26). *San Francisco Examiner-Chronicle,* p. A 10.

Yerkes, R. M. (1921). Psychological examining in the United States Army. In R. M. Yerkes (Ed.), *Memoirs of the National Academy of Sciences: Vol. 15.* Washington, DC: U.S. Government Printing Office.

Yerkes, R. M., & Dodson, J. D. (1908). The relation of strength of stimulus to rapidity of habit formation. *Journal of Comparative Neurology and Psychology, 18,* 459–482.

Young, P. T. (1961). *Motivation and emotion.* New York: Wiley.

Young, T. (1807). On the theory of light and colours. In *Lectures in natural philosophy* (Vol. 2, pp. 613–632). London: William Savage.

Younger, B., & Gotlieb, S. (1988). Development of categorization skills: Changes in the nature or structure of infant form categories? *Developmental Psychology, 24,* 611–619.

Yudkin, M. (1984, April). When kids think the unthinkable. *Psychology Today,* pp. 18–20, 24–25.

Z

Zadeh, L. A. (1965). Fuzzy sets. *Information Control, 8,* 338–353.

Zahn-Waxler, C., & Radke-Yarrow, M. (1982). The development of altruism: Alternative research strategies. In N. Eisenberg-Berg (Ed.), *The development of prosocial behavior* (pp. 109–138). New York: Academic Press.

Zajonc, R. B. (1968). Attitudinal effects of mere exposure. *Journal of Personality and Social Psychology, Monograph Supplement, 9* (2, Part 2), 1–27.

Zajonc, R. B. (1980). Feeling and thinking: Preferences need no inferences. *American Psychologist, 35,* 151–175

Zajonc, R. B. (1984). On the primacy of affect. *American Psychologist, 39,* 117–129.

Zanchetti, A. (1967). Subcortical and cortical mechanisms in arousal and emotional behavior. In G. C. Quarton, T. Melnechuk, & F. O. Schmitt (Eds.), *The neurosciences: A study program.* New York: Rockefeller University Press.

Zborowski, M. (1969). *People in pain.* San Francisco: Jossey-Bass.

Zeigarnik, B. (1927). Uber das leehalten von Erledigten und unerleighten Handbegen. *Psycholische Forschung, 9,* 1–85 [Classic research on task tensions from uncompleted tasks].

Zelnick, M., & Kantner, J. F. (1980). Sexual activity, contraceptive use and pregnancy among metropolitan-area teenagers: 1971–1979. *Family Planning Perspectives, 12,* 230–237.

Zelnik, M., Kim, Y. J., & Kantner, J. F. (1979). Probabilities of intercourse and conception among U.S. teenage women, 1971–1976. *Family Planning Perspectives, 11,* 177–183.

Zettle, R. D. (1990). Rule-governed behavior: A radical behavioral answer to the cognitive challenge. *The Psychological Record, 40,* 41–49.

Zilboorg, G., & Henry, G. W. (1941). *A history of medical psychology.* New York: Norton.

Zimbardo, P. G. (1970). The human choice: Individuation, reason, and order versus deindividuation, impulse, and chaos. In W. J. Arnold & D. Levine (Eds.), *Nebraska Symposium on Motivation, 1969.* Lincoln, NE: University of Nebraska Press.

Zimbardo, P. G. (1975). On transforming experimental research into advocacy for social change. In M. Deutsch & H. Hornstein (Eds.), *Applying social psychology: Implications for research, practice and training.* Hillsdale, NJ: Erlbaum.

Zimbardo, P. G. (1990). *Shyness: What it is, what to do about it* (Rev. ed.). Reading, MA: Addison-Wesley. (Original book published 1977)

Zimbardo, P. G., Andersen, S. M., & Kabat, L. G. (1981). Induced hearing deficit generates experimental paranoia. *Science, 212,* 1529–1531.

Zimbardo, P. G., & Leippe, M. (1991). *The psychology of attitude change and social influence.* New York: McGraw-Hill.

Zimbardo, P. G., & Montgomery, K. D. (1957). The relative strengths of consummatory responses in hunger, thirst, and exploratory drive. *Journal of Comparative and Physiological Psychology, 50,* 504–508.

Zimbardo, P. G., & Radl, S. (1981). *The shy child.* New York: McGraw-Hill.

Zola, I. K. (1973). Pathways to the doctor—from person to patient. *Social Science and Medicine, 7,* 677–689.

Zubeck, J. P., Pushkar, D., Sansom, W., & Gowing, J. (1961). Perceptual changes after prolonged sensory isolation (darkness and silence). *Canadian Journal of Psychology, 15,* 83–100.

Zucker, R. S., & Lando, L. (1986). Mechanism of transmitter release: Voltage hypothesis and calcium hypothesis. *Science, 231,* 574–579.

Zuckerman, M. (1979). Sensation seeking and risk taking. In C. E. Izard (Ed.), *Emotions in personality and psychopathology.* New York: Plenum.

Zuckerman, M. (1990). Some dubious premises in research and theory on racial differences: Scientific, social, and ethical issues. *American Psychologist, 45,* 1297–1303.

ACKNOWLEDGMENTS

PHOTO CREDITS

Unless otherwise acknowledged, all photographs are the property of Scott, Foresman. Page abbreviations are as follows: T—top, C—center, B—bottom, L—left, R—right.

CHAPTER 1

1	Gerard Vandystadt/Photo Researchers
5	Mark Antman/The Image Works
8	Sidney Harris
12T	Courtesy of WGBH Boston
12B	The Bettmann Archive
13	From *Punch's Almanack for 1882*
15T	Pete Turner/The Image Bank
15B	Courtesy of WGBH Boston
21	Gary Bistram/The Image Bank
22	David Muench

CHAPTER 2

27	*The Times,* Trenton, NJ; Photo: Michael Mancuso
32T	Sidney Harris
33	Sidney Harris
35	Jerry Howard/Positive Images
36	Sidney Harris
38	Rich Friedman/Black Star
39T	P. Breese/Gamma-Liaison
39BLR	Christopher Springmann
40	Louise Carter
48	Jeff Albertson/The Picture Cube
50	Jonathan L. Barkan/The Picture Cube

CHAPTER 3

55	Ken Keyman/Stock Boston
56	Courtesy of WGBH Boston
57	By permission of the Darwin Museum, Down House
61T	David Muench
61B	Dan Bosler/Tony Stone Worldwide
62	Omikron/SS/Photo Researchers
63T	Vol. 238, 1989/*Science*
63B	Giraudon/Art Resource, NY
64	Martin Rogers/Stock Boston
66	Warren Anatomical Museum, Harvard University Medical School
67	Montreal Neurological Institute
68	Dan McCoy/Rainbow
69T	Steven E. Petersen, Washington University School of Medicine, St. Louis
69B	Dan McCoy/Rainbow
91	Jim Pickerell/Tony Stone Worldwide

CHAPTER 4

103	Jim Pickerell/Tony Stone Worldwide
105	John W. Verano/National Museum of Natural History/Smithsonian Institution
109R	From *Mind Sights* by Roger N. Shepard. © 1990 by Roger N. Shepard. Reprinted with permission of W. H. Freeman and Company
111	Peter Fronk/Tony Stone Worldwide
112	Rhoda Sidney/The Image Works
114	© 1977 J. Allan Hobson and Hoffman-La Roche Inc./Courtesy DREAMSTAGE
121	Chronicle Features, San Francisco
122	Courtesy Stephen LaBerge
124	Courtesy of WGBH Boston
127	Mike Maple/Woodfin Camp & Associates
130L	P. Chock/Stock Boston
130R	R. D. Ullman

CHAPTER 5

135	D. McKay
138	Greenlar/The Image Works
141L	From *A Child Is Born,* New York: Dell, 1977, p. 42. Lennart Nilsson/Bonnier Fakta
142	Courtesy of WGBH Boston
143	Diana O. Rasche
144	John Chiasson/Gamma-Liaison
145	Bibliothèque Nationale
147	Courtesy Dr. Lew Lipsitt
148T	Vic Bider/Tony Stone Worldwide
148B	Dr. Alan Fogel, University of Utah
151	Courtesy of WGBH Boston
154	George Ancona
158	Courtesy of WGBH Boston
162L	Peter Menzel/Stock Boston
162C	George Godwin/Monkmeyer Press Photo Service
162R	Robert Mayer/Tony Stone Worldwide
164ALL	Marcia Weinstein
165	Courtesy of WGBH Boston
169	Thomas McAvoy © 1955/Life Magazine Time Warner Inc.
173	Universal Press Syndicate. Reprinted with permission. All rights reserved.

CHAPTER 6

179	Mary Kate Denny/Photo Edit
184	Andrew Holbrooke/Black Star
186T	Miro Vintoniv/The Picture Cube
186BL	James Chimbidis/Tony Stone Worldwide
186BR	Christopher Langridge/Sygma
191	Bob Daemmrich
193	Genaro Molina from *A Day in the Life of California*
196	Harley Schwadron

200ALL   Courtesy of WGBH Boston
202   Copyright 1976 Universal Press Syndicate. Reprinted with permission. All rights reserved.
203   Chat Slattery/Tony Stone Worldwide
205   Bob Daemmrich/The Image Works
207   Dan White from *A Day in the Life of California*
209   Bob Daemmrich/The Image Works

CHAPTER 7
213   Brown Brothers
214   Courtesy of WGBH Boston
215   Stephen Dalton/Photo Researchers
229T   Ken Briggs/Photo Researchers
229B   National Portrait Gallery, London
230   Fritz Goro © 1944/Life Magazine Time Warner Inc.
234   Courtesy of WGBH Boston
237ALL   From Frisby, J., *Seeing: Illusion, Brain, and Mind.* Oxford University Press, 1980. The Kobal Collection/SuperStock International
244   Photoreporters
247T   J. Andanson/Sygma
250ALL   Courtesy Dr. Daryl Tanelian
251   Fuji Photos/The Image Works

CHAPTER 8
255   Courtesy of WGBH Boston
265T   "Gestalt Bleue" by Victor Vasarely. Courtesy the artist
265BL   M. C. Escher Heirs, Collection of C. V. S. Roosevelt, Washington, D.C./Cordon Art-Baarn-Holland
265BR   "Slave Market and the Disappearing Bust of Voltaire," oil, 1940, Salvador Dali Museum, St. Petersburg, Florida
266   NASA
275   Peter Fronk/Tony Stone Worldwide
276   Joe Sohm/The Image Works
283   Esao Hashimoto/Earth Scenes
286   Holt Studios/Earth Scenes
288   Susan Schwartzenberg/The Exploratorium for Scott, Foresman
290T   Dr. Peter Thompson, University of York, England
295   From *Mind Sights* by Roger N. Shepard. © 1990 by Roger N. Shepard. Reprinted with permission of W. H. Freeman and Company
296T   From *Mind Sights* by Roger N. Shepard. © 1990 by Roger N. Shepard. Reprinted with permission of W. H. Freeman and Company

CHAPTER 9
301   Courtesy of WGBH Boston
302   Yoav Levy/Phototake
303   Universal Press Syndicate. Reprinted with permission. All rights reserved.
304   Courtesy John Hopkins University
306   The Bettmann Archive
311   Dr. Philip G. Zimbardo
312T   Courtesy of WGBH Boston
312B   Official U.S. Navy Photograph
314   Barbara Van Cleve/Tony Stone Worldwide
317   Chronicle Features, San Francisco
318   Richard Wood/The Picture Cube
320T   Flip Nicklin/Nicklin & Associates/Ocean Images
320B   Jacob H. Bachman

321   Hank Morgan/Discover Publications/Family Media
324   Yerkes Primate Research Center, Emory University
328   Copyright © 1985 American Psychological Association. Reprinted with permission from *Psychology Today* magazine.
333ALL   Courtesy Stuart Ellis, Ph.D., California State University, San Bernadino
334   Norman Baxley/Discover Publications/Family Media
335   Chronicle Features, San Francisco

CHAPTER 10
344   Sidney Harris
346   Flilp Chalfant/The Image Bank
354   LRN/Southern Light
358   Ellis Herwig/The Picture Cube
359   Courtesy of WGBH Boston
368   William Hubbell/Woodfin Camp & Associates
369   Reprinted by permission of United Feature Syndicate, Inc.
371L   Bob Andres/Times Tribune
371R   AP/Wide World
374L   Ira Wyman/Sygma
374R   Martin Rotker/Phototake

CHAPTER 11
379   G. Rancinan/Sygma
380   Washington Post Writers Group. Reprinted with permission.
382T   Stephen Sherman
383T   Sidney Harris
383B   Courtesy Professor David Rumelhart
385L   Les Stone/Sygma
385R   Bob Daemmrich/Stock Boston
386   Courtesy of WGBH Boston
389   Vol. 239, Jan. 8, 1988, p. 163/*Science*
390T   Courtesy of WGBH Boston
390B   Endel Tulving, *American Scientist,* July-Aug. 1989, p. 365, Photo: Dr. David Bryant, Northeastern University, Boston
394ALL   *Psychological Science,* Vol. I, No. 2, March 1990. Published by The American Psychological Society
401   Sidney Harris
402   Joe Feingersh/Tom Stack & Associates
413   Courtesy of WGBH Boston
416   Sidney Harris
417   Leslie Illingworth/Courtesy The National Library of Wales
418   Louise Carter

CHAPTER 12
423   Jay Mather/Sacramento Bee/Sygma
424   Chuck Gardner/Shooting Star
425ALL   Rich Clarkson/*Sports Illustrated*
429   Johnny Johnson/DRK Photo
431L   Joyce Wilson/*Animals Animals*
431R   Robert Brenner/Photo Edit
432T   Mike Powell/ALLSPORT USA
434   Courtesy of WGBH Boston
435   Kobal Collection/SUPERSTOCK
444   © 1983, Punch Publs., Ltd./Reprinted by permission, Los Angeles Times Syndicate
453   Courtesy of WGBH Boston

688	Robert Nebecker
690	The Prado, Madrid/Giraudon/Art Resource, NY
691L	Will McIntyre/Photo Researchers
698	Mary Kate Denny/Photo Edit
700	Richard Hutchings/InfoEdit

LITERARY CREDITS

CHAPTER 1

9 Figure 1.1. From "The Changing Face of American Psychology: A Report from the Committee of Employment and Human Resources," by A. Howard et al., in *American Psychologist,* Vol. 41, pp. 1311–27. Copyright © 1986 by the American Psychological Association. Reproduced by permission. Figure 1.2. From *1989 APA Directory,* compiled by the Office of Demographic Employment and Educational Research. Copyright © by the American Psychological Association. Reproduced by permission.

CHAPTER 3

60 Figure 3.2. From *Human Evolution: An Illustrated Introduction,* by Robert Lewin. Copyright © 1984 by W. H. Freeman and Company. Reprinted by permission.
71 Figure 3.4. By Lynn O'Kelley.
72 Figure 3.5. By Lynn O'Kelley.
73 Figure 3.6. By Lynn O'Kelley.
95 Figure 3.21. By Lynn O'Kelley.
98 Figure 3.24. From *The Harvey Lectures,* Series 62, by R. W. Sperry. Copyright © 1968 by Academic Press. Reprinted by permission of the author and the publisher.

CHAPTER 4

116 Figure 4.3. From "Ontogenetic Development of the Human Sleep-Dream Cycle," by H. P. Roffwarg et al., in *Science,* April 1966, Vol. 152, No. 9, pp. 604–19. Copyright © 1966 by AAAS. Reprinted by permission of the American Association for the Advancement of Science.
119 Figure 4.4. By Lynn O'Kelley. Redrawn from illustration by M. E. Challinor in "Images of the Night," by Kiester, in *Science,* May/June 1980.

CHAPTER 5

139 Figure 5.1. From *The First Two Years,* by Mary M. Shirley. Reprinted by permission of the University of Minnesota Press.
140 Figure 5.2. By Lynn O'Kelley. Redrawn from *The Brain,* by W. M. Cowan. Copyright © 1979 by W. H. Freeman and Company. Reprinted by permission.
148 Table 5.2. From p. 18 of *Child Development,* by L. P. Lipsitt and H. W. Reese. Copyright © 1979 by HarperCollins Publishers. Reprinted by permission of the publisher.

152 Figure 5.5. From "Human Cerebral Hemispheres Develop at Different Rates and Ages," by R. W. Thatcher, in *Science,* Vol. 236, pp. 1110–13. Copyright © 1987 by AAAS. Reprinted by permission of the American Association for the Advancement of Science.
167 Figure 5.9. From "Representing the Existence and the Location of Hidden Objects: Object Permanence in 6- and 8-Month-Old Infants," by Renée Baillargeon, in *Cognition, 23* (1986), pp. 21–41. Reprinted by permission of the author and North-Holland Publishing Company.

CHAPTER 6

187 Table 6.2. Adapted from *The Adolescent: A Psychological Self-Portrait,* by Daniel Offer, Eric Ostrov, and Kenneth I. Howard. Copyright © 1981 by Basic Books, Inc. Reprinted by permission of the publisher.
188 Figure 6.1. From p. 225 of *Psychopathology,* edited by D. Magnusson and A. Ohman. Orlando, Fla.: Academic Press, 1987. Reprinted by permission of Academic Press.
194 Table 6.4. From "A Conception of Adult Development," by D. J. Levinson, in *American Psychologist,* Vol. 41, pp. 3–13. Copyright © 1986 by the American Psychological Association. Adapted by permission.
195 Table 6.5. From *Adaptation to Life,* by George Vaillant. Copyright © 1977 by George E. Vaillant. Reprinted by permission.

CHAPTER 7

216 Table 7.1. Adapted by permission from p. 254 of *The Encyclopedic Dictionary of Psychology,* 3rd ed. Copyright © 1986 by the Dushkin Publishing Group, Inc. Reprinted by permission of the author.
218 Table 7.2. From *New Directions in Psychology,* by Roger Brown, Eugene Galanter, and Eckhard H. Hess. Copyright © 1962 by Holt, Rinehart and Winston, Inc. Reprinted by permission of Dr. Eugene Galanter.
221 Table 7.3. From *Introduction to Psychology,* 10th ed., by Atkinson et al. Copyright © 1990 by Harcourt Brace Jovanovich, Inc. Reproduced by permission of the author.
222 Figure 7.4. From *Sensory Communication,* by W. A. Rosenblith. Copyright © 1961 by the Massachusetts Institute of Technology. Reprinted by permission of MIT Press.
223 Figure 7.6. From *Brain, Mind, and Behavior,* Revised ed., by Floyd E. Bloom and Arlyne Lazerson. Copyright © 1985, 1988 by the Educational Broadcasting Corporation. Reprinted by permission of W. H. Freeman and Company.
228 Figure 7.10. Adapted from *Seeing: Illusion, Brain and Mind,* by John P. Frisby. Copyright © 1979 by John P. Frisby. Reprinted by permission of Oxford University Press.
241 Figure 7.20. From *The Science of Musical Sounds,* by D. C. Miller. Macmillan Company, 1926. Reprinted by permission of Case Western Reserve University.
243 Figure 7.22. From *Theory of Hearing,* by Ernest Glen Weaver. Copyright © 1949 by John Wiley & Sons, Inc. Reprinted by permission of the author.

CHAPTER 8

263 Figure 8.5. From *Fundamentals of Sensation and Perception,* by M. W. Levine and J. Shefner. Reprinted by permission of Michael W. Levine.
270 Figure 8.8. From "The Effect of Inattention on Form

Perception," by I. Rock and D. Gutman, *Journal of Experimental Psychology: Human Perception and Performance, I.* Copyright © 1981 by the American Psychological Association. Reproduced by permission.

271 Figure 8.9. From "Features and Objects in Visual Processing," by Anne Triesman, in *Scientific American,* November 1986. Copyright © 1986 by Scientific American, Inc. All rights reserved. Reprinted by permission.

272 Figure 8.10. From "Features and Objects in Visual Processing," by Anne Triesman, in *Scientific American,* November 1986. Copyright © 1986 by Scientific American, Inc. All rights reserved. Reprinted by permission.

273 Figure 8.11. From *Cognitive Psychology and Information Processing: An Introduction,* by Roy Lachman, Janet I. Lachman, and Earl C. Butterfield. Reprinted by permission of the authors and Lawrence Erlbaum Associates, Inc.

282 Figure 8.20. From "Impossible Objects: A Special Type of Visual Illusion," by L. S. Penrose and R. Penrose, in *British Journal of Psychology,* 1958, Vol. 49, p. 31. Reprinted by permission of The British Psychological Society.

285 Figure 8.22. From *Sensation and Perception,* by Stanley Coren, Clare Porac, and Lawrence M. Ward. Copyright © 1979 by Harcourt Brace Jovanovich, Inc. Reprinted by permission of the publisher.

287 Figure 8.24. Adapted from Figure 38 of "The Perspective of a Pavement," in *The Perception of the Visual World,* by James W. Gibson. Copyright © 1950 and renewed 1977 by Houghton Mifflin Company. Adapted by permission of the publisher.

292 Figure 8.28a. From *Droodles,* by R. Price. Copyright © 1953, 1980 by Price Stern Sloane, Inc., Los Angeles. Figure 8.28b. From *The Logic of Perception,* by I. Rock. Copyright © 1983 by the Massachusetts Institute of Technology. Reprinted with permission.

293 Figure 8.29a. From "Representation and Recognition of the Spatial Organization of Three-Dimensional Shapes," by D. Marr and H. K. Nishihara, in *Proceedings of the Royal Society of London,* 1978, p. 200B. Reprinted by permission. Figure 8.29b. From "Recognition by Components: A Theory of Object Recognition," by I. Biederman, in *Computer Vision Graphics and Image Processing,* 1985, p. 32. Reprinted by permission.

CHAPTER 9

308 Figure 9.2. From *Psychology,* by William Buskist. Copyright © 1991 by HarperCollins Publishers, Inc. Reprinted by permission.

309 Figure 9.3. Reprinted by permission of HarperCollins Publishers, Inc.

310 Figure 9.4. From *Principles and Methods of Psychology,* by Lawson, Goldsten, and Musty. Copyright © 1975 by Oxford University Press, Inc. Reprinted by permission.

314 Figure 9.5. From *Psychology,* by William Buskist. Copyright © 1991 by HarperCollins Publishers, Inc. Reprinted by permission.

315 Figure 9.6. From "Predictability and Number Pairings in Pavlovian Fear Conditioning," by Robert A. Rescorla, in *Psychonomic Science,* Vol. 4, No. 11. Reprinted by permission of the Psychonomic Society, Inc. Figure 9.7. From *Psychology,* by William Buskist. Copyright © 1991 by HarperCollins Publishers, Inc. Reprinted by permission.

319 Figure 9.9. From *Introduction to Psychology,* by

Christopher Peterson. Copyright © 1991 by HarperCollins Publishers, Inc. Reprinted by permission.

331 Figure 9.11. From "Learned Association Over Long Delays," by Sam Revusky and John Garcia, in *The Psychology of Learning and Motivation,* Vol. IV, edited by Gordon H. Bower. Orlando, Fla.: Academic Press, 1970. Reprinted by permission.

334 Figure 9.12. From "Degrees of Hunger, Reward and Non-reward, and Maze Learning in Rats," by E. C. Tolman and C. H. Honzik, in *University of California Publication in Psychology,* Vol. 4, No. 16, December 1930. Reprinted by permission of the University of California Press.

CHAPTER 10

349 From *Human Memory: Structures and Processes,* 2nd ed., by Roberta Klatsky. Copyright © 1975, 1980 by W. H. Freeman and Company. Reprinted by permission.

350 Figure 10.3. Adapted from "The Information Available in Brief Visual Presentations," by George Sperling, in *Psychological Monographs: General and Applied,* Vol. 174, No. 11, Whole No. 498. Copyright © 1960 by the American Psychological Association, Inc. Adapted by permission of the author.

355 Figure 10.5. From "Short-Term Retention of Individual Verbal Items," by Lloyd R. Peterson and Margaret Jean Peterson, in *Journal of Experimental Psychology,* September 1959, Vol. 58, No. 3. Copyright © 1959 by the American Psychological Association, Inc. Reprinted by permission of the authors.

356 Figure 10.6. From Figure 1 of "High Speed Scanning in Human Memory," by Saul Sternberg, in *Science,* Vol. 153, pp. 652–54, August 5, 1966. Copyright © 1966 by AAAS. Reprinted by permission of the author and the American Association for the Advancement of Science.

362 Figure 10.7. From "Remembering Odors and Their Names," by T. Engen, in *American Scientists,* 1987, Vol. 75, p. 498. Reprinted by permission of Sigma Xi, The Scientific Research Society.

364 Figure 10.9. From "Two Storage Mechanisms in Free Recall," by Murray Glanzer and Anita R. Cunitz, in *Journal of Verbal Learning and Verbal Behavior.* Copyright © 1966 by Academic Press, Inc. Reprinted by permission of the author and the publisher.

372 Figure 10.10. By Lynn O'Kelley.

375 Figure 10.11. By Lynn O'Kelley.

CHAPTER 11

379 Text reprinted by permission of Edith Eva Eger, Ph.D.

381 Figure 11.1. From *Cognitive Psychology,* 3rd ed., by Robert L. Solso. Copyright © 1991 by Allyn and Bacon. Reprinted with permission.

388 Figure 11.3. From *Cognitive Psychology,* 3rd ed., by Robert L. Solso. Copyright © 1991 by Allyn and Bacon. Reprinted with permission.

393 Figure 11.6b. From *British Journal of Psychology,* 72, pp. 499–503. Reprinted by permission of The British Psychological Society.

395 Figure 11.8. From "Retrieval Time from Semantic Memory," by Collins and Quillan, in *Journal of Verbal Learning and Verbal Behavior,* Vol. 8, pp. 240–47. Copyright © 1969 by Academic Press, Inc. Reprinted by permission.

399 Figure 11.11. From *Cognitive Psychology,* 3rd ed., by Robert L. Solso. Copyright © 1991 by Allyn and Bacon. Reprinted with permission.

400 Figure 11.12. From *Cognitive Psychology,* 3rd ed., by

Robert L. Solso. Copyright © 1991 by Allyn and Bacon. Reprinted with permission.

403 Figure 11.13. From *How to Solve Problems: Elements of a Theory of Problems and Problem Solving,* by Wayne A. Wickelgren. Copyright © 1974 by W. H. Freeman and Company. Reprinted by permission.

408 Figure 11.14. From *Protean Behavior: The Biology of Unpredictable Behavior,* by Driver and Humphries, 1988. Reprinted by permission.

409 Figure 11.15. From *Protean Behavior: The Biology of Unpredictable Behavior,* by Driver and Humphries, 1988. Reprinted by permission.

CHAPTER 12

427 Figure 12.2. From *Animal Motivation: Experimental Studies on the Albino Rat,* by C. J. Warden. Copyright © 1931 by Columbia University Press. Reprinted by permission.

432 Figure 12.4. From *Psychology,* 3rd ed., by Rathus. Copyright © 1987 by Holt, Rinehart and Winston, Inc. Reprinted by permission.

441 Figure 12.6. From p. 207 of *Human Sexualities,* by J. H. Gagnon. Copyright © 1977 by HarperCollins Publishers, Inc. Reprinted by permission.

451 Figure 12.8. Adapted from *Human Motivation,* by Bernard Weiner. Copyright © 1980 by Bernard Weiner. Reprinted by permission of the author.

CHAPTER 13

462 Figure 13.1. Reprinted by permission of the author and the publisher from "Crying Behavior in the Human Adult," by William H. Frey, II, Ph.D. et al., in *Integrative Psychiatry,* September/October 1983. Copyright © 1983 by Elsevier Science Publishing Company, Inc.

464 Figure 13.2. From "A Language for the Emotions," by Robert Plutchik, in *Psychology Today,* February 1980. Copyright © 1980 by Sussex Publishing. Reprinted by permission.

467 Figure 13.3. From *Psychology,* 3rd ed., by Rathus. Copyright © 1987 by Holt, Rinehart and Winston, Inc. Reprinted by permission.

476 Table 13.2. Adapted from Table 3, p. 475, of "The Minor Events Approach to Stress: Support for the Use of Daily Hassles," by Kerry Chamberlain and Sheryl Zika, in *British Journal of Pscychology,* 1990, Vol. 81. Reprinted by permission.

479 Table 13.3. Adapted from p. 333 of *Decision Making: A Psychological Analysis of Conflict, Choice, and Commitment,* by I. L. Janis and L. Mann. Copyright © 1977 by The Free Press, a Division of Macmillan, Inc. Adapted with permission of The Free Press.

483 Figure 13.7. From Figure 7.10 of *Psychology,* by Michael S. Gazzaniga. Copyright © 1980 by Michael S. Gazzaniga. Reprinted by permission of HarperCollins Publishers, Inc.   Table 13.4. From Table 6.1, p. 147, of *Health Psychology,* by Feuerstein. New York: Plenum Publishing Corporation, 1986. Reprinted with permission.

494 Table 13.7. From "Healthy Peopie 2000" in *Center for Disease Control Morbidity and Mortality Reports,* October 5, 1990, Vol. 39, p. 695. Published by the Department of Health and Human Services.

495 Table 13.8. Adapted from *Monthly Vital Statistics Report,* January 1991. Published by the Center for Disease Control.

497 Figure 13.9. From *Health and Human Services,* Office of Disease Prevention and Health Promotion.

498 Figure 13.10. From "AIDSweek," *San Francisco Examiner-Chronicle,* August 4, 1991, p. 32.

CHAPTER 14

514 Figure 14.2. From *The Inequality of Man,* by H. J. Eysenck. Copyright © 1973 by Hans J. Eysenck. Reprinted by permission of the author.

CHAPTER 15

551 Figure 15.1. From *Wechsler's Measurement and Appraisal of Adult Intelligence,* 5th ed., by J. D. Matarazzo. Copyright © 1972 by Oxford University Press, Inc. Reprinted by permission.

554 Figure 15.2. From p. 161 of *Way Beyond the IQ: Guide to Improving Intelligence and Creativity,* by J. P. Guilford. Buffalo, N.Y.: Barely Limited, 1977. Reprinted by permission of the author.

558 Table 15.1. From "Familial Studies of Intelligence: A Review," by T. J. Bouchard, Jr., and M. McGue, in *Science,* 1981, Vol. 212, pp. 1055–59. Copyright © 1981 by the AAAS. Reprinted by permission of the American Association for the Advancement of Science.

559 Figure 15.3. From "Achievement and Social Mobility: Relationships Among IQ Score, Education and Occupation in Two Generations," by Jerome H. Waller, in *Social Biology,* September 1971, Vol. 18, No. 3. Copyright © 1971 by The American Eugenics Society, Inc.

560 Figure 15.4. Adapted from "I. Q. Test Performance of Black Children Adopted by White Families," by S. Scarr and R. A. Weinberg, in *American Psychologist,* 1976, Vol. 31, pp. 726–39. Copyright © 1976 by the American Psychological Association. Adapted by permission of the author.

563 Figure 15.5. From *The Minnesota Multiphasic Inventory (MMPI).* Copyright © 1943 and renewed 1970 by the University of Minnesota. Reprinted by permission of the University of Minnesota Press.

CHAPTER 16

589 Figure 16.3. From *The Obedience Experiments: A Case Study of Controversy in the Social Sciences,* by A. G. Miller. Copyright © 1986 by Praeger Publishers. Reprinted by permission of Greenwood Publishing Group, Inc., Westport, Conn.

593 Figure 16.4. Adapted from "Bystander Intervention in Emergencies: Diffusion of Responsibilities," by Darley and Latane, in *Journal of Personality and Social Psychology,* 1968, Vol. 8, No. 4, pp. 377–84. Copyright © 1968 by the American Psychological Association. Adapted by permission of the author.

604 Figure 16.5. From "An Experimental Study of Apparent Behavior," by F. Heider and M. Simmel, in *American Journal of Psychology,* 1944, Vol. 57, pp. 243–59. Reprinted by permission of the University of Illinois Free Press.

CHAPTER 17

620 Figure 17.1. From p. 9 of *Mental Health for Canadians: Striking a Balance.* Minister of National Health and Welfare, 1988.   Figure 17.2. From p. 9 of *Mental Health for Canadians: Striking a Balance.* Minister of National Health and Welfare, 1988.

631 Table 17.2. From "Multiple Personality Disorder: Phenomenology of Selected Variables in Comparison to Major Depression," by R. Schults, B. G. Braun, and R. P. Kluft, in *Dissociation,* 1989, Vol. 2, p. 45.

633 Table 17.3. From *Abnormal Psychology,* by David L. Rosenhan and Martin E. P. Seligman. Copyright © 1984 by W. W. Norton & Company, Inc. Reprinted by permission of W. W. Norton & Company, Inc.

642 Figure 17.4. From pp. 72–80 of *Archives of General Psychiatry,* 1984, Vol. 41, by Rosenthal et al. Reprinted by permission.

643 Table 17.5. From *Mortality,* 1989. National Center for Health Statistics, Washington, D. C.

646 Table 17.6. From *Diagnostic and Statistical Manual of Mental Disorders,* 3rd ed., Revised. Copyright © 1987 by the American Psychiatric Association. Reprinted with permission.

648 Figure 17.5. From "Genetic Theories and the Validation of Psychiatric Diagnosis: Implications for the Study of Children of Schizophrenics," by Daniel R. Hanson et al., in *Journal of Abnormal Psychology,* 1977, Vol. 86, pp. 575–88. Copyright © 1977 by the American Psychological Association, Inc. Reprinted by permission of the authors.

649 Figure 17.6. From *Schizophrenia Genesis,* by Guttesman. Copyright © 1991 by W. H. Freeman and Company. Reprinted by permission.

CHAPTER 18

674 Table 18.1. From *The Practice of Behavior Therapy,* 2nd ed., by J. Wolpe. Copyright © 1973 by Pergamon Books Ltd. Reprinted with permission.

678 Figure 18.1. From p. 603 of *Journal of Abnormal Psychology,* Vol. 94, by Cook et al. Copyright © 1985 by the American Psychological Association. Adapted by permission.

679 Figure 18.2. From "Modeling Therapy," by Albert Bandura. Reprinted by permission of the author.

681 Table 18.2. Adapted from *Modern Clinical Psychology: Principles of Intervention in the Clinic and Community,* by Sheldon J. Korchin. Copyright © 1976 by Sheldon J. Korchin. Reprinted by permission of Basic Books, Inc., Publishers.

683 Figure 18.3. From p. 69 of *Panic,* 1988, by A. Agras.

695 Figure 18.4. From pp. 555–58 of *American Journal of Psychiatry,* 1979, Vol. 136, by Weissman et al. Reprinted with permission.

697 Figure 18.6. From Figure 1, p. 976, of "NIMH Treatment of Depression Collaborative Research Program," by I. Ilkin et al., in *General Psychiatry,* Vol. 46. Reprinted by permission.

NAME INDEX

A

Aaron, A., 328
Abelin, T., 43
Abelson, R. P., 370, 397, 601
Abramson, 640
Abramson, L. Y., 328, 603
Accornero, N., 249
Acker, L. E., 312
Ackerman, D., 213, 214, 239, 247
Adams, J., 398, 405, 686
Adams, J. A., 359
Adams, M., 576
Adams, W. G., 576
Ader, Robert, 301, 484
Adler, 447
Adler, Alfred, 524
Adler, J. E., 375
Adler, N. E., 474
Adler, N. T, 440
Adorno, T. W., 585
Affleck, G., 489
Agras, S., 673
Ahearn, F. L., 477
Ahern, G. L., 462
Ainsworth, M. D. S., 169, 171, 195
Aitken, D. H., 249
Akhtar, S., 635
Albee, G. W., 699
Alden, L. E., 191
Alderfer, C., 454
Aldrete, J., 104
Alex, M., 309
Alexander, J. K., 496
Alger, C. F., 611
Alicke, M. D., 582
Alker, H., 199
Allen, A., 517
Allen, B. P., 613
Allen, C. R., 641
Allen, J. G., 656
Allison, T., 115
Allport, D. A., 274
Allport, Gordon, 511, 512-14, 516-17, 580
Allport, G. W., 274, 599
Allred, E., 560
Als, H., 148
Alstatt, L., 312
Alterman, A. I., 534
Altman, I. A., 609
Amabile, T., 603
Amaral, D. G., 342
Ames, A., 267
Anastasi, A., 568

Andersen, S. M., 202
Anderson, J. A., 98, 407
Anderson, J. R., 343, 361
Anderson, W. F., 62
Andrasik, F., 679
Andreason, N. C., 68
Andrus, D. E., 414
Anisfeld, M., 353
Annis, H. M., 191
Antelman, S. M., 239, 438, 485
Antoni, M. H., 498
Antrobus, John, 112, 118, 121
Appenszeller, G., 373
Arendt, H., 587
Aristotle, 11, 401, 465-66
Armstrong, D. M., 106
Armstrong, Edward, 447, 601
Arnold, K. D., 199
Aron, 463
Aronson, Elliott, 600-601, 610
Arthur, R. J., 474
Asch, Solomon, 582-83, 587
Aserinsky, E., 113
Asher, S. R., 678
Ashton, P. T., 531
Atkinson, 221
Atkinson, R. C., 107, 221, 363
Atkinson, R. L., 221
Averbach, I., 351
Averill, J. R., 465
Ayllon, T., 324, 677
Azrin, N. H., 324

B

Bachman, J. G., 187
Backevalier, J., 373
Backus, Jim, 619
Baddeley, A. D., 352, 360
Bader, B. C., 699
Baer, J. S., 191
Bahrick, H. P., 205
Bahrick, P. O., 205
Baillargeon, R., 165
Balakrishnan, S., 613
Baldwin & Baldwin, 332
Bale, S. J., 642
Ballisteros, M., 268
Balsam, P. D., 334
Baltes, M., 201, 204, 553
Baltes, P. B., 201, 204, 553, 560
Bandura, Albert, 18, 332-33, 343, 489, 493, 527, 529-31, 533, 677-78, 682
Bane, A. L., 497
Bane, M. J., 184
Banks, M. S., 143

Banks, W. P., 256, 268
Banks, William, 570
Banuazizi, A., 578
Banyai, E. I., 124
Barash, David, 303
Barber, T. X., 124
Barcona, E., 547
Bard, Philip, 466
Barinaga, M., 68, 494, 642
Barker, J. L., 461
Barker, L. M., 332
Barlett, D. L., 506
Barnes, D. M., 649
Baron, A., 318
Baron, L., 485
Baron, S. H., 580
Barrett, K. C., 169
Barston, J. L., 402
Barthe, D. G., 640
Bartlett, Sir Frederick, 367
Bartoshuk, L., 248
Basseches, M., 197
Bateson, Gregory, 651
Batey, R., 547
Batson, C. D., 593
Baum, A., 476, 484
Baumeister, R. F., 469, 577
Baumrind, D., 47, 199
Bayley, N., 141
Baylor, D., 233
Bazerman, Max H., 419, 611
Beach, F., 430, 439, 443
Beardslee, W. R., 477
Beatty, W. W., 173
Beck, Aaron T., 279, 637, 640, 683
Beck, J., 268, 269, 273
Becker, M. H., 493
Beecher, H. K., 31
Beers, Clifford, 666
Beethoven, Ludwig van, 214
Begab, M. J., 55
Begg, I., 361
Begley, S., 119
Behr, S. E., 346
Bekerian, D. A., 368
Belinger, D., 560
Bell, A. P., 445, 446
Bell, I. R., 699
Bellack, A. J., 678
Bellak, L., 645
Bellugi, U., 353
Bem, Daryl, 603
Bem, D. J., 221, 517, 518, 529
Bem, S., 530
Benedict, Ruth, 187, 430
Beniger, James, 22

Bennett, B. M., 268
Bennett, P. J., 143
Bennett, William, 50-51
Benson, H., 125-26, 500
Bentler, 128
Beradelli, A., 249
Bereiter, C., 406
Berganza, C. E., 652
Berger, M. M., 685
Berglas, S., 533
Bergman, K., 207
Bergman, L. R., 187
Berk, L. S., 459
Berkeley, G., 267
Berkman, L. F., 490
Berkowitz, L., 532
Berlyne, D. E., 276, 431
Bernard, Claude, 104
Bernard, L. L., 430
Berndt, T. J., 190
Bernstein, 142
Bernstein, D. A., 621
Bernstein, I. L., 332
Bernstein, M., 332
Berry, J. W., 42
Best, M. R., 332
Bettleheim, B., 186
Betz, E. L., 454
Bhatnagar, S., 249
Bieber, I., 446
Bieber, T. B., 446
Biederman, I., 293
Bielski, R. J., 639
Bigelow, H. J., 66
Billig, M., 599
Billings, A. G., 488
Binet, Alfred, 549-51, 569
Bini, G., 249
Binkley, S., 114
Birbaumer, N., 500
Bird, 393
Birnbaum, D., 471
Bitner, R., 104
Bitterman, M. E., 326
Bjork, R. A., 275, 489, 500
Black, I. B., 370, 375
Blake, William, 127
Blakemore, C., 48, 237
Blaney, 471
Blass, Elliott, 146, 147
Blass, E. M., 147
Blehar, M., 169
Bleuler, M., 647
Blight, J. G., 611
Blinder, B., 295
Block, J., 173
Bloom, F. E., 250

Bloom, J. R., 124, 494, 686
Blos, P., 187
Bly, Robert, 22
Bohm, L. C., 203
Bolger, N., 476
Bond, C. F., 370
Bond, L. A., 182
Bongiovanni, A., 321
Booth-Kewley, 500, 501
Bootzin, R. R., 117, 672
Boring, 241
Borke, H., 163
Borkovec, T. D., 117
Bornet, A. R., 191
Bornstein, P. A., 8, 22
Borod, C., 462
Borton, 165
Botvin, G. J., 493
Botwinick, J., 204
Bouchard, T. J., 515, 558, 559
Boudreau, L. A., 656
Bourguignon, E., 667
Bourne, E. J., 182
Bourne, L. E., Jr., 392
Bower, Gordon H., 354, 359,
    366, 464, 470-71, 531, 678
Bower, S. A., 678
Bowers, J. M., 368
Bowers, K. S., 124
Bowers, M. B., Jr., 623
Bowlby, J., 169, 170
Bowles, C. A., 484
Boyd, J. H., 629, 631, 633, 643,
    645, 655
Boyes-Braem, P., 393
Brackbill, Y., 169
Braginsky, B., 545
Braginsky, D., 545
Braine, M. D. S., 160
Bransford, J. D., 358, 366
Braun, R. G., 630, 632
Brazelton, T. B., 148
Breggin, P. R., 691
Brehm, J. W., 602
Breland, Keller, 330
Breland, Marion, 330
Brennan, P., 362
Brenner, M. H., 477
Breo, D. L., 636
Bressler, S. L., 95, 388
Brett, J. F., 474
Breuer, Joseph, 519-20, 669
Brewer, M. B., 599
Briand, 275
Bridgeman, B., 228
Bridwell, L. G., 454
Brief, A. P., 474
Briggs, Isabel, 565
Brim, O. G., 180
Brislin, R. W., 42
Britten, K. H., 238
Broadbent, D. E., 110, 272-73
Broca, Paul, 65, 66, 68, 94
Brockett, D. R., 370

Brody, E. B., 560
Brody, N., 560
Brody, R. A., 611
Brody, R. V., 249
Broman, S. H., 559
Bromley, 533
Bronte, L., 200
Brotzman, E., 590
Broverman, D. M., 654
Broverman, I. K., 654
Brown, A. L., 406
Brown, A. M., 558
Brown, B., 486
Brown, C. C., 99
Brown, G. W., 474
Brown, J. D., 412, 500
Brown, J. S., 439
Brown, L., 22
Brown, R., 156, 590
Brown, Y., 584
Brownell, K. D., 438
Bruner, Jerome S., 164, 365,
    382, 391
Brunswick, A. F., 128
Bryant, B. P., 246
Buchanan, W., 312
Buck, R., 465
Buehler, A., 43
Buhler, Charlotte, 181, 182
Bullimer, P., 275
Bullock, T. H., 86
Bulman, J. R., 489
Bundlach, R. H., 446
Brunelleschi, 285
Burk, J. P., 535
Burke, J. D., 207, 629, 631, 633,
    634, 645, 655
Burke, M. J., 474
Burkhart, J. E., 199
Burrows, G. D., 124
Bush, George, 50-51
Bushnell, M. C., 251
Buss, David, 442
Butcher, J. N., 534, 535, 562,
    564
Butcher, M. G., 146
Butterfield, E. C., 396
Buzan, T., 98
Bykov, 313
Byrne, D., 443, 444
Byrne, R. M. J., 401
Byrnes, D. L., 364

C

Caddell, J. M., 485
Caggiula, A. R., 485
Cairns, R. B., 151
Calambokidis, John, 418
Calhoun, L. G., 485
Calkins, M. P., 203-204
Camerino, M., 209, 484
Campbell, D. T., 580
Campbell, F. W., 237

Campbell, P. W., 237
Campbell, R. G., 437
Campion, J., 229
Campos, J. J., 141
Cann, A., 485
Cannon, Walter, 431, 436, 466,
    481
Cantor, N., 366, 533, 602
Cantril, H., 596
Caplan, P. J., 627
Caplow, 193
Caporeal, L. R., 621
Capos, J. J., 169
Carey, S., 158
Carlsmith, J. M., 465, 603
Carlson, C. C., 312
Carlsson, A., 650
Carlton, J., 244
Carmichael, L., 140, 152
Carnes, Patrick, 447
Carone, P. A., 636
Carpenter, G. C., 148
Carpenter, J., 251
Carpenter, P. A., 387
Carrel, M. R., 455
Carrigan, S., 644
Carskadon, M. A., 114, 118
Carstensen, Laura, 206
Cartwright, R. D., 114, 115
Cartwright, S., 655
Carver, C. S., 218, 275, 488, 577
Case, R. S., 165, 167
Casey, Bill, 591
Caspi, A., 518, 529
Cassidy, J., 169
Catania, J. A., 498
Cattell, Raymond B., 553-54
Catterall, W. A., 87
Ceaucescu, Nicolae, 171
Cervone, D., 414
Chamberlain, K., 475, 476
Chapman, J. A., 364
Chapman, M., 199
Chapman, P. D., 550
Chapman, R. M., 364
Charack, G., 276
Charaton, F., 474-75
Charcot, Jean, 622
Charen, Mona, 606
Chase, William G., 355
Chasnoff, Ira, 144
Chawlisz, K., 466
Cheek, D., 104
Cheek, J. M., 6
Chemiakin, Mikhail, 654
Chen, K., 141
Cherkin, A., 104
Cherry, E. C., 110, 273
Chi, M. T. H., 167
Chilman, C. S., 189
Chilmonczyk, B. A., 478
Chipuer, H. M., 515
Chmiel, N. R. J., 274
Chomsky, Noam, 156, 381-82,

407
Chorost, S., 478
Chorover, S., 655
Christal, 516
Christensen, 609
Chung, C. S., 495
Church, J., 158
Churchland, P. S., 105, 383
Cicchetti, D., 115
Clancey, M., 469
Clark, D., 207
Clark, E. E., 22
Clark, E. V., 155
Clark, H. E., 155
Clark, Kenneth, 598-99
Clark, L. F., 488
Clark, M., 599
Clarkson, F. E., 654
Clausen, J. A., 655
Clayman, C. B., 244
Cleckley, H. A., 629
Cleek, M. B., 193
Clementz, B. A., 649
Clonginger, Robert, 535
Cloninger, 130
Cloninger, C. R., 64
Coates, Thomas, 498, 499
Cobb, S., 490, 493
Coch, L., 608
Coe, W. C., 124
Cofer, C., 428
Cohen, B. S., 34
Cohen, Nathan, 301, 484
Cohen, R. E., 477
Cohen, S., 484, 490
Cole, H. W., 388
Coleman, 644
Coleman, R. M., 113
Collier, G., 438
Collins, J. F., 695
Collins, K., 168
Columbus, Christopher, 266
Conger, J. C., 678
Conger, J. J., 190
Connell, S. I., 129
Conrad, R., 353
Conte, G., 642
Conte, H. Q., 522
Cook, K. V., 172-73
Cook, M., 677
Cook, S. W., 445
Cookerly, J. R., 687
Cooper, A. M., 627
Cooper, L., 293
Cooper, L. A., 361, 397
Corbett, Mike, 423-24
Coren, 262
Coren, S., 215
Coriell, A. S., 351
Cork, R. C., 346
Cosmides, Leda, 19, 407, 409
Costa, P. T., Jr., 501, 565
Courchesne, E., 388
Cousins, Norman, 49-51, 459

Covington, Martin, 452
Cowan, P., 473
Cowan, P. A., 473, 624
Cowan, W. M., 140
Cowles, J. T., 323
Cowley, G., 692
Cox, P. D., 452
Cox, P. W., 291
Coyne, J., 694
Coyne, J. C., 491, 533
Craighead, W. E., 641
Craik, F. I. M., 364
Craik, K., 131
Crandall, R., 46
Crapo, L., 77
Crawley, J. N., 89
Cresler, D. L., 680
Crick, Francis, 115-16
Cristol, A. H., 673, 694
Critelli, J. W., 32
Crosby, F. J., 195
Cross, P., 412
Cross, S., 533
Crowder, R. G., 349, 365
Cruccu, G., 249
Crutchfield, R. A., 584
Csikszentmihalyi, M., 110, 190, 454
Culbertson, S., 326
Culliton, B. J., 62
Culver, C., 96
Cumming, E., 206
Cunitz, A. R., 365
Cunningham, J. W., 569
Curtiss, S., 153
Cushing, 163
Cutillo, B. A., 95, 388
Cutler, W. B., 247
Cutting, E., 268, 287
Cutting, J., 283

D

Dackman, L., 266
D'Agostino, P. R., 218
Dahlstrom, L. E., 562
Dahlstrom, W. G., 562
Dain, H. J., 446
Dakof, G. A., 491
Dali, Salvador, 265
Dallenbach, K. M., 370
Dalrymple, S., 590
Damon, 533
Dandis, E. M., 555
Darley, J. M., 592
Darley, John, 592, 593-94, 608
Darwin, Charles, 13, 58, 63, 350, 428, 468, 469, 519, 541
Davert, E. C., 123, 558
David, H. P., 474
Davidson, M., 677
Davidson, R., 462
Davidson, R. J., 388, 443
Davies, D. L., 696

Davis, I. P., 190
Dawes, R. M., 413
Dawkins, Richard, 19
Dawson, K. E., 469
Day, R. S., 361
D'Azevedo, W. L., 353
de Baca, P. C., 324
De Boysson-Bardies, B., 158
DeCasper, A. J., 156-57, 320
DeCharms, R. C., 449
Deci, E. L., 454
Decker, S., 491
Decker, S. N., 145
De Fries, J. C., 145
Delgado, 461
Delishi, C., 62
DeLoache, Judy, 385, 406
DeLongis, A., 476, 488
Dembrowski, T. M., 501
Dement, W. C., 113, 114, 116, 117, 118
Dennerstein, L., 124
Dennett, D. C., 110, 407
Deregowski, J. B., 295
DeRivera, J., 465
Derrick, A., 644
Descartes, René, 17, 63-4, 76, 105, 380, 401
Desimone, R., 238
Deutch, D., 275
Deutch, J. A., 275
Deutsch, C. P., 560
Deutsch, M., 560, 582, 607
De Valois, Karen, 236-37
De Valois, Russell, 233, 236-37
Devereux, G., 667
Devine, J. V., 324
Devine, P. G., 218
DeVos, G. A., 186
Dewey, John, 13
Dhruvarajan, V., 182
Diamond, D., 683, 691
Diamond, J., 34, 60
Diamond, J. M., 692
Diamond, M. J., 124
Diamond, W. D., 580
Dickman, H., 486
Diener, E., 46, 466
Dietrich, N., 506
Dillon, K. M., 459
DiLollo, V., 350
Dince, P. R., 446
Dinges, D., 116
di Padova, C., 547
Dishman, R. K., 497
Dittrich, J. E., 455
Dixon, 205
Dixon, N. F., 217
Dixon, R. A., 560
Doane, J., 651
Dodson, J. D., 432
Dohrenwend, B. P., 474
Dohrenwend, B. S., 474
Dollard, J., 312, 527

Dombek, C. E., 129
Domjan, M., 332
Donchin, E., 41, 352, 388
Donovan, J. M., 534
Dowis, R. T., 257
Downs, A. C., 172
Doyle, J. C., 95, 388
Draguns, J. G., 652
Drellich, M. G., 446
Dremer, M. W., 446
Dreyfus, C. F., 375
Driver, J., 274
Drosnin, M., 506
Drugan, R. C., 483
Dryfoss, J. G., 184
DuBois, P. H., 562
Dudycha, G. J., 516
Duncan, 107
Duncan, B. L., 4
Duncan, G. H., 251
Duncker, K., 404
Dunkel-Schetter, C., 488, 490
Dunn, J., 158
Dunnette, M. D., 455
Dunning, D., 412
Dutton, 463
Dweck, C. S., 435
Dwyer, T., 547
Dyer, C. S., 491

E

Eagleston, J. R., 481, 501
Easton, P., 68
Ebbinghaus, Hermann, 11, 344, 370
Eby, W. C., 459
Eccles, John, 106
Edwards, 696
Edwards, A. E., 312
Edwards, B., 98
Edwards, G., 696
Edwards, K. L., 534
Edwards, N., 603
Efron, R., 98
Egeland, J. A., 641, 642
Eger, Edith Eva, 379, 410-11
Egeth, H. E., 275, 368
Ehrlich, B. E., 692
Eichmann, Adolf, 586
Eimas, 155
Einstein, Albert, 555
Eisenberg, N., 199
Ekman, P., 206, 469
Ekstein, R., 652
Ekstrand, M. L., 498
Eliade, Mircea, 662
Elkin, I., 695
Elliott, Jane, 599-600
Ellis, Albert, 624, 683
Ellsworth, P. C., 466
Ellwood, D. T., 184
Eme, R., 188
Emerson, Ralph Waldo, 2

Emery, G., 637, 683
Emmelkamp, P. M. G., 675
Emmons, 110
Endler, N. S., 517
Eng, A., 493
Engen, T., 362
Engle, G. L., 493
Epstein, S., 517
Erdley, C. A., 218
Ericksen, C. W., 295, 655
Ericsson, K. A., 110, 355
Eriksen, 275
Erikson, E., 173, 174, 181, 188, 190, 192
Escher, M. C., 265
Eskenazi, J., 44
Esveldt-Dawson, K., 679
Evans, A. C., 251
Evans, F. J., 124, 125
Evans, J. S. B., 402
Evans, R. I., 497
Evans-Pritchard, E. E., 667
Eysenck, Hans J., 514-15, 694

F

Fairweather, G. W., 680
Fallon, 108
Falloon, I. R. H., 651
Fantz, R. L., 147, 151
Faraday, Michael, 397
Farah, M. J., 382
Farina, A., 656
Farley, Frank, 480
Farquhar, J. W., 7, 496
Faucheux, C., 584
Fay, R. E., 445
Fechner, Gustav, 11, 217, 220, 221-22
Fein, G., 118
Feinleib, M., 501
Feirtag, M., 83
Fernald, A., 99, 158
Ferrare, N. A., 490
Ferster, C. B., 39, 326, 327
Festinger, Leon, 412, 435, 601-603
Feuerstein, M., 483
Field, Tiffany, 55-56, 99, 249
Fields, H. L., 90
Fiester, S. J., 695
Fifer, W. P., 320
Fifield, J., 489
Fink, H., 31
Fink, M., 690
Finkel, S. E., 414
Fischman, M., 90
Fish, R., 251
Fisher, A. E., 438
Fisher, K., 611
Fisher, R. J., 608
Fisher, S., 524, 672
Fishler, K., 138
Fiske, S., 613

Fiske, S. T., 294, 397, 411, 601, 605
Flacks, R., 581
Flavell, J. H., 162, 163, 167, 406
Fleischman, P. R., 654
Fletcher, 241
Fletcher, G. J. O., 605
Fletcher, M. A., 498
Flood, R. A., 643
Flora, J. A., 499
Florian, V., 501
Fodor, 98, 407
Fogel, A., 148
Foley, V. D., 687
Folkman, S., 487, 488, 491
Fong, G. T., 533
Fontaine, G., 452
Ford, C. S., 439, 443
Forest, D. V., 652
Forgas, J. P., 360
Fotergill, L. A., 90
Foucault, M., 665
Fowler, H., 431
Fowler, R. D., 506
Frances, A., 627
Frank, J. D., 31, 694
Frank, Jerome, 31, 612, 694
Frank, L. R., 691
Franklin, D., 625, 627
Franklin-Lipsker, Eileen, 370
Franks, J. J., 358
Franz, C. E., 196
Fraser, S. C., 43
Fredman, G., 559
Fredrickson, B. L., 206, 209
Freed, W. J., 206
Freeman, F. R., 118
French, J. R. P., Jr., 608
Frenkel-Brunswick, E., 585
Freud, A., 181, 187
Freud, Sigmund, 5, 8, 16, 32, 109-10, 119, 120, 181, 192, 371, 386, 425, 430, 439, 519-25, 527, 532, 555, 622-23, 668, 669
Frey, W. H., II, 462
Frezza, M., 547
Frick, F., 401
Fridlund, A. J., 168
Fridman, J., 68
Fried, P. A., 478
Friedel, R. O., 639
Friedman, H. S., 500, 501
Friedman, M., 501
Friedman, S., 170
Friedman, W. F., 375
Friesen, W. V., 206, 469
Frieze, I. H., 452
Frijda, 460, 464
Frisby, 228
Fromkin, V. A., 387
Fromm, E., 123, 124
Fromme, K., 191
Frumkin, B., 353

Fry, William F., 459
Fukui, I., 158
Fuller, J. L., 62, 137, 423
Funt, Allen, 459, 581
Furman, W., 679
Furstenberg, F., Jr., 183
Futrell, D., 469
Fyer, A. J., 632, 638

G

Gabrielli, W. F., 535
Gage, F., 206
Gage, Phineas, 66
Gagnon, J. H., 443, 445
Galaburda, A. M., 94
Galambos, R., 388
Galanter, E., 218
Galizio, M., 318
Gallagher, D., 466
Gallagher, J. M., 161
Gallant, D. M., 535
Galluscio, E. H., 72
Galton, Francis, 541
Garber, J., 603
Garcia, John, 331-32, 335
Garcia, L. T., 47
Garcia y Robertson, R., 335
Gardner, Howard, 382, 555-56
Gardner, L. I., 170
Garfield, 122
Garland, H., 455
Garmezy, N., 171
Garner, W. R., 281
Garrett, M., 110
Garrison, V., 667
Gates, D. W., 291
Gawin, F. H., 90, 91
Gay, P., 16
Gazzaniga, M., 96, 106, 120
Gazzaniga, M. S., 98, 407
Gelade, 269, 271
Gelb, L., 656
Gelman, 167
Genovese, Kitty, 592
Gentry, W. D., 493
George, C., 170
George, J. M., 474
George, L. K., 629, 631, 633, 634, 645, 655
Gerard, H. B., 582
Gergen, K. J., 208
Gergen, M. S., 208
Gerhard, D. S., 641, 642
Geschwind, N., 94, 95
Gevins, A. S., 95, 388
Giannipiccolo, J. S., Jr., 555
Gibbs, J. C., 198, 199
Gibson, F., 191
Gibson, James, 266-67, 268, 276, 285
Gift, T. E., 645
Gilbert, D. T., 608
Gilligan, Carol, 195, 199

Gilligan, S., 471
Gilman, L., 636
Gilmore, R., 580
Ginns, E. I., 642
Girgus, 262
Giudice, S., 151, 164
Givens, A., 68
Glantz, S., 478
Glanzer, M., 365
Glaser, R., 484, 491
Glass, A. L., 406
Glass, D. C., 476
Glass, D. R., 695
Glass, G. V., 674, 695
Gliha, D., 656
Goddard, Henry H., 541, 556-57
Goethals, G. R., 469
Goethe, 187
Gold, P. E., 206
Goldberg, 517
Goldberg, S. R., 91
Goldfried, M. R., 694
Goldman, R., 438
Goldsmith, H. H., 169
Goldstein, A. M., 642
Goldstein, D. A., 498
Goldstein, M. J., 651
Goldston, S. E., 699
Goleman, D., 262
Gonzalez, A., 600
Goodale, W., 188
Goodall, Jane, 38
Goodenough, D. R., 290, 291
Goodkind, 131
Goodstadt, M. S., 191
Gopher, D., 276
Gorbachev, Mikhail, 592
Gordon, A., 438
Gordon, L., 539
Gorman, J. M., 638
Gotesman, I. I., 623, 649
Gotlieb, S., 394
Gottesman, Irving, 648, 650
Gottfredson, L. S., 560
Gottheil, E., 124, 494, 686
Gottlieb, G., 139, 168
Gough, 515
Gough, Harrison G., 565
Gould, J. L., 361, 540, 549
Gowing, J., 126
Graf, P., 345
Graham, J. R., 562
Graham, P., 559
Graliker, B., 138
Grallo, R., 560
Grand, H. G., 446
Granger, R. H., 335, 373, 374
Grant, P., 58
Graves, N., 590
Gray, C. R., 361
Gray, L., 662
Gray, W. D., 393
Greaves, C., 686
Green, D. M., 219

Greenberg, J., 455
Greenberg, L., 694
Greenberg, R. P., 524, 672
Greene, Bob, 539-40, 570-71
Greene, D., 454
Greenfield, P. M., 158, 164
Greenwald, A. G., 44, 45, 217
Greenwald, P., 478
Greenwood, M. M., 146
Greer, D. S., 388
Greif, E. B., 199
Grieger, R., 624
Griffin, D. W., 412
Grim, C. E., 477
Grinnell, A., 86
Grinns, E. I., 642
Gross, 144, 145
Gross, A., 465
Gross, M. C., 312
Grossman, M. I., 436
Gruen, R. J., 488
Gruenberg, E., 207
Grusec, J. E., 321
Guay, P. F., 312
Guerra, F., 104
Guetzkow, H., 611
Guilford, J. P., 554
Guillemin, R., 250
Guilleminault, C., 117
Gummerman, K., 361
Gunzenhauser, N., 99
Gurman, A. S., 687
Gutman, D., 269, 270, 273
Gynther, M. D., 565
Gynther, R. A., 565

H

Haas, H., 31
Haber, R. B., 361
Haber, R. N., 361
Hacker, A., 539
Haddow, J. E., 478
Hagen, E., 552
Hagen, J. W., 183
Hale, R. L., 550
Haley, J., 651
Hall, G. Stanley, 12, 187
Hall, J. L., 206
Hallowell, A. I., 670
Hamill, R., 415
Hamilton, D., 144
Hamilton, D. L., 367
Hamilton, W. J., 246
Hamlin, P., 438
Hammen, C. L., 640
Hammersmith, S. K., 446
Hancock, M. E., 471
Haney, C., 561, 570, 576
Hanlon, C., 156
Hanna, S. D., 477
Hansen, W. B., 497
Hanson, D., 648
Harackiewicz, J. M., 371

Harary, K., 131
Harber, K. D., 476
Haritaos-Fatouros, M.,
Harlow, H. F., 170, 171, 431
Harlow, M. K., 171, 431
Harrington, G., 540
Harris, 142
Harris, B., 311
Harris, P., 257
Harris, T. O., 474
Harrison, N. L., 461
Harrour, P., 104
Hart, 533
Hart, R. A., 398
Hart, S. N., 184
Hartfelder, G., 31
Hartmann, E. L., 115, 116
Hartshorne, H., 199, 516
Hartup, W. W., 195, 679
Harvey, P. H., 60
Hass, A., 189
Hastod, A. H., 656
Hastorf, A. H., 596
Hatfield, E., 188
Hathaway, Starke, 562
Havis, J., 497
Hayes, D., 610
Hayes-Roth, B., 385, 398
Hayes-Roth, F., 385
Haygood, R. C., 392
Haynes, S. G., 501
Hazan, C., 195
Heath, A. C., 65
Heather, N., 696
Hebb, Donald O., 65, 137, 336,
   373, 460
Hebel, S. K., 129
Hecht, A., 692
Heider, Fritz, 429, 435, 601,
   603-604
Heinroth, J. C., 666
Helzer, J. E., 207
Henderson, N. D., 180
Henkin, R., 247
Henning, 247
Henry, G. W., 621, 665
Henry, W. E., 206
Heppenheimer, T. A., 381
Hering, Ewald, 232
Herold, E., 112
Herren, R., 96
Hersen, M., 678, 679
Hersh, S. M., 587
Herz, M. J., 373
Heslin, R., 444
Hess, E. H., 224
Hess, W., 67
Hester, 696
Heston, L. L., 648
Hetherington, E. M., 168
Higa, W. R., 312
Higgins, T., 528
Hilgard, E. R., 11, 108, 123, 124,
   125, 558

Hilker, R. R., 479
Hille, B., 87
Hillis, W. D., 387
Hillyard, S. A., 388
Hiner, S. L., 474
Hinkle, L., 436
Hinson, R. E., 313
Hinton, G. F., 98, 407
Hippler, A. A., 186
Hippocrates, 511, 514
Hirsch, E., 438
Hirsch, J., 540
Hirst, W., 276
Hitch, G., 352
Hite, Shere, 49
Hitler, Adolf, 541, 585
Hoban, T. M., 642
Hobson, J. A., 120, 121
Hochberg, J., 266, 282
Hodges, J., 152
Hoelzel, Russ, 418-19
Hoffman, D. D., 268
Hoffman, E. L., 580
Hoffman, Martin, 199, 460, 465
Hoffman-Ahern, C., 462
Hofling, C. K., 590
Hofstede, G., 42
Hogness, D. S., 233
Holahan, C. J., 488, 490
Holden, C., 324
Holen, M. C., 365
Holland, Jimmie, 494
Hollister, L. F., 124
Holloway, M., 95
Holmes, 126
Holmes, T. H., 474
Holyoak, K. J., 406
Homme, L. E., 324
Hong, H-W, 168
Honzig, C. H., 333
Honzik, M. P., 180
Hook, L. H., 584
Hopson, J. L., 90, 440
Horne, 115
Horn, J. L., 554
Horney, Karen, 672
Hornstein, H. A., 607
Horowitz, R. M., 183
Hosobuchi, Y., 250
Hostetter, A. M., 641
Houghton, J., 656
House, J. S., 490
Housman, D. E., 641, 642
Hovland, C., 585
Howard, K. I., 9, 187, 188, 190,
   668
Howarth, E., 514
Hrubec, Z., 64
Hubbard, R. W., 459
Hubel, D., 234
Hubel, David, 15, 235-36, 279
Huggins, G. R., 247
Hughes, Howard, 507-509
Hughes-Fulford, Millie, 491

Hughes, J., 90
Hulicka, I. M., 200
Hull, Clark, 430
Hultsch, 205
Hume, David, 267, 329
Humphrey, N. K., 140
Humphreys, 107
Hunt, Earl, 549, 554-55
Hunt, M., 380, 386, 577
Hunt, W. A., 493
Hunter, J. E., 569
Hunter, R. F., 569
Hurlburt, R. T., 110
Hurt, C. A., 345
Hurvich, L. M., 233
Huston, A. C., 333
Hutchins, D., 104
Huxley, Aldous, 127
Hyman, 321
Hyson, R. L., 483

I

Ian, S. A., 459
Illes, J., 388
Imber, S. D., 695
Imhof, P. R., 43
Inhelder, B., 163
Insel, P. L., 493
Insko, C. A., 580, 582
Ironson, G., 498
Irwin, M., 535
Isen, A., 465
Itard, J., 143, 145
Izard, Caroll E., 464

J

Jackson, D. D., 651
Jacob, F., 92
Jacobs, B. L., 89, 166, 233
Jacobs, R. C., 580
Jacobsen, B., 648
Jacobson, L. F., 597
James, 22
James, Henry, 12, 465
James, William, 12, 13, 105,
   107, 126, 142, 430, 532, 603
Jameson, D., 233
Janerich, D. T., 478
Janis, Irving L., 401, 417, 479,
   496, 499, 611
Janowitz, H. D., 436
Janz, N. K., 493
Jardine, R., 65
Jeannerod, M., 229
Jenkins, 364
Jenkins, C. D., 501
Jenkins, J. G., 370
Jennings, Peter, 469
Jensen, A. R., 365
Jessor, Richard, 190
Jodelet, D., 399
Joffee, J. M., 699

Johanson, C., 90
John, E. R., 68, 388
John, O. P., 516
Johnson, D. L., 123
Johnson, D. M., 393
Johnson, G. B., 523
Johnson, J. E., 499
Johnson, J. H., 474
Johnson, M. K., 358, 366
Johnson, R. A., 462
Johnson, T. D., 168
Johnson, Virginia, 441, 444
Johnson-Laird, P. N., 131, 401
Johnston, 128
Johnston, J., 187
Jones, 129
Jones, B. M., 547
Jones, E. E., 533, 656
Jones, Ernest, 519
Jones, Jim, 587
Jones, Mary Cover, 547, 673
Jones, S. S., 168
Jonides, J., 275, 276
Jordan, D. S., 265
Jordan, T. G., 560
Jorgenson, D. O., 455
Joyce, L., 87, 117, 623
Julesz, B., 269, 279
Jung, Carl, 16, 181, 182, 465,
   512, 524, 532, 565-66
Just, H. A., 387

K

Kaba, H., 362
Kabat, L. G., 202, 239
Kaemmer, B., 562
Kagan, Jerome, 38, 141, 171,
   180
Kahneman, Daniel, 276, 411,
   413-16, 419, 602
Kaij, L., 64
Kalat, J. W., 85, 309
Kalish, R. A., 209
Kallmann, F. J., 647
Kalnok, M., 206
Kamin, Leon J., 314-15, 540
Kandel, E. R., 92
Kanizsa, G., 268
Kanter, J. F., 190
Kaplan, J., 47
Kaplan, N., 169
Karno, M., 629, 631, 633, 634,
   645, 655
Karon, B. P., 671
Karraker, K. H., 173
Kasl, S. V., 493
Kastenbaum, R., 208
Kastrup, E. K., 129
Katz, D., 599
Katz, L., 48
Katz, L. B., 367
Kaushall, P. I., 342
Kay, D. W. K., 207

Kazdin, A. E., 673, 674, 695
Keane, S. P., 678
Keane, T. M., 485
Keats, J., 509
Keen, S., 112, 609
Keesey, R. E., 438
Kegeles, S. M., 498
Keir, R., 677
Keita, G. P., 643
Kekulé, F. A., 397
Keller, Helen, 213-14, 218, 223
Keller, S. E., 209, 484
Kellerman, H., 522
Kelley, Harold H., 604
Kellman, 166
Kelly, George, 527-28, 531
Kelsoe, J. R., 642
Kemp, M., 285
Kemper, T. L., 94
Kenge, 288
Kennedy, J. G., 469
Kennedy, John F., 417
Kennedy, S., 484
Kennedy, W. A., 559
Kennel, J., 169
Kenney, M. D., 169
Kesey, Ken, 691
Kessler, R. C., 333, 476
Kessler, S., 647
Ketterer, R. F., 699
Kety, S. S., 648
Keverne, E. B., 362
Kidd, K. K., 641, 642
Kiecolt-Glaser, J. K., 484, 491
Kieffer, S. N., 636
Kiely, M., 478
Kierulff, S., 630
Kiess, H. O., 359
Kiester, 121
Kihlstrom, 125, 533
Kihlstrom, J. F., 109, 346, 371
Kilmann, P. R., 690
Kimmel, H., 500
Kimura, Doreen, 95
Kin, H. E., 485
King Ismail, 442
King, R. G., 590
Kinsey, Alfred, 441, 445
Kintsch, W., 361, 393
Kippax, 333
Kirkpatrick, Jeanne, 591
Kivlahan, D. R., 191
Klag, M. J., 477
Klassen, A. D., 445
Klaus, M., 169
Klein, 275
Klein, D. C., 699
Klein, G., 291
Klein, R. E., 171
Klein, R. H., 685
Klein, T. P., 185
Kleinginna, A. M., 460
Kleinginna, P. R., 460
Kleitman, N., 113

Klerman, G. L., 627, 695
Klima, E. S., 353
Kling, A., 73
Klinger, E., 112
Klinger, M. R., 217
Kluckhorn, C., 667
Kluft, R. P., 630, 632
Knapp, J., 188
Knight, G. J., 478
Kniskern, D. P., 687
Knox, V. J., 125
Kobasa, Suzanne, 479
Kobre, K. R., 147
Koch, R., 138
Kocherty, J. P., 695
Koelling, R. A., 331
Koenig, D. E., 580
Koeske, R. D., 167
Koff, E., 462
Koffka, Kurt, 268
Kohlberg, L., 172, 197, 198, 199
Köhler, Wolfgang, 268, 334-35
Kohn, 34
Kohut, Heinz, 671-72
Kolata, G., 438
Kolb, B., 140, 152
Kolb, L. C., 130
Kondo, T., 118
Konner, M. J., 464
Kopta, S. M., 9, 669
Korlinsky, P. E., 9, 668
Korn, A. W., 18
Korn, J., 46
Kornreich, M., 694
Koss, M. P., 444
Kosslyn, S. M., 361, 397-98
Kostaerlitz, H. E., 90
Kraemer, H. C., 124, 494, 686
Kraepelin, Emil, 622
Kraft, Conrad, 255-56
Krajicek, D., 256, 268
Kramer, D. A., 560
Kramer, M., 629, 631, 633, 634,
    645, 655
Krank, M. D., 313
Krasner, L., 337, 651
Kraus, S., 249
Krause, M. S., 9, 668
Kraut, A. M., 662
Krebs, J. R., 60
Kreitler, H., 493
Kreitler, S., 493
Krett, 183
Krieger, A., 247
Krieger, L. M., 244
Krinsky, L. W., 636
Kristjansson, E. A., 478
Kritchevsky, M., 342
Ksir, C., 90
Ku, L. C., 189
Kübler-Ross, E., 208
Kubovy, M., 268
Kuczmierczyk, A. R., 483
Kuhar, M. J., 91

Kuhn, T. S., 33
Kuipers, A., 675
Kuipers, P., 460
Kulik, J. A., 490, 598
Kuller, L. E., 477
Kunda, Z., 598
Kurtines, W., 199

L

La Barre, W., 670
Labbe, E. E., 483
LaBerge, Stephen, 122
Labouvie-Vief, G., 197
Lacey, H., 329
Lachman, J. L., 396
Lachman, R., 108, 396
Lackner, J. R., 110
La Framboise, Teresa, 644
La Gamma, E. F., 375
Laing, R. D., 654
Laitsch, K., 677
Lalonde, 155
Lamb, M. E., 169
Lamb, R. J., 91
Lambert, A. J., 275
Lambo, T. A., 667
Landis, K. R., 490
Lando, L., 87
Lane, H., 145
Lang, P. J., 674
Lange, Carl, 466
Langer, E. J., 203
Langer, Ellen, 489-90, 584, 602
Langlois, J. H., 172, 395
Langs, R., 669, 670
Langseth, M., 462
Laperriere, A., 498
Larson, R., 190
Lashley, Karl, 372
Latané, B., 577, 592, 593
Latto, R., 229
Lau, R. R., 528
Laudenslager, M. L., 483
Lawler, E. E., 455
Lawley, H. J., 247
Lawley, J. J., 247
Lawrence, C. P., 414
Lawton, M. P., 203
Lazar, J. B., 656
Lazarus, Richard S., 460, 466,
    474-75, 479, 487, 488, 491
Lazovik, A. D., 674
Le May, M., 94
Leask, J., 361
Leber, W. R., 695
Leberman, R. P., 646
LeBon, G., 412
Lebow, R. N., 611
LeDoux, Joseph, 462
Lee, F., 451
Lee, J. W., 459
Leerhsen, C., 686
Leff, H. L., 296

Leger, D., 329
Lehman, D. R., 491
Leippe, M., 499
Leirer, V. O., 367
Leiter, M. P., 501
Lemert, E. M.,
Lenneberg, E. H., 156
Lennon, R. T., 550, 553, 560
Lepper, Mark R., 411, 454
Lerner, R. M., 188
Leslie, C., 570
Levenson, R. W., 206
Leventhal, H., 460, 466
Levi, Primo, 379
Levine, J. D., 90, 251
Levine, M. W., 217
Levine, M., 405, 654
Levine, Martin, 447
Levinson, B. W., 104
Levinson, Daniel, 193, 194
Levis, D. J., 585, 674
Levi-Strauss, C., 667
Leviton, A., 560
Levy, J., 96
Levy, L. H., 566
Lewin, Kurt, 131, 429, 434, 585-
    86, 602, 607
Lewine, R. R., 645
Lewinsohn, P. M., 640
Lewis, 516
Lewis, C., 669
Lewis, J. E., 459
Lewy, A. J., 642
Li, P., 41
Liberman, R. P., 646
Lieber, C. S., 547
Lieberman, 491
Lieberman, L. R., 654
Lieberman, M. A., 685
Liebert, R. M., 526
Liebowitz, M. R., 638
Liem, J. H., 651
Liem, R., 477
Lifton, R. P., 581
Light, L. L., 205
Lindhagen, K., 148
Lindsley, D. B., 461
Lindvall, D., 206
Lindzey, G., 559, 566
Linton, M., 362
Lippitt, R., 585-86
Lipsitt, L. P., 146, 147, 149
Lipsitz, A., 580
Liskow, B. I., 535
Little, M. I., 701
Liu, T. J., 217
Livesley, 533
Livingstone, M., 234
Locke, B. Z., 629, 631, 633, 634,
    645, 655
Locke, John, 110, 143, 267
Lockhart, R. S., 364
Loehlin, J. C., 515, 559
Loevinger, J., 544

Loftus, Elizabeth F., 367-68
Logan, G., 277
Lombardo, J. P., 312
Londer, R., 675
London, K. A., 189
Long, R. T., 642
Loomis, A. L., 113
Lorch, M. P., 462
Lorenz, K., 168
Lovibond, S. H., 576
Lovinger, 129
Luborsky, L., 295
Lubow, R. E., 309
Luchins, A. S., 404
Luker, K. C., 417
Lumsdain, A., 585
Luria, Z., 4, 172
Lykken, D. T., 462, 558, 559
Lynch, G., 335, 373, 374
Lynch, J. J., 249
Lyons, N., 199

M

Maas, James, 118
Maccoby, E. E., 168, 172, 173, 496
MacDonald, R. R., 191
Mace, W. M., 267
Mack, J. E., 477
MacLean, Paul, 70
MacLeod, C., 637
Maddi, S., 433
Maddi, S. R., 479
Magnusson, D., 187, 517
Maher, B., 202
Maher, Brendan A., 652
Mahler, H. I. M., 490, 535
Mahler, Margaret, 651, 671
Maier, N. R. F., 404
Maier, S. F., 483
Maier, Steven F., 328
Main, M., 169, 170
Maisiak, R., 188
Majewska, M. D., 461
Major, B. N., 474
Malamut, B., 373
Malamuth, N. M., 444
Malatesta, C. Z., 206
Malitz, S., 690
Maloney, M. P., 540
Maltzman, I. M., 697
Mandel, J., 499
Mandler, G., 345, 363, 464, 466
Mandler, J., 165, 167
Manfredi, M., 249
Mann, L., 479
Manning, C. A., 206
Manschreck, T. C., 202
Marcel, A. J., 107, 218, 258
Marco, C. A., 501
Marcus, A. D., 370
Marek, G. R., 369
Marentette, P. A., 156

Marks, I., 95, 680
Markus, H., 533, 602, 656
Marlatt, G. A., 191, 696, 697
Marler, P., 361
Marler, P. R., 246
Marmar, C., 694
Marr, D., 279, 293
Marrett, S., 251
Marsella, A. J., 667
Marshall, G. D., 467
Marshall, J., 228
Marshall, M., 217
Martin, C. H., 312
Martin, G., 333
Martin, G. A., 251
Martin, J. A., 148, 168
Martin, N. G., 65
Marx, Groucho, 237
Maslach, Christina, 467, 501
Maslow, Abraham, 18, 192, 429, 433, 454, 525
Mason, J. W., 483
Mason, W. A., 169
Masters, J. C., 148
Masters, William H., 441, 444
Masuda, M., 474
Matarazzo, J. D., 492, 493, 494, 542, 568
Matarazzo, J. K., 542
Mathews, A., 637
Matisse, Henri, 622
Matossian, Mary, 621
Matson, J. L., 679
Matthews, K. A., 501
Maugh, T. H., II, 114
May, M. A., 199, 516
May, Rollo, 18, 525, 684
Mayer, D. J., 90
Mayer, R. E., 382, 391
Maynard, R. F., 680
Mayr, E., 303
Mayseless, O., 584
Mazur, J., 322
McAdams, D. D., 195
McAuley, E., 452
McCabe, K., 47
McCarley, R. W., 114, 120, 121
McCarthy, J. E., 394
McCauley, M. H., 566
McClelland, David, 434, 449-50
McClelland, D. C., 196, 567
McClellend, J. L., 336-37, 383
McClintock, M. K., 246
McCloskey, M., 368
McConaghy, N., 675
McCormick, D. A., 373
McCoy, E., 183
McCrae, R. R., 565
McCrary, J. W., 364
McCraven, V. J., 112
McCulloch, Warren S., 381
McCully, J., 313
McDougall, William, 430
McFarlane, Robert, 591

McGaugh, J. L., 335, 373, 374
McGinnis, J. M., 494
McGlashan, T. H., 125
McGrath, E., 643
McGue, M., 515, 558, 559
McGuire, R. J., 532
McGuire, W. J., 532, 601
McKay, G., 490
McKean, K., 250
McKinley, J. R., 562
McKinnon, W., 484
McKneally, M. F., 478
McLoughlin, V. A., 559
McMahon, S., 547
McNeil, B. J., 416
McPherson, K. S., 557
Mead, Margaret, 187, 430
Meador, B. D., 684
Meany, M. J., 173, 249
Medin, D. L., 392
Medolago, L., 249
Meehl, Paul E., 413, 567, 648
Mees, H., 325
Mehler, B., 540
Mehrabian, A., 465
Meichenbaum, Donald, 489, 491, 682
Meier, R. P., 154
Melamed, M. R., 478
Meltzer, H. Y., 623, 652
Meltzoff, 165
Meltzoff, J., 694
Melzack, Ronald, 250-51
Menzel, E. M., 334
Meredith, M. A., 227
Merrill, M. A., 551
Merton, R. K., 598
Mervis, C. B., 392, 393
Mesmer, Franz, 622
Meyer, A. J., 497
Meyer, D. R., 431
Meyer, E., 251
Meyer, M. M., 652
Meyer-Bahlburg, H. F. L., 446
Meyers, C. E., 555
Mezzich, J. E., 652
Michael, J., 677
Middleton, J., 667
Milavsky, J. R., 333
Milgram, Stanley, 6, 47, 399, 585, 587
Milich, R., 621
Millar, K., 104
Miller, A. G., 587
Miller, D. T., 656
Miller, J. D., 49
Miller, L., 534
Miller, N. E., 48
Miller, Neal, 327-28, 527
Miller, P. Y., 189
Miller, S., 642
Miller, T. I., 695
Miller, W. R., 696
Milner, B., 364

Milojkovic, J. D., 412
Mineka, S., 677
Minke, K. A., 312
Mintz, J., 651
Minuchin, S., 688
Mischel, 529
Mischel, Walter, 366, 517, 527, 528-29, 531
Mishkin, Mortimer, 344, 373
Mitchell, T. P., 455
Mithison, Graeme, 116
Mittelmark, M. B., 497
Miyake, K., 141
Miyamoto, T., 246
Moar, I., 334
Moehle, D., 580
Molnar, J. M., 185
Monahan, J., 699
Moncrieff, R. W., 246
Moniz, Egas, 689
Montague, A., 249
Montague, W. E., 359
Montana, Joe, 432
Montgomery, G., 76
Montgomery, K. D., 431
Moon, Sun Yung, 49
Moore, C. A., 291
Moore, G. I., 398
Moore, Pat, 200
Moore, T. E., 217
Moos, R., 488
Moos, R. H., 488, 490
Morgan, A. H., 123, 125, 558
Morgan, B. A., 90
Morgan, N. H., 388
Morgane, P. S., 115
Moriarity, Tom, 594
Morin, S., 189
Morris, H. R., 90
Morris, L. A., 31
Morrison, M. A., 191
Morton, J., 349
Moscovici, Serge, 584, 585
Mosher, W. D., 189
Moskowitz, B. A., 155
Motley, M. T., 521
Movahedi, S., 578
Mowrer, O., 155
Mowrey, D. D., 677
Muehlenhard, C. L., 445
Muir, M. S., 449
Mullen, B., 577
Müller, Johannes, 65, 223
Muller, P., 43
Mullin, B., 469
Mullin, P. A., 275
Munroe, R. L., 668
Munsterberg, Hugo, 29
Munzio, J. N., 116
Murnen, S. K., 444
Muroff, M., 669
Murphy, J. M., 653
Murray, 333
Murray, Henry, 434, 449, 567

Muskin, P. R., 632
Mussen, P. H., 199
Mussolini, Benito, 585
Myers, I. B., 512
Myers, J. K., 629, 631, 633, 634, 645, 655
Myers, Peter, 565
Myers, R. E., 96

N

Nagel, E., 34
Napier, B. J., 459
Nason, Susan, 370
Nathans, J., 233
Natsoulas, T., 108
Naus, M. J., 359
Naus, M., 108
Nauta, W. J. H., 83
Navon, D., 276
Neale, M. A., 419
Needleman, H., 560
Neese, R. M., 468
Neisser, U., 276, 349
Neitzel, 621
Neligan, 144
Nelson, R. E., 641
Nelson, R. K., 22
Nelson, Z. P., 677
Nemeth, C. J., 584
Neuman, K. F., 32
Newcomb, 128
Newcomb, T. J., 601
Newcomb, T. M., 516, 580-81
Newell, Allen, 110, 381, 402
Newell, J. D., 47
Newman, O., 636
Newport, 154
Newsome, W. T., 237-38
Newton, Isaac, 229
Nguyen, M. L., 444
Nguyen, T., 444
Nhat Hanh, T., 126
Nicasio, 117
Nichol, S. E., 649
Nicholas, M., 462
Nichols, M. P., 452, 688
Nichols, P. I., 559
Nickel, E. J., 535
Nicoll, C., 48
Nietzel, M. T., 621
Nisbett, R. E., 411, 415, 438, 454, 587, 602, 605
Nishihara, H. K., 293
Nisseri, M. J., 275
Nixon, S. J., 535
Nobles, W. W., 7, 624, 667
Noel, R. C., 611
Nolen-Hoeksema, Susan, 643
Noonberg, R., 328
Norman, 517
Norman, Don A., 274, 387, 396
Norris, W., 665
Norton, R., 547

Nungesser, L. G., 499, 686
Nurius, P., 533
Nuttin, J., 449

O

Oaster, T. R., 365
Odbert, H. S., 511, 516
Oden, M. H., 150
Oden, S., 678
Oeltjen, P. D., 569
Offer, D., 187, 188, 190
Ogrocki, P., 491
Olin, B. R., 129
Ollendick, T. H., 679
Olson, J. M., 412
Olton, D. S., 328, 334
Olver, R. R., 164
Olweus, Dan, 698
O'Malley, P. M., 187
Omenn, G. S., 64
Oppel, J. J., 262
Opton, E. M., 587
O'Reilly, C. A., 454
Orkand, R., 86
Orlando, N. J., 680
Orlos, J. P., 188
Orne, M. T., 123, 125
Ornstein, P. A., 359
Ornstein, R. E., 98, 107, 204, 214, 407
Ornstein, S., 455
Oros, C. J., 444
Orr, T. B., 566
Orvaschel, H., 207
Osborne, R., 418
Osherow, W., 581
Oskamp, S., 608
Ostrov, E., 187, 188, 190
O'Sullivan, Chris, 445

P

Page, S., 654
Paivio, A., 359, 361, 397
Palmer, S. E., 267, 282
Palomaki, G. E., 478
Paplos, D. F., 623
Paplos, J., 623
Pappas, A. M., 183
Pappenheim, Bertha, 669
Pare, E. B., 237
Park, B., 599
Parke, R. D., 168, 173
Parks, S. H., 490
Parks, T., 282
Parloff, M. B., 695
Parmley, W. W., 478
Parsons, O. A., 535
Pass, J. J., 569
Passonant, P., 117
Pauker, S. G., 416
Paul, S. M., 89, 461, 642
Pauls, D. L., 641, 642

Pavelchak, M. A., 411
Pavlov, Ivan, 17, 32, 305-307, 309, 310, 313, 314-16, 337
Paykel, E. S., 485
Peake, P., 517, 528
Peake, P. K., 414
Pear, J., 333
Pearlstone, Z., 363
Pearson, J., 104
Pearson, T. A., 193
Peele, Stanton, 447-48, 696
Pelletier, L., 112
Pelz, E. B., 608
Pendery, M. L., 697
Penfield, Wilder, 67, 373
Penick, E. C., 535
Penick, S., 436
Pennebaker, James, 476, 500
Perenin, M. T., 229
Perkins, D. V., 654
Perlin, S., 644
Perlman, D., 496
Perls, Fritz S., 686
Perolt, A., 444
Perone, M., 318
Perron Boren, M. C., 326
Pershod, D., 635
Persons, J., 697
Persons, J. B., 627
Pert, C., 89
Peter Schure, E., 460
Petersen, S. E., 275
Peterson, C., 501
Peterson, L. R., 354
Peterson, M. J., 354
Petit, C., 130
Petitto, L. A., 156
Petri, H. L., 373
Petti, T., 679
Pettigrew, T. F., 599
Pfaffman, C., 248
Pfeiffer, C., 489
Phares, E. J., 549, 567
Phillips, L., 365
Piaget, Jean, 151-52, 161, 162, 163, 181, 196, 197, 198, 381, 411
Picasso, Pablo, 296, 555
Piccione, C., 123
Pierce, C. M., 590
Pifer, A., 200
Piliavan, I. M., 592
Piliavan, J. A., 592
Pilisuk, M., 490
Pilkonis, P. A., 695
Pinel, Phillippe, 622, 666
Pines, M., 152
Pittenger, J. B., 267, 268
Plato, 11, 412
Pleck, J. H., 189
Plomin, R., 10, 62, 515, 559
Plous, S., 414, 609
Plutchik, Robert, 460, 463, 464, 522

Pollard, P., 402
Pomerantz, J., 268
Poppel, E., 228
Poppen, P. J., 199
Porras, J. I., 454
Porter, L. W., 455
Posner, M. I., 269, 275, 277
Posner, Michael, 390
Post, F., 239
Postman, L., 365
Powell, B. J., 535
Powell, L. H., 481
Powley, T. L., 438
Pozzato, G., 547
Prakash, C., 268
Pratkanis, A. R., 44
Pratt, W. F., 189
Premack, David, 324
Prescott, P. A., 157
Prescott, S., 190
Press, G., 342
Preti, G., 247
Price, R., 292
Price, R. H., 699
Prichep, L. S., 68
Pritchard, R. D., 455
Proffitt, D., 283
Proshansky, H. M., 608
Proust, Marcel, 362
Provenzano, F. J., 4, 172
Psotka, J., 361
Pulkkinen, A. J., 478
Pushkar, D., 126
Putnam, F. W., 630-31

Q

Quattrone, G. A., 414, 599
Queen Elizabeth, 423
Quindlen, A., 144
Quinna, 8, 22

R

Rabbie, J. M., 599
Rabinowitz, F. M., 139
Rabkin, J. G., 656
Rachman, S., 443
Radke-Yarrow, M., 199, 200
Radl, S., 678
Radloff, C. E., 469
Rae, D. S., 629, 631, 634, 645, 655
Ragsdale, N., 138
Rahe, D., 679
Rahe, R. H., 474
Raiffa, H., 419
Rakic, P., 82
Raleigh, Sir Walter, 423
Ramon Garcia, C., 247
Ramón y Cajal, S., 65
Rapoport, J. L., 634, 638
Rath, W. R., 185
Ray, O., 90

Ray, W. J., 388
Rayman, P., 477
Raymond, J. S., 495
Rayner, Rosalie, 311
Read, M. R., 535
Reagan, Ronald, 342, 469, 591, 606
Reaves, C. C., 276
Reese, H. W., 149
Reeves, A., 96
Regier, D. A., 207, 629, 631, 633, 634, 645, 655
Rehm, L. P., 641
Reid, D. K., 161
Reilly, B., 146
Reisenzein, R., 467
Reiser, B. J., 370
Rende, R., 10, 62
Rescorla, R., 309, 314, 328, 336
Rest, J. R., 198
Reston, N. J., 342
Restrepo, D, 246
Revkin, A. C., 29
Reyhen, J., 124
Reynolds, C. P., 484
Reynolds, J. E., 129
Reznick, 141
Rheingold, H., 122
Rheingold, H. L., 172-73
Rich, S., 558
Richardson-Klavern, A., 275
Rickert, E. J., 324
Riddle, D., 189
Rieder, R., 648
Rifkin, A. H., 446
Rifkin, B., 309
Riggs, J. M., 533
Riordan, C. A., 469
Rips, 401
Risley, T., 325
Ritz, M. C., 91
Roach, A. H., 375
Roberts, T. B., 526
Robertson, I., 696
Robins, L. N., 207, 629, 631, 633, 634, 645, 655
Robinson, M. J., 469
Robles, R., 218
Robson, M. J., 237
Rock, I., 268, 269, 270, 273, 283, 290
Rockmore, M., 668
Rodin, Judith, 203, 484, 489-90, 592, 607, 608
Roediger, H. L., 345, 365
Roehrs, T., 118
Roffwarg, H. P., 116
Rogers, Carl R., 18, 434, 525-26, 532, 664, 684
Rogers, R. W., 493
Roggman, L. A., 395
Rohrer, J. H., 580
Roohey, M. L., 651
Rorer, L. G., 567

Rorschach, Hermann, 566
Rosch, E. H., 392, 393, 395
Rose, S., 89
Roseman, I. I., 466
Rosenbaum, L., 486
Rosenbaum, M., 669, 685
Rosenbaum, R. M., 452
Rosenberg, M. J., 601
Rosenberg, S., 533
Rosenfeld, P., 469
Rosenhan, David L., 619, 622, 633, 654
Rosenkrantz, P. S., 654
Rosenman, R. F., 501
Rosenthal, 597
Rosenthal, D., 648
Rosenthal, R., 30, 597
Rosenzweig, M. R., 8
Ross, D., 332
Ross, J. S., 202
Ross, L., 587, 605
Ross, Lee, 411, 412, 415, 602, 603, 605
Ross, R. T., 555
Ross, S. A., 332
Rossier, J., 250
Roth, S. H., 474
Roth, T., 118
Roth, W. T., 493
Rothbart, M., 599
Rothman, D. J., 666
Rotter, Julian, 429, 435
Rounsaville, E. S., 695
Rousseau, Jean Jacques, 143
Rowland, N. E., 438
Rozee, P., 295
Rozelle, R. M., 497
Rozin, P., 107, 108, 167
Rubens, W. S., 333
Rubin, B. K., 478
Rubin, J. Z., 4, 172
Rubin, Theodore, 668
Ruitenbeek, H. M., 671
Rumelhart, David E., 336-37, 383, 396
Ruse, M., 446
Rush, A. J., 683
Russell, D., 452
Russell, J. A., 608
Russell, S., 48
Russell, Sir Bertrand, 28
Russo, N. F., 474, 643
Rutter, M., 152, 171
Ryan, S. M., 483
Ryan, W., 605
Rychlak, J., 18
Rymer, 104

S

Saarinen, T. F., 399
Sachs, O., 258
Sack, R. L., 642
Sackheim, H. A., 690

Salmon, D. P., 72
Salovey, P., 471
Salzman, C., 691
Salzman, C. D., 238
Samuelson, W., 414
Sanchez-Craig, M., 191
Sanders, D. H., 680
Sanders, M. D., 228
Sanders, R. S., 124
Sanford, R. N., 585
Sansom, W., 126
Santa, J. L., 406
Sapolsky, R. M., 99, 249, 481
Sarason, I. B., 474
Sarbin, T. R., 124
Sarnoff, I., 599
Satir, Virginia, 688
Savage, C. W., 223
Sawin, D. B., 173
Sawyer, J., 567
Scardamalia, C., 406
Scarr, S., 559, 560
Schachter, Stanley, 428, 438, 466
Schacter, D. L., 275, 345, 346
Schaef, Anne Wilson, 534-35
Schaie, K. W., 197, 201, 205, 206
Schanberg, Saul, 55, 99
Schank, R. C., 397
Scheier, M. F., 488, 577
Schelkun, P. H., 478
Schell, A., 560
Scherer, K. R., 461
Schieffelin, 159
Schilling, E. A., 476
Schimek, J. G., 295
Schleifer, S. J., 209, 484
Schmidt, W. E., 321
Schneider, G. E., 228
Schneidman, Edwin, 643, 644
Schniederman, N., 498
Schreiber, F., 629
Schreiner, L., 73
Schulsinger, F., 648
Schultz, R., 208, 630, 632
Schulz, R., 203, 491
Schunk, D. H., 452
Schwartz, B., 329
Schwartz, G. E., 462, 470
Schwartz, Mark, 447
Schwartz, R. D., 461
Schweder, R. A., 182
Schweinhart, L. J., 560
Scott, 144
Scott, J. P., 152, 619
Scott, R. A., 655, 656
Scovern, A. W., 690
Seager, C. P., 643
Segal, N. L., 558, 559
Sejnowski, T. J., 383
Selby, J. W., 485
Selfridge, O. G., 294
Seligman, Martin E. P., 328, 417,

452-53, 485, 501, 552, 598, 603, 619, 622, 633, 638, 640
Selye, Hans, 482, 483
Serling, R. J., 675
Shaffer, 636
Shaffer, L. H., 277
Shaffer, R. E., 95
Shafii, M., 644
Shakespeare, William, 116, 357, 555
Shapiro, 126
Shapiro, A. K., 31
Shatz, M., 159
Shaver, P., 195
Shaw, B. F., 683
Shaw, George Bernard, 597
Shaw, J. C., 267, 268, 381
Shea, M. T., 695
Sheehy, G., 195
Sheffield, F., 585
Shefner, J. M., 217
Sheingold, K., 369
Sheldon, William, 512
Shepard, Roger N., 265, 267, 283, 361, 397
Shepp, B., 268
Sher, K. J., 535
Sheridan, C. L., 590
Sherif, C., 576
Sherif, Muzafer, 579
Sherman, J., 584
Sherman, M., 656
Sherrington, Sir Charles, 65, 306
Sherrod, K., 170
Shields, J. L., 501
Shiffrin, R. M., 107, 363
Shinn, M., 180, 185
Shockley, William, 558
Shor, R. E., 123, 124
Shoulson, I., 206
Showers, C., 602
Shuckit, M. A., 535
Shumate, M., 251
Shuttleworth, E. C., 491
Siegel, B., 499
Siegel, J. M., 206, 474
Siegel, Shephard, 313
Siegelman, M., 445
Siegler, R. S., 165, 167
Siever, Michael, 447
Silber, S., 159
Silver, R., 485
Silverman, L. H., 523
Silvers, R. C., 454
Simmel, E. C., 180
Simon, 19
Simon, H. A., 110
Simon, Herbert, 18, 380, 381, 402, 415, 549
Simon, W., 189
Simpson, E. E. L., 198
Sinclair, J. D., 348
Singer, J. L., 112
Singer, J., 466

Sinnott, J. D., 405
Siple, P. A., 353
Sjoberg, B. M., 124
Sjørstrøm, L., 438
Skinner, B. F., 17, 39, 305, 317-18, 322, 326, 327, 332, 337, 676
Skolnick, A., 171
Skolnick, P., 89
Sladek, J. R., 206
Sloane, R. B., 673, 694
Slobin, D., 160
Slovic, P., 411, 414, 417, 602
Smith, 533
Smith, C. A., 466, 470
Smith, D., 685
Smith, E. E., 221, 392
Smith, G., 436
Smith, J. H., 158
Smith, M. L., 674, 695
Smith, R., 218
Smith, R. A., 582
Smith, R. S., 172
Smith, T. W., 90
Smith, Y. M., 229
Smuts, A. B., 183
Snell, J., 419
Snidman, N., 141
Snow, C. P., 586
Snow, R., 257
Snyder, C. R., 277
Snyder, Mark, 412, 533, 598
Snyder, R. C., 611
Snyder, S., 89
Snyder, S. H., 623, 650
Sobel, D., 204, 214
Sobell, L., 696-97
Sobell, M., 696-97
Socrates, 11
Sokol, M. M., 540
Solomon, D. S., 496
Solomon, M. R., 580
Solso, R. L., 382, 394
Sonenstein, F. S., 189
Sorensen, R. C., 189
Sotsky, S. M., 695
Souza-Silva, K., 414
Sox, H. C., Jr., 416
Spangenber, E. R., 44
Spearman, Charles, 551
Speicher, C. E., 491
Spelke, E. S., 165, 166, 276
Spence, M. J., 156-57
Sperling, George, 350, 362
Sperry, Roger, 15, 96, 106
Sperry, R. W., 70, 96
Spiegel, D., 124
Spiegel, David, 494, 686
Spiegler, M. D., 526
Spiro, R. J., 366, 367
Spitz, R. A., 170
Spitzer, R. L., 643
Spong, Paul, 418-19
Spooner, W. A., 386

Sprecher, S., 188
Spuhler, J. N., 559
Squire, L. R., 72, 342, 345, 373, 375, 690
Squire, S., 691
Staats, A. W., 312
Stairs, D., 469
Stalin, Joseph, 414
Stampfl, T. G., 674
Staples, F. R., 673, 694
Starling, A. K., 40
Stedman, 636
Steele, C. M., 533
Steele, J. B., 506
Stein, B. E., 227
Stein, J. M., 638
Stein, M., 209, 484
Steinhorst, R., 324
Steininger, M., 47
Steinmetz, J., 603
Stenberg, C., 169
Steriade, M., 114, 121
Stern, M., 173
Stern, W., 550
Stern, W. C., 115
Sternberg, Robert, 386, 549, 555
Sternberg, Saul, 355-57, 362
Stevens, J., 661
Stevens, S. S., 222
Stevenson, 159
Stevenson, J., 559
Stewart, J., 173
Stipp, D., 610
Stipp, H. H., 333
Stone, C. A., 158
Storms, M. D., 443, 446
Strachan, A. M., 651
Strack, F., 533
Straub, E., 530
Straus, M. A., 485
Strauss, J. S., 645
Strickland, B. R., 643
Strodtbeck, F. L., 584
Stroebe, M. S., 208
Stroebe, W., 208
Stromeyer, D. F., 361
Strong, Edward K., 568
Strong, Sue, 328
Stroop, J. R., 277
Strube, 501
Stuart, R. B., 677
Styron, William, 639
Suchman, Anthony, 301
Sullivan, Annie, 213, 218
Sullivan, Harry Stack, 671
Suls, J., 501
Summers, M., 666
Sundberg, N. D., 568
Suomi, Steven, 142, 171
Sussex, J. N., 641
Svenson, 412
Swann, W. B., Jr., 412, 533, 598
Swazey, J. P., 691
Sweeney, J. A., 649

Sweet, M. D., 499
Swets, J. A., 219, 489, 500
Swinder, D. V., 580
Syme, S. L., 484, 490
Szasz, Thomas S., 654, 663, 666

T

Tajfel, H., 599
Talbot, J. D., 251
Tannehill, R. S., 95
Tannenbaum, P. H., 601
Targ, R., 131
Tarter, R. E., 534
Tata, P., 637
Taylor, Janet A., 427
Taylor, Shelley E., 294, 411, 412, 488, 491, 492, 493, 500, 582, 601, 602, 605
Teasdale, J. D., 328
Teeter, J. H., 246
Teicher, M. H., 146, 147
Tellegen, A., 558, 559, 562
Temoshok, L., 499
Templin, M. C., 158
Tenney, Y. J., 369
Tenopyr, M. L., 569
Terman, Lewis, 150, 541, 550-51, 557
Terpin, M., 547
Tharp, Twyla, 555
Thatcher, Margaret, 290
Thatcher, R. W., 151, 164
Thibaut, J. W., 580
Thigpen, C. H., 629
Thoma, S. J., 198
Thomas, B., 506
Thomas, D., 233
Thompson, D. A., 437
Thompson, K., 686
Thompson, R. F., 204, 311, 335, 373, 375
Thompson, Richard, 373
Thompson, W. D., 478
Thomson, D. M., 360
Thomson, J. C., 209
Thoresen, C. E., 501
Thorndike, Edward, 316-17, 334, 337, 550
Thorndike, R. L., 552
Thorndyke, P. W., 398
Thornton, E. M., 669
Thornton, J. C., 209, 484
Tice, D. M., 469
Tierney, W. M., 474
Tipper, S. P., 274
Titchener, Edward, 12, 105, 110, 215
Tizzard, B., 152
Tolman, Edward C., 333-34, 398, 426
Tomie, A., 334
Tomkins, R. D., 129
Tomkins, S., 465, 467

Tompkins, C., 491
Tompkins, R. D., 465
Toner, J. P., 440
Tooby, J., 319
Torrey, E. F., 650
Toscanini, Arturo, 369
Totten, M. C., 459
Townsend, J. T., 357
Treisman, 271
Treisman, Anne, 269, 272, 274
Treisman, Urie, 597-98
Trevarthen, C., 96, 148
Triandis, Harry C., 42, 182, 451, 556, 652, 666, 667
Trinder, J., 117
Triplett, Norman, 577
Trivers, 442
Troiden, Richard, 446-47
Tronick, E., 148
Trotter, R. J., 452
Tsuang, M. T., 623
Tuason, V. B., 462
Tucci, C., 478
Tuller, D., 455
Tulving, E., 108, 110, 343, 344, 346, 360, 363, 390
Tupes, 516
Turnbull, Colin, 288-89
Turner, C. F., 445
Turvey, M. T., 267, 268
Tversky, Amos, 411, 413-16, 602
Tversky, B., 361, 399
Tyler, L., 540, 551
Tyler, L. E., 512, 568

U

Ullmann, L. P., 651
Umberson, D., 490
Underwood, B., 370

V

Vaillant, G. E., 193-95, 196, 501, 696
Valenstein, E. S., 690
Valle, V. A., 452
Valsinger, J., 151
Van Berkel, C., 249
Van Boemel, G., 295
Vandenbos, G. R., 671
Vandermey, R., 623
Van Gogh, Vincent, 214
Van Wagener, William, 96
Varela, L. R., 478
Vasarely, Victor, 265
Vasari, G., 285
Vaughan, E., 417
Verma, S. K., 635
Verma, V. K., 635
Vernon, P. E., 552
Vesanen, K., 43
Vietze, P., 170

Vivano, F., 451
Vogel, S. R., 654
Volberg, 636
Voltaire, 265
von Békésy, Georg, 15, 243
von Helmholtz, Hermann, 11, 232, 243, 266, 287
von Hofsten, C., 148
Vonnegut, Kurt, 645
Vonnegut, Mark, 645
Von Neumann, 381
Vroom, V. H., 455

W

Wack, J. T., 203
Wade, J., 582
Wagner, R. A., 309, 336
Wahba, M. A., 454
Waldvogel, S., 371
Walker, L., 199
Walker, R. A., 151, 164
Wall, S., 169
Wallace, A. F. C., 667
Wallach, L., 671
Wallach, M. A., 671
Wallis, C., 249
Walsh, R. N., 662
Walters, C. C., 321
Wanous, J. P., 569
Ward, C., 605
Ward, L. M., 215, 608
Ward, M. P., 540
Warden, C. J., 426
Warington, E. K., 228
Warren, D. L., 414
Warwick, D. P., 581
Washburn, A. L., 436
Wasser, S. K., 40
Waters, E., 169
Watkins, J. T., 695
Watkins, L. R., 90
Watkinson, B., 478
Watkinson, N., 104
Watson, John, 304-305, 311
Watson, John B., 17, 105, 142
Watterlond, M., 127
Weakland, J. H., 651
Webb, R. B., 531
Webb, W. B., 115
Weber, Ernst, 220
Webster, J., 474

Wechsler, David, 552
Weick, K. E., 609
Weikard, D. P., 560
Weil, A. T., 112
Weinber, M. S., 446
Weinberg, M. S., 445
Weinberg, R. A., 560
Weinberger, Casper, 591
Weinberger, J., 196
Weinberger, N. M., 335, 373, 374
Weiner, B., 452, 603
Weiner, J., 648
Weiner, M. J., 600
Weinstein, N. D., 412, 417, 419
Weintraub, J. K., 488
Weisel, T. N., 235-36
Weisenberg, M., 251
Weiskrantz, L., 228, 229
Weiss, P., 191
Weiss, R. F., 312
Weiss, S. M., 493, 501
Weisse, C. S., 484
Weissman, M. M., 207, 643
Weissman, W. W., 491, 695
Weitzman, B. C., 180, 185
Welkowitz, J., 462
Wellens, A. R., 218
Wellman, H. M., 159
Wellman, Mark, 423-24
Welsh, H. G., 562
Wender, P. H., 648
Werker, 155
Werner, D., 445
Werner, E. E., 172
Wertheimer, Max, 268, 280
West, 205
West, L. J., 697
Wever, E. G., 243
Whelton, P. K., 477
Whipple, K., 673, 694
Whitbourne, S. K., 200
White, C. A., 666
White, M. D., 666
White, Ralph, 585-86
White, R. M., 388
Whitlow, Tommy, 575-76
Whittinghill, J. R., 644
Wicklund, R. A., 602
Widiger, T. A., 567
Wiebe, D. J., 480
Wienske, K., 436

Wiesel, Torsten, 15, 279
Wig, N. H., 635
Wiggins, J. S., 541
Wilbur, C. B., 446
Wilcox, K. J., 558
Wilcoxin, L. A., 674
Wilder, D. A., 599
Williams, 333
Williams, J., 478
Williams, J. B. W., 643
Williams, J. H., 172
Williams, L. B., 189
Williams, T., 22
Williams, Ted, 347
Willis, S. L., 205
Wills, T. A., 488
Wilson, E. D., 96
Wilson, E. O., 446
Wilson, G. T., 695
Wilson, J. M., 361
Wilson, M., 493, 580
Wilson, T. D., 415
Wingerson, L., 63
Wingert, P., 570
Wingfield, A., 357, 364
Wise, S. P., 238
Witkin, H. A., 290
Wittinger, R. P., 205
Woklestein, B., 677
Wolf, K., 170
Wolf, M., 324
Wolman, C., 697
Wolpe, Joseph, 674
Wood, D., 491
Wood, D. W., 495
Wood, P. D., 496
Woodruf-Pak, D. S., 204, 311
Woods, D. L., 388
Woodworth, Robert, 430
Workman, B., 371
Worthington, E. L., Jr., 251
Wortman, C. B., 489, 491
Wortman, E., 485
Wright, 529
Wright, F. E., 600
Wright, Jack, 517
Wundt, Wilhelm, 11, 12, 57, 105, 110, 215, 384
Wurf, E., 533
Wurtman, R. J., 152
Wyatt, G. E., 474
Wynne, L. C., 651

Y

Yalom, I. D., 686
Yantis, S., 276
Yarrow, L., 173
Yates, B. T., 678
Yeh, 275
Yeltsin, Boris, 592
Yerkes, R. M., 432
Yerkes, Robert, 550
Yolles, S. F., 636
Yorkston, N. J., 673, 694
Young, Sir Thomas, 232
Younger, B., 394
Yudkin, M., 477

Z

Zadeh, L. A., 393
Zahn-Waxler, C., 199, 200
Zajonc, R. B., 460, 467-68, 531, 577, 602
Zaman, M. B., 478
Zanchetti, A., 461
Zanna, M. P., 412
Zeckhauser, R., 414
Zeiss, R. A., 486
Zeitlin, G. M., 388
Zelnik, M., 190
Zetin, M., 342
Zettle, R. D., 333
Zick, J., 499
Zika, S., 475
Zilboorg, G., 621, 666
Zimbardo, P. G., 6, 123, 190, 202, 239, 431, 467, 489, 499, 545, 576, 618, 634, 678, 700
Zimering, R. T., 485
Zimmerman, R. R., 170
Zola-Morgan, S., 72, 342
Zubeck, J. P., 126
Zucker, R. S., 87
Zuckerman, 432
Zuckerman, M., 433, 559

SUBJECT INDEX

A

A-B-A design, 43
Abnormal behavior, 619-21
    determining, 653-56
    historical perspective, 621-22
Absolute threshold, 217-18
Accommodation, 161-62, 224-25
Acetylcholine, 89, 120
Achievement motivation, 449-55
Achievement test, 568
Acquisition, 308
Action potentials, 86, 216
Acute stress, 480-81
Addiction, 21, 128
Addiction to gambling, 636
Addictive personality, 535
Additive color mixture, 230-31
Adolescence, 185-92
    identity formation in, 181
    and occupational choice,
        190-92
    social relations in, 190
Adoption studies, 515
Adrenal cortex, 481
Adrenaline, 13
Adrenal medulla, 481
Adrenocorticotrophic hormone
    (ACTH), 481
Adulthood, 182, 192-200
    stages of, 193-95
    tasks of, 192-93
Affective disorders, 638-42
    bipolar disorders, 638-39
    sex differences in depression,
        643-44
    unipolar depression, 639
Afferent neurons, 83
Afferent systems, 216
Age, as independent variable in
    development studies, 136
Ageism, 200
Aggression, 19-20, 586-87
Agoraphobia, 634
AIDS, 497
    prevention of, 498
    risks of, for drug abusers,
        128
Alcohol, 130
    and college students, 191
    and women, 547
Alcohol dehydrogenase, 547
Alcoholic personality, 534-35
Alcoholics Anonymous, 685-86
Alcoholism, 130, 534-35
    genetics of, 64-65
    therapy for, 696-97

types of, 535
Algorithm, 406
    Darwinian, 407, 409
All-or-none law, 86
Alzheimer's disease, 203, 207,
    373-74
Ambiguity, 262, 63
    in art, 266
    and perception, 262-63
American Psychological
    Association (APA), 8
    and ethics, 46
    founding of, 12
American Psychological Society
    (APS), 8-9
American Sign Language (ASL),
    154
    and language acquisition,
        154
Ames room, 287-88
Amnesia, 341, 345-46
    anterograde, 341
    psychologically caused, 371
    retrograde, 341
Amphetamines, 130
Amplitude, of sound, 240
Amygdala, 72-73, 372
    and emotion, 461
    role of, in memory, 373
Analysis, levels of, 3
    statistical, of data,
        APPENDIX—1–10
Analytic psychology, 524
Anchoring bias, 413
Androcentric bias, 524
Androgens, 439
Animal Liberation Front, 47
Animal rights activists, 47
Animals
    instincts in, 429-30
    learning by, 407-408
    operant conditioning of, 302,
        316-28
    sexual arousal in, 431
Animistic thinking, 163
Animus/anima, 104, 524
Anorexia, 188, 438
Anterograde amnesia, 341
Antianxiety drugs, 692
Anticipatory anxiety, 632
Anticipatory coping, 487
Anticipatory grief, 209
Antidepressant drugs, 691-92
Antipsychotic drugs, 691
Antisocial personality disorder,
    629
Anvil, 242

Anxiety, 522
Anxiety disorders, 631-38
    agoraphobia, 634
    behavioral model, 637
    biological model, 637-38
    causes of, 635-38
    cognitive model, 637
    generalized anxiety disorder,
        631-32
    obsessive-compulsive
        disorder, 634-35
    panic disorder, 632
    phobic disorder, 633-34
    psychodynamic model, 635-
        37
    social phobia, 634
Aplysia, 67
Apparent motion, 283
Appetitive conditioning, 310
Applied psychologist, 10
Applied psychology, 10-11
Aptitude test, 568
Aqueous humor, 224
Archetype, 524
Archival research, 546
Arousal, incentives and optimal,
    428-31
Arousal theory, 431-33
Artificial intelligence, 256, 383
Asch effect, 582
Assimilation, 161-62
Association cortex, 75
Astrocytes, 84
Attachment, 168-72
    reasons for, 170-72
Attachment needs, 433
Attentional processes, 269-77
Attention
    definition of, 107
    functions of, 272-75
    as gateway to consciousness,
        275
    mechanisms of, 275-77
    resource allocation, 275-77
    response selection, 274-75
    as sensory filter, 272-74
Attitudes, and behavior, 612-13
Attributional styles, 452-54
    optimistic, 453
    pessimistic, 453
Attribution theory, 435, 603
Auditory awareness, during
    anesthesia, 104
Auditory cortex, 75, 243
Auditory nerve, 243
Authority, obedience to, 587-92
Autistic thinking, 401

Autocratic leaders, 586-87
Autohypnosis, 123
Autokinetic effect, 579
Automaticity, in information
    processing, 277
Autonomic nervous system
    (ANS), 79, 461
Availability heuristic, 413-14
Average, APPENDIX—5
Aversion therapy, 675-76
Aversive conditioning, 310
Axon, 83

B

Backward conditioning, 308
Backward masking, 351
Bait shyness, 331, 438
Barbiturates, 129-30, 692
Bar graph, APPENDIX–4
Base rate, 6
Basic level, 395
Basilar membrane, 242-43
Behavior
    definition of, 3
    experimental analysis of,
        317-18
    observable, 305
Behavioral confirmation, 533,
    598
Behavioral contract, 676
Behavioral data, 4
Behavioral genetics, 10, 515
Behavioral gerontology, 200
Behavioral measures, 37
    of anxiety disorders, 637
    of psychopathology, 623-24
    of unipolar depression, 640-
        41
Behavioral neurophysiology, 238
Behavioral observation, 37, 385
Behavioral psychology, 305,
    484-85, 518, 623-24, 672-80
Behavioral rehearsal, 678
Behavior analysis, 305
    applied, 337
Behavior genetics, 137
Behaviorism, 17, 304-305, 381
Behavioristic approach, 16-17,
    19
Behavior modification, 672
Behavior therapies, 663, 672-80
Belief-bias effect, 401-402
Bem Sex-Role Inventory (BSRI),
    APPENDIX—2
Bennington College, 580
Benzodiazepines, 692

Bereavement, 208-209
Bias
  androcentric, 524
  anchoring, 413
  avoiding, 34-35
  expectancy, 29-30
  external influences, 28-29
  in IQ tests, 560-61
  observer, 29
  personal, 29
  in research, 28-32
Biased assimilation, 411-12
Binocular cues, 284-85
Binocular disparity, 284
Biofeedback, 327-28, 500
  training, 327
Biological approach, 15, 19
  to mental disorders, 623
  to unipolar depression, 641-42
Biological clock, 113
Biological marker, 649
Biological model of anxiety
  disorders, 637-38
Biological needs, 433
Biological psychology, 9-10
Biological senescing, 182
Biomedical model of health and
  illness, 493
Biomedical therapies, 662, 688-92
  chemotherapy, 691-92
  electroconvulsive therapy,
  689-91
  psychosurgery, 689-91
Biopsychology, 56
Biopsychosocial model of health,
  492-93
Bipedalism, 59
Bipolar cells, 226
Bipolar disorders, 638-39
Birth cohorts, 150
Blindsight, 228
Blind spot, 226
Blocking, 315
Blood-brain barrier, 84
Body image, 188
Bottom-up processing, 260
  of perception, 292-93
Botulism, 89
Brain
  activities of, 74-76
  damage to, 66
  as dynamic system, 99
  electrical stimulation and
  recording, 67-68
  link between behavior and
  activities of, 63-76
  organization of memory in,
  372-73
  relationship between mind
  and, 104
  structures of, 69-73
Brain imaging, 390,

Brain scans, 68
  CT scanner, 68
  magnetic resonance imaging
  (MRI), 68
  PET scanner, 68
Brain stem, 120
Brain waves, 387-89
Brightness (color), 230
Brightness contrast effect, 234
Broca's area, 76
Bulimia, 188, 438
Bullies, 698-99
Bystander intervention, 591-94

C

Caffeine, 131
Calcium, and memory, 374
California Psychological
  Inventory (CPI), 515, 565
Calpain, and memory, 374
Cannabis, 129
Cannon-Bard theory of emotion,
  466
Cardinal traits, of personality,
  513
Case study, 510
Catch trials, 219
Catecholamines, 89
Catharsis, 669-70
  in psychoanalytic therapy,
  669
Causal prediction, 7
Central core, 70-71
Central nervous system (CNS),
  79
Central tendency, measures of,
  45, 000
Central traits, of personality, 513
Centration, 163
Cerebellum, 71, 372, 373
Cerebral cortex, 70, 73-76, 94,
  372, 373
Cerebral dominance, 94-95
Cerebral hemispheres, 73, 96
  functioning independently,
  96
Chaining, 325
Chemoreceptors, 216
Chemotherapy, 691-92
Childhood, changing conceptions
  of, 183-84
Chlorpromazine, 691
Chromosomes, 61, 137-38
Chronic stress, 480-81
Chronological age (CA), 136,
  549
Chunk, 353-54
Chunking, 353-54
  and long-term memory, 358
Circadian rhythms, 113
Classical conditioning, 302, 306-16
  basic processes of, 307-10

role of contingency and
  informativeness in, 314-16
Classification of psychological
  disorders, 625-27
Client-centered therapy, 526
Clinical psychologist, 8-9, 665
Clopazine, 691
Cocaine, 90, 130, 144
  and the central nervous
  system, 91
  crack, 90, 144
Cochlea, 242
Cochlear nucleus, 243
Codeine, 508
Cognition, 17, 332, 380
Cognitive Abilities Test (CAT),
  552
Cognitive appraisal, of stress,
  477
Cognitive approach, 17-18, 19
Cognitive behavior modification,
  681-82
Cognitive bias, 412-15
Cognitive development, 161-67
  assimilation and
  accommodation, 161-62
  evolutionary perspective,
  407-10
  information-processing
  approach, 167
  modern perspectives on, 164-67
  Piaget's contributions to, 161
  schemes, 161
  stages in, 162-64
Cognitive dissonance, 435, 602
Cognitive economy, 392
Cognitive map, 333, 398
Cognitive model, 382
  of anxiety disorders, 637
  of psychopathology, 624
  of unipolar depression, 640
Cognitive needs, 433
Cognitive processes, 380
Cognitive psychology, 10, 381-82
Cognitive restructuring, and
  dealing with stress, 489-90
Cognitive science, 382-83
  and intelligence, 554-56
  neuroscience, 383
Cognitive social-learning theory,
  528-31
Cognitive strategies,
  modification of, to deal with
  stress, 489-90
Cognitive style, 295
  levelling versus sharpening,
  295
  of work motivation, 455
Cognitive therapy, 663, 681-84
  for depression, 683
Cohort efforts, 201
Coincidence, 41

Collective unconscious, 524
Collectivism, 451
Color
  afterimages, 231
  complementary, 230
  contrast effects of, 234
  wavelength of light, 230
Color blindness, 231
Color circle, 230
Color vision
  molecular basis of, 233
  opponent-process theory of,
  232
  trichromatic theory of, 232
Common fate, law of, 281
Community psychologist, 9
Community support groups, 686
Componential intelligence, 555
Compulsions, 635
Compulsive personality disorder,
  634
Computational model, 407
Concept formation, 392
Concepts, 392
  critical features approach to,
  392
  hierarchical organization of,
  395
  prototype approach to, 392
Concrete operational stage, 163-64
Conditional response (CR), 307
Conditional stimulus (CS), 307
Conditioned reinforcer, 325
Conditioned social behavior,
  312-14
Conditioning, 17
  operant, 302, 316-28
Conduction deafness, 243
Cones, 225-26
Conformity, 582
  versus independence, 582-85
Confounding variable, 35
Connectionism, 335-37
Consciousness, 107-10
  as aid to survival, 107
  alteration, 104
  changing scientific status of,
  106
  characteristics of alternate
  and extended states of, 129-31
  development of, 131
  everyday changes in, 111-21
  extended states of, 122-31
  levels of, 108
  ordinary versus
  extraordinary, 131
  and research approaches, 110
  and self-awareness, 108
Consciousness alteration, 122-23
Consensual validation, 108
Conservation, 164
Consistency paradox, 516-18

causes of, 517
Consolidation, and memory, 373
Constant habitat, 303
Constitutional factors, 141
Constructions of reality
  cultural, 107-108
  personal, 107-108
Construct validity, 544
Contact comfort, 170
Context, 264-65, 293
Context dependence, 360
Contextual intelligence, 555
Contingency management, 673, 676-77
Control condition, 42-43
Controlled-drinking controversy, 696
Controlled procedures, 35
Convergence, 284-85
Coping, 487
Cornea, 224
Corpus callosum, 73, 96
Correlational methods, 41-42, 510, 541
Correlation coefficient, 41, APPENDIX-6
Correlation vs. causation, 41
Cortex, and emotions, 462
Counseling psychologist, 9, 664
Counterconditioning, 673-75
Countertransference, 670
Covariation principle, 604-605
Crack, 130-31, 144
Cranial nerves, 247
Crash, 91
Creationism, 13
Crime, and antisocial personality disorder, 629
Criterion performance, 345
Criterion validity, 543
Critical period, 152
Critical set point, 438
Critical thinking consumer checklist, 51
Critical thinking skills, 28
Cross-cultural research, 42
Cross-sectional research design, 150, 510-11
Cupboard theory, of attachment, 170
Cultural anthropologist, 667
Cultures, individualist vs. collectivist, 451
Cutaneous senses, 248

D

Darwin's evolutionary theory of emotion, 468
Data, 4
  statistical analysis of, 45, APPENDIX—1–10
Data-driven perception, 297
Date rape, 444-45

sexual scripts and, 445
Daydreaming, 111-12
Deafness
  conduction, 243
  nerve, 243
Debriefing, 47
Decay, of memory, 369
Decibels, 241
Decision making, 410
  decision frames, 416
  ecological, 418-19
  nonrational factors in, 417
  psychology of, 415-19
Declarative knowledge, 341, 343
Declarative memory, 344
Deficiency motivation, 433
Delirium tremens, 126
Delta rule, 336-37
Delusion(s), 262
  in schizophrenia, 646
Demand characteristic, 590
Dementia, 203
Democratic leaders, 586-87
Demographics, 200
Demonic possession, 621
Dendrites, 82-83
Dependence
  physiological, 128
  psychological, 128
Dependent variable, 7, 42, 308
Depressants, 129-30
Depression
  and the elderly, 207
  sex differences in, 643-44
  and suicide, 643-44
  unipolar, 639
Deprivation, 428
Depth cues, 284
  binocular, 284-85
  motion, 285
  pictorial, 285
Depth perception, 283-86
Descriptive statistics, 45
Determinism, 12, 32
Development
  continuity vs. discontinuity, 151-53
  normative investigations of, 149-50
  time-based research in, 150
Developmental age, 136
Developmental disabilities, 62
Developmental dyslexia, 145
Developmental psychology, 10, 136
  life-span approach to, 181
  research methods in, 150
  in social context, 184
Developmental stages, 151
Dichotic listening task, 110, 273
Difference threshold, 220-21
Differential reinforcement, 325
Direct observations, 37-38
Disasters, human reactions to,

477
Disclosure, healing power of, 500
Discriminative stimuli, 321, 325
Disease. See Illness
Disengagement theory, 206
Dishabituation, 150
Dispositional dominance, 605-606
Dispositional forces, 435
Dispositional variables, 7
Dissociation, 125
Dissociative disorders, 629-31
Dissonance theory, 602
Distal stimulus, 259
Distraction, 269
Divorce, 193
DNA, 137
Dominant genes, 137
Dopamine, 89
Dopamine hypothesis, and schizophrenia, 650
Double bind, 651
Double-blind control, 35
Down's Syndrome, 62
Drapetomania, 655
Dream(s)
  activation-synthesis theory of, 120-21
  causes of, 118
  content of, 119
  psychoanalytic theory of, 119
Dream analysis, 670
Drive(s), 424, 430
  manipulation of, 427-28
Drive theory, 428
  and learning, 430-31
Drug addiction, 90
Drug Policy Foundation, 50
Drugs
  effects of, on synapses, 90-91
  mind alteration with, 127
  therapeutic, 691-92
  war on, 50-51
DSM-III-R (Diagnostic and Statistical Manual of Mental Disorders, revised 3d Edition), 625-27
Dual-code model of memory, 361
Dual hypothalmic theory of hunger, 436-37
Dualism, 105
Duality of consciousness, 97
Duplex theory of memory, 363-65
Dying, process of, 208
Dynamic psychology, 424

E

Eardrum, 242
Eating. See also Hunger
  disorders associated with,

188, 438
  inhibition of, 438
  motivation of, 438
Echo, 349
Echolocation, 245
Ecological optics, theory of, 267
Ecology, 21
Ectomorphic type, 512
Educational psychologist, 10
Effect, law of, 317
Efferent neurons, 83
Efferent systems, 216
Ego, 520, 522, 668
Egocentrism, 163
Ego defense mechanisms, 522
  and emotion regulation, 488
Eidetic imagery, 361-62
Einstellung effect, 404-405
Elaboration, 346
Elaborative rehearsal, 354
  and long-term memory, 358
Elavil, 691
Electroconvulsive therapy (ECT), 689-91
Electrode, 67
Electroencephalograms (EEGs), 39, 68, 388
  for studying sleep, 113
Electromagnetic spectrum, 230
Emergent-interaction theory, 106
Emotion(s), 460-70
  basic, 463-64
  Cannon-Bard theory of
  central neural processes, 466
  Darwin's evolutionary theory of, 468
  definition of, 460
  experiencing, 461-64
  and facial expression, 468
  functions of, 464-65
  interpreting and labeling, 462-63
  James-Lange theory of body reaction, 466
  lateralization of, 462
  Lazarus-Schachter theory of cognitive arousal, 466-68
  misattributing arousal, 463
  neurophysiology of, 461-62
  theories of, 465-68
Emotional development, 168-75
Emotional expressions, universal, 468-70
Emotional stages, 208
Emotion wheel, 463-64
Empirical evidence, 3
Empirical investigation, 28
Empiricist, 143, 266
Encephalization, 59
Encoding, 346
  for long-term memory, 358-60
  in short-term memory, 353
Encoding specificity principle,

360, 366
Endocrine system, 76
Endomorphic type, 512
Endorphins, 89-90, 250
Engram, 371-72
Environment
    pollution and stress, 477
    structure and stress of, 491-92
Environmental psychologist, 10
Environmental psychology, 609-10
Environmental variables, 7
Epinephrine, 481
Episodic memory, 344
    serial position effect in, 364-65
Equanil, 692
Equity theory, of work
    motivation, 455
ERG theory of work motivation,
    454
Erogenous zones, 249, 520
Eros, 520
Erotic stimuli, 441, 444
Error analysis, 386-87
Esteem needs, 433
Esthetic needs, 434
Estrogen, 78, 439
Ethical standards, guidelines for,
    46
Ethics, in psychology, 7
Ethologists, 468
Etiology, 622-23
Eugenics, 541
Event-related potential (ERP),
    387
Evoked potential, 387
Evolution, 57
    cultural, 60, 65
    human, 59-60
Evolutionary approach, 18-19,
    20
Evolutionary psychology, 14
Evolutionism, 13
Excitatory synapses, 87
Excitement phase, 441
Exercise, 497
Existential-humanistic therapies,
    663, 684-88
Existentialism, 18
Expectancy, 455
Expectancy theory, of work
    motivation, 455
Experience-sampling method,
    110
Experiential intelligence, 555
Experimental condition, 42
Experimental methods, 42-45
    disadvantages of, 44
Experimental psychology, 10
Explanatory style, 452
Ex post facto experimental
    design, APPENDIX–2

Exposure therapy, 675
Extinction, 91, 309
Extraversion, 514
Extrinsic motivation, 454
Eyelid conditioning, 310-11
Eye movement, recording of,
    387
Eyewitness testimony, 367-68

F

Face validity, 544
Factor analysis, 510
False beliefs, perseverance of,
    411-12
Family therapy, 686-88
Fat cells, and obesity, 438
Feature-detection cells, 236
Feature-detection model, 236
Fechner's law, 222
Femininity, 172, APPENDIX—2–6
Fetal brain transplant, 206
Fetish, 443
Fetus, 140
Field dependence, 289-90
Field independence, 289-90
"Fight-or-flight" syndrome, 481
Figural goodness, 281
Figure-ground segregation, 234,
    238
Fixed-action pattern, 429
Fixed-alternative questions, 37
Fixed-interval (FI) schedules,
    327
Fixed-ratio (FR) schedules, 326-27
Flooding, 675
Flow, 454
Fodrin, 374
Forensic psychologist, 10
Forgetting, reasons for, 369-71
Formal operational stage, 164
Formal operational thought, 196
Forward conditioning, 308
Fovea, 226
Free association, 669
Free recall, 358
Frequency, of sound, 239-40
Frequency theory of pitch
    perception, 243
Freudian psychoanalysis, 519-24, 668-70
Freudian slip, 521
Freudian theory, criticisms of,
    522-24
Frigidity, 443
Frontal lobe, 73-74
Frontal lobotomy, 689-90
Functional fixedness, 404
Functionalism, 13
Functional pathology, 622
Functional psychologists, 428
Fundamental, 241
Fundamental attribution error,

605

G

Galvanic skin response (GSR),
    311
Gambling, addiction to, 636
Ganglion cells, 226
Gate-control theory of pain, 250-51
Gender, 172
Gender identity, 172
Gender roles, 172-73
Gender-role socialization, 172-73
Gender-role stereotypes, 172-73
General adaptation syndrome
    (GAS), 482-83
Generalization techniques, 673,
    679-81
Generalized anxiety disorder,
    631-32
Generalized fear reaction, 311
Generativity, 182, 193
Genes, 137
Genetic mapping, 62
Genetics, 61-65
Genital development, 141
Genotype, 58, 137
Germ cells, 137
Gestalt psychology, 267-68, 281
Gestalt therapy, 686
"g-factor," 551
Glandular control, of behavior,
    76-78
Glial cells, 84
Glucose, 206
Gonads, 439
Graded potential, 85
Group dynamics, 585
Group therapies, 685
Group think, 417
Growth motivation, 429, 433

H

Habitats, 58
    for the elderly, 203-204
Habitual criminal murderers,
    APPENDIX—1–10
Habituation, 150
Hallucinations, 136, 260
    in schizophrenia, 646
Hallucinogenic drugs, 128
Halo effect, 548
Hammer, 242
Hardiness, 479
Harmonics, 241
Hashish, 129
Health
    causes and correlates of
        illness, 500-501
    definition of, 493
    good health habits, 496

guidelines for, 502
    prevention and treatment of
        illness, 494-99
    promotion and maintenance
        of, 493-94
Health care
    biopsychosocial model of,
        492-93
    patient response to, 499-500
Health care system, formation of
    policies, 501-502
Health-oriented individuals, 493
Health psychologist, 10
Health psychology, 460, 492-503
Hearing, 239-45
    auditory system, 241-43
    loss of, and noise pollution,
        244
    loss of with age, 202-203
    physiology of, 241-43
    pitch perception, 243
    psychological dimensions of
        sound, 240-41
Hearing aid therapy, 202
Heart disease, 496
Hebbian learning, 336
Heredity, 57
Heritability estimate, 559
Hermann grid, 262
Heroin, 129
Hertz, 240
Heuristics, 406
Hidden observer, 125
Hippocampus, 72
    role of, in memory, 72, 373
Histogram, APPENDIX—4–5
Historical approach, to
    development, 183
HIV virus, 497
Holistic approach, 18
Homeopathic medicine, 29
Homeostasis, 73
Homosexuality, 445-46
    nature and development of,
        446
    and self-definition, 446
Hormones, 76
    influence of, on emotions,
        461
    steroid, 461
Hospice approach, 208
Hozho, 492
Hue (color), 230
Human behavior genetics, 62
Humanistic approach, 18, 20
Humanistic theories of
    personality, 525-27
    criticisms of, 526-27
Humanistic theory of growth
    motivation, 433-34
Human-potential movement, 685
Human sexuality, 440-42
Hunger, 436-38. See also Eating
    critical set point and, 438

and glucose levels, 437
human feeding patterns, 436-38
hunger pangs, 436
inhibitors of, 438
multiple-system approach to, 436
peripheral cues hypothesis of, 436
Hypnosis, 123
altered personal reality under, 124
and pain control, 124-25
Hypnotic induction, 124
Hypnotizability, 123
Hypothalamus, 72-73, 77, 227, 372
and emotions, 461
role of, in regulating hunger, 436-37
and stress response, 481
Hypothesis, 32
Hypothesis-driven perception, 297
Hysteria, 621
Hysterical conversion, 669

I

Icon, 349
Id, 521, 668
Identification, 522
and recognition, 258
Idiographic approach, 510, 519
Illness, 493
causes and correlates of, 500-501
prevention and treatment of, 494-99
Illness prevention, 494-95
Illusions, 260
lessons learned from, 262-66
in reality, 266
Illusory conjunctions, 271
Immediate memory span, 353
Implicit memory, 345
Implicit personality theory, 510
Implosion therapy, 674
Impotence, 443
Imprinting, 168
Incentive motivation, 428
Independent variable, 7, 35, 42, 308
Index variable, 136
Individualism, 451
Induced motion, 283
Industrial psychology, 10
Infancy period, 145
Infantile sexuality, 520
Infants
and drug exposure, 144
non-verbal communication in, 157
response and adaptation in,

146-47
social interactions in, 147-49
Inference, 5, 411
Inferential statistics, 45, APPENDIX-3
Inferential strategies, 411
Informational influence, 582
Information-gathering apparatus, 214
Information processing model, 382
Information processing, and mood, 470-71
Information, representation of, in memory, 360-62
Informativeness, 309, 315, 336
Informed consent, 46
Inhibitory synapses, 88
Initiation rites, 185
Inquisition, 621
Insanity, 653
Insight learning, 334-35
Insight therapies, 668
Insomnia, 117
Instincts
in animals, 429
in humans, 430
Instinct theory, 428
challenges to, 429-30
Instinctual drift, 330
Instrumentality, 455
Intellect, structure of, 554
Intellectual development, 152
Intelligence
componential, 555
contextual, 555
crystallized, 205, 553
definition of, 549
experiential, 555
fluid, 205, 553
and old age, 204-205
and problem-solving, 554-55
Intelligence assessment, 548-61
Intelligence quotient (IQ), 550
debate over testing, 556-57
group differences, 557
heredity versus environment, 558-60
use and misuse of, 556-61
Intelligence testing, 549-56. See also IQ tests
and groups, 552-53
historical context of, 549-50
IQ test scores of African-American children, 560
IQ tests, 550-56
validity and test bias in, 560-61
Interactionist perspective, 624
Interference, of memory, 369-70
Interfering variables, 6
Interjudge reliability, 548
Internal consistency, 543
Internalization, 580

Interneurons, 83
Interposition, 285
Interval schedule, 326
Intervening variable, 5
Interview, 37, 546
Intrinsic motivation, 454
Introspection, 12, 384
Intuitive psychologists, 604
Inverted U-shaped function, 431
In vivo therapy, 664
Ion channels, 87
IQ tests, 550-56
heredity versus environment, 559
scores of African-American children, 560
and statistical analysis, APPENDIX—7-8
Iris, 224
Irrationality, sources of, 412

J

James-Lange theory of emotion, 466
Jet lag, 113
Job analysis, 569
Job burnout, 501
Judgment, 410
Just noticeable difference (JND), 220

K

Killer whales, research on, 418
Kinesthetic sense, 245, 246
Kin selection, 446

L

Laissez-faire leaders, 586
Lamaze method of childbirth, 251
Language
acquisition of, 153-60
babbling, 155
and evolution, 60
grammatical skills, 160
overregulation in, 160
telegraphic-speech stage of, 160
vocabulary growth, 158-59
Language acquisition device (LAD), 156
Latent content, of dreams, 120
Lateral geniculate nucleus, 227
Lateral inhibition, 235, 262
Lateralization of emotion, 462
Laughter, medical benefits of, 459
Law of forward conduction, 83
Law of pragnanz, 281
Lazarus-Schachter theory of

emotion, 466
Learned helplessness, 328, 452-53, 640
Learning
and behavior analysis, 305
biofeedback, 327-28
biological constraints on, 329-32
chaining, 325
and classical conditioning, 302, 306-16
cognitive influences on, 332-35
and conditioned social behavior, 312-14
definition of, 303-304
and drug addiction, 313
evolutionary perspective on, 303
by insight, 334-35
and modern medicine, 302
observational, 332-33
operant conditioning and, 302, 316-28
and performance, 303
and reinforcement contingencies, 318-22
role of reinforcers in, 323
and stimulus discrimination, 310
and stimulus generalization, 209
study of, 302-305
Thorndike's law of effect, 317
Learning models, 335
Learning-performance distinction, 303-304
Learning and cognitive theories
criticisms of, 531-32
of work motivation, 455
Lens, 224
Lesioning, 427
Lesions, 66-67
Levels of processing theory of memory, 364
Libido, 520
Life-change units (LCUs), 474-75
Life cycle, genetic influences on behavior, 137-42
Life Experiences Survey (LES), 474
Life history, 546
Life-span development, 180-85
early life-span theories, 181
Limbic system, 70, 71-73
and emotions, 461
Linear perspective, 285
Lithium salt, 692
Locus of control orientation, 435, 451
Longitudinal prospective research, 196

Longitudinal research design, 150, 511
Long-term memory, 348
    encoding for, 358-60
    retrieval from, 362-63
    storage in, 360-62
Long-term potentiation, 374
Loudness, of sound, 240-41
LSD (lysergic acid diethylamide), 89, 128
Lucid dreaming, 122

M

Magnitude estimation, 222
Maintenance rehearsal, 354
Mandala, 524
Manic episode, 638
Manifest content, of dreams, 120
Manipulation drive, 431
Margin of error, APPENDIX–10
Marijuana, 129
Marital therapy, 686-88
Markers, 65
Masculinity, 172, APPENDIX—2–6
Masochism, 627
Mating, short term vs. long term, 442
Maturation, 139
McClintock effect, 246-47
Mean, 45, APPENDIX–5
Meaningful organization, role in long-term memory, 358-59
Mechanoreceptors, 216
Median, 45, APPENDIX–5
Medical model, of mental disorders, 622
Meditation, 125-26
Medulla, 71
Memory
    anatomy of, 371-73
    cellular mechanisms of, 374-75
    as constructive process, 365-68
    declarative, 344
    definition of, 343
    duplex theory of, 363-65
    encoding, 346
    episodic, 344
    failure of, 342
    information-processing view of, 343, 347-48
    integration of biology and psychology of, 375
    levels of processing theory of, 364
    long-term, 357-65
    neurobiology of, 371-75
    and old age, 205-206
    procedural, 343
    reasons for forgetting, 369-71

retrieval, 346
savings method, 345
semantic, 3434
short-term, 352-57
storage, 346
working, 352
Memory code, 352
Memory trace, 371-72
    decay of, 369
Menarche, 188
Mental age (MA), 549
Mental disorders, 631-38
    DSM-III-R classification system, 625-27
    major types of, 628-59
    stigma of, 655-56
Mental map, 398
Mental operations, 163
Mental processes, 3
Mental set, 294, 404
Mental shortcuts, 411
Mescaline, 127, 128
Mesomorphic type, 512
Metacognitive knowledge, 406
Method of loci, 359
Mid-life crisis, 182
Miltown, 692
Mind
    as communications channel, 272-74
    relationship between brain and, 104
Mind altering drugs, 127-28
Mind-body debate, 104-105
    across cultures, 106
Minnesota Multiphasic Personality Inventory (MMPI), 562-65, 000
    ego-overcontrol scale, 000
    revision of, 562-64
Minnesota Study of Twins Reared Apart, 515
Minority influence, 584-85
Misleading retrieval cues, 368
Mnemonics, 359-60
Mode, 45, APPENDIX–5
Monism, 105
Monoamine oxidase (MAO) inhibitors, 691
Mood-congruent processing, 471
Mood-dependent retrieval, 470
Moral behavior, 199-200
Moral development, 197-200
    gender differences in, 199
    stages of, 197
Morality, 197
Morality principle, 521
Moral reasoning, 197-99
Motherese, 157
Motion cues, 285
Motion perception, 283
Motion sickness, 246
Motivated forgetting, 370-71
Motivation, 424

achievement, 449-50
behavioral indicators of, 426-27
definition of, 424
and incentives, 428
intrinsic vs. extrinsic, 454
sexual, 439-49
understanding of, 424-28
Motivational concepts
    functions of, 425-26
    in research, 426-28
Motivational theories, 428-35
Motive(s), 424
    manipulation of, 427-28
Motor cortex, 74-75, 238
Motor neurons, 83
Motor set, 294
Multiple personality disorder (MPD), 629-31
Multiple sclerosis (MS), 86-87
Myelin sheath, 84
Myers-Briggs Type Indicator, 512, 565-66
Myopia, 225

N

Nanometers, 230
Narcissistic personality disorder, 629
Narcolepsy, 117
National Association for Mental Health, 697
National Institute of Health, 29
National Institutes for Mental Health (NIMH), 695
Nativist, 143, 266
Naturalistic observations, 38
Natural language mediators, 359
Natural selection, 57-58, 317
Nature, cross-cultural perspectives on, 22
Nature-nurture controversy, 14, 143-45
Necker cube, 263, 284
Need for achievement, 449-50
Needs hierarchy, 433
Need theories, of work motivation, 454
Negative afterimages, 231
Negative cognitive sets, 640
Negative correlation, 41
Negative reinforcement, 320
Negative reinforcer, 320
NEO Personality Inventory (NEO-PI), 565
Nerve deafness, 243
Nervous system, 76
    and conscious experience, 94-98
Neural impulses, rate of, 223
Neural networks, 92
Neuroadaptation, 91
Neurometrics, 68

Neuromodulator, 89
Neurons, 78, 82
    life and death of, 82
Neuropathic pain, 249-50
Neuroscience, 9-10, 56
Neuroscientists, 15
Neurotic disorders, 627
Neuroticism, 514
Neurotransmitters, 76, 87
    chemicals as, 89-90
Nicotine, 131
Nightmares, 121
Nodes of Ranvier, 86
Noise, 241
Noise pollution, 244
Nomothetic approach, 510
Nonconscious processes, 108-109
Non-REM sleep (NREM), 113
Norepinephrine, 89, 120, 481
Normal curve, APPENDIX–7
Normal distribution, APPENDIX–7
Normative influence, 582
Normative investigations, 149-50
Norm crystallization, 579
Norms, 149-50, 545
Nociceptive pain, 249

O

Obedience paradigm, 587-88
Obesity and dieting, 438
Objective behaviorism, 105
Objectivity
    in observation, 5
    problem of, 653-55
    safeguards for, 34-35
Object permanence, 163
Observational learning, 332-33, 529-30
Observer-report methods, 547-48
Obsessions, 635
Obsessive-compulsive disorders, 634
Obstruction box, 426
Occipital lobe, 74
Occupational Analysis Inventory, 569
Odor recognition, 362
Old age, 200-209
    cognitive changes in, 204-206
    dying process, 208
    myths about, 200-201
    new perspectives on, 201-202
    physiological changes in, 202-204
    and psychopathology, 207
    research approaches to, 201
Olfactory bulb, 246
Olfactory cilia, 246
One Flew over the Cuckoo's Nest, 691

One-word stage, 159-60
Open-ended questions, 37
Operant, 317
Operant chamber, 318
Operant conditioning, 302, 316-28
Operant extinction, 320
Operational definition, of variables, 34
Opiates, 129
Opinion surveys, 37
Opponent-process theory, 232-33
Optical illusions, 263-64
Optic chiasma, 227
Optic nerve, 227
Optic tract, 227
Optimal arousal, 431
Optimistic bias, 417
Organic pathology, 622
Organismic variables, 7
Organizational psychology, 454-55
Orientation constancy, 289
Orienting response, 307
Outward-inward directedness, 182
Overregularization, as language error, 160

P

Pain, 249-51
    acute, 249
    chronic, 249
    definition of, 249
    mechanisms of, 250-51
    neuropathic, 249-50
    nociceptive, 249
    psychology of, 251
Panic disorder, 632
Papillae, 247
Paradigm, 32-33
Parallel distributed processing models (PDP), 383
Parallel forms, 543
Parallel processing, 348
Parallel-processing scanning, 356
Parasympathetic division, 80
Parental investment, 442
Parietal cortex, 238
Parietal lobes, 74
Parkinson's disease, 89, 206
Partial reinforcement effect, 326
Partial-report procedure, 350
Participant modeling, 678
Passive smoking, 478
    effects of, 478
Pastoral counselor, 665
Pathology, 434
Patient, 663
Patient nonadherence, 499
Pattern recognition, 228
Pavlovian conditioning, 307

Payoff matrix, 220
PCP, 128-29
Peace psychology, 611-13
Perceived control, 489
Percept, 256
Perception, 215, 257
    artificial intelligence approach to, 268
    bottom-up process of, 260, 292-93
    closure in, 280
    constancy of, 287
    creatively playful, 295-96
    definition of, 257
    depth perception, 283-86
    figural goodness, 281
    figure and ground, 279-80
    Gestalt tradition, 257, 267-68
    Gibson's ecological optics, 267
    global process of, 258
    grouping in, 280
    Helmholtz's classical theory of, 267
    identification and recognition, 258, 292-97
    and illusions, 260
    influence of contests and expectations on, 293-94
    interpreting retinal images in, 258-60
    of motion, 283
    neuroscience perspective of, 256
    nurture and nature of, 266-68
    organizational processes of, 278-91
    recognition by components, 293
    reference frames, 281
    region segregation, 279
    role of personal and social factors in, 295
    and sensation, 257
    spatial and temporal integration, 282-83
    stages of, 257-58, 260
    task of, 256-57
    top-down process of, 260, 292-93
Perceptual constancies, 286-91
Perceptual grouping, principles of, 280-81
Perceptual organization, 278
Perceptual set, 294
Perceptual synthesis, 258
Peripheral cues hypothesis, 436
Peripheral nervous system, 79
Personal construct, 528
Personal construct theory of personality, 527-28
Personality
    and behavioral coherence, 518

the Big Five, 516
cognitive theories of, 527-32
comparing theories of, 534
the consistency paradox of, 516-18
definition of, 509
describing with traits, 512
field dependence in, 290
humanistic theories of, 525-27
idiographic approach to, 510
nomothetic approach to, 510
personal construct theory of, 527-28
psychodynamic theories of, 519-25
self theories of, 532-33
social learning theories of, 527-32
strategies for studying, 509-11
theories about, 511
type and trait theories of, 511-18
type categorizing of, 511-12
Personality assessment, 562-67
    objective tests, 562-66
    projective tests, 566-68
    statistical versus clinical prediction, 567
Personality disorders, 628-29
Personality inventory, 562
Personality psychology, 10, 509, 515
Person-centered therapy, 684-85
Personology, 567
Phantom limb phenomenon, 251
Phenomenological perspective, 596
Phenomenologists, 18
Phenotype, 58, 137
Phenylketonuria (PKU), 138
Pheromones, 246, 440
Phi phenomenon, 283
Phobic disorder, 633-34
Phonemes, 155
Photographic memory, 361
Photons, 230
Photoreceptors, 216, 225-26
Phylogenic scale, 138
Physical growth, 138
Physiological measures, 39
Physiological psychology, 15
Physiological stress reactions, 480-84
    emergency reactions to external threats, 481-82
    general adaptation syndrome, 482-83
    psychoneuroimmunology, 483-84
Pinna, 242
Pitch, of sound, 240
Pitch perception

frequency theory of, 243
place theory of, 243
volley principle of, 243
Pituitary gland, 78, 481
Placebo control, 35
Placebo effect, 31, 301
Placebo therapy, 694
    in pain management, 251
Place recognition, 228
Place theory of pitch perception, 243
Pleasure principle, 521
Polarity, of cell, 85
Pollution, and stress, 433
Polygenic characteristics, 137
Pons, 71
Ponzo illusion, 286
Positive afterimages, 231
Positive correlation, 41
Positive illusions, and well-being, 500
Positive reinforcement, 319
    extinction strategies of, 677
    strategies of, 676-77
Positive reinforcer, 319, 324
Postformal thought, 197
Post-Freudian theories, 524-25, 670-72
Postsynaptic membrane, 87
Posttraumatic stress disorder (PTSD), 485
Poverty, effect of, on intellectual functioning, 559-60
Power function, 222
Preattentive processing, 269-72
Preconscious memories, 109
Predicted response, 7
Predictions, 6-7
    scientific, 6
Prefrontal lobotomy, 689-90
Prejudice, 599
Premack principle, 324
Prenatal listening experience, and language acquisition, 156-57
Prenatal period, 140
Preoperational stage, 163
Presynaptic membrane, 87
Primary appraisal, and stress, 479
Primates, naturalistic observations of, 40
Priming effect, 345
Proactive interference, 370
Problem solving, 402-405
    finding the best search strategy, 405-406
    understanding the problem, 403-404
    well-defined and ill-defined problems, 402-403
Problem-solving intelligence, 554-55
Procedural knowledge, 341, 343

Procedural memory, 343
Processing, in short-term memory, 353-55
Progesterone, 440
Propanediols, 692
Proposition, 360-61
Proximal stimulus, 259
Proximity, law of, 280
Proximity-promoting signals, 169
Prozac, 692
Pseudomemory, 394
Psilocybin, 128
Psychiatric social worker, 664-65
Psychiatrist, 8, 665
Psychic determinism, 519-20
Psychic energy, 430, 520
Psychoactive drugs, 128
   varieties of, 128-31
Psychoanalyst, 8, 665
Psychoanalytic approach, 663
Psychoanalytic theory, 522-24
Psychodelic drugs, 128
Psychodynamic approach, 15-16, 19
Psychodynamic model
   of anxiety disorders, 635-37
   of psychopathology, 623
   of unipolar depression, 640
Psychodynamic personality theories, 519-25
Psychodynamic therapies, 668-72
   Freudian psychoanalysis, 519-24, 668-70
Psychogenic amnesia, 629
Psychological adolescing, 182
Psychological approaches, to mental disorders, 623-24
Psychological assessment
   definition of, 540
   history of, 541
   and intelligence, 548-61
   methods of, 542-48
   political and ethical issues in, 569-71
   purposes of, 541-42
   reliability of, 543
   sources of information for, 545-48
   standardization of, 545
   validity of, 543
Psychological autopsy, 509
Psychological diagnosis, 618
Psychological disorders
   classification of, 625-27
   historical perspectives of, 621-22
   major types of, 628-59
   nature of, 618-25
Psychological models, of mental disorders, 622
Psychological research, 32

   conducting, 36-45
Psychological stressors, 481
Psychological stress reactions, 484-86
   behavioral patterns of, 484-85
   cognitive effects of, 486
   emotional aspects of, 485-86
Psychological test, 42, 546
Psychology
   current perspectives of, 14-20
   definition of, 3
   descriptions in, 4-5
   environmental, 609-10
   goals of, 4
   historical foundations of, 11-12
   peace, 610-13
   as social science, 3
Psychometric function, 217
Psychometrics, 542, 553-54
Psychoneuroimmunology, 460, 483-84
Psychopathological functioning, 618
Psychopathology
   behavioral model of, 623-24
   cognitive model of, 624
   etiology of, 622-24
   psychodynamic model of, 623
   psychological approaches to, 623-24
Psychopharmacology, 9-10
Psychophysical scales, constructing, 221-23
Psychophysics, 217-21
Psychosocial dwarfism, 170
Psychosocial stages, 173, 181-82
   developmental tasks at, 181
Psychosomatic blindness, 295
Psychosomatic disorders, 482
Psychosurgery, 689-91
Psychotherapy, 662-63
Psychotic disorders, 627
Psychoticism, 514
Puberty, 185, 188
Punisher, 320
Punishment, 320
   conditions of, 321
   consequences of, 321
Pupil, 224
Pure tones, 240
Pygmalion effect, 597

Q

Questionnaire, 37

R

Radical behaviorism, 305
Randomization, 43

Range, 45, APPENDIX–6
Rape, aftershock of, 485
Rapid eye movement (REM), 113
Rapid eye movement (REM) sleep, 113
   deprivation of, 114
Rapport, 37
Rational-emotive therapy, 683
Ratio schedule, 326
Reaction formation, 522
Reaction time, 386
Realistic thinking, 401
Reality principle, 522
Reasoning, 401-10
   deductive, 401-402
   inductive, 402
Recall, 347
Receptive field, 235
Receptor molecules, 108
Recessive genes, 137
Reciprocal determinism, 529
Recognition, 347
Reference frames, 281
Reference group, 580
Reflexes, 304, 306
Refractory period, 86
Rehearsal, 354
Reinforcement contingency, 318-22
Reinforcement, schedules of, 325-27
Reinforcers, 319
   positive, 319
   properties of, 323-24
Rejection reflex, 438
Relapse, 493
Relaxation response, 500
Reliability
   interjudge, 548
   of psychological tests, 543
   of research findings, 35
   test-retest, 543
Religious ecstasy, 126-27
Remembering, 343, 348
Repeated reproduction, 367
Representativeness heuristic, 413, 415
Repression, 522
   and memory, 371
Repressors, 295
Repressor-sensitizer continuum, 295
Reproductive phases, 182
Research
   analyzing data, APPENDIX—1–10
   becoming wiser consumers of, 48-51
   correlational , 36
   descriptive, 36
   ethical issues in, 46
   experimental, 36
   methods, 36-45

Range, 45, APPENDIX–6
psychological measurement, 36-41
   public verifiability of, 33
   with animals, 47
Residual stress pattern, 485-86
Resiliency, 180
Resistance, 670
Resistance to extinction, 308
Response, 4
Response bias, 218-19
Reticular activating system (RAS), 227, 461
Reticular formation, 71
Retina, 224, 225
Retrieval, 346
   from long-term memory, 362-63
   from short-term memory, 355-57
Retrieval cues, 362, 368
Retrieval failures, 370
Retroactive interference, 370
Retrograde amnesia, 341
Rhinencephalon, 246
Risk strategies, 416-17
Rites of passage, 185
Ritual healing, 667
Rod-and-frame test, 290
Rods, 226-26
Romanian orphans, 171
Rote learning, 345
Rule learning, 333
Rules, 333, 578

S

Saccule, 246
Safety needs, 433
Salem witchcraft trials, 621
Saturation (color), 230
Savings, 309
Scaffolding, 158
Scapegoating behavior, 587
Schemas, 294, 366-67, 395-96, 528
Schemes, 161
Schizophrenia, 617
   catatonic type, 647
   causes of, 647-52
   disorganized type, 646-47
   major types of, 646-47
   paranoid type, 647
   undifferentiated type, 647
   use of chlorpromazine in treating, 691
Schizophrenic disorders, 645-53
Scholastic Aptitude Test (SAT), 539-40
School and College Ability Tests (SCAT), 552
Science-coated journalism, 49
Scientific knowledge, 33-34
Scientific method, 3, 33
Scientific prediction, 6

Script, 397
Secondary appraisal, and stress, 479
Secondary traits, of personality, 513
Selective advantage, 59
Selective attention, 273, 351
Selective breeding, 57
Selective exposure, 412
Selective optimization with compensation, 201-202
Self, 509
Self-actualization, 434, 525
Self-awareness, 108
Self-concept, 532
Self-deception, 262
Self-efficacy, 530-31
Self-esteem, 533
Self-fulfilling prophesy, 412, 479, 598
Self-handicapping behavior, 533
Self-perception theory, 603
Self-report measures, 37
Self-report methods, 546-47
Self-serving bias, 605
Self theory, of personality, 532-33
  criticism of, 533
Semantic memory, 344
Semicircular canals, 246
Sensation, 215, 257
Sensitizers, 295
Sensorimotor stage, 162-63
Sensory adaptation, 223
Sensory coding, 223
Sensory development, 142-43
Sensory gating, 350, 351
Sensory knowledge, 214
Sensory memory, 348-52
  encoding for, 349-50
  storage, 350-51
Sensory neurons, 83
Sensory physiology, 216
Sensory processes, 214
Sensory psychologists, 215
Sensory register, 349
Sensuality, 214
Sequential research design, 150
Serial-exhaustive scanning, 356-57
Serial learning, 345
Serial position effect, in episodic memory, 364-65
Serial processing, 348
Serial reproduction, 367
Serial self-terminating scanning, 356
Serotonin, 89, 120
Set, 294
Sex, 172
Sex chromosomes, 61
Sex roles, APPENDIX—2-6
Sexual addiction, 447-48
Sexual arousal, 439-41

human, 441
  nonhuman species, 439-40
Sexual desire, 441
Sexual drive, 439
Sexual functioning, and old age, 204
Sexuality, 188-90
  human, 440-42
Sexually transmitted diseases, 497
Sexual motivation, 439-49
Sexual reproduction, 440
Sexual response
  and cognitive desires, 443
  role of fantasy in, 443
  role of touch in, 443
Sexual response cycle, 441
  excitement phase of, 441
  orgasm phase of, 441-42
  plateau phase of, 441
  resolution phase of, 442
Sexual scripts, 443-44, 445
Sexual synchrony, 440
Shamanism, 661-62
Shape constancy, 289
Shaping, 325
  by successive approximations, 324
Short-term memory, 205, 348, 352-57
  encoding in, 353
  processing in, 353-55
  retrieval of information from, 355-57
  storage in, 353
  transferring sensory information to, 351-52
Signal detection, theory of, 219-20
Significant difference, APPENDIX-8
Similarity, law of, 281
Simultaneous conditioning, 308
Sine waves, 239
Situational behavior observations, 546
Situational forces, 435
Situational variables, 7
Situationism, 577
Size constancy, 287
Size/distance relation, 285
Skewed distribution, 000
Skin, cutaneous senses in, 248-49
Sleep
  cycle of, 114
  patterns of, 114-15
  reasons for, 115-16
Sleep apnea, 117
Sleep disorders, 116-18
Sleep spindles, 114
Smell, 246-47
Smoking, 7, 131, 302, 496-97
  passive, 478

Social categorization, 599
Social changes, and old age, 206
Social-cognitive motivational theories, 434-35
Social context, 576
Social development, 168-75
Social facilitation, 577
Social imitation, 527
Social interest, and language acquisition, 154-55
Socialization, 168-72
  of gender roles, 172-73
Social learning, 527
Social learning theories of personality, 527-32
Social-learning theory, 435
Social learning therapy, 677-79
Social loafing, 577
Social norms, 579
Social perception, 601
Social phobia, 634
Social problems, solving, 607-13
Social psychology, 10, 576
  social relevance of, 606
Social Readjustment Rating Scale (SRRS), 474
Social reality, 595-606
  definition of, 596
Social roles, 577-78
Social rules, 577-78
Social situations, 577-94
Social support networks, and dealing with stress, 490-91
Soma, 83
Somatic nervous system, 79
Somatosensory cortex, 75
Somatotypes, 512
Sound localization, 245
Soviet coup attempt, 592
Spatial and temporal integration, 282-83
Spatial-frequency model, 237
Species-specific behavior, 330
Speech perception abilities, and language acquisition, 155
Speech production abilities, and language acquisition, 155
Spinal cord, 79
Split-brain surgery, 96
Spontaneous recovery, 309
Spontaneous remission effect, 694
Spoonerism, 386
Sports psychologist, 11
Spreading activation theory, 387
Stages of mourning, 209
Standard deviation, 45, APPENDIX-6
Standardization, 34, 545
Stanford-Binet Intelligence Scale, 550, APPENDIX-8
Stanford Heart Disease Prevention Program, 7
Stanford Prison Experiment,

575-76, 578, 588, APPENDIX—1-10
Stanford Shyness Survey, APPENDIX-2
State dependence, 360
Statistical analysis, 45, APPENDIX—1-10
  correlation coefficient, APPENDIX-6
  frequency distribution, APPENDIX-3
  intervals, APPENDIX-5
  margin of error, APPENDIX-10
  mean, APPENDIX-5
  measure of central tendency, APPENDIX-5
  measures of variability, APPENDIX-6
  median, APPENDIX-5
  mode, APPENDIX-5
  normal curve, APPENDIX-7
  normal distribution, APPENDIX-7
  range, APPENDIX-6
  rank order, APPENDIX-4
  significant difference, APPENDIX-8
  skewed distribution, APPENDIX-7
  standard deviation, APPENDIX-6
  t-test, APPENDIX-8
Statistics. See also Statistical analysis
  descriptive, APPENDIX-3
  how to mislead with, APPENDIX—9-10
  inferential, APPENDIX-3
Status quo, 585
Stereotype effect, 548
Stereotyping
  of gender-roles, 172-73
  of sexual behavior, 439
Steroid(s), 481
Steroid hormones, influence of, on emotions, 461
Stigma, problem of, 655-56
Stimulants, 130
Stimulation, 428
Stimulation deafness, 244
Stimulus, 4, 216
Stimulus contrast, 235
Stimulus discrimination, 310
Stimulus generalization, 309
Stimulus-response (S-R) connection, 316-17
Stirrup, 242
Storage, 346, 350
  in long-term memory, 360-62
  in sensory memory, 350-51
  in short-term memory, 353
Storm and stress view of adolescence, 186-87

Strain, 472
Stress
  acute, 480-81
  and catastrophic events, 476-77
  chronic, 480-81
  coping strategies for, 488-89
  definition of, 472
  and low-level frustrations, 474
  physiological stress reactions, 480-84
  primary appraisal of, 479
  psychological stress reactions, 484-86
  role of cognitive appraisal in, 477
  secondary appraisal of, 479
  sources of, 473
Stress moderator variables, 477-80
Stressors, 472
  chronic societal, 477
  major life, 473-74
  physical, 481
  psychological, 481
  reappraising, 489
Striatum, 372
Strong-Campbell Interest Inventory, 568
Stroop task, 277
Structuralism, 12
Subconscious awareness, 109
Subjective contours, 280
Sublimation, 522
Subliminal perception, 217
Subtractive color mixture, 231
Success and failure, attributions for, 451-52
Sucking, 146
Sudden murderers, APPENDIX—1–10
Suicide, and depression, 643-44
Superego, 521, 668
Superior colliculus, 227
Supernatural, belief in, APPENDIX—9–10
Surveys, 37
Swedish Adoption/Twin Study on Aging, 515
Sybil, 629
Syllogism, 401
Symbolic representation, 131, 161
Sympathetic division, 80
Symptom substitution, 673
Synapse, 87
Synaptic cleft, 87
Synaptic transmission, 87-89
Synaptic vesicles, 87
Systematic desensitization, 674

T

Tasks of adolescence, 187-92
Taste, 247-48
  qualities of, 247
Taste-aversion learning, 330-31
Taste buds, 247
Tay-Sachs disease, 62
Telegraphic speech, 160
Temperament, 511-12
Temporal cortex, 238
Temporal focus, 14
Temporal lobe, 74
Tension reduction, 430-31, 527
Terminal buttons, 83
Testosterone, 78
Test-retest reliability, 543
Texas Adoption Project, 515
Texture gradients, 285
Thalamus, 71
Thalidomide, 138
Thanatos, 520
Thematic Apperception Test, 434, 567
Theory, 32
Therapists, cross-cultural perspective of, 664-65
Therapy, 662-63
  behavior, 672-80
  biomedical, 688-92
  cognitive, 681-84
  entering, 663
  existential-humanist, 684-88
  goals of settings of, 663-64
  historical and cultural contexts of, 665-67
  implosion, 674-75
  kinds of, 662-63
  psychodynamic, 668-72
Thermoreceptors, 216
Think-aloud protocols, 110, 384-85
Thinking. See also Cognitive skills
  definition of, 391
  means of studying, 384-90
  mental structures for, 391-99
  studying, 380-84
Thorazine, 691
The Three Faces of Eve, 629
Three-term contingency, 321-22
Thyroid gland, 481
Thyrotrophic hormone (TTH), 481
Tiennamen Square, 590
Timbre, of sound, 241
T-lymphocytes, 484
Tofranil, 692
Token economies, 324
Tolerance, 128, 313
Top-down processing, 260
  of memory, 357
  of perception, 292-93

Total situation, 581
Touch, 248
  and sexual response, 443
Trace conditioning, 308
Traits, 512
  and heritability, 514-15
Transactional perception, 267
Transcendence, needs for, 434
Transduction, 215-16
Transference, 670
Trial-and-error, learning by, 317
Tricyclics, 691
T-test, 000
Twins
  dizygotic, 64
  monozygotic, 64
Two-word stage, 160
Tympanic membrane, 242
Type A behavior syndrome, 501
Type T personality, 480
Type and trait theories
  criticisms of, 518
  of personality, 511-18

U

Unconditional positive regard, 526
Unconditional response (UR), 307
Unconditional stimulus (US), 307
Unconscious, 109-10, 520-21
  and mental processes, 109
  and personality, 520-21
Unconscious inference, 267, 287
Unipolar depression, 639
Utricle, 246

V

Valence, 455
Validity
  construct, 544
  criterion, 543
  face, 544
  of psychological tests, 543
  of research findings, 36
Valium, 130, 692
Variability, measures of, 45, APPENDIX–6
Variable, 32
  dependent, 7
  dispositional, 7
  environmental, 7
  independent, 7
  interfering, 6
  organismic, 7
  situational, 7
Variable-interval (VI) schedules, 327
Variable-ratio (VR) schedules, 327

Variation, 58
Vase/faces illusion, 263-64
Veridical view of reality, 256
Vestibular sense, 245-46
Violence, on television, 333
Visible spectrum, 230
Vision
  bipolar cells, 226
  color, 229-33
  form, depth, and movement, 233-38
  ganglion cells, 226
  human eye, 224
  loss of with age, 202
  pathways to the brain, 227-29
Visual afterimage, 231
Visual cortex, 75, 227
Visual imagery, 359
Visual mental imagery, 397
Vocational interests and aptitudes, assessment of, 568-69
Volley principle of pitch perception, 243

W

Wason Selection Task, 409
Wavelength, 230
Weber's constant, 221
Weber's law, 220-21
Wechsler Intelligence Scales, 552
Wellness, 493
Wernicke's area, 75-76
Whole-report procedure, 350
Wisdom, 204
Witchcraft, 621
Withdrawal, 91
  symptoms of, 128
Woodworth Personal Data Sheet, 562
Word associations, use of, in personality testing, 566
Working memory, 352. See also Short-term memory
Work motivation, 449-55
  cognitive theories of, 455
  equity theory of, 455
  ERG theory of, 454
  expectancy theory of, 455
  need theories of, 454
  and organizational psychology, 454

Y

Yerkes-Dodson law, 432
Young-Helmholtz trichromatic theory, 232
Youth, 182